C

CHRISTINA TREE, a ~~written more than 700 articles on New England~~ *Boston Globe* over the past 25 years, and continues to be a regular contributor. She is the author of *How New England Happened* and coauthor of several other current New England guides, including *Best Places to Stay in New England* and the exhaustive "Explorer's Guides" to Maine, New Hampshire, and Vermont. She is the editorial consultant for this guidebook.

RENÉ BECKER is restaurant critic and food editor of *Boston Magazine,* and writes on wine for *Worth Magazine*. His articles on Boston restaurants have appeared in various magazines, including *Food & Wine.*

PATRICIA BROOKS, a state resident since 1956, has received the Governor's Tourism Council Travel Achievement Award for her voluminous writings about Connecticut in *Travel & Leisure, Travel Holiday, Bon Appétit, Vogue,* and many other national magazines, as well as for her restaurant and country-inn guidebooks. Since 1977 she has been the restaurant reviewer for the Connecticut section of *The New York Times,* with the entire state as her beat.

KIMBERLY GRANT, a freelance travel writer and photographer, is coauthor of *Best Places to Stay in New England* and has contributed to several national guidebooks. A lifelong resident of Massachusetts, she resides in Boston and makes frequent trips to the Cape.

CYNTHIA HACINLI, a resident of Portland, served as restaurant critic for *The Maine Times* from 1988 to 1990 and now writes about food and travel for such publications as *The New York Times,* and *Travel & Leisure, Yankee,* and *Philadelphia* magazines. She is also the author of *Down Eats: The Essential Maine Restaurant Guide.*

CYNTHIA W. HARRIMAN is a longtime resident of Portsmouth. Her travel articles have appeared in the *Washington Post,* the *Chicago Sun-Times,* and the *San Francisco Examiner,* and she is the author of *Take Your Kids to Europe.*

ANN KEEFE writes on international travel from her home in the eastern Monadnock village of Lyndeborough.

JIM McINTOSH writes frequently about travel and culture in northern New England. For eight years until 1990 he was the editor of *Magnetic North* magazine, a quarterly that celebrated the history and natural attractions of the White Mountains. An 18-year resident of the mountains, he lives in Franconia.

PHYLLIS MÉRAS is the travel editor of the *Providence Journal*.

B. J. ROCHE writes about western Massachusetts for the *Boston Globe* and is an adjunct instructor of journalism at the University of Massachusetts at Amherst. Her work has appeared in the *Washington Post, The New York Times,* and the *Chicago Tribune,* and in *Travel & Leisure, Country Journal,* and *New Woman* magazines.

WILLIAM G. SCHELLER is a Vermont-based travel writer with 18 years' experience. A contributing editor to *National Geographic Traveler,* he is also a frequent contributor to *Islands* magazine and to the *Washington Post Magazine*'s special travel issues. He is the author of 20 books, many on travel subjects; his 1981 *Train Trips: Exploring America by Rail* was a Thomas Cook Award finalist.

JAN STANKUS is a freelance writer who has lived in Boston for 19 years. She is the author of *How to Open and Operate a Bed & Breakfast Home* and coauthor of *How to Be Happily Employed in Boston.* She has also contributed numerous articles and photographs to Boston and Cambridge newspapers and written children's fiction.

MIMI STEADMAN, formerly the executive editor of *The Original New England Guide* and assistant editor of Maine's *Down East* magazine, is a coauthor of *Maine, An Explorer's Guide* and author of *One Hundred Country Inns in Maine.* She is director of Mimi Steadman & Company, a small advertising agency specializing in the worldwide yachting industry, and lives by the sea in the heart of Maine's Midcoast.

SARA WIDNESS is a partner in Kaufman/Widness Communications, a New York–based public relations firm. Previously she worked as a journalist and marketing communications specialist in New England, developing an affinity for the region's many roads seldom taken.

THE BERLITZ
TRAVELLERS GUIDES

THE BERLITZ TRAVELLERS GUIDE TO NEW ENGLAND

ALAN TUCKER

General Editor

BERLITZ PUBLISHING COMPANY, INC.
New York, New York

BERLITZ PUBLISHING COMPANY LTD.
Oxford, England

THE BERLITZ TRAVELLERS GUIDE
TO NEW ENGLAND

First published as
The Berlitz Travellers Guide
to New England 1993

Berlitz Trademark Reg U.S. Patent and Trademark Office
and other countries—Marca Registrada

Published by Berlitz Publishing Company, Inc.
257 Park Avenue South, New York, New York 10010, U.S.A.

Distributed in the United States by
the Macmillan Publishing Group

Distributed elsewhere by Berlitz Publishing Company Ltd.
Berlitz House, Peterley Road, Horspath, Oxford OX4 2TX, England

ISBN 2-8315-1717-6
ISSN 1062-3655

Designed by Beth Tondreau Design
Cover design by Dan Miller Design
Cover photograph by Fred M. Dole/f/stop Pictures
Maps by Ortelius Design
Illustrations by Bill Russell
Copyedited by Amy Hughes and Benjamin Spier
Fact-checked by Charles Pappas
Edited by Lisa Leventer

Printed in the United States of America
1   3   5   7   9   10   8   6   4   2

THIS GUIDEBOOK

The Berlitz Travellers Guides are designed for experienced travellers in search of exceptional information that will enhance the enjoyment of the trips they take.

Where, for example, are the interesting, out-of-the-way, fun, charming, or romantic places to stay? The hotels described by our expert writers are some of the special places, in all price ranges except for the very lowest—not just the run-of-the-mill, heavily marketed places in advertised airline and travel-wholesaler packages.

We are *highly* selective in our choices of accommodations, concentrating on what our insider contributors think are the most interesting or rewarding places, and why. Readers who want to review exhaustive lists of hotel choices as well, and who feel they need detailed descriptions of each property, can supplement the *Berlitz Travellers Guide* with tourism industry publications or one of the many directory-type guidebooks on the market.

We indicate the approximate price level of each accommodation in our description of it (no indication means it is moderate in local, relative terms), and at the end of every chapter we supply more detailed hotel rates as well as contact information so that you can get precise, up-to-the-minute rates and make reservations.

The Berlitz Travellers Guide to New England highlights the more rewarding parts of the region so that you can quickly and efficiently home in on a good itinerary.

Of course, this guidebook does far more than just help you choose a hotel and plan your trip. *The Berlitz Travellers Guide to New England* is designed for use *in* New England. Our writers, each of whom is an experienced travel journalist who either lives in or regularly tours the city or region he or she covers, tell you what you really need to know, what you can't find out so easily on your own. They identify and describe the truly out-of-the-ordinary restaurants, shops, activities, and sights, and tell you the best way to "do" your destination.

Our writers are highly selective. They bring out the significance of the places they *do* cover, capturing the personality and the underlying cultural and historical resonances of a city or region—making clear its special appeal.

This edition of *The Berlitz Travellers Guide to New England* is full of reliable information. We would like to know if you think we've left out some very special place. Although we make every effort to provide the most current information available about every destination described in this book, it is possible too that changes have occurred before you arrive. If you have an experience that is contrary to what you were led to expect by our description, we would like to hear from you about it.

A guidebook is no substitute for common sense when you are travelling. Always pack the clothing, footwear, and other items appropriate for the destination, and make the necessary accommodation for such variables as altitude, weather, and local rules. Of course, once on the scene you should avoid situations that are in your own judgment potentially hazardous, even if they have to do with something mentioned in a guidebook. Half the fun of travelling is exploring, but explore with care.

ALAN TUCKER
General Editor
Berlitz Travellers Guides

Root Publishing Company
350 West Hubbard Street
Suite 440
Chicago, Illinois 60610

CONTENTS

MAPS

THE
BERLITZ
TRAVELLERS
GUIDE TO
NEW
ENGLAND

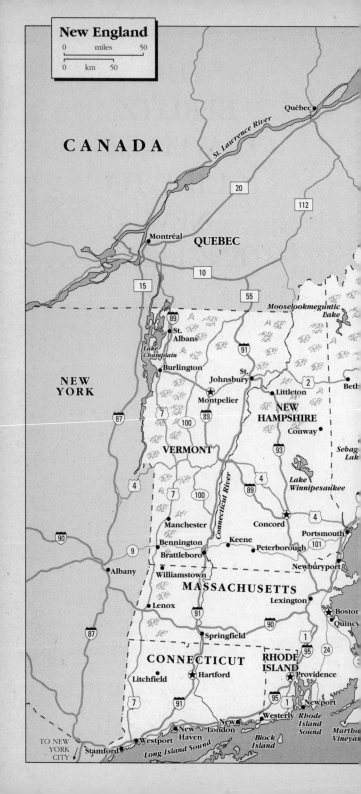

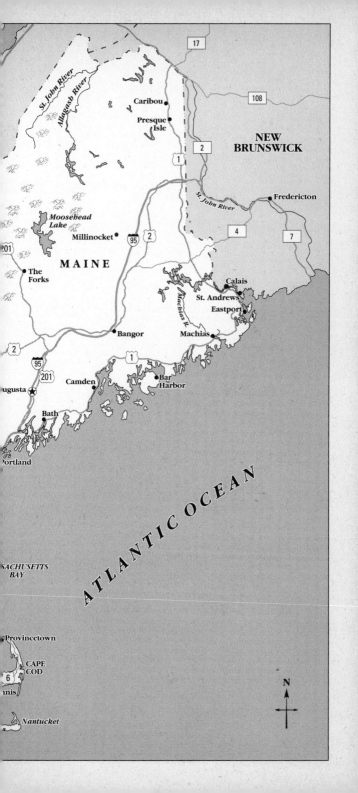

OVERVIEW

By Christina Tree

Over the past 25 years Christina Tree has written more than 700 articles on New England travel for the Boston Globe, *for which she continues to be a regular contributor. She is the author of* How New England Happened *and coauthor of several other current New England guides, including* Best Places to Stay in New England *and the exhaustive "Explorer's Guides" to Maine, New Hampshire, and Vermont. A resident of Concord, Massachusetts, she is the editorial consultant for this guidebook.*

Measuring New England's miles by the usual yardstick—an interesting city here, a resort town there—will not work. The six states that occupy the northeastern corner of the United States pack more variety into less space than any other region of the country, and the worst mistake a traveller can make is to try to go too far too fast.

To a degree the variety is topographical. The area is divided by two major mountain chains, innumerable hills, myriad lakes, and bays and inlets created by 6,000 miles of convoluted coastline. Humorist Keith Jennison has observed:

> Vermont may not look very big as states go.
> But if you got a flatiron and pressed it out,
> It would be as big as Texas.

Press it out and New England as a whole might equal a good chunk of the West, but as it stands all six states could fit handily within the borders of Texas. It's impossible, however, to imagine them as one uniform entity. Maine is totally different from New Hampshire, which could never be confused with Vermont, and so on.

New England's crinkly surface has served to keep its communities apart and self-sufficient, but topography hasn't been the only differentiating factor. The region's history and culture—who settled where and when—has a lot to do with how the New England states vary in look and feel, and even within the individual states layerings of history have created a tangible diversity that's unusual in America.

History and Culture

Boston, for instance, is a mix of glass high rises, mellow 19th-century brick, and a smattering of 18th-century buildings. In neighboring Cambridge a line of mansions built by pre-Revolutionary merchants stands just beyond the trendy boutiques and bookstores of Harvard Square, while less than a dozen miles to the west the same fields, and many of the houses, that were there in the 1700s still flank the road down which minutemen chased English regulars from Concord back to Lexington on April 19, 1775. Within an hour's drive of Boston it's possible (traffic permitting) to walk the sands of vast, dune-backed beaches (Duxbury Beach to the south and Crane's Beach on the North Shore), the mammoth courtyards of Lowell textile mills, the 18th-century streets of Portsmouth, New Hampshire, the shore path past moored lobstering boats in York Harbor, Maine, or the heady architectural mélange of styles that is Benefit Street in Providence, Rhode Island.

Still, it's what these six northeastern states share, rather than how they differ, that makes them New England. As early as 1789 geographer Jedidiah Morse observed that the states east of New York had "the general name of New England" and "several things" in common, such as "their religion, manners, customs, and character." And in 1947 John Gunther noted in *Inside U.S.A.* that "Every school child knows what the six New England states are, and what is the knifelike boundary of the whole." New England has its share of fast-food outlets and neon strips, but—both superficially and on a deeper level—the region reflects, to a remarkable degree, the three centuries that have shaped it.

THE NATIVE AMERICANS

Scant trace remains, on the other hand, of the 70,000 or so Native Americans said to have been living in the region when the first European settlements took root in the 1630s, although a few 10,000-year-old pictographs, tools, and human remains have been unearthed in Maine and Massachusetts. By the 17th century these people were known generally as Algonquian Indians and were divided into ten tribes whose members lived in villages of roughly 100 people each; they migrated between inland winter settlements and summer camps on the shore.

These New England natives taught the European newcomers how to plant corn, beans, tobacco, and squash; how to dig for clams; and how to make snowshoes, sleighs, maple sugar, and canoes. For this kindness—and the loss of their land—they were repaid with trinkets, alcohol, disease, and the unwelcome attentions of the military and missionaries. A last-ditch attempt to dislodge the white men (called King Philip's War, after the Narragansett chief who led the Native Americans) obliterated most Indian villages in southern New England (Connecticut, Massachusetts, and Rhode Island) by the close of the 1670s, while the French and Indian Wars did the same in northern New England (Maine, New Hampshire, and Vermont) by the close of the 1760s. Although the official number of Native Americans has increased in recent decades, the most palpable Native American legacy remains on the region's maps: names like Winnipesaukee, Penobscot, and Narragansett, not to mention Connecticut and Massachusetts.

THE EARLY SETTLERS

The first substantial European settlement on Massachusetts Bay was on the south shore at present-day Plymouth, established in 1621 by the Pilgrims, a group of separatists who had been barred from exercising their religious beliefs in England. The first group of Puritans, another sect opposed to the Church of England but committed to "purifying" it from within, arrived in Salem in 1629. That the land around Massachusetts Bay was settled by people who had come for religious rather than economic reasons has affected the look and outlook of all New England in many real ways, ranging from the early and sustained commitment to education (New England today is home to America's highest concentration of preparatory schools and colleges) to the distinctive look of the region's villages to the unusual importance placed on town lines and town government.

The members of the religious sects who settled Massachusetts Bay believed that any man, however humble, could be mightier in God's eyes than a king, an attitude that was reflected in the shape of their towns: Each was arranged around a "common" on which all men shared rights to pasture their animals. It also carried over into government: Major decisions were made at an annual town meeting at which every man had a say, and the town itself, rather than the county, was (and remains) the prime New England political unit. To this day New England town lines are marked more clearly than elsewhere in the country, and the town meeting, involving residents of all the villages within each town, remains a forum for often heated debate.

Ironically, both the Pilgrims and the Puritans were themselves so intolerant of later arrivals that subsequent religious refugees, especially those who came as congregations led by their ministers—thus the name Congregational—quickly "hived off" and founded their own communities. In 1636 the Reverend Thomas Hooker and his flock left Cambridge, Massachusetts, to found the state of Connecticut, and Roger Williams, seeking escape from all religious bigotry, led the first white settlers into Rhode Island.

The situation in northern New England was very different. Several fishing posts had already been established along the Maine coast before the Pilgrims arrived, and throughout the 17th century and well into the 18th northern New England continued to be settled by fishermen, adventurers, and entrepreneurs rather than religious groups.

AFTER THE REVOLUTION

It wasn't until after the American Revolution that residents of southern New England—which was getting crowded by New World standards—settled northern New England, attempting to turn the wilderness there into a carbon copy of the gentrified countryside they had left. Happily, the architecture from this period (the 1790s to the 1830s), now known as Federal style, is particularly graceful.

The unsung hero responsible for the architectural look of much of rural New England today is Asher Benjamin. A builder from the western Massachusetts town of Greenfield, Benjamin was keenly aware of the need for a "do-it-yourself" guide to the new architectural styles being introduced in Boston by Charles Bulfinch (who was greatly influenced by Scottish architect Robert Adam). In 1796 Benjamin wrote *The Country Builder's Assistant,* which was followed by six more books that resulted in the construction of thousands of homes and hundreds of churches—the distinctive three-story houses and high-steepled churches that remain the pride of New England villages.

New England still may be best known for the leadership role its inhabitants played in 1775 against the British, but, with the exception of a scattering of buildings in its oldest towns and cities, New England's ubiquitous tidy white-clapboard buildings are not Colonial, but distinctly Federal. While the small mills, shops, and modest houses of these old communities have long since disappeared, residents have almost always managed to preserve, as they would the formal portrait of a 19th-century forebear, the Federal-era church and mansions that typically surround a common.

THE INDUSTRIAL ERA

Like cocoons, these villages burst abruptly and forever in the 1840s, as New Englanders streamed west along the newly opened Erie Canal and then, in the mid- and late 19th century, along the railroads, earning a reputation as "industrious Yankees" wherever they went. Those who remained in New England tended to move from their native farms and villages to the new communities burgeoning around textile mills and train depots.

Until the 1840s New England's Puritan-Yankee heritage remained essentially undiluted, but in the late 19th century the combination of hard times in French Canada and throughout Europe (beginning with the Irish potato famine) and the need of burgeoning Yankee mills for cheap labor altered this picture dramatically. By 1850 one out of every ten New England residents was foreign-born, and in the ensuing decades hundreds of thousands of Irish arrived, followed by an equal number of French-Canadians and thousands of Italians, Poles, Germans, Lithuanians, Russian Jews, and Portuguese. The impact of this mass immigration on New England was greater than on any other single region of the country.

A small percentage of the early Irish arrivals found their way to northern Maine, where they helped found Aroostook County's present potato industry, but relatively few first-generation immigrants could afford to buy the region's languishing farms.

THE RESORTIFICATION OF NEW ENGLAND

As New England fields ceased to be cultivated and as the old villages stagnated, however, the rural landscape began to be perceived as "romantic," and the old whaling ports, such as New Bedford and Nantucket, eclipsed by the development of the petroleum industry and by the new railroads, were seen as picturesque. On Martha's Vineyard the unsolicited crop of summer visitors seemed God-sent (literally): It all began in 1835 with a Methodist meeting in an old oak grove on the high bluffs, seven bumpy miles from the distractions of Edgartown. By the 1870s the annual camp meeting had evolved into Cottage City, the country's first summer resort development (in today's Oak Bluffs), complete with a mammoth hotel, a chapel, shaded streets, and parks.

If in the 1830s New England was America's first finished corner, by the 1840s it was on the way to becoming America's first resort region. At that time landscape artists, among them Thomas Cole and Frederick Church, began painting and etching the rugged cliffs of Maine's Mount Desert Island and the dramatic peaks and passes of New Hampshire's White Mountains, while Henry David Thoreau, Nathaniel Hawthorne, and Ralph Waldo Emerson passionately described the landscape from the Berkshires to Provincetown to Maine's north woods. These painted and written pictures appealed to a country in need of escape from the smoke and noise of the new industrial era.

After the Civil War New England's "resortification" gained momentum. The scenery was more popular than ever, and much of New England—the deserted farms and cellar holes as well as the mountains and seacoast—was considered romantic. At the same time new rail lines, trolleys, and steamboats put every part of New England within reach. The wealthy elite of Philadelphia, Cleveland, and Chicago, as well as New York and Boston, built elaborate summer "cottages" in Newport, Rhode Island, in Bar Harbor, Maine, and in the Berkshires of western Massachusetts. Vast wooden summer hotels sprouted on Maine's lakes, along the length of the New England coast, on offshore islands, and seemingly on top of every major mountain.

In 1869 the Mount Washington Cog Railway began jolting passengers up the nearly perpendicular wall of New England's highest mountain (as it still does), leaving them there to choose from two rival hotels. Up to 70 trains a day stopped at Fabyan's Station near the base of the cog railway, and guest rooms in the half-dozen nearby hotels totaled 1,500.

The grand hotels catered to the rich, but this was also the first era in American history when everyone—postmen and schoolteachers as well as bankers—began taking vacations. In northern New England the state agricultural departments teamed up with the railroads to produce the region's first guidebooks, and thousands of farms were encouraged to take in guests. Coastal boarding houses and religious "camp meetings" also served working folk who sought to gather by "the waters."

In New England resort towns this period—which ended abruptly with World War I—is fondly labeled the Golden Era. After the war, and with the proliferation of the automobile, Americans tended to tour the country rather than sit out the summer at a resort or on a farm. New England's big summer hotels closed one by one.

This regional fall from favor continued during and after World War II. True, urbanites flocked to the motels and cottages that sprouted like mushrooms on Cape Cod and along Maine's south coast beaches, but many of Maine's lake resorts all but disappeared once their rail service ceased, as did the many coastal resorts at the tips of peninsulas that had been served by steamboats. In Vermont out-of-staters bought up big farms for peanuts; in New Hampshire the grand White Mountains hotels stood shuttered like so many wooden ghosts, while those that survived catered to the older generation. Port cities like Newburyport and Newport drowsed so deeply that no one troubled themselves to tear down their seemingly worthless old buildings.

THE PRESERVATION OF NEW ENGLAND

Then in the 1960s, as in the 1860s, New England was rediscovered. Country inns, the older the better, lured New Yorkers on weekends. Hundreds of city dwellers rehabilitated decrepit inns and created new ones throughout Connecticut, the Berkshires, and Vermont. Younger urban and suburban refugees flocked to communes in Vermont or moved to bargain-priced farms in western Massachusetts and rural Maine.

This back-to-the-earth movement gathered steam throughout the 1970s, and today a significant percentage of political and financial movers and shakers in both Maine and Vermont are relatively recent transplants. In the early 1970s New England's old seaports—Newport, Rhode Island; New Bedford, Newburyport, and Salem, Massachusetts; Portsmouth, New Hampshire; and Portland, Maine—also attracted their share of preservation-minded entrepreneurs, eager to restore reasonably priced old houses and to open shops and restaurants in spiffed-up waterfronts.

Next the preservationists turned to New England's all-but-abandoned mill towns and cities. The brick city of Lowell, Massachusetts, the nation's first planned urban area, became a National Historical Park, and the industrial and immigrant history of a number of other Massachusetts mill cities was dramatized in Heritage State Park visitors' centers.

The second resortification of New England accelerated in the 1980s. Ski areas in Maine, New Hampshire, and Vermont became year-round self-contained resorts with 18-hole golf courses, elaborate sports facilities, and hundreds of condominium units. Country inns continued to multiply and thousands of bed-and-breakfasts opened across the region, many of them in rural places that had supported inns a century ago. New England's bigger cities—from New Haven and Providence to Portland and Burlington—also regained their appeal, and a dozen major new hotels opened in Boston.

The boom years are over for now, but this time it seems that the tourist tide will not recede. In every New England state tourism now ranks as the number one or two industry. For the visitor this means more to do and see, and a far wider choice of year-round lodging options than existed a decade ago. From Boston, where you can now choose from some 20 major downtown hotels and a number of B and Bs, to Maine's remote Washington County and Vermont's Northeast Kingdom, the choice of places to stay in New England has never been broader.

A Geographical Overview

New England is old in geological as well as human terms. Vermont's Green Mountains date back more than 400 million years, and 75 million years later New Hampshire's White Mountains appeared in the shape of molten granite. The surface of the region continued to tilt and shift over the ensuing millennia up until a mere 10,000 to 12,000 years ago, when receding glaciers etched the peculiarly ragged coastline, the thousands of lakes, and the boulder-strewn uplands familiar to us today; later a vast glacial lake receded, leaving the rich bottomland of the Connecticut River Valley.

The six New England states are bounded on the east by the Atlantic Ocean, on the north by Canada, and on the west by Lake Champlain (Vermont's "west coast") and New York State, which also forms the southern boundary. The Connecticut River, which runs 409 miles from the springs that are its source in northernmost New Hampshire to Long Island Sound, is the region's one uniting feature, flowing through four of the six states. Cape Cod, a narrow, 65-mile-long hook-shaped peninsula, is the single most distinctive feature in 6,000 miles of coast that becomes especially ragged—riddled with coves and island-spotted bays beloved by sailors—northeast of Portland.

New England's mountains are all part of the Appalachians, a system that extends southwest across the East from Newfoundland, Canada, to North Carolina. They are traversed by the **Appalachian Trail**, the longest continuous hiking path in the world, extending 2,050 miles from Springer Mountain in Georgia to Mount Katahdin in Maine's Baxter State Park. The trail enters New England from New York State at Bulls Bridge in western Connecticut and continues up through the Berkshires and into southern Vermont, where it follows the ridge of the Green Mountains to Killington Peak before cutting eastward into New Hampshire. There the trail runs across the Presidential Range of the White Mountains (and over Mount Washington, at 6,288 feet the region's highest peak) and on up through the Mahoosuc Range of western Maine, across Sugarloaf Mountain and the Bigelow Range, through the Upper Kennebec Valley, and, finally, through virtual wilderness to Baxter State Park in the middle of the state, which is as far north as most visitors to the state go.

New England's best-known mountain ranges are Vermont's **Green Mountains**, running the entire 160-mile length of the state (traversed by the **Long Trail**, which also runs the length of the state), and New Hampshire's **White Mountains**, which extend diagonally northeast across northern New Hampshire, beginning with Mount Moosilauke near the Connecticut River and continuing beyond Evans Notch in western Maine.

Perhaps because Maine has no name for its mountains, most people don't consider them as impressive as they really are. Maine's highest peak, Katahdin, after all, is 5,268 feet high, and the mountains march all the way from the White Mountains National Park area west of Bethel up through the Mahoosucs, the Rangeley, Longfellow, and Bigelow ranges, on up through the north woods to the Katahdin Range.

Aside from its coast and mountains, Maine's distinguishing features are its north woods (some 6.5 million acres of woodland owned by lumber companies), New England's single largest lake (Moosehead), and two mighty rivers—the Kennebec, flowing southwest out of Moosehead Lake, and the Penobscot, which begins north of Moosehead and flows south along the eastern fringe of the woodland and down through the rolling farm country of "mid-Maine." Maine's capital city, Augusta, marks the head of navigation on the Kennebec River, as Bangor does on the Penobscot. The northernmost stretch of vast woodland and open, rolling farm country to the east is Aroostook County, bordering the wooded New Brunswick back country along the St. John River.

The Traveller's New England

New England divides naturally in two parts as well as six. Northern New England—Maine, New Hampshire, and Vermont—is an entity unto itself, accounting for almost five-sixths of the region's land but less than one-third of its population. With the exception of a dozen small, 19th-century mill cities in Maine and New Hampshire, this is the rural New England pictured in *Yankee* magazine, peopled by self-sufficient individuals (many of them urban transplants) in touch with the land.

Visitors with only a week for the entire region tend to shortchange northern New England. Boston, after all, demands at least a couple of days, and a ferry ride to Nantucket, a concert in Newport (Rhode Island), maybe dinner in

Portsmouth (New Hampshire), and an overnight across the Piscataqua River in Kittery or York (Maine) barely leaves time to stop by Mystic Seaport (Connecticut).

Many Americans, of course, explore New England sporadically, throughout a lifetime. Shepherded as youngsters by their parents to see "where it all began," they may return as students to discover the summer scene on the Cape and Vineyard, maybe to honeymoon in a country inn, and later to rent a cottage on a Maine lake where their children learn to swim and row; the children themselves may return to perfect their nautical skills at a Maine or New Hampshire summer camp.

The following overview of the six New England states attempts to highlight not only those areas of obvious interest to visitors but also more special, out-of-the-way regions. In addition we've described several interstate itineraries, as you may not want to limit yourself to state (or national) borders.

CONNECTICUT

While New Yorkers tend to drive up the western edge of Connecticut through the rural, if gentrified, Litchfield Hills to the cultural mecca of the Berkshires in Massachusetts and to Vermont's Champlain Valley, most everyone else follows the more obvious route (Interstate 95) northeast along Long Island Sound. Connecticut's so-called Gold Coast—really New York City exurbia—stretches from New York to New Haven, which is itself worth a stop if only to visit Yale University and its museums, and perhaps to take in a show at the Long Wharf Theatre. In Madison, just a half hour's drive east along the shore from New Haven, is dune-backed Hammonassett State Beach, with good birding and walking as well as swimming in the calm waters of the Sound. The shore town of Mystic, another half hour up I-95 and just west of the Rhode Island border, harbors two of the state's most-visited attractions: Mystic Marinelife Aquarium and Mystic Seaport, a re-creation of the 19th-century seaside village.

Perhaps more appealing to many are the less-travelled corners of the state, like the rolling Litchfield Hills in the northwest, where sophisticated inns welcome visitors in exquisite small towns like Canaan, West Cornwall, and Litchfield itself, a gathering of 18th-century mansions. The landscape in Connecticut's northeasternmost sector—the so-called Quiet Corner—is similar to that in the northwest; here the communities of handsome old wooden villages bear the names Woodstock, Pomfret, and Brooklyn. Inns and bed-and-breakfasts are also scattered along the Lower Connecticut River Valley, the oldest route to northern New England, and one that still works.

The Connecticut River Valley

A trip up the Connecticut River Valley might begin with an overnight stay at Old Saybrook Point (where the river meets the Sound), followed by a day or two in the picturesque old river towns of Essex, Ivoryton, and East Haddam, the last the home of the Victorian-era Goodspeed Opera House, which stages American musicals. The sizable city and state capital, Hartford, farther upriver, has fallen prey to many of the problems that beset urban areas nationwide, but it does have a couple of attractions to recommend it. The 1842 Wadsworth Atheneum is an exceptional art museum whose holdings span some 5,000 years, and Mark Twain's 1870s mansion may well be the most interesting historical house in all New England.

Continue north across the Massachusetts state line to Springfield, an old (settled 1636) city with an impressive collection of small museums (historic, art, and science) and home to the Basketball Hall of Fame. In the college town of Northampton, 20 miles (32 km) north of Springfield, survey the Main Street crafts shops and the outstanding collections of the Smith College Museum of Art, and have lunch in one of the town's many restaurants. For a second overnight, bed-and-breakfasts are plentiful in the hill towns just to the west and north along the river.

Just 10 miles (16 km) or so over the Vermont line is the gateway city of Brattleboro, a good place to shop and get something to eat; from here continue north on I-91 along a particularly scenic stretch of the highway that parallels the river. Before you get to the mid-valley towns of Woodstock and Hanover, detour up the toll road to the top of Mount Ascutney, yielding panoramic views of the river valley and of lakes and mountains in both central Vermont and New Hampshire. Spend a day between Woodstock, Vermont, and Hanover, New Hampshire, the former a Vermont resort town where the sport of skiing first made an impact on the state, the latter the home of Dartmouth College. Continue on up through the Upper Valley towns—there are plenty of good places to stay on either side of the river—and at St. Johnsbury turn either west toward Burlington or east toward the White Mountains and I-93 back to Boston.

RHODE ISLAND

Rhode Island, New England's—and the country's—smallest state, is home to the region's largest resort: **Newport**. With its genuine Colonial neighborhood and more than 100 opulent 19th-century summer mansions, Newport continues to attract yachters, socialites, and music lovers (for summer jazz, folk, and chamber-music festivals). But because Newport is situated on a narrow peninsula—technically it is an island—the traffic can be dreadful in summer, especially during one of the city's many festivals. Try to come midweek or off-season; Newport is pleasant in spring as well as fall, and month-long "Christmas in Newport" festivities make it particularly appealing in December.

Providence, the state capital, has profited from its status as New England's second city. Handsome 18th- and early-19th-century wooden houses, the kind that in downtown Boston were long ago replaced by high rises, still line the narrow streets on College Hill, which is also home to Brown University and the Rhode Island School of Design. Stroll down Benefit Street, which was laid out in the 1750s, perhaps stopping at the 1851 Providence Athenaeum and at the School of Design's Museum of Art; then get a taste of the student life in the cafés along Thayer Street. While the downtown area has seen better times (it is currently undergoing much renovation), you might want to at least stop in at the Arcade, built in 1828 as the country's first enclosed shopping mall; and at the McKim, Mead & White State House, which boasts the second-largest unsupported dome in the world (after St. Paul's in Rome).

Block Island and the Connecticut/Rhode Island Shore

Accessible by boat from Montauk at the tip of Long Island, New York; from New London, Connecticut; and from Newport and Port Galilee, Rhode Island, as well as by air, Block Island is a low-key retreat with a number of Victorian hotels, all booked solid for most of the summer. It's easier to get a room in September.

East of Mystic and the picturesque old fishing village of Stonington, Connecticut, the shore is fringed with white sand, much of it in the form of beautiful barrier beaches, along Block Island Sound. Unfortunately, most of this sand is backed by private beach cottages, and public strands like East Beach at the Ninigret Conservation Area in Charlestown offer limited parking. The Victorian-era village of Watch Hill offers the surest access to sand and lodging.

MASSACHUSETTS

Boston

When it comes to gracefully mixing soaring glass and concrete with the mellow brick past, few American cities can match Boston. Boston has managed to retain a vital, walkable downtown and one of the world's oldest (slow but safe) subway systems. Visitors are encouraged to walk a total of two miles along the so-called Freedom Trail from the Boston Common, a large inner-city park where Puritans once pastured their cows and where British militia trained, past downtown Revolutionary landmarks like Old South Meetinghouse and Faneuil Hall Marketplace, and on through the still residential North End, where Paul Revere's house, still in the family, is now open to the public. Along the way there's plenty of good shopping, and more shops along Newbury Street in the city's 19th-century Back Bay neighborhood and around Harvard Square across the Charles River in **Cambridge**.

Appealing during the winter theater and concert season, Boston is equally memorable in spring, when the magnolias bloom along Commonwealth Avenue, and in summer, when the waterfront quickens with strollers, café life, harbor excursion boats, and ferries to Provincetown, at the tip of the Cape.

The Boston area's population (more than half a million in 1990) is still far greater than the total of all the other New England states, excepting Connecticut (which can be included in this equation if we disregard its southernmost towns and cities, satellite communities of New York City). Boston remains the region's major port—air as well as sea—and its political and intellectual hub.

Cape Cod and the Islands

In Massachusetts summer is, of course, the season for the beaches of Cape Cod and the islands of Nantucket and Martha's Vineyard. Together these resort areas offer the lion's share of the region's public sand. But in New England even beach resorts are historic: Communities like Edgartown, on Martha's Vineyard, and Nantucket Town could still serve as backdrops for a whaling movie set in the 1820s.

Cape Cod and the Islands are mobbed in summer, further plagued by weekend access problems as beach-goers try to squeeze over the two four-lane bridges that span the canal that separates the Cape from the mainland. Most of these are Bostonians and New Yorkers rather than visitors from any farther away, and most are renting houses rather than staying in inns, which tend to be very expensive in July and August. All this doesn't mean you shouldn't come, but beware of weekends. June, September, and October are the best times to visit; prices and crowds are down, and the weather is still good.

The Other Massachusetts

A case can be made that Massachusetts is visited by fewer tourists than is any other New England state. Two regions, Boston and the Cape and Islands, constitute just one-third of the state's area (but three-fourths of its people). The rest of the state—which includes historic North Shore towns like Salem, Gloucester, and Marblehead as well as the whaling port of New Bedford to the south of Boston—gets incredibly shortchanged. All of it, that is, except for the small piece of the southern Berkshire Mountains that's equated with music (Tanglewood, the summer home of the Boston Symphony Orchestra, is in the Berkshire town of Lenox), theater, and dance in July and August, when it is deluged with New Yorkers.

Even the northern Berkshires, with two outstanding art museums—the Clark Art Institute (32 Renoirs and a great collection of 19th-century American art) and the Williams College Art Museum, both in Williamstown—receives relatively little notice.

It's not that we think every corner of Massachusetts is worth exploring. For example, aside from its art museum and the Higgins Armory, Worcester is a quick study, as are most of the other tired old mill towns whose reasons for existence died in the late 19th century. There are also pockets as forgotten as anything to be found in the farthest corners of Maine.

On the other hand, the so-called "hill towns" west of the Connecticut River Valley and east of the Berkshires have changed remarkably little since the 1820s, and harbor an unusual number of writers, artists, and, especially, craftspeople—in fact this area is frequently cited as one of the largest concentrations of craftspeople in the country. The artists' work is showcased in the outstanding lineup of galleries in Northampton and in rural cooperatives like those in Leverett, just north of Amherst, and Shelburne Falls, on the Mohawk Trail (Route 2). The hill towns are set in a landscape of humped mountains that's as beautiful as the Berkshires or southern Vermont and that offers its share of summer music and theater, as well as a number of inns, bed-and-breakfasts, and farms, most of them opened in the past ten years.

The cultural heart of western Massachusetts is "the Five College Area," so named for the five campuses (Amherst, Hampshire, Smith, and Mount Holyoke colleges and the University of Massachusetts) scattered over the valley floor in Northampton, Amherst, and South Hadley. The tripling of the student body during the 1970s and early '80s at the University of Massachusetts in Amherst has dramatically affected this area, as thousands of graduates have stayed on, opening restaurants and shops in the valley or settling in the hill towns.

VERMONT

Of all the New England states Vermont has best managed to project the image of unspoiled, essentially rural scenery, and of the classic village with white-clapboard houses and steepled churches, a funky general store (a wheel of Vermont cheddar on the counter), and a comfortable old inn with requisite white columns and gourmet meals.

It's not that there isn't an ugly strip here and there—for example, there are the stretches of Route 7 south of Burlington and Route 5 north of Brattleboro and the piece of road between Montpelier and Barre. But in contrast to New Hampshire, where both the people and the pollution are clustered in the Merrimack Valley while the mountains are off to the north, Vermont's mountains run down the length of an essentially rural state. Burlington (with 7 percent of Vermont's population), on Lake Champlain in the northwest corner, is Vermont's only real city. And even it is easily accessible and welcoming to visitors, with shops concentrated in the (car-free) Church Street Marketplace area and a waterfront with a boathouse and rental boats for paddling out onto Lake Champlain.

While purists complain that Vermont was over-gentrified in the 1980s, the Green Mountain State has nonetheless managed to recharge its economy while preserving its landscape, creating the country's most tasteful road signs (no billboards) and setting national environmental standards for ski resort expansion.

Aside from Stowe, Manchester, and Woodstock, Vermont claims no resort towns. More than any other New England state it succeeds in dispersing visitors evenly throughout its length and width—to explore back roads in search of artisans, antiques shops, and that certain something that historian Ralph Nading Hill articulates in his *Yankee Kingdom*. Vermont's serene white towns, Hill writes, have become a universal symbol of nostalgia, of belonging somewhere.

Foliage season aside (see Useful Facts, below), Vermont's lodging prices vary with the nature of the community and the degree to which it caters to skiers or summer people. As an extreme example of this practice, in the town of Manchester inns on the upland side of town, nearest to Bromley and Stratton ski areas, rates are higher in winter than in summer, while on the western fringe of town the opposite situation holds. What many people don't realize is that Vermont's ski areas represent a great value to travelling families in summer:

The condominiums that cluster at the mountain's base offer all the amenities at a fraction of what they cost in winter, and prove to be a far better value than the inns, most of which cater to couples. Farms also represent a great alternative for families, and a chance to meet Vermonters.

Generally speaking, the most visited parts of Vermont coincide with ski resorts, along the length of the Green Mountains from Wilmington and West Dover (Mount Snow) in the south up through Killington and Woodstock in Central Vermont, and from there up through Sugarbush and Stowe to Jay Peak (mobbed on winter weekends by skiers from Montreal) in the far north.

If you are looking for legendary Vermont farmscapes you'll find some around ski towns, but the chief patches are south of Middlebury, north of Burlington, in the Chelsea–Tunbridge area south of Montpelier, and in the high, rolling plateau around Craftsbury in the Northeast Kingdom (the remote northeastern corner of the state).

There is no single strategy for exploring Vermont. Back in the 1930s a skyline highway like the one in the Blue Ridge mountains was proposed for Vermont that would have cut just beneath the peaks of Killington and Sugarbush. After a year or so of heated debate the proposal was defeated by a general vote in the state. The feeling was that Vermonters didn't want to make their state that accessible. Perhaps that's one reason that Interstate 89, a 1970s phenomenon, doesn't really seem to serve any of the obvious places besides Montpelier and Burlington. The two most travelled roads in the state are Route 9, running east–west between Brattleboro and Bennington, and Route 100, which runs almost the entire length of the state. Rather than follow either of these highways exclusively, we recommend cutting back and forth across the state through high "gaps" in the mountains, slicing across Vermont's narrow width for a quick and dramatic sense of its variety.

NEW HAMPSHIRE

Because of the state's high mountains and dense forests, in the 17th century New Hampshire's settlement was limited largely to the coastal Portsmouth area; in the 18th century settlers moved slowly into the Merrimack Valley and up the Connecticut River. In the 1770s the inhabitants of the towns along both the Vermont and New Hampshire sides of the Connecticut River still felt far enough from everywhere else to attempt to form a state of their own ("New Connecticut").

During the Industrial Revolution in the mid- and late 19th century European immigrants swarmed into the new brick cities of Manchester, Concord, and Nashua to work in the mills powered by the river; this area, along with the state's abbreviated coast, still accounts for two-thirds of New Hampshire's residents.

New Hampshire's long-beaten "tourist trail" is clearly defined. The usual route is north up Route 16 from the coast to North Conway (known for its outlet shopping), up to the top of Mount Washington (New England's highest peak), and back down the western side of the White Mountains through dramatic Franconia Notch and then I-93 south to Boston, perhaps with a stop at one of the magnificent lakes in the central part of the state.

New Hampshire was the most heavily touristed of all the New England states in the 19th century, but for much of the 20th century—from the time its old summer hotels began closing in the 1930s until the '80s—it offered relatively few appealing places to stay beyond this narrow trail. The hundreds of bed-and-breakfasts that have opened throughout the state within the past decade have changed that situation, but so far the travelling public really hasn't noticed.

New Hampshire's winter ski resorts—such as Waterville Valley, Cannon, Wildcat, and Loon Mountain—tend to be flooded on weekends by Bostonians; midweek they are relatively empty, offering savings well below most rates at similar Vermont resorts. And as in Vermont the peak season is fall, for the foliage. Here, too, prices tend to be higher on the state's narrow tourist trail, specifically North Conway and the Route 302–Route 116 tour around Mount Washington that the state's tourism bureaus advise everyone to drive.

If you're looking to avoid the tourist trail, visit the exquisite villages, inns, mountain trails, and summer concerts in the Monadnock Region, in the southwestern corner of the state; the sleepy old river towns of the Upper Connecticut Valley, such as Lyme, Orford, and Haverhill; and the so-called Western Lakes region, which includes Sunapee and Newfound lakes.

The White Mountains and the Northeast Kingdom
On one possible interstate itinerary you might travel from Boston up I-93 through the spectacular chasm of Franconia Notch in New Hampshire's White Mountains, taking the time to do some hiking and to stay at one of the many inns and bed-and-breakfasts in the Franconia area. You could then continue on (it's just a half hour) to St. Johnsbury in Vermont's Northeast Kingdom, stopping to visit the Fairbanks Museum and Planetarium, with its huge collection of mounted wildlife and ethnographic pieces, and the St. Johnsbury Athenaeum and Art Galley, home to Albert Bierstadt's *Domes of Yosemite* (and much more). After lunch here you might head up through

Danville and Greensboro to Craftsbury Common, considered by many to be the state's most picturesque farming community, then down to the famous ski town of Stowe, 45 minutes to the southeast.

MAINE

If you have only a week or less to visit New England, it's best not to try to get too far "down" (north and east, that is) Maine's coast; all you will do is get bogged down in traffic on Route 1. Between them the Yorks and Kittery Point on the south coast offer a fair sampling of what the Maine coast is about, so it makes sense to cut west across southern New Hampshire from the coast on scenic Route 4/202, stopping in the antiquing center of Northwood for lunch, and pick up I-93 north to Franconia, as suggested above. If you have a week or more to devote exclusively to Maine, however, the coast and interior of the state offer numerous possibilities.

Coastal Maine

The ironic thing about Maine is that despite its huge dimensions more than half its tourists never explore beyond the 50-mile stretch of coast south of Portland. A large percentage of those who do tend to keep to a narrow and frequently crowded tourist trail that consists of resort villages—Kennebunkport, Boothbay, Camden, and Bar Harbor—spaced like stepping stones along the coast.

Our advice is to stray off Route 1 as quickly as you can. Explore at least one of Maine's many peninsulas and one island. Go beyond Bar Harbor to find coastal Maine as it was three decades ago. Hike in the inland wilderness that's Baxter State Park, drift out on Rangeley or Moosehead Lake to watch moose feeding at dusk, and try white-water rafting through Kennebec Gorge. Mid-Maine is relatively dull, but the way to the north woods and the Upper Kennebec is through Augusta, which does have an outstanding state museum.

Exploring Maine in any depth requires a real time commitment. You need a couple of days, preferably a week, to explore a peninsula, and to take only a day trip to an island like Monhegan is to miss what it is about. Mount Desert Island, much of which is given over to Acadia National Park, also demands several days, time to hike its numerous trails, to paddle or bike, and to take a boat ride as well as to drive the scenic Park Loop Road. To continue down east through the lobstering villages of Washington County (as far east as you can get in the United States) and on to the islands of Passamaquoddy Bay (the mouth of the St. Croix River, which divides the United States from Canada), requires still another couple of days at least.

Inland Maine

Varied and vast, inland Maine is underrated, perhaps because its magnificent mountains are less well known than their Vermont and New Hampshire counterparts. The mountains serve as backdrops for numberless lakes; those in southwestern Maine tend to be surrounded by summer "camps" (the local name for private cottages as well as children's programs), but farther north only the odd "sporting camp" interrupts the greenery (Maine's sporting camps, usually consisting of a group of cabins around a central lodge, are spotted throughout the north woods). Access to campsites along the Allagash Wilderness Waterway and in Baxter State Park, public preserves within this private fiefdom, is strictly limited.

Off-season Maine

Maine has a very short "high" season—July and August—and many coastal inns and inland sporting camps are open only from June through early September. Late September can be a great time to come; it's still warm but less crowded, and lodging rates are lower. Maine's foliage season is also a relatively well-kept secret; in western Maine especially there are plenty of maple and other foliage trees as well as firs. Maine's two big ski resorts, Sugarloaf/USA and Sunday River, are both routinely rated among the nation's top ski destinations, but, because of the way the roads run (to Boston rather than New York), they are relatively less crowded than comparable Vermont resorts.

Combining Maine with New Brunswick and/or Quebec

The route to Quebec City is up the Kennebec Valley, Maine's white-water rafting center. The scenic route to New Brunswick is along the coast of Washington County to Campobello Island or across Passamaquoddy Bay via small ferries from Eastport to the resort area around St. Andrews, New Brunswick. You can also take an overnight ferry either from Portland or Bar Harbor to Yarmouth, Nova Scotia.

USEFUL FACTS

When to Go

New England changes dramatically with each season. From late December to March, skiing at dozens of northern New England ski resorts is guaranteed by the world's largest concentration of snow-making equipment. Cross-country skiing is also reliable at a half-dozen resorts with well-groomed trails.

March is the month that divides northern from southern New England. In Maine, Vermont, and New Hampshire, March is synonymous with moderate snowfall, spring skiing, and maple sugaring (tapping maple trees), while in Boston and points south it's just windy, cold, and bleak. In April, however, southern New England begins to bloom, while "up-country" it's still "mud season." May brings spring flowers throughout the region, and on Memorial Day weekend (the last of the month) state parks and many rural museums officially open for the summer.

The best time to visit New England is between June and October. In June wild roses bloom on Cape Cod, and by early July summer music and theater festivals are in full swing throughout New England. August is the traditional month for exploring Maine, from its north woods lakes to island coves. Weather remains dependable through September—a quiet month, when lodging is easier to come by and cheaper than in either summer or "foliage season"—those weeks during which much of the rest of the country heads northeast to see the hills turn red and gold.

"Foliage" is both the region's most famous and its most misunderstood season. Foliage season rates, imposed by many inns throughout New England, begin in mid-September and extend through mid-October, but the color itself does not necessarily comply. In northern Vermont and in New Hampshire's White Mountains leaves begin to turn at higher elevations around the middle of September and "peak" by the last weekend of the month. By Columbus Day (the second weekend in October) color is usually brightest in central and southern Maine, New Hampshire, and Vermont and in the hill towns of western Massachusetts. Connecticut hills are usually at their brightest the following week. (Maine, incidentally, offers its share of fall colors, but its resort towns—from Bethel on the western edge of the White Mountains to such beach towns as Kennebunkport—are relatively uncrowded.)

The three-day Columbus Day weekend aside, visitors should be able to find lodging during foliage season. A few Vermont towns are particularly well equipped to meet the increased demand, and their respective chambers of commerce can help place visitors in private homes when inns and motels are filled (Middlebury, Tel: 802/388-7951; Woodstock, Tel: 802/457-3555; and St. Johnsbury, Tel: 802/748-3678).

Boston, with its theaters, museums, galleries, and shops, is a lively winter city, and its elaborate First Night celebrations—the New Year's Eve parade, fireworks, continuous live entertainment, and free public transit—have been copied by cities throughout the country.

In the Berkshires of western Massachusetts the liveliest six weeks of the year are July through mid-August, when Tanglewood has its season and the Boston Symphony Orchestra resides in Lenox, playing frequent concerts. Most inns insist on three- or four-day weekend reservations during this period.

What to Wear

New England weather is famously fickle, changing frequently. In winter snow and rain are likely, along with clear, cold (below freezing) days; in summer temperatures can soar, then suddenly dip when the wind changes. Rain gear, sweaters, and sturdy, comfortable shoes are advisable year-round. Traditionally Yankees have been "tweedy" rather than chic, adopting styles set by the region's many college campuses rather than by New York or Paris.

Entry Documents

The United States requires a passport and visitor's visa or long-term visa of visitors from Europe, Australia, and New Zealand. Canadians and Japanese need only proof of citizenship.

Arrival at Major Gateways by Air

Boston's **Logan International Airport** (Tel: 617/567-5400) is New England's air hub and is served by 54 airlines, including some 16 foreign national airlines. British Airways, Virgin Atlantic, TWA, and Northwest fly from London; Qantas, Northwest, American, and Continental fly from Sydney; Air Canada services Montreal, Halifax, and Toronto; and Delta services Montreal. Hourly shuttle service to New York is offered by USAir and Delta, and to Washington by USAir.

Logan is just 3 miles (5 km) northeast of downtown Boston, linked to the city by the **MBTA** (Massachusetts Bay Transportation Authority, better known as the T) and by the Airport Water Shuttle as well as by taxis and vans. The subway is the fastest way into town, especially during rush hours. Free airport buses stop at every terminal and shuttle passengers to the MBTA's Airport station on the Blue Line; from there it's a ten-minute ride to downtown Boston.

A free van also circles among the terminals and connects with the **Airport Water Shuttle** (Tel: 617/439-3131), unquestionably the most dramatic way to approach Boston. The boat, which takes just 7 minutes to reach Rowes Wharf on the downtown waterfront (handy to the financial district), costs $7 and runs every 15 minutes Monday through Friday from 6:00 A.M. to 8:00 P.M. and Sundays from noon to 8:00 P.M.

Taxis are usually plentiful at Logan and cost from $15 to $20 to downtown Boston and Cambridge; while there's no official cab-sharing program, doubling up with other passengers is common.

Vans, which also stop at all terminals and drop off passengers at most downtown Boston hotels, cost from $5.50 to $6.50. For details about ground transportation, Tel: (800) 23-LOGAN.

About a dozen car-rental firms are represented at the airport, but Boston is no place to drive if you can avoid it. Rent a car only when you are ready to leave the city.

Burlington International Airport (Tel: 802/863-2874), a gateway to Vermont ski areas, is served from most U.S. cities via United Airlines, USAir, Continental, Northwest Airlink, and Delta Connection. **Manchester Airport** (Tel: 603/624-6539) offers quick access to New Hampshire ski areas from Washington, Philadelphia, and Chicago via United Airlines and USAir. **Portland International Jetport** (Tel: 207/773-8462) in Maine receives direct flights from Chicago, Newark, Philadelphia, and Washington, via Delta, Continental, United, and USAir, and from Boston via Delta, Continental, and USAir. **Bradley International Airport** (Tel: 203/292-2000), in Windsor Locks, Connecticut, serves the Hartford/Springfield area, receiving flights from most U.S. cities and Toronto via Air Ontario, American, Continental, Delta, United, and USAir. **T.F. Green State Airport** (Tel: 401/737-4000), in Warwick, Rhode Island, receives flights from New York, Chicago, Philadelphia, Baltimore, Washington, D.C., Atlanta, Detroit, Orlando, and Raleigh via American, Continental, Delta, Northwest, USAir, and United Airlines.

Departure
The standard $6 departure tax is charged upon leaving the United States by air.

Arrival by Train
Amtrak (Tel: 800/872-7245) stations in Boston and New Haven, Connecticut, have been splendidly restored, but service is limited to the Eastern Corridor (Boston, New York, Philadelphia, Washington, D.C., and major points between), with connections available to Florida, Chicago, and Montreal. (It is easier to get to Montreal by train from New York City, which has two direct trains a day, than from Boston.) New Haven's Union Station is also served by frequent **Metro-North Commuter Railroad** (Tel: 212/532-4900) trains from New York City and is a good place to pick up a rental car (Thrifty Car Rental is not far away; Tel: 203/562-3191) if you want to explore New England from Connecticut.

Arrival by Bus

Boston has no one central bus terminal. **Greyhound Bus Lines** (Tel: 617/423-5810), at 2 South Station, on Atlantic Avenue where it meets Summer Street, serves New York City and Albany, New York, with connections to points west. (See "Travel within New England," next, for more information on bus travel in the region.)

Travel within New England

For foreign visitors determined to see America without driving long distances, Amtrak's **USA Rail Pass** (available to overseas visitors, not Canadians or Mexicans) offers unlimited train travel in the country for 45 days (Tel: 800/872-7245).

Boston is the East Coast departure point for **Green Tortoise** buses (Tel: 617/265-8533 or 800/227-4766), one of the most inexpensive and unconventional ways to travel across America. Departing twice monthly, May through October, these refitted sleep-in buses meander across the country for 10 or 14 days, following either a southern route through New Orleans and the Grand Canyon (spring and fall) or a northern course via Chicago, South Dakota's Badlands, and several other national parks during summer months. In 1992 the 14-day trip cost $349 per person, plus $81 for food.

Within New England it's difficult to explore the region by train or bus, but it can be done. **Vermont Transit** (Tel: 800/451-3292) links most major Vermont towns with Boston's Greyhound terminal (at 2 South Station) and Logan Airport.

Concord Trailways (Tel: 617/426-8080), based at Boston's Peter Pan/Trailways Station, 555 Atlantic Avenue (across from South Station), serves most New Hampshire cities and resort areas; Concord also accesses the "high huts" maintained by the Appalachian Mountain Club for hikers in the White Mountains. **Peter Pan Bus** (Tel: 617/426-8557 or 800/237-8747) serves much of western Massachusetts, and **Bonanza Bus Lines** (Tel: 401/751-8800 or 800/556-3815) serves Boston's Back Bay/South End train station as well as Providence, Rhode Island, and connects with the **Steamship Authority** ferries (Tel: 508/540-2022) out of Woods Hole, Massachusetts, to the islands of Nantucket and Martha's Vineyard. **Greyhound** buses (Tel: 617/423-5810) travel to Portland, Maine, but the Portland terminal is not within walking distance of downtown attractions or the **Prince of Fundy Cruises**' passenger/car ferry to Yarmouth, Nova Scotia (Tel: 207/775-5616).

Out of Boston, the **Bay State Cruise Company** (Tel: 617/723-7800) offers seasonal day trips to Provincetown on the tip of Cape Cod (as well as whale-watching, Boston Harbor, and other cruises).

Note that Logan Airport is also the hub for small airlines serving the rest of the region, including Cape Cod, Nantucket, and Martha's Vineyard in Massachusetts; Burlington, Vermont; and Portland, Rockland, and Bar Harbor, Maine. Cape Air serves Hyannis, Martha's Vineyard, and Nantucket, in Massachusetts (Tel: 800/352-0714), and Continental Express serves Bar Harbor, Maine (Tel: 617/569-8400).

Driving

More than 50 car-rental agencies are represented in the Boston area, and it pays to shop around. These generally require an international driver's permit and that the motorist be 25 or older. Seat belts are required for all front-seat passengers in Connecticut and for children aged 12 and under in Massachusetts and Maine.

A car is the last thing you need in Boston, which is a walking city, one unusually well served by a clean, safe public transportation system (the MBTA), which offers special three- and nine-day "Tourist Passports." To truly explore the rest of New England, however, a car is necessary. From Boston interstate highways radiate north (I-93 to New Hampshire and Vermont and I-95 to Maine), west (Route 90, the Massachusetts Turnpike), and south (I-95 to Connecticut and New York City).

Accommodations

New England is known for the variety of its independently owned lodging places: grand 19th-century resorts, country inns, farms, bed-and-breakfasts, motels, and cottages.

Boston's dozen or so luxury hotels offer discounted and family rates in summer and on weekends. All are within walking distance of downtown sights or the T (subway). There are also a number of bed-and-breakfasts in the Boston and Cambridge area; see the Accommodations section of that chapter, below. Rather than drive into Boston, however, you may also want to consider staying in Salem or in Concord, both with access to downtown Boston via commuter rail. Note that there are also excellent places to stay in some of New England's smaller cities, notably in Hartford, Connecticut; Portland, Maine; and Burlington, Vermont.

A number of mansions turned inns in **Newport** constitute the lion's share of interesting places to stay in Rhode Island, while **Connecticut** inns, found primarily along the coast and in the Litchfield hills, are priced for the New York market.

Motels and inns in **Massachusetts** beyond Boston are concentrated in the primary tourist destinations of Cape Cod and the islands of Martha's Vineyard and Nantucket. In western Massachusetts, Berkshire County, especially around the town of Lenox (where Tanglewood is the summer home of the Boston Symphony Orchestra), also offers a wide variety of lodging choices, as does the Cape Ann town of Rockport (accessible from Boston by train). The *Massachusetts Bed and Breakfast Guide,* published by the Massachusetts Office of Travel and Tourism (Tel: 617/727-3201), describes B and Bs throughout the state.

Vermont is known for its country inns scattered throughout the state (rental cottages and condominiums are described in the booklet *Four Season Vacation Rentals,* available from the Vermont Travel Division; Tel: 802/828-3236), and **New Hampshire** for its two surviving old White Mountain resorts, the Balsams in Dixville Notch and the Mount Washington at Bretton Woods. Self-contained ski areas in both Maine and Vermont offer reasonably priced, condominium-style bases from which to explore in summer.

Inns and B and Bs abound along the coast of **Maine** from Kittery to Bar Harbor, but reservations are necessary in July and August. Note that prices in Maine tend to be lower outside such well-known resort towns as Ogunquit, Kennebunkport, Boothbay, Camden, and Bar Harbor. A brochure describing farm B and Bs is available from the Maine Department of Agriculture, State House Station 28, Augusta, ME 04333; Tel: (207) 289-3491. Rental cottages throughout the state are detailed in the annual booklet *Maine, Guide to Camp and Cottage Rentals,* available from the Maine Publicity Bureau; Tel: (800) 533-9595 or (207) 582-9300.

In this book we do not attempt to include every acceptable inn and bed-and-breakfast. Two outstanding guidebooks that do are *Best Places to Stay in New England,* by Christina Tree and Kimberly Grant; and *America's Wonderful Little Hotels and Inns, New England,* by Sandra W. Soule.

See also "For Further Information," below.

Telephoning

The international country code for the United States is 1. The area code for Boston and immediate suburbs is 617; for other eastern Massachusetts towns 508; for western Massachusetts 413; for Vermont 802; for Maine 207; for New Hampshire 603; for Connecticut 203; and for Rhode Island 401.

Local Time

New England is in the eastern standard time zone and observes daylight saving time from November through April. The area is three hours ahead of Los Angeles and San Francisco, two hours ahead of Denver and Calgary, and one hour ahead of Chicago and Winnipeg; it is five hours behind

London and 15 hours behind Sydney. (The Canadian provinces of New Brunswick and Nova Scotia are one hour ahead of New England.)

Currency

Foreign currency may be exchanged for U.S. dollars at the BayBank branches in Terminals D and E at Boston's Logan Airport. The exchange rate is equal to that at other BayBank branches throughout the Boston area. The Bank of Boston branches also exchange a wide range of currencies, as does the Cambridge Trust Company, 1336 Massachusetts Avenue in Harvard Square.

The exchange rates vary; for large transactions it's wise to also check the rates offered by Thomas Cook Currency Services (Tel: 617/426-0016), an exchange broker at 160 Franklin Street, or with American Express (Tel: 617/723-8400), 1 Court Street, both in downtown Boston.

Most larger shops and restaurants throughout New England accept credit cards, especially VISA, MasterCard, and American Express. To report lost or stolen credit cards, to make balance inquiries, or for other matters, call American Express, Tel: (800) 528-4800; MasterCard, Tel: (800) 223-9920; VISA, Tel: (800) 336-8472. Traveller's checks are also widely accepted, although a surprising number of establishments are reluctant to honor them. To report lost or stolen traveller's checks, contact American Express, Tel: (800) 221-7282; BankAmerica, Tel: (800) 227-3460; Interpayment (Barclays), Tel: (800) 221-2426; Cooks, Tel: (800) 223-7373; or VISA, Tel: (800) 227-6811. Bankcard holders who subscribe to the Cirrus and Plus networks (instant cash) will find outlets throughout New England.

Electric Current

Current in the entire United States is 110/120 volts, 60 cycles. Foreign-made appliances may require adapters and North American flat-blade plugs.

Business Hours and Holidays

Business hours are generally 9:00 A.M. to 5:00 P.M. Monday through Friday; banks tend to open and close earlier, and many are open Saturday mornings. Shopping malls, department stores, convenience stores, and supermarkets are generally open seven days a week, but many smaller stores still close on Sundays. In Massachusetts and Connecticut liquor cannot be sold in stores on Sundays (nor after 8:00 P.M. Saturdays in Connecticut).

Government agencies, banks, and post offices close for a number of national holidays: New Year's Day (January 1);

Martin Luther King's birthday (the first Monday after January 15); Presidents' Day, honoring George Washington and Abraham Lincoln (observed on a Monday in mid-February); Memorial Day (last Monday in May); Independence Day (July 4); Columbus Day (second Monday in October); Veterans Day (November 11); Thanksgiving Day (fourth Thursday in November); and Christmas Day (December 25). In addition there are local holidays: Both Evacuation Day (March 17), which also happens to be St. Patrick's Day, and Patriots' Day (the first Monday after April 19), which coincides with the Boston Marathon, are widely observed in and around Boston. In Vermont state offices and some businesses close August 17 in observance of Bennington Battle Day.

Safety and Security Precautions
Boston has its share of street crime and more than its share of auto theft. Lock your car at all times and do not cross Boston Common at night. Thanks to the city's large student population, the subways are, however, relatively well used and safe at night.

Experiencing New England
Three organizations, two based in New England and one world-wide, offer alternative means of exploring the region. The most famous of these is the **Appalachian Mountain Club** (AMC), founded in 1876 to blaze and map hiking trails through the White Mountains of New Hampshire. The nonprofit AMC maintains eight alpine huts, each ranged a day's hike apart along mountain trails, and each offering hearty meals as well as bunks so that hikers need carry only daypacks. The AMC also offers nominally priced meals and lodging at its Pinkham Notch Base Camp at the eastern base of Mount Washington; the camp is also the starting point for daily guided hikes as well as a year-round program of workshops on topics ranging from watercolor and photography to canoeing, kayaking, and backpacking. Contact the AMC at P.O. Box 298, Pinkham Notch Camp, Gorham, NH 03581; Tel: (800) 262-4455 or (603) 466-2721. (See also the New Hampshire chapter, below.)

The **Maine Windjammers** also bears special mention; each of the dozen two-masted (and one three-masted) schooners offers a sense of the Maine coast and its islands simply unattainable by any other means (unless you own your own yacht). Don't confuse these vessels with their Caribbean counterparts: Drinking, while permitted, is not encouraged, and passengers are invited (although not pressured) to help peel potatoes for the chowder, tidy up in the galley, and to hoist the anchor and haul in the sails. The schooners tend to be captained by their owners and their spouses, most of whom have restored or built the craft from scratch. Rates are reasonable. For details, contact the Maine Windjammer Association, P.O. Box 317, Rockport, ME 04853, Tel: (800) 624-6380; or Windjammer Wharf, 70 Elm Street, Camden, ME 04843, Tel: (800) 999-7352 or (207) 236-3520.

Elderhostel is the third group, a world-wide organization begun in New England that offers a wide range of accommodations and academic programs at 135 New England locations—from backwoods cabins in Maine to some of New England's most prestigious campuses—designed for active, intelligent travellers aged 60 and over (spouses may be any age, but companions must be at least 50 years old). Elderhostel's headquarters are at 75 Federal Street, Boston, MA 02110; Tel: (617) 426-7788. For registration and general information, Tel: (617) 426-8056.

For Further Information

The **Greater Boston Convention & Visitors Bureau** (Prudential Tower, Suite 400, P.O. Box 490, Boston, MA 02199; Tel: 617/536-4100) publishes a guide to the city. The **Massachusetts Office of Travel and Tourism** (100 Cambridge Street, 13th floor, Boston, MA 02202; Tel: 617/727-3201 or 800/447-MASS, ext. 500) offers separate guides to attractions, hotels, and bed-and-breakfasts, as well as a calendar of events. The office will also advise you as to securing more detailed information from the state's 13 regional councils.

The **Connecticut Department of Economic Development** (865 Brook Street, Rocky Hill, CT 06067-3405; Tel: 203/258-4200 or 800/CT-BOUND) gives out the *Classic Connecticut Vacation Guide and Map*.

The **Rhode Island Tourism Division** (7 Jackson Walkway, Providence, RI 02903; Tel: 401/277-2601 or 800/556-2484) puts together visitors' packages of brochures, maps, and a calendar of events.

The **Maine Publicity Bureau**, Hallowell, ME 04347; Tel: 207/582-9300 or 800/533-9595) publishes *Maine Invites You,* a general, 300-page guide, and distributes *Inns and Bed and Breakfasts, Historic Homes and Museums, Hunting and Fishing Guide, Camp and Cottage Guide,* and a calendar of events. The publicity bureau maintains 32-year-round information centers, including those on I-95 at Kittery, just off Route 1 in Yarmouth, on I-95 in Hampden near Bangor, in Calais, and in Houlton. Travel brochures are also available to the state's 19 distinct travel districts.

The **New Hampshire Office of Travel and Tourism Development** (Box 856, Concord, NH 03302; Tel: 603/271-2343) publishes *The Official New Hampshire Guidebook,* describing attractions, events, and lodging in the state. New Hampshire also maintains information centers along its major highways, I-89 and I-93.

The **Vermont Travel Division** (134 State Street, Montpelier, VT 05602; Tel: 802/828-3236) publishes a semiannual calendar of events and guides; they also distribute the annual *Vermont Traveler's Guidebook* to attractions and lodging, an excellent road map, and the *Four Season Vacation Rentals* guide.

For information about the Canadian Maritime Provinces accessible from Maine, contact the **New Brunswick Department of Tourism and Culture** (P.O. Box 6000, Fredericton, N.B. E3B 5H1, Canada; Tel: 506/453-2444) and the **Nova Scotia Department of Tourism & Culture** (P.O. Box 456, Halifax, N.S. B3J 2R5, Canada; Tel: 902/424-4171).

—*Christina Tree*

BIBLIOGRAPHY

Social History and Public Affairs

GEORGE AIKEN, *Senate Diary: January 1972–January 1975* (1976). In this firsthand account of the Watergate years, the late and much-loved Vermont statesman reveals a great deal about his vanishing breed of wise, up-country Yankees.

CLEVELAND AMORY, *The Proper Bostonians* (1947). The original field guide to the Lowells, Cabots, Forbeses, and other Boston Brahmins, and still the best look at the ways in which New England's aristocracy exerted its moral, intellectual, and commercial influence upon the region.

BENJAMIN A. BOTKIN, *A Treasury of New England Folklore* (1947). Botkin's great trove was collected just before television and interstate highways commenced the homogenization of New England; it preserves everything from quaint turns of phrase to legends of the supernatural.

KEVIN RICHARD CASH, *Who the Hell Is William Loeb?* (1975). The life and machinations of the late publisher of the *Manchester Union Leader* provide a fascinating commentary on New Hampshire's political culture.

ROBERT P. TRISTRAM COFFIN, *Maine Doings* (1950). The Pulitzer Prize–winning poet looks back fondly at the saltwater farm of his Maine youth—at a world of lobster boats, fresh raspberries, Latin learned at the fireside, and tomcats named Calvin Coolidge.

JUDSON HALE, *Inside New England* (1982). Hale, the veteran editor of *Yankee* magazine, takes a droll view of his fellow New Englanders, recording regional quirks and characteristics now endangered by the homogenization brought on by mass media and interstate migration.

TAMARA K. HAREVEN AND RANDOLPH LANGENBACH, *Amoskeag: Life and Work in an American Factory-City* (1978). Hareven's collected oral histories, coupled with Langenbach's stark photos, document the heyday and decline of the largest textile enterprise on earth. In the process, the authors ably chronicle the immigrant experience in urban New England.

NAT HENTOFF, *Boston Boy: A Memoir* (1986). The jazz historian and social critic recalls his boyhood in Boston's Roxbury neighborhood during the 1930s and '40s.

J. ANTHONY LUKAS, *Common Ground: A Turbulent Decade in the Life of Three American Families* (1985). The 1970s school busing crisis wrenched Boston as had no other controversy since the days of the abolitionists. Here, Lukas takes a street-level view of the decade and its volatile racial politics.

PERRY MILLER, *The New England Mind: The Seventeenth Century* (1939) and *The New England Mind: From Colony to Province* (1953). Harvard's Miller, the greatest scholar of New England intellectual history, here traces the workings of the Puritan mind and its evolution into the practical yet idealistic instrument that helped forge the nation.

SAMUEL ELIOT MORISON, *One Boy's Boston: 1887 to 1901* (1962). Morison's delightful reminiscence of growing up on Beacon Hill in the 1890s, comfortable in his grandfather's house and the society of privileged equals.

HELEN AND SCOTT NEARING, *Living the Good Life* (1954). Preachy and pious enough to make one turn to a life of wretched excess, the Nearings's account of simple homesteading was a bible for the back-to-the-landers who emigrated to up-country New England in the 1960s and '70s—and who stayed to help change the region's politics and persona.

NEAL R. PEIRCE, *The New England States* (1976). Although the region's social and political circumstances have changed somewhat since Peirce combed the six states John Gunther–style, his portrayal nonetheless helps explain how things got the way they are today.

KENNETH ROBERTS, *Trending into Maine* (1938, 1944). The author of *Northwest Passage* returns to his native Maine in these essays on local traditions—farming, fishing, shipbuilding, lobstering, and small-town life. Look for the edition illustrated by N. C. Wyeth.

JOE SHERMAN, *Fast Lane on a Dirt Road: Vermont Transformed, 1945–1990* (1991). How the 20th century finally caught up with Vermont: Sherman chronicles the Green Mountain State's passage from pastoral backwater to trendy exurbia.

MARION L. STARKEY, *The Devil in Massachusetts* (1949). One of the best explications of the strange and deadly Salem witch hysteria of 300 years ago.

Literature and Literary History

LOUISA MAY ALCOTT, *Little Women* (1869). Alcott's classic of New England girlhood in the mid-19th century sheds light on the mores and family dynamics of the era, as well as on the circumstances of Alcott's upbringing in Concord, Massachusetts, as the daughter of the transcendentalist philosopher and educator Amos Bronson Alcott.

THOMAS BAILEY ALDRICH, *The Story of a Bad Boy* (1870). The "Rivermouth" of Aldrich's semi-autobiographical tale is his hometown of Portsmouth, New Hampshire; here he lives out an idyll of a boyhood not at all bad by modern standards. The Aldrich home, by the way, still stands on the grounds of Portsmouth's Strawbery Banke restoration.

VAN WYCK BROOKS, *The Flowering of New England, 1815–1865* (1936). Literary New England during the golden years from 1815 to 1865: the transcendentalists, the abolitionists, and such great names as Hawthorne, Longfellow, and Holmes.

———, *New England Indian Summer, 1865–1915* (1940). Brooks reviews New England culture and literature during the latter half of the 19th century, when the tone was set by William Dean Howells, Henry James, Emily Dickinson, Francis Parkman, and Henry Adams.

CAROLYN CHUTE, *The Beans of Egypt, Maine* (1985). A novel portraying the stark realities of the trailer-and-tarpaper culture of present-day interior Maine: It's a long way from Kennebunkport.

RALPH WALDO EMERSON, *Nature* (1836). In many ways, Emerson's essay was the inaugural text of the transcendentalist movement, New England's first native school of philosophy and literature. Emerson saw divinity in nature, and saw each individual soul as part of an "oversoul."

ROBERT FROST, *New Hampshire* (1923). The title poem of this volume is a long monologue in which Frost proclaims the persona by which the world knew him best: "I choose to be a plain New Hampshire farmer."

————, *North of Boston* (1915). Masterpieces in the New England vernacular: "Mending Wall," "After Apple-Picking," "The Death of the Hired Man," and others, in which Frost proved Yankee plain speech a fit vehicle for poetry.

JOHN GARDNER, *October Light* (1976). Gardner's central characters, the crusty Vermont farmer James L. Page and his stubborn, independent sister Sally, are archetypes of Yankee contrariness; the novel's Vermont passages make wading through the surrealistic subplot worthwhile.

NATHANIEL HAWTHORNE, *The Blithedale Romance* (1852). Based upon Hawthorne's experience with the utopian Brook Farm community near Boston, this novel looks into the quest for human perfectibility that has always been part of the New England mind. (Hawthorne remained unconvinced.)

————, *The House of the Seven Gables* (1851). The theme is guilt and expiation, the setting Salem, Massachusetts, where one of the author's own ancestors was a witch-trial judge.

————, *The Scarlet Letter* (1850). A cornerstone of the American literary canon, yes—but also a fascinating window on life in 17th-century New England.

————, *Twice-Told Tales* (1837, 1842). Many of the tales in this collection are based upon historical events in Colonial Massachusetts; in Hawthorne's hands they acquire his familiar dark gloss.

OLIVER WENDELL HOLMES, SR. *The Autocrat of the Breakfast Table* (1858). In these poems and essays, the man who coined the term "Boston Brahmin" captures the spirit and sensibility of the Hub's genteel classes during the mid-19th century.

WILLIAM DEAN HOWELLS, *A Modern Instance* (1882) and *The Rise of Silas Lapham* (1885). Boston in the '80s was a go-getter's town, where there were fortunes to be made and respectability to be relentlessly pursued. It all sounds familiar—but these were the 1880s and Howells has them down pat.

HENRY JAMES, *The Bostonians* (1886). James's novel of manners and sexual politics perfectly captures several enduring elements of Boston intellectual life, including a certain radical shrillness.

SARAH ORNE JEWETT, *The Country of the Pointed Firs* (1896) and *Deephaven* (1877). Jewett was Maine's voice in the

American regional literary movement of the late 19th century; in these books of sketches she portrays the down east yeomanry and faded gentry of her era.

JACK KEROUAC, *Visions of Gerard* (1958) and *Dr. Sax* (1959). Long before he emerged as the reluctant leader of the Beat movement Kerouac was a French-Canadian street kid in the fading mill town of Lowell, Massachusetts. In his Lowell books—these are two of the best—the old river city is a landscape of terror and wonder.

JOHN P. MARQUAND, *The Late George Apley* (1937). What Cleveland Amory did for the species at large, Marquand does for a single Boston patrician in this masterpiece of satirical fiction; it's still the best look at a lost world bounded by Beacon Hill, Back Bay, and Harvard Square.

HERMAN MELVILLE, *Moby-Dick* (1851). Far more than a high school *bête noire,* Melville's masterwork is a massively entertaining tale of the days of wooden ships and iron men; amid the metaphysics there are powerfully descriptive passages of life in the heyday of the Nantucket whaling trade.

ARTHUR MILLER, *The Crucible* (1953). Miller's powerful dramatic allegory, directed against McCarthyism in the 1950s, is set in the Salem of the witch trials.

EDWIN O'CONNOR, *The Last Hurrah* (1956). The fictional last word on big-city machine politics, O'Connor's novel draws freely from the career of Boston's legendary mayor James Michael Curley.

ROWLAND EVANS ROBINSON, *Uncle Lisha's Shop: Life in a Corner of Yankeeland* (1887). Robinson's phonetically spelled dialect writing isn't the easiest thing to read, but the effort is rewarded by the author's portrayals of Yankee and French-Canadian rustics of a century ago.

GEORGE SANTAYANA, *The Last Puritan: A Memoir in the Form of a Novel* (1935). Three centuries of New England puritanism stand behind Santayana's central character, in whom New England's bedrock moral philosophy might be said finally to have run itself to the ground.

UPTON SINCLAIR, *Boston* (1928). Published one year after the execution of Sacco and Vanzetti, Sinclair's novel features the two Italian anarchists as characters; the theme is the polarization between the establishment and radical elements in post–World War I Boston.

EDITH WHARTON, *Ethan Frome* (1911). Along with Eugene O'Neill's *Desire Under the Elms,* Wharton's book is one of the most powerful portrayals of the dark, unremittingly gloomy side of the New England psyche.

JOHN GREENLEAF WHITTIER, *Snow-Bound* (1866). Whittier's best poem is a long, sweet pastoral set at the hearthside of his Haverhill, Massachusetts, boyhood home. The poem defines old-time rural New England, as Currier and Ives never could.

THORNTON WILDER, *Theophilus North* (1973). Wilder, best known for his play *Our Town* (set in a place modeled after Peterborough, New Hampshire), here turns to the novel and a tale of life in Newport, Rhode Island, during its circa-1900 social heyday.

Nature

HENRY BESTON, *The Outermost House* (1928). In the tradition of Henry David Thoreau, Beston's work is a classic account of life lived in solitude, among the elements on the Great Beach of Cape Cod.

J. PARKER HUBER, *The Wildest Country: A Guide to Thoreau's Maine.* A modern author's tribute to Thoreau, retracing Thoreau's journeys through the Maine backcountry (see *The Maine Woods,* below) in words and black-and-white pictures.

NEIL JORGENSEN, *Guide to New England's Landscape* (1977). Drumlins, eskers, monadnocks, barrier beaches, and much more—a lucid, place-by-place explanation of the geologic and climatic forces that made New England look the ways it does.

PETER J. MARCHAND, *The North Woods* (1987). A detailed guide to the trees and forest plants of northern New England, and to the ecosystem of the great spruce-fir and hardwood-spruce woodlands that have dominated the region since the last Ice Age.

JOHN MCPHEE, *The Survival of the Bark Canoe* (1975). The peerless McPhee intertwines the tale of an authentic New England character, one of the last builders of birchbark canoes, with a narrative of a river trip—in bark canoes, of course—through the wilds of northern Maine.

HENRY DAVID THOREAU, *Cape Cod* (1865). Much to his taste, Thoreau found man and nature living on intimate terms in the Cape Cod of the 1850s. His descriptions of the great outer beach are exquisite, and should make us thankful for the stern preservationist hand of the Cape Cod National Seashore.

————, *The Maine Woods* (1864). Notes on three Maine canoe trips, distilled into one volume. This is still New England's great wilderness, and Thoreau is still one of its most perceptive visitors.

————, *Walden* (1854). One of the signature works of the contrary, individualistic New England mind, *Walden* has served as a declaration of independence for just about everyone who has ever set about breaking the bonds of convention. The pond remains, too, as one of the region's premier geographical icons.

Architecture

BAINBRIDGE BUNTING, *Houses of Boston's Back Bay: An Architectural History, 1840–1917* (1967). How did the Back Bay come to be, and how did it work in the days B.C.— before condos? Bunting's detailed account is a fascinating approach to sociology by way of architecture.

HERBERT WHEATON CONGDON, *Old Vermont Houses* (1940; 1968). An architect's guide to some outstanding (and many little-known) examples of two centuries of Vermont vernacular architecture, written to a layperson's understanding.

HENRY-RUSSELL HITCHCOCK, *The Architecture of H. H. Richardson and His Times* (1936). An appreciation of one of America's greatest architects, the master of the Romanesque Revival, who enriched New England's built environment with residences and libraries, churches and railroad stations.

RICHARD PILLSBURY AND ANDREW KARDOS, *Field Guide to the Folk Architecture of the Northeastern United States* (1970). A handbook to the architecture created by people who weren't architects, and a look at the many ways in which form has followed function in an unforgiving landscape.

SUSAN AND MICHAEL SOUTHWORTH, *A.I.A. Guide to Boston* (1984). A thorough and eminently readable tour of one of America's most architecturally eclectic cities, with anecdotes linking the social history of Boston to the progression of styles from 17th-century Colonial to contemporary office towers.

History and Biography

HENRY ADAMS, *The Education of Henry Adams* (1918). Although Adams's intellectual autobiography ranges far afield from his family's ancestral home, it contains revealing glimpses of Harvard life in the mid-19th century, and provides a first-hand view of the New England mind at work.

JAMES TRUSLOW ADAMS, *The Adams Family* (1930). The lives of four generations of that most distinguished of Yankee clans, the Adams family, exemplars all of the New England tradition of combining introspection and public service.

RICHARD D. BROWN, *Massachusetts: A Bicentennial History* (1978). Like its companion volumes in W. W. Norton's States and the Nation series, Brown's *Massachusetts* is a concise, readable account that chronicles the development of the state's personality as well as reviewing straight historical fact.

CHARLES E. CLARK, *Maine: A Bicentennial History* (1977). (See listing above under Richard D. Brown, *Massachusetts.*)

LUCY CRAWFORD, *History of the White Mountains* (1846). Written by one of *the* Crawfords, as in Crawford Notch, this is a mine of lore from the days when the New Hampshire north country had no palatial hotels or trains from Boston.

ESTHER FORBES, *Paul Revere and the World He Lived In* (1942). A lively and engaging history of Colonial and early republican America, built around the life of a hero more solid and admirable than the horseman of Longfellow's poem.

JOHN HARRIS, *Saga of the Pilgrims.* A simply told yet comprehensive chronicle, drawn from extensive reading of primary sources, of the migration of religious dissidents from England and the founding of the Plymouth colony.

THOMAS STARR KING, *The White Hills* (1859). Rev. King, a Unitarian minister, was one of America's first chroniclers of natural grandeur; this detailed history and description of New Hampshire north of Lake Winnepesaukee helped popularize the region among outsiders and remains a basic introduction to the White Mountains' geography and lore.

JOHN P. MARQUAND, *Lord Timothy Dexter* (1925) and *Timothy Dexter Revisited* (1960). Dexter was a wealthy and eccentric figure in Marquand's hometown of Newburyport, Massachusetts, circa 1800; in recounting Dexter's foibles, the novelist tells much about coastal New England in its Federalist heyday.

WILLIAM G. MCLOUGHLIN, *Rhode Island: A Bicentennial History* (1978). (See Richard D. Brown, *Massachusetts,* above.)

ELIZABETH FORBES MORISON AND ELTING E. MORISON, *New Hampshire: A Bicentennial History* (1976). (See Richard D. Brown, *Massachusetts,* above.)

SAMUEL ELIOT MORISON, *Builders of the Bay Colony* (1930). The Brahmin historian, master of a style at once anecdotal and magisterial, writes about the men who made Colonial Massachusetts.

CHARLES T. MORRISSEY, *Vermont: A History* (1981). (See Richard D. Brown, *Massachusetts,* above.)

FRANCIS PARKMAN, *Montcalm and Wolfe* (1884). Parkman, arguably America's greatest writer of historical narrative, devoted much of his career to chronicling the struggle between France and England for Colonial dominance in North America. In this volume, and in *A Half-Century of Conflict* (1892), he tells of the pivotal events that assured British hegemony, and of the role New Englanders played in the triumph over France.

DAVID MORRIS ROTH, *Connecticut: A Bicentennial History* (1979). (See Richard D. Brown, *Massachusetts,* above.)

WILLIAM G. SCHELLER, *New Hampshire: Portrait of the Land and Its People* (1988). The Granite State's past and present, in words and color photographs.

New England Cookery

DOROTHY BATCHELDER, *The Fishmonger Cookbook* (1988). New England's original and most essential culinary resource (after all, a wooden codfish hangs in the Massachusetts State House), given a respectful treatment by a Boston-area fish store proprietor.

JUDY GORMAN, *Judy Gorman's Breads of New England* (1991). The hearty, traditional breads of the region, many of which date back to the days of beehive ovens in Colonial hearths.

MARGARET D. MURPHY, *The Boston Globe Cookbook: A Collection of Classic New England Specialties* (1990). Classic New England recipes updated to reflect contemporary dietary wisdom; no doughnuts fried in lard, but plenty of Yankee flavor.

CLARISSA SILITCH, ED. *Yankee Church Supper Cookbook* (1980). The cuisine of rural and small-town New England, as exemplified by the dishes served at the region's church suppers: stick-to-your-ribs fare, with nary a nouvelle influence.

CAROLINE SLOAT, ED., *Old Sturbridge Village Cookbook.* More than 100 recipes, dating from the 18th and early 19th centuries and carefully revised for modern application, as served at the popular Massachusetts attraction.

SANDRA TAYLOR, ED., *The Best Recipes from New England Inns* (1991). The past two decades have seen a renaissance of New England innkeeping, and inn kitchens have been at the center of the revival. Truth be told, these recipes would probably shame the creations of Colonial hostelers.

Guidebooks

APPALACHIAN MOUNTAIN CLUB, *Massachusetts and Rhode Island Trail Guide*. The Boston-based AMC regularly updates this guide to long and short trails in these two heavily urbanized states, where visitors are often surprised to find hiking opportunities in bucolic settings close to major cities.

————, *Maine Mountain Guide*. AMC correspondents contribute detailed and timely information to this guide to mountain trails throughout the Pine Tree State, including the wilderness fastness of Baxter State Park and its magnificent Mount Katahdin.

————, *River Guide: New Hampshire/Vermont; River Guide: Maine;* and *River Guide: Massachusetts, Connecticut, and Rhode Island*. Arranged by watershed in each region, graded according to degree of difficulty, and regularly updated, these are the most comprehensive guides to New England waterways for canoeists and kayakers.

————, *White Mountain Guide* and *Guide to Mount Washington and the Presidential Range*. These are the oldest and most reliable guides to the trails and topography of New England's loftiest peaks. In addition to frequently revised details contributed by an extensive network of hikers and climbers, the guides contain full information on the AMC's own system of White Mountain huts for overnight lodging.

LYN AND TONY CHAMBERLAIN, *Cross-Country Skiing in New England* (1992). Currently in its third edition, this is a comprehensive guide to the commercial ski touring facilities and open-to-the-public trails of the region.

BERNICE CHESLER, *Bernice Chesler's Bed & Breakfast in New England* (1984). If it has quilts and muffins, Bernice Chesler has been there. The 450 listings in this guide, cross-indexed by name and state, include not only the likelier establishments in the countryside, but also many of the better B and Bs in the burgeoning urban market.

WAYNE CURTIS, *Maine: Off the Beaten Path* (1992). The idea of the Globe Pequot Press's Off the Beaten Path series—which also includes titles on Connecticut, Massachusetts, New Hampshire, and Vermont, all by different authors—is to cover the attractions conventional guidebooks frequently overlook. Some are offbeat in the extreme; some are monuments to the eccentricities of single individuals. All of the books make for good armchair reading.

GREEN MOUNTAIN CLUB, *Day Hiker's Guide to Vermont.* An invaluable guide to the trails of the Green Mountain State, many of them little known. The pocket-size book includes full information on automobile access to trails, degree of maintenance (or lack thereof), views, and even sources for drinking water.

———, *Guide Book of the Long Trail.* A superbly detailed, section-by-section guide to Vermont's Massachusetts-to-Quebec footpath, with maps, mileage tables, and information on each of the backcountry overnight facilities maintained by the GMC. The Mount Mansfield section includes coverage of all of the side trails that crisscross the mountain and its environs.

JOHN HARRIS, *Boston Globe Historic Walks in Old Boston* (1989) and *Historic Walks in Cambridge* (1986). Harris, an old Boston hand, knows every corner of Beacon Hill and the Back Bay, the narrow alleys and Colonial graveyards of downtown Boston and the North End, and the campuses of Harvard and Radcliffe. His routes are paved with anecdotes and steeped in history.

MIRIAM LEVINE, *A Guide to Writers' Homes in New England.* From Mark Twain's elaborate Hartford mansion to the Concord haunts of Emerson, Alcott, and Hawthorne, this is a handbook to the most fertile fields of literary America. All of the places described are open to the public.

EDWARD MULLEN AND JANE GRIFFITH, *Short Bike Rides on Cape Cod, Nantucket, and the Vineyard* (1991). The Cape and Islands are probably the most popular cycling territory in New England: The terrain is gentle, the towns and inns are close together, and the sea is never far off. This book features 34 rides, all off main traffic routes. (The publisher, Globe Pequot Press, also offers similar guides covering Connecticut, Rhode Island, and the Boston/central Massachusetts area.)

SUSAN P. SLOAN, ED., *Sloan's Green Guide Antiquing in New England* (1991). Up-to-date information on 2,500 antiques shops, antiquarian booksellers, flea markets, and the like, accompanied by suggested itineraries linking the richest antiques-hunting grounds in all six states.

CHRISTINA TREE, *Maine, An Explorer's Guide* (with Mimi Steadman, 1993), *New Hampshire, An Explorer's Guide* (with Peter Randall, 1991), *Vermont, An Explorer's Guide* (with Peter Jennison, 1992). The Explorer's Guides offer in-depth region-by-region descriptions of the northern New England states, detailing activities, lodging, dining, and shopping options.

————, *How New England Happened* (1976). This historical guide to the region draws the reader through time and space, describing things to see and do as each sight illustrates a phase in one evolving story.

CHRISTINA TREE AND KIMBERLY GRANT, *Best Places to Stay in New England* (1992). This is a lodging guide organized not geographically but by type of accommodation, such as "Grand Old Resort" or "Family Find." Some 350 places to stay are described, and cross-referenced in an appendix with categories like "Pets Welcome," "Horseback Riding," and "Golf."

—*William G. Scheller*

CONNEC-TICUT

By Patricia Brooks

A state resident since 1956, Patricia Brooks has received the Governor's Tourism Council Travel Achievement Award for her numerous writings about Connecticut in Travel & Leisure, Travel/Holiday, Bon Appetit, Vogue, *and many other national magazines, as well as for her restaurant and country-inn guidebooks. Since 1977 she has been the restaurant reviewer for the Connecticut section of* The New York Times, *with the entire state as her beat.*

The name "Connecticut" evokes images of pleasant, up-scale, well-tended towns in the minds of people who have never even been to the state. (Its benign reputation no doubt derives somewhat from scores of movies—*Christmas in Connecticut* comes to mind—in which fashionable, affluent couples are always escaping from frantic Manhattan to a restful farmhouse in the wooded wilds of Connecticut.) At the same time, travellers often overlook Connecticut in planning a trip to New England. Perhaps because of its proximity to New York City, the state often is not considered part of New England.

But Connecticut is very much New England, with the requisite village greens and steepled churches, stone fences, covered bridges and country inns, storybook farms and antiques shops, auctions and county fairs, historic houses and monuments, country roads and rolling hills. In short, everything that gives New England its identity as a region can be found in Connecticut—and more.

Among the state's numerous attractions are Mystic Seaport, an authentic 18th- to 19th-century seaside village; Mark Twain's house, in Hartford, one of the country's most unusual 19th-century homes; the Goodspeed Opera House, in

East Haddam, a musical-comedy theater in a 19th-century opera house; the Yale Center for British Art, in New Haven, the only British art museum in the country; the Nathan Hale Family Homestead, in Coventry, the family home of America's alleged first spy; and Gillette Castle at Hadlyme, a medieval-style castle towering above the Connecticut River. And that's just a partial inventory.

MAJOR INTEREST

Fairfield County (Southwestern Connecticut)
Pretty, well-groomed villages
Greenwich: Bruce Museum, historic houses, and fashion and gift shops
Stamford: Whitney Museum of American Art
New Canaan: historical society's old village complex
Ridgefield: Aldrich Museum of Contemporary Art and Colonial-era Keeler Tavern
Danbury: Scott-Fanton Museum
Norwalk: Lockwood-Mathews Mansion, Maritime Center, and SoNo shopping and dining district
Westport: shopping and dining in lovely riverside town

New Haven
Historic New Haven Green
Yale University museums and architecture
The Long Wharf Theatre

The Eastern Shore
Guilford: historic houses
Madison: Hammonasset Beach State Park
Connecticut River towns of Essex and Chester
Gillette Castle
East Haddam: Goodspeed Opera House and restored mill village of Johnsonville
Old Lyme: Florence Griswold House
New London: historic houses, Monte Cristo Cottage, Eugene O'Neill Theater Center, and Lyman-Allyn Art Museum
Groton: USS *Nautilus* submarine
Mystic Seaport and Marinelife Aquarium

The Quiet Corner (Northeastern Connecticut)
Norwich: Leffingwell Inn
Lebanon: Trumbull House and town common
Willimantic: Windham Textile and History Museum
Canterbury: Prudence Crandall Museum
Brooklyn: Golden Lamb Buttery
Woodstock: Roseland Cottage

Coventry: Caprilands Herb Farm and Nathan Hale
  Homestead

Hartford and West Hartford
Nook Farm: Mark Twain and Harriet Beecher Stowe
  houses
Wadsworth Atheneum art museum
Center Church and the Ancient Burying Ground
Old State House, Bushnell Park, and State Capitol
Museum of American Political Life

Hartford Environs
Historic houses in Old Wethersfield and Newington
Old New-Gate Prison and Copper Mine
Simsbury: Massacoh Plantation
Farmington: Hill-Stead Museum and Stanley-Whitman
  House
New Britain Museum of American Art

Litchfield Hills (Northwestern Connecticut)
Litchfield: village green and 18th-century houses
White Flower Farm
White Memorial Conservation Center
Handsome towns of Lakeville and Salisbury
Norfolk Chamber Music Festival
Kent's art galleries
Macedonia Brook and Kent Falls state parks
Washington: Institute for American Indian Studies
Lake Waramaug

Connecticut, though the country's third smallest state in area, is blessed with a shoreline that stretches 105 miles from New York State to Rhode Island, with scores of coves, inlets, and harbors. There is much to see in this coastal area. State parks with superb beaches for wandering (even in the off-season) hug the shoreline; antiques shops and historic homes proliferate in the shore towns of Greenwich, Norwalk, Guilford, and New London; Stamford and New Haven have wonderful museums; and Stonington, Mystic, New London, Groton, Essex, and Norwalk are charming nautical towns.

The state's main river and namesake—from an Indian word meaning "beside the long river"—flows from Canada along the Vermont–New Hampshire border and through Massachusetts and central Connecticut, past Hartford, before emptying into Long Island Sound. The Dutch first explored the rich valleys along the Connecticut River in the early 17th century, but it was Puritans from the Massachusetts Bay Colony who began settling them in the 1630s. Through the centuries Connecticut welcomed new arrivals, many of

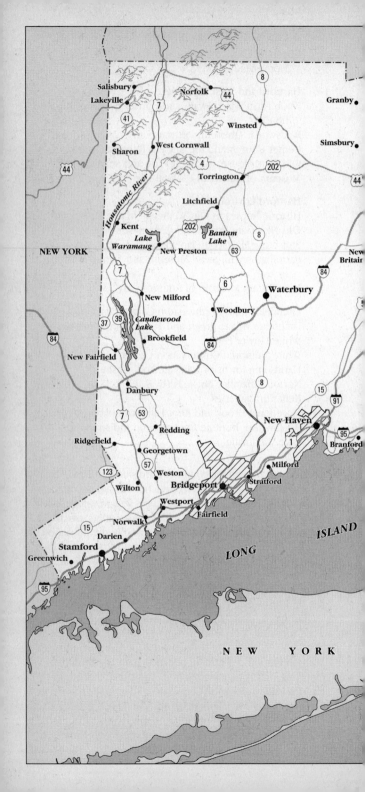

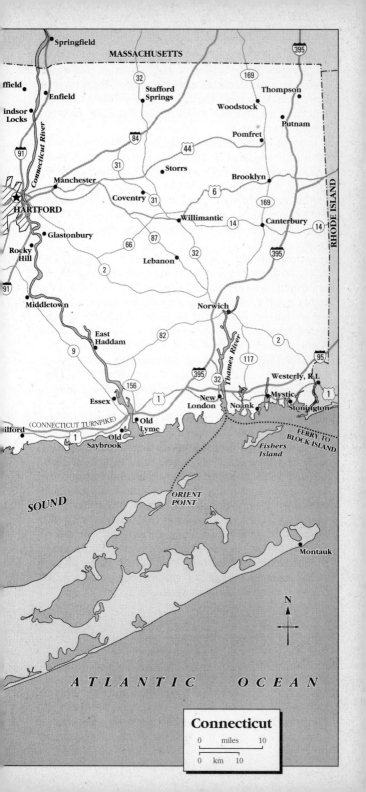

whom, in the 19th and early 20th centuries, found work in the factories of the thriving boating, armament, and textile industries in Connecticut's many river towns. Today many of those factories are idle, but the towns have retained a peaceful charm and, through typical Yankee ingenuity, have become tourist magnets.

A bonus for the traveller is that geographically Connecticut is relatively small. In a few hours you can cross the state, and in a week, if you insist on racing, you can visit most of the major sights, though it would take far longer to explore the state in depth. Even the cities are manageable: The largest city, Bridgeport, has a population of less than 142,000, and many of the other important cities are less than a third that large.

For convenience, Connecticut's sights are grouped below by region, beginning with Fairfield County at the southwestern corner, close to New York City, a section often called the Gold Coast because of the many estates and manorial homes tucked into its woods and along its shore. After a short detour inland up the Connecticut River valley, we continue northeast along the coast to the Rhode Island border. The route then leads into the northeastern corner—the so-called Quiet Corner—and from there west to Hartford and the central points around it, ending up in the Litchfield Hills, in the rural northwest.

If you are travelling from New York to Boston (or the reverse), you might pay special attention to the Connecticut Shore and Quiet Corner sections and select among the towns and attractions along or near this speedy, direct highway. If you are planning a short weekend outing from New York City, Philadelphia, or Boston, your best approach would be to home in on a specific area, perhaps the Litchfield Hills or the Quiet Corner. A business traveller to Hartford or New Haven, with a little extra time for day trips, will want to turn first to Hartford and Environs or the Connecticut Shore, while a vacationer with time for a leisurely ramble can pick and choose throughout the chapter, noting the ease of covering the entire state in a week.

FAIRFIELD COUNTY

Sprawling Fairfield County encompasses the southwestern corner of Connecticut. It is bordered by New York State on the west, Long Island Sound on the south, the Housatonic River on the east, and stretches north past New Fairfield to a narrow point of wooded farmland. Its shoreline from Greenwich east to Southport (just west of the city of Fairfield) is known as the Gold Coast because of the mansions and estates and the vast wealth located here.

One of the wealthiest counties in the United States, Fairfield is known for the company it keeps; scores of celebrities in the arts and media, along with titans of industry and finance, have homes here, drawn by the privacy that the county's many quiet, wooded towns provide. Because so many county residents work in New York City, it is said that Fairfield County residents consider Mario Cuomo their governor and Albany their capital. *The New York Times* is the newspaper of choice in this corner of the state, as *The Hartford Courant* is elsewhere. New York–style nightlife, on the other hand, is not a county—nor, in fact, a Connecticut—specialty, although a few towns (notably Stamford, Norwalk, Westport, Danbury, and Bridgeport) have at least a clutch of night spots with live jazz and other music.

Two routes cross lower Fairfield County from New York State: Route I-95, which more or less follows Long Island Sound, and the hilly, narrow, and far more scenic Route 15 (called the Merritt Parkway here, then the Wilbur Cross Parkway north of Stratford), which roughly parallels I-95 inland. Listed on the National Register of Historic Places, the tree-lined Merritt Parkway is a lovely drive, especially in spring and fall.

A third route that parallels the others, Route 1 (also known as the Boston Post Road, the historic stagecoach road that ran between New York and Boston 200 years ago) is a stop-and-go route that bottlenecks at traffic lights and slows with heavy local traffic. It is not recommended except for necessary travel within a particular town. When the Post Road was carved out of the wilderness, the area's first towns naturally sprang up along its length: Fairfield in 1639, Greenwich in 1640, Stamford in 1641, Westport in 1648, and Norwalk in 1651.

Visitors from New York City can easily explore Fairfield County and other parts of Connecticut by train or by train and rental car. Metro-North trains (the New Haven line) from Grand Central Station stop at 16 towns on the Connecticut shore, where connections are available to 16 inland towns, such as New Canaan, Wilton, Bethel, Danbury, and Waterbury. New Yorkers who like to weekend in Connecticut find it less stressful and considerably cheaper to take a train from the city to Stamford and pick up a rental car there (less than a block from the train station).

FAIRFIELD'S WESTERN SHORE
Greenwich

Affluent Greenwich, home to CEOs and former New Yorkers in business and the arts, is the most sophisticated Fairfield County town (a point with which residents of nearby Westport will argue). The town is peppered with vast estates and beautiful houses, hidden from view along wooded, well-kept "country lanes" located between the Merritt Parkway and Route 1, and tucked into coves along the water in neighborhoods protected by security guards. The casual visitor to Greenwich is pretty much restricted to the long commercial stretch of Route 1 (here called Putnam Avenue) and a hilly, six-block-long, one-way street called Greenwich Avenue, which begins at Putnam Avenue and descends to Railroad Avenue (and the Metro-North station). These streets are lined with scores of chic shops, art galleries, and gourmet food stores, as well as several of the county's finest restaurants. Shopping and dining may be highlights of a visit to Greenwich, but there are cultural attractions here as well.

Bruce Museum and Hurlbutt Gallery

The Bruce Museum, at 1 Museum Drive, south of the turnpike and just east of Greenwich Avenue (exit 3 off I-95), is located in a mid-19th-century house on 35 wooded acres atop a cliff overlooking Long Island Sound. The building was deeded to the town in 1904 by textile merchant Robert Moffat Bruce so that it could be converted to a museum. (Ironically, the only object in Bruce's "collection" was a clamshell.) The museum's holdings include late-19th- and 20th-century paintings of the Cos Cob school of American Impressionism (Elmer Livingston MacRae, J. Alden Weir, Leonard Ochtman, and others), a small collection of decorative arts, and wildlife dioramas that include birds and animals of the area. Perhaps of greater interest are the changing art exhibits, which often feature avant-garde works. Special museum events include an **outdoor crafts festival** (the third weekend in May) and an **outdoor arts festival** (Columbus Day weekend). (The museum has been closed for a renovation and expansion that will double its size; it is due to reopen in September 1993.)

The **Hurlbutt Gallery**, on the second floor of the Greenwich Library at 101 West Putnam Avenue, holds eight well-chosen exhibitions a year, ranging from ancient to contemporary art. Tel: (203) 622-7947.

Historic Houses

There are two old houses in the Greenwich area open to the public. **Putnam Cottage**, at 243 East Putnam Avenue, was built around 1692 and served as a tavern during the Revolutionary War. American Revolutionary general Israel Putnam made an audacious getaway from the cottage in 1779, just a step ahead of British troops. Note the cottage's rare scalloped shingles, huge fieldstone fireplaces, herb garden, and restored barn. Tel: (203) 869-9697.

The Colonial saltbox **Bush-Holley House Museum**, at 39 Strickland Road, south off Route 1 in Cos Cob (east of Greenwich), was the home of a prosperous 18th-century farmer named Bush (no relation to the former president), and is thought to have been built in 1732. The house was later owned by the Holley family, whose daughter married the artist Elmer Livingston MacRae. The house then became an informal art colony, and in 1912 its members formed the American Society of Painters and Sculptors, which organized the infamous 1913 Armory Show that introduced Post-Impressionistic (i.e., Modern) art to America and shocked the old New York art establishment. Galleries here today display works by Childe Hassam, John Henry Twachtman, and MacRae himself; sculptures by John Rogers; pottery by Leon Volkmar; and some rare pieces of Colonial furniture and wallpaper with the tax stamp of King George II. Tel: (203) 869-6899.

SHOPPING IN GREENWICH

Greenwich Avenue is chockablock with nationally known shops such as Laura Ashley (at number 321), Banana Republic (number 325), The Limited (number 200), and Pier 1 Imports (number 225), but it has many small shops and boutiques as well. **Betteridge Jewelers** (number 117) is a second-generation family-owned store with fine antique and custom-made jewelry and silver. **Tuscany** (number 360) sells unusual gifts and home accessories from Italy; the **Complete Kitchen** (number 118) has a wide assortment of kitchen wares; **Hoagland's of Greenwich** (number 175) carries unusual gifts; **Richards of Greenwich** (number 350) specializes in high-quality menswear; and **Eurochasse** (number 398) features horsey attire and hunting equipment.

Elements, an unusual shop at 14 Liberty Way, a block east of Greenwich Avenue between Lewis and Elm streets, specializes in museum-quality handicrafts, such as elegant bowls, woodwork, jewelry, and some clothing. **Razooks** at 45 East Putnam Avenue (Post Road) has top-of-the-line designer clothes, while **La Calèche**, across the street at number 40, sells French antiques and paintings. **Consign It**, 115 Mason Street (parallel to Greenwich Avenue to the east), is a clothing resale shop.

DINING AND STAYING IN GREENWICH

Two of Greenwich's best restaurants are on Greenwich Avenue: Terra, at number 156, and Bertrand, at number 253. **Terra** is a long, narrow storefront transformed into a Tuscan country villa, with decorative lunettes, a terrazzo floor, and a ceiling painted to resemble the sky. Although the restaurant can be noisy, the northern Italian food is superb. Tel: (203) 629-5222.

Bertrand, whose chef-owner, Christian Bertrand, was the executive chef at Lutèce in New York City for almost 12 years, is housed in a Neoclassical building designed in 1917 by F. A. Wright, creator of the Oyster Bar in New York's Grand Central Station. Inside, the brick-and-tile vaulted ceiling and Roman arches evoke an airy, spacious ambience, Mediterranean in spirit. The food is a mix of nouvelle and classic French, expertly prepared. Sautéed sea scallops with lobster coral in a light curry sauce with fresh pasta is just one of the many exceptional dishes on the menu. As in all of Greenwich's best restaurants, prices are among the highest in the county. Bertrand closes for two weeks in August. Tel: (203) 661-4459.

All Greenwich Avenue restaurants are not as costly as Terra and Bertrand. Less expensive ethnic restaurants worthy of attention include **La Maison Indochine**, upstairs at number 107, offering the food and decor of Vietnam with a dash of France (Tel: 203/869-2689); **C'est Si Bon**, at number 151, an attractive French bakery–specialty food store with a café (Tel: 203/869-1901); and **Abis**, at number 381, a Japanese restaurant, with a tatami room, serving sushi and other delicacies (Tel: 203/862-9100).

Just east of Greenwich Avenue, at 61 Lewis Street, is **Restaurant Jean-Louis**, a tiny, quietly elegant French restaurant that has built a national reputation for its excellent nouvelle cuisine. The four-course *menu dégustation* is the best value here, and the wine list is exceptional. Dinner only; reservations essential; Tel: (203) 622-8450.

There are three other notable northern Italian restaurants in Greenwich besides Terra. **La Strada**, at 48 West Putnam Avenue, serves such regional Italian specialties as risotto Milanese, linguine with pesto, salmon in green-peppercorn glaze, and tuna carpaccio. Marbleized pilasters and beams, crystal chandeliers, and well-spaced tables create an elegant ambience that suits the menu (and the prices). Tel: (203) 629-8484.

Housed in a 1908 stone building at 554 Old Post Road number 3 (off Route 1 on the western edge of town), **Bella Luna** resembles a Tuscan farmhouse, with an Italian kitchen that doubles as a bar and trattoria and a more formal dining room upstairs. Especially recommended are the veal grilled rare and served over wild mushrooms on toasted bread topped with mascarpone cheese, and grilled bluefin tuna in a tangy pesto vinaigrette with roasted pine nuts. Desserts change weekly; the poached pear stuffed with brandy-infused mascarpone in a white-wine sauce is ambrosial. Tel: (203) 862-9555.

A more informal and moderately priced northern Italian restaurant is **Centro**, housed in a converted brick felt mill facing a dam over the Byram River in the Glenville area, at 328 Pemberwick Road, between Glenville Road and Buena Vista Drive. The European-style pizzas, homemade pastas, and desserts are terrific. Tel: (203) 531-5514.

The **Homestead Inn**, at 420 Field Point Road, situated atop a loop of land called Belle Haven that juts into Long Island Sound, is another of Greenwich's top restaurants, and an inn as well. A 1799 house and barn with Victorian additions, the Homestead is an oasis of privacy and comfort; each guest room is furnished with Early American antiques and folk art. The dining room is especially delightful; in winter ask to be seated in the main room near the roaring fire, while in warm weather you might prefer the glass-enclosed porch overlooking the lawn and gardens. The French menu features such pleasures as sautéed striped bass in choron sauce (tomato-based béarnaise) and sweetbreads with chanterelles in a Madeira sauce; the dessert trolley is irresistible. Tel: (203) 869-7500.

Another comfortable, if less atmospheric, hotel is the **Hyatt Regency** on Route 1 in Old Greenwich, a small town wedged between Greenwich and Stamford. Off the lobby is a four-story, glass-roofed atrium with a garden of flowering plants, towering trees, walks, and a small waterfall. Winfield's, an active bar and restaurant in the atrium, is a cheerful place for breakfast or lunch or the buffet brunch on Sundays. Just off the atrium is Conde's, a small, sedate restaurant with American, Japanese, Chinese, and Italian specialties. Tel: (203) 637-1234.

Stamford

Ten minutes east up the turnpike from Greenwich is Stamford, which in 15 years has attracted branches of more than

20 Fortune 500 companies and is third nationally behind New York City and Chicago as a corporate center. About 1,500 companies of more than 50 employees now have their corporate headquarters in this town of 108,000. This influx of businesses has brought many new restaurants and four major hotel chains to town. While downtown Stamford is now a scaled-down concrete, steel, and glass canyon of high-rise office buildings, there is one ameliorating attraction: the **Whitney Museum of American Art**.

The Fairfield County branch of the New York City museum is housed in a spacious, high-ceilinged gallery in the Champion International building on Champion Plaza, at Atlantic Street and Tresser Boulevard. (The building's free parking lot is accessible from Tresser.) While there are no permanent exhibits here, the museum puts on five major shows a year (usually nine or ten weeks long), with accompanying gallery talks, tours, and occasional live musical performances, all free of charge. Tel: (203) 358-7652. The Champion reception area across the lobby also has some interesting art exhibits (also free).

The **First Presbyterian Church**, at 1101 Bedford Street (Atlantic Street turns into Bedford), designed by Wallace Harrison in 1958, resembles a giant concrete-and-glass fish—so much so that it is known as the "fish church" (and sometimes as the "holy mackerel"). The brilliant colors of the church's stained glass are more apparent from inside, where the biblical scenes (the work of Gabriel Loire of Chartres) evoke the mystery of a Gothic cathedral. The 56-bell carillon tower was added in 1968. Free outdoor concerts are held here every Thursday evening in July.

Stamford Museum and Nature Center

The Stamford Museum and Nature Center is north of the city center at 39 Scofieldtown Road (at High Ridge Road), ¾ mile (1¼ km) north of exit 35 off the Merritt Parkway. Children can feed ducks and geese here and watch farm (and some wild) animals being fed in a rustic landscape with a tiny pond. There are also nature trails; a museum with art, Connecticut Indian, and natural-history exhibits; and a planetarium with a 50-minute show on Sundays at 3:30 P.M. A small gift shop stocks the inexpensive items children like. Tel: (203) 322-1646.

STAYING, DINING, AND THE ARTS IN STAMFORD

Several downtown hotels make comfortable overnight stops. The **Holiday Crowne Plaza** is centrally located and convenient to the Stamford Town Center, a big shopping mall at 100 Greyrock Place, where Paul Mazursky filmed Woody Allen and Bette Midler in *Scenes from a Mall*. Macy's, J. C. Penney, Victoria's Secret, Saks Fifth Avenue, Banana Republic, and Eddie Bauer are among scores of stores in the mall.

The **Sheraton Hotel and Towers**, a handsome modern property popular with businesspeople because of its proximity to I-95 (exit 7), is located in a small industrial park near the railroad station, a short drive from the city center. Relatively quiet at night, the hotel is not far from Stamford Landing, an attractive marina overlooking the western branch of Stamford Harbor. In the marina complex, at 78 Southfield Avenue, is **Dolce**, a very good northern Italian restaurant with a stunning view of the harbor. Tel: (203) 325-8369.

The **Radisson Tara Hotel**, with a spacious, lively lobby and bar, is on Summer Street, around the corner from First Presbyterian (the "fish church"), near the Ridgeway Plaza shopping center, and a short drive from some of the city's best restaurants, which are farther south on Summer Street. The nearest one is **Kotobuki**, at number 457, serving wonderfully fresh sushi, sashimi, and Japanese specialties rarely found in the area. Check the daily specials. Tel: (203) 359-4747.

The premier Stamford restaurant for special occasions is **Amadeus**, at number 201, an elegant, mirrored place with a Continental menu that changes with the seasons. Such dishes as Culibiac of fresh salmon and schnitzel à la Vienna might be offered, along with superlative Viennese desserts. Reservations are essential; Tel: (203) 348-7775. On the same block (between Broad Street and West Park Place) are two very good, moderately priced ethnic restaurants: **Meera**, at number 227 (Tel: 203/975-0479), with well-spiced, attractively prepared Indian food; and **Hacienda Don Emilio**, at number 222 (Tel: 203/324-0577), featuring better-than-usual Mexican dishes. All three restaurants are right around the corner from the **Palace Theatre**, at 61 Atlantic Street, home of the Stamford Center for the Arts, New England Lyric Operetta, Stamford Symphony Orchestra, Connecticut Grand Opera, Stamford Chamber Orchestra, and Connecticut Ballet Theatre. The theater is closed from July to September. For a schedule of events, Tel: (203) 323-2131.

Next door to the Palace is **Il Forno**, a brand-new Italian restaurant at 45 Atlantic Street. The dining space suggests a piazza in an Italian village, with walls painted to resemble the façades of buildings surrounding the piazza. Reasonably priced specialties include carpaccio, *insalata capricciosa,* and rabbit with wild mushrooms. Tel: (203) 357-8882.

If you have a yen for barbecue (which is not easy to find in Connecticut), try **Harry's TX Barbecue & AZ Grill**, at 934

Hope Street, where the woodsmoke-infused ribs and briskets sizzle with flavor. Tel: (203) 348-7427.

UPPER FAIRFIELD COUNTY
New Canaan

Exit 36 north off the Merritt Parkway leads to the inland town of New Canaan, a pleasant place to overnight, about 10 miles (16 km) northeast of Stamford. At the corner where Park Street joins Oenoke Ridge is a tiny triangle of land known as God's Acre because of the three churches that border it. God's Acre and the town's informal slogan, "Next station to heaven" (it's the last stop on a spur line of Metro-North running from Stamford), have given New Canaan a reputation for pomposity among its neighbors. But in fact it's like many other Connecticut towns of 20,000 or so inhabitants, if considerably more affluent than most.

Main Street runs through town, turning into Oenoke Ridge at its northern end. Perpendicular to Main is the main shopping street in town, Elm Street (running one way from Main to the train station), with many elegant shops, several small eateries, delis, banks, and the town's only movie theater. The **Whitney Shop** (at number 100), known for high quality gifts and clothes, **New Canaan Book Shop** (number 59), and **Bob's Sports** (96 Park Street, across from the station), with a wide selection of sporting clothes, shoes, and gear, are magnets for shoppers.

On the east side of Oenoke Ridge, at number 13, is the **New Canaan Historical Society**, a complex of five historic buildings, two of which were moved from elsewhere in town, with seven museums: the Town House (the original town hall, built in 1825 on this same site), which contains the Cody Pharmacy (in operation from 1845 to 1965 on Main Street) and a costume museum with changing exhibits; the 1761 Hanford-Silliman House, on its original site (with a collection of quilts, samplers, and pewter of the same period as the house); the Rock School (a 1799 one-room schoolhouse); the Tool Museum and Print Shop, featuring tools and printing equipment of early local tradesmen; and the 1878 Rogers studio, where sculptor John Rogers (1829–1904) worked until his death, using many local residents as models for his so-called Rogers Groups. Tel: (203) 966-1776.

Two blocks north of the historical society, at 144 Oenoke Ridge, is the **New Canaan Nature Center**, with more than 40 acres of meadows, woods, ponds, nature trails, and a marsh boardwalk. In addition, there are a small exhibition center with hands-on displays and a gift shop; a solar greenhouse; a maple-sugar shed and cider house (with seasonal demonstrations); and herb and wildflower gardens. The grounds are open dawn to dusk. Tel: (203) 966-9577.

Silvermine Guild Arts Center

Nestled in the woods between New Canaan and Norwalk, to the southeast, at 1037 Silvermine Road, is the Silvermine Guild Arts Center, an art school with changing exhibits by county artists and craftspeople. The center holds a juried art show called Art of the Northeast each summer, with work by artists from all over New England, and a juried print show of national scope in the spring of even-numbered years. Tel: (203) 966-5618.

STAYING AND DINING
IN THE NEW CANAAN AREA

On the east side of Oenoke Ridge, between the nature center and the historical society, are two village inns (both within walking distance of the town center). The 1740 **Roger Sherman Inn**, at 195 Oenoke Ridge, a prime example of an early Connecticut central chimney house (though today much altered), originally belonged to Roger Sherman, a Connecticut jurist and the only man to sign all four documents on which the United States was founded: the Articles of Association in 1774, the Declaration of Independence in 1776, the Articles of Confederation in 1777, and the Constitution in 1788. Sherman's niece and her minister husband also lived here; the minister's Bible was once kept where the bar is now. The main dining room is rather formal; the smaller, cozier room in the rear has genuine Tiffany glass panels, a fireplace with delft tiles, and walls festooned with painted ivy. The classic French food is prepared with flair. The inn's 10 guest rooms were recently refurbished with an English country look and queen- or king-size beds. Tel: (203) 966-4541.

Next door is the **Maples Inn**, a well-kept, rambling frame house with a wraparound Victorian porch on spacious, maple-shaded grounds. Now a bed-and-breakfast, it has been renting units to corporate families relocating to this area while they are househunting. Furnished in period antiques, the guest rooms all have lace-draped four-poster canopy beds.

Within the past five years New Canaan has blossomed into a restaurant town. **L'Abbée**, at 62 Main Street, has a tiny, beautifully appointed dining room and a takeout shop. The Continental food is exquisite, especially the desserts. Tel: (203) 972-6181. For a simple meal of pasta or fresh seafood, try the pint-size **Bluewater Café**, at 15 Elm Street, on the town's two-block-long main shopping street. Reservations are essential; Tel: (203) 972-1799. **Gates**, at 10 Forest Street, is informal and lively, especially on weekend evenings when there's live music in the bar. Tel: (203) 966-8666.

Around the corner from the Silvermine Guild Arts Center (see above) is **Silvermine Tavern**, a quintessential country inn dating to 1767 and overlooking a gushing waterfall on the Silvermine River, complete with swans and ducks. There are six guest rooms above the tavern and four more across the road above the country store. Many have canopied beds and some have balconies over the river. Note the unevenness of the dining room's old brick floor, as well as the walls hung with vintage apothecary signs, farm implements, and other antiques. The inn is known for its sticky buns and all-you-can-eat Sunday brunches. The terrace is a lovely place to enjoy a drink in warm weather, but you'll want to head to New Canaan or Norwalk (covered further below) for dinner.

Ridgefield

A worthwhile side trip from New Canaan leads you north to prosperous Ridgefield and the **Aldrich Museum of Contemporary Art**. Take Route 123 (Smith Ridge Road) north from New Canaan, then head east on Route 35 into Ridgefield (about a 20-minute drive).

Ridgefield's wide main thoroughfare, Main Street (Route 35), is lined with beautiful old white clapboard houses. The museum is housed in one of them, at number 258, recognizable by the contemporary sculptures on its front and side lawns. The interior of the grand old house has been transformed into spacious, high-ceilinged galleries with track lighting, the better to display the many changing exhibits, and there's a sculpture garden out back. Tel: (203) 438-4519.

Just up Main Street, at number 132, is the 18th-century **Keeler Tavern**, dating from 1732, a museum with Colonial-era furnishings, a small gift shop, gardens, and an impressive history: The tavern was reputedly the local Revolutionary War headquarters for the rebels (note the British cannonball still lodged in one wall). During a 45-minute, anecdote-packed guided tour, a costumed volunteer relates how Jérôme Bonaparte, Napoleon's brother, dined here in 1804 on his way back from his honeymoon with his American wife in Niagara Falls. In 1907 Cass Gilbert, architect of the U.S. Supreme Court building in Washington, D.C., bought the tavern for his summer home, adding a garden house and rose garden. Closed in January. Tel: (203) 438-5485.

Of all Fairfield County towns, Ridgefield probably has the

largest number of antiques shops, at last count upward of 20. Among those of special interest are the **Red Petticoat**, at 113 West Lane (Route 35), with seven rooms of old furniture and reproductions; the **Ridgefield Antiques Centre**, at 109 Danbury Road, featuring folk art, quilts, and furniture from 35 dealers; and the **Ridgefield Antique Shoppes**, at 197 Ethan Allen Highway (Route 7), a number of individual shops selling everything from old buttons to country cabinets.

DINING AND STAYING IN RIDGEFIELD

Ridgefield has a number of fine restaurants, both elegant and casual. **Gail's Station House**, at 378 Main Street, is a homey (if noisy) hangout with a menu as eclectic as the decor. The home-baked items are especially good, and Sunday brunch is very well done here. Tel: (203) 438-9775.

The newish **Hay Day Café**, at 21 Governor Street (east off Main Street between Market Street and Bailey Avenue), resembles an old-fashioned Victorian hotel dining room and is attached to a wonderful fresh-foods market and deli and a wine shop of the same name. Hay Day has other outlets on Route 1 in both Greenwich and Westport, but this is the only one with a dining room. The food is New American; try the smoked duck with cranberries or grilled polenta with wild mushrooms. Tel: (203) 438-2344.

Café Natural, at 3 Big Shop Lane, off Bailey Avenue, is an informal lunch spot serving freshly made food, including delicious soups. David Letterman, who lives in neighboring New Canaan, sometimes eats here. Tel: (203) 431-3637. In the cellar level of the same small shopping complex, whose entrance is around the corner, is **Sam's Grill**. Whitewashed walls, wood posts and beams, and banquettes form a romantic backdrop for some imaginative cooking. Marinated chicken satay, grilled eggplant pizza, and fire-roasted game hen are some of the selections. Tel: (203) 438-1946.

The **Inn at Ridgefield**, a comfortable old clapboard house at 20 West Lane (just off Main Street), features classic Continental fare with a New American twist. Tel: (203) 438-8282. Next door is the **West Lane Inn**, a lovely place to spend the night. The inn has elements of a comfortable upper-class English home, with floral prints and hunting scenes, wall sconces, and thick carpets. A few guest rooms have fireplaces. There are heated towel racks in each bath; some baths have bidets.

Another local inn with a sophisticated restaurant can be found east of the center of town. Take Route 35 northeast to Route 7, turn south on 7; the second road on the right (west) leads you to the **Stonehenge Inn**, with gracious rooms, spacious grounds frequented by ducks and geese, and a trout pond. Longtime area residents swear by the restaurant's polished renderings of French classics and turn out in droves for the fixed-price Sunday brunch. Tel: (203) 438-6511.

Danbury

Danbury, the hat-making capital of the country until the 1950s, when people stopped wearing hats, is less than 10 miles (16 km) north of Ridgefield on Route 7. The Danbury Fair Mall (at the intersection of Route 7 and I-84), the area's largest shopping mall, lures shoppers from all over the county.

A traditional blue-collar town long in decline, Danbury had a spurt of progress in recent years when Union Carbide built its corporate headquarters here and other corporations followed suit. Although the local economy is still dicey, the town has become a mix of professionals and workers, with an influx of immigrants from Southeast Asia and South America. This makeup has added spice to Danbury's burgeoning restaurant scene, which is livelier and lower-priced than that of any other town in the county, despite a one-block-long Main Street that closes up at night.

Danbury Scott-Fanton Museum and Charles Ives Home

In downtown Danbury, at 43 Main Street, the Scott-Fanton Museum has an outstanding collection of vintage American quilts, textiles, and embroideries that is sometimes displayed, as well as a permanent exhibition of hat-industry memorabilia, and period furniture. Tel: (203) 743-5200. The museum also runs the Charles Ives Home, in town at 5 Mountainville Avenue, which was opened to the public in 1992. Inside the 1790 house in which Ives, a 20th-century composer, was born, visitors can see the parlor, with the piano Ives learned to play on, the bedroom where he was born, and other rooms with furnishings from the Ives family. Tel: (203) 778-3540.

Charles Ives Center for the Arts

Each summer, from late June to mid-September, the town honors Ives by hosting outdoor concerts (some free of charge)—chamber music, symphony, modern, jazz, Dixieland, blues, Latin, and country—at the Charles Ives Center for the Arts, on Western Connecticut State University's Westside campus, on Mill Plain Road. Tel: (203) 797-4002.

DINING IN DANBURY

Danbury has no shortage of decent restaurants, and all are inexpensive. For Middle Eastern and vegetarian specialties, try **Sesame Seed**, at 68 West Wooster Street (Tel: 203/743-9850); for inventive Cuban and Caribbean fare there's **Rumba**, at 52 Pembroke Road on the edge of town (Tel: 203/746-7093); for home-cooked Italian food and delicious fresh baked goods head to **Bentley's Restaurant**, at 1C Division Street (Tel: 203/778-3637); and for fiery Thai dishes, there's **Bangkok**, in Nutmeg Square Plaza on Newton Road (Tel: 203/791-0640). In the center of town, **Ciao! Café**, at 2B Ives Street, is this minute's trendy spot; Tel: (203) 791-0404. For hot jazz and other live music, check out the schedule at **Tuxedo Junction**, next door at 2 Ives Street; Tel: (203) 748-2561.

Brookfield and New Fairfield

Seven miles (11 km) or so northeast of Danbury via Route 7 is the turnoff to Brookfield, a small, essentially rural community. The **Brookfield Craft Center**, at 286 Whisconier Road (Route 25), offers classes, frequent craft exhibits, and a retail shop; Tel: (203) 775-4526.

If you take Route 7 just a few miles east from Danbury to Route 37 and follow that north 5 or 6 miles (8 or 10 km) more, you'll come to New Fairfield. The **Candlewood Playhouse**, at the junction of Routes 37 and 39, is a summer theater with professional productions of Broadway musicals; Tel: (203) 746-6557. Four miles (6½ km) north of New Fairfield (off Route 37 to Route 39) are the heavily overbuilt and, in summer, overcrowded **Candlewood Lake** and the more relaxing, less popular **Squantz Pond State Park** on a western finger of the lake, where there are hiking, picnicking, boating, fishing, and swimming.

South to Norwalk

The stretch of Route 7 south from Danbury to Norwalk is heavily congested at peak morning and evening hours, thanks to the office complexes along this two-lane road. A more scenic, alternate route south is Route 53 from Danbury through its bedroom suburb of Bethel to Route 58. This winding, wooded road takes you past **Putnam Memorial State Park** and **Collis P. Huntington State Park**, whose facilities include hiking and horseback trails, picnicking, and fishing. Continuing directly south will bring you to the Merritt Parkway at the first Bridgeport exit. If you're up for a detour, make a right turn from Route 58 at Redding Ridge onto Route 107 west, which joins Route 7. About 4 or 5 miles (7 or 8 km) south on Route 7, make a left turn to **Cannon Crossing**, a small complex of shops housed in pre–Civil War buildings tucked between the refurbished Cannondale Railroad Station and the Norwalk River in Wilton. **St. Benedict's Guild**, in the old station, has unusual Latin American imports, clothes, artworks, and cards.

FAIRFIELD'S EASTERN SHORE
Norwalk

Norwalk, whose population of 78,000 includes South Norwalk, East Norwalk, and Rowayton (all three are on Long Island Sound), has grown from a low-profile, smallish light-industry and commuting town to a bedroom community for medium-level executives in Greenwich and Stamford corporations. Although the Route 1 commercial strip winds up and down through town, Norwalk has many quiet residential neighborhoods and is a comfortable, family-minded community. Its biggest achievement has been the conversion of a decayed area of South Norwalk into the town's liveliest, most intriguing section, known as SoNo (from *So*uth *No*rwalk).

To avoid in-town traffic, swing onto I-95 from Route 7 and take exit 15 in South Norwalk. The Lockwood-Mathews Mansion is just to the north, at 295 West Avenue.

Lockwood-Mathews Mansion Museum
This magnificent 50-room château, built in 1864 for financier LeGrand Lockwood, is now a museum of Victorian furnishings and artifacts, with three or four exhibits per year that relate to the period. A one-hour guided tour leads you through the 18 rooms that have been restored so far. Superb craftsmanship is evident throughout the house in the coffered ceilings, parquet floors, inlaid woodwork and paneling, tiled fireplaces, gilded arches, and the 42-foot-high octagonal rotunda with etched skylight, painted ceilings, and frescoed walls. The gift shop has some intriguing Victorian-style gifts. Closed mid-December to mid-February. Tel: (203) 838-1434.

Maritime Center at Norwalk
Follow West Avenue seven blocks south (the name changes to Main Street), then turn left on Washington Street (under the railway overpass) and left again on North Water Street (the first traffic light), just before the Stroffolino Bridge, which leads over the Norwalk River to East Norwalk. On the right is Norwalk's newest sight, the Maritime Center, in a

large, restored, red-brick 19th-century ironworks factory fronting the river. The center has hands-on exhibits for kids, an aquarium with 20 tanks and a seal pool, a touch tank, special nautical exhibits, and an IMAX theater. Guided harbor tours are given in summer. Tel: (203) 852-0700.

Adjacent to the center is **Hope Dock**, from which you can take a 30-minute ferry ride to three-acre **Sheffield Island**, the outermost of Norwalk's 13 islands and home of the Sheffield Island Lighthouse, a ten-room granite edifice built in 1868 (tours of the lighthouse are given in summer). You can picnic on the island and enjoy a wide-angle view of Norwalk Harbor and the Sound. Boats run on weekends from Memorial Day to June 30, daily from July 1 to Labor Day. Tel: (203) 838-9444.

SONO

The two restored blocks of Washington Street that you passed on your way to the Maritime Center constitute SoNo. Attractive shops, art galleries, bars, and restaurants are located on the ground floors of the street's restored 19th-century buildings (many with ornate façades, cornices, and mansard roofs), which have been converted to office space and condominiums. The condos have been snapped up by young professionals working in nearby towns, which accounts for SoNo's lively weekend night scene (some of the bars feature live bands). SoNo is anchored by the **Rattlesnake Bar & Grill**, a casual restaurant and bar at the corner of Washington and North Main streets, and **Donovan's**, a popular, old-fashioned bar at the corner of Washington and North Water streets (138 Washington). Exercise caution in this area late at night.

The **Brookfield/SoNo Craft Center**, at 127 Washington Street, sells handicrafts by local artists. On the first weekend in August Washington Street is blocked off and lined with craft and art booths set up for the **SoNo Arts Celebration**. (Many artists work in lofts in the vicinity.) Also in the neighborhood is the area's only avant-garde movie theater, **SoNo Cinema**, at 15 Washington Street (west of South Main). Tel: (203) 866-9202.

Dining in SoNo

For refreshment in the neighborhood, drop by **La Provence**, at 86 Washington Street, serving excellent, moderately priced Mediterranean food in a Provençal setting—dried herbs and wildflowers, lace curtains, lattice-covered walls, ladder-back chairs—that evokes the French countryside. Tel: (203) 855-8958.

Around the corner in a nicely restored, high-ceilinged old

building at 18 South Main Street is **Miche Mache**, a restaurant with highly creative American Continental cooking, reasonable prices, and an exuberant bar scene. Try the Atlantic Amber, an exceptional beer made by the New England Brewing Company, a local microbrewery. Tel: (203) 838-8605.

If you retrace your steps north on West Avenue, it becomes Wall Street in Norwalk proper. You'll see on your left **Mesón Galicia** (between Knight and High streets). Housed in a renovated red-brick trolley barn, this charming restaurant, with whitewashed walls, ceramic plates, and other accoutrements, feels like a Spanish inn. The varied assortment of fresh seafood and *tapas* is mouth-watering, the Spanish wine list extensive. Tel: (203) 866-8800. Diagonally across from Mesón Galicia at 41 Wall Street is **Ganga**, a modestly priced Indian restaurant with many authentic South Indian specialties and an extremely welcoming staff. Tel: (203) 838-0660.

NORWALK CENTER

Continue on Wall Street up the sharply curving hill and you'll come to a major intersection with the **Norwalk Green** on the left. Make a right on East Avenue, which brings you to **City Hall**, at number 125, said to have the largest collection of WPA (Work Projects Administration) murals in the country. The 26 carefully restored murals detail Fairfield County life during the Great Depression.

Follow East Avenue north (before it crosses Route 1) and, on the north end of Norwalk Green, you'll see the Gothic form of **St. Paul's Church on the Green**, the fifth church on the site since 1737. Note the old stained-glass window and exquisite needlepoint prie-dieux in its Lady Chapel. Open daily by appointment; Tel: (203) 847-2806.

Shopping in Norwalk

There are two excellent outlet stores in Norwalk center: **Dansk Designs**, at 60 Westport Avenue (Route 1), for modern housewares; and **Villeroy & Boch**, at 75 Main Street, for fine china.

On Route 1 (Westport Avenue) east of Norwalk, toward Westport, on the right (south) side at number 100, is **Stew Leonard's Dairy & Animal Farm**, which has been called the "Disneyland of supermarkets." Stew Leonard's has grown from a modest farm store in 1969 into a huge, warehouse-like, nationally-known grocery with an astonishing variety of food products at reasonable prices. There is a petting zoo in the vast parking lot.

Westport

Westport, 5 miles (8 km) east of Norwalk, has been called Beverly Hills East, in reference to the numerous artists, writers, and TV and movie personalities who live in the town's many wooded and secluded areas away from the bustle of the commercial center. (Some, such as longtime residents Paul Newman and Joanne Woodward, are frequently spotted in local shops and restaurants.)

A small town of approximately 25,000, Westport straddles the Saugatuck River between the Merritt Parkway and Long Island Sound. Many sheltered inlets and sandy coves along the water, several town beaches, and the wild beauty of Sherwood Island State Park are within its domain. As recently as the mid-1940s Westport's landscape was covered with onion fields and farmland. Now it is a bustling, high-energy town of commuters, professionals, and small-business owners. Westport's main shopping, theater, restaurant, and motel thoroughfare is Route 1, which runs east–west through town, but the most interesting and unusual shops are on a couple of blocks of Main Street between Route 1 and Belden Place.

Westport's main draw lies in browsing through the many smart gift shops, clothing boutiques, antiques shops, and art galleries on the Post Road East and Main Street. The **Remarkable Book Shop**, at 177 Main Street, stocks all the current books and a selection of offbeat gifts. On a single block of the Post Road East are three shops of special interest: **Artafax**, at number 139, with stylish contemporary household accessories and gifts; **Papago**, at number 135, with colorful Southwestern crafts; and **American Classics**, at number 239, with witty examples of antique folk art. The **Save the Children Federation Craft Shop**, at 54 Wilton Road (on the west bank of the Saugatuck), has a large selection of handicrafts from some 22 states and 38 countries.

The rustic **Westport Country Playhouse**, just off the Post Road East in Powers Court, is one of the older summer theaters in the eastern United States; it features a new show and cast each week from mid-June to mid-September. The playhouse also has a children's theater, with two daytime performances every Friday during the summer. Tel: (203) 227-5137.

Just behind the theater in the same complex is a popular restaurant called **Sole e Luna**. Its spacious dining rooms, with a wood-burning oven at the entrance, suggest a northern Italian farmhouse, as do such sterling dishes as the *tavola fredda* (cold table of antipasto) and stuffed quail polenta. Tel: (203) 222-3837.

The **Levitt Pavilion for the Performing Arts**, an outdoor

amphitheater along the Saugatuck off Jesup Road (behind the Westport Library), stages 50 free musical and theatrical events from late June to late August. During 1993, the pavilion's 20th anniversary, there will be 60 shows, 57 of them free. Tel: (203) 226-7600 for the schedule.

A block from Main Street is the well-appointed, English-style **Cotswold Inn**, a quiet bed-and-breakfast with a restful garden. The inn is within walking distance of the Christ and **Holy Trinity Episcopal Church**, at 75 Church Lane, which bears a marker commemorating Washington's 1775 visit.

DINING IN WESTPORT

Westporters like to eat out, and the many restaurants along the Post Road give them plenty of opportunities. Heading east toward Fairfield, you'll come first to **Panda Pavilion**, at 1300 Post Road East, where some of the area's best Szechwan food is served in a spacious freestanding building; Tel: (203) 255-3988. Next comes **Amadeo's**, a small, informal, always crowded northern Italian restaurant, at 1431 Post Road East, with delicious pasta dishes, such as gnocchi alla Sorrentina, and a delicious chocolate cake; Tel: (203) 254-9482. **Fuddruckers**, a chain restaurant at 1495 Post Road East, specializes in burgers and is a popular place with families because of the moderate prices, informal atmosphere, and solid American fare; Tel: (203) 255-5960. Formal and French, **Le Chambord**, 1572 Post Road East, serves classic dishes. The prix-fixe dinners offer exceptional value; Tel: (203) 255-2654. (See also Sole e Luna, above.)

What is probably Westport's best restaurant, **Da Pietro**, is several blocks south of the Post Road, at 36 Riverside Avenue, across from the Saugatuck River. Superb northern Italian dishes are served in a minuscule space seating just 22 diners. Risotto alla pescatore, tortellini with Gorgonzola, and poached Norwegian salmon in sorrel sauce are among the best selections. Tel: (203) 454-1213.

SHERWOOD ISLAND STATE PARK

With more than 200 acres of marshes, woods, and a sandy beach, nearly two miles long, fronting Long Island Sound, Sherwood Island State Park (take exit 18 off I-95) offers facilities for picnicking, hiking, biking, softball, and swimming.

Fairfield

To the east, Westport almost melts into Fairfield, as each coastal town does with the next. Aside from several good restaurants along a tiresome commercial center (Route 1/the Post Road), the very old town of Fairfield (settled in 1639) is now mainly a residential community whose homes, ranging from manorial to modest, are tucked into the wooded countryside. Fairfield's **Dogwood Festival** takes place in the affluent Greenfield Hill section of town (south of the Merritt Parkway) in early May, when more than 30,000 trees are in flower—a dazzling sight. The five-day festival is celebrated on the Greenfield Hill Congregational Church green (exit 20 off I-95, then north on Bronson Road to 1045 Old Academy Road), with live music, sales of herbs and flowers, art, crafts, and antiques, picnic lunches, and walking tours past the historic homes and gardens that line the green. The beautiful white-spired church, dating to 1726, served as a lookout for George Washington's troops during the Revolutionary War.

If you head south on Bronson Road you'll come to Route 1, where there are several agreeable restaurants. **Centro Ristorante & Bar**, for pizzas, pastas, and scrumptious desserts, is ensconced in an exuberantly painted, airy space with a cozy bar, at 1435 Post Road. Tel: (203) 255-1210. Just east, at 1229 Post Road (between Unquowa Place and Beach Road), is **Spazzi**, currently a hot (and sometimes noisy) spot popular for its *focaccia,* pastas, pizzas, and northern Italian dishes. The trompe l'oeil wall and columns add a witty reminder of Italy. Tel: (203) 256-1629.

Still farther east, Fairfield flows into Bridgeport as the Post Road becomes Fairfield Avenue. **Arizona Flats**, at 3001 Fairfield Avenue, at the corner of Gilman Street, specializes in imaginatively prepared, Mexican-accented Southwestern cuisine. Tel: (203) 334-8300.

Bridgeport

Connecticut's largest city, with almost 142,000 residents, Bridgeport has problems similar to those of any large urban area: unemployment, pollution from its remaining factories, crime, drugs, and homelessness. But that shouldn't deter you from the handful of worthwhile sights in this once-prosperous city. The city sprawls from the Merritt Parkway to the Sound, and the sights of interest span its length.

The **Discovery Museum**, at 4450 Park Avenue (at Geduldig Street), is just a mile south of exit 47 off the Merritt Parkway, but can also be reached from Route 1 going north (left turn). The museum has about 100 hands-on exhibits for children, as well as a planetarium and a *Challenger* space exhibit. Tel: (203) 372-3521.

If you retrace your route south on Park Avenue, cross Route 1, make a left turn on State Street, continue five short blocks to Main Street, then make a right turn onto Main, you'll find the **Barnum Museum**, at number 820 (exit 27A off I-95). P. T. ("There's a sucker born every minute") Barnum, the legendary 19th-century circus promoter and entrepreneur, lived in and loved Bridgeport. When he died in 1891 he left $100,000 for the museum, a three-story domed and turreted Byzantine–Romanesque Revival building. The exhibition space has recently been renovated and expanded, with a special wing designed by Richard Meier. Among the many fascinating objects are a scale model of a three-ring miniature animated circus (with some 4,000 hand-carved performers, animals, and wagons) and 36-inch-tall Tom Thumb's brown velvet suit. Tel: (203) 331-1104.

Very near the museum, at 121 Wall Street (between Main and Middle streets), is **Ralph 'n Rich's**, which serves very good Italian food in a high-ceilinged, nicely appointed dining room; Tel: (203) 366-3597. Three blocks north, at 263 Golden Hill Street (across from City Hall), is the **Downtown Cabaret Theater**, a tiny space with much-acclaimed musical revues. Tel: (203) 576-1636.

Before leaving Bridgeport you might meander down to **Captain's Cove Seaport**, a marina at 1 Bostwick Avenue (exit 26 off I-95) on Cedar Creek, which leads to Black Rock Harbor and Long Island Sound. In the marina—along with shops, a fish market, and a massive, mass-feed seafood restaurant (open March to October)—is a replica of the 22-gun British frigate HMS *Rose,* a Revolutionary War ship that sank in Georgia's Savannah River in 1779. From the harbor there are full-day cruises across the Sound aboard the *China Clipper* (Tel: 203/334-9256) and, on weekends from May to mid-October, 14-mile narrated cruises along the shoreline aboard *Island Girl* (Tel: 203/334-9166).

East to Stratford

If a yearning for real ribs and barbecue overwhelms you as you motor east on I-95, turn off at exit 31 at the Bridgeport-Stratford line. Near the exit, at 1785 Stratford Avenue (at Honeyspot Road), is **Stick to Your Ribs**, a onetime hamburger stand with barbecued food so authentic it attracts aficionados from New York to Boston. This is a no-frills kind of joint: Place your order, pick up your smoky, richly blackened ham, spareribs, or beef brisket, and munch at a picnic table or in your car. Tel: (203) 377-1752.

Bridgeport melts into **Stratford**, a boat-building shore town with many inlets and marshes, separated from neighboring Milford on the east by the Housatonic River, which flows into the Sound. There's not much reason to pause here: Stratford's Shakespeare Memorial Theatre, the town's major draw, unfortunately remains closed as of this writing.

NEW HAVEN AND THE EASTERN SHORE

The stretch of southern Connecticut from New Haven northeast to the Rhode Island border contains some of the state's most popular attractions, including the museums of New Haven and Mystic Seaport. Eastern shore towns such as Guilford, Madison, Old Lyme, and Stonington are especially active in summer. Our itinerary follows the shore, with a detour inland up the Connecticut River to the little river towns of Essex, Chester, and East Haddam.

Milford

Founded in 1639 by 15 Puritan families from England and nestled in Milford Harbor, Milford, 8 miles (13 km) east of Stratford on I-95, has more charm than is evident from a fast drive-by. Speeding along the interstate, you'd never guess that Milford is a lovely little residential town of woods and shore. That's its happy little secret.

The town of about 50,000 residents has been wise enough to restrict its commercial areas to the long swath of Route 1, which cuts through Milford like an extended shopping mall. This leaves intact the core of the quiet old town of Colonial houses, which extends from the long rectangular town green down to Milford Harbor and the rocky coast along the Sound.

Take exit 38 off I-95 and follow High Street southeast for eight or nine blocks (two blocks south of the green) to the Milford Historical Society's **Wharf Lane Complex**, three restored 18th-century houses open to the public as a museum. The gray frame Eells-Stow House in the center, dating to 1700, is the oldest; to its left is the shingled 1780 saltbox Stockade house (moved from another site), and to the right rear is the 1785 barn-red Bryan-Downs House, another saltbox, now the repository of some 4,000 Native American artifacts. Open Wednesday and Sunday afternoons from Memorial Day to Columbus Day; Tel: (203) 874-2664.

The restaurant **Scribner's**, at 31 Village Road (reached by way of Chapel Street, off Route 162 on the eastern edge of town), not far from the beach at Merwin Point, is widely known for its moderately priced fresh seafood. Tel: (203) 878-7019.

NEW HAVEN

Continue 12 miles (19 km) or so east on I-95 to New Haven, leaving the highway at exit 47, which leads to Route 34 and the city center. It is also possible to take Metro-North's New Haven line from Grand Central Station, in New York City, and then get a taxi in New Haven to the green, from which you can tour much of the city on foot.

A full day in New Haven will give you a sense of this venerable city of about 130,000, situated on a triangle of land where the West, Mill, and Quinnipiac rivers flow into New Haven Harbor. New Haven has come a long way from the original settlement of Quinnipiac, which was bought in 1638 from the Quinnipiac Indians for a few coats, hatchets, and knives by Pilgrims from Boston, lured here by the promising harbor, with the intention of combining the shipping trade with a model religious colony.

This "model" colony was a theocracy in which only church members could vote and make decisions; the basic laws were biblical. The more lenient Dutch in New York dubbed them blue laws, alluding to such "true blue" zealotry— penalties for breaking the Puritan code were severe. So many offenses were committed that, as one historian noted, "it is a wonder one pair of stocks on Market Street [the green] was enough." When New Haven joined the more democratic Connecticut Colony in 1665, theocracy was discarded.

Today New Haven is a modern city with many problems, chiefly related to the usual urban trilogy of drugs, crime, and unemployment. Even the ivy-covered retreat of Yale University, located in the central core of the city, has seen muggings and other serious crimes, though a visitor walking through the campus and the nearby downtown streets in the daytime has little to worry about.

Touring New Haven

NEW HAVEN GREEN

A walking tour of New Haven will take you within a few short blocks from the town's earliest buildings on the green to present-day New Haven, where Yale University serves as the vortex of good theater, dining, and shopping. Fortunately, most of the city's attractions are within walking distance of each other, so you would be advised to park your car in a lot near the green or the Yale campus and proceed on foot. Begin your walk at the New Haven Green, a 16-acre square that served as the central section of the original nine town squares laid out by the Pilgrims. Divided by Temple Street, the square is bordered by Elm Street on the north, Church on the east, Chapel on the south, and College on the west.

City Hall (1862), facing the green on Church Street, epitomizes the High Victorian style, noted for its polychrome limestone-and-sandstone façade. Down the street at the corner of Court and Church streets is the monumental Greek Revival **Post Office and Federal District Court**, designed in 1913 by James Gamble Rogers, architect of many of Yale University's Gothic Revival buildings.

On the green along Temple Street you'll find three historic churches, all built between 1812 and 1815: **United Church on the Green** (also called North Church because it's northernmost), in the style of St. Martin-in-the-Fields in London, with a Federal-style interior; the Georgian-style **First Church of Christ** (also known as Center Church), with the remains of a Colonial-era burial ground in its crypt; and **Trinity Church on the Green**, one of the first Gothic-style churches in America.

YALE UNIVERSITY AND ENVIRONS

A couple of blocks west of the green at 1080 Chapel Street, at the corner of High Street (across from the Yale campus), is the **Yale Center for British Art**, a stunning stainless-steel and poured-concrete structure built in 1977, the last work of architect Louis I. Kahn and a gift to Yale from Paul Mellon. The interior, a handsome mix of polished steel and wood with a four-story-high atrium and a series of skylights, forms a strong backdrop for a comprehensive collection of British paintings, prints, drawings, and rare books. Exhibits, which are always of British art, change frequently. The center's small gift shop features offbeat British books and art gifts. Tel: (203) 432-2800. **Atticus Bookstore-Café**, next to the Yale Center for British Art at number 1082, is a comprehensive bookshop with a tiny dining area serving soups, sandwiches, and delectable desserts and muffins; it's open until midnight every day.

One block west, on the northern corner of Chapel and York, is an earlier (1953) building by Kahn, the **Yale University Art Gallery**, housing a top-flight collection of European, Asian, African, pre-Columbian, and contemporary American painting and sculpture. One of the finest medium-size art museums in the country, it also boasts a choice collection of early American furniture and decorative arts. Tel: (203) 432-0600. The unusual contemporary building across the street on the north side is the **Yale School of Art and Architecture**, designed in the mid-1960s by Paul Rudolph and controversial in its time. (The church across from the gallery on the south side houses the Yale Repertory Theatre; see "The Performing Arts," below.)

While the above-mentioned museums are just off campus, Yale as an entity forms a rough "J," with the base at Chapel Street between Park and Temple, and the top of the J at Highland Street between Mansfield and Loomis Place. At 120 High Street (a block north of Chapel, on the campus) is the Gothic-style **Sterling Memorial Library**, designed by James Gamble Rogers. Among the treasures housed in the library are a Gutenberg Bible and illuminated medieval manuscripts. Across the street, at 121 Wall Street, you will find a translucent marble gem, the **Beinecke Rare Book and Manuscript Library**, designed by Skidmore, Owings & Merrill in 1963, with a softly glowing interior and an austerely beautiful sunken garden by Isamu Noguchi.

Additional Yale buildings to look for on campus are Philip Johnson's **Kline Biology Tower** on Hillhouse Avenue and the **Yale School of Organization and Management**, whose rebuilding was done in part by Edward Larrabee Barnes, at the corner of Hillhouse and Sachem Street. Free one-and-a-quarter-hour walking tours of the Yale campus leave from the Yale Visitor Information office in Phelps Gate (between Chapel and Elm) at 10:30 A.M. and 2:00 P.M. weekdays, and at 1:30 P.M. weekends. Tel: (203) 432-2302.

Other landmarks in the vicinity include **Mory's**, a private club frequented by generations of Yalies, located in a Federal-style house at 306 York Street (between Elm and Wall); and the **Grove Street Cemetery**, 227 Grove Street, at the north end of High Street, with an 1845 Egyptian Revival gate that is considered a model of its type. The cemetery contains the graves of Eli Whitney, Charles Goodyear, Samuel F. B. Morse, Noah Webster, and other notable local residents. **Connecticut Hall**, near College and Chapel, is Yale's oldest building (1750); Nathan Hale, Noah Webster, and President William Howard Taft studied here.

A couple of additional attractions are near one another. Yale's **Peabody Museum of Natural History**, at 170 Whitney Avenue (on the eastern edge of the campus at Sachem Street), contains a large collection of Connecticut flora, fauna, and Native American artifacts, as well as other geological and scientific materials. Tel: (203) 432-5050.

The **Yale University Collection of Musical Instruments**,

just south of the Peabody Museum at 15 Hillhouse Avenue, houses more than 850 musical instruments dating from 1550 to 1900 from various cultures, including violins by Stradivarius and Stainer. Concerts and guided tours (by appointment) are also given here. Closed July and August. Tel: (203) 432-0822.

DINING AND STAYING IN NEW HAVEN

The three blocks of Chapel Street between Park and College contain many attractive shops and a cluster of good restaurants in a wide price range, though most are moderate, as befits a college town. There's even a convenient lodging place, the **Inn at Chapel West**, a well-restored Victorian mansion, now a bed-and-breakfast with ten suites done in period style.

From west to east on Chapel, the best places to eat include **Saigon City**, at number 1180 (Tel: 203/865-5033), for such excellent Vietnamese dishes as lime chicken and ginger squid; and **Scoozzi Trattoria and Wine Bar**, next door to the Yale Repertory Theatre at number 1104 (Tel: 203/776-8268), a trendy Italian restaurant especially strong on pasta.

Chapel Street's crème de la crème is **Robert Henry's**, at number 1032. This exceptional restaurant—one of Connecticut's best—features Continental cuisine inside the apricot-hued walls of the former Union League Club, on a site where jurist Roger Sherman's house once stood. The dining room, with its gaslit fireplace, huge windows, and well-spaced tables, has a simple elegance, matched only by the food. Dinner only; reservations are suggested. Tel: (203) 789-1010.

Bruxelles, at 220 College Street, is another popular restaurant, with both high-decibel and high-tolerance levels for children. The decor in this restored two-story town house is stunning black-and-white high-tech with bars on both floors and an open rotisserie on the lower level. The delicious food is New American; try the goose liver royale, spinach bow-tie pasta with pesto, grilled tuna steak, and any of the marvelous desserts. Tel: (203) 777-7752.

Pizza fans insist that no visit to New Haven is complete without a thin-crust white-clam pie at Sally's or Pepe's, both on Wooster Street in the Italian section, just east of the city center. (Wooster runs parallel to Chapel Street, one block south.) **Sally's Pizza** is at number 237 (Tel: 203/624-5271), **Frank Pepe's Pizzeria** is at number 157 (Tel: 203/865-5762), and both are the absolute pinnacle of pizzas. Be prepared to wait in line for a table.

Azteca's, at 14 Mechanic Street (off State Street at Lawrence Street), is noted for its creative, reasonably priced Southwestern and Mexican cuisine; Tel: (203) 624-2454. New

Haven's newest hot ticket is **Bagdons**, at 9 Elm Street (corner of State), with a black-and-white interior and New American cooking; Tel: (203) 777-1962.

THE PERFORMING ARTS

Across the street from the Yale University Art Gallery on the south side is an old church, converted some years ago to the **Yale Repertory Theatre**, one of the leading theaters of its kind in the country. In recent years the plays of Athol Fugard, August Wilson, and many other once-unknown playwrights premiered at the Yale Rep, later going to Broadway. The season runs from October through May. Tel: (203) 432-1234.

College Street, recently rejuvenated (and with several good shops), is home to the **Shubert Performing Arts Center**, featuring touring productions of plays, music, and dance; Tel: 203/562-5666. The **Long Wharf Theatre**'s schedule (September to June) of professional productions often features high-profile Broadway or Hollywood actors. The theater is located at 222 Sargent Drive (take exit 46 off I-95); Tel: (203) 787-4282.

The **Yale Cabaret**, at 217 Park Street (west of and parallel to York Street), stages innovative, often irreverent productions from September to May in an informal setting where you can eat and imbibe while watching the performance. Yale Summer Cabaret runs from mid-June to early August at the same address. Tel: (203) 432-1566.

Artspace, at 70 Audubon Street, a short brick-lined thoroughfare between State Street and Whitney Avenue (three blocks north of the green), is a large, active center of the visual, performing, and literary arts, with frequently changing exhibits, concerts, and other live performances—the cutting edge of what's new and original in this part of the state. Tel: (203) 772-2377.

THE SHORE TOWNS

The shore towns of Stony Creek, Guilford, Madison, Clinton, and Old Saybrook were sleepy backwaters until recent decades, when their quiet greens, marshlands, rocky coves, sandy beaches, and fine old Colonial and Victorian houses began to attract commuters from New Haven. Generally speaking, though, these towns are still quiet most of the year—but not in summer, when New Yorkers and others head for their summer getaways (the streets of Madison are especially clogged during this season). It is worth noting, though, that except for Hammonasset State Park at Madison, the various town beaches, like beaches throughout Connecti-

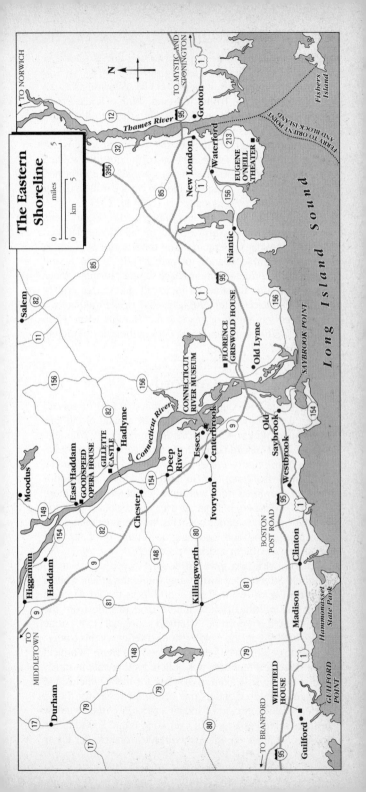

cut, are restricted to town residents and guests staying at local inns or hotels.

Heading east from New Haven on I-95, follow signs at exit 51 to the **Shore Line Trolley Museum**, south of Route 1 at 17 River Street in East Haven. One of 20 restored trolleys from 1904 to 1939 takes visitors on an hour-long ride on an old trolley line through salt marshes and woods a few miles east into Branford. There's time at the end of the ride for a walking tour of the shop where trolleys are restored and refurbished and of the car barns housing some 100 vintage trolleys dating to 1878. Hours vary seasonally. Tel: (203) 467-6927.

Less than 5 miles (8 km) east of Branford via Route 146 is **Stony Creek**, the departure point for 45-minute narrated cruises from May to September on the *Sea Mist II* of the 35 offshore **Thimble Islands**, private islands in the Sound where a few fortunate families have summer homes. Dinner cruises are also available spring to fall, and foliage cruises run in mid-October; Tel: (203) 481-4841. While waiting for a cruise, you can lunch or snack at the **Thimble Island Café**, which faces the water and town dock at the end of Thimble Island Road.

Guilford

Scenic Route 146 continues for 5 miles (8 km) or so into Guilford, which was settled in 1639 by a band of Puritans from Surrey, England, led by the Reverend Henry Whitfield. The 16-acre **Guilford Green** in the town center was modeled after a 17th-century English common and hasn't changed much since that time. The **Guilford Handcraft Exposition** is held on the green on a weekend in mid-July, when more than 130 craftspeople from all over the region display and sell their products under vast tents. It's a big regional event, with music, food, and lots going on. A number of attractive gift shops line the west side of the green.

As you drive into town on Route 146 you will come to Whitfield Street. A left turn brings you to the green, while a right turn leads two to three short blocks to Old Whitfield Street, off of which, on Whitfield Lane (a mile from the green), is the Reverend Whitfield's original 1640 stone house—New England's oldest stone dwelling of this type.

The three-story Whitfield house, now the **Henry Whitfield State Historical Museum**, was built of local granite in sturdy Tudor Gothic style both as a house for the Whitfields and their nine children and as one of five fortresses for the 25 settler families in case of Indian attacks. A corner window upstairs served as a lookout over Long Island Sound to the Indians' summer encampments in the marshes. For all its austere simplicity, the house's interior is a beauty, especially the 33-foot-long, 15-foot-wide great hall, with a fireplace at each end, 30-inch-wide pine panels, wide oak floorboards, leaded casement windows, and 17th-century furnishings. The most historic piece is a 1650 oak panel-back chair that belonged to William Leete, known for hiding two of the regicides of King Charles I who had fled to the Colonies from England. Note also the 1726 tower clock, believed to be the oldest in the country. Tel: (203) 453-2457.

Back on Old Whitfield Street, make a left (heading south) and you'll quickly come to **Guilford Point** with its scenic marina. Beyond, over a short bridge, facing a rocky shore, you can park and fish.

The barn-red **Hyland House**, with mullioned windows, one block east of the green at 84 Boston Street (at the corner of Graves Street), serves as a fine example of Colonial construction, dating to 1660 with a lean-to added in 1720. Interesting features include a chamfered overhang at the second-story level and an original casement window. Open June to September; Tel: (203) 453-9477.

Another historic house is the circa 1774 **Thomas Griswold House**, farther along at 171 Boston Street (a.k.a. Route 146, which runs along the south side of the green), at the corner of Lovers Lane. It's a white saltbox owned by one family for more than 200 years. Original furniture, wallpaper, and fireplace moldings are of special interest, along with costumes and exhibits depicting 300 years of Guilford life. A forge, ox sling, and hundreds of original farm implements are kept in a blacksmith shop in the barn. Open mid-June to October; Tel: (203) 453-3176.

Return to the north side of the green, to Broad Street, and continue west one block to **Fair Street**, on the right, which for a single block is a hodgepodge of homes that includes pre-Revolutionary, Italianate Gothic, early Victorian, and an octagonal Late Victorian. All in all there are some 84 houses in Guilford built between 1700 and 1776 and 41 more built before 1810, making this one of the best preserved of all New England towns.

DINING AND SHOPPING IN GUILFORD

Guilford boasts one fancy restaurant, **Whitfield Alley**, a rather dress-up place serving first-rate French food, at 63 Whitfield Street (set back from the green on a short, brick-lined alley). Dinner only; Tel: (203) 458-8457.

There are several informal dining spots, also along the green, with the best being the **Bistro on the Green**, a high-ceilinged, all-white place at 25 Whitfield Street. Everything is freshly made, and the salads, soups, pastas, and desserts are superb. Breakfast and lunch are served daily, dinner only Thursday through Saturday; Tel: (203) 458-9059. The **Greene Gallery**, next door, has the same ownership and a wide range of intriguing gifts, M. A. Hadley pottery, and antiques.

Also on the west side of the green is **Cilantro**, serving sandwiches, sorbets, and gelato; and just behind the green at 51A Whitfield Street (rear) is **Tastebuds**, a pastry shop with good scones, muffins, sandwiches, salads, and take-out items for picnicking.

Madison

East of Guilford Route 146 turns into Route 1 (the Post Road), with Madison just 4 miles (6½ km) beyond. Madison's main drag, the Post Road, is relieved by a pretty green where there are free band concerts at 6:30 P.M. on weekend evenings in summer. But what Madison is really about is beaches: There are two beautiful town beaches, which you have access to if you're staying in town, and the spectacular Hammonasset Beach State Park, about a mile east of the town center on the Post Road (well posted).

Driving from town, you'll come first to **West Wharf Beach** (south of the Post Road at the end of Wharf Road). Overlooking the beach and a rocky ledge is the **Madison Beach Hotel**, a large, rambling, old-fashioned gray clapboard hotel with white trim, whose guest-room balconies overlook the beach and the stone breakwater. The hotel, open from March through December, affords its guests beach access. The Wharf, a restaurant connected to the hotel, is convenient, but there are other, better places to eat in town (see below). If you follow Middle Beach Road West eastward, past some grand old beach homes, to Middle Beach Road, you'll find the smaller **East Wharf Beach**.

Return to the Post Road via East Wharf Road and head east a few blocks to reach **Hammonasset Beach State Park** (exit 62 off I-95). This beautiful public facility consists of 930 acres of woods, marshes, duck ponds, and ballfields, and a two-mile stretch of sandy beach. Hiking, swimming, fishing, scuba diving, picnicking, jogging, barbecuing, bird-watching, boating, and camping can all be enjoyed here. The park's Meigs Point Nature Center has a kite-flying field, another expanse of beach with a stone breakwater you can walk on, and an open-sided pavilion with picnic tables.

If it isn't beach weather when you're in Madison, you might visit two early homes that are open to the public. The **Deacon John Grave House**, at Academy and School streets (take exit 61 south), is an early timber-framed Colonial dating back to circa 1685. Open mid-June to October and by appointment; Tel: (203) 245-4798. The **Allis-Bushnell House** (circa 1785), at 853 Post Road (Route 1), is known for its fine antique furniture, toys and dolls, period rooms, and four corner fireplaces. One of the house's former owners, Cornelius Bushnell, was a wealthy shipbuilder who underwrote the construction of the ironclad ship *Monitor,* which battled the Confederate *Merrimac* in 1862. The house contains *Monitor* and other ship memorabilia. Open May to September and by appointment; Tel: (203) 245-4567.

When hunger strikes, consider the colonnaded **Café Lafayette**, at 725 Boston Post Road, for classic French specialties such as escargots de Bourgogne or coq au vin (Tel: 203/245-2380); or **Friends & Company**, a casual place at 11 Boston Post Road, with excellent breads and quiches and delicious desserts (Tel: 203/245-0462).

Clinton and Westbrook

Madison drifts into Clinton, 3 miles (5 km) east, another attractive shore town, with a town beach that is open to the public. The 1789 **Stanton House**, at 63 East Main Street (Route 1), contains the site of the first Yale University classroom, a parlor with its original 1825 French wallpaper, a bed slept in by the Marquis de Lafayette (on a visit in 1824), many antiques, and Staffordshire china. An authentic general store is attached to the house's east wing. Open from June to September; Tel: (203) 669-2132.

From Clinton it's about 4 miles (6½ km) east to Westbrook (exit 65 off I-95) and the **Water's Edge Inn and Resort,** a resort complex with a luxurious hotel, spacious grounds overlooking the Sound, and a restaurant specializing in seafood prepared New American style. The tiered dining room affords splendid views of the water. There's an outdoor dining room open during the summer that faces the water and a private sandy beach. The inn offers spacious guest rooms as well as villas near the water. There are two swimming pools (indoor and outdoor), two tennis courts, and a spa on the grounds. Tel: (203) 399-5901.

Old Saybrook

Less than 5 miles (8 km) east of Westbrook is Old Saybrook, a bustling shore town on the western side of the mouth of the 400-mile-long Connecticut River. The Saybrook Colony of 1635 was one of the first English settlements in New England, but there's not much left to remind you of it today.

For views of Old Saybrook's marshes, sheltered coves, and shoreline, make a loop on Route 154 around Saybrook

Point. At the point where the Connecticut River and Long Island Sound meet is a new conference center/spa called the **Saybrook Point Inn**, with a comfortable hotel and a restaurant on a colorful, boat-filled marina. Some of the ample guest rooms, furnished with 18th-century reproductions, face the water. The hotel is geared to small business meetings and conferences (which is why so many of the guests sport name tags).

Farther along on the route around Saybrook Point, at 350 Main Street, stands the imposing **General William Hart House**, the Georgian home of a prosperous merchant-politician. The house, thought to have been built in 1767, has many fine architectural touches, eight corner fireplaces, most of the original wainscoting, lovely antiques, Colonial gardens, and a period herb garden. Open mid-June to mid-September and late November to mid-December; Tel: (203) 388-2622.

THE LOWER CONNECTICUT RIVER VALLEY

If you enjoy shunpiking, the Connecticut River valley is a perfect area for it. A leisurely drive, weaving back and forth across the river as far north as Middletown (30 miles round trip), can easily take two full days, with an overnight, perhaps, at the Griswold Inn in Essex. The sights along the way include two scenic river towns (Essex and Chester), a vintage railway, a unique castle-home, a prestigious regional theater, numerous art galleries and workshops, a university, and several excellent restaurants and charming inns. (We cover Hartford and its environs, in the Connecticut River Valley north of Middletown, in a separate section below, after northeastern Connecticut.)

Essex

Take exit 69 from I-95 to Route 9 north, then exit 3 east into Essex, a well-preserved New England village with a population of nearly 6,000 and a lovely terrain of sheltered coves and hills. A shipbuilding center since Colonial days, Essex, then known as Potapotoug, built and launched Connecticut's first Revolutionary War battleship, the 300-ton *Oliver Cromwell,* in 1776.

Essex social life centers on the **Griswold Inn**, across from the pretty marina at 36 Main Street. The inn, dating to 1776, was commandeered by the British when they took over the town during the War of 1812 (and subsequently burned every vessel in the village shipyard). "The Gris," as it is widely known, is famous for its gargantuan "hunt breakfast" every Sunday (reservations essential; Tel: 203/767-1776), its St. Patrick's Day revels, December holiday festivities (special game dinners and evening musical events), and nightly live music and singalongs in the Tap Room.

Antiques adorn the inn's four dining rooms, each of which follows a different decorative theme. The "Library" is especially cozy for breakfast. The inn's nine guest rooms are small and simply furnished, many with old brass beds, hooked rugs, and other touches of Americana. There are other larger rooms and suites in the annex, the Hayden House next door, and the Garden Suite across the street, for a total of 25 units. The General Trumbull Suite in the annex has a spacious book-lined sitting room and exposed beam ceilings.

Shops and art galleries line Main Street, at the foot of which (a block from the Gris) is the **Connecticut River Museum**, located in a riverfront park at Steamboat Dock. Exhibits include nautical displays, model boats, paintings, and a full-scale working replica of the first American submarine, *The Turtle*. River cruises depart from here as well. Tel: (203) 767-8269.

The white clapboard **Pratt House**, one block north of Main at 20 West Avenue, takes its name from Lieutenant William Pratt, who at age 17 played a leading role in defeating the Pequot Indians after the Fort Pequot massacre in the Saybrook settlement in 1637. Although the house was begun in 1700, most of it dates to the mid-18th century, displaying fine elements of Connecticut Colonial architecture: feather-edge sheathing, narrow paneling, and hand-hewn oak and chestnut beams. Among the many early American antiques in the house is a large collection of courting mirrors, so called because they were brought back from China by seamen as gifts to their lady friends. The small mirrors are distinguished by their Chinese-style painted glass crests and borders. Open by appointment only, June through August; Tel: (203) 767-0681 or 767-1191.

If you head back to Route 9 you'll come to the **Valley Railroad** depot on Railroad Avenue, just one block from exit 3. A vintage steam train, pulled by a 1924 steam locomotive called Old 97, leaves from the depot on a 12-mile round-trip ride through backwoods to the town of Chester (for which see below) and back. You can detrain in the town of Deep River for an hour-long **riverboat ride** and catch a later train back to Essex; the entire train-and-boat excursion takes about two and a half hours. The cars of the Valley Railroad are all handsomely restored originals and include a 1908 Chicago & Northwestern car and a 1926 Jersey Central commuting car with mahogany siding, gold-leaf lettering, and thick, royal blue plush seats. Open May through October, and December; Tel: (203) 767-0103.

DINING AROUND ESSEX

There are two delightful places to dine just outside of Essex, but within Essex Township. **Fine Bouche**, a country French restaurant in an old farmhouse at 78 Main Street in **Centerbrook**, 1 mile (1½ km) west of Essex Center via Route 602, offers superb food and a superior wine list. Prices are reasonable, especially for the pre-theater prix-fixe dinner offered during the scheduled run of the Goodspeed Opera House in East Haddam (see below). Tel: (203) 767-1277. The pastry shop in the rear called **Sweet Sarah's** sells mouthwatering desserts—the marjolaine is a dream—candies, breads, and ice creams.

A mile closer to Essex on the same road, in **Ivoryton** (named for the ivory imported here for the making of piano keys), is the **Copper Beech Inn**, an 1898 Victorian house tucked behind an enormous copper beech tree at 46 Main Street. The inn's dining rooms are impeccable, as is the French food served here. There are also 13 pretty guest rooms in the house and the carriage house on the grounds. Some are furnished with Queen Anne, Chippendale, and Empire pieces and with canopy or four-poster beds; several have fireplaces. Tel: (203) 767-0330. (Farther along Ivoryton's Main Street is the **Ivoryton Playhouse**, a summer theater going strong since the 1930s; Tel: 203/767-8348.)

Chester

From Essex follow Route 9 northwest to exit 6, then take Route 148 east to Chester, another winning one-street river town. Chester is a pleasant place to browse, especially at the **Connecticut River Artisans Cooperative**, at the corner of Spring and Main streets, with weaving, pottery, baskets, and other crafts for sale.

The **Goodspeed-at-Chester/Norma Terris Theatre** (an offshoot of the Goodspeed Opera House in East Haddam), which showcases original musicals, is housed in a converted knitting-needle factory on West Main Street. The season runs from May through November. Tel: (203) 873-8664.

After a matinee or before an evening performance—or just for a leisurely dinner in a romantic setting—Chester's finest dinner spot is **Restaurant du Village**, at 59 Main Street. With its lace curtains, pretty dining room, cozy barroom, and robust and delicious country French fare, it offers a little touch of France in Connecticut. Dinner only. Tel: (203) 526-5301.

Route 148 heads east to the river and the old Chester **car ferry**, which holds ten cars at a time for the four-minute crossing to Hadlyme. This ferry service, which dates to 1769, is one of the last two on the river (the other is Rocky Hill–Glastonbury, farther north).

Just reopened is the **Inn at Chester**, about 3 miles (5 km) west of exit 6. The inn's rooms are rather motel-like, but its post-and-beam restaurant combines rustic charm with New American cooking.

Hadlyme

On the east side of the river your first stop in Hadlyme should be at **Gillette Castle State Park**, perched atop high cliffs overlooking the river. This dramatic site so appealed to Hartford-born actor-playwright William Gillette when he first sighted it from his yacht in 1913 that he immediately snapped up 122 acres on which to build his retirement home, choosing one of the lofty tree-covered hills known as the Seven Sisters, 2,000 feet above sea level. (From 1899 until his death in 1937 Gillette was famous for his Broadway stage portrayal of Sherlock Holmes. It was he who added the deerstalker cap and Inverness cape to Holmes's image.)

Gillette named the house the Seventh Sister and modeled it on a Rhine castle, complete with two- to four-foot-thick granite walls, turrets, and balconies. It took five years (from 1914 to 1919) and more than one million dollars to complete—a vast sum at the time. When it was finished there were 24 rooms, each with flamboyant touches that contribute to the place's idiosyncratic charm. All the doors, no two of which are alike, are fitted with wooden locks operated by hidden springs. The 30-by-50-foot living room resembles a stage set, with an 18-foot ceiling, a hand-carved white-oak balcony around two sides, a floor-to-ceiling field-stone fireplace, and baronial furniture (mostly designed by Gillette himself). A series of mirrors gave Gillette a view from his bedroom of the living room below, permitting him to make a "grand entrance" at an appropriate moment. A secret panel in the study provided him with a quick escape from unwanted visitors.

Gillette left instructions to his executors not to let the property fall into "the hands of some blithering saphead who has no conception of where he is or with what surrounded." The state bought it in 1943 and has added 62 acres, with tables for picnicking and more than seven miles of hiking trails. Open Memorial Day to Columbus Day; Tel: (203) 526-2336.

East Haddam and Environs

Four miles (6½ km) north of Gillette Castle on Route 82 is East Haddam, a sleepy place with a bustling past. It was founded in 1662 by a group of settlers who paid the local Indians 30 coats (worth about $100) for it and Haddam, on the other side of the river. In time East Haddam became an active mill town and shipbuilding center, supplying many vessels to the rebels in the Revolutionary War.

A local resident, steamboat magnate William Goodspeed, created a stir in 1876 when he decided to build a five-story Italianate Victorian theater, using shipwrights to create his vision of the Paris Opera House—mansard roofs and all— overlooking the river, with a landing for his boats at the lower level. At the time the ornate **Goodspeed Opera House** was derided as "Goodspeed's folly." It is still the tallest wooden structure on the 400-mile length of the Connecticut River, and its lavish central staircase leading from the lobby up to the theater and the long curved bar remain. (The balcony off the bar area affords a wide-angle view of the river and Goodspeed Landing below.)

But Goodspeed had the last laugh, in spite of his critics. He lured Minnie Maddern Fiske, Josh Billings, Henry Ward Beecher, and entire Broadway casts to perform at his opera house. Goodspeed steamers brought New Yorkers to see the shows and to spend the night at the Gelston House, a hotel in a similar style next door.

After its owner's death the Goodspeed Opera House de-clined, and was destined for the wrecker's ball in 1959. Rescued, it was splendidly restored and reopened in 1963 as a venue for musicals, both originals and revivals, and has been successful ever since. *Annie, Man of La Mancha,* and scores of other hits debuted at the Goodspeed and later went on to national acclaim. The Goodspeed season runs from April through December; tours are offered in summer. Tel: (203) 873-8664 for information; 873-8668 for the box office.

The **Gelston House**, another Victorian gem, has also had its ups and downs. Recently repurchased by the Goodspeed Opera House, it is expected to reopen as a restaurant in 1993. A few doors down the same street, at 8 Norwich Road, is **The Seraph**, a home accessories, antiques, and handicrafts shop ensconced in another imposing Victorian house.

The one-room **Nathan Hale Schoolhouse**, where Hale

taught briefly in the winter of 1773–1774, is just one block up the hill from the Goodspeed, at 33 Main Street. The single room contains two benches, a desk, and fireplace, and from the hilltop there is a sweeping view of the valley and river. Open weekend afternoons in summer and by appointment; Tel: (203) 873-9547.

Less than a mile east of the Goodspeed is **Bishopsgate Inn**, a 19th-century house turned into a cozy bed-and-breakfast. The inn has just six guest rooms, all with private baths and four with working fireplaces.

At the western end of the East Haddam Bridge (the longest swing bridge in the country) on Route 82 (at 1 Marine Park in Haddam) are the two 400-passenger cruise vessels of **Camelot Cruises**, which offers various cruises (including lunch and dinner cruises) down the Connecticut River as far as Essex. A cruise is an idyllic way to see the beauty of the river, with Gillette Castle looming above tawny bluffs and magnificent greenery around each turn of the river. Operating March through December; Tel: (203) 345-8591.

If you continue north on Route 9 to Route 81 on this side of the river, look for signs to the **Sundial Herb Garden** at **Higganum**, where you can enjoy a lovely prix-fixe high tea Sunday afternoons at 3:00 and the gardens and shop weekends from 10:00 A.M. to 5:00 P.M. Reserve for tea; Tel: (203) 345-4290.

JOHNSONVILLE

Three miles (5 km) north of the Goodspeed Opera House via Route 149 is Johnsonville, a restored Victorian mill village with seven buildings that are open for two-hour tours every Wednesday from June through September. (You may stroll the grounds year-round.) The buildings—the old Johnson home with its Victorian furnishings, Gilead Chapel, a clock and toy museum, a mill office, a company store, the Hyde Schoolhouse, and a livery stable (with an extensive horse-drawn vehicle collection)—are in pristine condition. You can picnic on the grounds or buy a picnic lunch from the Red House in the village and enjoy it outside by the pond or in the eatery's modest Garden Room. The Johnsonville gift shop is open year-round and stocks old-fashioned Christmas items during the holiday season. Tel: (203) 873-1491.

AMASA DAY HOUSE

Two miles (3 km) farther north along Route 149 is the town of **Moodus**. Right at the junction of Routes 151 and 149 is the

1816 Amasa Day House, a large white frame house sur-rounded by a white picket fence. The house boasts rich architectural details, hand-stenciled floors and stair risers, handsome furniture (Chippendale, Duncan Phyfe, Sheraton, and Empire), and accoutrements (Canton and Staffordshire ware, needlework) that belonged to three generations of the Day family. Also on the grounds is a museum run by the East Haddam Historical Society. Open mid-May to mid-October; Tel: (203) 873-8144.

Middletown and Environs

About 12 miles (19 km) upriver from Haddam via Route 9 is Middletown, once an industrial mill town and important river port for trade with the West Indies. Its long, wide Main Street, many of whose shops are closed, reflects the town's decline in recent decades, although there is still some light, diversified industry. For visitors the magnet is **Wesleyan University**, which was established in 1831 by Methodists, but has flourished as a leading nonsectarian university since then. On the campus is the **Center for the Arts**, designed by Kevin Roche, which has changing contemporary art and crafts exhibits. The **Davison Art Center**, a Greek Revival building nearby on High Street, has a large print and photo-graph collection in addition to special exhibits of contempo-rary art by students, faculty, and big-name national artists. Tel: (203) 347-9411.

The **Wesleyan Potters, Inc.**, at 350 South Main Street (Route 17), is one of the best handcraft centers in the state. Its shop features all crafts, including especially pottery. The guild is open all year, but its annual craft sale, held from just after Thanksgiving until mid-December, is a big event in the area. Tel: (203) 347-5925.

About 8 miles (13 km) southwest of town via Routes 66 and 157 is **Wadsworth Falls State Park**, with a scenic water-fall and overlook, picknicking spots, hiking trails, swimming, fishing, and cross-country skiing in winter. About 3 miles (5 km) farther south at the junction of Routes 157 and 147 is **Lyman Orchards**, a complex that includes orchards where you can pick your own apples in the fall; an 18-hole public golf course; the restaurant **Green Fields** (open only for lunch, Tuesday through Friday), serving sandwiches, salads, and light meals; and the large **Apple Barrel Farm Store**, where in the fall you can buy as many as 20 different varieties of apples. Tours of the farm and orchards (free of charge) leave from the store. Tel: (203) 349-3673.

EAST TO RHODE ISLAND

From the mouth of the Connecticut River and Old Saybrook it is less than 30 miles (48 km) on I-95 east to the Rhode Island border, but that distance is punctuated with many interesting sights, beginning with Old Lyme, just across the river, and concluding with Stonington, near the state line.

Old Lyme

Old Lyme's scenic location, at the meeting of the Connecticut River and Long Island Sound—with a number of tiny islands, coves, and inlets and a mix of marshland and sandy beach—has long made it a favorite summer retreat for artists. But the village's many imposing 18th- and 19th-century mansions attest to its earlier prosperity, when it was home to many sea captains during the peak of the sailing era. The stately homes lining the tree-shaded streets, the town's sleepy attractiveness, and beautiful **White Sands Beach** make Old Lyme a favorite escape (especially in summer).

The **Florence Griswold House**, one of the town's fine old houses, a late Georgian (1817) mansion at 96 Lyme Street (a block from exit 70 off I-95), belonged to Captain Robert Griswold. In the 1890s, years after his death, Griswold's daughter Florence began taking boarders. One was Henry Ward Ranger, a New York landscape painter who visited in 1899. He loved the marshy vistas and sea views, the picturesque village, and the summer light, and he returned the next summer with fellow artists who were equally enchanted. Thus was born the Old Lyme Art Colony, with American Barbizon its reigning style.

From 1901 to 1936, when Florence Griswold died, the house drew many artists in summer. The boarders, from Childe Hassam to Willard Metcalf and Walter Griffin, covered the walls of the dining room and mahogany door panels with 40 works. A panel above the fireplace called *The Fox Chase,* by Henry Rankin Poore, is a narrow, eight-foot-long landscape with amusing portraits of his fellow artists. All in all, the permanent collection contains some 900 works by more than 130 artists who lived at the house or in the area. Tel: (203) 434-5542.

Next door is the **Lyme Art Association**, built in 1922 by the artists on land donated by Miss Griswold. The gallery features changing exhibitions.

STAYING AND DINING IN OLD LYME

Directly across the street is the **Old Lyme Inn**, a handsome white clapboard house from the Empire period (1850) that makes a comfortable overnight choice, with an exemplary kitchen and attractive Victorian antiques throughout. Note the enormous 19th-century stained-oak bar and marble fireplace in the bar. The hand-painted murals in the entrance hall add a welcoming touch. Another first-rate overnight or dinner option is the **Bee and Thistle Inn**, across Lyme Street at number 100, in a nicely restored house dating to about 1756. The 11 attractive guest rooms have period wallpaper and fishnet-canopy or four-poster beds.

If you follow Route 156 east (or the quicker I-95 to exit 72), you'll come to **Rocky Neck State Park** at East Lyme, with a good beach for swimming and fishing, hiking and cross-country ski trails, camping, and picnic facilities.

New London

It is a little more than 10 miles (16 km) on I-95 from Old Lyme east to New London (exit 84). This deep-water seaport on the Thames (rhymes with "James") River dates to 1646 as part of the Massachusetts Bay Colony and was once one of the busiest whaling ports in the world.

Although the city has been disjointed by some unfortunate urban planning (or lack thereof), a few remnants of the whaling days remain, along with a number of worthy sights within walking distance of each other. A drive south along Huntington Street (just south off exit 84) takes you past **Whale Oil Row** (between Federal Street and Governor Winthrop Boulevard), a lineup of four majestic colonnaded Greek Revival houses built in 1830 for wealthy whale-oil merchants.

One block south of Whale Oil Row (a right turn) is the short pedestrians-only Captain's Walk, at the end of which is the **Nathan Hale Schoolhouse**, a tiny (22-by-28-foot), heavily restored two-story school building where Hale taught for 16 months before enlisting in Washington's Army in 1775. Open mid-June through August; Tel: (203) 426-3918.

Return to Huntington and head south two blocks, then turn left on Coit. Just off the corner of Coit and Hempstead Street is the **Joshua Hempsted House**, the oldest surviving house (1678) in town and one of the few 17th-century houses left in Connecticut. It miraculously escaped the burning of the town by Benedict Arnold. On the same grassy enclosure (part of the original 1645 land grant) is the gambrel-roofed **Nathaniel Hempsted House**, the home of Joshua's grandson (built in 1759). One of only two mid-18th-century buildings of dressed granite extant in Connecticut, it has unusual two-foot-thick block walls. Both houses are open mid-May to mid-October; Tel: (203) 443-7949.

The 21-room **Shaw Mansion**, four blocks from the Hempsted houses at 11 Blinman Street (corner of Bank Street), is New London's other granite house. Built in 1756 for a prosperous shipping merchant named Captain Nathaniel Shaw, it hosted George Washington, General Nathaniel Greene, Nathan Hale, and the Marquis de Lafayette at various times. During the Revolution the house served as the naval war office for Connecticut, and the first naval expedition under Congress was fitted out here in 1776. The house has unique paneled cement fireplace walls, as well as many original furnishings and portraits. It now houses the **New London County Historical Society**, open weekday afternoons from April through October. Tel: (203) 443-1209.

Eugene O'Neill's boyhood home, the restored Victorian-style **Monte Cristo Cottage**, set back from the road at 325 Pequot Avenue (reached via Bank Street west to Howard, then southwest to Pequot), is now a research library. Some of the playwright's belongings are on display, including his desk and a table used in the original Broadway production of *Long Day's Journey into Night.* Open mid-April to mid-December. Tel: (203) 443-0051.

Less than 5 miles (8 km) southwest on Route 1 is the **Eugene O'Neill Memorial Theater Center**, at 305 Great Neck Road in Waterford—it's easier and shorter to approach from New London than from I-95—a workshop for budding playwrights that stages readings of new plays in July and August. Tel: (203) 443-5378.

A few blocks west of Monte Cristo Cottage at the foot of Ocean Avenue is **Ocean Beach Park**. In addition to the beach, facilities include a playground, a triple water slide, a swimming pool, a picnic area, miniature golf, an arcade, and a wonderful, old-fashioned boardwalk. From the beach you'll have a good view of the New London lighthouse. Open from late May through Labor Day.

North of the entrance to I-95 via Route 32, at 625 Williams Street, is the Neoclassical **Lyman-Allyn Art Museum**, whose holdings include early American silver; Far Eastern, Greco-Roman, European, and native art of various cultures; and dolls and dollhouses. Also on the grounds is the **Deshon-Allyn House**, the Federal-style home of a whaling captain, with period furnishings; open by request. Tel: (203) 443-2545 for both.

Across the road from the Lyman-Allyn Museum is the **U.S. Coast Guard Academy**, home of the 295-foot-long square rigger *Barque Eagle.* You can visit the ship when it is in port, and watch a cadet parade on Fridays in spring and fall. Tel: (203) 444-8270. Ferries from the New London pier at Ferry Street (off Water Street, which runs north from the railroad station) leave for Block Island, Fishers Island, and Orient Point on Long Island.

STAYING AND DINING IN NEW LONDON

Just off Route 32 at 265 Williams Street is the **Queen Anne Inn**, a bed-and-breakfast installed in a well-restored 1903 turreted Victorian house. The eight guest rooms are furnished with antiques that complement the floral-patterned wallpaper, stained-glass windows, and polished woodwork throughout the house.

For dinner, try **Ye Olde Tavern**, at 345 Bank Street (west of the Shaw Mansion), whose medium-priced steaks are good (skip the inferior seafood offerings). Tel: (203) 442-0353. Spicy Thai dishes can be found at **Bangkok City**, at 123 State Street. Tel: (203) 442-6970.

From New London you can head north via Route 32 to Norwich and the northeastern corner of the state (the Quiet Corner, discussed below), but there are still a few more sights of interest along the coast between New London and the Rhode Island border.

Groton

Across the Thames from New London is Groton, where many of the world's submarines are built. The first diesel-powered sub was built here in 1912, the first nuclear-powered one in 1955. The USS *Nautilus,* part of the **USS Nautilus Memorial Submarine Force Library and Museum**, the U.S. Navy's official submarine museum, can be boarded (take exit 86 off I-95, then go north on Route 12). Tel: (203) 449-3174.

Groton has an excellent Lebanese restaurant called **Diana**, at 970 Fashion Plaza, on Poquonnock Road (exit 85 off I-95). There's nothing fancy about this family-run place, but the food is authentic, portions are generous, and prices are moderate. Tel: (203) 449-8468.

Mystic

Just 5 miles (8 km) or so east of Groton on I-95 is Mystic, containing two of Connecticut's most visited attractions. As you turn off the highway at exit 90 you'll see signs for the first, **Mystic Marinelife Aquarium**, at 55 Coogan Boulevard. In addition to more than 6,000 sea creatures in the aquarium, there are performances by dolphins, sea lions, and whales; Tel: (203) 536-3323. Next door is **Olde Mistick Village**, a complex of appealing shops.

Mystic Seaport, 2 miles (3 km) south via Route 27, is a historic village on the Mystic River as well as the country's largest maritime museum and one of Connecticut's biggest tourist attractions. Sprawling over 17 acres, the village is beautifully maintained; a half-day visit will reveal as much as you can absorb about 18th- and 19th-century seaport life. For information, Tel: (203) 572-0711.

The seaport includes three majestic 19th-century vessels (a whaling ship, a fishing schooner, and a training ship) that can be boarded, period houses, shops, a working shipyard, a children's museum, some 400 small vessels, and seasonal activities. From May through October the coal-fired steamboat *Sabino* takes passengers on river cruises.

From Whaler's Wharf, at 7 Holmes Street, you can take dinner cruises on weekends and one- to five-day coastal excursions on one of two schooners, the *Mystic Whaler* and *Mystic Clipper,* from May through October. (Tel: 203/536-4218 or, in-state, 800/243-0416.) The *Sylvina W. Beal,* an 84-foot schooner, has two- and three-day and weekend windjammer cruises to other spots in New England (Tel: 203/536-8422 or 800/333-MYSTIC), and the *Voyager,* a traditional windjammer schooner, offers two- and three-day cruises to Newport, Block Island, and (across the Sound) Sag Harbor (Tel: 203/536-0416).

DINING AND STAYING IN MYSTIC

Mystic has two fine choices for spending the night. The **Inn at Mystic**, down the road from Mystic Seaport, perches atop a hill above the Mystic Motor Inn (on the same property). The inn is a 1904 Colonial Revival house where, when it was privately owned, Lauren Bacall and Humphrey Bogart reportedly spent part of their honeymoon. The views of Fishers Island Sound from several of the five spacious guest rooms (some with fireplaces and Jacuzzis) are spectacular. On the same grounds is **Flood Tide**, a polished restaurant that serves Continental fare and has water views. Tel: (203) 536-8140.

The **Mystic Hilton** is another convenient, if predictable, overnight choice, with an excellent dining room called **The Mooring**, serving New American fare in a high-ceilinged, dramatic setting. Tel: (203) 572-0731.

For fresh lobster, follow Route 215 southwest about 5

miles (8 km) to **Noank** and **Abbott's Lobster-in-the-Rough**, a no-frills spot in a little cove at 117 Pearl Street. The buttery lobster rolls and fresh lobster are memorable. Open daily from the first Friday in May to Labor Day, weekends after that to October 12; Tel: (203) 536-7719.

Stonington

From Mystic follow Route 1 east into Stonington, a sleepy shore town and harbor popular in summer with city folk. Connecticut's last commercial fishing fleet still sails from the harbor. The village's sole historical sight is the **Old Lighthouse Museum**, built in 1823 and moved to its present location at 7 Water Street in 1840. It is now a museum that presents a full history of the community, with whaling and fishing gear, Stonington-made firearms, and stoneware. Tel: (203) 535-1440.

Stonington's Water Street is lined with handsome 18th- and 19th-century houses and charming shops. Notable is **Quimper Faïence** at number 141, an outlet for the hand-painted Breton ceramics, run by its sole U.S. distributors. From the foot of Water Street you'll have wide-angle views of Fishers Island and Little Narragansett Bay. **Harborview**, a French restaurant with many seafood dishes, is a popular dining choice, at 60 Water Street. Tel: (203) 535-2720.

For a more memorable dining experience try **Randall's Ordinary**, in North Stonington (exit 92 off I-95 to Route 2, then northwest ⅓ mile/½ km). Moderately priced prix-fixe dinners are prepared on the open hearth from historic recipes—including Thomas Jefferson's for bread pudding laced with brandy. Parts of the house date to 1685, when it was built by a farmer named John Randall. It has been an inn since 1987 but looks as it must have in Randall's time. If you spend the night, request one of the three rooms in the main house; they are more atmospheric than the twelve in the restored (and transplanted) 1819 barn, which handles the overflow, and some have working fireplaces. Dinner reservations are essential, as space in the three tiny dining rooms is limited, and there is only one seating, at 7:00 P.M. Tel: (203) 599-4540.

North of Connecticut's easternmost shore is the northeastern part of the state, known as the Quiet Corner. To enter this area backtrack west on I-95 past New London to I-395, then head north to Norwich.

THE QUIET CORNER

The Quiet Corner of Connecticut begins in the northeast, where Massachusetts and Rhode Island meet, rolls south along I-395, its major thoroughfare, to Norwich, and stretches west as far as Storrs and Willimantic. This was one of the earliest parts of the state to be settled by Europeans, and Norwich, settled in 1659, was one of the first towns chartered in Connecticut.

Although located in what once was a thriving industrial area in the 19th century, the factories of the northeast have been empty for many years. Ironically, the area's long neglect has contributed to its touristic interest because so much of the past has been preserved rather than updated. Village greens—such as those in Thompson, Pomfret, Woodstock, and Brooklyn—look much as they have for centuries. This region of gently rolling hills, woods, ponds, streams, and tiny lakes has some memorable sights (mostly historic houses), several excellent restaurants and country inns, antiques shops that haven't been picked clean, and generally lower prices than elsewhere in the state.

The recent opening of a casino in Ledyard holds promise that this so-called Quiet Corner may be on the brink of both economic recovery and touristic discovery. In the meantime, though, the thoughtful visitor who enjoys scenic drives with a dash of history will want to add this part of Connecticut to the itinerary, planning a leisurely three days here. The best times to visit are spring, when the fields and woods are newly green, and fall, when the maples are in full autumn splendor.

The first night of a tour of the Quiet Corner might be in Norwich, where the Shetucket and Yantic rivers merge to become the Thames. From Norwich you can make a day's loop through Lebanon, Willimantic, and Canterbury, and spend your second night in Brooklyn. The third day should lead to Thompson, Pomfret, and Woodstock, with a possible overnight in Woodstock. Then it's on to Storrs, Manchester, and, perhaps, Hartford, discussed following this section.

Norwich

Norwich, about 10 miles (16 km) north of New London via Routes 32 and 52 (or the more scenic Route 12 along the Thames River north from Groton), was a prospering small city by 1766, when it opened the colony's first paper mill.

During the 18th and 19th centuries Norwich was an industrial center, due partly to its prime location at the head of the Thames River, with textile and other mills. Today Norwich, a small city of about 37,000, is more of a backwater than it was when Benedict Arnold was born here (at Washington Street and Arnold Place). It has two main attractions today, the Slater Museum and the Leffingwell Inn.

The **Slater Museum**, on the campus of the Norwich Free Academy at 108 Crescent Street, has an intriguing collection of traditional Asian and African art, American art and furnishings from the 17th through the 20th century, and numerous changing exhibitions. Tel: (203) 887-2506.

The **Leffingwell Inn**, a two-story restored Colonial that is really two small saltboxes joined by an addition at the rear, is at 348 Washington Street. The oldest section dates to 1675, the next to 1701, and the third between 1730 and 1765. The interior of the inn has never been remodeled, which makes it something of a rarity and of great interest to architects, preservationists, and antiques collectors.

Christopher Leffingwell, an entrepreneur who built the first paper mill in Connecticut, was a major supplier for the Continental Army. News of the battles of Lexington and Concord first reached Norwich through reports made to him. His Tavern Room, with its heavily shuttered windows, was the scene of many Revolutionary War conferences and secret meetings.

The inn, including the George Washington Parlor (where Leffingwell entertained the general at breakfast on April 8, 1776), contains many fine examples of late-17th- and 18th-century furniture, among them Chippendale chairs and a Queen Anne tea table set with valuable china. Note also the samples of locally made silverware and the Mohegan Indian succotash bowl carved from pepperidge tree burl with wolf-head handles (the wolf is a Mohegan symbol). Open mid-May to mid-October and by appointment; Tel: (203) 869-9440.

Native American Sites

You'll notice a number of Indian names in the Norwich area, and you might want to spend a few hours visiting the sights that are reminders of the Mohegan presence. At the **Mohegan Burial Ground**, on Sachem Street off Route 32, is an 1840 obelisk honoring the burial site of Uncas (who died around 1683), a great Mohegan chief who was a friend of the first English settlers.

Yantic Falls, off Yantic Street, is the site of Indian Leap, where, according to legend, a band of Narragansett, fleeing from the Mohegan during the Battle of Great Plains in 1643, were driven over the rocks and into the chasm below.

About 5 miles (8 km) south of town via Routes 32 and 2A is **Fort Shantok State Park**, the site of another battle between the Narragansett and Mohegan, this one in 1645. The Mohegan retreated to their fort and would have been starved out had provisions not been smuggled in by their English allies, enabling Uncas and his men to drive the Narragansett out once and for all. The park is open year-round for hiking and picnicking.

Tucked into the woods a short drive east of Fort Shantok State Park (via Route 2A to 117 north, then Route 2 southeast), and about 10 miles (16 km) southeast of Norwich, is the **Manshantucket Pequot Reservation**, the location of **Foxwoods High Stakes Bingo and Casino**, Connecticut's first casino, Indian owned and open 24 hours a day. Discreet turquoise-coral markers along the wooded roads point the way. The casino's **Pequot Grill** serves reasonably priced steaks, chops, and other grilled meats. Tel: (203) 885-3000.

STAYING IN NORWICH

The most luxurious overnight choice in this part of the state is the **Norwich Inn, Spa & Villas** on Route 32. The Norwich is a 1929 inn that was totally renovated and upgraded in 1983 by Edward J. Safdie, owner of the Sonoma Mission Inn & Spa in Sonoma, California. The public rooms are elegant, while the guest rooms have a sort of cultivated rustic chic. The inn's Prince of Wales Room features a hearty New American menu, with many game dishes, but lighter spa fare is available as well. The spa, which adjoins the inn, has both an indoor and outdoor pool.

Lebanon

About 10 miles (16 km) northwest of Norwich (via Route 2 to exit 25, then along Route 87 for about 6 miles/10 km) is Lebanon, a wonderfully tranquil village with a mile-long, 160-acre common, where French hussars trained before joining Rochambeau on his march to Yorktown, Virginia. The handsome **Congregational Church** at the western corner of the common was designed by the artist John Trumbull in 1807. Constructed entirely of brick, even the pillars, it is something of a rarity.

Facing the common on West Town Street are four historic properties. The nine-room **Governor Jonathan Trumbull House** (1740) belonged to John Trumbull's father, who was governor of Connecticut both before and after the Revolutionary War. The house, a mansion in its time, has three stone chimneys that serve three rooms before merging into one in the attic. There is also a secret room where Trumbull worked, guarded by a sentry, while hiding from the English, as well as many of Trumbull's furnishings. The staff tells fascinating anecdotes. Open May 15 to October 15. Tel: (203) 642-7558.

Behind the house, moved from elsewhere in town, is the tiny **Doctor William Beaumont Homestead**, the birthplace of Dr. William Beaumont, the "father of gastric-digestion physiology," in 1785. The house is furnished with old-time medical implements, and one room is set up as an early-19th-century doctor's office. Open from May 15 to October 15. Tel: (203) 642-7247.

Also on the Trumbull property is the **Wadsworth Stable**, a Neoclassical structure built in the 1730s and moved from Hartford. Washington and others kept their horses here. (The stable is rarely open to the public.) Two doors farther along the same street is a barn-red, two-room frame building that served as the **war office** of Governor Trumbull. The structure is remarkable for its modest size, especially when you consider the military activity and efforts to secure supplies that took place in this area in 1780, during the last phases of the war. Open mid-May to mid-October; for information, call Jean MacArthur, Tel: (203) 423-2263.

Willimantic

From Lebanon take Route 207 east about 3 miles (5 km) to North Franklin and then head north along Route 32 for another 7 miles (11 km) into Willimantic, a delightful little town that is the largest of the four boroughs of Windham (whose total population is 22,000), just to the east.

Long known as "thread city" because of the longtime presence and influence of the American Thread Company in town, Willimantic has diversified in recent years with a variety of light industries. Its bustling Main Street, which parallels the Willimantic River, has recently been revitalized, with signage and storefronts made to resemble the period from 1880 to 1910. The **Jillson House Museum**, at 627 Main Street, is a mill owner's home that was built in 1825 from stone quarried on the banks of the Willimantic River; it's filled with period furniture and historical artifacts. Open Sundays in July and August, and for special exhibitions and by appointment; Tel: (203) 456-2316. For a light, casual lunch of soup, sandwiches, or quiche, drop by **Victorian Lady**, just up the street at 877 Main Street; Tel: (203) 456-4137.

Of perhaps greater interest than the Jillson Museum is the **Windham Textile and History Museum**, which consists of two buildings a few blocks away at 157 Union-Main Street, across from the abandoned, forlorn-looking factories of the

American Thread Company (which moved to South Carolina in 1985). An hour-long tour begins at the mill's fire station, where old tools and equipment are displayed and demonstrated. The old company store, the second building, today houses the re-created rooms (with authentic articles and furnishings) of a mill agent's Victorian home and, in contrast, the lodgings of a mill-working family. The mill, which began operation in 1854, relied on succeeding waves of immigrants for its work force, so each year the workers' rooms in the museum are changed to depict a different immigrant group, from Irish to French-Canadian to Polish and so on; the museum plans to cover 11 of the 25 ethnic groups that worked in the mill. In 1993 native-born Yankee workers will be featured. Tel: (203) 456-2178.

Canterbury

From Willimantic drive 13 miles (21 km) east on Route 14 into Canterbury, a pretty small town with a classic New England green, where Prudence Crandall, a remarkable Quaker schoolmistress who ran the first school for "young ladies and little misses of color" in the United States, made her home.

Prudence Crandall Museum

The 13-room Prudence Crandall Museum, a handsome, well-restored 1805 Federal structure at the junction of Routes 14 and 169, was Crandall's home and school. When Crandall opened her girls' school here all her students were white. In 1832 she admitted Sarah Harris, the 20-year-old daughter of a free black family in town, causing the exodus of many white students. Undaunted, Crandall kept the school open for black girls and women, the first such institution in Connecticut, if not New England. The subsequent uproar led to an infamous state law that forbade any school for "colored persons who are not inhabitants of the state." Crandall was arrested and imprisoned briefly in the county jail in nearby Brooklyn.

The school was continually vandalized, garbage and eggs were thrown at it, and someone attempted to set it on fire. One September night in 1834 a screaming crowd, armed with clubs and iron bars, surrounded the Crandall house and broke 90 windowpanes. Fearful for her girls' safety, Crandall closed the school, sold the house, and moved to the Midwest, where she continued to teach and to advocate abolitionism. In 1886, at age 84, she received an official apology, along with a $400 yearly pension from the Connecticut legislature, for the "cruel outrages" she had endured. She died four years later in Elk Falls, Kansas.

It took another 80 years for the state to buy and restore Crandall's home. It is now, fittingly, a museum dedicated to the history of African Americans and women and to the local history of northeastern Connecticut. The ground-floor rooms are furnished as they might have been in the 1830s, and there are changing exhibits as well as a black history research library. Interesting architectural features include pilasters, intricate cornices, and nine fireplaces. Open mid-January to mid-December. Tel: (203) 546-9916 or 566-3005.

Brooklyn

Brooklyn, 7 miles (11 km) due north of Canterbury via Route 169, is a quiet little town, so small and off the beaten track that most Nutmeggers (as residents of this, the Nutmeg State, call themselves), other than those in nearby towns, are unaware that there *is* a Brooklyn, Connecticut. Near the intersection of Routes 169 and 6 in the town center is the **Trinity Episcopal Church**, an undistinguished 19th-century edifice made of gray stone. But from the inside, especially on a sunny day, the stained-glass windows are magnificently luminous. Three are indisputably by Louis Comfort Tiffany. Tiffany's family lived in this area for more than two centuries, his father a prominent mill owner.

Brooklyn was the burial place of General Israel Putnam, who is said to have given the command at Bunker Hill in 1775, "Don't fire until you see the whites of their eyes." Putnam's trail winds throughout this northeast corner (and south as far as Greenwich), but his career began and ended in Brooklyn. A statue of him on horseback on the green in the center of town commemorates his many heroic deeds; his remains are buried beneath the statue. Also on Brooklyn's tranquil, Currier & Ives green are the white frame **Unitarian Universalist Church**, dating to 1771, and the town hall.

One mile (1½ km) north of town via Route 169, in a seemingly out-of-the-way spot, is the **New England Center for Contemporary Art**. Housed in a big, high-ceilinged barn, the gallery holds changing exhibitions of international art; theatrical performances are given in the barn in July and August. The center is open from May to November. Tel: (203) 774-8899. Across from the center stands a restored 1750 saltbox that now houses **Tannerbrook**, a small (only two guest rooms), pleasingly outfitted bed-and-breakfast.

Another mile farther north along Route 169 is the sign for the **Golden Lamb Buttery**, at Hillandale Farms, a sophisticated restaurant on a farm. You may begin your meal with cocktails on a hayride over fresh-mown fields, dodging sheep, ponies, and cows. A prix-fixe Continental dinner follows in the smartly decorated, high-ceilinged converted barn. During the meal a folksinger/guitarist strolls from table to table. It may sound a bit hokey, but it's done in a low-key way that makes for a memorable evening. In warm weather lunch is served on the deck. Reservations are essential, and no credit cards are accepted (although checks are). Open late May to January 1. Dinner Fridays and Saturdays only, at 7:00 P.M.; lunch Tuesday through Saturday. Tel: (203) 774-4423.

The **Brooklyn Fair**, the oldest continuous agricultural fair in the United States, is held the weekend before Labor Day on the fairgrounds on Route 169.

Pomfret

About 7 miles (11 km) north of Brooklyn on Route 169 is Pomfret. On the way there you might stop at **Sandra Lee's Herbs and Everlastings** (Route 97 in Pomfret Center, just south of Pomfret), where you can walk through two acres of gardens and field-grown everlastings; or at **Pomfret Antique World** (Routes 44 and 101), a huge enterprise, with dozens of dealers showing their wares in a 15,000-square-foot space (closed Wednesdays).

Pomfret itself is a delightful eye blink of a town with a handsome green, the Pomfret Preparatory School, and the stately, steepled 1715 **First Congregational Church**. The Vanilla Bean Café, housed in an old barn at the intersection of Routes 169, 44, and 97, is *the* spot in Pomfret, for students, faculty, and townsfolk alike. This is a casual self-serve place, with homemade soup, fresh muffins, sandwiches, and salads (and beer and wine). Tel: (203) 928-1562.

A gracious place to spend the night in Pomfret is **Cobbscroft**, on Route 169, a house constructed between 1800 and 1890. The inn has just three guest rooms: One is a suite with a fireplace and a gold-plated bathtub; the second has an attached extra room with a single bed; and the third has antique beds and pretty stenciling on the walls. Thomas and Janet Cobb, the owners, are an artist and a ceramist, respectively. Mr. Cobb's paintings decorate the rooms and are exhibited for sale in the old barn gallery on the grounds.

Putnam and Thompson

Route 44 east brings you in just 5 miles (8 km) to Putnam and the **Bradley Theater**, at 30 Front Street, whose schedule includes theater, concerts, and variety shows. Tel: (203) 928-7887.

Just a bit farther east on Route 44, then north on Routes 21 and 193, is Thompson, another old town (1693) with a beautiful green bordered by a classic, steepled New England church and a town hall dating to 1842. On the edge of the green is the **Vernon Stiles Inn**, which is of greater interest for its history and antique furnishings than its food, though lunches here, in front of a wood-burning fireplace, can be cozy. Closed Tuesdays; Tel: (203) 923-9571.

Thompson seems to be the very model of New England virtue today, but its 19th-century history is anything but virtuous. Situated near both the Rhode Island and Massachusetts borders, the town—with the inn as a magnet—attracted fugitives, liquor salesmen, and eloping couples evading the more stringent laws of the neighboring states. Captain Vernon Stiles, a justice of the peace, was the inn's landlord. When Thomas Dorr, unofficially elected governor of Rhode Island and instigator of Dorr's Rebellion in 1841 (a protest against a voting restriction in the Colonial Charter), had to flee the state, he headed for Thompson. He subsequently escaped capture at the Vernon Stiles by using the complicated back stairways of the inn.

Not everyone who visited Thompson was an outlaw or runaway. In 1824 the Marquis de Lafayette spent the night at the Vernon Stiles, an event commemorated on the inn's sign ever since.

The Vernon Stiles is no longer open to overnight guests, but for them there is the **Lord Thompson Manor**, a bed-and-breakfast on 66 acres on Route 200, a comfortable Victorian mansion furnished with fin-de-siècle antiques. Four of the nine guest rooms are truly enormous, the others perfectly adequate, and all look out onto beautiful wooded grounds.

Woodstock

Perhaps the most important stop on a Quiet Corner itinerary is Woodstock, about 10 miles (16 km) west of Thompson via Route 193 south to 171 west, then north on Route 169. Dominating this little jewel of a town is the huge grassy Woodstock Common. Woodstock's biggest attraction is Roseland Cottage, but this unhurried, old-fashioned town makes a peaceful base for exploring the area.

Local antiques and craft shops include **Windy Acres** on Route 171, the **Scranton's Shops** complex at the junction of Routes 171 and 169, and **Robin's Nest Studio** at 269 Child Hill Road (off Route 169). The **Woodstock Fair**, the largest agricultural fair in the state, with family entertainment and handicrafts, as well as the usual farm animals and equipment, is held every Labor Day weekend and attracts thousands. The fairgrounds are on Route 171.

Roseland Cottage

Facing the Woodstock Common is Roseland Cottage, recognizable by its vibrant bubblegum-pink color, dark green shutters, and brown trim ("all the colors you'd find in a rose," the house guides explain). The cottage is Gothic Revival in style, with Gothic windows, gables, finials, chimneys and chimney pots, intricate gingerbread detailing, and a pitched roof. The Society for the Preservation of New England Antiquities (SPNEA), which owns the house, considers it one of the most important surviving examples of the style in New England.

The "cottage"—really a large, rambling structure—was built in 1846 as a summer home for Henry Bowen, a local boy who made good in New York as a silk importer and the publisher of an antislavery newspaper called *The Independent*. Bowen showed off a bit to his home-town folks by commissioning New York architect Joseph Collins Wells (designer of the First Presbyterian Church in Greenwich Village, Manhattan) to build the house and by hiring New York cabinetmaker Thomas Brooks to make the Gothic Revival furniture, most of which is still in place. The cottage was so named for Mrs. Bowen's love of roses.

In the guest book are the names of Bowen's friends: Henry Ward Beecher, Ulysses S. Grant, Rutherford B. Hayes, Benjamin Harrison, and William McKinley. Many came on the Fourth of July, a big occasion in mid-19th-century-Woodstock, with torchlight rallies, fireworks, and fiery oratory. President Grant's arrival in 1870 was announced by a volley of cannon fire. (Grant may have been disappointed that the strongest drink served at the Bowens' was rose-tinted fruit punch. Bowen was an ardent advocate of temperance; Grant most assuredly was not.)

The Bowen house is of course interesting for its historical associations, but it is fascinating in and of itself. Bowen's descendants lived in the house until 1968, when SPNEA bought the property. SPNEA has kept the place pretty much as it was in Bowen's day; it still offers a rare, authentic portrait of 19th-century Gothic interior design. In the south parlor, which is separated from the north parlor by a Gothic arch, is a Minton-tiled bird scene hand-painted on the fireplace, and in both parlors is stained glass from Italy. Among the items to look for as you tour the house are the Gothic designs on interior door panels; the cathedral window in the writing room; porcelain door handles inside and out; Chinese wallpaper designs; many pieces of Gothic Revival furniture; an original Thonet chair from Vienna; and the pink, gold, and white Limoges porcelain (with the Bowen monogram) on the great oval dining room table. Oliver Wendell Holmes and Harriet Beecher Stowe dined at this table, consuming great quantities of chicken salad that Bowen had shipped from New York.

The heavily embossed wall covering that resembles tooled leather in the downstairs rooms is called Lincrusta Walton, a pressed wood-pulp fabric that is rare in the United States but was widely used in Victorian England. The process was invented in Stamford, Connecticut, by the same man who invented linoleum.

The upstairs bedroom where Presidents Hayes, Harrison, and McKinley slept (at different times, of course) in a huge Empire-style bed affords excellent views of the formal parterre garden, laid out in 1850 with dwarf hedging.

Be sure to leave time to wander Roseland's grounds. Originally six acres, the property is now three, with several outbuildings, an ice house, an aviary, and a huge carriage barn. Inside the barn is Bowen's bowling alley, one of the first private alleys in the country and the oldest surviving, with his original wooden pins. (Rumor has it that Ulysses Grant threw a strike on his first attempt, then declined to try again.)

If you visit in late spring or midsummer you'll be treated to a garden vibrant with peonies, asters, roses, impatiens, begonias, snapdragons, phlox, goat's beard, heliotrope, hydrangeas, lemon lilies, and geraniums, all planted in the style in which Bowen originally arranged them (known as ribbon planting), surrounded by a boxwood hedge. A tiny Greek-temple gazebo stands to the side. Lilacs, a tulip tree, hemlocks, and other plantings, many of which are descendants of the originals, grace the grounds. Every other Friday during the summer, twilight concerts are held on the lawn, and afternoon tea is served every second and fourth Wednesday from 2:00 to 4:00 P.M. The house is open from Memorial Day through mid-October; Tel: (203) 928-4074.

The Common

Across from Roseland Cottage on the town common is a marker relating that 13 men (one a Bowen ancestor), known as the 13 goers (an archaic word for travellers), came from Roxbury in the Massachusetts Bay Colony to build a settlement here in 1686. One of the town's famous personages, the marker continues, was Jedediah Morse, who wrote the first text published in this country on American geography, entitled *Geography Made Easy,* in 1784. Diagonally across the common is the old white clapboard house where Bowen was born. His gravestone is in the **Woodstock Hill Cemetery** across the common.

DINING AND STAYING IN THE WOODSTOCK AREA

A cheerful place for an overnight stay and/or dinner (or Sunday brunch) is the **Inn at Woodstock Hill**, an imposing old house turned inn at 94 Plaine Hill Road, in South Woodstock. The 19 guest rooms are individually decorated and pleasingly color-coordinated. There is a mini-suite with a four-poster canopy bed. The house itself is listed on the National Register of Historic Places. Tel: (203) 928-0528.

Another dinner option is the **Harvest at Bald Hill** (corner of Routes 169 and 171), a romantic, softly lit place with a sophisticated menu. The lobster bisque, chicken madrigal, and seared peppered sirloin are excellent. The wine list has won awards for its depth and complexity. Tel: (203) 974-2240.

If you are on a slow travel track, take time to drive a bit farther west (about 18 miles/29 km via Route 171 west and north, then another 10 miles/16 km west on Route 190) to **Stafford Springs**. There you'll find **Chez Pierre**, a country French restaurant lodged in a Victorian home, at 111 West Main Street. The hearty fare is authentically Gallic, and chef-owner Pierre Courrieu stocks a superb wine cellar. Tel: (203) 684-5826.

Storrs

The distance from Woodstock to Storrs is about 20 miles (32 km) via Route 169 south then Route 44 west. On Route 44 (just west of the junction of Routes 44 and 169, 2 miles/3 km south of Pomfret center) is the entrance to **Mashamoquet Brook State Park**. Among the park's hiking trails is the Wolf Den Trail, which leads to the wolf den where Israel Putnam is said to have slain the last wolf in Connecticut. You can also picnic, fish, and swim at the park.

Continuing west from the park on Route 44, then 44A, you make a right onto Route 195 just beyond Mansfield and head south about 2 miles (3 km) to reach Storrs. Route 195 runs right through town and is chockablock with collegiate-type shops and fast-food joints. Turn left off 195 to where the real interest lies, the **University of Connecticut** (UConn, pronounced "Yukon") campus, which dominates this little town of 12,000 and has several interesting attractions.

Facing each other on the campus are the **William Benton Museum of Art** (Tel: 203/486-4520; closed late December to late January), with an impressive collection of 3,000 American and European paintings of the 19th and 20th centuries, and with changing thematic exhibits; and the **Connecticut State Museum of Natural History** (Tel: 203/486-4460), with permanent exhibits on Connecticut woodland Indians, Connecticut minerals, and birds of prey, as well as changing exhibits.

While on campus, sample the fresh, homemade ice cream at the **UConn Dairy Bar**, on Horsebarn Hill Extension. There are usually about 34 flavors to choose from, made from the cream of the UConn Agricultural School's cows (UConn began in 1881 as an agricultural land-grant college).

Also on the campus are the **Nutmeg Summer Theater**, with professional productions, and, in the same building, **UConn Nutmeg Theater**, which stages university productions. Tel: (203) 486-3969. In fall, winter, and spring **Jorgensen Auditorium**, at 2132 Hillside Road in Mansfield, just north of Storrs, features touring companies in dance, music, and theater. Tel: (203) 486-4226.

For lunch or dinner in Storrs you might try the **Altnaveigh Inn**, a lively establishment at 957 Storrs Road known for its high-quality Angus beef. The six guest rooms in this 1734 farmhouse are simple but well kept. Tel: (203) 429-4490.

Coventry

Five miles (8 km) south of Storrs via Routes 195 and 275, Coventry has three claims to fame: Caprilands Herb Farm, just off Route 31 at 534 Silver Street; the Nathan Hale Homestead, at 2299 South Street; and the Strong-Porter House, family home of Hale's mother, across South Street from the Hale Homestead.

Caprilands Herb Farm is an 18th-century farmhouse and barn surrounded by herb gardens that are laid out in specific decorative motifs according to the plants included, such as the Silver, Medieval, Shakespeare, Colonial, and Saints gardens. The grounds also include 50 acres of woods, meadows, and pastures. Special herb lunches are served in the small rooms of the old farmhouse.

Caprilands was created by Adelma Grenier Simmons, a pixieish lady of indeterminate years who turned a goat farm (hence the name, *capri* being derived from the Latin word for goat) into prosperous herb gardens. Always garbed in a cape, she gives such lively lectures on herbs and herb lore that every scented bit of greenery assumes a personality of its own. Simmons's aphorisms include "Silver rosemary is good for mind and memory, and tasty in tea, but if you don't like that, you can wash your hair in it," and "Bay leaf is a perfect city companion; it resists pollution and likes people."

Devotees, mostly women, travel great distances to spend a day at Caprilands, attend a lecture, browse the gardens, buy plants, and enjoy lunch in the farmhouse, where every dish is accented by a different herb. Lectures are given Monday through Saturday at noon; Caprilands is open every day. Tel: (203) 742-7244.

The name **Nathan Hale Homestead** is somewhat misleading, as this sturdy, ten-room barn-red farmhouse was built by Hale's brothers and father, Deacon Richard Hale, in 1776, the year the 21-year-old Nathan was hanged by the English as an American spy. Nevertheless, the house, erected after the elder Hale made his fortune in farming and livestock, serves as a prime example of a prosperous farm home of the era. It does contain a few of Nathan's belongings, including his army trunk, his boyhood "fowling piece," mounted above the fireplace in the dining room, and his Bible and silver shoe buckles (in the parlor).

The house has a center hall, new in Connecticut at that time, which allowed for a more formal, gracious arrangement of the unusually large rooms.

The Hale family's affluence is most apparent in the parlor, with its fine wood paneling, a portrait of Nathan's brother John, and a Queen Anne tea table set with English lusterware in front of the brick fireplace. The farm remained in the Hale family until 1832. Open mid-May to mid-October. Tel: (203) 742-6917.

The **Strong-Porter House**, across the road from the Nathan Hale Homestead (a combination ticket can be bought for both houses), was built in 1730 by a prominent local man, Captain Joseph Strong, whose oldest daughter, Elizabeth, married Richard Hale in 1746 and bore him 12 children, of whom Nathan was the sixth. The house displays local artifacts and memorabilia. Also on the grounds are a carpenter's shop, carriage shed, and barn. Open weekends mid-May to mid-October.

SHOPPING AND DINING
IN THE COVENTRY AREA

Take some time to do a little antiques browsing in the numerous shops along Coventry's Main Street (Route 31). The inventory at **New Coventry Antique Center & Loft**, in an old church at 1141 Main Street, ranges from furniture to linens to old bottles. The **Coventry Flea Market**, at the junction of Routes 31 and 275, is held on Sundays.

For a more sophisticated alternative to a lunch at Caprilands, drive 10 miles (16 km) west on Route 31 to Route

44 into **Manchester**. **Cavey's**, a first-rate Continental restaurant at 45 East Center Street here, is a two-leveled affair: On the lower floor is Cavey's excellent French restaurant, a formal place decorated in Belle Epoque style; the cuisine is *haute,* and only dinner is served. The ground level is light, sunny, and Mediterranean in spirit, with delicious northern Italian fare at both lunch and dinner. Tel: (203) 643-2751.

From this part of the Quiet Corner, so idyllic for meandering and casual exploring, it is a short and easy ride (just 10 miles/16 km west from Manchester on I-384/I-84) into the modern, bustling, big-city ambience of Connecticut's capital, Hartford.

HARTFORD AND ENVIRONS

There are various ways to explore this north-central region of Connecticut, centered on the Connecticut River, but most convenient is to use Hartford as a base, making day trips in all directions from here. As the Hartford area was one of the earliest settled, there are a number of intriguing historical sights within a 10- to 15-mile radius of the city, and a good highway system extends north–south (I-95) and southwest–northeast (I-84).

HARTFORD

For a city its size (population about 140,000), Hartford has a lot going for it, despite its stodgy reputation as "insurance capital of the nation." As the state capital and, consequently, the source of Connecticut's political and economic agenda, it is the focus of statewide attention.

Hartford's roots go deep, having been established by the Saukiog Indians along the Connecticut River. In 1633 the Dutch established a trading post on the river and called it the House of Good Hope. Around the same time, the Reverend Thomas Hooker, learning of the abundance of furs and timber there, led a group of 100 independent-spirited people from the Massachusetts Bay Colony to settle in the Hartford area. Those from Dorchester established a trading post in the Windsor area to the north, while those from

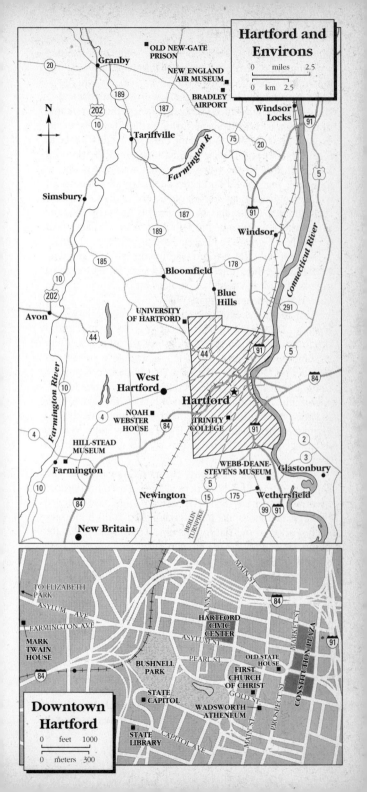

Hartford and Environs

0 miles 2.5
0 km 2.5

N

OLD NEW-GATE PRISON
Granby
NEW ENGLAND AIR MUSEUM
20
189
202
187
BRADLEY AIRPORT
10
Windsor Locks
91
Tariffville
75
20
5
187
Farmington R.
Simsbury
91
189
Windsor
185
178
Connecticut River
202
10
Bloomfield
291
Avon
Blue Hills
44
UNIVERSITY OF HARTFORD
44
91
5
Farmington River
10
West Hartford
Hartford
84
NOAH WEBSTER HOUSE
4
84
TRINITY COLLEGE
91
2
HILL-STEAD MUSEUM
WEBB-DEANE-STEVENS MUSEUM
Glastonbury
3
4
Farmington
10
5
175
Wethersfield
84
Newington
15
99
91
BERLIN TURNPIKE
New Britain

Downtown Hartford

0 feet 1000
0 meters 300

TO ELIZABETH PARK
ASYLUM AVE.
FARMINGTON AVE.
MAIN ST.
MAIN ST.
84
MARKET ST.
91
MARK TWAIN HOUSE
HARTFORD CIVIC CENTER
ASYLUM ST.
CONSTITUTION PLAZA
PEARL ST.
OLD STATE HOUSE
84
BUSHNELL PARK
FIRST CHURCH OF CHRIST
PROSPECT ST.
STATE CAPITOL
GOLD ST.
WADSWORTH ATHENEUM
MAIN ST.
STATE LIBRARY
CAPITOL AVE.

Watertown settled in Wethersfield to the south, thus sparking a continuing controversy as to which town was actually the first in the state to be settled.

Hooker dubbed *his* settlement New Town, after the Massachusetts town now called Cambridge, where the group came from. It was later renamed Hertford, which eventually evolved into Hartford. In 1638 the three settlements joined to form the Hartford Colony, coming together at the Hartford meetinghouse. A governing document was drawn up the following year, called Fundamental Orders of Connecticut, which many historians consider to be one of the world's first constitutions. The Dutch were ousted in 1654. By 1662 the Hartford Colony became officially the Colony of Connecticut with a charter granted by England's Charles II. Much later, on September 20, 1780, George Washington and the Comte de Rochambeau, the French commander, met for the very first time in Hartford to plan their strategy for beating the British and ending the Revolutionary War.

What really put Hartford on the map was the insurance business. During the 18th century groups of men in Hartford began insuring losses on shipping vessels lost at sea. There is some evidence that the first fire insurance policy was issued in 1794 by the Hartford Fire Insurance Company. Later, as the shipping business declined, the Hartford insurance companies concentrated on selling fire insurance, making good on disasters all over the country, including the San Francisco earthquake of 1906. There are now some 35 to 40 insurance-company headquarters in the greater Hartford area.

As the insurance business prospered, so did the city. Colonel Samuel Colt, born here in 1814, started his Hartford firearms factory in 1855. The factory's blue, star-spangled dome, which looks like that of a displaced Turkish mosque, adds sparkle to the Hartford skyline. Legend has it that the dome was a gift from an Ottoman sultan in gratitude for the success of Colt products against his enemies.

Hartford's golden age, though, was the late 19th century, when the city was a literary and cultural oasis between New York and Boston. When Samuel Clemens (hereafter in these pages referred to by his pen name) first visited in 1869, he called Hartford "the best built and the handsomest town I have ever seen. . . . They have the broadest, straightest streets . . . and the dwelling houses are the amplest in size, and the shapeliest, and have the most capacious ornamental grounds about them." Twain put his money where his mouth was and built a home here, which he lived in from 1874 to 1891, a period he considered the happiest of his life.

The poet Wallace Stevens moved to Hartford from Pennsylvania in 1916 to make his livelihood in the insurance business and lived in the city, writing his poems in his spare time, until his death in 1955.

Like many cities Hartford has had its ups and downs, as the once-thriving city center deteriorated and many professionals and white-collar workers fled to quieter, safer suburbs. A 1960s revitalization spree gave the city **Constitution Plaza**, a complex of high-rise office buildings connected by a series of plazas and an elevated walkway; the **Phoenix Life Insurance Building** (on the plaza), a blue-green all-glass tower called "the boat" for its elliptical shape; and I. M. Pei's residential and office complex **Bushnell Tower**, on Gold Street. Every year from the day after Thanksgiving through December there is a **Festival of Lights** on Constitution Plaza.

In 1975 the **Hartford Civic Center** was built downtown on more than seven and a half acres west of Constitution Plaza, with a food court, some 50 shops, a coliseum for sporting and musical events, an underground parking garage, and an indoor link to the Sheraton Hotel.

All this urban renewal has given Hartford a psychic boost (though the trade-off is that very little of old Hartford remains in the city center except for a few fine old brownstones) and has led to new office complexes, restaurants, and a first-rate repertory theater, the **Hartford Stage Company** (Tel: 203/525-5601). Although the last decade has brought the usual big-city problems of unemployment, the decline of peripheral neighborhoods, and increased crime, Hartford remains a magnet for visitors, with many things to see and do, especially by day. (At night use the same caution exercised in any big city.)

The major sights of downtown Hartford—the Wadsworth Atheneum, Center Church, the Old State House, the Civic Center, and the Butler-McCook Homestead—are all within a few blocks of one another and just a few blocks east of Bushnell Park and the State Capitol. The Mark Twain and Harriet Beecher Stowe houses are just outside the city center. To reach them you need to drive or take a bus west on Asylum, which runs into Farmington Avenue. Attractions in West Hartford, discussed following the Hartford section, are best reached by car.

Downtown Hartford

For a large city, the center of Hartford is surprisingly compact, especially the areas of touristic interest. It is easiest to park your car and proceed from sight to sight on foot.

WADSWORTH ATHENEUM

Founded in 1842 by local philanthropist Daniel Wadsworth and opened officially in 1844, the Wadsworth Atheneum, at 600 Main Street, is the nation's oldest continuously operating public art museum. The original Gothic Revival building is a gray stone marvel of towers, leaded windows, and battlements. Through the years—with the largess of other donors and patrons, among them Elizabeth Colt, Samuel Colt's widow, and J. P. Morgan, whose family roots were in Hartford—four buildings were added to house the ever-expanding collection.

Gifts to Wadsworth by his friend Thomas Cole and other painters of the Hudson River School form the nucleus of the Atheneum's American collection. Hartford-born Frederic Church, encouraged by Mark Twain to become a painter over his businessman father's objections, contributed a number of outstanding works to the museum.

Other standouts among more than 40,000 pieces of art—spanning some 5,000 years and displayed in five buildings—are works from the Renaissance, Baroque, and Impressionist (both French and American) periods and from the European decorative arts in the J. Pierpont Morgan collection. There are also two magnificent rooms, one mid-18th-century, the other Victorian, that were rescued from local homes facing demolition.

Of contemporary interest are the Atheneum's Amistad Foundation collection of African-American art and artifacts, two new galleries exhibiting the works, history, and culture of African Americans; and the Matrix Gallery, which exhibits the work of new artists. Outside the Atheneum is a monumental red-steel sculpture, *Stegosaurus,* by the late Alexander Calder, once a Connecticut resident. Tel: (203) 278-2670.

CENTER CHURCH AREA

Just a short stroll north along Main Street at the corner of Gold Street is Center Church, Thomas Hooker's **First Church of Christ**. In its yard Connecticut ratified the United States Constitution in 1788. The present church (the fourth on the site), which dates to 1807, was modeled after St. Martin-in-the-Fields in London and has five windows by Tiffany. The church runs a series of musical programs and lectures open to the public. Tel: (203) 249-5631.

Behind the church is the grassy **Ancient Burying Ground**, where Hooker, Joseph and Jeremiah Wadsworth (active during the American Revolution), and other notables are buried. The carved headstones, some of which date to 1640, are used by craftsmen for making stone rubbings. Certain epitaphs are treasures: "As I am now/So will you be/Prepare for

Death/And follow me," was answered on a neighboring tombstone with these lines: "To follow you/I'm not content/ Until I know/Which way you went." Note the **Founders' Monument**, erected in the 1940s, which lists the names of Hartford founders.

Outside the church grounds, on the grass along Gold Street, are 36 huge boulders. These did not fall off a quarry truck; they form a "sculpture" by Carl Andre called *Stone Field,* a source of local controversy. Perhaps a more uplifting sight is the silhouette of the church steeple reflected in the shimmering gold panels of Financial Plaza (better known as the Gold Building).

Across Main Street is the 527-foot-high **Travelers Tower**, the highest man-made observation point in Connecticut, built on the site of Sanford's Tavern, which was the scene of the legendary Charter Oak incident (see below). Free tours are available from May to October. Tel: (203) 277-2431.

OLD STATE HOUSE
Just three blocks north of Center Church, smack in the middle of modern downtown Hartford and visible as you come off I-91 at exit 31, is one of the city's oldest edifices, the Old State House. At 800 Main Street, just west of Constitution Plaza, is the handsomely refurbished structure, built in 1796 by Charles Bulfinch before he rebuilt the U.S. Capitol in Washington, D.C. It is considered one of the finest examples of Federal architecture in the country.

The venerable brick-and-brownstone building has seen its share of history. Seven U.S. presidents (two Adamses, Monroe, Jackson, Polk, Johnson, and Grant) have climbed the massive staircase that dominates the central hall, and in 1814, at the Hartford Convention, 26 New England state representatives met to air their complaints about the lack of naval protection in the War of 1812. In 1834 in the gracefully columned courtroom, Prudence Crandall (see The Quiet Corner, above) was convicted of flouting a state law that deemed it illegal to open a school for "colored persons who are not inhabitants of the state." Just five years later the courtroom witnessed another trial with a far different outcome: Slaves who mutinied and seized the Spanish ship *Amistad* were freed and the ship impounded.

The Old State House is closed for restoration until 1995, and its Visitor Information Center, with an attractive gift shop, has moved across the street for the duration. Once the renovation is complete visitors will be able to see the beautifully proportioned rooms, especially the Senate Chamber, with its Gilbert Stuart portrait of George Washington and many antiques. Tel: (203) 522-6766.

Just outside the Old State House, at Main Street and Asylum Avenue, there is a year-round **open-air market** where farmers from nearby areas bring fresh produce every Monday, Wednesday, and Saturday from 10:00 A.M. to 2:00 P.M.

BUTLER-McCOOK HOMESTEAD

South of the Old State House, at 396 Main Street, at Capital Avenue, is the Butler-McCook Homestead. While historic homes are no rarity in New England, what is especially interesting about this one is that, first, it is the only 18th-century house left in Hartford's center; and, second, it was occupied by a single family for four generations (from 1782 to 1971).

John James McCook, an Episcopal priest and professor at Trinity College here, was best known for his ground-breaking work in sociology and urban studies. As other prosperous families moved westward to the Asylum Hill area or out of town, it was McCook's wish to keep "the family together in the old surroundings," which left a treasure trove for visitors today. Among the many artifacts on the homestead is a small but fine collection of Japanese armor, Colonial-era pewter plates and stoneware, and Victorian toys and artifacts—even a Victorian garden. Tel: (203) 522-1806.

Lunch in Downtown Hartford

Wadsworth Atheneum's **Museum Café** is a congenial spot overlooking the Gengras Sculpture Court; tea is served in the café on Sunday afternoons. Tel: (203) 728-5989. An inexpensive lunch alternative is to pick something up at the ethnic food booths at the nearby Civic Center; **Gaetano's Café**, on the second floor of the Civic Center, is a more casual annex of **Gaetano's Ristorante**. The café, just to the right inside the restaurant door, is a good place for pastas, salads, and sandwiches. The restaurant proper is more expensive and offers more elaborate Italian fare such as pollo pomodoro and saltimbocca. Its window tables provide a nice view of the busy street scene below. Tel: (203) 249-1629.

(See also Dining in Hartford, below.)

State Capitol Area

BUSHNELL PARK

A few blocks west of the city's commercial core, and only three blocks south of the Civic Center, the Bushnell Park area is bustling with legislators, business people, and tourists. Bushnell Park, a well-manicured tract of land dotted with some 150 varieties of trees, is a 40-acre park designed in 1853 by Frederick Law Olmsted, a Hartford resident renowned for his design of New York City's Central Park. The park was named for the Reverend Horace Bushnell, a famed local reformer, preacher, and civic leader who helped secure the land for a public park. When the city of Hartford purchased it in 1854, it set an example that began a national trend to city-owned parklands. It is now a national landmark.

The **Bushnell Park Carousel** is a wonderful merry-go-round made in 1914, complete with 48 hand-carved horses, two ornate "lovers' chariots," and music provided by a refurbished Wurlitzer Band Organ. Operating times depend on the weather. Tel: (203) 246-7739.

STATE CAPITOL

The imposing Gothic Revival Connecticut State Capitol, designed by Richard Upjohn in 1879 and recently refurbished, is on the south side of Bushnell Park on Capitol Avenue. Its gold-leafed dome dominates the downtown landscape. Guided tours of the marble and granite building (conducted by the League of Women Voters weekdays year-round and also on Saturdays in summer; Tel: 203/240-0222) show off the imposing interior, with its hand-painted marble columns; the carved walnut paneling and colorful Gothic stained-glass windows of the house of representatives; and the oak woodwork and famous, ornately carved Charter Oak chair (see below) of the state senate.

CONNECTICUT STATE LIBRARY

Across Capitol Avenue is the Connecticut State Library, housing the **Colt Collection of Firearms** (more than 1,000 in all) and the original 1662 **royal charter** for the state. The story of Connecticut's royal charter and the so-called Charter Oak is fraught with intrigue.

When James II became king of England in 1685 he decided to unite the New England colonies into a single entity, with Sir Edmund Andros as the royal governor—an arrangement opposed by Connecticut officials. Andros came to Hartford to retrieve the royal charter issued by the previous king, Charles II, and met with local officials at Sanford's Tavern (where Travelers Tower is now).

The evening the charter was to be handed over, someone blew out the candles at the crucial moment. In the ensuing confusion Captain Joseph Wadsworth spirited the charter away and hid it in a large, hollow oak tree, known ever after as the Charter Oak until it was felled by a storm in 1856. (The "grandchild" of the Charter Oak can be seen on the Center Church grounds.) Andros managed to take over the state for two years, but in 1688, when James II was deposed, Andros was ousted. In 1689 the original royal charter was retrieved and a century later used as a model for the United States Constitution.

MARK TWAIN HOUSE

If you have time to visit just one sight in Hartford, it should be the Mark Twain House in Nook Farm, one mile west of the Civic Center via Farmington Avenue, at 77 Forest Street. Anyone who grew up on *The Adventures of Tom Sawyer* or *The Adventures of Huckleberry Finn* will delight in this house, in which Twain wrote both books and five others during the 17 years he spent here.

What makes the Mark Twain house so special is the spirit it evokes of the author himself. It is thoroughly eccentric, from its rambling three-story "steamboat Gothic" exterior—enhanced with decorative designs in red and orange brick, turrets, gables, balconies, and porches—to the extraordinary carved-wood mantelpiece, extending from floor to ceiling, that he brought back from Ayton Castle in Edinburgh, Scotland, for his library.

Twain spent $131,000 on the house, a fortune at the time (1874). The architect was Edward Tuckerman Potter, but the house seems thoroughly Twain's, especially the Mississippi steamboat-like shape, the dressing room that resembles a boat's wheelhouse, and the "ombra," the family name for the open porch designed like a riverboat deck.

Louis Comfort Tiffany's firm was hired to decorate the house, and Tiffany's touches remain in the Easter-lily glass panels at the front door, the silvery, geometric stenciled wall designs, and the stenciled "riverboat" dining room doors that fold back. (Twain's wife, Livy, did not like the doors, so Tiffany stenciled them to make them "disappear.")

The house's uniqueness was noted by the author himself in a poem called "This is the house that Mark built." The first stanza says:

> These are the bricks of various hue
> And shape and position, straight and askew,
> With the nooks and angles and gables too,
> Which make up the house presented to view,
> The curious house that Mark built.

Twain procured many of the furnishings on his European travels. The richly carved four-poster bed in the master bedroom, rife with three-dimensional wooden cherubs, was bought in Venice in 1878. Twain claimed that he and Livy slept in the bed backward so they could better admire the ornate headboard. There are 12 carved and tiled fireplaces in the 19-room house (Livy collected tiles and they can be seen throughout). Above the Tiffany-tiled fireplace in the dining room is a window, because Twain supposedly liked the conceit of watching a fire and a snowstorm at the same time (the flues of the chimney go off to the side).

While the house and its idiosyncrasies speak for themselves, the tour guides have been well briefed. Anecdotes about Twain's Nook Farm life unfold, making even the least knowledgeable visitor feel a kinship with the author.

For all the pleasures this cheerful house holds for the visitor, it had an unfortunate ending for the owner and his family. Financial woes made it impossible to keep up; the Twains closed the house in 1891 and left on a lengthy money-raising lecture tour. While they were away their daughter Susie returned to Hartford for a visit, was stricken with spinal meningitis, and died at age 24, supposedly in the Mahogany Room (named for the African mahogany bed and bureau Livy commissioned and had embedded with Wedgwood tiles), the same ground-floor guest bedroom that William Dean Howells had christened the Royal Chamber when he stayed there in happier times. The house subsequently filled Livy with such sadness that she refused to live there again, and it was sold in 1903.

Yet during Twain's years in Hartford, visitors to the city and his house read like a Who's Who of 19th-century American cultural life: William Dean Howells, Thomas Nast, Thomas Bailey Aldrich, Joel Chandler Harris, George Washington Cabell, Henry Ward Beecher, and William Gillette. Gillette, who originated the role of Sherlock Holmes on Broadway, had roots at Nook Farm. His father bought the 100-acre wooded tract, on the western edge of Hartford by the Park River, that was called The Nook. Little by little he sold off parcels to friends; in time his Nook Farm became *the* fashionable residential section of town. Charles Dudley Warner, editor of *The Hartford Courant* and collaborator with Mark Twain on *The Gilded Age,* lived nearby; Harriet Beecher Stowe was Twain's closest neighbor. A later Nook Farm owner was Katharine Hepburn's father.

Through time Hartford has swallowed up the neighborhood, and the Twain and Stowe houses are all that's left of Nook Farm. Fortunately, both are impeccably preserved.

HARRIET BEECHER STOWE HOUSE
The Harriet Beecher Stowe house, adjacent to the Twain house on Farmington Avenue, is fascinating in its own right and also reflects the strong personality of its owner. Built in 1871, the simple, well-proportioned house typifies late-

19th-century "cottage" architecture, with many gingerbread details.

Mrs. Stowe had a flair for decorating, and many of her ideas were advanced for the time. It was she who influenced the light, airy feel of the Twain house's conservatory. In fact, a book she wrote on home decorating was as widely read as her novel *Uncle Tom's Cabin*. She used plants extensively throughout her house, draping German ivy as frames around the windows. Her rooms were lighter and airier than in most Victorian homes, with big windows, floral wallpaper, and an asymmetrical floor plan.

The Stowe family lived in the house until Mrs. Stowe's death in 1896; many of the Victorian furnishings that remain in the house were hers, such as the tufted Victorian sofa, two Gothic walnut chairs with red velvet seats, a fine American Chippendale mahogany side chair, and a drop-leaf Empire mahogany table (on which she wrote parts of *Uncle Tom's Cabin*). Mrs. Stowe also painted, and the long, narrow oils on either side of the Gothic bookcases in the front parlor are some of her many works.

During the Christmas holidays both houses are decorated in the Victorian manner, with evergreen garlands and trees festooned with popcorn and cranberry chains, antique ornaments, and red velvet ribbons and bows.

A visit to the two houses takes about one and a half hours; the Twain house alone takes approximately 50 minutes. There's a gift shop on the grounds with a full selection of books by Stowe and Twain, as well as other memorabilia. One ticket will admit you to both houses; guided tours only. Tel: (203) 525-9317.

ELIZABETH PARK

Six blocks north and west of the Mark Twain and Harriet Beecher Stowe houses is 90-acre Elizabeth Park (take Woodland Avenue north to Asylum Street and turn left toward Prospect Avenue), with some 14,000 rosebushes and more than 900 varieties of roses. This was the first city-owned rose garden in the United States, the gift in 1894 of Charles M. Pond, a wealthy descendant of early Hartford settlers, who named the park after his wife. Outdoor concerts are held here in summer, and there's ice skating (with skate rentals) on the pond in winter when it's cold enough.

THE GOVERNOR'S MANSION

Across from the park, at 990 Prospect Avenue (at the corner of Asylum), is the State of Connecticut's 19-room Governor's Mansion. Governor and Mrs. Lowell Weicker have opened it to the public Tuesday, Wednesday, and Thursday mornings, by prearrangement only. This is only the second time in Connecticut's history that the stately brick Georgian Revival house has been made accessible to the general public; the first time was for a tea party in 1945. Built in 1908, it was a private home until purchased as the official residence in 1943. Of the public rooms on display, the parlor has the finest antiques—a 1780 walnut highboy, a Queen Anne corner chair, two Meissen porcelain vases—all on loan from the University of Connecticut's Benton Museum. Call the governor's office to arrange a visit; Tel: (203) 566-4840.

The Arts in Hartford

An art lover will find much of interest in Hartford besides the Atheneum. Right in Bushnell Park, at the eastern tip near Bushnell Tower, is the **Pump House Gallery**, a Tudor-style building, where works of Connecticut painters, sculptors, photographers, and craftspeople are exhibited and sold. The **Widener Gallery**, open during the academic year, at the Austin Arts Center of Trinity College, less than a mile south of the capitol, has changing monthly exhibits of contemporary art. **Artworks Gallery**, at 30 Arbor Street (off Capitol Avenue, a few blocks south of the Mark Twain House), is an artists' cooperative, showing contemporary works by area artists. There are several art galleries downtown, such as **100 Pearl Street Gallery**, at 100 Pearl Street, featuring works by local artists.

Nightlife in Hartford

Downtown Hartford is the focus of most nightlife in greater Hartford. The critically acclaimed **Hartford Stage Company**, at 50 Church Street, a block west of the Civic Center's north end, performs both new plays and classics from fall to late spring. Playwright Edward Albee once premiered two short works here before taking them to New York. For information, Tel: (203) 527-5151.

The **Bushnell Memorial Auditorium**, across from the State Capitol at 166 Capitol Avenue (corner of Trinity), maintains a steady schedule of rock and classical music concerts, theater, dance, opera, and other events. Tel: (203) 246-6807.

Hartford's National Hockey League team, the Whalers, plays at the **Coliseum**, in the Hartford Civic Center, as does, on occasion, the Boston Celtics basketball team. Rock concerts are also held at the Coliseum. Tel: (203) 727-8010.

Hartford offers a variety of options for a cozy evening of music, pub crawling, or dancing. The **Russian Lady**, in a historic building at 191 Ann Street, features live bands; in warm weather the rooftop garden is a refreshing spot. Tel: (203) 525-3003. Union Place, north off Asylum, jumps at night with live music, at **Bopper's**, number 22 (Tel: 203/549-5801); and **Bourbon Street North**, number 70 (Tel: 203/525-1014). The newest hot spot is the **Municipal Café** at 485 Main Street (Tel: 203/527-5044).

Hartford's first—and, to date, only—brew pub is the **Hartford Brewery**, at 35 Pearl Street, where you can sample suds made on the premises and lunch, snack, or have a late evening pick-me-up, and play darts, pool, pinball, chess, or backgammon. Tel: (203) 246-BEER.

The restaurant **Brown, Thomson & Company**, inside a 19th-century building designed by Henry Hobson Richardson at 942 Main Street, has a lively after-work bar scene and is better for hanging out than for food, though the Sunday brunch here is pleasant. Tel: (203) 525-1600.

Dining in Hartford

Hartford offers a wide range of dining choices, but even its most expensive restaurants are moderate by big-city standards, with entrées priced generally under $20, even at the finest restaurants. At many ethnic places a complete meal can cost between $15 and $20, often less.

Frank's Restaurant, across from the Civic Center at 185 Asylum Street, is *the* hangout for political honchos when the state legislature is in session. Frank's does a yeoman job with traditional Italian specialties and Sunday brunch. Tel: (203) 527-9291.

Among the many casual places handy to downtown are the **Congress Rotisserie**, at 7 Maple Avenue (Tel: 203/560-1965), with moderately priced grilled dishes and snack items for "grazing"; **Max on Main**, at 205 Main Street (Tel: 203/522-2530), the current "in" place, with American bistro dishes; **Peppercorn's Grill**, at 357 Main Street (Tel: 203/547-1714), popular for business lunches and leisurely Italian dinners; and **Capitol Fish House**, at 391 Main (Tel: 203/724-3370), with first-rate seafood.

For ethnic food there's **Truc Orient Express**, 735 Wethersfield Avenue (a southern extension of Main Street), with delicate and tasty Vietnamese dishes. Tel: (203) 296-2818. At 360 Franklin Avenue, **Shish Kebab House of Afghanistan** is an inexpensive sleeper serving well-seasoned Afghan specialties similar to Indian food, but without the incendiary spiciness. Tel: (203) 296-0301.

Franklin Avenue, an offshoot of Maple Avenue, which itself is an offshoot of Main Street in the south of the city, was once the heart of Italian Hartford but has been in a long

decline. Despite the many boarded-up and decaying buildings, you'll still find scores of Italian bakeries and restaurants
here. Arguably the best place along this stretch is **Carbone's
Restaurant**, at number 588, which combines quiet decor,
well-spaced tables, and soft music with classic Italian dishes
(such as fettuccine alla carbonara and chicken Parmigiana)
with attentive service.

Farmington Avenue, a long commercial strip, has many
restaurants. At number 964 in West Hartford (see below), the
Panda Inn is an attractive Chinese restaurant known for such
specialties as black bean sizzling seafood and lamb pot in
spicy tea sauce. Tel: (203) 233-5384. Others of interest are
Assaggio at number 904, a somewhat fancy Italian place, with
homemade pastas, wood-fired pizzas, and many Italian-style
grilled dishes (Tel: 203/233-4520); and **Edelweiss** at number
980, for German-Swiss specialties (Tel: 203/236-3096).

Staying in Hartford

The most deluxe accommodations in downtown Hartford
can be found at the **Goodwin Hotel**, in a handsome 1881
red-brick building just across from the Hartford Civic Center. The hotel's romantic dining room, **Pierpont's**, features
competently prepared New American specialties. As a historic building, the hotel's exterior can't be altered, but the
interior is all new; the spacious, well-lighted rooms are
handsomely decorated in a traditional style, with reproductions of antiques, and the bathrooms have been done in red
marble. Despite the downtown location, the rooms are surprisingly quiet, especially those on the top (fifth) floor.
Afternoon tea is served in the lobby, and the Lounge is
popular for late evening drinks.

The **Sheraton Hartford Hotel** is an extension of the Civic
Center and is accessible directly from the center. Its location
is handy to the Hartford Stage Company and all the downtown sights.

WEST HARTFORD

Hartford melts into West Hartford, which is wedged between
Route 44 on the north and I-84 on the south and southwest.
West Hartford is home to the University of Hartford, the
Greater Hartford campus of the University of Connecticut,
and St. Joseph College. The impetus for a visit, despite stop-
and-go traffic, consists principally of two intriguing sights:
the Museum of American Political Life and Noah Webster's
House.

Museum of American Political Life

This newish (1989) museum is located in the Harry Jack Gray Center of the University of Hartford, at 200 Bloomfield Avenue (Route 189), just 4 miles (6½ km) west of the heart of Hartford (take Route 44 west from downtown, turn right on Route 189, and right again to the university).

Exhibits at this fascinating museum include a 70-foot-long wall with a time line of each U.S. president's place in history, complete with events of the time, and memorabilia from every presidential campaign from 1792 to 1988.

There are also displays of campaign artifacts: curios (such as the paper fan with the printed message "I am a fan of Ronald Reagan," and a golf ball with Spiro Agnew's face), bumper stickers, more than 5,000 campaign buttons, and posters. Television screens let you select political commercials by topic (issues, leadership, endorsements, anti-opponent ads) and watch old presidential speeches. The exhibition's finale is a life-size re-creation of an old-time political torchlight parade. To absorb the highlights of this 70,000-item collection requires about two hours. Tel: (203) 768-4090.

The same building also houses the **Joseloff Gallery** (with contemporary art exhibits), the University Bookstore, and the **Lincoln Theater**, which hosts visiting theater companies (Tel: 203/768-4228).

Noah Webster's House

The 18th-century Noah Webster's House, at 227 South Main Street (seven blocks north of exit 41 off I-84, just past the Rockledge Country Club), was the birthplace (in 1758) of the teacher/lexicographer who compiled the first American dictionary, called *A Compendious Dictionary of the English Language,* in 1806. The story is told that when Webster was working on this book, his wife discovered him in his study locked in an embrace with a young servant. "Noah, I am surprised," said his wife. "No, my dear," he replied, "I am surprised, you are astonished."

Webster's small red clapboard farmhouse contains some rare period furniture, back-to-back hearths, and herb gardens. It is also home to the **West Hartford Historical Society**, which mounts changing exhibitions. Closed Wednesdays. Tel: (203) 521-5362.

Science Museum of Connecticut

The Science Museum of Connecticut, at 950 Trout Brook Drive (about three blocks north of exit 43 off I-84; from

Noah Webster's House, go north to Park Road, then east to Trout Brook Drive, which parallels South Main Street, and north two blocks), has a small zoo, a planetarium, a marine-life touch tank, and the Discovery Room, an exhibit geared especially to children two to seven years old. The museum hosts frequent travelling exhibitions as well. Tel: (203) 236-2961.

Sarah Whitman Hooker Homestead

At 1237 New Britain Avenue (southeast corner of South Main Street, exit 41 off I-84), this well-restored home, named for a local Revolutionary War heroine, showcases three periods of early Connecticut domestic architecture from 1720 to 1807 and houses an outstanding collection of early-19th-century Staffordshire ware. Open Mondays and Wednesdays; closed in August. Tel: (203) 523-5887.

SOUTH OF HARTFORD

Just 4 miles (6½ km) south of Hartford are Newington (reached via Route 314 or Maple Avenue) and Wethersfield (via Wethersfield Avenue, a right turn off Main Street, or I-91 to exit 26), which melt into one another. Just east of Wethersfield is Glastonbury, and to the southeast is Rocky Hill. These towns are within the Hartford orbit, and it is possible to visit all four on a day trip. (If you have time for just one quick side trip from Hartford, Old Wethersfield should be it.)

Old Wethersfield

Most compelling to visitors is Old Wethersfield, the historic district of Wethersfield, an affluent Hartford suburb. Wethersfield was settled in 1634, giving it an edge over Windsor (which was first a trading post) as the state's first settlement, though a formal purchase of the land from the Wongunk Indians wasn't effected until 1636. The nomadic Wongunks called the area Pyquag (which means "cleared land") and considered it their home base.

By the late 17th century Wethersfield was a thriving Connecticut River port, but in the next century floods changed the river's course and left the town high and dry, its surroundings suitable only for farming.

The town really entered the history books May 21, 1781, when General George Washington arrived to confer with the commander of the French fleet, the Comte de Rochambeau, who had just come down from Newport, Rhode Island, to discuss joint strategy for ending the Revolutionary War. Over the next five days, in a meeting known as the Yorktown Conference, the two planned the final campaign against the British that indeed ended the war at Yorktown, Virginia, four months later.

Especially of interest in Wethersfield today are the dozen or so blocks along Main and Broad streets and Hartford Avenue, which are lined with houses that date to the 17th, 18th, and 19th centuries—a virtual primer of American architecture. Each historic house has a marker with the original owner's name and the date of construction. In all there are 150 pre-1820 houses still privately owned in town. Seven others, restored and outfitted with period furnishings, are open to the public. Note, though, that some of the seven are open only from mid-May to mid-October, others by appointment. Telephone numbers are provided below so you can check before visiting.

A useful first stop in Wethersfield is the red-brick **Old Academy** (1804), at 150 Main Street, headquarters of the Wethersfield Historical Society, to pick up brochures about the town. Once a female seminary (hence the name Old Academy), the handsome building also has served as the town hall, a library, and an armory. Tel: (203) 529-7656.

Webb-Deane-Stevens Museum
Diagonally across Main Street are three old clapboard houses that together constitute the Webb-Deane-Stevens Museum. Viewed together, the three houses show three different lifestyles in 18th-century America: those of a wealthy merchant, a diplomat, and a tradesman. A single tour takes in all three houses. Open May through November. Tel: (203) 529-0612.

Most impressive (and important) in the gracefulness of its interior details and elegance of its furnishings is the **Webb House** in the center, built in 1752 by a local merchant named Joseph Webb. Washington conferred with Rochambeau in the south parlor, which still bears its authentic bright green wood paneling (the map on the conference table belonged to Benjamin Franklin), and slept in the front bedroom facing the street. The deep red flocked wallpaper was hung especially for his visit.

To the left of the Webb house is the **Deane House**, built in 1766 by Silas Deane, who married Webb's widow. Deane's career was a classic American success story: The son of a blacksmith, he was educated at Yale, became a lawyer, was a member of the First Continental Congress, and served as commissioner to France, securing arms and supplies for the Continental Army. John Adams was among Deane's distinguished guests here.

The **Stevens House**, to the right of the Webb, was built in 1788 by Isaac Stevens, a saddler and leather tanner. More modest than the other two, the house was lived in for 170 years by the same family.

Other Historic Houses

Another landmark, at 249 Broad Street, is the **Buttolph-Williams House**, a rare example of a grand, shingled early-18th-century house (ca. 1710–1720). Medieval in character, it contains a fully furnished 18th-century New England kitchen. Open from May through October. Tel: (203) 247-8996.

The **Captain James Francis House** (1793), at 120 Hartford Avenue, has the furnishings of seven generations, spanning 170 years, of the same family. The house is open on Saturday afternoons from May 15 to October 15 and by appointment; Tel: (203) 529-7656. The **Hurlbut-Dunham House**, at 212 Main Street, is an 1804 house, later Victorianized, that belonged to a local sea captain. It will be open to the public beginning in 1994; Tel: (203) 529-7656.

The **Meeting House of the First Church of Christ**, at 250 Main Street, was built in 1761 and is believed to be the only brick Colonial meetinghouse left in the region. In 1774, after visiting Wethersfield, John Adams noted in his diary: "We went up to the steeple of the Meeting House, from whence is the most grand and beautiful prospect in the world." The church was long known as "the meetinghouse that onions built" because funds for the building were raised by taxing the main local crop. Note the original hand-carved pulpit; an old **burying ground**, with 17th-century headstones, is in the rear. Tel: (203) 529-1575.

DINING AND STAYING IN OLD WETHERSFIELD

Plan on having dinner at **Standish House**, at 222 Main Street, a handsomely restored 1787 house with polished wood floors, brass chandeliers, and dining rooms on two floors. The menu is New American, the setting Colonial. (Open for dinner only.) Tel: (203) 721-1113.

For spending the night there's a cheerful bed-and-breakfast just down the street, the **Chester Bulkley House**, a sturdy brick Greek Revival with five guest rooms, nicely restored in 1989. The beautiful "antique" dolls throughout the house are made (and sold) by the proprietor.

Newington

Neighboring Newington lives at a fast 20th-century pace as a bustling, self-contained suburban center. It differs from Old

Wethersfield, which is isolated in something of a time warp, and its two attractions are tucked into modern residential and commercial neighborhoods. The **Kellogg-Eddy Museum**, at 679 Willard Avenue, is a post-Revolutionary (1808) house noted for its handcrafted woodwork, especially the elaborate detailing of the fireplace mantels. The house was built by Captain Martin Kellogg III, a prosperous farmer-businessman who was a lieutenant general in the state militia and member of the state senate. The museum features changing exhibits of antique toys, quilts, and costumes. Open weekends; Sundays only in January and February. Tel: (203) 666-7118.

The **Enoch Kelsey House**, at 1702 Main Street, is a plain frame house with a center chimney, the original fireplaces, and a beehive oven, built in 1799 by a farmer-tinsmith. What makes it special are the four charming trompe l'oeil paintings discovered on the parlor walls underneath the wallpaper, the hand-painted borders in both the parlor and dining room, and the sprightly floral designs painted on the upstairs walls. Open May through October and by appointment. Tel: (203) 666-7118.

Glastonbury and Rocky Hill

Glastonbury, east of Wethersfield across the Connecticut River, is reached by the William H. Putnam Memorial Bridge right off I-91 as you head northeast. A more scenic route (possible only from April to early November) is via the **Rocky Hill–Glastonbury Ferry**, south on Route 160. Since the mid-17th century there has been public transport over the river at this site, making this the oldest continuously operating ferry in the country. The tugboat-towed carrier barge holds 20 people, plus cars and vans. The ride takes four minutes.

One of Glastonbury's two historic houses open to the public is the 1755 **Welles-Shipman-Ward House**, at 972 Main Street. A two-story, center-chimney Colonial, it has a huge kitchen fireplace, elaborate paneling and molding in the parlors, and an herb garden. Open Sundays May through October, excluding July, and by appointment. Tel: (203) 633-6890. The other is the **Museum on the Green**, at Main and Hubbard streets, adjacent to the old town cemetery, which dates to 1690. A brick house that once served as the old town hall, it is now a museum containing Native American artifacts, glass- and silverware, items from America's first soap factory, and changing exhibits. Open Mondays and Thursdays and by appointment. Tel: (203) 633-6890.

One of the state's most enjoyable bed-and-breakfasts is in

Glastonbury: **Butternut Farm**, a restored 1720 house furnished with Early American antiques. There are just five
guest rooms, two with canopied beds. Goats and chickens
graze in the back yard, and almost everything served at
breakfast comes from the premises, including goat's milk,
eggs, and homemade jams.

For a change of pace from visiting historic houses, hop
the ferry back across the river and head south about 4 miles
(6½ km) to **Rocky Hill** (exit 23), another suburban community and home of **Dinosaur State Park**, where you can hike
the nature trails, picnic, cross-country ski, and inspect dinosaur tracks that date back to the Jurassic period, 185 million
years ago. Visitors are allowed to make plaster casts of the
dinosaur prints.

NORTH OF HARTFORD

It is less than 15 miles (24 km) north from Hartford on I-91
to the Massachusetts state line toward Springfield, but in
those few miles are several sights of interest.

NEW ENGLAND AIR MUSEUM

Some years ago a tornado wrought terrible damage on the
collection of the New England Air Museum in Windsor
Locks, north of Bradley International Airport. (From exit 40
off I-91, go west on Route 20 for 2 miles/3 km, then north on
Route 75 for just 1¼ miles/2 km.) The grounds still have a
temporary look, but more than a dozen U.S. military planes
are parked here, including the type of B-29 bomber that
dropped the atom bomb. On display inside a huge hangar
are some 42 aircraft dating from 1909 to the present, as well
as numerous engines, propellers, and other aviation-related
artifacts.

To experience the challenge of flying the world's first
commercially produced supersonic jet fighter, climb into the
MB-22 flight simulator cockpit module of the North American F-100C Super-Sabre (subject to availability), the plane in
which Air Force pilots trained in radio navigation and low-
altitude bombing in the late 1950s and early '60s. The museum is instituting new hours in 1993; call for specifics; Tel:
(203) 623-3305.

HATHEWAY HOUSE

Less than a mile (1½ km) north of the air museum via Route
75 in Suffield is the Hatheway House, a Colonial shaded by a
300-year-old sycamore tree. The house, maintained by the
Antiquarian and Landmarks Society, is a classic Revolutionary

War–era home, constructed between the years 1760 and 1795. Note the three rare original French hand-blocked wallpapers of the 1780s (and one reproduction). Open May 15 to October 15. Tel: (203) 668-0055.

OLD NEW-GATE PRISON
AND COPPER MINE

Old New-Gate Prison, south on Route 75, then about 7 miles (11 km) west on Route 20 in East Granby, was originally a copper mine dating to 1707. The site was converted in 1773 to a prison that held many Tories during the Revolutionary War; it later became the first state prison. You can wander through the underground caves where prisoners were kept. Open mid-May through October. Tel: (203) 653-3563.

Windsor and East Windsor

As you head back on I-91 south to Hartford, take a detour at exit 37 to Windsor, considered one of the three earliest Connecticut settlements and today a thriving Hartford sub-urb. A drive south along Windsor's Palisado Avenue (Route 159) leads past a handful of venerable houses, including, at number 778, the **Oliver Ellsworth Homestead** (Ellsworth was instrumental in establishing the country's bicameral legislature at the Constitutional Convention in 1787 and was later a chief justice of the Supreme Court). Owned and operated by the Connecticut Daughters of the American Revolution, the house, which has its original wallpaper and many of Ellsworth's furnishings, is open from May to mid-October. Tel: (203) 688-8717.

Other stops along Palisado include the **Lieutenant Walter Fyler House**, at number 96, one of the oldest surviving frame houses in Connecticut, from 1640, with many furnishings and artifacts of early settlers; the **Dr. Hezekiah Chaffee House** across the street, scheduled to open in mid-1993 (Tel: 203/688-3813 for both houses); and the **First Church in Windsor**, at number 75, a 1794 Georgian building with a cemetery dating to 1644 and sporting one of the oldest gravestones in the state.

Just 3 miles (5 km) away in East Windsor, at 58 North Road (exit 45 off I-91), is the **Connecticut Trolley Museum**, which offers a short nostalgic trip into the not-so-distant past, with displays of some 50 trolley cars from 1894 to 1949. Open year-round; weekends only, September to May. Tel: (203) 623-7417.

WEST OF HARTFORD

The **Farmington Valley**, to the west and southwest of Hartford, is a lush and fertile landscape of rolling hills, farmland, and woods, following the serpentine north–south V-shaped route of the Farmington River. The valley's most sparkling jewel is the historic town of Farmington, now a prosperous Hartford suburb. When planning a visit to the Farmington Valley area, it is wise to check in advance with the Farmington Valley/West Hartford Visitors Bureau, at 41 East Main Street, Avon (Tel: 203/674-1035), to see what specific history-oriented tours are being offered in a particular season. Several tour groups in the area run two-hour, half-day, full-day, and evening candlelight dinner tours in historic homes that are not normally open to the public.

Avon

Ten miles (16 km) west of Hartford along a fairly commercialized stretch of Route 44 is the town of Avon. One reason to stop here would be to visit the **Farmington Valley Arts Center**, off Route 44 at 25 Arts Center Lane. Twenty studios, open at each artist's inclination, are housed here in a former explosives plant. Also on the premises is the **Fisher Gallery Shop**, where you can see juried art shows and buy one-of-a-kind handicrafts. The shop's annual November-to-December holiday sale is a much-anticipated event.

Another reason to stop in Avon is the new **Horse Cavalry Museum**, at Riverdale Farms, on Route 10/202 (north off Route 44). The museum honors the cavalry from the Revolutionary War to the present, with all sorts of American and European artifacts, from uniforms, sabers, and pistols, to a saddle and plow that belonged to General Israel Putnam. Open weekends only; Tel: (203) 676-8926.

Every Thursday evening, from 7:30 to 10:00 P.M., the **First Company Governor's Horse Guards**, the oldest cavalry unit in continuous service in the nation (1778), drill and train in mounted and dismounted formations at the Horse Guard State Park on Route 167 (off Avon Road). Visitors may watch the drills and tour the stables.

On Route 44 is **Max A Mia**, a lively, moderately priced trattoria. The pastas, gourmet pizzas, risotto, and other northern Italian specialties attract crowds of local professionals for lunch and dinner. Tel: (203) 677-6299.

Simsbury

About 5 miles (8 km) north of Avon on Route 10/202 is Simsbury, another Hartford suburb of ancient lineage, founded in 1660. Much of the town sprawls along a single main street—Hopmeadow Street, named for the hops grown here for the early distillers in the area—lined with historic buildings. The **First Church of Christ Congregational**, which was built in 1832, was damaged by fire in 1965 and restored.

Head up Hopmeadow to the **Massacoh Plantation**, the Simsbury Historical Society's enclosed complex of buildings and displays that depict 300 years of local life. On the grounds are a replica of an old meetinghouse (1683), the Captain Elisha Phelps House and Tavern (1771), a schoolhouse (1740), an icehouse, the 1795 Hendricks Cottage, a Victorian carriage house, and exhibits of farm and industrial implements. Open afternoons, May through October. Tel: (203) 658-2500.

Simsbury also has a notable inn, the **Simsbury 1820 House**, with 34 comfortable guest rooms (some with four-posters) and a dining room furnished with New England antiques. A signature dish of the New American menu is a delicate pear-and-scallop bisque. Guests are encouraged to have dessert and coffee upstairs in the lounge before a toasty fire.

If you have time before continuing on to Farmington, you might turn east off Route 202 onto Route 185 (halfway back to Avon) to **Talcott Mountain State Park**, which has a variety of hiking and bike trails and a picnic area. Talcott Mountain rises 875 feet above the Farmington River and is a popular launching pad for hang gliders. For far-ranging views of the area (especially lovely in the fall), climb the 120 steps to the top of the **Heublein Tower**, a Bavarian-style edifice built in 1914 as a country retreat for Gilbert F. Heublein, a marketer of wines and spirits. Later it was owned by the *Hartford Times* (now defunct), which staged various gala parties here, with guest lists that included Ronald Reagan, General Omar Bradley, Frank Lloyd Wright, and Dwight D. Eisenhower (who was urged to run for president while at a tower party). To reach the tower follow a hiking trail 1¼ miles (2 km) from the parking area at the ridge of the mountain.

Farmington

From Simsbury head back through Avon and continue another 7 miles (11 km) or so south on Route 10 to Farmington, a charming, affluent little town on the surging Farmington River. The river, popular with canoeists, fishermen, and bird-watchers, begins in the Berkshire hills in Becket, Massachusetts, ripples south to Farmington, then turns abruptly north and runs in a northeasterly direction until it joins the Connecticut River in Windsor. The Farmington Valley also attracts hang gliders and hot-air balloonists (at least six companies offer balloon rides in the area).

A left turn (east) off Route 10 onto Mountain Road in Farmington leads to the **Hill-Stead Museum**, at number 35, one of the most intriguing properties in the area.

Theodate Pope, a young woman who in the 1890s attended Miss Porter's School, a fashionable preparatory school still here on Route 10, fell in love with the Farmington area and persuaded her parents to retire here on a 150-acre "gentleman's farm." They in turn gave her free rein in designing the Colonial Revival house, which she did with the help of the famous New York architectural firm McKim, Mead & White, between 1899 and 1901. (The name "Hill-Stead" was intended to suggest a farmstead on a hill.)

Theodate Pope married John Wallace Riddle and moved into the house in 1916. When she died, childless, in 1946, her will stipulated that nothing in the house was to be changed, added to, or labeled—in effect, to keep it looking as "lived in" as in her lifetime. Her hats and silk gowns still hang in the bedroom closet. The house, frozen in time, is a remarkable example of what might be called an American version of Edwardian taste and sensibility. Architecturally handsome, the house has a wonderful collection of early French and American Impressionist paintings—including works by Degas, Manet, Monet, Cassatt, and Whistler, among others—as well as fine antique furniture and decorative arts.

The very first painting the Popes bought, Monet's *View of the Bay* (1888), still hangs above the drawing-room mantel. The fine furniture includes a Biedermeier sofa in the library and a Chippendale secretary in the parlor bedroom. The guided house tour lasts exactly one hour, and then you are free to wander through the beautifully kept grounds and fields. A pre-1925 sunken garden was recently reconstructed. Tel: (203) 677-9064.

As you head west along Mountain Road from the Hill-Stead Museum, turn right onto High Street. At number 37 is the **Stanley-Whitman House**, a Colonial home (ca. 1720) and a well-preserved example of the framed overhang style of New England architecture. The interior has been restored and furnished in 18th-century style. From time to time special crafts demonstrations and exhibits are held in the house. Open April through October. Tel: (203) 677-9222.

DINING IN FARMINGTON

For lunch or dinner with a river view head to **Apricots**, a favorite of the locals. Overlooking the river at 1593 Farmington Avenue (Route 4), in an attractively decorated former trolley barn, the restaurant serves creative regional American cuisine. The downstairs pub, which serves snacks and light meals, goes strong day and night and often features live piano music. Tel: (203) 673-5405.

New Britain, Bristol, and Waterbury

These three small cities once prospered mightily as industrial centers: New Britain as a hardware center with more than 100 different plants, Bristol as a leading producer of clocks, and Waterbury as the brass capital, making all kinds of small products for America's homes and offices. All are working-class, blue-collar towns, with melting-pot populations whose ancestors were part of the late-19th-century immigration from Europe. New Britain's largely Polish heritage is celebrated in late September with the Dozynki Polish Harvest festival, while Waterbury residents have their Italian Festival the last weekend in July.

From Farmington continue south and east about 6 miles (10 km) to New Britain via Routes 10 and 372. The **New Britain Museum of American Art**, at 56 Lexington Street, exhibits works by 18th- to 20th-century American artists, including Gilbert Stuart, John Singer Sargent, Winslow Homer, Andrew Wyeth, Maxfield Parrish, and many others, with some 5,000 works in all. Thomas Hart Benton's murals *The Arts of Life in America* are on permanent display. Tel: (203) 229-0257.

A good place to sample some of New Britain's best Polish food is at **Rena's**, 270 Broad Street, where the barley soup, *schav* (sorrel soup), pierogi, and stuffed cabbage are hearty and satisfying. Tel: (203) 224-2166.

In **Bristol**, 5 miles (8 km) west of New Britain via route 372, the draw is the **American Clock and Watch Museum**, in an 1801 house at 100 Maple Street. The collection of more than 1,700 American-made clocks and some 1,250 watches includes pieces by Seth Thomas, Eli Terry, Daniel Burnap, and many others. Tel: (203) 583-6070. Bristol is also home to the **New England Carousel Museum**, with exhibits of antique merry-go-round horses displayed in a restored turn-of-the-century factory. Tel: (203) 585-5411.

About 12 miles (19 km) southeast of Bristol is **Waterbury** (I-84 west is the fastest route), the urban center of the

Naugatuck Valley. For the visitor Waterbury's chief attraction is the recently rejuvenated **Mattatuck Museum**, housing a range of exhibits depicting the human side of the area's industrial history (inventive visual displays make it more interesting than it sounds). The museum building was formerly the Masonic Temple on the green, but a new entrance and interior renovations by architect Cesar Pelli have given it renewed verve and style. Tel: (203) 753-0381.

One of the city's best Italian restaurants, at 457 West Main Street, bears the curious name **No Fish Today**, a reference to the Prohibition era, when speakeasies put up a "No Fish Today" sign in their windows as a message to customers that a liquor shipment had just arrived. The name has nothing to do with this casual storefront restaurant, whose forte is bounteous portions of Italian seafood dishes at modest prices. Tel: (203) 574-4483.

From Waterbury it's a quick ride back to Hartford (via I-84 northeast) and almost as fast to Litchfield (via Route 8 north to Harwinton, then west on Route 118), gateway to the northwestern territory known as the Litchfield Hills.

THE LITCHFIELD HILLS

The town of Litchfield, the heart of Litchfield County, is only about 40 miles west of Hartford on the map, but light-years away in spirit. Until the past 15 years or so this northwestern corner of the state, bordered by New York and Massachusetts, was as sleepy as its northeastern counterpart, the Quiet Corner. Tucked into the foothills of the Berkshire and Taconic mountains and anchored by the Housatonic River, this bucolic landscape of woods, rolling hills, rambling farms, stone fences, state parks, and quintessential New England villages was peopled largely by dairy farmers, preparatory-school students and faculty, a few artists (the late Alexander Calder being the most famous), and writers (such as Arthur Miller and William Styron).

Then, after a 1978 *New York* magazine article comparing real estate prices here with those in other New York exurbs, Litchfield County was "discovered" by Manhattan's fashionable and famous.

Tired of the Hamptons, eager for space and solitude, the likes of Meryl Streep, Henry Kissinger, Tom Brokaw, and

Mike Nichols bought weekend properties sprawling through secluded woodlands. Yet aside from sending real estate prices skyward and leading to the gentrification of some local shops and an infusion of new restaurants, the influx hasn't caused much of a change in the area. Those who visit Litchfield County do so for the understated attractions of lovely scenery, country inns, antiques shops, and village fairs, and for the outdoor pursuits of hiking, camping, cross-country skiing, and various sports on the Housatonic. The showiest sight around is the spectacular foliage display each October.

Although Torrington (population 33,687) is the largest city in Litchfield County, with plenty of small-city bustle, all sightseeing roads in the area lead to tiny Litchfield (population 8,365), the imperative stop on any exploration of the Litchfield Hills.

From Litchfield you can easily spend a week meandering through the entire northwest territory, stopping night by night at a series of delightful village inns. If, however, you prefer a single home base, Litchfield itself would be a comfortable choice; the itineraries laid out below follow this second alternative, allocating a day each for exploring the byways north, west, and south of Litchfield. Keep in mind that much of the pleasure of the Litchfield Hills rests in just poking around, making your own discoveries. This is not possible on a rushed, superficial day trip.

LITCHFIELD

Settled in 1720 by third-generation New Englanders, Litchfield was throughout the 18th century a bustling stagecoach stop between Albany and Hartford, and Boston and New York. In 1732 iron ore was discovered in the area and settlers flocked to the Litchfield Hills—also called the Western Lands—to open and work in foundries. The area became a veritable arsenal for the American Revolution, with the promise of becoming as bustling an industrial center as Birmingham, England.

By 1810 Litchfield was the fourth-largest settlement in Connecticut, a center of mills, tanneries, and forges. But by the mid-19th century, as railroads bypassed the area and water-powered industry concentrated in the river valleys (especially the Naugatuck), Litchfield and the surrounding villages settled into the role of a scenic backwater. Its golden age ended, the town was left with many handsome mansions and not much commercial wealth to maintain them. The lack

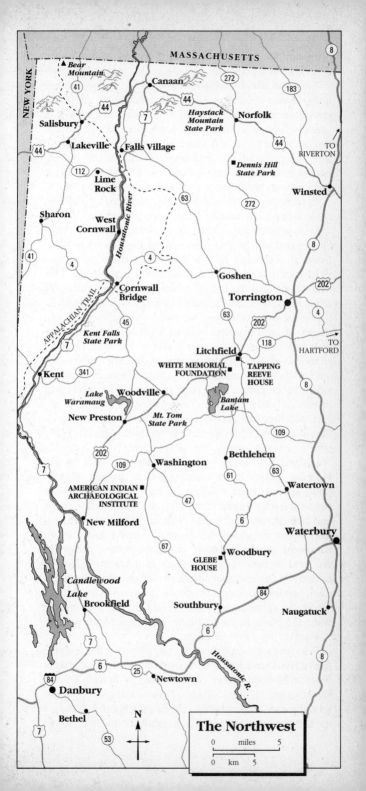

of money for "improvements," however, is the reason the town is so well preserved.

Today Litchfield's wide streets—the better for carriage traffic in past centuries—shaded by canopies of trees; dozens of imposing 18th-century white-clapboard houses; a classic village green that looks much as it did when it was laid out in the 1770s; and a tranquil air all suggest a cohesive past. To preserve this ambience owners of the historic houses have tucked their garages out back, and parking is forbidden on North Street, the most picturesque in town.

In some ways Litchfield promises more than it delivers. Aside from its immediate visual appeal as a true, lived-in 18th-century village, where Ethan Allen, Harriet Beecher Stowe, and her brother Henry Ward Beecher were born, many of Litchfield's historic homes are closed to view— unless you plan your visit for the annual **Open House Tour** (the second Saturday in July), when five handsome homes (a different group each year) are open to the public. Unfortunately, the town is then so jammed with tourists that a visit doesn't afford a true sense of Litchfield's serenity.

At other times of the year a visit to Litchfield means a chance to absorb the atmosphere of the 18th century (but with 20th-century amenities, of course). From the majestic village green radiate streets that run along the four cardinal directions (and so are rather prosaically named North, South, East, and West streets). On the northeast side of the green is the colonnaded, white-spired **Congregational Church** (1829), with a two-story portico. Across the green, at the corner of South and East streets, is the **Litchfield Historical Society Museum**, a 1900 brick building with a modern addition housing a fine, small collection of Early American paintings (including some minor masterpieces by Ralph Earl from the late 18th century) of the elite of Litchfield's golden age. Also displayed throughout the museum's seven galleries are handsome period furniture, costumes, pottery, decorative arts, and depictions of the village as it was in 1820. The museum's tiny gift shop proffers well-chosen educational toys, puzzles, books, and redware pottery by Guy Wolf of Woodville in the style of the Hervey Brooks 19th-century ware exhibited in the museum. Open mid-April to mid-November. Tel: (203) 567-4506.

One historic house open to the public is the **Tapping Reeve House and Law School**, surrounded by a white picket fence at 82 South Street, on the corner of Wolcott. On the vast lawn are a house dating to 1773 and a simple, one-room schoolhouse (1784) where Judge Tapping Reeve established the first law school in America. Its graduates included Aaron

Burr (Reeve's brother-in-law and first student), John C. Calhoun, three Supreme Court justices, a dozen governors, and more than 50 members of Congress. Take a look at the period furnishings and attractive garden. Open mid-April to mid-November. Tel: (203) 567-4501.

Just opposite, at number 89, is the **Oliver Wolcott, Sr., House**, a plain 1734 clapboard structure where George Washington, the Marquis de Lafayette, and Alexander Hamilton were, at various times, entertained. Wolcott, a signer of the Declaration of Independence, was also a governor of Connecticut. A historic event took place behind the house: A bronze statue of King George III, trundled from New York City on an oxcart, was melted down to make bullets for the American Army during the Revolutionary War. The property is now privately owned and so can be viewed only from the street.

A drive along South and North streets leads past almost 30 of Litchfield's most impressive Colonial houses. Sinclair Lewis noted in the 1920s that the "only street in America more beautiful than North Street in Litchfield is South Street in Litchfield." Just north of the green on the west side of North Street (Route 63) is a large clapboard house with a Neoclassical entryway, Doric columns, and a widow's walk. Constructed in 1760, it was formerly Sheldon's Tavern, a local landmark during Revolutionary War times, where Washington actually did spend the night, when on his way to West Point. (Not open to the public.) Farther up North Street, at the corner of Prospect, a marker indicates the former site of the Beecher house, birthplace of both Harriet and Henry Ward. (The house has since been moved farther north on Route 63 and is now part of a school.)

SHOPPING IN LITCHFIELD

One of the pleasures of meandering through Litchfield is shopping, especially for antiques. **Thomas McBride Antiques**, right next to the town hall at 62 West Street, specializes in furniture, silver, accessories, and American and European paintings. Closed weekends, except by appointment; Tel: (203) 567-5476. The **Litchfield Auction Gallery**, on Route 202 one mile (1½ km) west of the green, sells 18th- and 19th-century American pewter and decorative arts, with an auction approximately every three weeks. Tel: (203) 567-3126. A bit farther west on the same road is **Donald W. Linsley**, one of the most comprehensive antiques shops in the area.

If you're an old- or rare-book aficionado, stop in at the **John Steele Book Shop**, at 15 South Street. Across from it is the entrance to Cobble Court, a quaint brick-lined mews with several attractive shops, among them **Cobble Court Bookshop**, **Kitchenworks**, **Litchfield Exchange**, and **Curtis Hanson Gallery**.

Many art galleries have begun to open in Litchfield of late, most of them featuring the work of local artists. A number are located on West Street facing the green. The **Litchfield Art Guild**, on the second floor at 33 West Street, is a cooperative of ten artists. **P. S. Gallery** has shows of various regional artists.

DINING AND STAYING IN LITCHFIELD

The place for local celebrity watching—and also, not incidentally, for terrific, original food and homemade peasant bread—is the **West Street Grill**, at 43 West Street facing the green. Henry Kissinger, Sam Waterston, Philip Roth and Claire Bloom, Bill Blass, and Susan Saint James all dine here. Open for lunch and dinner. Tel: (203) 567-3885. For takeout, the **Litchfield Food Company** is almost next door.

If you want to immerse yourself completely in the 18th century, stay overnight at the **Toll Gate Hill Inn**, ensconced in a 1745 farmhouse listed on the National Registry of Historic Places, 2½ miles (4 km) east of town on Route 202. Eight of its charming guest rooms, which are spread out among the inn, a schoolhouse annex, and an outbuilding, have fireplaces. Lunch and dinner (open to guests and nonguests) are served in the two period dining rooms, with fireplaces and exposed-beam ceilings; the food is snappy and contemporary. Sunday brunch, with live music, is a popular event with locals. Tel: (203) 567-4545.

AROUND LITCHFIELD

White Flower Farm

Three to four miles (5 to 6 km) south of the green on Route 63 is White Flower Farm, famous among serious gardeners for its beautiful flower catalogues. You can see a wide variety of the finest houseplants, shrubs, and perennials (but you can buy them only by mail order) and wander through ten acres of dazzling gardens (in season, of course). Another 25 acres of fields are filled with flowers and shrubs. Open from late April to late October.

Haight Vineyard and Winery

One mile (1½ km) east of Litchfield, off Route 118 at 29 Chestnut Hill Road, is the Haight Vineyard and Winery, which offers tours, complimentary tastings, and a vineyard walk. Also on the premises are picnic tables and a gift shop. The weekend before the Fourth of July a popular food fair called "A Taste of Litchfield Hills" is held at the winery. Tel: (203) 567-4045.

White Memorial Conservation Center

Just outside of town to the west off Route 202 is the White Memorial Conservation Center, the state's largest nature preserve; the 4,000-acre park is laced with 35 miles of nature trails and encompasses much of **Bantam Lake**. The trails are popular with hikers, mountain bicyclists, horseback riders, and, in winter, cross-country skiers, yet so vast is the woodland you're hardly aware of sharing it with anyone but deer, beavers, and game birds. It's also possible to explore part of the preserve by canoe from the lake. The **White Memorial Conservation Center**, also on the preserve, has nature displays, dioramas, a library, and a small gift shop. Tel: (203) 567-0857.

THE NORTHWEST CORNER

From Litchfield one day's outing might take you north toward Lakeville, Salisbury, Canaan, and Norfolk, with a possible detour east to Riverton before you return to Litchfield. (Take Route 63 for 6 miles/10 km north to Goshen, follow Route 4 west for 9 miles/14½ km to Cornwall Bridge, then go north about 17 miles/27 km on Route 7.) If you want more time to shop and browse, you'd best allow two days, staying overnight at Salisbury.

Cornwall Bridge and West Cornwall

Cornwall Bridge and West Cornwall are tiny villages about 5 miles (8 km) apart on Route 7, tucked into a scenic wooded and hilly terrain bordered by the Housatonic River. Between the two villages is **Housatonic Meadows State Park**, where boating, fishing, hiking, picnicking, and cross-country skiing can be enjoyed.

The **Cornwall Bridge Pottery Workshop**, at the junction of Routes 4 and 7, is a working pottery with a showroom by the side of the road. You can take a look at the 40-foot-long wood kiln, watch potter Todd Piker at work, and perhaps pick up some of his Asian-looking bowls, plates, or platters.

West Cornwall is a sleepy one-street village with one of the state's two drive-through **covered bridges**, in continuous operation since 1837. Made of native oak, it is noted for its intricate latticework truss. (The other bridge is near New Milford; see below.)

Near the bridge is an informal lunch stop (also serving dinner and Sunday brunch) called **Freshfields**, with a deck overlooking Mill Brook, a rushing stream. Tel: (203) 672-6601. Across from Freshfields is the **Cornwall Bridge Pottery Store**, an outlet for Todd Piker's stoneware and an excellent crafts shop full of other handcrafts, toys, and clothing. Barbara Farnsworth's two-floor **bookshop**, in a vintage Masonic hall on West Cornwall's short main street, contains a tantalizing array of old, rare, and out-of-print books. Works on gardening and horticulture—some 1,500 volumes—are a specialty. The shop is open only on Saturdays and Sundays.

Clarke Outdoors, right on Route 7, offers three- to four-hour, ten-mile canoe, kayak, and raft trips on the Housatonic, April to October. They also rent canoes, kayaks, and other equipment, and offer shuttle service to the river. Tel: (203) 672-6365.

Falls Village and Lime Rock

Falls Village, about 7 miles (11 km) north of West Cornwall via Routes 7 and 126 west, hosts **Music Mountain**, a summer chamber-music festival that runs from mid-June to mid-September (Tel: 203/824-7126). There's nothing much to detain you in this tiny river village aside from **R & D Emerson Books**, at 103 Main Street, a shingled former church with stained-glass windows, a vaulted ceiling, and aisles with rare, out-of-print, and just plain old books on many subjects. Open Thursday to Monday afternoons.

Falls River is the departure point for **Riverrunning Expeditions**' day-long canoe, kayak, and raft trips down the Housatonic to Cornwall Bridge, mid-March through October. Two-day trips and 14-mile voyages on the upper Housatonic can also be arranged. Canoe, kayak, and raft rentals are available. Tel: (203) 824-5579.

If it's the sports-car racing season (May to September) you might stop at Lime Rock Park in **Lime Rock**, about 6 miles (10 km) north and west of West Cornwall on Route 112. Paul Newman and Tom Cruise have competed on the 1.53-mile track. For racing dates, Tel: (203) 435-0896.

Lakeville

A classic Connecticut town, Lakeville (west on Route 112 from Lime Rock, then north on Route 41) is best known for the Hotchkiss Preparatory School, but it also claims **Lake Wononscopomuc**, the deepest spring-fed lake in the state, popular for swimming, boating, and fishing for rainbow trout and lake salmon.

Serenely peaceful Lakeville had its 15 minutes of fame in the 18th century. The village, incorporated in 1740, grew up around a blast furnace, the Furnace Village Forge, owned by Revolutionary War patriot Ethan Allen, a Litchfield native. The furnace, along with forges and mines in nearby Salisbury, was used to cast the guns for the USS *Constitution,* as well as many arms for the Americans in the Revolutionary War.

Overlooking the site of the old blast furnace, which was dismantled in 1843, on Route 44 is the **Holley-Williams House,** built in 1768 and added on to in 1808 by John Milton Holley, a local ironmaster, whose descendants lived in the house until 1971. Because of this continuity the house retains many of the original touches, such as the windows, the hand-carved woodwork, and a curved staircase. On the grounds are several of the original outbuildings and a carriage house that now displays antique tools and a model of an iron forge. Open weekend afternoons, July through early October and by appointment. Tel: (203) 435-2878.

In Lakeville's center is the **Methodist Congregational Church,** built in 1816. The congregation was founded in 1791, making it the oldest Methodist congregation in New England.

The **Wake Robin Inn**, at the top of a winding driveway on Route 41 in Lakeville, has ample rooms and a good, if pricey, dining room called **Savarin**, with knowledgeably prepared French fare. Service, however, is erratic.

The town of **Sharon**, 5 miles (8 km) south of Lakeville on Route 41, has a lovely village green and many handsome 19th-century houses and mansions.

Salisbury and Mount Riga

Salisbury, 2 miles (3 km) north of Lakeville at the junction of Routes 41 and 44, is an old town, first settled permanently by the Dutch in 1720, but incorporated by the English as Salisbury (after the English cathedral town) in 1741, just ten years after the first iron-ore beds were discovered in the vicinity. Since the last mine closed in 1917 the area has sputtered along on farming, sporadic tourism, and as a vacation retreat for the affluent from New York and Boston.

Salisbury has no famous landmarks but a number of handsome ones: the rose-red brick **Old Academy Building** (1833), with a distinctive belfry (now the circuit court); a Federal-style **Congregational Church** (1800) with a Palladian window and a whale weathervane; and the stone Gothic **Scoville Memorial Library** (1895).

There are also many fine 19th-century houses and a number of gift and antiques shops in the village. The **Salisbury Antiques Show** (a big event) is held on the green the first weekend in October before Columbus Day. For lunch, homemade snacks, or afternoon tea, try **Chaiwalla** (which means "tea maker" in Sanskrit), a restful place on Main Street (Route 44). Tel: (203) 435-9758.

Salisbury is home to several comfortable inns. **Ragamont Inn**, at 10 Main Street, serves delicious Swiss specialties at lunch (weekends only) and dinner (Wednesday through Sunday); the outdoor dining area is separated from the street by a thick hedge, which makes it quite private. The few guest rooms here are too Spartan to be recommended. Open May through November. Tel: (203) 435-2372.

The **White Hart**, on the green at the junction of Routes 41 and 44, is a lumbering frame building with a long history as an inn. Its floral-patterned guest rooms, recently renovated, are very attractive if small. Perhaps the inn's best feature is its restaurant, **Julie's New American Sea Grill**, which specializes in seafood dishes prepared in New American style. The Garden Room bustles at lunch, and the cozy taproom is a local favorite for a late-evening snack and a nightcap.

Another lodging choice in the Salisbury area is **Under Mountain Inn** (north on Route 41, almost as far as the Massachusetts line), a restored 18th-century farmhouse with antiques-filled rooms. The British touches on the menu, such as steak-and-kidney pie and bangers, reflect the owner's heritage. Tel: (203) 435-0242.

Just north and west of Salisbury is the **Mount Riga** area, with **Bear Mountain**, at some 2,300 feet the highest peak in the state. At the summit of the mountain you'll have views of three states (Connecticut, Massachusetts, and New York); the hour-long hike is especially lovely in the fall. To reach the hiking trails to Bear Mountain and neighboring **Bald Peak**, turn off Route 44 by the town hall onto Factory Street/ Washinee Street. Follow this road for 1 mile (1½ km), past the Old Burying Ground (dating to 1741), where you'll reach a fork. Make a sharp left, then at the next fork bear left up a narrow gravel road (closed after the first snowfall until spring). At the top of the hill, facing Lake Wononscopomuc, bear right to reach the hiking trails. It's a ten-minute walk to the 2,010-foot-high summit of Bald Peak. A mile beyond is the entrance to the Bear Mountain trail, from the start of which it's about an hour's climb to the summit. At the top is a 30-foot-high stone monument, which you can climb for even greater views.

The **Appalachian Trail** crosses Route 44 in Salisbury, having wound its way into Connecticut from Webatack, New York (near Route 55, 2½ miles/4 km west of Gaylordsville), then along the Housatonic past Kent, Cornwall Bridge, Falls Village, and Salisbury, from which it continues northward to Massachusetts.

Canaan

You might loop back to Litchfield through Canaan, 6 miles (10 km) east of Salisbury on Route 44. The least charismatic of the villages in this corner of the state, Canaan is more commercial than most. Still, it too has certain attractions. The **Cannery Café**, at 85 Main Street, is a modest, old-fashioned storefront restaurant that dishes up meals with an authentic Cajun accent (the owners, husband and wife, formerly cooked in New Orleans). Tel: (203) 824-7333.

At **Canaan Union Station** (1872), a cupola-topped Victorian depot on Route 44, you can board a car of the **Housatonic Railroad** from Memorial Day through October for a leisurely 5- to 25-mile-per-hour ride (two and a half hours in all) to Cornwall Bridge and back, following the Housatonic's twists and turns, past Falls Village (Tel: 203/824-0339). The ride provides an open window onto a leafy landscape of aspen, oak, birch, and maple, an unfettered natural terrain once pockmarked by mine shafts, smoldering charcoal pits, and iron forges—in short, a miracle of century-long reforestation.

Norfolk

Norfolk, 7 miles (11 km) east of Canaan on Route 44, is another historic village in the Berkshire foothills, with a noteworthy green and a year-round population of about 2,000. The population reaches about 2,500 each summer during the **Norfolk Chamber Music Festival** (formerly called Yale at Norfolk), held on weekend evenings from June through early August (Tel: 203/542-5039).

The concerts are held on the Ellen Battell Stoeckel estate, at the junction of Routes 44 and 272. Stoeckel and her husband, Carl, had strong ties to Yale University and established as their legacy the Yale School of Music and Art on spacious, hilly grounds. The open-sided, redwood-paneled Music Shed (seating 1,200), in a pastoral setting behind the manor house, has admirable acoustics. Before the concerts visitors are free to picnic and stroll the grounds.

Summer concerts have long been part of Norfolk life. In the early 1900s Jean Sibelius made his only visit to the

United States, at Stoeckel's request. Later Ralph Vaughan Williams conducted the American premiere of his symphony *Pastoral* in Norfolk.

Between concerts you might take a stroll around the trapezoidal Norfolk Green; the Battell Fountain on the green was designed in 1899 by architect Stanford White. The 1814 **Church of Christ** is next door to the **White House**, in which some of the Yale Summer School of Music and Art activities are held. Interesting exhibits are often held in the sprawling brownstone **Norfolk Library**, designed in the style of Henry Hobson Richardson; and the **Norfolk Historical Museum** (in the former Norfolk Academy, ca. 1840) contains a small collection of Connecticut-made clocks and memorabilia of Norfolk's history (open mid-June to mid-October). Both the library and museum are on the green.

Just a half mile east of the green is an immaculately kept bed-and-breakfast, **Greenwoods Gate**, a Federal-style frame house with just three spacious suites, each furnished with antiques. One is on three levels and has a whirlpool, another has a bay window and a seven-foot-long claw-footed bathtub, and the third has a sitting room.

NORFOLK AREA PARKS

There are three state parks in the Norfolk area. You can hike and picnic at **Haystack Mountain State Park** (north on Route 272); the view from the stone tower here encompasses Long Island Sound, New York State, and the Massachusetts Berkshires. **Campbell Falls State Park**, 6 miles (10 km) farther north, is a popular place for fishing, hiking, and picnicking; some of the trails lead past beautiful misty cascades. **Dennis Hill State Park**, south on Route 272, is a magnet for cross-country skiers, hikers, and picnickers. The stone observation towers afford views of three states.

Riverton

Riverton, 13 miles (21 km) east of Norfolk via Routes 44 east, 8 north, and 20 northeast, is best known as the home of the Hitchcock chair. Lambert Hitchcock opened his first chair factory here in 1820. The original brick building, across the river from Main Street (Route 20), now doubles as a showroom and the **Hitchcock Chair Factory Outlet**, where you can purchase modern versions of Hitchcocks, with stenciling, rush seats, and other handiwork. The factory itself is not open to the public.

The **Hitchcock Museum**, housed in the 1829 Old Union Church in the village center, displays many rare Hitchcock pieces and other decorated 19th-century furniture. Open April through December; Tel: (203) 738-4950.

Many of Riverton's handsome Colonial houses have been converted into gift shops, factory outlets, and eateries. The liveliest time for a visit is during the annual **Riverton Fair**, the second weekend of October.

Riverton also offers a historic place to stay, the **Old Riverton Inn**, better for its atmosphere than its food. The inn dates to 1796, when it was a stagecoach stop between Boston and Albany. Grindstones embedded in the original floorboards, fireplaces, hemlock beams, and antique furnishings signal the inn's age. The guest rooms are old-fashioned, but four-poster canopy beds, old prints on floral-papered walls, and the uneven floors provide a certain idiosyncratic charm.

Winsted and Torrington

Route 8 south to Route 202 brings you back to Litchfield via Winsted and Torrington. These two towns, larger and more commercial than the villages to the northwest, were once thriving manufacturing centers, Winsted for clock making, hardware, and diverse products, Torrington for its many brass products. Both towns have suffered the region-wide manufacturing decline over recent decades. **Jessie's**, a casual Italian restaurant at 142 Main Street in Winsted, is a good choice for zesty pizzas and pastas. In warm weather you can dine on the patio. Tel: (203) 379-0109.

Torrington, Litchfield County's largest town, is noted more for its industry than its tourism, though its most famous native son had a profound effect on American history: The abolitionist John Brown was born here in 1800. His house still stands but is not open to the public.

If you find yourself in Torrington in the evening you might look into the schedule of Torrington's Art Deco **Warner Theater** (Tel: 203/489-7180) or **Nutmeg Ballet**, which performs at the Warner (Tel: 203/482-4413). The theater also features touring companies and guest concerts by such names as James Taylor. For lunch or dinner, **Le Rochambeau**, at 46 East Main Street, is a decent, moderately priced choice, with a wide selection of traditional French dishes. Tel: (203) 482-6241.

SOUTH TO "BURY" COUNTRY

For a day of antiquing and shunpiking, a second excursion from Litchfield might lead you south to the quiet towns of Bethlehem, Woodbury, and Southbury.

Bethlehem

Bethlehem, 8 miles (13 km) south of Litchfield via Routes 63 and 61, is a somnolent village that leaps briefly to life in mid-December, when it stages a Christmas festival of arts, crafts, hayrides, and lights.

Bethlehem's main attraction is the **Abbey of Regina Laudis** (on the south edge of town on Flanders Road), home to an order of cloistered Benedictine nuns. A shop on the grounds offers for sale handmade gift items, herbs, cheeses, and ice cream, all made by the nuns. Of more interest, though, is **Pax Creche**, an elaborate Nativity scene with 80 18th-century porcelain figures. It is displayed in a windowless building ¼ mile (½ km) before the entrance to the abbey. Open from April through mid-January.

Woodbury

Woodbury, 8 miles (13 km) south of Bethlehem via Routes 61 and 6, is a delightful, gentrified village, one of two major antiques centers in the Litchfield Hills. (The second is Kent, which we discuss below.) With a population of slightly more than 1,000, Woodbury sometimes seems to have more antiques shops than people—there are some two dozen on Main Street alone. Just a few of those are **Grass Roots Antiques**, at 12 Main Street, selling a wide variety of 18th- and 19th-century glass, china, silver, prints, paintings, and rare books; **Gerald Murphy Antiques, Ltd.**, in a Greek Revival house at 60 Main Street, specializing in English and American furniture of the 17th to 19th centuries; and **Hamrah's Oriental Rugs**, at 115 Main Street, showing antique rugs, including Persian, Aubusson, and needlepoint pieces.

Other than shopping, the reason to come to Woodbury is to visit the **Glebe House Museum** (ca. 1750), the home (or "glebe") of the Episcopal minister during the Revolutionary War. The gambrel-roofed, post-and-beam saltbox contains the original pine paneling and many of the furnishings, including quilts, chairs—even an 18th-century mousetrap. The restored garden, with 600 feet of ten-foot-deep borders and myriad flowering shrubs and annuals, was designed in 1926 by the English garden architect Gertrude Jekyll. Indeed it is the only example of her work left in the United States. The garden looks its best from July through September. The house is open from April through early December; the grounds are open year-round. Tel: (203) 263-2855.

Three miles (5 km) off Flanders Road (south via Route 6) is the **Flanders Nature Center**, where you can wander the nature and wildflower trails, visit the sheep farm, and observe seasonal events such as maple-syrup tapping.

Southbury

Five miles (8 km) south of Woodbury, Southbury is reached by a section of Route 6 called the Grand Army Highway of the Republic because it was a major thoroughfare used by Washington, Lafayette, and Rochambeau during the Revolutionary War. Rochambeau led his troops through Woodbury and Southbury to join Washington in the decisive battle of Yorktown.

Southbury is the home of **Heritage Village**, one of the country's oldest and most successful condominium complexes–cum–retirement communities. On its grounds are some interesting shops, along with the **Timbers on the Green,** a high-ceilinged, loftlike restaurant in the Heritage Inn that is especially popular for Sunday brunch. Tel: (203) 264-8325.

Sunday brunch at **Bacci's**, at 900 Main Street South, is accompanied by harp music. Dinner is even more romantic; the well-prepared Piemontese and other northern Italian specialties are served in a gracious room with a fireplace. Tel: (203) 262-1250.

KENT AND ENVIRONS

Another excursion, providing a mix of antiquing, sightseeing, and hiking through wooded parklands, leads west of Litchfield to Kent, south to New Milford, northeast to Washington, and back to Litchfield. It is possible to do this loop in a single day, but, as everywhere in this scenic area, you'll sacrifice much of the pleasure of discovery if you travel at such a clip. Antiquers could browse away an entire day in Kent alone. Plan accordingly.

Kent is less than 20 miles (32 km) from Litchfield (via Route 202 southwest, then west on Route 341 at Woodville), but the road curves and twists through some compelling scenery. Kent itself consists of 49 square miles of breathtaking terrain, though you'd never guess it from the few heavily commercial blocks that constitute the town center along Route 7. Tucked into the outskirts are the Kent Preparatory School (founded in 1906) and the houses of a number of artists, writers, and celebrities, such as Henry Kissinger and Oscar de la Renta.

Artists have been coming to Kent since the 1920s, charmed by its remote and wooded beauty. But in the last 10 to 15 years

Kent has been "discovered," and its increasingly crowded center is clogged on summer weekends with tourists and artistic types browsing through the galleries and hoping to spot some celebrities.

There are six art galleries in Kent and a dozen antiques shops. The **Kent Art Association Gallery**, on Route 7, features four juried art shows per year; for information, Tel: (203) 927-3989. **Kent Antiques Center**, located behind Kent Station Square, houses a number of shops. Also in the station is **Stosh's**, a good spot for sandwiches, ice cream, and homemade cookies. The center is open year-round, but only on weekends January through March.

Another bright spot for lunch, afternoon tea, or takeout items is **Cobble Cookery**, a deli/gourmet food shop in the spiffed-up Kent Green shopping complex, just off Route 7. In warm weather you can eat outside. Tel: (203) 927-3393.

The **Sloane-Stanley Museum**, located in a weathered New England barn on the site of the old, defunct Kent Furnace (1826), which operated for 70 years (and whose ruins are still visible on the grounds), exhibits artworks by artist-writer Eric Sloane, along with his sizable collection of Early American tools. Open from mid-May to mid-October. Tel: (203) 927-3849.

The **Appalachian Trail** winds north through Kent. To reach it, drive west on Route 341 (just off Route 7 at St. Andrew's Church), cross the bridge over the Housatonic, and turn right on the river road. At the fork follow the right branch about 2½ miles (4 km) to a parking lot, where you can leave your car while hiking. It is about an eight-mile hike along the river to Cornwall Bridge through beautiful woodlands along the well-marked trail.

Macedonia Brook State Park, also reached via Route 341 west, has playing fields, streams, a brook, and a rocky gorge, and attracts hikers, fishermen, picnickers, cross-country skiers, and campers.

Just 5 miles (8 km) north of Kent on Route 7 is **Kent Falls State Park**, another popular spot for great numbers of weekend campers and hikers, who climb the steps by the falls to gaze down on the cascades.

New Milford

Following the Housatonic River through Bulls Bridge (whose **covered bridge** dates to the Revolutionary War), Route 7 winds its way southeast from Kent 14 miles (22 km) to New Milford, whose bustle belies its small population of 23,500. Home to the Nestlé Corporation and Kimberly-Clark, New

Milford is also something of a supply source for the smaller towns and villages of the Litchfield Hills.

The area outside New Milford is mostly farmland, while the lengthy town green is flanked by a number of stately buildings. The red brick town hall stands on the site of the home of Connecticut jurist and politician Roger Sherman, who had a cobbler shop in town at one time. The white frame **Village Hardware Store** across the green was built in 1837 and was at one time an Episcopal church.

A mile (1½ km) before the turnoff to Route 202 into New Milford, on the left side of the road, is **Maison LeBlanc**, a white Colonial house where country French food is served in two cozy dining rooms, each with a fireplace. Tel: (203) 354-9931. Another good restaurant in the New Milford area is **Rudy's**, just north of town on Route 202. Gemütlich Alpine ambience, complete with maps of Switzerland and cowbells, will either enchant or dismay you, but the Swiss food is skillfully prepared and prices are fair. Tel: (203) 354-7727.

As you swing north on 202 watch for a right-hand turnoff to Upland Road and signs for the **Silo**. The dream project of bandleader Skitch Henderson and his wife, Ruth, the Silo is a combination country kitchen store, cooking school, art gallery, and craft center, all housed in the former stables and barns of Hunt Hill Farm, a dairy farm nestled in rolling hills. Tel: (203) 355-0300.

Washington

From New Milford Route 202 north to Route 109 leads, after various scenic twists and turns up and down hills dense with hemlock, into Washington Depot and, 1 mile (1½ km) south via Route 47, Washington, snuggled in the watershed of the Shepaug River.

Washingtonians claim their town was the very first named after the general and also the first to be incorporated after the Declaration of Independence. The pretty village green is dominated by the steepled **First Congregational Church meetinghouse**, rebuilt in 1801, the third on the site of a 1742 church.

Across from the church, in the same clapboard building as the post office, is the **Green General Store**, which serves breakfast, lunch, and snacks; a small selection of local baskets and pottery is also sold here.

On the east side of the green, next to the Gunn Memorial Library on Wykeham Road, is the **Gunn Historical Museum**. Housed in a 1781 clapboard structure with a classic central hall, the small museum contains Colonial pewter and silver, costumes, Indian baskets, tools, toys and dollhouses, rare books, paintings, and autographs of George Washington, Thomas Jefferson, and others (only copies are displayed; the original autographs are kept elsewhere). Closed January and early February. Tel: (203) 868-7756.

The **Institute for American Indian Studies**, off Route 47 south of town via Route 199 and Curtis Road, is a research center for indigenous New England peoples that has attracted worldwide attention. Indian tribes, including the Wampanoag, Pequot, and Paugussett, lived in this area before the European settlers arrived. Other Native Americans were here for more than 8,000 years.

The institute features exhibits of artifacts, contemporary art, and documents about many of these peoples, including 18th-century documents in which the Schaghticoke begged the Connecticut General Assembly to let them retain their land. Also on the grounds are a longhouse outfitted with baskets, pots, and deerskins; the Quinnetukut Habitats Trail, a quarter-mile woodland loop that reflects the changing environment of the past 10,000 years; a prehistoric rock shelter; and a reconstructed 17th-century Indian village and gardens. Tel: (203) 868-0518.

The **Mayflower Inn**, on Route 47, is set in 28 acres on a hilltop at the end of a steep, twisting, rhododendron-lined drive. Recently renovated, this magnificent English-style country hotel is a perfect retreat for a special weekend. There is a heated outdoor pool on the beautifully landscaped grounds as well as an indoor pool and fitness center. The genteel dining room serves imaginative, well-presented New American dishes with a regional emphasis. Guest rooms are lavish, outfitted with antiques, canopy beds, marble bathrooms, luxurious Frette bed linens, and thick Turkish-towel robes. Tel: (203) 868-9466.

For a lunch break on your way back to Litchfield stop at the **Pantry**, on Titus Square in Washington Depot, a small, casual place serving homemade breads, soups, salads, and delicious desserts. From Washington Depot head northeast on Route 109, then north on 209 past Bantam Lake to 202 east to Litchfield.

LAKE WARAMAUG

Another way to enjoy the Litchfield Hills, especially if you're visiting in spring, summer, or fall, is to make Lake Waramaug your base instead of Litchfield (but reserve *well* in advance in season). This tiny (nine miles in diameter), crystalline, spring-fed lake is the second-largest natural lake in the state.

To get there take Route 45 a short distance north from the one-street town of New Preston, which is 12 miles (19 km) southwest of Litchfield on Route 202.

An idyllic vacation spot, the lake is ringed with wooded hills. There are four inns on the lake, three of which we recommend highly, so you can dine happily at a different place each night and spend the days exploring Kent, New Milford, Washington, and Litchfield, or swimming, boating, and lazing at the lake. The road around the lake is fairly flat, which makes it ideal for cycling. (The road changes names several times: On the eastern shore it's the East Shore Road/Route 45, on the north it's North Shore Road, and on the west and south it's first Lake Waramaug Road, then West Shore Road.)

If all that's not enough, **Mount Tom State Park** is just 4 miles (6½ km) east on Route 202. There's swimming and fishing in the park's pond, picnicking alongside it (perhaps on takeout from the Pantry in Washington Depot), and a one-mile hiking trail that leads to a 1,325-foot observation tower with commanding views as far as Long Island Sound and the Catskills (especially rewarding during the foliage season).

One story goes that Lake Waramaug was named after a Schaghticoke chief who died in 1736. ("Waramaug" is also said to mean either "good fishing place" or "valley of 100 hills"—take your pick.) According to a legend, Waramaug's people put stones on his grave in tribute, while his enemies added stones to keep the chief's spirit from escaping. Unfortunately, no one seems to know where the grave is.

STAYING IN LAKE WARAMAUG

One mile (1½ km) north from New Preston on East Shore Road is **Boulders Inn**, with a tiered, tree-shaded terrace overlooking the lake for dining in warm weather. The inn's guest rooms are comfortable, and some of the adjacent cottages have fireplaces.

The front guest rooms of the **Hopkins Inn**, a modest 1847 farmhouse on a hill on Hopkins Road (north off North Shore Road), have grand views of the lake. Perhaps the best reason to come here is for the Swiss-Austrian cuisine, knowledgeably prepared by chef-owner Franz Schober. Lake breezes are best caught on the tree-shaded flagstone terrace (used in summer only). The inn's extensive wine list includes a few selections from **Hopkins Vineyard**, down the road—no relation to the Schobers' inn, but the winery welcomes visitors and offers wine-tastings and self-guided tours.

One-quarter mile (½ km) farther down North Shore Road is the **Inn on Lake Waramaug**, the lake's largest, most rollicking lodging place. It has grown from a 1795 house (the main building) to a small resort with several outbuildings, its own minuscule beach, tennis courts, and an indoor heated swimming pool. There are also hiking trails and horseback riding in the area. The inn hosts a raft of special activities each season, from an old-fashioned Frog Jump Jamboree the first weekend in July to Live Turkey Olympics around Thanksgiving. On warm summer days you can dine alfresco on the terrace facing the lake.

(A fourth inn on the lake, Birches Inn, is considerably more rustic and the food and service can be erratic. It is located 3 miles/5 km from New Preston.)

DINING IN LAKE WARAMAUG

There are two very good informal restaurants in the vicinity. **Doc's Pizzeria & Trattoria**, on Route 45 and Flirtation Avenue (where the lake drive begins), is a casual place with ambrosial northern Italian food at reasonable prices. Bring your own wine; no credit cards accepted; erratic hours. Tel: (203) 868-9415.

New and making a real splash is **The Café**, tucked away on the bottom floor of a stone building in the center of New Preston. A variety of Tuscan peasant dishes with a nouvelle twist are served in one tiny, flagstone-walled room, decorated with intriguing oddments. Save room for dessert. Tel: (203) 868-1787. Upstairs is a delightful gift shop called **Rigamarole**, with antiques and folk art.

For a slightly more elaborate occasion—though no place in the area demands really formal attire—there's **Le Bon Coin**, a country French restaurant in the Woodville section of Washington, 5 miles (8 km) east of New Preston via Route 202. Tel: (203) 868-7763.

GETTING AROUND

Connecticut can be reached by air, train, bus, or car. The only major airport is **Bradley International Airport** (Tel: 203/627-3000), at Windsor Locks, 10 miles (16 km) north of Hartford. American, Continental, Delta, Northwest, TWA, United, and USAir all serve Bradley daily. United, United Express, USAir Express, and Continental Express fly into **Tweed–New Haven** (Tel: 203/787-8283), located southeast of the city near East Haven. Business Express, Continental Express, and USAir Express fly to **Igor Sikorsky Memorial Airport** at the eastern tip of Bridgeport. **Groton–New London** is served by Action Airlines, Continental Express, and USAir Express commuter flights. Most major car-rental agencies have facilities at or near these airports.

By Car

Four interstate highways link Connecticut with its neighboring states and connect with U.S., county, and local roads throughout the state: I-95 runs along the entire Connecticut coast linking New York, Providence, and Boston; I-91 leads from north of Springfield down through Hartford to New Haven; I-84 leads east from New York State (Newburgh, Brewster) to Danbury and northeast through Hartford up to Sturbridge, Massachusetts; and I-394 enters Connecticut's northeastern corner from Worcester, Massachusetts, at Thompson, and continues south through Norwich, connecting with I-95 in Waterford.

Touring by car is not just the best way to get around Connecticut, it's virtually the *only* way to cover the smaller towns and move with ease from town to town and to sights within a town or village. In Connecticut (as anywhere these days) it is advisable to lock your car when leaving it and, especially in Bridgeport, Hartford, and New Haven, not to leave valuables visible or even *in* the car for any length of time.

By Train

Metro-North New Haven line commuter trains leave regularly (usually hourly) from Grand Central Station in New York City and stop in all the coastal towns from New York to New Haven, with connecting service inland (such routes as Stamford–New Canaan, South Norwalk–Danbury, and Bridgeport–Waterbury). Tel: (203) 773-0869 for Metro-North in New Haven or (212) 532-4900 in New York City.

Many New Yorkers who travel in Connecticut avoid New York's steep rental-car rates by taking Metro-North to Stamford and renting a car at one of the companies across the street from the station and north along the I-95 exit. Car-rental agencies include **Hertz**, at 74 North State Street (Tel: 800/654-3131 or 203/324-3131); **Budget**, at 28 Guernsey Avenue (Tel: 800/527-0700 or 203/325-1535); and **Avis**, at 10 Guernsey (Tel: 800/331-1212 or 203/359-2910).

Amtrak trains from Boston's South and Back Bay stations and New York's Pennsylvania Station make stops in Mystic, New London, Old Saybrook, Windsor Locks, Windsor, Hartford, Berlin, Meriden, Wallingford, New Haven, Bridgeport, and Stamford. Amtrak also links at New Haven with service to Hartford and Springfield, Massachusetts. Amtrak's New England Express between Boston and New York makes very few stops, one of which is in New Haven; seats must be reserved in advance. Tickets for unreserved trains can be purchased in the station at least 30 minutes before departure. Senior citizens receive a 15 percent discount on tickets. Tel: (800) USA-RAIL.

By Bus
Regularly scheduled interstate service to most points in Connecticut is provided by **Greyhound/Trailways Bus Lines** (Tel: 203/547-1500) and **Bonanza Bus Lines** (Tel: 800/556-3815).

Within major cities (Hartford, New Haven, Bridgeport, Stamford) there are public buses, but to see the various spread-out sights nothing matches a car for both speed and convenience.

Special Tours
Connecticut does not attract mass tourism (which adds to its charm), but there are a number of small companies offering specialized, unusual, and sometimes customized tours to various places and sights of interest. Some of the area tourism commissions have special packages of their areas. The Waterbury Convention and Visitors Commission, at 83 Bank Street, for instance, has six three-day tours, summer and fall, with such themes as "Fall Foliage" and "Classic Carousel Country." Tel: (203) 597-9527.

Heritage Trails Tours in Farmington offers two-hour, half-day, and full-day tours of the Hartford–Farmington area daily year-round. These include ten-person customized minibus tours, Hartford city tours, self-drive auto tours with cassette tapes, and walking tours of Farmington. Especially popular are their candlelight dinner tours of historic houses and museums in the area. Tel: (203) 677-8867.

Canton-based **Unique Auto Tours** offers four- to seven-day tours by antique Rolls-Royce or Bentley or 1950s Cadillac, June to November. Tel: (203) 693-0007. **Quiet Wanderings** in Scotland, Connecticut, features horseback tours, camping tours, and a tour called "Canoe Nature Trip for Wildlife Observation and Photography." Tel: (203) 456-4145.

ACCOMMODATIONS REFERENCE
Unless otherwise noted, the rates given below are projections for 1993 for double room, double occupancy. As prices are subject to change, always double-check before booking. Connecticut state and hotel tax (12 percent) is extra. The area code for all of Connecticut is 203.

Fairfield County (Southwestern Connecticut)
► **Cotswold Inn.** 76 Myrtle Avenue, **Westport**, CT 06880. Tel: 226-3766. $175–$225; Continental breakfast included.

▶ **Holiday Crowne Plaza**. 700 Main Street, **Stamford**, CT 06901. Tel: 358-8400. $59–$89.

▶ **Homestead Inn**. 420 Field Point Road, **Greenwich**, CT 06830. Tel: 869-7500. $127–$175; Continental breakfast included.

▶ **Hyatt Regency Hotel**. 1800 East Putnam Avenue (Route 1), **Old Greenwich**, CT 06870. Tel: 637-1234. $89–$250.

▶ **Maples Inn**. 179 Oenoke Ridge, **New Canaan**, CT 06840. Tel: 966-2927. $65–$150; apartments $175–$225; Continental breakfast included.

▶ **Radisson Tara Hotel**. 2701 Summer Street, **Stamford**, CT 06905. Tel: 359-1300. $115–$135 weeknights; $69–$115 weekends.

▶ **Roger Sherman Inn**. 195 Oenoke Ridge, **New Canaan**, CT 06840. Tel: 966-4541. $100 weeknights; $120 weekends; Continental breakfast included.

▶ **Sheraton Hotel and Towers**. 1 First Stamford Place, **Stamford**, CT 06902. Tel: 967-2222. $69–$130; full breakfast included.

▶ **Silvermine Tavern**. 194 Perry Avenue, **Norwalk**, CT 06850. Tel: 847-4558. $80–$92; Continental breakfast included.

▶ **Stonehenge Inn**. Route 7, **Ridgefield**, CT 06877. Tel: 438-6511. $90–$200; Continental breakfast included.

▶ **West Lane Inn**. 22 West Lane, **Ridgefield**, CT 06877. Tel: 438-7323. $135–$145; Continental breakfast included.

New Haven, the Lower Connecticut River Valley, and the Eastern Shore

▶ **Bee and Thistle Inn**. 100 Lyme Street, **Old Lyme**, CT 06371. Tel: 434-1667. $64–$115.

▶ **Bishopsgate Inn**. 7 Norwich Road, **East Haddam**, CT 06423. Tel: 873-1677. $75–$100; full breakfast included.

▶ **Copper Beech Inn**. 46 Main Street, **Ivoryton**, CT 06442. Tel: 767-0330. $105–$165; Continental breakfast included.

▶ **Griswold Inn**. 36 Main Street, **Essex**, CT 06426. Tel: 767-1812. $80–$165; Continental breakfast included.

▶ **Inn at Chapel West**. 1201 Chapel Street, **New Haven**, CT 06511. Tel: 777-1201. $175; Continental breakfast included.

▶ **Inn at Mystic**. Routes 1 and 27, **Mystic**, CT 06355. Tel: 536-8140. $55–$160.

▶ **Madison Beach Hotel**. 94 West Wharf Road, **Madison**, CT 06443. Tel: 245-1404. $50–$130; Continental breakfast included.

▶ **Mystic Hilton**. 20 Coogan Boulevard, **Mystic**, CT 06355. Tel: 572-0731 or (800) 826-8699. $129–$149.

▶ **Old Lyme Inn**. 85 Lyme Street, **Old Lyme**, CT 06371. Tel: 434-2600. $95–$140; Continental breakfast included.

▶ **Queen Anne Inn.** 265 Williams Street, **New London**, CT 06320. Tel: 447-2600. $78–$155; full breakfast and afternoon tea included.

▶ **Randall's Ordinary.** Route 2, **North Stonington**, CT 06359. Tel: 599-4540. $85–$135; Continental breakfast included.

▶ **Saybrook Point Inn.** 2 Bridge Street, **Old Saybrook**, CT 06475. Tel: 395-2000 or (800) 243-0212. $110–$190.

▶ **Water's Edge Inn & Resort.** 1525 Boston Post Road, **Westbrook**, CT 06498. Tel: 399-5901. $140–$200.

The Quiet Corner (Northeastern Corner)

▶ **Altnaveigh Inn.** 957 Storrs Road, **Storrs**, CT 06268. Tel: 429-4490. $45–$60; Continental breakfast included.

▶ **Cobbscroft.** 349 Pomfret Street (Route 169), **Pomfret**, CT 06058. Tel: 928-5560. $65–$80; full breakfast included.

▶ **Inn at Woodstock Hill.** 94 Plaine Hill Road, **South Woodstock**, CT 06267. Tel: 928-0528. $75–$140; Continental breakfast included.

▶ **Lord Thompson Manor.** Route 200, **Thompson**, CT 06277. Tel: 923-3886. $75–$110; full breakfast included.

▶ **Norwich Inn, Spa & Villas.** Route 32, **Norwich**, CT 06360. Tel: 886-2401. $85–$200 weeknights; $100–$215 weekends.

▶ **Tannerbrook.** 329 Pomfret Road (Route 169), **Brooklyn**, CT 06234. Tel: 774-4822. $65; full breakfast included.

Hartford and Environs

▶ **Butternut Farm.** 1654 Main Street, **Glastonbury**, CT 06033. Tel: 633-7197. $65–$85; full breakfast included.

▶ **Chester Bulkley House.** 184 Main Street, **Old Wethersfield**, CT 06109. Tel: 563-4236. $65–$75; full breakfast included.

▶ **Goodwin Hotel.** 1 Haynes Street, **Hartford**, CT 06103. Tel: 246-7500 or (800) 922-5006. $159–$224; suites up to $629.

▶ **Sheraton Hartford Hotel.** 315 Trumbull Street, Civic Center Plaza, **Hartford**, CT 06103. Tel: 728-5151. $99–$130.

▶ **Simsbury 1820 House.** 731 Hopmeadow Street, **Simsbury**, CT 06070. Tel: 658-7658 or (800) TRY-1820. $85–$135; Continental breakfast included.

The Litchfield Hills (Northwestern Connecticut)

▶ **Boulders Inn.** East Shore Road (Route 45), **New Preston**, CT 06777. Tel: 868-0541. $125–$175 off-season; $225 in season; full breakfast and dinner included.

▶ **Greenwoods Gate.** 105 Greenwoods Road East, **Norfolk**, CT 06058. Tel: 542-5439. $135–$195; breakfast included.

▶ **Hopkins Inn.** 22 Hopkins Road, **New Preston**, CT 06777. Tel: 868-7295. $122–$194 off-season; $138–$229 in season;

includes breakfast and dinner. Closed January 2 to mid-March; no credit cards.

▶ **Inn on Lake Waramaug**. 107 North Shore Road, **New Preston**, CT 06777. Tel: 868-0563 or (800) 525-3466. $122–$154 weeknights; $154–$194 weekends; full breakfast and four-course dinner included.

▶ **Mayflower Inn**. Route 47, **Washington**, CT 06793. Tel: 868-9466. $190–$275; suites $285–$475.

▶ **Old Riverton Inn**. Route 20, **Riverton**, CT 06065. Tel: 379-8678. $65–$150; full breakfast included.

▶ **Toll Gate Hill Inn**. Route 202, **Litchfield**, CT 06759. Tel: 567-4545. $110–$175; Continental breakfast included.

▶ **Under Mountain Inn**. 482 Undermountain Road (Route 41), **Salisbury**, CT 06068. Tel: 435-0242. $160–$190; full breakfast and dinner included.

▶ **Wake Robin Inn**. Route 41, **Lakeville**, CT 06039. Tel: 435-2515. $95–$145; suites $250.

▶ **White Hart**. Village Green (junction of Routes 41 and 44), **Salisbury**, CT 06068. Tel: 435-0030. $110–$135.

RHODE ISLAND

By Phyllis Méras

Phyllis Méras is the travel editor of the Providence Journal.

Forty-eight miles long by 37 miles wide, Rhode Island is the nation's smallest state. For the visitor, however, it is among the richest in historic, architectural, and scenic attractions. And despite its diminutive size, Rhode Island—squeezed between Narragansett Bay, which cuts it almost in two, and the Atlantic Ocean, which borders it to the south—has more than 400 miles of shorefront. Shellfish and finfish thrive in its clear waters; surf crashes against rocky headlands. Inland, apple blossoms and dogwoods nod along its roads in spring, and in autumn its maples, ashes, locusts, birches, and beeches turn crimson and gold.

Although legend has it that 11th-century Vikings were the first white men to occupy the fertile lands that are today's Rhode Island, it wasn't until 1636 that European settlers came to stay. (However, the explorer Giovanni da Verrazano passed by what is now Block Island in 1524. Finding that the wooded island reminded him of the Greek island of Rhodes, he lent the future state its name.) They were led by Roger Williams, a clergyman banished from the Massachusetts Bay Colony for his liberal thinking. So it is not surprising that the country's first synagogue was built in Newport and its first Baptist church in Providence. Sadly, although Roger Williams always maintained good relations with the Native Americans, the colony's record in Indian affairs is flawed: In 1676 during King Philip's War the bloodiest battle against them in New England was fought on Rhode Island soil, in the Great Swamp near West Kingston. But, on a more positive note, one hundred years later Rhode Island's independent-minded colonists were the first in the New World to declare for freedom from the English Crown, on May 4, 1776.

In the mid-1600s Rhode Islanders lived by farming and fishing. In the late 1600s, as production exceeded local needs, the colony began to trade, mainly in rum (made in Rhode Island), molasses, and slaves. The Industrial Revolution began in America in Rhode Island when Samuel Slater established a water-powered cotton-spinning mill in Pawtucket, on the Blackstone River north of Providence, in 1793. The textile industry grew rapidly, and mills thrived the length of the Blackstone river valley (it wasn't until the 1920s, with the shift of the textile business to the South, that Rhode Island lost its hold on the industry). In the 18th and 19th centuries maritime fortunes were made in Providence, Newport, Warren, and Bristol, and many homes built with their profits still stand in these towns.

In the first half of the 18th century America's first summer colony was established in Newport after wealthy plantation owners from the Carolinas and the West Indies, seeking relief from the sultry heat of those southern climes, discovered the cool breezes of Narragansett Bay. They were followed in the late 19th century by the millionaires of the railroad, mercantile, and mining age—Vanderbilts, Astors, and Berwinds—who built villas and mansions to rival the palaces of Europe along the cliffs of Newport overlooking the sea. It was in the Newport Casino a little more than a century ago that American lawn tennis was inaugurated.

For the outdoorsman, the sportsman, the nature lover, the historically minded, Rhode Island (properly, the State of Rhode Island and Providence Plantations) has much to offer.

In addition to its capital city of Providence and its turn-of-the-century summer resort of Newport, there are many lesser-known attractions: the cozy Colonial towns of Wickford and Kingston; Block Island, at the base of Long Island Sound; golden-sand beaches on the southern shore; the perfect New England common in Little Compton; Portsmouth's topiary gardens; and some 15 miles of woodland trails in the Norman Bird Sanctuary in Middletown. And always, Narrangansett Bay's waters sparkle invitingly for the yachtsman. The state has more than 120 beaches open to the public, seven state-owned campgrounds (and dozens more in private or municipal hands), and seven wildlife sanctuaries. Block Island, lying as it does directly in the path of the Atlantic flyway for birds, is said to welcome more avian visitors than any other spot on the Eastern seaboard.

Newport, at the mouth of Narragansett Bay, was the state capital in Colonial days and today is one of the world's leading yachting centers. For more than 50 years, from 1930 until

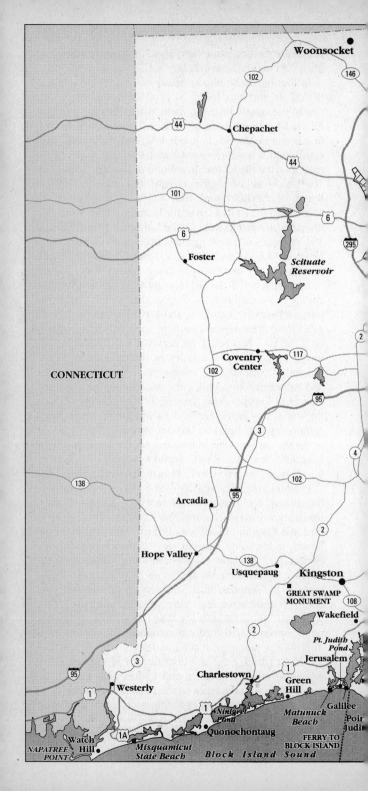

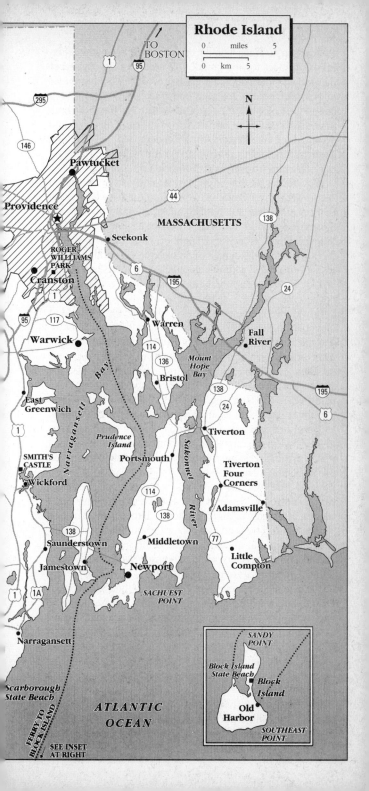

1985, when Australia won the cup, it was the site of the America's Cup races for the grandest of sailing yachts. But other national and international regattas are still held each summer in Newport waters, bringing both yachtsmen and yachting fans to the Colonial city's restored waterfront, lined with boutiques and restaurants, and its narrow streets of pink, red, and powder blue 18th-century houses. Among Newport's cultural attractions is the Newport Music Festival, which draws chamber musicians from around the world each summer.

Providence, the state capital, was known from the end of World War II through the 1970s as the costume-jewelry capital of the nation. That star has fallen lately, but the city is in the throes of a revival and today is characterized by its many different ethnic groups and neighborhoods. The College Hill section is rich in distinguished architecture; Federal Hill is the city's "Little Italy," with the attendant restaurants and shops; and the recently renovated waterfront is lined with pubs and outdoor cafés.

Providence is home to Brown University, the third oldest university in New England and seventh oldest in the country, and the Rhode Island School of Design, one of the nation's most prestigious art schools—which frequently hosts outstanding art exhibitions and lectures. Providence is also the site of the award-winning Trinity Square Repertory Company, where the fare ranges from Shakespeare and Molière to Sam Shepard and aspiring young American playwrights.

The visitor to Rhode Island would do best spending three to four days in the capital and making day excursions to such points as the Blackstone river valley to the north, Wickford on the west side of Narragansett Bay, and Bristol and Warren on the east side. Another three to four days could be spent headquartered in Newport, and from there exploring Portsmouth, Middletown, and Jamestown. Either Providence or Newport could be used as a center for touring Tiverton and Little Compton, in the eastern part of the state, while beach aficionados will wish to position themselves in South County, in the southern part of the state.

We begin our coverage in Providence, then go to South County and trace its Block Island Sound and Narragansett Bay shorelines. Next we cover eastern Rhode Island, beginning with Bristol, then Portsmouth and Middletown, east to Little Compton, and then to Newport. Lastly, we go to the state's islands: Jamestown and Block Island.

MAJOR INTEREST

Providence

College Hill, especially 18th- and 19th-century houses
along Benefit Street, and Brown University

Restaurants and shops of the Harbor District and
  Fox Point
Downtown: Arcade and State Capitol
Federal Hill's Little Italy
Roger Williams Park and Zoo

Pawtucket: Slater Mill historic site

South County
Wickford: Smith's Castle, 18th-century architecture,
  delightful old town
Saunderstown: Gilbert Stuart birthplace
Kingston: picturesque village with 18th- and 19th-
  century architecture
West Kingston: the Great Swamp
Beaches, especially Watch Hill, Ninigret Pond (for
  windsurfing), and Narragansett

Bristol
Mid-19th-century mansions
Colt State Park
Blithewold Gardens and Arboretum
Haffenreffer Museum of Anthropology
Herreshoff Marine Museum

Portsmouth and Middletown
Second and Third beaches
Norman Bird Sanctuary

Little Compton and Tiverton
Sakonnet Vineyards
Little Compton Commons
Goosewing Beach

Newport
Colonial Newport: Touro Synagogue, Trinity Church,
  Fort Adams State Park
Bowen's and Bannister's wharves' shops and
  restaurants
Ocean Drive and the mansions
Newport Casino and Tennis Hall of Fame
Cliff Walk

Jamestown

Block Island
Unspoiled beaches
Bird-watching and fishing
Bicycling and walking

PROVIDENCE

It was in January 1636 that reformer-clergyman Roger Williams of the Puritan Massachusetts Bay Colony learned that colony officials were making secret arrangements to have an English vessel take him away. He was too outspoken in his criticism of the way the colony was being run and too staunch a supporter of the rights of Indians, whom most colonists feared. So Williams and a companion, Thomas Angell, fled into the woods, hoping to find an inviting place to settle outside the colony.

It wasn't until spring that they reached a location that pleased them, a spot along the banks of the Seekonk River (the Blackstone River becomes the Seekonk south of Pawtucket), where East Providence lies today. So delighted were they with the site that they sent word back to Massachusetts Bay friends that they would welcome any who wished to join them in establishing a more charitable and hospitable settlement. Refugees began to arrive, but construction of houses had barely begun when word came from the governor of the Plymouth Bay Colony that they were intruding on his land. So they packed their belongings into their canoes and headed westward across the river. As they neared the opposite bank a band of Indians appeared on a rock outcropping. Although Williams had mingled with the Indians and got along with them, his canoeful of followers watched nervously as their leader paddled toward the tribesmen on the overlook. But with the greeting, "What cheer, Netop [friend]," the Narragansett Indians welcomed the newcomers to their land. The settlers paddled off to search out the perfect place for their home. The site they found here at the northern reaches of Narragansett Bay Williams named Providence in gratitude for God's "providence" to him in his distress. It would ever afterward, he announced, be a refuge for others who were oppressed.

By 1660 Providence had 1,000 settlers and 75 houses. By 1680 it had a wharf, and its days of prosperity had begun. Today, with a population of 150,000, it is one of New England's largest cities, and architecture historians maintain it is the only living example of almost all phases of American architecture.

On College Hill's streets tall brick and clapboard mansions proclaim the wealth that shipping brought to the city in the 18th and 19th centuries. Among the early merchants were the brothers James and Obadiah Brown. James's sons, John, Nicholas, Moses, and Joseph, all brought wealth and renown to the "small town at the head of Narragansett Bay."

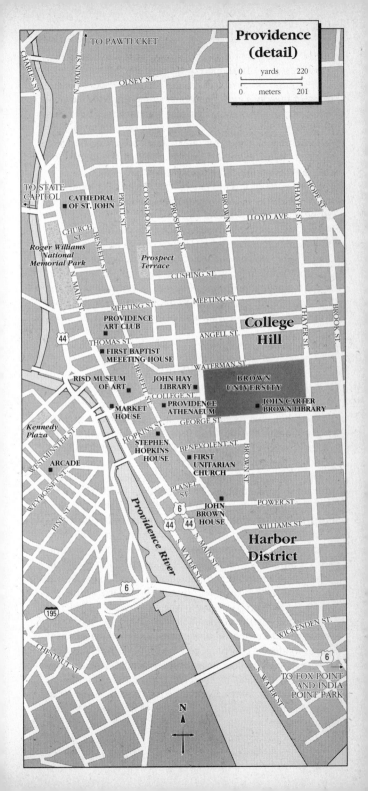

0   yards   220

0   meters   201

TO PAWTUCKET

CHARLES ST.

OLNEY ST.

N. MAIN ST.

TO STATE
CAPITOL

CATHEDRAL
OF ST. JOHN

CHURCH ST.

PRATT ST.

CONGDON ST.

PROSPECT ST.

BROWN ST.

THAYER ST.

HOPE ST.

LLOYD AVE.

BROOK ST.

Roger Williams
National
Memorial Park

BENEFIT ST.

N. MAIN ST.

Prospect
Terrace

CUSHING ST.

MEETING ST.

MEETING ST.

College
Hill

44

PROVIDENCE
ART CLUB

THOMAS ST.

ANGELL ST.

FIRST BAPTIST
MEEETING HOUSE

WATERMAN ST.

RISD MUSEUM
OF ART

BENEFIT ST.

JOHN HAY
LIBRARY

COLLEGE ST.

BROWN
UNIVERSITY

THAYER ST.

MARKET
HOUSE

PROVIDENCE
ATHENAEUM

JOHN CARTER
BROWN LIBRARY

GEORGE ST.

Kennedy
Plaza

WESTMINSTER ST.

HOPKINS ST.

STEPHEN
HOPKINS
HOUSE

BENEVOLENT ST.

BROWN ST.

ARCADE

FIRST
UNITARIAN
CHURCH

WEYBOSSET ST.

PINE ST.

PLANET
ST.

POWER ST.

6

44   44

JOHN
BROWN
HOUSE

WILLIAMS ST.

Providence River

S. MAIN ST.

S. WATER ST.

Harbor
District

6

195

CHESTNUT ST.

WICKENDEN ST.

6

TO FOX POINT
AND INDIA
POINT PARK

S. WATER ST.

N

John, a merchant and shipbuilder, sent the first Rhode Island vessel to China, thereby opening the profitable China trade. Joseph became an architect and was responsible for many of the city's most handsome structures. Nicholas provided land and money to help start the university that bears the family name, and Moses donated land for a Quaker school that was named for him; with an eye to the development of industry, he also helped establish the first cotton mill in America in neighboring Pawtucket.

Those parts of this old city of major interest to the traveller are discussed below: College Hill (sometimes referred to as the East Side), home of Brown University, Rhode Island School of Design, and numerous 18th- and 19th-century houses; the recently restored Harbor District along the Providence River, which separates College Hill from downtown; the downtown area, now undergoing massive renovation and reconstruction; Federal Hill, with its Italianate mansions and fine restaurants, west of downtown; and Victorian, 430-acre Roger Williams Park, south of Providence on the Cranston line.

College Hill

It was on the east side of today's city, at North Main and Smith streets, that Roger Williams and his companions erected their first dwellings near a spring revealed to them by the Indians. Today a small park, the original well, and the visitor center (Tel: 401/528-5385) of the **Roger Williams National Memorial** mark the site.

Opposite it, at 271 North Main Street, rises the brown and gray Episcopal **Cathedral of St. John**. Built in 1810 by Providence architect John Holden Greene, who took his inspiration from Charles Bulfinch of Boston, the cathedral combines a basically Georgian-style stone structure with a wooden "Carpenters' Gothic" tower and "Carpenters' Gothic" decoration ("Carpenters' Gothic" is a 19th-century North American style of wooden architecture ornamented with Gothic Revival fretwork). In the early-18th-century graveyard beside St. John's, Edgar Allan Poe is said to have proposed to Providence widow and poet Sarah Helen Whitman. The couple met when Poe came to lecture at Brown University, after which followed correspondence, courtship, and the proposal. Mrs. Whitman accepted, and the couple became engaged, but Poe's penchant for drink, and her parents' opposition to the union, resulted in the breaking of the engagement. It is believed, however, that she was the inspiration for both "To Helen" and "Annabel Lee."

BENEFIT STREET AND
LOWER COLLEGE HILL

Church Street leads uphill from North Main to Benefit Street, so named because it was to be of "benefit" to residents as a back street when it was put down in the 1750s. All along the street stand imposing, handsome 18th- and 19th-century dwellings. At 109 Benefit Street is the 1810 **Sullivan Dorr House**, built for a merchant in the China trade and one of Providence's grandest Federal mansions—its façade is said to be a copy of Alexander Pope's villa at Twickenham, England. Though it is today privately owned, even from the outside the house gives a clear indication of the wealth of the city's merchant princes in the early 19th century.

Just a block above the Dorr House, on Congdon Street (which runs parallel to Benefit), is a little park at **Prospect Terrace**, marked by a statue of Roger Williams looking down on the city he founded. Usually the park affords fine views of downtown and the State House dome, but with downtown Providence being extensively rebuilt, its river being diverted, and new bridges under construction, the view from the terrace is largely of cranes and construction materials.

If you head back down the hill on Meeting Street to the right, and then turn right again along Benefit, you'll see more of the pink and chocolate-brown 18th-century houses for which the street is famous. If instead you turn left on Benefit, then right downhill on Thomas, you'll come upon the red-brick **Providence Art Club** at number 11, built in 1791 for Seril Dodge, Providence's first jewelry maker. It was here that Seril's brother, Nehemiah, developed the gold-plating process that made Rhode Island a major jewelry center. From time to time art exhibitions, open to the public, are held here. Tel: (401) 331-1114.

The half-timbered **Fleur-de-Lys Building**, next door, was constructed in 1886 as a studio for Rhode Island artist Sidney Burleigh, who was responsible for much of its stucco decoration. It continues to house artists' studios.

At the foot of the hill, across Thomas Street at 75 North Main, is the tall, graceful **Meeting House of the First Baptist Church in America**, designed in 1775 by Joseph Brown and topped with a 185-foot steeple. The church, which copies one of several alternative designs for St. Martin-in-the-Fields in London, succeeded two earlier ones that had been used for Baptist worship in Providence ever since Roger Williams founded the congregation in 1639. Happily for the church, its builders were out-of-work ship's carpenters, unemployed because of the closure of the port of Boston after the Boston Tea Party. Their knowledge of masts and rigging enabled them to build the steeple with sufficient sway to keep it from being blown down in either the gale of 1815, which devastated Providence, or the hurricane of 1938. Roger Williams's church was the first Baptist church in America and continues to be the mother church for all United States Baptists.

Its circumspect interior (where Brown University's baccalaureate and commencement are held each year) is pale green, with enormous columns barely touched with gold. Illuminating it is a Waterford glass chandelier that glows iridescently, said to have been lighted for the first time in 1792 for the wedding of the architect Joseph Brown's niece, Hope, to Thomas Poynton Ives. In the early 19th century the shipping firm of Brown and Ives was "known and respected in the Orient and throughout the marts of Europe, wherever their ships bore in honor the flag of the United States."

Turn right on North Main Street to see, above the 20th-century storefront at number 118, the striking 18th-century Georgian brick façade of the **Joseph and William Russell House**, one of the first grand houses of Providence (privately owned). To the left on North Main Street, at South Water and College streets, is a square red-brick building with fanlights known as the **Market House**. Now part of the Rhode Island School of Design, the house was designed by Joseph Brown in 1775 on a bank of the Providence River so that produce could be delivered directly by ship. In the years just before and during the Revolutionary War it was a center of resistance to British rule, and in March 1775 300 pounds of tea from China were removed from ships tied up here and burned in response to the British tea tax. A plaque on the wall marks that site, while a second plaque shows the height to which floodwaters rose during the terrible hurricane of 1938. As part of the recent downtown renovation project, the riverbed has been rechanneled in this area.

Recross North Main Street, climb College Street, and turn left on Benefit Street to reach (at number 224) the red-brick **Museum of Art at the Rhode Island School of Design**, which is particularly rich in Newport silver, French Impressionist painting, and ancient Egyptian and Asian art. Its Charles L. Pendleton Collection contains many pieces by 18th-century Newport cabinetmakers John Goddard and Job Townsend, as well as English furniture of that period. Continental and Chinese export porcelain is exhibited in adjoining **Pendleton House**, a hip-roofed structure built, as lawyer-collector Pendleton stipulated, in Georgian style to display his gift properly. (Closed Mondays; Tel: 401/331-3511.) The exterior of the Pendleton House is not unlike the striking brick **Handicraft Club**, a Federal-style mansion built for banker and cotton merchant Truman Beckwith in 1828 by John

Holden Greene, much to the dismay of Beckwith's family, who considered the location, at 42 College Street, "out in the sticks." (It is, however, actually a copy of the Pickman House in Salem, Massachusetts, and was designed by Salem native Edmund Willson.) Pendleton House's grand and gracious interior, rich in mahogany woodwork, imitates Pendleton's own home, the now privately owned 1790s **Captain Edward Dexter House**, nearby at 72 Waterman Street.

Across Benefit Street from Pendleton House and to the right, at number 251, is the 1856 Greek-Doric **Providence Athenaeum**, founded as a subscription library in 1851. Among its treasures are a hand-illustrated elephant folio of John James Audubon's work and an 1801 ivory miniature by Newport artist Edward Malbone that is regarded as the most valuable such miniature in the United States. The library also displays watercolors and drawings by 19th-century African-American artist Edward Bannister. It is said that in the alcoves here Poe and Sarah Whitman whispered and passed love notes, and Providence-born gothic novelist H. P. Lovecraft skulked. Benefit Street was one of Lovecraft's favorite grounds for prowling after dark as he sought inspiration for his tales of horror and the fantastic. The five tall brick houses next door, called **Athenaeum Row**, were built in 1845 and are among the city's first row houses (all are privately owned).

The little red house on the far side of Benefit Street, where Hopkins Street runs down the hill, is the **Governor Stephen Hopkins House**, home of one of Rhode Island's two signers of the Declaration of Independence and brother of Esek Hopkins, the first admiral of the U.S. Navy. Governor of the Rhode Island colony ten times, chief justice of its superior court, and the first chancellor of Brown University, Stephen Hopkins was responsible for Brown's being moved from Warren, where it was founded, to Providence. Hopkins was in his late 60s and afflicted with palsy at the time of the signing of the Declaration; seeking to control his shaking fingers as he wrote his name, he is said to have assured onlookers, "My hand trembles, but my heart does not."

Hopkins was a Quaker and so lived unostentatiously; it is said that when George Washington came to visit him in 1776 neighbors feared that the general would not be entertained in grand enough style, so they arrived with their best linens and china—all of which were promptly returned unused by Hopkins's uncompromising daughter, who remarked that if the simplicity of her father's house was good enough for him, it was good enough for General Washington. The Hopkins house and garden are open Wednesday and Saturday afternoons and by appointment. Tel: (401) 751-1758 or 884-8337.

On Benefit Street at the corner of Benevolent rises the tall, gray stone **First Unitarian Church**. In its tower tolls the largest bell (2,500 pounds) ever struck at Paul Revere's foundry. John Holden Greene, the church's architect, considered the gracefully proportioned Federal structure his masterpiece. (The marvelous John Brown House is nearby on Power Street, but we'll return to it after a tour of Brown University.)

BROWN UNIVERSITY AND ENVIRONS

If you head up Benevolent Street and turn left at the first corner onto Prospect Street, the extensive campus of Brown University will come into view. The privately owned redbrick **Candace Allen House**, at 12 Benevolent Street, was designed by John Holden Greene for Zachariah Allen, who hoped to console his heartbroken daughter with the house after her fiancé was killed in the War of 1812.

On Prospect Street between College and George streets sprawls the modern **John D. Rockefeller, Jr., Library**, also known as the Rock, Brown's general library (as opposed to its science library). Just across College Street is the marble-faced **John Hay Library**. Named for the Brown alumnus of the class of 1858 who became secretary of state under Presidents William McKinley and Theodore Roosevelt, the John Hay was the university's main library from 1910 until 1964, but today it houses special collections.

Of most interest among these collections are 5,000 toy soldiers and miniature figures that include a 20th-century Indian army with caparisoned elephants, Nazi motorcyclists of 1934, a royal cortege accompanying Elizabeth II and the Duke of Edinburgh, the coronation of Edward VII, Zulu warriors of 1879, Napoleonic troops, Roman legions, and Japanese samurai. The library also contains drawings, watercolors, and manuscripts related to military history.

Less accessible to the general viewer are more than 500,000 pieces of sheet music dating from the 18th-century to the present day and the Lincoln Manuscript Collection, including some 950 items, many of which were signed by the president. To view these, as well as other manuscripts owned by the museum (among them several by H. P. Lovecraft), you need to ask specifically for the item you wish to see. Tel: (401) 863-2146.

Across Prospect Street and through the wrought-iron **Van Wickle Memorial Gates** is Brown's oldest building, the redbrick **University Hall**, built in 1770 and modeled after Princeton's Nassau Hall. In Revolutionary War days there was no other place in the city to quarter Colonial troops, so University Hall became a barracks for them and their French allies.

Behind University Hall stretches the **college green.** Across the green, at the end of the right diagonal footpath, is the stolid **John Carter Brown Library,** containing the first printed accounts of Christopher Columbus's arrival in America as well as early editions of Amerigo Vespucci's *Mundus Novus,* which led to the naming of the New World after him. Tel: (401) 863-2725.

When you leave the John Carter Brown Library turn right, and right again, through the leafy lower campus to reach **Thayer Street.** Both commercial and intellectual, this is Providence's version of Harvard Square: a mix of book and music stores, fast-food restaurants, and shops catering to college students. (Most of the dining is of the deli and chili sort, but **Adesso's,** at 161 Cushing Street, at the corner of Thayer, serves California-style hearth-baked pizza and good pasta at moderate prices.)

POWER – BENEFIT – SOUTH MAIN

If you turn left upon leaving the John Carter Brown Library and head straight along Brown Street to Power, you will see more of the city's impressive architecture. The **Thomas Poynton Ives House** (private), an orange-red brick mansion at 66 Power, was built in 1806 for Thomas Poynton Ives and his wife, Hope (at whose wedding the First Baptist Church chandelier was first lit). With its impressive white portico and marble lintels and windowsills, it is one of the city's most handsome early homes, a fine representative of the city's wealth at the turn of the 19th century.

Also on Power Street, in the direction of Benefit Street, is another imposing brick mansion, at number 52. This is the **John Brown House,** which John Quincy Adams called "the most magnificent and elegant private mansion that I have seen on this continent."

Joseph Brown designed the house for his shipowner brother John but died before it was completed in 1786. From the hilltop location John Brown had an unimpeded view of the harbor into which his laden vessels sailed, bringing home tea, silk, china, and lacquer ware from the Far East, for he was the most prosperous merchant in Providence at the time. It is said that he owed his success to having abandoned the slave trade after deciding it was far easier to carry canisters of tea and boxes of silk than human beings, who needed food and water. During the Revolution Brown provided ships from his shipyard to the fledgling American navy and cannon from the family foundry to the army.

Inside this historical museum are exquisite Queen Anne, Hepplewhite, Sheraton, and Townsend and Goddard pieces;

Chinese export ware; Sandwich glass; and Staffordshire earthenware. In the coach house is a chariot that was made in Philadelphia in 1782, reportedly the earliest "fancy" vehicle made in this country.

Half hidden behind a wall at 357 Benefit Street (toward Williams Street), the imposing yellow **Colonel Joseph Nightingale House** is said to be the largest frame house in America. It was built in 1792 for a successful merchant and sold in 1814 to the Brown family. From 1932 until the mid-1980s the roof held a curious cagelike structure said to have been constructed after the Lindbergh baby was kidnapped in 1932 so that the Brown children could play outdoors in safety, for theirs was one of the richest families in the nation. (When John Nicholas Brown was born in 1900, the New York *Post* described him as "the world's richest baby.") The house is now undergoing reconstruction that will transform it from the private residence it has been for generations to a scholars' study center with offices and sleeping quarters for researchers doing work in Providence.

At 66 Williams Street is another striking dwelling, the 1810 brick **Edward Carrington House**, especially interesting for its pillared portico with delicate floral carving and its cobblestone courtyard on Power Street. It is not open to the public. If you return to Benefit and turn right toward Planet Street you'll see the turreted, red-brick Victorian **Burnside Mansion**, spilling out over the brick sidewalk. Its original inhabitant was Civil War general Ambrose Burnside, whose facial hair gave rise to the word "sideburns."

At the foot of Planet Street boutiques and restaurants line the far side of the revived old thoroughfare of South Main Street (see Shopping and Dining, below). Also down here, on South Main between Benevolent and George streets, is the gold-leaf-and-copper-domed **Old Stone Bank**, whose brass and marble banking hall, richly paneled and adorned with historic portraits, is one of the handsomest and best preserved of its period in the nation. On the College Hill side of South Main Street, at number 110, are the striking Federal-style **Benoni Cooke House**, a sister to the Handicraft Club, and the wedding-cake-style **Joseph Brown House**, at number 50, with a gracefully curved white pediment.

The newly renovated **Harbor District**, south along South Main Street on the banks of the Providence River, is now the site of numerous bars, restaurants, and galleries. See Shopping and Dining, below.

FOX POINT

The coffee bars, foreign restaurants, print shops, galleries, and socialist/feminist bookshop on Wickenden Street, Fox

Point's main thoroughfare, have transformed what was only a few years ago a predominantly Portuguese area of bakeries, fish markets, and noisy bars into an upscale enclave for college students and other young people. (The restaurants of the Wickenden Street area are discussed below.) The dramatist and vaudevillian George M. Cohan was born in this section of the city in 1878. (To get to Fox Point from the university, follow South Main, Hope, or Brook streets south to Wickenden.)

As this book went to press, the entrance to the new East Bay Bicycle Path was under construction beneath the Washington Bridge to East Providence. This scenic 12½-mile-long bayfront pathway follows an old railway route, passing through woods and edging back yards all the way to Bristol.

Downtown Providence
and Federal Hill

If you turn to the right along South Main Street at the foot of Planet, go back to the Market House, and cross the river on College Street, you'll see an enormous sculpture of a turbaned **Turk's Head** glowering from the building at 1 Turk's Head Place, where Westminster meets Weybosset Street. This 1913 building is so embellished because the early 19th-century house that previously stood on the site had on its porch a similar figurehead from a ship.

For the aficionado of 19th-century, turn-of-the-century, and Beaux Arts commercial architecture, there are any number of buildings to admire on a stroll in the heart of the city. During the city's renovation project, however, much of the downtown's retail space has been empty, giving an air of desolation. Even the venerable **Arcade** on Westminster Street has had difficulty finding tenants for its upper floors during the renovation. Nonetheless, the Arcade is one of the highlights of a visit to Providence. Built in 1828, it was listed in *Guyot's Geography* in 1930 as one of the "Seven Wonders of the United States." The inspiration for the structure was the church of the Madeleine in Paris. Providence banker and investor Cyrus Butler envisioned such a design for a covered shopping arcade with handsome colonnaded façades at either end. But he faced problems in realizing its construction.

Although Butler owned half the land on which he wished the building to be constructed, two other men owned the rest. They were willing to have the shopping arcade on their land, but they wanted a say in how it would look. As a result, two different architects were hired for the construction— one for each end. Happily, both admired the Greek Revival style and there was no altercation until it came to façades. One architect chose a series of stone panels to decorate his pediment; the other favored a simple triangle. Consequently, there is a triangular pediment on the Arcade's Westminster Street side and panels on its Weybosset Street side. Both architects, however, agreed on 22-foot-tall monoliths to support the pediments. At the time of the building's construction these 12- to 15-ton pillars were the largest monoliths in the country. To haul each from the quarry in Johnston, Rhode Island, took more than a dozen yoke of oxen.

In addition to its pillars, architectural high points of the Arcade include the ironwork on its upper stories and the cantilevered stairs between the street and the second floor, for they have no visible means of support.

Today, much overhauled and refurbished, the Arcade's ground level is largely devoted to fast-food restaurants, and its second level to clothing boutiques, gift stores, and a bookshop. A seller of puzzles and board games is among the top-floor tenants.

RHODE ISLAND STATE HOUSE

On the other side of town, beyond Kennedy Plaza and the railroad station, rises the white marble dome of the turn-of-the-century capitol building. The dome is the second-largest unsupported dome in the world, exceeded in size only by that of St. Peter's in Rome. The building's architects were the prestigious New York firm of McKim, Mead & White.

Notable works of art displayed in the State House include a full-length portrait of George Washington by Rhode Island native Gilbert Stuart and a portrait of Civil War general Ambrose Burnside by Emanuel Leutze, the German immigrant artist noted for his painting *Washington Crossing the Delaware*.

FEDERAL HILL

From the heart of the downtown area Sabin Street leads southwest past the Rhode Island Convention Center, still under construction at press time, and the Providence Civic Center, where rock concerts, circuses, and sporting events are held. Atwells Avenue runs to the right off Sabin Street (which leads into Broadway) up Federal Hill. A cement archway topped with a pineapple—symbolizing hospitality—marks the start of the city's old Italian section, with bakeries, butcher shops, cheese and pasta stores, restaurants, and cafés. (The New England Mafia is said to be headquartered here.)

Although there are some interesting turn-of-the-century and early-20th-century structures in Federal Hill, most are now funeral parlors or commercial buildings; nonresidents of the area visit largely to dine here. (See Shopping and Dining, next.)

Shopping and Dining in Providence

COLLEGE HILL

Right at the foot of College Hill, at 7 Steeple Street, the **New Rivers Restaurant** offers cuisine from around the world at fairly high prices; the menu includes the chef's suggestions for wines to accompany each dish (Tel: 401/751-0350). On North Main Street, near the Joseph and William Russell House, are the **Accident or Design Bookstore**, with fine art books, and, at number 128, the **Bluepoint Oyster Bar**, popular with businesspeople for its fine drinks, extensive wine list, and fresh seafood served in informal but sophisticated surroundings. In summer a trellised dining area is set up on the sidewalk (Tel: 401/272-6145). **Angel's**, at 125 North Main, serves Italian and Mediterranean-style grilled dishes and has an impressive old mahogany bar. Prices are on the high side (Tel: 401/273-0310).

On the other end of the street are **L'Elizabeth's**, at 285 South Main Street, a toney place for coffee and cake or an after-dinner drink (Tel: 401/621-9113); and **Ichidai**, at 303 South Main, for Japanese food (Tel: 401/483-3660). **Amsterdam's Rotisserie**, a trendy establishment at 76 South Main, specializes in spit-roasted chicken, crisp duckling, and exotic desserts (Tel: 401/331-5770). **Hemenway's**, a warehouse-like seafood restaurant across from the Old Stone Bank, serves every sort of oyster you can imagine (Tel: 401/351-8570). The **Cactus Grill**, at 566 South Main (Tel: 401/434-0616), is a new place specializing in Mexican food.

Shops on South Main include the **Opulent Owl**, at number 295, for interesting kitchen items, and **Comina's**, at number 245, for jewelry and gifts.

HARBOR DISTRICT

At the foot of Planet Street, South Main Street leads under the Route 195 overpass to one of the city's newest attractions, **Corliss Landing**. On the bank of the Providence River, the landing is lined with the renovated buildings of the old Providence Steam Engine Company, built between 1845 and 1895 and now housing bars with live music, restaurants, and galleries. The nationally acclaimed restaurant **Al Forno**, right next to Corliss Landing at 577 South Main Street, attracts diners from all over with its superb wood-grilled chicken and meats (Tel: 401/273-9767).

Guests at the riverfront **Hot Club**, a bar and grill nearby at 575 South Water Street, at India Point (from where ferries leave daily in summer for Block Island), can sit outdoors in good weather for a riverside view of the cityscape: the smokestacks of the Narragansett Electric Company, the iron-work Point Street Bridge, the towers of the Citizens' Bank Building, and the old Rhode Island Hospital Trust.

FOX POINT

The **Coffee Exchange**, at 207 Wickenden Street, is popular for its pastries and fresh-roasted coffee, sold by the pound or served by the cup on its porch in summer. Slightly less casual is **Café Zog**, on the corner of Wickenden and Brook, renowned for its French breakfast puffs. The **Wickenden Street Pub**, at 320 Wickenden Street, serves beers from around the world, while the **Taj Mahal** (Tel: 401/331-2442), at number 230, and the **Taste of India** (Tel: 401/421-4355), at number 221, both offer excellent and cheap curries and papadums. For sushi, try the **Tokyo Restaurant** (Tel: 401/331-5330), at 231 Wickenden Street; for vegetarian dishes, the neat and bright **Extra Sensory** (Tel: 401/434-3920), at number 388.

Neighboring Hope Street's eateries include **Guido's** (Tel: 401/273-5812), a comfortable hole-in-the-wall at 100 Hope Street that shares space with **Big Alice's** ice cream parlor; and **Rue de L'Espoir**, at 99 Hope, with a French-bistro flavor and popular "small plates"—two or three of which will make a varied and satisfying meal (Tel: 401/751-8890).

DOWNTOWN AND FEDERAL HILL

For a community of Providence's size, its downtown restaurants are few and far between. The upstairs dining room of **Pot au Feu**, a French restaurant at 44 Custom House Street, offers an inviting prix-fixe menu in the moderate to expensive range, while the smaller room on the ground floor serves lower-priced offerings (Tel: 401/273-8953).

Capriccio's, at 2 Pine Street, is an expensive and formal Italian restaurant (Tel: 401/421-1320). **Leo's**, at 99 Chestnut Street, is a favorite for Sunday brunch—try the waffle topped with strawberries, raspberries, and whipped cream—or hot chili on a cold night (Tel: 401/284-3541). Also in this immediate neighborhood is the **Down City Diner**, at 151 Weybosset Street (Tel: 401/331-9217), with imaginative three-course meals for $10 and a World War II ambience.

On the other side of the city, the former Union Station now houses a leading downtown restaurant called the **Capi-**

tal Grille, a pricey businesspersons' place specializing in steaks (1 Cookson Place; Tel: 401/521-5600).

Camille's Roman Garden, at 71 Bradford Street, at the start of Federal Hill, is situated in a large 1865 Italianate house that has been a restaurant since 1925. It is a typical old-style Italian restaurant with statues and private dining rooms behind trellises on which "grow" artificial grapevines. The southern Italian cooking and the service, however, are almost unfailingly excellent—and prices are high (Tel: 401/751-4812).

In a mansard-roofed 1870s house at 120 Atwells Avenue is the **Old Canteen**, a restaurant since 1928. Its decor is less flamboyant than that of the Roman Garden, its service black-tie impeccable. Also expensive, its southern Italian cuisine is well prepared (Tel: 401/751-5544).

Small, new, and less expensive is bistro-like **L'Epicureo's**, squeezed into one room beside Joe's Quality Market at 238 Atwells Avenue (Tel: 401/454-8430). **Little Pastiche**, at 1 Sprague Street on the hill, is a favorite for coffee and pastries.

Staying in Providence

As with Providence's restaurant scene, accommodations in the downtown area—or anywhere in Providence, for that matter—are limited, though a Westin Hotel is scheduled to open in August 1994 in the Rhode Island Convention Center. The **Omni Biltmore**, a venerable (1922) structure in a good, central location on Kennedy Plaza, was recently renovated, but it is distinctly lacking in charm. The food in the hotel's Stanford restaurant is fair. There is a **Holiday Inn** at 21 Atwells Avenue, also an excellent downtown location. The **Providence Marriott**, at Charles and Orms streets, not far from the State House, is the liveliest of Providence's hostelries. Top-40 bands frequently play at its lounge, Cahoots, and its dining room, Stacy's, serves better-than-average fare. Although the location is not central, it is not too long a walk to College Hill or downtown.

Overlooking India Point Park in the Harbor District is the **Days Hotel**, a new, moderately priced hotel on the waterfront. Its outside is very plain, but the interior is neat and pleasant. It has a small restaurant called the India Point Café.

Just about the only Providence accommodation with any charm is the 11-room **Old Court Bed & Breakfast**, at 144 Benefit Street, near the Rhode Island School of Design. The red-brick 1863 main building has 12-foot ceilings, and its rooms are decorated with Victorian furnishings.

Providence After Dark

Amsterdam's Rotisserie, a restaurant (discussed above) at 76 South Main Street, is the venue for blues music on Sunday evenings and jazz on Mondays (Tel: 401/331-5770). Not far away, at 575 South Water Street (one block west of South Main), set along the banks of the Providence River, is the **Hot Club**, a perfect place to while away a summer evening (Tel: 401/861-9007).

The **Last Call Saloon**, at 15 Elbow Street (corner of Chestnut), is crowded and loud, but the blues music is very good (Tel: 401/421-7170). For quieter tastes the **Music Room**, a piano bar at 1060 Hope Street, more than fills the bill (Tel: 401/454-7043). **Sh'Boom's**, at 108 North Main Street, specializes in 1950s, 1960s, and early 1970s music and dancing (there's a disc jockey); the dancing moves outdoors on summer weekends (Tel: 401/751-1200). Big band jazz resounds on weekends at **Victoria House**, at 23 Rathbone Street (Tel: 401/273-7450).

Bori's Tavern, at 287 Taunton Avenue in East Providence, offers nightly live jazz, blues, and country music (Tel: 401/434-9670).

Roger Williams Park and Zoo

Off I-95 at the Providence–Cranston line are the ponds, gardens, and winding roadways of Roger Williams Park. The original 102 acres of farmland, woods, and swamp were a gift to the city from Roger Williams's great-great-great-granddaughter Betsey in 1871. Seven years later the city commissioned a landscape architect to transform the woodland into a park, and in 1890 another 320 acres were added.

Today there are rowboats to be rented for outings on its lakes; paths for cycling and jogging; a carousel; concerts on the shores of Roosevelt Lake; greenhouses and gardens to explore; a French-château–style **museum of natural history** filled with local flora and fauna; a **planetarium**; and a **zoo** with polar bears, penguins, sea lions, zebras, elephants, and giraffes. Established in 1872, it is one of the oldest zoos in the country. The little red clapboard **Betsey Williams Cottage**, built in 1773 for Betsey's father, James, contains a few early-19th-century items.

Rhode Island Public Transit Authority (RIPTA) runs buses to the park from Kennedy Plaza downtown; take the number 20, Elmwood Auburn bus. For bus information, Tel: (401) 781-9400; for the park and zoo, Tel: (401) 785-9450.

PAWTUCKET

The former textile center of Pawtucket, whose name means "the place by the waterfall," is Providence's northern neighbor in the Lower Blackstone Valley. Unfortunately, the exodus of textile mills to the South since World War II has seriously damaged the economy of the city. Its historic Slater Mill, however, where its textile importance began, is alone worth the trip here. To get to Slater Mill from Providence take I-95 north to exit 28, turn left off the exit ramp, continue straight across Main Street Bridge, then turn right on Roosevelt Avenue (about 8 miles/13 km in all).

The site comprises a number of structures and buildings, among them **Slater Mill** (1793) itself, where you can still witness machines spinning, weaving, and knitting; the **Wilkinson Mill** (1810) next door, an authentic machine shop where you can hear the rush of the Blackstone River driving the wheel to produce the mill's power; and the quaint **Sylvanus Brown House** (1758), once the home of a millwright and carpenter who worked at the mill, and furnished with his early-19th-century belongings.

Samuel Slater, for whom Slater Mill is named, grew up on a farm in Derbyshire, England. The Industrial Revolution was dawning as he reached his teens in the 1780s, so he was apprenticed to the partner of Richard Arkwright, the inventor of the spinning frame, which used water power to produce cotton thread, thereby doing away with a great deal of human labor. During his apprenticeship Slater is said to have memorized (perhaps unintentionally) the plans of his employer's spinning machinery, and when he decided to emigrate to America a few years later he took the plans along with him "in his head." (Because of English fears that plans of their machinery would leave the country, Slater had to disguise himself as an agricultural laborer to get passage.)

Of course, interest in textile manufacture was increasing in the New World, and Pawtucket was already a spinning center. So it was that Slater made his way to Rhode Island. He impressed the wily businessman Moses Brown, who hired him to improve machinery he had purchased. In 1793 Slater and his Rhode Island employers—Moses Brown, his son-in-law William Almy, and his nephew Smith Brown—together built a new mill (the one that stands today) with the perfected machinery based on the water-powered machinery Slater had seen. In 1810 the Wilkinson Mill was built beside it as a machine shop.

SOUTH COUNTY

South County, which begins 16 miles (26 km) south of Providence, is actually a nickname for Washington County, which includes the southernmost part of the state (and, technically, Block Island, which we cover separately, below). It starts south of East Greenwich and stretches along the western shore of Narragansett Bay, along Block Island Sound, and to the Connecticut border. To get here, leave Providence on I-95 south and take exit 9 in East Greenwich to Route 4, which becomes Route 2, a relatively rural route. (Route 1, a long commercial strip, also leads to South County from south of Providence.)

South County is quintessential Rhode Island: The beaches here are endless, seabirds dive offshore, mergansers and mallards inhabit the ponds, and fat green trawlers chug into harbors at dusk. In spring silver herring—locally called buckeyes—fight their way up the streams. White clapboard houses line oak-shaded streets.

It was to South County in 1636, soon after he had settled Providence, that Roger Williams came to build a trading post for dealing with the Native Americans. It was also in South County, four decades later, that the bloodiest battle of the Indian wars in New England was fought.

Wickford

Roger Williams established a trading post on what today is Route 1, 1½ miles (2½ km) north of Wickford village, right on Narragansett Bay. Always a friend to the Indians, Williams compiled the first dictionary in the Narragansett tongue. In return the sachem Canonicus sold him a site that the Indians called Cocumscussoc (marked rock) on which to build, and Canonicus's wife presented Williams with an island on which to graze his goats. Though only a plaque marks the location of that first trading post, nearby rises **Smith's Castle**, a 1678 reconstruction of the garrison–trading post that Richard Smith erected in 1640 on property sold to him by Williams to raise money for a trip back to England.

Some years later relations between the colonists and Indians soured, and King Philip's War, named for the leader of the Wampanoag tribe, broke out. It was in the original Smith's Castle that in December 1675 soldiers of the Massachusetts and Plymouth Bay colonies and of Connecticut, along with a few Rhode Islanders, planned the war against the Indians. And from the same garrison they set out for their merciless slaughter of the Indians in the Great Swamp Fight (see below).

While the soldiers were gone the Indians burned the garrison to the ground, and when the white men returned, bearing their dead and wounded, only smoldering embers remained. A tablet marks the common grave of those who died (40 soldiers). Two years later the destroyed garrison was replaced and whatever remained of it incorporated into the new structure.

In the next century Daniel Updike, a prominent lawyer and socialite who had inherited it, added onto the garrison extensively so that there would be plenty of room for both living and entertaining. With its elegant paneling, Smith's Castle today is a fine example of the "plantation" houses that stretched along the Rhode Island shore from Wickford to Westerly in the 18th century. Both Benjamin Franklin and Lafayette are said to have been guests here.

WICKFORD VILLAGE

Pretty little Wickford village is south of the castle. White and yellow clapboard houses with fanlights and gleaming brass knockers, and handsome red-brick buildings line its streets, which were laid out in 1707. From the time of its founding until the Revolution the village prospered, for from its snug harbor sloops full of goods crossed the bay to Newport for transferral to ships bound for the West Indies. But when the British occupied Newport at the mouth of Narragansett Bay, all shipping stopped. Dry years followed, but once the war ended, cattle and sheep were again driven up from Connecticut to be shipped out of Wickford to the West Indies.

Wickford remained a bustling community until the invention of the steam vessel and the train in the first half of the 18th century. Then it began to be passed by, to the sorrow, at that time, of its citizenry, and to the delight, today, of those who live along its old-fashioned Main Street and its narrow, meandering waterfront lanes.

Simple, white-framed **Old Narragansett Church** (Old St. Paul's), at 60 Church Lane, built in 1707, is the oldest Episcopal church building north of Virginia. For the best vantage point approach it from across the Greenway, where the names of former pastors and church benefactors are cut into a stone pathway. Where the path ends on Church Lane stands the church, its gracefully arched windows flanking its double doors.

Because of the community's enthusiasm for the church and their sizable donations toward its construction, Queen Anne, the ruler of England at the time, presented the parishioners with a silver baptismal font (in which the artist Gilbert Stuart was baptized) and a silver Communion service that is still used on special occasions. St. Paul's notable features include its box pews, its upstairs gallery for plantation slaves, and its wineglass pulpit. The old church has never been wired for electricity and is now used only for services in July and August and on special occasions. It is open to visitors on Friday, Saturday, and Sunday afternoons in summer. (Since 1847 Wickford has claimed another **St. Paul's**, a white and brown "Carpenter's Gothic" church built across Main Street from the Greenway. Here all but summer services are held.)

It's said that during the tenure of one of its more notorious ministers, the Reverend James McSparran, the old church's pulpit had to be enlarged as the reverend's girth increased. But it was for his loyalty to the Crown before and during the Revolution that Dr. McSparran is particularly known. Because he refused to omit prayers for George III from his services, American patriots closed St. Paul's, and Continental troops were housed in it.

The church originally stood on Shermantown Road in neighboring North Kingstown; only after the Revolution was it moved to its present site. This sparked considerable dissension among the parishioners. Because there was such strong sentiment against a move, those favoring it waited until one of the coldest January nights to have the church towed off to its new location. The frightful cold, they hoped, would keep parishioners opposed to the move at home in their beds (they were right).

If you return to Main Street and turn left you'll come to the **harbor**. Nowadays, instead of turkeys, salt fish, sheep, and cheese (Rhode Island cheese was considered the best in the country at the end of the 18th century), quahogs are unloaded here from broad-beamed quahog damming skiffs, which moor alongside sleek yachts.

DINING IN WICKFORD

Peaches, at 16 West Main Street, is a moderately priced restaurant with especially good fresh fish and Jamaican-style jerk pork; the desserts are exceptional. Bring your own wine; Tel: (401) 294-3323. For lunch try the **Wickford Gourmet**, at 31 West Main Street, which offers sandwiches on homemade bread and imaginative salads and desserts. Just out of Wickford village at 7355 Post Road in North Kingstown, the **Red Rooster Tavern** has attracted diners for two decades with its lovingly prepared Continental cuisine; Tel: (401) 295-8804.

Saunderstown

The hamlet of Saunderstown, just 7 miles (11 km) south of Wickford via scenic Route 1A, claims the 18th-century **Silas Casey Farm**, actually a plantation of the kind that extended everywhere in South County in those days, and the **Gilbert Stuart Birthplace**, the home in which the acclaimed portrait artist was born in 1755. The Casey farm now houses three museum rooms furnished in 19th-century style, and is open to the public Sunday afternoons from June 1 to September 30. Tel: (401) 294-2868.

The barn-red hip-roofed Gilbert Stuart Birthplace, in a lovely, peaceful spot beside the Mattatuxet River on Gilbert Stuart Road, was constructed by Stuart's father, also named Gilbert Stuart, who came to America from Scotland with Dr. James Moffatt, a Newport physician (also Scottish), who hoped to develop a snuff mill here. Tobacco was a thriving crop in Rhode Island in those days, and Stuart was an able millwright. It was hoped that the combination of Stuart's skills and the good tobacco would bring prosperity to both Moffatt and Stuart. Trusting that it would, Stuart married a Newport woman and built this structure, which combined a mill and kitchen on the lowest level with living accommodations for the family above, which by then included Gilbert Stuart, Jr.

But the mill was not a success, and when the younger Gilbert was ten his family moved to Newport. Stuart later became the most famous portrait artist in New England and painted three studies of George Washington, one of which appears on the dollar bill.

The furnishings in this house-museum represent the period of Gilbert Stuart's youth but they did not actually belong to the Stuart family. Sadly, there are no genuine Gilbert Stuart paintings on display here; in the mid-1950s the paintings the house owned were stolen and have never been recovered. The snuff mill is still in operation. Open April 1 to November 1; Tel: (401) 294-3001.

Kingston Village and Environs

Picturesque Kingston village, site of the University of Rhode Island, is about 6 miles (10 km) southwest of Saunderstown. Head south on Route 1A and go right on Bridgetown Road, a wooded, winding road that crosses Route 1 and eventually becomes Mooresfield Road and then Route 138, the main street of Kingston.

In the 18th century this attractive little community of

green- and black-shuttered white clapboard houses was known as Little Rest, for in those days this was one of the seats of the Rhode Island General Assembly, which, when it was in session, was a place of "little rest." Another story has it that soldiers on their way to the Great Swamp Fight stopped here to catch their breath. In any case, today, despite the presence of the main campus of the University of Rhode Island, the village remains a quiet, restful place, rich in historic and architectural highlights; its only business establishments are a service station and a general store.

The little Cape Cod cottage on Route 138 that now serves as the headquarters of the **Fayerweather Craft Guild**, where crafts demonstrations are held in the summer, is one such historic structure. It was built in 1820 by the village blacksmith, the son of a slave from one of the plantations that extended along the shores of Rhode Island in the 18th century. The guild is open from mid-May to mid-December (closed Mondays), when crafts are made and sold there.

Another early building, though largely reconstructed, is the yellow clapboard **Helme House**, constructed in 1802 as a lodging house and later turned into a bank. It is now used as a museum by the South County Art Association, with the works of some 400 contemporary artists on display.

In another, unrelated Helme House (destroyed in a fire in 1910) an 18th-century silversmith named Samuel Casey tried his hand at counterfeiting to recoup some of his losses after suffering a spate of misfortunes. But he was found out, tried, found guilty, and sentenced to be hanged. Friends, however, helped him to escape from jail and he was never seen again.

The building from which he escaped, down the road from the Helme House, no longer stands, but was situated across the road from the gray stone **Washington County Jail**, which operated as a jail from 1858 to 1956. Today its downstairs cells, with their cast-iron doors, and the jail keeper's quarters may be visited. The upstairs rooms formerly occupied by women prisoners now contain displays of toys and antique furniture.

Just beside the jail is the simple, Federal-style **Kingston Congregational Church**, built in 1820. On the same side of the street as the church and jail and almost directly across from the Kingston Free Library stands a grey clapboard private house that, when it housed the **Kingston Inn**, was the setting for much merriment. Many a merchant and traveller tarried here to wet his whistle in the 18th and 19th centuries, and even briefly into the 20th century. Now a private home, it may be viewed only from the outside.

The tall, tan and gray **Kingston Free Library**, topped with a cupola, is as imposing today as it was when it served as the

Kings County Courthouse after it was built in 1775. From 1776 until 1853 it also served as one of the five statehouses of Rhode Island, with government officials convening here periodically. (The other communities where they met were Providence, Newport, East Greenwich, and Bristol.) It has been a library since 1894.

If you are an aficionado of railroads, turn right from the library parking lot onto Route 108 and continue on that until you reach Route 138. Turn left onto Route 138 and drive another 2 miles (3 km) or so and you'll come to little **Kingston Station**, with its potbellied stove, dark wooden benches, creaky floors, and an old-fashioned teller's wicket. Built in 1875 to replace an earlier station, it is among the oldest rail depots in the world still serving its original purpose.

When you leave Kingston Station return to Route 138, turn left (west) and continue until you reach Dugway Road. If you then turn right you will come to a picturesque stone mill that has stood on the same spot since 1830. No longer in operation, this former woollen mill now houses **Peter Pots Pottery**. Inside, in addition to an old waterwheel, is a wide assortment of vases, plates, cups, and pots made and sold on the premises.

If you turn right on Route 138 onto Glen Rock Road from Peter Pots Pottery you will arrive shortly in **Usquepaug**, 4 miles (6½ km) west of Kingston, at the **Kenyon Mill**, where corn, wheat, rye, and oats are ground. The cornmeal ground by the huge stones is the specialty here, for white cornmeal has long been favored for Rhode Island johnnycakes, flat cornmeal cakes that were properly known as journey cakes in Colonial days and were carried in saddlebags for on-the-road eating. Today they are served in a number of restaurants around the state, slathered with butter and frequently with maple syrup; sometimes they are accompanied by fresh tomato slices. The mill-ground meal is sold at a gift shop across the road from the mill, and tours are available by appointment in summer; Tel: (401) 783-4054.

THE GREAT SWAMP

From the mill take Route 138 east for about 1½ miles (2½ km) and turn right onto Route 2 about a mile before West Kingston and you will see the entrance road to the **Great Swamp Monument**. This stone obelisk with its surrounding stone markers commemorates the troops of the Massachusetts and Plymouth Bay colonies and Connecticut who fought in the Great Swamp Fight of December 19, 1675.

After the gathering at what is now Smith's Castle at Cocumscussoc (see Wickford, above), Colonial forces, led by an Indian guide who had turned against his people, attacked the winter camp that the Narragansetts had built in the center of this swamp. The colonists suspected that the Wampanoag warriors of their enemy King Philip were being sheltered here. Ordinarily the Indians' fort would have been inaccessible, for though it was on solid ground itself, it was surrounded by swampy lands. But December of 1675 was unusually cold, and the swampy ground had frozen; a blizzard notwithstanding, the white men made their way across it. Indian arrows pelted them, but they managed to set fire to the fort. Out from the flames ran not only Wampanoag warriors but their wives and children. Enraged by Wampanoag attacks on their own settlements, the white men mercilessly slaughtered all they could. By nightfall the Indians within the fortification had been virtually wiped out. The colonists were undeniably the victors, but they, too, had suffered losses—40 men were dead and 150 wounded.

When you leave the monument, turn right on Route 2 and continue to the **Great Swamp Management Area** sign on the right, just before the first traffic light. There are five miles of walking trails in this 2,895-acre swampland of holly and rhododendron, white oak, red maple, tupelo, pin oak, and many varieties of berry bushes. Mink, raccoon, deer, foxes, hawks, ospreys, owls, black and wood ducks, pheasant, woodcocks, and grouse are among the inhabitants here, and both hunting and trout fishing are permitted in season. Canoeing offers the best opportunities for viewing the swamp; the Division of Fish and Wildlife in Wakefield can supply details. Tel: (401) 789-3094.

To return to Providence go back to Route 138 and turn right; continue to Route 1, turn left (north), and follow signs for Providence. If you'd like to visit the island of Jamestown, follow the signs to the Newport Bridge. But first, we proceed to South County's beaches.

SOUTH COUNTY BEACHES

Rhode Island indeed merits its nickname the Ocean State, for along the South County shore between Watch Hill to the west and Point Judith to the east are some 20 miles of beaches on Block Island Sound, offering surf swimming for the experienced. North of Point Judith another six miles of more sheltered beaches, suitable for novice swimmers, edge Rhode Island Sound. Most of the county's beaches are open to the public (though generally there is a parking fee and sometimes a beach fee as well); parking is on a first-come first-served basis. Some beaches have bathhouses and food concessions and amusements, while others offer simply sea and sand, wrack and dunes, fish and shorebirds.

Added attractions along this stretch of Rhode Island are the marshes and wildlife preserves where swans, wild ducks, Canada geese, and egrets feed, and hawks soar.

The Western Beaches

Half-mile-long **Napatree Point** is the westernmost of the beaches of the southwestern part of the state. Houses once sat on this narrow strip of sand, but now all are gone, victims of hurricane winds and waves. A spit of sand remains, washed on one side by Block Island Sound, on the other by Little Narragansett Bay. The beach here is good for walking and beachcombing, but visitors should bear in mind the fragility of the sands. The surf along the sand spit's south side is rough, but the bay on the north side is sheltered (there are no lifeguards, however). Parking for Napatree Point is at neighboring Watch Hill Beach, but parking spaces may be in short supply in summer.

Watch Hill is a quiet resort colony of weathered shingled Victorian "cottages" overlooking the sea and arcaded shops offering both fishing tackle and high fashion. The painted horses of what is said to be the nation's oldest carousel, built in New York in 1879, go round and round in an outdoor pavilion. The beach itself is relatively free of undertow, the waves small. There are public bathhouses.

To reach Watch Hill and Napatree Point from Providence, follow I-95 south to the Westerly–Hopkinton exit and continue south on Route 3 for about 3½ miles (5½ km). Then go left (east) on Route 78 to the traffic light at the junction of Routes 78 and 1, straight on the Westerly Airport Road to Route 1A, then right to Watch Hill. Because salt ponds are scattered all along the southern Rhode Island coast, reaching the beaches means zigzagging from Route 1A down to the shore, then returning to 1A and going down again to the next beach.

Off Route 1A on Atlantic Avenue is seven-mile-long **Misquamicut State Beach**, the state's largest, with water slides, lifeguards, bathhouses, moderate surf, and, at the eastern end, clam bars, video games, nighttime dancing, motels, and Atlantic Beach Park, popular with teenagers. If you continue to the right along Atlantic Avenue you'll come to the small, family-owned **Dunes Park Beach**, beside the Weekapaug Breachway, with a lifeguard, bathhouses, and a snack bar beside a mobile home park. There is good fishing from the rocks in this neighborhood, at both the Weekapaug and the

Quonochontaug breachways, for flounder, bluefish, and striped bass.

DINING AND STAYING
ALONG THE WESTERN BEACHES

There is casual dining in Watch Hill at the **St. Clair Annex**, which prides itself on its ice cream, on Bay Street. Steaks, chops, and seafood are offered at the bubble-gum pink 1950s-style **Olympia Tea Room**, with its old-fashioned soda fountain and waitresses in frilly aprons, also on Bay Street (Tel: 401/348-8211). Seafood is the specialty at the **Ocean House**, at 2 Bluff Avenue overlooking Block Island Sound (Tel: 401/348-8161); and steaks and seafood balance the menu at the **Watch Hill Inn**, at 50 Bay Street overlooking Little Narragansett Bay (open only in summer; Tel: 401/348-8912).

Back in Westerly (north from Watch Hill on 1A or northwest from Weekapaug along Route 1), the cozy, old-fashioned **Shelter Harbor Inn** offers both the finest seasonal fare and attractive accommodations overlooking the Atlantic. The charming, gray-shingled, red-shuttered **Weekapaug Inn**, on Quonochontaug Pond in Weekapaug, has breezy, spacious public areas and prettily decorated guest rooms (no TVs or phones). The food is simple and wholesome; no liquor is served, but you may bring your own.

Ninigret and Charlestown

East of Quonochontaug, abutting the Ninigret Conservation Area, is **Blue Shutters Town Beach**, rough but good for surfing, with lifeguards and food concessions. Three-mile-long **East Beach**, part of the conservation area, is one of Rhode Island's least frequented beaches. The water can be rough, however; the drop-off is sudden and the lifeguard is positioned at one end of the beach. If you would rather walk than swim, it is ideal. There are neither bathhouses nor concessions and parking is limited at East Beach, so it is wise to arrive early in the morning in summer.

Just behind East Beach is **Ninigret Pond**, home to mute swans and mallards; conditions on the pond are ideal for windsurfing, and there is a sandy area for children. **Ninigret National Wildlife Refuge**, a 404-acre wildlife sanctuary on Ninigret Pond, has sand trails and attracts migrant water birds.

The next beach to the east is **Charlestown Town Beach**, with lifeguards and smooth, fine sand but no concession stands. Unfortunately, the summer houses here have crept rather close to the beachfront. The surf is moderate to heavy, with some undertow. There is plenty of parking, however, and the beach is pleasant for walking.

There are state camping areas in Charlestown at the **Charlestown Breachway** (Tel: 401/364-7000), with a small beach and jetty fishing for blues, bass, and tautog; at the **Ninigret Conservation Area** (Tel: 401/322-0450), on Ninigret Pond adjacent to the wildlife refuge; and at **Burlingame State Park**, on Route 1 (Tel: 401/322-7994), in a wooded area right on Watchaug Pond—one of the most popular campgrounds in the state (no reservations are taken, but you can check in advance on general availability). All three are open from mid-April to late October.

DINING AND STAYING
IN THE CHARLESTOWN AREA

The **Charlestown Lobster Pot**, on Route 1 beside the Land Harbor Inn, prides itself on its moderately priced seafood served in a converted 18th-century house (Tel: 401/322-7686). Among the best bets at **Wilcox Tavern**, on Route 1 near the Westerly line, are the roast beef dinner and the sautéed lobster; the tavern's eclectic decor changes according to the whims of the decorator. Tel: (401) 322-1829.

If you're really famished head for the **Nordic Lodge**, at 176 East Pasquisett Trail, with an all-you-can-eat menu including lobsters, clams, and shrimp for $34.95 on weekends. Open Memorial Day through November; Tel: (401) 783-4515.

For overnights there's the **Willows Resort** in Charlestown, set on 20 acres above Ninigret Pond. The complex includes a motel, apartments, cottages, tennis courts, and a swimming pool. Breakfast and dinner are offered; open Memorial Day to Columbus Day.

South Kingstown Beaches

Green Hill beach in South Kingstown has moderate waves, good for surfing and bodysurfing, but limited parking. Roy Carpenter's, the South Kingstown Town Beach, and Matunuck Beach, all with lifeguards and concessions, cluster together as you continue east. **Roy Carpenter's Beach** is largely a family beach, with moderate surf, bathhouses, lifeguards, and many summer cottages. Right near the beach, on Card's Pond Road, is the **Theatre-by-the-Sea**, a breezy, old-fashioned summer playhouse where Tallulah Bankhead, Carol Channing, and Groucho Marx once trod the boards (performances only in summer; Tel: 401/789-1094).

The new **South Kingstown Town Beach** has lovely golden sand, lifeguards, and snack bars, and the surf is moderate to heavy. Similar to South Kingstown and almost adjoining it is **Matunuck Beach**; summer cottages clutter the approach to it. East of Matunuck down Succotash Road is **East Matunuck State Beach**, a teenagers' favorite with moderate surf. Still farther down Succotash Road on the western side of Point Judith Pond is **Jerusalem**, a modest beach and fishing community that's relatively free of commercialism.

DINING AND STAYING IN THE SOUTH KINGSTOWN AREA

Captain Jack's, overlooking the Succotash Salt Marsh, at 484 Succotash Road in Wakefield, serves genuine clear Rhode Island clam chowder; the dessert menu is filled with items bearing such enticing names as "Rocky Mountain butterscotch cream pie." While you eat, if you're keen eyed, you may be able to see little green and great blue herons feeding in the marsh. Tel: (401) 789-4556. There's good casual dining in Jerusalem at **Jim's Dock**, popular with sportfishermen. You can watch the boat traffic going up and down Point Judith Pond from here. Down Salt Pond Road in Wakefield (north of Matunuck Beach) is one of South County's finest— and most expensive—restaurants, the **South Shore Grille**, where gas-fired grilling is the specialty and the waterfront view is phenomenal. Tel: (401) 782-4780.

For charming overnight accommodations, the **Admiral Dewey Inn** in South Kingstown is the place to stay. Nearly a century old, but recently renovated, the antiques-filled inn is a bona fide example of the wood-shingled boarding houses of Matunuck at the turn of the century. It is on the National Register of Historic Places.

Galilee

Narragansett County's beaches are the next inviting ones along the South County shore. From Jerusalem drive up Route 1, then down Old Point Judith Road around Point Judith Pond to get to Galilee (a 9-mile/14½-km drive).

Sunset is the ideal time for a visit to the fishing port of Galilee, for then the trawlers, nets swinging from their rigging, come through the narrow channel into Point Judith Pond with their catches. Legend has it that the little port got its name around the turn of the century from a Nova Scotia fisherman who settled here and felt it was appropriate, with the abundance of fish being brought into port, to call it after the Sea of Galilee, where Jesus's disciples fished. From Galilee a ferry leaves almost every hour for the hour-and-fifteen-minute trip to Block Island (discussed below), 12 miles off Point Judith. In addition, the 65-foot *Southland* offers one-and-three-quarter-hour harbor cruises from Galilee.

The protected **Salty Brine State Beach** at the Galilee breakwater is an ideal spot for swimming with small children, as the waters are calm, there is little undertow, and a lifeguard is on duty. Unfortunately, the beach backs onto a parking lot. **Roger W. Wheeler State Beach**, sometimes called Sand Hill Cove Beach, up Sand Hill Cove Road from Galilee, is another good beach for children, with lifeguards and a play area, calm water with no undertow, and a gradual drop-off.

DINING IN THE GALILEE AREA
Two popular waterfront restaurants in the Galilee area are **George's of Galilee**, 25 Sand Hill Cove (Tel: 401/783-2306), a Narragansett institution with clam cakes, chowder, and seafood platters; and **Champlin's Seafood**, on Great Island Road (Tel: 401/783-3152), with outdoor dining. Where Point Judith Road meets Ocean Road is **Aunt Carrie's**, another informal oceanfront restaurant that is a Rhode Island mainstay for clam cakes and fish-and-chips (Tel: 401/783-7930).

Scarborough State Beach and Narragansett

Scarborough State Beach, the busiest beach in the state and very popular with teenagers, is the next beach to the north. Though the areas for surfing and bodysurfing are limited, they are first-rate, but the drop-off is abrupt. There are a boardwalk, lifeguards, gift shops, a pavilion, and concessions aplenty.

The stretch of Ocean Road (Route 1A) that leads from Scarborough State Beach to Narragansett Pier is lined with multichimneyed, weathered-shingle "cottages." In the 1880s, when there was both a railroad station and a steamboat stop here, Narragansett Pier was a flourishing summer place that attracted wealthy vacationers from all parts of the country, who bathed in the ocean, enjoyed picnics in sylvan retreats, and danced the nights away. *The New York Times* described Narragansett then as "an American watering place in the truest sense of the term." A stone and shingle casino was built here by Rhode Island State House architects McKim, Mead & White, but in September 1900 a fire destroyed all but the stone towers and the archway of the structure, putting an end to pier merrymaking. Today the remaining archway houses the **Narragansett Chamber of Commerce**.

The white sands of **Narragansett Town Beach** are lapped by waves that roll in at an angle that makes them long, smooth, and nearly ideal for surfers. Parking is limited, however, so it is wise—especially on a sunny weekend—to get here early. A few hundred yards up a dirt road opposite the beach is the **South County Museum**, displaying local artifacts from the days when this was plantation land.

DINING AND SHOPPING
IN NARRAGANSETT

Across the street from the beach is the **Pier Marketplace**, housing more than two dozen gift shops, restaurants, and galleries. **Basil's**, a formal French restaurant at 22 Kingstown Road (Tel: 401/789-3743), and **Spain**, a Spanish provincial restaurant at 1 Beach Street (Tel: 401/783-9770), are both recommended. Next door to the chamber of commerce is the **Coast Guard House** restaurant, where diners can sit outside and look across Narragansett Bay at the flashing lights of Brenton Reef Tower and Beavertail Light at the tip of James-town. Whether or not you choose to eat here—the menu emphasizes seafood—you should stop by for a late-afternoon postswim drink and the spectacular view. Open for lunch and early dinner; Tel: (401) 789-0700.

BRISTOL

It was on this green peninsula lapped on the west by Narragansett Bay and on the east by Mount Hope Bay that the Wampanoag Indians hunted and fished and lived content-edly in the early days of the 17th century. Then the colonists came and the Wampanoags sold them their land; by 1680 very little of the peninsula still belonged to the Wampanoag. Where they had hunted, fences and houses began to appear, and the settlers from the Plymouth Bay Colony sought to impose their laws.

At this time Metacom (King Philip) became the leader of the Wampanoag tribe. Seeing his people dispossessed and the woods he loved destroyed enraged King Philip, so, with the help of neighboring tribes, he sought to drive out the white man. King Philip's War ended with the massacre of hundreds of Indians in the Great Swamp Fight near West Kingston (see above), and with Philip's death a few months later at the hands of a turncoat Indian.

With Philip gone, the settlers prospered. The town of Bristol was built and soon established as a valuable port town with a deep harbor. At the time of the Revolution, 50 of its vessels were involved in the West Indian trade. Although the British did some damage here during the war, the wily Yankee traders of Bristol soon put the town to rights, and an increasingly brisk foreign trade—this time with Europe and England as well as the West Indies—developed. Commerce faltered somewhat in the War of 1812, but Bristol profited by privateering; when the war was over, the men of Bristol turned their abilities to the whaling trade. It was during this period, from 1825 to 1846, that many of the impressive white mansions that line Bristol's streets were constructed.

To reach Bristol from Providence take I-195 east to the Barrington–Seekonk exit, and bear right on Route 114, which follows the Barrington River south. If you have time for a brief detour, bear right on Water Street in **Warren**, south of Barrington, where there are a number of second-hand and antiques shops, open on an irregular basis and offering items of varying quality. Also in Warren, at 125 Water Street, is the 1795 **Nathaniel Porter Inn**, with moderately priced fare in an attractive, old-fashioned setting (Tel: 401/ 247-0244). Cruises of Narragansett Bay on the *Bay Queen* leave from 461 Water Street; Tel: (401) 245-1350.

AROUND IN BRISTOL

To continue to Bristol follow Route 114 south to **Colt State Park**, which is about 2 miles (3 km) north of the center of town. Two bronze bulls by the French sculptor Isidore Bonheur mark the main entrance to the 455 acres of Colt State Park, where azaleas bloom in the spring and roses perfume the summer air. Fishermen cast from the shore into Narragansett Bay; hikers and joggers have miles of trails to hike and run; and picnickers will find plenty of meadows for spreading their blankets.

The park also has a working farm called **Coggeshalle Farm and Museum**; to reach it continue on Route 114 past the main entrance and turn right on Poppasquash Road, edging past Bristol Harbor and Marina. Follow tree-shaded Poppasquash for 1 mile (1½ km) to the sign for the farm and turn right. Here, in stalls and yards, are cows, chickens, pigs, and horses—all breeds that might have existed in the late-18th-century period the farm represents. Costumed farm-hands go about daily tasks of that era. For open hours, Tel: (401) 253-9062.

If you return to Route 114 (Hope Street) and turn right you'll see on your left a three-story dwelling with columns. Called **Linden Place**, it was designed in 1810 by the post-Colonial architect Russell Warren, one of the designers of Providence's Arcade, for Bristol planter General George DeWolf. In 1825, when his sugar crop in Cuba failed, DeWolf fled Bristol, leaving behind many creditors who had happily lent him money in his profitable days. When they discovered that he was gone, they broke into the mansion and stole whatever they could. After changing hands a number of times the house was occupied by Theodora DeWolf, George's daughter, after the Civil War. It is now a museum open to the public Wednesday, Saturday, and Sunday afternoons from Memorial Day to Columbus Day; Tel: (401) 253-0390.

All along Bristol's parallel Hope and High streets are imposing Victorian and Federal houses constructed in the town's shipping heyday (all are privately owned, and not open to the public). These include the clapboard **Joseph Reynolds House**, where the young Lafayette is said to have stayed, on northern Hope Street at number 956; the **James DeWolf House**, at 56 High Street, a striking Federal structure that was the property of a slave trader; the Greek Revival **Governor Francis Diamond House**, at 617 Hope Street, designed, like Linden Place, by Russell Warren; the Victorian **Codman-Dixon House**, with a Mansard roof, at 42 High Street; the 1800 **Herreshoff House**, at 142 Hope Street; and the mid-19th-century **Octagonal House**, at 42 High Street. Russell Warren's own house is at 86 State Street.

Other notable structures are the First Baptist Church, on High Street, built in 1814; the 1854 Bristol County Court House, which some attribute to Russell Warren, also on High Street, opposite Court Street; and the Renaissance-style Customs House, on Hope Street, dating from 1857. The **Bristol Historical and Preservation Society Museum and Library**, at 48 Court Street, in the former county jail, built of ship's ballast in 1828, has further information about Bristol's architectural highlights; Tel: (401) 253-7223.

At the corner of Hope and Burnside streets, at 7 Burnside, is the **Herreshoff Marine Museum**, built on the site of the old Herreshoff Manufacturing Company, which from 1861 into the 1940s was one of New England's leading boat-design and boat-building companies. Forty-five full-scale Herreshoff boats, ranging in size from an eight-foot skiff to a sixty-foot sailing yacht, are displayed in its Hall of Boats, and exhibits recount the history of the company that built more America's Cup defenders than any other yard in the world. Open May through October, except Mondays; Tel: (401) 253-5000.

Bristol claims the oldest Fourth of July parade in the United States. Independence Day was first celebrated here in 1785, and the first parade took place in 1865 and has been an annual event ever since. The parade now draws an audience of 250,000.

Dining in Bristol

If sightseeing has whetted your appetite for food, there are a number of possibilities in Bristol. **Redlefsen's Rotisserie and Grille**, at 425 Hope Street, is a plank-floored, casual Norwegian place that is fine for weekday dining but can be noisy on Saturday nights (Tel: 401/254-1188). The **Golden Goose Delicatessen**, at 365 Hope Street, serves thick sandwiches and filling soups (Tel: 401/253-1414), while the **S. S. Dion**, a simple, friendly restaurant at 520 Thames Street, overlooking Bristol Harbor (Tel: 401/253-2884). The **Lobster Pot**, at 120 Hope Street, has unsurpassed views of Narragansett Bay; Tel: (401) 253-9100.

SOUTH OF TOWN

Blithewold Gardens and Arboretum, south of town on Route 114, cover 33 acres that extend to Narragansett Bay. In addition to the somewhat usual floral specimens such as daffodils (spring) and velvety roses (summer), the arboretum includes a seaside rock garden, a Japanese water garden, a bamboo grove, an 85-foot giant sequoia, and a house built in 1907 by Brown University graduate Augustus Van Wickle, who became a Pennsylvania coal baron. Tel: (401) 253-2707.

To get to the **Haffenreffer Museum of Anthropology**, upon leaving Blithewold turn right on Route 114 (Ferry Road) and then left on Metacom Avenue at Roger Williams College. In the 17th century the Haffenreffer's setting was the site of the Wampanoags' summer encampment, and the museum is rich in arrowheads, masks, and ceremonial headdresses of North American Indians, as well as Inuit carvings, African jewelry, and South American Indian artifacts. Tel: (401) 253-8388.

To continue on to Aquidneck Island (Portsmouth, Middletown, and Newport), turn left on Metacom Avenue from the Haffenreffer Museum and follow Route 136/114 south across the Mount Hope Bridge.

PORTSMOUTH AND MIDDLETOWN

The Mount Hope Bridge links Bristol and the Rhode Island mainland with Aquidneck (Peace) Island, the site of the communities of Portsmouth, to the north; Middletown, in the center; and Newport, occupying the southern end. About 3 miles (5 km) beyond the bridge, Cory's Lane branches off Route 114 on the right and passes **Portsmouth Abbey**, a preparatory school with extensive grounds open to visitors and a striking modern church, notable for its stained glass and the Richard Lippold crucifix held in place by a radiating pattern of thin gold wires.

At the end of Cory's Lane are the **Green Animals Topiary Gardens**, where some 80 objects, animals, and birds, including camels, giraffes, elephants, lions, and bears, have been fashioned from California privet, yew, and English boxwood. Also on the grounds is a small **museum of Victorian toys**, in a white clapboard former summer dwelling on the shore of Narragansett Bay. The gardens and museum are open from the end of April until the beginning of November, weekends from November 29 through December 22, and every day from December 26 to 30; Tel: (401) 683-1267. Except for the gardens, Portsmouth Abbey, and a handful of restaurants, Portsmouth today, sadly, is largely strip malls sprawled along Route 138.

For dining in Portsmouth, the **Sea Fare Inn** is a fine but pricey ($60 a person) restaurant housed in an elegant Victorian mansion at 3352 East Main Road (Tel: 401/683-0577). **Fifteen Point Road**, at that address, is more moderately priced and offers broiled chops, steaks, and seafood (Tel: 401/683-3138).

If you turn right on Route 114 at the top of Cory's Lane you'll come to **Prescott Farm** and its windmill, on the left in **Middletown**. It was in this farmhouse, in 1777, that the detested English general Richard Prescott was routed out of a love nest by Colonial soldiers during the British occupation; he was taken prisoner and eventually exchanged for an American major general.

Although the farmhouse is not open to the public, there is a small **museum** of Colonial furniture and artifacts in the guardhouse where British troops were billeted, and ducks and geese wander the grounds. Although today's Middletown is largely suburban residential areas and malls, it is also the site of the 450-acre **Norman Bird Sanctuary**, on Third Beach Road, with 15 miles of walking trails. The local fauna here includes egrets, herons, thrashers, rails, woodcocks, rabbits, red foxes, ducks, swans, and the ubiquitous Canada geese. In spring dogwoods and apple trees bloom along the trails; in summer cornflowers and honeysuckle are in flower, while the maples turn crimson and the oaks golden in fall.

Middletown claims several interesting rock formations, including the enormous **Hanging Rock** in the bird sanctuary and **Purgatory Chasm** on Second Beach Road. The chasm overlooks quiet, sandy **Second Beach** below the **Sachuest Point National Wildlife Refuge**. Although wave conditions vary, of course, from day to day, Second Beach is a favorite for swimming. The grounds of **St. George's School** on Purgatory

Road afford a spectacular view of the beach. This venerable preparatory school was founded in 1896 by the Reverend Hugh Dinan, an Episcopal priest who later converted to Catholicism and founded the Roman Catholic Portsmouth Priory (now Portsmouth Abbey, discussed above).

Third Beach, about 1½ miles (2½ km) northeast of Second Beach on a cove of the Sakonnet River, is used by surfers and windsurfers more than swimmers. Though neither of these beaches is technically in Newport, Newporters consider them their own.

To reach Newport from Third Beach take Routes 114 and 138 south; for Providence, take Third Beach Road north to Mitchell's Lane to Route 138 and follow the signs north. Our route takes us east across the Sakonnet River to Little Compton and Tiverton before concluding a tour of Aquidneck Island with Newport.

LITTLE COMPTON AND TIVERTON

Across the Sakonnet River from Aquidneck Island are Little Compton and Tiverton, settled by Captain Benjamin Church, the Plymouth Bay colonist who masterminded the war against Wampanoag chief King Philip. Both communities were once part of the Plymouth Bay Colony. Of picturesque Little Compton it is said that if the mossy stone fences that border Little Compton's tree-shaded roads and rich green pastures were laid end to end, they would reach to Boston and back.

Situated as it is at the end of a peninsula, with no bridge linking it directly to anyplace else, Little Compton remains as unspoiled as its evocative original Indian name—which translates as "haunt of the wild goose"—suggests. Grapevines and wild roses tumble over its walls; its meadows rise and fall soothingly. The Atlantic rumbles on its southern shore, while the Sakonnet River lies to the west. The steeple of its white clapboard Congregational church reaches toward the sky above the town commons. The town's lone inn (discussed below) is quaintly down-at-the-heels, and residents like it that way. Little Compton seems to be set back in time, and many call it the loveliest spot in Rhode Island. (A few years ago, filmmakers seeking the perfect New England setting for the movie version of the John Updike book *The Witches of Eastwick* asked to use Little Compton; residents fiercely turned down such an inappropriate request.) Tiverton, just north of Little Compton on the same peninsula, has not, unfortunately, escaped the bulldozers and construction of developers, though Tiverton Four Corners, its historic crossroads, retains some of its old charm.

To get to Tiverton and Little Compton from Bristol, cross the Mount Hope Bridge (Route 114/136), which links the Rhode Island mainland with Aquidneck Island, go straight on Boyd Lane, and follow signs to Route 138. At 138 turn left toward Fall River, Massachusetts. Cross the Sakonnet River Bridge and take the exit to Route 77 south. Turn right on 77 south and you'll pass through Tiverton, with the Sakonnet River coming into view every now and then, and Nonquit Pond and Sin and Flesh Ponds just below the bridge.

TIVERTON

At Tiverton Four Corners, where everyone stops at the outdoor stand for a top-heavy cone of **Gray's** ice cream, stands the big yellow Federal-style **Soule-Seabury House** in a yard shaded by elms. All around the house Captain Cornelius Soule, a China-trade sea captain, planted trees he brought back from his travels. But that was nearly 200 years ago, and few of them still stand. As for the structure itself, it has long since passed out of family hands and now houses offices. Up West Main Road a bit is the birthplace of another seafaring man of whom Tiverton is proud—Robert Gray, who claimed the Columbia River for the United States, opening the Northwest to further exploration and settlement.

The inviting aroma of coffee and baked goods wafts from the **Provender Gourmet Take Out Store** in the 1875 former A. P. White Store on the northwest side of the Corners, with its mansard roof, cupola, and a big front porch. The light and airy **Virginia Lynch Art Gallery**, which specializes in contemporary painting and sculptures, is upstairs.

If you go straight ahead at the Corners on West Main (Route 77) toward Little Compton you'll pass Mill Pond, a complex of gardens and shops housed in a refurbished mill and surrounding a courtyard. Among the stores here are **Country Cabin**, with patchwork items and stoneware; **Nonquit Interiors**, a design shop; a cozy bookstore; a garden shop; and a children's shop.

Two miles (3 km) farther down West Main is **Country Harvest**, a restaurant with traditional American cuisine in the evenings and Sunday brunches; there are fine views of the Sakonnet River below (Tel: 401/635-4579).

LITTLE COMPTON

Just about half a mile (1 km) over the town line in Little Compton is the sign for the **Sakonnet Vineyards**, on the left, at 162 West Main Road. Guided tours allow you to observe grape growing, harvesting, and wine making in the appropriate seasons, and a shop on the premises sells sparkling America's Cup white as well as more sedate red wines. Tel: (401) 635-8486.

When you leave the vineyard turn left again on winding Route 77 (which becomes Sakonnet Point Road) to reach **Sakonnet Point**, where fishing boats come in with their catches early in the morning; sailboat racers heel and tack on late summer afternoons. The funky old **Stone House Club**, on Sakonnet Point Road, a gold fieldstone structure that sits above Round Pond, is, except for a bed-and-breakfast or two, the only accommodation in Little Compton. Basically a fashionably musty private club, the Stone House admits non–club members for overnights and meals for an additional fee (dinner is served only on Fridays, Saturdays, and Sundays). Rooms are just the sort you would find in your great-aunt's summer house—old prints askew on the walls, a claw-foot bathtub down the hall, patched cracks in the plaster—but the setting would be hard to match anywhere. The club sits among windswept fields of tiger lilies and Queen Anne's lace, where ospreys, Canada geese, and great blue herons fish the blue-green ponds.

Within walking distance, or a five-minute ride by car, is a dirt road that leads to the unofficial bird sanctuary of **Wilbour's Woods**. Deep within the woods off Swamp Road is a monument hand hewn by the colonists to honor the sachem Awashonks, a friend to the first white settlers of the peninsula, who promised them that her Sakonnet tribe would not assist King Philip in his war. It was indeed a member of her tribe who killed the Wampanoag chief.

If you turn left when you leave the woods and take the first left onto South of Commons Road you'll come to the **Little Compton Commons**, with its tall white church and slate stones marking, among others, the grave of Elizabeth Pabodie, the daughter of John Alden and Priscilla Mullens and the wife of William Pabodie, Little Compton's first town clerk. Also on the commons is the **Commons Lunch**, known for its crisp, paper-thin johnnycakes and a favorite with locals for Sunday brunch.

To reach **Goosewing**, the Little Compton town beach, from the commons follow South of Commons Road to Brownell, turning left (east) onto Brownell, then right (south) onto South Shore Road, which ends at the beach parking lot. Goosewing is an unspoiled stretch of oceanfront backed by quiet farmland.

From Goosewing you might head to **Adamsville**, a village of white farmhouses along stone-fence–lined fields and hills, just this side of the Massachusetts border. Adamsville is the site of a monument to the Rhode Island Red, an exceptional layer and a good-tasting chicken, first bred in Little Compton in 1854. Retrace your route on South Shore and turn right (east) onto John Sisson Road, then left onto Long Highway, until you reach Coldbrook Road, the third major turn on the right. In Adamsville is **Abraham Manchester Restaurant & Tavern**, a popular stopping place for lunch (Tel: 401/635-2700); in its early days it was a general store. Also in Adamsville, on its Main Street, are **Stonebridge Dishes**, a sprawling shop selling a variety of pottery, and the quaint **F. A. Simmons General Store**.

At **Gray's Mill**, a stone's throw away from Abraham Manchester's in Westport, Massachusetts, Rhode Island flint corn—the correct kind for Rhode Island johnnycakes—has been stone ground since 1750 and is sold in the mill shop on weekends.

The quickest route back to Providence from Adamsville is to go right upon leaving Abraham Manchester's tavern and then turn immediately right again on Route 81 (Crandall Road) and on up to Route 24 north just over the Fall River, Massachusetts, line. This leads to I-195 west back to Providence.

NEWPORT

Newport, the "grande dame" of Rhode Island, occupies the southernmost tip of Aquidneck Island (just take Route 114 from Providence through Bristol, Portsmouth, and Middletown). It is the sailing capital of the world as well as one of the nation's most elegant summer resorts; in the 18th century it was the wealthiest port on the East Coast. The slave trade prospered; molasses was imported from the West Indies, distilled into rum in Rhode Island, and returned in exchange for slaves. Some 50 Newport vessels participated in this triangular trade, and it is said that the streets and the bridges of Newport in Colonial days were largely paid for by the tax on imported slaves.

A more laudable part of Newport's history is its founding in 1639, like Providence, by religious refugees from the Massachusetts Bay Colony. In Newport Quakers and Jews were allowed to worship as they chose, and many a 17th-century Jew found haven here from persecution in Portugal, the Netherlands, and the Dutch West Indies. Jewish settlers became an important part of the community, involved in the slave and molasses trades and in whaling.

Newport was occupied by the British during the American Revolution and suffered greatly when they not only cut down its trees for firewood but tore down nearly 500 houses

Newport and Environs

| 0 | miles | 2 |
| 0 | km | 2 |

TO PROVIDENCE

N

Colt State Park

Bristol

114 136

MT. HOPE BRIDGE

138

Tiverton

Sakonnet

Portsmouth

GREEN ANIMALS TOPIARY GARDENS

Prudence Island

114

138

77

Tiverton Four Corners

NARRAGANSETT BAY

PRESCOTT FARM

River

JAMESTOWN BRIDGE

138

N. MAIN RD.

E. SHORE RD.

Conanicut Island

NEWPORT BRIDGE

138

Middletown

Little Compton

NORMAN BIRD SANCTUARY

Third Beach

Jamestown

138A

Easton Beach

Second Beach

77

Fort Wetherill

Newport

SAKONNET POINT

BEAVER NECK

ATLANTIC OCEAN

Newport

| 0 | yards | 880 |
| 0 | meters | 805 |

NEWPORT BRIDGE

138 114

Goat Island

WASHINGTON SQUARE

BROADWAY

HAMMERSMITH FARM

Fort Adams Park

BOWEN'S WHARF

BANNISTER'S WHARF

TOURO ST.

THAMES ST.

MEMORIAL BLVD.

COLONY HOUSE

TOURO SYNAGOGUE

Brenton Cove

HARRISON AVE.

WELLINGTON AVE.

NEWPORT CASINO

Brenton Point State Park

138A

Easton Beach

OCEAN AVE.

BELLEVUE AVE.

RUGGLES AVE.

ROSECLIFF

THE BREAKERS

Bailey's Beach

CLIFF WALK

N

as well, for the same purpose. Churches were used as stables and British troops were garrisoned in private homes. From 1776 until 1779 the redcoats were everywhere in the city. Then, to the delight of the Newporters, came the Americans' allies, the French, whose courtliness during their year-long stay has never been forgotten.

It took a while, however, for Newport to recover from the ravages of that war and the War of 1812. But by the mid-1830s plantation owners of the South and the West Indies, who had always enjoyed Narragansett Bay's cool summer climate, began to build homes here. Newport, the summer colony, was launched, and by the turn of the century it was thriving. In Newport's heyday as a summer resort, however, at the turn of the century, it was largely the high society of New York and Boston who built villas and "cottages" along the frothing Atlantic and organized balls, gala picnics, and grand dinner parties.

Today many of these private clifftop dwellings are open to the public, though many 18th-century houses in town, dazzlingly restored by millionaire Doris Duke a few decades ago, can be viewed only from the outside. There is Newport's waterfront to visit, too. The tattoo parlors and dingy bars that studded the waterfront not long ago (there is a naval base at Newport) have been replaced with stylish gift and clothing shops, restaurants, and outdoor cafés.

Colonial Newport

To visit the Colonial part of the city, turn right off Broadway (West Main/Route 114 becomes Broadway in Newport) when you see the white-towered gray stone city hall. Take Marlborough Street to 23 America's Cup Avenue, where there is a parking lot behind the Newport Gateway Visitors' Center. (Parking on the streets of the city is virtually impossible.)

THE WASHINGTON SQUARE AREA
Proceed on foot across America's Cup Avenue. On the right, at the foot of Washington Square, is the Georgian **Brick Market**, the main town market in the 18th century and due to open as a museum of the history of Newport in 1993.

Colony House
At the top of Washington Square rises the red-brick Colony House (constructed between 1738 and 1741), trimmed with white balconies and balustrades. This impressive structure, designed by Richard Munday, architect of Newport's Trinity Church, served as capitol of both the colony and then the

state of Rhode Island and Providence Plantations off and on into the 19th century. From its balcony the coronation of George III was announced with fanfare in 1760, but from the same balcony 16 years later an enthusiastic crowd heralded Rhode Island's Declaration of Independence, two months before the other colonies declared theirs. During the Revolutionary War Colony House served as a hospital for both French and British soldiers, and in it, in 1781, George Washington and the French marshal Comte de Rochambeau met to lay plans for the Yorktown campaign, which subsequently ended the Revolution.

Earlier in the history of Colony House, in 1756, it is said, the first lecture on medicine and dentistry in America was delivered by the Scottish-born physician Dr. William Hunter. The building is occasionally open to the public; Tel: (401) 846-2980.

Wanton-Lyman-Hazard House

Just up Broadway from Colony House, at number 17, is the Wanton-Lyman-Hazard House, with its steeply pitched roof and central chimney. Built in 1675, it is the oldest dwelling in Newport. Before the Revolution this was the home of Martin Howard, the Crown's stamp master, who was so hated for his imposition of the detested stamp tax that his effigy was dragged through the streets and burned by patriotic Newporters and his house raided and almost destroyed. They even made an attempt to haul down the chimney with ropes. Howard himself, meanwhile, fled to a British ship in the harbor and never returned to Newport. The house later suffered damage by the patriots when it became the property of a Tory, Governor Joseph Wanton. During the year of the French occupation of Newport, the pretty daughter of the house, Polly Wanton, was much sought after by the French officers for her beauty, but she elected to marry an American, Major Daniel Lyman, instead.

Wanton-Lyman-Hazard House, decorated with period furniture, is open June through August from Tuesday through Friday or Saturday; Tel: (401) 846-3622.

Friends' Meeting House

Continue up Broadway and make a left on Marlborough Street to see the long, beige **Friends' Meeting House**, at the corner of Marlborough and Farewell streets. Built in 1699, it is the oldest Quaker meetinghouse in the country; today it displays Quaker dress and other memorabilia of the Society of Friends. Just up Farewell Street is the venerable White House Tavern; see Dining in Newport, below.

Newport Artillery Company

On the opposite (southern) side of Washington Square, at 25 Clarke Street (corner of Touro Street), is the armory of the Newport Artillery Company, housed in a 19th-century stone Greek Revival building. Today the armory is used to display a rich collection of weapons, flags, and uniforms from many lands, including World War II uniforms of Britain's Prince Philip and the late naval hero Lord Louis Mountbatten, uniforms of Queen Elizabeth's guards, and a uniform that once belonged to the late Egyptian president Anwar Sadat.

HISTORIC HILL

Touro Synagogue

Just up Touro Street from the artillery company headquarters is the white and brown Touro Synagogue, set at such an angle at 85 Touro that the ark faces Jerusalem. The synagogue is named for Rabbi Isaac Touro, who founded it, and is the oldest synagogue in North America.

In 1658 a number of Spanish-Portuguese Jewish families, believed to have emigrated from Barbados, in the British West Indies, settled in Newport. In the early days of their settlement they worshiped in private homes, but as more and more Jews arrived over the next century—fleeing the Inquisition and the ravages of the Lisbon earthquake of 1755—it was decided that a genuine house of worship was in order. In 1763 this building, which combines the Georgian architecture of its day with elements of Portuguese and Spanish synagogue style, was erected. The designer for the graceful brick structure was Peter Harrison, architect of the Brick Market. In the simple gray interior, 12 Ionic columns representing the 12 tribes of Israel support the galleries, and 12 Corinthian columns extend from the galleries to the ceiling.

It is said that Thomas Jefferson, visiting Newport as secretary of state with Washington in 1790, was so impressed with the design that he incorporated elements of it into Monticello, the capitol building in Richmond, and the University of Virginia. As for Washington, it was in this synagogue that he proclaimed that America "gives to bigotry no sanction; to persecution no assistance." The building is open 10:00 A.M. to 5:00 P.M. Sunday through Friday from June to Labor Day, and from 1:00 to 3:00 P.M. Sundays year-round. Services are held on Fridays at 6:00 P.M. in winter and on Saturdays at 9:00 A.M. and 7:00 P.M. in summer; Tel: (401) 847-4794.

Farther up Touro Street, behind a wrought-iron fence at the corner of Bellevue Avenue and Kay Street, is the Jewish **cemetery** where, among others, Judah Touro, a son of Rabbi Isaac Touro, is buried. Among his legacies are Newport's

Touro Park (discussed below), and Boston's Bunker Hill Monument, to which he made contributions.

Redwood Library

Beyond the cemetery, if you bear right onto and cross Bellevue Avenue, you will see the Redwood Library, erected in 1748 and the oldest library building in continuous use in the country.

Though the building appears to be made of pink stone, it is actually constructed of wooden blocks sanded and painted to give the appearance of stone. A path around it leads through a small botanical garden of holly trees, maples, and beeches; a lacy fern-leaf beech shading the walk has managed to survive northeasters and hurricanes ever since 1835, when it was brought across the Atlantic from England. Inside, hanging above the sunny reading alcoves, are paintings by Rhode Island native Gilbert Stuart and Robert Feke, Charles Wilson Peale, and Rembrandt Peale. There are also a sculpture of Benjamin Franklin by Jean Antoine Houdon and furniture by 18th-century Newport craftsmen Job Townsend and John Goddard.

Touro Park

A curiosity diagonally across the street from Redwood Library is the tower of clamshell mortar and stones in Touro Park, now believed to have been part of a windmill built in the 17th century by Rhode Island governor Benedict Arnold (grandfather of the traitorous general). It has also been speculated, however, that Portuguese seamen built the tower. The fact that its arches correspond to the points of the compass is the basis for this belief. A third theory proposes that the tower is an 11th-century Viking construction. Henry Wadsworth Longfellow reinforced this idea in his poem "Skeleton in Armor," wherein a Norse warrior is said to have erected it for his wife, and when she died he buried her beneath it. James Fenimore Cooper mentioned it, too, in his novel *The Rover.*

Trinity Church

Across the park, down Mill Street, and to the right on Spring soars the 150-foot spire of Trinity Church (at the corner of Church Street). The spire dominates not only the neighborhood's chocolate-brown, mustard-yellow, and barn-red Colonial houses, but indeed the whole waterfront. Atop its weather vane gleams the gilded miter of a bishop of the Church of England.

Legend has it that in Revolutionary War days (the church was built from 1725 to 1726), when the British redcoats damaged every other building in the city in some fashion, only Trinity was spared, out of deference to the Church of England miter that the patriots had neglected to take down.

The church was designed by Newporter Richard Munday, who also designed Colony House. The inspiration for Trinity was Old North Church in Boston, which had been based on the architectural style of Christopher Wren. Of particular interest in Trinity's interior are the monument donated by Louis XVI honoring Admiral d'Ansac de Tenney, who died in Newport when he and his fleet came to the aid of the rebels; the wineglass pulpit, believed to be the only one still standing in its original position in a church in America today; two Tiffany windows; a pew in which George Washington, Queen Elizabeth II, Princess Margaret, and Bishop Desmond Tutu of South Africa have all sat; and wall memorials to Commodore Oliver Hazard Perry, hero of the Battle of Lake Erie in the War of 1812, and his brother Commodore Matthew Perry, who opened Japan to the world, and to Alfred Gwynne Vanderbilt, who drowned when the *Lusitania* went down at the start of World War I. The Trinity Church organ, which came from England, was said to have been tested by George Frideric Handel before it was sent to America.

THE WATERFRONT AREA

A couple of blocks west on Mill Street from Trinity Church is the **Thames** (pronounced "thaymes") **Street** waterfront; across America's Cup Avenue you will see the gray and white shops and restaurants of 19th-century **Bowen's Wharf**. Farther to the left, as you face the waterfront, the red-brick and white-clapboard buildings of **Bannister's Wharf** stretch out into the harbor. At its marina are moored the grandest of sailing yachts. From Bannister's Wharf you can take a water taxi to Fort Adams State Park and the Museum of Yachting (see below).

Long Wharf

North of Bowen's and Bannister's, along America's Cup Avenue, is Long Wharf, which has a long pedestrian mall. If you have not yet visited the Green Animals Topiary Gardens in neighboring Portsmouth (discussed above), you can take the 1912 wooden coach of the **Old Colony & Newport Railway** from the historic Newport Depot, just north of Long Wharf at 14 America's Cup Avenue, to the gardens. The coach travels along Narragansett Bay, past the Newport Naval Base, and through wild grape and blackberry tangles. In the evening the **Newport Star Clipper Dinner Train** follows the same route, but with a four-course dinner offered aboard. For reservations, Tel: (401) 849-7550, (800) 462-7452 from outside Rhode Island, or (800) 834-1556 within the state.

Hunter House

Right on the water several blocks north of Long Wharf on Washington Street is Hunter House, a Late Colonial residence (1748) filled with mahogany and walnut Townsend-Goddard furniture.

In Newport's heyday as a port, a captain or two occupied this residence; consequently, the lintel of the front door is marked by a pineapple. Genuine pineapples, symbols of hospitality, were put outside a front door whenever a captain came home from a voyage.

The house's walls, which were painstakingly painted with turkey feathers to look like cedar or rosewood paneling, and the wooden mantels painted to look like marble are among the decorative highlights here. A painting of a dog by a young Gilbert Stuart hangs over the mantelpiece. The house is open daily in summer, weekends in April and October. Tel: (401) 847-7516.

Ocean Drive and the Mansions

The area of Newport south of downtown is ringed by the famous 10-mile-long (16-km) route known as Ocean Drive, along which are perched some of New England's grandest mansions, known to their wealthy turn-of-the-century owners as "cottages." Along this beautiful road gray shingled mansions and imposing châteaux perch on rocks, seagulls wheel over rocky inlets, and small boats bob offshore. Beach grass, cattails, and tall marsh fragomytes sway in the sea wind.

The mansions that are open to the public are all open from at least April 1 to November 1. Some stay open all year, others during the Christmas season. Most are run by the Preservation Society of Newport County, which offers discount combination tickets for its mansions (for information, Tel: 401/847-1000).

Note that no stretch of this road is actually called Ocean Drive; the loop comprises Harrison Avenue, Ridge Road, Ocean Avenue, and Bellevue Avenue. Our coverage follows a counterclockwise route, beginning just south of downtown Newport and continuing around to Bellevue Avenue, just east of downtown.

FORT ADAMS STATE PARK

Just before Ocean Drive begins its magnificent loop is Fort Adams State Park, on a peninsula of land jutting northward that encloses Newport Harbor. To get here pick up your car from the lot on America's Cup Avenue and head back through town; when the avenue turns away from the waterfront, bear right and continue on lower Thames Street, then turn right on Wellington Avenue. You'll pass **King Park**, where the first French troops coming to the aid of the colonists in the Revolution landed, and then the **Ida Lewis Yacht Club**, named for the indomitable lighthouse keeper who manned the tower that was perched on its rock for 32 years in the 19th century (it was dismantled and incorporated into the Newport Yacht Club); she is credited with 18 rescues from her rowboat.

After the yacht club Wellington bears left to Halidon Avenue; make a right onto Harrison Avenue, which brings you to the entrance of 18th-century Fort Adams State Park. The hillsides of the park's spacious grounds are set with many earthworks of the old fort, and the view back across Brenton Cove toward Newport Harbor is spectacular.

William Brenton, for whom the cove is named, is believed to have first fortified the spot with two cannon to protect himself from pirates soon after his arrival from England in 1639. Later colonists posted lookouts on Brenton Point, and in May 1776 the citizens of Newport, fearful of the British, began to construct earthworks on the site. They were too late, and within seven months they were forced to abandon their fortifications to the British. In 1779, when the British left Newport, they did their best to destroy the fort, but in 1799 it was reconstructed and dedicated to President John Adams.

On and off over the years Fort Adams has been allowed to fall into disrepair and then been restored. During Dwight D. Eisenhower's presidency, when the fort became a national park, he liked to vacation in the Victorian house on the grounds. Today, however, the fort itself has been deemed unsafe for visitors and the Eisenhower house is used only for special occasions. But there is good fishing here, and fine picnic sites and safe swimming at Brenton Cove. In the **Museum of Yachting**, at the north end of the park, are photographs and paintings of famous yachts and a history of the America's Cup races.

HAMMERSMITH FARM

If you turn right back onto Harrison Avenue when you leave the fort you'll soon see the sign to turreted, weathered-shingled Hammersmith Farm, on Ocean Drive. It was on Hammersmith's grounds overlooking Narragansett Bay that the wedding reception of Jacqueline Bouvier and John F. Kennedy was held on September 12, 1953, following their marriage at St. Mary's Church on Spring Street. The 28-room farm, now a house-museum, was built in 1887 by John W. Auchincloss and inherited by his grandson, the late Hugh Auchincloss, who was Jacqueline Bouvier's stepfather.

While the mansions of Newport's Gilded Age are over-whelmingly grand by most contemporary standards, Ham-mersmith Farm, though large, seems livable. The house is sunny and airy, and it is not difficult to visualize little Caro-line and John-John Kennedy romping outside while their parents and grandparents enjoyed the cocktail hour. The gardens, originally laid out by Frederick Law Olmsted, de-signer of New York's Central Park, are not to be missed either. Open from April to mid-November, and at Christmas time; Tel: (401) 846-0420.

OCEAN AVENUE

From Hammersmith Farm head south along Ridge Road and Ocean Avenue. About 3½ miles (6 km) beyond Hammer-smith, turn right to get to the **Inn at Castle Hill**, where Sunday-morning brunch on the lawn is a special affair. The inn's grounds afford spectacular ocean views. While the Inn at Castle Hill is open year-round, its restaurant, serving lunch, dinner, and Sunday brunch, is open only from Easter week through October.

South of the inn back on Ocean Avenue is **Brenton Point State Park**, a fine spot for picnicking, where fishermen cast their lines off the rocks into the sea and children fling their kites into the air. The contemporary monument to the Portu-guese explorers here is a controversial curiosity.

Gooseberry Beach, farther east along Ocean Avenue, is a quiet, protected, public beach that is exceptional for chil-dren. Not open to the public is sandy Bailey Beach (just east of Gooseberry), one of the most exclusive enclaves of New-port society and, at the turn of the century, known for its idiosyncratic bathers. One, it is said, always carried a green parasol as protection from the sun; another sported a white boater for the same purpose when he was in the water.

BELLEVUE AVENUE

Belcourt Castle

If you turn right immediately after Bailey Beach, then left onto Bellevue Avenue and left again when Bellevue turns, you will soon see, on the left, Belcourt Castle, the extrava-gant mansion fashioned after a hunting lodge of French king Louis XIII. The castle was built in 1892 for then-bachelor and horseman Oliver Hazard Perry Belmont by Richard Morris Hunt, one of the most popular architects in Newport in the 1890s. One wing of the castle served as a stable where, it is said, Belmont's horses slept on their own embroidered linens. Hunt, much enamored of the Middle Ages, created a ballroom of the period of Henry IV and an Italianate banquet hall with stained-glass windows and a hand-carved staircase that copied one of Francis I's. After socialite Alva Smith Vanderbilt was divorced from William K. Vanderbilt she married Belmont, and Belcourt Castle became the setting for many a grand event. Today Belcourt is open to the public as a museum. Among the displays of Oriental rugs, art, and antiques from around the world is a copy of the 23-karat gold Portuguese royal coronation coach, whose original is in Lisbon's coach museum. Open year-round (except for two weeks in February); Tel: (401) 846-0669.

(Though it is not open to the public, 18th-century English mansion–style **Clarendon Court**, on the water side of Belle-vue Avenue opposite Rovensky Park, achieved notoriety in recent years when it was the home of Sunny and Claus von Bülow.)

Marble House

Next up the avenue on the right is Marble House, the mansion in which Alva Smith Vanderbilt lived before she became the mistress of Belcourt. This $11 million gift from her husband, William (given to her when they were still in love), contains some 500,000 cubic feet of marble: purple, black, white, yellow, and pink. The mirrored walls of its Gold Salon were inspired by similar decor at Versailles. According to one story, in the house's heyday Alva Smith Vanderbilt (by then Mrs. Belmont, but she had won Marble House in the divorce settlement) gave a famous dinner party in the Gold Salon for 100 socialite dogs, accompanied by their masters and mistresses. The menu consisted of liver and rice, dog biscuits, and fricassee of bones. (In another version of the tale Mrs. Stuyvesant Fish is the hostess and Crossways, now a condominium, is the site of the dinner.) Richard Morris Hunt was, again, the architect. The red-and-gold Chinese teahouse on the back lawn was one of Alva Smith Vanderbilt's favorite places for entertaining. Open year-round; Tel: (401) 847-2445.

Beechwood

Beechwood is the next major mansion past Marble House along Bellevue Avenue. This stuccoed brick structure was built in the 1850s, but its interior was much redesigned by Mrs. William (Caroline) Backhouse Astor after her husband bought it for her in 1880. She added what was then the largest ballroom in Newport so she could assemble "The 400"—the select members of society—for dances; and with the help of the ingenious Ward McAllister, inaugurator of picnics aboard yachts and elaborate breakfast parties, and social director Harry Lehr (whose idea the dogs' dinner party was), she planned many extravaganzas here. Closed in January; Tel: (401) 846-3772.

Rosecliff

To the right (north) is Rosecliff, the backdrop for several scenes in the 1974 film *The Great Gatsby,* starring Robert Redford. Designed by Stanford White, architect also of the State House in Providence, Rosecliff claims as progenitor the Grand Trianon at Versailles. The mansion was built in 1902 for Mrs. Herman (Tessie) Oelrichs, whose father, James Graham Fair, an Irish immigrant, was among the discoverers of the Comstock Lode of silver in Nevada. When Tessie Fair married Oelrichs, an agent for the North German Lloyd Steamship Line, her father's gift to the couple was a check for $1 million. Rosecliff's 40 rooms include the largest ballroom (72 feet long) in Newport. Mrs. Oelrichs, despite her humble origins, became one of Newport's leading hostesses. One of Rosecliff's most famous balls was the White Ball, to which all women were asked to come in white with their hair powdered, all men in black. In addition to the ballroom, the heart-shaped staircase and the Court of Love, designed by Augustus Saint-Gaudens after Marie Antoinette's Court of Love, are particularly arresting. Open April 1 to December 1; Tel: (401) 847-5793.

The Breakers

From Rosecliff continue north along Bellevue Avenue to Ruggles Avenue and turn right, then left on Ochre Point Avenue; soon you'll see the wrought-iron gates of the Breakers on the right. This time Richard Morris Hunt turned to northern Italian villas for inspiration for this grandest of all the Newport mansions. It was built in 1895 for Cornelius Vanderbilt II, the brother of William K. and grandson of Commodore Cornelius Vanderbilt, who amassed the family fortune in shipping and railroads. Because the original mansion that occupied this spot burned in 1893, Vanderbilt insisted that no wood be used in the construction of the replacement and, as still another safety measure, had the heating plant placed in a separate building. The 70 rooms of the Breakers are made of stone, marble, and alabaster.

Sparing no expense to create the home he wished, Vanderbilt had the entire Music Room, including its columns, fireplace, and coffered ceiling, constructed in France, broken down, and shipped here to be fitted together again. The spacious dining room gleams with red marble columns topped by bronze capitals and glitters with crystal chandeliers and wall sconces. As many as 200 guests can be received at one time in the stone Great Hall, which truly lives up to its name. One long glass wall affords a view of the ocean beyond, for which the Breakers is named.

The Breakers' owner was to enjoy all its beauty and opulence for only one year. At the age of 53, Cornelius Vanderbilt suffered a stroke from which he died three years later. Open April 1 to December 1; Tel: (401) 847-6543.

Château-Sur-Mer

Back on Bellevue is Château-sur-Mer, a turreted Victorian "cottage" of Fall River granite. The original house was built in 1852 for William S. Wetmore, who made his money in the China trade. But that house simply became the core of the existing structure, fashioned by Richard Morris Hunt in 1872 for George Peabody Wetmore, William's son. Château-sur-Mer is notable for its solidity, its fine ballroom, its extravagant carving, and its stucco moldings resembling wood. Open year-round; Tel: (401) 847-0037.

The Elms

Turn right on Bellevue Avenue to the Elms (on the left), probably the grandest of the turn-of-the-century Newport residences after the Breakers. The Elms was built, however, not for a man of inherited wealth, but for the son of a German immigrant cabinetmaker and his wife. Edward Julius Berwind of Philadelphia attended the U.S. Naval Academy in 1865, served in the navy for some years, then left it to make millions in the coal-mining business and, as it turned out, to supply the coal that ran the ships of the U.S. Navy. It was this coal-mining money that bankrolled his palatial stone villa.

True to his humble beginnings, Berwind selected as architect a fellow Philadelphian, a relatively unknown and untravelled young man named Horace Trumbauer. His lack of experience notwithstanding, Trumbauer managed to create this graceful 18th-century–style château, imaginatively combining some of the best elements of the Château d'Asnières outside Paris with those of Versailles. The conservatory, indeed, resembles Versailles' Hall of Mirrors. Inside are exquisite paintings, furniture, porcelains, and tapestries. Open year-round; Tel: (401) 847-0478.

Kingscote

From the Elms turn left on Bellevue, then left on Bowery for a look at Kingscote, a lacy Gothic Revival villa, pretty rather than grand. It was built in 1839 after a design by an English cabinetmaker turned architect, Richard Upjohn. Its owner was a Georgia plantation man, George Noble Jones. Later Stanford White made some alterations in it. In contrast to most of the Newport "cottages," Kingscote is made largely of wood. Items of particular interest here are China-trade imports, Tiffany glass, and furniture by 18th-century cabinetmakers Job Townsend and John Goddard. Open to the public; Tel: (401) 847-0366.

Newport Casino and Cliff Walk

NEWPORT CASINO AND INTERNATIONAL TENNIS HALL OF FAME

To get to this brick and shingle landmark at 194 Bellevue Avenue (designed by McKim, Mead & White), turn left from Kingscote back onto Bowery; go left again at the corner onto Bellevue and continue to the ornate, red-brick Audrian building, with its grimacing heads and green lattice-work.

According to local legend, the casino came into being after a disagreement between newspaperman James Gordon Bennett, Jr., and officials of an exclusive men's club, the Newport Reading Room (Bennett was incensed when a friend he had lured into riding his horse into the foyer of the Reading Room was censured). In retaliation Bennett ordered the construction of this complex of grass tennis courts (the oldest public tennis courts in the world), grandstands, a ballroom, a restaurant, a lawn-bowling facility, a theater, and a courtyard; and it became almost as exclusive. The United States National Lawn Tennis Championships were held here annually from 1881 until 1915, when the tournament was moved to Forest Hills, New York.

All facilities are still in use today, with the addition of the **International Tennis Hall of Fame**, a museum of tennis memorabilia, and **Canfield House**, a pleasant, moderately priced restaurant (Tel: 401/847-0416). Beside it on the corner of Memorial Boulevard and Bellevue Avenue is the Victorian **Travis Block** of old-fashioned gift, linen, and clothing shops. The block was designed by Richard Morris Hunt.

CLIFF WALK

Go out the Memorial Boulevard exit of the casino and continue down (east, toward the ocean) Memorial Boulevard to the end (you can do this on foot or pick up your car and look for a parking place on the boulevard). There, at the head of **Easton's** (a.k.a. First) **Beach**, begins the three-mile-long Cliff Walk, which wends its way above the thudding sea and below the lawns and gardens of the mansions. Unfortunately, storms do a little more damage to the walk each winter, making it, in some sections, unsafe to pass. But the areas that you can traverse afford fine views of Easton's Beach and Middletown in the distance, the white sails of yachts, and the multicolored sails of windsurfers defying the waves. (The rollers of Easton's Beach are said to be among the best on the eastern seacoast for windsurfing.) There are several places along the walk where, if you are weary of being windblown or of the uneven terrain, you can return to Bellevue Avenue by city streets.

Alternatively, you can walk back to Memorial Boulevard and head down to Easton's Beach. The beach, on the Atlantic between the Cliff Walk and the Esplanade of Middletown, is open to the public for only a parking fee; it lost considerable sand in the 1991 hurricane, however. (Although Second and Third beaches are technically in Middletown, Newporters frequent them as their own. See Middletown, just above.)

Dining in Newport

WHARF AREA

Bannister's Wharf

The casual **Black Pearl Tavern** is a good choice for chowder and hamburgers, or for heartier fare. In summer there is outdoor dining that is ideal for people-watching. The elegant Commodore Room here serves fine (and expensive) French cuisine (Tel: 401/846-5264). The **Clark Cooke House**, next door, also features good, expensive French food and game that it raises itself. From its upper deck there is a 180-degree view of Newport harbor (Tel: 401/849-2900).

Bowen's Wharf

Le Bistro is yet another French restaurant, though more moderately priced than either the Commodore Room of the Black Pearl or the Clark Cooke House. The top floor affords lovely views of the harbor (Tel: 401/849-7778).

The **Chart House**, a member of a nationwide chain, also has wonderful views and moderate prices (Tel: 401/849-7555). Another restaurant right on the waterfront, in the old New York Yacht Club, is the **Mooring**, with fine views of the harbor and a moderately priced menu of fish and meat dishes. The **Mooring Canteen** serves the same menu, but in a more casual dining room and at even lower prices (Tel: 401/846-9740).

Thames Street

Elizabeth's, at the Brown and Howard Wharf (several wharves south of Bannister's), serves inexpensive family-style combination platters for two (poultry and fish, meat and fish). The decor is whimsical—no two antique chairs are alike—and there is outdoor dining in summer. Bring your own wine or beer (Tel: 401/846-6862).

The atmosphere of the **Brick Alley Pub**, at 140 Thames Street, is casual, the clientele young, and the fare light—largely soups and sandwiches (Tel: 401/849-6334). **Christie's**, at 351 Thames, is likely to be crowded, but it's a relaxed place with live music and an outdoor bar with a view of the harbor. Lobster is a specialty here, but it and other seafood items are expensive (Tel: 401/847-5400).

At 527 Thames Street, **Scales and Shells** is a fast-paced, moderately priced California-style fish restaurant; your dinner is grilled right in the dining room, and any manner of dress will do here (Tel: 401/846-3474). There's also **Pezzuli's**, at 673 Thames Street, an informal Italian restaurant featuring such imaginative dishes as ginger fettucine and sautéed liver with grilled radicchio and anchovy-mustard sauce (Tel: 401/846-5830). For outdoor family dining try the **Shore Dinner Hall**, on Waite's Wharf off lower Thames Street.

WASHINGTON SQUARE AND MARLBOROUGH STREET

The **Wave Café**, at 22 Washington Square, though small and inclined to be crowded, is a good place for coffee and cake or for a first-rate lunchtime soup. **Yesterday's**, at number 28, also offers good, moderately priced pub food—chicken wings, Mexican standbys, burgers; it also has a wine bar.

On Marlborough Street, not far from the Friends' Meeting House, is the **Whitehorse Tavern**, established in 1673 and one of Newport's most expensive restaurants. Dine here on Chateaubriand in winter by a roaring fire. It's the perfect place to celebrate something special, such as a birthday or anniversary (Tel: 401/849-3600).

At 19 Charles Street, between Washington Square and Marlborough Street, is **La Petite Auberge**, a snug little French restaurant in a Colonial house. A bistro menu is offered outdoors in summer (Tel: 401/849-6669).

Staying in Newport

If you plan to stay overnight in Newport—and a three-day visit is none too long for sightseeing—there are cozy bed-and-breakfasts in Colonial houses and Victorian "cottages" from which to choose.

The **Cliffside Inn**, housed in a 12-room, antiques-filled Victorian at 2 Seaview Avenue, is less than a three-minute walk from the Cliff Walk and about five minutes from

Easton's Beach. The ten spacious guest rooms of the Georgian-style **Francis Malbone House** are furnished with Queen Anne reproductions. It is also centrally located, at 392 Thames Street, and has a dining room for breakfast and inviting parlors. **Hydrangea House** is a six-room Victorian bed-and-breakfast not far from the Tennis Hall of Fame, quiet and off the beaten track at 16 Bellevue Avenue. Owned by former antiques dealers, Hydrangea House is decorated with an eclectic array of antiques from different periods. There is a contemporary-art gallery on the premises; breakfast is served in the gallery.

When the **Sanford Covell Villa Marina** was erected in 1869, it was called the most elegantly finished house in Newport, with walls of butternut and ebony, walnut trim, frescoed ceilings, stained glass, and gold- and silver-leaf decorations. Many of these features are still in place in this harbor-front, stick-style, eight-room house with a wrap-around porch overlooking Newport Harbor.

Though the **Victorian Ladies** is on a busy street, at 63 Memorial Boulevard, it is also near the sea and the Cliff Walk, and it has tucked-away gardens and a courtyard. Also near the Cliff Walk is the elegant **Elm Tree Cottage**, a French country–style bed-and-breakfast at 336 Gibbs Avenue.

Then there are the full-scale hotels. The atrium at the **Newport Marriott**, right on Long Wharf, brings the outdoors inside. With 320 rooms, this is Newport's largest lodging facility. The hotel's dining room, the G. W. Sea Grill, specializes in seafood. The **Newport Harbor Hotel and Marina**, formerly the Treadway, is right on America's Cup Avenue. A renovation has recently been completed, giving it a fresh and nautical air. **Waverley's**, the popular restaurant and night spot that used to be Checker's, is here, with live music on weekends.

The 253-room **Newport Islander Doubletree Hotel**, on Goat Island, reached from downtown Newport by a short causeway, is pleasantly removed from Newport's bustle. There is live entertainment in its old Mug Lounge year-round and in the Sunset Café in the summer, and dining in its Windward Room.

Finally, there is the **Hotel Viking**, which was in Newport's ascendancy *the* place to stay. The old section of the hotel, built in the Federal style in 1820, is still receiving guests, but there is also a modern wing with spacious, up-to-date accommodations. Among the hotel's facilities are the Vanderbilt Restaurant, with fine dining; the Top of Newport, a cocktail lounge with views of the city; and two other lounges, the Skull and the Torch, with live music on weekends.

Shopping in Newport

You can't really escape the shopping scene in Newport: Where once there were ships' chandleries along the wharves, today there are souvenir and gift shops, scrimshanders, stylish boutiques, and tee-shirt vendors. Among those with more unusual offerings are the antiques stores along Franklin and Spring streets; the **Griffon Shop** of antiques and "found treasures" at the Newport Art Museum, at 76 Bellevue Avenue; a genuine **Army & Navy Surplus Store**, at 262 Thames Street; **Thames Glass Inc.**, at 688 Lower Thames Street; **Rue de France**, selling French linen, lace, and gifts at 78 Thames Street; the **Linen Shop**, at 196 Bellevue Avenue; and **Newport Needleworks Ltd.**, at 210 Bellevue Avenue.

Carroll Michael & Co. Pharmacy, at 115 Bellevue Avenue, is an apothecary shop that smells invitingly of potpourri and hard-to-find perfumes, while **Cabbages & Kings**, at 214 Bellevue, is an old-fashioned gift shop featuring fine china and crystal.

For nautical sorts, **Team One**, at 547 Thames Street, and **J. T.'s Ship Chandlery**, at number 364, offer foul-weather gear and other clothing for the out-of-doors; at the **Armchair Sailor Bookstore**, 543 Thames Street, customers can sip coffee or browse among nautical charts and new and old books about the sea. Flags and pennants are for sale at **Ebenezer Flagg**, 65 Touro Street, and **Flying Colors**, at 468 Thames.

Newport after Dark

On summer weekends, when the yachtsmen are in town, Newport swings after dark. There's live rock 'n' roll music at **One Pelham East**, at the corner of Thames and Pelham (Tel: 401/847-9460); the **Landing**, on Bowen's Wharf (Tel: 401/847-4514); **Surf's Up**, at 91 Long Wharf (Tel: 401/846-0936); and at the **Deck**, on Waite's Wharf (Tel: 401/847-2211).

For dancing there is an old standby, the **Daisy**, at the Clark Cooke House on Bannister's Wharf (Tel: 401/849-2900). Other dance clubs include **Christie's**, at 351 Thames (Tel: 401/847-5400), and **Tickets Lounge**, in the Marriott Hotel on Long Wharf (Tel: 401/849-1000).

Jazz lovers will find their sort of music being played at **Waverley's** in the Newport Harbor Hotel, right on the harbor at 49 America's Cup Avenue (Tel: 401/847-9000). In summer there are the **Newport Jazz Festival**, two weeks in mid-July with jazz musicians of international renown performing in the city's mansions (Tel: 401/846-1133); the **Newport Folk Festival**, at Fort Adams State Park in late July (Tel:

401/847-3709); and the **Newport Music Festival**, classical music held in the mansions in July (Tel: 401/846-1133).

For theater you have a choice between the **Rhode Island Shakespeare Theater**, which also performs works other than Shakespeare (Tel: 401/849-7892), and the **Newport Playhouse and Cabaret Restaurant**, at 102 Connell Highway, near the Newport Bridge (Tel: 401/848-7529).

Sports in Newport

There are, of course, innumerable opportunities for boat rentals and fishing excursions in this city by the sea. **Sail Newport**, in Fort Adams State Park (Tel: 401/846-1983 or 849-6117), and **Jo-World Sailing School**, at the Perry Mill Wharf (Tel: 401/849-9642), both offer sailing instruction. Once you pass Sail Newport's course you can then rent boats from them. Rentals and charters are offered by: **America's Cup Charters** (Tel: 401/489-5868), **Antique and Classic 12-Meter Association** (Tel: 401/847-5007), and **Island Yacht Charters** (Tel: 401/849-4820). Those who wish to spend a day on the water—and $6,000—can charter the 120-foot *Shamrock* with a full crew; she holds up to 20 passengers (Tel: 401/849-4060).

For more ordinary souls, the *Bay Queen* (Tel: 401/245-1350) and the *Viking Queen* (Tel: 401/847-6921) offer motorboat trips at more reasonable prices. *Fishin' Off* (Tel: 401/849-9642) has charter fishing boats.

The finest of wooden sailing yachts parade annually at the **Classic Yacht Regatta**, on Labor Day weekend.

The International Tennis Hall of Fame's 13 grass courts (Tel: 401/849-3990) as well as the city courts are all open to the public. To see the greats of tennis play, plan to be in Newport in July, when the **Miller Lite Hall of Fame** men's tournament is played, followed by the **Virginia Slims Tournament**; for information, Tel: (401) 849-3990.

Bicycles are for rent at various locations, and there's golf at the **Green Valley Country Club** at 371 Union Street (Tel: 401/683-2162).

JAMESTOWN

Jamestown (a.k.a. Conanicut, as it was originally known), the nine-mile long, one-mile-wide island at the mouth of Narragansett Bay, is just west of Newport across the Newport Bridge. (To get there from Portsmouth and points north, bear right off Route 114 onto Route 138 and follow the Newport Bridge signs.)

In 1657 a group of Newporters that included Benedict Arnold, the grandfather of the Revolutionary War traitor, purchased Conanicut from the Narragansett Indians for 100 English pounds "payable in wampum." It was not long before their sheep were grazing the island. The sheep are gone now, and bridges link the island with Saunderstown on the west bay shore and with Newport on the east, but much of Jamestown is still a quiet, rural place where the fragrance of wild rose is carried by the salt air.

In the mid-19th century, when it was still a genuinely isolated place, Jamestown was a favorite retreat of the well-to-do of Philadelphia, Washington, and New York, and some of their grand dwellings still stand along its country roads. A good way to see the houses, as well as the other sights of the island, is to take East Shore Road north once you have crossed the bridge and to stay on it after it becomes North Road. Where North Road recrosses Route 138 is the **Old Windmill**, a 1789 gristmill that has been restored. Though no longer operating, it is a pretty spot, open to the public on summer weekends.

If you continue looping around to the south, North Road becomes Southwest Avenue and leads to sheltered **Mackerel Cove**, with its small **beach** encircled by turn-of-the-century shingled cottages. At the southernmost point of the island, at the end of Beavertail Road, where the waters of Rhode Island Sound splash the gray rocks, the first lighthouse in Rhode Island was built in 1749. Its successor has been flashing warning signals since 1856. The rocks here are inviting to fishermen, sunbathers, and picnickers alike in the warm seasons.

A somewhat drier spot for a picnic is **Fort Wetherill**, perched atop the cliffs that overlook Newport across the East Passage of Narragansett Bay. With its carefully tended lawns, its paths for strollers, and the view of the boats that come and go below, the fort is an enticing place to spend a sunny afternoon. (Just retrace your steps on Beavertail and continue east on Hamilton, then south on Walcott.)

Fort Wetherill Road leads from the fort north to Jamestown, the business center of the island, which consists of a little main street with an impressive, old-fashioned marine hardware store, restaurants, and a gift shop. (Any serious shopping is done across the bridge in Newport.) The **Bay Voyage Inn**, right on the water on Canonicus Road, was barged in from its original site in Middletown. Its brunches, served year-round, are quite popular; Tel: (401) 423-2100.

You can return to Providence from Jamestown by taking Route 138 west to Saunderstown and Route 1 north, following the signs to the capital.

BLOCK ISLAND

Twelve miles off Point Judith (the southeastern corner of South County) and 14 miles off Long Island's Montauk Point, this is a nearly 11-square-mile island of blackberry vines and bayberry bushes, rolling hills and headlands, sea- and song-birds, and ponds (one for every day of the year), and thundering ocean. Red-roofed white farmhouses sprawl on its hilltops, though few today are still the homes of farmers, for Block Island is, above all, a summer community now. Its year-round population of 800 swells to 10,000 as seasonal visitors come to enjoy its largely unspoiled beaches, vistas, and harbors.

Because Block Island is situated directly under the Northeast flyway, it is said that more varieties of birds pass by here than anywhere else in New England. Offshore, in the clear green waters, swim bluefish, bass, and giant tuna. Yachtsmen from all parts of the Northeast put into New Harbor, while day-trippers sun at Old Harbor's Crescent Beach. Canoeists, sailors, and sea kayakers can rent boats at **Oceans and Ponds**, just outside Old Harbor on Ocean Avenue.

This little island's separateness and beauty have earned it the nickname "the Bermuda of the North." The Narragansett Indians who lived on the island before the Europeans came called it Manisses—Island of the Little God.

In 1524 the explorer Giovanni da Verrazano reported the island to be rich in woodlands and not unlike the Greek island of Rhodes. (It was from this comparison, indeed, that the state gained its name.) But Verrazano apparently did not put in himself. The Dutch explorer Adriaen Block is believed to have been the first white man to set foot on the island (in 1614), and so it bears his name.

Block Island has not always been as peaceful as it is today. In the early days of white settlement there were bloody encounters with the Indians; later came attacks by privateers. Then there were the "mooncussers," who lured unsuspecting mariners to the island's shoals and then looted their wrecked vessels. And nature herself has often proved an enemy: In the 1938 hurricane Block Island was virtually cut in two by the sea, and all her fishing fleet was lost.

But on summer days when the beach roses are in bloom, and in the fall when the bittersweet is red and gold and the stripers and bluefish are striking, such violent times are forgotten. Then the Interstate Navigation Company (Tel: 401/783-4613) ferries from Providence, Newport, Galilee, and New London arrive daily at Old Harbor, on the island's east side, and the Montauk Ferry *Jigger III* (Tel:

516/668-2214) and the Montauk Express *Viking* (Tel: 516/
668-5709) sail into New Harbor, on the west coast of Block
Island, from Montauk.

Old Harbor

Old Harbor is a lovely seaside town with charming Victorian
houses and hotels with dormers, turrets, and gingerbread
trim. Before the federal government constructed a breakwater at Old Harbor in the 1870s, Block Island's income derived more from farming than from fishing or tourism, for
there was no natural harbor for boats. But after the breakwater was built, both fishing and tourism thrived, and hotels
quickly rose in the newly created port.

STAYING IN OLD HARBOR
Several Victorian structures still stand—though they have
undergone many reconstructions—and welcome visitors.
Note that most hotels and facilities on Block Island are open
only in season, generally May to October.

The **National**, built in 1888, is one of the old hotels.
Opposite the ferry landing on Water Street, it has undergone
extensive renovation and is the most up-to-date of Block
Island's older hotels. It also has three restaurants: **Soli's**, a
Japanese steak house (Tel: 401/466-5400); **Hemingway's**,
serving American cuisine on the porch as well as inside (Tel:
401/466-5400); and the **Block Island Burrito Company**,
which sells Mexican take-out for beachgoers. Four-and-a-
half-mile-long **Crescent Beach**, with lifeguards and a changing pavilion, begins diagonally across the street.

On Spring Street, near Water Street Square, is the mansard-
roofed **Manisses**, another of the older hotels in Old Harbor.
The Manisses makes the most of its Victorian origins with
plenty of bric-a-brac and flowered Victorian wallpaper. The
hotel dining room, which serves French, American, and Italian dishes, is quite good. **Spring House**, also on Spring Street,
was built in the 1850s but has expanded since. It's a big, old-
fashioned white frame structure with a long front porch,
exceptional ocean views, and an inviting bar called **Victoria's
Parlor**, a dark, cool, quiet space. The **1661 Inn**, yet another
hostelry on Spring Street, is a quiet, romantic getaway just
outside Old Harbor. It serves a delicious brunch and has
superb views of the ocean.

Up on High Street is another restored Victorian, the **Atlantic Inn**, also with views of the water. Its dining room serves
good food and wine, while light fare is available in its annex.

Old Harbor also claims a good number of bed-and-
breakfasts. **Rose Farm Inn**, removed from the bustle of Old

Harbor, has ten cozy rooms decorated with Victorian antiques; and the eight-room Victorian **Hardy Smith House**, some of whose rooms boast views of both Old and New harbors, provides a homey look at island life.

DINING IN THE OLD HARBOR AREA

There are plenty of restaurants from which to choose in Old Harbor. The **Corn Neck Country Kitchen** on Corn Neck Road (Tel: 401/466-5059) is a homespun place for breakfast coffee and pastry and local gossip (it serves dinner on weekends). Also on Corn Neck Road, in Bridgegate Square, is **Capizzano's Pizza**, a favorite with children. **Ernie's** (Tel: 401/466-2473), on Water Street, is another good breakfast spot, where you can sit out on the deck and watch the ferry come in. The fried fish sandwiches at **Finn's** (Tel: 401/466-2473) are incomparable, especially if you consider their low prices. **Ballard's** (Tel: 401/466-2231) is a reliable standby for take-out steamers and fried clams to eat on Ballard's Beach.

At the **Airport Restaurant**, just west of Old Harbor (Tel: 401/466-5468), youngsters can enjoy watching the planes come in, while oldsters sample the meaty lobster salad sandwiches and the crisp johnnycakes. (The Block Island airport is 2 miles/3 km west of Old Harbor.)

For fine dining in Old Harbor, **Winfield's** seafood is the freshest of the fresh (Tel: 401/466-5856). **McGovern's Yellow Kittens**, which occupies the other half of the building (Tel: 401/466-5855), features live music and dancing until 2:00 A.M. weekends, and at lunchtime you can dine outside on the porch to the accompaniment of a guitarist.

New Harbor

Yachtsmen tend to make New Harbor, on the other (northwest) side of Harbor Pond from Old Harbor, their port of call. A modern yacht basin with docks, three marinas, and a few restaurants, New Harbor has two inns: the **Narragansett Inn** and **Samuel Peckham Tavern**. The Narragansett Inn is an old-fashioned Victorian structure with a wrap-around porch and a spectacular view of New Harbor across the street. It also has a few cottages with two bedrooms and kitchens. Sam Peckham's is a 17-room, air-conditioned (unusual for Block Island), family-oriented place. It has a pool and is just minutes from the New Harbor docks.

Dead Eye Dick's, right down at Payne's Dock here, serves fresh seafood outside on the deck (Tel: 401/466-2654). The **Oar** (Tel: 401/466-7753) has the best-stocked bar on all of Block Island, along with signed oars from virtually every crew that has put in here in recent years; breakfast and lunch are also served. If you are interested in a harbor tour rather than in dining, the launch servicing yachtsmen will take you around for a minimal fee.

Around the Island

Although the ferries from Galilee and New London carry cars, a bicycle is the ideal way to see Block Island; rentals are available in Old Harbor. By car or bicycle, the first major site outside Old Harbor is **Mohegan Bluffs**, reached by taking Spring Street to Southeast Light Road, about 2 miles (3 km) south. These sandy bluffs, which rise 150 feet above the Atlantic, take their name from the war party of 40 Mohegan Indians who were driven off them by Block Island's Indians in the 16th century. Southeast Point Lighthouse has served as a beacon to mariners since 1875. There is a swimming beach below the bluffs.

If you follow the Mohegan Trail west from the bluffs to Lakeside Drive, you'll see on your left **Rodman's Hollow**, a glacial depression that stretches down to the sea. It is at its most spectacular in May when the shadbush that fills the hollow is in bloom; were it not for the season you might think it was a snowbank you were seeing. Leave your bicycle here and pick up the Greenway walking trail through the shad and the bayberry; in the fall season you may hear pheasants calling as you walk by. You can head either west toward **Dickens Farm** or south to the precipitous headland of **Black Rock Point**, where the Atlantic churns over dark rocks and Block Islanders do much of their fishing for striped bass and bluefish (take care not to be swept off the rocks by the often thunderous sea). Dickens Farm is a 40-odd-acre bird sanctuary owned by the Block Island Conservancy. It was a gift of the late Elizabeth Dickens, a grade-school teacher who lived to be nearly 100, known as the "bird lady" and the mother of conservation on Block Island. Guided tours are available.

For a fine view of both the Southeast and North lighthouses, as well as of neighboring New York (Long Island), Connecticut, and Massachusetts on a clear day, return to the center of the island, pick up your bicycle, and head west on Beacon Hill Road until you reach 210-foot-high Beacon Hill. It is said that in Revolutionary War days a barrel of tar was put atop Beacon Hill and set on fire whenever a lookout saw a group of deserters fleeing here from the mainland as a signal to fellow islanders to prepare to drive the new arrivals off.

From Beacon Hill turn back east to Old Harbor, where you can either call it a day or head north on Corn Neck Road to **Clay Head**, soaring above New Harbor. An ideal vantage point for watching Block Island sailboat races, it is also the start of a nature trail known as the Maze—through blackberry bushes.

Corn Neck Road continues to the northern end of the island, to **Settlers' Rock** at Cow Cove, where Block Island's first white settlers landed in 1661 and the first cow to come to the island swam ashore.

Sandy Point, the northernmost point of the island, is a wildlife preserve where herring and black gulls and terns nest; cormorants are often sighted on the rocks offshore. Although the old North Light here no longer operates, it brings to mind many a maritime drama of the past: It was off Sandy Point in the 18th century that the ill-fated ship *Palatine* either was lured to destruction or ran aground of her own accord. But however it happened, legend has it that the results were gruesome indeed. Laden with Dutch emigrants seeking religious freedom in the New World, the vessel, according to one account, was tossed about by midwinter storms. As the food and water supply began to diminish, the seamen mutinied, killing the captain and demanding unconscionable sums of the passengers for what food and drink remained. One after another, almost all the passengers died or went mad with hunger. Finally the crew, who by this time had taken all that there was to take, abandoned the ship.

With no one at her helm, the *Palatine* drifted onto the shoal to the north of the point. Island "wreckers" sighting her went out to loot the ship. They found virtually no goods left, but they did find 16 passengers, whom they brought to safety. The wreckers then made an effort to bring the vessel into a cove, but a new storm interfered, so they set fire to the *Palatine* and turned her adrift. Only then did they discover that there was one more passenger on the vessel: a madwoman, whose dying screams echoed across the sea.

A story less charitable to the islanders claims they enticed the ship onto the reef by extinguishing the old North Light and substituting a light on the neck of a horse sent to graze. Seeing the light, the *Palatine* put in toward what her passengers thought was safety, only to be wrecked, plundered, and set afire and adrift.

The poet John Greenleaf Whittier's "The *Palatine* Light" relates the macabre incident, and to this day, it is said, a murky vision of a blazing ship presages bad storms here.

GETTING AROUND

By Car

The swiftest approach to **Providence,** the Rhode Island capital, for travellers from New York and the New London,

Connecticut, area is on Interstate 95, the major thruway spanning the south-central part of the state. If you prefer to go first to **Newport**, exit 3 off I-95 connects with Route 138, which crosses the Jamestown and Newport bridges and leads into Newport. Route 138 meanders through the countryside and passes through the 18th-century village of Kingston, home of the University of Rhode Island.

To get to the Rhode Island **beaches** from the south, take Route 1, which connects with Route 1A.

Routes 6 and 101 are two scenic, wooded routes from the Hartford area to Providence. From Worcester, Massachusetts, Route 146 will take you to the capital; from Boston, I-95; from Cape Cod and New Bedford, Massachusetts, I-195.

Within the state there are three possible routes between Providence and Newport. The most direct route is to take I-195 east to Fall River, then pick up Route 24 to Portsmouth and continue on Route 138 south to Newport. To see the communities on the east side of Narragansett Bay you can take I-195 east to Seekonk, then Route 114 through Barrington, Warren, and Bristol, and across the Mount Hope Bridge to Portsmouth, Middletown, and Newport (once over the Mount Hope Bridge, you can also take Route 138).

For an itinerary that takes you through the communities along the west side of Narragansett Bay—East Greenwich, Wickford, and Saunderstown—follow I-95 south from Providence to Route 4 and turn east on Route 401 to Route 1 south. Pick up scenic Route 1A at Wickford and follow it along the coast, or turn east again on Route 138 across the Jamestown and Newport bridges ($2 toll) to Newport.

To reach picturesque Little Compton from Providence, I-195 west leads to Route 24 in Fall River, Massachusetts, which, in turn, connects with Route 77 south through Tiverton to Little Compton.

By Bus
You can reach Providence from Boston, Cape Cod, New York, and Connecticut points on **Bonanza** (Tel: 800/556-3815 or 401/781-8800), and from New York and Connecticut points on **Greyhound** (Tel: 401/454-0790).

Within the state, the Rhode Island Public Transit Authority (RIPTA) has limited service from community to community and to the beaches in summer. Information is available by calling (800) 224-0444 or (401) 781-9400, weekdays from 9:00 A.M. to 5:00 P.M.

By Train
There is Amtrak service from both New York and Boston to Providence (Tel: 800/USA-RAIL) and limited commuter ser-

vice run by the Massachusetts Bay Transportation Authority
(MBTA) (Tel: 617/227-5070).

By Boat

Ferries run in summer from New London, Connecticut,
Providence, Newport, and Galilee to Block Island with the
Interstate Navigation Company (Tel: 401/783-7328 or 401/
673-4613), and from Montauk, New York, with Viking Ferry
Lines (Tel: 516/668-5709) or *Jigger III* (Tel: 516/668-2214). In
winter the only service is from Galilee.

By Air

There are both commuter and nonstop jet airline service
into Providence's Theodore Francis Green State Airport
from New York, Chicago, Philadelphia, Baltimore, Washington, D.C., Atlanta, Detroit, Orlando, and Raleigh via American, Business Express, Continental, Delta, Northwest, USAir,
and United airlines. Block Island Airport is served by New
England Airlines from Westerley, Rhode Island.

Sightseeing Services

Sightseeing tours of Providence are offered by the **Providence Preservation Society**, 21 Meeting Street (Tel: 401/831-
7440). Tours of Newport are offered by **Newport on Foot**
and **Viking Land Tours** (Tel: 401/847-6921; motor-coach and
boat tours). Tickets for both operations are sold through the
Newport Gateway Visitors Center, 23 America's Cup Avenue
(Tel: 800/326-6030 or 401/849-8098).

Information on travel to and within the state is available
for visitors entering from the south at the **Rhode Island
Welcome Center** (Tel: 401/539-3011 or 3012) on I-95 north,
6 miles (10 km) north of the Connecticut line in Richmond,
Rhode Island, daily. In Providence, visitors' centers are located at the **Roger Williams National Memorial**, on North
Main Street (Tel: 401/528-5385), open daily; and the **Greater
Providence Convention and Visitors Bureau**, 30 Exchange
Terrace in downtown Providence (Tel: 401/274-1636), open
weekdays. In Newport the **Newport Gateway Visitors Center**, open daily, is at 23 America's Cup Avenue (Tel: 800/326-
6030 or 401/849-8098).

For beachbound visitors, the **Narragansett Chamber of
Commerce** is in the old McKim, Mead & White archway on
Ocean Road (Tel: 401/783-7121); the **Charlestown Information Center**, on Routes 1A and 1 (the Ninigret exit; Tel: 401/
364-3878); the **Westerly Chamber of Commerce** (Tel: 401/
596-7761), at Merchants' Square on Route 1A (open weekdays and weekend mornings); and the **South Kingstown
Chamber of Commerce** (Tel: 401/782-2801), at 328 Main

Street in Wakefield (open daily from 10:00 A.M. to 2:00 P.M.). The **Block Island Chamber of Commerce** (Tel: 800/383-2474 or 401/466-2982), at the Old Harbor ferry landing, is open from 9:00 A.M. to 4:00 P.M. daily in summer.

ACCOMMODATIONS REFERENCE

Unless otherwise noted, the rates given below are projections for 1993 for double room, double occupancy. As prices are subject to change, always double-check before booking. Rhode Island's 7 percent sales tax and 5 percent room tax are extra. The area code for all of Rhode Island is 401.

Providence

▶ **Days Hotel**. 220 India Point, **Providence**, RI 02903. Tel: 272-5577 or (800) 325-2525. $80–$115.

▶ **Holiday Inn**. 21 Atwells Avenue, **Providence**, RI 02903. Tel: 831-3900 or (800) 465-4329; Fax: 751-0007. $85–$95.

▶ **Old Court Bed & Breakfast**. 144 Benefit Street, **Providence**, RI 02903. Tel: 751-2002; Fax: 272-6566. $65–$135.

▶ **Omni Biltmore**. Kennedy Plaza, **Providence**, RI 02903. Tel: 421-0700 or (800) THE-OMNI; Fax: 421-0210. $89–$174.

▶ **Providence Marriott**. Charles and Orms streets, **Providence**, RI 02904. Tel. and Fax: 272-2400 or (800) 228-9290. $72–$156.

South County

▶ **Admiral Dewey Inn**. 668 Matunuck Beach Road, **South Kingstown**, RI 02879. Tel: 783-2090 or (800) 457-2090. $60–$120; includes breakfast.

▶ **Shelter Harbor Inn**. 10 Wagner Road, **Westerly**, RI 02891. Tel: 322-8883 or (800) 468-8883; Fax: 322-7907. $82–$102.

▶ **Weekapaug Inn**. 15 Taylor Lane, **Weekapaug**, RI 02891. Tel: 322-0301. $300; includes three meals.

▶ **Willows Resort**. 5310 Old Post Road, **Charlestown**, RI 02813. Tel: 364-7727. $75–$150.

Little Compton

▶ **Stone House Club**. 122 Sakonnet Point Road, **Little Compton**, RI 02837. Tel: 635-2222. $48–$110; nonmembers pay an additional $20 per stay.

Newport

▶ **Cliffside Inn**. 2 Seaview Avenue, **Newport**, RI 02840. Tel: 847-1811. $95–$205; includes breakfast and hors d'oeuvres.

▶ **Elm Tree Cottage**. 336 Gibbs Avenue, **Newport**, RI 02840. Tel: 849-1610 or (800) 882-3ELM; $80–$300; includes breakfast (this is a non-smoking inn).

▶ **Francis Malbone House.** 392 Thames Street, **Newport**, RI 02840. Tel: 846-0392; Fax: 848-5956. $85–$225; includes breakfast.

▶ **Hotel Viking.** One Bellevue Avenue, **Newport**, RI 02840. Tel: 847-3300; Fax: 849-0749. $69–$199.

▶ **Hydrangea House.** 16 Bellevue Avenue, **Newport**, RI 02840. Tel. and Fax: 846-4435 or (800) 945-4667. $65–$135 (this is a non-smoking inn).

▶ **Newport Harbor Hotel and Marina.** 49 America's Cup Avenue, **Newport**, RI 02840. Tel: 847-9000 or (800) 995-2558; Fax: 849-6380. $75–$215.

▶ **Newport Islander Doubletree Hotel.** Goat Island, **Newport**, RI 02840. Tel: 849-2600; Fax: 846-7210. $80–$250.

▶ **Newport Marriott.** Long Wharf, **Newport**, RI 02840. Tel: 849-1000 or (800) 228-9290. $99–$229.

▶ **Sanford Covell Villa Marina.** 72 Washington Street, **Newport**, RI 02840. Tel: 847-0206. $75–$195.

▶ **Victorian Ladies.** 63 Memorial Boulevard, **Newport**, RI 02870. Tel: 849-9960. $125–$165.

Block Island

▶ **Atlantic Inn.** High Street, **Block Island**, RI 02807. Tel: 466-5883; Fax: 466-5678. $55–$165.

▶ **Hardy Smith House.** High Street, **Block Island**, RI 02807. Tel: 466-2466. $40–$115.

▶ **Manisses.** Spring Street, **Block Island**, RI 02807. Tel: 466-2421 or 466-2063; Fax: 466-2858. $55–$240.

▶ **Narragansett Inn.** Ocean Avenue, **Block Island**, RI 02807. Tel: 466-2901 or (800) 225-2449. $95–$125 (with bath).

▶ **National.** Water and Dodge streets, **Block Island**, RI 02807. Tel: 466-2901 or (800) 225-2449. $139–$180.

▶ **Rose Farm Inn.** Roslyn Road (off High Street), **Block Island**, RI 02807. Tel: 466-2021. $55–$155.

▶ **Samuel Peckham Tavern.** New Harbor, **Block Island**, RI 02807. Tel: 466-2439 or 466-2567. $95–$150.

▶ **1661 Inn.** Spring Street, **Block Island**, RI 02807. Tel: 466-2421 or 466-2063; Fax: 466-2858. $55–$300; includes breakfast.

▶ **Spring House.** Spring Street, **Block Island**, RI 02807. Tel. and Fax: 466-5844. $55–$225; includes breakfast.

Bed-and-Breakfasts

▶ **Bed & Breakfast of Rhode Island,** 38 Bellevue Avenue, **Newport**, RI 02840, offers a free reservations service for bed-and-breakfast accommodations statewide. Tel: 849-1298.

BOSTON
AND
CAMBRIDGE

By Jan Stankus

Jan Stankus is a freelance writer who has lived in Boston for 18 years. She is the author of How to Open and Operate a Bed & Breakfast Home *and coauthor of* How to Be Happily Employed in Boston. *She has also contributed numerous articles and photographs to Boston and Cambridge newspapers and written children's fiction.*

W e shall build a city upon a hill. The eyes of all people are upon us.

—*John Winthrop*

When people think of Boston, what usually comes to mind first is its role in the birth of a nation. The history of this part of the world did not exactly begin 360-some years ago—Indians had, after all, occupied what they called the Shawmut for countless years because of the good fishing—but the coming of the European settlers (the Reverend William Blaxton in 1624 and then the Puritans led by John Winthrop in 1630) changed the face of this land forever. In this "city upon a hill" (named after Boston, England, whose name is a shortened version of St. Botolph's Town, for the founder of a local monastery), there's a story beneath every cobblestone, behind every shuttered window, along every widow's walk: tales of the Boston Massacre and the infamous Boston Tea Party, the lanterns in the Old North Church and Paul Revere's midnight ride, escaped slaves and the fight for abolition and women's rights, public hangings on the Boston Common, as well as the

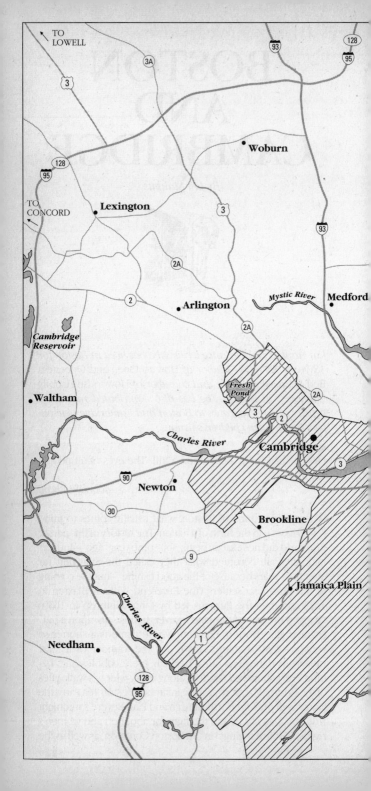

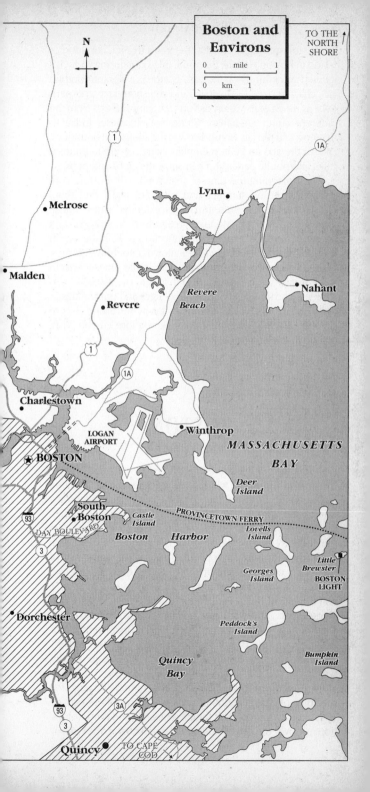

Boston and Environs

TO THE
NORTH
SHORE

N

0   mile   1

0   km   1

1

1A

Melrose

Lynn

Malden

Revere

Revere
Beach

Nahant

1

1A

Charlestown

LOGAN
AIRPORT

Winthrop

★ BOSTON

MASSACHUSETTS
BAY

Deer
Island

93

South
Boston

Castle
Island

PROVINCETOWN FERRY

DAY BOULEVARD

Lovells
Island

3

Boston   Harbor

Little
Brewster

Georges
Island

BOSTON
LIGHT

Dorchester

Peddock's
Island

Bumpkin
Island

Quincy
Bay

93

3A

3

Quincy

TO CAPE
COD

Great Molasses Explosion and the ghost that haunts Georges Island in Boston Harbor. But you'll miss a lot during your visit if you dwell entirely on the past. Boston is a vibrant, youthful city, characterized by diversity, and you should try to experience as much of its variety as you can. Sample foods from the different cultures—Italian, Chinese, Vietnamese, Indian—that now call the city home, browse the shops and boutiques, take in the arts and entertainment, hang out in the outdoor cafés and public parks, and patronize the clubs and pubs.

When planning the time of year you'll visit Boston, consider that during summer and early fall you'll find tours offered frequently, museum hours extended (most museums are closed on Mondays regardless of season), and outdoor activities turning neighborhoods like the North End, Newbury Street, and Chinatown into block parties. Boston's compact size and efficient rapid transit system make it easy to get around. And thanks to the 250,000 or so students enrolled at the array of colleges and universities in the area, it's also a casual city. As far as wardrobe is concerned, just about anything goes. So explore all you wish, and go in comfort.

BOSTON

Our coverage of Boston begins in the Downtown area, near the Boston Common, where we explore some of the landmarks dating from the time of the early European occupation of the land. Government Center, Faneuil Hall Marketplace, and the Common follow, after which we proceed up the slope to elegant Beacon Hill, once home to early-19th-century society and Boston's free black community. Two of the city's ethnic neighborhoods come next: Chinatown, which is situated just behind the Downtown shopping area, and the Italian North End, a short distance from Faneuil Hall Marketplace. Afterward, we visit the Waterfront, also near Faneuil Hall Marketplace, which offers opportunities for excursions to the Boston Harbor Islands, Charlestown Navy Yard, and the John F. Kennedy Library and Museum. Finally, we go to the Back Bay: Beginning at the Boston Public Garden, adjacent to the Common, we continue through the carefully planned landfilled area where members of late-19th-century society built their homes. We end our exploration just over the line dividing the Back Bay from the Fenway at the oldest ballpark in the country, Fenway Park. Cambridge, Boston's most famous neighbor, follows.

MAJOR INTEREST

Downtown
Old Granary Burying Ground
King's Chapel and Burying Ground
Old South Meeting House
Old State House
Faneuil Hall Marketplace

Boston Common, start of the Freedom Trail

Beacon Hill
Charming neighborhood of 19th-century houses
Massachusetts State House
Chestnut and Acorn streets
Nichols House Museum
African Meeting House, highlight of the Black Heritage Trail

Chinatown
Shopping and dining
Festivals

North End
Haymarket Square
Little Italy
Paul Revere House
Old North Church
Copp's Hill cemetery

The Waterfront
Long Wharf and excursion boats
Central Wharf's New England Aquarium
Museum Wharf's Computer and Children's museums

Boston Harbor Islands
Georges Island's Fort Warren

Charlestown Navy Yard
USS *Constitution* (a.k.a. Old Ironsides)

John F. Kennedy Library and Museum

Back Bay
Boston Public Garden and Swan Boats
Residential streets of Beacon, Marlborough, and Commonwealth Avenue
Shopping on Newbury Street
Copley Square Plaza: John Hancock Tower, Trinity

Church, Boston Public Library, and New Old South
Church
Prudential Center's Skywalk
Institute of Contemporary Art

Fenway
Museum of Fine Arts
Isabella Stewart Gardner Museum
Fenway Park, home of the Red Sox

DOWNTOWN

Downtown Boston offers countless diversions within a compact sector that is easily explored on foot. The main entrance of the Park Street MBTA, or "T," station (Green and Red lines) is just steps away from the information booth on Boston Common where you can pick up a free map to help guide your explorations (see Getting Around, below). A stroll through the busiest streets of Boston's "Hub"—as the Downtown area is called—will give you a taste of contemporary Boston, for this is the center of business and government activity, with the attendant offices, shops, and restaurants that cater to the crowds of people who frequent the area. You will also discover people, places, and events that occupy a niche in American history: Paul Revere, Captain Kidd, Mother Goose, Faneuil Hall, and the Boston Massacre, to name just a few.

PARK AND TREMONT STREETS
Begin your stroll along Tremont Street, which runs along the eastern boundary of the Boston Common. ("Tremont" derives from "tri-mountain," which referred to the three hills that originally rose above the Common before two were used for landfill and the third, Beacon Hill, was shortened.)

Park Street Church
At the corner of Tremont and Park streets is "the most interesting mass of brick and mortar in America," at least according to Henry James. Built in 1809, the Park Street Church is noted for a number of "firsts," beginning with its role as the first Trinitarian church established after Unitarianism had gained popularity in the city. (Its adherence to orthodox Puritan doctrine gave rise to many "fire and brimstone" sermons that some say lent the corner of the Common opposite the church the nickname "Brimstone Corner.") The church was also the place where abolitionist William Lloyd Garrison made his first public speech against slavery on July 4, 1829. On Independence Day three years later the song "America," written by a

young seminary student, was first sung here. Park Street Church was also the site of the first Sunday school and the first prison aid society in America.

Finally, a Sunday morning in November 1895 marked the first—and probably only—case in documented history in which a man of God was swept off his chair by a wall of water. It seems that some overzealous workman, in defiance of the laws of the Sabbath, was hard at work digging a tunnel for Boston's modern-day T system when he hit a water main. The ruptured pipe spewed muddy water through the second-story windows of the church (right above the main door), breaking them and covering everything inside with brown gook—including the sermon the minister had been preparing and the minister himself. The Reverend Isaac J. Lansing was heard to condemn America's first rapid-transit system as the work of the Devil.

During July and August you may visit the church's sanctuary (it's on the second floor) Tuesday through Saturday from 9:00 A.M. to 3:30 P.M., or attend services at 9:00 or 10:45 A.M. Sundays. During the rest of the year guests are welcome to attend Congregational services on Sundays at 9:00 A.M., 10:45 A.M., or 6:00 P.M., but the church is not open for tours.

Old Granary Burying Ground

The Old Granary Burying Ground, next door to the Park Street Church on Tremont Street, occupies land that was once part of the Common (as does its neighbor). Set aside as a burying ground in 1660, the parcel was later named for the sprawling wooden barn constructed between the graveyard and the rest of the Common in 1737 to store the town's grain. Among the 2,300 buried here beneath slate markers, many etched with winged skulls or hourglasses (symbols of mortality), are individuals who played roles of distinction in Boston's history. Among them are John Hancock, Samuel Adams, and Robert Treat Paine, three "Sons of Liberty" and signers of the Declaration of Independence, along with Paul Revere, Peter Faneuil, Judge Samuel Sewell, religious martyr Mary Dyer (her grave is unmarked), and the five victims of the Boston Massacre (their marker can be seen from the sidewalk to the far right of the gate).

Benjamin Franklin's parents are also buried here. Their granite obelisk, which dominates the center of the yard, was fashioned by Solomon Willard, who also designed the graveyard's granite gateway and the Bunker Hill Monument in Charlestown. The Franklin monument you now see replaced the original one set there by the Franklins' youngest and most famous son; he composed the epitaph that is inscribed on the bronze tablet on the monument's face. The final resting place

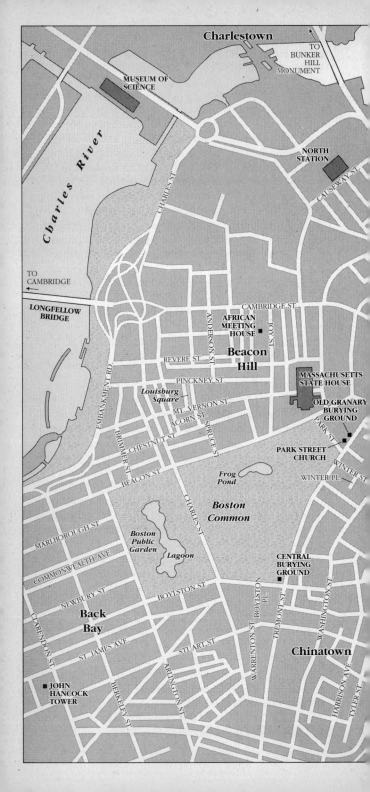

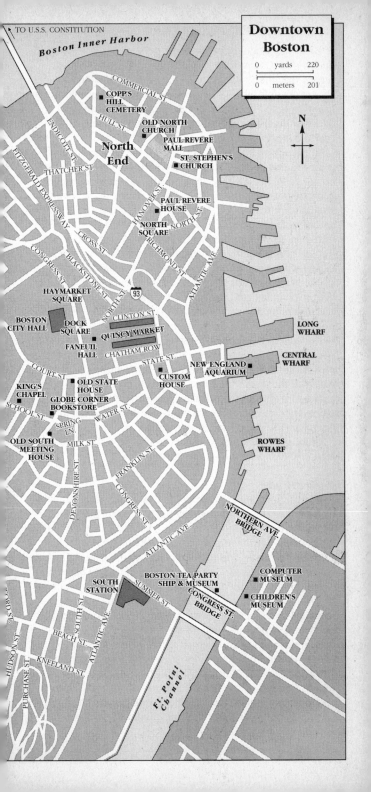

of Benjamin Woodbridge, the only person ever killed in a duel on the Common, is near the fence. One historian observed that the graveyard couldn't have accommodated a greater possible distance between the remains of the unfortunate young man and those of Peter Faneuil, who had helped the other duelist, a relative, to escape on a British man-of-war after the incident.

To anyone taking stock of how small the graveyard really is for the number of people buried here, it should come as no surprise that two or three dearly departed often lie beneath one headstone. Mary Goose is a case in point. Beneath her marker are Mary, her husband, Isaac, and his second wife, Elizabeth Foster Goose. Elizabeth is often referred to as Mother Goose, though scholars continue to dispute her authorship of the children's rhymes that appear in *Songs for the Nursery, or Mother Goose's Melodies.* The Goose gravestone stands next to that of Thomas Fleet, Elizabeth's son-in-law and the publisher who printed the book.

Sticklers for accuracy should also be warned that a headstone may or may not designate the true resting place of the individual named on it, because of a rearrangement of the stones in the mid-19th century. Some speculate that an overly meticulous caretaker found it easier to maintain a yard in which all the stones were lined up neatly in rows instead of scattered within individual family plots. (A preference for symmetry rather than accuracy was not uncommon among caretakers of Boston's older graveyards.)

Old Granary is open to visitors daily from 8:30 A.M. to at least 3:30 P.M. (later during the summer).

Parker House

Farther north along Tremont, at the corner of School Street, is the Parker House, a hotel established in 1855, though the current structure was built in 1927. If you walk through the hotel lobby you'll see glass cases containing memorabilia from bygone days. Through the hotel's doors have walked celebrities of all types: Charles Dickens, who stayed here on one of his visits to the States; John Wilkes Booth, who came to town to see his brother, Edwin, perform in a play at the Boston Theater just ten days before the assassination of Abraham Lincoln; members of the Saturday Club, an informal literary circle that included Ralph Waldo Emerson, Nathaniel Hawthorne, and Henry Wadsworth Longfellow; and Ho Chi Minh and Malcolm X, who both worked here as waiters (though not at the same time). In the Last Hurrah bar and grill downstairs, local political deals have sometimes served as the main fare, the fine points worked out on cocktail napkins.

King's Chapel

Across from the Parker House, at 58 Tremont Street, is King's Chapel, whose original wooden structure was erected in 1689 amid much protest from the Puritan colonists. The royal governor of the time, Sir Edmund Andros, insisted on establishing an Anglican church in Boston, but the Puritans refused to sell him any land to do so. The governor then seized part of the graveyard that had occupied the land here for some 50 years and ordered the house of worship constructed despite the controversy, making King's Chapel the first Anglican church in New England.

In 1749 the granite structure you see today was built around the wooden building that already stood here so as not to interrupt the schedule of services (when it was completed, the old church was dismantled and thrown out the windows of the new). This construction also was met with much hostility from the townsfolk, who reportedly threw dead animals and garbage during the ceremony held to lay the cornerstone. Funds were always a problem, and the steeple that had been included in the original design was never built. After all the fuss, many of the parishioners left town when the British army evacuated Boston in 1776—and less than ten years later King's Chapel became the first Unitarian church in America.

Guests are welcome to visit the interior today, which retains the traditional box pews (in contrast to those in other churches of the era, these are upholstered). Note the spacious governor's pew (along the aisle on the right side) with its canopy, chairs, and table—rather like a small drawing room. King's Chapel possesses the largest bell ever cast in Paul Revere's foundry, and it is still rung today (on the bill Revere wrote "the sweetest bell we ever made"). The story goes that Revere agreed to give the church an exceptionally good price if, in return, the bell would be rung upon the occasion of his funeral (it was). Although it is impossible to get a good look at the bell, which is inside the tower, if you show up on Sunday at around 10:45 A.M. or Wednesday at 11:55 A.M., right before services, you'll get to hear its sweet tone.

The church is open to visitors Tuesday through Saturday from 10:00 A.M. to 4:00 P.M. in the summer; and Tuesday through Friday until 2:00 P.M. and on Saturdays until 4:00 P.M. off-season.

King's Chapel Burying Ground

Adjoining the church is King's Chapel Burying Ground, Boston's first and oldest graveyard, predating King's Chapel by nearly half a century. The land was once owned by a

Puritan settler named Isaac Johnson, whose last wish was to be buried in a corner of his garden—and so he was, in 1631. As other members of the new colony aged in the months and years that followed, their final wish was to be buried near their good friend Isaac Johnson. Eventually the town made a decision to set aside the plot of land as an official burial ground, noting for the record, "Brother Johnson's garden is getting to be a poor place for vegetables."

Though you won't find a headstone for Johnson here today, there are numerous others—though they are not in any order that makes sense except to the neatniks who realigned them around 1850. In the center of the yard you will find a plaque marking the burial of William Dawes, the "midnight rider" neglected by history. Although Longfellow did not make him famous for his efforts (supposedly "Revere" presented more rhyming options than his compatriot's name), Dawes is here honored posthumously for his role as a messenger sent from Boston to Lexington to sound the warning that the British were coming.

If you take the path to the right from the gate and follow it to the left around the intriguing-looking well (actually a subway vent), you will come upon the marker for Elizabeth Paine, a Puritan woman said to have been branded with an "A" (for "adulteress") after bearing the child of her minister. If the story sounds familiar, it's because Nathaniel Hawthorne used this real-life drama to fashion his tale about Hester Prynne in *The Scarlet Letter*. Also buried on the grounds is John Winthrop, first governor of Massachusetts (his tomb is off to the left from the gate). It is sometimes said that Captain Kidd is buried in this graveyard as well (there is no stone here bearing his name), but he was most likely laid to rest in England, where he was found guilty of piracy and sentenced to death. Kidd's job had been to capture pirates off the coast for the royal governor in Boston in the 1690s, but presumably he took to the life instead (though he denied it to the end). Legend has it that anyone who knocks on the stones of King's Chapel three times and whispers, "Captain Kidd, for what were you hanged?" will receive his answer: "Nothing."

The graveyard is open daily from 8:30 A.M. to 3:30 P.M. (usually later in summer).

SCHOOL AND WASHINGTON STREETS

Old City Hall

Along School Street, just behind King's Chapel, is Boston's Old City Hall, which served in this capacity for 104 years until 1969, when the new City Hall was built and the old structure was converted to offices and a restaurant. The location is important because it marks the site of the first public school in America, Boston Latin School, founded in 1635 (the school still exists but is now on Louis Pasteur Avenue).

The statue in the courtyard on the left is a tribute to Benjamin Franklin, who attended Boston Latin for a time. (Although Franklin moved to Philadelphia as a teenager, Boston likes to claim him as its own whenever possible.) Sculptor Richard Saltonstall Greenough intended his 1856 work to capture the dual nature of the great man's face—the left side "philosophical and reflective," the right side "funny and smiling." You can decide which expression is more appropriate for the statue's current position as the centerpiece of **Ben's Café**, which now occupies Old City Hall's plaza. Surrounded by outdoor tables topped with cheerful striped umbrellas, his head is bent at just the right angle to survey the diners who come and go. The statue of Josiah Quincy, second mayor of Boston, in the opposite courtyard, stares straight ahead as if to say he does not care that he has been left out of all the fun. Ben's Café is operated by Maison Robert, an acclaimed French restaurant located inside Old City Hall.

Globe Corner Bookstore

Farther down School Street, at number 1 (at the corner of Washington Street), stands the Globe Corner Bookstore, housing Boston's most comprehensive selection of travel guidebooks to New England and the world. The current building occupies the site of the home of Anne Hutchinson, who was banished from the colony in 1638 because her "heretical" beliefs went against strict Puritan dogma. (She preached that salvation could be had without obedience to church and state.) Governor John Winthrop called this mother of 14 "a woman of haughty and fierce carriage, a nimble wit and active spirit, a very voluble tongue, more bold than a man, though in understanding and judgment inferior to many women." In 1915 a statue of Hutchinson was placed in front of the State House (where it still stands), but it was not until 1945 that the city retracted the edict of banishment against her. The current building, dating to 1718 (replacing Hutchinson's after it burned down), became in the mid-1800s the office of Ticknor & Fields, successful publishers of the best talent of the time (in part because Jamie Fields believed authors should be paid). The office became a popular gathering place for the literati of the day: Hawthorne, Dickens, Longfellow, Emerson, and Oliver Wendell Holmes (whose desk sits in the window). Nevertheless,

Fields was known to make a mistake or two on occasion; after reading a story by Louisa May Alcott he advised her that she would do well to remain a teacher.

Old South Meeting House

The Old South Meeting House, at 310 Washington Street (catercorner to the Globe Corner Bookstore), is located on the site of the original meetinghouse built in 1669 by a dissident group of Puritans as their place of worship (in what was then the south end of Boston). The earlier structure was plain and had no steeple (in keeping with the group's rejection of the pomp and circumstance they found in churches other than their own "purified" version) and in fact did not resemble a church so much as it did a barn. But when the first building was razed and a new one erected just 60 years later, in 1729, somehow a little of that pomp crept onto the drawing board and the resulting meetinghouse actually resembled a church, steeple and all. It remained, however, a meetinghouse, not only providing space for worship but also accommodating town gatherings too large for Faneuil Hall. The best known of these was one held December 16, 1773, when 5,000 people jammed into the space to rally against the tea tax. The Sons of Liberty went directly from the meeting to Boston Harbor to attend to the latest shipment of tea from England—and the rest, as they say, is history. (The front pews are outfitted with earphones through which you may hear a reenactment of the meeting.)

Old South Meeting House suffered considerable indignities when the British occupied Boston between October 1775 and March 1776, quite probably because of the role the meetinghouse had played as a forum for the American "hotheads." The pulpit and pews were taken out and burned for fuel, then dirt and gravel were strewn over the floor so that British soldiers could use it as a riding school. After the British evacuated, Old South's interior was restored; the meetinghouse subsequently managed to survive two fires, one in 1810 when the roof caught fire, the other in 1872 when the great Boston fire devastated 65 acres of downtown businesses and homes nearby.

In 1875 a new Old South Meeting House was built in the Back Bay, leaving the earlier building up for sale and possible destruction. Ralph Waldo Emerson, Wendell Phillips, and Julia Ward Howe joined Boston philanthropist Mary Hemenway to save Old South. Afterward, the Old South Association formed and to this day remains the building's caretaker. Old South continues its role as a meetinghouse where the community comes together to discuss controversial subjects, listen to lectures, hear music, and attend dramatic performances. Visitors are invited to come inside (for a small fee) to view the interior and look at the displays of memorabilia from Boston's past. The uppermost gallery near the roof has tiers of seats where church member Phillis Wheatley, America's first published black poet, would have been sitting in the late 1700s, in the section reserved for slaves and young boys. (A first edition of Wheatley's book of poems is on display.)

SPRING LANE

Directly across Washington Street from the Globe Corner Bookstore is a narrow, red-brick pedestrian walkway called Spring Lane. While there is not much to see today along this short passageway except for a few plaques affixed to the buildings, at one time this was a center of town activity: the site of the Great Spring that provided water for the people of Boston for nearly two centuries until it ran dry in the early 1800s (though it is reported that it made a brief appearance some years later in the basement of the post office on Milk Street). When in 1630 the Reverend William Blaxton invited the Puritans to join him on the peninsula we have come to know as Boston, it was not because he wanted the company. Rather, he did so for humanitarian reasons, because the brackish water in nearby Charlestown, the Puritans' first settlement, was making people ill. Blaxton reserved the spring in Beacon Hill's Louisburg Square for himself and extended an invitation to the others to come and use the other spring, whose location no doubt seemed a safe enough distance from his homestead. Come they did, crowding out the reverend and building a city.

COURT AND STATE STREETS

Old State House

If you walk through Spring Lane and turn left onto Devonshire you will come to the Old State House on your left (the State Street MBTA station, Orange and Blue lines, is beneath the building), directly across from the Boston National Historical Park Visitor Center at 15 State Street. The area around the Old State House was the focus of early town life, a place for buying and selling and punishment. The Puritans erected their pillory, stocks, and whipping post in this busy place to publicly chastise transgressors (the first victim was the carpenter who made the tools of punishment—for charging too much).

Today the Old State House is a museum administered by the Bostonian Society (which was hurriedly formed in 1881 when the city of Chicago tried to purchase the building with the intention of moving it, brick by brick, to the shores of Lake Michigan as a tourist attraction). There was first a town hall on this site, built in 1657 to house a meeting place, library, armory, and court chambers. When the wooden structure burned it was replaced in 1713 by the more fire-resistant brick building you see today, though the interior was consumed by flames in 1748.

As the seat of royal government, the town hall provided the venue for lively argument as the British imposed taxes and further trade restrictions upon the colonists. It was here that patriot James Otis argued in 1761 against the Writs of Assistance, search warrants used to ferret out smuggled goods. This was a speech in which "the child Independence was born," according to John Adams. Be sure to visit the council chamber on the second floor where the arguments took place and peer through the window to see the balcony on which the Declaration of Independence was read on July 18, 1776 (an event that is reenacted here every Fourth of July). Colonists marked the joyous occasion in part by ripping down the symbols of the Crown from the town hall (the lion and unicorn that decorate the exterior today are replicas); the symbol of the new country, the American eagle, was added later.

From the balcony you can also see where the Boston Massacre occurred, in what is now the traffic island directly below. (A copy of the engraving Paul Revere made of the event is displayed near the window.) Other artifacts here include a coat belonging to John Hancock, which may have been the garment he wore for his inauguration as first governor of the Commonwealth of Massachusetts (ironically, the style and color—crimson—echo those of the uniforms that had been worn by the much-hated "bloodybacks"). You'll also find a tricornered hat, tea from the Boston Tea Party, a musket and sword from the Battle of Bunker Hill, along with other Revolutionary War objects and domestic items that trace the political, economic, social, and cultural life of the city from the early 17th century to the present.

The Boston Massacre

You'll miss the site marker for the Boston Massacre unless you keep your eyes to the pavement as you walk east from the Old State House and into the busy intersection at State and Devonshire streets. Set into the small traffic island is a circle of cobblestones whose diameter approximates the length of one impossibly tall colonist laid head to boot. It was here on the bitterly cold evening of March 5, 1770, that Hugh White, a lone British sentry, exchanged words with a young local apprentice. The situation escalated as dozens of colonists—some reportedly drunk and armed with clubs—tramped through the snow to surround the man. Fed up with the continuing British occupation of Boston and angry over the killing of a young boy by a Loyalist merchant only weeks before, the crowd hurled taunts at the red-coated sentry, followed by rocks, oyster shells, and chunks of ice. Eight British soldiers came to White's aid. What happened next depends on whom you wish to believe. If you listen to the red-coated sentry who appears every March near the site as part of the National Park Service's commemorative tour, the incident was a terrible accident and nothing more. Outnumbered by an angry mob, the British soldiers were pushed and struck until, somehow, a gun went off. The shot triggered more shots, and when it was all over five colonists lay dead or dying in the snow. The first to fall was the six-foot-two Crispus Attucks, a slave who had run away from his owner 20 years before. Having found work as a sailor, he was in Boston waiting to ship out again. The other colonists killed by British bullets were Patrick Carr, James Cauldwell, Samuel Gray, and Sam Maverick.

If you prefer Paul Revere's version, the British shot down innocent colonists in cold blood, including Attucks, a huge and no doubt an intimidating presence who some say was the ringleader. Prints from Revere's engraving depicting the event as he saw it were widely circulated. These days historians pretty much agree with the redcoat's interpretation, but back in 1770, with the colonists' sympathy for the victims compounded by the mood of the times and a little help from Revere's propaganda, the "accident" was transformed into a "bloody massacre." And so the Boston Massacre became one of the rallying points that drove the colonists along the road to revolution.

CONGRESS STREET

Government Center and Boston City Hall

From the traffic island walk north along Congress Street a short distance and you will come to Government Center's expansive brick plaza (on your left). The centerpiece is a massive, top-heavy concrete and brick building that looks as if it was fashioned to withstand just about any adversity short of nuclear war: Welcome to Boston City Hall. Designed in what is known as the "brutalist" architectural style, the ten-acre complex actually won a design award, yet some locals continue to criticize their "new" City Hall, which was built in the 1960s. ("It looks like the box Faneuil Hall came in," was one architect's complaint.)

To its credit, one goal the overall design does accomplish,

and quite effectively, is public access. Rallies and demonstrations are held here just as often as on the Boston Common; thousands of commuters crisscross the open space each day as they go to and from work (the Government Center MBTA station—Green and Blue lines—is located on the plaza); area workers bring their lunch here in pleasant weather; and free cultural events are held on the outdoor stage. Every summer the public is invited to enjoy concerts of popular contemporary music on Wednesday evenings at 7:30 and "oldies" groups on Saturdays at 7:00 P.M. If you're looking for a good spot to view the fireworks on New Year's Eve as part of Boston's First Night celebration, you won't find any better than the plaza.

Visitors are also welcome to come into the lobby area of City Hall to look around between 8:00 A.M. and 5:00 P.M. weekdays (there's an information desk just inside to the left of the entrance). The lobby doubles as an exhibit area, so most of the time you will find displays of sculpture, jewelry, artifacts, architecture, photographs, or paintings. (For more information on exhibits and scheduled outdoor events, call the main City Hall number at 617/635-4000.) In addition, occasional exhibits featuring Boston artists or arts organizations are sponsored by the Mayor's Office of Arts and Humanities (Tel: 617/635-3245). These are held at the Scollay Square Gallery, located off the main lobby to the left.

Before Government Center was paved over with red bricks in the 1960s, the area was a tangle of narrow streets leading down to old Dock Square (where Faneuil Hall stands). Once part of the original waterfront settlement, over time Scollay Square (as Government Center was then called) was transformed into what Bostonians nicknamed the Combat Zone, characterized by all-night theaters (of the peepshow variety), bars, tattoo parlors, and prostitutes. (When construction began on the new City Hall, the Zone relocated next to Chinatown, where it exists today in spite of continuing protests from the Asian community.)

Before leaving Government Center's plaza, take a look at the one respectable survivor from the old Scollay Square days: the immense steaming kettle that hangs above a doorway at the head of Court Street (opposite the Government Center MBTA station). Fashioned in 1873 as a trademark for the Oriental Tea Company, the 227-gallon kettle is now a landmark.

Faneuil Hall Marketplace

Across Congress Street from City Hall is the Faneuil Hall Marketplace, which hosts an estimated 50,000 visitors every day. The park-like plaza includes historic Faneuil Hall and three long market buildings: Quincy in the center, flanked by North and South markets. The marketplace offers a variety of restaurants, outdoor cafés, and food stalls with a smorgasbord of treats from around the world; and shops and pushcarts loaded with everything imaginable for sale— all against the backdrop of a continual festival featuring musicians, magicians, and psychics. In the evenings especially, there are only two places in the Boston area to find a "scene," with lots of people, entertainment, food, and the unexpected: Harvard Square is one; the other is Faneuil Hall Marketplace.

As you come down the stairs from Government Center and cross Congress Street you'll see Anne Whitney's statue of Samuel Adams at Dock Square, home of Faneuil Hall Marketplace. The statue holds an honored position in front of Faneuil Hall, where Adams, the "Father of the Revolution," was known to lend his mind and voice so many times to the cause of independence. Successful merchant Peter Faneuil gave Faneuil Hall to the city in 1742 with the idea that it would be a central marketplace, a concept so controversial at the time (many Bostonians preferred that vendors continue selling house to house) that his proposal squeaked by with just enough votes to approve it. The hall's ground floor was used for selling produce and goods (as it is today), but the second floor's meeting hall—which eventually made the place famous as the "cradle of liberty"—was added almost as an afterthought (some historians believe it was tacked on to make the building, and its central marketplace, more palatable). It was here that the colonists proclaimed that there should be "no taxation without representation" and spoke most vehemently against the Sugar Act, the Stamp Act, and the Townshend Acts. In the 19th century the hall served as the venue for speeches by abolitionists William Lloyd Garrison, Frederick Douglass, and Wendell Phillips (though not much is ever said about the fact that the hall was funded in part by Peter Faneuil's profits from the slave trade). Today the hall is still used as a public forum for political rallies, meetings, spelling bees, and concerts. When not in use, the hall is open to the public every day from 9:00 A.M. to 5:00 P.M.; Boston National Historical Park rangers (Tel: 617/242-5642) give a short talk about the building and its history every half hour, as well as free guided tours from Patriot's Day (mid-April) through late November.

Inside Faneuil Hall, G. P. A. Healy's painting *Webster's Reply to Hayne* dominates the area behind the stage. Measuring 30 by 16 feet, the painting, which shows Daniel Webster speaking before the U.S. Senate, contains portraits of 130 senators and other men of distinction from that time. The work was commissioned in 1842 by King Louis Philippe of France, who had spent some time in Boston teaching French. The clock in the back of the hall was paid for by the pennies of Boston schoolchildren and presented as a gift to the city in 1850. (Their names were placed inside the clock's case, to be opened 100 years later, in 1950.) Made by David Davis and Edward Howard in the Boston neighborhood of Roxbury, the clock still runs on its original eight-day, weight-driven mechanism, which was tooled and assembled by hand.

Outside the building, one of Faneuil Hall's more interesting features is the grasshopper vane atop the cupola, a design selected by Peter Faneuil himself and crafted by Shem Drowne out of copper and gold leaf in 1742 (its eyes are glass doorknobs). It has been called a symbol of trade, and is said to be a copy of one of six grasshoppers that stood above the first London Exchange (built in 1574). Whatever its meaning, the grasshopper has become a symbol of Boston over the two and a half centuries since it was first placed atop Faneuil Hall (it is said that during the War of 1812 suspected spies were asked to identify the shape of the city's most famous vane). The variations in brick color on the building's exterior reveal that Faneuil Hall was smaller as originally built; an addition and other modifications were designed by architect Charles Bulfinch in 1806.

The plaza with the three long market buildings behind Faneuil Hall represents a risk that turned into a commercial success beyond anyone's wildest imagination—and not just once, but twice. In 1824 Boston's mayor, Josiah Quincy, proposed building an extension to the central market at Faneuil Hall, an idea that was met with considerable opposition because it required a major landfill project (the water's edge pretty much came up to Faneuil Hall in those days). But the mayor's persistence paid off and his dream was accomplished in only one year, with the sale of the new land providing the funds for the project and then some.

Nearly a century and a half later, though, the buildings and the area around them had deteriorated, and architect Benjamin Thompson was hired to restore the marketplace to its original concept while incorporating modern touches. Faneuil Hall Marketplace reopened in 1976. Today you can stroll through the central Quincy Market building much as Bostonians did in the past, stopping to look at merchandise on display in the pushcarts in the Bull Market (where entrepreneurs rent carts by the week). In the central corridor food has been sold since the place first opened in the 19th century. Hang out in a café; relax on a park bench; drop by **Durgin Park** (in the North Market building), a restaurant "founded before you were born"; or just enjoy the entertainment. (For more on Faneuil Hall Marketplace and Quincy Market, see Shops and Shopping, below.)

BOSTON COMMON

If the Reverend William Blaxton had had his way, he most likely would have continued his life of happy isolation from the civilized world he had left behind in the 1620s. His hospitality to the Puritan settlers who arrived in the New World a few years after he did led to entirely too much company for his taste. By 1634 Blaxton's homestead, in the center of modern Boston, had become so populous that he felt compelled to move on; for 30 pounds sterling he sold the bulk of the land he had claimed as his own to the newcomers (they had already taken the rest) and headed for the wide open spaces of Rhode Island. (He is said to have returned only once, astride his bull and scouting for a wife.) The settlers promptly laid out Blaxton's land, approximately 50 acres, as "a place for a trayning field" for soldiers and for "the feeding of cattell."

Prime real estate in the heart of any city always risks development. But thanks to a town order passed in 1640, most of Blaxton's property was reserved as a common field for use by all. The order still stands, making the Boston Common the oldest public park in America. These days, though, the only time you might see any "cattell" is during an occasional dairy festival. What you will find is an **information booth** right on the edge of the Common at Tremont Street, near the MBTA's Park Street station (with both Red Line and Green Line service). Here you can pick up a free map, sign up for trolley tours, or embark on your own walking tour of the **Freedom Trail** (just follow the red brick pathway; for more specific information on the Freedom Trail, see Getting Around, below). Set back from the booth is a park ranger station; from here rangers conduct free tours of the Common and other areas of Boston from mid-April to early November.

(Across Charles Street, on the western side of the Common, is the Boston Public Garden, which may seem to be just more of the Common. It was in fact created by landfill; we cover it separately, below.)

The Great Elm
Just behind the park ranger station to the left is a plaque in the ground marking the site of the legendary Great Elm. There are different accounts of just how large the tree

actually was (some say 100 feet tall, others say 72 feet with a 100-foot spread), but everyone agrees that it was indeed massive.

Already standing when the Puritans arrived, the elm went on to play a grisly role in Boston's history until it finally blew down in a storm in 1876. It was here that the Puritans punished those who broke their strict code of rules with death by hanging, with a rope slung over one of the tree's sturdy limbs. Transgressions included adultery (two lovers were executed in 1643), witchcraft (Anne Hibbens was the victim of such an accusation, suffering her assigned punishment here in 1656), theft (in the late 1700s Rachell Whall lost her life for stealing a bonnet), and joining a prohibited religious sect (after a last-minute reprieve at the gallows tree and banishment from the colony in the mid-1600s, Mary Dyer chose to return to face sure death as a martyr for her Quaker beliefs).

Flagstaff Hill

Nearby is the highest point on the Common, Flagstaff Hill. Because of its height and the Common's military history, the hill was selected as the site for the **Soldiers and Sailors Monument**, a 70-foot granite sculpture by Martin Milmore erected in 1877 to honor the men of Boston who had died for their country during the Civil War. The hill had been a favorite British camp during the Revolution, causing local boys, who had their own ideas about the best use of the hill, to complain to General Thomas Gage that his men were destroying their snow slides. The dispute was settled peaceably when Gage ordered his troops not to interfere with the boys' sledding in the future.

Frog Pond

At the foot of Flagstaff Hill is the Frog Pond, so named, it is said, because no frog has ever been seen anywhere near it. Of the three ponds that used to provide drink for the cattle that roamed here, this shallow body of water is the only one remaining. It enjoys its place in history as the inspiration for James Russell Lowell's "Ode to Water" and as the focal point for the contempt Edgar Allan Poe felt for his birthplace (he referred to Boston as "Frogpondium"). These days it provides a place for kids to splash and wade in the summer months—when there's water in it, that is; nearby is an enclosed playground.

Robert Gould Shaw Memorial

If you walk up the stairs leading to Beacon Street and outside the gate (the State House is just across the street),

you will find the Robert Gould Shaw Memorial by Augustus
Saint-Gaudens, which honors the 54th Regiment of Massachusetts Infantry, the first unit of free black soldiers to fight
in the Civil War. The regiment's odyssey, which culminated
in the 1863 battle at Fort Wagner in Charleston, South
Carolina, where Shaw and many under his command died, is
depicted in the 1989 film *Glory*.

Brimstone Corner

At the corner of the Common where Park and Tremont
streets meet (across from the Park Street Church) is Brimstone Corner, so named because a quantity of brimstone was
stored in the basement of the church during the War of 1812
(though some historians say the name derived from the fiery
sermons emanating from the pulpit). Today most sermons
on this corner are delivered by orators of the soapbox
variety, who lecture passersby on matters of religion and
politics, competing for attention with an assortment of street
vendors, musicians, panhandlers, and an occasional sword
swallower.

Elsewhere in the Common

Every square foot of the Common seems to have historical
significance; you could spend a great deal of time wandering at will and making discoveries. Between the Park Street
T station entrance and the information booth, for example,
is the **Brewer Fountain**, a bronze reproduction of the
Parisian fountain displayed at the 1855 Paris Exposition.
Along Tremont Street is the 1888 monument to the victims
of the **Boston Massacre**, while the **Founders' Monument**
(depicting the Reverend William Blaxton with the newly
arrived Puritans) stands near Beacon Street.

During your exploration you will no doubt come across
a picturesque bandstand near Flagstaff Hill encircled by
walkways and benches. This is the **Parkman Bandstand**,
which these days sees little use. At the corner of Tremont
and Boylston streets is the **Central Burying Ground**, one of
the oldest cemeteries in Boston, dating to the mid-1700s.
(The gates are sometimes locked; to enter you must first go
to the ranger station near the information booth or phone
the rangers; Tel: 617/522-2639.) Here lie some of the participants in the Boston Tea Party along with many British
soldiers who fell during the Battle of Bunker Hill. The most
famous inhabitant is painter Gilbert Stuart, known for his
portraits of the first U.S. presidents (he is said to be buried
inside Tomb 61, although it does not bear his name). It is
perhaps no accident that located directly across Boylston

Street from this serene spot is the edge of the Theater District (discussed below) and the most raucous singles scene in the city. After all, who is less likely to complain about the loud music and laughter emanating from the clubs until the wee hours than the residents who repose here?

BEACON HILL

With its gas street lamps (burning day and night), narrow cobblestone streets, and lovely 19th-century red-brick houses adorned with ornamental railings and lavender window glass, the historic district of Beacon Hill is one of the most picturesque neighborhoods in the country. A stroll through Beacon Hill—the only hill remaining of the three that originally stood here (the other two were leveled when the settlers needed them for landfill)—will give you a true sense of what New England charm is all about. To get here, take the MBTA's Green Line or Red Line to the Park Street station and walk up the slope of the Boston Common until you reach Beacon Street, which borders the northern edge of the Common.

BEACON STREET

Massachusetts State House
A good place to begin your exploration is the oldest building in this part of the city, the Massachusetts State House, which has served as the commonwealth's seat of government since 1798. (You can't miss it; just look for the golden dome at the northeastern summit of Beacon Street.) Originally gray shingle, the dome was sheathed in copper by Paul Revere in 1802. It was changed back to a dark gray when it was discovered that the bright copper dome served as an outstanding target for British ships in the harbor. In 1861 the dome was painted gold, and since 1874 has been covered in 23-karat gold leaf. Located in John Hancock's former cow pasture, this new building replaced the original State House (still standing at the corner of Washington and State streets; see above) as a larger, more elegant home for the center of government.

Go up the steps to enter through the doors on the left or the right. (The big double doors in the center are opened on only three occasions: when the governor leaves the State House for the last time at the end of his term, when the president of the United States or a visiting foreign head of state enters on official business, and when Massachusetts regimental flags are being returned from war.) Just inside the door at the entrance to Doric Hall is **Visitor Services** (Tel: 617/727-3676). Free guided tours of the interior are offered continuously on weekdays from 10:00 A.M. to 4:00 P.M., but you are also welcome to pick up a flyer for a self-guided tour and wander around on your own.

Doric Hall (named for the architectural style of its ten columns) is the oldest part of the State House, designed by architect Charles Bulfinch (an addition was finished in 1895). Every inch of the building contains a statue, mural, or piece of memorabilia. Of special note are the marble statue of an army war nurse and patient sculpted in 1914 by Bela Pratt to honor the women of the North after the Civil War (located in Nurses Hall); the stained glass window at the main staircase illustrating the series of state seals over the years (the oldest example, at the top of the central window, depicts a rather odd British notion of a Native American—in a grass skirt and voicing the plea "Come over and help us"); the "Sacred Cod" hanging in the house of representatives (when staff members of the *Harvard Lampoon* "codnapped" the wooden sculpture in 1933, the house refused to meet until its good-luck charm was returned); the "Holy Mack-erel" riding atop the massive chandelier in the senate cham-ber (the senate's version of the "Sacred Cod"); and the controversial $100,000 clock sculpture hanging in the Great Hall on the second floor (it was purchased in 1990, at a time when many people felt the state didn't have any money to spare, although funds had been set aside in 1986 for the purchase). If you happen to notice a statue with exception-ally shiny shoes, you've found the statue of Roger Wolcott. The story goes that one woman rubbed her state lottery ticket over the former governor's shoe for luck one day, then won $1 million; people have been giving the statue a shoe shine with their lottery tickets ever since.

There is much to see outside the building as well, includ-ing statues of former U.S. president John F. Kennedy, orator Daniel Webster, educator Horace Mann, and Civil War gen-eral Joseph Hooker. Also here are statues of two religious martyrs, Anne Hutchinson and Mary Dyer (Anne was ban-ished, while Mary was hanged on the Boston Common). Outside near the back entrance is a tall column that serves as a perch for a golden eagle. Created by Charles Bulfinch, the monument (which reaches to the original height of Beacon Hill before some 60 feet of it was carted away for landfill) is located on the site where the warning beacon that gave the hill its name once stood. (The bucket of pitch that hung from atop the pole was never set afire; the contraption blew down in 1789.)

The Bull & Finch Pub

At some point during your exploration take a short walk from the State House down Beacon Street to number 84, one of Boston's most visited attractions ever since the barmaid Carla started insulting customers more than a decade ago in a bar made famous on the television show "Cheers." The Bull & Finch Pub (Tel: 617/227-9605), whose name is a play on Charles Bulfinch's surname, indeed played host in the early 1980s to producers who declared it the perfect prototype for the situation comedy they were planning. Fans of the show (and occasionally cast members) have been dropping by for a burger and a brew ever since. Although there are structural differences between the two places, and the waitresses here are much friendlier than Carla, the essence of a Boston neighborhood watering hole is the same. You'll most likely have to wait to get inside.

CHARLES STREET

Close by is Charles Street, which runs more or less north to south through the "flats" of Beacon Hill. Walk along Charles and you'll see a good number of interesting antiques and craft shops, businesses, and restaurants, many of which advertise their services with big cutout signs: an oversized spool of thread for a tailor, a giant key for a locksmith, and a replica of a human spine edging the sign of a chiropractor. The origin of this visual form of advertising dates to the days when only a small percentage of the population could read.

SPRUCE AND CHESTNUT STREETS

Between the State House and the Bull & Finch Pub, at the corner of Spruce Street, a plaque affixed to 50 Beacon Street marks the location of the apple orchard (and possibly the dwelling) once owned by Rev. William Blaxton. Boston's first European settler, Blaxton loved to saddle his pet bull and ride through the land that the Indians called Shawmut (loosely translated as "living waters," which may have been a reference to the springs).

South Slope

Walk up Spruce Street to enter the maze of streets on the so-called South Slope, the part of Beacon Hill associated with wealth and the upper class. The homes here are privately owned and not open to the public, but visitors enjoy strolling through this section to view the architecture. Spruce will take you to Chestnut Street (parallel to Beacon), which has lovely ornamentation, such as elaborate wrought-iron railings and lamps.

Number 29A, a house that dates to 1800, is one of the

earliest mansions built on the hill. The front door faces the side courtyard rather than the street; peek through the gate for the full effect. This structure displays a number of purple panes of glass that have become associated with the look of Beacon Hill. These days the purple windows are a status symbol, but the color is actually caused by a defect in the process of glass making. It began with an 1818 shipment of glass to Boston from Europe that was found to contain too much manganese oxide, which turns purple upon exposure to the sun. One of the more notable occupants of this house was the famous Shakespearean actor Edwin Booth, who was living here when his brother, John Wilkes Booth, assassinated Abraham Lincoln. Horrified, Edwin stole out of town, and his play—about a murderer haunted by his crime—closed down.

Also located on Chestnut Street are the three Swan houses, at numbers 13, 15, and 17, commissioned by Hepzibah Swan as wedding gifts to her daughters. Designed by Charles Bulfinch, these houses are considered prime examples of the Federal style: characterized by a flat façade with slender columns at the doorway and recessed arches around the first-floor windows. During the Civil War number 13 was the home of Julia Ward Howe, a human rights activist best known for her authorship of "The Battle Hymn of the Republic." She also initiated "Mother's Day for Peace," a day she intended to be reserved for mothers to demonstrate their commitment to world peace. (The Swan houses are now privately owned.)

Acorn Street

From Chestnut walk along Willow so that you can enjoy the view down Acorn Street, which branches off Willow to the left. Photographs of vintage Beacon Hill often feature Acorn's narrow cobblestone roadway cutting a rough path between rows of Federal-style, red brick carriage houses. Although Acorn is the narrowest street on the hill, it apparently adheres to the old Colonial city planning regulation that a street be wide enough for two cows to pass each other without rubbing bellies. (Passageways between houses had to be able to accommodate the width of one cow and the height of a boy with a basket on his head.)

MOUNT VERNON STREET

Nichols House Museum

If you continue straight on Willow you'll come to Mount Vernon Street, where visitors are welcome to tour the mansion at number 55 (the only home on the hill open to the public), designed by Bulfinch. This is the Nichols House Museum, established by the will of Rose Standish Nichols, one of the first female American landscape architects and a founder of the Women's International League for Peace and Freedom.

Nichols's home for 75 years, the house is an authentic period mansion rather than a restoration. The rooms retain Nichols's personal belongings and treasures, which include needlework and her own hand-fashioned furniture as well as items brought back from her world travels. There are also three sculptures by Nichols's uncle by marriage, Augustus Saint-Gaudens.

The house is shown by guided tour; for the schedule, Tel: (617) 227-6993.

LOUISBURG SQUARE

Connecting Mount Vernon with Pinckney Street is Louisburg Square, a neighborhood within a neighborhood where the traditions of Christmas caroling and placing seasonal candles in windows began. The park here was made famous by Robert McCloskey in his 1941 children's book *Make Way for Ducklings,* in which Mrs. Mallard considered the place unsuitable for habitation as "there was no water to swim in."

The houses that surround the private park (residents have keys to the gate and are responsible for the park's upkeep) have long been associated with the comings and goings of literati, royalty, politicians, and others in the public eye. The house at number 10 was once the home of Louisa May Alcott; number 20 provided the venue for the wedding of Jenny Lind, the "Swedish Nightingale," and her pianist-conductor, Otto Goldschmidt; numbers 4 and 16 were residences of William Dean Howells, an editor of *The Atlantic Monthly;* and number 19 (the first building erected in the square, in 1834) was the home of Boston mayor Frederick Walker Lincoln when he hosted a reception for the young prince of Wales (later King Edward VII).

PINCKNEY STREET
AND THE NORTH SIDE

Louisburg Square is bordered on one side by Pinckney Street, which acts as the unofficial dividing line between Beacon Hill's elegant South Slope and its North Slope, once nicknamed "Mount Whoredom" because its proximity to the water—and therefore sailors—made it a perfect location for brothels. Nevertheless, the North Slope developed a history apart from its reputation as a red-light district as it became home to the free-black community during the 19th century. The first slaves were brought to Boston in 1638, and slavery was abolished statewide by a Massachusetts Supreme Court ruling in 1783. By 1820 Boston's black population numbered nearly 1,700, almost 4 percent of the total population. The **Black Heritage Trail** is centered on the North Slope; tours of the 15 sites are offered regularly from mid-April through early November by the National Park Service (see Getting Around, below).

Number **62 Pinckney Street** (where it meets Anderson Street) was the home of George Hillard, a U.S. commissioner whose job was to issue warrants for fugitive slaves, and his abolitionist wife, who supposedly hid slaves in the house without (some historians say with) his knowledge. The Hillard home, now privately owned, is thought to have been a stop on the Underground Railroad because of the later discovery of a false ceiling in a closet that led to an attic cubbyhole, where two plates and two spoons were found. If you happen to be exploring the hill toward the end of the day, stand in front of the house and look down Pinckney Street toward the river—it's one of the best spots in all of Boston to view the sunset.

African Meeting House

The treasure of the Black Heritage Trail is the African Meeting House, home of the **Museum of Afro-American History** (Tel: 617/742-1854). Located at 8 Smith Court, a side street off Joy Street (which runs perpendicular to Pinckney), the structure is the oldest standing African-American church building. Although they were welcome to attend local churches, blacks were confined to the galleries (from where it was hard to hear the sermon) and held no voting privileges, so they raised funds to construct a separate place of worship. Completed in 1806 almost entirely by black labor, the African Meeting House became an important center of religious, educational, and political activities—giving rise to its nickname "Black Faneuil Hall." It was here that abolitionist William Lloyd Garrison founded the New England Anti-Slavery Society and the 54th Regiment recruited volunteers.

While examining the displays in the meetinghouse, note that the ceiling arch in the main hall runs north to south for optimum acoustics, allowing anyone who happens to be seated in the galleries to hear the proceedings with no trouble. The building is open daily from 10:00 A.M. to 4:00 P.M.

CHINATOWN AND THE
THEATER DISTRICT

Boston's Chinatown, estimated to be the tenth-largest Asian community in the country, is first and foremost a neighborhood. More than 8,000 people with roots in China, Hong Kong, Taiwan, Burma (now Myanmar), Macao, Vietnam, Thailand, Laos, and Cambodia live and work here, while thousands more commute here to shop for special food and personal items, eat in favorite restaurants, utilize a wide range of multilingual human services, and enjoy the social benefits of being part of a multifaceted Asian community. Other Bostonians and tourists like to come here for the food, especially dim sum, but also to view the public art, participate in cultural festivals, shop (this is the place to find tiger balm, ginseng root, kimonos, and folding fans), and experience an active community where tradition holds strong.

To enter Chinatown's commercial area you might walk east on Boylston Street from its intersection with Tremont (at the southeastern corner of Boston Common, location of the Boylston MBTA station), then turn right on Washington and left onto Beach. But be forewarned that this route cuts through parts of town that are at best unpleasant and at worst unsafe. If you're travelling alone, the better route is through the official Chinatown gateway: Take the Red Line to South Station, then traverse the rather confusing section of streets cut by the John F. Fitzgerald Expressway (I-93); the best strategy here is to walk down Atlantic Avenue (where it parallels the train yard), turn right onto Beach Street, then walk straight ahead until you come to the giant archway guarded by four huge marble lions. The **China Gate** was a gift to the people of Boston by Taiwan in honor of the U.S. bicentennial in 1976, though the structure was not completed until 1982, after the necessary funds had been raised.

As you explore Chinatown you'll notice just how compressed the neighborhood is, considering the large number of people it accommodates. This is because city developers in the 1950s and 1960s were hardly kind when it came to plotting routes for the expressway and the Massachusetts Turnpike, which essentially cut Chinatown's landmass in half and demolished more than 1,000 units of housing at a time when the population was rising rapidly. One Chinatown historian points out the irony of positioning the large red letters "Welcome to Chinatown" along the top edge of the Chinese Merchants Association Building, at 20 Hudson Street, at the corner of Kneeland (it's the building with the large green and red pagoda on its roof). This beautiful structure, ornamented with panels showing figures from the Taoist tradition, was literally sliced in half in the name of progress shortly after it was erected in 1952.

Indeed, the evolution of Boston's Asian community, whose history spans more than a century, has been beset by difficulties. Chinatown, for example, has the dubious distinction of having suffered the largest immigration raid ever executed in the United States. (Only one of the 258 people corralled on October 11, 1903, was unable to produce the required proof of legal residence.) These days the neighborhood is grappling with the persistent efforts of the nearby Tufts Medical Center to expand farther into the community, plus the consequences of the relocation of the Combat Zone (Boston's red-light district) next to Chinatown in the 1960s. (Exploring the area alone during the daytime or early evening is fine, but late-night visits to restaurants, some of which stay open until 3:00 A.M., are best made in groups.)

The struggle of Chinatown to retain its community identity is conveyed in the 1986 mural painted in part as a protest at 34 Oak Street on a location originally eyed by Tufts as part of its intended expansion. A collaboration between artists Wen-ti Tsen and David Fichter, with the help of community leaders and residents, the design for *Unity/Community* grew out of the troubled history of Asian immigration to Boston from the mid-19th century to the present. Today the building, home to the Asian Resource Workshop and a nursery school, remains as much a part of the community as ever.

Around in Chinatown

Walk down Beach and meander at will onto Oxford, Hudson, Tyler, and Harrison streets to discover bakeries selling delicious pastries (cakes of nuts or rice, steamed buns filled with pork or curried beef, and cookies with walnuts or almonds, as well as fortune cookies by the sack); restaurants with bilingual and sometimes trilingual signs and menus (English, Chinese, and Vietnamese, for example); grocery stores with bean thread, dried mushrooms, and poultry so fresh the heads may still be attached; and specialty shops selling Chinese-language magazines and videos and Chinese herbs, clothing, and fabric. Many of the buildings are decorated with bright red, green, and gold, and with architectural motifs drawn from Asian cultures. Occasionally you'll see a small mirror affixed to the outside of a building, said to discourage evil spirits who are so uncomely they frighten themselves with their own appearance.

Many of the earliest Chinese residents came here in the late 1870s to work as laborers in the construction of the Pearl Street telephone exchange near South Station. **Ping On Alley** (now a narrow walkway off Beach Street behind the Imperial Tea House) was the site where Chinatown's first inhabitants made their homes in tents. By 1890 there were approximately 200 Chinese living in the area, only six or seven of whom were women, as the Chinese Exclusion Acts helped create what was essentially a bachelor society of laborers. It wasn't until after World War II—and the repeal of the restrictive acts in 1943—that Chinatown was able to become a home to families in the traditional sense.

OXFORD STREET

A short distance up Oxford Street (near Ping On Alley) you will find a small park with a few benches. On the wall of a building here is the giant **Chinatown Heritage Mural**, completed in 1988 by Wen-ti Tsen, assisted by Yuan Zuo, to highlight the fine Asian collection at Boston's Museum of Fine Arts. The mural is "a copy of a copy," according to Tsen; the original 11th-century work by Chinese painter Fan K'uan was lost, but the copy rendered on silk by Wang Yun in the 17th century is part of the museum's collection. The mural, called *Travel in the Mountain Landscape,* depicts a spiritual journey, as illustrated by the two paths suggested in the mural: one, an easier, more common way, leading to the village; the other, the less travelled, leading to the mountaintop—and enlightenment.

TYLER STREET

Much of Chinatown is built on landfill; the water's edge used to be at the intersection of Beach and Tyler, a location that holds particular significance for admirers of Phillis Wheatley, the first published African-American poet. In 1761 a frail, sick child no more than seven years old arrived at this site (formerly a wharf) on the ship *Phillis* and was sold to Susannah and John Wheatley. Encouraged to learn to read and write, the young girl soon impressed those who knew her with her skillfully crafted verses. Her book *Poems on Various Subjects, Religious and Moral* was published in England in 1773 with a foreword signed by important Bostonians of the day (including John Hancock) attesting that this young black female slave had indeed penned the work within its pages.

The small red-brick building at 12 Tyler Street (the one advertising Sunrise Travel) was the place where Sun Yat-sen is said to have raised funds and planned his strategy in 1905 to establish the Republic of China.

The Quincy School

Those interested in the history of education should take a short walk down Tyler to number 90, once the home of the Quincy School (look for a red-brick building with a statue of Confucius near the entrance). Founded in 1847 and named for Boston's second mayor, Josiah Quincy, this school was the first to separate students into 12 classrooms based on age and level of achievement (it was also the first to provide an individual seat and desk for each student). The new Quincy School, a nationally recognized bilingual elementary school (two blocks away at 885 Washington Street), was opened in the mid-1970s, and the Tyler Street building now serves as a community center and the offices of *Sampan,* Boston's Chinese newspaper.

FESTIVALS

Chinese New Year, which usually falls in February, is celebrated with music, parades, and special programs of dancing and martial arts. The **August Moon Festival**, usually the third Sunday of the month, has a street party atmosphere with outdoor entertainment; moon cakes are served for good luck.

The Theater District

Just south of the Boston Common is Chinatown's next-door neighbor, a three-block area known as the Theater District. Boston enjoys a lively nightlife, and much of the activity takes place here (the nearest MBTA stop is the Boylston station on the Green Line, at the corner of Tremont and Boylston streets). Any night of the week a visitor can find a variety of theater or dance productions at the theaters located here, which include the Wang Center and the Emerson Majestic Theater, among others. Visitors should note that the Theater District is also home to the Combat Zone, with its peep shows and unsavory elements. (See Nightlife, below, for specific dance and theater listings.)

NORTH END

One of the oldest settlements in Boston (and before the Revolution the most fashionable), the North End couldn't help playing a part in the events that shaped America. It was here that Paul Revere was born and lived most of his life. And it was here that two signal lanterns were hung to warn the colonists that the British were indeed coming, and that their route was by water. (A sign inside the North End's Old

North Church, made famous in Longfellow's poem "Paul Revere's Ride," reads: "Remember: If it weren't for Old North Church, you might be making donations in pound notes.") The chance to visit sites where great moments in history occurred is just one of the reasons to visit the North End; another is the opportunity to enjoy the distinctive character of Boston's Little Italy, with its restaurants and cafés. Over the centuries people representing a variety of cultures have called this section of the city home, among them Portuguese, Jews, Irish, and, most recently, Italians. So it is the Italian influence that continues to predominate despite gradual changes caused by gentrification.

HAYMARKET SQUARE

The best place to begin your exploration is Haymarket Square, which most Bostonians consider part of the North End, though the expressway slices it off from the rest of the neighborhood. The insular quality of the North End is nothing new, as it was once set apart by a pond (now filled in) and a creek that ran along the route of Blackstone Street. In the early days, in fact, the parcel of land was referred to as "the island of Boston." Take the T (Orange or Green line) to Haymarket station, walk south along Congress Street toward City Hall, then turn left onto Hanover, one of the North End's main thoroughfares. (Don't even think about driving into the area; streets are narrow and congested, and parking is impossible.)

If you visit on a Friday or Saturday, the section of Hanover located in Haymarket Square will be crowded with pushcarts full of fresh produce in a **farmers' market** tradition that has been going strong since the early settlement days (in the distant past hay was also sold here, hence the name).

Before following Hanover in the direction of the expressway, take a minute to walk down Marshall Street (on the right) and around the corner of the red-brick building that houses **Boston Stone Gift Shop** to its side entrance. Set against the base of the building is a worn millstone resting atop a rough piece of stone that bears the inscription "Boston Stone 1737." Brought from England in 1635, the stone was used as a paint millstone by Thomas Child, a painter who operated his shop nearby. For a reason that no one has been able to determine with any certainty (though perhaps in imitation of the London Stone), it is said that the millstone may have been the marker for the center of town from which distances were measured (the State House dome, on Beacon Hill, now holds that honor). Whether the stone ever actually performed this function is in dispute, but people like to repeat the story.

The flavor of what the town must have been like in the 17th century survives right in this city block. Take a look down the narrow, winding lanes and note the **Union Oyster House**, at 41 Union Street; a restaurant since the early 19th century, the 1714 building originally housed a dry-goods shop and was once home to the *Massachusetts Spy,* a Whig party newspaper published from 1771 to 1775. This was also the place where future French king Louis Philippe gave French lessons during his exile. At 10 Marshall Street is the **Ebenezer Hancock House** (now occupied by lawyers), which was owned by John Hancock's younger brother, paymaster for the Continental army.

Continue down Hanover Street to the crosswalk over Blackstone Street (named in honor of William Blaxton, Boston's first settler), then just follow the trail of garbage—bronzed garbage, that is, created by local artist Mags Harries—that leads across the street to the pedestrian walkway underneath the expressway. Then follow the red-brick path of the Freedom Trail over Cross Street and around the corner to Hanover. (See the Getting Around section for more on the Freedom Trail.)

HANOVER STREET

The main commercial street in the North End, Hanover is lined with shops that reflect the Italian culture. You can get cannoli or calzone in a bakery, eat pizza or pasta in a *ristorante,* linger over a *cappuccino* in **Café Paradiso**, at number 255, or **Café Pompei**, at number 280, buy a pasta machine or espresso pot, or cull Italian designer clothing and jewelry closeouts in a shop appropriately named **Liquidazione**, at number 228.

On the sidewalk you'll probably have to work your way around clumps of men engaged in animated *conversazione* while women, their elbows propped on windowsills, watch them (and everybody else) from second-story windows. On summer weekends the streets come alive with neighborhood *feste* featuring processions (where money for charity is pinned to the statue of an honored saint), music, dancing, games, and, of course, food. Hanover Street also provides an ideal reference point for exploring the historic sites in the area—and if you happen to get lost you can always follow the Freedom Trail's red-brick path back to Haymarket.

NORTH SQUARE

Paul Revere House

One of the main attractions in the North End is the Paul Revere House (follow the red-brick path to the right off

Hanover down Richmond and then left up North Street). Located at 19 North Square, the house was nearly 100 years old when Paul Revere purchased it in 1770 a few months before the Boston Massacre. It had been built on the site of another home, first occupied by a sea captain named Kemble. That poor man was sentenced by the Puritans to two hours in the stocks for what they considered lewd behavior: Upon returning from a three-year voyage, he kissed his wife on the steps of their house—on a Sunday, no less. The house, which then passed to the Reverend Increase Mather, burned down in 1676 and another was built in its place in 1680 and sold to a wealthy merchant named Robert Howard.

Decades later when Revere moved in there were three floors (today there are two and a half), providing ample space for Revere's growing family, which would eventually total 16 children by his two wives, first Sara Orne (who died after the birth of their eighth child) and then Rachel Walker. During the 30 years he owned this house, from the age of 35 to 65, Revere was truly a man of all trades, working as a silversmith fashioning fine bowls and silverware, casting bells (there is one on display in the courtyard), making copper spikes and bolts for the USS *Constitution* (he would later provide the copper plating for the ship's hull as well), practicing as a dentist of sorts (it is said that when his friend Joseph Warren fell at the Battle of Bunker Hill, Revere was able to identify the body by the dental work he had done), and acting as express rider for the cause of independence.

The exterior of the house has been restored to its original 17th-century appearance, and exhibits the architectural fashion of Robert Howard's day; note the second-floor overhang with pendant drops at the corners, the diamond window casements, and the dozens of decorative nails in the front door (at that time nails were very expensive). Inside, visitors are welcome to tour the rooms, which have been outfitted in part with some of the Revere family's possessions. The house has been operated as a museum by the Paul Revere Memorial Association since 1908. Tel: (617) 523-2338.

The association also conducts year-round guided tours of the adjacent **Pierce/Hichborn House** (built about 1711, the structure is considered an excellent example of the symmetrical style that characterized early Georgian architecture) and summer walking tours of sites associated with Paul Revere (among them are the former locations of his shop and the tavern where he conspired with other Sons of Liberty).

Mariner's House

The Second Church of Boston—the original "Old North," which the British tore apart for firewood in 1776—once stood at the head of the North Square triangle. On your way up North Street, take note of the Mariner's House (built in 1838), at 11 North Square, which is said to be so well funded that retired mariners who stay here need pay only four dollars per week for the privilege. (The octagonal cupola on its roof allows residents a view of the water.) Though visitors may not explore the interior of this private building, if the door happens to be open—as it often is in fine weather— take a peek at the private garden within.

A short walk up Garden Court to number 4 will bring you to the birthplace of Rose Fitzgerald Kennedy. Then turn left on Fleet Street to return to Hanover.

PAUL REVERE MALL

A short distance down Hanover and on the left is Paul Revere Mall, directly across from **St. Stephen's Catholic Church**. Originally called the New North Meeting House—and of Congregational denomination at that time—this was the house of worship attended by Paul Revere and his family. Built in 1714, the structure was redesigned in 1804 by architect Charles Bulfinch, making it the last Bulfinch-designed church remaining in Boston.

If you stand at the entrance to the mall (and no closer) you will see one of the best photographic compositions in Boston: the statue of Paul Revere mounted on a horse against the backdrop of the Old North Church's spire and framed by a line of trees on either side. While it provides a pleasant passageway to Old North Church, the mall itself— with its spacious red-brick plaza, numerous benches, and flower urns—is an enjoyable place to relax for a while. Buy a slush from a vendor, eavesdrop on the *conversazione* around you, check out who's winning at cards or checkers, watch kids racing in circles around the fountain's edge (it's always dry), or feed the perpetually hungry pigeons before walking through to the other side of the mall and up the stairs to the entrance of Christ Church—what we know as Old North.

Old North Church

Built in 1723, Christ Church is the oldest church building in Boston; despite the thousands of visitors who come here each year (admission is free but donations are encouraged), it is not a museum at all but a working church of Episcopal denomination with Anglican roots. This was indeed the place where sexton Robert Newman, at the request of his friend Paul Revere, hung two lanterns in the steeple (at 191 feet the tallest in town) on the night of April 18, 1775, to signal that the British would be heading for Concord by a water route. After giving the signal—a momentous occasion that most likely lasted all of about 20 seconds—Newman beat a hasty retreat out the window you see in the front of the church, but he was later caught and jailed by the British. (This window was discovered behind a wall by a workman only a few years ago.)

Though we have come to associate this church we call Old North with Paul Revere because of the event that sent him on his famous midnight ride, he did not worship here; however, as a young teen he organized a guild with a half-dozen friends to ring the eight bells in the steeple that are still sounded today for services (these days students from the Massachusetts Institute of Technology do the honors). Later in life Revere would cast an estimated 100 bells in his foundry.

The famous steeple, incidentally, is not the original but a replacement built in 1955; its two predecessors were destroyed by high winds.

The interior of the church has been restored to its early appearance with original, candle-lit chandeliers, a wooden clock on the back wall that has kept time for more than two and a half centuries (it runs a little fast), the first pipe organ ever built in America (note the four trumpeting angels in the loft—controversial booty from a pirate ship), and box pews with chin-high wooden walls, so constructed to keep in the heat generated by foot warmers and, in extremely cold weather, the family dog.

Church staff members are always on hand to answer questions and give a short talk about the history of the church, and they are sure to caution you to walk gently in deference to the more than 1,000 former parishioners who lie buried in the 37 crypts just under the floorboards. The church is open daily to visitors from 9:00 A.M. to 5:00 P.M.

Next door to the church is the **Old North Museum and Gift Shop**. A small section in the back contains a display of memorabilia from America's early history: a musket from the Battle of Lexington, the sword of Colonel Robert Gould Shaw (commander of the 54th Regiment from Massachusetts portrayed in the film *Glory*), and a strand of George Washington's hair donated by his godson (it's blond). Among the items for sale are copies of Paul Revere's bell-ringing contract with the church.

COPP'S HILL

From directly in front of the church follow the Freedom Trail up Hull Street to the top of the hill. The gate for one of the oldest graveyards in the city, Copp's Hill, is on your right (open every day until sunset). But before you enter, take a look across the street at number 44, a house reputed to be the narrowest in Boston (about ten feet wide). With frontage enough for only one shuttered window, the home is rumored to have been built in the early 1800s out of spite—to obstruct the view of a feuding neighbor.

If you have never visited an old New England cemetery, Copp's Hill, with its winding brick paths and stately trees—and its estimated 10,000 burials—is an excellent example. Winged skulls and an occasional family coat of arms decorate tombstones that date to the mid-1600s—though markers have been moved around so much over the years (and sometimes stand three deep) that there is little correspondence between the name on a stone and the location of the earthly remains. The earliest tombstone dates to 1625 and marks the burial place of a Plymouth settler whose body was brought here by her husband (the Puritans did not settle Boston until 1630).

While there has been some vandalism over the years, the tumble of cracked, eroded markers is more the result of centuries of New England weather than mischief. Daniel Malcolm's tombstone (1769; located just off the center path) was vandalized by British soldiers who used it for target practice, most likely because the merchant had been well known for opposing British-imposed taxes. Note the right eyeball on the winged skull, which one sharpshooter managed to hit dead center. Copp's Hill is also the final resting place for Old North Church sexton Robert Newman; Edmund Hartt, builder of the USS *Constitution;* the Reverends Increase, Cotton, and Samuel Mather; and approximately 1,000 slaves and free blacks who lived in the first black community in the area (called New Guinea), which was situated on the north slope below Charter Street.

At the bottom of Copp's Hill are the Charles River and, just beyond, Charlestown (home of the USS *Constitution* and the Bunker Hill Monument, discussed below); it was from the foot of the hill that Paul Revere was rowed across the water to begin his famous ride on the night of April 18, 1775. If you happen to smell a faint odor of something sweet in the air, it's because not far from here occurred the Great Molasses Explosion, one of the most unusual disasters in history. Just above Commercial Street, west of North End Park, there once stood an enormous tank 50 feet high and 282 feet in girth. On January 15, 1919, it contained almost two and a half million gallons of molasses waiting to be distilled into rum—overfilled by some 200,000 gallons, according to a subsequent investigation. At 12:41 P.M. neighbors heard a series of sharp explosions as the rivets popped, then a rumbling noise as one whole side of the tank flew into the park and a 50-foot-high wave of molasses rolled down Commercial Street at an estimated 35 miles per hour, engulfing all in its path. According to the *Boston Globe* report of the incident, "Firefighters drowned in the sugary mire, horses were trapped like flys to flypaper and were shot by police. Survivors had to be cut from their clothing, and buildings were ripped from their foundations." When it was over, the toll was 21 dead, 150 injured, dozens of horses lost, and damage exceeding $1 million (a successful damage suit held the company accountable). It took a week to recover all the bodies and weeks more to clean up the mess—though some residents of the area claim that the sickly sweet smell has never quite disappeared.

THE WATERFRONT

Over the centuries the Boston shoreline has edged away from what was once the town center, as a combination of landfill and silt accumulation has extended the city seaward, but through it all the ever-changing waterfront has played a major role in city life. Shipping no longer dominates the activity here as it did in the past; at one time there were an estimated 80 wharves jutting into the water to facilitate the comings and goings of boats laden with bananas, rum, spices, cloth, furniture, and other imports, with codfish as a key export. Today that type of trade has been largely replaced by recreation. Museums, hotels, restaurants, and excursion-boat operations intermingle with apartments and offices, some refashioned from the old granite warehouses that formerly housed commercial goods.

STATE STREET

A good place to begin a stroll along Boston's waterfront is the top of State Street, which was once known as "the great street to the sea." (Pick up a free HarborWalk map for easy reference at the National Park Service Visitor Center across from the Blue Line's State Street station.) In the 19th century the water was closer to the town center, which is why the **Custom House** (notable for its tall tower) is situated where it is on State Street. Now surrounded by buildings, it was once right at the water's edge, built on 3,000 piles at the head of the dock between two of the major wharves (Long and Central). A glance reveals that it was constructed in two phases: The granite Greek temple with a dome and fluted columns (each a solid piece weighing 42 tons) was completed in 1847; the 29-story tower was finished in 1915 and made the building the tallest skyscraper in New England. The tower also served as a symbol of government's disregard for its own rules: The city had established a 125-foot height restriction for buildings, which the 495-foot tower flagrantly exceeded.

LONG WHARF

If you continue walking down State Street and cross Atlantic Avenue you'll come to Long Wharf. Built in 1711, the wharf (the longest in the city) once stretched approximately one-third of a mile, beginning at the top of State Street. The length has since been cut by landfill, but its role in Boston's history has not diminished. A major site of trade activity during the 18th century, Long Wharf was also the place where the British landed when the time came to put the Colonial "hotheads" in their place. (The British also evacuated from here after their defeat.)

Today there's a public park with benches and telescopes on the cobblestone plaza at the very end of the wharf, a pleasant place to catch a cool breeze on a hot day. The huge granite building that dominates the farthest point near the water served as a customs station but now houses offices and residences. Nathaniel Hawthorne served as a customs inspector here while working on *Twice Told Tales* in his spare time. Behind the former customs station a branch of the Chart House chain of restaurants occupies a former brick warehouse dating to the mid-1700s. The oversized nuts and bolts protruding from the outside walls of the building were added later to hold iron bars in place that help support the building as it settles (note the cracks and uneven fall of bricks beneath the windows).

But the main attraction on the wharf in the summertime is the line-up of **excursion boats** waiting to take passengers on tours of the inner and outer harbor (and all the way out to the Boston Harbor Islands, which we discuss below), on whale watches, and to the Charlestown Navy Yard (also discussed in the pages that follow). For more specific information, see Getting Around, below.

CENTRAL WHARF

New England Aquarium

Just south of Long Wharf is Central Wharf, home of the New England Aquarium. The 45-foot wind sculpture on the plaza,

Echo of the Waves, was constructed by Susumu Shingu to suggest the movements of water.

More than 70 exhibit tanks fill the aquarium's galleries, but the centerpiece is the 187,000-gallon ocean tank—one of the largest of its type in the world—that rises four stories to offer a sort of theater-in-the-round view of the sea turtles, moray eels, sharks, and tropical fish that live inside. Other popular exhibits are the man-made tide pool with its own tides (kids are welcome to climb on the rocky shore and touch the starfish and horseshoe crabs that dwell here), the floating sea lion pavilion, and the outdoor harbor seal pool (some of the playful residents came to the aquarium as orphaned pups who were rescued and raised by the staff).

The aquarium is open daily throughout the year from 9:00 A.M. to at least 5:00 P.M., with longer hours on Thursdays and in summer; Tel: (617) 973-5200. The Aquarium's boat, *Voyager II,* runs daily whale-watching excursions from April through October; Tel: (617) 973-5277.

ROWES WHARF

Walking a bit farther south along the waterfront will bring you past India Wharf to Rowes Wharf, once owned by merchant and revolutionary patriot John Rowe. It is reported that Rowe was the troublemaker who planted the question in the minds of the angry colonists gathered at the Old South Meeting House the evening of the Boston Tea Party: "Who knows how tea will mingle with salt water?" (He is also said to have asked the captain of one of the controversial ships laden with tea—which happened to be docked at his wharf—to move the vessel to another wharf, as he didn't want any trouble.) Rowe is credited with presenting the "Sacred Cod" to the Massachusetts House of Representatives, in whose chamber the wooden sculpture has hung for good luck ever since.

Rowes wharf was completely redesigned in 1987 to house the Boston Harbor Hotel (see Accommodations, below), offices, and condominiums in a striking complex that features a six-story arched passageway to the water. The plaza has an outdoor restaurant and café in the summer and a dock for the Logan Airport Water Shuttle and other commuter boats.

BOSTON TEA PARTY SHIP
AND MUSEUM

If you proceed south along Atlantic Avenue to the Congress Street intersection you'll come to the site of three of Boston's most unusual museums. (The nearest MBTA stop is

South Station on the Red Line.) Griffin's Wharf, the original site of the Boston Tea Party, is no longer in existence; however, the Boston Tea Party Ship and Museum at the Congress Street Bridge manages quite effectively to capture the essence of the real thing in spite of its change of venue. Visitors may explore the *Beaver II,* a full-scale working replica of one of the original ships involved in the "party" on a December night in 1773, and may even hurl a bale of "tea" into the water. On the Sunday closest to December 16, the anniversary of the Boston Tea Party, the *Beaver II* is the stage for a reenactment of the colorful event that quickened the onset of the Revolution with the battle cry: "Taxation without representation is tyranny!"

The ship is open to visitors daily from 9:00 A.M. until dusk; Tel: (617) 338-1773.

MUSEUM WHARF

Computer Museum

Across the Congress Street Bridge is Museum Wharf, home of the Computer Museum and the Children's Museum. If you do nothing more than take a stroll through the giant walk-through desktop computer that occupies the fifth and sixth floors, a visit to the Computer Museum, at 300 Congress Street, will be rewarding no matter how computer literate you may or may not be. Roll the five-foot-high trackball (if you can muster the strength) to engage the computer program; called the "World Traveler," the program sets up a series of interactive questions and answers about geography. Elsewhere in the museum, denizens of the Smart Machines section will estimate your height (though on occasion lopping off a good quarter-inch for unknown reasons) and spell your name in blocks by means of a robotic arm (which sometimes has a bit of trouble with the alphabet). Other hands-on exhibits allow you to use a computer to paint a picture, compose a song, fly a plane, or haggle over the price of potatoes. The museum store in the lobby is a good place to seek out the perfect gift for your favorite hacker.

The world's only museum devoted solely to computers is open daily, except Mondays, from 10:00 A.M. to 5:00 P.M. In summer the museum stays open an extra hour every day, and on Fridays until 9:00 P.M.; Tel: (617) 426-2800.

Children's Museum

Next door is the Children's Museum, established in 1913 by a group of university and classroom teachers who believed that learning need not be confined to the classroom. If you're travelling with kids, the Children's Museum may save your vacation, as its three floors of exhibits are guaranteed to keep any child from infancy to age 15 happily occupied for hours. To locate specific exhibits pick up a free map at the entrance or use the computers set up on each floor. For parents with small children, the best place to start is the second floor, where you can park your stroller or borrow a baby backpack if you need one.

Overall, the Children's Museum specializes in exhibits that are hands-on; kids are *supposed* to touch everything. There are climbing environments and play spaces for different age groups; organized activities for tots, such as finger painting and collage making; a dance floor with a video screen onto which images of the dancing children are projected; and an area called Studio 10/15, a private haven for kids aged 10 to 15, where they can learn how to write song lyrics, record music videos, try different arts and crafts, or just hang out for a while. Exhibits are multicultural; dolls come in all human shades, and hopscotch games are written out in Chinese, Italian, and other languages. The museum has a shop on the first floor; the Recycle Room, on the second floor, sells used items, some for as little as a nickel apiece. Summertime brings plenty of outdoor activities, too: miniature golf, magicians, jugglers, clowns, drummers, and traditional dance troupes from different cultures.

The museum is open daily in the summer from 10:00 A.M. to 5:00 P.M.; closed Mondays from September to June. Hours are extended on Fridays year-round to 9:00 P.M. (when admission is also discounted). Tel: (617) 426-8855.

BOSTON HARBOR ISLANDS

Just off the coast of Boston is a group of 27 islands that beckon visitors with their colorful history, involving pirates, buried treasure, shipwrecks, unsolved murders, and ghosts. Catch a boat at Long Wharf (near the Blue Line's Aquarium station) for a 90-minute narrated tour of the islands (note that park rangers and volunteers from Friends of the Boston Harbor sometimes disagree on details of history rendered as fact by the captains). **Bay State Cruise Company** (Tel: 617/ 723-7800) stops at Georges Island, where you may disembark and do some exploring. Then you might take a later boat back to the mainland or, in summer, take a water taxi (also operated by Bay State Cruises) from here to one of the other islands that permit visitors. Boats operate from mid-April through mid-October. Lovells, Peddocks, Grape, and Bumpkin islands have very basic camping facilities (there are restrooms, but food and water must be brought along).

For the most part, the Boston Harbor Islands are uninhabited, and therefore lack creature comforts. For more information about camping in the Boston Harbor Islands State Park (and about the islands in general), call the Metropolitan District Commission; Tel: (617) 727-5215.

GEORGES ISLAND

Georges Island provides a marked contrast to the over-developed Boston waterfront you left behind at the wharf. The island is named after its former owner, John George, a Boston merchant who lived in the late 1600s (there's no apostrophe in the official name, which tends to unsettle grammarians and copy editors). The island is well prepared for visitors, with walking tours, a snack bar, restrooms, and maps of the fort that occupies a good chunk of its area.

Fort Warren

Fort Warren served during the Civil War as a prison for captured Confederates, which created the circumstances for the story of "the Lady in Black," the island's ghost. Her name was Melanie Lanier; her husband, Samuel Lanier, was a Confederate soldier incarcerated on the island. Determined to free him, Melanie disguised herself as a Union soldier and rowed over to the island, where, the story goes, the two were reunited but were caught when trying to escape. Melanie tried to resist capture with the gun she had brought along, but accidentally killed her husband instead. Brought to trial and sentenced to be hanged as a spy, Melanie requested that she be dressed as a lady at the end, so black fabric was found for her to fashion a garment. Her troubled spirit has reportedly haunted the island ever since.

Visitors may examine the prisoners' living quarters, where Samuel Lanier and his compatriots were confined, and other features of the fort. Especially rewarding on a hot day is searching out the fort's "cold room" (it's also a dark room, so bring a flashlight). Enter through the brick archway at the southeastern corner of the parade ground; once inside the archway head toward the doorway cut into the right-hand corner of the room. Go down the hall (where it begins to get really dark), feeling along the left-hand wall until you come to an opening. Go through the entranceway and push open the gates that lead into the cold room. Enjoy.

LOVELLS ISLAND

Lovells Island, a short water-taxi ride from Georges, has a beach for swimming, piers for fishing, camping facilities, and a very friendly rabbit population. Although it was rejected as the site for the Statue of Liberty, the island had earlier had a brush with fame when the *Magnifique,* a French man-of-war, sank offshore in 1782. Because its Boston pilot was blamed for the incident, the American government felt compelled to compensate the French for the loss with a new ship, the *America.* (John Paul Jones, an American naval hero who had been promised the ship, promptly resigned his post.) There were rumors that the *Magnifique*'s treasure had been lost, and one day a resident of Lovells actually uncovered a few gold coins while digging in his garden. The story goes that upon returning from a brief absence shortly afterward the owner discovered that there was a deep hole in his garden and his hired help had disappeared. Many people accepted this as proof that the *Magnifique* treasure had been found and spirited away. Still, visitors usually keep an eye out for gold coins when walking on the island's beach.

CASTLE ISLAND

Castle Island, the closest of the group to Boston, is now a peninsula since its connection by landfill to the mainland in 1891. The pentagonal fort claiming the bulk of the landmass is **Fort Independence**, one of America's oldest (1834) military fortifications and the inspiration for Edgar Allan Poe's story "The Cask of Amontillado." Although the events remain unsubstantiated, it is said that while Poe, a young soldier, was stationed here in 1827, he heard gossip about an officer who had been walled up and left to die. Long after Poe's death, a skeleton was supposedly discovered behind a wall during renovations.

Castle Island is popular in summer as visitors come to tour the fort or sun on the beach. If you're driving, take exit 17 (South Boston/Dorchester) off the Southeast Expressway, turn left onto Columbia Road, then right at the rotary onto Day Boulevard. Or take the City Point bus from Broadway, South, or Dudley station.

CHARLESTOWN NAVY YARD

A water shuttle operated by Boston Harbor Cruises (Tel: 617/227-4320) from Long Wharf runs from mid-April to mid-October to the Charlestown Navy Yard, which served the United States Navy for 174 years and is now a member of the Boston National Historical Park system.

The major attraction here is the USS *Constitution,* which dates to 1797. The frigate, constructed of oak, cedar, pitch pine, and locust wood, earned its nickname "Old Ironsides" in the War of 1812 when she engaged the British frigate HMS

Guerrière in a victorious battle. When shots from the enemy made no impression on the *Constitution*'s outer planking, one of the British sailors was heard to shout, "Huzza! Her sides are made of iron!" Still a member of the fleet of the U.S. Navy, the *Constitution* is the oldest fully commissioned warship in the world. Visitors are invited to explore the ship, which is currently manned by 46 active-duty sailors. The ship and the **USS Constitution Museum** (Tel: 617/426-1812), which tells the story of the frigate's past, are open daily from 9:00 A.M. to 6:00 P.M. in the summer; in winter closing time is 4:00 P.M., in spring and fall 5:00 P.M.

Also berthed in the Navy Yard is the USS *Cassin Young,* which served from 1943 to 1960. It was named for Captain Cassin Young, who was awarded the Medal of Honor at Pearl Harbor. Park rangers conduct regular tours of the ship, which is representative of those destroyers built in Charlestown in the early 1940s.

BUNKER HILL PAVILION AND MONUMENT

Charlestown is also the home of the Bunker Hill Pavilion and Monument. The pavilion is located just outside the Navy Yard. Go out Gate 1 (next to Building 5) and walk about 200 yards up Water Street. Here you can enjoy a 30-minute audio-visual presentation of the Battle of Bunker Hill (Tel: 617/241-7575).

The monument is a short walk from the Navy Yard. Head toward the massive granite obelisk by walking up Adams Street and turning right onto Winthrop Street, which curves to the top of Breed's Hill, where the Battle of Bunker Hill was actually fought. It was here that the patriots constructed a fortification of earth and timber literally overnight to prepare for the onslaught of British soldiers on June 17, 1775. Though the battle was technically a British victory, the patriots killed or wounded nearly half of their attackers, resulting in a major blow to enemy morale. The monument, which was built between 1825 and 1842, has an observatory at the top. If you climb the 294 steps leading up to it you will be rewarded by a view of the harbor, the City of Boston, and nearby Bunker Hill. Tel: (617) 242-5641.

JOHN F. KENNEDY LIBRARY AND MUSEUM

The Boston Harbor Cruises water shuttle (Tel: 617/227-4320) from Long Wharf, which operates mid-April to mid-October, offers easy access to the John F. Kennedy Library and Museum, located at Columbia Point in Dorchester, one of Boston's neighborhoods. If you are driving from Boston, take the Southeast Expressway to exit 15, then follow the signs for the University of Massachusetts and JFK Library. By public transit, take the Red Line to the JFK/UMass station, where a free shuttle bus runs to the library every half hour between 9:00 A.M. and 5:00 P.M.

Dedicated to the memory of John Fitzgerald Kennedy, the 35th president of the United States, the library was built with donations from millions of people and presented to the U.S. government in 1979. The half-hour biographical film provides a context for the displays, which trace the personal and professional life of the president. Exhibits include a replica of the Oval Office, furnished with the rocking chair Kennedy favored. Photographs, audio tapes, letters, and hundreds of other objects that evoke Kennedy's memory fill out the collection. A special section is devoted to the career of JFK's brother Robert. The John F. Kennedy Library and Museum is open daily from 9:00 A.M. to 5:00 P.M.; Tel: (617) 929-4523.

BACK BAY

If you began your explorations of Boston along the meandering cow paths of Beacon Hill, the Back Bay will come as a pleasant, orderly surprise. Unlike the original section of Boston, which encompassed the Shawmut Peninsula (where bovines are blamed for creating the paths that determined the twists and turns in the streets), the newer Back Bay was laid out on paper before any streets were built. (The only construction here had been Mill Dam, built in 1818, which ran along what is now Beacon Street, then known as Dam Road.) The reason for the uncharacteristic foresight rests on one factor alone: The entire Back Bay was under water and had to be filled before it could be developed. Before this was accomplished, Boston proper ended at what is now Charles Street, at the western edge of Boston Common. (When the British piled into boats on the night of April 18, 1775, to launch their attack on the Patriots, they were rowing through the waters of the Back Bay.) The landfill project began after a development plan was adopted in 1857, and for the next 30 years gravel was brought in by train from the suburb of Needham and dumped into the water, beginning at the edge of Boston Common.

The result of the planned development of the Back Bay neighborhood is a grid formed by five parallel streets running the length of the eight-block rectangle (Boylston,

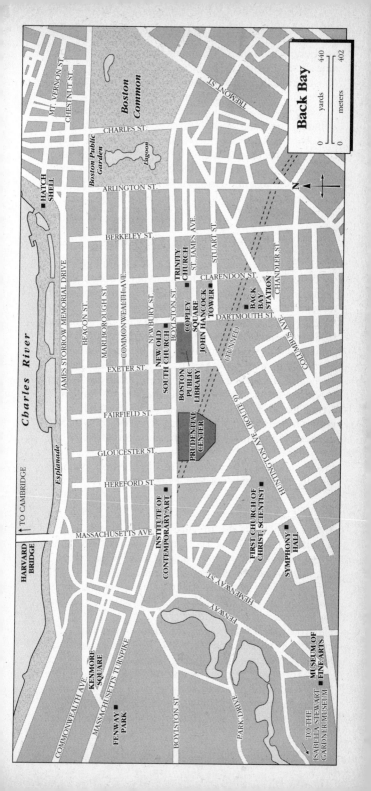

Back Bay

yards 0 440

meters 0 402

N

Charles River

Boston Common

Boston Public Garden

Lagoon

Hatch Shell

Esplanade

TO CAMBRIDGE

HARVARD BRIDGE

MT. VERNON ST.

CHESTNUT ST.

CHARLES ST.

ARLINGTON ST.

BERKELEY ST.

CLARENDON ST.

DARTMOUTH ST.

EXETER ST.

FAIRFIELD ST.

GLOUCESTER ST.

HEREFORD ST.

MASSACHUSETTS AVE.

JAMES STORROW MEMORIAL DRIVE

BEACON ST.

MARLBOROUGH ST.

COMMONWEALTH AVE.

NEWBURY ST.

BOYLSTON ST.

ST. JAMES AVE.

STUART ST.

TREMONT ST.

CHANDLER ST.

COLUMBUS AVE.

HUNTINGTON AVE. (ROUTE 9)

HEMENWAY ST.

FENWAY

PARK DRIVE

BOYLSTON ST.

MASSACHUSETTS TURNPIKE

COMMONWEALTH AVE.

KENMORE SQUARE

TURNPIKE

TRINITY CHURCH

COPLEY SQUARE

NEW OLD SOUTH CHURCH

JOHN HANCOCK TOWER

BOSTON PUBLIC LIBRARY

PRUDENTIAL CENTER

BACK BAY STATION

INSTITUTE OF CONTEMPORARY ART

FIRST CHURCH OF CHRIST, SCIENTIST

SYMPHONY HALL

FENWAY PARK

MUSEUM OF FINE ARTS

TO THE ISABELLA STEWART GARDNER MUSEUM

Newbury, Marlborough, Commonwealth, and Beacon) and nine streets crossing the width (Arlington, Berkeley, Clarendon, Dartmouth, Exeter, Fairfield, Gloucester, and Hereford streets, and Massachusetts Avenue).

The best way to explore the Back Bay is to begin at Arlington Street and work your way southwest to Massachusetts Avenue, locally known as Mass. Ave. Take the Green Line to the Arlington stop or, if you're walking from Beacon Hill, simply cross over Charles Street from the Boston Common into the adjacent Boston Public Garden, which was the first parcel of land to be filled and developed.

Boston Public Garden

There was a time when all 24 acres of the Boston Public Garden was referred to as "the marsh at the bottom of the Common." Thanks to the landfill project that slowly extended the dimensions of the city, and the petitions of Horace Gray (an iron heir and professed lover of camellias), the section of land now bounded by Charles, Beacon, Arlington, and Boylston streets was set aside for use as a botanical garden as early as 1837, but it wasn't until 1859 that a law was passed guaranteeing that no building could ever be erected in this section. Landscape architect George Meacham laid out plans for a formal garden with flower beds (America's first tulips, imported from Holland, were planted here) and paths loosely modeled after a French park. More than a century and a half later, in the midst of a city congested with buildings and too much traffic and what at times seems like entirely too many people, this beautiful, quiet refuge remains.

THE LAGOON

The centerpiece is the irregularly shaped lagoon (so designed to make it look larger than it is, just under four acres), where four swans—named Castor, Pollux, Romeo, and Juliet—and countless ducks swim every summer. The best view of the lagoon is from the tiny suspension bridge (long ago dubbed the "Bridge of Size") that carries the garden's main path over the water.

If you visit between April and October you'll have the opportunity to take a ride on one of Boston's famous **Swan Boats**, which have been gliding across the lagoon since 1877. The boats were the brainchild of Robert Paget (the Paget family still operates the business), who had been rowing passengers around the lagoon but wanted to find a way to conceal the new paddle-box mechanism he had adopted to power the crafts. His answer came from the opera *Lohengrin,* in which a knight saves his princess by crossing a river in a boat pulled by a swan. Paget added the silhouette of a swan and the Swan Boats were born.

AROUND IN THE GARDEN

The natural beauty of the garden is accented with many statues and monuments. Near the Arlington Street gates is a 38-foot-tall memorial to **George Washington**, who is shown astride his horse (Thomas Jefferson called Washington the best horseman of his era). The statue was unveiled for the Fourth of July festivities in 1869. Another notable monument is that of the **Good Samaritan**, near Beacon Street, erected to commemorate the first use of ether in the world (in an operation at Boston's Massachusetts General Hospital).

But the garden's most popular sculpture these days is the family of ducks that can be found tramping through the grass near the corner of Beacon and Charles streets. The bronze **Mrs. Mallard and her eight ducklings** (Jack, Kack, Lack, Mack, Nack, Ouack, Pack, and Quack), fashioned by local artist Nancy Schon, were placed here in 1987 in tribute to Robert McCloskey's 1941 children's story *Make Way for Ducklings,* the tale of a family of ducks that comes to live on the island in the middle of the lagoon.

The Streets of the Back Bay

After visiting the Public Garden, you'll need to decide which of the Back Bay's five parallel streets to stroll along—an easy decision to make depending upon whether your primary interest lies in history, architecture, or shopping. As it developed in the late 19th century, the Back Bay became the fashionable place to live, with a definite pecking order. It is said that the "old rich" chose to live on Beacon Street, the "old poor" on Marlborough, the "new rich" on Commonwealth, and the "new poor" on Newbury. Although many of the lovely houses that were built then still stand, they have been converted from single-family homes to other uses. These days Beacon, Marlborough, and Commonwealth are primarily residential—apartments and condominiums interspersed with private clubs and college dorms; Boylston and Newbury are lined with stores, restaurants, and offices. While the charm of 19th-century architecture remains, Back Bay inhabitants are no longer defined by their streets. Today students and working professionals can be found living next door to the old rich.

BEACON AND MARLBOROUGH STREETS

Beacon and Marlborough streets provide some fine examples of 19th-century architectural features: Classical Revival bowfronts, Victorian Gothic gingerbread gables, and Queen Anne wrought-iron fencing and ornamentation. Across from the Boston Public Garden starting at River Street are six white houses at numbers 70 through 75 Beacon Street that were built in 1828 along the Mill Dam, making them the oldest structures in the Back Bay. The mansion at 53 Marlborough Street (on the corner of Berkeley) was the family home of sculptor Katherine Lane Weems, who created the group of dolphins in front of the New England Aquarium. In 1961 she donated the building to the **French Library**, whose purpose is to provide information about the culture and language of France and French-speaking nations. The library presents lectures, art and photography exhibitions, French musical performances, films, and language classes, and sponsors a Bastille Day party every July 14. Tel: (617) 266-4351.

COMMONWEALTH AVENUE

Commonwealth Avenue (usually called simply Comm. Ave.) shows off some of the best planning done for the Back Bay. The key feature of this grand residential street, which was patterned after the wide boulevards of Paris, is its central mall, a park-like stretch of greenery that begins at the Public Garden and runs the entire length of the Back Bay. The mall contains varieties of elm (some of which have been lost to disease), maple, green ash, and sweet gum trees, among others. Over the years statues of famous men have been placed in the mall, including Leif Eriksson, Alexander Hamilton, and William Lloyd Garrison.

NEWBURY STREET

Newbury Street, lined with three- to five-story red-brick houses featuring bay windows and ornamental brickwork, is the Back Bay's showcase retail area. If your time is limited—or if your favorite activity is shopping—this is the street to explore. Its residential character was altered soon after the turn of the century, when the advent of the automobile allowed people to move to the suburbs, and the street was transformed into an exclusive shopping area, now full of galleries, boutiques, and salons, as well as restaurants and cafés, such as the elegant **29 Newbury Street Restaurant**, at Arlington Street, and the **Harvard Bookstore Café**, at number 190 (at Exeter Street). (For a discussion of Newbury Street's many shops, see Shops and Shopping, below.)

The latest attraction on the street is a 60-by-60-foot trompe l'oeil mural painted on the side of the building that houses the **DuBarry Restaurant**, at the corner of Dartmouth and Newbury streets. Completed in 1991, the mural is a result of a design contest among local art schools (the winner was Joshua Winer, a student at the Massachusetts College of Art). It took 17 painters, 70 models, and the cooperation of the community to make this café scene in 19th-century France come to life. The unfurled banner that reads "Laissez chaque homme exercer l'art qu'il connait" (Let every man practice the art he knows) provides the theme for this fictional café. Rubbing elbows in the mural are famous Bostonians from throughout the city's history (John F. Kennedy, Crispus Attucks, John Hancock, Babe Ruth, Julia Ward Howe, Mary Baker Eddy, Edgar Allan Poe) along with Madame DuBarry (the French adventuress who is the namesake of the restaurant) and a host of others. An identification key to the mural is usually available from the attendant at the parking lot it faces.

BOYLSTON STREET

Boylston Street, dominated by offices and shops, lacks the charm of Newbury Street and Commonwealth Avenue but does provide direct access to Copley Square, with its pleasant plaza area surrounded by Trinity Church, the John Hancock Tower and Observatory, and the Boston Public Library. Boylston Street has a number of well-known stores, such as F.A.O. Schwarz, at Berkeley Street, and the department stores Lord & Taylor and Saks Fifth Avenue, at the Prudential Center, as well as the Institute of Contemporary Art, at number 955 (see below).

Copley Square

Before beginning your exploration of Copley Square (easily reached by the Green Line to the Copley stop or by walking southwest along Boylston Street from the Public Garden), take a few minutes to sit down on one of the park benches in the plaza to get your bearings and enjoy the surroundings.

Named for Boston painter John Singleton Copley, this leftover space between streets was eventually transformed into a public plaza that has had different faces over the years. The Copley Square Plaza you see today is the result of a much-needed metamorphosis in the 1980s. To say it has no critics would be untrue, although the consensus is that the new village-green style is far more hospitable than the design it replaced, which was not unlike an empty concrete swimming pool. Much of the current criticism is directed at the overly complicated fountain with its 12 spouts and un-impressive duo of mini-obelisks. It seems the fountain works only sometimes, at other times functioning mainly as an obstacle course for accomplished skateboarders. Even so, the daredevil kids are fun to watch, and the open lawn attracts other entertaining elements as well, such as sunbath-ers, would-be musicians, and toddlers chasing belligerent pigeons. But the best feature of the plaza is that it is ringed by four architectural landmarks—the John Hancock Tower, Trinity Church, Boston Public Library, and New Old South Church.

JOHN HANCOCK TOWER AND OBSERVATORY

Completed in the 1970s, the John Hancock Tower, at 200 Clarendon Street, is one of the newer members of the collec-tion of notable buildings here. It has been applauded for its modern design (by I. M. Pei and Associates) that does not detract from its 19th-century neighbors; rather, the glass walls of the 62-story tower (Boston's tallest building) reflect the magnificence of the structures around it. From certain van-tage points the tower appears two-dimensional, more a frame for the sky itself than part of the earthbound city beneath.

In its early years this architectural wonder was plagued with problems. Its construction disturbed the area's tempera-mental landfill, causing shifts in the ground level that threat-ened nearby structures. (At one point the Hancock pur-chased the Copley Plaza Hotel next door, a move some say was motivated by a desire to avoid a lawsuit of the type filed—and won—by Trinity Church for damage done to its foundation during the Hancock's construction.) Soon after the tower was completed some of its 10,344 mirrored panes of glass began popping out and sending shards plummeting to the pavement below. For a time the tower was partially covered with plywood sheets (and nicknamed "the plywood palace") until an expensive reconstruction was eventually completed, much to the relief of pedestrians who frequent the area. Today the building's skin is continually monitored for even the slightest imperfection.

The **John Hancock Observatory** (Tel: 617/572-6429), lo-cated on the 60th floor, is one of the city's most visited attractions. Open daily from 9:00 A.M. to 11:00 P.M. (on Sundays it opens at 10:00 A.M.), the deck affords an unparal-leled view of up to 100 miles on a clear day. A recorded narrative by architectural historian Walter Muir Whitehill helps visitors pick out the Boston Public Garden, State House, and other notable sites. A sound-and-light show entitled "Boston 1775" is presented in an adjoining room. If you don't have the patience to last through the entire presentation (about 15 minutes) recalling the Boston Tea Party, Paul Revere's ride, and the Battle of Bunker Hill, do watch at least the very beginning or ending to see the striking contrast between the size of the old Shawmut Peninsula and today's Boston, which is built largely on landfill.

The Old John Hancock Insurance Company Building

In the shadow of the tower, at 175 Berkeley Street, is the old John Hancock Insurance Company building, easily identifiable at a distance by its weather beacon, which looks somewhat like an enormous hypodermic needle jutting upward from a miniature step pyramid. The beacon, composed of hundreds of red and blue lightbulbs, was shut down in the mid-1970s to conserve energy but was turned back on in 1983 and has been showing its colors ever since, 24 hours a day. Sadly, many Bostonians have no idea what the various signals indicate, but you will if you remember this verse:

> Steady blue, clear view
> Flashing blue, clouds due
> Steady red, rain ahead
> Flashing red, snow instead.

(Incidentally, flashing red in summertime means that the Red Sox game at Fenway Park has been canceled.) At a height of approximately 495 feet (its sister tower measures 790 feet), the smaller Hancock property was the second-tallest structure in the city when it opened in 1949 (it ranks 15th now).

TRINITY CHURCH

Set off at one end of Copley Square Plaza is Trinity Church, widely considered Henry Hobson Richardson's crowning achievement. The architect's original plans for the central tower had to be scaled down to minimize the weight of the structure, which is supported by 4,502 wooden piles driven into the landfill beneath. To prevent them from rotting, the piles must be kept saturated—at one time a boat was kept in the basement as a floating monitor of the water level.

Trinity was the only Anglican church in Boston that did not close its doors during the American Revolution. Its first building, at another location, burned in the Great Fire of 1872; the Richardson building opened in 1877. The church's most famous rector was Phillips Brooks, a colorful figure who wrote "O Little Town of Bethlehem" and was known for his fondness for fast horses and food (he weighed about 300 pounds), as well as his rapid-fire sermons (he once was clocked at 213 words per minute). The sculpture of Brooks by Augustus Saint-Gaudens on the Boylston Street side of Trinity has drawn criticism because the rector looks more important than the gentleman standing behind his left shoulder—Jesus Christ.

Visitors are welcome inside the church and can pick up a free guide to its decorative features right inside the door. To view the famous trio of stained glass windows by John LaFarge, walk all the way inside the church, turn around, and look up at the back of the nave; they are immediately recognizable by the predominance of brilliant blue glass. Home of the 70-member Trinity Church Choir, the church has also become well known over the years for its magnificent music at services and concerts, all open to the public. For information, Tel: (617) 536-0944.

BOSTON PUBLIC LIBRARY

Opened in 1852, the Boston Public Library was the first free public lending library in the United States. After being housed in two other locations, it opened for use in its Copley Square home (opposite Trinity) in 1895. Designed by Charles Follen McKim (who had apprenticed under Trinity's architect, H. H. Richardson, and was a principal of the New York firm of McKim, Mead & White), the library was intended to be a marriage of art and architecture in the tradition of an Italian Renaissance palazzo.

Inside the older half of the library (the less interesting, utilitarian newer half was added in the late 1960s), visitors will find paintings, sculptures, and dioramas on display among the volumes. Murals by Pierre Puvis de Chavannes adorn the walls of the grand staircase; in the third-floor Sargent Gallery, John Singer Sargent's *Judaism and Christianity* (considered an undertaking historical in nature by the artist, an atheist) is showcased in dark, moody lighting. McKim wrapped the building around a serene inner courtyard, and planned to donate a larger-than-life bronze by Frederic MacMonnies called *Bacchante and Child* for the courtyard's fountain as a memorial to his wife, Julia. A library art commission considered the statue inappropriate and rejected it—not over the question of artistic merit or nudity (the woman was au naturel), but because the subject was holding a bunch of grapes and thus the statue was obviously a "monument to inebriation." The commission agreed to a temporary installation for review of the sculpture, but the controversy (and widespread amusement) that ensued prompted McKim to withdraw his gift, donating it instead to the Metropolitan Museum of Art in New York City. A replica, however, was presented to Boston's Museum of Fine Arts, which at that time stood catercorner to the library (where the Copley Plaza Hotel now stands), and Copley Square got its "monument to inebriation" after all (until the museum later relocated and took the controversial statue along). For the library's centennial in 1995, efforts are underway to return the statue (or a copy) to its intended home.

Free tours of the Boston Public Library are offered daily except Fridays and Sundays; Tel: (617) 536-5400.

NEW OLD SOUTH CHURCH

Before leaving Copley Square, take a look at the church on the corner of Boylston and Dartmouth streets. The oldest structure in the square, it was built in 1874 as the new home for the congregation that had been located in the Old South Meeting House—hence its rather contradictory name, New Old South Church. The tower you see was once considerably taller (246 feet), but when its slight tilt gradually widened to a three-foot angle, it was dismantled stone by stone and rebuilt with steel reinforcements, but shorter. Note the tombstone fragments on the wall of the arcade at the foot of the tower. One stone belongs to John Alden, son of Pilgrim settlers John and Priscilla Alden and a member of the congregation of Old South Meeting House.

PRUDENTIAL CENTER

The atmosphere of the Skywalk on the 50th floor of the Prudential Center's tower is very different from that of the John Hancock Observatory, although both exist to offer a bird's-eye view of Boston and its surroundings. (The Prudential—known here as "the Pru"—is the structure west of Copley Square that looks like a giant computer chip; enter through the Prudential Center complex at 800 Boylston Street.) There's none of the hoopla here that you find at the Hancock, no narrated history, no rows of photographs with lengthy captions (only a few unobtrusive maps and directionals). The Skywalk feels almost like a park, with plants, tiled floors, and park benches—the kind of place that makes you want to linger. The Prudential's observation deck here is not as high as the Hancock's, but being closer to the city below allows for more detail to be seen with (or without) a telescope (if there's a game on you can make out the Red Sox at Fenway Park). And there's one unforgettable sight that can best be seen from the vantage point of the Skywalk—the John Hancock Tower itself.

The Skywalk (Tel: 617/236-3318) is open daily from 10:00

A.M. to 10:00 P.M. except Sundays, when it opens at noon. The 52nd floor has a restaurant and bar called Top of the Hub.

INSTITUTE OF CONTEMPORARY ART

Farther up Boylston Street, at numbers 941 and 955, is a building constructed in the mid-1880s to serve as fire station, police station, and stable. The fire station remains, but the police station and stable have been replaced by the Institute of Contemporary Art, which was first established in 1936 and relocated here in 1976 (making this museum the only one in town with jail cells in its basement).

Over the years the ICA has brought contemporary art to Boston with frequently changing exhibits, films, and performances—sometimes in spite of attempts to censor the more controversial fare (such as the Robert Mapplethorpe photography exhibit a few years ago). Tel: (617) 266-5151.

BOSTON ARCHITECTURAL CENTER

If you walk just beyond the ICA onto the Patrolman James B. O'Leary Bridge and turn around you'll have a good view of the building that houses the Boston Architectural Center (founded in 1889 as the Boston Architectural Club). When its new home here at 320 Newbury Street was dedicated in 1966, the expectation was that its one blank, windowless, five-story wall would soon be abutted by other buildings, and thus hidden. But in 1977 trompe l'oeil artist Richard Haas was hired to address the problem with an enormous mural (85 feet wide by 65 feet tall—one of the largest murals in the country) depicting the interior of a Neoclassical building with a central dome. If you look closely at the detail you'll see that mysterious characters appear to be stalking one another; note the figure in the doorway on the upper left on his way to the top of the rotunda, and the foot disappearing through a closing door at the upper right of the dome. Those interested in architecture are welcome to visit the changing exhibits displayed on the first floor of the BAC. Tel: (617) 536-3170.

THE CHRISTIAN SCIENCE CENTER

At the edge of the Back Bay (a short walk down Mass. Ave. from its intersection with Boylston Street, near the Green Line's Hynes Convention Center station) is the world headquarters of the First Church of Christ, Scientist, which was founded by Mary Baker Eddy in 1879 on the basis of her belief that will, mind, religious faith, and psyche played a strong role in matters of personal health and well-being. The 15 acres here include a pleasant plaza area and various church buildings, including the original church and its extension, the administration and Sunday school buildings, and the offices of the *Christian Science Monitor*.

Even if you're not a believer take a few minutes to go inside the **Mapparium**, a 30-foot stained glass globe with a glass bridge running through the center that enables visitors to view the world from the inside. Designed by the architect of the Christian Science Publishing Society (building on your left as you enter the grounds from Mass. Ave.), the globe's 608 panels depict the political boundaries of the world at the time of their construction in the early 1930s. A short talk is given right inside the globe every 15 minutes from 9:30 A.M. to 4:00 P.M., Tuesday through Saturday.

You are also welcome to take a free guided tour of the original church (constructed in 1894), which quickly became too small for the rapidly growing congregation, prompting the construction of the impressive, domed extension (the glassed-in front was added later). Note the hand-carved quotations from the Bible and Mary Baker Eddy's book, *Science and Health*, on the walls, the lovely stained glass windows (fashioned in Boston), and the intricate mosaics and frescoes that decorate the walls. Tours are offered Tuesday through Saturday from 10:00 A.M. to 4:00 P.M.; Tel: (617) 450-3790.

Before leaving the grounds of the mother church, walk along the lake-size reflecting pool connecting the administration building (the tall tower) and the Sunday school building (the crescent), which functions as part of the air-conditioning system for the complex. Though swimming and wading in the sheet of water is prohibited, the tricky reflection will convince you that people strolling on the opposite side of the pool are actually immersed to the knees in defiance of the signs—or at the very least walking on water. In truth, only a few gulls break the rules; anyone else who wants to get wet is invited to splash about in the fountain that punctuates the Belvidere Street end of the pool.

SOUTH END

The Boston neighborhood known as the South End borders the Back Bay on its southern side. For most of the 19th century the home of diverse groups of immigrants, today the neighborhood has become the chosen residence for many young professional Bostonians, who have lovingly restored the brick bowfront town houses built in the mid-1800s. Primarily a residential district, with the city's largest gay population and a lively ethnic and economic mix, the South End is also home to some fine restaurants and the **Boston Center for the Arts**, located in the **Cyclorama Building**, at 539 Tremont Street, built in 1884. The building's dome (now hidden from outside view) once housed Paul Philippoteaux's 400-by-50-foot cyclorama painting of the Battle of Gettysburg (now displayed at Gettysburg National Military Park). The Boston Center for the Arts hosts art exhibitions, dance performances, theatrical productions, music, carnivals, and festivals; for a recorded listing of events, Tel: (617) 426-7700.

FENWAY

While the Back Bay is usually touted as a success in urban planning, the Fenway, west of the Back Bay, is another story—not that intentions were not as lofty or plans as grand. It's just that after development of this newly land-filled area began in the 1890s nobody seemed to take control of the whole picture. So today there is a mishmash of hospitals, colleges, student housing, and low-income dwellings wrapped around a lovely park designed by landscape architect Frederick Law Olmsted. Still, the Fenway is home to three institutions of special interest to visitors: the Museum of Fine Arts, the Isabella Stewart Gardner Museum, and Fenway Park, home of the Red Sox.

MUSEUM OF FINE ARTS
The best way to get to the Museum of Fine Arts, at 465 Huntington Avenue (Route 9), is to take the Green Line's "E" train to the Museum stop, just past Northeastern University. Upon alighting, look for the statue of an Indian astride a horse (Cyrus Dallin's *Appeal to the Great Spirit*), which has stood in front of the museum since 1913. (If you drive, you can use a garage parking lot on Museum Road across from the West Wing entrance.)

From its humble origins on the top floor in the Boston Athenaeum, incorporated in 1807, the Museum of Fine Arts has grown into one of the five largest art museums in the country. The collection had grown so large by the 1860s that the Athenaeum, primarily a library, could no longer accommodate it, so an act of legislature in 1870 established a separate museum to be housed in its own building (on the site of today's Copley Plaza Hotel) in Art Square, later renamed Copley Square, while the Athenaeum, at 10½ Beacon Street, remained a library. But soon the continually expanding collection outgrew even this building. The Fenway was selected for construction of the museum's new, bigger home, which was opened in 1909. Ever growing, the museum has continued to increase its exhibition area, the most recent addition being the 1981 West Wing, with its special exhibition gallery, auditorium, museum shop, and restaurant. Today the museum operates nine curatorial departments for its permanent collection of one million objects: Classical; Asiatic; Ancient Egyptian, Nubian, and Near Eastern; European Decorative Arts and Sculpture; American Decorative Arts and Sculpture; Paintings; Prints, Drawings, and Photographs; Textiles and Costumes; and Contemporary. Among the artists represented here are El Greco, van Gogh, Renoir, Cézanne, Copley, Picasso, and O'Keeffe.

Although the museum has had a long-standing predilection for European cultures, it has many excellent holdings outside the Western realm. Of special interest is the Old Kingdom art and sculpture yielded by the Egyptian department's joint excavations with Harvard University (a collection said to be rivaled only by that in Cairo's Egypt Museum). In addition, the Nubian collection, considered the most significant outside the Sudan, finally has been awarded its own permanent gallery space, though the artifacts have been in the MFA's possession since a joint MFA-Harvard expedition saved them from the impending flooding caused by the first Aswan Dam in the early 1900s. Included in the collection on display are solid gold jewelry, bows and arrows, and the world's first known upholstered chair. Another recent departure from the museum's European slant is the construction of Tenshin-En, the Garden of the Heart of Heaven, dedicated in 1988. Designed by Kinsaku Nakane of Kyoto, Japan, the garden combines the style of Zen temple gardens of 15th-century Japan with elements of the New England landscape (rocky coastlines, gentle hills).

The MFA is open Tuesday through Sunday from 10:00 A.M. to 4:45 P.M., Wednesdays until 9:45 P.M. Admission is free on Wednesdays from 4:00 to 9:45 P.M. Guided tours (at no extra charge beyond museum admission) through all the collections are conducted Tuesday through Friday at 10:30 A.M. and 1:30 P.M., Wednesdays at 6:15 P.M., and Saturdays at 11:00 A.M. and 1:30 P.M. Tel: (617) 267-9300.

ISABELLA STEWART GARDNER MUSEUM

When Isabella Stewart Gardner was around there was never a dull moment. She was always finding new ways to scandalize the ever-so-proper Boston Brahmins who dominated the social scene in the late 19th century. There are endless stories (many of which may be apocryphal) about the New York–born heiress, wife of the wealthy John Lowell Gardner. It is said that she once wore a Red Sox cap to the symphony, liked to take strolls with a lion cub, sometimes greeted guests from a branch of the mimosa tree in front of her Beacon Street house, and wound diamond-studded wires into her hair so that they wiggled like antennae when she moved her head. The portrait by her friend John Singer Sargent—in which Gardner is clad in a low-necked gown with a shawl wrapped about her hips—outraged her contemporaries' Victorian sense of propriety.

It is entirely fitting that the unorthodox "Mrs. Jack" came up with a unique way to share her private 2,000-piece collection of paintings, sculptures, tapestries, furniture, rare books, ceramics, and stained glass with the public. (She was especially fond of Italian Renaissance paintings, including the work of Raphael, Titian, and Botticelli.) Shortly after her husband passed away she built an elaborate home fashioned after a Venetian palazzo on what was then newly filled swampland in the Fenway area of Boston. Taking an apartment on the top floor for her living quarters (where she stayed until her death in 1924), she decorated the remaining floors with her treasures, filled the magnificent central courtyard with flowering plants, and opened her museum on January 1, 1903, with Champagne, doughnuts (her favorite indulgence), and a concert by 50 musicians from the Boston Symphony Orchestra. Today visitors can enjoy the legacy of this unusual woman much as she intended, for her will explicitly prohibits any tampering with her displays.

Gardner did not, however, anticipate the events of the night of March 18, 1990, when two thieves posing as police officers gained entry into the museum and proceeded to help themselves to 12 paintings, including Rembrandt's *The Storm on the Sea of Galilee* and Vermeer's *The Concert*. To date, the stolen artwork—estimated to be worth in the neighborhood of $200 million—has not been recovered. In September 1992 another event unforeseen by Gardner occurred when museum officials (with court approval) opened a new gallery on the ground floor near the gift shop and café. A space for temporary exhibitions, the small gallery will favor shows that relate to some aspect of the Gardner collection.

The museum, at 280 The Fenway (a short walk from the rear of the Museum of Fine Arts), is open Tuesday through Saturday from 11:00 A.M. until 5:00 P.M.; Tel: (617) 566-1401. Because Gardner felt that flowers and music were the natural accompaniments for the visual arts, you can expect to find the interior courtyard bedecked in seasonal flowers (grown in the museum's greenhouse) and possibly music in the air from the regularly scheduled concerts from September through May; for concert information, Tel: (617) 734-1359.

FENWAY PARK

The third key attraction in the Fenway section of Boston is just as much a museum in its own right, though of a different sort than the Gardner and Fine Arts museums. Fenway Park, home field of the Boston Red Sox, was opened on April 20, 1912, and is the oldest ballpark in the country still in use (along with Tiger Stadium in Detroit). The value of the 34,000-seat park is not just that America's favorite game is played here, but that it is played under the purest conditions, as the park remains true to its heritage. There's no Astroturf here; the game is played on a fresh green lawn lovingly tended by grounds keeper Joe Mooney, who has made its care his life's work. Those who are used to attending games in other ballparks will be immediately struck by the intimacy here, due to the close proximity of seats to the action. The scoreboard—a rare hand-operated model—is a throwback, too.

As a continuously operating ballpark for some 80 years, Fenway Park has hosted its share of memorable moments. It was the scene of the only two American League one-game playoffs—in 1948 against Cleveland and 1978 against the Yankees. That the Sox didn't win either playoff came as no surprise to those who believe in "the curse of the Bambino." The Boston Red Sox, it is said, are eternally cursed (and so will never again win another World Series) because former owner Harry Frazee, in order to finance his passion, which was producing Broadway shows, sold pitcher Babe Ruth to the Yankees in 1920. Some frustrated fans point to the numbers displayed above the grandstands—9, 4, 1, 8 (actually the numbers of retired baseball greats Ted Williams, Bobby Doerr, Joe Cronin, and Carl Yastrzemski)—as an ironic reminder of the date (September 4, 1918) of the final game in the last series the Sox did win.

Of course, the park has seen some truly fine moments as well, such as Carlton Fisk's home run in the bottom of the 12th inning during a game in the 1975 World Series; and some odd occurrences, too, as when a seagull dropped a three-pound fish onto the pitching mound during a game in 1942, barely missing the head of startled pitcher Ellis Kinder.

If you want to attend a Red Sox game, plan ahead if you can, as games are well attended and often sold out. Check with the box office for schedule and ticket information (Tel: 617/267-8661), or come 90 minutes early and take your chances with unreserved bleacher seats ($7 in cash) or scalpers. Coming early has its advantages, as you might get to watch batting practice, guaranteed to send a few balls soaring over the net that is slung above the Green Monster, the imposing wall in left field. And while people are settling into their places, scan the right-field bleachers for the seat painted bright red; Ted Williams's longest home run demolished the straw hat of the occupant of this very chair, which now holds a place of honor in this "museum" of baseball.

The best way to get to the ballpark is to leave your car wherever it is and take the T, as the few private parking lots in the area fill quickly. Take the Green Line to the Kenmore station, walk up Comm. Ave. to where it meets Brookline Avenue, then follow the crowds up Brookline for a few blocks until you come to the ballpark. Then enjoy the game as it's been played here for more than eight decades.

CAMBRIDGE

Even though it is separated from Boston by nothing more than a river, Cambridge has an identity quite distinct from that of its larger neighbor. The feeling is different on this side of the water, more, well, daring. Cambridge is where the new takes root before the world (and sometimes Boston) may be ready for it, whether it involves scientific breakthroughs or poetry slams. The trailblazing spirit that has come to characterize what some call "the city across the river" is suggested by its original name—Newtowne—though the spirit these days surely manifests itself in ways the Puritan founders never intended. Yet there is a small-town feel to the place, with a strong sense of community and tradition, which is sometimes at odds with the more progressive elements.

Instead of the small but noticeable number of proper grandes dames in hats and white gloves and the countless executives in business suits that are typical of Boston, here you are more likely to see mothers in mismatched outfits shopping with their kids or young professionals sporting the "Cambridge chic" style preferred by those who must dress up (sort of) for work. There are rumpled professors (among them a few Nobel Prize winners) and blue-jeaned students caught up in future thoughts, plus colorful characters who are known here by sight, if not always by name. There's Brother Blue (always decked out in ribbons and butterflies) telling stories to anyone who will listen, or Lee Kidd (always in black) striding toward the Naked City Coffeehouse with an armload of poems, or Mary (just Mary, no last name)—babushkaed, bespectacled, and perennially short of cash—

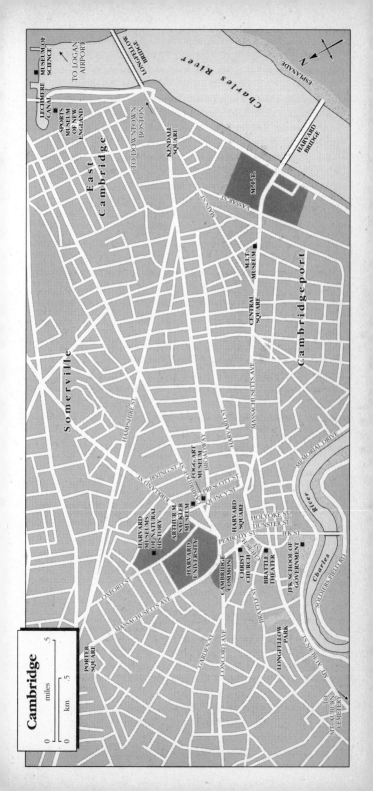

wheedling her way into whatever dance performance is on the calendar for the day. Mix its cast of characters into the concoction of bookstores (there are more bookstores in Cambridge than in any other city in the country), restaurants, and shops that reflect the vast ethnic diversity of the city; a history that features some of the most famous people and events from early Colonial America until the present time; two of the most respected universities in the world, Harvard and the Massachusetts Institute of Technology, and you'll have a glimmer of what Cambridge is all about.

We begin our coverage in what may be called the heart and soul of Cambridge, Harvard Square, with a look at the square itself, along with the Cambridge Common, John Fitzgerald Kennedy Park, and the Charles River—saving Harvard University, which is adjacent to the square, for later. Then we proceed along Brattle Street to the Longfellow House and Tory Row, followed by a short bus trip to Mount Auburn Cemetery, just outside of Harvard Square. We finish the area with an in-depth tour of Harvard University and its museums.

Next, in Cambridgeport, just east and south of Harvard Square, we concentrate on the Massachusetts Institute of Technology campus and museums. Finally, we head to the up-and-coming "CambridgeSide" area of East Cambridge to see the CambridgeSide Galleria, the Sports Museum of New England, and the Museum of Science.

MAJOR INTEREST

Harvard Square
Street performers

Cambridge Common Area
God's Acre burying ground
Christ Church
Radcliffe College

Brattle Street
Tory Row houses, including Longfellow House

Mount Auburn Cemetery

Boat rides on the Charles River

Harvard University
Harvard Museums of Cultural and Natural History, including Botanical Museum
Harvard University Art Museums: Fogg Art Museum, Busch-Reisinger Museum, and Arthur M. Sackler Museum

Massachusetts Institute of Technology
MIT Museum

East Cambridge
Sports Museum of New England
Museum of Science

HARVARD SQUARE

In the center of Harvard Square stands a 21-foot granite sculpture. Its creator, Dmitri Hadzi, named it "Omphalos" (Greek for "navel"), signifying the center of the universe— and certainly there are times when Harvard Square seems to be exactly that. Stand here and you can feel the thrum of activity all around you: Harvard students hurrying to class (or to the **Boathouse**, a favorite hangout on J. F. Kennedy Street, for a beer instead); street performers vying with one another for attention, and a few dollars, from passersby; visitors, armed with cameras, filling the air with the sounds of languages from every continent; down-on-their-luck souls hawking the publication *Spare Change* or panhandling for whatever they can get.

Start your explorations at the **Cambridge Discovery** infor-mation booth on the small central plaza a short distance from *Omphalos*. (It's the tiny structure shaped like a cake right in front of the main entrance to the MBTA Red Line's Harvard station.) You can pick up a map, sign up for a walking tour, and get answers to questions concerning just about anything here. Trolley tours also leave from the plaza. **Out of Town News**, located inside (and outside) the kiosk, is stocked with newspapers and magazines from around the world. This central plaza is bordered on two sides by Massa-chusetts Avenue, the main street that runs through the square. Other key streets are Brattle, Garden, Church, and Mt. Auburn.

A good place to engage in one of the favorite pastimes in the square—hanging out—is at the Holyoke Center's **Au Bon Pain** café, right across Dunster Street. Get yourself a café au lait and croissant at the counter, then find an outdoor table with a good view and watch the passing parade.

The scene is at its liveliest on summer evenings, when street performers claim every available nook and cranny to entertain the throngs of people who come to the square. Wander through the streets and you'll see a wide variety of acts: a juggler on a tightrope, a band from the Andes, an a cappella group from Harvard, street theater and poetry per-formed by a gaggle of local creative misfits called Fire of

Prometheus, local yarn-spinner Brother Blue telling tales, fire eaters, magicians, and musicians playing rock, blues, folk, reggae, you name it—all hoping you'll enjoy their work enough to pitch a few coins their way at the end of a set.

DAWES ISLAND

If you walk north from the information booth along Mass. Ave. and cross Garden Street you'll come to a tiny traffic island called Dawes Island where brass horseshoes are embedded in the sidewalk. These mark the route that the other midnight rider took to Concord and Lexington to sound the warning that the British were coming. William Dawes was the rider that history—or, more specifically, Henry Wadsworth Longfellow, in his poem "Paul Revere's Ride"—neglected to immortalize. While Revere chose the Charlestown route to deliver the message the night of April 18, 1775 (the date on the sidewalk, April 19, is the date of the battle, not the ride), Dawes went by way of Cambridge. He was only partially successful in his mission: It is said that after escaping from the British soldiers who intercepted him, he rode smack into a tree limb and was knocked unconscious. If you're in town the day of the Boston Marathon (Patriots' Day, the third Monday in April; see Celebrations and Special Events, below), come by for a reenactment of the ride by one of the patriot's descendants.

Across Mass. Ave., on the grassy traffic island to your right, is a statue of antislavery activist Charles Sumner, a U.S. senator who throughout the Civil War urged President Lincoln and his fellow senators to emancipate the slaves, the sooner the better. With sentiments on both sides of the issue running high, a South Carolina congressman beat Sumner so severely with his cane that it took him more than three years to recover fully. (It is said that Sumner's attacker received as gifts more than 120 new canes to replace his broken one from those who supported his views.)

The Sumner statue was sculpted by Anne Whitney, who was the victim of discrimination of another sort. After Whitney won a competition to sculpt a statue of the senator, in which the entries were anonymous, committee members reversed their decision and gave the award to another artist—a man—when they learned that the winner they had initially chosen was a woman. Years later the statue you see here was made from the model that had legitimately won the competition in 1875.

CAMBRIDGE COMMON AREA

Just beyond Dawes Island is the Cambridge Common, where the roaming of cattle has been superseded over the years by the wanderings of the human species. Some people come here for peace and quiet, others because they have nowhere else to go. If you walk along the Garden Street edge (the common's southern border) you'll come to an important-looking tree encircled by a fence. The tablet next to it reads "Under this tree Washington first took command of the American Army July 3rd, 1775." But don't believe it. The original elm, which ended up in the middle of a busy street after the growing city claimed a good piece of the common's pastureland for development, managed to survive the fumes and vibrations of traffic until 1923. The young tree now honored as the **Washington Elm** was actually grown from a cutting of the original.

The Cambridge Common's history goes back to 1631, when this parcel of land was first set aside for grazing cattle. The site of another famous tree is marked with a stone slab along the edge of the common nearest Mass. Ave. The **Election Oak** is where annual public elections were held in Colonial days. In the center of the common is the **Soldiers' Monument**, dedicated in 1870 to the soldiers and sailors from Cambridge who lost their lives in the Civil War.

Much of the common's history, though, is not commemorated by plaques and statues, such as public debates over religious freedom and military maneuvers (a two-story naval barracks was erected here during World War I), protests and peace gatherings in the 1960s, and the traditional Harvard commencement festivities of years past.

GOD'S ACRE

Backtracking to the corner of Mass. Ave. and Garden Street, you will come upon an ancient graveyard guarded by an iron fence. This is God's Acre, the oldest cemetery in Cambridge, which dates to 1635. If the side gate next to Christ Church, at Zero Garden Street, is open (it's often padlocked to discourage vandalism) you may go right in. If not, the church sexton can let you inside the grounds. Buried here are some of Harvard's earliest presidents, soldiers from the Revolutionary War, and a number of once-prominent local citizens, including Dexter Pratt, the blacksmith mentioned in the Longfellow poem "The Village Blacksmith." It is estimated that there are seven times more bodies buried here than there are headstones; who is buried inside the "mystery mound" near the fence where Mass. Ave. meets Garden Street is anybody's guess. Over the years many of the grave markers have been defaced by weather or vandals. Probably one of the worst offenders was George Washington, who, in need of bullets for his militia, had the metal nameplates mounted on some of the stones removed and melted down for the cause of freedom.

The stone located just inside the fence at the Mass. Ave. and Garden Street intersection inscribed with "Boston 8 miles 1734" on one side and "2¼" on the other is not a tombstone, but rather a milestone. The conflicting information on its two faces may represent one of the first documented cases of recycling in the city of Cambridge. One side reports the distance to Boston by a land route in the year 1734. When a bridge was later built over the Charles River, greatly shortening the distance between the two cities, the stone was simply flipped over and the new information recorded. (The initials "A. I." belong to the stonecutter.)

CHRIST CHURCH

Christ Church, at Zero Garden Street, lost its organ pipes for the same cause for which the residents of God's Acre lost their metal nameplates during the Revolution. But it's unlikely the patriots thought twice about confiscating anything from the church; in fact, they probably enjoyed the irony. After all, it was an Anglican church, built by local Tories (British sympathizers) in 1761, only 15 years before the Revolution (they found the long trip—eight miles back then—to worship in Boston's King's Chapel too arduous). Although as many as 90 percent of the Cambridge population in the years just before the Revolution had Puritan roots and considered Cambridge their home, the other 10 percent—the wealthy (their wealth primarily due to lucrative Caribbean plantations)—considered England their real home. Predictably, most of this Tory congregation was forced to flee Cambridge in 1774 when trouble began, and no regular church services were held in Christ Church for 16 years. For a time Christ Church was used as a barracks by the patriots, and George and Martha Washington worshiped here on New Year's Eve 1775 (the two had a fife-and-drum military escort to pew 93, located front left).

Visitors are invited to explore the interior. Just to the right of the inside doorway (through the front doors in the vestibule area) is a bullet hole that is thought to date from an incident that occurred when the church was reopened for a funeral in 1778 after a British prisoner named Richard Brown was accidentally shot by a sentry. Despite the solemn occasion, anti-British sentiment overwhelmed the townspeople, who ransacked the church, smashing windows and destroying the pulpit; it's more than likely that at least one weapon was discharged in the confusion.

The church is usually open daily from 9:00 A.M. to 5:00 P.M., but be aware that the place is not a museum but an active parish (Episcopalian) and community center. In addition to church sermons and homeless and day-care services, Christ Church is the venue for what has to be the most ambitious language-study program in the country and perhaps the world—the Intercontinental Foreign Language Program, known for its decalingual course, in which students can learn ten languages at once.

RADCLIFFE COLLEGE

A short walk west along Garden Street will bring you to the gate that leads into Radcliffe Yard (just past the intersection of Garden Street and Appian Way on the left). Founded in 1879 as the Society for the Collegiate Instruction of Women, the school was named for Anne Radcliffe, who was the first woman to donate a scholarship to Harvard (in 1643). For years Harvard professors would teach a course at the all-male institution on one side of the square, then cross the street and teach the exact same course to Radcliffe students. Although the education always has been virtually the same for both sexes, instruction did not become coeducational until after World War II.

Feel free to walk through the yard and look around. Of special note is the **Schlesinger Library**, which retains the most extensive collections of materials pertaining to women's studies in the country. Its culinary collection, which includes the papers of Cambridge resident Julia Child, is unsurpassed. Walk through the opposite gate and cross Brattle Street to number 76, the president's house; to the right is a path leading to a fountain next to a residence hall. While there have been many notable women who have attended Radcliffe (Gertrude Stein and Adrienne Rich among them), probably none of them is more admired than Helen Keller, who completed her studies though she was unable to see or hear. The fountain was dedicated by Keller to her teacher, Anne Sullivan, to commemorate the moment when the young child made a connection between the word "w-a-t-e-r" being finger-spelled by Sullivan onto one of her hands and the liquid she felt splashing onto the other.

CHURCH STREET

The **Harvard Square Theater**, on Church Street, a short street that connects Brattle Street and Mass. Ave., features first-run films, as well as the *Rocky Horror Picture Show* every Saturday night at 12:15 A.M.—just get in line behind Charlie Chaplin to purchase your ticket. Chaplin is part of the trompe l'oeil mural painted in 1983 as a compromise solution when the local neighborhood association objected to remodeling plans that called for a marquee that would jut into the street. The marquee façade has such realistic touches as pigeons roosting on the eaves.

Before or after a movie you might want to stop by **Steve's Ice Cream** (also called the Church Street Café) across the street from the theater at 33 Church. If you've been ordering nuts, M & Ms, and jelly beans mixed in with your ice cream for the last decade or so, you have Steve to thank—though you won't find him on the premises anymore. He sold his business in the late 1970s to someone else (whose name wasn't even Steve). Later he decided he wanted to open his own Steve's again and fought in court for the right to use his own name (he lost). The building at 33 Church Street used to be a jail (note the bars on the side windows).

JOHN FITZGERALD KENNEDY PARK

For a respite from the bustle of the square you might find a bench on the wide lawn in John Fitzgerald Kennedy Park, adjacent to Harvard's John Fitzgerald Kennedy School of Government on J. F. Kennedy Street, south of Harvard Square. The fountain, dedicated to America's 35th president (one of six to have graduated from Harvard), spills a continuous sheet of water over quotations excerpted from Kennedy's address before the Massachusetts Legislature on January 9, 1961, eleven days before his inauguration as president. The fountain serves as a perpetual reminder of the values inscribed on the granite: integrity, courage, judgment, and dedication.

THE CHARLES RIVER

The Charles River is just across Memorial Drive from JFK Park, bordering one edge of Harvard Square with benches and enough grass on its banks to attract its share of sunbathers in the summertime. On Sunday afternoons the usually busy Memorial Drive is blocked off to traffic, so you can stroll a riverbank free of exhaust fumes (the ban on cars leaves plenty of pavement available for cycling and roller-skating). This stretch of the river is generally more lively than JFK Park; one of the more popular activities here is rowing, a major college sport in the city. You'll find dedicated athletes out on the Charles as early as 6:00 A.M. Every October teams from around the world compete in the **Head of the Charles** race, the largest rowing event in the world, which attracts thousands of fans to the banks of the river to cheer on their favorite teams. You may see the losers strip off their shirts and hand them to the winners, a tradition said to be the origin of the cliché about losing one's shirt.

The Boston side of the river is every bit as festive as the Cambridge side, with the added feature of the **Hatch Memo-**

rial Shell, an outdoor performance space that hosts free concerts, dance performances, and films. The Boston Pops' Fourth of July concert here attracts more than a million people every year.

BRATTLE STREET

LONGFELLOW HOUSE AND PARK

Along Brattle Street, which runs due west from Harvard Square, are seven houses that were occupied by wealthy Tories (hence the street's nickname, Tory Row)—that is, until the onset of the Revolution sent their owners packing. About a 15-minute walk from Harvard Square at 105 Brattle is the Longfellow House, which has been preserved as a historic monument and is open to the public. (It's the yellow house with black shutters on the right just beyond the Episcopal Divinity School.)

Originally built by Tory John Vassall as a country home in 1759, the house served as George Washington's military headquarters for about ten months in 1775 and 1776 after the Tories had left town. The mansion later became the residence of Henry Wadsworth Longfellow, who rented a room here after he had accepted a teaching appointment at Harvard. He later became the owner when the house was given to him and his bride as a wedding gift from his new wife's father, and he lived here 45 years in all. The interior has been preserved from the time that Longfellow and his descendants lived here, and the family's original furnishings, paintings, and personal belongings remain. Longfellow was a poet so beloved that he often received gifts from admirers; one such gift in the drawing room is a piece of embroidery woven with feathers and human hair. Because he never forgot that his abode had once provided shelter for "the father of our country," he placed various tributes to Washington throughout his home, including sculptures, reliefs, and a coat of arms (red, white, and blue, with stars and stripes, it is said to have suggested the design for the American flag).

The tour begins at the visitors' center in the back of the house, where you can buy a copy of the guide to the premises written by Henry Wadsworth Longfellow Dana (the poet's grandson, who lived here until 1950), with a rundown of some of the personal items you will see on the tour. You can also purchase individual copies (in folders) of Longfellow's most famous poems, including "The Village Blacksmith," "Paul Revere's Ride," "The Children's Hour," and *Song of Hiawatha*. In Longfellow's study, which Washington had used as his office and where the poet wrote much of his work, you will see what's left of the "spreading chestnut tree" mentioned in "The Village Blacksmith." After the tree was felled the schoolchildren of Cambridge pooled their pennies to pay for the creation of a fashionable armchair, carved with horse-chestnut leaves and lines from the poem, out of the wood. Longfellow was so touched that he wrote "From My Arm-Chair" and gave copies to the children as thanks for their gift.

Before leaving the grounds, walk behind the visitors' center and enter the garden through the fence. Longfellow laid out the flower garden in the shape of a lyre in 1845, later enlarging it, adding more flowerbeds and paths. The centerpiece is a sundial that bears one of the poet's favorite mottoes from Dante's *Purgatorio:* "Pensa che questo di mai non raggiorna" (Think that this day will never dawn again). In the summertime the garden and adjoining lawn provide an idyllic setting for Sunday afternoon classical music concerts and poetry readings (call for schedule). Guided tours of the house are conducted daily between 10:00 A.M. and 4:30 P.M. (the last tour begins at 4:00) by the National Park Service. Tel: (617) 876-4491.

After leaving the Longfellow House take a walk across Brattle Street to **Longfellow Park**. John Vassall's estate extended clear down to the Charles River, with an unobstructed view from the front porch. The long expanse of lawn is still here, though numerous houses have been built around it over the years.

ALONG TORY ROW

Among Brattle Street's other Tory mansions (all marked with blue oval plaques) is that at **number 94**, which belonged to Henry Vassall (John's uncle) and was used as a hospital during the Revolution and a prison of sorts for the traitor Benjamin Church. (What looks like a British flag hanging out front is actually one of the earliest American flags.) At number 149 is the **Lechmere-Riedesel House**, whose alterations entailed lifting the entire structure to add a first floor (the large central window on the second story used to be a door). The house itself was moved from its original location to its current position on the corner of Riedesel Avenue, named for Baron Riedesel, a Hessian officer serving in the British army who was imprisoned with his wife here in 1778 and 1779.

The **Hooper-Lee-Nichols House**, at number 159, dates to 1685, but many alterations (including the addition of a third story) were made in the years that followed; it is now the home of the **Cambridge Historical Society**, which conducts occasional guided tours of Tory Row (Tel: 617/547-4252). At number 175 is the **Ruggles-Fayerweather House**, built in 1764 and used as a military hospital during the Revolution; some of the wounded from the Battle of Bunker Hill were brought here. For a time in the 19th century the building housed a private school for boys; James Russell Lowell was among the prominent Bostonians educated here.

As you return on Brattle to Harvard Square, take a look at number 56, the **Blacksmith House**, once the home of Dexter Pratt, who was the subject of Longfellow's "The Village Blacksmith." Owned by the Cambridge Center for Adult Education since 1972, it not only provides classroom space for courses as varied as Tai Chi, Introduction to Pagemaker, and Writing Children's Literature, but also offers a scenic outdoor café setting where the foot-weary can enjoy a cup of coffee and a torte. A bit farther down the street, between the Café of India and Clothware, is a stone marker indicating the location of the "spreading chestnut tree" under which the "village smithy" stood in Longfellow's poem. Despite some protest, the famous tree was chopped down in 1870—either because its low-hanging branches were knocking the heads of people riding by in carriages or simply as a victim of the city's expansion. Its wood was then used to make the chair in Longfellow's study.

Brattle House, at number 42, is also owned by the Cambridge Center for Adult Education, and is used for offices and classrooms. Built in 1727 by the wealthy Tory William Brattle, Brattle House later became the temporary home of feminist Margaret Fuller when she moved here with her father in 1832.

Next to Brattle House at number 40 is **Brattle Hall**, built in 1889 by the Cambridge Social Union (which later changed its name to the Cambridge Center for Adult Education). Brattle Hall has long housed some of the area's most popular hangouts (denizens of the hall had feared that recent renovations would change things, but their fears happily have turned out to be unfounded). The hall's **Algiers Coffee House** (Tel: 617/492-1557) was recently cited as the best place in town to bring a first date; it's intimate, with lots of atmosphere (especially upstairs), but no one minds if you arrive unaccompanied and read a book as you sip your coffee. The murals alone in the **Casablanca Restaurant and Bar** here (the subject will come as no surprise) are reason enough to find an excuse to walk through the restaurant and back to the bar for a cocktail (Tel: 617/876-0999). Brattle Hall also houses the **Brattle Theater**, which specializes in vintage films. Now used primarily for film showings, in the past the theater hosted numerous theatrical productions, including some by Harvard students in the days when such activities were discouraged on campus. T. S. Eliot, Paul Robeson, and E. E. Cummings were among those who performed here. The theater gained a reputation for backing the arts and artists no matter what, and in the 1950s those who found themselves blacklisted were still welcome here. Such liberal attitudes helped give rise to the nicknames still applied to Cambridge on occasion: the People's Republic of Cambridge and Pinkotown.

MOUNT AUBURN CEMETERY

To visit the Mount Auburn Cemetery, at 580 Mount Auburn Street, west of Harvard Square and south of Brattle Street, hop onto the Watertown Square bus (number 71), which runs west along Mount Auburn Street from the square usually every 10 to 15 minutes (board in the underground bus terminal at the Harvard Square MBTA station or along the route).

Mount Auburn, which opened in 1831, is America's first so-called garden cemetery, the brainchild of Dr. Jacob Bigelow, who decided to meet the need for more burial ground in a way that also satisfied his love for botany. The 170 acres have been landscaped with fountains, monuments, flowering shrubs, and plants, as well as an estimated 600 types of trees and 200 species of birds. Stop by the cemetery office to pick up maps to the greenery and the location of grave sites of some of the more notable people (including Julia Ward Howe, Mary Baker Eddy, Henry Wadsworth Longfellow, and Phillips Brooks) among the 82,000 buried here. The cemetery gates open by 8:00 A.M. every day and close at 7:00 P.M.

HARVARD UNIVERSITY AND MUSEUMS
The University

Harvard Square derives its name from the school founded here in 1636 by the Massachusetts Bay Colony General Court: Harvard University, the oldest institution for higher learning in the country. Visitors are welcome to explore the grounds on their own or to take a free tour (lasting about an hour and conducted by Harvard students) starting from the **Harvard Information Center** (Tel: 617/495-1573), at 1350 Massachusetts Avenue in Holyoke Center (across from the Old Harvard Yard near Au Bon Pain café). During the academic year tours are offered weekdays at 10:00 A.M. and 2:00 P.M. and on Saturdays at 2:00 P.M. From June through August tours leave at 10:00 and 11:15 A.M. and at 2:00 and 3:15 P.M. Monday through Saturday; additional tours are given at 1:30 and 3:00 P.M. on Sunday. (You can also pick up a flyer for a self-guided walking tour here.)

OLD HARVARD YARD

A good place to start a tour of Harvard is Old Harvard Yard, the oldest part of the campus. There are a number of entrances, but if you go through **Johnston Gate** (a work by Charles F. McKim, who also designed the Boston Public Library, located across Mass. Ave. from the Charles Sumner statue), take a look at the inscription. After the Colonists had taken care of the basics in their new land—building their homes and churches and setting up a civil government—one of the next things they "longed for and looked after was to advance learning and to perpetuate it to posterity."

If you've come through Johnston Gate, to your immediate left is **Harvard Hall**, the third of three structures on this site to bear that name (the first two were destroyed by fire). The second building contained a physics lab where Ben Franklin liked to work and provided a home for John Harvard's extensive book collection, which was destroyed in 1764 by the second fire—except for a single volume. Apparently a certain overachiever had surreptitiously removed a book to peruse overnight. After the fire the student returned the sole survivor of the valuable collection to the president of the college—who thanked the young man and then promptly expelled him for breaking the rules.

On the other side of Harvard Hall are two of the oldest dormitories on campus, Hollis and Stoughton. Notice the round depressions in the brick sidewalk that runs in front of the buildings: Legend says that students used to heat cannon-balls in their fireplaces to help generate warmth in the winter and then toss them out the windows come spring onto the sidewalk below. A number of famous historical figures have resided in the Old Yard's dorms over the years, among them Ralph Waldo Emerson, Henry David Thoreau, E. E. Cummings, and John F. Kennedy. George Washington's troops were housed here during the Revolutionary War, which accounts for the leftover cannonballs.

The most popular attraction inside the Old Yard is the **bronze statue** located in front of University Hall (directly across from Johnston Gate). It is easily identified by the tourists taking pictures of one another in front of it and by the inscription on its base: "John Harvard, Founder, 1638." The piece, however, exhibits a few characteristics that inspired its reputation as "the statue of the three lies." First, the school was founded in 1636, not 1638; second, the founder was the General Court, not John Harvard; and last, the fine-looking man you see is Sherman Hoar, a Harvard student who modeled for sculptor Daniel Chester French (the school's benefactor, after all, was long dead when the statue was cast in 1884). If you lightly scrape the gentleman's boot with your fingernail, you might discover a waxy residue. Every fall the statue receives a protective coating to make it easier to clean, as it is sometimes the butt of practical jokes.

The gate in the northern perimeter of Old Harvard Yard leads to the **Science Center**, whose resemblance to an old-fashioned bellows camera is not accidental—or at least that is what visitors are told, as Edwin Land (founder of Polaroid and inventor of the Land camera) funded the building. In front of the Science Center is the Tanner Fountain, a curious assortment of 159 mist-enshrouded boulders strewn about the grass and asphalt. Installed in 1984, the wet, rocky landscape is a favorite place for students to sit and read, kids to frolic in the spray, and dogs to roll in the mud.

The large building that evokes the feeling of a Gothic cathedral just to the right of the Science Center is **Memorial Hall** (familiarly known as "Mem Hall"), dedicated in 1874 in honor of the Harvard students and alumni who had served on the Union side in the Civil War (this one-sided view has been the subject of controversy ever since). Visitors may enter the main hallway to view the names of the soldiers inscribed on the walls and to see the stained glass windows (some of which came from the famed Tiffany and LaFarge studios). **Sanders Theater**, a venue for numerous musical performances, poetry readings, and lectures, is housed here. Martin Luther King, Jr., Spike Lee, and Dr. Ruth Westheimer are just a few of the speakers who have addressed audiences at Sanders; Tel: (617) 495-1000.

NEW HARVARD YARD

Back inside the enclosure, walk behind University Hall into the open, grassy area known as New Harvard Yard (or Tercentenary Theatre), where Harvard graduations are held rain or shine. The massive building with the dozen columns on your right is the **Widener Library**. With 3.2 million volumes (more than five miles of books), it is one of the largest libraries in the United States. The $2 million library was financed by the mother of Harvard graduate Harry Elkins Widener—who died on the *Titanic* in 1912—but with the stipulation that every Harvard student be taught to swim (according to today's students, this is no longer enforced). Students also say a second stipulation was that ice cream (Harry's favorite food) had to be served at least once a day (sources say it is served often, if not every day).

Directly across from the library is **Memorial Church** (a.k.a. Mem Church), which welcomes visitors. Listed on the inside right-hand wall are the names of those Harvard students and graduates who died in World War II; through the doorway in this wall is a room dedicated to those who died in World War I, while on the left-hand wall of the church are several plaques with names of casualties from the wars in Korea and Vietnam.

Occupying one end of New Harvard Yard is a red-brick building with terra-cotta detail, **Sever Hall**, designed by Henry Hobson Richardson, architect of Boston's Trinity Church. An acoustical anomaly allows people standing on either side of the center archway to hear one another's whispers perfectly—unless a third person stands between them. (The brick for Sever Hall came from the clay pits of the nearby Porter Square section of Cambridge; note the rounded bricks used to build the front columns.)

Behind Sever Hall is a gate that leads to Quincy Street and the **Carpenter Center for the Visual Arts**, at number 24, the only building in North America designed by Le Corbusier. Harvard has been much criticized for keeping this architectural masterpiece at such a low profile; however, the public is welcome inside the building to attend any of the films shown here. Schedules are available at the center or from the Cambridge Discovery booth in Harvard Square; Tel: (617) 495-4700.

The Museums

HARVARD MUSEUMS OF CULTURAL AND NATURAL HISTORY

Harvard University operates nine museums with diverse holdings, but the main question from visitors always seems to be, "Where are the glass flowers?" The **Botanical Museum**, located inside the complex that houses the Harvard Museums of Cultural and Natural History, at 24 Oxford Street (a short walk beyond the Science Center), is the home of Harvard's most popular exhibit. The 3,000 glass models of plants in the Ware collection were made from 1887 to 1936 by artists Leopold Blaschka and his son Rudolph, originally for the purpose of teaching botany. Their imitation of nature is in some cases so good that it took some convincing for one agriculturist with a half century of experience raising strawberries to concede that the berries he was viewing in their various stages of growth and decay were, indeed, modeled in glass and not the genuine article somehow cleverly coated with a miracle preservative.

Inside the same complex are the **Mineralogical and Geological Museum**, with its extensive collection of gems and minerals (some in raw form, others polished and cut or sculpted), in addition to ores and meteorites; and the **Museum of Comparative Zoology**, which features such rare and unusual specimens as whale skeletons, the largest turtle shell ever found, a horned dinosaur skull, and the golden pheasants presented to George Washington by the Marquis de Lafayette in November 1786 (when they perished a few months later, they were stuffed for posterity).

The fourth museum housed in the complex is the **Peabody Museum of Archaeology and Ethnology**, the oldest museum in this hemisphere devoted entirely to the disciplines featured in its name. Of special interest here are the Hall of the North American Indian and the collections that focus on Central and South American Indian cultures. On display are numerous Kachina dolls, models of pueblos (Acoma, Taos, and Chaco Canyon), and a Navajo sand painting.

For general information on all museums housed in the Museums of Cultural and Natural History complex, Tel: (617) 495-3045. Exhibits are open Monday through Saturday from 9:00 A.M. to 4:30 P.M. and Sundays from 1:00 to 4:30 P.M.; the admission price allows entrance to all five museums.

SEMITIC MUSEUM

Across the street from the rear of the Museums of Natural History, at 6 Divinity Avenue, is the Semitic Museum, founded in 1889, closed in 1942 because of the war, and reopened in 1982. The museum houses materials promoting knowledge of Semitic languages and history. Open Monday through Friday; Tel: (617) 495-3123.

THE ART MUSEUMS

The Harvard University art museums, located in three buildings near the corner of Quincy Street and Broadway, include the **Fogg Art Museum**, which is home to masterpieces by Fra Angelico, Rembrandt, Monet, Renoir, van Gogh, and Picasso, as well as sculpture by Rodin; the **Busch-Reisinger Museum**, containing one of North America's leading collections of German Expressionist art, with pieces by Klee and Kandinsky; and the **Arthur M. Sackler Museum**, which displays ancient Chinese jades, Persian and Indian miniatures, and Japanese prints and ceramics.

Hours for all three are Tuesday through Sunday from 10:00 A.M. to 5:00 P.M.; Tel: (617) 495-9400.

CAMBRIDGEPORT

Cambridgeport, which occupies the central swath of the city of Cambridge (east and south of Harvard Square), is an odd mixture of working-class homes, budget shops, city government offices, and the campus of the Massachusetts Institute of Technology. This is the most culturally varied area of Cambridge; an estimated 70 languages are spoken by its various residents. Take the Red Line to the Central Square stop, then walk either east or west on Massachusetts Avenue; you will immediately notice the cultural diversity, as reflected in the flags of different nations suspended from streetlight poles and in the restaurants specializing in cuisine from India, the Middle East, and Italy as well as other regions of the world.

Massachusetts Institute of Technology

The MIT campus draws many visitors to Cambridgeport for its architecture, museums, and public art. The campus straddles Mass. Ave., stretching for about a mile along the Charles River into both East and West Cambridge. The best way to get here from Harvard or Central Square is to take the number 1 Dudley bus, which stops right in front of the Rogers Building at 77 Mass. Ave. (the structure with double sets of pillars), or take the MBTA Red Line to Central Square and walk for 15 minutes or so east along Mass. Ave. There are metered parking spaces available here and a lot at the corner of Vassar Street, but this is a busy area and parking is not always available.

Go first to MIT's **Information Center**, just inside the lobby of the Rogers Building and to the right in room 7-121 (Tel: 617/253-4795), to pick up a free map of the campus (you'll need it) or to take a free, student-guided tour that lasts about an hour and a half. Tours are offered weekdays at 10:00 A.M. and 2:00 P.M. If you have the time, do take the tour, as the campus is so large and so confusing to anyone unfamiliar with its seven miles of interconnecting corridors that it typically takes freshmen a couple of weeks to figure out how to get from one class to the next without getting lost. If you choose to wander around on your own, keep in mind that buildings are commonly referred to by number rather than name, so just look at any room number to find out where you are. The figure preceding the hyphen always designates the building; the Information Center, for example, is in building 7.

While you're inside the rotunda of building 7 take a quick look on the left wall for the plaque dedicated to William Barton Rogers, who founded the institution in 1861. Then head for the passageway directly across from the entrance to the building: This is what MIT students call the infinite corridor; it runs for at least a mile and will lead you through building 3 and into building 10.

Where the corridor widens go through the doors on the right into the expansive grassy area known as **Killian Court**. This is the oldest part of the campus, dating to 1916, when the school moved here from its previous location in Boston. From here you can see the Pantheon-inspired dome atop building 10 (which houses the engineering library) and examine the two sculptures on display in the yard: Henry Moore's *Three-Piece Reclining Figure* and Michael Heizer's *Guennette*. Go back inside building 10 and continue down the infinite corridor until you find, on your left, the **Compton Gallery**, which showcases changing exhibits that illustrate an interaction between art and science. Right outside the exhibit area is a glass case containing items that constitute a brief MIT history. Open weekdays; Tel: (617) 253-4444.

The **Hart Nautical Galleries**, displaying models of various sailing vessels and covering 1,000 years of nautical history, can be reached from the rotunda in building 7 by way of the corridor that leads off to the right past the Information Center. A "replica" of the *Santa María,* flagship of Christopher Columbus's fleet in 1492, has sails, rigging, and a square stern—a shape that was not actually in use until the following century. An especially ominous-looking model is the one of a 1591 Korean warship called *Turtle* (although its enclosed deck pierced with iron spikes is more suggestive of a porcupine). To further the vessel's terrifying effect its sailors used a mixture of sulfur and saltpeter to create fumes that poured from its dragon-shaped head. Open weekdays; Tel: (617) 253-5942.

Cross Mass. Ave. outside building 7 to enter the west side of the campus, where student activities are concentrated. Straight ahead is the **Kresge Oval**, an oval-shaped lawn edged by a few buildings of particular interest. To the right is the student center, the **Julius Adams Stratton Building** (named after MIT's 11th president), which houses a variety of shops and services for students (visitors, too, are welcome) and a museum shop. Also on the edge of the oval is **Kresge Auditorium**, designed by architect Eero Saarinen in the mid-1950s, which houses two theaters. The roof is one-eighth of a sphere and rests on only three points (the walls of the building were constructed after the roof was finished). Saarinen was also the designer of the small **Kresge Chapel** opposite the auditorium (the chapel's doors are usually open, and visitors may enter). The moat surrounding the round red-brick chapel reflects patterns of light onto the low arches at its outside base and the interior rim. A multi-piece screen at the altar creates a waterfall effect with light from the skylight above it.

If you walk a short distance on Mass. Ave. from the MIT campus to the Charles River you'll come to the **Harvard Bridge**, which opened in 1891. Proposals to rename the bridge for MIT because of its proximity to the relocated campus were decried by members of the MIT community who felt that the bridge was so poorly designed that the name would not do justice to an institution that prides itself on its knowledge of engineering. If you walk onto the bridge (it's safe, thanks to a recent overhaul), in addition to a beautiful view of Boston you will discover that marked in paint on the sidewalk at regular intervals are units of measurement unique to MIT called "Smoots." There was a time when many MIT students lived across the bridge on the Boston side of the river and had to make the trek to campus in all kinds of weather. One day an upperclassman at a fraternity decided it was high time that students be able to judge just how much farther they had to go to get to class, so he measured the bridge in "pledge lengths," using five-foot-six-inch-tall pledge Oliver Reed Smoot. The marks on the bridge, which measures 364.4 Smoots and one ear, are repainted every year by the new pledge class.

Walk back up Mass. Ave. beyond the MIT campus for about ten minutes to reach the Main Exhibition Center of the **MIT Museum**, at number 265 (look for the red door set back from the street). You might begin your visit with a computer quiz just beyond the reception desk. You probably won't know most of the answers, as the questions are based on MIT history and trivia, but the quiz is a quick way to learn a few interesting tidbits about MIT before making a foray into the main exhibit areas. There are changing exhibitions as well as a half-dozen permanent displays. The sign near an exhibit of light sculptures warns of mild electrical shock if two people touch a plasma globe simultaneously but also reassures: "This exhibit is not dangerous to your health." Crazy After Calculus highlights some of the top pranks pulled by MIT students over the years. The museum shop sells myriad appealing scientific curios and souvenirs.

The museum is open Tuesday through Friday from 9:00 A.M. to 5:00 P.M., and on Saturday and Sunday from 1:00 to 5:00 P.M.; Tel: (617) 253-4444.

EAST CAMBRIDGE

Not so long ago there wasn't much of a reason to go out of the way to visit East Cambridge. But that's changed. Today this part of the city is home to the Sports Museum of New England and is the point of departure for excursion boats that cruise along the Charles River. In addition, Boston's Museum of Science is close by.

Much of the activity in this area is centered around the **CambridgeSide Galleria**, a mall accessible by means of the Green Line to the Lechmere stop or the Galleria's own shuttle bus from Kendall station on the Red Line. Although primarily an indoor suburban-type shopping mall (its three levels have more than 100 stores and restaurants), the Galleria has a wonderful outdoor space. Its semicircular design hugs the Lechmere Canal's lagoon and the surrounding plaza to create a public park and outdoor café area. Summer evenings are graced by free outdoor music concerts featuring top local names in blues, rock, country, and folk. For further information, Tel: (617) 621-8666.

But you don't have to settle for a view of the lagoon from across your café table (although the view is indeed lovely). The **Charles River Boat Company** makes it possible to get right out there on the water in craft ranging from paddleboats to excursion boats, which depart hourly every day between noon and 5:00 P.M. in the summer (there are special dinner cruises, too). Tel: (617) 621-3001.

SPORTS MUSEUM OF NEW ENGLAND

On the first floor of the Galleria is the Sports Museum of New England. Opened in 1987 in Boston and relocated to its larger space here in 1992, the museum is dedicated to honoring the achievements of professional and amateur athletes in all sports in the six New England states. Among the displays of memorabilia are the 1970 Stanley Cup Player Trophy, awarded to Bobby Orr for scoring the winning goal (in overtime) that clinched the Boston Bruins' first cup in 29 years; a swimming trophy won by Eva Morrison, considered by some to be the greatest female marathon swimmer of all time (she is also credited with saving 52 people from drowning); a baseball bat used in the first World Series (1903), won by the Boston Red Sox; the oldest tennis racket in America; plus full-size wooden sculptures of Bobby Orr and Larry Bird. Educational programs are also held at the museum, and occasionally sports celebrities put in an appearance.

The museum (whose chairman is former Celtics guard David Cowens) is open from 10:00 A.M. to 9:30 P.M. daily, except Sundays, when doors open at noon and close at 6:00 P.M. Tel: (617) 787-7678.

MUSEUM OF SCIENCE

Although its address is in Boston, the Museum of Science is just a short distance from the Cambridge city line and is easily included in an exploration of the East Cambridge area. The museum is located just across the street from the Green Line's Science Park station or a short walk from the CambridgeSide Galleria and the Sonesta Hotel. (Parking is available in the museum's garage.)

Founded in 1830 as the Boston Society of Natural History, the museum houses more than 400 permanent exhibits and hosts a series of outstanding travelling exhibits throughout the year. Some of the more popular attractions include the Human Body Discovery Space, which features a human skeleton riding a bicycle, and the Live Animal Stage, with guest appearances by porcupines, snakes, owls, and an eight-foot-long, 50-pound boa constrictor. Don't miss the Thomson Theater of Electricity, where the world's largest electrostatic generator, capable of generating 2½ million volts of electricity, produces indoor lightning bolts for the museum's most hair-raising performance. The museum's Omni Theater presents films on the largest screen in New England (a four-story-tall wraparound) that allow you to experience the thrill of floating over Niagara Falls in a hot-air balloon or peering inside an erupting volcano. The museum's **Charles Hayden Planetarium** (Tel: 617/523-6664) will take you on a journey to the heavens.

Exhibits are open Tuesday through Sunday from 9:00 A.M. to 5:00 P.M. (also open Mondays in the summer); and until 9:00 P.M. on Fridays (hours are sometimes extended on weekends as well). The museum is free Wednesday afternoons from 1:00 to 5:00 P.M. from September through May. Planetarium and Omni Theater presentations have varying schedules and separate admission fees. Tel: (617) 723-2500.

CELEBRATIONS AND SPECIAL EVENTS

Below is a month-by-month listing of the most popular celebrations and events that are held in the Boston area every year without fail—some for more than 100 years. Still, they represent only a fraction of what there is to see and do. Specifics about these and other events can be found in the Calendar section of the Thursday *Boston Globe* or in the

Travel Planner booklet available from the Greater Boston Convention & Visitors Bureau. Call the bureau for up-to-the-minute details of any of the listings that appear below; Tel: (617) 536-4100.

January. Boston's **First Night Celebration**, a tradition since 1975, draws thousands of costumed revelers into the city every New Year's Eve to enjoy more than 100 different events involving dance, theater, mime, film, and music. The day begins with a parade and ends with fireworks. And afterward, your ride home on the T is free, compliments of the city of Boston.

On New Year's Day those with hangovers might find a dip with the **L Street Brownies** a sobering experience. Since 1904 swimmers have been taking their annual plunge into the icy Boston Harbor from the L Street Bathhouse in South Boston. Join them if you dare.

February. Just when the winter blahs are setting in, the **Boston Festival** comes to the rescue with its ongoing, month-long festival of arts and entertainment (from Valentine's Day to St. Patrick's Day). In 1992 there were dog-sled races on the Boston Common, an ice-carving competition, and a public skate at the Boston Garden, home of the Boston Bruins. Discounts at restaurants, museums, hotels, and retail stores are part of the deal, too.

March. A reenactment is held each year on the anniversary of the **Boston Massacre** (March 5, 1770), when Crispus Attucks, a former slave, and four others were killed just outside the Old State House by British soldiers.

The **St. Patrick's Day Parade** begins at 1:00 P.M. in South Boston on the Sunday before March 17, the date, coincidentally, when the British left town in 1776. (To get there, take the MBTA Red Line to the Broadway station.)

The theme of the **New England Spring Flower Show**, the oldest continuing flower exhibition in the country (staged by the Massachusetts Horticultural Society for 130 years), changes every year. The 1992 show included the creation of a lavish indoor tropical rain forest, complete with rain, thunder, and lightning; the theme of the 1993 show is "Through the Garden Gate." It's scheduled for March 6 through March 14 at Bayside Exposition Center, 200 Mount Vernon Street, Dorchester, a short walk from the Red Line's UMass/JFK Library station (or a shorter ride on the special shuttle bus from the T station right to the door).

April. The **Swan Boats**, a tradition since 1877, return to the Boston Public Garden's lagoon in mid-April, where they float through September.

The third Monday in April, Patriots' Day, is the day of the **Boston Marathon**, the oldest marathon in the United States (run since 1896), drawing athletes from all over the world. The race begins at noon at Hopkinton Common and finishes 26.2 miles later in front of the Boston Public Library in Copley Square in the Back Bay. The entire weekend is filled with related events, from carbo-loading the night before to sightseeing tours and sports clinics.

Patriots' Day commemorates the beginning of the American Revolution. Activities include reenactments of the rides of Paul Revere and William Dawes, and the hanging of the lanterns in the Old North Church.

May. The **Ducklings Day** parade from the State House to the Public Garden is held every May by the Historic Neighborhoods Foundation to honor Robert McCloskey's classic story *Make Way for Ducklings,* written in 1941.

On the third Sunday in May, when the biannual **Art Newbury Street** is held, Boston's most fashionable street is closed to traffic for an open house of its many galleries. (Also held one Sunday in September.)

June. **Bunker Hill Day**, named for a battle that never happened (the battle was actually fought on June 17, 1775, on Breeds Hill), is commemorated on the Sunday before June 17 with an 18th-century military encampment that includes inspection of arms, maneuvers, and open-fire cooking at the Charlestown Navy Yard, in Charlestown.

The **Dragon Boat Festival**, held on a Sunday in late June, celebrates the summer solstice with boats disguised as dragons racing from the Harvard Bridge to the Charles River Esplanade, a public park where there are martial arts demonstrations, Chinese folk dances, arts and crafts displays, and poetry readings in memory of Zhou dynasty poet Chu Yuan.

July and August. Boston's **Fourth of July** celebration, known as **Harborfest**, is perhaps the country's best, with more than 120 activities throughout the city over a five-day period. The annual **Boston Pops** concert, held at the Hatch Memorial Shell on the Charles River Esplanade at 7:30 P.M., is typically attended by a million or so patriots. (Some fans camp out the night before to get a good place on the lawn for the concert or rent a boat to moor nearby on the Charles River.) The Pops' version of the *1812 Overture* finale under the open sky uses real cannon and accompanies an elaborate display of pyrotechnics.

July and August are the months for the **North End Italian Festas**, held nearly every weekend to honor a designated saint with the blessing of the statue and procession through the streets, followed by food, games, and entertainment.

A number of **free outdoor concerts** by the Boston Pops are offered during July and August at the Hatch Memorial Shell; there are **free films** here, too, usually on Friday nights, as well as occasional dance performances. At City Hall Plaza once or twice a week the stage is occupied by artists who perform contemporary music, anything from '60s rock 'n' roll (Lou Christy performed in 1992) to Motown to country.

The largest Chinese festival of the year, the **August Moon Festival**, is held at the end of the summer to celebrate the coming of autumn, with traditional dances and foods—such as moon cakes for good luck.

September. On the third Sunday in September **Art Newbury Street** holds the second installment of its biannual celebration of art (the first takes place in May) by closing off the street and holding an open house at its numerous galleries.

October. Crews from all over the world compete in the **Head of the Charles Regatta**, held the next to the last Sunday in October. Each of the 18 events has 40 boats competing in three-mile races from the Boston University Bridge to the Park Reservation area (near the WBZ studios). More than 3,000 people participate, including the 1972 U.S. Olympic rowing team members, who have vowed to race every year until they come in last.

November. The **Veterans Day Parade** begins at 1:00 P.M. on Commonwealth Avenue at Hereford Street in the Back Bay and ends at Columbus Avenue and Dartmouth Street.

December. A reenactment of the **Boston Tea Party** (which occurred on December 16, 1773) is held every year on its anniversary beginning at 5:30 P.M. with a rally and parade from Old South Meeting House to the Tea Party Ship (at the Congress Street Bridge) for a mock tea dumping by costumed participants.

The **Boston Common Holiday Lights** ceremony includes carolers, speakers, and the lighting of some 25,000 bulbs draped on the Boston Common's trees the week before Christmas.

GETTING AROUND

We say the cows laid out Boston. Well, there are worse surveyors.

—*Ralph Waldo Emerson*

Arrival and Departure by Air

The runways at Logan International Airport, which is situated less than 3 miles (5 km) from downtown Boston, extend to water's edge, creating the perfect set-up for a grand aerial view of Boston Harbor and the city skyline. Look for the golden dome of the Massachusetts State House and the glass walls of the John Hancock Tower.

If you have questions about getting from the airport to your destination, go to the **Public Information Booth** on the lower level of the airport near the baggage claim area. Or ask one of the roving Airport Ambassadors, identifiable by the question mark on their lapels. Information is also available from Logan's 24-hour ground-transportation hot line; Tel: (800) 23-LOGAN or (800) 262-3335 TDD.

Taxis from the Airport. As the airport is only a few miles from Boston and Cambridge, the convenience and comfort of a taxi are well worth the few extra dollars. Taxis are dispatched continually to pick up passengers waiting in the designated line right outside the baggage claim area. The fare is metered, and a small amount is added to cover the toll if the route takes you through the Callahan Tunnel, which it probably will. First-time visitors are advised to read the posted rates. For points in Boston expect to pay up to $15 for the trip, plus tip; for Cambridge you'll pay up to $20 or more.

The taxi ride from the airport to Boston or Cambridge could take anywhere from 15 or 20 minutes to an hour or more, depending on traffic. The tunnel connecting the airport to the city invariably clogs at rush hour.

Car Rental. Car-rental booths are on the lower level of each terminal. If you are planning to rent a vehicle out of habit rather than need, however, be forewarned that parking in Boston and Cambridge is severely limited and getting around without a car is quite easy and enjoyable. If you are planning an out-of-town excursion, it might be a better idea to rent a car just for that day after you are settled into your hotel.

Public Transportation. An economical and efficient way to get to the city from the airport is the Massachusetts Bay Transit Authority system, commonly known as the T. For the time being, travelling by subway with heavy luggage is difficult; future MBTA plans call for the addition of a baggage car to address this problem. Free airport shuttle buses connect all terminals on a nine-minute circuit that includes a stop at the MBTA's Airport station on the Blue Line. (Get the number 22 or 33 bus; the number 11 does not stop at the T station.) The price of a token (85¢) will take you inbound to downtown Boston (about a seven-minute ride) and on into Cambridge via connections on the Green, Orange, and Red lines.

Water Shuttle. If your destination is Boston's financial district or Waterfront area, a good transportation option is the Airport Water Shuttle. The cross-harbor trip takes only seven minutes, meets no rush-hour traffic, costs only $7, and on a beautiful day can be a glorious experience. The shuttle

operates every 15 minutes on weekdays from 6:00 A.M. to
8:00 P.M., and every 30 minutes on Sundays and national
holidays from noon to 8:00 P.M. There is no service on
Saturdays, the Fourth of July, Thanksgiving, Christmas, or
New Year's Day. The airport's free shuttle bus connecting all
terminals also stops at the Logan Airport dock; tickets may be
purchased on the boat. For recorded information, Tel: (617)
330-8680.

The shuttle's point of arrival in the city is Rowes Wharf, on
Atlantic Avenue (Boston Harbor Hotel fronts the wharf).
South Station, with Amtrak and MBTA Red Line service, is a
few blocks south from Rowes Wharf. There are usually a few
taxis waiting at the entrance to the Boston Harbor Hotel.

For Wheelchair Users. For passengers who use wheelchairs,
the options for getting from the airport to your destination
include renting a car equipped with hand controls, arranging
for a wheelchair taxi to meet you, or contracting with a private
service for the use of a chair car. Hand-controlled cars can be
reserved in advance (two weeks is recommended) from Avis,
Hertz, Budget, and National car-rental companies. **Veterans
Taxi**, based in the nearby suburb of Newton, has a fleet of six
wheelchair taxis to service Greater Boston and the western
suburbs; Tel: (617) 527-0300 or (800) 442-7554. For referrals
and information about chair cars, call the **Information Center
for Individuals with Disabilities**; Tel: (617) 727-5540 (voice
and TDD) or (800) 462-5015 (within Massachusetts).

The airport provides one lift-equipped **Accessible Shuttle
Van** to take passengers to other terminals, parking areas, the
water shuttle, and the nearby Hilton Hotel. Tel: (617) 561-
1770 to arrange for the van to pick you up, or use the
automatic ring phone in the baggage claim area. Some
airport shuttle buses are also wheelchair accessible (look for
the HP symbol adjacent to the rear door of the bus).

The MBTA station at the airport is not wheelchair accessible at present, although there are plans to accomplish this in
the indefinite future. (The entrance to the subway platform
is down a flight of stairs; there is a single escalator running
up.) The Airport Water Shuttle is accessible, though problems are posed depending in part on the tide (high tide is
best), and it is probably more trouble than it is worth unless
you are staying at the Boston Harbor Hotel, which is located
right at the Boston-side dock.

Arrival by Rail

Trains for nationwide service arrive and depart from either
South Station, which connects with the MBTA Red Line, or
the Back Bay/South End station, with connections on the

Orange Line. In addition to Amtrak service (Tel: 617/482-3660 or 800/USA-RAIL), commuter-rail service operated by the MBTA (sometimes called the Purple Line) carries passengers from as far away as 60 miles to these two terminals and North Station, on the Green Line (Tel: 617/722-3200 or 800/392-6100).

After years of neglect **South Station**, on Atlantic Avenue where it meets Summer Street (Tel: 617/482-3660), has been completely refurbished, and its massive central space is now airy and bright with inviting café tables and chairs and a half-dozen food purveyors. South Station is close to the Financial District and Chinatown, and a short walk from Downtown Crossing's shopping area. The Red Line provides connections to points in Cambridge, including Harvard Square. The Greyhound Bus Terminal is also here.

The **Back Bay/South End** station, at 145 Dartmouth Street (Tel: 617/482-4400), is not as elaborate as South Station, but it is pleasant and has an interesting history. Located on the edge of the South End where it meets Copley Square, the station was the terminus for many trains from the southern United States, which carried blacks coming north in search of employment during the first half of the 20th century. Many of these newcomers went to work on the railroads as members of the Brotherhood of Sleeping Car Porters, the first black union in America. This station is dedicated to A. Philip Randolph, a Boston porter who was the union's chief organizer; there is a statue of Randolph in the station and a history of the union on the walls. The Back Bay/South End station is a short walk from Copley Square and the many hotels clustered in the area. The MBTA Orange Line stops here and connects with the Red and Blue lines for points throughout Boston and Cambridge.

North Station (in serious need of renovation) does not have interstate connections but is the point of departure for commuter-rail service to points north of Boston as well as connections to the Green and Orange lines. Commuter rail is convenient for travelling to the North Shore's Salem or Rockport.

Arrival by Bus

If you are arriving in Boston by bus, most likely you will end up at the **Greyhound Bus Terminal**, at South Station, on Atlantic Avenue where it meets Summer Street (Tel: 617/423-5810), as most of the private bus lines use this terminal. Connections can be made here for train and Red Line service. Boston's second bus terminal, the **Peter Pan/Trailways Station**, at 555 Atlantic Avenue (Tel: 617/426-8557 or 800/237-8747), is near South Station, for rail and Red Line service.

Getting Around on Foot

The best way to really *see* the Boston and Cambridge area is on foot. Boston and Cambridge are both delightfully compact, perfect for explorers with a pair of comfortable shoes, a map (pick one up at the information booth on the Boston Common or the Cambridge Discovery booth in Harvard Square), and a sense of adventure.

There are a few points to note when orienting yourself in the city. Downtown Boston is referred to as "the Hub" for a very good reason: Streets form sort of a wheel pattern radiating not from one center, but from several. This confusing pattern is blamed on the cows of centuries past, whose paths became Boston's earliest streets. Still, knowing the names of a few main streets—Tremont, Beacon, Washington—can help guide a disoriented pedestrian through the maze left by the cattle that once roamed the land.

The Back Bay, built on landfill, was a planned neighborhood, laid out as a long rectangle with one narrow edge bordering the Public Garden, the other ending with Massachusetts Avenue. One of the longest streets in the country, Mass. Ave. is the main thoroughfare running through the city of Cambridge.

While you're hoofing it around Boston, remember that the notoriously discourteous Boston driver is no myth: Boston has one of the highest rates of pedestrian fatalities in the nation. You'll be fine if you use caution, looking both ways even if you do have the walk light.

Getting Around by Public Transportation

For the price of a token (currently 85¢, with discounted fares for children, senior citizens, and persons with disabilities), a visitor can travel to destinations in the metropolitan Boston and Cambridge area quickly and easily on the rapid transit system operated by the Massachusetts Bay Transportation Authority (MBTA). Using the T can save you the unnecessary expense of a taxi and eliminate the hassle of driving and parking a car in a congested city. Daily service begins at around 5:00 A.M. and ends at around 12:30 A.M., with trains running every few minutes (a wait longer than ten minutes is unusual). Trains are of course crowded at rush hour, but, even so, the T is preferable to the alternatives. For information, Tel: (617) 722-3200 or (800) 392-6100.

Mastering the MBTA system is simple. First, pick up a color-coded map; the MBTA information booth inside the Park Street station and the tourist information booth on the Boston Common always have plenty. The subway trains and trolley cars operate along four lines designated by color: red, green, blue, and orange. The term "inbound" means you are headed for downtown Boston (the main station, Park Street, is the inbound terminus for the Green and Red lines). "Outbound" means you are heading outward from the downtown area. You can transfer from one line to another underground without paying an additional fare. There is no one station where all four lines converge, which means you may have to ride just one stop on one line to pick up the line you want. Rapid transit stations are designated by a sign with a large black T on a white background. Some stations are wheelchair accessible, some are not. The MBTA also operates buses with wheelchair lifts by advance arrangement on its regular routes. Tel: (800) LIFT BUS; (617) 722-5415 TDD.

Just a few of the destinations that can be reached easily by means of the T are: Logan Airport, Boston Common, Boston Public Garden, the Old State House, Faneuil Hall Marketplace, Newbury Street, the Museum of Science, Harvard Square, the Boston Tea Party Ship, the New England Aquarium, and Filene's Basement.

The MBTA has expended some effort to make its stations more pleasant than the usual underground station. Musicians are invited to perform at various T stops for what is a tough, though captive, audience. There are also artworks integrated into the architecture of certain stations. An enormous bronze hand reaches from the ceiling between the Red Line trains at Park Street station; hanging in the space between the inbound and outbound platforms at the Kendall Square station is a musical sculpture by Paul Matisse called "The Kendall Band," which people waiting for trains can "play" by pulling handles on the platform walls.

For those who intend to rely heavily on public transportation to get around, the MBTA sells two Boston Passport passes good for unlimited travel on the T and the buses (see below); currently a three-day pass costs $8 for adults, while a seven-day pass costs $16 for adults (children aged 6 to 11 pay half price). (At 85¢ per ride, you would need to use the three-day pass at least 10 times and the seven-day at least 19 times for the purchase to be justified.) Passes can be purchased at the three rail stations (North, South, and Back Bay), the tourist information booth on the Boston Common, and a few MBTA stations, including the Airport and Harvard Square. Tel: (617) 722-3200 or (800) 392-6100.

The MBTA's underground train lines are supplemented by the authority's bus system, which serves areas not covered by the four train lines. A bus ride costs 60¢, exact change. Buses operate on a daily schedule from approximately 5:00 A.M. to 12:30 A.M.

Getting Around by Car

The best advice when it comes to exploring Boston and Cambridge by car is *don't*. If you've come to the area by car, do yourself a favor and leave it safely parked at your hotel, then set out on foot or use the T to get around. If you insist upon driving, take note of the following local idiosyncrasies: Rotaries and merging lanes are commonplace, so be prepared to cut and be cut in the flow of traffic. Boston drivers are aggressive and cavalier (they often don't use their turn signals). If you want to get anywhere you'll have to be likewise—but keep an eye out for Boston pedestrians, who are equally aggressive and cavalier.

It is no accident that parking is a nightmare—the limited number of parking places (many of which are assigned to residents) is seen as a deterrent to increasing congestion. Consequently, motorists are reduced to fighting over the few available spaces. Again, the best advice is to forget driving altogether. Nevertheless, there may be a time when you'll need to take a car to the city. Be sure to find out if your hotel provides parking and at what price. One of the larger parking areas in downtown Boston is the **Prudential Center Garage** (at the Prudential Tower Building); in Harvard Square there's the **University Place Garage** (near the Charles Hotel, at 124 Mount Auburn Street).

Getting Around by Taxi

Taxis are often a good solution to getting somewhere that is off the beaten paths of subway lines and buses. They are plentiful, available any time of the day or night (they're especially useful after the T shuts down at around 12:30 A.M.), and reasonably priced.

Taxis typically line up in front of major hotels and at the main entrance to the Harvard Square subway station in Cambridge; otherwise a cab is just a phone call away. A few of the main companies in Boston are **Checker** (Tel: 617/536-7000), **Yellow Cab** (Tel: 617/536-3600), and **Town Taxi** (Tel: 617/536-5000); in Cambridge, try **Yellow Cab** (Tel: 617/547-3000) and **Ambassador Brattle Taxi** (Tel: 617/492-1100).

Wheelchair Taxis. In 1990 **Veterans Taxi** (based in the suburb of Newton) acquired a vehicle that carries two wheelchairs (it was the first taxi company in the state to do so). Now the company operates a fleet of six wheelchair taxis that service all of metropolitan Boston and the western suburbs. Standard taxi rates are charged for service. It's always recommended to call in advance to reserve one of the accessible vehicles for the day and time desired. Tel: (617) 527-0300 or (800) 442-7554.

Organized Walking Tours

Rangers from the **Boston National Historical Park** offer a variety of free walking tours, talks, and programs. The mainstay is the **Freedom Trail** tour, but there are also guided tours of the Black Heritage Trail and an occasional "Remember the Ladies" tour, which highlights women of note in Boston's history (the Freedom Trail, the Black Heritage Trail, and the Boston Women's Heritage Trail are discussed below in the section Self-Guided Tours). In addition, costumed characters help re-create events of the past, such as the Boston Massacre and Paul Revere's ride. A dozen or so tours are given daily in the summer, leaving from the visitors' center at 15 State Street; the rest of the year there are only occasional tours. Rangers also conduct tours and programs at historical park sites, including the USS *Cassin Young*, the Bunker Hill Monument, and Faneuil Hall. Tel: (617) 242-5642.

The **Boston Park Rangers** offer free nature and history walks in different areas of the city throughout the year. Walk and talk with a ranger to learn about the Boston Common or the Boston Public Garden, hike (or bike) the seven-mile stretch of Boston's parks called the Emerald Necklace, study the art and architecture of the Back Bay, hear about the women who played a part in "women's herstory," or visit Boston's historic burying grounds. Activities for kids include meeting a ranger's horse and a reading of the classic children's book *Make Way for Ducklings.* Tel: (617) 522-2639.

Discovering Boston Walking Tours specializes in customized private tours (and occasional public tours) led by Will Holton, a Northeastern University sociology professor, and his staff of guides—all educators who emphasize the social history of Boston. Favorite tours are of the North End, South End, Beacon Hill, the Waterfront, the Back Bay, Charlestown, and the Freedom Trail. Tel: (617) 323-2554.

The **Boston Women's Heritage Trail** (publisher of the *Boston Women's Heritage Trail* guide booklet) conducts walking tours by arrangement in the Downtown area, the North End, Chinatown, Beacon Hill, and the Boston neighborhood of Jamaica Plain (south of Roxbury), pointing out sites associated with such notable women in Boston's history as Amy Beach (the first woman to write a symphony), Mother Mary Joseph Rogers (founder of the Maryknoll Sisters), and Louisa May Alcott (best known for her book *Little Women*). Tel: (617) 522-2872.

The **Women's Heritage Foundation**, founded by the former director of the Boston Women's Heritage Trail, also conducts regularly scheduled walking tours during the summer and occasional trolley tours (see below) that focus on the history of women in Boston. Tel: (617) 731-5597.

The **Eliza Spencer Gallery**, at 54 Canal Street, conducts a walking tour of selected Newbury Street art galleries, where current exhibitions are viewed and discussed. The tour visits four prominent galleries with an optional stop for tea at the Ritz-Carlton Hotel. Tel: (617) 742-1400.

Cambridge Discovery, a nonprofit information service, leads regularly scheduled walking tours of Cambridge during the summer and by appointment for both individuals and groups at other times of the year. Tours leave from its tiny information booth in the center of Harvard Square (look for a structure that resembles a large birthday cake). Tel: (617) 497-1630.

The **Cambridge Historical Society** offers a series of Sunday walks during the month of May. Historical Society members take participants on strolls down Tory Row, along upper Brattle Street, and through East and North Cambridge. Tel: (617) 547-4252.

Trolley Tours

Boston Trolley Tours (the "blue trolley") operates 100-minute tours beginning at 9:00 A.M. every day of the year; visitors may board (or reboard) at any of its 16 stops (major hotels and sites). Driver/guides tell stories about Boston's history as they take guests along the Waterfront, through the North End, the Back Bay, Chinatown, Beacon Hill, and Charlestown. This is the only trolley line in Boston with wheelchair-accessible trolleys. Tel: (617) TROLLEY.

Old Town Trolley Tours (the "original orange and green trolley"), part of the national Historic Tours of America chain, conducts 90-minute narrated tours of Boston covering more than 100 points of interest in the Back Bay, Chinatown, Beacon Hill, the North End, the Waterfront, and Charlestown. Guests may board (or reboard) at any of the 15 stops. Sixty-minute tours are offered in Cambridge daily between 9:00 A.M. and 4:00 P.M., departing from the Cambridge Discovery booth in Harvard Square. Tel: (617) 269-7010.

The **Gray Line** operates 90-minute narrated tours of Boston's Freedom Trail in its open-air double-decker buses, which is sort of like riding in a convertible (glass tops are installed on cloudy days). Participants may board and reboard at any of the 14 stops along the route. The company also operates a comprehensive three-hour tour of Greater Boston, plus tours of Cape Cod, the New England seacoast, Salem, and Plymouth, and a combination tour of Lexington, Concord, and Cambridge. Tel: (617) 426-8805.

Sleuth & Co. offers the **Twilight Mystery Tour**, a 90-minute sunset drive along a route that features Boston's most notorious crime spots. The tour guide adds a few entertaining insights for guests by assuming the identities of the different villains. Tel: (617) 542-2525.

Limousine Tours

If you feel like seeing the sights in style, **Commonwealth Limousine Service** will be more than happy to accommodate with its fleet of Cadillac and Lincoln stretch limousines featuring a uniformed chauffeur (dressed in hat, gloves, and three-piece black suit), air conditioning, complimentary bar, stereo cassette system, TV, phone, and moon roof. (Luxury sedans and vans are available, too.) Boston's only licensed sightseeing limousine service, the company can suggest itineraries that explore historic Boston and Cambridge, Lexington and Concord, the North Shore, and Cape Cod and the Islands, or will otherwise customize your tour to your every desire. There is a minimum of three hours per booking. (For a special occasion, prices aren't nearly as high as you'd expect.) Tel: (617) 787-5575 or (800) 558-LIMO.

Self-Guided Tours

While some visitors prefer the convenience and comfort of trolley tours that stop at the sites along the **Freedom Trail**, walking the route (or some of it) at your own pace on a pleasant day can be an adventure in itself. Maps are available at the information booth on the Boston Common and at the Boston National Historical Park Visitor Center at 15 State Street. Just follow the red line painted on the pavement from the Boston Common to Bunker Hill; along the way you'll see Faneuil Hall, Paul Revere's house and the Old North Church, the Old State House, and more. Tel: (617) 536-4100.

Visitors who use wheelchairs have the option of signing up for Freedom Trail tours on the accessible trolleys of Boston Trolley Tours, but can also put together their own self-guided **Boston by Wheelchair** tour with the help of the *Sightseeing in Boston* publication available free from the Information Center for Individuals with Disabilities (Tel: 617/727-5540 voice; 617/345-9743 TDD). Accessible sites included are the Boston Common, the State House, the Boston National Historical Park Visitor Center, Faneuil Hall Marketplace, and the Bunker Hill Monument. Also noted in the publication are accessible parking places, T stops, drinking fountains, and rest rooms. In addition, *Choices: A Cultural Access Directory,* sold by Very Special Arts Massachusetts, lists access information for museums, theaters, and historical sites (Tel: 617/350-7713 voice; 617/482-4298 TDD). Call early to get copies of these publications sent to you in advance of your trip. One cautionary note about putting together your own self-guided tour: Many public sites are now accessible to wheelchairs, but many of the streets and sidewalks in between are rough going.

Although occasional guided tours are conducted by the Boston National Historical Park rangers and others (see Organized Walking Tours, above), most of the time visitors are on their own when it comes to following the footsteps of the women who are honored on the **Boston Women's Heritage Trail**. The booklet published by the trail's founders outlines four different walking tours of Boston: Downtown, the North End, Chinatown, and Beacon Hill. Among the women featured are Phillis Wheatley (the first published black female poet), Mary Dyer (a Quaker hanged on the Boston Common for her religious beliefs), Mother Goose (author of children's nursery rhymes), and Julia Ward Howe (author of the "Battle Hymn of the Republic" and initiator of Mother's Day). The booklet is usually available at the information booth on the Boston Common and at the Boston National Historical Park Visitor Center at 15 State Street, but if you want to be sure you'll have one in hand when the time comes, advance orders are filled by the Boston Women's Heritage Trail. Tel: (617) 522-2872.

Guided tours of the **Black Heritage Trail** are conducted by the Boston National Historical Park from mid-April through early November and by arrangement at other times. But visitors are also welcome to pick up a map from the park's Visitor Center at 15 State Street or the Museum of Afro-American History, at 46 Joy Street on Beacon Hill, to explore the history of Boston's 19th-century African-American community on their own. The map shows sites located primarily on the north slope of Beacon Hill, including the African Meeting House (the oldest black church still standing in the United States), the Robert Gould Shaw and 54th Regiment Memorial (which commemorates the bravery of the first free black regiment that fought for the North in the Civil War), and the Lewis and Harriet Hayden House (a station on the Underground Railroad). Tel: (617) 742-5415.

The information booth in Harvard Square operated by Cambridge Discovery supplies visitors with maps for various walking tours of Cambridge. **Cambridge During the Revolution** includes Christ Church (an Anglican Church that got caught in the crossfire when sentiment turned away from England) and the Harvard University buildings used for barracks during the American Revolution. **Old Cambridge Walking Guide** points out 30 historic sites such as the Washington Elm on the Cambridge Common (where George Washington took command of the Continental Army in 1775) and the site of the "spreading chestnut tree" immortalized by Henry Wadsworth Longfellow. Many famous events that took place in and around Harvard Square are covered by these two walking tours. For those who enjoy looking at typical homes built in the styles favored in the 19th century (many are Greek Revival), there's the **East Cambridge Walking Guide**. Now in development is the **Cambridge African American Heritage Trail**, which will identify about 20 sites associated with prominent African-American educators, abolitionists, writers, politicians, and others, such as W. E. B. DuBois (the first black man ever to receive a Ph.D. from Harvard and principal founder of the NAACP in 1903) and Lewis and Milton Clarke (escaped slaves on whose lives Harriet Beecher Stowe based the character of George Harris in *Uncle Tom's Cabin*). Tel: (617) 497-1630.

The **HarborWalk** trail, marked by a blue line on the pavement, takes visitors to sights important in Boston's maritime history, starting at the Boston National Historical Park Visitor Center at 15 State Street, once known as "the great street to the sea." On the route are the Custom House, Long Wharf (Boston's principal wharf since 1711), the Boston Tea Party Ship and Museum, and the New England Aquarium on Central Wharf. Maps are available at the visitors' center and at the information booth on the Boston Common. Tel: (617) 242-5642.

Harbor Tours and Whale Watches

Bay State Cruise Company, at the RED Ticket Office on Long Wharf, offers a 55-minute inner harbor sightseeing cruise with an optional stop at the USS *Constitution,* sunset and lunch cruises, plus whale watches and daily sailings to Georges Island, Nantasket Beach on Boston's South Shore, and Provincetown on Cape Cod. This company also operates a water shuttle to other harbor islands from Georges Island. Boats operate from mid-April to mid-October. Tel: (617) 723-7800.

Boston Harbor Cruises, at One Long Wharf, offers both public and private excursions, including whale watches, a cruise to the USS *Constitution,* and 90-minute sightseeing cruises that explore the old and new of Boston Harbor. They also operate a water shuttle to the John F. Kennedy Library. Boats operate from mid-April to mid-October. Tel: (617) 227-4321.

The harbor cruises of the **Spirit of Boston**, at the Boston Harbor Hotel on Rowes Wharf, offer an abbreviated version of a cruise ship experience, with live entertainment, full-service bars, lobster luncheons, and dinner cruises. The captain's narration highlights such landmarks as Castle Island, Bunker Hill, the USS *Constitution,* and the Old North

Church. Boats operate from April to December. Tel: (617) 569-4449.

The **New England Aquarium** sponsors whale-watching cruises from April to October aboard their vessel *Voyager II,* which leaves from Central Wharf near the Aquarium. Experienced naturalists explain whale behavior and identification, point out sea birds and marine life, and relate the history of Boston Harbor and its islands. Sightings of finback and humpback whales are guaranteed—if you don't see any you are issued a rain check. Each sailing lasts four to five hours. Tel: (617) 973-5277.

Helicopter Tours

Business Helicopters takes visitors on helicopter tours that fly over the State House, Fenway Park, the Bunker Hill Monument, the USS *Constitution,* and Boston Harbor. Flights depart from the Boston City Heliport, at 31 Fargo Street in South Boston, which is a short taxi ride from South Station. Tours are offered in summer from 10:00 A.M. to 4:00 P.M.; each flight lasts eight to ten minutes. Note that the company requires a minimum of four passengers per flight. Tel: (617) 423-0004.

For Further Information

The walk-in **Boston National Historical Park Visitor Center** (Tel: 617/242-5642) offers Boston information, free guided walking tours (donations welcome), rest rooms, and a bookstore that contains an interesting assortment of titles relating to area history, life in the Colonies, and the American Revolution and its major players. An eight-minute slide show, hidden in a back corner of the second floor, can be activated at will. The visitors' center, located at 15 State Street next to the Old State House (at the State Street T stop), is open weekdays from 8:00 A.M. to 5:00 P.M., and weekends from 9:00 A.M. to 5:00 P.M. Hours are extended to 6:00 P.M. from Memorial Day weekend through Labor Day.

The **Boston Common Visitor Information Center**, operated by the Greater Boston Convention and Visitors Bureau (Tel: 617/536-4100), is located on the Tremont Street side of the Boston Common (near the Park Street station). Open daily from 8:30 A.M. to 5:00 P.M., the booth provides a variety of free brochures, and staff members will answer whatever questions you might have about planning your visit.

The **Cambridge Discovery Information Booth**, a tiny structure that bears an uncanny resemblance to a cake, sits at the mouth of the main entrance to the Harvard Square T station. The small space is packed full of information organized so efficiently that if the volunteer doesn't already know the answer to your question, he or she can find it easily. Here are brochures, maps, bus schedules, even tax forms and Red Sox schedules, all for the asking, some free of charge. Cambridge Discovery also offers walking tours of the Harvard Square area. Hours are Monday through Saturday from 9:00 A.M. to 5:00 P.M., Sundays from 1:00 to 5:00 P.M. In late spring and summer the booth stays open an hour later. Tel: (617) 497-1630.

—*Jan Stankus*

ACCOMMODATIONS

Finding a comfortable, well-situated place to stay in Boston or Cambridge is easy enough if you plan ahead. Although it may be hard to believe that at times all of the 14,000 rooms in the area's three-dozen or so hotels are completely booked, be forewarned that this can and does happen—during college graduation time every spring, during fall foliage season, on the July 4 holiday weekend, and whenever a special event or major convention is held in town. So do reserve in advance, especially if you intend to visit during one of these peak times.

If your trip is a spontaneous one, however, and you have not made advance reservations, as a last resort you can head for the **Boston Welcome Center**, at 140 Tremont Street (across from the Boston Common), or the **Cambridge Discovery Information Booth**, in the center of Harvard Square. Both outfits offer an on-the-spot reservations service, with some discounted rates as well. (Be advised that both usually close at 5:00 P.M., though the Welcome Center is open until 7:00 P.M. and the Cambridge Discovery Information Booth until 6:00 P.M. during the summer.)

Visitors to the Boston area can expect to find all the usual comforts and amenities, but at rates that are among the highest in the country. Projected room rates for 1993 indicate doubles running as high as $210 to $380 per night in the luxury hotels, and $365 to $785 or more for suites, depending on the degree of luxury you desire. Moderate-to-expensive hotels are projected to charge between $110 and $200 for doubles. Lower rates are available for special weekend packages (always ask), which often include such money-saving extras as complimentary breakfast, dinner for two at the hotel's restaurant, a bottle of Champagne, theater or Red Sox tickets, First Night and Boston Festival buttons (for free admission to events), an MBTA visitor pass (for free public transportation), free parking, or discounts on major attractions.

Besides standard hotels, the Boston and Cambridge area has a number of bed-and-breakfasts and a few small inns for those who prefer more personal accommodations. While some of the more luxurious B and Bs can cost more than $100 per night for a double (including breakfast, of course), many more offer a reasonably priced alternative in the $60 to $95 range. Some B and Bs are accessible only through their reservation service agency; others advertise directly to the public.

The discussion that follows includes only well-located accommodations. The Back Bay and environs (Beacon Hill, the South End, the Fenway), the Waterfront, and Harvard Square are recommended for their proximity to just about everything of interest to a visitor. Unless otherwise indicated, rates given below are projections for double rooms, double occupancy, for 1993. As rates are subject to change, always check before making reservations. State and city taxes combined add another 9.7 percent to the bill.

The telephone area code for Boston and Cambridge is 617.

Boston

BACK BAY AND ENVIRONS

Staying at one of the many hotels and several bed-and-breakfasts in the Back Bay section of Boston positions you within easy walking distance of such major attractions as the Public Garden; Newbury Street, with its numerous shops and restaurants; and the John Hancock Observatory. The MBTA's Green Line stops in the Back Bay area include the Arlington, Copley, Prudential, and Hynes Convention Center/ICA stations. The Orange Line stops at the Back Bay/South End station on Dartmouth Street, as does the commuter-rail line serving points outside of Boston.

Boston Public Garden Area

In the Back Bay neighborhood closest to the Boston Public Garden (near the Arlington T station) there are two luxury hotels, the Ritz-Carlton and the Four Seasons, as well as the more moderately priced Boston Park Plaza Hotel. The Beacon Hill Bed & Breakfast is a short walk down a charming street on the other side of the Public Garden.

"We are ladies and gentlemen serving ladies and gentlemen" is the credo that the staff of the **Ritz-Carlton** lives by. Guests have come to expect, and appreciate, the strict etiquette and formal elegance that set the tone at Boston's premier hotel: the polite "Good afternoon" that greets them in the hallways, the white-gloved elevator operators, the cobalt-blue goblets that match the original chandeliers, the jacket-and-tie requirement in the dining room. For six decades this prestigious hotel has welcomed royalty (such as King Hussein, Prince Charles, and the Aga Khan) and celebrities (Elizabeth Taylor and Gary Cooper, among others).

The Ritz-Carlton's graciously appointed suites have woodburning fireplaces and views of the Public Garden (complimentary ice skates are provided in winter for those who wish to venture out onto the frozen lagoon). Furnished in classic French Provincial style, all rooms are lovely, regardless of whether they are situated in the older wing or the 1981 addition (which has the same decor but larger bathrooms). Amenities include weekday-morning limousine service to selected areas and 24-hour room service. While health-club facilities are available on the premises, guests are also given complimentary access to the outstanding facilities and pool at Le Pli, at the Heritage, just down the street at 28 Arlington Street. Guests who arrive by car may park in the hotel's own garage nearby.

The formal Dining Room, which has a fine reputation, requires proper dress, while the Café is more casual. The Bar at street level is an elegant meeting place. If you choose to stay elsewhere but find yourself in the mood to be treated as a lady or gentleman, dress in your finest and stop by between 2:30 and 5:00 P.M. for tea in the Lounge, when you can sample the cucumber finger sandwiches and the best scones in town.

15 Arlington Street, Boston, MA 02117. Tel: 536-5700 or (800) 241-3333; Fax: (617) 536-1335. $260–360; suites $785–$2,075.

For a luxury establishment, the **Four Seasons Hotel** is curiously relaxed and unpretentious, the kind of place where you can wear jeans and not worry about breaking the dress code. Kids are made to feel comfortable here, too, with toys and games, kid-size robes, and peanut-butter-and-jelly sandwiches on the menu, which doubles as a coloring book. And in a city that can sometimes seem provincial, the hotel's international atmosphere is welcome (members of the staff speak more than 50 languages among them).

The amenities intended to make your stay as pleasant as possible include 24-hour concierge and room service, free limousine rides downtown, a health club and pool, and valet parking. Although the hotel has no outside space of its own, the Public Garden acts as its front yard. A room with a garden view costs more, but you'll be able to open your windows onto one of the most beautiful sights in the city. For those who'd like to do more than view the greenery from across Boylston Street, the Four Seasons staff will prepare a picnic basket or supply a bag of peanuts to feed the squirrels. As the theater district is virtually in the hotel's back yard, special theater packages are offered frequently. There's also a fixed-price theater menu at the hotel's celebrated French restaurant, **Aujourd'hui**, so that guests can enjoy dinner and still make the curtain—a courtesy that should not be taken lightly, considering the often slow service at many other theater-district restaurants.

200 Boylston Street, Boston, MA 02116. Tel: 338-4400 or (800) 332-3442; Fax: (617) 423-0154. $250–$340; suites $365–$400.

Every spring the Saunders family, current owners of the **Boston Park Plaza Hotel & Towers**, arranges for the Public Garden swans (Romeo, Juliet, Castor, and Pollux) to be brought from their winter home in Maine to their Boston habitat a block from the hotel, which explains the logo (a swan and its reflection) that appears throughout the property (even on the doorknobs). First opened in 1927 by Ellsworth Milton Statler, the hotel has always played a significant role in the Boston scene. Franklin D. Roosevelt, John F. Kennedy, Richard Nixon, and Michael Dukakis have campaigned on the premises. This grand hotel has long had a reputation for providing modern amenities at reasonable prices. It was the first hotel to put a radio in every guest room and to install valet doors (still there) in a deliberate effort to minimize the need for tipping. The hotel continues to offer affordable accommodations but also offers luxury-class amenities on the Plaza Towers floor: express check-in, a concierge, a private elevator, complimentary Continental breakfast, and a cozy lounge.

Although the neighboring Four Seasons obscures the Park Plaza's views of the Public Garden, the Park Plaza's large complex offers guests easy access to parking (in a garage across the street), foreign currency exchange, language interpreters (in 26 languages), and airline ticket offices. Also on the premises are a popular **cabaret theater** (ask about hotel packages that include free tickets) and the **Legal Seafoods** restaurant. For children, the hotel's Cub Club program provides free swan boat tickets, a story hour, and picnics in the park. The hotel also offers special "family double/double" rooms with two double beds and two bathrooms. Finally, you might rest easier here knowing that the hotel's operations follow an aggressive recycling and waste-reduction program.

64 Arlington Street, Boston, MA 02117. Tel: 426-2000 or (800) 225-2008; Fax: (617) 426-5545. $125–$175; Plaza Towers $150–$195.

Beacon Hill

Just down the street from the Bull & Finch Pub in Beacon Hill, the model for the television show "Cheers," the **Beacon Hill Bed & Breakfast** is situated in a quiet neighborhood just a few minutes' walk from the Boston Common and Public Garden, the Freedom Trail, the Arlington and Park Street T stations, restaurants, and downtown businesses. Built in 1869, the grand, six-story Victorian brick row house features high ceilings, massive doors, marble fireplaces (now solely decorative), and original moldings, as well as crystal chandeliers that once adorned a Loire château. Each of the three guest rooms is exceptionally large, even by Victorian standards, and has a private bath. Host Susan Butterworth serves delicious breakfasts of homemade granola, coffee cake, and French toast in the spacious dining room overlooking the Charles River. A caterer by profession, Butterworth trained at La Varenne in Paris and lived for many years in France, where she acquired expertise in the language as well as the cuisine. Discounted parking is available in a nearby garage. Smokers might be happier elsewhere, as this is a smoke-free home.

27 Brimmer Street, Boston, MA 02108. Tel: 523-7376. $100–$120 (includes breakfast).

Copley Square/South End

In the heart of the Back Bay at Copley Square is the elegant Copley Plaza Hotel, while just a few blocks west are the moderately priced Copley Square and Lenox hotels. Bed-and-breakfast accommodations are available at the Terrace Townehouse, which is just a short walk south of Copley Square in Boston's South End neighborhood, and at Newbury Guest House, a B and B on nearby Newbury Street. This part of the Back Bay is convenient to the Back Bay/South End station, with commuter-rail and Orange Line service, and the Green Line's Copley station.

A pair of gilded, three-ton lions guard the entrance of the **Copley Plaza Hotel**, moved here after decades of duty at the former Kensington Hotel on Boylston Street. Preserving Boston history seems to come naturally to this "Grande Dame," which was built in 1912 on the original site of the Museum of Fine Arts (now in the Fenway section of the city). The hotel's opulent decor reflects the best of old Boston, when debutantes sporting gardenia corsages would arrive with their escorts to attend tea dances in the Oval Room— which has seen more weddings than Trinity Church next door. Though the tea dances are no more, the hotel recently reopened its **Tea Court**, which has been attracting business types, among others, for tea and scones. A quiet old Boston atmosphere prevails in the intimate, book-filled **Library Bar**, made for quiet conversation, while the **Plaza Bar** features live jazz in the evening. The hotel has two popular restaurants, the formal **Plaza Dining Room** and the casual **Copley's Restaurant and Bar**, which displays caricatures of celebrities on the walls.

The massive archways and ceilings have been newly gilded in 24-karat gold (note the "skylight" above the reception desk, a square of frescoed sky in a painted window frame), and all guest rooms have been refurbished with marble bathrooms and reproductions of antique furniture. The best rooms are the spacious corner suites that afford views of the Copley Square Plaza out front. Guests are invited to use the hotel's valet parking service, car service to the financial district, and complimentary privileges at a nearby spa with a lap pool, aerobics classes, and massage.

138 St. James Avenue, Boston, MA 02116. Tel: 267-5300 or (800) 8-COPLEY; Fax: (617) 247-6681. $210–$260; suites $280–$375.

Despite its location in the busy Back Bay just a block from Copley Square, the small, family-owned **Lenox Hotel** is often compared to a country inn. This is the kind of place where you can come inside from a chilly New England day and warm yourself beside a crackling fire in the lobby's inviting lounge area. Rooms and suites are decorated in Colonial, French Provincial, and oriental styles, and 13 of them have wood-burning fireplaces. Opened in 1900—when the site of the Lord & Taylor next door was a railroad yard and trains used to back right up to the horseshoe-shaped hotel to unload passengers—the Lenox was hailed as "Boston's Waldorf-Astoria." Today the owners (the Saunders family, local Boston hoteliers who also own the Park Plaza and Copley Square hotels) promote its "affordable elegance," a trait that also extends to the reasonably priced **Upstairs Grill**, a fine restaurant with the atmosphere of an English manor house. Also on the premises is **Diamond Jim's Piano Bar**, a popular gathering place for amateur and professional singers, with an open mike. Guests may take advantage of valet parking and an adjacent garage, as well as the hotel's limousine service to and from Logan Airport.

710 Boylston Street, Boston, MA 02116. Tel: 536-5300 or (800) 225-7676; Fax: (617) 267-1237. $135–$215; corner rooms with fireplaces $235; suites $350.

In 1891 it cost one dollar for a night's stay at the **Copley Square Hotel**, then the only hotel in Copley Square and one of the few public buildings with electric lights and telephones. More than 100 years later, the small, informal hotel, which has recently completed a total renovation (the ninth since the property was purchased in 1948 by the Saunders family), is still offering bargain rates. The octagonal corner rooms are the most desirable for the space and view, but all rooms are comfortable and proffer the basics as well as a few extra touches, such as coffeemaker, hair dryer, and cable television.

The hotel is home to the **Original Sports Saloon**, a former hangout of the Boston Braves. Established in 1904, the saloon has what some say are the best ribs in town, along with an assortment of sports memorabilia, including a row of bleacher seats, a version of "the Green Monster," a papier-mâché bust of Bobby Orr, and original drawings of sports figures by Pulitzer Prize–winning cartoonist Paul Szep embedded in all the tabletops. On the bottom level of the hotel is what some consider one of the most romantic restaurants in Boston, the **Café Budapest** (featured in *Housesitter,* a 1992 movie with Goldie Hawn and Steve Martin; see the Dining section, below). The restaurant's space was once a club that attracted such jazz legends as Billie Holiday and Louis Armstrong.

Reduced-rate parking is available in a garage adjacent to the hotel. The closest T station is the Prudential, for Green Line service.

47 Huntington Avenue, Boston, MA 02116. Tel: 536-9000 or (800) 225-7062; Fax: (617) 267-3547. $120–$145.

The **Terrace Townehouse**'s black cat Nellie keeps pretty much to herself, though you may catch her napping on the couch in the library, where afternoon tea is served to guests of this South End bed-and-breakfast. On nice, warm days host Gloria Belknap serves tea—which often includes scones hot from the oven—on the roof deck, from which you can enjoy the view of the Back Bay and beyond. Situated on a quiet residential street lined with rows of Victorian town houses and brick sidewalks, this restored 1870 B and B has four guest rooms furnished with antiques. Breakfast, which is brought to your room in the morning, is served on antique china with crystal and silver (a bathrobe is provided to get you into the breakfast-in-bed mood). There are no televisions here, and no smoking. There's also no on-street parking, but several parking lots and car-rental offices are nearby. The Terrace Townehouse is two blocks east of Copley Square's Green Line station.

60 Chandler Street, Boston, MA 02116. Tel: 350-6520. $105–$140.

If you like to be where the action is, **Newbury Guest House** couldn't be better located. One step out the door and you're part of the endless parade of people along Boston's most fashionable street. A four-story town house built in

1882 as a private residence, the 15-room guest house has been carefully restored and furnished in Victorian style by the owners, a friendly father-and-son team. The original stained glass and polished wooden floors have been preserved, and paintings by local artists grace the guest rooms. A Continental breakfast buffet is served in the homey parlor or, in good weather, on the patio. Rates for rooms, each with private bath, are based in part on how many steps you're willing to climb (rooms on the top floor cost the least). You might also note that while front rooms afford great views of Newbury Street, the rooms facing the alley are significantly quieter. There is limited parking in the back for a small fee, but be sure to reserve a space in advance. Positioned in the central section of the eight-block street, between Fairfield and Gloucester, this B and B is close to Copley Square and the Green Line.

261 Newbury Street, Boston, MA 02116. Tel: 437-7666 or (800) 437-7668; Fax: (617) 262-4243. $85–$145.

Upper Back Bay and Fenway

At the western edge of the Back Bay (near the Hynes Convention Center/ICA Green Line station) are the newly refurbished Eliot Hotel and, just beyond the Back Bay in the area known as the Fenway, the American Youth Hostel.

When you first enter the **Eliot Hotel** (near the west end of Newbury Street), it may take a moment to remember what country you're in; the style, atmosphere, and clientele of this small, family-run, all-suites hotel, built in 1925 by the family of former Harvard president Charles Eliot (it's right next to the Harvard Club), are decidedly international. While suites in most hotels usually provide at most an extra sitting area, those in the Eliot (all newly redone with Italian marble in the baths and French doors in the bedrooms) have kitchenettes outfitted with a microwave and a refrigerator or minibar stocked with drinks. The hotel's **Eliot Lounge** is a famous runners' bar where survivors of the Boston Marathon congregate after the big race. Athletes from all over the world stop in to say hello to bartender (and former marathoner) Tommy Leonard, who established the post-run party tradition in the early 1970s. International flags, photos, and other sports memorabilia, including the running shoes of Joan Benoit Samuelson and Bill Rodgers, decorate the walls and ceiling. Parking is available.

370 Commonwealth Avenue, Boston, MA 02215. Tel: 267-1607 or (800) 44-ELIOT; Fax: (617) 536-9114. Suites $175 (a few double rooms are available for $145).

People of all ages (and of various income levels) stay in

the **American Youth Hostel**'s inexpensive, dormitory-style rooms, which are usually outfitted with three bunk beds each and a fan (there is no air conditioning). Because the AYH is part of an international peace organization, the emphasis is on making connections among people, so any night of the week there are organized outings to blues or comedy clubs, Faneuil Hall Marketplace, Red Sox games (the AYH purchases 1,000 tickets every season), walking tours, the symphony, or lectures. In addition, hostelers need only show their AYH receipt to receive discounts at nearby restaurants (mainly of the fast-food variety), museums (including the Museum of Fine Arts and the Computer Museum), facilities at the YMCA, and a nearby parking lot.

Take the Green Line to the Hynes Convention Center/ICA stop and walk west on Boylston Street, then left on Hemenway to reach the hostel. One note of caution: While the hostel itself is an oasis of friendship and goodwill and has taken security measures within and without the building—Boston's Guardian Angels, a citizen peacekeeping force, patrol regularly—the property is situated on a side street running behind a somewhat unsavory city block. Stay alert if you're walking alone.

Because of the great demand for lodging in season, only AYH members are permitted to stay at the Boston hostel (memberships are $25 for adults, $35 for families); nonmembers may stay here off-season for an additional nightly fee.

12 Hemenway Street, Boston, MA 02115. Tel: 536-9455; Fax: (617) 424-6558. $7–$10 per person for members; $3 surcharge for nonmembers.

FANEUIL HALL AND THE WATERFRONT

In addition to the Back Bay area, Faneuil Hall Marketplace and the Waterfront are especially desirable locations for lodging. Across the street from the marketplace, the Bostonian Hotel couldn't be better placed for visitors who like to be right in the middle of things. Access to much of the rest of the city is provided by the Green Line from nearby Government Center station. A short distance from the marketplace, right at the harbor's edge, is the luxurious Boston Harbor Hotel. The Blue Line's Aquarium station is right on the harbor, and South Station (for Red Line, Amtrak, and commuter-rail service) is a few blocks south.

The **Bostonian Hotel**, a warm, friendly establishment, recently replaced one of its trademark green-and-white-striped awnings with a yellow-and-white one in honor of a pair of house finches that nested in the window box of one of the suites. Some of the hotel's rooms are so close to the Haymarket that guests have been known to pitch money down to an obliging vendor who in turn heaves a cantaloupe up to the balcony. (Guests are entitled to discounts at certain Faneuil Hall shops.) Along with the standard amenities (including a VCR, minibar, and a telephone in the bathroom), some rooms have a wood-burning fireplace, a bidet, an oversized tub or Jacuzzi, and an exercise bicycle. On chilly days complimentary cider and cookies are served by the fireplace in the intimate lobby. Note the original paintings of the marketplace by New England artist Gracia Dayton, which were commissioned exclusively for the hotel. The hotel's acclaimed **Seasons Restaurant** has a view of the golden dome of Faneuil Hall.

At Faneuil Hall Marketplace, North and Blackstone streets, Boston, MA 02109. Tel: 523-3600 or (800) 343-0922; Fax: (617) 523-2454. $159–$235; suites $355–$550.

Those who come to town by private yacht needn't think twice about which of Boston's luxury hotels to select, as there is only one that provides guests with a private dock: the **Boston Harbor Hotel**, built on Rowes Wharf as part of a larger office and condominium complex surrounding an impressive 80-foot archway and copper-domed rotunda. A public plaza contains the hotel's marina, an outdoor restaurant and café (open in season), and docks for tour boats and the Airport Water Shuttle. While the hotel offers amenities expected of a luxury accommodation (plush robes, slippers, hair dryers, minibars), guests will especially appreciate the spacious rooms with windows that open for fresh air, plus a desk and separate dressing area. If you're not totally distracted by the view from your room (the harbor on one side, the city skyline on the other), you might take advantage of the full-service health club (with a 60-foot lap pool, exercise classes, sauna, and massage), the on-site business center, or the elegant **Rowes Wharf Restaurant**, overlooking the harbor. There's also a permanent exhibit of antique maps and charts of early New England (with originals dating back to the 15th century) in the Magellan Gallery on the first floor. The New England Aquarium and Faneuil Hall Marketplace are just a short walk to the north, and if you've forgotten your camera, one will be provided by the hotel.

Pet owners will be happy to know that their dogs and cats are not just tolerated here but rather considered part of the family. Your companion will be welcomed with an amenity basket (including biscuits and a pooper scooper for dogs, catnip toys for felines), plus a list of local contacts should walking, grooming, medical attention, or even psychoanalysis be required.

The hotel is, of course, ideal for those arriving from the airport by water shuttle (the trip takes about seven minutes). By car take the Harbor Tunnel to Route 93/3 south, exit at High and Congress streets onto Purchase Street, then turn left onto Atlantic Avenue. Rowes Wharf Parking Garage is adjacent to the hotel.

70 Rowes Wharf, Boston, MA 02110. Tel: 439-7000 or (800) 752-7077; Fax: (617) 330-9450. $225–$375; suites $340–$1,600.

Cambridge

Because the Cambridge/Boston area is so compact and the MBTA so efficient, you can find accommodations right in busy Harvard Square and still get around to see the sights in the rest of Cambridge and nearby Boston with no trouble at all. "The square" is the best place in Cambridge for easy access to the Harvard Square station on the Red Line as well as walking and trolley tours of the city (see Getting Around, above). At one edge of the square, close to the river, is the luxurious (and expensive) Charles Hotel; nearby is the moderately priced Harvard Manor House, the closest you can get to a motor inn in this part of Cambridge. Across from Cambridge Common (the square's back yard) is the lovely, traditional Sheraton Commander, while rooms at the new Inn at Harvard at the other edge of the square are priced more or less the same as those at the Harvard Manor House. Budget travellers will like the Irving House, located just a few blocks from Harvard Yard, with the lowest prices in this most desirable area. The Royal Sonesta Hotel is an excellent choice in eastern Cambridge, near the Museum of Science and the Green Line's Lechmere station.

Stories abound at the **Charles Hotel** about celebrities who have stayed here since the 1985 opening. (Jack Nicholson, clad in just his bathrobe, locked himself out of his room one day; Bill Murray threw a wild party that pretty much trashed the place.) Cambridge's "hotel to the stars" is at once luxurious and casual. Among its amenities are valet parking, 24-hour room service, and complimentary use of **Le Pli**, a full-service spa with an indoor heated lap pool set in a sunny, glassed-in deck. The **Regattabar**, site of an award-winning annual jazz festival (January through April), has showcased dozens of jazz greats, among them Stan Getz, Chick Corea, and Dizzy Gillespie. Also on the grounds are an indoor/outdoor bar fronting the plaza, the gourmet restaurant **Rarities**, and the **Bennett Street Café**, which serves a Sunday brunch so popular the hotel doesn't dare promote it.

1 Bennett Street, Cambridge, MA 02138. Tel: 864-1200 or (800) 882-1818; Fax: (617) 864-5715. $209–$259; suites $375–$1,400.

The **Harvard Manor House**, not far from the Charles Hotel at the corner of Mount Auburn and Eliot streets, couldn't be more centrally located. Restaurants, shops, and a park-like traffic island where street musicians perform nightly are right outside. A basic motor-inn style prevails in this former Treadway Inn (built in the 1960s): Rooms are plain but clean and comfortable, with a few amenities, such as color television and air-conditioning. Overall, you won't find much to write home about—except for the nightly rates, which are among the lowest for hotels in the square. For morning coffee there's a small café on the lowest level (the entrance is outside), but you might want to walk across the street to the Café Paradiso for cappuccino and a croissant at one of the outdoor tables. Parking is plentiful (but not free).

110 Mount Auburn Street, Cambridge, MA 02138. Tel: 864-5200 or (800) 458-5886. $113.

If you stand directly in front of the **Sheraton Commander Hotel** you'll see that the structure resembles a large, red-brick letter "H," which is said to stand for Harvard, located just on the other side of Cambridge Common. The establishment is close to the site of the elm tree on the Common where George Washington first took command of the American Continental Army in 1775; hence, the hotel was christened the Commander in 1926 when it opened. A statue of the commander stands at the entrance, while inside a diorama commemorates the event with minuscule soldiers in front of a tiny tree.

For many years the Commander was a residential hotel, which accounts for the range of room shapes and sizes (some suites have a magnificent sitting and dining area, complete with a cherry-wood table large enough to hold Thanksgiving dinner for your entire extended family). The decor throughout reflects the charm of a past era, with such genteel and authentic touches of luxury as hand-cut crystal chandeliers. Favored by people who like the feel of being in "old Cambridge," the hotel has hosted various celebrities visiting the area, among them Bob Hope, John Lennon and Yoko Ono, and Dr. Ruth Westheimer. On the premises are a restaurant and lounge, as well as a small fitness room and tiny sun deck; parking is also available. A monthly newsletter publishes information about current events (cruises, book fairs, Red Sox games).

16 Garden Street, Cambridge, MA 02138. Tel: 547-4800 or (800) 325-3535; Fax: (617) 868-8322. $150; suites $200.

The **Inn at Harvard**, which opened in 1991 on the site of a former gas station and parking lot, has its critics, many of whom got into the act before ground was ever broken. Compromises between Harvard University (the owner), community groups, the fire marshal, and architect Graham Gund resulted in a finished product that has been likened by some to a camel produced by a committee that set out to design a horse. Unless you look closely, it's hard to tell that the structure is even a hotel at all. Nevertheless, its primary appeal is its location at the eastern edge of Harvard Square (the less noisy edge), catercorner to Harvard Yard. Its guest rooms are pleasant and more affordable than those in the square's showplace hotel, the Charles, and the walls are graced with portraits of prominent Bostonians, on loan from the Fogg Museum. The hotel's atrium has drawn critics, too. Functioning as a combination breakfast room, lounge and work area, library, and chess and backgammon game room, it seems to be trying to please everyone at once. But light coming through the glass roof infuses the entire space (a 3,250-square-foot area) with a marvelous atmosphere. Parking is available.

1201 Massachusetts Avenue, Cambridge, MA 02138. Tel: 491-2222 or (800) 528-0444; Fax: (617) 496-5020. $109–$179.

The **Irving House** is as friendly and funky as a college dormitory. Guests like to hang out in the lounge, reading (books are provided rather than TVs) or talking. Furnishings are functional rather than aesthetically pleasing, current events are posted on a central bulletin board, and messages are taped to the wall.

Originally a two-family home built in 1893 in the Colonial Revival style, the Irving House was later converted to a lodging house, known most recently as the Kirkland Inn. Since purchasing the property in 1990 to operate it as a guest house for budget-minded travellers, Rachael Solem has been restoring and brightening the 44 guest rooms with fresh, light colors and polishing the original hardwood floors. While there are spacious doubles here, some with private baths, nearly half the rooms are no-frills singles and doubles that share bathroom facilities. In the morning guests are invited to help themselves to a complimentary Continental breakfast of muffins, croissants, fresh fruit, and coffee served in the lounge or, in pleasant weather, on the two large porches. Students love the place—as do couples and families—partly for the low prices but also for the location: The Irving House sits on a quiet residential street just a few blocks from Harvard Yard and the Harvard Square T stop. Off-street parking is provided, but you must reserve a space in advance.

24 Irving Street, Cambridge, MA 03138. Tel: 547-4600; Fax: (617) 661-6246. $45–$75.

Sometimes it's worth going a little out of the way to seek certain rewards. The **Royal Sonesta Hotel**, situated on the banks of the Charles River in up-and-coming East Cambridge, is one such reward. While it's not in Harvard Square, the hotel has a wonderful riverside location; guests can jog or bicycle along the Charles (ask about jogging maps and free use of bikes in the summer) and take in perhaps the best view from any hotel of the river and the Boston skyline. A few steps away is the CambridgeSide Galleria shopping mall (home of the Sports Museum of New England), with outdoor café tables, free evening concerts, and a boat concession offering rides on the river in spring and summer. The Sonesta's shuttle and the mall's Ride the Wave van (both free), plus the proximity of the Green Line's Lechmere station, make up for the slightly out-of-the-way location.

The Sonesta's postmodern look is refreshing, especially when you consider that many Boston-area hotels—even newer ones—go to such great lengths to look old. The collection of contemporary artwork throughout the twin towers includes some notable pieces, such as Jonathan Borofsky's *Flying Man with Briefcase* suspended overhead inside the front entrance. The hotel's health spa is one of the best in town, with a sauna, Jacuzzi, aerobics classes, massage, manicures and pedicures, and an inviting swimming pool (with a retractable roof). The spacious guest rooms are priced according to view, and some suites come equipped with a kitchenette and a small triangular balcony. Wheelchair users will appreciate the gradual slopes that have been incorporated into the overall design for easy access to **Davio's** restaurant (noted for its northern Italian cuisine) and other public spaces. The hotel also offers organized activities for children and babysitting services.

5 Cambridge Parkway, Cambridge, MA 02142. Tel: 491-3600 or (800) SONESTA; Fax: (617) 661-5956. $160–$205; suites $270–$635.

BED-AND-BREAKFAST RESERVATIONS SERVICES

If you'd like to stay in a residential area somewhat out of the mainstream of the city, your best bet may be a bed-and-breakfast. In addition to those discussed above, numerous B and Bs in both the Boston and Cambridge neighborhoods are represented by the reservations services listed below.

Arline Kardasis and Marilyn Mitchell founded **Bed and Breakfast Associates Bay Colony Ltd.** in 1981, when B and Bs were beginning to emerge as a popular lodging choice in the United States. Today their reservations service represents a wide variety of hosts who live and work in the Boston and Cambridge area (and beyond). Among the accommodations available in Cambridge are a spacious Victorian home near Harvard whose owners (a biochemist and a biophysicist) speak four languages between them; and a large family-oriented Colonial (owned by an illustrator and an economics consultant) with skylights and a deck, as well as a playroom and a fenced yard for kids. In Boston are a Beacon Hill penthouse with a rooftop balcony and private bath with Jacuzzi, a restored 20-room Victorian inn (also on Beacon Hill) that is wheelchair accessible, and a Back Bay apartment with a working fireplace and full kitchen in an owner-occupied brick town house.

P.O. Box 57166, Babson Park Branch, Boston, MA 02157. Tel: 449-5302 or (800) 347-5088; Fax: (617) 449-5958. $50–$135.

Host Homes of Boston, a reservations service founded by director Marcia Whittington 11 years ago, also represents B and Bs in Boston, Cambridge, and outlying areas. Those on Beacon Hill include a coach house (originally constructed to house 12 coaches and staff) converted to a private home in 1890 and located on a quiet gas-lit street. A private, genteel club in the Back Bay features rooms with fireplaces and antiques. Among the B and Bs in Cambridge is a 100-year-old Victorian home just off Brattle Street, which before the Revolution was known as Tory Row for the wealthy British sympathizers who lived along it.

P.O. Box 117, Waban Branch, Boston, MA 02168. Tel: 244-1308; Fax: (617) 244-5156. $55–$105.

—Jan Stankus

DINING

Boston is no longer the home of only the bean and the cod. The restaurant boom that hit in the 1980s—and shows no sign of slowing down—changed the Hub irrevocably. Quahog chowder is still widely available, but fish houses have taken a back seat. And, sadly, almost all the star chefs—and would-be stars—have eschewed the regional theme. Italian is the hottest flavor, the *trattoria* the preferred venue. Other ethnically influenced eateries are proliferating wildly. The newest and most popular restaurants offer something akin to "world beat" cuisine, a dizzying blend of cooking styles as disparate as Mexican, Thai, and Moroccan under one roof.

With a few notable exceptions, the bastions of fine dining in Boston are the better hotels. Elsewhere, white-tablecloth restaurants, popular during the high-flying eighties, have given way to a plethora of noisy bistros. Unfortunately, good crisp service has become a rare commodity. But both Bostonians and Cantabrigians are in love with fun, boisterous eateries that emphasize gutsy flavors, chuck-wagon portions, and at least the appearance of good value.

The Boston area is an expensive place in which to live and, especially, to eat. What is locally considered a modest dinner, including drinks and tip, usually comes to around $25 a person. At middle-range restaurants, the most common variety in Boston, dinner runs about $30 to $40 a person. Expect to pay $75 a person, and sometimes more, at the Hub's top restaurants. Exact prices are usually not quoted in the discussions that follow, but general expense levels are often indicated in the restaurant descriptions.

Although Boston is a very proper town, Bostonians and their Cambridge counterparts have never been slaves to fashion. Coats and ties are required and jeans are banned at the Ritz-Carlton and a few other hoity-toity establishments, but in this notoriously unstylish town just about anything goes. Clubs seem to be much more concerned with dress than restaurants.

Reservations are always a good idea at area restaurants, and are essential for weekend nights. The best-known restaurants fill up quickly when conventions are in town. Because Bostonians tend to eat dinner early, it may be easier to come by a reservation in the late evening—but not too late. Most restaurants stop serving as early as 9:30 P.M. on weekdays and rarely serve past 10:30 P.M. on weekends. Chinatown, where many local chefs and their staffs go after work, is the best place to find something to eat after 11:00 P.M.

The following is a selective review of popular Boston and Cambridge restaurants. First we discuss the "top circle" of restaurants, which are located in Boston, with one exception. We then talk about hotel dining before moving on to a discussion of restaurants by neighborhood and type, first in Boston and then in Cambridge.

The telephone area code for Boston and Cambridge is 617.

Boston

THE TOP CIRCLE

Bostonians have never been seduced—at least for long—by chefs obsessed with froufrou. Yankee sensibility can't stand much fluff. The first-tier, or most celebrated, Boston-area restaurants offer earthy fare, although the prices are aimed at the heavens. Expect to pay between $50 and $75 a person for a full dinner, including drinks, tip, and tax. Reservations are essential on weekend evenings.

At **Jasper's**, 240 Commercial Street in the North End, the bean and the cod are a matter of ecclesiastical discussion. Chef and owner Jasper White, the dean of Boston chefs, is a leading proponent of New England cookery. White gives four-star treatment to picnic-table classics: feathery codcakes with lightly dressed bitter greens; salmon-trout fillet grilled just past translucency and served on a ragout of broad white beans, fresh artichokes, and tomato; grilled maple-glazed quail and spicy duck sausages with parsnip purée and asparagus; and baskets of Boston brown bread.

Anyone looking for the Hub's best fish house can stop searching at Jasper's. More than half the menu is seafood, and White's raw shellfish selection—usually tiny Wellfleet littlenecks and Belon oysters from Maine—is unparalleled in town. Jasper's waterfront restaurant is quiet and sophisticated, with heavy polished silver, fine linen, red lacquered chairs, indirect lighting, and fresh flower arrangements. The only major flaw here is the rather weak and overpriced wine list. The service, however, is first-rate. Tel: 523-1126.

Biba, at 272 Boylston Street in the Back Bay, is the domain of Lydia Shire, who in her way is Jasper White's equal, not to mention his friend and former sous-chef. Shire's way, however, is completely different. The second-floor "food hall" is an unusual 150-seat room with intricate inlaid-wood trappings, exotic upholstery, and a ceiling of boldly colored, hand-painted geometric designs. (The street level houses a toney saloon; see Bars, below.) Window seats afford a stunning view of the Public Garden. The real stunner, however, is usually Shire's eclectic menu: wood-roasted goat with toasted layered pastry of black olives and white beans; grilled potato and caviar pizza; foie gras salad with field peas, sprouted radish, and chopped fried chicken hearts; steamed lobster and cold-water mussels with warm brandade in hot fennel broth. The trick here is to order several appetizers and share larger dishes. Unfortunately, the notoriously slow service can be aggravating, and the din can make polite conversation among four people impossible at certain tables. The wine list, including many wines by the glass, changes often and is usually very good. Reservations, especially for weekends, should be made well in advance. Tel: 426-7878.

L'Espalier, also in the Back Bay, at 30 Gloucester Street, is an anachronism in Boston, but one that lovers of formal dining, haute cuisine, and professional service will enjoy.

The location, a posh Back Bay town house, fits the style of L'Espalier perfectly, as do the crisp linen, polished silver, and tuxedoed waiters. Chef and co-owner Frank McClelland consistently produces polished dishes that please rather than amaze: a sautéed foie gras, avocado, and yellowfin tuna sandwich with pineapple vinaigrette; grilled Maine lobster with white-truffle-creamed potatoes; grilled corn and red pepper salad; roast loin of lamb in molasses, mustard, and pecan crest with grilled black olive and red pepper tart. The wine list is pricey but studded with jewels. L'Espalier is perhaps the only Boston restaurant that offers a tray of fabulous French and native cheeses for dessert. The three-course prix fixe dinner is about $56. Tel: 262-3023.

Hamersley's Bistro, opened in 1987, was the first restaurant in Boston to offer high-quality food in a casual atmosphere. The small storefront bistro, downtown at 578 Tremont Street, looks out on a rather dismal urban street scene. But inside there's a cherry glow, due in no small part to the crowd of sophisticated regulars. The simple trappings will change when Hamersley's moves up the street to larger, more fashionable digs adjacent to the Boston Ballet. Let us hope that the soul-satisfying food will remain the same. Chef and owner Gordon Hamersley cooks an earthy blend of country French and New England cuisines. The menu changes at least six times a year and perfectly reflects the regional food seasons: hearty cassoulet with rich duck confit in the winter; roasted cod tail with spicy sausage and kale in the spring; grilled bluefish with corn relish in late summer; and in the fall succulent skate sautéed with brown butter and capers. At Hamersley's there is a strong sense that dishes are cooked, rather than merely assembled at the last minute as they are at most restaurants these days. The wine list fluctuates in quality and the prices are a little high, but there are always a few good bottles. Service is very good. The restaurant does not permit smoking. Tel: 267-6068.

Olives, at 10 City Square in Charlestown, is perhaps the most popular restaurant in Boston. One important reason is chef and owner Todd English's inspired cooking, which is loosely based on Mediterranean cuisines. Hardwood fire is the key cooking element at Olives; the spit-roasted chicken, leg of lamb, and pork loin chops are sensational. Salad of wood-grilled prosciutto and bitter greens or grilled calamari are also great. Many dishes arrive on huge, overflowing Spanish or Italian platters, sometimes too big for the tiny tables. English's weakness is his tendency to overdo everything. But without question Olives is also a place to see and be seen. On most nights casually dressed diners wait up to two hours at the bar for one of the tightly packed tables in the sparely decorated dining room. Conversation and background rock and roll create an awesome din. Service is fast, sometimes too fast, and tables are turned on average about every one and a half hours. Tel: 242-1999.

Representing the top circle on the Cambridge side of the Charles is contemporary Italian Michela's; see Cambridge, Eclectic, below.

HOTEL DINING

Boston's most exclusive hotels, always at the fore of the restaurant boom, spawned many top chefs who left to open their own restaurants and bistros. Still, a few hotels offer some of the city's best food as well as its finest formal dining.

With its captivating view of the Public Garden and its elegant decor, **Aujourd'hui**, on the second floor at the Four Seasons Hotel, 200 Boylston Street in the Back Bay, is easily one of Boston's most luxurious restaurants. There is no dress code, which is one reason rock stars favor this establishment, but almost all men wear a jacket and tie. Chef Michael Kornik is a whiz kid in the kitchen, producing lively and creative dishes like warm salad of roast squab with blackberry vinegar, roasted pears, and spiced pecans; and crispy halibut with taro root, baby arugula, and blood oranges. The wine list is good enough, but pricey; service can be a little less sharp than you would expect from one of Boston's most expensive restaurants. Be prepared to spend up to $100 a person, including wine and tip. Tel: 338-4400.

From the street you can only glimpse or just imagine the beauty of those great Back Bay houses. But at the **Plaza Dining Room**, at the Copley Plaza Hotel, 138 St. James Avenue, the glory that was old Boston completely surrounds you. The high vaulted ceiling is simply gorgeous with its molded plaster trappings, intricately carved dark wood trim, and crystal chandeliers; two gargantuan Chinese vases are always filled with exotic flowers. The room is small enough to be cozy but large enough to allow intimate conversation—much like one of the proper clubs up on Beacon Hill. The light is soft but unfortunately too bright to be romantic. The other drawback is the food, which is merely satisfactory. Still, this is Boston's most beautiful public dining room, and the wine list holds a few absurdly undervalued bottles. So order what sounds appealing and enjoy the atmosphere. Tel: 424-0196.

The **Ritz Bar** at the Ritz-Carlton Hotel, 15 Arlington Street, still offers the best martini in town and the coziest environment in which to drink, although you must be appropriately attired (coat and tie for men, and no jeans after 5:00 P.M.).

The **Ritz Dining Room** is a lovely setting for dinner, as are all the Ritz dining rooms. But the old-line Ritz Continental cuisine is outrageously overpriced. Tel: 536-5700.

Only a handful of restaurants in the entire country have produced more winning chefs than **Seasons**, at the Bostonian Hotel, 9 Blackstone Street in the North End. Jasper White, Lydia Shire, and Gordon Hamersley figure prominently on that all-star list. Anthony Ambrose, the current executive chef, has not yet achieved the success of his predecessors, but he clearly has the potential. Sometimes his craftsmanship isn't quite up to his ideas, but when everything comes together Ambrose makes heavenly food: silky sweet-potato soup with garlicky croutons; exquisite shiitake-mushroom terrine; sautéed loin of venison with latikia-and-pear glaze and turnip-and-celeriac tartlet (latikia is an aromatic Turkish spice). The all-American wine list needs pruning. Waiters, dressed in European-style suits rather than tuxedos, are efficient. Tel: 523-4119.

For sheer elegance and romance, the **Julien**, at the Meridien Hotel, 250 Franklin Street, downtown, is difficult to beat. The room, with a towering gilded ceiling and five crystal chandeliers, was once the Members Court of the old Federal Reserve Bank—a true temple to money patterned after a Renaissance Roman palazzo. The brocaded banquettes are the most romantic spots, and the miniature table lamps couldn't cast a more flattering light. The service, provided by an essentially European-trained staff, is perfectly understated.

The food is as French as anyone could expect to find in Boston. The menu is created three or four times a year by Marc Haeberlin, the chef of L'Auberge de L'Ill in Alsace. Although few could match Haeberlin's finesse, chef André Chouvin does a very good job executing the neoclassic dishes day to day. The fresh foie gras with truffle, a menu constant, is a pricey but sumptuous treat that shouldn't be missed. Soups and consommés are also superb. Expect unusual treatments, such as Maine lobster meat wrapped in crispy phyllo and served with an ethereal butternut squash sabayon. The pricey wine list needs tending. The Julien also serves lunch weekdays. Tel: 451-1900.

Boston Harbor is less than pristine, and a close examination is not advised, but from the elegant surroundings of the **Rowes Wharf Restaurant**, in the Boston Harbor Hotel, at 70 Rowes Wharf, the water looks downright beautiful, especially at sunset. The large dining room with lush walnut paneling and crisscrossed ceiling beams and the attentive, brass-buttoned waiters could make you think you were aboard a luxury liner. Chef Daniel Bruce, a favorite of Julia

Child, produces thoughtful dishes that reflect New England and taste good to boot—braised striped bass served in delicate fish broth with native baby turnips, carrots, sugar-snap peas, and asparagus. The hotel is justifiably famous for its annual vintners' dinner series, which runs from January through April (it may run an extra month in 1993). Bruce creates special meals around selected wines from some prestigious winemakers—Joe Heitz, Josh Jensen, and Giovanni Puiatti are some recent examples. Tel: 439-3995.

The hotels, especially the Meridien, Boston Harbor, and Four Seasons, also offer the best brunches in Boston. The prices are all around $35 per person.

THE NORTH END
Tourists and natives alike flock to the North End for dinner, although the reasons are not altogether obvious. Of course, the North End is immensely important historically, but the Old North Church and Paul Revere's house are closed at night, and the streets are usually dirty. The century-old rehabilitated apartment buildings are rather unattractive. And the restaurants aren't particularly good, or even cheap. Still, the North End is the most easily lovable neighborhood in town.

After almost 80 years of occupation the North End remains an essentially Italian-American neighborhood. The Italian language is commonly heard on the streets and in the shops, *caffès*, and restaurants. Unfortunately, there is no mistaking any North End restaurant for a Florentine or Roman trattoria. The 70-plus eateries crammed into this tiny community can be succinctly characterized as red-sauce palaces. Some may look a little fancier than others and charge more, but no North End restaurant dinner rises above the level of pleasant. Expect to pay between $20 and $40 a person with drinks and tip.

With that in mind, it is possible to have a delightful, or at least fun, meal in Boston's North End. Without doubt the afternoon is the best time to experience this unusual American neighborhood, where many shop owners still live down the street and their best customers are their neighbors.

Italian
Galleria Umberto, at 289 Hanover Street, opens at about 11:00 A.M. and closes when the last of the pan pizza and calzone have been sold, usually by 2:00 or 2:30 P.M. The lunch-bucket fare is served in a cafeteria-style hall, but it's fun. Try the *arancini,* orange-size deep-fried rice balls stuffed with stew. But beware: One arancino can be more filling than it looks. Tel: 227-5709.

Few would ever suspect that the savory pies at **Circle Pizza**, a dumpy little joint at 361 Hanover Street, would vie for top North End honors. Nonetheless, the flavorful and chewy crust is slightly thicker than the standard Boston issue and the sauce is sweet. This is a good spot for a quick and cheap lunch. Tel: 523-8787. But the North End pizzeria nonpareil is the nearly legendary **Pizzeria Regina**, at 11½ Thacher Street. The tiny place, from the well-worn wooden booths to the pressed-tin ceiling, looks and feels every bit its more than 50 years of hard service. But Regina rocks and rolls, especially before hockey or basketball games at the Boston Garden, a short walk away. A long wait in line (outside) is de rigueur most evenings, and don't expect to find anything other than pizza—no salad and no cannoli here. The thin-crust pizza is better some nights than others, but it is always good. The beer is served cold, just like the red wine, and the gum-chewing waitresses are just right. Tel: 227-0765.

Most North End Italians have humble roots in either Campania or Abruzzo, where lentils, beans, and potatoes are staples. Rather than heaping piles of ersatz puttanesca sauce, savvy North End diners opt for peasant dishes from those regions, such as thick braised pork chops finished with vinegar-marinated red and yellow peppers and chunky roasted potatoes. This sort of cooking is the specialty at **Massimino's Cucina Italiana**, at 207 Endicott Street. Ordering family style here is rewarded with large platters of simple but tasty food at very reasonable prices. Tel: 523-5959.

Seafood

Although the North End is almost surrounded by water, seafood is all but missing on most menus here. Only two restaurants specialize in seafood, and both happen to be among the neighborhood's best eateries.

Everybody's favorite, judging by the ever-present line, is the **Daily Catch**, at 323 Hanover Street. The chalkboard features all the usual suspects—linguine with clam sauce and mussels marinara—but the real star here is calamari prepared in every imaginable fashion. The crowd goes nuts for the heaping platefuls of crispy golden rings of tender fried squid. Warning: The Daily Catch is small and no one leaves without smelling a bit like garlic and olive oil. Tel: 523-8567.

Giacomo's, at 355 Hanover Street, is at times more popular than the competition down the road. The pretty exposed-brick room and checkered tablecloths, as well as the ventilation fans, explain the difference. Also, the squid is almost as good, specials always include grilled fish, and the food is slightly more refined. A good example is the fettucine with salmon and sun-dried tomatoes in a light cream sauce. Tel: 523-9026.

Caffès

Many North end restaurants (Giacomo's and the Daily Catch, for example) do not serve dessert—all the more reason to while away the later evening in a local caffè watching the world pass by. The original **Caffè Vittoria**, at 296 Hanover Street, is charming, with its tile floor, old photos of the neighborhood, and bevy of Italian grandfathers discussing world problems over espresso for hours. No American-style coffee is served. Ask for a "short one" if you want a strong espresso. Vittoria also serves reasonably good *gelati* and cannoli, and the jukebox features many old Frank Sinatra and Italian pop songs. Tel: 227-7606.

CHINATOWN

Chinatown is a confusing mess of tiny streets almost constantly clogged with people. The oldest families of this burgeoning community came from Canton, a large coastal city with a cuisine renowned for seafood dishes with subtle spicing and exquisite flavor combinations. That is good enough reason to avoid Chinatown's chile-hot Szechwan or Hunan meat-based dishes. Unfortunately, exquisite food is near impossible to find in this neighborhood, which is among the filthiest in Boston. And although many restaurants here stay open until 4:00 A.M., this is no place to get lost at night. Still, a few Chinatown restaurants are worth the visit, but bring cash because many don't accept credit cards.

Chau Chow, at 52 Beach Street, is a little jewel, despite the formica tabletops and the beer cooler in the middle of the room. Don't pay any attention to the colored construction paper with Chinese characters hanging above the mirror, unless you have a yen for chewy large intestines. Instead, try the salted unshelled jumbo shrimp; the coating of salt, hot chile pepper, and some other magical spice is thoroughly addictive. Other great dishes include whole steamed bass delicately scented with ginger; unshelled crab knuckles and claws in ginger and scallion sauce; and Swatowese dumplings in rich broth. Tel: 426-6266.

Almost every Chinatown eatery serves pork and watercress soup, but **Hoy Yeung Ting**, at 13A Hudson Street, makes about the best. The slightly bitter, peppery watercress is added to clear meat broth at the last second, so the color is bright green and the flavor is distinct. Other treats here are hot pots—old battered, banged-up, blackened earthenware pots bearing any of several savory bubbling-hot concoctions, such as beef with ginger and scallion or lamb Cantonese style. Tel: 426-2316.

Ocean Wealth, at 8 Tyler Street, allows diners to pick their own live prawns, frogs, Pacific scallops, lobsters, and Dungeness crabs (the feistiest are always the best). This extremely popular restaurant, which is a very stylish place for Chinatown, specializes in Pacific seafood. One of the most esoteric and frightening species offered regularly, and stored live in a tank near the front door, is geoduck (pronounced "gooey-duck"), giant clams with 18-inch necks. The taste is similar to abalone; the black bean version is excellent. Tel: 423-1338.

Dim sum is available at many Chinatown restaurants from 9:00 A.M. to about 3:00 P.M. None warrants a special trip, but dim sum addicts may find satisfaction at the **Golden Palace**, at 14 Tyler Street (Tel: 423-4565). Everybody in the Chinese community seems to turn out on Sunday for dim sum, and waits can be long then.

BEACON HILL AND THE BACK BAY

For most people, including Bostonians, Beacon Hill and the Back Bay define the character of this grand old city on the Massachusetts Bay: the cobblestone streets, antique gas lamps (now electric), and fantastic Victorian and Edwardian town houses. Over the years, though, many restaurateurs have tried and failed to bring upscale food to the Back Bay, Boston's wealthiest neighborhood. But for reasons unknown, only L'Espalier, mentioned above (see Top Circle), has succeeded. Most restaurants located in this chic shopping mecca are satisfying and perhaps good rather than stellar, but several stand out nonetheless.

Classic Boston/Romantic

At the foot of Beacon Hill, along postcard-perfect Charles Street, there are a couple of restaurants that capture Boston's charm of the last century. Perhaps the Hub's most romantic lunch spot is **Another Season**, at 97 Mount Vernon Street. The intimate dining rooms, colorful murals, white tablecloths, and unobtrusive service contribute to the mood—it seems no one speaks much louder than a whisper here. Dinner, too, can be romantic. Chef and owner Odette Bery, perhaps Boston's first top-rank female chef, prepares contemporary dishes based on cuisines from around the world. Tel: 367-0880.

On a brisk autumn or winter night in Boston there's nothing so appealing as ducking into the **Hungry i**, at 71½ Charles Street—and duck is literally what most adults must do to avoid bumping their heads on the low, arched entrance. The narrow little restaurant is quaint and cozy, complete with a blazing fire in winter, exposed-brick walls hung with polished copper pots and bowls, antique plates and other knickknacks, a wood-beamed ceiling, and fresh flowers. The slightly expensive menu is short and sweet, with such dishes as prune and rabbit turnovers; rack of lamb roasted with fresh rosemary and whole garlic bulbs; and thin slices of black-pepper-crusted venison sautéed and flambéed with Cognac. The brief wine list is excellent and fairly priced. During the summer months the nighttime garden dining in back is perfectly delightful. Tel: 227-3524.

Italian

Boston's most theatrical restaurant, **Rocco's**, at 5 Charles Street South, is appropriately within the boundaries of the Theater District. With all the restaurant's visual tricks and puns, Salvador Dalí would feel right at home in this cavernous space. A sweeping two-story-high faux-stone arch holds up nothing and leads to nowhere; the ceiling is painted with cupids and angels; odd sculptures skulk in corners; plaster rabbits, chickens, and pigs sit on the tables; and theatrical curtains hang everywhere, as if the whole place were a stage. The food is well above North End standard, but still a hodgepodge of Italian cuisines: linguine with clam sauce, lasagne, gnocchi, chicken cacciatore, osso buco. The wine list, featuring hard-to-find Italian reds and whites, is exceptional. Tel: 723-6800.

    Ristorante Toscano, at 41 Charles Street, is a very popular restaurant, although the attraction is by no means clear to everyone. Many Beacon Hill residents love it, as they do convenience. The Tuscan-style steak is excellent and veal dishes can be very good here. Tel: 723-4090.

Seafood

Legal Seafoods stores and restaurants are famous in part because Julia Child shopped at the original store in Cambridge when she began "The French Chef" television series. With seafood sales of more than 50 tons a week, Legal is no longer the little neighborhood fishmonger near Julia's house. The Park Square location in the Park Plaza Hotel (35 Columbus Avenue), the flagship of the nine-restaurant chain, unfortunately has the longest waits for tables and the slowest and most confused service. Still, simple grilled and broiled fish can be excellent, but the prices are high. Tel: 426-4444. The branch at Copley Place, 100 Huntington Avenue, seems to do a better job. Tel: 266-7775.

Japanese

Boston's most authentic Tokyo-style sushi bar is **Gyuhama**, at 827 Boylston Street. Japanese women in traditional garb, some of whom don't speak English well, are wonderfully attentive in this rather stark yet pleasant subterranean get-away. Singles may sit at the bar (the chef at the far right, near the kitchen, is usually the top man, and the best). Two small rooms have tables for two or four; larger groups doff their footgear and sit in the private rooms in the back. On Friday and Saturday nights after midnight the lights are turned down, the music is turned up, the prices are almost doubled, and the normally sedate Gyuhama turns into a rock 'n' roll sushi bar. Tel: 437-0188.

Steaks

Come to Boston, the home of the most important fish market on the eastern seaboard, for a great steak? In a word, no. In general, the beef in New England does not compare with the Midwest, or probably anywhere else, for that matter. It should come as no surprise then that the best steak available in these parts comes from **Morton's of Chicago**, at 1 Exeter Plaza (on Boylston Street at the corner of Exeter). The steaks here are as tender and flavorful—and portions as big—as anyone could desire. Unfortunately, the dining room, which resembles a stuccoed cave, has little character or charm. Tel: 266-5858.

Boston does have a couple of very good places to eat a steak, including the **Capital Grille**, at 359 Newbury Street. The fancy Capital bar, with a polished marble floor, dark mahogany, cut frosted glass, and miles of shiny brass, is perhaps the most masculine watering hole in town. The rest of the restaurant is much the same, with red leather uphol-stery, Gainesborough-style hunt scenes, and a giant moose-head. The dry-aged steaks are good but not great, and the wine list, heavy on Bordeaux and California Cabernet Sauvignon, is massive and overpriced. Tel: 262-8900.

The other good Boston steakhouse is **Grill 23**, at 161 Berkeley Street. This super-masculine retreat features a decid-edly New England look with a beautiful molded plaster ceil-ing, marble columns, dark wood and brass trim, and a hand-some bar. The food and the service are good, but the din in this cavernous space can overwhelm normal conversation. The wine list is also clunky and overpriced. Tel: 542-2255.

Newbury Street Cafés

Newbury Street is at once Boston's chic-est, most tawdry, cheapest, most sophisticated, and most uncouth thorough-fare. Haute couture boutiques, third-hand clothing stores, flashy hair salons, frozen yogurt shops, and fine art galleries share this always-crowded street. All of which makes people-watching from a café table outside **29 Newbury Street Restaurant**, at 29 Newbury Street, a perfect spring, summer, or fall activity. The small bar inside is very popular among some of the sophisticates who shop (or wish they could) across the street at Giorgio Armani. Lunch and dinner, either alfresco or in the two rows of very private booths inside, can be just the thing if you want something light. Tel: 536-0290.

The advertising crowd convenes for lunch and after-work cocktails and perhaps dinner just up the street at **Papa Razzi**, 271 Dartmouth Street. The reasonably priced fare is essentially gussied-up pastas and pizza—California pizza with fresh and sun-dried tomato, goat cheese, mozzarella, and basil; and fusilli with a light tomato and mushroom sauce. Dinner is slightly more expensive than lunch. Tel: 536-9200.

INSTITUTIONS

Seafood

Boston has a few restaurant institutions famous well beyond city limits. Some are best avoided, such as the **No Name** restaurant, at 15½ Fish Pier. Years ago this restaurant had no name but served flapping fresh fish picked straight off the boats unloading literally next door. Well, the best days of the Fish Pier are long gone, and the institutionalized No Name isn't worth the trip. The same is generally true of **Anthony's Pier 4**, at 140 Northern Avenue. This huge, rambling building on Boston Harbor affords a nice view of the water—and that's about it. Wine enthusiasts occasionally trek out to Anthony's to pick the few remaining cherries from the once-stellar list.

Jimmy's Harborside, a bit farther out at 242 Northern Avenue, is almost as famous as Anthony's and a much better deal, although the view of the water from the warehouse-like restaurant isn't as good. The chowders and grilled or broiled fish steaks and fillets are good and usually well turned out. Tel: 423-1000.

Classic Boston

Durgin Park, in the Faneuil Hall Marketplace, still cranks out the same old tired New England–style dishes, such as Yankee pot roast, prime rib, boiled lobster, chowder, and Indian pudding. The fact that Durgin Park has been cranking for more than 160 years makes the place special, at least in some eyes. And through all those years, the kitchen has had only five chefs. Diners sit at long communal tables and allow surly waitresses to slap down their food and dish out abuse.

If you have the right attitude, though, the place can be fun. Tel: 227-2038.

Locke-Ober Café, at 3 Winter Place (off Winter Street downtown), still may be Boston's most famous restaurant. Since 1875, when Frank Locke joined his Wine Room to Louis Ober's Restaurant Parisienne, the resulting café has drawn the rich, famous, and notorious to its beautiful fin-de-siècle dining rooms. Dining at the Men's Bar and Café, with its hand-carved mahogany detail and gleaming silver steam trays, is a special experience. The Ober Room is reminiscent of a Newport mansion. Locke-Ober draws mostly a business crowd, especially at lunch. The food, which dates to the era of roaring Newport, disappoints by today's standards. Moreover, the rack of lamb and châteaubriand are among the most expensive in town. Still, anyone with a fondness for "old Boston" may be charmed. Tel: 542-1340.

Some consider **Café Budapest** in the Copley Square Hotel (90 Exeter Street in Back Bay) to be one of Boston's most romantic restaurants. But others, mainly the under-40 crowd, find the lavishly decorated, almost-all-pink dining room to be amusing rather than pretty. The cold cherry soup, goulash, chicken paprika, and other Central European classics fail to impress at least some Hungarian visitors, especially those conscious of price—the Café Budapest is one of the more expensive restaurants in town. To make matters worse, the wine list is completely Hungarian. Tel: 734-3388.

French

The first serious French restaurant in town, back when Julia Child was just getting going on television, was **Maison Robert**, now at 45 School Street in the Old City Hall building. For years, budding Francophiles zipped over to Maison Robert after Julia's show to see and taste the real thing up close, whether it was *steak au poivre flambé* or *sole de la Manche meunière*. Lucien Robert's daughter, Andrée, now runs the kitchen and has spruced up the offerings. But basically she's sticking with the classics. Sadly, the kitchen is uneven. The informal dining room here, **Ben's Café**, does a little bit better, and dining on the terrace during the summer, either at lunch or dinner, is thoroughly delightful. Tel: 227-3370.

Cambridge

While fashionable Bostonians traipsed around to the new chic-for-a-week restaurants throughout the eighties, staid Cantabrigians seemed perfectly content to crunch granola and occasionally trudge to the two or three worthwhile restaurants on their side of the Charles River. What visitors to the area must understand is that some Cantabrigians never set foot in Boston for *any* reason, or even travel much past Harvard Square, unless they are on the way to the airport or Martha's Vineyard. So when the restaurant scene in Boston proper stalled momentarily after the stock market crash a few years ago, more than a few people (mostly Bostonians) were shocked to see restaurants opening left and right in Cambridge, where the Birkenstock sandal and the clog have never gone out of style. Bostonians were probably more surprised at how much cheaper and livelier these new restaurants were.

ECLECTIC

The **Blue Room**, at 1 Kendall Square, in many ways is typical of the new Cambridge restaurant: boisterous crowd, formica tabletops, bistro-style service, wood-fired cooking, and strong flavors. At the Blue Room you may be just as likely to use chopsticks as knives and forks. The menu is inspired by cuisines as disparate as Mexican, Greek, Indonesian, Vietnamese, and even American. The traditional soup-to-nuts approach doesn't play here; the menu encourages sharing small and large dishes. Chefs and owners Stan Frankenthaler, Cary Wheaton, and Chris Schlesinger change the menu often, but you can expect starters such as Persian spice–rubbed smoky duck, tender enough to fall off the bone, served with a warm earthy potato and chick-pea stew and a sweetish chutney made from dried fruit. One of the most popular large dishes is the slow-roasted tea-soaked chicken served with Szechwan-spiced beans and grilled oriental eggplant. For dessert try the delicious Mexican chocolate-filled corn pancakes. The Blue Room is clearly not a fine dining experience, but there's no question that it is an experience. Tel: 494-9034.

A little farther up the road is another hip new Cambridge joint, **Daddy O's Bohemian Café**, at 134 Hampshire Street. The two chefs and owners, Paul Sussman and Ellis Seidman, have broken new ground, of sorts, with their jazzy beatnik motif and distinctive American cuisine. In addition to the hardwood-grilled pork chops and grilled vegetable platters, Daddy O's also serves light and lacy potato latkes, the best in greater Boston. This funky little neighborhood bistro is a fun Cambridge side trip. Tel: 354-8371.

The granddaddy of new-wave Cambridge restaurants is the **East Coast Grill**, at 1271 Cambridge Street. Owners Chris Schlesinger and Cary Wheaton, who also are Blue Room co-owners, turned a dying storefront luncheonette

into a nationally known restaurant. Although he has authored an award-winning cookbook, *Thrill of the Grill,*
Schlesinger is perhaps best known for his Inner Beauty hot
sauce, a mustard-colored concoction made dangerous by
scotch bonnets peppers, the fieriest chile of all. "This is not
a toy, this is serious," warns the label. Inner Beauty is the
key ingredient in the grill's infamous "Pasta from Hell,"
which will slow even the most macho chile-eaters. The
eclectic menu also features Boston's best barbecued ribs
and North Carolina–style pulled pork. Rambunctious is the
best description for the crowd at this 48-seat hot spot. The
no-reservations policy, in force Sunday through Thursday,
usually means long waits at the bar, by the door, or outside.
Tel: 491-6568.

In a small district commonly known as Artificial Intelligence Alley, at 1 Athenaeum Street, **Michela's** fortifies brainy
Cantabrigians with contemporary Italian-style cooking. The
overhauled ink factory that houses Michela's may be a little
difficult to find, but taxi drivers usually know the way. Enter
the restaurant through the caffè, which offers a very different
and less expensive menu, or the cozy bar. Michela's white-
tablecloth dining room—done up in creamy yellows, ocher,
purple, umber, and green—manages to be chic despite
exposed ceiling pipes and ducts. A playful mural of Siena
covers the back wall. The talented chef, Jody Adams, is
capable of turning out wonderful food, although sometimes
she misses. Her talent really shows in such slow-cooked
dishes as braised and grilled veal breast stuffed with pista-
chios and mortadella; or roasted salt and fresh cod fillets
wrapped in *pancetta.* Owner Michela Larson keeps an eye
on the kitchen as well as the dining room and often chats up
customers. Service in the restaurant is good, but long waits
are possible in the caffè. The wine list is also good, but
suffers from too many options. Tel: 225-2121.

SPANISH

Anyone who doubts that Cantabrigians really do like to have
a good time should go to **Dalí,** which straddles the
Cambridge–Somerville line at 415 Washington Street. This
large, rambling building isn't just a restaurant, it's a quick
trip to Spain. The bar near the entrance is crowded with
Spanish earthenware bowls and platters overflowing with
large home-cured olives, garlicky potato salad, two-inch-
thick omelets, and husky loaves of bread—all standard *tapas*
fare and available on small plates. Dangling overhead are
Spanish-style dried hams, ropes of fresh garlic, bouquets of
herbs, and sides of salt cod. All that food will be cut down as

needed and cooked or sliced and eaten. Throughout the three windowless rooms the walls are hung with homey Spanish memorabilia, creating the atmosphere of a country inn. In addition to a long list of *tapas,* which changes daily, Dalí offers some traditional Spanish dishes. The succulent braised rabbit has an enchanting flavor of cinnamon, juniper berries, and Sherry vinegar. And Sherry is spoken here: The *fino* is served well chilled. The all-Spanish wine list is exceptional and fairly priced. For any aficionado of Spain Dalí is a must—one of the most authentic Spanish restaurants in the country. Tel: 661-3254.

BRAZILIAN
Cantabrigians' attitudes about multiculturalism translate directly to their restaurants. It's almost as if a group from Harvard and MIT looked around and said, "We have no Brazilian food." Suddenly, in 1991, Cambridge became home to the only *churrascaria* in the area: **Pampas**, at 928 Massachusetts Avenue. This is a South American–style all-you-can-eat restaurant where waiters come to the table about every three minutes with a long sword filled with wood-fired roast meats—pork leg, turkey, duck, beef, lamb, chicken hearts, goat, rabbit, sausages. For the protein-deprived, Pampas is nirvana, but the salad bar, filled with Brazilian salads, is also outstanding. Pampas is a unique experience and great for families. Tel: 661-6613.

HARVARD SQUARE
The pickings are slim in Harvard Square. **Upstairs at the Pudding**, at 10 Holyoke Street, is a favorite for faculty members and others who live around the Square. The Ivy League dining-hall decor appeals to some, especially parents of students. The food, often described as Northern Italian, also has its devotées. Service can be good, although distinctly Cantabrigian—a unique mélange of socially awkward, condescending, and always politically correct. Prices are high. Tel: 864-1933.

The **Harvest**, at 44 Brattle Street, is a Cambridge institution that has wonderfully benefited all restaurant-goers in greater Boston. During more than 15 years of continuous service (the restaurant closes only for Christmas), Harvest has launched a bevy of top chefs, including Lydia Shire and Chris Schlesinger. Since the beginning quality has swung wildly from stellar to mediocre. Lately the self-conscious food hasn't measured up to the high prices. In the past, **Ben's Corner Bar & Café** here offered less fuss and much better value than the restaurant, but it has also slipped (see

Bars, below). Too bad. But that's the story of the Harvest and that's why it is always worth a try. Tel: 492-1115.

—René Becker

NIGHTLIFE AND ENTERTAINMENT

Puritanical beginnings and prudish Brahmin dictates made "Boston nightlife" an oxymoron for many years. After all, this is the city that banned Cole Porter's "Love for Sale." Even during the eighties the hottest restaurants stopped serving after 10:00 P.M. on weekend nights, and that holds true today. But Boston nightlife is booming.

Boston and Cambridge are overgrown college towns, and students always have some money, so there are plenty of bars and clubs geared to the 20-to-30 age group. There is something for just about everyone else here too. The trick is to know when your crowd hits what place. On Wednesday nights a particular club may cater to a Champagne-drinking Euro-clientele, while on Saturday nights the same club will be filled to the rafters with big-hair suburban girls and their boyfriends in acid-washed jeans, and gays may take over on Sunday nights. Every Monday the cycle begins anew. Clubs are more than happy to tell you exactly what the crowd is like on any given night. Most bars, on the other hand, attract basically the same crowd every night.

Some clubs and bars stay open until 2:00 A.M., the legal limit, but others still ask for last call at 1:00 A.M. or earlier. Some serve food, especially those connected to restaurants, but many don't. What follows is an arbitrary list of some Boston and Cambridge bars and clubs. One or more of the many other establishments out there may fit your specific needs. This list is merely an introduction, a jumping-off point.

The telephone area code for Boston and Cambridge is 617.

BARS

Back Bay
The Back Bay is quickly becoming one big bar scene. The action started several years ago and continues at **Biba**, 272 Boylston Street. The street-level saloon, below Lydia Shire's posh second-floor restaurant (see Top Circle in the Dining section, above), attracts a toney but occasionally obstreperous crowd. On Friday and Saturday nights you can barely see the terra-cotta floor, burnished woodwork, copper-topped bar, or other fancy trappings through the masses, most of

whom fall between ages 30 and 50. Not everybody wears Armani and drinks Veuve Cliquot, the house pour, but this is usually the flashiest crowd Boston can muster. Tel: 426-7878.

Marais, only a few doors away at 116 Boylston Street, stole some of Biba's thunder when it opened in 1992. Although named for the trendy Paris neighborhood, this Marais attracts a wannabe crowd that probably wouldn't know the difference between the Left Bank and the Right. Still, the old French posters, authentic Paris knickknacks, and mile-long marble-top bar make for a snazzy saloon. The crowd is usually two or three deep until the bitter end Thursday through Saturday nights. The better option is to sit across from the bar at bistro-style tables, snack on appetizers, and watch the action. Full dinners are available, but this is not a prime dining destination. Tel: 482-7799.

The bar and café at nearby **Rocco's**, 5 Charles Street South, pulls in a more sedentary post-theater crowd. You can actually hear the taped background music here—the Gypsy Kings, Jimi Hendrix, Leonard Cohen, Little Feat—and women need not fear wolves. This is the place to get comfortable with a large group or just one friend. (See also Dining, above.) Tel: 723-6800.

This may be Back Bay Boston, but cactus does grow at the **Cottonwood Café**, 222 Berkeley Street (at St. James Street). The Postmodern Southwestern design is slick and colorful: aqua tablecloths, lavender napkins, teal chairs, persimmon trim, and purple neon. The margaritas are excellent (strong), and the bar food—chips and salsa, cowboy pot-stickers, chile-pepper-hot snakebites—tastes good enough. A young secretarial crowd in dresses and running shoes comes straight from work on Thursdays and Fridays. Later in the evenings the clientele turns a bit older and looks a little more urbane. Tel: 247-2225.

South End

The **St. Cloud**, at 557 Tremont Street, is slightly off the beaten track, in more ways than one. The South End is by far Boston's most eclectic neighborhood, and nowhere is that more evident than at the St. Cloud. Tweedy professorial types stand shoulder to shoulder with bicycle messengers, dancers (Boston Ballet is around the corner), and Chanel-suited art dealers. Most important, everyone talks to each other here, a rare event in stoic Boston, and lone women feel completely safe at the bar. The reason is probably bartender Robert Gerard—he can make anyone feel at home. Talk to him, or he'll talk to you. The St. Cloud, which serves pretty good food, is Boston's best bar for dining alone—no matter who you are. Tel: 353-0202.

Cambridge

Ben's Corner Bar & Café, at the Harvest restaurant (44 Brattle Street; see Dining, above), has been Harvard Square's premier watering hole for more than a decade and a half. No youngsters wander into this grown-up playground. Harvard professors and graduate students mix it up with townies most nights until very late in a comfortable, if slightly dated, atmosphere (Marimekko upholstery). Thursdays seem particularly good for the over-50 crowd. The food at the café can be tasty, and is generally a better value than that at the hoity-toity restaurant, although quality has been uneven of late. Tel: 492-1115.

For something altogether different, try the **Miracle of Science**, at 321 Massachusetts Avenue, a funky little corner bar a strong Frisbee throw from MIT. Despite the proximity and the moniker, Science, as the regulars call it, has nothing to do with higher learning—unless you find Jane's Addiction and other rockers edifying. The simple grilled fare—burgers, chicken and shrimp skewers with salsa, and hummus—is a step above most bar food. The crowd is unpretentious and around 30. Tel: 868-ATOM.

Jamaica Plain

If you're Irish, or you just have smiling eyes and a taste for Guinness on tap, then a trip to Boston wouldn't be complete without a visit to at least one of the area's Irish pubs. The Boston area's large number of Irish emigrés, legal and illegal, enjoy a proper pour, and that's what they get at **Brendan Behan's**, at 378 Centre Street in Jamaica Plain, a largely Hispanic Boston neighborhood. Although difficult to find and of late with no telephone, this is the real thing. Take the number 39 Forest Hills bus from Copley Square, or take a cab. Another option in the same general vicinity is **Doyle's Café**, at 3484 Washington Street, also in Jamaica Plain. Although the thought may cross your mind, do not order pizza at Doyle's. Instead, have a burger with your brew (25 of them on tap, including Guinness). And Scotch aficionados take note: Doyle's offers 33 single-malts. A fun place whether you're Irish or Lithuanian. Tel: 524-2345.

CLUBS

Since at least the late 1950s Boston has been a center for cutting-edge music in a variety of genres, including folk, jazz, and especially rock. The reason is the incredible concentration of colleges and universities—more than 80 institutions in the vicinity. As long as there are students here, the music clubs and bars will surely flourish. Here's a selective sampling of live-music venues around Boston and Cambridge, followed by comedy clubs and places to dance.

Jazz

Boston had a very lively jazz scene about 30 years ago. Considering the talent that lives here (Gary Burton, Pat Metheny, and a host of others) and the new talent at the schools here (Berklee and New England Conservatory), it's amazing that more jazz isn't available at local bars. But there's the rub: Boston's jazz bars have gone the way of the bean and the cod. The few jazz outlets around are relatively new.

The **Regattabar**, on the third floor in the ritzy Charles Hotel, at 1 Bennett Street, Cambridge, is the best and, sadly, only venue for top players. Most nights, Tuesday through Saturday, you can expect first-rate jazz in a quiet, casually sophisticated setting where everyone wants to listen to the music. Tel: 937-4020. The newest comer, **Scullers**, in the Guest Quarters Suite Hotel at 400 Soldiers Field Road (a stone's throw from Cambridge in Brighton), has aggressively promoted their jazz program, which features very good native and national players. The environment is comfortable and dress is casual. Tel: 783-0811.

Ryles, at 212 Hampshire Street in Cambridge, is always worth a look for jazz, blues, and even world-beat stuff. One act plays upstairs in a clubby room, while the other plays downstairs on a smaller stage. Tuesday is open-mike jazz night. Tel: 876-9330.

If you'd just like to listen to good jazz (without the club atmosphere), check the schools for student and teacher recitals, which are almost always free, and upcoming concerts. See the Classical Music section, below, for a list of area music schools.

Rock, Blues, and Other Music

The **Rat**, at 528 Commonwealth Avenue (in Boston's Kenmore Square), has a time-honored tradition of presenting alternative, head-numbing rock 'n' roll for those who love paste-white faces and dyed black hair. The name above the entrance is Rathskeller, but "rat" seems so much more appropriate for this dingy basement club. Much fun for the right crowd. Tel: 536-2750.

For raucous, blue-jeans-and-leather rock 'n' roll, the place to go is **Bunratty's**, at 186 Harvard Avenue in Allston, the community between Brookline and Cambridge, not far from Boston University. (Take the "B" train on the Green Line to Harvard Avenue.) This down-and-dirty saloon is nothing more than a large room with a bar and lots of underground music every night from local and touring bands. The cover varies with the act. Tel: 254-9804.

R & B and blues fans should head directly to **Harper's Ferry**, at 158 Brighton Avenue in Allston (walk a few blocks from Bunratty's to Brighton Avenue and turn left). The room is big and so is the crowd Thursday through Sunday, when national-level players take the stage. Local bands play on Mondays. The acoustic jam on Tuesdays and electric blues jam on Wednesdays also can be interesting. The music begins at 9:30 every night; the cover varies. Collared shirts are required. Tel: 254-9743 or 254-7380.

The **Tam**, 1648 Beacon Street in Brookline, west of Boston, is such a respectable place that neighborhood families often come here for a tasty home-style dinner before the music starts at 10:00 every night. The music, which ranges from folk to jazz, often rocks—but never too hard. The Tam is a very comfortable club, especially for those with a touch of gray. Take the "C" train on the Green Line to Washington Street. The Tam is across the street. Tel: 277-0982.

Every night, but especially on weekends, a host of musicians set up microphones and little portable amplifiers in just about every nook and doorway in **Harvard Square**. They play their hearts out for the crowd that moves along from stage to stage, stopping for a song here or an entire set there. The musicians, who compete in front of a jury for the right to perform in the square, can be surprisingly talented. Along with the jugglers and storytellers also performing, these Harvard Square musicians offer some of the best, and certainly cheapest, entertainment in the entire Boston area. A warm spring, summer, or fall night wandering around the square is an experience that's hard to beat.

Of course, there's always the option of listening to music in one of the square's legendary coffeehouses. In the world of folk music, the name **Passim** is hallowed. This Harvard Square coffeehouse, at 47 Palmer Street, has fostered such famous folkies as Joan Baez, Bob Dylan, Joni Mitchell, and, more recently, Tracy Chapman. Tel: 492-7679. Just a stone's throw away from Passim, the **Nameless Coffeehouse**, at 3 Church Street in Cambridge, has also been providing good folk music lately. Tel: 864-1630.

But Cambridge today offers much more than folk music for the Birkenstock crowd. The **Middle East**, a funky dive at 472 Massachusetts Avenue near Central Square in Cambridge, is perhaps the hippest of all area hangouts, at least for those who wear Dr. Martens boots and have several earrings or perhaps a nose ring. The inexpensive restaurant up front serves decent tabbouleh and hummus to the hipoisie until at least 1:00 A.M., later on weekends. The music, which starts at 8:30 P.M. in the back room, brings new meaning to the term eclectic: Various sorts of jazz dominate on Mondays; expect rock in myriad forms (but always progressive) on Sundays and Tuesday through Friday; Saturdays are reserved for acoustic and international music. The cover varies. Tel: 354-8238.

T. T. the Bear's Place, at 10 Brookline Street, Cambridge, is another popular venue for local and national progressive rock bands. The café side of the club features Caribbean and West Indian food. The cover varies. Tel: 492-0082.

Within walking distance of Central Square, about halfway to Harvard Square, is Cambridge's premier Irish bar and another laudible music venue, the **Plough and Stars**, at 912 Massachusetts Avenue. The musical diet ranges from bluegrass to folk-rock. The television is tuned to international soccer matches on Saturday afternoons. There is no cover charge. Tel: 492-9653.

Comedy

Comedy is very big in Boston, which is in itself funny because Bostonians are inherently stodgy and stoic—or at least they work hard at convincing you they are. Nonetheless, greater Boston has given birth to some hilarious comedians and a few area clubs have launched careers. Both Jay Leno and Steven Wright started at **Stitches**, 835 Beacon Street in the Back Bay, Boston's foremost laugh shop. Tel: 424-6995. The local branch of the famous New York club **Catch a Rising Star**, at 30B J. F. Kennedy Street in Harvard Square, features hot natives on the way up and national acts who are holding steady. Tel: 661-9887 or 661-0167. Another club worth checking out is **Nick's Comedy Stop**, at 100 Warrenton Street in the Theater District, a three-block area south of the Boston Common. Tel: 482-0930. You can expect to wait in line and pay a cover at all these places.

Dancing

If you like dancing to Motown or just good old-fashioned rock 'n' roll, get a blaster and find a well-lit spot on the Common—the dance clubs of Boston are not meant for you. Most dance clubs are concentrated in two areas, Boylston Place and Ted Williams Way (still called Lansdowne Street by everybody). Discerning the difference between the clubs here can be difficult, even if you're on the inside. Be aware that the crowd does change from night to night at almost every club.

Boylston Place, a lively alley in the heart of the Theater District and therefore the center of Boston, has become a nightlife mecca. The newest addition is **Esmé**, a dance club attached to Marais, at 116 Boylston Street (see Bars, above). While Marais is modeled after a bistro, Esmé is supposed to resemble a turn-of-the-century Parisian bordello. Alas, red velvet is as gaudy today as it was then, and the dance floor is tiny. But there's plenty of space at the bar for aging oglers. Jackets and ties are the rule at Esmé, which is open Wednesday through Saturday. Tel: 482-3399.

The next theme disco along the way is **Zanzibar**, at 1 Boylston Place. The motif throughout the two-story building is tropical, and the bar at the club's Cannibal Lounge serves frozen cocktails. Jackets and ties are in order for men, most of whom are in their thirties or a little older. DJs play contemporary music most nights. Tel: 451-1955.

For something a little younger and livelier, try **Avenue C**, at 25 Boylston Place. The long room with black walls looks like a storage space, which is what it was originally. But the twenties crowd couldn't care less as long as the progressive/ alternative tunes (the stuff played on college radio stations) are played loudly and there's room to dance. Alternative bands play live on Thursdays. No sneakers, jeans, or tee-shirts. Tel: 423-3832.

The other, and bigger, collection of clubs is on **Lansdowne Street**, which runs along the backside of Fenway Park. Lansdowne, which is only a five-minute walk from bustling Kenmore Square, has been renamed Ted Williams Way, in honor of the near-legendary Boston baseball player. It's not clear whether Ted would appreciate the honor if he saw the throng of outrageous partygoers traipsing nightly from club to club on his street. In the shadow of the infamous Green Monster, Fenway's 60-foot left-field wall, lies the anchor of this club mecca, **Avalon**, at 15 Lansdowne Street. Avalon is by far the biggest of the clubs and the most elaborate—dramatic light and smoke effects, huge dance floor, and bars on every level. Thursday night is Euro-night at Avalon, when a large group of Boston's foreign students, many of whom are relatively wealthy, take over. The suburban crowd moves in on Friday and Saturday nights, and on Sunday nights Avalon is the biggest gay club in Boston, with lots of funky dancing. As usual, no jeans, sneakers, or tee-shirts are allowed (though jeans are allowed on Thursdays). Tel: 262-2424.

While the competition is tight, **Venus de Milo**, at 11 Lansdowne Street, may be the funkiest club on the street. The decor has been described as Neoclassical, Postmodern, and sixties revival. Who can see enough in the dark to really know—or care? The music can be eardrum-crushing, whether it's rare-culture music on Thursdays, techno-music on Fridays, or funk and disco throwback on Saturdays. The dancers are frenetic, especially the women in cages. Jeans are okay here, but not baseball caps. Tel: 421-9595.

There are a few other prominent clubs scattered around town, but only one of them attempts to promote a multiracial atmosphere: the **Cotton Club**, at 965 Massachusetts Avenue. Like all the other big clubs, the Cotton Club offers different nights to fit varying tastes. R & B is featured on Saturdays. On Thursday nights a live reggae band rocks the first-floor dance room, while house music plays upstairs. On Fridays the place becomes the Cat Club. Jeans not allowed. Tel: 541-0101.

M-80, at 969 Commonwealth Avenue, is perhaps the most notorious club in town these days. On Wednesday and Saturday nights the small club is packed with rich, sometimes super-rich, Saudi Arabians, South Americans, Japanese, and even a few Europeans. Champagne is the common beverage, as well as toy: Moët et Chandon White Star is used for spraying; Dom Pérignon is for drinking. The music is aptly classified "Eurohaus." The dance floor is small, so everyone eventually dances on the tables. Never go before midnight, and don't bother to go at all on Friday nights. Tel: 254-2054.

CLASSICAL MUSIC

Boston is something of a paradise for the classical-music lover. The city may not have as many groups and ensembles as, say, New York, but there may be more first-rate live classical music available per capita here than in any other city in America. Boston is a major stop on the international performance circuit, but the city has considerable talent in its own back yard. The Boston Symphony Orchestra (BSO), under the direction of Seiji Ozawa, is undeniably one of the world's great ensembles. Boston is also a leading center in the early-music and original-instrument movement. For choral music, it's tough to beat—the Handel & Hayden Society, the nation's oldest choral group, is just one of many at every level of professionalism.

Opera in Boston hasn't been the same since Sarah Caldwell's company folded a few years ago. Still, the Boston Lyric Opera is slowly coming up to snuff, and the Boston Opera Association is working on new concert collaborations with the BSO. And then there are the Composers in Red Sneakers, whose occasional concerts always create interest and sometimes stir controversy. If you wear red sneakers to the concerts, admission is free.

Therein lies another Boston advantage. Hearing great music in Boston need not cost a fortune, or even a nickel. Inexpensive rush seats for the BSO are available on the day of the performance. Throughout the year there is a wealth of free concerts and recitals in churches and at the area's many music schools. For instance, no admission is charged for the New England Conservatory of Music's annual faculty recital every September, which is a stellar event.

What follows is a very selective list of schools and various performing ensembles based in Boston. (The telephone area code for Boston and Cambridge is 617.)

Symphony

Boston Symphony Orchestra, 301 Massachusetts Avenue, Boston. Tel: 266-1492. The orchestra sponsors the Boston Pops, which performs April through June.

Early Music

Boston Baroque (formerly known as Banchetto Musicale), P.O. Box 380190, Cambridge. Tel: 641-1310.

Choral

Handel & Hayden Society, 300 Massachusetts Avenue, Boston. Tel: 266-3605.

Cantata Singers, 729 Boylston Street, Boston. Tel: 267-6502.

Emmanuel Music, Emmanuel Church of Boston, 15 Newbury Street, Boston. Tel: 536-3555. This unusual group, under the able direction of Craig Smith, presents a Bach cantata with outstanding singers and instrumentalists at each Sunday-morning service. They also offer an annual AIDS benefit and a Mozart birthday concert in January.

Opera

Boston Lyric Opera, 114 State Street, Boston. Tel: 248-8660.

Boston Opera Association, 4 Copley Place, Suite 140, Boston. Tel: 437-1316.

Chamber Music

Pro Arte Chamber Orchestra, 1950 Massachusetts Avenue, Cambridge. Tel: 661-7067.

Boston Chamber Music Society, 286 Congress Street, Boston. Tel: 422-0086.

Isabella Stewart Gardner Museum, 280 The Fenway, Boston. Tel: 566-1401. The chamber-music program at the Gardner Museum offers some exceptional music in one of Boston's greatest treasures.

New Music

Boston Musica Viva, 25 Huntington Avenue, Boston. Tel: 353-0556.

Composers in Red Sneakers is a loose-knit consortium that has no fixed address or concert schedule. It happens when it happens. Watch newspapers for concert announcements, or call 527-3171.

Music Schools

New England Conservatory of Music, 290 Huntington Avenue, Boston. Tel: 262-1120.

   Boston Conservatory of Music, 8 The Fenway, Boston. Tel: 536-6340.

   Longy School of Music, 1 Follen Street, Cambridge. Tel: 876-0956.

   Boston University School of Music, 855 Commonwealth Avenue, Boston. Tel: 353-3345.

   Berklee School of Music (Berklee Performance Center), 136 Massachusetts Avenue, Boston. Tel: 266-1400, ext. 261.

THEATER

Boston was once one of the great theater towns in this country. But decades have passed since Boston provided Broadway with a steady stream of hits. Today the Shubert Theater and occasionally the Wang Center present the touring editions of the Broadway smash hits, but the real stuff of theater can be found at the little houses attached to the universities. The most prominent is the American Repertory Theater (ART) at Harvard University. Under the direction of Robert Brustein, ART has produced some ground-breaking works by the likes of Sam Shepard, David Mamet, Robert Wilson, and Don Delio. The other theaters listed below offer a wide variety of plays.

   American Repertory Theater, Loeb Drama Center, Harvard University, 64 Brattle Street, Cambridge. Tel: 547-8300.

   Charles Playhouse, 74 Warrenton Street, Boston. Tel: 426-6912.

   Hasty Pudding Theater, 12 Holyoke Street, Cambridge. Tel: 495-5205.

   Huntington Theater Company, Boston University Theater, 264 Huntington Avenue, Boston. Tel: 266-0800.

   Lyric Stage, 140 Clarendon Street, Boston. Tel: 437-7172.

   Shubert Theater, 265 Tremont Street, Boston. Tel: 426-4520 or (800) 233-3123.

   Strand Theater, 543 Columbia Road, Dorchester, Tel: 282-5230.

   Wang Center, 268 Tremont Street, Boston. Tel: 482-9393.

DANCE

Boston enjoys a lively dance scene. Boston Ballet, under the direction of Bruce Marks, is now one of the nation's premier companies and boasts an impressive bevy of international soloists. Dance Umbrella is New England's largest presenter of modern dance. Lately the Umbrella has also produced a wide variety of ethnic dance troupes from Asia, Africa, and America. Mobius, a small presenter, offers the most avant-garde dance and performance art in Boston. If you are in the area during the summer months, look for interesting performances from talented choreographers at Harvard University's Summer Dance program.

Boston Ballet, 19 Clarendon Street, Boston. Tel: 695-6950.

Dance Umbrella, 380 Green Street, Cambridge. Tel: 492-7578.

Mobius, 354 Congress Street, Boston. Tel: 542-7416.

—René Becker

SHOPS AND SHOPPING

The shops of Boston and Cambridge are an exciting mix of the old and the new, the conservative and the avant-garde. Some have been around for more than a century and have histories nearly as compelling as that of the Boston Tea Party. Others are new concerns, outlets for well-known chains as well as small, independent ventures put together by local entrepreneurs; some "stores" are nothing more than push-carts wheeled out in the morning and wheeled back in at night.

Though many think of the Boston and Cambridge area as the premier place in New England to buy clothing—and rightly so—it is also a rich source for arts and crafts. The arts community here is as energetic as any in the world. At least a half dozen "artists' colonies"—warehouses converted into low-rent lofts—hum like beehives all year round. Visit open studios at various colonies and arts-and-crafts fairs (check local newspapers for current listings) to get a glimpse at what is about to happen rather than what has already reached the mainstream. The main showplace for established artists, past and present, is Boston's Newbury Street, which is lined with more than 40 galleries. Twice a year (the third Sundays in May and September) the street is closed off for **Art Newbury Street**, a celebration when galleries open their doors to welcome visitors with music and good cheer.

There are probably more bookstores per square mile in Boston and Cambridge than anywhere else in the country. What is striking is that most are independently owned and operated, and they have a tendency to specialize—in mysteries, world revolution, multicultural children's books, poetry, travel, New Age.

Though a dedicated shopper can ferret out some good buys in almost any of the local commercial areas, the place to go shopping in Cambridge is Harvard Square, while in Boston it's Faneuil Hall Marketplace, the Back Bay (especially Newbury Street and Copley Place), Downtown Crossing, and Chinatown.

Many shops are open daily, although Sunday hours start at noon instead of 10:00 A.M. Closing time at small operations depends upon the store, the location, the season, and the whim of the owner. Some may close as early as 5:00 or 6:00 P.M., while others stay open as late as 9:00 P.M. Department stores usually stay open until 7:00 P.M. Monday through Saturday and are open Sundays as well. Some bookstores remain open later than most other shops, but smaller bookstores may have odd closing days, such as Mondays or Tuesdays.

Boston

FANEUIL HALL MARKETPLACE AND THE HAYMARKET

Where to begin is the shopper's dilemma here. Faneuil Hall Marketplace has 125 individual shops in addition to numerous pushcarts, restaurants, and cafés. There is often free outdoor entertainment as well, and the people-watching is the best in town. Stores here are open later than elsewhere in Boston, until 9:00 P.M. every day except Sundays, when closing is at 6:00 P.M.; restaurants and pubs remain open even later.

Getting to the marketplace, between City Hall and the Waterfront, is easy by subway. It's a short walk from the Green Line stop at Government Center or the Orange Line at Haymarket. If you're determined to ignore good advice and drive a car into this hectic, congested area, head for one of the two nearby lots that offer discounts with validation of purchase: **Safe Harbor Parking**, at the Government Center garage on Congress Street (directly across from Faneuil Hall), or **75 State Street Parking**.

The marketplace consists of three long buildings: **Quincy Market**, in the middle, with food stalls and pushcarts; and **North Market** and **South Market**, both full of shops, on either side. Adventurous souls undoubtedly will be happy just wading right into the scene and exploring the vast selection of shops, and the many pleasant distractions, at random. If you'd rather be more selective, check the directory on the cobblestone plaza between Quincy Market and South Market. There's also an **Information Center** in the south canopy of Quincy Market in the winter and at entrance 3 of the South Market in the summer.

Quincy Market

Although there are 22 proper restaurants and outdoor cafés in Faneuil Hall, many shoppers prefer to head for the center colonnade of Quincy Market. In keeping with its traditional roots as a produce and retail food center, this part of the complex features 40 stalls with food from around the world. You'll find New England fare (chowder, lobster, Boston baked beans) alongside foods with a more international flavor (tacos, pork fried rice, *gelato*), as well as the old standbys that might satisfy a hungry but fussy kid (hot dogs, pizza, jelly beans).

Under the glass canopies on either side of the colonnade, and lined up outside as well in warm weather, are wooden pushcarts displaying constantly changing merchandise. Called the **Bull Market** (after the bull atop Quincy Market's weather vane), the fleet of pushcarts sells artwork and specialty items—hats, tee-shirts, earrings, note cards, scarves, suspenders, clocks, and the like. Browsing here is half the fun; the other half is talking with the artisans who rent the carts, usually a week at a time, to sell their wares. A few years from now the more successful of these entrepreneurs may be renting store space in the marketplace.

North Market

The North Market has a higher turnover rate than the South Market, so don't be surprised to discover that a shop listed in the central directory is nowhere to be found. Still, there are some long-term residents who have helped define the diverse character of the marketplace. **Durgin Park** is one of these. The restaurant is well known not only for its longevity ("established before you were born"—actually 1826), but also for its outspoken staff, who can dish out more orders to their customers than they receive (and they won't accept your credit cards either).

Among the novelty shops in the marketplace is **Hog Wild** (second level, entrance 7), a 14-year-old store (one of the earliest tenants of the North Market building), featuring porcine designs and slogans imprinted on tee-shirts, men's briefs, bumper stickers, and piggy banks. The **Little Lefty Shop**, a small section within a store called **Personal Impressions** (second level, entrance 8), offers sinistral instruments such as scissors, can openers, and corkscrews as well as measuring cups with the gradations placed where they can be read easily by those who see the world from the other side.

South Market

On the ground level of South Market is **Frillz** (entrance 4), which specializes in white and cream-colored skirts, blouses, camisoles, dresses, and petticoats hand-painted by local artists in the store's studio in Boston. More than a dozen years ago artist Carol Lewis rented a pushcart in the Bull Market to sell her hand-painted tuxedo blouses, noted for their striking tulip, rose, and tiger lily designs. Now Lewis owns three stores, two in the marketplace and one in Copley Place.

Decorative decoy making, which reached its peak in the 1820s, is the only true, purely American folk art, according to Sarah Codd, resident artist and proprietor of **Migrations** (second level, entrance 3). She and her father, Peter Codd, a master carver of worldwide stature, craft much of the work here—loons, quail, owls, mallards, puffins, and whistling swans—which is now sought out by collectors more than hunters. Prices range widely, from $44 to $600, and there's always a "duck of the month" special.

Daniel Kiracofe, owner and resident artist of **Boston Scrimshanders** (second level, entrance 3), bills his shop as "two hundred years behind the times," which would put us back in the 1700s when whalers were beginning to engrave designs on ivory as a way to pass idle hours. Although the shop carries rare collectibles from scrimshaw artists of the past who used whale and elephant ivory, Kiracofe, who hand-engraves much of the store's modern inventory (brooches, bracelets, earrings, bolo ties, tie tacks, and knives), seeks out alternative sources of raw material for himself—prehistoric mammoth and walrus ivory and African elephant ivory taken from animals that have died of natural causes. He donates a portion of sales to game reserves.

Haymarket

As long as you're in the neighborhood, take a walk over to the Haymarket, just north of Faneuil Hall. Long ago, around the time George Washington came to Boston with his troops, hay was sold for horses here. Today the place is an active open-air marketplace on Fridays, Saturdays, and Sundays (best selection before 7:30 A.M.) where Bostonians come to buy fresh fruits and vegetables, meat, and cheese at wholesale prices. Tables and pushcarts are heaped high with produce, but don't touch the displays unless you want to be scolded by the vendors, who insist on selecting the individual items themselves—sometimes a source of argument between buyer and seller. To get a sense of the place at its busiest, go toward the end of the day on a Friday or Saturday, when prices are lowered to sell off perishables before the market shuts down.

NEWBURY STREET

Although Newbury Street, with its red-brick town houses, chic outdoor cafés, and numerous art galleries, exudes its own distinctive charm, it has been called Boston's Rodeo Drive, for its raison d'être seems to be to indulge a shopper's greatest fantasies. You can indulge yours in the 300 stores that line the eight-block area in Boston's Back Bay, just west of the Public Garden, whether your interests lie in fashion, art, or just about anything else: books, antiques, gifts, novelties, candy, entertainment.

Fashion

If fashion is your priority, be assured that shops are numerous, varied, and, regardless of style, relentlessly upscale (even the resale shops). Adventurous and exceptionally energetic shoppers should simply start at one end of the street and work their way down, perhaps stopping from time to time for sustenance at one of the 30 cafés and restaurants along the way.

The more conservative end of the street is that closest to the Boston Public Garden near the Ritz-Carlton Hotel. Here you'll find **Burberry's**, at number 2, for classics that are always in style; **Brooks Brothers**, at number 46, for perfectly tailored suits; and **Laura Ashley**, at number 83, for dresses, skirts, and blouses in country prints. **Margaretta**, at number 85, features hand-loomed sweaters of exquisite quality that have been featured on the covers of *Elle* and *Glamour* magazines. Designed by the store's eponymous owner, the sweaters are handmade in New England, Scotland, and Great Britain. Also at this end of the street, at number 93, is **Kakas Furs**, a family-owned business begun in 1858 that lately has garnered unwanted attention as the former workplace of the late Charles Stuart, certainly one of Boston's most notorious elements.

A couple of newer tenants noted for their fashions for both men and women are also at this end of the street: the Milan-based designer **Giorgio Armani**, at number 22, and **Joseph Abboud**, number 37, owned by a Boston native who began his career at the nearby **Louis, Boston** (at the corner of Newbury and Berkeley streets), a four-floor men's store made up of "salons within a salon," with hair- and skin-care products, fragrances, and a café as well as fine clothing that runs the gamut from business suits to casual wear.

Newbury Street also has its wild side, but that aspect is kept as far away as possible from its more conservative denizens. Those who favor a trendier, avant-garde look should start at the far end of the street, all the way up by Massachusetts Avenue, next to the Hynes Convention Center/ICA Green Line stop. **Urban Outfitters**, on the corner, carries casual, playful wear, and **Allston Beat**, at number 348, is known for funky but chic denim and leather articles.

How to dress well in a recession is a problem addressed by **Déjà Vu**, an upscale consignment shop at number 222 that specializes in "gently worn" women's clothes and accessories. The two owners are very selective about the merchandise they sell here, accepting only those items that bear major designer labels with a retail value of at least $300. Markdowns are made to one-third of the value or better, so a discriminating bargain-hunter can find some real buys here—a $650 Escada jacket for $150, for example, or a $350 Chanel blouse for $150.

Galleries

Shoppers interested mainly in visiting art galleries face the same dilemma as fashion mavens: so much to see, so little time. To help narrow your focus, visit any of Newbury Street's 40 galleries and pick up a free *Gallery Guide,* which contains brief descriptions of all the galleries (with a map), as well as listings of current exhibits.

Gallery Naga, inside the Church of the Covenant at number 67, was founded in 1977 by a group of Boston artists for the purpose of showing the best of Boston painting. The gallery also stages occasional studio furniture exhibitions.

The **Society of Arts and Crafts**, at number 175, the oldest craft organization in the United States (founded in 1897), exhibits and sells works of more than 300 contemporary American craft artists. The downstairs gallery presents a continually changing array of works in all media (jewelry, wood, cloth, pottery, glass, furniture). The two galleries upstairs feature special exhibits, such as works created around a set theme. (On your way up the stairs take a look at the narrative and photographic display about the SAC on the wall.)

On the other side of the street, at number 158, is another prominent Boston gallery. Founded in 1879, the **Copley Society of Boston** is the oldest art association in America, with a focus on contemporary visual arts, primarily painting, photography, and sculpture. Today the society represents more than 700 artists in the United States and abroad, sponsors awards and scholarships, and conducts educational programs in the community.

At number 162 is the gallery operated by the **Guild of Boston Artists**, a nonprofit association of painters, sculptors, and printmakers founded in 1914, emphasizing contemporary artwork that affirms a faith in the enduring beauty of nature. The Front Gallery contains the paintings and sculpture of members (membership is limited to 70 artists), while special exhibits are shown in the back-room President's Gallery, whose double-paned ceiling makes this area one of the best in the city for viewing artwork under natural light.

For a real change of pace stop by **Starving Artist**, at number 224, a gallery/boutique that couldn't be more different from the traditional Guild. Founded by artist Rick Lange to showcase the work of "Boston's finest unknowns," the place feels more like the Hard Rock Café than a gallery, with the music of local bands blasting in the background (their recordings are sold here). Jewelry, paintings, clothing, sculptures, and more are brought here by local artists to be sold on consignment, and the work and the atmosphere challenge the conservative (some say stuffy) reputation of Newbury Street.

Books, Antiquities, and Miscellanea

Though art and fashion predominate on Newbury Street, there are also numerous shops dealing in other types of merchandise. **Waterstone's**, the branch of the British bookstore occupying the old Exeter Street Theater (originally a Spiritualist church), feels a bit like a London drawing room, with deep red rugs and heavy wooden bookcases. In its current incarnation the theater encourages a decorum little practiced when the stage was set for raucous midnight showings of the *Rocky Horror Picture Show* here in the 1970s. Boston's largest (and neatest) bookstore, Waterstone's has found a place for everything literary, and supplements its excellent selections with numerous readings and book signings and a regular Sunday-afternoon story hour for kids. At 26 Exeter Street, the entrance is just a few steps from Newbury Street next to T.G.I.Friday's, a chain restaurant and singles hangout. The building still looks like a theater from the outside, but the days when *Rocky Horror* fans flung toast at the stage here are long gone.

The owner of **The Gods**, the only antiquities dealer in Boston, has a special fondness for the Egyptian cat goddess Bast, so there are usually a few statues of regal felines interspersed among the other 100 or so deities from religions past and present (paganism, Hinduism, Druidism, and Christianity, to name a few) that reside in the shop, at number 253. The store carries reproductions and also has a display case filled with genuine antiquities, including iridescent glass beads from ancient Rome in modern jewelry settings, Egyptian amulets, small statuettes, and a 3,000-year-old mummified baby crocodile.

The **Nostalgia Factory**, at number 336, is devoted to memorabilia from the near and distant past (granny glasses, stock certificates, campaign buttons), but the 23-year-old store is known primarily as the repository of the largest collection of original old advertisements in the United States—more than 1 million at last count. The shop's clients include companies researching their own advertising past, ad agencies seeking authentic period looks, and collectors and dealers.

Although the mammoth **Tower Records** at the corner of Newbury Street and Mass. Ave. seems to be ruled by Boston's youth who hang out here sampling new music on the video preview screens, there's a lot of diversity here, both in music and in customers. *The Life of Irving Berlin* might be displayed next to *Sting: A Biography* in the first floor's book section. On the two floors above, the CDs, tapes, 12-inch singles, and 45s are divided into well-stocked sections devoted to every imaginable taste in music. Students and teachers from the nearby Berklee College of Music frequent Tower for inspiration, as do dance teachers trying to stay one step ahead of their students. There's a second, smaller store in Harvard Square, but it hasn't got the cultural mix that gives this one its edge.

If you want to continue exploring shops along Newbury Street but feel compelled to sit down and relax for a while, two literary dens offer a way to satisfy both desires. The outdoor terrace of the **Harvard Bookstore Café**, at number 190, is the perfect place for a tired shopper to enjoy a cappuccino or light meal while watching the endless fashion parade on the sidewalk. (The hostess will come find you among the bookcases when your table is ready.) Farther up the street, at number 338, is the **Trident Bookstore Café**, whose indoor space is a quiet, unhurried refuge; the Trident offers an eclectic assortment of literary magazines and New Age titles, with espresso and vegetarian chili on the menu. Popular with writers as well as readers, the café also serves as a venue for occasional Sunday-afternoon poetry readings.

BOYLSTON STREET

Although eclipsed by Newbury Street's scope and grandeur, Boylston Street (which runs parallel to Newbury) nevertheless has a few stores that offer merchandise that cannot easily be found elsewhere. Across from the Boston Public Garden near the Four Seasons Hotel is a building called the **Heritage on the Garden**, which houses such shops as **Escada**, **Hermès of Paris**, the **Waterford Wedgwood Store**, and **Arche Shoes**, known for its line of comfortable pumps.

In contrast to the relatively new shops at the Heritage, several Boston landmark stores line the next block. "A little something from Shreve's" is the understated way some Bostonians have of referring to an impeccable item, perhaps in crystal or silver, from **Shreve, Crump & Low**. Founded in 1796, the store went through a series of changes in both name and location until 1930, when it moved to its present imposing site at 330 Boylston Street, on the corner of Boylston and Arlington. Always a dealer of fine jewelry, Shreve's also became known for its antiques when owner Charles Crump began scouting abroad in 1869 for pieces to bring back for his store. Stationery, giftware, and china can also be found here, but of particular interest is the store's exclusive Boston series of jewelry, which includes sterling silver pins of the Boston Public Garden, its swan boats, and the ducklings made famous by Robert McCloskey's children's book *Make Way for Ducklings*.

Beneath the gilded swan at 356 Boylston Street is the store owned and operated by the **Women's Educational & Industrial Union** since the nonprofit social service organization was first established in 1877 by Louisa May Alcott, Julia Ward Howe (author of "The Battle Hymn of the Republic"), and other prominent Boston women. Now, as then, proceeds from sales go to support the union's mission to advance opportunities for women and to help Boston's needy. Exuding a sense of New England refinement, the store consists of five shops featuring some unusual and one-of-a-kind items. There are a needlework shop, the oldest of its kind in the country, selling fine yarns and hand-painted canvases produced in its own design studio; a children's shop, with hand-knit sweaters by local designers; and a gift shop, featuring the union's own cookbook with recipes from Bostonians past and present, among other items. Ask for a copy of the union newsletter for notices of slide shows, day trips, and other events.

Farther up the street, at number 440, is **F.A.O. Schwarz**, recognizable by the 12-foot-tall, 6,000-pound bronze teddy bear standing at the entrance. The Boston branch of the toy store founded by Frederick August Otto Schwarz in 1862 has the irresistible but pricey assortment of toys (a $7,000 Ferrari) and the amusement-park atmosphere (a talking bear imparts directory information, and a tree delivers friendly promos in rhyme) that have become the hallmarks of the Schwarz chain. Personalized shopping and delivery services are unusual extras here, and the rest rooms on the second floor are a welcome amenity.

Fine women's clothing is the draw at the venerable **Lord & Taylor**, 760 Boylston Street. Be sure to check L & T's window displays to see if the yearly sale on Clinique makeup and facial-care products is underway. The store is located at the street edge of the **Prudential Plaza**, a complex of shops that is currently undergoing major renovations and tenant turnover. You will be rewarded for maneuvering through the construction, however, by the high-quality women's clothing at the elegant **Saks Fifth Avenue**.

COPLEY PLACE

Copley Place complex, in the Back Bay's Copley Square, behind the Boston Public Library, is hardly the kind of mall where teenagers roam looking for something to do, or where budget shoppers stalk markdowns. Stores with names like Gucci, Tiffany, Louis Vuitton, and Armani define the strictly upscale scene here (the refreshment stand at the movie theater serves cappuccino). The complex, which houses more than 100 shops, offers ample parking and a direct connection (via skywalks) with the Boston Marriott and Westin hotels. Although some shops have extended hours, most are open from 10:00 A.M. to 7:00 P.M. Monday through Saturday and from noon to 5:00 P.M. on Sundays.

Those who enter the complex at the Westin Hotel, on the corner of Huntington and Dartmouth streets (behind the Boston Public Library near the Copley Green Line station), arrive by way of an escalator that cuts through the center of a waterfall. At the top of the escalator is **New England Sampler**, which sells regional crafts and specialty foods in the Yankee tradition: Nantucket lightship baskets, scrimshaw cuff links and tie clips, beeswax molds (in such forms as potatoes, asparagus, and corn), needlepoint pillows, quilts, chutney, plum sauce, maple sugar, and cranberry honey. Across the skywalk is an information booth (there are two more at the other entrances to the mall) that provides a useful directory of all the shops and their whereabouts, as well as the location of rest rooms.

The shops on the first floor are arranged along wide hallways that meet at a central atrium with a 60-foot waterfall as its centerpiece. On this level is **Traveldays**, a bookstore with a good selection of travel books about destinations around the world in addition to extensive sections on Boston and New England. **Noah's**, also on the first floor, is a toy store carrying some of the more unusual puppets on the market (rhinos, owls, hippos) and a collection of soft dolls that includes not only Raggedy Ann and Andy but also their black counterparts Rags and Patches (handmade in nearby Dorchester by a local artist). Elsewhere on the first floor are **Gucci**, for fine leather bags and shoes for both men and women, and **Beylerian**, for men's better suits and sweaters.

On the second level is an official "Cheers" outlet with sweatshirts, tee-shirts, and mugs, as well as several stores devoted to women's fashions. A **Frillz** store (the original is in Faneuil Hall Marketplace) sells blouses and dresses hand-painted with floral designs in addition to flowery jewelry. **Liz Claiborne** features its own popular line of scarves, jackets, pants, dresses, handbags, and belts, while **Cignal** (which has a shop on Newbury Street as well) offers trendy men's and women's clothing. **Compagnie International Express** is a real find for women who enjoy comfortable, casual, yet stylish clothes that are fun to wear.

The three-story **Neiman-Marcus** can be entered from any level of the mall. Nicknamed Needless Markup by some Bostonians who claim they can find the same merchandise elsewhere at lower prices, the store has its fans, who love the selection and live for the sales.

DOWNTOWN

The center of activity in downtown Boston—the area from Boston Common to Government Center—is in Downtown Crossing (a compact retail district located one block east of the Common; easily accessible by MBTA Red and Orange lines). The atmosphere along the pedestrian walkway through Washington and Summer streets is festive, with pushcart vendors selling sweatshirts, tee-shirts, toys, scarves, and jewelry (not to mention fried dough and teriyaki), and with benches for shoppers to rest on between wanderings while enjoying a snack or listening to the street musicians.

Right at the intersection of Summer and Washington streets is a store where many who work nearby choose to spend their lunch hours: **Filene's Basement**, a totally different world from **Filene's**, the upscale department store upstairs. Down here the price tags are dated; the longer an article remains in the store, the cheaper it becomes. There's no pretense here, no fancy displays, no accessorized mannequins. Although there are now branches elsewhere in Massachusetts and around the country, they are mere shadows of the original, where the courtesy that dedicated Basement shoppers show one another is rivaled only by that of Boston drivers. Don't be surprised if somebody rips the sweater you're examining right out of your hands or lifts up her skirt and shimmies into a pair of slacks right in the aisle. Stranger things have happened in the country's oldest bargain store (founded in 1908). Upstairs in Filene's there are public rest rooms on the fourth floor (the only ones in the area).

Across the street, at number 429, is **E. B. Horn & Co.**, a jewelry and gift store founded in 1839 and owned and operated over the century and a half since by two families: the Horns and the Finns, three generations each. Diamond rings, watches, silver tea services, pewter flasks, and pins and necklaces from the estate jewelry collection are among the items sold here.

Off Summer Street behind the **Jordan Marsh** department store (which, like Filene's, has a basement full of bargains) is **Matthew F. Sheehan Co.**, at 22 Chauncy Street. Established in 1907 by an Irish immigrant, the store grew from its humble beginnings with just a few statues and rosaries in stock into one of the largest suppliers of religious books and articles in the country today. The section devoted to Bibles is so extensive that there's a guide for selecting the one that's best for you (the store offers a selection of zippered Bible covers, too).

Just a short walk down Franklin Street, which borders one side of the huge Filene's building, is the oldest retail store in the Commonwealth of Massachusetts—and perhaps the nation, although this honor is hotly contested. When Benjamin Franklin wanted a couple of trunks for his trip to France as the new U.S. ambassador to that country, he came here, as did the Pony Express when saddles were needed to outfit its stable of horses. Founded in 1776, **London Harness** (at number 60) still caters to travellers' needs with its stock of suitcases and bags, but the sole pigskin saddle is kept on display more out of nostalgia than to meet the demands of today's shoppers (and there's not a harness in sight). The store's warm scent of leather, the friendly clerks, and the high ceilings and polished floors seem from a more genteel era. Leather binders, wallets, briefcases, globes, chess sets, wind and weather indicators, and framed sets of cigarette cards are also sold.

On the other side of Washington Street, Franklin becomes Bromfield Street, where the tiny **Bay State Coin Co.**, at number 31, trades in old coins, stamps, toy trains, political buttons, comic books, autographs, World Series pins (a 1915 Red Sox pin went for $3,200—on sale), baseball cards, and memorabilia.

The **Watch Hospital**, across the street at number 40, is a combination repair shop and jeweler specializing in watches. Customers take a number and line up for service (minor repairs are done while you wait); time is of the essence, as it has been in this family business for nearly 50 years. There's also a discounted stock of Timex, Citizen, Casio, Pulsar, and Swatch watches.

If you follow Washington Street toward Government Center you will come to the **Globe Corner Bookstore** (at School Street). This is the place to find books about Boston to further enrich your stay (such as Charles Bahne's *The Complete Guide to Boston's Freedom Trail*). If travel is your passion you could easily spend an afternoon browsing through the store's vast selection of books about the city, New England, and the wider world.

CHINATOWN

One member of the Chinese community in Boston commented on the most unusual "store" he had ever seen in the area: an orange Pinto parked at the corner of Beach and Kneeland streets every weekend. The owners would open the trunk and sell homemade egg rolls out of it. Eventually the trunk turned into a storefront, stocking videos instead of egg rolls. This is just one example of the entrepreneurial spirit that thrives in Chinatown (which is just a short walk from South Station, on the MBTA's Red Line).

One of the best fabric stores in the city in terms of quality, selection, and price is **North End Fabrics/Harrison Textile**, at 31 Harrison Avenue. In addition to the staples, the shop carries such special goods as silks and laces, as well as a quantity of remnants. If buttons or trimmings are needed to match a purchase, **Windsor Button** is a short walk from Chinatown at 35 Temple Place, a side street connecting Washington and Tremont. On the way you'll pass **Nam Buk Hong Chinese Herbs**, at 75 Harrison, in case your supply of ginseng needs replenishing.

Boston Costume, at 69 Kneeland Street, on the edge of Chinatown, is the place to pick up a feather boa to complete your ensemble for First Night or outfit yourself for Halloween. Owned by the Bertolino family for half a century, Boston Costume may well be the largest store of its kind in the world, with 50,000 masquerade and theatrical costumes for rent or sale. If your heart is set on a popular character, such as a Teenage Mutant Ninja Turtle, be advised to call and reserve it in advance, just to be sure you don't have to settle for a Purple People Eater. Tel: (617) 482-1632.

Cambridge

HARVARD SQUARE

When it comes to shopping in the city of Cambridge, Harvard Square is the center of activity, with dozens of shops within easy walking distance of the Red Line's Harvard Square stop. The square is a mecca for book lovers, though many other shoppers come here to poke around in stores featuring the work of local artists or selling clothing and specialty items. The square is geographically so compact that it's just as efficient and perhaps more fun to stroll around and visit stores as you happen upon them than to follow a strict itinerary.

Books

Wordsworth and Barillari Books are two large discounters offering great prices on tens of thousands of new books.

Wordsworth, at 30 Brattle Street, west of Harvard Square, provides a literary escape from the jugglers, fire-eaters, and folk singers performing nightly on the outdoor plaza directly across the street from the store. (For cards and calendars look for **Wordsworth Abridged** up the street at number 5.) **Barillari Books**, which serves espresso along with its reduced prices, is at 1 Mifflin Place on Mount Auburn Street at the western edge of the square's commercial district. Guests of the neighboring Charles Hotel can take advantage of Barillari's "room-service books," an idea dreamed up by the hotel's owner and his friend playwright David Mamet, whereby the hotel concierge delivers books to your room.

On the opposite edge of Harvard Square, at 76A Mount Auburn Street, is **Schoenhof's Foreign Books**, opened in 1856 by Carl Schoenhof, an importer of German books for Boston's German community. But what began as a one-language store has become a repository for the literature of more than 40 countries in 192 languages. The store (which now has a second outlet in Washington, D.C.) is well known for its extensive stock of books and tapes for language students, but holdings also include original-language material representing both the classics and more contemporary literature.

J. F. Kennedy Street, which runs through the center of the square toward the river, is home to several specialty bookstores. The volunteer in charge for the day at **Revolution Books**, downstairs at number 38, may be wearing one of the tee-shirts or buttons sold here with strong personal and political statements. The store is one of a dozen or so independently operated bookstores around the country that were inspired by the Revolutionary Communist Party in the late 1970s. There are, of course, books dispensing political dogma here, including the requisite works by Marx and Mao, but the well-stocked sections go beyond any strict party line.

Palm readings, energy healings, and handwriting analyses are just a few of the features of the psychic fair held every Saturday at **Seven Stars**, 58 J. F. Kennedy Street. The rest of the week, as luck (or fate) may have it, those who stop by may or may not find the psychic in residence for an impromptu reading. Although crystals and other stones are sold here, they are being crowded by the store's growing collection of New Age books, the most comprehensive in the city: astrology, the insights of Shirley MacLaine and Robert Bly, health and healing, Native American history and lore, the prophecies of Nostradamus, and more. The shop is open until 10:00 P.M. every night.

Directly behind the **Harvard Book Store**, which is at 1256

Mass. Ave. and has a good selection of used books downstairs, is **Grolier Poetry Book Shop**, at 6 Plympton Street. Be prepared to step over the resident dog and squeeze in, sideways perhaps, between walls of bookcases and boxes of new releases waiting to be shelved. Packed into the tiny space are more than 14,000 titles, ranging from mainstream to obscure, along with an audiotape collection of works by Marge Piercy, Dylan Thomas, and other notables, plus a few surprises (such as Vincent Price reading Percy Bysshe Shelley). Established in 1927, the store has specialized exclusively in poetry since 1974, when the current owner, Louisa Solano, took it over. Many of the photographs displayed above the bookshelves are candid shots taken by relatives and friends of contemporary poets—Allen Ginsberg and Adrienne Rich among them—who have spent some time themselves shuffling through the crowded store and participating in readings sponsored by Grolier (held in a larger space nearby on the Harvard campus about twice a month from September to May).

Fashion

Clothing shoppers can turn up some interesting booty in Harvard Square. **Calliope**, at 33 Brattle Street, is strictly for kids, with great stuffed animals (and vegetables) along with delightful, if somewhat pricey, clothes, such as raincoats that transform children into small blue dinosaurs or yellow ducks.

For more than 20 years **Oona's**, a self-described "experienced clothing" store at 1210 Mass. Ave., has dealt in army jackets, Indian print skirts, funky coat pins, and leather jackets for less than $10. For a few dollars more you can own the vintage prom dress of your dreams. Named after the owner's daughter, Oona's now has a second location at 1110 Boylston Street in the Back Bay.

Arts, Crafts, and Esoterica

Artists Naomi Kahn and Steve Gallagher, the owners of **Toucan**, take some real chances with the artwork they place on consignment. Their shop is located on the second floor of **The Garage**, a shopping complex at 36 J. F. Kennedy Street that also houses other enticing stores with out-of-the-ordinary clothing, accessories, and artwork. More than 150 artists, many on the cutting edge, show their work at Toucan. Polka-dotted chairs, driftwood jewelry boxes, weird creatures, funky hats, and clocks fashioned from computer disks and CDs are some of the items sold here. Toucan also serves as the official outlet for *Squawk* magazine (aptly termed by one reader "an open mike in print"), published by the Naked City

Coffeehouse, which, in Brigadoon-like manner, appears once a week at the Old Cambridge Baptist Church so that local poetic souls can share their inspirations.

Imaginative gifts can also be found at **Details**, located down a flight of stairs at 40 Brattle Street. (Sharing the same address is the renovated Brattle theater complex, which houses the popular **Algiers Coffeehouse** and the **Casablanca** bar and restaurant.) Among the handcrafted items at Details are picture frames fashioned out of aluminum by a couple of local architectural students, and delicate wire baskets produced by a Maine company called Burt's Bees. The bath-products section features a shelf devoted to the Kama Sutra line of oils and balms.

Follow the pachyderm prints on the sidewalk from Eliot Street up Winthrop Street until you reach number 106, **Good Good the Elephant**, named for an enigmatic phrase the owner's grandmother used when she was especially pleased. The shop carries a vast assortment of playful gewgaws: mood rings, rubber bugs in a plastic bug bag that can double as a lunch box or purse, temporary tattoos, and *Star Trek* wristwatches (the *Enterprise* makes one full voyage every minute). But what the store is famous for is its selection of rubber stamps from more than 30 different companies, plus its own Good Good line. The staff here also custom-designs stamps, holds stamp-making classes, and operates a rubber-stamp library.

Passim Coffee Shop and Gallery, nearby at 47 Palmer (downstairs from a branch of the **Globe Corner Bookstore**, which specializes in books about travel), is known primarily for its owner's friendship with such Beat Generation moguls as Allen Ginsberg, an old college roommate who still stops by from time to time. The place is very much a part of the folk scene (a tradition continued when Passim moved into the space formerly occupied by Club 47), providing a venue for intimate nighttime concerts by visiting folk artists. During the day Passim provides the visitor with a place to relax over a cup of coffee and examine the variety of artwork displayed wherever there's room: photographs, porcelain bells, hand-carved and -painted wooden feathers, silver earrings, and the like. Although some items are made by local artists, most come from such distant lands as Bali.

Around the corner, at 59A Church Street, is the **Cambridge Artists' Cooperative**, a spacious, two-floor craft gallery owned and run by 20 local artists and exhibiting the work of more than 100 American artisans. New items (in wood, ceramics, fiber, leather, and more) are continually being added to the inventory of works by the co-op regulars, such as the colorful cast-paper masks, jewelry, and sculptures by Barbara Fletcher and the delicate glass creations by Cape Cod artist Patricia Marlborough.

Although it is named for its address, **10 Arrow Gallery/ Shop** is nevertheless a little hard to find—but worth the effort for anyone with an interest in contemporary American crafts. Walk down Bow Street, which begins its curve at the Baskin Robbins at 1230 Mass. Ave., to where Arrow Street (usually not marked here because its sign gets stolen every year as part of a collegiate prank) shoots straight off to the left at St. Paul's church. Opened in 1972 by sisters Betty Tinlot and Ruth Walkey, 10 Arrow specializes primarily in wood and metal crafts, though ceramics and glass can be found here as well. The owners are partial to furniture, such wrought-iron items as fireplace pokers and candleholders, wooden and ceramic bowls, and jewelry.

The oldest continuously operating store in Harvard Square, **Leavitt & Peirce**, at 1316 Mass. Ave., seems to exist in a time warp, recalling the style and atmosphere of the era in which it was founded (1883) by partners Fred Leavitt and Wallace Peirce. The two ran the establishment not just as a tobacco store, which it remains, but also as a part of Harvard student life, sort of an unofficial club for young gentlemen. Although undergraduates would come here to purchase some of the store's own tobacco blend (which an employee mixed in a cake box), they mainly wanted to hang out in the billiard room upstairs. For years the store was the only ticket outlet for Harvard football games, which explains the sports memorabilia on exhibit today—trophies, old photos of Harvard teams, hockey sticks, and footballs with scores on them, including the one used in Harvard's only Rose Bowl appearance, in 1920. In the location of the former billiard room is a chess parlor set up on a narrow balcony overlooking the main floor. Despite the strict smoking regulations in the city of Cambridge, the store somehow manages to maintain the parlor as a place where patrons can rent one of the five chess tables (for a dollar an hour) to have a quiet smoke and perhaps even play chess. The "cake box" brand is still available here along with many other tobacco blends, in addition to snuff, cigars, pipes, cigarette boxes, lighters, spittoons, men's toiletries, and chess sets—all guarded by the wooden cigar-store Indian that used to stand outside until he lost his left arm in a scuffle. The trademark lady in blue hovers above the front door, the handle of which is in the shape of a large, silver-colored pipe.

At the **Harvard Cooperative Society**, at 1400 Mass. Ave., in the heart of the square, the cashier will most likely ask if you have a "Coop number," distributed to individuals associated with the extended Harvard community for participation in the discount program. Informally called the Coop (as in chicken), the store was founded in 1882 by Harvard students as a response to prices too high for their lean pockets. Then the issue was coal, but the needs of students continued to grow with time, so in 1920 the Coop's main building was constructed on the site of the former courthouse (which was the scene of much activity in the days preceding the American Revolution). Currently the Coop's two buildings stock kitchen utensils and appliances, clothing, books, records and tapes, bath products, cards, and much more. This is the place to buy mugs, sweatshirts, and tee-shirts with the Harvard insignia. The Coop also has a public rest room on the second floor, the only one in the square.

BEYOND HARVARD SQUARE

Those who take the trouble to go north of Harvard Square to Porter Square, southeast to Central Square, or beyond will find specialty bookstores, educational toys, Japanese imports, music, art supplies, and antiques. Walk or drive to Porter Square or Central Square from Harvard via Mass. Ave. or take the MBTA Red Line one stop in either direction.

Porter Square

Just beyond the Porter Square MBTA station is the **Children's Workshop**, at 1963 Mass. Ave. Founded by a former kindergarten teacher more than a decade ago, the store specializes in safe, interesting toys meant to educate and stimulate young minds. The bins in the back left corner contain an ever-changing stock of low-priced, recycled items purchased in bulk from the Children's Museum. Visit the store late on a Saturday morning and you may find a magician, folksinger, or storyteller performing in the back room.

On the lower level of the same building is the **Book Cellar Café**, an affiliate of the Avenue Victor Hugo used bookstore on Newbury Street in Boston, with a selection of resale merchandise and refreshments.

If your favorite reading material is a good mystery, you must visit **Kate's Mystery Books**, at 2211 Mass. Ave. There is usually ample metered parking this far northwest of Porter Square, but if you're on foot you can make it to Kate's in about five minutes from the Red Line's Porter Square stop. You can't miss the place: Look for the mysterious silhouetted figures in the windows. This 1863 Victorian also carries the distinction of once having been demolished by a runaway bus. Inside, feline shapes from the owner's black cat collection line the tops of the bookcases, one of which is a hidden entrance to an office (Robert Parker, author of the *Spenser: For Hire* series, helped build the cases). Books are grouped into such categories as "Strong Women" and "Cyberpunk," with special sections for New England authors and settings and another for autographed books. The store, which opened on Friday the 13th in May 1982, has become a favorite meeting place for local mystery writers and hosts numerous book-signing parties.

Central Square and Beyond

A short walk southeast on Mass. Ave. from Harvard toward Central Square will bring you to another bookstore of note: **Savanna**, a tiny store at number 856 specializing in multicultural books for children and young adults. It's the only one in Boston and Cambridge that emphasizes books about African-American children.

Nearby at 862 Mass. Ave. is **Kikyo Imports**, which sells hand-sewn men's and women's silk kimonos and *haori,* jackets worn over a long kimono. Most items are from the 1940s and 1950s, and are beautiful to wear or display as wall hangings.

Pearl, right in the heart of Central Square, at 579 Mass. Ave. (one stop from Harvard Square on the Red Line), calls itself "the world's largest art, craft, and graphic discount center." One of more than a dozen outlets around the country, Pearl is a mammoth two-level smorgasbord of supplies for the artist and craftsperson: clay, dried flowers, paint, brushes, tools, glue—you name it.

Another store worth visiting in this neighborhood is **Cheapo Records**, at 645 Mass. Ave. (near Woolworth's). While there are numerous retailers selling new CDs and tapes throughout the Boston and Cambridge area, and even a few dealing in used records, Cheapo is the place other stores send customers whenever they can't fill a request for vintage albums or 45s. The specialty here is blues, and the price, as you might guess from the name, is usually right.

More than 100 independent dealers in antique and vintage merchandise can be found in a mall located just a two-block walk northeast from Lechmere station on the Green Line: the four-story **Cambridge Antique Mart**, at 201 Monsignor O'Brien Highway. An unbelievably wide range of collectibles is housed under this roof, including toys, jewelry, furniture, clothing, posters, silverware, musical instruments, books, and more. Closed Mondays.

On the opposite side of Lechmere station is the **CambridgeSide Galleria**, a mall designed around a picturesque lagoon where shoppers can enjoy a snack at outdoor tables and then top off their day with a cruise down the Charles River. The mall contains many shops, but the main draw here is **Lechmere Sales**, where a variety of small appliances and household gadgets are sold at reasonable prices. There's an inexpensive parking garage at the mall for the convenience of shoppers lugging home toasters, microwave ovens, and electric can openers.

—Jan Stankus

BOSTON ENVIRONS

By B. J. Roche, Christina Tree, and Kimberly Grant

B. J. Roche, who contributed the North Shore and Merrimack Valley sections herein, also wrote the Central and Western Massachusetts chapter of the book. Christina Tree, the editorial consultant for this guidebook, contributed much of the Maine chapter of the book as well as the West of Boston section of this chapter. Kimberly Grant wrote Cape Cod and the Islands in addition to her section here on South of Boston.

Styled the "Hub of the Universe" by 19th-century writers, Boston remains the workaday hub of four distinct regions: the North Shore, the Merrimack River Valley, south of Boston, and the Lexington–Concord area, generally referred to as west of Boston.

On the North Shore old families, old money, and the purest of Massachusetts accents prevail. The old seaports here remain much as they were in their heydays: the decades just prior to the Revolution for Marblehead; the Federal era for Salem and Newburyport; and the late 19th century for Gloucester, still a major fishing port.

The Merrimack River Valley, northwest of Boston, is best known as the site of America's first planned mill cities, a story dramatized by the Lowell National Historical Park.

The area west of Boston is typical New England countryside. Battle Road, route of the early days of the Revolution, remains resolutely rural; Concord is a lovely old town; and the rolling orchards of the Nashoba Valley seem far from the city.

South of Boston includes the South Shore, with its very old and elegant seaside towns, such as Hingham and Cohasset, and beach-fringed, cranberry bog–studded Plymouth County, the Pilgrims' old colony. Bristol County, with its old industrial fishing towns of New Bedford and Fall River, lies to Plymouth County's west.

Each of these regions has its own distinct character and thus offers visitors its own particular rewards. A traveller wishing to explore eastern Massachusetts in depth will want to visit all four areas, spending a few days in each.

THE NORTH SHORE

Once a collection of feisty fishing and shipbuilding towns and seaports, the North Shore of Boston is now one of the state's tonier residential areas, stretching along the coast from Marblehead, 17 miles north of Boston, through Salem, Gloucester, Rockport (these last two on Cape Ann, the state's "other" cape), and Essex to Newburyport, on the New Hampshire border. All of these places played important roles in the fight for the nation's independence and in the development of New England's 18th- and 19th-century economy, yet each has its own identity, which in some cases is still emerging.

Marblehead, once a rough-hewn fishing and sailing town, has become a Boston suburb, while Salem's old tanneries and factories have given way to a tourism industry focused on witchcraft and the city's past as an important seaport.

Gloucester is struggling to remain Cape Ann's only major fishing town; its diverse population of Portuguese and Italian families, Yankees, and bohemian artists gives it a flavor unique to the North Shore. Rockport, farther out on Cape Ann, seems content with its status as a resort town, with numerous shops and galleries, while Essex, an old shipbuilding and clamming community farther inland, has evolved into the North Shore's antiques center.

At the region's northern reaches is Newburyport. Much of Newburyport's waterfront and business district—some 16 acres of the downtown area—was destroyed by fire in 1811 and rebuilt in the then-current Federal style. Partially demolished in the 1960s and early 1970s, Newburyport's waterfront is now a preservationist's dream, with one of the largest collections of restored Federal-style architecture in the country.

What all these places have in common is a history of independence and enterprise dating to the 17th century and

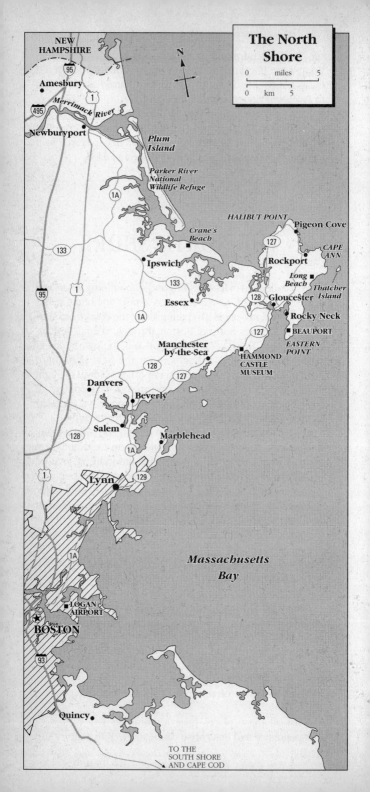

NEW HAMPSHIRE

N

95

Amesbury

1

Merrimack River

495

Newburyport

Plum Island

1A

Parker River National Wildlife Refuge

133

HALIBUT POINT   Pigeon Cove

127

Crane's Beach

95

1

Rockport

CAPE ANN

Long Beach

Thatcher Island

Ipswich

133

128

Essex

Gloucester

1A

127

Rocky Neck

BEAUPORT

EASTERN POINT

Manchester by-the-Sea

HAMMOND CASTLE MUSEUM

128

Danvers

127

Beverly

Salem

1A

Marblehead

Lynn

129

128

1

Massachusetts Bay

1A

LOGAN AIRPORT

★ BOSTON

93

Quincy

TO THE SOUTH SHORE AND CAPE COD

the arrival of the first English settlers. Salem's port served as one of the only shipping routes to Europe during the Revolutionary War, and it was a crew from Marblehead that rowed George Washington across the Delaware on Christmas night 1776 in the victorious Battle of Trenton, thereby earning the town the title "birthplace of the American navy."

In the mid-19th century train and steam-ferry connections from Boston opened up the North Shore for tourism. Marblehead, Rockport, and Gloucester became favorite resorts, and Marblehead in particular became one of the yachting centers of the East Coast. Hotels, camps, and cottages sprang up along the shore to cater to visitors, and the wealthy from up and down the East Coast built elegant seaside estates. Many of these still stand along Route 127 in Pride's Crossing and Manchester-by-the-Sea, on Eastern Point Road in Gloucester, and on Marblehead Neck.

Visitors to this area will find the past commemorated and celebrated in historic houses, buildings, and museums, and in delightful old residential neighborhoods. Furthermore, these towns are all set against the backdrop of the sea. Indeed, you're never far from the ocean in various guises: rocky coves, crashing breakers on the craggy coast, windswept ranges of sand dunes.

If sea blue is the dominant color, there are also contrasting patches of green. The salt marshes of Essex and Ipswich have a wild, expansive beauty, and working farms still dot Route 133 between Essex and Ipswich and Route 1A between Beverly and Newburyport.

Though there is much to see and do on the North Shore, the area is compact, and all towns are easily accessible from one another. Gloucester and Rockport have the largest range of accommodations, but if you're seeking out a small inn or hotel, you'll find one just about anywhere on the North Shore.

MAJOR INTEREST

Old New England seaside towns
Beaches

Marblehead
Old Town and harbor
Antiques and specialty shops
Marblehead Neck

Salem
Peabody and Essex Museum
Essex Institute Museum Neighborhood
Witch House

Chestnut Street's Federal-style houses
The Salem Witch Museum
Maritime Museum and Pickering Wharf
House of the Seven Gables

Gloucester
Hammond Castle Museum
Rocky Neck art colony
The Sleeper-McCann House
Ocean views from Bass Rocks
Whale watching

Rockport
Picturesque town wharf
Shops and galleries on Bearskin Neck
Halibut Point State Park

Essex
Antiques shops

Newburyport
Custom House Maritime Museum
Federal-style homes
Plum Island and Parker River National Wildlife
   Refuge

While it's possible to cover the major "sights" of the North Shore in a long day trip from Boston, you'll need at least three to four days to explore the area adequately. If you're travelling in summer be sure to schedule some beach time—Gloucester, Ipswich, and Newburyport have some of the best beaches in New England.

MARBLEHEAD

"That here is plentie of marble stone ... our plantation is from hence called Marble Harbor," wrote Francis Higginson in 1629; hence the town's name, Marblehead (the accent is on the last syllable). Higginson, one of a group of Cornwall and Channel Island fishermen who settled here on a plantation of Salem, was mistaken about the rocky outcroppings that border the harbor. But no matter—Marblehead's natural deep-water harbor has served the town well throughout its history, especially during the Revolution. Even today it is a major attraction for the yachting set that gathers here each July for Race Week, a series of sailboat races sponsored by the town's yacht clubs.

Marblehead is an easy, though not very scenic, 17-mile (27-km) drive north from Boston. Take the Callahan Tunnel out of town and follow Route 1A (locally referred to as "the Lynnway") through Revere and the old industrial city of Lynn. There follow Route 129 north along the coast through the residential seaside town of Swampscott and on to Marblehead.

Marblehead's historic district is called the **Old Town**, which is woven with crooked, narrow streets lined with Colonial houses, each of which seems to have a tale to tell (and a plaque to tell it). Many of these houses have only an alley-wide view of the harbor between them; occasionally you'll come upon a set of stairs leading down into another neighborhood. In the old days the Old Town's streets were mere cowpaths and the Cornwall fishermen, noted (and often cursed) for their independent ways, ruled. While the Puritans of Salem had come to the New World to find freedom of religion, those who settled in Marblehead came to catch fish, and the town soon gained a reputation for drunken ungodliness. In 1648 Salem cut the heathen town loose.

Around in Marblehead

The best way to indulge in Marblehead's charms is to walk through the Old Town. Follow Route 129 (here Atlantic Avenue) into town and turn right onto Washington Street and park the car. (If you don't find a parking spot here, continue on Washington Street to Penni's supermarket, on your right, where you can park all day for $4. If you continue straight on Atlantic you'll come to the chamber of commerce's information booth at 62 Pleasant Street, open weekdays; Tel: 617/631-2868.) Begin your tour on Washington Street at **Abbot Hall** (housing the historical commission and the town clerk's office), which stands just above the town common, used for militia training during the Revolution. Here in the Selectmen's Room is Archibald M. Willard's *The Spirit of '76,* an enduring image of the Revolutionary War and a symbol of American patriotism. The painting was given to the town in 1880 by General John Devereaux, whose son was the model for the drummer boy.

Stroll down Washington Street past several period homes and, near the bottom of the hill, you'll come to two historic houses that help illustrate the lives of Marblehead's wealthy 18th-century shipowners. The stately **Jeremiah Lee Mansion**, at 161 Washington Street, built in 1768, was described by a Boston newspaper at the time as "the most elegant and costly furnished home in the Bay State Colony." Today the Georgian-style home is considered one of the best examples of such architecture in the country. Headquarters of the Marblehead Historical Society, it is decorated with portraits and furnishings of the day, including many items connected to Marblehead history, such as works by local primitive artist J. O. J. Frost (1852–1928), a kind of coastal Grandma Moses who did not begin painting until he was nearly 70 and used ordinary house paint in his works. The house is open mid-May to mid-October.

Just around the corner at 8 Hooper Street is the **King Hooper Mansion**, a Colonial-era home built in 1728, with a three-story façade that was added on 20 years later. The home of Robert Hooper, a shipowner nicknamed "King" by his sailors, it is now home to the Marblehead Arts Association, which uses it for exhibitions and public events. (Open from 1:00 to 4:00 P.M. daily, except Mondays.)

Next walk down Hooper Street toward Union Street, at the corner of which is another Marblehead house with a story: The **Lafayette House** (privately owned), whose lower corner was cut out to prevent carriages and wagons from swiping it as they turned the corner (legend says that it was altered specifically to allow the Marquis de Lafayette to pass when he visited in 1824). Follow Union down to Front Street, turn left, and continue a few blocks to the entrance to **Crocker Park**, which affords the best views of Marblehead harbor.

Follow Front Street to the **Phillip T. Clark Public Landing**, named for a town harbormaster who died in 1968. Just off the landing, at 63 Front Street, is **The Driftwood**, a local fishermen's greasy spoon, with cheap breakfasts and lunches and lots of atmosphere. If you prefer a little more decorum, keep walking for several blocks down Front Street to **The Barnacle**, at number 141, an old clam shack that has been upgraded to full restaurant status, offering great seafood chowder, lobster, and fried and broiled seafood—and the best view of the harbor of any restaurant in town (Tel: 617/631-4236).

Just beyond is **Fort Sewall**, whose earliest incarnation was erected by the British in the early to mid-1600s and used as a defense and training grounds by colonists during the Revolution. Today its grounds are a public park (there's not much left of the actual fort) overlooking the harbor, a peaceful, leafy spot to picnic.

On your way back up Front Street bear right onto Circle Street. Number 19 is the privately owned **Skipper Ireson House**, once home to the famous Captain Ireson, whose crew was charged with failing to help a disabled vessel. The event was chronicled, albeit somewhat inaccurately, in John

Greenleaf Whittier's poem, "Skipper Ireson's Ride," published in 1857:

> The strangest ride that ever was sped
> Was Ireson's out from Marblehead!
> Old Floyd Ireson, for his hard heart,
> Tarred and feathered and carried in a cart
> By the women of Marblehead.

Circle Street loops back to Front; follow Front three blocks to State Street, where you'll find two more popular places to eat: The **Sail Loft**, at 15 State Street, is a favorite with the sailing crowd; its downstairs bar serves mile-high drinks, while the upstairs restaurant serves steaks and seafood. Tel: (617) 631-9824. Just across State Street at number 12, the **King's Rook** is a more sedate coffeehouse with an old tavern atmosphere. Beer and wine are served and the menu consists of homemade soups, sandwiches and light meals, and good desserts. Tel: (617) 631-1255.

At the head of State Street, at Washington, is the yellow and white **Old Town House**, built in 1727 on the site of Marblehead's first jail. You might now head up Washington Street and perhaps browse in the antiques and specialty shops on this stretch. **Old Town Antiques Cooperative**, at number 108, offers the wares of several dealers (closed Wednesdays), while **Marblehead Handprints**, at number 111, specializes in gifts and accessories. A few blocks up at number 148 is **O'Rama's**, for antique linens and vintage-style lingerie.

If you are in need of picnic supplies, **Ambrosia**, at 9 Pleasant Street, just off Washington Street, has gourmet take-out sandwiches. Next door, **Much Ado Books** has a good selection of used books, with a focus on marine and yachting subjects.

Gourmands make the trip from Boston to **Rosalie's**, one block off Pleasant Street at 18 Sewall Street in downtown Marblehead. The menu features northern Italian specialties and includes veal Giorgio, veal rolled and stuffed with Dijon mustard, Gruyère, onions, prosciutto, and cream sauce; and chicken Francesca, a sautéed breast of chicken with a Grand Marnier and mushroom sauce. It's expensive, but worth the splurge. Tel: (617) 631-5353.

Most visitors to this area choose to stay in Salem, which has a larger range of accommodations than Marblehead. But if you fall in love with the Old Town here, the **Harbor Light Inn**, at 58 Washington Street, is an excellent choice. Within walking distance of most of the town's sights, it's a small and elegant place, built in 1712 but renovated and updated with all the modern comforts.

MARBLEHEAD NECK

Head out of town on Route 114 and turn left onto Ocean
Avenue to reach the causeway out to Marblehead Neck, the
peninsula on the opposite side of Marblehead Harbor from
the city proper that is home to Marblehead's upper crust.
Bear right at the end of the causeway and stay on Ocean
Avenue for 2 to 3 miles (3 to 5 km) and you'll come to Castle
Rock (good for climbing) on your right. Here you can get a
breathtaking view of the Atlantic, and a peek at **Carcassonne**,
a gothic-looking castle built in the 1930s by patent-medicine
heir Lydia Pinkham Gove (it's still a private residence).
Follow Ocean Avenue all the way out to Chandler Hovey
Park and the Marblehead Lighthouse at the tip of the peninsula, a good spot for a picnic, with great views of Old Town
across the harbor.

SALEM

The city of Salem, 7 miles (11 km) northwest of Marblehead
on Route 114, is best known for one of the most notorious
periods in American history. Here in 1692 hundreds of men,
women, and children had their neighbors put on trial as
practicing witches and wizards. Suspicions and accusations
fell on more than 150 people in several North Shore towns,
including Marblehead, Gloucester, and Topsfield. Fourteen
women and five men were eventually hanged; several more
died in jail.

The original accusations began in Salem Village (now the
town of Danvers), at the home of the Reverend Samuel
Parris. Parris's West Indian slave, Tituba, was said to have
enchanted the minister's nine-year-old daughter, Elizabeth,
and her eleven-year-old cousin, Abigail, with fortune telling.
In early 1692 the girls began to have fits, and the village
doctor concluded that they were under the influence of
witchcraft. Coerced by their elders, the girls named three
women as witches: Tituba, Sarah Good, and Sarah Osburne,
and later, 71-year-old Rebecca Nurse. Soon other villagers
became "afflicted," and the hysteria and accusations spread.
By June the trials had begun, and in July, August, and September 19 people were hanged, and one man, Giles Cory, was
crushed to death under a weight of rocks that were piled
atop him to force him to give evidence; he remained mute.

Though some historians attribute the convulsions to er-
got, a rye fungus, it has never been determined what actually
caused the fits. One thing for certain is that the witchcraft
phenomenon has become a cottage industry in Salem,
which bills itself as "The Witch City." There seems to be a

psychic on every corner on the blocks that border Derby Street, and Halloween is a major event here, celebrated with parties in Salem's bars and restaurants and public activities in the museums.

Salem's later history is more distinguished. In the years between the American Revolution and the War of 1812 the city had a fleet of 185 vessels trading with the West Indies and the Orient; indeed in some parts of the world Salem was better known than any other American city. After the war, however, Salem's commercial star faded, to be replaced by an industrial base. In the mid-19th century paint and shoe factories and tanneries opened, drawing immigrant labor that helped create the city's ethnic mix. Today the city relies on a state college, a hospital, small industry, and tourism for its job base.

Around in Salem

The **Salem Heritage Trail**, marked by a red line on the sidewalks, links most of Salem's sights. Start your walking tour at the centrally located Museum Place Mall (just off Washington Street) at the **Peabody and Essex Museum**, the oldest continuously operating museum in the country and the largest on the North Shore. The Peabody was founded in 1799 by the East India Marine Society to preserve the collections of "natural and artificial curiosities" gathered by Salem sea captains during their travels. With a fantastic, well-presented collection of paintings, models, porcelain, furniture, and oddities from around the world (masks from South Pacific islands, natural history exhibits), the museum amply chronicles Salem's maritime history and its prominent role in the 19th-century China trade. The gift and book shop has a nice selection. Open daily; Tel: (508) 745-9500.

Across the mall at 132 Essex Street, the **Essex Institute Museum Neighborhood**, now a part of the Peabody and Essex Museum, includes on its grounds the 17th-century John Ward House, the Georgian Crowninshield-Bentley House (1727), and the Federal-era Gardner-Pingree House (1804), this last the work of Samuel McIntire, a local master craftsman and architect. The institute also has three floors of galleries that provide a look at the fashions and furnishings of 17th-, 18th-, and 19th-century Salem. Children will especially enjoy the toys and old dollhouses. Tel: (508) 744-3390.

Head north along the mall and cross Washington Street to the restored **Witch House**, at 301½ Essex Street. Built in 1642, and still sitting in its original location, this was the home of magistrate Jonathan Corwin, who held pretrial investigations of some of the accused "witches" in a sitting room upstairs. Closed December 1 to March 15; Tel: (508) 744-0180.

Continue up Essex Street past the early-19th-century **First Church** on your right. Just next door, at 318 Essex Street, is the **Ropes Mansion**, built in 1720 and later owned by Nathaniel Ropes, a Superior Court judge, and, later, his son, a successful merchant. The gambrel-roofed house is noted for its collection of family heirlooms spanning two centuries and its formal gardens, laid out in 1912. Open daily June to October. At the Ropes Mansion, cross and turn left down Cambridge Street. **Hamilton Hall**, at the corner of Cambridge and Chestnut, designed by Samuel McIntire in 1805, is a private house where a debutantes' ball is held every spring.

Chestnut Street, Salem's grandest thoroughfare, was designed in 1796 at the request of wealthy merchants and sea captains. These local aristocrats had the street built 60 feet wide and then lined it with three-story Federal and Greek Revival mansions landscaped with formal English gardens. One typical Federal home open to the public is the **Stephen Phillips Memorial Trust House**, at number 34. The family home of the descendants of a wealthy 19th-century shipmaster, the house retains many original furnishings, including an extensive set of porcelain, furniture, and decorative items gathered from all over the world. Open late May to mid-October (closed Sundays); Tel: (508) 744-0440.

Circle back to Essex Street and stop in at **Crow Haven Corner**, at number 125, a shop owned by Jody Cabot (the daughter of Laurie Cabot, Official Witch of Salem), with crystals, books, and all kinds of potions guaranteeing everything from wealth and fame to a good love life.

At the foot of Essex Street turn left on Hawthorne Boulevard and walk a few blocks up to the **Salem Witch Museum**, at 19 Washington Square. A half-hour-long dramatization of the history of the witchcraft trials, with life-size stage settings, special lighting, and narration, re-creates Salem's infamous era. Open daily; Tel: (508) 744-1692.

A right turn off Essex down Hawthorne Boulevard leads to Derby Street and **Pickering Wharf**, a complex of shops and restaurants on the waterfront, and the **Salem Maritime National Historic Site**, a complex of buildings that includes the Custom House, where Nathaniel Hawthorne once worked. (The **Custom House Gallery**, just across Derby Street, has a good selection of Colonial-style gift items, including Jamestown blown glassware.)

The 17th-century **House of the Seven Gables**, the inspiration for Hawthorne's 1851 novel, is just a few blocks up Derby Street at 54 Turner Street. Built in 1668 by a wealthy

Salem merchant, the house has steep-pitched roof that is typical of the period, but historians have yet to determine the purpose of the hidden staircase inside. Hawthorne was said to have been inspired to write the novel on his many visits to the house, which was owned at the time by his cousin Susan Ingersoll. To see the interior of the house as well as the one adjacent in which Hawthorne once lived you must join an organized tour. Tel: (508) 744-0991.

DINING IN SALEM

There are several good restaurants on Derby Street near Pickering Wharf. **Tammany Hall**, at 208 Derby Street, has good chowder, salads, and sandwiches. Just across Derby Street at number 197 (at Pickering Wharf) is the **Crystal Chamber and Café**, where you can get sandwiches and salads and pick up a crystal and have a reading in the back room.

In Salem Center, **Red's Sandwich Shop**, housed in a 1698 meeting place at 15 Central Street, is a local favorite for breakfast or lunch. Just across the mall, behind the visitors' center at 43 Church Street, the **Lyceum Bar and Grill** serves excellent New American lunches and dinner, with items like grilled chicken breast with a chile lime sauce and black-bean corn relish; baby-back ribs with sweet potatoes; and lobster and scallop ravioli with roasted corn butter. Prices are reasonable, and the atmosphere is refined. Tel: (508) 745-7665.

Nathaniel's, in the Hawthorne Hotel on Salem Common, is another fine choice for dinner, with beef, seafood, and poultry dishes. You might try the Chicken Dundee, a chicken breast cooked in a Scotch cream sauce. Tel: (508) 744-4080.

STAYING IN SALEM

Built in 1925 and restored in the 1980s, the six-story **Hawthorne Hotel** is the largest and most centrally located of Salem's lodgings. It has 89 rooms, some of which overlook Salem Common, where Revolutionary militiamen once drilled. Rooms are decorated with reproductions of 18th-century furniture. The Hawthorne has a pleasant, small-hotel feel; the elegantly appointed lobby is a great place for morning coffee.

Two small bed-and-breakfasts are located just off Salem Common. The **Inn at Seven Winter Street** is a ten-room Victorian home built in 1870 and recently restored. While Victorian decor can be dark and heavy, this inn has a light and spacious feeling. Rooms are individually decorated with period pieces, and some have working fireplaces and canopied beds. Across the street in a restored Greek Revival home is the **Amelia Payson Guest House**, a homier bed-and-breakfast option with four rooms, including a studio with a kitchenette. Both are non-smoking inns.

Across the city center at 7 Summer Street, the 22-room **Salem Inn** is a handsome Federal-style brick inn built in 1834 by sea captain Nathaniel West. It's just across the corner from the Witch House and a stone's throw from Chestnut Street, with its magnificent rows of Federal homes. The Salem Inn has the feel of a small inn with the amenities of a hotel—including a restaurant, telephones and televisions in all rooms, and working fireplaces in some. Three family suites consist of two guestrooms and an equipped kitchen. The shady and secluded brick courtyard is a pleasant place to enjoy your Continental breakfast, which is included in the price of a room.

Northeast from Salem

Upon leaving Salem, follow Route 1A north until you reach **Beverly**. The **North Shore Music Theater** in Beverly presents plays, concerts, and musical performances in a theater-in-the-round, at 62 Dunham Road, just off Route 128. Their season is April through December; Tel: (508) 922-8500.

Bear right in Beverly onto Route 127, a scenic road that hugs the coast, and follow it into **Pride's Crossing**, whose railroad depot was built (with separate benches for Democrats and Republicans) to serve the private railroad cars of the wealthy families that used to summer in the luxurious estates along the coast. If you're travelling directly north to Newburyport, you can continue on Route 1A, which winds through the horse country of Wenham and Hamilton and on through Ipswich and Rowley. If you're in a hurry, take Route 114 from Salem to I-95 and zip north.

Manchester-by-the-Sea, about 7 miles (11 km) east of Beverly on Route 127, is a good place to stop for lunch, but first you might pause at **Yankee Pedlar Antiques**, on the right as you enter town, for a browse through its collection of furniture, prints, and collectibles. On Manchester's harbor, **Masconomo Park**, with its white bandstand and stacks of lobster traps, provides a scenic setting for a picnic; stop across the street for lobster and seafood takeout at **Captain Dusty's**, an old lobster shack that's a Manchester landmark (open from May to mid-September).

A right turn off Route 127 on Hesperus Avenue (follow signs for Magnolia) brings you to the **Hammond Castle Museum**, a medieval-looking castle that was once the home of inventor John Hays Hammond, Jr. Today the castle houses Hammond's eclectic collection of medieval art and artifacts, and concerts and other special events are held here throughout the year. Tel: (508) 283-2080. Gloucester, on the southern shore of the neck of **Cape Ann**, is just another 7 miles (11 km) northeast on Route 127.

GLOUCESTER

Fishing was the raison d'être of Gloucester almost from the town's beginnings in the 1620s at what is now Stage Fort Park. In the 1920s Clarence Birdseye gave the industry a boost when he refined the process of packaging frozen fresh haddock; consequently Gloucester's harbor is lined not only with wharves but warehouses and fish-processing plants. (Today these plants are likely to be processing foreign fish to sell to McDonald's.) Though overfishing and depletion of stocks are threatening the centuries-old industry, Gloucester remains an active, if struggling, fishing port. Parts of Gloucester may not be as pretty as other towns on the North Shore, but, unlike most, Gloucester retains a significant working-class population.

As you enter Gloucester along Route 127 you'll come to one of its best-known sights, *Man at the Wheel,* a bronze sculpture of a New England fisherman at his steering wheel commissioned in 1923 to honor "They that go down to the sea in ships." Just across the street, at 25 Western Avenue, is the **Boulevard Ocean View Restaurant**, an informal place favored by locals for its reasonably priced Portuguese dishes and fried seafood. Try the kale soup or lemon sole.

With its proximity to Stellwagen Bank, a fertile feeding ground for whales and dolphins, Gloucester has become one of the world's best **whale-watching** centers. More than a dozen boats leave daily from early spring to late fall from the wharves downtown along Rogers Street, Main Street, and East Main Street, and at the Cape Ann marina on Essex Avenue. They include **Cape Ann Whale Watch**, Tel: (508) 283-5110; **Capt. Bill & Sons Whale Watch**, Tel: (508) 283-6995; **Seven Seas Whale Watch**, Tel: (508) 283-1776; and **Yankee Whale Watch**, Tel: (800) WHALING. (Walk one block up from the wharf to **Virgilio's Italian Bakery** at 29 Main Street for hefty submarine sandwiches to take along on your trip.)

If you have a hankering to sleep at sea, try a bunk-and-breakfast aboard the *Adventure,* a double-masted, 121-foot knockabout schooner docked in Gloucester harbor near the city's center. **Gloucester Adventure, Inc.**, a nonprofit group trying to restore the boat, offers overnight accommodations on the *Adventure* in the summer and fall. For information, Tel: (508) 281-8079.

If you're in town the last weekend in June, don't miss **Saint Peter's Fiesta**, the most enduring Italian festival on the North Shore. For three days downtown Gloucester becomes an extravaganza of food and festivities, an old-fashioned fishermen's celebration, with the traditional greased pole competition, a blessing of the fleet, parades, and music.

Gloucester is also home to playwright Israel Horovitz, founder and director of the **Gloucester Stage Company**, which presents theatrical works by Horovitz himself as well as other authors. The theater is located at 267 East Main Street, out toward Rocky Neck. The season runs from May through September; Tel: (508) 281-4099.

ROCKY NECK

Having gone through downtown Gloucester, follow the signs to Eastern Point and Rocky Neck, one of the oldest art colonies in the country, with more than 20 different galleries, shops, and restaurants stretching out onto the water. With its snug harbor and colorful bungalows and galleries, Rocky Neck has provided inspiration for such artists as Winslow Homer, Childe Hassam, Fitz Hugh Lane, and the brothers Maurice and Charles Prendergast.

The **Lobster Pond**, at 121 East Main, on the way to Rocky Neck, serves lobster-in-the-rough as well as good fried seafood and chowder; Tel: (508) 281-3001. The **Rudder**, at 73 Rocky Neck, is a restaurant and raw bar on the water that draws an occasionally rowdy clientele; Tel: (508) 283-7967. Up the street at 51 Rocky Neck, the **Studio Deck and Lounge** offers outdoor dining on the water and has a piano bar at night; the menu includes pasta, seafood, chicken, and steaks. Tel: (508) 283-4123.

In the summer Rocky Neck is the center of Cape Ann's nightlife. The **Outrigger** has live music featuring R & B bands from Boston (Tel: 508/281-4998). In downtown Gloucester, at 40 Railroad Avenue, the **Rhumbline** features local bands (Tel: 508/283-9732).

EASTERN POINT

Continue on toward Eastern Point and the **Sleeper-McCann House** (sometimes called Beauport), at 75 Eastern Point Boulevard overlooking Gloucester Harbor. The summer home of interior designer Henry Davis Sleeper, Beauport was under construction from 1907 through 1934, and is made up of a hodgepodge of architectural details Sleeper saved from houses that were being demolished around New England and Europe. Later he decorated each room in a distinctive style, and used the home to entertain and woo clients. It's a house full of whimsy, from its hidden passageways and false doors to Sleeper's extensive collections of amber glass and majolica to the home's pièce de résistance, the Chinese Room, with a soaring pagoda ceiling and hand-made Chinese wallpaper. Open mid-May to mid-September; a concert series is held on the grounds during the summer. Tel: (508) 283-0800.

BASS ROCKS

Loop back toward Gloucester and take a right onto Atlantic Road (Alt. 127) out to Bass Rocks for spectacular views of the ocean crashing up against the broad, flat-rocked shoreline. The twin lighthouses off the coast are on **Thacher Island**, named for one Anthony Thacher, who was shipwrecked there in 1635, the first known wreck to have occurred off the Massachusetts coast. Thacher is one of the last islands to still have working lighthouses; you can visit on summer week-ends and climb the towers. Boats leave from Rockport's T-Wharf; for information, Tel: (508) 546-2326.

Bass Rocks Ocean Inn, at 107 Atlantic Road, offers motel-style accommodations on a bluff overlooking the ocean, with a pool, a billiard room, and a game room in the main house, a handsome white Colonial Revival structure known as the Wedding Cake House. The decor is nothing special, but for those who like falling asleep with the waves breaking just out the window, this is the place.

ROCKPORT

Rockport was actually once part of Gloucester, but was incorporated as a separate town in 1840 with the booming of its granite industry. Today this pretty resort town out on the northeastern coast of Cape Ann (follow either Route 127 or coastal 127A from Gloucester) is known for its art galleries, shops, and inns. It can get crowded here in the summer, and like the other towns on the North Shore it is best seen on foot.

Art galleries are the thing in Rockport. Your best starting point is the **Rockport Art Association Gallery**, at 12 Main Street, which houses works by most local artists as well as others from around New England. Next follow Main Street down the hill, turn right, and take your first left to T-Wharf (named for its shape), where you'll get the best view of Rockport's most famous landmark, Motif #1, a red fishing shack decked out with colorful lobster buoys. The shack is a New England icon, and one of the most painted and photo-graphed sights in the country—hence its "title." The building was partly destroyed by a storm in 1978, but townspeople quickly had it rebuilt.

Rockport is paved with shops. Some worth checking out include **London Ventures**, at 2 Dock Square, for contemporary crafts and jewelry. Up Main Street, at number 37, the **Madras Shop** will appeal to bargain hunters looking for women's clothing. **New England Goods**, at 32B Main Street, offers crafts, ceramics, and offbeat items made in New England.

After a stop for saltwater taffy at **Tuck's Candies**, at 7 Dock Square, walk a block up to **Bearskin Neck**, once the town's commercial center and today its main tourist promenade. Old fishing shacks here have been converted into dozens of small specialty shops selling everything from miniatures and crystals to tee-shirts and artworks of varying quality. Follow South Road out to the end of the neck (it's a short walk) for expansive views of the sea.

Many visitors never get farther than Rockport's downtown, but if you follow Route 127 north out of town you'll wend your way up through **Pigeon Cove**, a more rustic and, in some places, rural part of town. Follow signs to the left to the **Paper House** (52 Pigeon Hill Street), a strange bit of kitsch if ever there was one: a small house whose walls and furnishings—even the curtains—are made from old newspapers, some dating back to the 1920s.

Continue north on Route 127 to **Halibut Point State Park**, a nature reserve with paths that lead down to the ocean. The path from the parking lot takes you to the old granite quarry that created Rockport's fortunes a century ago. The bird life here is bountiful, and the juxtaposition of the quarry, now filled with water, and the ocean beyond, is breathtaking.

DINING IN ROCKPORT

There are lots of options for having a meal in Rockport. The **Hannah Jumper** on Wharf Road serves sandwiches and seafood with a view of the water from the warren of shops on Tuna Wharf. (The **Appledore III**, a 56-foot schooner, embarks on one-and-a-half-hour ocean trips from Tuna Wharf. The tours run from May to mid-October; tickets are available at the wharf or by reservation, Tel: 508/546-9876.) You'll have to squeeze into **Flav's Red Skiff**, at 15 Mount Pleasant Street, just off Dock Square, but this local favorite serves the best breakfasts in town. At the other end of town, at 18 Beach Street, the **Peg Leg Restaurant** is a good choice for lunch or dinner, serving lobster, seafood, and specialties like scallop pie; Tel: (508) 546-3038.

If you've worked up an appetite hiking at Halibut Point, follow Route 127 farther to Folly Cove and the **Lobster Pool**, overlooking the water at 329 Granite Street, for lobster-in-the-rough and other seafood. If you prefer a sit-down meal, try the **Folly Cove Pier Restaurant** next door at number 325; Tel: (508) 546-6568. Both are open in season.

STAYING IN ROCKPORT

Thanks in part to the crusading of Hannah Jumper, who led the Women's Raid of 1856 that destroyed every cask of liquor in town, hotels and restaurants in Rockport still serve no liquor. Most places, however, do allow you to bring your own wine, beer, or liquor, and they'll provide setups. Rockport's status as a dry town has prevented large-scale chain-motel development; nearly all of its lodgings are individualized and privately owned.

On the way to Rockport, just over the Gloucester line off Route 127A, is the **Chicataubut Inn**, smack on Long Beach, a mile-long stretch of narrow, sandy beach on the eastern side of Cape Ann. All 13 of the pine-paneled rooms have private baths. The Chicataubut has the decor and ambience of a family camphouse, simple, informal, and utilitarian. Request a room on the ocean side. Open from May to October.

Two smaller inns are set on the rocky shoreline just outside Rockport. At 131 Marmion Way, just off Route 127, **Seacrest Manor** is an elegant, English-manor–style inn. Some of the eight rooms have views of the water. **Eden Pines Inn**, on Eden Road just off Route 127A south of Rockport Center, offers more casual, spacious accommodations directly on the water; some rooms have fireplaces (open in summer only).

Closer to the center of town, at 173 Main Street, the **Sandy Bay Motor Inn** is a good choice for those who prefer less expensive motel-style accommodations. There are an indoor pool, a whirlpool, and a sauna. The homey, old-fashioned **Peg Leg Inn**, with 33 rooms spread among five early-American homes, is on the edge of Rockport Center across from Front Beach. The front porch of the main inn, which overlooks the ocean, is a pleasant place to enjoy morning coffee.

Pigeon Cove has some fine bed-and-breakfasts, including the **Ralph Waldo Emerson Inn**, set on a bluff overlooking the ocean. Housed in a classic New England Greek Revival building with a long front porch, the Emerson has a downstairs parlor and 36 rooms spread over three floors. There are a heated saltwater pool, a whirlpool, and a sauna. Open May through October and weekends in April and November.

Just up the road, at the entrance to Halibut Point State Park, is **Old Farm Inn**. The main house, built in 1799, has ten rooms, and there are additional quarters in the Barn Guesthouse and Field Cottage; the Fieldside suite has a fully equipped kitchen and two large bedrooms. Set on five acres of grounds, the inn gives you the feeling of really being away from it all, yet you're only ten minutes from town.

Essex

Antiques hunters will want to follow Route 127 the rest of the way around Cape Ann to Route 128, and from there head northwest on Route 133 to Essex, an old shipbuilding town on an inlet of Ipswich Bay whose Main Street is lined with antiques shops. Two good ones in downtown Essex are **Main Street Antiques**, at 44 Main Street, and the **White Elephant Shop**, at number 32. Stop for lunch in Essex at **Woodman's**, where, according to legend, the fried clam was invented in 1916, when Lawrence (Chubby) Woodman threw a few clams into kettles he was using to fry chips. It's a casual, rustic spot, and a good place to indulge a craving for fried seafood.

From Essex continue north along Route 133 to Route 1A, a pretty, rural stretch of road that leads directly north to Newburyport.

NEWBURYPORT

Just 20 years ago, Newburyport, an old shipbuilding city at the mouth of the Merrimack River, faced the urban renewal wrecking ball. But preservationists launched a stiff campaign, and today the city is a shining example of what can be accomplished with historic restoration. Newburyport is said to have the largest collection of Federal-style buildings in the country, built by merchants and sea captains who grew wealthy trading with Europe and the Far East.

The Federal style of architecture, which developed between 1790 and 1830, is characterized by its symmetry in design, spare use of decoration on its façade, and, in this region, an early version of the hipped roof. On the North Shore the major architects of the Federal era were Charles Bulfinch (who designed Boston's Faneuil Hall) and Samuel McIntire. This area's Federal-style building boom was fueled by the increasing wealth of shipowners and sea captains, many of whose homes were built by former ship's carpenters.

Today Newburyport's architectural mix is fascinating, from the old sea captains' mansions along High Street (Route 1A) to the brick façades of the restored shops that line State Street, Newburyport's main thoroughfare. Natural attractions can be found at Plum Island and the Parker River

National Wildlife Refuge, with its dunes, beaches, and salt marshes just a few miles from downtown Newburyport.

When you arrive in Newburyport, turn right off Route 1A onto State Street and park the car at one of the municipal lots at the end so you can explore the town on foot. At the Firehouse Theatre, an old fire station converted into a theater and gallery space at the end of State Street, stroll down to the boardwalk, where the Merrimack's waters mix with the Atlantic. Next head up Water Street to the granite **Custom House Maritime Museum** (at number 25), built in 1835 by Robert Mills, who designed the Washington Monument. The museum's upstairs, from which there are views of the harbor, is modeled after an old ship, complete with giant steering wheel. Open from April to December 23. Nearby is one of Newburyport's best antiques shops, the **Ice House Marketplace**, housing the collections of dozens of dealers in two buildings along Water Street.

From the water Federal Street leads inland through some of Newburyport's older neighborhoods and back up to High Street (Route 1A), with its dignified three-story mansions, some with widow's walks on their roofs, from which wives could search the seas for their husbands' ships. The three-story brick Federal-style **Cushing House**, at 98 High Street, was built in 1808 for a sea captain named John Cushing. Cushing's son Caleb was Newburyport's first mayor and the nation's first ambassador to China (although his official title was Envoy Extraordinary Minister Plenipotentiary). Today the house and its fantastic collection of furnishings, artwork, and Oriental cabinets and curios acquired in the China trade are owned by the Newburyport Historical Society. Tours are offered between May and October; the rest of the year the house is open by appointment; Tel: (508) 462-2681.

Turn right onto State Street just a block up and plan to dawdle in the many shops on the blocks that run down to the water. **Fowler's News** is the only Art Deco holdout on the street (number 17), with a soda fountain and luncheonette that serves some surprisingly good natural foods. Across the street, the **Olde Port Book Shop** stocks old books, lithographs, and prints from many different dealers.

DINING IN NEWBURYPORT

Newburyport is full of good restaurants of all types and price ranges. **The Mall** (pronounced "mal"), at 140 High Street (corner of Green), is a solid favorite for burgers, Mexican food, and grilled seafood (Tel: 508/465-5506). Just off State Street, at 13 Middle Street, is **The Grog**, a Newburyport institution for burgers, sandwiches, and Mexican food (Tel: 508/465-8008). A few blocks up Middle Street at number 25,

Middle Street Foods is a good place for lunch, with a reasonably priced and eclectic menu that includes items like shrimp curry, burritos, and gourmet sandwiches. You can also get take-out food for picnics here (Tel: 508/465-8333).

At 55 Water Street, the **Starboard Galley** will satisfy your yen for seafood in a casual setting (Tel: 508/462-1326). **David's**, at the Garrison Inn, is a highly acclaimed restaurant offering such gourmet fare as tenderloin of beef with wild mushrooms and Madeira sauce, roasted game hens with garlic and *fines herbes,* and ragout of sea scallops, baby vegetables, and mushrooms in a Madeira cream sauce. Tel: (508) 462-8077.

Scandia Restaurant, at 25 State Street, serves New American dishes in an informal atmosphere. The menu changes seasonally, with an emphasis on seafood in the summer and game and meats in fall and winter. Dishes include swordfish Provençal, lobster and veal sautéed with capers and lemon, roasted boneless duck with vodka peach glaze, and rack of lamb Dijonnaise. Tel: (508) 462-6271.

STAYING IN NEWBURYPORT

Most of Newburyport's lodgings are located within walking distance of downtown. A portrait of Queen Elizabeth II stands on the mantel at the **Windsor House** (38 Federal Street), testimony to the innkeepers'—Judith and John Harris—love of anything English. This is a small, six-room Federal-style inn built as a combination residence/ship's chandlery in 1786. The inn is decorated with antiques throughout, and some rooms retain the original exposed beams. Hearty English breakfasts are served in the kitchen; the dining room still has the home's original paneling and wide-plank pine floors. Closer to State Street, the **Essex Street Inn** is an old rooming house with 16 large and simply decorated rooms. This inn is nothing fancy, but it has modern amenities and is well located.

Just off High Street on Green Street, the **Clark Currier Inn** has eight elegantly appointed rooms in a beautiful Federal home built in 1803. The formal front parlor has an ornate mantel carved by Samuel McIntire, the renowned 19th-century craftsman and architect from Salem. Some rooms have fireplaces (nonworking) and balconies. In good weather you can take your breakfast in the inn's gazebo in the back yard.

For those who prefer full-service lodgings, the **Garrison Inn**, at 11 Brown Square (at the intersection of Titcomb and Pleasant streets, three blocks off State), offers 24 rooms in a recently renovated Federal-style hotel. Each room has a different detail, such as exposed brick or beams, and some have working fireplaces.

Plum Island

At its south end Water Street becomes the Plum Island Turnpike, leading in just 3 miles (5 km) or so to Plum Island and the **Parker River National Wildlife Refuge**, certainly the highlight of any trip to Newburyport. Visited by Samuel de Champlain in 1601 when he was exploring the coast north of Boston, Plum Island was so named in the 1630s by settlers who found an abundance of beach plums there in the late summer. Today one of the few natural barrier beach-dune complexes left in the Northeast, the island is an area of expansive salt marshes and grass-studded dunes. In spring and fall it's a popular bird-watching spot; more than 300 species stop at the refuge on their seasonal migrations. A 7-mile (11-km) drive winds through the refuge, and swimming and picnicking are allowed in designated areas.

NORTH SHORE BEACHES

The best beaches on the North Shore can be found on Cape Ann and in Ipswich and Newburyport (Plum Island). Bring bug repellent along with your tanning lotion, as voracious greenheads can sometimes be a problem in midsummer.

Visitors to **Singing Beach** in Manchester, on Route 127 between Salem and Cape Ann, can park at the beach lot or the train station for $15 a day—or the small free lot across from the station—and walk up the road to the beach. Singing Beach is accessible by train from Boston, so many people come up for the day.

Cape Ann has 22 beaches, ranging from wide expanses of sand to quiet rocky coves. **Good Harbor** and **Wingaersheek** are the largest and most popular beaches in Gloucester; public parking for nonresidents is $10 a day. Get there before 9:30 A.M. on a midsummer day—spaces fill up fast.

Cranes Beach Reservation, Route 1A in Ipswich (north of the junction with Route 133 from Essex), is one of the finest beaches in New England, with a five-and-a-half-mile stretch of sandy beach and natural dunes. A parking fee as high as $10 per day is charged on summer weekends (lower weekdays and off-season).

The beaches of **Plum Island** near Newburyport are also generally open to the public for a fee, although they may be closed at times from April 1 to June 30 to protect nesting birds, such as the piping plover.

THE MERRIMACK VALLEY

Like the Connecticut River in western New England, the Merrimack, which flows from New Hampshire through the region northwest of Boston to the Atlantic, was once a thriving thoroughfare. In the 17th and 18th centuries lumber was ferried downriver to shipbuilders along its banks. In the early 19th century industrialists harnessed its power to ignite an American Industrial Revolution, and factory cities such as Lowell and Lawrence were born along the river's banks.

By the end of the 19th century a proliferation of competing textile mills, followed by the Depression, led to the factories' eventual decline, and today they exist only as museums: in Lowell as the Lowell National Historical Park and in Lawrence as the Lawrence Heritage State Park.

Both Lowell and Lawrence are easy day trips from Boston. Take Route 93 north for about 23 miles (37 km) and then follow Route 495 for 10 miles (16 km) south to the Lowell connector. Lawrence is just 20 miles (32 km) northeast of Lowell on Route 495. Another possibility is to visit the Merrimack Valley after a tour of the region west of Boston (see below); from the Fruitlands Museums in Harvard follow Route 495 north for about 17 miles (27 km).

LOWELL

Lowell's story begins in the 1820s, when wealthy Bostonian Francis Cabot Lowell travelled through the textile factories of England and memorized the mechanisms of the power loom. Once back Stateside he convinced his business partners to build a textile mill in what was then Chelmsford, at the 32-foot Pawtucket Falls on the Merrimack River.

Lowell died before his plans could be realized, but in 1822 the Merrimack Manufacturing Company was established in the town that bears his name. Dozens of cotton manufacturing companies soon followed, powered by a network of canals that took advantage of the steep drop in the Merrimack. (Canals played a large role in the local economy, and for a decade or so the Middlesex Canal, built in the early 19th century, carried freight and passenger traffic between Lowell and Boston.) The city was incorporated in 1826, and by 1848 Lowell, with row upon row of red-brick mill buildings, had become the largest industrial city in America.

The factories created wealth for their owners, but they also had a great impact on the poorest of New Englanders. Hundreds of farmgirls left their families in New Hampshire, Vermont, and Maine to move to Lowell. There, they lived together in boarding houses and worked 13-hour days, six days a week, in hot, deafening mills surrounded by often dangerous machinery. They also gained a measure of independence, however, and, in many cases, educational and cultural opportunities they would not have had otherwise. Few returned to the farm.

The terrible working conditions and low wages eventually led to labor strife in the mills, and by the 1850s the owners were replacing the mill girls with immigrants eager to work in their new country.

In the end Lowell became a victim of its own success. Other textile mills began to spring up wherever there was water power, including upriver in Manchester, New Hampshire. The market became glutted, prices fell, and increasing labor disputes eventually led to the industry's demise in the city. The last of the big mills shut down in the mid-1950s, closing the book on Lowell's prosperity.

In the 25 years that followed Lowell went into a steep decline. But in the late 1970s preservationists seeking to revitalize the city restored some of the old industrial architecture and ultimately established the **Lowell National Historical Park**. The park now includes more than five miles of canals, operating gatehouses, brick mill complexes, housing, and commercial structures. Tel: (508) 459-1000.

Start your tour at the visitor center on Market Street (free parking behind the building) and pick up maps and information about the city. Park Service guides offer tours, which include a boat ride on one of the canals in summer, or a ride on a replica of a 1919 trolley car to the **Old Suffolk Mill**, one of the city's original textile mills, opened in 1831. Here you'll see how the turbine technology developed in Lowell in the 19th century used water to power the gears, leather belts, and pullies that powered the looms.

Three blocks away the **Boott Mills**, a re-creation of a weave room with more than 90 operating looms in a mill originally constructed in 1836, is the newest addition to the park.

Followers of the Beat Generation will want to walk one long block east of the Boott Mills to **Jack Kerouac Park**, where there's a monument to one of Lowell's best known residents. Stone markers are inscribed with excerpts from

Kerouac's works, with a focus on passages that refer to the city of Lowell, which Kerouac called "Galloway" in his books. One features these lines from "Mexico City Blues":

> Wild men
> who kill
> have karmas
> of ill.

Lowell's large ethnic population means an abundance of good ethnic restaurants. The **Melting Pot**, just across the hall from the visitor center, is a food-mall operation with Greek, Chinese, and Mexican offerings. Just across from the visitor center at 207 Market Street is the **Athenian Corner**, a family-run Greek restaurant serving huge souvlaki sandwiches (one will serve two people) and other traditional Greek dishes. Try the *skordalia,* mashed potatoes with garlic, vinegar, and olive oil; and the egg-lemon soup (Tel: 508/458-7052). The **Dutton Street Grille**, at 91 Dutton Street, two blocks from the visitor center, offers burgers and sandwiches for lunch, as well as a somewhat more elaborate dinner menu (Tel: 508/458-9191).

Lowell hosts a number of special events throughout the year, the best of which is the **Lowell Folk Festival**, a three-day celebration of food and dance and musical performances held the last weekend in July.

LAWRENCE

Lawrence, about 20 miles (32 km) northeast of Lowell on Route 495, was founded in the 1840s as a planned mill city, complete with a large common and elm-lined streets. As in Lowell, the boom years faded with the mills' insatiable demand for labor, which was supplied by thousands of immigrants from no fewer than 40 countries.

Follow Route 495 north to the Marston Street exit and follow the signs to the **Lawrence Heritage State Park**. Set in a former canal-side boardinghouse (ca. 1840), the park features multimedia exhibits that dramatize the city's history, including the 1860 collapse of the five-story Pemberton Mill—a disaster that claimed the lives of 88 people—as well as the 1912 Bread and Roses Strike involving some 30,000 workers. Tel: (508) 794-1655.

WEST OF BOSTON

In American history Lexington and Concord loom as large as Boston itself. Every American schoolchild learns of the events of April 19, 1775, the day local "minutemen" first stood their ground against the British. It is the second skirmish of that day—the one at the North Bridge in Concord—that is recognized as the opening salvo of the American Revolution, largely because that's the way Ralph Waldo Emerson, a Concord resident, wrote it:

> By the rude bridge that arched the flood,
>   Their flag to April's breeze unfurled,
> Here once the embattled farmers stood,
>   And fired the shot heard round the world.

This opening verse of Emerson's "Concord Hymn," written in 1836, has long been accepted as gospel, along with "Paul Revere's Ride," which appeared in *Tales of a Wayside Inn*, written by Henry Wadsworth Longfellow in 1861. But Lexington and Concord continue to dispute where the Revolution actually began, and national park rangers here tell visitors that Paul Revere never did reach Concord with the news that the British were coming.

Some visitors head west from Boston looking for historic shrines, others for literary ones. They find both. The historic can be found in Minute Man National Historical Park's Battle Road—the four-mile road over which the redcoats marched from Lexington to Concord, and over which they later retreated—and the North Bridge area at the road's Concord end. The literature of the day is evoked at a number of places: again, at Concord's North Bridge, where Emerson's poem is mounted; in the neighboring Old Manse, where both Emerson and Nathaniel Hawthorne lived; and in houses and sites associated with Henry David Thoreau, Bronson Alcott, and Alcott's daughter Louisa May.

What surprises visitors today about the Lexington–Concord area—which includes the adjacent towns of Sudbury, Lincoln, and Harvard—is how much of the natural beauty conveyed in the writings of Concord's eminent 19th-century authors remains. Walden Pond, which Thoreau transformed into both a literary and ecological icon, remains a renewing place to walk, fish, and swim, and Concord's three rivers—the Sudbury, the Assabet, and, formed by the other two, the Concord—are still accessible by boat.

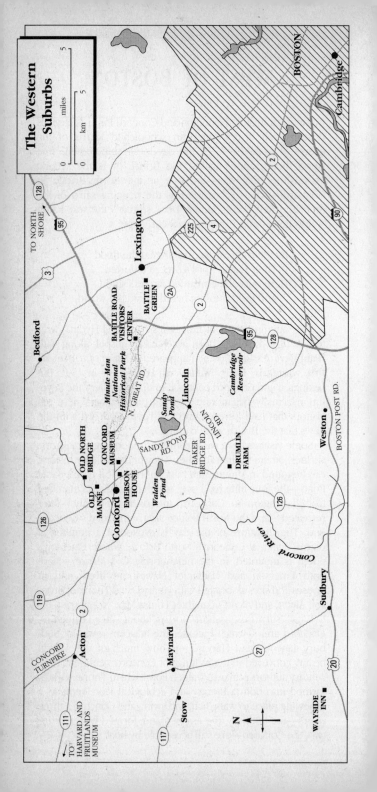

The Western Suburbs

miles 0 — 5

km 0 — 5

128

TO NORTH SHORE

95

3

Bedford

Lexington

BATTLE ROAD VISITORS' CENTER

BATTLE GREEN

2A

225

4

2

95

128

90

BOSTON

Cambridge

Minute Man National Historical Park

N. GREAT RD.

OLD NORTH BRIDGE

CONCORD MUSEUM

OLD MANSE

EMERSON HOUSE

Concord

Walden Pond

Sandy Pond

SANDY POND RD.

Lincoln

BAKER BRIDGE RD.

LINCOLN RD.

DRUMLIN FARM

Cambridge Reservoir

Weston

BOSTON POST RD.

126

126

Concord River

Sudbury

119

2

Acton

CONCORD TURNPIKE

Maynard

Stow

27

20

117

WAYSIDE INN

TO HARVARD AND FRUITLANDS MUSEUM

111

N

MAJOR INTEREST

Natural beauty
History of the American Revolution
Gathering place of 19th-century literati

Lexington
Museum of Our National Heritage
Battle Green
Buckman Tavern, gathering place for minutemen

Concord
Old North Bridge battle site
Authors' houses: Old Manse (Emerson and Haw-
    thorne), Emerson House, and Orchard House
    (Alcotts)
Concord Museum, town historical collection
Thoreau Lyceum
Walden Pond
Canoeing on the Concord River

Lincoln
Gropius House, home of Walter Gropius of the Bau-
    haus school
DeCordova Museum and Sculpture Park
Codman House, Georgian-era mansion
Drumlin Farm Education Center and Wildlife
    Sanctuary

Sudbury
Longfellow's Wayside Inn

Harvard
Fruitlands Museums

In its loop around Boston, Route 128 divides few towns
more decisively than Lexington and Concord. Lexington,
within the Boston area code (617), is a solid suburb, while
Concord, half the size of Lexington and a long-distance call
from Boston (area code 508), remains a small town that city-
dwellers visit to swim, canoe, bike, walk, and to buy
farmstand flowers and produce. (Concord and Lexington,
incidentally, do not border each other; Lincoln intervenes,
but you barely notice, so low-profile is that old-money
community.)

Concord continues to conjure up the spirits of the literati
who found inspiration here in the 19th century. Emerson,
while less widely read today than his Concord colleagues,
was the center and mentor of the literary circle that included
Thoreau, Nathaniel Hawthorne, Louisa May Alcott, and her
father, Amos Bronson Alcott. It has been noted that Emer-

son's Harvard address, "The American Scholar," and his slim book *Nature* were the opening shots of America's struggle for intellectual independence in the 1830s.

Nature presents Emerson's philosophy of **transcendentalism**, a philosophy that differed strongly from the Puritan preoccupations with guilt and sin on which New England had been founded. Transcendentalism expressed the belief that man can intuitively comprehend truth and beauty, with an unprecedented (at least in America) importance on the contemplation of nature, as described in Thoreau's classic, *Walden*.

Among the most evocative of Concord's literary shrines is Walden Pond, which, like the Concord River, remains much as it was when Thoreau wrote of it. Take the time to walk around the pond and, if possible, to canoe the river he described so well.

The town of Lincoln claims New England's largest contemporary-art museum, the DeCordova Museum and Sculpture Park, and two architecturally noteworthy houses maintained by the Society for the Protection of New England Antiquities (SPNEA): Codman House, an 18th-century mansion, and Gropius House, designed in 1938 by Walter Gropius, founder of the Bauhaus school of art and architecture. On the outskirts of Lincoln the Massachusetts Audubon Society maintains Drumlin Farm, the first place many Boston children visit to see domestic and wild animals. The nearby town of South Sudbury claims the venerable Longfellow's Wayside Inn, serving travellers for nearly three centuries. In the orchard town of Harvard, west of Concord, Fruitlands Museums includes the farmhouse described in Louisa May Alcott's *Transcendental Wild Oats*.

TOURING THE LEXINGTON – CONCORD AREA

While you can cover the major sights in Lexington and Concord in one day, it's wise to take several days to savor the area's many attractions. But if you do have only one day, don't try to squeeze everything in—choose the sights that interest you most and explore them thoroughly. (Note that most of the sights in this area are seasonal and are open generally from mid-April through mid-October.)

If you're out this way on **Patriots' Day**, April 19, celebrated on the closest Monday, expect reenactments of the skirmishes at Lexington and Concord, and other special events.

Our coverage begins in Lexington, at some of its Revolutionary War sites. We then head west along "Battle Road" through Minute Man National Historical Park to Concord.

There we find the homes and haunts of the Concord literati and pick up the trail of the Revolution again. Next we go south of Concord to an art museum and some important historic houses in Lincoln and Sudbury, and then west through the lovely Nashoba Valley, the highlight of which is Fruitlands, site of Bronson Alcott's experiment in communal living.

LEXINGTON

Lexington today is a sprawling suburb, but its Revolutionary-era sites and museums, shops, and restaurants are all conveniently strung out along Massachusetts Avenue, the main thoroughfare (known as "Mass. Ave.").

Take Route 2 west from Boston to Route 4/225 (Mass. Ave.), which leads right into Lexington. Your first stop in town might be the **Museum of Our National Heritage**, at 33 Marrett Road (Route 2A), just off Route 4/225. The museum offers constantly changing exhibits in several galleries, as well as films, lectures, and a multimedia dramatization of events leading to the Revolution. Tel: (617) 861-6559.

A little farther up Mass. Ave. is the **Munroe Tavern**, at number 1332, an early-18th-century inn that a British earl, Lord Hugh Percy, appropriated on April 17, 1775. Earl Percy arrived in Lexington that afternoon with 1,000 fresh men and cannon, giving the retreating troops a chance to rest. Wounded redcoats were treated here. The 18th-century furnishings include a table upstairs at which George Washington dined when he toured these already-historic sites during his presidency.

Now head up Mass. Ave. to **Battle Green**, as Lexington Common is known today, a large, grassy triangle with a statue of a minuteman at its head, where the town's old meetinghouse once stood. A granite marker erected by townspeople in 1799—the earliest monument to the American Revolution—names the eight men, seven from Lexington, who died as "the first victims of the sword of British Tyranny and oppression." (Details of the encounter are outlined in the Battle Road section, below.)

Across from the green on Hancock Street is **Buckman Tavern**, which looks much as it did when the colonists assembled there in the predawn hours of April 19, 1775. Costumed guides recount the history of the building, and point out such details as an 18th-century fireplace in the taproom and a door with a 1775 bullet hole. Open mid-April through October. The Lexington Chamber of Commerce

Visitors' Center (with public restrooms), next to Buckman Tavern at 1875 Massachusetts Avenue, dispenses information about lodging and dining in the area; Tel: (617) 862-1450.

In 1886 the town salvaged the 18th-century **Hancock-Clarke House**, just up Hancock Street at number 36. It was in this parsonage that John Hancock and Samuel Adams happened to be sleeping when Paul Revere roused them. The house, now a museum, is furnished with Revolutionary War exhibits and artifacts. Open mid-April through October. (Buckman Tavern, the Hancock-Clarke House, and Munroe Tavern are operated by the Lexington Historical Society; Tel: 617/861-0928.)

DINING IN LEXINGTON

Clothing stores, bookstores, and restaurants line downtown Massachusetts Avenue and adjacent streets for several blocks east of Battle Green. **Sweet Peppers**, right off Mass. Ave. at 20 Waltham Street (three blocks from the Green), is the area's favored Italian trattoria, with dining areas on two brightly painted floors. Its extensive menu features items ranging from pastas and pizzas to such specials as grilled shrimp with fennel-flavored mushrooms and tomato. It can be busy in the evenings, but reservations are not accepted for fewer than five people; Tel: (617) 862-1880.

The **Yangtze River Restaurant**, just a block or so up Mass. Ave. from Battle Green at 25 Depot Square, serves a menu of basic Chinese dishes as well as spicy Szechwan, lamb, and low-cholesterol steamed dishes; Tel: (617) 861-6030. The **Lemon Grass**, at 1710 Mass. Ave., serves Thai food (Tel: 617/862-3530), while the **Versailles Restaurant**, at number 1777, specializes in classic French and Continental fare, like veal à la crème and duck à l'orange. Reservations are advised; Tel: (617) 861-1711.

BATTLE ROAD

Follow the signs for Battle Road west from Battle Green and across Route 128 into **Minute Man National Historical Park**, which lines both sides of Battle Road all the way to Concord. The **Battle Road Visitor Center**, 2 miles (3 km) west of Lexington's Battle Green, is one of two such facilities operated by the park. (The other is the North Bridge Visitor Center, in a separate part of the park north of Concord Center.) The center offers a good overview of the historical sites in this area, with an audiovisual presentation and plenty of printed information on hours, fees, guided tours, demonstrations, and special events. (The center opens at 8:30 A.M., so if you've gotten an early start from Lexington or Boston it can be your first stop.) For information, Tel: (617) 862-7753.

The visitors' center shows a short film about the events of the spring of 1775, by which time 4,000 soldiers of the British army—commanded by Major General Thomas Gage—had occupied Boston for a year. For their part, the Continental Congress had voted to raise an army of 18,000 men. Gage had received orders from London to arrest the rebel leaders Samuel Adams and John Hancock, and to put down the "rude rabble" before they became an army. Gage decided to begin by confiscating the rebel arms that he knew to be stockpiled in Concord. It was a maneuver that depended on secrecy, but Bostonians heard word that the elite grenadiers and light infantry were being mustered and surmised their mission.

On the morning of April 16 Boston patriot Paul Revere rode out to Lexington to warn Adams and Hancock of the impending raid. He returned to Lexington around midnight on April 18 with firm news that the redcoats were on their way. Yet, when 700 redcoats under the command of Lieutenant Colonel Francis Smith marched into Lexington at five o'clock on the morning of April 19, only 77 men—half the town's adult male population—had assembled to face them. Undaunted, Captain John Parker gave his troops, the so-called minutemen, his now-famous order: "Stand your ground! Don't fire unless fired upon! But if they mean to have a war, let it begin here."

Realizing how badly outnumbered they were, however, Parker ordered his men to disperse. A shot was fired—by which side is still unclear. The British soldiers, despite orders to stop, began firing at the backs of the Americans, and eight minutemen were killed.

As you continue west through the park on Battle Road (Route 2A) you'll pass a turnoff marking the spot where Paul Revere was surprised by two British officers as he headed for Concord at about 1:00 A.M. on April 19. Luckily two other patriots, William Dawes, Jr., who, like Revere, had ridden out from Boston, and Dr. Samuel Prescott of Concord, who had been courting his sweetheart in Lexington, were riding far enough behind Revere to avoid capture. Dr. Prescott succeeded in spreading the alarm to Concord.

About half a mile (1 km) west of the turnoff is the entrance to **Virginia Road**, a narrower piece of the original highway along which some of the bloodiest fighting took place as the British retreated. The restored 18th-century **Hartwell Tavern** here hosts frequent demonstrations of 18th-century crafts and games and periodic historical reenactments in summer.

Battle Road/Route 2A splits shortly thereafter. Route 2A

forks left; you should bear right on Battle Road (which technically becomes Lexington Road here) for Concord. Since its founding in 1957 Minute Man National Park has been gradually rolling back the look of this stretch of the busy highway. Some 150 houses have been demolished, but the old stone walls, a vast area of farmland, and nearly two dozen 18th- and 19th-century homes remain. The park plans to gradually reclaim over the next decade as much farmland as possible and lease historic houses to farmers.

Sadly, one of the buildings due for future demolition is the **Willow Pond Kitchen**, a genuine 1950s roadhouse on Lexington Road just east of Meriam's Corner (the corner of Lexington and Old Bedford roads). The Willow Pond has deep wooden booths and red-checked curtains and serves steamers, fried fish, baked beans, the cheapest lobster around, and draft beer in frosted mugs. Currently owned by the park service, it's doomed when former proprietor Peter Sowkow, who still manages the restaurant, retires.

At Meriam's Corner itself, the striking 18th-century **Meriam House** (not open to the public) was the site of a skirmish between colonists and the British, sparking a running battle as the redcoats retreated back down the road toward Lexington.

CONCORD

"Concord is the oldest inland town in New England, perhaps in the States, and the walker is peculiarly favored here."

Thoreau's description of his home town still holds almost 150 years later; Concord is old, and looks it. Anthropologists maintain that this site has been populated for 10,000 years. Its fields had been cleared by generations of Indians, and the town is said to have been the first settled by whites above tidewater (1635).

Concord Center's three commercial blocks and its shaded residential streets have changed remarkably little since the mid-19th century. Although the town, which includes the depot neighborhood around the railroad station and the old mill village of West Concord on the other side of Route 2, has grown dramatically in recent years, there is little evidence of this in the Center. And Concord still harbors an unusual number of scholars and writers.

TOURING CONCORD

On the way to Concord from Lexington and the Battle Road you might want to stop at the Hawthorne, Alcott, or Emerson houses and the Concord Museum on the eastern edge of Concord Center; or you might continue through Monument Square right to the North Bridge area, which also marks the terminus of the Battle Road. The neighboring Minuteman National Park headquarters serves as an information center for both Concord's historical and literary landmarks. If you have time to tour only one historic house in town it should be the Old Manse, adjoining the North Bridge, as it figured in the events of April 19, 1775, as well as in the lives of Emerson and Hawthorne.

From the North Bridge area return to Monument Square, turn right down Main Street, and park your car (town lots are posted). Stroll up into the Old Hill Burying Ground and down by the shops and restaurants along Walden and Main streets (be sure to look into the library).

After touring Monument Square pick up your car and drive up to Sleepy Hollow Cemetery to visit "Author's Ridge," then head for Walden Pond. On the way you might want to stop at the Thoreau Lyceum in Concord Depot and, if time still permits and the weather cooperates, rent a canoe and paddle up the Concord River from South Bridge back to Old North Bridge.

CONCORD AUTHORS' HOUSES AND CONCORD MUSEUM

As you drive west on Battle Road toward Concord Center, the 18th- and 19th-century houses begin to thicken along Lexington Road. Not far past Meriam's Corner are two of the homes of the so-called Concord authors: the Wayside, Nathaniel Hawthorne's home before his death, and Orchard House, where Louisa May Alcott wrote *Little Women*. (Note that each of the houses and the museum charges its own fee, and there are no combination tickets.)

In the 1870s and 1880s the Concord authors enjoyed a national status currently reserved for film stars. In an 1869 newspaper article Alcott, who detested all the publicity, satirized this phenomenon that drew "pilgrims to the modern Mecca." She proposed that a hotel be built featuring "Walden water" and "Hawthorne's pumpkins," and furnished with "Alcott's rustic furniture, the beds made of Thoreau's pine boughs, and the sacred fires fed from the Emersonian woodpile." She suggested that telescopes be made available for guests to study "the soarings of the Oversoul."

The Wayside, at 455 Lexington Road, was the home of the Alcotts when Louisa May and her sisters were children (it was then called Hillside). Hawthorne, who moved in in 1860, named the house the Wayside, symbolic of his wish to just sit, observe, and describe. He added a tower study that he did not live long enough to enjoy, as he died of cancer at the age of 59. The house, currently maintained by the park service, was restored by Harriett Lothrop, who also acquired and restored neighboring Orchard House. Lothrop was known as Margaret Sidney, author of the children's book *The Five Little Peppers*.

Orchard House, right next door to the Wayside at 399 Lexington Road, was the setting for Alcott's *Little Women* and remains one of the most interesting 19th-century houses open to the public in New England. (It's actually two 18th-century houses that Bronson Alcott combined into a home for his family in 1858.) Alcott wrote her best-seller here in 1868, a chapter a day, at the desk set between the windows in her upstairs bedroom. She was known as "wise owl" by her family, and her room has two owls painted by Louisa's sister May, an accomplished artist whose studies she financed.

The rest of the house is filled with May's pictures: sketches on doors, mantels, and walls as well as framed watercolors and oils. It's also filled with the spirit of Louisa's father, Bronson Alcott, who, while never a financial success—he ultimately became Concord's superintendent of schools at $100 per annum—was considered a brilliant education reformer, advocating a learning approach that fostered physical and spiritual development as well as mental. At the age of 80 he established the Concord Adult Summer School of Philosophy in the fanciful building called Hillside Chapel constructed for that purpose in his back yard. It still offers summer programs for both adults and children. Orchard House is open year-round, closed weekends from November through March; Tel: (508) 369-4118.

A little farther west is the **Concord Museum**, at 200 Lexington Road, at its junction with the Cambridge Turnpike. One of the country's oldest town historical collections, the museum is a surprisingly grand institution for a town of 15,400. Its collection includes Indian artifacts, 18th-century furniture made in Concord, Revolutionary mementos (including one of the two lanterns said to have been hung for Paul Revere in Boston's Old North Church), and an exhibit on the Concord authors, featuring Emerson's entire study and a number of Thoreau's belongings, such as his flute and his snowshoes. Upstairs is a series of period rooms from 1680 to 1890, arranged in chronological order. The museum is open year-round; Tel: (508) 369-9609.

The **Emerson House** is across from the Concord Museum, at 1 Cambridge Turnpike. Ralph Waldo Emerson was already known for his unorthodox views when he moved into this

square white house with his second wife, Lidian, in 1835. He
lived here until his death in 1882. Scattered about the house
are many of Emerson's personal belongings, including walking sticks and the chair designed by Thoreau with a drawer
for Emerson's gloves. The writer's aeolian harp still sits on
the windowsill of his study, its music produced by the wind.
Open Thursday through Sunday and holidays from mid-
April to mid-October; Tel: (508) 369-2236.

OLD NORTH BRIDGE

Lexington Road ends in Monument Square, a busy five-way
crossroads that forms the center of Concord Center. Note
the wine-red house on the left as you enter the square
(corner of Main Street). This is **Wright Tavern** (1749), which
the redcoats commandeered as they marched into town that
April 19. Most of the Continental provisions had been moved
from Concord, but the British troops found 500 pounds of
musket balls—some of which they set fire to.

We will return to Monument Square and Wright Tavern
later, but for a sense of where Concord patriots were standing when they saw this fire, drive through the square and
out Monument Street to the **Major John Buttrick House**. This
massive brick mansion capping the rise above North Bridge
today serves as **Minute Man National Historic Park** headquarters, offering a slide show, an extensive bookshop, and
restrooms (Tel: 508/369-6993).

It was from this rise that the Concord patriots saw the fire
set by the British in front of Wright Tavern. "Will you have
them burn the town down?" one of the minutemen, Joseph
Hosmer, is said to have asked, provoking the 400 or so
patriots gathered here, who had come from nearby Acton
and Bedford as well as Concord. The order was given to
advance, and the 100 or so redcoats at North Bridge, in turn,
withdrew, pulling up planks of the bridge behind them. In
the standoff that followed, the Continental militia wounded a
dozen British soldiers, three mortally. Unaccustomed to this
kind of resistance, the British soldiers panicked and retreated hastily to town.

From the park headquarters walk down through the terraced gardens overlooking the river and on through the
quiet meadow to the **Old North Bridge**, a recent reproduction built on the site of that skirmish. Various displays
dramatize the battle that took place here. The **Minuteman
statue** at one end of the bridge, commissioned by Emerson
for the centennial of the battle, was fashioned by an as-yet-
unknown 23-year-old Concord sculptor named Daniel Chester French, who did the work for free. French went on to
become one of the era's most famous sculptors; he is per-

haps best known for his statue of Abraham Lincoln, which sits in the Lincoln Memorial in Washington, D.C.

The Old Manse

The nearest house to the Old North Bridge is the Old Manse, built in 1770 by William Emerson, the town's fiery patriot-minister, grandfather of Ralph Waldo Emerson. (William Emerson's wife, Phebe, was the sister of the Tory who told the British where patriot arms were stored.) The Reverend Emerson, who became the country's first army chaplain, died on the way home from Ticonderoga, and Phebe Emerson eventually married the next minister.

For Ralph Waldo Emerson, who was just 11 years old when his father died, this house became a second home, and he lived here four separate times in his life. Nathaniel Hawthorne rented the house and brought his bride, Sophia Peabody, here on their wedding day in July 1842. Hawthorne later described their three years here in *Mosses from an Old Manse*. The author felt great empathy for this already historic house, with its "glimmering shadows that lay half asleep between the door of the house and the public highway ... a kind of spiritual medium, seen through which the edifice had not quite the aspect of belonging to the material world." The Hawthornes' first child, Una, was born here, and scratched on a window pane in the upstairs study are the words: "Una Hawthorne stood on this window sill January 22, 1845 while the trees were all glass chandeliers, a goodly view which she liked much, tho' only ten months old."

Today the Old Manse's parlors are filled with 18th- and 19th-century furniture—a mahogany writing desk, side chairs, a rosewood Steinway grand piano—while the upstairs study is furnished to reflect the way it looked in 1830, when Emerson wrote his essay *Nature* here. The Old Manse is open April to November (closed Tuesdays); Tel: (508) 369-3909.

It's a short walk from the Old Manse back to Monument Square, but you might want to reposition your car in one of the lots off Main and Walden streets.

THE MONUMENT SQUARE AREA

The logical place to begin a walking tour of Concord is Monument Square, the hub of Concord Center. Named for the granite Civil War commemorative obelisk on its small common, the square is ringed by an eclectic mix of public and commercial buildings.

Note the **Colonial Inn** on the north side of Monument Square, with wicker chairs and rockers on its porch, an inviting taproom that serves a light lunch and tea, and a more formal dining room featuring such traditional American fare as roast beef and chicken pot pie. In the evening the inn sometimes presents jazz or folk music. (See Staying West of Boston, below, for information on the Colonial Inn's accommodations.) Next door to the inn, at 15 Monument Street, is a branch of the **Nature Company**, carrying birdhouses, telescopes, minerals, books, and a wide variety of other items having to do with nature.

The brick, mansard-roofed house on the south side of the square, now the rectory of St. Bernard's Catholic church, was once the sheriff's house. The jail in which Thoreau spent one night in 1846 "for refusing to recognize the right of the state to collect taxes from him in support of slavery" stood next door (a plaque marks the spot). This episode, described in Thoreau's "Civil Disobedience," has been cited frequently since the Vietnam War.

Old Hill Burying Ground, next to St. Bernard's, affords an overall view of Concord Center. The town looks much as it did in 1775, as illustrated in the "Doolittle" print on view at the Old North Bridge Visitor Center in Minute Man Park (see above) that was sketched from this spot. The old headstones and Wright Tavern are just as pictured, but the old millpond just off Main Street is gone.

Downtown Concord Center

Wright Tavern (see the Old North Bridge section, above), at the corner of Monument Square and Main Street, now houses a mix of businesses, including the **Concord Chamber of Commerce**, which dispenses a handy map/guide to the town that includes a listing of shops and restaurants; Tel: (508) 369-3120.

At the next corner turn left on Walden Street, where you will find two options for a meal. The **Walden Station Restaurant**, occupying a former fire station at number 24, is a dimly lit place with booths and good sandwiches. Dinner entrées range from mussels and pasta to shrimp and vegetable crêpes to chicken Thoreau. (Thoreau surely would approve of the shiitake mushrooms in this dish, but the Boursin cream sauce is questionable.) Tel: (508) 371-2233.

The **Concord Cheese Shop**, in business since 1860 at 29 Walden Street, sells take-out soups and delicatessen fare as well as many types of cheeses. You can bring your picnic to the small park around the corner on Heywood Street, behind the Concord Chamber of Commerce information booth (closed mid-October through mid-April), which is staffed by knowledgeable volunteers. Local historian Dan Harper leads free walking tours from the booth on Friday and Sunday afternoons, and other licensed guides offer tours (for a fee) at 1:00 P.M. on Saturdays, Sundays, and holidays.

Walk back the two blocks to Main Street. The **Milldam Store**, at 57 Main Street, is a source of reasonably priced sandwiches and local gossip. The basement-level **Concord Gourmet Deli**, at 32 Main Street, serves Greek pastries (baked fresh daily), gyros, and lamb balls in pocket bread, but has limited seating. **Perceptions**, down the street at number 67, is known throughout the Boston area for its unusual clothing, jewelry, and crafts. The **Concord Bookshop**, next door at number 65, has a general-interest selection with a focus on New England subjects. The **Barrow Bookstore**, at number 79, specializes in local-interest and children's books and is an inviting place to browse.

The **Concord Free Public Library**, at the corner of Main Street and Sudbury Road, is a larger, blander version of the Victorian building dedicated on this spot by Emerson in 1873. The three-story atrium within remains intact, and contains marble busts and books of the Concord authors. The Trustees Room is hung with 19th-century portraits, and a second-floor gallery mounts changing exhibits of art and photography. The large special collections room, with its trove of original and rare material, is a mecca for American-history and literature scholars from throughout the world.

Sleepy Hollow Cemetery

Before heading to the Thoreau Lyceum and Walden Pond you might want to visit Sleepy Hollow Cemetery. The cemetery is less than half a mile from Monument Square, north of the Old Hill Burying Ground, on Bedford Street, but you may want to drive; sidewalks are scarce and the cemetery itself is quite large.

Like Mount Auburn Cemetery in Cambridge, Sleepy Hollow is known for its lovely park-like landscaping. In the cemetery's Authors' Ridge are the remains of the Alcott, Thoreau, and Emerson families, as well as those of Nathaniel Hawthorne. Interestingly enough it's Emerson's grave, rather than Thoreau's, that is marked by a natural, uncut stone. Thoreau in death, as he was in life, is surrounded by his family.

Henry David Thoreau died of consumption May 6, 1862, at the age of 44, in the family house on Main Street (between Belknap and Thoreau streets). Later the house was sold to the Alcotts; it is now private. But it would be inappropriate to look for Thoreau's spirit in a house. Replicas of the cabin he built at Walden Pond can be seen at the Thoreau Lyceum and at Walden Pond, our next two stops.

CONCORD DEPOT

The **Thoreau Lyceum**, the comfortably cluttered headquarters of the Thoreau Society at 156 Belknap Street in Concord Depot (Belknap is the second left off Main Street after the library), is the best place to learn about the naturalist. Curator Anne McGrath conducts informal tours, and one entire room is filled with publications by or about Thoreau (in Concord the writer's name is pronounced with the stress on the first syllable). The Lyceum is open April 1 through December, with sporadic hours in January and March; Tel: (508) 369-5912.

The Old Concord Depot itself, back up Belknap and to the right on Thoreau Street, remains a stop on the commuter-rail line from Boston. The station is now home to a complex of shops and, upstairs, a restaurant called **Aigo Bistro**. Both the decor (which includes a brightly colored mural by Concord artist Jane Damon) and the cuisine (dishes such as grilled stuffed squid and braised lamb shanks with rosemary and chick-pea polenta) are drawn from Provence. Desserts are made fresh every day. Aigo serves lunch and dinner (closed Mondays); Tel: (508) 371-1333.

Across the way at 71 Thoreau Street, **New London Style Pizza** serves the area's best pizza. The former freight station, at number 68, now houses **Coggin's**, an exceptional bakery that carries a variety of coffees as well as muffins, breads (try the almond poppy-seed bread), and stuffed croissants, all baked on the premises daily. The old freight room is filled with tables and chairs, a good place to read some Thoreau before heading for Walden Pond, about 2 miles (3 km) southeast via Thoreau Street and Walden Street (Route 126).

WALDEN POND

Walden Pond is now a Massachusetts State Reservation, readily accessible except on hot summer weekends when its parking lot fills with Bostonians seeking solace from the heat at the pond's beach (with bathhouse). On such days it's best to wait until evening to walk the ten minutes from the entrance to the wooded spot where Thoreau built a cabin in 1845. "I went to the woods," he explained, "because I wished to live deliberately, to front only the essential facts of life, and see if I could not learn what it had to teach, and not, when I came to die, discover that I had not lived."

It was during his two years at Walden that Thoreau wrote *A Week on the Concord and Merrimack Rivers,* a book that endows the river with the same symbolism he later conferred on the pond. You may want to peruse a copy while lazing on the river.

THE CONCORD RIVER

It's an hour's paddle to Old North Bridge and back from South Bridge, location of the **Concord Canoe Service** boathouse, at 502 Main Street (between Route 2 and Concord Center on Route 62; Tel: 508/369-9438). But there's no need to go the whole way. Except for a few old houses that dot the banks of the river, this journey through Concord Center (you are just off Main Street) is unrelentingly green: woods, gardens, and flood meadow as far as the eye can see. You might want to go just as far as Egg Rock, the point at which the Sudbury and Assabet rivers join to form the Concord.

LINCOLN

The houses in Lincoln are sequestered up leafy drives, set in their fields behind stone walls. The few commercial shops cluster around the depot. From Concord Center, Lincoln's historic houses and art museum are a short, pleasant ride. Head south on Walden Street (Route 126); less than 1 mile (1½ km) south of Walden Pond, turn left onto Baker Bridge Road.

The **Gropius House**, at number 68, was built in 1938 by the innovative modern architect Walter Gropius, founder of Germany's Bauhaus school of art and architecture, for his family while he was teaching at Harvard. This fascinating home combines such traditional New England elements as clapboard and fieldstone with glass bricks and welded steel. The furniture (some by Marcel Breuer, designer of the famous cane and tubular-steel Breuer chair) and furnishings are carefully integrated works of art. Even from the inside you are aware of the surrounding orchards and fields. Open Friday through Sunday from June 1 to October 15; open one weekend a month from November to May; Tel: (617) 259-8843.

Continue east on Baker Bridge and bear right on Sandy Pond Road to the **DeCordova Museum and Sculpture Park**, at number 51. The museum, housed in a castle-like mansion set in 35 stately acres, features frequently changing exhibits of modern art in addition to works from its 1,800-piece permanent collection. On weekends from July 4 through Labor Day concerts are held on the grounds, which overlook Sandy Pond and include an extensive sculpture garden. Tel: (617) 259-8355.

Not far from the DeCordova is one of the area's most splendid mansions, **Codman House** (follow Sandy Pond Road east to Lincoln Road and turn right; Codman Road is the next right and less than a mile away). Built in the early 18th century but substantially enlarged and altered in the

1790s, Codman House is one of New England's finest Georgian-period mansions, set in an elaborate Italianate garden on 16 acres of sloping grounds. Rooms, which vary by period, include splendid detailing. Like the Gropius House, Codman House is owned by the Boston-based Society for the Preservation of New England Antiquities (SPNEA). Open June 1 through October 15; Tel: (617) 259-8843.

Drumlin Farm Education Center and Wildlife Sanctuary, at the corner of Lincoln Road and Route 117, is a great antidote to historic houses and museums, especially if you have children in tow. The 180-acre former estate, now maintained by the Massachusetts Audubon Society, encompasses pastures, fields, woodlands, and ponds. Among the animals here are cows, horses, mules, sheep, goats, pigs, poultry, hawks, and woodchucks. Closed Mondays; Tel: (617) 259-9807.

SUDBURY

From Concord take Route 126 south to the town of Wayland on Route 20; from there follow signs west to South Sudbury and the **Wayside Inn**, an 18th-century tavern billed as "America's oldest operating inn." It was already so creaky in 1861, the year Longfellow visited, that he called it "Hobgoblin Hall." The Cambridge poet used it as a setting for his *Tales of a Wayside Inn,* a collection of poems, one of which begins: "Listen my children and you shall hear / Of the midnight ride of Paul Revere."

In 1923 Henry Ford bought the inn and conducted a search for some of the furnishings described in Longfellow's *Tales;* he also put some of the poet's personal belongings in the inn. Ford acquired some 3,000 acres of surrounding land as a fitting frame for the picture and assembled historic buildings from the area, including the red schoolhouse attended by "Mary and her little lamb," a general store, and a gristmill. (The inn now sits on 106 acres, and many of the structures are no longer on its property.) The inn's restaurant, specializing in traditional New England fare, is always busy; Tel: (508) 443-1776. (See Staying West of Boston, below, for information on the inn's guest rooms.)

THE NASHOBA VALLEY

Just west of Concord lies the rolling, open orchard country of the Nashoba Valley. The valley's town of Harvard, west of Concord on Route 2 and then 2 miles (3 km) south on Route 110, is the home of **Fruitlands Museums**, at 102 Prospect Hill

Road (follow the signs from Route 110). Fruitlands is a complex of museums surrounding the 18th-century farmhouse in which Bronson Alcott and his family and several friends attempted to establish a "New Eden" in 1843. The group aimed to be a self-sufficient community and to exploit neither man nor beast; they practiced vegetarianism and refused to use cotton—raised by slaves—silk, or wool. Unfortunately, the communards proved to be far more adept with their heads than their hands, neglecting to harvest what they had sown, and dissolved after only seven months.

Fruitlands comprises four permanent exhibitions: the farmhouse; an American Indian display; a Shaker house; and a picture gallery. The farmhouse is now a museum of the transcendental movement, with pictures, books, and relics of Emerson, Alcott, and other leaders of the movement in America. The gallery, up the hill, contains some fine early-19th-century portraits and late-19th-century New England landscapes by the likes of Thomas Cole, Albert Bierstadt, and Frederick E. Church. The 1790s Shaker house was the first to be opened to the public. Fruitlands' unusual collection was amassed by Boston blueblood Clara Endicott Sears in the first half of the 20th century.

The extensive property overlooks a spread of hill and valley. The view can be enjoyed from the **tearoom**, open for lunch and tea (10:00 A.M. to 4:00 P.M.) and Sunday brunch. Open mid-May to mid-October (closed Mondays); Tel (508) 456-3924.

The exceptionally handsome center of **Harvard** is a couple of miles south on Route 110. You can return to Concord via Route 111, which runs east out of town. If you'd like to see more of the valley, drive 5 miles (8 km) farther south through orchards on Route 110 then 2 miles (3 km) east on Route 117 to the **Nashoba Valley Winery and Orchards**, at 100 Wattaquadoc Hill Road, off Route 117 in Bolton. Visitors may pick their own fruit and sample fruit wines made of cranberry, blueberry, peach, pear, and apple. The winery is open year-round, but fruit-picking is, of course, seasonal; Tel: (508) 779-5521. To return to Concord, follow Route 117 for about 12 miles (19 km).

Staying West of Boston

The accommodations in this area, which include several wonderful old inns as well as more run-of-the-mill hotels, can make a handy base not just for excursions in the Lexington–Concord region but also for trips to Boston by commuter rail.

LEXINGTON

Wedged unobtrusively between shops on Massachusetts Avenue in the center of Lexington, the **Battle Green Motor Inn** is an outstanding value. Each of its 96 rooms, which are grouped around a skylit pool, is furnished with Colonial reproductions.

The **Sheraton Tara Lexington Inn**, a low-rise, ivy-covered brick motor inn on extensive grounds, is conveniently located just west of the center of town, on Route 2A just off Route 128 (not far from Minute Man Park's Battle Road Visitor Center). Rooms are furnished in reproduction antiques, and amenities include the Cracker Barrel Tavern, serving light fare, an outdoor pool, and an exercise room. (Ask about special summer packages.)

CONCORD AREA

The **Colonial Inn**, at 48 Monument Square in Concord Center, a rambling gray clapboard landmark dating—in its various parts—from 1716 to 1961, remains one of the area's most attractive places to stay. Rooms in the main inn are furnished with antiques to go with the low ceilings and wide floorboards, while those in the newer, air-conditioned Prescott Wing are boxier but have country touches like quilts and flowery paper. Suites, with a bedroom or two, a kitchen, and sitting room, are also available on a daily basis.

The **Hawthorne Inn**, east of Concord Center at 462 Lexington Road, is an 1870s house with seven guest rooms furnished with antiques, handmade quilts, and original artwork. Guest and public rooms are well stocked with local-interest reading materials, and guests meet around the breakfast table.

A handsome 19th-century house, **Garfield House** is within walking distance of both North Bridge and downtown Concord. Hostess Beth Dawson greets guests in her expansive kitchen and offers a choice of two homey rooms with private baths. There is no common space here, however, and breakfast is served on a tray.

The **Anderson-Wheeler Homestead**, at 154 Fitchburg Turnpike (Route 117) in Concord, is a century-old working farm overlooking fields and wetlands. Owned by a Concord family, it offers five bedrooms, some with working fireplaces and one with a canopy bed, and a family suite of two rooms sharing a bath on the top (third) floor.

The **Colonel Roger Brown House**, at Damonmill Square in West Concord, is an 18th-century house with its original paneling and six-over-six windows. The furnishings are comfortable, not antiques, and amenities include central air-conditioning, phones, private baths, and access to facilities at the neighboring Concord Fitness Club.

About 15 minutes west of Concord in Stow, **Amerscot House** dates to around 1734 and retains much of its original paneling and a number of hearths. Rooms range from a family space with bunk beds to a suite with a canopy bed and Jacuzzi. All have private baths and small TVs. Breakfast is served in a glassed-in area where the owners grow plants. This is a nonsmoking inn.

SUDBURY

Longfellow's Wayside Inn, just off Route 20 in Sudbury, is best known as a historical sight and a restaurant, but the ten guest rooms upstairs are attractively furnished and remarkably reasonably priced. All have small sitting areas and private baths and are effectively separated from the noise and bustle of the inn.

SOUTH OF BOSTON

The story of the Pilgrims, who settled this coastal region in 1620, barely requires an introduction. Hardly a traveller passes south of Boston without making his or her own pilgrimage to see how and where their search for a better life and religious freedom began. Boston's South Shore, the region between Boston and the Cape Cod Canal, which stretches approximately 55 miles (88 km), isn't as charming as Boston's North Shore, but it's still worth a few meandering detours.

Just south of Boston, Quincy, the South Shore's most populous city, was the birthplace of two American presidents. On the coast just north of Plymouth is Duxbury, a quiet, dignified town of historic patrician homes (and the area's best beach). Plymouth and the coastal communities off Route 3A are typically sandwiched between a visit to Boston and Cape Cod.

The fate of Bristol County, tucked between Rhode Island and the South Shore in southeastern Massachusetts, has always been tied to water. Fall River, now quite industrial, is famous for a floating memorial to World War II victims. Fall River's other attractions—shopping outlets—are housed in dozens of former textile mills (which were powered by an abundant water supply). New Bedford, the largest whaling port in the world in the 19th century, today boasts the largest fishing port in the country and a beautifully restored water-

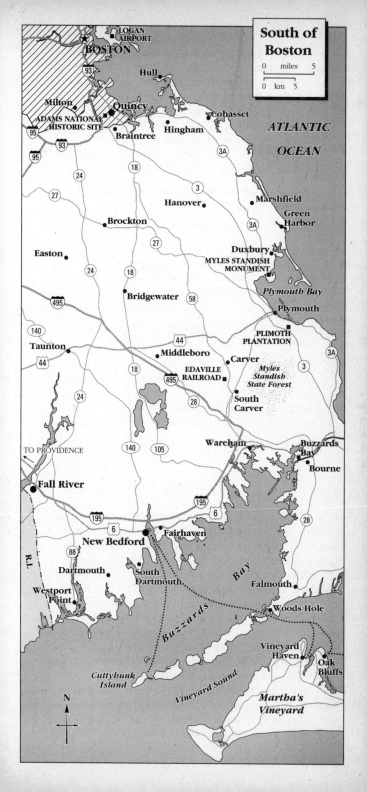

South of Boston

0 miles 5
0 km 5

front district. South of these two cities lies a small pocket of seaside farmland, quiet coves, and shaded roads. Bristol County is easily visited on the way from Newport, Rhode Island, to Cape Cod.

Either of these two distinct areas south of Boston—the South Shore and Bristol County—can be visited, if you're short on time, in one very long day.

MAJOR INTEREST

Quincy: Adams National Historic Site and related historic houses

Duxbury: Nine-mile barrier beach

Plymouth
Plimoth Plantation, open-air museum
Mayflower II, replica of the *Mayflower*
17th- and 18th-century houses

Fall River
Old textile mills housing shops and factory outlets
Battleship Cove, armada of retired ships

New Bedford
Federal-style and Victorian houses on County Street
Historic waterfront district
Seamen's Bethel, old mariners' church
New Bedford Whaling Museum

Cuttyhunk Island

QUINCY

Most people bypass Quincy, just a few miles south of Boston, thinking of it principally as a traffic-choked commuter town. But it has had an interesting past. Granite from dozens of local quarries was used to build the Bunker Hill Monument in Charlestown (in 1842) and America's first commercial railway, at about the same time. Quincy shipyards produced the only seven-masted schooner ever built, and many World War II navy vessels were built here (the General Dynamics Shipyard remains active). Both industries attracted diverse ethnic populations, which remain in the city today.

Quincy is the only town in America that was the birthplace of two presidents, John Adams, who served from 1797 to 1801, and John Quincy Adams, 1825 to 1829. Exit 8 off I-93 south from Boston brings you to the **Adams National Historic Site**, at 135 Adams Street. John and Abigail Adams purchased this impressive house (built in 1731) in 1787, and over the next 140 years four generations of Adamses lived here. The house expanded from seven to twenty rooms. Especially noteworthy is the rich mahogany in the paneled room and the magnificent Stone Library, built in 1873 and housing the personal library of John Quincy Adams. The stunning formal English gardens were established in the mid- to late 1800s. You'll have to take the informative park service tour to go inside the property. Tel: (617) 773-1177; open mid-April to mid-November.

American history and architecture buffs will enjoy exploring Hancock Street, Quincy's principal thoroughfare, about two blocks east of the Adams National Historic Site. At the intersection of Adams and Hancock streets, the Gothic Revival **Adams Academy** still educates students in accordance with the stipulations and principles set forth in John Adams's will (Adams died in 1826, but the school was not functioning until 1872). The academy is now home to the Quincy Historical Society, with exhibits on the city's industrial history open to the public year-round. Several of the historic homes on Hancock Street were lived in by Abigail Adams's relatives, members of the prominent Quincy family; the houses, open primarily in the summer, are all along the Quincy Historical Trail, a mile-long tour of 21 sights marked by a brown line in the sidewalk. The **Dorothy Quincy Homestead**, at 1010 Hancock Street (a half block north of the academy), is a Georgian Colonial homestead with beautiful gardens. Its oldest section was built in 1686. Open May through October; Tel: (617) 472-5117.

A half block south of the academy, at the corner of Coddington and Washington streets, is the **Thomas Crane Public Library**, designed in the Romanesque style by Henry Hobson Richardson, foremost architect of his time. Another half block south, at 1306 Hancock, is the **United First Parish Church**, an impressive Greek Revival structure made from Quincy granite, where the presidents and their wives are buried.

At the end of Hancock Street, where Franklin Street and Quincy Avenue intersect, is a **cairn** that marks the spot from which Abigail Adams and her son John Quincy looked to the north watching smoke rise from Charlestown, eight miles northwest, and listening to musket shots from the Battle of Bunker Hill (in Charlestown). On Franklin Street, a few long blocks from the Adams National Historic Site, you can visit the modest Colonial saltbox houses, aptly named the **John Adams Birthplace** (number 133), built in 1681, and the **John Quincy Adams Birthplace** (number 141), built in 1663, where our second president was born in 1735 and our sixth (son of the former) in 1767, respectively. Tel: (617) 773-

1177. The John Adams Birthplace contains reproduction furnishings, based on an actual list of his parents' possessions, from his boyhood years. The John Quincy Adams Birthplace houses reproductions from the time of Adams's early years during the Revolutionary War.

SOUTH FROM QUINCY

From Quincy you can head south on Route 3 or the slower Route 3A (our route). Initially Route 3A is altogether unscenic, passing through some congested suburban sprawl, until you get to the lovely coastal town of **Hingham**, 6 miles (10 km) east of Quincy. Hingham's Main Street, just west of Route 3A, is lined with shady elm and maple trees and 18th- and 19th-century buildings. The **Old Ship Church**, at 90 Main Street, is the oldest standing meetinghouse from the original 13 colonies, built by ship's carpenters in 1681. The great curved frames of the roof resemble a ship's hull turned upside down. The **cemetery** behind the church affords a nice view of the harbor.

From the harbor rotary on Route 3A, take Summer Street east to Martin's Lane and follow the signs for **World's End**, a pretty little peninsula covered with paths crossing meadows and hillsides, landscaped by Frederick Law Olmsted. From World's End backtrack to Hingham and follow signs for Nantasket. Just north of Nantasket, at the end of another solitary peninsula in the town of Hull, is a restaurant frequented by Bostonians who pride themselves on appreciating out-of-the-way places. **Saporito**, at 11 Rockland Circle, serves hearty, imaginative northern Italian dinners in a charming little bungalow. Securing a reservation is worth the trouble; Tel: (617) 925-3023.

Four miles (6½ km) east of Hingham via Route 3A is **Cohasset**, a lovely coastal village of patrician houses surrounding a town green. Cohasset is home to a small **Maritime Museum** housed in an 18th-century former ship chandlery on Elm Street (Tel: 617/383-6930). Ship models, scrimshaw, whaling implements, and other seafaring memorabilia are on display from June to September. The **South Shore Music Circus** (119 Ripley Road; Tel: 617/383-1400) attracts formerly big-name entertainment to its theater-in-the-round from June to early September. From Cohasset continue south along the shore road toward **Scituate** harbor; along this 6-mile (10-km) stretch of flat coastline you'll pass a beachfront summer community before reuniting with Route 3A south.

Duxbury

From Route 3 take Route 14 east to Duxbury; if you're on Route 3A, take St. George Street into Duxbury Village, about 25 miles (40 km) south of Quincy. This peaceful and aristocratic town, filled with wealthy sea captains' homes, was settled in 1627 by Myles Standish and other Pilgrims who needed land to raise their cattle.

The **John Alden House**, at 105 Alden Street, was built by one of those Pilgrims in 1653. John Alden and his eventual wife, Priscilla Mullens, were typical of the settlers who came to America on the *Mayflower.* John became a cooper, and Priscilla's family was among those who died during Plymouth's harsh first winter. The couple's friendship with Myles Standish gave rise to the romantic triangle recounted in Henry Wadsworth Longfellow's poem *The Courtship of Miles Standish.* The house, open to the public from late June to early September, features period furnishings and a massive central chimney. Tel: (617) 934-6001.

Turn left at the flagpole at the end of St. George Street to reach the **King Caesar House**, an imposing Federal mansion built in 1807 that belonged to Ezra Weston II, one of America's wealthiest men and Duxbury's foremost shipbuilder and merchant, thus dubbed "King Caesar." The interior contains fine detailing, a painting of Daniel Webster, the original French wallpaper in the front parlors, and furniture of the period. The house, open to the public on a limited schedule in the summer, has an interesting exterior that makes it worthwhile to visit even if you can't get inside. Tel: (617) 934-6106.

If you turn right at the flagpole you'll come to Snug Harbor, a fashionable summer community, and the **Winsor House Inn**, on Washington Street. Reasonably priced, light fare is available at lunch, while the dinner menu consists of pricier Continental and American dishes. Meals are served in a dark English-style pub, in the low-ceilinged dining room (with fireplaces), or, in good weather, outside on the patio. The 1807 house offers three guest rooms upstairs decorated with antiques and reproductions; all rooms have private baths.

Turn left at the makeshift rotary at the end of Washington Street to reach the **Myles Standish Monument**, from which there is a sweeping view of Plymouth, Cape Cod Bay, and Provincetown, at the tip of the Cape. The monument rises 130 feet in tribute to New England's first commissioned military officer.

For access to Duxbury's sandy, nine-mile barrier **beach**, the best in the area (with lifeguards, concession stands, and a bathhouse), head back through the rotary to Route 3A and follow that north to Route 139 toward Green Harbor in Marshfield. Otherwise take Route 3A south to Route 3 to Plymouth. Both routes are about an 8-mile (13-km) drive.

PLYMOUTH

The town of Plymouth, home to New England's first permanent settlement, takes its visitors seriously. It has to: 1.5 million of them come every summer. You can rest assured that the area's lodging and dining choices are more than adequate, considering the number of people who pass through. Still, don't expect to find any culinary stars or beautifully restored inns—just the basics.

Go first to Plimoth Plantation, while you still have energy. Then head back to the center of town, where there is a visitor information booth just south of the rotary on the waterfront. Most sights are clustered on the waterfront and Main Street, within walking distance of one another. A public trolley connects them in the summer. (Most of the historic houses are closed from late November through June.)

PLIMOTH PLANTATION

Take exit 4 off Route 3, 3 miles (5 km) south of town (if you are driving north from Cape Cod, take exit 5), to the open-air museum of Plimoth Plantation, where costumed "interpreters" reenact the dress, manner of speech, and chores of life in 1627. A stockade fence surrounds the cluster of small houses where you can watch "Pilgrims" grind corn, bake bread, salt fish, shear sheep, and make candles and clapboards. All the gardens, paths, straw-thatched roofs, and buildings are historically accurate; even the animals are genetically similar to those the Pilgrims would have raised. Also on the site is a re-creation of the summer campsite of a Wampanoag Indian, with narration by a costumed interpreter.

Admission to the plantation is steep, but you get your money's worth; spend a few hours to do it justice. Open mid-April to November 29; Tel: (508) 746-1622.

After you get a sense of Colonial life in 1627, head into town (via Route 3 north to Route 44) to get a glimpse of what life was like when the Pilgrims first landed in 1620.

THE PILGRIMS

In 1620 a group of religious separatists, after unsuccessfully attempting to reform the Church of England, decided to emigrate to America to avoid persecution. The *Mayflower*, carrying 102 passengers intent for Virginia, landed in Provincetown, at the tip of Cape Cod, two months later. After five weeks exploring the tip of the Cape and Cape Cod Bay, they set out for what is now Plymouth. The site was blessed with a good harbor, a source of fresh water, high ground that could be defended, and fields that had been cleared and abandoned by the Indians. **Plymouth Rock**, generally regarded as the debarkation point where the Pilgrims stepped ashore, is not much more than a cracked boulder with "1620" emblazoned on it, enshrined in a grand Greek Revival granite enclosure on the beach at Water Street.

The Pilgrims' first winter was harsh, and they had inadequate supplies and no livestock. Half their number died of scurvy, pneumonia, and influenza. To hide their dwindling numbers from the Indians, it is said that the Pilgrims buried their dead at night in unmarked graves on **Cole's Hill**, just above the rock. In commemoration of the very small band of Pilgrims who survived their first winter in the New World, a procession is held at 5:00 P.M. on Fridays in August, with a historically accurate number of townspeople representing the surviving Pilgrims.

In the spring of 1620 (possibly 1621) the Indians befriended the Pilgrims and taught them to hunt, fish, and cultivate indigenous crops. After a bountiful fall harvest they all sat down to a three-day feast, the forerunner of Thanksgiving. There is disagreement among scholars of settlements in Plymouth, Jamestown, Virginia, St. Augustine, Florida, and San Elizario, Texas, as to where the first Thanksgiving took place. Nonetheless, Thanksgiving is celebrated mightily in Plymouth. Plimoth Plantation, for example, offers three dining choices: a buffet, a 17th-century multi-course meal, and an authentic Victorian dinner. (The traditional Thanksgiving as we now celebrate it in America began during Victorian times.) The Plymouth Chamber of Commerce puts on a public dinner serving 1,200 or so at Memorial Hall; reservations are required for all dinners (Tel: 508/746-3377).

Mayflower II

Adjacent to Plymouth Rock is a replica of the same type of vessel as the original *Mayflower* (no one knows exactly what the *Mayflower* looked like), the *Mayflower II,* built in England in the 1950s and sailed across the Atlantic. Surprisingly small (just 104 feet in length) and with very cramped quarters, the ship gives you an indication of the courage and dedication required of its original passengers. The *Mayflower II* is operated by Plimoth Plantation, and it too has costumed interpreters aboard representing historical figures. A character named Governor John Carver might tell you about how he helped draw up the Mayflower Compact, under which the Pilgrims agreed to live by democratic principles. Democratic principles or not, the colony was able to survive, in part, thanks to a treaty signed by Massasoit, a powerful Wampanoag chief, ensuring peace between the two groups. After just a few short years Plymouth was a thriving colony, and by 1637 the colony had several thousand inhabitants. (The *Mayflower II* is open from April through November.)

Around in Plymouth

From the *Mayflower II* head up North Street to begin a tour of other points of interest. The **Plymouth National Wax Museum**, atop Cole's Hill at 16 Carver Street, contains 26 life-size dioramas with 180 wax figures telling the Pilgrims' story. Open mid-February through November; Tel: (508) 746-6468. To the right on Winslow Street, the **Mayflower Society Museum** is the headquarters for the General Society of Mayflower Descendants, but is open to the public. The elegant home, built in 1754 and remodeled in the late 19th century, features a "flying staircase" (so named because it has no visible means of support), formal gardens, and period rooms filled with 17th- to 19th-century furnishings. Open Memorial Day to mid-October; Tel: (508) 746-2590.

Almost across the street, the **Spooner House** (1749), at 27 North Street, was home to the Spooner family, makers of rope and twine, for 200 years. The interior of the richly furnished merchant's house displays many of the family's belongings and thus provides a splendid representation of the changes Plymouth has seen over two centuries. Open late May to mid-November; Tel: (508) 746-0012.

Turn left on Main Street, which becomes Sandwich Street, to reach the **Pilgrim Howland House**, at number 33. Built by the son of two original Pilgrims in 1667, it is the only surviving house in Plymouth where Pilgrims are known to have lived. (The elders lived with their son as they aged.) The house is filled with furniture dating from 1667 to 1750. Open from Memorial Day to mid-November; Tel: (508) 746-9590. Farther on, at 119 Sandwich Street, the **Harlow Old Fort House** (1677) was built with hand-hewn timbers from the original Plymouth fort on Burial Hill. Demonstrations of candle-making, dyeing, and weaving are given here. Open late May to mid-November.

Retrace your steps and turn left on Summer Street to reach the **Richard Sparrow House** (1640), the oldest dwelling in town; pottery is now made on the premises (demonstrations are occasionally given by the Plymouth Pottery Guild) and is sold in the gift shop. The house is open from

Memorial Day until Thanksgiving; the shop remains open until December 24. To the right on School Street, **Burial Hill** contains gravestones, including Governor William Bradford's, dating back to the original colony. There's a nice view out to the sea from here.

Retrace your steps back to Main Street and head north (left) until Main becomes Court Street. The **Pilgrim Hall Museum**, at 75 Court Street, contains more original Pilgrim artifacts and furnishings than any other place in the country. Items on hand include the wicker cradle of a baby born aboard the *Mayflower,* Governor Bradford's Bible, and some of Myles Standish's swords. Dating to 1824, it's the nation's oldest continuously operating public museum. Open year-round; Tel: (508) 746-1620.

Head down to the waterfront via Chilton Street, where **Captain John Boats** takes passengers out to Stellwagen Bank, where whales come to feed in the summer. The trip takes four hours; boats run from mid-April through October (Tel: 508/746-2643). Of the self-serve seafood places on the water, try **McGrath's**, on Water Street, offering lunch and dinner year-round.

A few doors down, at 225 Water Street, is the **Cranberry World Visitors' Center**, where you can take a look at a demonstration cranberry bog. The cranberry is Massachusetts's largest agricultural crop, and half the nation's cranberries come from this region. The area's sandy soil and acidic marshy areas are perfect habitats for the little red berry. Ocean Spray Cranberries, Inc., a nationwide cranberry co-operative of 800 growers, operates this center, which is open from May through November (Tel: 508/747-2350).

Head back toward the rotary to see the **Antiquarian House** (1809), a Federal-style home at 126 Water street filled with porcelain from the China trade and featuring an interesting 19th-century kitchen. You have now come almost full circle; the *Mayflower II* is a few blocks ahead of you.

To witness the colorful cranberry harvest, primarily from mid-September through mid-October, drive the back roads in and around **Carver**, about 7 miles (11 km) southwest of Plymouth via Routes 44 and 58. In South Carver, on Cranberry Road, is the **Myles Standish State Forest**, with more than 15,000 acres for camping, swimming, biking, and picnicking.

DINING AND STAYING IN PLYMOUTH

Plymouth's most atmospheric restaurant is **Station One + 1**, at 51 Main Street. Richly decorated with mahogany, crystal, and brass, it's in the old fire station; the extensive menu features American and Continental food. Tel: (508) 746-1200.

As for lodging in Plymouth, **Pilgrim Sands Motel**, on Route

3A close to Plimoth Plantation, has 64 rooms, some of which are oceanfront, and an indoor-outdoor pool. A five-minute walk from Plymouth Rock, the **John Carver Inn** has 79 attractive hotel-like rooms, all with air conditioning, telephone, and color TV, and an outdoor pool.

FALL RIVER

From the 1870s to the late 1920s, with the help of a natural harbor and easily harnessed water power, Fall River (about 30 miles/48 km southwest of Plymouth, 50 miles/80 km south of Boston, and 20 miles/32 km southeast of Providence, Rhode Island) enjoyed its heyday as a major textile manufacturing center. But when the textile industry moved to the South in the late 1920s, Fall River's prosperity declined, and the town went into receivership for the next ten years. The last mill shut down in 1965, and nowadays most of the old five- and six-story granite **mills** (accessible from I-195; follow the billboards) can be visited. Clustered within a five-block area, the visually impressive mills have found new life: They now contain more than 60 manufacturers' outlets (many of which are self-contained malls), where shoppers can realize savings on everything from designer labels to factory seconds in clothing accessories, housewares, crystal, luggage, and linen.

Housed in a former mill-owner's mansion, the **Fall River Historical Society Museum**, at 451 Rock Street, offers a perspective on the opulent side of the textile industry. Fall River's most notorious citizen, Lizzie Borden, who was accused of murdering her parents with an axe, also merits an exhibit here. (Lizzie was acquitted, and the crime never solved.) Closed January and February; Tel: (508) 679-1071. (To get to the museum, take Route 24 north from I-195 to Route 6/Presidents Avenue; head west on Route 6 and turn left onto Rock Street.)

BATTLESHIP COVE

Fall River's other major draw is also right off I-195 (take exit 5 and follow the signs). This small armada of retired floating ships serves as a memorial to the state's 13,000 World War II victims. The enormous battleship USS *Massachusetts,* also known as "Big Mamie," required a crew of 2,300 and logged more than 225,000 miles of service off North Africa and in the Pacific without losing one crewman. You can wander the top deck, where a Japanese suicide submarine invites inspection, and tour the nine decks below. Sandwiches are available in the wardroom.

A PT boat, one of only two of this type used in World War II, is more modest in size but not in the fear it instilled: Because of its speed and maneuverability, it was capable of firing torpedoes at close range. The USS *Lionfish,* which carried 20 torpedoes, is typical of the submarines used in World War II. The destroyer USS *Joseph Kennedy,* named after the eldest Kennedy brother, who was killed during a volunteer air mission in 1944, served in Korea, Vietnam, and the Cuban blockade. The cove is open every day, year-round.

Marine Museum

The region's maritime past is depicted in photographs at the adjacent Marine Museum. Exhibits of the luxurious Fall River steamship *Pilgrim,* which carried a crew of 200 to serve 1,000 passengers, are fascinating. The *Pilgrim* carried wealthy vacationers to their summer "cottages" from Boston and New York for 70 years, until 1937. The most popular exhibit here is a one-ton scale model of the *Titanic,* created in the 1950s for a film.

South of Fall River

The area south of Fall River is usually ignored by visitors, so if you take a little time to explore it you'll belong to a select group. The network of indirect roads is not very well marked, so be prepared to get lost in some of the prettiest seaside farmland in the state.

Ten miles (16 km) south of Fall River via Route 88 from I-195 east are the picturesque little towns of **Westport Central Village** and **Westport Point.** The toney yachting community of Padanaram Village in **South Dartmouth** (east of the Westports and about 14 miles/22 km southeast of Fall River) supports two fine restaurants. The gourmet **Bridge Street Café,** at 10A Bridge Street, is a bit overpriced for the area. The menu emphasizes, but is not limited to, fresh fish. Open for lunch and dinner daily, except Mondays, in the summer (open limited hours in winter); Tel: (508) 994-7200. **Le Rivage,** 7 Water Street, specializes in French cuisine and is open year-round for lunch and dinner. The $17 prix-fixe menu is a good deal (Tel: 508/999-4505).

Follow Bridge Street over the water, turn left on Smith Neck Road, and continue for 3 miles (5 km) to **Salt Marsh Farm** (no sign—watch for the mailbox). Even if you decide not to stay overnight at the farm, this is a nice drive. The 250-year-old Colonial, set on 90 wooded acres, offers two guest rooms, comfortably furnished with antiques, each with a private bath and separate stairway. After the full breakfast guests can enjoy the peacefulness of the hay fields and organic gardens, or use the farm's bicycles and ride to the nearby town beach (private).

Before heading to New Bedford, families might enjoy the **Children's Museum**, at 276 Gulf Road in South Dartmouth, just south of New Bedford. Housed in a huge old dairy barn, it's filled with lots of hands-on exhibits, including a walk-in kaleidoscope; outside are 50 acres of trails. Tel: (508) 993-3361.

NEW BEDFORD

In his novel *Moby-Dick* (1851), Herman Melville described New Bedford as "perhaps the dearest place to live in all New England . . . Nowhere in America will you find more patrician-like houses." It's easy to imagine that that was true when New Bedford was the whaling capital of the world. Just ten years after whaling was introduced to New Bedford by a Nantucket seaman (in 1765), 50 ships were sailing out of the port. By the 1830s New Bedford had 329 ships, while Nantucket had only 88. More than 10,000 seamen would sail on vessels out of New Bedford by the time the industry began to decline in the 1860s.

Though much of New Bedford, just 10 miles (16 km) east of Fall River on I-195, is dilapidated today, there's still a great deal to recommend this city: a working waterfront, old mills, and mansions on the hill. Many of the Federal-style and turreted Victorian houses that Melville referred to still stand on **County Street**, parallel to the waterfront along the crest of a hill. Wealthy merchants and whaling captains built here, and when that industry died textile-mill owners moved in. Chief among the houses, the 22-room **Rotch-Jones-Duff House & Garden Museum**, at 396 County Street, was built in 1834 for a Quaker whaling merchant by Richard Upjohn. The extensive formal gardens are magnificent, and afternoon tea is served here (Tel: 508/997-1401).

THE HISTORIC WATERFRONT DISTRICT

New Bedford was known for cod fishing, shipbuilding, whaling, and textiles. Today the principal industry is again fishing; piers are filled to capacity with fleets. The historic waterfront district, ten blocks of cobblestone streets that are adjacent to the city's original ten acres, caters to both visitors and fishermen. **Whale** (Waterfront Historic Area League), at 13 Centre Street, is a nonprofit preservationist organization responsible for much of the district's restoration. Informative, free, one-hour walking tours led by volunteer guides begin from the visitor center at 47 North Second Street. You can take your own tour of the waterfront district, County Street, or Acushnet Heights with the help of excellent pamphlets prepared by the New Bedford Preservation Society and available at the visitor center.

Less than a block away from the visitor center on Johnny Cake Hill, the **Seamen's Bethel** was a requisite stop for mariners about to set sail. Inside this sailors' church is the preacher's pulpit, resembling the bow of a whaleboat, described in *Moby-Dick*. The walls are lined with memorials to sailors who died at sea. Both the Bethel church and the Greek Revival U.S. **Custom House**, at the corner of Second and William streets, have been in use since 1834.

New Bedford Whaling Museum

This excellent museum, across the street from the Seamen's Bethel at 18 Johnny Cake Hill, tells the story of New Bedford's whaling days. They began in the 18th century when a Nantucket seaman, carried out to sea and assumed lost, eventually turned up with a captured sperm whale in tow. This single event led to the construction of larger vessels that could be outfitted for the long voyages necessary to hunt profitable sperm whales. (The sperm whale was a source of such rare substances as spermaceti, used for candles; a pure oil from a cavity in the head; and ambergris, used for perfume.) Whale processing took place along the side of the ship, with seamen working on planks suspended above sea level. Among the products harvested from whales was blubber melted down into an oil that produced a bright, clean light; meat, for food; and baleen (the 19th-century "plastic"), used to fashion corsets and umbrellas.

Life at sea was rugged and harsh. Quarters, for a typical crew of 15 to 20, were cramped; food was bad and the danger of being capsized or attacked by a whale was omnipresent. When whale populations began to decline, seamen were forced to stay at sea for up to four or five years in search of the behemoth. Captains, usually accompanied by their families on these voyages, rarely turned home until all the barrels on board were filled with oil.

The museum's scrimshaw collection is among the finest in the world; of particular note are a meticulously detailed sleigh and birdcage. Other fine exhibits include a half-scale model of the *Lagoda,* a fully rigged whaling ship, and two sections of an 1848 panoramic painting by Russell Purrington that was originally more than a half-mile long, depicting a whaling voyage around the world.

On the pier across the street from the historic district you can see the lightship *New Bedford,* one of dozens of lightships that protected ships along coastlines where it was too dangerous to build lighthouses. The *Ernestina,* which you should board if she's in port, has had many incarnations as the oldest remaining Grand Bank fishing schooner: the only ship afloat that explored the Arctic under full sail, she also transported many New Bedford immigrants from the Cape Verde Islands off the coast of Africa. In winter and spring the *Ernestina* is a training ship and excursion vessel in the Atlantic and the Caribbean.

DINING AND STAYING IN
NEW BEDFORD

In the historic district, at 41 William Street, **Freestone's** is the most convenient place to eat in the area. A casually upscale atmosphere pervades this restored 19th-century bank build-ing with mahogany woodwork and a working fireplace. The kitchen puts out dependable burgers as well as a full course seafood dinner. Open for lunch and dinner daily; Tel: (508) 993-7477.

The most convenient place to stay in town is on the pier, a few blocks south of the lightship *New Bedford.* The **Durant Sail Loft Inn** offers 16 undistinguished but neat and spacious rooms, half of which face north to the fishing fleet. The manager, Michael DeLacey, is one of New Bedford's most enthusiastic, knowledgeable, and committed supporters. The Portuguese food at **Lisboa Antiga,** which shares the same granite counting house as the Sail Loft, is consistently authen-tic; don't expect much atmosphere though. The bar is popular with fishermen after work. For Portuguese food for the uniniti-ated palate, **Antonio's** fits the bill. About a mile (1 ½ km) from the waterfront historic district off Route 18, at 267 Coggeshall, Antonio's serves lunch and dinner daily; Tel: (508) 990-3636. Portuguese from the Azores, after coming in contact with whaling ships that plied their waters, arrived here in the mid-1800s. In early August New Bedford hosts the largest Portu-guese feast in America, the **Feast of the Blessed Sacrament.** This is followed by the **Seafood Festival** in mid-August, which coincides with the spectacular **Blessing of the Fleet.**

Davy's Locker, near the ferry terminal, delivers the best seafood in town. The atmosphere is nothing to write home about, but the prices are moderate. It's about 1 mile (1½ km) from the piers and the historic district; take Route 18 along the waterfront, turn left onto Cove Street, and right onto East Rodney French Boulevard. Tel: (508) 992-7359.

Poverty Point

Poverty Point, just a few miles east of New Bedford in Fairhaven, affords the best view of New Bedford. From Route 6, turn left onto Main Street and left onto Oxford Street (on Poverty Point). From a grassy plot at the end of the street, **Edgewater Bed & Breakfast** overlooks New Bedford and the bay. The five guest rooms, all with private bath, are spacious and have water views. The view from the living room will make you feel as though you're on a ship. If instead you turn right onto Main Street from Route 6, you'll pass stately homes and eventually come to **Fort Phoenix**, a pre-Revolutionary site where it is said that the first naval engagement of the Revolution took place.

Cuttyhunk Island

Fourteen miles off the coast of New Bedford and just two miles long and less than a mile wide, Cuttyhunk is the westernmost of the 16 Elizabeth Islands, which separate Buzzards Bay and Vineyard Sound. Bartholomew Gosnold built the Bay State's first English settlement here in 1602. Today Cuttyhunk is best known as a haven for bass fishing; guides, their boats, and tackle are available for hire. Its rocky shoreline is not for sunbathers, however. With just 90 or so houses, a seasonal general store, a summer population that soars to only 400 from 40 year-rounders, Cuttyhunk, with its rolling landscape and sandy roads, attracts visitors who wish to truly escape from it all.

The only place to stay on the island is the **Allen House**, with two cottages and 12 clean and simple guest rooms (all with shared baths). The house is closed from early October to late May; lunch and dinner are available on the wrap-around porch. (The only other place to get food is the **Vineyard View Bakery and Restaurant**.) The island is dry, so bring your own wine.

Cuttyhunk is accessible via the M/V *Alert* (Tel: 508/992-1432), which sails on a limited schedule from the New Bedford pier across from the historic district. It is possible to take the 90-minute morning ferry (no cars), hike around for a few hours, and return in the afternoon.

GETTING AROUND

The North Shore

Massachusetts Bay Transit Authority (MBTA) buses 450 and 455 run regularly all day from Haymarket in Boston to downtown Salem; to get to Marblehead, take bus 441 or 442.

Commuter trains link Boston's North Station with Salem, Beverly, Rockport, Manchester, and Gloucester, although the Gloucester station is not within walking distance of any of the sights. In summer and early fall the train is an excellent option for day trips to Salem or Rockport from Boston. The ride to Rockport is especially pretty, and you won't have parking hassles when you get there. For MBTA bus and rail information, Tel: (800) 392-6100 or (617) 722-3200.

The North Shore as a whole is best approached by car, however. Salem, in the heart of the area, is about a 40-minute drive from downtown Boston and less from Logan Airport, which is served by all major automobile rental companies. Route 128 is the quickest route to Salem and Cape Ann, while Route 1A goes directly from Boston to Marblehead. If you're driving from Boston to Newburyport, I-95 is the most direct route.

Summer is the most popular time to visit the North Shore, but even then the weather can be rainy and cool one day, hot and breezy the next. Many restaurants, hotels, and museums in the area, especially on Cape Ann, are seasonal, so it's a good idea to call ahead before you go out of your way to visit something.

For more information, contact any of the chambers of commerce in the region: **Marblehead Chamber of Commerce**, 62 Pleasant Street, P.O. Box 76, Marblehead, MA 01945, Tel: (617) 631-2868; **Salem Chamber of Commerce**, 32 Derby Square, Salem, MA 01970, Tel: (508) 744-0004; **Cape Ann Chamber of Commerce**, 33 Commercial Street, Gloucester, MA 01930, Tel: (508) 283-1601 or (800) 321-0133; Fax: (508) 283-4740; **Rockport Chamber of Commerce and Board of Trade**, 37 Hodgkins Road, P.O. Box 67A, Rockport, MA 01966, Tel: (508) 546-6575 or (508) 546-5997 (year-round); **Greater Newburyport Chamber of Commerce and Industry**, 29 State Street, Newburyport, MA 01950, Tel: (508) 462-6680; Fax: (508) 462-6680.

West of Boston

Concord Depot is 20 miles (32 km) west of downtown Boston, accessible from North Station in Boston and Porter Square in Cambridge by MBTA Commuter Rail. For information, Tel: (800) 392-6100 or (617) 722-3200. In Concord, however, the sights are too far-flung from the depot to be covered entirely on foot, so a car is necessary.

It's also possible to take a bus from the MBTA station in Cambridge to Lexington's Battle Green, but there is no public transportation between Concord and Lexington. If you are a seasoned bicyclist (and can handle some 20 miles on trafficked, narrow roads), you might take advantage of the rental bikes available from **Lincoln Guide Service**, 152 Lincoln Road, across from the railroad station in Lincoln (they also rent skis and Rollerblades); Tel: (617) 259-1111.

The **Gray Line**, a Boston-based bus company, offers a three-hour tour of Lexington, Concord, and Cambridge (Tel: 617/426-8805). This is strictly a drive-through tour: out Mass. Ave. through Cambridge to Lexington's Battle Green, where there's a 30-minute stop, then on to the North Bridge for another 30-minute stop.

By car you can follow this same route west along Mass. Ave. (billed as "The Ride of Paul Revere"), but it takes a fraction of the time (10 to 15 minutes instead of half an hour) to take Route 2 west from Cambridge to Lexington.

South of Boston

Driving is the only practical way to see the major and minor towns south of Boston. Plymouth is a 45-minute drive southeast of Boston; the Cape Cod Canal is just 20 minutes farther. From the Cape Cod Canal west to New Bedford takes 30 minutes, while Fall River is another 20 minutes west. The trip from Fall River to Newport or Providence takes less than half an hour. Both Fall River and New Bedford are about a 50-minute drive due south of Boston.

If you choose public transportation, **Plymouth & Brockton** buses (Tel: 508/746-0378) connect Plymouth to Boston and Hyannis (Cape Cod). **American Eagle** (Tel: 508/993-5040 or 800/453-5040) operates buses from Boston to New Bedford, while **Bonanza Bus Lines** (Tel: 617/720-4110 or 800/556-3815) links Fall River to Boston. **Cape Air** (Tel: 508/693-0505 or 800/352-0714) flies from New Bedford to Martha's Vineyard and Nantucket.

You can ferry from towns south of Boston to Cape Cod and Martha's Vineyard. **Martha's Vineyard Ferry** (Tel: 508/997-1688) carries passengers (no cars) from New Bedford to the Vineyard three times a day during the summer, less frequently in the late spring and early fall. The trip takes 90 minutes. **Cape Cod Cruises** (Tel: 508/747-2400) operates a daily morning boat from Plymouth to Provincetown from late June to early September.

For additional information about New Bedford and Fall River, contact the **Bristol County Convention and Visitors Bureau**, 70 North Second Street, P.O. Box 976, New Bedford, MA 02741; Tel: (508) 997-1250. For additional information on Plymouth and the smaller towns north of it, contact the **Plymouth County Development Council**, P.O. Box 1620, Pembroke, MA 02359, Tel: (617) 826-3136; or the **Plymouth Area Chamber of Commerce**, 91 Samoset Street (Route 44), Plymouth, MA 02360, Tel: (508) 746-3377.

ACCOMMODATIONS REFERENCE

Unless otherwise indicated, the rates given below are projections for 1993 for double room, double occupancy. As prices are subject to change, always double-check before booking. Ask about packages, especially in the off-seasons; many lodgings offer deals on two- or three-night stays.

The North Shore

▶ **Amelia Payson Guest House.** 16 Winter Street, **Salem,** MA 01970. Tel: (508) 744-8304. $65–$85.

▶ **Bass Rocks Ocean Inn.** 107 Atlantic Road, **Gloucester,** MA 01930. Tel: (508) 283-7600. $75–$120; includes cold breakfast buffet.

▶ **Chicataubut Inn.** Long Beach (off Route 127), **Rockport,** MA 01966. Tel: (508) 546-3342. $63–$105.

▶ **Clark Currier Inn.** 45 Green Street, **Newburyport,** MA 01950. Tel: (508) 465-8363. $65–$95.

▶ **Eden Pines Inn.** Eden Road, **Rockport,** MA 01966. Tel: (508) 546-2505. $80–$120; includes breakfast.

▶ **Essex Street Inn.** 7 Essex Street, **Newburyport,** MA 01950. Tel: (508) 465-3148. $55–$145.

▶ **Garrison Inn.** 11 Brown Square, **Newburyport,** MA 01950. Tel: (508) 465-0910; Fax: (508) 465-4017. $69.50–$130.

▶ **Harbor Light Inn.** 58 Washington Street, **Marblehead,** MA 01945. Tel: (617) 631-2186; Fax: (617) 631-2216. $75–$185.

▶ **Hawthorne Hotel.** Salem Common, **Salem,** MA 01970. Tel: (508) 744-4080; Fax: (508) 745-9842. $79–$120.

▶ **Inn at Seven Winter Street.** 7 Winter Street, **Salem,** MA 01970. Tel: (508) 745–9520. $75–$165.

▶ **Old Farm Inn.** 291 Granite Street (Route 127), **Rockport,** MA 01966. Tel: (508) 546-3237. $65–$98; includes Continental breakfast.

▶ **Peg Leg Inn.** 2 King Street, **Rockport,** MA 01966. Tel: (508) 546-2352. $55–$105; includes Continental breakfast.

▶ **Ralph Waldo Emerson Inn.** 1 Cathedral Avenue (Route 127), Pigeon Cove, **Rockport,** MA 01966. Tel: (508) 546-6321. $71–$117.

▶ **Salem Inn.** 7 Summer Street, **Salem,** MA 01970. Tel: (508) 741-0680; Fax: (508) 744-8924. $85–$125; includes breakfast.

▶ **Sandy Bay Motor Inn.** 173 Main Street, **Rockport,** MA 01966. Tel: (508) 546-7155; Fax: (508) 546-9131. $56–$158.

▶ **Seacrest Manor.** 131 Marmion Way, **Rockport,** MA 01966. Tel: (508) 546-2211. $76–$102; includes full breakfast.

▶ **Windsor House.** 38 Federal Street, **Newburyport,** MA 01950. Tel: (508) 462-3778; Fax: (508) 465-3443. $59–$115; includes breakfast.

West of Boston

▶ **Amerscot House.** 61 West Acton Road, **Stow**, MA 01775. Tel: (508) 897-0666; Fax: (508) 897-2585. $80–$95; includes full breakfast.

▶ **Anderson-Wheeler Homestead.** 154 Fitchburg Turnpike, **Concord**, MA 01742. Tel: (508) 369-3756. $65–$75; suite $145.

▶ **Battle Green Motor Inn.** 1720 Massachusetts Avenue, **Lexington**, MA 02173. Tel: (617) 862-6100, (800) 322-1066 (in MA), or (800) 343-0235 (outside MA). $45–$70.

▶ **Colonel Roger Brown House.** 1694 Main Street, **Concord**, MA 01742. Tel: (508) 369-9119 or (800) 292-1369; Fax: (508) 369-1305. $65–$75; includes buffet breakfast.

▶ **Colonial Inn.** 48 Monument Square, **Concord**, MA 01742. Tel: (508) 369-9200 or (800) 370-9200; Fax: (508) 369-2170. $95–$125.

▶ **Garfield House.** 41 Monument Street, **Concord**, MA 01742. Tel: (508) 369-8540. $55–$60; includes breakfast.

▶ **Hawthorne Inn.** 462 Lexington Road, **Concord**, MA 01742. Tel: (508) 369-5610. $85–$160.

▶ **Longfellow's Wayside Inn.** Wayside Inn Road, **Sudbury**, MA 01776. Tel: (508) 443-1776; Fax: (508) 443-2312. $86; includes breakfast.

▶ **Sheraton Tara Lexington Inn.** 727 Marrett Road, **Lexington**, MA 02173. Tel: (617) 862-8700; Fax: (617) 863-0404. $75–$139.

South of Boston

▶ **Allen House. Cuttyhunk**, MA 02713. Tel: (508) 996-9292. $85; includes Continental breakfast.

▶ **Durant Sail Loft Inn.** 1 Merrill's Wharf, **New Bedford**, MA 02740. Tel: (508) 999-2700; Fax: (508) 990-7863. $78–$88.

▶ **Edgewater Bed & Breakfast.** 2 Oxford Street, **Fairhaven**, MA 02719. Tel: (508) 997-5512. $60–$80.

▶ **John Carver Inn.** 25 Summer Street, **Plymouth**, MA 02360. Tel: (508) 746-7100 or (800) 274-1620. $45–$105.

▶ **Pilgrim Sands Motel.** 150 Warren Avenue (Route 3A), **Plymouth**, MA 02360. Tel: (508) 747-0900. $70–$108.

▶ **Salt Marsh Farm.** 322 Smith Neck Road, **South Dartmouth**, MA 02748. Tel: (508) 992-0980. $65–$75; includes breakfast.

▶ **Winsor House Inn.** 390 Washington Street, P.O. Box 2133, **Duxbury**, MA 02331. Tel: (617) 934-0991. $65–$90; includes breakfast.

CAPE COD AND THE ISLANDS

MARTHA'S VINEYARD AND NANTUCKET

By Kimberly Grant

Kimberly Grant, a freelance travel writer and photographer, is coauthor of Best Places to Stay in New England *and has contributed to several national guidebooks. A lifelong resident of Massachusetts, she resides in Boston and makes numerous trips to the Cape.*

In the mid-1800s Henry David Thoreau, one of Cape Cod's earliest tourists, remarked that the sparse beauty of this arching peninsula—"the bared and bended arm of Massachusetts"—would not appeal to travellers. But today Cape Cod and its island neighbors, Martha's Vineyard and Nantucket, are arguably the East Coast's most popular seaside resorts. The combination of sandy beaches, picturesque harbors, local historical museums, fine art galleries, and fresh seafood lures more than 14 million visitors a year.

The Cape Cod peninsula, boasting more than 300 miles of shoreline, begins about an hour's drive south of Boston and extends out to sea in its familiar bent shape for another 70 miles. Just five miles off the Cape's south coast lies Martha's Vineyard, while Nantucket is stranded 30 miles out to sea. Cape Cod and the Islands were formed about 20,000 years ago when the region was covered by a retreating ice sheet. Some of the area's most notable topographic features—

among them sandy shores, dunes, cliffs, and moors—were left in its wake.

The mainland and the Islands share a similar history with regard to the original Native American inhabitants and, later, the Pilgrims; the industries of whaling and fishing; the onslaught of 20th-century tourism; and a lingering provincialism (each town thinks the sun rises and sets over it and not its neighbor ten miles away). But while the Cape, Martha's Vineyard, and Nantucket do share some characteristics, they are remarkably unlike considering their proximity, common history, and mutual dependence on the sea. In fact, the communities on the Cape are themselves distinct and insular places, and it behooves the traveller to recognize the differences. (There are Cape Cod residents who haven't been off-Cape in a half dozen years, and who won't venture to Hyannis, its busiest community, during the summer unless it's a matter of life or death.)

Visualize the Cape Cod Canal, a deep man-made waterway that separates the Cape from the mainland, as the shoulder of Thoreau's "bared and bended arm," Chatham as the elbow, and Provincetown, at the tip of the peninsula, as the fist. That part of the peninsula known as the Outer (or Lower) Cape extends from Chatham to Provincetown, and includes the long stretch of coastline protected as Cape Cod National Seashore. Sandwich, just east of the Cape Cod Canal on Cape Cod Bay (the inner side of the peninsula's crooked arm), is a stable year-round community; many residents commute into Boston every day. Barnstable, Yarmouth Port, Dennis, and Brewster, all east of Sandwich on the bay side, have been populated recently by an influx of young professionals, as well as older professionals enjoying a comfortable retirement in 200-year-old houses. (These small classic cottages—usually a story and a half with shingles that turn a silvery-gray when exposed to the elements—are omnipresent on the Cape.)

Orleans, on the inside of the "elbow," provides a buffer between the undeveloped and overdeveloped Cape, gently absorbing both. Patrician, genteel Chatham on the Cape's south shore has managed to insulate itself from Hyannis, just to the west. The Cape's share of fast-food joints, tacky souvenir shops, miniature golf courses, condominium complexes, and strip malls are concentrated along, but not limited to, Route 28, which connects Chatham, Hyannis, and Falmouth, at the soutwesternmost corner of the peninsula. Falmouth accommodates both affluent summer residents and a growing year-round community, including fishermen and employees of the town's many commercial establishments. Next door, Woods Hole is primarily a scientific community and the terminus for ferries to the Islands.

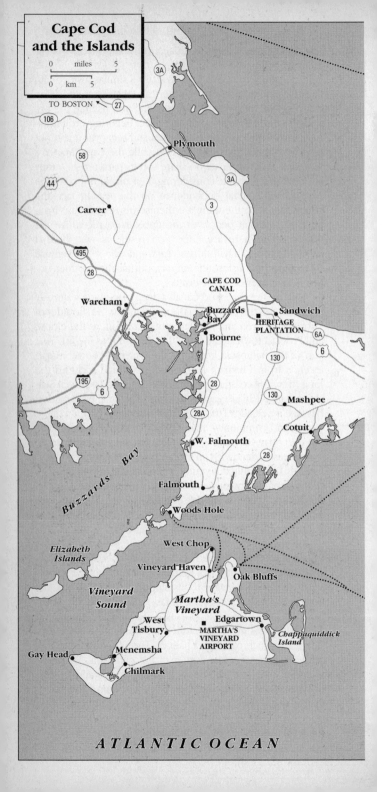

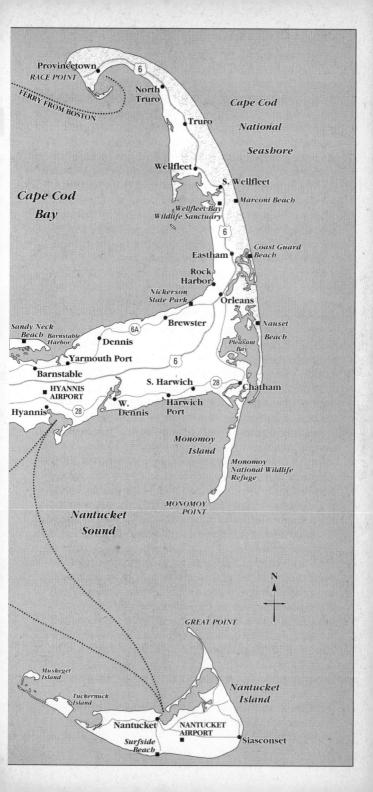

The Outer Cape is the Cape of the visitor's imagination. Here are spectacular beaches, thousands of acres of pristine coastline and forest, quiet coves, and towering windswept dunes, much of it protected as part of the National Seashore. And at the tip of the peninsula is artsy and independent Provincetown, Cape Cod's most cosmopolitan community.

Despite the Cape's tremendous allure, there's nothing like pulling away from the mainland on a ferry, leaving one of the nicest summer resorts in New England for another. Similarities exist between "the Vineyard" and Nantucket: Both have fine, long, sandy beaches, both have remarkable places to stay and undeveloped natural resources. But each has a distinct personality, too; longtime visitors tend to love one or the other. The same probably will be true for you.

Martha's Vineyard is the more casual island, and because of its size it offers more distractions and attractions. The town of Oak Bluffs has an almost carnival-like atmosphere, with its unusual gingerbread houses. Vineyard Haven combines peace and quiet with the benefit of services. Edgartown, filled with fine (and expensive) shops and sea captains' houses, draws a sophisticated crowd. "Up-island," the southwestern corner of the island, remains tranquil and sparsely populated; the dramatic seaside clay cliffs at Gay Head are here. The Vineyard also draws more celebrities (among them Carly Simon, James Taylor, Walter Cronkite, and Mike Wallace) and celebrity-watchers than Nantucket.

Nantucket is smaller and therefore more convenient for touring. Nantucket town, the main town, is picturesque and historic. Cobblestone streets pave the way between pricey antiques shops and art galleries. Gas lanterns light streets that lead to restored 17th- and 18th-century houses, now inns or historical museums. Nantucket town has so many fine restaurants that some two-week visitors, having of necessity made reservations months in advance, eat in a different restaurant every night. The only other town of interest is quiet Siasconset, picture-perfect with its profusion of rosebushes and restored fishermen's cottages. Discreet summer visitors tend toward quiet, catered cocktail parties behind closed doors and beyond the rolling heaths.

If you have to make a choice between the Vineyard and Nantucket, and you have time for only a day trip from the Cape, let it be to Nantucket.

MAJOR INTEREST

Cape Cod
Sandwich Village's 17th-century houses and Heritage Plantation

Nickerson State Park in Brewster
Cape Cod National Seashore
Wellfleet's oysters and art galleries
Provincetown's funky mix of artists and locals
Chatham's grace and gentility
Monomoy National Wildlife Refuge
Falmouth's town green

Martha's Vineyard
Vineyard Haven's tranquil harbor
Gingerbread cottages in Oak Bluffs
Sea captains' houses in Edgartown
Chappaquiddick Island's beaches
Menemsha Harbor at sunset
Cliffs and beach at Gay Head

Nantucket
Whaling Museum
Historic houses and buildings
Restaurants
Siasconset's unspoiled scenery
Bicycling

CAPE COD

The fast-paced traveller could see Cape Cod in a couple of days, but it would be a superficial and exhausting trip. To enjoy the Cape's natural beauty, to explore its picturesque towns, and to taste the bounty of the sea, spend at least a week here. One method of exploring is to base yourself in the middle of the Cape and take day trips to and fro, but that could mean an hour's drive each way every day. Or you could make your way along the peninsula, staying in a different area every night, as we do here: Travel out along Route 6A, skirting Cape Cod Bay, then head north on Route 6 to Provincetown, then travel back along the south shore on Route 28. The best plan might be to combine the two approaches.

From Boston it takes an hour (in light traffic) to reach either of the two high, elegant bridges that cross the Cape Cod Canal. Use the Bourne Bridge if you're coming from the south and heading to Falmouth or the Islands; use the Sagamore Bridge if you're coming from Route 3 in the north and heading to the bay side, Hyannis, or the Outer Cape. In the summer expect bumper-to-bumper traffic heading to the Cape on Fridays and Saturdays and heading off-Cape on Sundays; it's not uncommon for 100,000 cars to cross the canal daily.

Because the Cape's configuration is long and thin, with just two or three roads running the length of it, the towns situated along those roads tend to spill one into the other. This is especially true of the communities along Route 6A, which skirts Cape Cod Bay, and along Route 6 on the Outer Cape.

Summertime visitors make a beeline for the Cape's beaches, many of which, though, restrict parking to permit holders in the summer. If you'll be based in one town, consider heading to its town hall or recreation center to purchase a weekly or seasonal beach-parking permit. The beaches owned by the National Seashore charge a parking fee (you can pay by the day or buy a pass). The beaches themselves are free of charge and open to all, and you can bike or walk to any beach. Many beaches stop checking permits after 4:00 P.M. (and don't check at all on rainy days), so if you prefer to be at the beach when everybody else is in town, there's your chance.

Generally, the protected waters of Cape Cod Bay are shallower and calmer than those of the outer shores, without the dangerous ocean surf. Beaches exposed to Nantucket Sound (on the Cape's south side) are warmer, while beaches on the east coast, exposed to the mighty Atlantic, have good surf, cold water, and a formidable undertow.

The highest of high season officially begins on Memorial Day (late May) and continues through Labor Day (early September), although the month of June—especially before school lets out—is relatively quiet here. Venturing to the Cape in the spring and fall (commonly referred to as the "shoulder seasons") yields lower room rates, less traffic, uncrowded beaches, and good crisp air. Oftentimes there is a brief period of summer-like weather in late October and early November—Indian summer—which is glorious on the Cape. Although Cape Cod has seen a fair amount of snow in recent winters, it is still generally mild, and snow disappears quickly. The majority of Cape establishments are seasonal, but enough restaurants and hostelries remain open all year in each town. Many of the minor attractions and the fancier restaurants close after Labor Day or by mid-October, reopening again in late May or June. When a major sight is not open year-round it has been so indicated in the text that follows.

FROM SANDWICH TO ORLEANS

Route 6, the major highway that runs the length of the Cape from Sandwich to Provincetown, is strictly utilitarian along the stretch eastward to Orleans (it's a little more picturesque on the Outer Cape). But Route 6A, which runs parallel to it on the Cape Cod Bay side, is quieter, more scenic, and less trafficked. Nearly all the inns, restaurants, and sights mentioned below are visible, or easily accessible, from this two-lane road, which stretches 32 miles (51 km), ending at the Orleans rotary. The six towns discussed below are fairly evenly spaced, every six or seven miles or so, along Route 6A, and tend to run one into another.

Sandwich and Environs

Just 56 miles (90 km) southeast of Boston, Sandwich is often bypassed by travellers in a hurry to get somewhere else. But Sandwich is really a microcosm of all the Cape has to offer: a tight-knit community, quaint town green and village center, and an interesting history told in its small museums. Still graceful and charming, it's the oldest town on the Cape, settled in 1627. The numbers above residential doorways (many of them in the 1600s) designate the year the house was built, not the street number.

In the center of town, among a pretty cluster of Colonial buildings, the restored **Hoxie House**, built circa 1637, may be the oldest house on the Cape. It's a good example of a traditional saltbox, a one-story lean-to whose steep roof resembles an old-fashioned box of salt, and is decorated with late-17th-century furnishings. The house is set on lovely Shawme Pond (home to hundreds of duck, geese, and swans), which supplies the power for the **Dexter Grist Mill**, built in the 1650s; cornmeal is still ground and sold daily in season. (Both the house and the mill are open from mid-June to early October; Tel: 508/888-1173.)

Next door, the **Thornton W. Burgess Museum** (Tel: 508/888-4668) displays original illustrations of the children's classic *Peter Cottontail*. Burgess, who said "It's a wonderful thing to sweeten the world which is in a jam and needs preserving," was born in Sandwich in 1874. The "Old Briar Patch" made famous by him as the home of Peter Cottontail is honored at the **Green Briar Nature Center & Jam Kitchen**, 2 miles (3 km) east at 6 Discovery Hill Road (off Route 6A in East Sandwich). The center has a network of nature trails and a delightfully old-fashioned kitchen that has been selling cranberry conserve, beach-plum jelly, and other preserves for more than 80 years.

Sandwich Glass Museum

In the mid-19th century Sandwich was synonymous with superb glassmaking, specifically a delicate, lacy glass pressed in the same type of three-part mold used by the ancient Romans and prized for its subtle colors. Deming Jarves opened his Boston & Sandwich Glass Company in 1825, and by 1850 some 500 people were employed, including skilled European craftsmen. (A labor dispute caused the company to fold in 1888.) To appreciate this highly valued glass, head to the Sandwich Glass Museum, at 129 Main Street, where you'll find a vast array of glass in all styles and colors, as well as dioramas explaining how the glass was made, and learn the interesting fact that sand of the fine quality required to make Jarves's glass had to be shipped in from New Jersey (closed in January; Tel: 508/888-0251).

You can watch master glassmakers blow glass at **Pairpoint Crystal**, the oldest glassworks in America, in Sagamore, 3 miles/5 km west of Sandwich on Route 6A.

Heritage Plantation

A mile (1½ km) southwest of town on Grove Street is Heritage Plantation, formerly the estate of a horticulturist. The plantation encompasses 76 acres of rhododendrons (in bloom from mid-May to mid-June) and more than 1,000 varieties of trees, shrubs, and flowers. American folk art and artifacts are housed in the plantation's impressive buildings of different architectural styles, including a round Shaker barn like the one in Hancock, Massachusetts. The automobile collection includes Gary Cooper's 1931 Duesenberg; the military collection contains a firearm used by Buffalo Bill Cody and 2,000 miniature lead soldiers representing three centuries of American military units; and the art museum boasts an extensive collection of Currier & Ives prints and wooden decoys. Open mid-May to mid-October; Tel: (508) 888-3300.

Sandy Neck Beach

All along Route 6A here are cranberry bogs, salt marshes, old Indian cemeteries, scrub oak and pine trees, little fishing ports, farm stands, pottery shops, and other cottage industries. About 10 miles (16 km) east of Sandwich off Route 6A, just before the Barnstable town line, is Sandy Neck Beach (off the road of the same name). This oasis of dunes and hollows includes an eight-mile-long barrier beach that protects Barnstable Harbor. Although the beach is open year-round to four-wheel-drive vehicles, it's this area's best. Plenty of parking is available (for a fee), and permits for over-sand vehicles may be purchased at the entrance booth. (Early Cape settlers started whaling when whales beached themselves on sand spits like this. Then townspeople would set out for the beach to boil blubber in "tryworks," or caldrons.)

STAYING IN SANDWICH

Centrally located on Main Street, the **Dan'l Webster Inn** offers 47 rooms and suites decorated with reproduction Colonial furnishings. Each room has air conditioning, cable television, telephone, and private bath; there's an outdoor pool on the premises as well. The **Summer House,** on the other side of the street, is the town's nicest bed-and-breakfast. Only one of the five simple rooms has a private bath, but other amenities include a full breakfast, afternoon tea, a glassed-in sun porch, and a hammock in the back yard.

Barnstable

Barnstable's official municipal boundaries are far-reaching. Bustling Hyannis, to the south, is within its township, and so is West Barnstable Village, the center of which is little more than a shop selling stoves and toy trains, a country store, and a train depot. The area was settled in 1639 by a band of separatist parishioners, and thus the West Parish Congregationalist Church, on Route 149, is probably the oldest of its kind in the country. Its church bell was later cast by Paul Revere. Whale-watching excursions are offered from Barnstable's harbor, but don't take one from here if you're planning to go on to Provincetown; the boat ride takes too long.

STAYING IN BARNSTABLE

Arguably the most romantic place to stay on Cape Cod is the **Charles Hinckley House** on Old Kings Highway (a.k.a. Route 6, or Main Street) in Barnstable. Each of the four rooms has private bath, Oriental carpets, fluffy pillows, a down comforter, antiques, a fireplace, and wide-plank floorboards; fresh fruit, bottled water, and freshly cut flowers are set out for new arrivals. Superb breakfasts prepared by Miya Patrick, who is also a caterer, include fresh breads and fruits, coffee in a silver service, and, perhaps, scrambled eggs with salmon and pan-fried new potatoes with capers. The living room has stacks of good magazines and Sherry on hand.

   Beechwood, just east on Route 6A, is a Victorian guesthouse with six light and airy guest rooms, with brass, canopy, or carved beds and private baths with claw-footed tubs.

Rocking chairs sit under the shade of a mighty beech tree. A full country breakfast is included in the price of a room.

Yarmouth Port

Yarmouth Port looks quiet, and it is, with only a few diversions worthy of brief stops. The **Parnassus Book Store**, on Route 6A right in town, is crammed from floor to ceiling with an eclectic and intelligent selection of books; they even spill outside under an awning on the side of the building. The Greek Revival **Captain Bangs Hallet House**, down the street, is filled with Far Eastern treasures obtained during the captain's numerous voyages in the late 19th century. Behind the house are more than 50 acres with botanical trails and a handsome, inviting garden. More or less across the street, the **Winslow Crocker House**, also open to the public (limited hours), contains a fine collection of Early American furnishings. Both houses are open seasonally.

DINING AND STAYING
IN YARMOUTH PORT

Two of Yarmouth Port's more interesting restaurants are like night and day. **Abbicci**, at 43 Main Street, offers a strictly Italian menu. Lunch (moderately priced) and dinner (more expensive) offerings include risotto Milanese and baked penne with four cheeses, *pancetta,* asparagus, and fennel. The interior is chic and sophisticated, with a black slate bar, white linens and china, and contemporary collages hung next to enlarged sections of a map of Italy. (Tel: 508/362-3501.) **Jack's Outback** (behind the small complex at 161 Main Street) has an open kitchen, and menu items are posted on the wall on pieces of paper. The service isn't nearly as surly and gruff as it was before Jack's moved into this new building, but the place is still a local institution. Write your own order and put it on the counter to be served.

Inns in Yarmouth Port, like restaurants, cover a broad spectrum. **Wedgewood**, a finely restored 1812 maritime attorney's home on Main Street, is upscale and sophisticated, yet relaxing. Of the six rooms, four have fireplaces and two are suites with private screened-in porches; a full breakfast is included. Nestled in the woods, **Lane's End Cottage**, a 300-year-old home, offers three simple but thoughtfully furnished rooms. Each has a firm mattress, plenty of hot water, a rocking chair, and books; one has a fireplace and private terrace. The first floor conjures up images of Grandmother's house. A full breakfast is served on the tranquil back patio.

Almost any left turn off Route 6A leads to the ocean. A particularly scenic drive begins on Church Street just after the New Church; take it to Thatcher Shore Road, where a dirt road leads to the bay. Continue to Water Street and cross the one-lane bridge, under which the tide comes rushing in and out. Farther along Route 6A, but still in Yarmouth Port, **One Centre Street Inn** offers seven rooms, most with private bath, and a bountiful buffet breakfast. Rooms are tastefully furnished and accented in period colors. This is a good place for families, as the innkeepers have young ones of their own. At the end of Centre Street (which intersects Route 6A), about 1¼ miles (2 km) past the inn, is **Gray's Beach**, with a long boardwalk that extends a quarter mile out into the marshes.

Dennis

Dennis provides a unique perspective of the Cape's topography that will bring to life the "bared and bended arm" analogy. On a clear day the view from **Scargo Hill Tower**, reached by turning right onto Old Bass River Road next to the town green off Route 6A, extends some 80 miles, taking in the entire peninsula. More than 20,000 years ago the region was covered by glaciers. When they withdrew, leaving enormous moraines that are now Cape Cod, Martha's Vineyard, and Nantucket, huge chunks of ice were stranded. These formed kettle holes, now freshwater ponds that make classic swimming holes, round and deep at the center. You'll see a number of these inland ponds from atop the tower.

STAYING AND DINING IN DENNIS

The **Four Chimneys Inn** is across from one such pond. The large, well-priced guest rooms have a summery feel to them, with natural wood or semigloss floorboards. Most of the nine rooms have a private bath. On the back roads of town, the **Isaiah Hall B&B Inn**, an 1857 farmhouse and converted carriage house, offers 11 rooms, 10 of which have a private bath. Frequent guests include the actors and actresses who perform in the light comedies at the **Cape Playhouse** (summers only; Tel: 508/385-3911); it's just around the corner, off Route 6A.

The **Red Pheasant**, in a historic building on Route 6A, is a good place to try the traditional New England version of seafood chowder: milk based, with corn, potatoes, scallops, and cherrystone clams. The Red Pheasant grills swordfish nicely and is also adept with game and veal. The wine list is superb in both selection and price. Dinner only; reservations recommended; Tel: (508) 385-2133.

Brewster

The beach scene in Brewster is typical of that of other towns on the bay. Beaches are family-oriented, and at low tide you can walk out two miles, exploring tide pools in the flats. Although Brewster has no harbor, it's said to have been home to more sea captains, masters, and mates than any other town its size. Their homes are not open to the public (though some have been converted to inns), but you will notice them if you take a few minutes to drive around the back roads off Route 6A.

Stony Brook Road leads to the **Herring Run and Stony Brook Grist Mill**. Take a right turn off Route 6A immediately after crossing the Brewster town line to reach the mill; its parking lot is visible from the intersection of Stony Brook and Setucket roads. In this very picturesque little area a waterwheel in the brook powers machinery that grinds corn into meal (the mill is open only in summer). If you're here in April you'll have a real treat: foot-long herring, also called alewives, run upstream through a series of fish ladders to spawn in the freshwater ponds where they were hatched. The mill is open only in the summer.

Retrace your tracks back to Route 6A and venture 1 mile (1½ km) farther east to find the **Cape Cod Museum of Natural History**, with hands-on exhibits for children, including a working beehive, as well as nature walks and talks about native salt-marsh flora and fauna. Tel: (508) 896-3867.

Nickerson State Park
Once the personal hunting and fishing preserve of railroad magnate Roland Nickerson, Nickerson State Park consists of 1,955 acres with trails, wooded campsites (the best on the Cape; no reservations accepted; Tel: 508/896-3491), and freshwater ponds for fishing and swimming. The park is located at the eastern edge of town on Route 6A, just a few miles from the center of Brewster.

The **Cape Cod Rail Trail**, a 20-mile-long, eight-foot-wide paved bicycle trail, passes through Nickerson. Once the bed of the Penn Central Rail Road, the trail begins in South Dennis and links up with trails at the National Seashore in Eastham (construction is expected to begin in spring 1993 to extend the trail into South Wellfleet). Many people start at Nickerson because of the convenient parking and the bike-rental shop (seasonal). Another bike-rental shop, **Idle Times**, on Route 6 in Eastham, is open year-round, but closed

Tuesdays and Wednesdays. The generally flat trail—also used by joggers and horseback riders—passes through dunes, ponds, scrub pine, a horse farm, and cranberry bogs.

STAYING AND DINING IN BREWSTER

Unknown to many visitors simply because it is off the beaten path, **High Brewster** offers fine food and lodging. The 1738 homestead consists of four guest rooms and three dining rooms with low ceilings, ladder-back chairs, and burnished barnboard walls. Highly regarded American country dinners are served at a fixed price. You might also have a drink before dinner on the three and a half acres of grounds overlooking a tranquil pond. Three quaint private cottages with complete kitchens on the property are rented by the week. Overnight guests receive a full breakfast. To reach High Brewster turn right onto Stony Brook Road from Route 6A just after crossing the town line, then right onto Setucket Road.

A couple of miles east on Route 6A, the **Captain Freeman Inn** overlooks Brewster's town green and its classic country store. Recently completely renovated, the inn's 12 rooms are varied: Luxury suites have a whirlpool, fireplace, and video-cassette player; regular rooms have a private bath and Victorian reproduction furnishings; and three rooms, available only in the summer, share one bath. Full breakfast and use of the pool are included in the rate.

Another mile farther east is the **Old Sea Pines Inn**, built in 1907 as the School of Charm and Personality for Young Women. Of its 21 rooms, five were converted from dormitory rooms (two of those have twin beds) and share baths; others have brass, iron, or wooden beds. The adjacent North Cottage building is more like a motel. Common space in the main building includes a large living room with a fireplace, wraparound porch, and enclosed porches where a full breakfast is served.

Brewster boasts some of the Cape's best restaurants. The **Bramble Inn & Restaurant**, on Route 6A in the center of town, offers a fixed-price menu; service and dress are formal, the cuisine New England (Tel: 508/896-7644). For fine (and pricey) French nouvelle, **Chillingsworth**, 2449 Main Street, is hard to beat. The chef/owner's classic haute cuisine is influenced by American nouvelle. Though service is sometimes less impressive than the superb cuisine, you'll dine amid elegant 18th-century furnishings. Open for lunch and dinner; Tel: (508) 896-3640.

For a quick and informal meal of fresh fish, the nearby **Brewster Fish House**, 2208 Main Street, is consistently good. Lobster is usually on the menu as are such saltwater fish as flounder, sole, cod, and scrod (young cod or salmon, often the catch of the day). Open for lunch and dinner; Tel: (508) 896-7867.

Orleans

Orleans, at the intersection of Routes 6 and 6A (and Route 28, which runs along the Cape's south shore), has two aspects: a quiet seaside town along both the bay and ocean and a boisterous commercial crossroads where numerous shops, bars, and quick-stop restaurants provide necessary conveniences. The most picturesque parts of town are around Rock Harbor, on Cape Cod Bay, and the inlets of **Little Pleasant Bay**, formed by a long barrier beach on the ocean side of town. **Nauset Beach**, with ample parking, changing facilities, lots of youth, and a good clam shack, extends for some 15 miles along the Atlantic Ocean.

Orleans was named after the duc d'Orléans (Louis Philippe, later king of France), who visited in 1797 while in exile after the French Revolution. Orleans is also connected to Brest, France: 4,000 miles of underwater telegraph cable were laid in 1879, honored by the **French Cable Station Museum** (41 South Orleans Road; open only in summer). The museum contains all the Morse code equipment that was in use until 1959, when the cable station was closed.

DINING AND STAYING IN ORLEANS

Orleans residents have always made their livelihood from deep-sea fishing and harvesting shellfish. In Rock Harbor, home to one of the Cape's largest charter-fishing fleets, **Cap't Cass** is a particularly quaint seafood shack offering clams, lobster, and other seafood for sit-down lunches and dinners. The specialty is lobster, which are brought up in the restaurant's own traps. Clams are classified as littlenecks (the smallest, containing the most tender meat), cherrystones (about 2½ inches in diameter and often minced for clam chowder), quahogs (pronounced "CO-hog"; hardshelled, fist-size things, often stuffed, cut, and fried, or used in stews and chowder), or steamers (soft-shelled, longneck clams, usually steamed, hence their name).

In the center of Orleans at the corner of Route 6A and Cove Road, the **Land Ho! Tavern** is a fun local hangout, good for lunch or a casual dinner, serving fried fish, burgers, chowder, and kale soup (Portuguese style). At 212 Main Street in East Orleans, on the way to Nauset Beach, **Kadee's Lobster & Clam Bar** serves very fresh lobster and fish at reasonable prices. Eat in a casual indoor setting, outside under umbrellas, or get your order from a takeout window;

lunch and dinner are served. Lobster, usually boiled and served with butter sauce, is also found in lobster rolls and lobster chowder. **Fancy's Farm**, across the street, has good baked items and picnic fixings.

Right down the street, the **Nauset House Inn**, one of the best places to stay in the area, is just a ten-minute walk from **Nauset Beach**. Some of the 14 rooms have private decks, more than half have a private bath, and a few are quite large. Common space includes a comfortable living room and a large greenhouse/conservatory; there are plenty of lawn chairs on the grounds.

THE OUTER CAPE

Route 6A joins Route 6 in Orleans, from which point they run up the spine of the Outer Cape as a single road until North Truro, where they split again. The distance from Eastham, the next town north, up to Provincetown is 29 miles (46 km). The Cape is so narrow here that each town occupies the entire width, first Eastham, then Wellfleet (including South Wellfleet), then Truro and North Truro, and finally Provincetown. The gems of the Outer Cape are the pristine National Seashore, a ruggedly beautiful stretch of long sandy beaches along the Atlantic, and artsy Provincetown. There's nothing else quite like these places in the United States.

Cape Cod National Seashore

In 1961 President John F. Kennedy, passionate about the ocean and recognizing the inherent value of these historic lands, set aside this 43,500-acre preserve that stretches 40 miles from Chatham Light (at the Cape's "elbow") to the lighthouse at the tip of Provincetown, encompassing much of Eastham, Wellfleet, and Truro. At present the National Seashore actually owns only 27,000 of those acres; the remaining are owned by the various towns or the Commonwealth of Massachusetts. Two visitors' centers, one in Eastham (open year-round; weekends only from January to mid-February), the other in Provincetown (closed from Thanksgiving to late March), anchor the seashore and provide a wealth of information, including how unusual geological processes shaped the Cape. The nature trails around both centers are accessible year-round; beaches and trails are discussed within the towns that follow.

Remember, you can park at National Seashore beaches for a daily fee, or, for longer stays, purchase a beach pass.

Many beaches within the Seashore's boundaries are operated by the town and thus require a resident parking sticker. Parking fees and stickers are required only in season and before 4:00 P.M.

Eastham

The first stop on our tour of the Outer Cape is the **Fort Hill** area, a good introduction to the National Seashore. A panoramic view of Nauset Marsh opens before you; a two-mile walking trail leads down into the Red Maple Swamp, filled with aromatic bayberry and red maples, especially beautiful in the fall. To the south you'll see the break in the sand where Orleans' Nauset Beach ends and Eastham's Coast Guard Beach begins (the latter discussed below). The **Edward Penniman House**, which you'll pass on the right, was built for a successful New Bedford whaling captain in 1867. The cupola is dramatic; vintage photographs are displayed inside. Reservations are often needed to visit the house; Tel: (508) 255-3421.

The Wampanoag Indians occupied Cape Cod for nearly 3,500 years before the Pilgrims arrived in 1620. The two groups first encountered one another in Eastham (pronounced "east-HAM," not "EAST-um"), at the aptly named First Encounter Beach, on the bay. At this "first encounter" Myles Standish and his exploration party from the *Mayflower* were attacked with arrows and fired back with muskets; surprisingly, there were no casualties, and subsequent meetings were more peaceful. The Wampanoag were understandably hostile to the intruders, because the last English settlers they encountered had kidnapped some of them to sell in Spain. A plaque at the beach commemorates this meeting. To get to First Encounter Beach, turn off Route 6 at the Cape's oldest **windmill**, dating to 1793. In case you're wondering if you missed Eastham's town center, there really isn't one. Eastham is more or less spread out along the highway.

Beaches and Ponds

Eastham has two beautiful beaches: **Nauset Light Beach** (not to be confused with Nauset Beach in Eastham), with a picturesque lighthouse, and **Coast Guard Beach**. (Coast Guard Beach was the setting for *The Outermost House,* Henry Beston's account of his year living on the beach; see the Bibliography.) Both beaches are beyond the Salt Pond Visitors' Center (closed late December to mid-February; Tel: 508/255-3421) off Route 6, from which there's a bucolic view of Salt Pond. **Salt Pond** was originally a freshwater "kettle" before the ocean broke through and connected it to Nauset Marsh and the Atlantic. At the visitors' center there are interpretive exhibits and educational films, including one on the site of a prehistoric Indian settlement (occupied ca. 8,000 to 1,000 B.C.) discovered accidentally in 1990 on Coast Guard Beach. A film shown every half hour, *The Sands of Time,* describes how the coastline is constantly being re-worked as currents carry sands northward and deposit them at the tip of Provincetown, how five acres of land a year are lost because of shifting sands and erosion, and how tena-cious plants stabilize fragile dunes against wind erosion and human assaults.

STAYING IN EASTHAM

Eastham offers two fine places to spend a night or two. The very Victorian **Overlook Inn**, on Route 6 just 3 miles (5 km) north of the Orleans rotary, has ten distinctive guest rooms, all with private bath. Common rooms are filled with Nige-rian art, a handsome pool table, Winston Churchill memen-tos, and large paintings by the innkeeper's son. Afternoon tea and a full breakfast are included; bike trails pass the back door.

A mile (1½ km) southeast of the Orleans rotary (where Routes 28, 6, and 6A meet), near Rock Harbor, the **Whale-walk Inn** offers 12 well-appointed guest rooms, suites (some with a kitchen), and a quaint saltbox cottage on the peaceful grounds. Decor and baths have been nicely updated, but traditional elements of a sea captain's home remain. A full breakfast is served on the quiet patio.

Wellfleet

South of Wellfleet Center on the bay side, just over the town line from Eastham, is the **Wellfleet Bay Wildlife Sanctuary**, operated by the Massachusetts Audubon Society. Within the 1,000 acres of woods and marshlands, the din of traffic and the hordes of tourists recede. The sanctuary offers bird-watching tours of Monomoy National Wildlife Refuge (see Chatham, below), boat tours of Pleasant Bay (between Chatham and Orleans), Cape Cod Bay, and Nauset Marsh, and seal-watching trips in the winter. Tel: (508) 349-2615.

On the Atlantic side in South Wellfleet are Marconi Beach, Marconi Station, and the Atlantic White Cedar Swamp Trail. One of the seashore's finest, and one of the few remaining of its kind, the **Atlantic White Cedar Swamp Trail** passes through stands of pitch pine, scrub oak, and beach grass; a portion of the trail is actually a boardwalk suspended over the swamp. The trail opens onto the old road to the **Marconi Wireless Station**, from where Nobel prize–winning Italian physicist Guglielmo Marconi transmitted the world's first wireless message in 1903, an official communiqué between President Roosevelt and King Edward VII of England. Only the concrete foundations of the station's original 200-foot towers remain, the victims of storms and dune erosion. **Marconi Beach** is a broad, sandy, cliff-backed beach run by the National Seashore.

Farther north on Wellfleet's Atlantic coast are **Lecount Hollow**, **White Crest** (popular with surfers), **Cahoon Hollow**, and **Newcomb Hollow** (considered the best beach by locals) beaches, all accessible along Ocean View Drive, reached off Route 6 by Lecount Hollow or Cahoon Hollow roads in South Wellfleet and Long Pond, Gross Hill, or Gull Pond roads up by Wellfleet center. These last three roads lead to some of Wellfleet's wonderful freshwater ponds. Traditionally, Fleetians hit the beaches at midday and then head to the ponds in late afternoon to wash off the sand and salt.

Wellfleet Center, less than two miles wide in parts, is a rare place around here, a town little touched by tee-shirt and souvenir shops. The streets in Wellfleet Center, off Route 6 just south of the Truro town line, are lined with art galleries and antiques shops, and the town remains a vibrant summer artists' colony. On Saturday evenings in season some of the 20-odd galleries, which line Commercial Street between Main Street and the pier, host receptions with the artists. Many of Wellfleet's visitors come for the entire summer, lending a distinctly non-transient feel to the quaint town. Wellfleet's active, working harbor also tempers the influence of summer visitors; it's an omnipresent reminder that art and commerce can coexist. Wellfleet boasts the only church in the world, the **First Congregational Church** (on Main Street), that keeps ship's time: Two bells signify one, five, and nine o'clock; four bells designate two, six, and ten o'clock; six bells ring at three, seven, and eleven o'clock; and eight bells mean it's four, eight, or twelve o'clock. To make it even more complicated, bells are struck on the half hour, too.

Great Island, west of town in Cape Cod Bay, is no longer an island. As recently as 1831 it did stand alone, but currents created sandbars that eventually connected it to the mainland. Because of soft sand, the eight-mile (round trip) foot trail here is the National Seashore's most strenuous. The drive out from the center of town on Commercial Street, past the pier, and on around the harbor on Chequesset Neck Road is pretty. In 1982 Billingsgate Island, off the tip of Great Island (its visibility depends on the tide), yielded an archaeological find, an 18th-century pirate ship, called the *Whydah*. (The Provincetown Museum, discussed below, displays findings from the ship.)

Oysters and Clams

Wellfleet has been famous for oysters since 1606, when French explorer Samuel de Champlain tasted them and promptly named the harbor Oyster Port. After 1770, when the beds inexplicably died out, oysters were brought up from Chesapeake Bay and bedded here. Today Wellfleet leads New England in the cultivation of oysters. The oysters grow on the surface of the sand, and at low tide the harbor is active with commercial shell fishing. Oysters, also found in Chatham, are usually eaten raw here, freshly "shucked," or on the half shell with a bit of lemon and tangy horseradish seafood sauce. Oyster aficionados prefer oysters plucked from colder winter waters rather than the warm waters of summer, hence the adage that you should eat oysters only in months with an "r" in them.

Wellfleet may be the place you experience an authentic New England clambake. Prepared on a sandy beach as the Native Americans did it, a clambake is quite a time-consuming undertaking. This is basically how it's done: Dig a huge but shallow pit in the sand, start a fire with charcoal and wood in the pit, then clear away the burning wood and place rocks on the charcoal. Place a layer of seaweed on the hot rocks; add layers of live lobsters, clams (dug that morning), and ears of corn and potatoes wrapped in foil or cheesecloth; top that with another layer of seaweed. The back-yard approach is simpler: Add a few inches of clean seawater to a large pot, bring it to a boil, put live lobsters on the bottom, and cover them with a layer of seaweed. Then add ears of corn, more seaweed, and a layer of soft-shell clams (steamers). The whole concoction is ready when the steamers open. Dip your clams into the leftover broth to wash off any sand still clinging them, then dip them in melted butter. Small contained fires are permitted on the beach, but you must contact the Wellfleet Fire Department to discuss the details.

DINING AND STAYING IN WELLFLEET

If you'd rather have someone else do the cooking, visit the **Bayside Lobster Hutt**, in town on Commercial Street. The former oyster shack offers self-serve, informal dining indoors at picnic tables. Choose your own lobster from the tank and accompany it with corn on the cob, steamers, or something from the raw bar. Bring your own wine or beer. Keep in mind that before lobsters shed their shells in the early summer they are difficult to break open. In August, though, a lobster's shell is thin and can be pried open without tools.

The best choice among finer restaurants is **Aesop's Tables** on Main Street, serving New American cuisine in six dining rooms in an old summer mansion. They also serve a popular Sunday brunch and have a quiet, intimate bar upstairs. Open from mid-May to mid-October; Tel: (508) 349-6450. **Cielo**, a gallery/café on East Main Street, seats just 16 people a night for a fixed menu of New American cuisine. Cielo overlooks a marsh and is best appreciated for an à la carte lunch. Dinner by advance reservation only; Tel: (508) 349-2108. In the summer you can get a casual, moderately priced lunch or dinner at the **Flying Fish Café** on Briar Lane, right off Main Street. Year-round you can dine with the locals at the **Lighthouse Restaurant**, on Main Street, which is famous for its blueberry muffins. The lunch and dinner menu is varied and inexpensive; the kale soup is always good and hearty.

The **Holden Inn**, in the center of town on Commercial Street, offers inexpensive, basic rooms (no frills) with and without bath. On Main Street just off Route 6, the **Inn at Duck Creeke** has 25 well-priced, pleasant rooms (with shared or private bath) in three different buildings. Two rooms in the inn's Carriage House have exposed barnboard and cathedral ceilings. Third-floor rooms in the main house are smaller, more rustic, and air conditioned out of necessity.

Truro

Truro and North Truro are sleepy little towns, with three-quarters of their combined area owned by the National Park Service. On the back roads around here the landscape is rather wild and barren. **Pamet Harbor**, on the bay side, is particularly pretty at dusk. Off North Pamet Road, on the opposite side of Route 6, the **Cranberry Bog Trail** affords a close-up view of the berry that has such an important role in the traditional Thanksgiving dinner. The quiet center of Truro is home to **jams, inc.**, right off Route 6, which sells upscale treats like pâté, rotisserie chicken, imported cheese, and Chardonnay. Professionals who summer in the big houses on the bay flock here to pick up *The New York Times*.

The Pilgrims almost settled in Truro after Myles Standish discovered a cluster of Indian homes and a cache of Indian corn in the area now called Corn Hill. Standish plundered the stash, but upon meeting the owner a year later he promptly paid for the corn. In North Truro at **Pilgrim Heights**, Pilgrim Springs Trail leads to the site where it is believed the Pilgrims first found fresh water in 1620. The

Atlantic waters off Truro are some of the most treacherous for boats on the Cape, which is why the U.S. government chose it as the site for the Cape's first lighthouse, Highland Light (1797). The present light was rebuilt in 1857 after dunes crumbled underneath it; today it is again threatened by erosion. The beaches at **Head of the Meadow** in North Truro are among the Cape's finest.

There isn't much in the way of restaurants or accommodations in Truro, which remains relatively unspoiled. **Adrian's**, on Route 6A, which branches off from Route 6 in North Truro, is a homey, popular breakfast place. The **Truro Motor Inn**, on Route 6 in North Truro, has 36 inexpensive, no-frills rooms and housekeeping cottages, as well as a pool.

Just before you reach Provincetown, enormous sand dunes begin to infringe on the highway. The drama of this sight never recedes, even after you have made countless approaches. There's an extensive network of trails for overland four-wheel-drive vehicles; dune tours can be arranged at **Art's Dune Tours** (Tel: 508/487-1950), a good way to see how dunes are shaped and reshaped by the winds. (In winter the dunes sometimes drift across the road, and in very high winds blowing sand can blast the paint right off your car.)

Off to the left, on Route 6A (visible from Route 6), are tiny, identical cottages all in a row on the bay. On the opposite side, lines of gulls perch atop the dune straddling Pilgrim Lake and the Atlantic shore.

PROVINCETOWN

Provincetown is many things to many people. Gays and lesbians congregate openly; AIDS benefits and women's crafts stores are visible and well supported. The quality of light has attracted artists for almost a century, and today there are more than 30 galleries, ranging from traditional to avant-garde. Pastel portrait artists eke out a living here, as do owners of crystal and leather shops. Tee-shirt emporiums vie for visitors' dollars with sophisticated clothing boutiques; tawdry bars abut trendy cafés. Portuguese from the Azores and Cape Verde Islands fish the waters and bake wonderful breakfast treats. Female impersonators share the streets with families eating saltwater taffy. Sun and beach worshipers revel in the sand that surrounds them on three sides.

Wintertime in "P-town" brings a keen sense of isolation to the 4,000 or so hardy souls who choose to brave the damp cold, unemployment, and loneliness. It's a chilly but peaceful time to visit; a few good restaurants and lodging places remain open year-round. In summer the town's population swells more than tenfold, and the place doesn't feel so remote—about 100 miles from Boston overland or 40 miles across the bay on the Boston–Provincetown boat (see Getting Around, below)

In July and August the main, one-lane, one-way thoroughfare, **Commercial Street**, becomes nearly impassable, with cyclists, rollerskaters, window shoppers, and a steady stream of cars going nowhere slowly. (Do yourself a favor and park in one of the central lots right away; there are lots on the wharves and next to the Pilgrim Memorial Museum.) About three miles from one end to the other, the street skirts the bay and is home to most of the town's tourist facilities. Bradford Street runs parallel to it. The town, just a few blocks wide, takes about five minutes to traverse—and more than an hour to stroll the length of along Commercial Street. The East End (east of MacMillan Wharf) is home to writers, artists, and galleries, while the West End has fine 18th- and 19th-century houses and is closer to the dunes at the tip of the Cape. For the establishments that follow, the number in parentheses corresponds to the establishment's location on Commercial Street; our coverage goes from east to west. (Note that many places do not accept credit cards.)

THE ARTS IN PROVINCETOWN

Artists from New York's Greenwich Village came to Provincetown in the early 1900s, and in 1914 the **Provincetown Art Association and Museum** (460) was established. The permanent collection consists of 1,600 pieces of American art by artists who have worked in town. The museum also mounts special exhibits of its more than 800 member-artists. Call for hours in the off-season; Tel: (508) 487-1750. More fine shows are held at the **Fine Arts Work Center**, 24 Pearl Street. The center has an auction in August, but otherwise the art displayed is not for sale. Pick up a copy of the *Provincetown Gallery Guide,* dispensed at most of the galleries and at the chamber of commerce, to help pinpoint your specific interests—be they abstract, impressionistic, or realistic works—before setting off to explore Provincetown's galleries.

Playwrights Tennessee Williams and Eugene O'Neill worked in Provincetown in their early years. O'Neill's close association with the Provincetown Players began in 1916, when *Bound East for Cardiff* was produced. Rebelling against the rigid dictates of Broadway, the Provincetown Players came into existence about the same time that Provincetown was becoming a prestigious artists' colony, attracting the likes of John Dos Passos and Sinclair Lewis.

SHOPPING IN PROVINCETOWN

Shopping and art often go hand in hand in Provincetown. Intersperse gallery-hopping with visits to some of the interesting shops along Commercial Street: **Llama** (382) sells international folk art, kilims, and African tribal masks and musical instruments; the **Susan Baker Memorial Museum** (379) hawks irreverent tee-shirts, prints, and other objects created by the owner (still very much alive); **Northern Lights Leather** (361) offers fine leather jackets, bags, and belts; and **Impulse** (188) displays kaleidoscopes, American crafts, and jewelry. Usually by mid-October shops begin their end-of-the-season sales, which can yield substantial savings.

MACMILLAN PIER

"Cape of the Cod" got its name when English explorer Bartholomew Gosnold, exploring the coast from Maine to Narragansett Bay in 1602, saw "the great store of cod-fish" teeming off its shallow, sandy banks. Fishing soon became the backbone of the area's economy; fishermen were even exempt from military service. Cod, because it lent itself to being salted and preserved, was the area's most important fish, and was adopted as the symbol of the Massachusetts Bay Colony. Today a stuffed and mounted codfish, representing the importance of cod fishing, hangs in the State House in Boston.

One hundred years ago more than 60 wharves lined the harbor in Provincetown; today there are three. Fishing fleets come into the harbor at MacMillan Wharf in the late afternoon to unload the day's catch. In late June the **Blessing of the Fleet**, a religious celebration in which boats receive a priest's blessing (with seafood feasts, festivities, and lots of locals from all over the Cape in the streets and bars) honors fishermen, their families, and the town's history.

In the mid-1800s Provincetown was America's third largest whaling center, after New Bedford and Nantucket. While the schooners and whalers have been replaced by motorboats and yachts, ships still set out from MacMillan Wharf in search of the leviathans. The **Dolphin Fleet**, sailing from mid-April to October, has naturalists on board and offers the best trips. Reservations should be made a few days in advance in the summer; Tel: (800) 826-9300 or (508) 349-1900. Occasionally whales can be seen with the naked eye from the Coast Guard Station or Race Point (discussed below).

The chamber of commerce (Tel: 508/487-3424), located on MacMillan Wharf, carries the *Provincetown Gallery Guide,* maps, and information on the historical society's walking tours.

HISTORIC PROVINCETOWN

The *Mayflower* Pilgrims, blown off their original course, first touched American soil (or sand, in this case) in Provincetown on November 21, 1620. After spending five weeks here they decided the area was too rugged and sandy and headed to what is now Plymouth. A small plaque at the traffic rotary where Commercial Street ends commemorates their time here. The most visible tribute to their arrival is the granite **Pilgrim Memorial Monument**, modeled after the Torre del Mangia in Siena and completed in 1910. To reach the monument from Commercial Street, walk up Gosnold Street to Winslow Street and look up; you can't miss it, perched atop High Pole Hill. Climb the 252-foot-high tower for a 360-degree view of the natural landscape; on a clear day you can see all the way to Boston Harbor.

At the base of the monument, the small but excellent **Provincetown Museum** (Tel: 508/487-1310) houses a diorama of the *Mayflower,* whaling artifacts, and photographs of the burgeoning artists' and writers' communities here. The museum's conservation laboratory is examining the plunder from an 18th-century pirate ship, the *Whydah,* recently retrieved from waters off Wellfleet. Cannon, jewels, and pirate clothing from the ship are on display at least through 1993, but Tampa, Florida, has been awarded the rights to display the *Whydah,* and how much of the ship's legacy will remain in Provincetown is uncertain. Editorialists in Boston would have you believe that Boston lost its bid for the *Whydah* to be docked in the Charlestown Navy Yard because of political infighting and a lack of support and cohesion within Boston's business community.

Topped with an octagonal belfry and therefore a prominent landmark, the old Center Methodist Church, at Commercial and Center streets in the center of town, houses the **Heritage Museum**, filled with maritime items, Victorian artifacts, and a large model of the *Rose Dorothea,* a Grand Banks fishing schooner. Open mid-June to mid-October; Tel: (508) 487-7098.

Toward the west end of Commercial Street at number 72, the **Seth Nickerson House**, built in 1746 (the oldest in town, and now privately owned), typifies Cape Cod architecture. It's interior was built with materials scavenged from shipwrecks.

From 1818 until 1876 there was a fishing settlement out at **Long Point**, at the peninsula's very tip. After it was abandoned the houses were floated across the harbor on barges to Provincetown. Today a number of houses in town sport a little blue plaque bearing the likeness of a house on a barge to signify their history.

RACE POINT BEACH
AND THE PROVINCE LANDS

The Cape Cod National Seashore encompasses the entire tip of Provincetown. Route 6 leads directly to Race Point Beach and the Province Lands Visitor Center. You can also drive out from the west end of Commercial Street, circling around past Herring Cove Beach and on to Race Point.

The **Province Lands Visitor Center** (closed late December to mid-February; Tel: 508/487-1256) maintains extensive nature and bicycle trails. The eight-mile bike trail, the seashore's steepest and most beautiful, traverses forests, bogs, long stretches of moors, and dunes. Dunes encroaching on forests are visible from an observation tower. Bicycles can be rented in town.

Race Point Beach, complete with lighthouse, and **Herring Cove Beach** are two of the Cape's finest. This is the only area on the eastern seaboard where you can watch the sun set over the ocean (from bay beaches in Eastham, Wellfleet, and Truro you can see it sink into Cape Cod Bay).

STAYING IN PROVINCETOWN

High tide reaches the lower deck of the **Watermark Inn** (603), perhaps the nicest place to stay in Provincetown. The ten contemporary suites have plenty of windows or sliding glass doors for taking in the view of the sunset. Some also have a kitchenette, private deck, skylights, angled ceilings, and a loft. The **Ship's Bell Motel** (586), closed in the winter, has 23 rooms (all with private bath), efficiencies, and apartments, some with views and balconies. The **Windamar House** (568), in a nicely restored mid-19th-century home, has six tasteful rooms sharing three baths, and two apartments available by the week. Front rooms have views of the water across the street. **Surfside** (543) has 84 motel-style rooms, a quarter of which are on the beach. The heated pool and four-story brick buildings that straddle Commercial Street are quite noticeable in a town of small-scale operations.

Frank Schaefer has been welcoming artists, writers, and anyone who appreciates Provincetown into his **White Horse Inn** (500) since the early 1960s. A bohemian sensibility pervades the 12 rooms (most with shared baths), decorated with more than 300 paintings and sculptures by local artists; the six studio apartments are eclectically furnished. The **Hargood House** (493), one of the few places on the water, has 19 one- and two-bedroom apartments. Many have water views and decks, and all have private entrances and share the green lawn and lounge chairs above the beach.

At the western end of Commercial Street, the **Masthead** (31–41) has rooms overlooking the water, and one-, two- and three-bedroom apartments and cottages. All of the individualized units share the private beach and broad lawn. **Land's End Inn** (22) is an 1890s summer house furnished with Victorian antiques. There are 16 rooms, all with private bath. The living room showcases an extensive glass collection and the solarium is filled with plants. The view from the inn's large lawn and small lily pond encompasses dunes, bay, and harbor. During the summer a seven-night stay is requested.

DINING IN PROVINCETOWN

The following tour of restaurants begins back in the East End. Go to **Pucci's Harborside** (539; Tel: 508/487-1964) for unsophisticated, solid American food and meal-size appetizers; entrées are moderately priced. Two struggling artists began **Ciro & Sal's** (just off Commercial Street at 4 Kiley Court; Tel: 508/487-0049) in a brick cellar accented with Chianti bottles almost 40 years ago. To this day the very popular old standby serves substantial portions of reliable Italian fare (dinner only). It's usually crowded, and there's often a wait, even with reservations. **Pepe's Wharf Restaurant** (371; Tel: 508/487-0670), in the same family for 25 years, offers nicely prepared seafood for lunch and dinner. The **Mews Restaurant** (359; Tel: 508/487-1500), tucked away on the beach, is a quiet, intimate place with good Continental food and fine service.

Stop at one of the **Portuguese Bakeries** (338 and 299) for authentic sweet breads (Portuguese sweet bread, that is—not sweetbreads) and pastries. One flight up from the street (and thus often overlooked) is **Café Edwige** (333; Tel: 508/487-2008), a popular breakfast place with outstanding danishes. The dinner menu emphasizes seafood, and it's all well priced, sophisticated, and creative. Across the street, the highly visible **Café Blasé** (328; Tel: 508/487-9465) serves expensive coffee and mediocre food. Don't let the giant neon lobster in front of the **Lobster Pot** (321; no reservations) deter you from waiting in the long hallway to have fresh, simply prepared seafood overlooking the beach. Lunch specials are reasonable.

The interior of **Napi's** (7 Freeman Street; Tel: 508/487-1145) is as eclectic as the menu is extensive and the food tasty. The best place in Provincetown for vegetarians, Napi's also happily accommodates special diets. Napi's is open for dinner in the summer and all three meals in the winter. **Stormy Harbor** (277; Tel: 508/487-1680), a nondescript place across from the town hall, serves steaming hot Italian dishes with homemade sauces. Takeout sandwiches rolled on Lebanese bread are the specialty at the branch of the **Box Lunch** hidden in the Whaler's Wharf shopping complex (237).

The dinner menu changes weekly at **Front Street** (230; Tel: 508/487-9715), which may be the best restaurant in town. The limited Continental and Italian menu always includes a pasta, a veal, a chicken, a meat, and a shrimp entrée. The casually elegant bistro in the basement is decorated with high wooden booths, exposed brick walls, and local artwork. Even if you don't get one of the few tables outside at **Café Express** (214; next to the New Art Cinema), the coffee is worth drinking inside or out. **Café Heaven** (199; Tel: 508/487-9639), a casual place with large canvases covering the walls, is popular for all three moderately priced meals. Frequented by a thirtysomething crowd of gay regulars and out-of-towners, the café serves a variety of salads, pastas, sandwiches, and soups. Across the street, **Spiritus** (190) serves rich baked goods and delicious cappuccino and pizzas. **Franco's by the Sea** (186; Tel: 508/487-3178) offers nicely prepared Italian, Cajun, and New American cuisine on the harbor, but the service can be a bit uppity.

Most visitors don't make it down as far as **Gallerani's** (133; Tel: 508/487-4433), and even if they did, the Naugahyde booths and wooden tables would probably scare them off. Locals, though, indulge in spicy Mexican omelets for breakfast and appreciate being able to order half portions at dinner. Grilled and Italian dishes are the most popular. Practically out on the moors, the **Moors Restaurant** (5 Bradford Street West; Tel: 508/487-0840) specializes in Portuguese food, such as *espada cozida* (swordfish in lemon juice, olive oil, and garlic) and *caldeirada a portuguesa* (crab, clams, mussels, shrimp, and fish in a tomato sauce with herbs and wine). Open for lunch and dinner.

THE SOUTH SHORE
Chatham

In the mid-1800s Chatham was the terminus of the railroad that brought wealthy vacationers to Cape Cod. That same railroad also transported local commodities such as salt and fish off the Cape. As a result, a lot of money flowed in and out of Chatham. Today it is a graceful and sophisticated place, a residential town that exudes gentility. At the "elbow" of Cape Cod, Chatham is a natural bridge between the solitude of the Outer Cape and the hubbub of the south shore.

From Orleans take Route 28 south 6 miles (10 km) to Chatham, passing pine forests and lovely Pleasant Bay. Once in Chatham, browse along Main Street, lined with fine and distinctive shops, art galleries, an **information booth** (Tel: 508/945-0342), and lodging places with neatly manicured lawns. In many ways Chatham embodies the great American myth or dream, depending on your politics. On Friday evenings in summer, townsfolk and visitors gather 5,000-strong at **Kate Gould Park** for concerts. Families picnic, children dance, and adults sing along while a brass band plays waltzes, bunny hops, and ballads. Meanwhile, Chatham's **Veterans Field** comes alive with minor-league baseball. There are ten teams in the Cape Cod Baseball League, and the games, like the band concerts, are free.

Head to the **Fish Pier**, one of the most active ports on the Cape, to watch the boats return in the late afternoon. Because local fishermen use small boats, they must return to shore each day. Accordingly, fish is as fresh as it gets—unless, of course, you try to catch something from the drawbridge on Bridge Street as the townfolk do. The scallops harvested in Chatham's waters tend to be large sea scallops; however, smaller and more delicate bay scallops, harvested in the late fall, are also available at the pier's fish market.

Chatham residents, more than those of many other towns on the Cape, are forced to contend with Mother Nature. A barrier beach sheltered Chatham's inner harbor and shoreline until 1987, when a violent storm destroyed a part of the beach. The Chatham Breakthrough, as it's called, is now a hotly debated issue, pitting environmental purists, who want to leave it as is, against property owners, who want to create some kind of new barrier. A northeaster (or "nor'easter," a coastal storm that develops north and east of the coastline, bringing heavy rains, tidal flooding, and gale-force winds) in June 1992 caused another break in the barrier beach, reminding residents yet again of the power of the sea that surrounds them on three sides. For a good vantage point head to **Chatham Light** (1878), overlooking Nauset Beach and Pleasant Bay. The current lighthouse was built after rough seas, eventually carrying away more than 200 feet of land, toppled two previous lighthouses.

MONOMOY NATIONAL WILDLIFE REFUGE

Naturalists will want to head to **Monomoy Island** (actually two islands constituting Monomoy National Wildlife Refuge), off the coast south of Chatham in Nantucket Sound. Nesting grounds and habitat for more than 300 species of birds, Monomoy is an important stopping spot for migrating waterfowl along what ornithologists call the Atlantic

Flyway. The two islands can be reached only by boat; ask at the information booth (Tel: 508/945-0594) or call the Massachusetts Audubon Society (Tel: 508/349-2615), whose naturalists lead tours. North Island, ten minutes from the mainland, supports broad stretches of tidal flats, sand dunes, and salt marshes that attract more than 10,000 birds in the late summer, including herons, terns, egrets, and the endangered piping plover. South Island, 30 minutes from shore, is full of freshwater ponds and thickets that harbor migrating ducks, owls, and deer. In the winter seals make their home here.

STAYING IN CHATHAM

Chatham boasts dozens of places to stay, most very pricey, many quite fine. One of the Cape's best resorts, tucked away on a secluded cove of Pleasant Bay, is the **Wequassett Inn**, offering traditional shingle-style cottages as well as upscale hotel rooms in 18 different buildings, many with private decks. Modest and unpretentious, the full-scale resort offers many amenities: tennis courts, an extensive sailing program, a heated swimming pool situated on a spit of land that juts out into the bay, and superb New England and Continental cuisine at its restaurant, **Square Top**.

Chatham Bars Inn, about a ten-minute walk from the center of the village, is one of New England's grand old resorts. Cottages and rooms are gracious, its lobby is accented with wicker and chintz, its verandah is long. Amenities include an outdoor heated pool, tennis courts, a private ocean beach, and a nine-hole golf course. The main dining room offers a fixed-price four-course dinner, while the tavern serves a lighter menu.

The Greek Revival **Captain's House Inn of Chatham**, a ten-minute walk from town on Old Harbor Road, is one of New England's top inns. Period antiques, pumpkin-pine floors, and four-poster beds grace the 16 rooms, all with private bath. You can rest assured that every detail has been considered here. The hosts, the Eakins, are happy to describe each of the rooms, all of which are highly recommended. English-style tea is served in the afternoon. Across the street, the **Moses Nickerson House**, a former sea captain's house built in 1839, is maintained with warmth and care. The seven rooms all have private bath, and the price of a room includes a full breakfast.

On Main Street, the **Cranberry Inn** has 18 completely renovated rooms, all light and airy and furnished with simple, tasteful antiques and reproductions. Modern comforts include television, telephone, and air conditioning. Quite a few rooms have a fireplace, private balcony, or beamed ceilings.

(See also "Chatham to Hyannis," below, for additional lodgings in the area.)

DINING IN CHATHAM

Chatham offers a similarly wide range of dining options. **Christian's**, at 443 Main Street, serves dinner year-round and lunch as well in the summer. A light menu is available on the deck (nice for after-dinner drinks too); a pub menu is served in the English bar; and there's more formal dining inside (Tel: 508/945-3362). Meals at the **Impudent Oyster**, at 15 Chatham Bars Avenue, are eclectic, innovative, international, and boisterous (Tel: 508/945-3545). **Oyster's Garden Café**, behind the Swinging Basket at 483 Main Street, is a little courtyard oasis open only for lunch.

Heading out of town a mile or two on Route 28 west toward Hyannis, stop and collect a picnic at **Fancy's Farm**, the **Pampered Palate**, or **Chatham Fish and Lobster**, all near each other. Or eat where the local fishermen do, at **Larry's P.X.** The place opens at 4:00 A.M., and fishermen begin and end their days here. Doughnuts, burgers, fried clams, and the like are on the menu. It's located in the Shop Ahoy Shopping Center, a strip mall on Route 28.

Chatham to Hyannis

There are few notable establishments between Chatham and Hyannis, a 40-minute drive west along Route 28. Most people will want to bypass this stretch and take Route 6 to Hyannis. Traffic on two-lane Route 28 out of Chatham begins to slow down as the number of shops, real-estate offices, miniature golf courses, and other services increases.

On Route 28 in **South Harwich**, 5 miles (8 km) from Chatham, the **House on the Hill** has three simple guest rooms, one of which has a private bath, and a comfortable deck and patio. The breakfast room, with a beehive oven, pine wainscoting, and handwrought door latches, is the centerpiece of the 1832 Federal farmhouse. A bit farther down the road pause at picturesque **Wychmere Harbor**, visible from the road and from a grassy knoll overlooking it.

In **West Dennis**, another few miles west on the shores of Nantucket Sound, the **Lighthouse Inn** embodies the spirit of old Cape Cod. The main building is the Bass River Lighthouse, surrounded by cottages, a private and protected beach, a pool, and tennis courts. Each of the 63 rooms has a private bath, television, refrigerator, and phone. All three meals are served in a large, open dining room (breakfast and dinner are included in the room rate; lunch is extra); all in all, this is a good find for families.

Hyannis

Hyannis gained fame as the location of the summer White House of President John F. Kennedy. Some visitors come to look at the simple memorial, a bronze medallion embedded in a fieldstone wall on Ocean Street, or to try to get past the guard who watches the "Kennedy Compound," an enclave of posh oceanside estates surrounded by hedges. But the Kennedys' summer home is not visible from the road or open to the public. The new **John F. Kennedy Hyannis Museum**, located in the Old Town Hall at 397 Main Street, displays 50 photographs of JFK with his family, cabinet members, and government officials, spanning the years from 1934 to 1963. The museum will be closed for renovation in the first half of 1993; for information, call the Hyannis Chamber of Commerce, Tel: (508) 775-2201.

Unquestionably, Hyannis remains the commercial hub of the Cape. There are certainly quieter places to spend a vacation, but if you're heading to Nantucket, this is the place to be. If you're pressed for time, Nantucket can be seen in one long day trip from Hyannis, but only if you take the first ferry over and the last one back. There are two docks in Hyannis: Ocean Street Dock (for Hy-Line ferries) and South Street Dock (for the Steamship Authority). For details, see Getting Around at the end of the chapter.

The Cape's early visitors escaped New York, Boston, and Philadelphia via the railroad. Today, the **Cape Cod Scenic Railroad** (Tel: 508/771-3788) operates between Hyannis, Sandwich, and the Cape Cod Canal. The commentary is rather corny, but the restored coaches and first-class parlor cars are nice. They also operate the **Cape Cod Dinner Train**, which makes the same run without commentary and serves an elegant multi-course dinner at tables for four.

Of the town's beaches, **Craigville Beach**, not particularly picturesque—and inundated with teens—is nonetheless a good bathing beach and the area's largest.

STAYING AND DINING IN HYANNIS

Sea Street boasts the best of Hyannis's restaurants and accommodations. The **Inn on Sea Street**, one of the few inns in the vicinity that accepts one-night reservations, has nine lovely antiques-filled guest rooms, most with private bath. Breakfast is more than generous, and a beach is within walking distance. Next door, on Gosnold Street, the **Old Crocker Barn** consists of two nicely renovated, fully equipped apartments in a converted barn, complete with horse stalls. At the end of Sea Street on the beach, the **Breakwaters** offers 16 neat and tidy one- and two-bedroom cottages, each with a private deck. At the other end of Sea Street, at 488 South Street, the **Roadhouse Café** serves moderately priced Italian and standard New England food for lunch and dinner; Tel: (508) 775-2386.

Hyannis to Falmouth

The drive from Hyannis to Falmouth on Route 28 also takes 40 minutes, and there is no alternate route. About 15 minutes west of Hyannis, the **Regatta of Cotuit**, housed in a 200-year-old Federal-style mansion on Route 28 near Route 130, is consistently voted among the Cape's top restaurants, with good reason. Dinner, served by candlelight, is romantic and elegant; service is friendly and knowledgeable; the wine list is excellent. The menu, which changes frequently, has quite a range. Seafood is the specialty, prepared with a variety of sublime sauces. Tel: (508) 428-5715.

Two miles (3 km) farther west on Route 28, **Mashpee** is home to the **Old Indian Meeting House** (1684), the oldest surviving church building on Cape Cod (open by appointment; Tel: 508/428-6133 or 477-0208). The simple, square wooden building with a plain steeple was probably the largest structure in the village when it was built. It housed a congregation of Native Americans converted to Christianity, among them preachers who were descendants of Massasoit, friend and benefactor to Pilgrims and other English colonists. Mashpee holds an annual powwow over the July Fourth weekend that is attended by 25,000 people. Tribes from all over the country gather here for ceremonies, dancing, and handicrafts demonstrations.

About 3 miles (5 km) farther in New Seabury (follow signs from the rotary), **New Seabury Resort** is a full-service complex with two 18-hole championship golf courses, 16 tennis courts, miles of beachfront, outdoor pools, a variety of dining options, and a host of other planned activities throughout the summer. Set on 2,000 acres, New Seabury offers about 170 units, ranging from rooms to studios to two-bedroom apartments. Its full-day camp program for children in summer makes it particularly suitable for families.

FALMOUTH

Falmouth, encompassing 44 square miles—the largest town on the Cape—has many distinct and far-flung districts. For the last 20 years or so East Falmouth has hosted the **Barnstable County Fair** from mid- to late July, attracting more than 150,000 people to its livestock shows, oxen pulls, and horticultural exhibits. The fair was first held in 1843 and has taken place every year since 1866. **Falmouth Heights** is a boisterous beach area known among college crowds. The commercial district of Falmouth can be ignored (except for one restaurant), but the **town green** cannot. It's one of the Cape's prettiest, set aside in 1749 for the enjoyment of all community members. Carefully planned and compact, its white 18th- and 19th-century wooden houses are dominated by the **First Congregationalist Church** spire, whose bell was cast by Paul Revere in 1797. From the green, the five-mile **Shining Sea Bicycle Path** runs to Woods Hole, following an old railroad bed.

Just off the green at 65 Palmer Avenue, the **Julia Wood House** (1790), operated by the Falmouth Historical Society, displays 19th-century furnishings. One room is dedicated to Katharine Lee Bates, a Falmouth resident and the composer of the hymn *America the Beautiful.* Open weekday afternoons in summer; Tel: (508) 548-4857.

DINING AND STAYING IN FALMOUTH

Mostly Hall, on the green, offers a full breakfast and six rooms with private bath. It is, indeed, "mostly hall," with a grand 13-foot entryway and long, shuttered windows. Furnishings are predominantly Victorian, elegant yet comfortable. A widow's walk, enclosed and used as a sitting room, caps the 1849 house. If Mostly Hall is full, the **Village Green Inn**, across the street, has comfortable and tasteful rooms, all with private bath.

Off Main Street in the center of town, the old-fashioned **Elm Arch Inn**, built in 1810 and operated by the same family since 1926, offers 24 inexpensive rooms, half of which have a sink in the room and share a bath. In addition to the main inn there's an annex with eight, more modern, rooms. As for dining on Main Street, **Laureen's**, at number 170, offers breakfast, lunch, and afternoon tea and finger sandwiches (Tel: 508/540-9104). The **Regatta of Falmouth By-the-Sea**, at the corner of Scranton and Clinton avenues overlooking the entrance to Falmouth Harbor, is a sister-restaurant to the Regatta in Cotuit. Slightly less expensive and less formal than the Cotuit location, it serves both lunch and dinner (Tel: 508/548-5400).

West Falmouth, off Route 28A, was originally settled by Quakers in 1661. Today it's still a refuge, a quiet place with a picturesque little harbor off Old Dock Road. The **Inn at West Falmouth**, a luxurious retreat with a landscaped pool, clay

tennis courts, and perfectly placed potted plants, offers nine
rooms with private bath. Some have balconies looking to the
sea, fireplaces, Jacuzzis, and marble tiling.

Woods Hole

Three miles (5 km) south of Falmouth via Woods Hole Road,
Woods Hole is devoted to a world-renowned scientific community studying marine life that includes the National Marine Fisheries Service and the Woods Hole Oceanographic
Institution. Established by a Rockefeller grant in 1930, the
institution studies the topography of the ocean floor and
ocean currents; its research vessels helped locate the *Titanic*. None of the facilities is open to the public except a
small **aquarium** (Tel: 508/548-5123) run by Marine Fisheries
at the end of the peninsula, and an exhibition center at the
Oceanographic Institution (Tel: 508/548-1400).

In addition to the international marine science world,
Woods Hole is known to vacationers travelling to the islands,
as ferries for Martha's Vineyard and Nantucket leave from
here. The **Fishmonger's Café**, at 56 Water Street, serves both
sets of people. Burgers, vegetarian dishes, and blackboard
fish specials are the norm in this rustic restaurant on the
water. Tel: (508) 548-9148.

Cape Cod Canal

Head north on Route 28 to the Bourne Bridge rotary and
follow signs for Mashpee, then Shore Road, then Aptucxet
Road for the **Aptucxet Trading Post and Museum**. (The trading post is about 15 miles/24 km north of Woods Hole and just
a mile from the rotary.) The original trading post was established in 1627 by the Pilgrims in order to trade with the Dutch
from New Amsterdam and the Wampanoag Indians. Fur,
sugar, and tobacco were traded; wampum served as the
currency. The present building has been reconstructed on the
foundations of the original. Tel: (508) 759-9487.

You've now come full circle; cross the canal that has
effectively severed you from the mainland. The seven-mile-
long Cape Cod Canal, dug from 1909 to 1914 between
Buzzards Bay and Cape Cod Bay, saves vessels travelling
between New York and Boston the distance of 100 miles at
sea. As far back as 1624 Myles Standish had the same idea to
avoid circumnavigating Cape Cod. Even George Washington
ordered a plan drawn up during the Revolutionary War.
Bourne Railroad Bridge, southernmost of the two bridges
that cross the canal, has a 544-foot span and is the second
highest vertical lift bridge in the world. It is raised and

lowered as needed using counterweights. To get a ship's-eye view, take a trip with **Cape Cod Canal Cruises**, whose boats leave from Onset Town Pier, on the south side of the canal. Tel: (508) 295-3883.

MARTHA'S VINEYARD

Visualize Martha's Vineyard, only five miles off the coast of Cape Cod directly across Vineyard Sound from Woods Hole, as a triangle: Vineyard Haven occupies the northern tip, Edgartown (and Chappaquiddick Island) the southeastern tip. Oak Bluffs, the other principal town, rests between the two. (Ferries come in to either Vineyard Haven or Oak Bluffs; see Getting Around, below.) "Up-island," the southwestern part of the Vineyard, consists of West Tisbury, Chilmark, Menemsha, and Gay Head. The island can be "seen" in two days, with mornings spent in town and afternoons spent sunning at the beach, driving back roads, or exploring nature preserves. Four or five days are ideal to experience the island, however, which is 100 square miles in area and 23 miles long across its hypotenuse (the south shore).

The Gulf Stream, though far east of the island, warms waters here to a moderate temperature into October. Though many of the island's beaches are private, especially up-island, plenty are easily accessible. Terrain between the down-island towns of Vineyard Haven, Oak Bluffs, and Edgartown is flat, while up-island, crisscrossed by stone walls and dotted with ponds and lakes, comprises rolling heaths and forests of oak and pine. Vineyarders, concerned with the environment, outside encroachment, and further development, have always been activists and independent people. They've adopted tough zoning and building laws and acquired land for preserves (and lately have voiced concerns about the proliferation of noisy mopeds used by careless riders). But their livelihood depends on the summer influx that increases the island population nearly tenfold (the year-round population of 11,500 swells to almost 100,000).

You'll need a car to tour the island efficiently. If you plan in advance you can schedule space for your own car aboard the ferry out of Woods Hole or rent a car on the island. Otherwise, you should be either a strong bicyclist or relaxed enough to take the slow public buses.

Unless otherwise noted, restaurants and lodging places discussed below are open year-round.

Vineyard Haven

In the 18th and 19th centuries seafaring vessels travelling south from Boston needed a place to resupply and take refuge. As a result, Vineyard Haven, also referred to as Tisbury, became an active seaport. When the Cape Cod Canal opened in 1914 and shipping channels were rerouted, tourism became the big industry. Today, even though Vineyard Haven is considered the island's commercial center (you'll notice the large oil and gas tanks at the far end of the harbor), there are plenty of reasons to stay behind while most of your fellow ferry passengers head elsewhere on the island. Though the town is quite small, Vineyard Haven's tranquil harbor boasts the greatest number of residential wooden boats in a New England harbor. Vineyard Haven is also quieter than Edgartown and Oak Bluffs because it's "dry" (that is, no alcohol is sold in town).

The chamber of commerce maintains an information office about a block south of the ferry terminal via Water Street on Beach Street; Tel: (508) 693-0085. On the way there you'll pass the **Black Dog Bakery**, on Water Street, selling strong coffee, muffins, and loaves of bread. The well-known **Black Dog Tavern**, around the corner and about 100 yards east on Beach Street Extension, is a dark room—crowded, casual, and noisy—with tables set close together and an exposed kitchen. There's also an enclosed porch right on the harbor. Inside or out, the fresh seafood here is quite good. No reservations are taken, but the tavern is open for three meals a day; Tel: (508) 693-9223. More than just a restaurant, though, the Black Dog has become something of a phenomenon, spawning a million-dollar industry selling tee-shirts and assorted paraphernalia (sold at the bakery).

If you head straight up Union Street from the ferry you'll come to **Main Street**, lined with small shops (including the wonderful **Bunch of Grapes Bookstore**) and restaurants. Among the island's best of the latter is **Le Grenier**, offering consistently fine creative French cuisine in an elegant, candlelit setting. Dinner reservations are essential in the summer; Tel: (508) 693-4906 (closed January and February). The informal patisserie downstairs offers breakfast and lunch in the sidewalk café.

A three-minute walk north along Main Street or the town beach leads to a green knoll called **Owen Park** and the **Lothrop Merry House**, an inn operated by a modern-day seafaring family, the Clarkes. Most of the seven comfortable, unpretentious rooms in this 18th-century house have unhindered views of the harbor, as the house's yard extends to their private beach, fronting the inner harbor. The Clarkes also expertly sail a newly outfitted 54-foot Alden ketch, **Laissez Faire**, taking passengers on day and evening cruises around the island. Special week-long charters may be arranged; Tel: (508) 693-1646. The owners' son Mark, a waterskiing instructor at **M.V. Ski**, in town, gets everyone from toddlers to retirees up out of the water and onto skis; Tel: (508) 693-2838.

A mile (1½ km) north on Main Street is the elegant **Thorncroft Inn**, a full-service inn with outstanding amenities, diligent service, and 13 impeccable guest rooms. Some rooms have working fireplaces and a Jacuzzi; all have private baths and central air conditioning. A stay at Thorncroft includes a full breakfast and afternoon tea. Take advantage of the multi-course lobster or filet mignon dinner served to house guests only, one of the nicest meals on the island. Farther along Main Street is **West Chop**, a quiet residential area, home to writers and television personalities. The lighthouse here is one of two that signals the entrance to the harbor; there's a good spot for watching the sun set around the bend from the lighthouse.

One of Vineyard Haven's public beaches is a well-kept secret. From Main Street (beyond Owen Park) take Daggett Avenue north about ¾ mile (1¼ km), where a lamppost and two dirt roads converge on the right. Take either road about 2½ miles (4 km) to **Tashmoo Beach**, a small, sandy beach with a strong current on which you can float into Lake Tashmoo or out into Vineyard Sound.

There's another beautiful beach in Vineyard Haven, but it's open only to residents or guests of **Lambert's Cove Country Inn**. To get here, head southwest along State Road and detour onto Lambert's Cove Road (on the right), a shady rural road that passes ponds, cleared fields, and stone walls. There couldn't be a more beautiful setting for the inn, amid apple orchards, perennial gardens, and spacious lawns. Lambert's Cove offers a variety of antiques-appointed guest rooms in the main 1790 farmhouse and in a converted barn and carriage house. Some rooms have private decks, one has a greenhouse sitting room, and all have private baths. The common living room is particularly spacious and inviting.

A mile (1½ km) out of town on State Road (before the Lambert's Cove detour) toward Gay Head is the unassuming **Louis' Tisbury Café**, with casual indoor dining in addition to a thriving takeout business. Specialties include homemade pasta and shrimp sautéed in garlic butter. Open for lunch and dinner; Tel: (508) 693-3255.

Oak Bluffs

From Vineyard Haven you might take scenic Beach Road 3½ miles (5½ km) east to Oak Bluffs, with a detour to **East Chop Lighthouse**. Otherwise take Beach Road to County Road, turn right, continue to Shirley Road, and turn right again, where you'll find the world's oldest **lobster hatchery** (established 1949). Thousands of tiny lobsters are hatched and raised here until they're deemed fit to plunge into the frigid Atlantic.

Oak Bluffs is a whimsical place, where religion and tourism mingle peacefully. In 1835 Methodists held revival meetings here in Wesleyan Grove, a secluded stand of oaks. Over the years thousands of worshipers came to a Methodist summer camp here and stayed in tents ringing the iron-covered tabernacle (built in 1879), still the center of worship today. Eventually tents were replaced by the hundreds of small, elaborately carved and flamboyantly painted gingerbread cottages that make up what is today called **Trinity Park**. Despite a mishmash of pastels, turrets, spires, and eaves, the effect is remarkably harmonious. Every August since 1869 Japanese lanterns have been strung from house to house for Illumination Night (the exact date is announced just a week in advance). Historically, wealthy African Americans have made their homes in Oak Bluffs; most recent among them is Spike Lee.

Smack in the center of town penny arcades and the **Flying Horses Carousel**, the oldest operational merry-go-round in the country, keep things lively. The carousel's 100-year-old-carved horses are trimmed with real horsehair and have rare animal figures inside their glass eyes.

STAYING AND DINING IN OAK BLUFFS

Two very different Victorian bed-and-breakfasts abut the dollhouse-like cottages in Trinity Park. The **Attleboro House** offers inexpensive, homey rooms (with shared baths) overlooking the harbor. Closed late September to late May. Gracious, antiques-filled guest rooms are found at the 19th-century **Oak House**, a five-minute walk from the center of town on Seaview Avenue. Oak paneling and furnishings fill the rooms, many of which have private porches and balconies with ocean views; all have private bath. Closed mid-October to mid-May. The 62 rooms at the Victorian-style **Wesley Hotel**, also overlooking the harbor, feature typical hotel conveniences—television, wall-to-wall carpeting—and uniform layouts; closed mid-October to April.

It's ironic that Oak Bluffs, with its religious history, is one of the island's two "wet" towns (the other is Edgartown).

David Cronin's piano playing draws crowds at **David's Island House**, on Circuit Avenue, a popular place for an after-dinner drink (lunch and dinner are also served); open May through September. Just up the street is **Linda Jean's**, an affordable family-style place serving standbys like hamburgers and a seafood platter with french fries, coleslaw, and rolls. A few doors beyond, the **Oyster Bar** is a boisterous, trendy, upscale bistro with an excellent wine list and tasty regional American cuisine. Oysters (obviously), a raw bar, and fresh seafood are the specialties. The atmosphere is just as enticing as the food: high tin ceilings, an exposed kitchen, and a 40-foot marble and oak bar. Closed mid-October through April; Tel: (508) 693-3300.

Across from the carousel, in the center of town, **Giordano's** serves pizza and what may be the best fried clams on the island; closed October through May.

OAK BLUFFS TO EDGARTOWN

Take Beach Road south out of Oak Bluffs along a narrow spit of land between Nantucket Sound and Sengekontacket Pond. This is a popular bike route, flat and just 5½ miles long, though the wind really kicks up here. Not surprisingly, windsurfers favor the area, too (the pond is warm and shallow for novice windsurfers; the Sound serves those with more experience). The beach, **Joseph Sylvia State Beach**, fronts Nantucket Sound and is a favorite with families. The limited parking is usually filled to capacity by late morning.

The inland Edgartown–Vineyard Haven Road, which by-passes Oak Bluffs, runs past **Felix Neck Wildlife Sanctuary**, a 350-acre waterfowl preserve affiliated with the Massachusetts Audubon Society with beach, marsh, nine miles of walking trails, and woodlands. Thanks to the efforts of island naturalists, osprey-nesting poles, visible as you drive in, have helped these large birds make a comeback in the area.

Edgartown

Edgartown, long a haven for the rich and famous, is the oldest settlement on the Vineyard. In 1642 it was purchased by the Mayhews, who set about converting the Indians to Christianity. By the early 19th century it was a flourishing whaling center said to have sent more captains to sea than Nantucket or New Bedford. As whaling ships grew larger, ships from Nantucket, unable to navigate the shallow waters and sandbars surrounding Nantucket harbor, docked in Edgartown.

Edgartown's main attractions are the pristine white houses surrounded by picket fences and profuse flowers. Many fine historical houses line Main Street from Pease's Point Way to the harbor, a few blocks to the east. Edgartown's most regal house was built in 1840 by whale-oil magnate Dr. Daniel Fisher, who supplied the country's lighthouses with Edgartown whale oil. The **Fisher House**, at 99 Main Street, will open to the public in June 1993. Exhibits are in the planning stages, and hours have not yet been set. For information, call or visit the Martha's Vineyard Historical Preservation Trust, next door at 89 Main Street; Tel: (508) 627-4440. The **Vincent House** (1672), on the same property, is the oldest house on the island; it is open to visitors and retains original woodwork, glass, and hardware, though no furniture. The **Old Whaling Church**, with impressive white pillars, is the best example of Greek Revival architecture on the island.

Off School Street (a block east of Pease's Point Way) at Cook Street, the Dukes County Historical Society (Tel: 508/627-4441) houses the **Vineyard Museum**, with 12 rooms of whaling and farming artifacts as well as the Fresnel lens used in Gay Head Lighthouse until 1952. The lens, with 1,008 prisms, used light from whale-oil lamps to create a beacon visible for 20 miles out to sea. Off South Water Street, the huge **pagoda tree** shading the Victorian Inn was brought as a seedling from China in the 19th century.

SHOPPING IN EDGARTOWN

Shopping and browsing are two of the prime activities in Edgartown; the small town center is filled with clothing, antiques, crafts, and other goods. The **Edgartown Art Gallery and Antique Shop**, at the Charlotte Inn (discussed below), is unrivaled in its offerings. At 29 Main Street, **Tashtego** sells a wide variety of carefully chosen household items. The **Scrimshander**, on lower Main Street, sells scrimshaw that has been carved on a "whalebone-*like*" material for those opposed to the killing of whales.

STAYING IN EDGARTOWN

Edgartown is best appreciated in the spring and fall when solitude is found on the beaches and lodging prices are reduced. (It's deserted in the winter and crowded in the summer.) Three fine inns are located on Pease's Point Way. The landscaped grounds of the **Point Way Inn** sport a professional croquet court and a gazebo, while the inn's 15 tastefully appointed guest rooms, each with private bath, feature layouts of all sizes and shapes. Nautical motifs and photographs of staff and guests fill the common rooms. Next door at the **Shiverick Inn** things are more formal, though not stuffy. The house, built in 1840 for the town physician, has been graciously restored. Many rooms have fireplaces and are furnished with 18th- and 19th-century American and English antiques. There's a small, private terrace in the back of the house. A block away, the **Captain Dexter House** was recently renovated top to bottom. It offers 11 spiffy rooms, all with private bath; closed November through April.

On South Summer Street, off Main Street, the **Charlotte Inn** remains the unrivaled jewel of the island's lodgings. The 21 guest rooms and three suites are impeccably furnished with fine art and priceless antiques. The grounds are stunning and the atmosphere is one of exclusivity.

North and South Water streets, overlooking the harbor, are lined with prosperous sea captains' homes from the 1820s and 1830s. On North Water Street, the best rooms at the **Daggett House** are in the main house and cottage, decorated in small-patterned paper, rich colors, and muslin curtains. The lawn sweeps down to the Chappaquiddick ferry and harbor. Rooms on the water are much nicer than those in the building across the street. The porch of the turn-of-the-century **Harbor View Hotel**, at the end of North Water Street, five blocks from the center of town, overlooks bluffs and the Edgartown Lighthouse, one of the island's five lights. The Harbor View recently underwent extensive renovations, and the 124 guest rooms are now quite luxurious. Amenities include a heated outdoor pool, tennis courts, room service, and a concierge.

DINING IN EDGARTOWN

Demanding diners have three choices in Edgartown. The exposed kitchen at **Savoir Fare**, 14 Church Street, executes a creative American menu sure to please any "foodie." The interior is light and airy. Closed November through April; Tel: (508) 627-9864. It's located in Post Office Square next to **Warriner's**, where you may dine on American cuisine in a paneled library with a fireplace and candles. Warriner's offers courteous service and an outstanding, reasonably priced wine list; Tel: (508) 627-4488. At **L'etoile**, in the Charlotte Inn (on South Summer Street), a slightly haughty wait staff serves contemporary French cuisine in lovely surroundings. A prix-fixe Sunday brunch and prix-fixe dinner are offered; Tel: (508) 627-5187.

As for the restaurants overlooking the harbor, you probably won't get a bad meal at any one of them, but none stands out, either. Celebrity-owned restaurants are all the rage in Edgartown. One of the latest, partially owned by Glenn Close and Boston Bruins hockey player Cam Neely, is **Decoy's** on Winter Street in the center of town, which serves California cuisine for lunch and dinner. Closed November through April; Tel: (508) 627-7665.

CHAPPAQUIDDICK AND EDGARTOWN'S BEACHES

Three of the Vineyard's nicest public beaches are close to Edgartown. One is on **Chappaquiddick Island**, five minutes away via the car-carrying ferry *On Time*. Keeping to no regular schedule, *On Time* runs whenever it's needed— which is, of course, on time. Chappaquiddick, which translates as the "separated island," is thickly wooded, with nothing more than large private homes and one main road. Parking for the island's unspoiled East Beach at the 500-acre **Cape Pogue Wildlife Refuge** is 3 miles (5 km) from the ferry. Walking on the dunes at Cape Pogue is discouraged because endangered seabirds nest there. (The nearby 200-acre **Wasque Reservation** is one of the best places on the island from which to surf fish.)

Otherwise head to sandy, three-mile-long **Katama Beach** (also known as South Beach), popular with surfers because of its two- to three-foot waves, though there are no facilities. It's an easy three-mile bike ride south along Katama Road from Edgartown, but if you drive note that the limited parking fills early.

One of the island's prettiest and most picturesquely situated beaches, **Lighthouse Beach**, has no on-site parking, but is within walking distance of Edgartown Center (walk five blocks east down North Water Street, to Starbuck's Neck in front of the Harbor Hotel, where you'll see the lighthouse). A final note about the waters off Edgartown: Though sharks are never sighted here, many people associate sharks with Edgartown, as it was featured as the town of Amity in the movie *Jaws*.

Up-Island

As you head southwest along State Road toward Gay Head from Vineyard Haven it becomes clear how the island got its name. There are indeed grapevines on Martha's Vineyard, though today there are far fewer (mainly cultivated varieties) than there were when Bartholomew Gosnold landed in 1602 and named the island after his daughter. **Chicama Vineyards**, to the left off State Road about 2½ miles (4 km) out of Vineyard Haven, offers tours and produces some mediocre wines but fine herbal vinegars. Also off State Road, just a bit farther along (bear to the right onto Indian Hill Road), is **Christiantown**, consisting of a monument, a little graveyard, and a church founded for the island's few converted Indians. **Cedar Tree Neck Wildlife Sanctuary**, more than 300 acres of headlands and trails with commanding views of Vineyard Sound, is farther along Indian Hill Road toward Vineyard Sound.

The **Blue Goose**, signposted just north of the intersection of State Road and North Road in West Tisbury, offers three rooms (one with private bath) and a dear little cottage next door. It's secluded and quiet, in a field by itself; closed December through mid-April.

Heading up-island from Edgartown, the Edgartown–West Tisbury Road passes through **West Tisbury**, dominated by an old-fashioned general store and the **Field Gallery**, with its large whimsical figurative sculptures standing out in a field, tempting you to stop and take a closer look. West Tisbury comes alive every Saturday morning during the growing season when the farmer's market is held (come before 10:00 A.M. for the best selection) and on one weekend in August when the Agricultural Society Fair is alive with blue-ribbon contests for everything from fiddling to jam making.

From the center of West Tisbury three pastoral roads— appropriately named North, Middle, and South roads—head southwest to Gay Head. All three roads lead to Chilmark's **Beetlebung Corner**, so named for a stand of trees from which "beetles" (mallets) and "bung" (wooden stoppers) were made. Here you'll find the **Feast of Chilmark**, a restaurant frequented by up-island summer people, featuring American cuisine in a gallery showing the photographs of Peter Simon. Closed Columbus Day through April; Tel: (508) 645-3553. Next door, an indulgence at **Chilmark Chocolates** never disappoints.

North Road and Menemsha

Take North Road toward Menemsha to find one very pricey and two moderately priced places to stay. **Captain R. Flanders' House** is situated on top of a knoll surrounded by 60 acres of farmland, with horses roaming in the fields; the living room has an expansive view. Simple country antiques fill the four guest rooms (two with private bath); the separate two-room suite with two fireplaces is lovely. You can also rent a complete house, which sleeps eight people, by the week. Open late May to mid-November.

Not all of the cottages at **Menemsha Inn and Cottages** are renovated or overlook the harbor, but all are quite charming: Their rather rustic exteriors belie the cozy, brightly lit rooms inside, marked by such touches as fresh wildflowers in jam jars. The sunsets over the Elizabeth Islands are spectacular from here. Rented by the week, the cottages sleep two to five people and are fully equipped for cooking (including a barbecue grill and picnic table outdoors); open

May to late November. The expensive rooms at the nearby
Beach Plum Inn are impeccable but simple. The clientele is
sophisticated, Menemsha Harbor is in the distance, and the
peace and quiet are calming. The inn's dining room (Tel:
508/645-9454) is respected for outstanding nouvelle Continental cuisine; a full breakfast is included in the price of a
room. Open mid-May to mid-October.

North Road ends in picture-perfect **Menemsha Harbor**, a
working harbor with stacks of lobster traps, fishing shacks,
and weathered shanties. Fishing boats have been docked
here by the same families for over 300 years, including
descendants of Thomas Mayhew, who purchased the island
in 1641. Buy some fresh fish at Larsen's or Poole's fish
market to take back to your cottage or pick up some fresh,
simply prepared takeout fish at the **Homeport Restaurant**
(Tel: 508/645-2679; open May to late October) on North
Road and watch the sun set over Dutchers Dock. There's a
popular sandy beach here, too.

Middle and South Roads

Middle Road out of West Tisbury passes the newly constructed **Breakfast at Tiasquam**, a secluded house with eight
carpeted guest rooms, 20 skylights, a two-story living room/
atrium, a spiral staircase, solid cherry doors, multilevel
decks, and hand-thrown pottery sinks. An extensive full
breakfast is included in the price of a room.

South Road out of West Tisbury passes perhaps the island's most beautiful beach, **Lucy Vincent Beach**. It's open
only to those with a parking pass, which you may obtain if
you're staying at an inn in Menemsha or Chilmark.

GAY HEAD

From Chilmark State Road, which runs south and then west
from Beetlebung Corner and which affords outstanding
views of Menemsha Harbor and Squibnocket Pond, head to
the cliffs at Gay Head, home to one of the state's two Indian
communities. (On the way, a detour down Lobsterville Road
to the right leads to a spot with an especially nice view of
Menemsha Harbor.) Park your car and walk past a row of
fast-food and souvenir shops to the vantage point overlooking the dramatic cliffs and lighthouse, first built in 1799 on
tribal lands. The 150-foot cliffs, a national landmark, mark
the terminus of the glacier that formed the island. Geologists
have discovered fossils more than a million years old along
the mile-long cliffs. (Please note: It is forbidden to remove
the multi-hued, striated layers of clay.)

The fine public beach here, **Moshup Beach**, is well suited
for a full day trip, as it takes 45 minutes to drive here from

Vineyard Haven or Edgartown and another 10 minutes to walk from the parking lot to one of the less crowded parts of the beach to the north. Generally, keep in mind that waters up-island tend to be about five degrees colder than those off other parts of the island. The **Outermost Inn** is well poised to take advantage of the seclusion: on the moors above the beach, looking toward the lighthouse and uninterrupted ocean and sky. Each of the seven large rooms has a picture window. Decor is stylish contemporary, with white walls, light wood, local art, and natural fabrics.

NANTUCKET

Nantucket, east of Martha's Vineyard, is 15 miles long and three miles wide. Nantucket town, small, with one-way streets—and not a single traffic light or parking meter—is best explored on foot, while the rest of the island is best toured by bicycle or four-wheel-drive vehicle. Carved by a glacier, "the faraway island" is covered with tree-studded moors, ponds, and rolling dunes. In pleasant contrast to Martha's Vineyard, most of Nantucket's beaches and moors are open to nonresidents, and no beach is more than a six- or seven-mile ride from town. Bike paths are excellent, but while the roads are predominantly flat, winds frequently make trips more difficult than they look. Other than Nantucket town, Siasconset (referred to simply as 'Sconset) is the only real "destination" on the island.

Visitors to Nantucket tend to be well-heeled city sophisticates who appreciate the fact that their island is more elitist than the Vineyard. No camping is permitted on the island and printed tourist information reminds people that bathing suits are not appropriate on Main Street and that noise levels should be kept to a minimum. Still, you don't have to wear designer clothes or drive a Range Rover to enjoy the island's superb architecture, unspoiled beaches, and fine dining.

Nantucket's year-round population of 7,000 swells to 45,000 during July and August. Try to visit in May and June, when well-tended gardens bloom profusely and wild roses blanket the island. In September and early October the Gulf Stream keeps the waters warm enough for swimming. Most of Nantucket's restaurants open seasonally and about half the inns remain open year-round; months of operation are noted below, unless an establishment is open year-round.

If you're visiting Nantucket on a day trip from Cape Cod (a very long one), climb the tower of Nantucket town's First Congregational Church for the view, take in some of the town's historic houses operated by the Historical Association, visit the Whaling Museum to appreciate the dangers of the industry that brought Nantucket its wealth, and take a tour of the island with **Gail's Tours** (Tel: 508/257-6557). If you can stay overnight, tack on a wonderful meal and bicycle trip to 'Sconset. If you have two or three nights, skip the tour and rent a Jeep to drive out to the dunes and beaches at Great Point, take a whale-watching excursion from Straight Wharf, listen to a band concert, and relax. Take a look at island-photographer Cary Hazlegrove's slide show, covering the changing moods and seasons of island life, shown weeknights in season at the Methodist Church on Centre Street.

Nantucket Town

Approach Nantucket Harbor by boat (as opposed to by plane) to best appreciate it. The ferry rounds **Brant Point**, headed by the country's second oldest lighthouse (1746). (Tradition dictates throwing a penny toward the light when you leave to ensure your return.) Brant Point is also known for the island's best surf fishing (for striped bass) and the strong current at nearby **Jetties Beach**, one of the town's two public beaches. The other, aptly named **Children's Beach** because it's well protected, is on the other side of the point, near Steamboat Wharf in town. Nantucket Harbor extends eastward from town for six miles, protected by a white-sand barrier beach called Coatue, which can be reached only by boat or four-wheel-drive vehicle. The harbor then curves north to **Great Point**, where an 1818 lighthouse warns boats against the treacherous sandbars of Nantucket Sound.

Nantucket town, its narrow streets paved with cobblestones and its uneven sidewalks with brick, is the focal point of the island. It's a dense but orderly maze of shops, inns, restaurants, 18th- and 19th-century architecture, and weathered and shingled houses. In interesting contrast to the one-and-a-half-story cottages prevalent on Cape Cod, you'll notice that Nantucket houses tend to be a full two stories high. The town has five wharves, the spiritual centers of the island.

The chamber of commerce (Tel: 508/228-1700), located on the second floor of the Pacific Club at the foot of Main Street (corner of Federal Street), sponsors two popular annual events that anchor the tourist season: the **Daffodil Festival**, held mid- to late April, and the **Christmas Stroll**, in early December. The Daffodil Festival includes an antique car rally that rolls out—passing thousands of blooming daffodils—to 'Sconset, where islanders gather for tailgate picnics. The Christmas Stroll is more commercial, but is still enchanting. Freshly cut trees decorated with ornaments made by the island's schoolchildren line the streets. Carolers stroll through the town, traditional holiday music is played in churches, Santa makes an appearance in a horse-drawn carriage, and numerous parties, antiques auctions, and fairs are held.

The Nantucket Historical Association (Tel: 508/228-1894) owns and oversees 14 historic properties (most open between late May and mid-October), which, if seen in chronological order, give an overview of the town's history. The association's brochure (readily available at the chamber of commerce and all the historic houses mentioned below) outlines an easy-to-follow walking tour; purchase a pass valid at all their buildings (including the Thomas Macy Warehouse; see below). Otherwise, consider taking a walking tour (Tel: 508/228-1062, by appointment) with Roger Young, a former town selectman full of interesting island lore.

STRAIGHT WHARF

Begin exploring at Straight Wharf, an extension of tree-lined Main Street. (The Hy-Line ferry docks here, while the Steamship Authority boats dock two blocks north at Steamboat Wharf.) Straight Wharf is home to **Nantucket Whalewatch** (Tel: 800/322-0013), an outfit that takes passengers out to sea from July through September. Deep-sea-fishing vessels and surf-casting boats are docked here as well. Next to them, former fishing sheds have been turned into shops and art galleries. The island's history, from farming to whaling to tourism, is told at the **Thomas Macy Warehouse** (also known as the Museum of Nantucket History). Next door, the **Artists' Association of Nantucket** is a good introduction to some of the island's superb artists, whose works are sold here. **Four Winds Craft Guild**, the last stop on the wharf, is said to carry the island's widest selection of lightship baskets. To while away the hours spent at sea protecting boats from dangerous offshore shoals, crew members of lightships began weaving baskets. Today the omnipresent woven creations come in all sizes, shapes, and price ranges.

WHALING AND
PETER FOULGER MUSEUMS

At Broad and South Water streets, the Whaling Museum is considered the nation's best after New Bedford's. Built as a candle factory in 1846, the museum now houses austere captains' portraits, a whale skeleton, equipment used to capture whales and process blubber, and an outstanding collection of scrimshaw, an art that sailors practiced on long voyages: They dried whale teeth or jawbones, polished them with sharkskin, then etched them with a simple knife or needle (scenes often followed nautical motifs), and, finally, rubbed soot or tobacco juice over the sketch to bring out the detail. Open May to mid-October.

Nantucket began its rise to whaling prominence after Nantucketers were taught open-boat (or "onshore") whaling in small vessels by the Algonquian Indians. In the early 1700s they began offshore whaling, roaming the expansive seas in search of the beasts. The discovery of sperm whales, which lived farther out at sea and yielded more oil than right whales (caught onshore), inspired shipbuilders to make bigger ships that could stay longer at sea. From 1740 to 1830 Nantucket reigned as the world's whaling capital; merchants and shipowners grew wealthy by selling oil in London and other cities. Nantucket's prominence declined as the ships became too large to navigate the sandbar forming at the mouth of Nantucket Harbor. (This coincided with the rise of New Bedford as the whaling capital.) When petroleum was discovered in Pennsylvania and the world became less dependent on whale oil, tourism took its place as Nantucket's principal industry in the late 1800s. At the same time the steamboat made the island more accessible.

Next door to the Whaling Museum, the **Peter Foulger Museum** is an active research center that depicts island life—through displays of paintings, drawings, furniture, and artifacts—as it was for farmers, artisans, Indians, Quakers, whalers, and traders.

HISTORIC NANTUCKET
Before beginning a tour of Nantucket's historic buildings, stop in at the efficient and well-stocked information bureau (Tel: 508/228-0925) at 25 Federal Street.

Emerson, Thoreau, and Frederick Douglass all spoke at the Great Hall of the Nantucket **Atheneum** (Nantucket Library), a beautiful 19th-century Greek Revival lecture hall off Federal Street. A few blocks to the northwest, at 62 Centre Street, is the **First Congregational Church** (1834); climb to the top for the best view of town and the harbor. A ten-minute walk to the northwest edge of town via Centre Street leads to Sunset Hill Lane and the Jethro Coffin House, familiarly known as the **Oldest House** (1686), a typical saltbox with a large central chimney and casement windows. Open to the public, it's a good representation of the austere life practiced by the island's first white settlers, who arrived in 1659 and purchased Nantucket from the Native Americans for 30 pounds and two beaver hats. (Two centuries later disease wiped out the Indians on the island.)

The Quaker movement, which established itself on Nantucket in the 1800s, exerted a strong cultural influence still visible in the island's simple, austere houses and in the strong character of Nantucketers. On Fair Street south off Main Street, the **Quaker Meetinghouse** (1838), where a dozen or so Quakers still meet, exemplifies this influence. The meetinghouse was the Nantucket Historical Association's first property, given to the association by one of the original founders in 1894. Attached to it is the **Fair Street Museum**, which houses changing exhibits of Nantucket's culture and arts. In 1994 this property will be the center-piece of the 100th anniversary celebration of the association.

A stroll up Main Street reveals some of Nantucket's best architectural jewels. Perhaps the most famous houses in Nantucket are the so-called **Three Bricks** (at numbers 93, 95, and 97), a trio of identical houses built in the 1830s by a wealthy whaler for his three sons. (You must be satisfied with a view of the exteriors; the houses are privately owned and not open to the public.) The very fine 1845 **Hadwen House** (96 Main Street), built for a merchant and candle maker, reflects the prosperity of whaling days. Its front columns and colossal scale resemble a Greek temple; its interior is richly decorated and filled with treasures. The Federal-style **Thomas Macy House** (99 Main Street) has perhaps the most handsome doorway in Nantucket.

A ten-minute walk down Pleasant Street (off Main) to South Mill Street leads to the **Old Mill** (1746), which still grinds corn into meal that can be purchased on the prem-ises. Farther west, off Vestal Street, the **Old Gaol** (1805) shows how seriously the town took its criminals; you may enter the four stone prison cells. The **Maria Mitchell Association**, also on Vestal Street, celebrates the distinguished achievements of Maria Mitchell, America's first woman as-tronomer. It consists of an observatory, a natural science museum, a science library, and Mitchell's birthplace, land-scaped with a wildflower and herb garden. Mitchell discov-ered an uncharted comet in 1847 while looking out from the roof of the Pacific National Bank, on Main Street, where her father worked. Tel: (508) 228-9190.

STAYING IN NANTUCKET TOWN

Nantucket town boasts a large number of fine inns, most no more than a ten-minute walk from the ferry. All rooms at all of the inns discussed below have private baths.

76 Main Street offers 12 bright and comfortable rooms in the main inn and six rather motel-like rooms behind the inn. Third-floor rooms are small but newly remodeled, while first- and second-floor rooms have high ceilings and dark woodwork. The manager is very knowledgeable about Nantucket politics and life.

The **Jared Coffin House**, a collection of six historic buildings from the mid-1800s on Broad Street, has 60 antiques-filled rooms with unusual configurations; most have a television. Common spaces are lovely, and a full breakfast is served.

Seven Sea Street, of new post-and-beam construction, has eight rooms off a center hallway. Braided rugs, Early American furnishings, and a television and refrigerator are standard amenities. There are also a rooftop widow's walk and a Jacuzzi.

The **Corner House**, on Centre Street, nicely restored to its 18th-century origins, is tastefully furnished with English and American antiques. The 15 rooms are quite varied: Some have cathedral ceilings, some are painted in period colors, and one is a stupendous suite. There is plenty of common space, indoors and out; afternoon tea is served.

Across the street, the **Anchor Inn** (open April through December) features 11 unpretentious rooms of all shapes and sizes, all furnished with comfortable antiques. The innkeepers are particularly helpful. There's a nice terrace off the house. The Anchor Inn also rents two large residences, fully equipped to accommodate four or five people.

The **Harbor House** is a large complex of beautifully landscaped buildings surrounding an 1880s summer house on South Beach Street. The 111 rooms and town houses are decorated with sophistication. The Harbor House offers off-season packages that are difficult for smaller properties to match.

The next batch of inns is on the perimeter of town, but still not more than a 15-minute walk from the wharves. **Ten Lyon Street Inn**, renovated from top to bottom, has seven rooms decorated with great flair. They are warm without feeling cluttered, sophisticated without being stuffy. Attention to detail is apparent from the carefully tended garden to the ironed cotton sheets; open mid-April to mid-December. The six luxurious guest rooms at **Centerboard Guest House** attract upper-crust urbanites. Rooms are romantic and comfortable, with television. **Cliff Lodge**, which sits atop a hill on Cliff Road, offers simple English country decor and a television in each of its 11 rooms. There are nice views from the roof walk.

There are also a few fine places to stay on the water. Packed tightly together, **Wharf Cottages**, on Swain's and Old South wharves, are popular with yacht owners who dock at the front door. The 28 cottages have a kitchen, sleep two to seven people, and need to be reserved well in advance. Open late May to mid-October. The **White Elephant Inn and Cottages**, open mid-May to mid-September, consists of 48 rooms and many one-, two-, and three-bedroom cottages. The White Elephant has the feeling of a resort, especially at the harborside pool, where guests can enjoy a fancy luncheon. The exclusive **Cliffside Beach Club**, a mile (1½ km) northeast of the center of town on Jefferson Avenue, offers 27 stylishly contemporary and bright rooms, suites, and apartments on a private beach. Open late May to mid-October.

DINING IN NANTUCKET TOWN

Dining in Nantucket can be a very serious and costly undertaking, and where you eat may be determined by where you can get a reservation. Many of the restaurants have two seatings in July and August; reservations are always advised.

At 1 South Beach Street, **Second Story**, so named because it's above an antiques store, is identifiable only by the shiny plaque on the door. This boisterous bistro serves a mix of Spanish, French, Cajun, and Thai dishes, some quite spicy, all well presented. The decor consists of mismatched chairs and silverware and local art on the walls. Open for dinner only, April through December; Tel: (508) 228-3471.

Straight Wharf gained fame through its original owner, Marian Morash, who co-wrote the *Victory Garden Cookbook* with Jim Crockett and Julia Child in the early 1980s. Reservations are difficult to get, but excellent appetizers are available at the bar if you just want to sample the food or have a light meal. Straight Wharf is renowned for its fresh fish as well as its wonderful way with produce, and the atmosphere is sophisticated yet casual. The restaurant also operates a fish market and gourmet shop called **Provisions**, also on Straight Wharf. Open for dinner only, from mid-June to mid-September; Tel: (508) 228-4499.

21 Federal (named for its address) offers traditional and creative American cuisine on a courtyard patio for lunch and in one of eight small dining rooms for dinner. One of the less pretentious places on the island, the restaurant has a country-elegant atmosphere. The convivial bar is popular with year-rounders, summer residents, and short-term visitors alike. Open April through December; Tel: (508) 228-2121.

Every night from late May to mid-October, **Company of the Cauldron**, at 7 India Street, offers a different prix-fixe dinner. It's a small, romantic place (with excellent breads and flower arrangements) with an atmosphere not unlike that of a small dinner party; Tel: (508) 228-4016. The chef-owner of **India House**, in a historic building at 37 India Street, is known for his pecan-glazed swordfish and the special lamb India House, a tenderloin rolled in Dijon mustard and honey, then in French bread crumbs and spices, and roasted and served with a béarnaise sauce. All dishes are consistently good here, and prices are slightly lower than at other comparable places. A lighter café menu is served in a garden to the accompaniment of classical music. Open for dinner and a fixed-price Sunday brunch, from April through December; Tel: (508) 228-9043.

The cuisine at **Le Languedoc**, at 24 Broad Street, is creative Continental, the atmosphere formal; dinner is served by hurricane lamp in four small rooms. Downstairs in the basement there's an informal café that serves some of the same appetizers offered upstairs, as well as lighter (and less expensive) fish, pasta, and burgers. There's a covered sidewalk café, too. Open for lunch and dinner, April through December; Tel: (508) 228-2552.

Housed in a 1709 building at 29 Fair Street, the **Woodbox** exemplifies historic Nantucket. Continental fare is featured; beef Wellington is a specialty. The restaurant is open for breakfast and dinner from June through Thanksgiving; Tel: (508) 228-0587. **American Seasons** has simple Southwest decor and prepares eclectic and contemporary American dinners. It's more affordable and a little more out of the way, at 80 Centre Street, than most. Closed in February and March; Tel: (508) 228-7111.

Less Expensive Dining
On the less formal and less expensive side, not requiring reservations, is the popular **Tap Room** at the Jared Coffin House (29 Broad Street; Tel: 508/228-2400), serving familiar American staples for lunch, between-meal snacks, and dinner. The **Brotherhood of Thieves**, at 23 Broad Street, packs in the crowds with burgers, hefty sandwiches, and very good thinly cut fries. Open for lunch and dinner all year except February.

For quick, inexpensive food try the **Espresso Café**, at 40 Main Street, serving tasty pizzas, soups, hearty stews, sandwiches, salads, and strong coffee. The **Downeyflake**, at Children's Beach, dishes out breakfast and lunch until late in the afternoon; the simple setting is appreciated primarily by year-rounders. Closed mid-November to mid-March; Tel: (508) 228-4533. At the end of Old South Wharf, **Morning Glory Café** puts out well-priced lunches and dinners from an open kitchen; most of the dining is outside. Open mid-April to mid-October; Tel: (508) 228-2212. A 15-minute walk northwest out of town, at 50 Cliff Road, **Something Natural** makes sandwiches worth the walk. Open mid-May to mid-October; Tel: (508) 228-0504.

Elsewhere on the Island

SIASCONSET

From the traffic rotary southeast of town, take Milestone Road east—past the world's largest working cranberry bog—to Siasconset (shortened to 'Sconset by islanders), 9 miles (14½ km) from Nantucket town. The island's second largest town and its easternmost settlement, 'Sconset consists of a general store, a rotary, a few restaurants, a private tennis club, and a beach. Its curving lanes are lined with fashionable, rambling shingle-style houses. In the late 1800s artists came this way in search of unspoiled scenery, and found it in 'Sconset. But almost two centuries before that, fishermen lived in one-room shacks on the water, which have since been enlarged to multi-room residential cottages surrounded by white picket fences, covered in late June (and again in September) by hundreds of roses. The road north to **Sankaty Head Lighthouse** affords views of the ocean, cranberry bogs, and deserted moors.

One of the island's best, priciest, and most romantic restaurants is 'Sconset's **Chanticleer**. Lunch is served in a rose-covered courtyard, while dinner is in one of three lovely dining rooms. The cuisine is classical French, the ambience one of exclusivity. Open mid-May to mid-October; Tel: (508) 257-6231. At the traffic rotary, **'Sconset Café** offers excellent, more casual lunches and dinners from May to September; Tel: (508) 257-4008. Or you might pick up a picnic lunch, lemonade, and ice cream at **Siasconset Market**, a general store, or a clambake to go at **Claudette's Box Lunch**; both are open late May to mid-October.

POLPIS ROAD

Polpis Road leads northeast from the traffic rotary at Nantucket town to the **Wauwinet**, the island's most expensive place to stay, with 35 rooms and five cottages (open late April through November). The remote location, manicured lawns, country antiques, and indulgent service are an unbeatable combination. The sun literally rises and sets over its private beaches on both the protected bay and the Atlantic.

It's easy to see how the ocean constantly changes the shoreline of the island out here. In the northeaster of October 1991, for example, Great Point, north of the inn, became an island for most of the winter when the ocean broke through a narrow section of beach known as the Galls. After currents gradually deposited more and more sand, the beach was again reconnected. Great Point is accessible via four-wheel-drive vehicle only. The Wauwinet's restaurant, **Toppers**, is one of the island's finest (non-houseguests are welcome for lunch and dinner and Sunday brunch). The New American food transcends expectations, while the service and setting, too, receive the highest praise; Tel: (508) 228-0145.

BEACHES

Windswept beaches exposed to the Atlantic Ocean on the south shore typically have one- to two-foot waves and a strong undertow. Beaches on the northern shore get seaweedy and have gentle waves, while those on the eastern shore, at 'Sconset, are similar but have a strong undertow. Among the first kind, **Surfside Beach** is the most popular, just 2½ miles (4 km) from Nantucket town via Surfside Road. Farther west, reached by Hummock Pond Road from Nantucket town, **Cisco Beach** is the least spoiled and is favored by surfers. **Madaket Beach**, white and sandy with clear surf, is 5½ miles (9 km) west of town along Cliff and Madaket roads. **Dionis Beach** is on the north shore a few miles west of town facing Nantucket Sound.

GETTING AROUND

Cape Cod

By Boat. Although Cape Cod is most accessible by car, a network of boats, buses, trains, and planes goes to the Cape as well. **Bay State Cruises** (Tel: 617/723-7800) operates a daily boat between Boston and Provincetown (three hours each way), from late May through early September. From Plymouth, **Cape Cod Cruises** (Tel: 508/747-2400 or 800/242-2469) also sails to Provincetown (one and a half hours). Neither accepts cars, but bikes are allowed.

By Bus. Bonanza (Tel: 617/720-4110 or 800/556-3815) operates buses from Boston to Falmouth and Woods Hole, and from New York and Providence to Woods Hole, Falmouth, and Hyannis. From Boston, **Plymouth & Brockton** (Tel: 508/775-5524) buses connect towns along Route 6A, Hyannis, and out to Provincetown. Plymouth & Brockton also offers local bus service to many smaller towns.

By Train. On Fridays in the summer only, **Amtrak** (Tel: 800/USA-RAIL) discharges passengers from New York City and Providence in Sandwich, West Barnstable, and Hyannis; it makes the return trip on Sundays.

By Air. The **Barnstable Municipal Airport** (Tel: 508/775-

2020) in Hyannis is the largest on Cape Cod. **Business Express/Delta Connection** (Tel: 800/345-3400) flies from Boston to Hyannis; **Northwest Airlink/Precision Air** (Tel: 800/225-2525) flies from New York to Hyannis; **Cape Air** (Tel: 508/771-6944 or 800/352-0714) flies from Boston to Hyannis with a layover in Martha's Vineyard. The **Provincetown Municipal Airport** (Tel: 508/487-0240) is also served by Cape Air.

For Further Information. Write to the chamber of commerce, Hyannis, MA 02601 (Tel: 508/362-3225) for specific information. Or stop in at one of their seasonal, well-stocked booths: at the Sagamore Bridge rotary and on the south side of the Cape Cod Canal on Route 28 in Bourne.

Martha's Vineyard

Getting to the Ferry. There are many ways to reach the Vineyard. Drive or take the bus to Woods Hole or Hyannis on Cape Cod. **Bonanza Bus Lines** (Tel: 401/751-8800 or, in New England, 800/556-3815) serves Woods Hole from Boston, Providence, and New York City. Be forewarned, however: While some buses appear to connect with the ferries, they are not guaranteed to do so. **Plymouth & Brockton** buses (Tel: 508/775-5524) serve Hyannis from Boston.

By Boat. The **Steamship Authority** in Woods Hole (Tel: 508/540-2022 for car reservations) operates frequent year-round service to Vineyard Haven and Oak Bluffs. It is the only company (from any port) that carries autos. It is imperative to have an auto reservation during the summer, but if you are unable to get one, the Steamship Authority has a "guaranteed standby policy." Effective from late May through mid-October, it guarantees transport of your car on a space-available basis if you are in the "standby line" by 2:00 P.M. Passage takes about 45 minutes.

Travellers without cars have a few choices for getting to the Vineyard. The **Island Queen** in Falmouth (Tel: 508/548-4800) makes the 40-minute trip daily from mid-May through mid-October. **Hy-Line** (Tel: 508/778-2600) operates boats from Hyannis for the one hour and 45 minute trip to Oak Bluffs from May through October. From New Bedford, **Martha's Vineyard Ferry** (Tel: 508/997-1688) operates a limited number of boats daily from mid-May through mid-October; the voyage takes almost two hours.

Public mooring facilities are available in Vineyard Haven, Oak Bluffs, Edgartown, and Menemsha for private boats.

By Air. **Cape Air** (Tel: 508/771-6944 or 800/352-0714) flies from Boston, Hyannis, and New Bedford. During the summer, **Continental** (Tel: 800/525-0280) flies seasonally from Newark, New Jersey. The Martha's Vineyard Airport, located in the center of the island, is 4 miles (6½ km) from Edgartown and 6 miles (10 km) from Vineyard Haven. Taxis meet every incoming flight, but car rentals are also available in the summer through All-Island Rental (Tel: 508/693-6868).

By Car and Bicycle. In some cases the best way to get around New England's largest island is by car. For longer stays (and a stay of any length up-island) a car is necessary for convenience and in-depth exploring. On the other hand a car is also necessary if you don't have much time. The island's leisurely pace and (mostly) gentle terrain also make it a good place for cycling. Bicycle routes between Edgartown, Vineyard Haven, and Oak Bluffs are flat; distances range from 3 to 7 miles (5 to 11 km). If you're exploring up-island, however, the terrain is very hilly and distances are significant. It's 20 miles (32 km) to Gay Head from Oak Bluffs or Vineyard Haven. In any event, there are numerous car-rental, moped, and bicycle agencies near the boat docks. (All the ferries mentioned above allow bicycles on board.)

Car-rental agencies include Adventure Rentals (Tel: 508/693-1959) in Oak Bluffs and Vineyard Haven, Budget (Tel: 508/693-1911) in Oak Bluffs, Hertz (Tel: 508/627-4727) in Edgartown, and Rent-a-Wreck (Tel: 508/693-8838) in Vineyard Haven. If you can secure an auto reservation on the ferry and plan to stay on-island for more than a few days, it is more cost-effective to bring your own car. Otherwise, rent. In the height of the season make a rental car reservation as early as possible.

Tours. Tour buses meet incoming ferries for a two-and-a-half-hour narrated tour; all buses stop at Gay Head cliffs. In the summer, public school bus–type vehicles travel between Vineyard Haven, Oak Bluffs, Edgartown, and Gay Head. They're dependable as long as you're not on a tight schedule. Bus service is more limited from early May to late June and from mid-September to mid-October, at which time it stops completely until early May.

For Further Information. Innkeepers are an invaluable source of information that you can exploit throughout your stay. The chamber of commerce (P.O. Box 1698, Vineyard Haven, MA 02568; Tel: 508/693-0085), not far from the ferry on Beach Street, prints a wealth of information.

Nantucket

By Boat. Take a bus (see the Vineyard section, above) or drive to Hyannis on Cape Cod. From Hyannis the **Steamship Authority** (Tel: 508/540-2022) offers daily service to Nantucket year-round; reservations (made well in advance) are essential for autos. **Hy-Line** (Tel: 508/778-2600) offers passengers-only service from Hyannis. The trip takes about one hour and 45 minutes.

By Air. Many airlines serve Nantucket: **Cape Air** (Tel: 508/771-6944 or 800/352-0714) from Hyannis via Martha's Vineyard and from New Bedford; **Island Air** (Tel: 800/248-7779) from Hyannis; **Nantucket Airlines** (Tel: 800/635-8787) from Hyannis; **Northwest Airlink** (Tel: 800/225-2525) from Boston and Hyannis; and **Business Express/Delta Connection** (Tel: 800/345-3400) from Boston and Hyannis. Nantucket's airport is 4 miles (6½ km) from town and is served by taxis. Car-rental agencies at the airport include Budget (Tel: 508/228-5666 or 800/527-0700) and National (Tel: 508/228-0300 or 800/227-7368).

By Car. Nantucket town is small and should be covered on foot. Much of the rest of the island can be toured easily by bicycle. You can rent a four-wheel-drive vehicle for dune travel. Essentially, you do not need a car on Nantucket unless you are staying for a long time or are staying at one of the few remote inns mentioned. There is no public transportation on the island, but taxis are plentiful.

For Further Information. The chamber of commerce (Main Street, Nantucket, MA 02554; Tel: 508/228-1700) publishes a very complete Nantucket guide; it's three dollars if you order it, but on the island it's free. The information bureau (25 Federal Street, Nantucket, MA 02554; Tel 508/228-0925) is also very helpful.

Inter-Island

Passengers can travel by boat between Martha's Vineyard and Nantucket from June to mid-September via **Hy-Line** (Tel: 508/778-2600 or 693-0112, on the Vineyard); the trip takes two hours. **Cape Air** (Tel: 508/771-6944 or 800/352-0714) flies between the islands. It is not possible to travel between the Vineyard and Nantucket with a car; visitors often bring a car to the Vineyard, leave it near the dock, and take the passenger ferry to Nantucket for a couple days.

ACCOMMODATIONS REFERENCE
Unless otherwise noted, the rates given below are projections for the 1993 high season for double room, double occupancy. As prices are subject to change, always double-check before booking. The area code for Cape Cod and the Islands is 508.

Cape Cod: Sandwich to Orleans

▶ **Beechwood.** 2839 Main Street, **Barnstable**, MA 02630. Tel: 362-6618. $110–$145; includes breakfast.

▶ **Captain Freeman Inn.** 15 Breakwater Road, **Brewster**,

MA 02631. Tel: 896-7481 or (800) 843-4664. $75–$185; includes breakfast.

▶ **Charles Hinckley House**. Old Kings Highway, P.O. Box 723, **Barnstable**, MA 02630. Tel: 362-9924. $119–$149; includes breakfast.

▶ **Dan'l Webster Inn**. 149 Main Street, **Sandwich**, MA 02563. Tel: 888-3623. $99–$175.

▶ **Four Chimneys Inn**. 946 Main Street, **Dennis**, MA 02638. Tel: 385-6317. $45–$90; includes breakfast.

▶ **High Brewster**. 964 Setucket Road, **Brewster**, MA 02631. Tel: 896-3636. $80–$160; includes breakfast.

▶ **Isaiah Hall B&B Inn**. 152 Whig Street, **Dennis**, MA 02638. Tel: 385-9928 or (800) 736-0160. $55–$98; includes breakfast.

▶ **Lane's End Cottage**. 268 Main Street, **Yarmouth Port**, MA 02675. Tel: 362-5298. $75–$95; includes breakfast.

▶ **Nauset House Inn**. 143 Beach Road, P.O. Box 774, **East Orleans**, MA 02643. Tel: 255-2195. $55–$95.

▶ **Old Sea Pines Inn**. 2553 Main Street, **Brewster**, MA 02631. Tel: 896-6114. $40–$85; includes breakfast.

▶ **One Centre Street Inn**. 1 Centre Street, **Yarmouth Port**, MA 02675. Tel: 362-8910. $50–$100; includes buffet breakfast.

▶ **Summer House**. 158 Main Street, **Sandwich**, MA 02563. Tel: 888-4991. $60–$75; includes breakfast.

▶ **Wedgewood**. 83 Main Street, **Yarmouth Port**, MA 02675. Tel: 362-5157. $105–$150; includes breakfast.

The Outer Cape

▶ **Hargood House**. 493 Commercial Street, **Provincetown**, MA 02657. Tel: 487-9133. $638–$1,200 weekly; $69–$139 daily (off-season only).

▶ **Holden Inn**. Commercial Street, P.O. Box 816, **Wellfleet**, MA 02667. Tel: 349-3450. $53–$63.

▶ **Inn at Duck Creeke**. Main Street, P.O. Box 364, **Wellfleet**, MA 02667. Tel: 349-9333. $60–$80.

▶ **Land's End Inn**. 22 Commercial Street, **Provincetown**, MA 02657. Tel: 487-0706. $98–$220.

▶ **Masthead**. 31–41 Commercial Street, **Provincetown**, MA 02657. Tel: 487-0523 or (800) 395-5095. Rooms $119–$142 nightly; apartments and cottages $863–$1,335 weekly.

▶ **Overlook Inn**. 3085 Route 6, P.O. Box 771, **Eastham**, MA 02642. Tel: 255-1886 or (800) 356-1121. $90–$110; includes breakfast.

▶ **Ship's Bell Motel**. 586 Commercial Street, **Provincetown**, MA 02657. Tel: 487-1674. $72–$172.

▶ **Surfside**. 543 Commercial Street, **Provincetown**, MA 02657. Tel: 487-1726. $80–$97.

▶ **Truro Motor Inn**. Route 6, P.O. Box 364, **North Truro**, MA 02652. Tel: 487-3628. $51–$61.

▶ **Watermark Inn.** 603 Commercial Street, **Provincetown**, MA 02657. Tel: 487-0165 or (800) 734-0165. $90–$245.

▶ **Whalewalk Inn.** 220 Bridge Road, **Eastham**, MA 02642. Tel: 255-0617. $90–$150; includes breakfast.

▶ **White Horse Inn.** 500 Commercial Street, **Province-town**, MA 02657. Tel: 487-1790. $60–$100.

▶ **Windamar House.** 568 Commercial Street, **Province-town**, MA 02657. Tel: 487-0599. $65–$85.

Cape Cod's South Shore

▶ **Breakwaters.** 432 Sea Street, **Hyannis**, MA 02601. Tel: 775-6831. $850 per week.

▶ **Captain's House Inn of Chatham.** 371 Old Harbor Road, **Chatham**, MA 02633. Tel: 945-0127. $119–$179.

▶ **Chatham Bars Inn.** Chatham Bars Avenue and Shore Road, **Chatham**, MA 02633. Tel: 945-0096 or (800) 527-4884. $150–$350.

▶ **Cranberry Inn.** 359 Main Street, **Chatham**, MA 02633. Tel: 945-9232 or (800) 332-4667. $112–$150.

▶ **Elm Arch Inn.** 26 Elm Arch Way, **Falmouth**, MA 02540. Tel: 548-0133. $55–$65.

▶ **House on the Hill.** 968 Main Street, **South Harwich**, MA 02661. Tel: 432-4321. $55–$65; includes breakfast.

▶ **Inn at West Falmouth.** P.O. Box 1208, **West Falmouth**, MA 02574. Tel: 540-6503 or 540-7696. $135–$185.

▶ **Inn on Sea Street.** 358 Sea Street, **Hyannis**, MA 02601. Tel: 775-8030. $70–$90; includes breakfast.

▶ **Lighthouse Inn. West Dennis**, MA 02670. Tel: 398-2244. $138–$220; includes breakfast and dinner.

▶ **Moses Nickerson House.** 364 Old Harbor Road, **Chatham**, MA 02633. Tel: 945-5859 or (800) 628-6972. $99–$149; includes breakfast.

▶ **Mostly Hall.** 27 West Main Street, **Falmouth**, MA 02540. Tel: 548-3786 or (800) 682-0565. $95–$105; includes breakfast.

▶ **New Seabury Resort.** Rock Landing Road, P.O. Box 550, **New Seabury**, MA 02649. Tel: 477-9111 or, in MA, (800) 999-9033. $190–$240.

▶ **Old Crocker Barn.** 278 Gosnold Street, **Hyannis**, MA 02601. Tel: 799-5807 or 785-0701. $650–$750 per week.

▶ **Village Green Inn.** 40 West Main Street, **Falmouth**, MA 02540. Tel: 548-5621. $90–$110.

▶ **Wequassett Inn.** Pleasant Bay, **Chatham**, MA 02633. Tel: 432-5400 or (800) 225-7125. $170–$400.

Martha's Vineyard

▶ **Attleboro House.** 11 Lake Avenue, **Oak Bluffs**, MA 02557. Tel: 693-4346. $45–$125.

▶ **Beach Plum Inn.** Menemsha, MA 02552. Tel: 645-9454. $130–$275; includes breakfast.

▶ **Blue Goose.** Old Courthouse Road, West Tisbury, MA 02575. Tel: 693-3223. $65–$75.

▶ **Breakfast at Tiasquam.** Middle Road, RR 1, Box 296, Chilmark, MA 02535. Tel: 645-3685. $105–$185; includes breakfast.

▶ **Captain Dexter House.** 35 Pease's Point Way, P.O. Box 2798, Edgartown, MA 02539. Tel: 627-7289. $120–$180.

▶ **Captain R. Flanders' House.** North Road, P.O. Box 384, Chilmark, MA 02535. Tel: 645-3123. $85–$150; house rentals $1,500–$1,600 weekly.

▶ **Charlotte Inn.** South Summer Street, Edgartown, MA 02539. Tel: 627-4751. $175–$295; suites $245–$450.

▶ **Daggett House.** 59 North Water Street, Edgartown, MA 02539. Tel: 627-4600. $130–$230; includes Continental breakfast.

▶ **Harbor View Hotel.** 131 North Water Street, P.O. Box 7, Edgartown, MA 02539. Tel: 627-7000 or (800) 225-6005. $195–$475.

▶ **Lambert's Cove Country Inn.** Lambert's Cove Road, RFD 422, Vineyard Haven, MA 02568. Tel: 693-2298. $110–$145.

▶ **Lothrop Merry House.** Owen Park, P.O. Box 1939, Vineyard Haven, MA 02568. Tel: 693-1646. $88–$155.

▶ **Menemsha Inn and Cottages.** North Road, Menemsha, MA 02552. Tel: 645-2521. $105–$220; cottages $675–$975 weekly.

▶ **Oak House.** Seaview Avenue, P.O. Box 299, Oak Bluffs, MA 02557. Tel: 693-4187. $110–$220.

▶ **Outermost Inn.** Lighthouse Road, RR 1, Box 171, Gay Head, MA 02535. Tel: 645-3511. $195–$220.

▶ **Point Way Inn.** Pease's Point Way and Main Street, P.O. Box 5255, Edgartown, MA 02539. Tel: 627-8633 or (800) 942-9569. $110–$225.

▶ **Shiverick Inn.** Pease's Point Way, P.O. Box 640, Edgartown, MA 02539. Tel: 627-3797 or (800) 723-4292. $165–$225.

▶ **Thorncroft Inn.** 278 Main Street, P.O. Box 1022, Vineyard Haven, MA 02568. Tel: 693-3333. $129–$299; includes breakfast.

▶ **Wesley Hotel.** 1 Lake Avenue, P.O. Box 2370, Oak Bluffs, MA 02557. Tel: 693-6611. $110–$140.

Nantucket

▶ **Anchor Inn.** 66 Centre Street, P.O. Box 387, Nantucket, MA 02554. Tel: 228-0072. $85–$135; apartments $1,120 weekly.

▶ **Centerboard Guest House.** 8 Chester Street, P.O. Box 456, Nantucket, MA 02554. Tel: 228-9696. $145–$245.

▶ **Cliff Lodge.** 9 Cliff Road, **Nantucket**, MA 02554. Tel: 228-9480. $100–$150.

▶ **Cliffside Beach Club.** Jefferson Avenue, P.O. Box 449, **Nantucket**, MA 02554. Tel: 228-0618. $230–$355.

▶ **Corner House.** 49 Centre Street, P.O. Box 1828, **Nantucket**, MA 02554. Tel: 228-1530. $85–$145.

▶ **Harbor House.** South Beach Street, P.O. Box 359, **Nantucket**, MA 02554. Tel: 228-5500 or (800) ISLANDS. $190–$240.

▶ **Jared Coffin House.** 29 Broad Street, P.O. Box 1580, **Nantucket**, MA 02554. Tel: 228-2400. $135–$170; includes breakfast.

▶ **Seven Sea Street.** 7 Sea Street, **Nantucket**, MA 02554. Tel: 228-3577. $145–$165.

▶ **76 Main Street.** 76 Main Street, **Nantucket**, MA 02554. Tel: 228-2533. $115–$135.

▶ **Ten Lyon Street Inn.** 10 Lyon Street, **Nantucket**, MA 02554. Tel: 228-5040. $120–$160.

▶ **Wauwinet.** Wauwinet Road, P.O. Box 2580, **Nantucket**, MA 02554. Tel: 228-8718 or (800) 426-8718. $250–$620; cottage $825 nightly; includes breakfast.

▶ **Wharf Cottages.** P.O. Box 1139, **Nantucket**, MA 02554. Tel: 228-4620 or (800) ISLANDS. $230–$295.

▶ **White Elephant Inn and Cottages.** Easton Street, P.O. Box 359, **Nantucket**, MA 02554. Tel: 228-2500 or (800) IS-LANDS. $145–$595.

Reservation and Rental Services

Provincetown Reservations System (Tel: 800/648-0364) secures hotel and inn rooms. The **Provincetown Chamber of Commerce** (Tel: 487-3424) publishes **Provincetown Discovery**, which includes long-term rentals.

Rooms on Nantucket and Martha's Vineyard can be found through **Martha's Vineyard and Nantucket Reservations** (Tel: 693-7200 or, in Massachusetts, 800/649-5671); **Nantucket Accommodations** (Tel: 228-9559) serves Nantucket only.

Weekly and monthly condominium, cottage, apartment, and house rentals can be sought on the islands through the following agencies. **Flanders Real Estate** (Tel: 645-2632) specializes in up-island stays on Martha's Vineyard of two weeks or more (houses and cottages only). **Martha's Vineyard Vacation Rentals** (Tel: 693-7711) is one of the few places that books one-week rentals. **Nantucket Vacation Rentals** (Tel: 228-3131) maintains listings of more than 300 cottages, apartments, and houses scattered all over Nantucket.

CENTRAL AND WESTERN MASSA-CHUSETTS

By B. J. Roche

B. J. Roche writes for the Boston Globe *about western Massachusetts and is an adjunct instructor of journalism at the University of Massachusetts at Amherst. Her work has appeared in the* Washington Post, The New York Times, *and the* Chicago Tribune, *and in* Travel & Leisure, Country Journal, New Woman, *and* Walking *magazines.*

As you leave the eastern part of Massachusetts you begin to ascend, imperceptibly at first, into the hills of the central and western parts of the state: the rolling uplands of central Massachusetts around Mount Wachusett and, beyond, first the Holyoke range and then the Berkshire Hills near the New York State border.

The pace is slower, the scale smaller in central and western Massachusetts. Yet the region has the best of both the urban and rural worlds; tucked into stretches of sometimes awe-inspiring landscape are pockets of sophistication and an abundance of cultural activities. The pleasures to be found here are varied, ranging from a picnic by a stream to a find in an out-of-the-way antiques shop to a discovery of old ways at one of the region's three village museums—to something new at a concert or a performance at one of many festivals and performance halls.

If you're an urban animal in search of the next club trend, or a foodie looking for the culinary cutting edge, central and western Massachusetts are not for you. The draw of this part of New England is its quiet and its countryside, its unpretentious villages and eclectic college towns. The biggest cities here—Worcester, Springfield, and Pittsfield—are not the area's best offerings, but they do have fascinating and sometimes quirky museums and good ethnic restaurants, established in the days when immigrants flooded the region to work in its now-rusting mills and factories.

Central and western Massachusetts is an excellent part of New England for those who enjoy the outdoors. There are nearly 90 state forests, recreation areas, and parks here, and dozens of public reserves owned by private environmental groups. The Appalachian Trail traverses the Berkshires, and the Mid-State Trail runs through central Massachusetts into New Hampshire. There are waterfalls, gorges, ponds, and lakes, and the Connecticut and Deerfield rivers offer fishing, boating, and rafting opportunities.

But even if your idea of an outdoor activity is hoisting a beer in a sidewalk café, you'll enjoy this region for its combination of rural beauty, easygoing attitudes, and Yankee sensibilities. Bring some comfortable shoes and casual clothes.

MAJOR INTEREST

Worcester's museums, especially the Worcester Art Museum
Old Sturbridge Village
Brimfield Outdoor Antique Shows

The Pioneer Valley (Connecticut River)
Springfield: Museums and Naismith Memorial Basketball Hall of Fame
College towns of Northampton and Amherst
Historic Deerfield

The Mohawk Trail
Scenic route along the Deerfield River, from Greenfield west to North Adams in the northern Berkshires

The Berkshires
Art and cultural offerings of Williamstown
Hancock Shaker Village, near Pittsfield
Lenox: Historic homes, Tanglewood, Shakespeare & Company summer theater

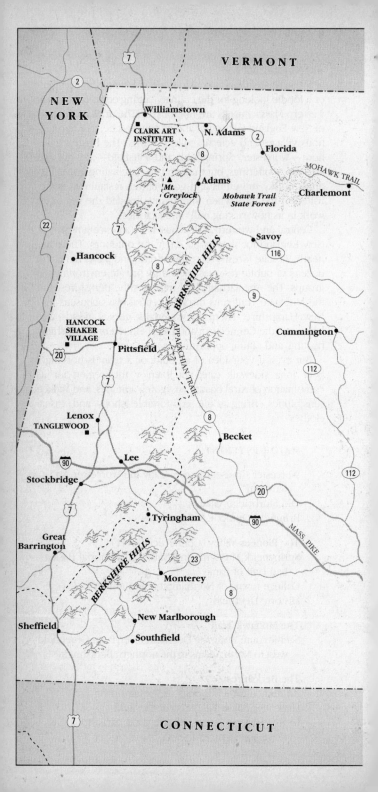

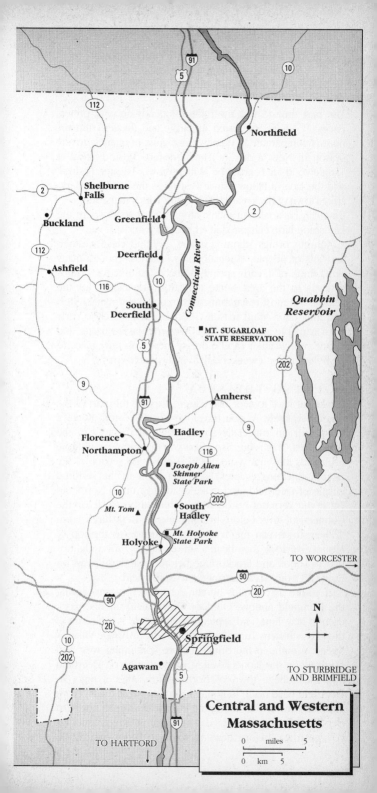

Central and Western Massachusetts

Stockbridge: Historic homes, Norman Rockwell Museum, Berkshire Theater Festival

Back-road drives and antiques shops

The best time to visit the region depends on your preferences. If you're interested in music and theater, summer here is comparable in quality if not quite in quantity to any season in New York City. The Berkshire Music Festival at Tanglewood in Lenox, the Williamstown Theater Festival, and the Jacob's Pillow Dance Festival in the southern Berkshires town of Becket are in full swing. Lunch in the summertime can be a takeout picnic along a back road where the landscape hasn't changed in a hundred years.

Autumn brings stunning colors, dry and clear weather, and lots of people, especially on weekends. Though many don't think of it, early spring can be a fine time for a quick getaway to the area. Some attractions are closed for the season, but most restaurants remain open, and many hotels and inns offer "mud season" specials. Early March to early April is maple sugaring time in western Massachusetts, and though the weather can be dreary there's no finer place to be holed up for a weekend than in a country inn.

TOURING THE AREA

It takes at least four or five days to explore this part of the state adequately. As you travel west from Boston, Route 2 makes for an especially scenic drive all the way to the Berkshires. This route also offers you the chance to visit the Fruitlands Museums (see the West of Boston section of the Boston Environs chapter), spend a night in the restored village of Deerfield, and make a side trip up to Northfield (near the Vermont border) and to take a boat ride on the Connecticut River before heading into the Berkshires. From Williamstown you might take an excursion to the top of Mount Greylock, then head south on Route 7 for a night or two in Lenox and Stockbridge before meandering east on Route 23 from Great Barrington to Springfield.

If you're an antiques hunter, schedule your trip during the Brimfield Antique Outdoor Shows, held for one week each in May, June, and September (Brimfield is just south of the Massachusetts Turnpike, not far from Sturbridge Village). Spend a night in Sturbridge before continuing west and north along the Pioneer Valley, concentrating on Deerfield and the college town of Northampton. After a night in Deerfield head north to Route 2, also known as the Mohawk Trail, and travel west along the Deerfield River to northern Berkshire County. Spend a day in Williamstown, yet another college town, before heading south to Lenox and Stockbridge. From there you can explore the "antiques alleys" of Sheffield and Egremont.

If your interests are of a more cultural bent you may want to begin in Worcester, spend a day at Old Sturbridge Village, and stay overnight in Sturbridge. The next day you might visit the museums of Springfield before heading to Northampton or Amherst for a night. Spend a morning in Deerfield before heading west along the Mohawk Trail to Williamstown. There you may want to stay overnight and visit museums or catch a play before heading south to Lenox and Stockbridge, where you should plan on at least a two-night stay. (Be sure to reserve tickets for performances early.)

History buffs will want to build a trip around the three museum villages in the region, each offering a look at a different time period in New England. Start at Old Sturbridge Village, head up to Deerfield, and wind up your visit in the Berkshires at Hancock Shaker Village.

Whatever your itinerary, don't schedule too much, and set aside some time to do nothing, because this is a great place to do it. Whether you laze away an afternoon by a waterfall in the middle of the woods or stretch out on a canopy bed with a good book, this region can renew you if you give it the time and pacing it deserves.

You'll need to book a room early if you're staying in Sturbridge during the Brimfield Outdoor Antique Shows in May, June, or September. In the college and prep-school towns of Amherst, Northampton, Deerfield, and Williamstown, rooms are booked a year ahead at graduation time in mid-May, so plan accordingly.

In the Berkshires, book early for a room during the summer Tanglewood season and during fall foliage season, which generally runs from mid-September to the third week in October. Also, it may be difficult to get a room for just one night in the summer, especially in the southern Berkshires. Many hotels and inns require a two- and sometimes three-night minimum on weekends when there is a performance at Tanglewood.

Our coverage begins in the central Massachusetts town of Worcester, 40 miles (64 km) west of Boston, and continues west from there to Old Sturbridge Village (with a good selection of accommodations and restaurants). We then zip along I-90 to the western Massachusetts city of Springfield at the foot of the Pioneer Valley and follow it (and the Connecticut River) north through the college towns of Northampton and Amherst and the historic town of Deerfield. Our route turns west again along the scenic Mohawk Trail (modern Route 2) to North Adams and Williamstown in the northern

Berkshires. Finally we head south through the old industrial city of Pittsfield to the cultural and pastoral delights of Lenox and Stockbridge in the southern Berkshires.

CENTRAL MASSACHUSETTS

Worcester

Located just 40 miles (64 km) west of Boston off the Massachusetts Turnpike, Worcester is the heart of central Massachusetts and the point of demarcation between eastern and western Massachusetts. A working-class city built on a series of hills, Worcester has given the country such diverse products as the valentine, the birth control pill, and the first NASA space suit. Perhaps more than any other city in New England, Worcester has a history of Yankee inventiveness and a population that reflects the region's immigration patterns over the past 200 years.

Early in its history Worcester was a hub for Revolutionary War activity. Isaiah Thomas moved his patriotic newspaper, *The Massachusetts Spy,* to Worcester in 1775 because he feared retribution from the Tories in Boston. Ten years later, after the war had been won, the farmers of Worcester lent their support to Daniel Shays, leader of the nation's first tax revolt.

Worcester's real flowering came in the 19th century, when thousands of workers in scores of mills cranked out products like wire, textiles, and even valentines for export all over the world. In 1875 the mayor dubbed Worcester the "City of Workshops"; and the place was, it seemed, bursting with inventors. Among their creations and developments were the fancy loom, which revolutionized the textile industry, and a wire manufacturing process. In fact, many of the products we take for granted—envelopes, for example— were made using Worcester inventions.

Today the mills that once employed immigrants from Canada and Europe are empty and abandoned or have been converted to other uses. With the exception of its upper-class residential neighborhoods, Worcester is not a particularly pretty city, despite perennial revitalization efforts. The city is much maligned in Massachusetts; one western Massachusetts rock group has as its signature song "Gotta Get Outta Worcester."

Despite its reputation the city does have some sights worth seeking out. It is home to seven colleges, including Holy Cross, Clark University, and Worcester Polytechnic Institute, and it has several small museums, launched in the 19th and early 20th centuries by Worcester's captains of industry.

The best way to tour Worcester is by car; the sights of interest are far-flung and sometimes hard to find. For a map and information, stop downtown at the Worcester County Convention° and Visitors Bureau at 33 Waldo Street; Tel: (508) 753-2920.

Mechanics Hall

Just around the corner from the visitors' bureau, at 321 Main Street, is Mechanics Hall, a source of great pride to the city. The Worcester County Mechanics Association, a group of skilled tradesmen and artisans, built the hall in 1857 as a venue for lecture series for the training of skilled laborers and for concerts.

With its sweeping staircases and richly decorated coffered ceiling, Mechanics Hall is considered by architectural historians to be the nation's finest pre–Civil War concert hall. It has served as the setting for such speakers as Dickens, Thoreau, and Emerson; Mark Twain and Teddy Roosevelt; and modern-day performers like Judy Collins and Itzhak Perlman. To this day the hall's acoustics are considered so fine that recording companies use it to record compact discs and tapes. Restored to its original magnificence in 1977, Mechanics Hall still hosts regular concerts, often free, on its 52-stop, 3,504-pipe organ, one of the largest in New England. For information, Tel: (508) 752-5608; box office, Tel: (508) 752-0888. The building is open on weekdays.

At the other end of the entertainment spectrum, but just a few blocks away, is the **Centrum**, a 14,000-seat arena built in 1980. Here you can see entertainers ranging from Anthrax to Bruce Springsteen to Frank Sinatra and Liza Minnelli. For information, Tel: (508) 798-8888; for tickets, Tel: (617) 931-2000.

Worcester Art Museum

As you head up Main Street to Highland Street, turn left and go two blocks to Lancaster Street. Two blocks down, at 55 Salisbury Street, is the Worcester Art Museum. Another good example of civic philanthropy, the museum was founded in 1892 by Stephen Salisbury III, a prominent businessman, "for the benefit of all the people."

If you make only one stop in Worcester, this should be it. Housed in an Italianate building, the museum is one of New England's best mid-size art museums, with some surprisingly innovative changing exhibitions, often photographic. Among the museum's 35 galleries is a broad sampling of works by American and European artists, including Bierstadt, Homer, Monet, and Gauguin, as well as antiquities from Egypt, Greece, and Rome. The museum also has a pleasant café that looks out onto a courtyard. Closed Mondays and holidays; Tel: (508) 799-4406.

Salisbury Mansion

Just up the hill at 40 Highland Street is the Salisbury Mansion; built in 1772, it served as the Salisbury family home until 1851. The house, which was moved in 1929 from its original location across from the city courthouse, is listed in the National Register of Historic Places. One of Worcester's few remaining 18th-century structures, the home is decorated in the fashion of the early 19th century and gives an idea of what life must have been like for one of Worcester's prominent upper-class families. The Worcester Historical Society also offers regular exhibitions on the decorative arts of the period. Open Thursday through Sunday from 1:00 to 4:00 P.M.; Tel: (508) 753-8278.

Historical and Higgins Armory Museums

Backtracking down Main, take a right onto Elm Street to reach the **Worcester Historical Museum** at 30 Elm, which offers a look at the city's more recent past, with a focus on its industrial, business, and ethnic history. Closed Mondays; Tel: (508) 753-8278.

Everyone in New England is a collector, it seems, and for industrialist John Woodman Higgins, the weakness was for armor. Higgins, who was president of the Worcester Pressed Steel Company, collected medieval and Renaissance armor and weapons until the collection grew too big for his home. In 1929 he built an industrial-cum-Art Deco building adjacent to his factory at 100 Barber Avenue, which later became the **Higgins Armory Museum**.

To get there, take Route 290 east to exit 20 and turn left onto Burncoat Street. At the second light, turn left onto Randolph Road and follow it until you come to the corner of Randolph and Barber. If the outside of the museum is an industrialist's sleek vision, the inside resembles a medieval castle, its great hall filled with examples of armor and weaponry from all over the world down through the ages, from a circa-1920s chain-mail flapper dress to a medieval set for a hunting dog. Children may try on pieces of armor in the Quest Gallery. Closed Mondays, except in summer; Tel: (508) 853-6015.

SHOPPING IN WORCESTER

Much of the shopping in Worcester has been relegated to the malls that keep sprouting up along Route 495. One exception can be found by travelling east on Route 9 toward the Shrewsbury line, at **Spag's**. Spag's is a bargain-basement Worcester institution, and a shopping experience not found in many places these days. Shoppers wander through several buildings filled with discount merchandise of all kinds, from tennis shoes (in odd sizes) to gardening equipment to groceries. Bring your own bags and an attitude.

NIGHTLIFE IN WORCESTER

In addition to concerts at Mechanics Hall or the Centrum, the colleges also have a full calendar of jazz, folk, drama, and dance performances. For listings of events, pick up a copy of the weekly *Worcester* magazine.

El Morocco, a restaurant at 100 Wall Street (discussed below), houses the **Nile Lounge**, a 100-seat venue that features big-name jazz performers; Tel: (508) 756-7117. The local alternative-rock crowd gathers across town at **Ralph's Chadwick Square Diner**, at 95 Prescott Street. Ralph's is youth democracy in action, a place where leather-clad rockers mix it up with college kids out on the town. There's live music, pool tables, and several bars; the diner serves good hamburgers. Tel: (508) 753-9543.

Gilrein's, at 802 Main Street, offers blues, jazz, and rock in a smoky bar atmosphere; Tel: (508) 791-2583. **Sir Morgan's Cove**, at 89 Green Street, had a brush with fame several years ago when the Rolling Stones tried out their act here in preparation for their world tour. This is the spot to see local rock bands. Tel: (508) 753-2188.

On the quieter side, in an old mill at 335 Chandler Street, **Tatnuck Booksellers** is a bookstore/gathering place featuring readings and some performances; Tel: (508) 756-7644.

STAYING AND DINING
IN WORCESTER

Worcester has all the major lodging chains, from the budget-priced Days Inn to the Marriott. Many visitors to the area stay in Sturbridge, a 20-minute ride away, and do Worcester as a day trip. If you choose to stay in Worcester, the **Beechwood Inn**, just off Route 9 at 363 Plantation Street, is a good bet. Located high on a hill near the University of Massachusetts Medical Center, the inn draws the medical and biotech travelling crowd. Its name is a bit deceiving: It's more like a hotel than a country inn, a round, five-story brick building with 58 spacious rooms, decorated with eclectic pine reproductions. Several of the junior suites have gas fireplaces, wing chairs, and sofas.

Even if you're not staying here, you should try the Beechwood's highly acclaimed restaurant, which offers New American dishes served by candlelight. Try the delicate butternut crab bisque and indulge in any of the homemade desserts, such as crème brulée or chocolate mousse–filled crepes. Tel: (508) 754-5789.

The influx of immigrants over the past century has left its mark on Worcester's restaurant scene. At 100 Wall Street, in a working-class neighborhood off Route 122 south, the **El Morocco** is an old-time Worcester institution, serving Lebanese and other Middle Eastern foods for lunch and dinner in a sprawling brick building overlooking the city. The walls are covered with photos from famous fans. Dishes include seafood, steaks, and such specialties as stuffed grape leaves, *hummus,* and *kibbe,* a spicy ground-lamb dish. (El Morocco's Nile Lounge is discussed under Nightlife, above.) Tel: (508) 756-7117.

Downtown at 144 Commercial Street, the **Thai Orchid** serves well-prepared Thai food in a contemporary setting; Tel: (508) 792-9701. Around the corner at 1 Exchange Place is **Legal Sea Foods**, the Worcester branch of the Boston-based restaurant chain. Just about everything is good here, including fried or broiled fish, crabcakes, and creamy New England clam chowder. There's even a lower-fat version of the chowder for those watching their weight. Tel: (508) 792-1600.

George's Coney Island, seven blocks down Main Street at 158 Southbridge Street, is a hot dog joint that dates to 1918. The decor, it seems, hasn't changed much since the 1950s, and lawyers and blue-collar workers sit shoulder to shoulder over dogs and Budweisers at lunchtime. Everybody orders more than one hot dog here, and they have them "up," that is, with everything on them: chili, onions—you name it; Tel: (508) 753-4362. The diner was perhaps one of Worcester's most popular and well-known inventions. Just up the street at 300 Southbridge is the **Miss Worcester Diner**, built by the Worcester Dining Car Company in 1919; Tel: (508) 752-1310.

Grafton

Follow Route 122 to Route 140 for about 8 miles (13 km) south of urban Worcester to the rural town of Grafton. Founded in 1735 and named for England's duke of Grafton, a Colonial sympathizer, the town has the only oval common in New England; North and South streets, just off the common, are lined with a wonderful collection of Federal and Greek Revival homes.

Turn onto North Street and follow the signs off the common to 11 Willard Street and the **Willard House and Clock Museum** for a look at the art of clock making in the 18th and 19th centuries. This handsomely restored red farmhouse displays 58 shelf and tall clocks made by the Willard brothers: Benjamin, Ephraim, Aaron, and Simon, considered among the finest New England clock makers. Willard clocks can still be found in the Supreme Court building in Washington, D.C., as well as in many buildings in the Boston area. Closed Mondays; Tel: (508) 839-3500.

Sturbridge

Travel west from Worcester for about 22 miles (35 km) on the Massachusetts Turnpike (I-90) to the town of Sturbridge. The not-so-pretty business district stretches along Route 20 west (also the town's main street). A turn east onto Route 131 brings you to the postcard-perfect Sturbridge Town Common, which once served as a drilling ground for Colonial militiamen, and today is ringed by beautiful Federal-style homes. There's an information booth operated by the Sturbridge Area Tourist Association at 380 Main Street, Route 20, in Sturbridge; Tel: (800) 628-8379 or (508) 347-7594.

Old Sturbridge Village

Old Sturbridge Village, located in the center of Sturbridge on Main Street (Route 20), is the highlight of any tour of central Massachusetts. The largest living-history village in the Northeast, Old Sturbridge is a model of a rural New England town in the 1830s, a time of transition in the countryside as mass-produced goods began to replace the old craftsmen. It provides a fascinating look at the time, from wool carding and sawmills, both powered by water, to the white-steepled **Center Meetinghouse** on the common and the **Knight General Store**, filled with goods from rum sold in bulk to ribbons and china from England.

More than 40 buildings have been moved here from all over New England; even the farm animals are representative of breeds raised in the 1830s. Informative interpreters dress in 19th-century clothes, and special events are held throughout the year for those interested in specific aspects of 19th-century New England life.

The village's **Museum Gift Shop and New England Bookstore** is among the best in the Northeast, with an extensive collection of books on regional history, gardening, food, and decorative arts. If you're interested in any aspect of New England history, no matter how arcane, you're likely to find a book on it here.

Just up the hill from Old Sturbridge Village is **Bethlehem in Sturbridge**, an animated diorama more than 50 feet in diameter with more than 800 figurines illustrating the birth of Christ. This obsessive labor of love by J. George Duquette draws hundreds of visitors at Christmas and Easter. For the schedule of shows, Tel: (508) 347-3013.

Old Sturbridge Village is open year-round; in fact, winter is a good time to come here. Local lodgings offer weekend packages then, and the museum has hands-on activities for visitors. Join a 19th-century housewife for tea and parlor games, or enjoy a meal prepared in the manner of the time. Tel: (413) 347-3362.

SHOPPING IN THE STURBRIDGE AREA

Seven miles (11 km) up Route 20 west is the sleepy country town of **Brimfield**, which undergoes a metamorphosis three times each year during the **Brimfield Outdoor Antique Shows**, the largest outdoor flea market and antiques show in the country. The six-day shows are held three times a year; the 1993 schedule is May 11–16, July 6–11, and September 7–12.

Up to 4,000 antiques and collectibles dealers display their goods, ranging from old postcards to glassware to furniture, in tents and buildings on a three-mile stretch of Route 20, Brimfield's main street. Dealers alternate on openings, and only on Fridays and Saturdays are all displays open. Some exhibitors charge admission to their tents, while others are free. The action begins officially at 8:00 A.M. and runs until 5:00 P.M. and sometimes sundown.

Some longtime patrons complain about the prices, which, they say, have steadily increased with Brimfield's popularity. Be prepared to dicker, and wear comfortable shoes and a sun hat. For more information, call the Quaboag Valley Chamber of Commerce in Palmer, Massachusetts; Tel: (413) 283-6149 or 283-2418. The *Brimfield Antique Guide,* a bi-monthly newspaper that publishes ongoing information about the shows, is available by subscription; write to Brimfield Publications, P.O. Box 442, Brimfield, MA 01010, or call (Tel: 413/245-9329). The *Brimfielder,* published by Worcester County Newspapers three times a year during the Brimfield season, also lists exhibitors. These publications are available at shops, restaurants, and hotels in the Sturbridge area.

Other antiques shops in Sturbridge are open year-round. The best is **Sturbridge Antique Shops**, 200 Charlton Road,

Route 20, ½ mile (1½ km) east of the Massachusetts Turn-pike and I-84. More than 75 dealers occupy two large floors here, selling everything from furniture to glassware and estate jewelry. While not as large, the **Showcase Antique Center**, on Main Street at the entrance to Old Sturbridge Village, offers antiques from a number of different dealers, including old toys, jewelry, and small goods. The **Antique Center of Sturbridge**, 426 Main Street, also houses the goods of several different dealers.

The **Shaker Shop**, at 454 Main Street, sells reproduction Shaker furniture and accessories, Early American stencils, and paints in Early American colors.

STAYING IN THE STURBRIDGE AREA

Sturbridge offers the largest number of accommodations between Worcester and the Pioneer Valley. Reservations are an absolute necessity during the Brimfield shows.

On Main Street in Sturbridge Center, the **Sturbridge Country Inn** offers nine rooms and suites in a Greek Revival mansion, each individually decorated with floral prints, quilts, and Early American reproductions. The good-size rooms have private baths, whirlpools in the tubs, and gas fireplaces, but be aware that the inn is on a busy street. Continental breakfast is included in the price of a room.

The Publick House Historic Resort is a group of lodgings set just across the road from Sturbridge Common. The resort's **Publick House Historic Inn**, on Route 131, is the nicest place to stay in Sturbridge, with 15 guest rooms and two suites, each furnished with reproductions of antique four-poster beds, canopies, brocade spreads, botanical prints, and ceramic Chinese lamps.

The Publick House Historic Inn was originally a tavern, opened in 1771 by Colonel Ebenezer Crafts to serve the coach trade in what was then a crossroads for travellers headed for Albany, Providence, and Boston. Crafts eventually left town and headed north, where he founded Craftsbury, Vermont, but his inn remains popular for its Colonial architecture and ambience. There's hardly a right angle to be found in the older part of the inn. (The inn's restaurant is discussed below.)

Chamberlain House, adjacent to the Publick House Historic Inn, has four newly renovated suites, while the **Country Lodge at the Publick House Historic Resort**, a short walk from the inn, offers motel-like facilities, with 96 guest rooms and three town-house suites, a swimming pool, and tennis courts, which are available to all Publick House Historic Resort guests.

High on a hilltop 1¼ miles (2 km) south of the Publick

House Historic Inn, the **Colonel Ebenezer Crafts Inn** is an eight-room bed-and-breakfast built in 1786. This is a smaller, more intimate inn, more like a family home, with a sitting room and grand piano, an outdoor swimming pool, and magnificent views to the west. The deep fireplace has a tunnel behind it that was used to hide slaves on the Underground Railroad.

The **Old Sturbridge Village Lodge** and the **Oliver Wight House** are located at the entrance to, and are run by, Old Sturbridge Village. The Oliver Wight House has ten guest rooms, nicely decorated in Federal-style period pieces, and modern amenities; the two Dennison Cottage suites are more spacious. The Village Lodge units offer comfortable, motel-style accommodations with a country decor.

DINING IN STURBRIDGE

The atmosphere of the **Publick House Historic Inn**'s dining room is enhanced by the low ceiling, wooden beams, and huge walk-in fireplace. Meals begin with a relish tray and an assortment of freshly baked rolls and breads, but save room for lobster pie, a traditional turkey dinner, or prime rib. Breakfasts here are large and hearty; in keeping with Colonial traditions, you can even have apple pie for breakfast. Route 131 on the Common in Sturbridge. Tel: (508) 347-3313.

A block away, at Haynes Street and Route 131, is **Crabapple's Eating and Drinking Place**, a more casual dining spot, with light lunches, dinners, and snacks, like *hummus,* burgers, sandwiches, pasta, and barbecued chicken. Full dinners are served in the evening, featuring duckling and broiled seafood. Brunch is served on Sundays. Tel: (508) 347-5559.

About a mile (1½ km) south of the Publick House Historic Inn on Route 131, **Rom's** is a local favorite for its reasonably priced Italian food. The dining room is huge, and often packed, especially on buffet night. Try the veal parmigiana and leave room for the strawberry ricotta pie. Tel: (508) 347-3349.

In the center of town at 502 Main Street, the **Whistling Swan** is a tonier choice, its formal dining room set in a Greek Revival mansion built in 1855 by Emory Lymon Bates, a Sturbridge businessman and politician, and restored in 1980. The kitchen specializes in American and Continental dishes, including grilled lemon chicken with mashed potatoes, herb-crusted rack of lamb, seafood, and steaks. Reservations recommended. The menu at the Whistling Swan's more casual **Ugly Duckling** loft is as adventurous, including pasta, seafood, and sandwiches like tenderloin *au poivre* served on sourdough bread with sautéed mushrooms. For both venues, Tel: (508) 347-2321.

The **Sunburst**, at 484 Main Street, is a good spot to regroup over a quick lunch; Tel: (508) 347-3097.

From Sturbridge it's a 10-mile (16-km) drive north on Route 9 to West Brookfield, but worth the 20-minute trip to the **Salem Cross Inn** there. The rambling wood-frame structure was built in 1705 as the home of Peregrine White, who was born on the *Mayflower;* it takes its name from the "Salem cross" etched in the front door latch to protect against witchcraft in Colonial days. Coincidentally, it is now run by a family named Salem. Traditional New England fare—beef, seafood, and lamb—is served here. The inn's Hearthside Suppers in the winter and Drover's Roasts in the summer are a lot of fun; the evenings include sleigh rides or hayrides on the 600-acre farm, and roast beef cooked on an antique spit in the walk-in fireplace, served family-style at long wooden tables. (No overnight accommodations here.) Tel: (508) 867-2345.

Leaving Sturbridge you'll head west to the Connecticut River Valley and Springfield, the largest city in western Massachusetts and our first stop in the Pioneer Valley.

WESTERN MASSACHUSETTS

THE PIONEER VALLEY

The Pioneer Valley—so called because this was an area of early settlement—is that portion of the Connecticut River Valley that stretches from Springfield north to Brattleboro, Vermont. The valley is narrow, especially west of the river, where you quickly climb into the Berkshire foothills and the many small hill towns of Hampshire and Franklin counties. Once a thriving farming and manufacturing region, today the Pioneer Valley supports five colleges and three preparatory schools in the upper valley, and five colleges in the Springfield area.

It's hard to overstate the importance of the Connecticut River to this part of the state. Besides endowing the region with fertile farmland and abundant waterpower, the river has served as an artistic inspiration since the settling of the area in 1635. Thomas Cole's famous painting *The Oxbow* portrays a view of the river from what is now Skinner State Park in Hadley.

As the isolated early settlements along the river began to grow, the region became the setting for the evolution of the uniquely American Connecticut River Valley style of architecture and design, which set the standards for 19th-century housing, churches, and public buildings around rural New England. Indeed, valley architect Asher Benjamin literally wrote the book on Early American architecture in 1806 with his builder's guide, *The American Builder's Companion: or A New System of Architecture Particularly Adapted to the Present Style of Building in the United States of America.*

The settlement of the region marked the English colonists' first forays into what was then thought of as the "wilderness" of interior New England. In fact, the settlements were not without peril; the villages were subject to attacks, particularly during the French and Indian War. More than half the inhabitants of the village of Deerfield were killed or taken captive by French Canadians and Indians in the Deerfield Massacre of 1704.

The Pioneer Valley was also the site of an early revolt that grew out of class tensions. In 1786 Daniel Shays led an armed movement by local farmers that shut down courts in protest of laws and policies that hurt them financially and would prevent them from having the vote. In September of that year 700 farmers attempted to seize weapons from the Springfield arsenal but were blocked by government soldiers. Markers commemorating battles and milestones in the revolt can be found all over western Massachusetts, from Worcester west to Sheffield.

Springfield

Springfield, 60 miles (96 km) west of Worcester via the Massachusetts Turnpike, was settled in 1636 by William Pynchon, a merchant and trader whose family also owned the lands that would later become Northampton, Deerfield, and Hadley. In the early 18th century the city developed an industrial base with the sawmills, gristmills, and brickmaking facilities that would propel it to manufacturing prominence in the region when the railroad arrived in the mid-19th century.

The city's textile and machine shops drew immigrants from French Canada, England, and Scotland; Irish, Italian, and Swedish labor added to the melting pot. Abolitionist John Brown lived in Springfield for two years during the

1840s, during which time the city was a stop along the Underground Railroad for hundreds of runaway slaves.

Springfield's population doubled between 1910 and 1920, testimony to its thriving factories and mills. The first American motorcycle was built here in the Indian Motorcycle factory (there's a museum devoted to Indian Motorcycles at 33 Hende Street), and the development of the Springfield rifle between 1901 and 1903 led to a thriving gun trade that has lasted nearly a century—Smith & Wesson continues to do business here. However, many local industries declined in the 1970s as companies moved south to take advantage of cheaper labor costs. Gradually the downtown area fell into decline as well, and Springfield is struggling to redefine its future.

Nevertheless, its collection of small museums offers a good introduction to the region and makes it worth spending a morning here before heading north to the upper valley or west to the Berkshires. The Greater Springfield Convention and Visitors Bureau has an information center, open weekdays, that offers maps, at 34 Boland Way, next to Baystate West mall in downtown Springfield; Tel: (413) 787-1548.

Court Square

A good place to start is in the city's downtown, at Court Square. Here you'll find **City Hall**, **Symphony Hall**, and the **Old First Church**, all bordering a shady green you'd expect to find in a more rural setting. After the destruction of the old City Hall by fire in 1905, city leaders embarked upon a master plan to build a replacement, along with a Municipal Auditorium (now Symphony Hall). The classic buildings, their columns and broad steps standing in contrast to the plain Puritan lines of the church, give a sense of different eras in the city's history. In the past, even presidents have passed this way. The body of former President John Quincy Adams lay in state in the sanctuary of the church in 1848 on its way back to Boston from Washington, and President William Howard Taft dedicated the City Hall and Municipal Auditorium buildings when they opened in 1913.

The Quadrangle

From Court Square, drive two blocks south on Main Street and turn left onto State Street. Two blocks up the hill, at State and Chestnut, is the Quadrangle, a small, shady green bordered by four museums and the Springfield Public Library. Like the museums of Worcester, those of the Quadrangle offer bite-size looks at the region's history and artistic heritage. Outside the entrance to the Quadrangle is Augustus Saint-Gaudens's statue *The Puritan;* placed here in 1899, it memorializes Deacon Samuel Chapin, one of Springfield's founders. The museums are open Thursday through Sunday from noon to 4:00 P.M.; for general information, Tel: (413) 739-3871.

The **Connecticut Valley Historical Museum** focuses on the history and culture of the valley since 1636, with examples of home life, decorative arts, and portraits by itinerant artists. There's an excellent exhibit on the evolution of the region's architectural styles, and even an example of one of Springfield's more enduring contributions to the nation— an early vacuum cleaner. Tel: (413) 732-3080. The **George Walter Vincent Smith Art Museum**, built in 1895 to house the collection of a local philanthropist, includes the Western world's largest collection of Chinese cloisonné, as well as an impressive array of Japanese arms and armor, screens, and ceramics. There's also a collection of 19th-century American paintings. Tel: (413) 733-4214. Next door is the **Springfield Public Library**, an Italian Renaissance building built in 1912; it was funded in part by philanthropist Andrew Carnegie, who paid for many local libraries in New England and elsewhere in the country. Today it is the second most active public library in New England.

Across the green is the **Museum of Fine Arts**, with a good selection of American, early modern European, and Impressionist works, including one of Monet's *Haystacks*. Perhaps the museum's proudest holding is local 19th-century artist Erastus Salisbury Field's huge and complex painting *Historical Monument of the American Republic*. Tel: (413) 732-6092. Children especially will enjoy the **Springfield Science Museum**, a multilevel structure with a Dinosaur Hall that has a full-size replica of a Tyrannosaurus rex and an African Hall with a real (stuffed and mounted) African elephant. It has one of the oldest (1937) American-built planetariums. Tel: (413) 733-1194.

The **Quad Café** serves lunches outdoors Monday through Friday during the summer. Just down the hill, at 5 Dwight Street, is **Montori & Company**, a fancy-food deli with good coffee, large sandwiches, and unusual salads.

Naismith Memorial Basketball Hall of Fame

Springfield's most enduring and widely recognized contribution to the world is the game of basketball. From the Quadrangle, drive down State Street toward I-91, cross under the highway, and take a left onto West Columbus Avenue to get to the Naismith Memorial at number 1150, overlooking the Connecticut River. The Naismith Memorial Basketball Hall of Fame offers a look at the history of the game, which was invented here by physical education instructor Dr. James

Naismith in 1891. It's a real treat for basketball fans, chock-full of photos, memorabilia, and videos. If you're a Larry Bird wannabee, try your skills at the "basketball fountains" or the Spaulding Shoot-Out, which allows you to shoot hoops of varying heights while standing on a moving sidewalk. Tel: (413) 781-6500.

Seasonal Events

The **Eastern States Exposition**, held the second Wednesday after Labor Day at the Eastern States Exposition grounds at 1305 Memorial Avenue across the river in West Springfield, is the largest agricultural fair in New England. The "Big E" is an extravaganza of food and exhibits from the six New England states, as well as nationally known country-music acts. It's brash, commercial, and a lot of fun. Its midway alone is worth the price of admission, featuring every kind of ethnic food available in the valley, from tofu hot dogs to fried chicken cooked by Baptist church ladies. Tel: (413) 787-0271 or 737-2443.

In late June more than 500 craftspeople from around the country are represented at the **American Crafts Council Crafts Fair**, also held at the fairgrounds. Simultaneous events are scheduled in the Northampton area in conjunction with the show. This year the fair will be open to the public June 25–27; for information, Tel: (413) 787-0271 or 737-2443.

Riverside Park

Also on the west side of the Connecticut River, at 1623 Main Street (Route 159) in Agawam, is Riverside Park, evidence that the old-fashioned amusement park lives on, despite the proliferation of Disney World clones. Riverside is home to the Cyclone, one of the country's largest roller coasters; rock concerts are held here in summer. Open every day in June, July, and August, and weekends in April, May, September, and October. Tel: (413) 786-9300.

STAYING AND DINING IN SPRINGFIELD

Accommodations in Springfield, though abundant, are mostly of the chain motel and hotel variety. Downtown are the **Sheraton Springfield at Monarch Place** and the **Springfield Marriott**, both with nice views of the river and full facilities like indoor pools and fitness clubs. For more moderately priced accommodations there's the **Ramada Hotel West Springfield** on Route 5, Riverdale Street, in West Springfield.

Springfield has some good, moderately priced restaurants, mostly in the downtown area near the Baystate West mall. Three blocks from Court Square, at 1688 Main Street, the **Sitar** serves superb Indian food; Tel: (413) 732-8011. A few blocks up, at 1390 Main Street, **Tilly's** is an informal place that serves as a watering hole for downtown business-people and shoppers. The setting is casual, with pine panel-ing and lots of plants—dine in booths or at a table. The **Student Prince and Fort Restaurant**, just off Main Street toward the bus station, at 8–14 Fort Street, specializes in German food, served in a beerhouse-style setting, decorated with hundreds of steins; Tel: (413) 734-7475.

For a special dinner travel across the river to West Spring-field and the **Storrowton Tavern**, which serves traditional New England fare in an authentic 19th-century tavern on the Eastern States Exposition grounds off Memorial Avenue; Tel: (413) 732-4188.

NIGHTLIFE AND ENTERTAINMENT

Come nightfall there are a few options in the city. **Stage West** offers contemporary theater in Columbus Center, on Bridge Street just off Main Street, in downtown Springfield. Closed during the summer. For information, call the box office; Tel: (413) 781-2340. The 7,000-seat **Springfield Civic Center**, at 1277 Main Street, hosts rock concerts as well as athletic and other events (Tel: 413/787-6600), while **Symphony Hall**, near Court Square downtown, holds lectures and performances by the Springfield Symphony Orchestra year-round; Tel: (413) 733-2291.

Four blocks north of Symphony Hall, at 1700 Main Street, the **Paramount Theatre** is an old theater, newly restored, that hosts rock performers and comedians; Tel: (413) 734-5874. The **Zone Art Center**, at 395 Dwight Street showcases contemporary and at times avant-garde performances, in-cluding readings, films, and theater; Tel: (413) 732-1995.

SKIING

The Holyoke range rises up on both sides of Interstate 91 as you head north from Springfield. Just off I-91 is **Mount Tom Ski Area & Summerside**, in winter a downhill ski area and in summer an "Alpine slide," where you ride the lift to the top and slide down a luge-like track in a small car. Mount Tom offers day and night skiing on 16 slopes and trails. Though a small mountain, it's popular with Pioneer Valley residents because of its proximity to I-91. Tel: (413) 536-0416 or 536-0516.

Northampton

It could be said that a city that once touted itself as the "Paris of New England" was asking for trouble, but Northampton (20 miles/32 km) north of Springfield on I-91), with its somewhat chic downtown and many cafés and restaurants, is as congenial a spot as you'll find in western Massachusetts. It is also the commercial/entertainment/dining hub of the region, making it a good home base to stay for a couple of days.

Like Portland, Maine, Northampton is a small city that revitalized itself in the 1980s with upscale shops and eateries. Its roots as a working-class town and the academic influence of the colleges in the area each gives the town substance and contributes to its urbane yet relaxed quality of life.

Noho, as it is sometimes called, occasionally draws some exaggerated media attention for the large number of lesbians who live here. (The *National Enquirer* dubbed it the "City Where Men Are Not Wanted" last year. It's not true, however—men are quite welcome!) In fact the city's tolerance and diversity make it one of the most interesting spots in western Massachusetts.

The Northampton vicinity is also home to a considerable community of craftspeople and artists, drawn to the area for its academic resources and its proximity to Boston and New York. They include illustrators Barry Moser and Leonard Baskin and artists Gregory Gillespie and Scott Prior. Randall Diehl immortalized an usher who runs the concession stand at one of the local movie houses; his portrait hangs in the Metropolitan Museum of Art in New York.

The city also counts among its famous residents Sylvester Graham, a health-food enthusiast whose innovations with flour led to the graham cracker, and Calvin Coolidge, who served as mayor and later became the nation's 30th president. Its most famous residents, however, are not even human. The Teenage Mutant Ninja Turtles were spawned by local cartoonists Peter Laird and Kevin Eastman. Their company, Mirage Studios, is located on a Northampton back street.

The Northampton chamber of commerce has an information center downtown on King Street, one block off Main; Tel: (413) 586-3178 or 584-1900.

Smith College

At the western end of the downtown area, the campus of Smith College is a good place to begin a walking tour of Northampton. Founded in 1871 by Sophia Smith as one of the first institutions of higher education for women in the country, the 125-acre campus is a deft combination of old and new buildings. **Paradise Pond**, so named after opera singer Jenny Lind dubbed the city the "Paradise of America," is the perfect place for a summer picnic.

From the ornate college gates that open onto Main Street

and face the downtown area, walk two blocks up Elm Street to the **Smith College Museum of Art**. The museum has an outstanding collection of 19th- and 20th-century American and European paintings, 17th-century Dutch paintings, and prints from the 15th through the 20th centuries. Among the many local artists represented here is Edwin Romanzo Elmer, who painted landscapes and portraits in the hill towns of Franklin County, just north of here. Closed Mondays and during January; Tel: (413) 585-2770. Walk back out to Elm Street and take a left past the Victorian houses that still serve as dormitories. Turn left and head down College Lane, where Paradise Pond will be on your right. To your left will be the **Lyman Plant House**, a sprawling complex of Victorian-era greenhouses that hosts the **Annual Bulb Show** in early to mid-March and the **Chrysanthemum Show** in November. Tel: (413) 585-2740.

As you walk back down Main Street toward the center of town, on your right at number 274 will be the restored **Academy of Music Opera House**, with a wonderfully ornate decor; movies are now shown here; Tel: (413) 584-8435. Next door is **Pulaski Park**, a good place to people-watch and enjoy a cone from **Bart's Ice Cream** across the street, or from **Herrell's**, a few blocks down in the basement of Thorne's Marketplace.

Agricultural Fairs

One of the reasons so many people like living in this city is its proximity to the country; indeed, Northampton is home to the oldest American agricultural fair in continuous existence. The **Three County Fair**, which starts the Friday before Labor Day, includes a midway, horse racing, and agricultural exhibits.

Other agricultural fairs worth visiting in the region include, in August, the **Cummington Fair**, about 30 miles (48 km) west of Northampton; in September, the **Franklin County Fair**, in Greenfield, 20 miles (32 km) north of Northampton; and the smallest and funkiest of them all, the **Heath Fair**, which takes place the third weekend in August in the hill town of Heath, about 35 miles (56 km) northwest of Northampton, off Route 2. (For a complete list of agricultural fairs in the state, contact the Massachusetts Department of Food and Agriculture, 100 Cambridge Street, Boston, MA 02202; Tel: 617/727-3000.)

STAYING AND DINING IN NORTHAMPTON

Accommodations in Northampton range from budget chain motels to the elegant **Hotel Northampton** on King Street, with spacious rooms and a richly decorated lobby. This is the most centrally located lodging in town, and also the priciest. Out on Route 9, just past Smith College, is another good choice, the **Autumn Inn**. It's more of a motel than an inn, but the rooms are comfortable and ample.

Northampton has an assortment of eateries in all price ranges and styles. For gourmet pizzas cooked in a wood-fired oven, try **Pizzeria Paradiso** at 12 Crafts Avenue, just off Northampton's Main Street. **Spoleto**, at 50 Main Street, is one of Northampton's best restaurants, offering northern Italian specialties in a contemporary setting, with white linens on tables that sometimes seem too close to each other. It's also very popular, so be prepared to wait on the weekends. Tel: (413) 586-6313.

Just around the corner, at 19 Strong Avenue, the **Eastside Grill** has an eclectic menu that ranges from burgers to Cajun. Try it for lunch; Tel: (413) 586-3347. At 150 Main Street in Thorne's Marketplace, **Paul & Elizabeth's** serves excellent natural foods in a light and airy setting; Tel: (413) 584-4832. **Curtis & Schwartz**, just up the block at 116 Main Street, serves big breakfasts, burgers, sandwiches, and salads, and full meals in the evenings; Tel: (413) 586-3278.

Though subject to change, of course, at press time the intellectuals' hot spot is a basement coffeehouse in an alley just behind Main Street. The **Haymarket Café** serves pastries along with big bowls of coffee and cups of espresso. Wear black and bring your own Gauloises.

NIGHTLIFE AND ENTERTAINMENT IN THE NORTHAMPTON AREA

Because of the presence of two clubs, both in the downtown area, Northampton is the focus of nightlife in western Massachusetts. The **Iron Horse Music Hall**, at 20 Center Street, is a small venue that hosts a wide range of music from folk to jazz to Afro-pop; Tel: (413) 584-0610. A few blocks off Pleasant Street, at 10 Pearl Street, **Pearl Street** is a larger club with a full dance floor that draws bigger names, like the Neville Brothers, and regional favorites, like NRBQ; Tel: (413) 584-7771.

Sheehan's Café, at 24 Pleasant Street just off Main, is a lively nightspot that features mostly local bands; Tel: (413) 586-4258. Around the corner at 23 Main Street is **Fitzwilly's**, the young professionals' hangout, with a menu and happy hour; Tel: (413) 584-8666. Try **Packard's**, on 14 Masonic Street, for a beer and a late-night snack; Tel: (413) 584-5957. Down beside the municipal parking garage at 11 Brewster Court, the **Northampton Brewery** is a microbrewery that serves sandwiches and meals; Tel: (413) 584-9903.

The so-called Five Colleges—the University of Massachusetts, Smith, Mount Holyoke, Amherst, and Hampshire—all located in the valley, offer regular schedules of concerts, plays, and performances of all kinds. UMass (see Amherst, below) in particular is strong on jazz; drummer Max Roach is on the school's academic staff. To find out what's going on when you're in town, pick up the weekly *Valley Advocate* or the *Daily Hampshire Gazette*.

In the classical vein, **Music in Deerfield** hosts concerts in the Brick Church at Deerfield (discussed below), October through April; Tel: (413) 772-0241. About 30 miles (48 km) northwest of Northampton, **Mohawk Trail Concerts** sponsors summer events on weekends in the white clapboard Federated Church on the Mohawk Trail in Charlemont (also discussed below); Tel: (413) 625-9511.

Northampton also has two movie theaters. The **Academy of Music Opera House**, at 274 Main Street, one of the last remaining one-screen theaters in New England, is the nicer of the two; Tel: (413) 584-8435. In the town's center, at 27 Pleasant Street, is the **Pleasant Street Theater**, which shows art films and documentaries; Tel: (413) 586-0935.

SHOPPING IN THE NORTHAMPTON AREA

Northampton and its environs offer some fertile antiquing territory. The **Antique Center of Northampton**, at 9½ Market Street, sells the wares of several dealers on two floors (closed Wednesdays). Halfway between Amherst and Northampton, the **Hadley Antique Center**, at 227 Russell Street (Route 9) in the farming town of Hadley, houses 70 dealers on two floors. The **Antique Center of Old Deerfield**, about 15 miles (24 km) north of Northampton right off I-91, sells antiques from 17 dealers.

The Northampton area is also the best part of western Massachusetts for finding crafts. The Ferrin Gallery at **Pinch Pottery**, at 179 Main Street in Northampton, has an outstanding collection of ceramics, jewelry, and other crafts from local craftspeople and from around the country. **Don Muller Gallery**, up the street at 40 Main, sells jewelry, glassware, and ceramics. Twenty-five miles (40 km) east of Northampton, **Leverett Crafts & Arts**, at 13 Montague Road in Leverett, offers ceramics, paintings, and textiles done by a group of 20 artists. In June and September the Memorial Hall Museum in Deerfield hosts the **Old Deerfield Craft Fairs**. In Shelburne Falls, off the Mohawk Trail at 1 Ashfield Street, **Salmon Falls Artisans Showroom** has pottery, carvings, glass, ceramics, photographs, and furniture by local artists. (Deerfield and Shelburne Falls are discussed further below.)

It was the renovation of an old department store into **Thorne's Marketplace**, smack in the middle of Northampton's Main Street, that launched the city's renaissance in the early 1980s, and the urban mall has proved to be a keeper, with some dozen or so shops ranging from a New Age bookstore to ultra-trendy fashion boutiques. There's probably nothing here that you really, truly need, but it's a lot of fun to wander the three floors of shops.

Two good bookstores in Northampton are the **Broadside**, at 247 Main Street, and the **Globe Bookshop**, at 38 Pleasant Street, the latter with a full selection of international periodicals.

AROUND NORTHAMPTON

A drive northwest of Northampton along Route 9 takes you to the rural hill towns of Hampshire County. The **William Cullen Bryant Homestead**, off Route 112 in Cummington, 19 miles (30 km) northwest of Northampton, is set on a sloping piece of farmland studded with old maple trees. The poet, who was a kind of bard of the Berkshires, lived in Great Barrington and spent his summers in retirement here. The house is a good example of an 18th-century farmhouse converted into a Victorian mansion, and most of the furnishings belonged to the Bryant family. Open weekends late June through Columbus Day; Tel: (413) 634-2244.

On your way back to town, stop at 99 Main Street, Route 9, in Florence for coffee and pie at the **Miss Florence Diner**, about 5 miles (8 km) east of Northampton center, a local favorite for 50 years, with cheap food and plenty of atmosphere. Tel: (413) 584-3137.

If instead of following Route 9 northwest you head northeast toward Amherst, take a right onto Route 47, which winds through the town of Hadley (see Shopping, above) to the **Joseph Allen Skinner State Park**, atop Mount Holyoke. The 390-acre park affords a spectacular view of the river, including the famous "oxbow." Hiking is permitted year-round; cars are allowed only May through November.

Amherst

Like Northampton, Amherst (5 miles/8 km northeast of Northampton via Route 9) is a college town, but with a little more emphasis on the colleges themselves. Amherst College, the University of Massachusetts, and Hampshire College lend a youthful feel to this old New England town; its picture-perfect common is still the site of many a demonstration.

The town was named for Lord Jeffery Amherst, a British

general who fought in the French and Indian Wars. Emily Dickinson lived here until her death in 1886, and Robert Frost was a professor of English at Amherst College off and on between 1917 and 1963.

In the 1960s and 1970s Amherst was a center of counter-culture whose downtown featured stores selling sandals and hippie paraphernalia. In the past decade franchises and chain stores have replaced many of the locally owned businesses and, as a result, Amherst's once-distinctive downtown now has a generic look to it. Still, it's a lively place to eat, browse, and people-watch. The town is often referred to as "the people's republic of Amherst" for its consistently liberal stances.

The **Amherst Common**, the town's physical center, is a good place to begin a tour. It's the site for all kinds of town activities, from farmers' markets and carnivals in the summer to the lighting of the large, sprawling "Merry Maple" tree at Christmas time. In the summer there's an information booth here run by the chamber of commerce; Tel: (413) 253-0700.

Three blocks down Main Street from the common, at 280 Main Street, is the **Emily Dickinson Homestead**, now a private residence. Guided tours of parts of the home, including the bedroom where Dickinson wrote most of her poetry, are provided by Amherst College, which owns the homestead, between March and November. Open times are limited and reservations strongly advised. Tel: (413) 542-8161.

Just up the hill from the Amherst Common is **Amherst College**, founded in 1821 by a group of scholars that included Noah Webster and Samuel Fowler Dickinson, Emily's grandfather. The 1,000-acre campus is a classic, with tall old maples and stretches of Greek Revival houses.

Across town, the **University of Massachusetts** is the flagship of the state system of public higher education. Once an agricultural land grant college, UMass has grown into a teeming academic hub with about 23,000 students. The 3,912-acre campus is an eclectic, and sometimes jarring, mix of the old and the new; for example, the modern skyscraper library sits alongside the 19th-century chapel.

At the UMass Fine Arts Center, designed by architect Kevin Roche, the **University Gallery** houses the school's impressive collection of 20th-century American works on paper, as well as changing exhibitions that focus mainly on contemporary art; closed during the summer. Tel: (413) 545-3670.

The center is also a regular stop on many touring companies' lists, featuring dance and classical, jazz, and rock music; Tel: (413) 545-2511. And if you're in the area in the summer, be sure to check out the **Bright Moments Jazz Festival**, which offers performances of jazz, salsa, and African music on three Thursdays in July on the lawn by the campus pond at UMass.

STAYING AND DINING IN AMHERST

The **Lord Jeffery Inn** is centrally located on the Amherst Common, a short walk from shops and restaurants in town as well as the Emily Dickinson Homestead. It's a gracious old building, with spacious common rooms with fireplaces and a good restaurant. Just down the street, at 599 Main Street, is the **Allen House Victorian Inn**, a Queen Anne–style house built in 1886, with three rooms in winter, five in summer. It's a little noisy because of the traffic coming into town, but nicely decorated with Victorian antiques; full breakfasts are served in a sunny dining room.

The **Campus Center Hotel**, a gray concrete tower, is the on-campus accommodation for the University of Massachusetts. The bland but reasonably good-size rooms have magnificent views of the campus on one side and the Berkshire Hills on the other. The **University Motor Lodge**, with standard motel–style rooms, is another good choice just a short walk from the campus.

Most of the restaurants that serve the student (and parent) trade are located on North Pleasant Street, not far from the town center. **Judie's**, at 51 North Pleasant Street, is always a good choice, whether you're seated in the back room or, better, in the sunny greenhouse that faces onto Amherst's busy main street. Giant popovers are the trademark here, and the kitchen turns out huge portions of eclectic fare. The desserts are wonderful. Good for dinner or a late-afternoon snack. Tel: (413) 253-3491.

Up the street at number 71, **Café DiCarlo** offers traditional Italian as well as some pricier, more unusual cuisine, such as fresh scallops in lobster saffron sauce. Tel: (413) 253-9300.

Just across the street and up a few blocks at 168 North Pleasant is the **Classe Café**, a popular lunchtime or coffee-break hangout for students, professors, and locals. Good vegetarian sandwiches, burgers, homemade soups, and shakes are served by sometimes laconic but always well-educated waitresses. Tel: (413) 253-2291.

The **Top of the Campus** restaurant at the UMass campus center offers a spectacular view of the valley, particularly during foliage season or at sunset any time of year. Tel: (413) 545-3216.

Head north along Route 116 about 9 miles (14½ km) to the outskirts of Sunderland for what the locals call a "wicked good deal" at **Bub's Barbeque**. Bub's is a favorite with the college crowd for its in-the-rough pork and chicken barbecue and all-you-can-eat hot and cold buffet, which includes sweet potatoes, baked beans, coleslaw, soup, and a variety of vegetables. Place your order and pick up your beer at the counter; eat at picnic tables indoors or out. Tel: (413) 259-1254.

SHOPPING IN AMHERST

As befitting a college town, Amherst is loaded with bookstores, all within a few blocks of one another and within walking distance of Amherst Common. The **Jeffery Amherst Bookshop**, facing the common at 55 South Pleasant, is one of the area's mainstays, specializing in local authors, including Emily Dickinson. **Food for Thought Books**, at 106 North Pleasant Street, offers selections on social change, gay and lesbian issues, and feminist politics. Also on North Pleasant, at number 19, **Wootton's Books** concentrates on art, philosophy, poetry, literature, and journals. Offerings at the **Sophia Bookstore**, 63 Main Street, include books on world religions, Middle Eastern issues, Asian studies, and some metaphysics.

NORTH FROM AMHERST

As you head north on Route 116 from Amherst, look back and you'll see a landscape that serves as a metaphor for the region: its past embodied in the tobacco barns in the foreground, its present in the skyscrapers of UMass in the middle ground. Though education is now a major industry in the upper valley, at one time it was agriculture that paid the bills; the fields along Route 116 were tilled with, among other crops, tobacco, which was strung up to dry in the long red barns that still dot the fields. Though development has encroached on much Massachusetts farmland, and many farmers are struggling, the fields along Route 116 are testimony to the endurance of agriculture and to the rich alluvial soil of the Connecticut River Valley.

You can get a real sense of the sweep of the river, as well as modern-day settlement patterns, by taking a drive to the top of **Mount Sugarloaf State Reservation**, just off Route 116 in South Deerfield, about 10 miles (16 km) northwest of Amherst. From here, with the Holyoke range visible to the south, you can get a sense of the geological evolution of this area, formed 14,000 years ago with the retreat of the last glacier. There are hiking trails and picnicking spaces on the mountain.

Turn right (north) from Route 116 onto Route 5 and 10 toward Deerfield. After about an eighth of a mile you arrive at the **Yankee Candle Company** in South Deerfield. Here you can dip your own candles, tour the candle-making factory, or browse through the rambling complex, which includes a year-round Christmas shop and a bakery/snack shop.

Deerfield

The fertile valley between the Connecticut and the Deerfield rivers seemed the perfect spot to settlers back in the 17th century. But the first white arrivals at Deerfield (about 15 miles/24 km north of Northampton and Amherst) didn't have an easy time of it. In 1675 a band of 1,000 Indians massacred 64 teamsters and soldiers who were carrying wheat to Hadley in what was later called the Attack on Bloody Brook. In 1704 nearly half the settlers were either killed or taken captive by French Canadians and Indians during what's come to be known as the Deerfield Massacre. The village was later resettled and became a thriving center of farming and commerce.

Today South Deerfield, three blocks off Route 5 and 10, is the town's main business district. But visitors come to see the site of the original settlement. Deerfield, 7 miles (11 km) north of South Deerfield on Route 5 and 10 (the village will be on your left—follow the brown and white signs), has been meticulously restored over the years. At its center is Deerfield Academy, the prestigious preparatory school founded in 1797.

In 1952 Mr. and Mrs. Henry Flynt, at the urging of renowned Deerfield Academy headmaster Frank Boyden, launched Historic Deerfield, Incorporated, with the intention of preserving the town to show the architecture and village environment in Colonial and Federal days. Today the collections of furnishings and decorative arts at Deerfield rank with the holdings of such better-known places as the Winterthur Museum in Delaware and Colonial Williamsburg.

What makes Deerfield special are its low-key ways and lack of commercialism. The town's main thoroughfare, lined with beautifully restored 18th- and 19th-century homes in muted blues, yellows, and whites, is called simply The Street. Strolling under old maples, past academy students clad in turtlenecks, khakis, and backpacks, you find yourself in another era—one without telephone poles or modern streetlights.

Memorial Hall Museum
From Route 5 and 10, take a left at the sign for Historic Deerfield, and turn right onto The Street. Take the next right onto Memorial Street and you'll come to Memorial Hall Museum, the best place to start any tour of Deerfield. The museum is one of the nation's oldest, inaugurated in 1880 by the Pocumtuck Valley Memorial Association. Town historian George Sheldon acquired and organized the collection by soliciting pieces from neighbors' barns and attics. As a result,

the museum is full of the accoutrements of everyday life in Deerfield: quilts, tinware, dishes, clothing, furnishings, paintings, textiles, and Native American artifacts.

Here you'll find the famous **Old Indian House Door,** taken from Ensign John Sheldon's 1698 home, which has the actual gashes in it from the French and Indian attack on Deerfield. The house was torn down in 1847, but the door serves as a reminder of the dangers faced by the early New England settlers. Open April 15 through November 15; Tel: (413) 774-7476.

On the third weekends of June and September the **Old Deerfield Craft Fairs** are held on the grounds of the museum.

Deerfield's Historic Houses

Turn right back onto The Street, and after ¼ mile you'll be in the center of Deerfield, near the Deerfield Inn and the offices of Historic Deerfield. There is no admission fee to walk the streets of Deerfield, but tickets are required for the guided tours of the 13 historic houses, each with its own history and emphasis. At the **Hall Tavern,** on The Street, you can get information and purchase a $10 general admission house-tour ticket, good for two consecutive days of tours in Historic Deerfield. The **First Church of Deerfield,** better known as the Brick Church, is diagonally across from Hall Tavern. Built in 1824, it illustrates the wealth and sophistication of the town in the early 19th century. Today **Music in Deerfield** hosts classical music concerts in the church from October through April; Tel: (413) 772-0241.

If you have the time and the interest, Historic Deerfield also offers educational programs, lectures, and workshops on furnishings and homemaking arts of the past, including hearthside cooking demonstrations and antiques and furniture workshops. For information, Tel: (413) 774-5581.

Tours of the homes last about 30 minutes. If your time is limited, be sure at least to visit the **Wells-Thorn House,** at the intersection of Memorial Street and The Street, which provides a sense of life in Deerfield over a span of 200 years up to the early Victorian era. The house, built in 1717 and the home of settler Ebenezer Wells, shows the architectural and decorative changes that took place as the village evolved from a frontier settlement to an active commercial center.

Also of interest are the **Sheldon-Hawks House,** the best-preserved 18th-century building in Deerfield, featuring New England furniture, English ceramics, and European brass; and the **Helen Geier Flynt Fabric Hall,** with quilts, costumes, textiles, and needlework as well as some period furniture.

SHOPPING IN DEERFIELD

The **Museum Store** at Deerfield, located on The Street next to the Deerfield Inn, has a good selection of gifts and books about Early American decorative arts, antiques, and customs. If looking at all those Early American interiors whets your appetite for antiques, drive about 1 mile (1½ km) north of town on Route 5 and 10 to the **Antique Center of Old Deerfield**, which houses antiques from some 20 different dealers (closed Mondays).

STAYING IN THE DEERFIELD AREA

The **Deerfield Inn** has a history of its own. Built in 1884, the inn was purchased in 1945 by the Flynts, who began an extensive renovation and expansion program and filled it with antiques acquired in their travels. In 1979 a grease fire destroyed the third floor but, remarkably, left the structure intact. A complete remodeling of the inn followed, along with construction of a south wing in 1981. The inn now has 23 deluxe guest rooms. Its restaurant serves contemporary American dishes in a warm and elegant setting.

Not far from Deerfield in the country town of Conway (just west of Route 5 and 10 on Route 116), the three-room **Merriams Bed and Breakfast** is set in a beautifully restored 1767 house with period furnishings. Mary makes quilts and Bob sells used and old books from his store out back. The Merriams' place is a rare B and B that welcomes children.

Just north of Deerfield in Greenfield (which is discussed below), the eight-room **Brandt House Bed and Breakfast** is a turn-of-the-century house in a quiet residential neighborhood on three and a half acres with tennis courts.

Northfield

Before the building of the interstate, Routes 5 and 10 were the main north–south highways for travellers, and some of the old compounds of motorists' cottages remain. Today Route 10 is a pleasant back route; if you follow it north from Deerfield for 16 miles (26 km) you'll end up in Northfield, a pretty farming village with a wonderful collection of Greek Revival, Federal, and Victorian Gothic homes lining its Main Street. The town is home to **Northfield Mount Hermon School**, founded in 1879 by Dwight L. Moody, a 19th-century evangelist whose followers would come up in the summers to hear him preach. A walking-tour guide is available at Town Hall or at the historical society on Pine Street, at the upper end of Main Street.

Located on the banks of the Connecticut River in Northfield, the **Northfield Mountain Recreation and Environmental Center** is a good place to learn about the geology, flora, and fauna of the Connecticut River Valley; mountain biking paths, camping, and bridle paths (no horses provided) are available. Northfield Mountain itself has some 25 miles of hiking and cross-country ski trails. For prices, Tel: (413) 659-3714; for snow conditions, Tel: (413) 659-3714.

From June until Columbus Day you can really get a sense of the beauty and power of the Connecticut River by boarding the **Quinnetukut II Riverboat**, which from late May to mid-October cruises a six-mile section of the river from the Riverview Picnic Area in Northfield to Barton Cove in Gill, where bald eagles, thought to be graduates of the eagle restoration program at the Quabbin Reservoir to the southeast, have begun to nest. It's a relaxing and educational ride; the narrator explains the geology and natural and cultural history of the river, including the legend of the French King rock, a huge formation in the middle of the river named for Louis XIV. The rock served as a landmark for Canadian troops, who camped out on the riverbank there in 1704 before invading Deerfield. Other cruises include one-hour family excursions; kids-only cruises with musicians and magicians; and sunset cruises with bands playing jazz, blues, country, and other types of music. Tel: (413) 659-3713.

If you'd like to stay a night or two, try the seven-room **Northfield Country House**, out in the woods but just 1 mile (1½ km) off Main Street. The 1901 English manor house, built by a follower of Dwight Moody, has the feel of an Adirondack retreat, with a large fireplace and a cherry-paneled dining room. There's a pool on the grounds as well as some pleasant nature trails.

THE MOHAWK TRAIL

The 38-mile (61-km) stretch of road that runs west from Greenfield (on Interstate 91 just north of Deerfield) to North Adams follows the basic route travelled by Indians along the Deerfield River to the Connecticut. Today this trail (modern Route 2) remains one of New England's most scenic roads, especially in the fall, when the mountains are splashed with colors.

After World War II this so-called Mohawk Trail became a nationally known tourist destination, lined with a dozen or so "motor courts," cabins where city folk would come and spend a week or two in the summer, and souvenir shops hawking "authentic" Indian crafts (many of them made by locals). By that time few Indians were left in the region, so entrepreneurs would pay Native Americans to come and spend the summer at their shops.

The old Mohawk Trail Drive-In is closed now, and the Trail, once the major route between Albany and Boston, has since been replaced by the faster and wider Massachusetts Turnpike (I-90). Once you leave Greenfield behind, the Trail is still largely undeveloped, and a few of the old motorists' cabins and souvenir stands remain.

If you have the time, a drive along the Mohawk Trail will take you back through a landscape that doesn't exist in many places anymore. For much of the ride the road follows the Deerfield and, later, the Cold rivers, winding past orchards, forests, and farms.

Greenfield

The Trail starts just east of Greenfield at the French King Bridge, a spot that affords one of the most striking views in all of New England: of the Connecticut River, of Vermont and New Hampshire to the north, and of farms rising up along the riverbanks. So valued is the view that the state has taken action to protect these lands from development.

Greenfield, the county seat, has all the trappings of civilization. With about 20,000 residents, Greenfield is the largest of the country towns in the region, and its downtown has a comfortable, 1950s feel to it, anchored by **Wilson's**, a small-scale department store the likes of which are fast disappearing in the Northeast. The Franklin County Chamber of Commerce provides information on the county from its office at 395 Main Street.

Just around the corner, on Federal Street, is one of the county's best restaurants, the **Green River Café**. It's a laid-back, sixties kind of place where everyone seems to meet for lunch. The vegetarian fare here ranges from basic rice and beans to more gourmet offerings, like pasta with smoked red pepper sauce. Some restaurants are bringing back the past in decor and style, but **Famous Bill's Restaurant**, just up the street, never left. It's the kind of place where waitresses call you "hon." The food is American—love it or leave it— but there's plenty of it at good prices. Tel: (413) 773-9230.

Several chain motels are clustered around the Route 2/ I-91 rotary in Greenfield. If you're planning a stay here, your better bet is to try a local bed-and-breakfast in the Shelburne Falls area, about 10 miles (16 km) west of Greenfield, to which we now turn.

West from Greenfield

Leaving Greenfield you'll head up into the hills of Franklin County, a region that poet Archibald MacLeish (who lived in nearby Conway) described as being on a "human scale." The hills are not quite the Berkshires, but you'll definitely feel your ears pop.

This is hillside dairy farm country (it's not much good for raising anything else), and where there are dairy farmers in New England, there are also maple sugarers. "Sugaring"— that is, tapping maple trees in the early spring, gathering the sap, and boiling it down into maple syrup—is an age-old tradition in western Massachusetts. The income from sugaring helps farmers buy the seed and repair the equipment they'll need for another season.

If you're in these parts in early spring, look for steam coming from the smokestacks of the small sugarhouses on the back roads, and stop in. The odds are good the farmer will welcome the company, and he'll likely have some fresh syrup for sale.

The Massachusetts Maple Producers Association offers a directory of 100 sugarhouses, and the Maple Phone (Tel: 413/628-3912) provides callers with an update on which houses are open to visitors. Call or write the Massachusetts Maple Producers Association, Watson Spruce Corner Road, Ashfield, MA 01330.

SHELBURNE

At **Gould's Sugar House** on the Mohawk Trail in Shelburne, just 6 miles (10 kms) west of Greenfield, visitors can watch the sap being "boiled" in the big evaporator downstairs in front of the restaurant. The smell is just this side of heaven, and you can chow down on waffles, pancakes, and corn fritters, each accompanied by syrup and a small bowl of dill pickles to cut the sweetness. Try sugar on snow, a seasonal treat made by pouring hot syrup on muffin-size snowballs. Closed during May and from November through February; Tel: (413) 625-6170.

Another unchic but satisfying spot in Shelburne is **Davenport's Maple Farm and Restaurant**, located high on a hill about 5 miles (8 km) north off Route 2. Davenport's offers a wider menu and views of the Davenport family's working farm. Dinner specials are inexpensive and filling. To find the place, just after you've entered Shelburne watch for a white clapboard church on your right and follow the signs up the hill. Closed late December through the end of January; Tel: (413) 625-2866.

SHELBURNE FALLS

With a turn-of-the-century downtown and an old iron trolley bridge spanning the Deerfield River, the village of Shelburne Falls looks a little like Bedford Falls, the fictional town in Frank Capra's classic film *It's a Wonderful Life*.

The village encompasses parts of Shelburne and Buckland, across the river; connecting the two sides is the 400-foot-long **Bridge of Flowers**, a former trolley bridge transformed by the local women's gardening club into a three-season garden. There's an information booth on the Shelburne side at the end of Bridge Street.

Follow the signs from Bridge Street to the **Glacial Potholes**, ancient plunge pools created 13,000 years ago by the Deerfield River. They are particularly dramatic in the spring, when the mountain runoff floods the riverbed. Originally called Salmon Falls, the plunge pools attracted the Mohawk and Pocumtuck Indians because the salmon and shad were slowed by the river drops of 64 feet here.

McCusker's Market, on the Buckland side of the bridge, has a good delicatessen with sandwiches and light meals. Just up the hill, **Salmon Falls Artisans Showroom** houses several shops selling crafts, ceramics, photographs, and furniture made by local artists.

In Ashfield, 6 miles (10 km) south of Buckland on Route 112, **South Face Farm** (Tel: 413/628-3268) and **Gray's Sugarhouse** (Tel: 413/625-6559) serve pancakes to visitors on weekends during the spring sugaring season.

Several bed-and-breakfasts offer accommodations in this area, including the **1797 House** in Buckland, and the **Bullfrog Bed and Breakfast** in South Ashfield, about 8 miles (13 km) south of Buckland. The 1797 House sits high on a hill facing Buckland's classic town green. Three double guest rooms are decorated with antiques and offer good views of the Berkshire foothills. Bullfrog, a 200-year-old home, offers four antiques-furnished guest rooms, a lovely garden, and, of course, a pond for the bullfrogs.

West from Shelburne Falls

West of Shelburne Falls the Trail is at its prettiest, as it winds its way along the Deerfield River past fields and farmland. In **Charlemont**, about 7 miles (11 km) west of Shelburne Falls, you'll see on your right the Academy at Charlemont administration building, built from local bricks in 1810 and recently restored. There are plenty of places by the river to stop and picnic, but if you get the urge to be out on the river itself, **Zoar Outdoor**, in a red farmhouse on your right just past

Charlemont Center, offers white-water rafting and canoe trips, as well as instruction in kayaking and rock climbing. Open April through October; Tel: (413) 339-4010.

At the time of its opening in 1876, the **Hoosac Tunnel**, about 11 miles (18 km) west of Charlemont, was one of the wonders of engineering, a five-mile-long tunnel drilled through Hoosac Mountain at a cost of $14 million and 195 lives. From Route 2, turn right at the sign that leads to Rowe to get to the eastern portal of the tunnel. You'll probably come across one of the many train buffs who make the pilgrimage from all over the Northeast to hang out and watch the few remaining trains come through, about four or five every day.

Head back to Route 2, where you resume the route west by crossing the Deerfield River. Just beyond the bridge on your left is the **Hail to the Sunrise Monument**, dedicated in 1932 in honor of the Mohawk Indians. Across Route 2 is **Mohawk Park**, with some of the old cabins that used to serve travellers. These days fishermen rent them by the season, from April through September; Tel: (413) 339-4470.

Two miles (3 km) beyond the monument is **Mohawk Trail State Forest**, one of four state parks in the immediate area, with trails and campsites on more than 6,400 acres spread along the Cold and Deerfield rivers. You're never far from the sounds of the river here, and there's even a stretch in this forest that Indians used to travel on their way to Deerfield. For those seeking a forest-primeval experience, there are five primitive log cabins for rent year-round, heated with wood stoves and plumbed with outhouses. Tel: (413) 339-5504. **Savoy Mountain State Forest**, about 8 miles (13 km) farther west along Route 2, has similar accommodations. The cabins are popular, and reservations are taken up to six months in advance; Tel: (413) 663-8469.

From here Route 2 winds along the Cold River, which flows from the Hoosac Range to the west. You'll travel through a deep gorge and up into the incongruously named town of **Florida** and **Whitcomb Summit**, at 2,173 feet the highest point along the Mohawk Trail. Drop a quarter into the slot of the telescope up here on a clear day and you can see as far as New Hampshire and Connecticut. The large body of water below is the Bear Swamp Reservoir, designed to feed a hydroelectric station. Ten miles (16 km) beyond Whitcomb Summit you'll come to the Hairpin Turn, which offers good views of North Adams and Williamstown to the west and the farms and fields of Vermont to the north.

If you follow the signs and take a quick right before you come to the center of the city of North Adams, you'll come to the **Natural Bridge State Park**, another of the region's geological wonders: a white marble formation with a stream rushing through it. The "bridge" is the result of millions of years of glacial erosion; the stream is estimated to cut through about one foot every 2,500 years. Over the past 150 years workers have etched their initials in the stone; some date to 1840.

North Adams

North Adams, 63 miles (101 km) west of Greenfield (still on Route 2, the Mohawk Trail, which continues to the New York State line), started out as a farming village and later evolved into a manufacturing center, powered by the waters of the Hoosac River. Today North Adams is a city in decline, with high unemployment and a Main Street marred by many empty storefronts. City and state officials are betting on an economic revival with the planned conversion of an empty mill complex to the north of Route 2 into the Massachusetts Museum of Contemporary Art, which would be the largest contemporary art museum in the world.

From Route 2, turn left and drive three blocks south on Route 8 to the **Western Gateway Heritage State Park**, one in a system of state-run urban parks. The complex includes shops, an antiques cooperative, and a small museum that documents in fascinating detail the political haggling over and eventual construction of the Hoosac Tunnel. Exhibits also tell the story of the growth of North Adams into the most important commercial center in Berkshire County and a vital railroad hub in the Northeast. The park attracts train enthusiasts from across the country. Open daily mid-May through October, Thursday through Monday the rest of the year; Tel: (413) 663-6312.

As you continue along Route 2 toward Williamstown you'll see a sign to your left for the road that takes you to the top of **Mount Greylock**, at 3,487 feet the state's highest mountain. Greylock has served as inspiration to many of the Berkshires' greatest poets and authors, including Herman Melville, who wrote *Moby-Dick* while viewing the mountain's whalelike shape from his farm in Pittsfield, 17 miles (27 km) to the south (see below). Greylock is crisscrossed by a number of trails of varying length and difficulty. Among the rare species of plant life found on Mount Greylock is, on the western face, a stand of 200-year-old red spruce trees that escaped the clear-cutting that denuded the Berkshires a century ago; these are now protected by state law. The state Department of Environmental Management offers interpretive programs during the summer at the summit and at the visitors' center in Lanesboro, about 16 miles (26 km) south of North Adams on Route 7; Tel: (413) 499-4262.

Bascom Lodge, at the top of the mountain, is a classic old rustic stone and timber building put up by the Civilian Conservation Corps in the 1930s, providing rustic accommodations (at about $50 a room) for hikers; the snack bar here affords breathtaking views. Family-style dinners are served each evening from mid-May to the end of October. Reservations must be made by noon each day; Tel: (413) 743-1591.

Williamstown

Just 6 miles (10 km) west of North Adams (you are still on Route 2) is Williamstown, the northern Berkshires' handsomest town and a good place to spend a day or two. Originally called West Hoosick, the town later changed its name to honor Colonel Ephraim Williams, a Revolutionary War hero who founded Williams College here in 1793.

Williamstown is a quintessential New England college town, with tree-lined streets, classic architecture with an emphasis on white clapboard and black trim, and lots of young people. Many alums are so enamored of the place that they retire here. The town also claims some famous residents, including actor Christopher Reeve, who cut his acting teeth at the Williamstown Theater Festival, author Joe McGinniss, and historian James MacGregor Burns; Cole Porter and Farah Diba Pahlavi, the widow of the shah of Iran, also once lived here.

The combination of old money and an academic environment makes Williamstown a toney place, and for such a small town it has some remarkable cultural resources, including the Williamstown Theater Festival, which is based in the summer at Williams College, and two nationally recognized art museums.

Williams College
The Williams College campus stretches along both sides of Route 2 as you enter town; the sights of interest are within walking distance of Williamstown's shopping district on Spring Street, to your left from Route 2. There's a public parking lot three blocks down Spring Street.

Walk back up to Route 2, turn right, and the **Williams College Museum of Art** will be one block up on your right. The museum's holdings, which focus on 19th- and 20th-century American art, include works by Grant Wood, Edward Hopper, and Andy Warhol (his last self-portrait). The museum also has one of the largest collections of works by New

England painters Charles and Maurice Prendergast, as well as an intriguing program of changing exhibits ranging from early photographs of American landscapes to the history of African masks. Closed Mondays; Tel: (413) 597-2429.

Directly across the street, behind the college chapel, is **Chapin Library**, on the second floor of Stetson Hall, a highlight of a visit to the college. Here you'll find original copies of the Declaration of Independence, the Articles of Confederation, the Constitution, and the Bill of Rights. Open weekdays; Tel: (413) 597-2462.

Between late June and the end of August the **Williamstown Theater Festival** takes over on the Williams campus. Such celebrities as Joanne Woodward and Paul Newman, Joan Van Ark, and Bianca Jagger have performed here in works ranging from Shakespeare to light musicals (on its Main Stage) and newer plays and works in progress (on the smaller Other Stage).

The late director Nikos Psacharapoulos cajoled many of his New York theater friends into directing and performing at Williamstown; as a result, WTF is a cut above most summer festivals. The relationship seems to be a symbiotic one: Many plays first presented here, by writers like A. R. Gurney, Ariel Dorfman, and others, end up in the theaters of New York City and London.

Main Stage performances generally sell out early, so reserve your tickets as far in advance as possible—the schedule is announced in mid-May. You can buy tickets or request a brochure by writing or calling the **Williamstown Theater Festival**, P.O. Box 517, Williamstown, MA 01267; Tel: (413) 597-3399. For tickets once you're in the area, call the box office at Tel: (413) 597-3400.

Elsewhere in Williamstown

Beyond the center of town Route 2 meets Route 7 at a rotary. Two miles (3 km) south of the rotary is the **Sterling and Francine Clark Art Institute**, whose collection includes more than 30 paintings by Renoir, among other French Impressionists, as well as works by Homer, Sargent, and Cassatt. The museum itself, opened in 1955, is a work of art, its exterior a classic white marble Greek façade. In summer the museum's café is a pleasant spot for lunch. Closed Mondays except holidays; Tel: (413) 458-9545.

Two miles (3 km) north of the rotary on Route 7, turn right onto Sand Springs Road for an old-time bathing experience at **Sand Springs Pool and Spa**. The place originally served as a campground for Indians from five nations, who believed that the naturally mild and alkaline waters here had medicinal value. A bathhouse was later built for health-conscious 19th-century travellers, and the place has been updated recently to include the largest outdoor hot tub in the state. Closed in winter; Tel: (413) 458-5205. The complex includes a 74° F natural-spring outdoor swimming pool, a toddlers' pool, and a whirlpool, along with a sauna, snack bar, and play space for children. The bathhouse is the original one built in the Victorian era.

STAYING IN WILLIAMSTOWN

Williamstown offers the best range of accommodations north of Lenox; some travellers even prefer to make the town their home base for ventures southward. It's a good idea to reserve a room early during foliage season, or in mid-May during the Williams College graduation weekend.

The **Orchards** offers the poshest lodgings in town. The hotel's 49 individually decorated rooms are among the finest in the Berkshires, with marble bathrooms, a sprinkling of antiques, and Oriental carpets; some of the rooms have fireplaces. Complimentary tea and savories are served every afternoon in the elegantly appointed living room, and turn-down services include chocolate chip cookies. The hotel's restaurant is also good. The only drawbacks here are that the hotel's grounds are practically nonexistent and that it's located on busy Route 2 across from a Burger King.

The **Williams Inn**, at the junction of northerly Route 2 and Route 7, near the campus, is the town's most centrally located hotel, within walking distance of nearly everything, with 103 rooms, two restaurants, and an indoor pool, Jacuzzi, and sauna. Rooms here are good-size and nicely decorated in Colonial reproductions and Waverly prints. The public spaces are old-money elegant, with big chandeliers, couches, and a fireplace, lending the hotel a comfortable and unpretentious ambience. There is a formal dining room and a more casual tavern serving light meals.

The **Maple Terrace Motel** draws repeat visitors for its near-town location and reasonable prices. With 14 rooms, two efficiency apartments, and a king-size suite with fireplace, it's an especially good choice if you're travelling with children. The decor is simple, but it's impeccably clean and there's a pool/picnic area behind the hotel that makes you feel as if you're really out in the country.

If you're looking for a past-life experience, **River Bend Farm Guest House** will take you there. The place was built in 1770 by Colonel Benjamin Simonds, one of Williamstown's founders, as a tavern. Innkeepers Dave and Judy Loomis have restored it, room by room, back to its Colonial basics, including foot-wide pine wall panels, large fireplaces, and sloping floors. Five bedrooms, decorated with four-poster beds and Oriental rugs, share two bathrooms. In keeping with the integrity of the house, the bathroom facilities, while adequate, may be Spartan for some. If you don't mind that, it's a great place to stay. Open April through November.

At the other end of town, in southern Williamstown, **Field Farm Guest House** is a departure from other local hostelries in that it prides itself on *not* being authentically old. Field Farm is a distinctly modern five-bedroom home set on 254 country acres and accented with art and sculpture. The house was designed in 1948 by Edward Goodell in the American Modern style. Rooms are simply furnished in modern or Scandinavian decor. All rooms have private baths, and four of the five have a splendid view of Mount Greylock. The house may not be everyone's cup of tea, but the setting, with a pool, tennis courts, nicely landscaped grounds dotted with sculptures, and 3½ miles of nature trails, is a knockout. It's tranquil and solitary, yet only a ten-minute drive to Williamstown.

DINING IN THE WILLIAMSTOWN AREA

As with most college towns, Williamstown has a wide range of restaurants, from student hangouts to places where Mom and Dad pay. **Michael's Restaurant & Pizzeria**, located on the south side of Route 2 just before you enter the town center, is a local favorite, serving Italian and Greek food, and, of course, great pizza. Try the vegetarian, with feta cheese, squash, eggplant, fresh tomato, black olives, and spinach. Closed Mondays; Tel: (413) 458-2114.

At 27 Spring Street, Williamstown's shopping street, the **Cobble Café** serves sandwiches that are a cut above the ordinary, with smoked meats and homemade breads, as well as salads and homemade soups. Though it has the look of a funky coffee shop, the café serves special dinners that include appetizers like pâté and smoked salmon and entrées such as steak *au poivre* and roast chicken with artichoke hearts. Reservations for dinner are appreciated; Tel: (413) 458-5930.

The **Hancock Inn**, a pretty half-hour drive on Route 43 through the countryside west of Williamstown, is worth the trip for gourmands in search of Continental cuisine served by candlelight. Innkeepers Chester and Ellen Gorski have made a reputation for themselves on their food, which includes such dishes as duckling in Port wine with figs, and filet mignon sautéed in shallots, red wine, and Cognac. Open Friday through Sunday, some Thursdays in summer. Reservations recommended; Tel: (413) 738-5873.

At the other end of the dining spectrum is the **Miss Adams**

Diner, at 53 Park Street in **Adams**, 6 miles (10 km) south of North Adams at the junction of Routes 8 and 116. The restored 1949 Worcester lunch car has an updated diner menu that includes vegetarian fare along with the old standards. The homemade bread pudding is wonderful. Open for breakfast and lunch; closed Mondays. Tel: (413) 743-5300.

For picnic supplies, the **Clarksburg Bread Company**, at 37 Spring Street in Williamstown, has the best selection of baked goods in the northern Berkshires, including home-made whole-grain breads, French bread, and sweets. Closed Sundays and Mondays. The **Store at Five Corners**, a gift and gourmet shop at the junction of Routes 7 south and 43, is one of the oldest operating businesses in America, dating back to the 1770s.

THE SOUTHERN BERKSHIRES
Pittsfield

About 20 miles (32 km) south of Williamstown on Route 7, Pittsfield was settled as Pontoosuc Plantation in 1752, incor-porated as the town of Pittsfield in 1761, and incorporated as a city in 1891. Although Pittsfield, named for British states-man William Pitt the Elder, lacks the aristocratic mien of the southern Berkshires, the city did claim its share of literary lights in its heyday. Oliver Wendell Holmes, Sr., father of the famous judge, made his summer home here in the mid-19th century, Longfellow honeymooned here after marrying a local girl, and Herman Melville wrote *Moby-Dick* while a resident of Pittsfield.

Whereas Lenox and Stockbridge, as we will see, were refuges for the wealthy, Pittsfield was the Berkshires' indus-trial center. In 1907 the city underwent a transformation with the establishment of the General Electric Company, which drew Jewish, Italian, Armenian, and African-American labor-ers. GE, along with the textile and paper industries, was responsible for creating a middle class in the Berkshires.

But in the past quarter century Pittsfield has fallen on hard times. Most of its textile factories have closed, and GE's work force has been reduced to less than half what it was 25 years ago. Though some attractive redevelopment has taken place downtown, many of the buildings that gave the area its character have fallen into disrepair and have been destroyed.

As a result, there's not much worth stopping for in the city, with the exception of the **Berkshire Museum**, at 39 South Street on Route 7 just south of Park Square. The museum's art collection includes a number of Hudson River school landscapes, and there are natural science and history exhibits as well. Closed Mondays except in July and August, when it is open every day. Tel: (413) 443-7171.

Hancock Shaker Village

Five miles (8 km) west of Pittsfield at the junction of Routes 20 and 41, Hancock Shaker Village illustrates and chronicles the history of the Shakers, the 18th- and 19th-century religious sect founded in England and made up in the United States of followers of Mother Ann Lee, who in 1774 fled the religious persecution of England and settled at Watervliet (then called Niskeyuna), near Albany. By 1800 most of the 19 Shaker communities in the Northeast, from Maine to Kentucky, had been formed, all based on tenets of celibacy, pacifism, separation from the world, simplicity, conservation of resources, and hard work.

Lee established the Hancock community in 1790. At its peak in about 1830 Hancock housed some 300 members in neat, white clapboard houses on some 1,200 acres of farmland. The Hancock settlement was known as the City of Peace; members made their living by making furniture, baskets, boxes, and textiles in winter, and by farming and selling seeds and medicinal herbs in summer.

By the mid-19th century between 6,000 and 10,000 men, women, and children belonged to the sect nationwide. But the Civil War and the arrival of the Industrial Age accelerated the group's decline—as did rules about celibacy. (It's hard to know what the Shakers would think about today's skyrocketing value of the furniture they made, with collectors willing to pay tens of thousands of dollars for a single piece.) The village fell into disarray in the 20th century as its members died off, and many of the buildings were sold or razed. In 1960, after the last of the Shaker residents here vacated the village, a group of local citizens established a nonprofit educational corporation and began restoration.

The 20 buildings of Hancock Shaker Village warrant a full day, both for the content of their exhibits and for their setting. The three-story round stone barn, the centerpiece of the village, was designed to increase the efficiency of feeding the cows. Meetinghouses, the machine shop, and the kitchen all illustrate how the Shakers went about their daily lives, and the herb gardens include species raised by Shakers more than 100 years ago. Special programs are scheduled regularly for both adults and children, including crafts workshops and demonstrations, Shaker family meals, and sleigh rides. Bring a picnic.

The village/museum is open daily for self-guided visits

from May 1 through October 31, from 9:30 A.M. to 5:00 P.M.
In April and November guided tours of the most important
buildings are given between 10:00 A.M. and 3:00 P.M. For
information, Tel: (413) 443-0188, or write P.O. Box 898,
Pittsfield, MA 01202.

Arrowhead

Literary history is one element of the Berkshires' cachet.
Tanglewood, the region's most famous institution, was named
after Nathaniel Hawthorne's *Tanglewood Tales*. Novelist Edith
Wharton made her home for a time in Lenox, and Hawthorne's friend Herman Melville wrote *Moby-Dick* not while
vacationing on Nantucket, but from his landlocked farm
called Arrowhead, at 780 Holmes Road, about 1¼ miles (2
km) east of Route 7 at the Pittsfield–Lenox line. (Take a left at
the London Fog outlet.)

Melville moved his family here from New York in 1850,
after the successful publication of his book *Typee* in 1846. He
completed *Moby-Dick* in the upstairs study here, looking
northward toward the Mount Greylock range, which he
thought resembled a huge whale. The home and grounds
are now owned by the Berkshire County Historical Society
and are open to the public during the summer months. The
tour, which may be of interest only to hard-core fans of
Melville, provides a glimpse of life in his day, including 19th-
century dress and furnishings. Open May through October;
Tel: (413) 442-1793.

Lenox

As you continue south on Route 7 from Pittsfield you'll travel
into the heart of the Berkshires. The small-town feel and the
physical beauty of the southern Berkshires—the rural landscape of fields and farmland, mountains and rolling hills, red
barns and stone fences—have always contributed to their
allure. But so, too, has the area's level of sophistication—
you can easily fill your evenings with a different concert,
play, or dance performance each night of the week.

There's not much going on in the southern Berkshires in
the winter months, which may be just the point if you're
looking for a good place to hibernate for the weekend. Most
inns and restaurants remain open, and many offer off-season
packages.

We first discuss the attractions of the towns of Lenox and
Stockbridge separately—historic homes, shops, and the
like—and then cover neighboring towns and back roads,

music and theater, and accommodations and restaurants of the Lenox–Stockbridge area.

Lenox, 8 miles (13 km) south of Pittsfield on Route 7, began its life as a farming village but was transformed in the middle of the 19th century when the town was "discovered" by Charles Sedgwick (a distant ancestor of Edie, the late protegée of artist Andy Warhol), who moved here in 1821. By 1846 the first of the cottages that became famous in the Gilded Age, Highwood, was being built by banker Samuel Ward. The literati were beginning to gather here as well, drawn to the area for its natural beauty. The rich and the writers mixed at house parties, balls, and rambles, like the famous 1850 picnic on Monument Mountain in Great Barrington, where Herman Melville, Nathaniel Hawthorne, and Oliver Wendell Holmes sipped Champagne from a silver mug in the pouring rain.

By then Melville had moved his family to Pittsfield from New York, and Holmes had inherited his family's Pittsfield estate. Hawthorne was staying at the Red House on the Tappan estate, which would later become the grounds of Tanglewood; he would complete *The House of Seven Gables* and parts of two other books here.

Other visitors included Henry James, who was a regular guest at Edith Wharton's home, The Mount (see below), William Lowell, Henry David Thoreau, and Samuel Longfellow, who found it difficult to write in such a soothing environment.

The 1880s saw the flourishing of the Gilded Age in the Berkshires, with the Harrimans, Biddles, Vanderbilts, Westinghouses, Carnegies, and others all trying to outdo one another by building ever more magnificent "cottages," one with as many as 100 rooms. By the turn of the century the hills around Lenox and Stockbridge were dotted with some 75 villas, palazzi, and mansions, each surrounded by manicured lawns and formal gardens, eventually earning the area the title "Inland Newport." Those days turned out to be fleeting, however, as the imposition of federal income taxes and the Great Depression soon led to the decline of these awesome, if sometimes overdone, residences. Today Lenox is a stately hybrid: a cross between a country hamlet and a retreat for both old- and new-moneyed Bostonians and New Yorkers.

The Route 7 strip leading into Lenox is nearly always jammed with traffic in summer, and much of the countryside leading into town has been paved with outlet stores and boutiques hawking their high-priced wares to visitors. (The Lenox Chamber of Commerce has its information center in the old Lenox Academy Building, on the right on Route 7A as you enter town from the north; Tel: 413/637-3646 or 800/25-LENOX.) For a respite, take a short drive off Route 7, off Dugway Road, to the **Pleasant Valley Wildlife Sanctuary**, which offers a quieter piece of the Berkshires along with educational trails and a small nature museum. The sanctuary, run by the Massachusetts Audubon Society, includes a beaver pond, hummingbird gardens, and meadows. It's a good spot for children, who will enjoy exploring its winding paths. Closed Mondays; Tel: (413) 637-0320.

HISTORIC HOMES OF LENOX

Many of the 19th-century cottages that made the area famous have been torn down or converted into inns or private schools. For example, Bellefontaine, the former estate of Giraud Foster (the inventor of clothing snaps) designed after the Petit Trianon at Versailles, is now home to Canyon Ranch in the Berkshires (discussed under Accommodations, below).

But some remain open to the public in various incarnations; you can see quite a few in Lenox in varying states of restoration and repair by strolling up Walker Street and bearing right onto Kemble. **Bassett Hall**, a Georgian Revival–style mansion once owned by Frederick Frelinghuysen, President Chester Arthur's secretary of the treasury, now houses **Charles L. Flint Antiques**, which specializes in country primitives. Just "next door" is **Springlawn**, built in Beaux-Arts style in 1902 and now empty; it's up for sale if you decide you like the place.

Follow Kemble Street 1¼ miles (2 km) southeast of Lenox Center to Plunkett Street and **The Mount**, the former summer home of Edith Wharton, the most spectacular of the houses open to the public. Wharton, dubbed the Lady of Lenox by Henry James, was an influential interior designer of the time. She built the house in 1902 and wrote two of her better-known works here—*Ethan Frome* in 1911 and *The House of Mirth* in 1905. Wharton wrote in bed in the mornings and dropped the pages on the floor for her secretary to type. She would spend afternoons with her many house-guests, conversing or strolling through her gardens.

Wharton worked on the interior design of the house with Boston architect Ogden Codman, Jr., with whom she also coauthored the book *The Decoration of Houses*. The 35-room white stucco mansion is currently being restored by Edith Wharton Restoration, Inc., which offers hour-long tours of the house and gardens, as well as special programs like the Edith Wharton Designer Showhouse, from Memorial Day weekend until late October. For information, Tel: (413) 637-1899.

(Shakespeare & Company stages dramatic performances here in summer; see Music and Theater, below.)

SHOPPING IN LENOX

Locals defeated an effort in the 1980s to build a designer outlet emporium similar to those in other New England tourist centers, which was probably good for the environment but bad for hard-core shoppers. There is a strip mall on Route 7 just north of town, which has a **Harvé Benard Outlet**, with some good values on men's and women's clothing, and **Laura's Scottish Tea Room and Bakery**, offering delicious Scottish scones and shortbreads.

Lenox Center doesn't have the kind of shopping scene that you'd associate with such a posh region. The central shopping and dining district that runs from the corner of Walker and Church streets has a lot of touristy places; nevertheless there are a few interesting shops as well. On Walker Street, **Evviva** sells contemporary women's clothing, including hand-painted silks. A few blocks down, at 76 Church Street, **Glad Rags** has a good selection of casual women's wear.

Two crafts shops here are also worth a look. **Annie Goodchild American Primitive!**, at 22 Walker Street, is a fun and unusual shop, with boldly colored furniture and paintings, while **Concepts of Art**, at 67 Church Street, sells stained glass, pottery, and handcrafted jewelry.

At the end of Church Street, take a left onto Franklin Street and pop into the **Ella Lerner Gallery**, at number 17. One of the area's oldest galleries, the Ella Lerner specializes in 19th- and 20th-century paintings, drawings, and prints, including works by Leonard Baskin, Käthe Kollwitz, and Salvador Dalí. Closed Tuesdays.

Picnic supplies for Tanglewood are available at **Nejaime's Lenox Wine Cellar** at 33 Church Street, but for a wider selection of foods drive up Route 7 to the Pittsfield city line to **Guido's Marketplace**, a collection of five stores that provide a full selection of deli, bakery, and produce.

Stockbridge

Stockbridge is the most popular town in the Berkshires; what draws people here is the small-town feel of its main street, with neatly kept Victorian homes and gardens, and, of course, the rambling Red Lion Inn (see Accommodations and Dining, below), which seems to anchor the town permanently in a simpler, bygone time. (Stockbridge's Laurel Hill Association, the oldest existing village improvement society in the United States, has helped preserve the town's rural character.) Many come to stay, including Seiji Ozawa of the Boston Symphony and Norman Rockwell, who lived here from 1953 until his death in 1978.

And don't forget Arlo Guthrie, who wrote his famous ballad "Alice's Restaurant" about a littering incident that took place after a party held at a now-defunct eatery owned by Alice Brock. Arlo lives with his wife and four children in nearby Washington, Massachusetts, and recently bought the old church in Great Barrington where the movie based on the song was made in the late 1960s.

Way before Guthrie and Rockwell, Stockbridge was a mission, started in 1739 by the Yale-educated Reverend John Sergeant to educate and "redeem" the local Mahican Indians. Fifty years later, their lands taken by settlers, the Mahicans moved on to an Oneida Indian reservation in New York State.

Stockbridge today is a bit of an icon, epitomizing our imaginary version of a small New England town, even though it is among the wealthiest in the Berkshires. Its scale is small, and you can walk to most of the sights here. In summer Stockbridge is best enjoyed on a weekday; even then, finding a parking space will be difficult. There is an information booth in the center of Main Street.

The front porch of the **Red Lion Inn**, right on Main Street, is a great place to relax and watch the passing traffic on a summer's afternoon. Begun in the early 19th century as a stagecoach stop between Boston and Albany, the inn is one of the oldest in New England. It was rebuilt in 1895 after a fire and today is the center of activity in Stockbridge—any time of year. (The Red Lion is discussed further under Accommodations and Dining, below.)

One block beyond, still on Main Street, is the **Mission House**, home of John Sergeant and his wife, Abigail, who was the daughter of Ephraim Williams, founder of Williamstown. The house was purchased by Mabel Choate and moved to its current location, where it was landscaped with an 18th-century–style herb and flower garden by celebrated landscape architect Fletcher Steele. The ornate front door of the house was carved in the Connecticut River Valley. Open in summers only; Tel: (413) 298-3239.

About 2 miles (3 km) southwest of the center of Stockbridge, on a 36-acre parcel of land off Route 183, is the **Norman Rockwell Museum** at Stockbridge (formerly in the Old Corner House in Stockbridge Center). The museum displays the world's largest collection of Rockwell paintings, including the *Four Freedoms,* and a rotating exhibition of hundreds of his other works. The artist's studio has been moved to the new site as part of the museum and is open six months of the year. Closed Thanksgiving, Christmas, and New Year's Day; Tel: (413) 298-4100.

STOCKBRIDGE'S HISTORIC HOMES

Just up Prospect Hill from Stockbridge center is **Naumkeag**, the Norman-style summer home of Joseph Hodges Choate, once an ambassador to England. Built in 1885, Naumkeag was designed by Stanford White and its extensive gardens laid out by Fletcher Steele. Open from late May to Labor Day; closed Mondays. Tel: (413) 298-3239.

Six miles (10 km) from Stockbridge Center, on Route 183 south, **Chesterwood** is another wonderful place to spend a morning. Sculptor Daniel Chester French, who created the seated Lincoln at the Lincoln Memorial in Washington, D.C., lived here in the summers from 1897 to 1931. The barn gallery houses castings of his works, while the studio illustrates the different stages of the creation of the Lincoln statue. Though not as elaborate as the grounds at The Mount in Lenox, the gardens here are beautiful, as are the nature trails where French used to wander with his daughter when he wasn't working. Open May through October, and for special events; Tel: (413) 298-3579.

The Back Roads of the Berkshires

The best way to really enjoy the Berkshires is to venture out into the countryside on one of the region's many back roads. Here you'll find the New England of calendars and postcards: fields and farmland, woods and meadows, streams and the trademark stone fences.

TYRINGHAM AND MONTEREY

Beginning in Stockbridge, follow Route 102 east and north to Lee, and then head southeast on Tyringham Road toward Tyringham, a real country village surrounded on three sides by mountains. Thanks to the fact that the railroad never quite made it this far, the Tyringham Valley is one of the least developed areas of the Berkshires, and is still home to dairy farms and orchards. In 1792 a Shaker colony was established here, eventually claiming more than 100 residents by 1852. Today many of the homes here are owned by "city people."

If you'd like to stay a night or two, the **Golden Goose Bed & Breakfast** is located in the center of town, at the heart of what limited action there is in Tyringham; it is discussed below, under Accommodations. There's hiking nearby at **Tyringham Cobble** (a "cobble" is what the locals used to call a rocky-topped hill) and swimming at **Upper Goose Pond** and another local swimming hole.

Farther down Main Road you'll come to the thatched-roof fantasy that was once the home of sculptor Sir Henry Hudson Kitson, who created the Minuteman statue in Lexington. Now called **Tyringham Galleries and Gingerbread House**, the place contains several rooms full of paintings, photographs, and etchings from contemporary artists around the country. The grounds are laced with nature trails and filled with sculptures.

About 2 miles (3 km) beyond you'll come to Monterey Road on your right, named for the village to the south that was once a part of Tyringham; **Monterey** was named in honor of General Zachary Taylor's battles in Mexico in 1847. The **Monterey General Store**, an old-fashioned country store with a deli, sells Monterey *chèvre,* a goat's-milk cheese made at nearby Rawson Brook Farm. The 10,500-acre **Beartown State Forest**, north of Route 23 on Blue Hill Road in Monterey, offers hiking, camping, and swimming in pristine, 35-acre Benedict Pond; Tel: (413) 528-0904.

SHEFFIELD, SOUTHFIELD, AND NEW MARLBOROUGH

Beginning in Great Barrington, which is 7 miles (11 km) south of Stockbridge on Route 7, follow Route 7 south 6 miles (10 km) to **Sheffield**, where the last battle of Shays's Rebellion was fought in 1787. Sheffield is the home of the oldest covered bridge in the state, still visible from a side road to your left off Route 7 before you enter the town.

Sheffield Pottery, on your right on Route 7 just north of town, sells a good selection of pottery and ceramic work by dozens of New England artists. Sheffield's main street is lined with nearly 20 antiques shops, excellent for browsing. Travel south on Route 7 and bear right onto Route 7A to visit the **Colonel Ashley House**, built in 1735 and the oldest dwelling in Berkshire County. Here you'll get a look at the furnishings, tools, and pottery used in everyday life by the well-to-do Ashley family in the 18th and 19th centuries. Open Memorial Day through Columbus Day; call for days and hours. Tel: (413) 229-8600.

Just around the corner is **Bartholomew's Cobble**, where you can hike and see an incredible array of wildflowers, other plant life, and geological outcroppings. The cobble is a good picnic spot, with the Housatonic River sweeping around its base and surrounding meadows, tended by a prominent local farmer named George Bartholomew in the 19th century.

Turn onto Maple Avenue, across from Memorial Park, and follow a winding country road through the village of Mill

River (where author Roy Blount makes his home) and on to **Southfield**. The Buggy Whip Factory, a renovated tannery on Main Street, houses outlet stores and the **Southfield Antiques Market**, as well as the **Boiler Room Café**, an innovative restaurant serving dishes like sorrel tarts, grilled bluefish with saffron aïoli, and fried Maine crabcakes. Call to be sure it's open; Tel: (413) 229-3105.

New Marlborough, just a few miles north of Southfield via Southfield–New Marlborough Road, is another old New England village with a common flanked on one side by the **Old Inn on the Green & Gedney Farm**, which is discussed under Accommodations, below. Route 57 takes you the 9 miles (14½ km) back to Great Barrington.

MUSIC AND THEATER IN THE SOUTHERN BERKSHIRES

With the increasing popularity of the Berkshires, tickets to all the performances discussed below go fast, so it's a good idea to reserve as soon as you've developed your itinerary.

Tanglewood

The decline of the Berkshires' Gilded Age in this century might also have brought about the decline of the region were it not for the **Tanglewood Music Festival**, which draws thousands of visitors to the area each summer. The summer home of the **Boston Symphony Orchestra**, Tanglewood, 1¼ miles (2 km) west of Lenox village on West Street, is one of the best-known classical music festivals in the world, and has been a performing venue for such conductors as the late Leonard Bernstein, Zubin Mehta, and Seiji Ozawa, the festival's current director. There are all kinds of opportunities to listen to music here, from the Saturday morning rehearsals in the shed to small chamber concerts on weeknights to performances by students at Tanglewood's summer music school.

What makes Tanglewood such a treat is its setting on a rolling 500-acre estate with lush lawns and towering evergreens. It's traditional here to bring a lavish picnic lunch or dinner and spread a blanket and enjoy. For ticket information in summer, Tel: (413) 637-1940; for program information, Tel: (413) 637-1666. From September to June information is available from the BSO's offices at Symphony Hall, Boston, MA 02115; Tel: (617) 266-1492.

Jacob's Pillow Dance Festival

This festival was founded in 1933 in the hills of **Becket** (12 miles/19 km east of Stockbridge Center via Route 102 to Route

8 north) by dancer Ted Shawn and his wife, Ruth St. Denis. Over the years artists like Agnes de Mille, Merce Cunningham, Mark Morris, and others have performed in this spectacular hillside setting, with both indoor and outdoor theaters and several studios. Jacob's Pillow continues to be a place where works in progress are honed and polished every summer from late June through September 1. Go early before the performance; the grounds—and the people—are beautiful. For ticket information, Tel: (413) 243-0745, or write to Box 287, Lee, MA 01238.

Shakespeare & Company

Under the direction of Tina Packer, Shakespeare & Company has come into its own in the past five years, producing innovative and often challenging interpretations of the works of the Bard in four different settings on the grounds of The Mount in Lenox (see above). The Mainstage Theater and the Court Theater, next to the Wharton house, present popular productions of Shakespeare's plays in the open air, while the new Stables Theater, in an old carriage house on the grounds of the estate, offers a series of plays by modern playwrights, as well as some Shakespeare. The company also presents adaptations of Edith Wharton's short stories in the Wharton Theater, which is actually the salon of the main house at The Mount. The season runs from late May to the first week in September. For tickets and information, write to The Mount, Lenox, MA 01240, or Tel: (413) 637-3353.

The Berkshire Theater Festival

Stockbridge's Berkshire Theater Festival (on Route 7 just north of Stockbridge Center), which runs from the end of June through August, features works by such playwrights as Christopher Durang and A. R. Gurney on the Mainstage, and newer works in production at the 99-seat Unicorn Theater housed in the Red Barn behind the playhouse. Tickets are available at the theater box office. For information after June 1, Tel: (413) 298-5576. Before June 1 Tel: (413) 298-5536, or write BTF, Box 797, Stockbridge, MA 01262.

Aston Magna Festival

The Aston Magna Festival offers baroque and classical music concerts at St. James Church in Great Barrington, 7 miles (11 km) south of Stockbridge on Route 7, on Saturdays in July and August. Single tickets for nonsubscribers are usually available in early July at the Aston Magna box office, at 323 Main Street, Great Barrington, and at Bill's Pharmacy, at 362

Main Street in Great Barrington. For ticket information, Tel: (413) 528-3595.

STAYING IN THE SOUTHERN BERKSHIRES

Lodgings in the southern Berkshires include chain motels, small bed-and-breakfasts, larger inns, and full-scale resorts, as well as some once-in-a-lifetime splurges.

Be prepared to spend more here for accommodations than elsewhere in central and western Massachusetts, and if you're travelling on a weekend in the summer you'll probably have to commit yourself for at least a two-night stay. Regular visitors tend to reserve their rooms in early spring, once they've bought their Tanglewood tickets, so the sooner you make your reservations, the better.

If you find yourself in the Berkshires on a weekend without a room, try the chamber of commerce information booths in Great Barrington, Lee, Lenox, Pittsfield, and Stockbridge. Staffers do not accept advance reservations, but they can help with last-minute lodging referrals.

First, the splurges.

Expensive

Like many of the old Berkshire cottages, **Wheatleigh** has a story behind it. Built in Stockbridge in 1893 as a wedding present to a daughter marrying into royalty, Wheatleigh is a paean to the 16th-century Florentine palazzo. Located on Hawthorne Road, a half mile (less than 1 km) off Route 183 between Lenox and Stockbridge, it was at one time a residence for Tanglewood artists but now serves as a retreat for frazzled Wall Streeters and others who can afford the luxurious accommodations. The 17 guest rooms, some with hardwood floors and nine with fireplaces, are grand and spacious. Some quibble about the chrome-and-glass decor in the public space downstairs, but with Tiffany windows and grounds with fountains and gardens designed by Frederick Law Olmsted, Wheatleigh has little to apologize for. The restaurant, also acclaimed and expensive, is discussed under Dining, below.

The Victorian-style **Apple Tree Inn**, located about a mile (1½ km) south of Lenox center on Route 183, is set on a hilltop within earshot of Tanglewood. It's less formal than Wheatleigh, with extensive apple orchards, rose gardens, and a spectacular view of the Stockbridge Bowl, a man-made lake. The main house has 14 rooms, some with fireplaces, while the more modern guest lodge has 21 rooms.

The **Old Inn on the Green & Gedney Farm**, in New

Marlborough, is a bit off the beaten track, about a 30-minute drive along country roads southeast from Great Barrington, but gourmands make the trip for a meal in the Old Inn's candle-lit dining room and an overnight in one of the rooms upstairs. The Old Inn has five restored bedrooms (two with a shared bath), that are Colonial to the point of being austere, though decorated with antiques and country furniture. Gedney Farm, about a mile (1½ km) down the road, is a newly converted 19th-century Norman-style barn with 15 guest rooms, some of which have fireplaces and whirlpool tubs.

Bed-and-Breakfasts

A short walk north from Lenox center, **Garden Gables Inn** is a pretty, 14-room country inn set on five acres, with gardens and a large outdoor swimming pool. Built as a private estate in 1780 and run as a country inn since the 1940s, Garden Gables has been renovated to keep the old nooks and crannies, but with modern comforts, including private bathrooms. The downstairs sitting rooms are charming and comfortable without being cloying. Highly recommended.

On the southern edge of Lenox Center but still within walking distance of town, the **Walker House** is an old, Federal-style mansion. The eight guest rooms, many with fireplaces, have canopy beds and lots of antiques; the decor of each room is centered around a different classical music composer. There's a nice, big screened-in porch for drinks in the evening, and pets are often welcome, but you must call to discuss and arrange this in advance.

Just across the way, the **Gables Inn** is another beauty, once the home of Edith Wharton while she was building The Mount. A rambling, Queen Anne–style mansion, the Gables Inn has 19 guest rooms and three suites, many done up in themes; some, for example, are devoted to past presidents and are decorated with presidential memorabilia. The new suites look like settings from a Ralph Lauren ad (innkeeper Frank Newton says Ralph copied him). An outdoor swimming pool, tennis court, and the proximity to town make this a good choice for the money.

Roeder House Bed & Breakfast is an 1856 Federal/Colonial–style farmhouse that has undergone a recent renovation. The six guest rooms are decorated to the hilt with period reproductions and antiques, canopy beds, and quilts. Roeder House draws an upscale urban clientele who value the place for its peace, quiet, and location, five minutes from Tanglewood and two minutes from Stockbridge, on Route 183 at the foot of Chesterwood.

South of Lenox on the way to Stockbridge on Route 7, the

Inn at Stockbridge is an elegantly appointed Georgian/ Colonial bed-and-breakfast, with eight guest rooms decorated with a mix of antiques and reproductions. The place has the feel of a country manor, with an outdoor pool and 12 acres of grounds; the common rooms are formal yet welcoming, with a baby grand, overstuffed chairs, and a big fireplace.

Closer to Stockbridge, on Yale Hill Road just off Route 7, behind the Berkshire Theater Festival, **Arbor Rose Bed & Breakfast** is a homey, more casual B and B, with a rose garden, an old sawmill, and small waterfalls in the back yard. There are five guest rooms, two with private bath.

Bear left off Route 7 onto Route 102 east and head for the village of South Lee and the **Historic Merrell Tavern Inn Bed and Breakfast**. Just 1 mile (1½ km) from Stockbridge Center, the three-story brick inn was built around 1794 and served as a stagecoach stop in the 19th century. Its nine guest rooms are decorated with colors and murals from that period and an astounding array of 18th- and 19th-century antiques, including canopy beds. Despite its faithfulness to the period, the Merrell Tavern is comfortable and accessible; you never feel as though you can't touch anything. (Note: This is no longer a tavern and serves no alcohol.)

In the country village of Tyringham (discussed above), the **Golden Goose Bed & Breakfast** is a 200-year-old house decked out in Victoriana. There are six guest rooms and a studio apartment with a separate entrance.

Full-Service Inns

If you prefer the amenities and atmosphere of a larger, full-service inn, the **Red Lion Inn**, on Stockbridge's Main Street, is a good choice. The inn has 108 rooms and suites, each decorated in period pieces, and its public spaces are adorned with Oriental rugs, lush flower arrangements, and antique couches. (The inn's dining room is discussed below.)

In Lenox Center, the **Village Inn** is another large hostelry with a small-inn flavor, and is the oldest inn in Lenox. Even though it has 32 guest rooms, there's still a personal feel to the place, which has a tavern and sunny dining room. Some of the rooms have fireplaces and four-poster beds, and all are individually decorated with country-style antiques and prints by Audubon and other artists.

Seven Hills Inn, originally known as Shipton Court, is a stucco, Tudor-style Berkshire cottage built in 1911. Accommodations here include the 38-room motel-style Terrace (closed in winter) and the 15-room Manor House, which is preferable. This is a big, sprawling place that draws regulars in the off-season; summer people like it for its location just 2 miles (3 km) east of Lenox Center. The dining room serves northern Italian and French cuisine, and a Modified American Plan (breakfast and dinner) is available.

Spa Hotels

About a mile (1½ km) from Lenox Center, **Canyon Ranch in the Berkshires** is the pricey eastern version of the Tucson-based health and fitness spa. It's housed at Bellefontaine, one of the fancier remaining Berkshire cottages, built to resemble the Petit Trianon at Versailles. Canyon Ranch's renovation has preserved the grandeur of the estate while adding spa amenities, like indoor-outdoor swimming pools and tennis courts, and hiking and skiing trails that meander through the estate's 120 acres of manicured grounds and woodlands. And, of course, a platoon of gourmet chefs, dietitians, fitness instructors, herbalists, massage therapists, and skin-care specialists awaits your call. You definitely pay for what you get here, but regular clients swear by the place.

An earthier spa not far from Lenox Center is **Kripalu Center**, a yoga retreat based in a dormitory-style former Jesuit monastery. The center offers nightly stays and week-long programs that include good vegetarian meals, kripalu yoga classes, and use of the spa's facilities, which include hiking trails and a private beach on Lake Mahkeenak.

DINING IN THE
SOUTHERN BERKSHIRES

Dinner in the chandeliered dining room at Lenox's **Wheatleigh** hotel (discussed above) is an extravagance, to be sure, but its original cuisine, prepared by chef Peter Platt, gets raves. The fixed-price dinner menu ($65 per person) includes such hors d'oeuvres as salad of Maine lobster in a mango ginger sauce and grilled loin of rabbit with shiitake mushrooms and tarragon sauce. Entrées include loin of veal with wild-mushroom-and-sweetbread ravioli, and roasted loin of Texas antelope with black huckleberries. The Grill Room (closed in winter) features a pared-down, more informal menu that includes sandwiches, grilled salmon, and Black Angus sirloin.

Two less expensive eateries are located on Route 7, the Pittsfield–Lenox Road. Right at the Pittsfield–Lenox line, **Dakota** serves moderately priced steaks, poultry, and seafood grilled and charcoal-broiled in a setting that recalls an Adirondack camp. Tel: (413) 499-7900.

Closer to Lenox, at 579 Pittsfield–Lenox Road, **Zampano's** is the new kid on the block, but already popular with locals for its wide range of dishes at reasonable prices, including sandwiches like veggie pockets and sweet sausage grinders. It also has a good salad bar and rotisserie-cooked chicken, which you may have packaged for picnics. Tel: (413) 448-8600.

In Lenox Center, the **Church Street Café**, at number 69, is one of the Berkshires' better restaurants. It's a casual bistro-style spot with a wide-ranging menu that includes Jamaican jerked chicken, Thai beef salad, and red-chile pasta with corn, peppers, cilantro, and jalapeños; Tel: (413) 637-2745. Down the street at number 83, the **Roseborough Grill** has a large menu. Among the better choices are chicken pot pie, grilled seafood, New England clam pasta, and Memphis-style ribs. Tel: (413) 637-2700.

Dinner at the **Red Lion Inn** is worth the high prices for the ambience in the light and elegant main dining room. If you're not in the mood for formality, you can have the same menu next door in the **Widow Bingham Tavern**, with its rough-hewn wood paneling and low beams. In either room, the bountiful dinner buffet served once a week in the off-season is a good deal. Tel: (413) 298-5545.

Great Barrington has become a bit of a diner's haven, with a couple of good restaurants serving Continental food at reasonable prices. At 293 Main Street, in the town's center, **La Tomate Bistro Provençale** offers a selection of pasta and Provençal specialties, like bouillabaisse and veal in Calvados sauce. The atmosphere is upscale yet casual, and the food is great. Reservations suggested on weekends; Tel: (413) 528-3003.

Across the street and one block up at 10 Castle Street, the **Castle Street Café** serves contemporary cuisine that ranges from burgers to steak *au poivre* and cassoulet of lamb. Excellent desserts and nice atmosphere in an old storefront; Tel: (413) 528-5244.

GETTING AROUND

If Boston isn't on your itinerary, you can fly into **Bradley International Airport**, near Hartford, Connecticut, which is 25 miles (40 km) south of Springfield. USAir and Continental Airlines fly into **Worcester Municipal Airport**.

The easiest and most practical way to explore this region is by car. Though buses connect the area with Hartford, Boston, and New York, getting around using public transportation can be difficult. Most of the major car-rental agencies have offices in Worcester and at Bradley International Airport. In Springfield, rentals are available from Enterprise Rent-A-Car (Tel: 413/785-5002) and Thrifty Car Rental (Tel: 413/783-9181).

Amtrak links Boston with Springfield and Worcester, and several trains run daily between Springfield and New York City via Hartford; Tel: (800) 872-7245.

Greyhound Bus Lines links the Worcester area with points north, including Boston, Newburyport, and Maine, as well as Springfield, Albany, and New York City; Tel: (508) 754-3247. **Peter Pan Bus Lines** connects Worcester, Springfield, Northampton, Greenfield, and Williamstown with Hyannis and Falmouth on Cape Cod, Boston, and New York City; Tel: (508) 753-1515, (800) 237-8747, or, in Massachusetts, (800) 322-0364. **Bonanza Bus Lines** connects Pittsfield with Springfield and New York City; Tel: (413) 442-4451 or (800) 556-3815. The **Pioneer Valley Transit Authority** provides public bus transportation in the Springfield area between Amherst and Northampton; Tel: (413) 781-7882.

Four companies offer inn-to-inn biking and walking tours in western Massachusetts: **Berkshire Hiking Holidays**, P.O. Box 2231, Lenox, MA 01240, Tel: (413) 499-9648; **Berkshire Walking Tours**, Box 383, Pittsfield, MA 01201, Tel: (413) 443-5017; **Vermont Hiking Holidays**, Box 750, Bristol, VT 05443, Tel: (802) 453-4816; and **Brooks Country Cycling & Hiking**, 140 West 83rd Street, New York, NY 10024, Tel: (212) 874-5151.

ACCOMMODATIONS REFERENCE

Unless otherwise noted, the rates given below are projections for 1993 for double room, double occupancy. (In the Berkshires section, the higher rate shown is for summer weekends and fall foliage season.) As prices are subject to change, always double-check before booking.

Worcester–Sturbridge

▶ **Beechwood Inn.** 363 Plantation Street, **Worcester**, MA 01605. Tel: (508) 754-5789. Reservations only; Tel: (800) 344-2589. $75–$100.

▶ **Chamberlain House at the Publick House Historic Resort.** Route 131 (on the common), **Sturbridge**, MA 01566. Tel: (800) PUBLICK or (508) 347-3313. Suites only, $85–$115.

▶ **Colonel Ebenezer Crafts Inn.** Fiske Hill, **Sturbridge**, MA 01566. Tel: 800-PUBLICK or (508) 347-3313. $69–$150.

▶ **Country Lodge at the Publick House Historic Resort.** Route 131 (on the common), **Sturbridge**, MA 01566. Tel: 800-PUBLICK or (508) 347-3313. $55–$95.

▶ **Old Sturbridge Village Lodge. Sturbridge**, MA 01566. Tel: (508) 347-3327. $55–$100.

▶ **Oliver Wight House. Sturbridge**, MA 01566. Tel: (508) 347-3327. $55–$100.

▶ **Publick House Historic Inn.** Route 131 (on the common), **Sturbridge**, MA 01566. Tel: 800-PUBLICK or (508) 347-3313. $69–$115; suites $99–$150.

▶ **Sturbridge Country Inn.** 530 Main Street, **Sturbridge**, MA 01566. Tel: (508) 347-5503. $69–$149; includes breakfast.

Pioneer Valley

▶ **Allen House Victorian Inn.** 599 Main Street, **Amherst**, MA 01002. Tel: (413) 253-5000. $45–$95 (includes full breakfast).

▶ **Autumn Inn.** 259 Elm Street, **Northampton**, MA 01060. Tel: (413) 584-7660. $82.

▶ **Brandt House Bed and Breakfast.** 29 Highland Avenue, **Greenfield**, MA 01301. Tel: (413) 774-3329. $85–$105.

▶ **Bullfrog Bed and Breakfast.** Route 116, **South Ashfield**, MA 01330. Tel: (413) 628-4493. $75 with shared bath; $85 with private bath.

▶ **Campus Center Hotel.** Campus Center, University of Massachusetts, **Amherst**, MA 01003. Tel: (413) 549-6000. $70.

▶ **Deerfield Inn.** Main Street, **Deerfield**, MA 01342. Tel: (413) 774-5587. $122–$140.

▶ **Hotel Northampton.** 36 King Street, **Northampton**, MA 01060. Tel: (413) 584-3100. $91–$132.

▶ **Lord Jeffery Inn.** 30 Boltwood Avenue, **Amherst**, MA 01002. Tel: (413) 253-2576. $80–$120.

▶ **Merriams Bed and Breakfast.** Newhall Road, **Conway**, MA 01341. Tel: (413) 369-4052. $65.

▶ **Northfield Country House.** School Street, P.O. Box 617, **Northfield**, MA 01360. Tel: (413) 498-2692. $50–$90.

▶ **Ramada Hotel West Springfield.** 1080 Riverdale Road, **West Springfield**, MA 01089. Tel: (413) 781-8750 or (800) 2-RAMADA. $69.

▶ **1797 House.** Charlemont Road, **Buckland**, MA 01338. Tel: (413) 625-2975. $60–$75.

▶ **Sheraton Springfield at Monarch Place.** One Monarch Place, **Springfield**, MA 01115. Tel: (413) 781-1010 or (800) 325-3535. $79–$145.

▶ **Springfield Marriott.** 1500 Main Street, **Springfield**, MA 01115. Tel: (413) 781-7111 or (800) 228-9290. $69–$99.

▶ **University Motor Lodge.** 345 North Pleasant Street, **Amherst**, MA 01002. Tel: (413) 256-8111. $52–$89.

The Berkshires

▶ **Apple Tree Inn.** 224 West Street, **Lenox**, MA 01240. Tel: (413) 637-1477. $95–$290.

▶ **Arbor Rose Bed & Breakfast.** 8 Yale Street, P.O. Box 114, **Stockbridge**, MA 01262. Tel: (413) 298-4744. $55–$150.

▶ **Canyon Ranch in the Berkshires.** Bellefontaine, 91 Kemble Street, **Lenox**, MA 01240. Tel: (413) 637-4400. $215–$350 per person, per night; includes meals and use of facilities (multiple-night stays are encouraged).

▶ **Field Farm Guest House.** 554 Sloan Road, **Williamstown**, MA 01267. Tel: (413) 458-3135. $75; includes breakfast.

▶ **Gables Inn.** 103 Walker Street, Route 183, **Lenox**, MA 01240. Tel: (413) 637-3416. $60–$195.

▶ **Garden Gables Inn.** 141 Main Street, **Lenox**, MA 01240. Tel: (413) 637-0193. $65–$175.

▶ **Golden Goose Bed & Breakfast.** Main Road, Box 336, **Tyringham**, MA 01264. Tel: (413) 243-3008. $60–$90.

▶ **Historic Merrell Tavern Inn Bed and Breakfast.** Main Street, Route 2, **South Lee**, MA 01260. Tel: (413) 243-1794. $75–$145.

▶ **Inn at Stockbridge.** Route 7 North, **Stockbridge**, MA 01262. Tel: (413) 298-3337. $75–$225.

▶ **Kripalu Center.** Box 792, Route 183 South, **Lenox**, MA 01240. Tel: (800) 967-3577. $56–$145 per person per night (includes three meals and all classes).

▶ **Maple Terrace Motel.** 555 Main Street, Route 2, **Williamstown**, MA 01267. Tel: (413) 458-9677. $44–$83.

▶ **Old Inn on the Green & Gedney Farm.** Star Route 70, **New Marlborough**, MA 01230. Tel: (413) 229-3131. $80–$225.

▶ **Orchards.** 222 Adams Road, **Williamstown**, MA 01267. Tel: (413) 458-9611. $135–$195.

▶ **Red Lion Inn.** Main Street, **Stockbridge**, MA 01262. Tel: (413) 298-5545. $95–$185.

▶ **River Bend Farm Guest House.** 643 Simonds Road, **Williamstown**, MA 01267. Tel: (413) 458-3121. $50–$60. Open April through November.

▶ **Roeder House Bed & Breakfast.** Route 183, Box 525, **Stockbridge**, MA 01262. Tel: (413) 298-4015. $110–$185.

▶ **Seven Hills Inn.** 100 Plunkett Street, **Lenox**, MA 01240. Tel: (413) 637-0060. $60–$270.

▶ **Village Inn.** 16 Church Street, P.O. Box 1810, **Lenox**, MA 01240. Tel: (413) 637-0020. $50–$160.

▶ **Walker House.** 74 Walker Street, **Lenox**, MA 01240. Tel: (800) 235-3098 or (413) 637-1271. $50–$150.

▶ **Wheatleigh.** Hawthorne Road, **Lenox**, MA 01240. Tel: (413) 637-0610. $110–$425.

▶ **Williams Inn.** 1090 Main Street, **Williamstown**, MA 01267. Tel: (413) 458-9371. $120.

VERMONT

By William G. Scheller

William G. Scheller is a Vermont-based travel writer with 17 years of experience. A contributing editor to National Geographic Traveler, *he is also a frequent contributor to* Islands *magazine and to the* Washington Post Magazine's *special travel issues. He is the author of 20 books, many on travel subjects; his 1981* Train Trips: Exploring America By Rail *was a Thomas Cook Award finalist.*

Back in the 1960s and 1970s a Yankee entrepreneur named Vrest Orton used his Vermont Country Store mail-order catalogue, *The Voice of the Mountains,* to project his favored image of Vermont and Vermonters: independent, self-reliant, and staunchly conservative in all matters, from their purses to their politics. Orton's dream landscape was the Republic of Vermont, cradle of Calvin Coolidge and all he stood for.

During the 1980s and 1990s the world (or at least that part of it that eats ice cream) has heard the Vermont gospel according to Ben and Jerry. The dessert moguls have traded heavily on their own image of Vermont: a clean, green, socially responsible sort of place, a peaceable kingdom in tie-dyed tee-shirts and Birkenstock sandals. This is the Vermont not of Calvin Coolidge but of Bernie Sanders, the state's independent socialist congressman.

It would be possible to discourse at some length on the ways in which these two Vermonts intersect, to a degree that might startle Ben, Jerry, the late Mr. Orton (whose family now publishes a still quaint but apolitical *Voice*), and the two politicians. But the really interesting question is why anyone who might consider buying a Vermont product would care all that much about the particular character of the place it came from. After all, barely one out of every 450 Americans

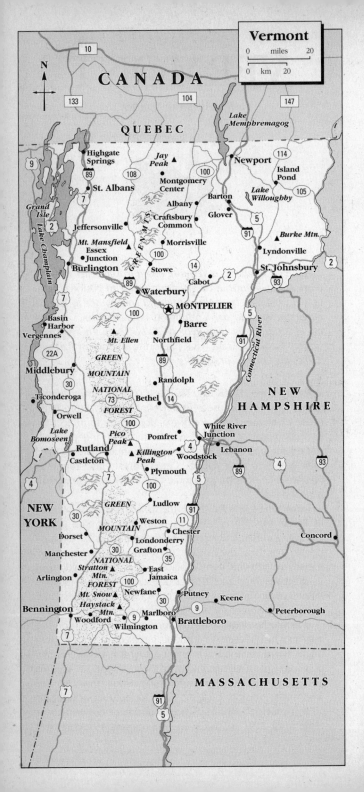

is a Vermonter. Why should Vermont, or Vermonters, loom so large in the popular imagination?

For one thing, Vermont is the most rural state in the Union, the state in which the smallest percentage of the population lives in what federal census-takers term an urban area. No matter that only a small fraction of Vermonters now works or lives on farms; rural life, in the American perception, is a wholesome and independent life, and if it has survived here for so long, this must be a wholesome and independent place.

Vermont stands apart even from the other New England states, which for all their history and tradition seem to have turned outward, to a greater degree, toward the wider world. Vermont, the one New England state without a seacoast, the one state in the region besides Maine not to have been among the original nation-building colonies, remains somehow different. In its brief fling at independence (there was indeed a "Republic of Vermont" in the 1770s and 1780s), Vermont seems to have embodied a wistful dream of yeomen at liberty in the fastness of their hills. Vermont is an American Switzerland, earning the comparison not because of its decidedly un-Alp-like mountains, but because it is tiny, self-contained, and often delightfully contrary. And what works for chocolate and watches will work for country stores and ice cream.

Vermont was the first frontier to have drawn settlers from the older, more densely populated parts of New England. In a sense, it was a colony of a colony, as the grants for many of its towns were issued by the Colonial governor of New Hampshire, Benning Wentworth. These "New Hampshire Grants" were the bone of contention when New York, Vermont's neighbor to the west, attempted to lay claim to the Champlain Valley and western Green Mountains in the early 1770s. The fierce resistance of Ethan Allen and his Green Mountain Boys was one wellspring of Vermont's spirit of independence, as was the frontier mindset of the settlers themselves. Vermont was further differentiated from its neighbors by having had no seat of Colonial aristocracy such as Boston, Newport, or Portsmouth, and no locus for the 19th-century concentration of industrial might, money, and political power such as Manchester, New Hampshire. It attracted individualists, to a land and a life that could be rigorous in the extreme. Beginning in the middle of the last century, as farming and self-sufficient village life went into decline, people became one of Vermont's major exports, but during the past 25 years the flow has reversed to such an extent that barely half of all Vermonters are now native-born. The newcomers often share the same individualistic spirit that built the old Vermont, even though their social and political agendas—particularly on matters such as land-use planning—frequently run counter to those of the natives. People move to Vermont to be able to live in the country and work in town, or to live *and* work in the country: This is prime territory for the "electronic cottage" that futurists claim will be the workplace of tomorrow. Others get involved in specialty farming (there's a couple in Lamoille County who raises llamas and Christmas trees) or in running inns. "Bob and I fell in love with this place, and it didn't take us ten minutes to decide we were getting out of advertising and leaving New York" seems to be part of the introduction whenever you stop at a Vermont bed-and-breakfast.

The land has always drawn outsiders to Vermont, whether for a weekend or a lifetime. It is a terrain of alternating hills and valleys, set between the broader valleys of New England's longest river (the Connecticut) and largest lake (Champlain). The Green Mountains extend in a straight line north to south along the center of the state, while an outlying range of isolated peaks crumples the landscape of the far northeast. Throughout Vermont, except among the most remote reaches of the Green Mountains, the balance of forest and open meadow creates a visual texture that makes agriculture—and particularly dairy farming—seem an improvement over raw nature. Rivers are mostly narrow and meandering; lakes, though few and generally small (except for Champlain), are often set like jewels in a circle of surrounding hills.

TOURING VERMONT

We have organized this chapter in terms of this varied terrain. The opening section covers the gentle hills and long-settled valleys of **Southern Vermont**, where resort towns such as Manchester and postcard villages like Weston have attracted generations of visitors. This is the Vermont of summer theater, of the Marlboro Music Festival, of ski resorts such as Bromley and Stratton, and of Bennington's sophisticated collegiate scene. Next, we venture into the **Champlain Valley**, Vermont's "coastal" region, with its rolling dairylands and apple orchards culminating in the lively city of Burlington. The valley offers the state's gentlest terrain for walkers, cyclists, and cross-country skiers, and the greatest range of possibilities for water-sports enthusiasts. The **Central Vermont** section covers the heart of the state, the Green Mountains from Rutland to the Canadian border. Here you'll find the state's most challenging hiking and cycling, some of the prettiest mountain villages, and the great alpine ski meccas of Killington, Stowe, and Jay. The following section explores the isolated **Northeast Kingdom**, where the Vermont of 50 years ago looms around each bend in the road. Finally, there's a section covering both the Vermont and New Hampshire portions of the upper **Connecticut River Valley** along Vermont's eastern border, a cradle of the Industrial Revolution that also contains one of America's great centers of learning, Dartmouth College.

Destinations in each section are linked along a recommended driving route, with options for side trips and alternate roads. It's easy, of course, to link tours of the sections, or cross from one to another and back with the use of a map. Who knows? A traveller might easily get carried away and try for membership in the "251 Club," an informal association of people who have set foot in every municipality, organized and unorganized, in Vermont.

Three of them, by the way, are accessible only by foot.

MAJOR INTEREST

Outdoor pursuits of skiing, hiking, bicycling, canoeing, and fishing
Antiquing
Foliage viewing
Summer theater

Southern Vermont
Downhill skiing: Haystack, Mount Snow, Stratton, Okemo, Bromley
Cross-country skiing: White House of Wilmington; Viking, Londonderry
Bennington Battle Monument
Fall foliage along the Molly Stark Trail
Hiking in Green Mountain Forest
Marlboro Music Festival
Summer theater, Weston and Dorset
Calvin Coolidge Birthplace, Plymouth Notch
Trout fishing on the Battenkill
Outlet shopping in Manchester
Hildene, Robert Todd Lincoln homestead, Manchester
Golf at the Equinox resort, Manchester

The Champlain Valley
Pick-your-own apple orchards, Shoreham
Revolutionary forts and battlefields, lower Champlain Valley
Touring campuses of Middlebury College and the University of Vermont
Crafts shops, Middlebury and Burlington
Morgan Horse Farm, Weybridge

Shelburne Museum and Vermont Mozart Festival
Ethan Allen Homestead, Burlington
Lake Champlain ferry rides
Swimming and boating on Lake Champlain

Central Vermont
Downhill skiing: Killington, Pico, Sugarbush, Mad
    River Glen, Suicide Six, Bolton Valley, Stowe, Smug-
    glers' Notch, Jay Peak
Cross-country skiing at Trapp Family Lodge
Fall foliage along Route 100 and the gap roads
Antiquing near Woodstock
State House and museums, Montpelier
Ben and Jerry's ice-cream factory, Waterbury
Hiking the Long Trail
Climbing Mount Mansfield
Canoeing on the Winooski, Lamoille, and Missisquoi
    rivers
Glider rides, Morrisville-Stowe Airport

Northeast Kingdom
Fairbanks Museum and Athenaeum art gallery, St.
    Johnsbury
Downhill skiing at Burke Mountain
Boating and fishing on Lakes Seymour, Memphre-
    magog, and Willoughby
Cross-country skiing at Craftsbury

Connecticut River Valley
Old Constitution House and American Precision
    Museum, Windsor, VT
Longest covered bridge, Windsor, VT–Cornish, NH
Saint-Gaudens National Historic Site, Cornish, NH
Quechee Gorge, VT
Dartmouth College campus, Hanover, NH
Peacham village (VT) in foliage season

SOUTHERN VERMONT

The southernmost quarter of Vermont typified, for many
years, the face shown by the state to the outside world. It was
the most readily accessible region to Boston and New York
before the interstate highways opened up northern Vermont
to short-term visitors, and, as such, it was the first of the state's

regions to suggest—and then struggle to fit—the Vermont stereotype. Nowadays, it isn't at all uncommon to hear northern Vermonters decry the prospect of their particular corner of paradise ending up "like southern Vermont," which they understand to mean overdeveloped, inundated with out-of-staters' second homes, and self-consciously adorable. To hear anyone from the Northeast Kingdom tell it, southern Vermont is a vast time-sharing resort complete with artificial maples that turn color on cue, where the only license plates you see are from Massachusetts or New York.

It isn't nearly that bad. To be sure, the southern Vermont landscape has a gentler, more manicured look than the counties up near the Canadian border; this is partly due to the tamer character of the terrain, partly to the fact that there *is* more money—both in- and out-of-state—on the land, and partly (see reason 2) to the church steeples being painted more frequently. But the state's southern counties are by no means hopelessly overbuilt, nor prettified to the point of theme-park perfection. Vermont's stringent development guidelines and environmental protection laws apply here as in the rest of the state, and the thousands of acres of wilderness in the southern portion of the Green Mountain National Forest are just as wild as their counterparts up north. You will see more out-of-state license plates than in northern Vermont, but if you didn't see any—well, you probably wouldn't be here.

Bennington

Vermont's southwest portal, just north of the Massachusetts border on Route 7, is at Bennington, the first town chartered (1749) in what is now Vermont. The name is derived from Benning Wentworth, the royal governor of New Hampshire who issued charters to townships throughout the region north of Massachusetts and west of the Connecticut River; thus the term "New Hampshire Grants" that was applied to the Green Mountain region in Colonial times. But to the west—particularly south of Lake Champlain—there was an indistinct boundary between the "Grants" and the colony of New York. After the settlement of Bennington in 1761, open hostility broke out between the settlers and surveyors from New York, who wished to establish Albany's hegemony over the region. These conflicts were the origin of the long feud waged against the "Yorkers" by Ethan Allen and his Green Mountain Boys, freedom fighters (or outlaws, depending on your point of view) whose efforts were eventually directed against the British and their Tory allies, and whose hard-won object was the independent Republic of Vermont, which was in turn accepted into the Union in 1791 as the 14th state. Bennington and its Catamount Tavern (the site of the now-vanished tavern is marked on Monument Avenue, west of downtown) were the informal headquarters of Ethan Allen and the Boys, and it was here that Allen plotted his dramatic 1775 seizure of Fort Ticonderoga.

But Bennington's place in Vermont history—and in the minds of Americans who have never been to the Green Mountain State—is forever associated with another battle, one that wasn't even staged on Vermont soil. The Battle of Bennington took place on August 16, 1777, in what is now the town of Walloomsac, just across the New York border. Here, the Continental Army's general John Stark defeated two detachments sent by British general John Burgoyne to raid American supplies at Bennington. The British foray was part of Burgoyne's plan to isolate New England from New York—a plan resoundingly thwarted six weeks later at Saratoga, in no small part because of Stark's success near Bennington.

Walloomsac may have had the battle, but Bennington has the monument. Rising from a gentle slope on Monument Avenue off Route 9 west of town, the **Bennington Battle Monument** was dedicated in 1891 and stands, at just over 306 feet, as the tallest structure in Vermont. An observation level, accessible by elevator, offers fine views at a point two-thirds of the way up the limestone obelisk; at ground level a diorama and exhibits of artifacts help explain the battle and the era in which it was fought. (Open daily from April 1 to November 1.)

OLD BENNINGTON

One mile (1½ km) west of Bennington proper, between the monument and the town on Route 9, the village of Old Bennington sits in serene, white-clapboarded repose along its Colonial green. Its landmark is the **Old First Church** (Congregational), a magnificent Palladian structure built in 1806 for a congregation organized in 1762, the year after Bennington's settlement. In the shadow of the tall white steeple, in a churchyard honored with the remains of dozens of Revolutionary soldiers and five Vermont governors, lies the family plot of the man who made the plain speech of up-country New England into a matchless poetic instrument. Robert Frost (1874–1963) rests beneath a slab bearing his own words: "I had a lover's quarrel with the world." Born in California, Frost had ancestral New England roots; late in his life, when he was a resident of Vermont, he was named by the legislature as the state's official poet laureate.

Just past the Old First Church on West Main Street (Route 9), on the way into downtown Bennington, the

Bennington Museum (Tel: 802/447-1571) is the region's premier institution devoted to arts, crafts, and cultural history. The folk artist Anna Mary Robertson Moses, better known as "Grandma Moses" (1860–1961), lived and painted just across the border in Eagle Bridge, New York, and the Bennington Museum now has the largest public collection of her work—in addition to the schoolhouse she attended as a young girl. Also on display is a flag carried at the Battle of Bennington, believed to be the oldest surviving Stars and Stripes; fine collections of American glass, landscapes, and portrait paintings; and more than 4,000 pieces of 19th-century Bennington pottery. (Long associated with sturdy, utilitarian pottery, the name "Bennington" survives in the work of today's local artisans, whose work is for sale at **Bennington Potters**, at 324 County Street in downtown Bennington.)

DOWNTOWN BENNINGTON

Downtown Bennington runs for only a couple of commercial blocks; as in most small Vermont cities, much of the nuts-and-bolts trade is carried on at mini-malls outside of town, leaving the old central blocks to a handful of banks, specialty shops (see especially Bennington Potters, noted above), and casual restaurants catering to the college trade (just outside Bennington is Bennington College, the small liberal-arts institution famous for high tuition and alumni novelists; and Southern Vermont College, known for its environmental programs).

Dining and Staying in Bennington

A local standby for the past 50 years is the **Blue Benn Diner** on North Street, a relic of the Formica age that remains popular by straddling retro and New Age cuisine: Here, cheeseburgers coexist with vegetarian enchiladas. Tel: (802) 442-8977.

For formal dining the choice in Bennington has long been the **Four Chimneys**, a stately white mansion located on the western outskirts of town at 21 West Road. The menu is classic, with subtle innovations such as beef Wellington laced with chestnuts, and the overall experience is akin to dining at the country estate of rich, gracious relatives. The Four Chimneys also has a few handsomely appointed guest rooms, so you can pretend that the relatives have asked you to spend the night. Or, for more modest quarters at an appreciably lower tariff, try the **Bennington Motor Inn**, at 143 West Main Street near the Bennington Museum. There is also a scattering of moderately priced motels along Route 9, east of town.

The Molly Stark Trail

Heading east out of Bennington, follow Route 9, better known as the Molly Stark Trail. Molly Stark was the wife of Battle of Bennington hero General John Stark, a New Hampshireman who followed this route to Bennington and who remarked, as the armies were about to clash, "There are the redcoats—they will be ours or tonight Molly Stark sleeps a widow." They were; she didn't. (General Stark, incidentally, is also credited with coining the motto that today appears on New Hampshire license plates: "Live Free or Die.")

The eastward route out of Bennington involves a quick change of mountain ranges. Southwest of Bennington, peaks such as Mount Anthony, which rises 2,340 feet, are part of the Taconic Range, which runs in a north–south direction in Vermont and New York (east of the Hudson River) and extends into Massachusetts' Berkshires. But as the Molly Stark Trail begins its sharp climb just a few miles east of Bennington, you will be heading into the worn and jumbled half-billion-year-old mini-cordillera of the Green Mountains, the spine of Vermont. Woodford, the next town past Bennington, contains—at an altitude of 2,215 feet—the highest village in Vermont. (Note the distinction: "Town" is the political designation; "village" is the actual settlement. One town can, and often does, contain several villages—as in the case of Wallingford, South Wallingford, and East Wallingford, all within the town of Wallingford.)

The Molly Stark Trail enjoys considerable cachet as a scenic route, and as such draws a considerable number of travellers during fall foliage season. The road *is* undeniably beautiful when the maples are in full flame, although the lushness of the roadside foliage comes at the expense of the great, rolling vistas that characterize byways farther to the north. At times—particularly in Woodford and Searsburg, along the western third of the trail—the impression is of not seeing the forest for the trees.

If you want to get in among the trees, though, break up your Molly Stark drive with a stop at **Woodford State Park**, 11 miles (18 km) east of Bennington. Woodford has full camping facilities (lean-tos and tent sites), a swimming beach and boat rentals on Adams Reservoir, and trout fishing; Tel: (802) 447-7169. There is also an easy, 2½-mile walking trail around the reservoir. Several more strenuous hikes originating on or near Route 9 in the **Green Mountain National Forest** are outlined in the book *Day Hikes in Vermont,* published by the Green Mountain Club (see Bibliography, above), and in the brochure "Day Hikes on the Manchester Ranger District of the Green Mountain National Forest," available from the

U.S. Forest Service Manchester Ranger District, R.R. 1, Box 1940, Manchester VT 05255 (Tel: 802/362-2307). The Long Trail/Appalachian Trail crosses Route 9 between Bennington and Woodford; for information on the trail and the Green Mountain Club that maintains it, see Central Vermont, below.

Roughly 15 miles (24 km) east of Bennington, a sign on the right side of the Molly Stark Trail proclaims the surrounding section of the Green Mountain National Forest as the **George D. Aiken Wilderness Area.** Putney native George Aiken (1892–1982) was arguably Vermont's greatest home-grown statesman. As governor (1937–1941) and U.S. senator (1941–1975), he was the conscience of the progressive wing of the Republican party, championing agriculture, conservation, and publicly owned electric utilities. Outside the state Aiken is chiefly remembered for his suggestion that the United States declare victory in Vietnam and bring the troops home, and for spending all of $17 on his last senate campaign. He could have been reelected, most Vermonters agree, without having gone to all that expense.

WILMINGTON

Wilmington, which lies just beyond the National Forest's eastern boundary, marks the midpoint on the Molly Stark Trail and the intersection with Route 100, the state's central north–south artery and the main street of its ski industry. Over its nearly 200-mile course between here and the Canadian border, Route 100 passes within a short distance of 14 major ski areas and connects dozens of picturesque villages and small towns. If you are planning to head north rather than stay on the Molly Stark straight through to Brattleboro, Route 100 is the choice that sticks closest to the Green Mountains. It meanders far more than the parallel alternatives, Routes 7 and I-91, and its traffic can be tediously slow; but as Ethan Allen said, "The gods of the valleys are not the gods of the hills."

Haystack and Mount Snow

Wilmington is not so much a destination in itself as it is a jumping-off point for the ski areas of Haystack and Mount Snow, immediately north along Route 100. Although they are five miles apart, the two resorts are connected—corporately and by a cross-country ski trail. Mount Snow lift tickets cover Haystack, but not vice versa.

Haystack (1,400-foot vertical drop) is one of Vermont's smaller full-service ski resorts, with a preponderance of intermediate trails among its 43 runs though with a new selection of short but steep expert slopes and a separate beginners' section. There are five chair lifts and a T-bar, and skiing schools for children as young as three. Tel: (802) 464-3333; for lodging information, Tel: (802) 245-SNOW. In summer the draw is the **Haystack Golf Club**, a fine 18-hole public course designed by Desmond Muirhead. Tel: (802) 464-8301.

Mount Snow (1,700-foot vertical drop) is nearly twice as big, with 77 trails (two-thirds of them intermediate), 15 chair lifts, and 62 miles of nearby cross-country routes. Here, the emphasis is on family skiing: ski school begins at age four, and the nonski nursery takes children as young as six weeks. In summer the resort offers the 18-hole public **Mt. Snow Golf Course**, a golf school, and mountain-bike rentals. Tel: (802) 464-3333 or (800) 451-4211.

Staying in the Wilmington–Dover Area

Thanks to the ski areas and its position astride the Molly Stark Trail, Wilmington features a concentration of comfortable inns. At the elegant and expensive end of the scale is the **White House of Wilmington**, an imposing Federal mansion just east of town on Route 9. There is a leather-and-brass country formality to the White House; guest rooms (several with fireplaces) have been beautifully restored without sacrificing their antique patina. The White House is by no means for downhill skiers only; the inn has its own system of cross-country trails, complete with rentals and instructions, and there are outdoor and indoor pools as well.

The **Nutmeg Inn**, on Route 9 near the Wilmington town center, offers private baths, king-size bedrooms and suites (some with fireplaces), and a full breakfast menu, along with a bring-your-own bar and private toboggan hill. The **Red Shutter Inn**, also on Route 9 on the outskirts of the village, features similar amenities (plus a fireplace suite with two-person Jacuzzi) as well as a pub and restaurant within its century-old premises.

For more moderately priced accommodations try the 24-room **Old Red Mill**, on Route 100 just north (and within walking distance) of the Wilmington town center, alongside the Deerfield River. With its tavern and small restaurant, the Red Mill offers an ambience more reminiscent of a cozy stop on a Colonial post road than a contemporary "destination" inn. The Red Mill might best be avoided during peak seasons (especially foliage time), however, because of its location at a busy intersection and popularity with bus tours.

The town of Dover, just north of Wilmington, is the actual location of the Mount Snow ski complex, and its village of West Dover is home to the bulk of the lodging establishments that cluster around the resort. In fact, West Dover's accommodations and other ski-related businesses have expanded so rapidly over the past three decades that the region is credited with having provided the impetus for passage in 1970 of Vermont's landmark environmental regulatory statute, Act 250. But Act 250 controls and guides development—it doesn't stop it. The foothills and former farmlands around Mount Snow continue to make up one of the state's fastest-growing regions. On the plus side, it's an area that offers a wide selection of places to stay.

One obvious choice, if proximity to Mount Snow itself is a desirable factor, is the sizeable condominium village at the base of the mountain. With their full housekeeping facilities along with the accessibility of summer as well as winter activities, the condos are a popular family option; central booking is handled by the SnowResorts Hospitality Group; Tel: (802) 464-2177 or (800) 451-6876; Fax: (802) 464-3808. For more traditional inn accommodations in West Dover, try the **Kitzhof Lodge**, on Route 100, which offers M.A.P. (Modified American Plan, i.e., breakfast and dinner included) rates and satisfying New England fare, private baths, and a congenial bring-your-own lounge; or the smaller and more elegant **West Dover Inn**, also on Route 100. Built in 1846, the West Dover offers eight handsomely decorated rooms, all with private baths and some with fireplaces. Full breakfast is included; other meals are available in the inn's excellent restaurant.

MARLBORO

Ten miles (16 km) east of Wilmington, as the Molly Stark Trail begins its descent toward the Connecticut River at Brattleboro, is the tiny hamlet of Marlboro. "Nonexistent" might seem the more appropriate word, unless you bear right off Route 9 and follow the signs for Marlboro College. Located 2 miles (3 km) south of the village, Marlboro is a small liberal-arts college whose reputation outside Vermont is overwhelmingly associated with the **Marlboro Music Festival**, held each year from early July through mid-August. Founded by pianist Rudolf Serkin and graced by the longtime residency of Pablo Casals, the festival has become, along with the Burlington area's Vermont Mozart Festival, the state's leading summer venue for classical music. For schedules and ticket information, Tel: (802) 254-8163.

Brattleboro

The Molly Stark Trail comes to its eastern terminus at Brattleboro, gateway city to Vermont for anyone arriving from points south on Interstate 91. "City" is actually a misnomer;

although its 12,000 inhabitants qualify Brattleboro as a city by Vermont standards, it is nevertheless chartered as a town, governed by representatives elected to town meeting.

Here, where the West River empties into the Connecticut, the first permanent settlement in what is now Vermont was established in 1724. That year saw the construction of Fort Dummer, named for the lieutenant governor of Massachusetts and intended as a bulwark against French and Indian attacks against the Bay Colony's settlement at Northfield, farther south along the Connecticut. The fort stood until 1763 (the site is now covered by the widened river north of the Vernon Dam), by which time a nearby village had grown up on lands granted by that master dispenser of real-estate largesse, Governor Benning Wentworth of New Hampshire. One of the grantees was a Colonel William Brattle; hence the town's name. Dummerston, which inherited the name of the old fort, is today the next town north.

The water power available at the confluence of the two rivers enabled Brattleboro to thrive as an early Vermont outpost of the Industrial Revolution. Throughout the late 19th and early 20th centuries the town's most important enterprise was the Estey Organ Company, manufacturers of the parlor organs around which Victorian families gathered. Brattleboro might have been driven to extinction by the advent of the phonograph had it not diversified its manufacturing base and exploited its natural position at the juncture of southern and northern New England. Today its largest employer is a wholesale grocery distributor—although a more typically Vermont cachet attaches to the downtown headquarters of the Holstein-Friesian Association. You may have seen dairy farms with signs proclaiming that their herds are registered Holsteins. Here, in Brattleboro, is where they're registered.

But despite this connection with rural tradition, Brattleboro today is essentially a vest pocket–size blue-collar town, prey to the suburban strip development that comes with being an exit on an interstate but nevertheless preserving a few busy blocks of its compact, red-brick downtown. One highlight of that downtown is the **Brattleboro Museum & Art Center**, housed in a restored 1915 railroad depot near the Connecticut River at the intersection of Main, Vernon, and Canal streets. The center features rotating exhibits of art and historical objects related to changing annual themes; one constant, however, is a handsome collection of Estey organs (open May through October; Tel: 802/257-0124).

Nearby, at 224 Main Street, the **Brooks Memorial Library** (Brattleboro Public Library) exhibits *The Prodigal Son,* a painting by Brattleboro native William Morris Hunt (1824–

1879). The town was also home to two important 19th-century architects: Hunt's brother, Beaux-Arts disciple Richard Morris Hunt (1827–1895), and William Rutherford Mead (1846–1928), of McKim, Mead & White fame. In the arts, however, perhaps the greatest name associated with Brattleboro is that of a foreigner who spent only four years here. In 1892 Rudyard Kipling settled with his Brattleboro-born wife at a nearby country house he named Naulakha; he wrote his *Just So Stories* here. But the great novelist and balladeer was gone by 1896, having stormed off in a huff after a bitter quarrel with his brother-in-law.

DINING AND STAYING
IN THE BRATTLEBORO AREA

Kipling, the arch-imperialist, would probably be drawn into many another quarrel if he were to return to today's Brattleboro and patronize a downtown institution called the **Common Ground**, a cooperatively owned restaurant at 25 Elliot Street that manages to preserve perfectly the countercultural climate of Vermont circa 1970. In those days, now-defunct Windham College, in nearby Putney, drew a sizable contingent of hip émigrés from outside the state, both as students and hangers-on. The Common Ground became the in-town eatery of choice of back-to-the-landers and rural New Leftists, and it still is. Walk up the stairs to the second-floor dining room, and the handbill-plastered walls will take you back to the heyday of the Woodstock Nation. But come for the food. Hearty and honest, it's a combination of whole-grain Americana and the cuisines of nations with low GNPs (the menu consists of fish and vegetarian dishes). The odd thing is, reason would dictate that the staff should all be 45 years old—how come a lot of them look so young? Either brown rice is better for you than anyone guessed, or the counterculture is taking on more than a few twenty-something recruits. Closed Tuesdays.

Unlike many northern New England towns its size, Brattleboro has an excellent downtown hotel. The **Latchis Hotel**, on Main Street, is a small, recently restored 1930s property with many of its original Art Deco touches intact. On the premises are a decent restaurant, featuring local ingredients prepared New American style; a three-screen cinema; and a tavern offering its own selection of craft-brewed ales. As downtown Brattleboro is big enough for a stroll (particularly recommended for browsing are the **Green Mountain Bookstore**, 29 High Street; **Book Cellar**, 120 Main Street; and **Vermont Artisan Designs**, 115 Main Street), the Latchis is a pleasant alternative to the motels out by I-91.

Putney

Another pleasant alternative, if you'd prefer not to stay in town, is the **Hickory Ridge House**, on a quiet road just outside of the village of Putney (Putney is 8 miles/13 km north of Brattleboro via Route 5 or I-91). Hickory Ridge occupies an 1808 Federal-style brick house set amid 12 acres of meadow and woods; three of its seven pretty, airy rooms have private baths, and four have fireplaces. Rates include full breakfast.

Putney itself offers plenty of opportunity for browsing in shops largely dating from, or at least owing their character to, the "colonization" of this area by urban refugees in the 1960s. On Westminster West Road, the **Silver Forest** carries distinctive jewelry and women's casual apparel, while **Carol Brown** specializes in an international array of handwoven and hand-printed fabrics by the yard: Irish linens, Chinese silks, Indonesian batiks, and the like. On Main Street there's **Basketville**, an emporium crammed with basketware of every description, along with wicker and rattan furniture.

Putney is also home to the **River Valley Performing Arts Center**, on River Road, the venue for the Whetstone Theater's spring-through-fall season of six or seven plays, as well as the Dodd classical music series and a full schedule of dance, folk, and jazz performances. Tel: (802) 387-4507.

If it's summertime, stop at **Curtis' Bar-B-Que** on Route 5 in Putney. Curtis is a transplanted southerner who must surely go home each winter to recharge at the roots of the religion of barbecue. His chicken and ribs are the real thing, slow-cooked outdoors and served with homemade sauce of your preferred intensity. Don't look for fancy premises; Curtis operates out of an old school bus parked in a roadside lot and surrounded by picnic tables.

Up the West River Valley

Route 30 follows the valley of the West River northwest out of Brattleboro, away from the Connecticut River Valley and into the foothills of the Green Mountains. The river, when you can see it from the road, appears fast and rocky, except in the dry doldrums of late summer; especially in spring (and especially after a winter of heavy snows), its vigor as it races beneath side-road covered bridges at West Dummerston and Townshend is a reminder that you are gaining altitude, heading toward its source in the Green Mountain National Forest above Weston. The West was one of the rivers involved in the catastrophic Vermont floods of 1927, the state's worst ever; today, at Townshend just north of Newfane, there is a dam and flood-control reservoir.

NEWFANE

Twelve miles (19 km) from Brattleboro is Newfane, one of the Vermont towns most representative of the stereotype of chaste white public and domestic architecture surrounding a classic village green. If the Newfane example seems extreme, almost to the point of being a stage set, the effect is partly the result of a particularly graceful **Congregational church** (1839), along with the 1825 Greek Revival **Windham County Courthouse** and the similarly styled **Four Columns**, a stately white mansion housing an inn of the same name. The Four Columns was built in the 1840s, in the Greek Revival style then in vogue in Vermont; if it looks almost too much like Tara, remember that its original mistress was in fact a southerner.

The 17-room inn (all but four rooms are in the original section; the rest are in an annex) is more like a small hotel than many Vermont country hostelries. Fireplaces, antiques, and brass beds abound, and the restaurant belies its bluff Colonial decor by offering a New American repertoire leaning heavily (but lightly) on Vermont-raised game and other local provender.

For more intimate lodging in a country rather than town atmosphere, the **West River Lodge** is a good choice. Located just outside Newfane, the small, antiques-furnished inn offers bed-and-breakfast or M.A.P. (breakfast and dinner plan) accommodations, along with English riding and instruction at its own stables.

Set aside an hour or so to browse among the handmade quilt selection in the **Newfane Country Store** and the oddments at the **Nu-Tique Shop** (open summer and fall) and the **Newfane Antiques Center** (all three are on Route 30). Newfane is also the site of Vermont's oldest and largest flea market, held on summer Sundays.

TOWNSHEND AND GRAFTON

Three miles (5 km) north of Newfane, bear left off Route 30 for the access road into **Townshend State Park**, at 856 acres southern Vermont's largest. The park offers tent sites and showers; there is no swimming beach, but several hiking trails include a strenuous one to the top of 1,680-foot Bald Mountain. The West River just below the Townshend Dam and the picturesque Scott covered bridge is also a good canoe put-in spot, with Class I and II rapids; this stretch of the river is described in the Appalachian Mountain Club's *River Guide: New Hampshire/Vermont* (see the Bibliography, above).

At Townshend Route 35 forks off to the right from Route 30. Follow Route 35 for 10 miles (16 km) north to **Grafton**, one of the most deliberately and meticulously restored villages in Vermont. "Restoration," in fact, may not be the proper word, because it is doubtful that any Vermont community was ever so free of ragged edges. The careful polishing that has made Grafton such a popular destination was accomplished not by the casual application of capital from mixed sources, but by the Windham Foundation, which, starting in the 1960s, undertook the preservation of virtually the entire town. You can visit an exhibit chronicling the restoration at the **Grafton Historical Society**, on Route 35 just south of town. Tel: (802) 843-2584.

Staying in Grafton

The general architectural flavor of Grafton is country Federal, and its centerpiece is the **Old Tavern at Grafton**, parts of which date to 1788. The 66-room tavern makes for a pleasant stopover or a destination in itself, with broad, rocker-filled porches, a pond for swimming, and antique furnishings. If the word "tavern" conjures up visions of a pint of ale between stagecoaches, you're on the right track—just eliminate the stagecoaches and add a cuisine that suggests what circa-1800 Vermont would have been like if the settlers had had goat's cheese, eggplant, and decent wine cellars. What they *did* have was a knack for cheese-making, and Grafton cheddar is still one of the finest in the state. Any of the local storekeepers will be happy to quarry you a chunk from the wheel on the counter.

As an alternative to staying right in the village, consider the **Inn at Woodchuck Hill Farm**, on Middletown Road 2 miles (3 km) west of town. Open between May and October, the inn occupies a 200-year-old farmhouse on 200 acres with spectacular mountain views. There are hiking trails on the property, along with a pond for swimming and an antiques shop in the barn.

CHESTER

If you continue north on Route 35 past Grafton, a 7-mile (11-km) drive will take you to Chester. Chester, which arranges itself along either side of a long, narrow green that divides Route 11, is notable for its numerous stone houses—oddly enough, a rarity in Vermont, given the state's prominence in the granite industry. Most of these early-19th-century structures are on North Street, off Route 11 on the right if you're heading west, although several are on Route 11 on the west side of town. Chester is also the home of the **National Survey** (downtown, on Route 11), a cartographic concern with a comprehensive inventory of topographical maps. If you plan on doing any backwoods hiking while in Vermont, here's the place to stock up on topos.

The best lodgings in Chester are at the **Inn at Long Last**, a rambling ark of a building in the center of town. With 30 rooms, the inn approaches the size of a small hotel; the library and other common rooms are cozy, and the sophisticated dining room offers such dishes as grilled chicken breast with avocado-tomato relish and pork tenderloin cooked in phyllo dough with sausage, pears, and sage.

The **Stone Hearth Inn**, on Route 11 in Chester, offers a less formal, lower-key environment than the big downtown inn; it's an 1810 house with ten nicely decorated rooms and suites, plus a licensed pub and billiard room.

If you've gone as far north as Chester, you'll probably want to take Route 11 west toward the villages and resorts of the south-central Green Mountains (which we cover below). If, on the other hand, you have stayed on Route 30 at Townshend, continue north for 6 miles (10 km) to East Jamaica and another of the choices reminiscent of Robert Frost's "The Road Not Taken." Here, Route 30 merges with Route 100, and the two routes remain one until the tiny junction hamlet of Rawsonville, 8 miles (13 km) to the northwest; this is the route we now take. Or you can shunt off to the left at East Jamaica and take Route 100 southwest through Wardsboro and (see above) the Mount Snow–Haystack Mountain area and an eventual reunion with the Molly Stark Trail at Wilmington.

STRATTON MOUNTAIN

At Rawsonville, bear left on Route 30 as it splits off from Route 100 and drive 2 miles (3 km) to the base entrance of Stratton, one of Vermont's biggest ski areas. Since its opening in 1959, Stratton has grown to typify the modern ski mountain as a combination of four-season sports facility, destination resort, and residential community. The raw materials were superb: At just under 4,000 feet, Stratton Mountain offered its developers the wherewithal for three skiing sections. The upper mountain (served since 1989 by a high-speed, 12-passenger gondola) offers both intermediate and expert runs; the lower mountain is largely for novices; and the "Sun Bowl" is an intermediate haven. In all, 11 chair lifts (plus the gondola) serve 92 slopes, and there are 32 kilometers (20 miles) of cross-country trails as well. Ski school begins at age three (ages six weeks through five years are accommodated at a day-care center), and there is a racing program for junior skiers. During bad weather skiers can stay limber at an indoor pool and tennis courts. For ski area information, Tel: (802) 297-2200.

In summer Stratton offers a golf school as well as tennis (Stratton is often a venue for pro tour events), horseback riding, and mountain biking. For golf school, Tel: (802) 297-2200; for all other summer activities, Tel: (802) 297-9393.

Needless to say, a recreational complex this big has to center around more than a base lodge and a parking lot. Stratton features an entire replica Austrian village of shops and restaurants at its base, as well as the 216-room **Stratton Mountain Resort** and slopeside condominiums. The resort is a full-service hotel, with a restaurant, lounge, sauna, and health spa; the slopeside condominiums have microwave ovens, refrigerators, wet bars, and coffeemakers. All in all, a far cry from the old rope tow.

Weston

If you bear right at Rawsonville and stay on Route 100 rather than go left on Route 30, a 16-mile (26-km) drive will take you to Weston, via South Londonderry and Londonderry (which we discuss below). Weston was one of the earliest small Vermont communities to take itself through the transition from quiet hill town to tourist destination; the Weston Playhouse (discussed below), its original attraction for visitors, dates to 1937. Its cachet grew along with the resorts at nearby Bromley and Stratton mountains, but development has been gradual enough so that—except on weekend afternoons in high summer or foliage season—it's possible to walk around Weston without reflecting on its status as one of Vermont's premier postcard towns. Here, even the institutions of tourism have a certain mellow patina.

For nearly half a century one of Weston's biggest draws has been the **Vermont Country Store**, right in the village on Route 100, established by writer and Weston native Vrest Orton as a tribute to a Yankee institution. Orton installed all the country store necessities—a penny-candy counter, a potbellied stove, shelves of calico yard goods—and built around them an inventory of practical items, old-fashioned and otherwise. Blessed with plenty of land out back, the place has expanded into something resembling a country department store, but the merchandise still tends toward the time-tested and reliable, from sturdy outdoor clothing to portable manual typewriters. The store's seasonal catalogue, *The Voice of the Mountains,* has over the years parlayed the cracker-barrel image into an enormous mail-order business.

The **Bryant House**, two doors down from the Country Store, is to lunch what the store's inventory is to mercantile

Americana. Chicken pie, homemade Indian pudding, and cob-smoked ham sandwiches are the order of the day in this refuge from "lite" dining, and the century-old German silver soda fountain alone is worth a visit.

The Weston town green, with its cast-iron railing and Victorian bandstand, is one of Vermont's loveliest. Facing the green are the white-pillared **Weston Playhouse** (performances from late June to Labor Day; Tel: 802/824-5288 for program information and tickets); and the **Farrar-Mansur House**, a 1797 tavern where Weston's first town meeting was held in 1800. The Farrar-Mansur is furnished as it would have been when that meeting took place, right down to the kitchen paraphernalia centered around a great open hearth. (Open daily Memorial Day to Columbus Day.)

"Downtown" Weston, within a few hundred yards of the green, offers an array of shops—places such as the **Bandstand**, selling books, art prints, and matted vintage magazine covers; the **Weston Toy Works**, featuring handmade wooden toys; the **Weston House**, purveyors of gorgeous goose down–filled quilts, comforters, and pillows; the **West River Jewelry Company**, with handmade craft jewelry; and, providing energy for the shopping sprint, the **Weston Fudge Shop**. Just north of the village proper on Route 100, the **Weston Bowl Mill** occupies an ancient wooden building where craftsmen fashion handsome bowls from solid hardwood. Prices for large bowls are considerable, as each incremental increase in size represents a cross-section of a larger tree, but the shop always offers a good assortment of seconds, which usually can be made serviceable and attractive with sandpaper, oil, and elbow grease.

STAYING AND DINING IN WESTON

The **Inn at Weston**, just south of the green, has been a local fixture under several owners for more than 40 years. In its present incarnation the inn offers comfortable lodging (the rooms in the older, front section are larger and have more character), an ambitious menu in the Vermont-Continental vein, home-baked breads, and, in the pub, a fieldstone fireplace that can annihilate ambition. Farther south on Route 100, and a three-minute drive from town, the **Colonial House Inn & Motel** features exactly that choice: rooms in the main house or a motel wing, reasonably priced and with hearty breakfasts and dinners available.

Ludlow and Plymouth

If you're heading north out of Weston—or if you have time for a 22-mile (35-km, one way) side trip before turning west toward Manchester—continue north on Route 100, bearing right 4 miles (6½ km) north of Weston toward Ludlow. (Near the Ludlow turnoff, at the intersection of Routes 100 and 155, a narrow side road leads off to the left and the **Weston Priory**, a small Benedictine establishment offering public Catholic services, many featuring the monks' beautiful choral singing. (Tel: 802/824-5409 for information.) Ludlow, 7 miles (11 km) farther along Route 100, is notable chiefly for a downtown factory complex turned into shops and restaurants (the fate of half of Vermont's manufacturing base, it seems) and **Okemo**, a medium-size ski area (eight chair and two surface lifts) with 70 trails divided among all ranges of abilities. Particularly convenient are the lessons available for ages three and up, and the slopeside **Okemo Mountain Lodge**, where all guest rooms have fireplaces.

Not quite as close to the slopes, but certainly close enough, the **Okemo Inn** (at the junction of Routes 100 and 103) has only 11 lovely rooms (all with private bath), yet offers a licensed lounge with a fireplace and a rate package that includes full breakfasts and candle-lit dinners. Five miles (8 km) north of Ludlow, on Route 100 near Echo and Rescue lakes, the **Echo Lake Inn** is an elegant restoration of an old country hotel, now featuring suites and condo units as well as inn rooms. There are tennis courts and an outdoor pool, a tavern and fine restaurant, a steam bath, and a selection of "ski and stay" packages with tickets to Okemo or Killington.

For a boy growing up in the 1870s in **Plymouth**, 12 miles (19 km) north of here via Routes 100 and 100A, Ludlow would have been the big city. So it was for Calvin Coolidge, 30th president of the United States, who was born in this tiny hamlet in 1872. Plymouth, which has been preserved in its entirety by the State of Vermont as the Plymouth Notch Historic District, is unique among American presidential birthplaces. Not only have the buildings Coolidge knew as a boy survived, they have survived almost exactly as they were when he knew them.

Plymouth Notch Historic District

The centerpiece of Plymouth Notch is **Coolidge Homestead**, a white clapboard house purchased in 1876 by Colonel John Coolidge, the president's father. Vice President Calvin Coolidge was visiting his boyhood home on August 3, 1923, when word arrived that President Warren G. Harding was dead. Coolidge hastily dressed and went down to the family sitting room. There, at 2:47 A.M. by the light of a kerosene lamp, he was sworn in by his father, a notary public. Like most of the other areas of the house, that room remains as it was when the oath was administered.

Across from the homestead is the general store Colonel Coolidge ran at the time of his son's birth; in the rear are the family's modest quarters. The museum store—with wooden counters the boy may have helped build—has shelves still stocked with late-19th-century merchandise. Nearby is a visitors' center and museum, a barn filled with antique carriages and farm equipment, and the **Wilder House**, childhood home of the president's mother. If you stop in at the restaurant in the Wilder House for a light country breakfast or lunch, you may be served some of the delicious cheddar cheese made at the **Plymouth Cheese Factory**, just up the road and open to the public. It was founded in 1890 by Calvin Coolidge's father and three other townsmen, and is owned today by the president's son John.

Plymouth Notch Historic District has just opened the 1924 summer White House office, in the old dance hall in the village. The district is open daily from mid-May through mid-October; Tel: (802) 672-3773.

The Londonderry Area

To continue a circuit of southern Vermont, return to Londonderry on Route 100 (it's about 35 miles/56 km south of Plymouth and just 6 miles/10 km south of Weston). Here, within a short drive of Weston's inns, are two of Vermont's favorite ski areas, one cross-country and one downhill.

SKIING

The **Viking Ski Touring Centre**, on Little Pond Road off Route 11 in Londonderry (east of the intersection with Route 100) has 40 kilometers (25 miles) of trails, three-quarters of them machine-groomed; skiing lessons and rentals, guided tours, a restaurant, an ice-skating rink, and on-site lodging are available. Tel: (802) 824-3933.

Nine miles (14½ km) on the other side of Londonderry via Route 11, in Peru, **Bromley Mountain** has attracted downhill enthusiasts for 56 years. Bromley has 35 trails, divided roughly equally among novice, intermediate, and expert; seven chair lifts; and two surface lifts. There's a congenial family atmosphere throughout (day-care starts at one month), and, as an added attraction, many of the slopes face south. This can shorten the spring season (although snow-making guns reach more than 80 percent of the trails), but it does cut down on bitter cold days. Tel: (802) 824-5522. The **Bromley**

Sun Lodge, a small hotel located near the base of the broad intermediate slope called the Lord's Prayer, may seem merely functional in appearance but offers great views (from the front rooms) and incomparable convenience for skiers.

DINING AND STAYING
IN LONDONDERRY

Both downhill and cross-country appetites can be dealt with in Londonderry at the **Mill Tavern,** an informal steak house with live entertainment (on Route 11 just east of Route 100; Tel: 802/824-3247); and at the small, comfortably elegant **Three Clock Inn,** where chef Heinrich Tschernitz upholds the traditions of Continental cooking; there are four exquisite rooms for overnight guests here as well (one block off Route 100 in South Londonderry; Tel: 802/824-6327). Just across the West River, on Route 100, the sedate and reasonably priced **Londonderry Inn,** a local institution for 50 years, offers comfortable European-plan lodgings; an ample breakfast buffet is a daily fixture, and a changing, imaginative American-Continental menu is presented nightly except Tuesdays.

Manchester

At Bromley Route 30 joins Route 11, and both commence a 6-mile (10-km) downhill run to Manchester, unofficial capital and liveliest community of this corner of Vermont. Manchester's cachet as a summer retreat dates back to railroad days; more recently, it has been a lodging, dining, and nightlife magnet for patrons of Bromley and Stratton. Over the past decade, however, Manchester has made a name for itself in much the same way as has Freeport, Maine: as a mecca for shoppers seeking designer names at bargain prices. The transformation was quick and deliberate; most of the shops occupy separate buildings or mini-malls built since the early 1980s. As you approach Manchester Center (quieter Manchester *Village* is 1 mile/1½ km south on Route 7) from the east on Route 11, you'll pass (or stop at) **Jones New York, Joan and David** shoes, **Ralph Lauren, Cole-Haan, J. Crew, Boston Traders,** and **Coach** leatherware; **Benetton** and **Harrington** (smoked hams and specialty foods) are on Route 7A at the town center; and **Timberland** and **Bass** outlets are on Route 7A just south of the intersection with Route 11. These are just a few of the bigger names, but they convey the idea.

Manchester's mercantile draw also includes a couple of homegrown names. **Northshire Bookstore,** on Main Street, is on anyone's list of the best half-dozen bookshops in the state; it excels in regional and children's titles and also has an excellent selection of tapes and CDs. On Route 7A just south of town, the **Orvis Company** maintains an august reputation as one of the world's most respected makers and purveyors of fly-fishing tackle. An Orvis rod—fiberglass, graphite, or one of the exquisite bamboo models made on the premises—is the né plus ultra of the fly-fisher's equipage. Orvis also features a line of sporting and leisure clothing in the country-squire-and-squiress mode, and offers comprehensive three-day courses in fly-fishing and upland game shooting (Tel: 802/362-3622). If you wish to try the action of an Orvis rod, you can use the private trout pond that students train on.

The river that runs through Manchester is the legendary Battenkill, one of the East's finest trout streams. Thanks to the river's proximity and the Orvis presence, the town is home to the **American Museum of Fly Fishing**, 1 mile (1½ km) south of town on Route 7A. The museum's collection of more than 1,000 rods (along with hundreds of reels and an encyclopedic assortment of flies) makes it possible to trace the very gradual evolution of a graceful, antique sport. Added attractions are a comprehensive library and exhibits of tackle owned by famous individuals: Winslow Homer took along more than his watercolors and brushes to the Adirondacks. The museum is open daily from May to October and on weekends the rest of the year; Tel: (802) 362-3300.

Another Manchester attraction worth a visit is the **Southern Vermont Art Center** on West Road, off Route 7A just south of town. Housed in a National Register Georgian Revival mansion, the center features rotating exhibitions in ten galleries, a 375-acre sculpture garden, a nature trail, and a performing-arts series. Open late May to late October; Tel: (802) 362-1405.

The turn of the century saw a spate of mansion building in the hills around Manchester. Perhaps the grandest of the era's Georgian Revival summer homes is **Hildene**, built by Robert Todd Lincoln—diplomat, cabinet secretary, railroad executive, and son of President Abraham Lincoln. Filled with the furnishings and personal articles used by Lincoln descendants until 1975, Hildene (on Route 7A, 2 miles/3 km south of Manchester) is open for guided tours of the interior and formal gardens from mid-May through October. Special attractions at Hildene include 15 kilometers (9 miles) of groomed cross-country ski trails (rentals available), and a program of candlelight tours through the exquisitely decorated house during Christmas week. For house tour and ski information, Tel: (802) 362-1788.

STAYING AND DINING
IN MANCHESTER

In all of New England only a handful of grand hotels remains from the days of private railroad cars, steamer trunks, and six-week sojourns. One of them is in Manchester Village, 2 miles (3 km) south of the town center. Behind the colonnaded façade of the **Equinox** stands a 224-year innkeeping tradition (the building's oldest section is the 1769 Marsh Tavern), recently revivified through a meticulous restoration undertaken by the hotel's new owners, Guinness Resorts. Using interior themes ranging from Federal (the entrance lobby) to High Victorian (the Mary Todd Lincoln Suite), Guinness's designers have managed to capture the style of smaller country inns; nevertheless, a lap-of-luxury resort hotel feeling pervades, thanks to indoor and outdoor pools, concierge and room service, a fitness spa, and elegant dining rooms. Most accommodations are in the main building, although a cluster of adjacent town houses offers suites with fireplaces.

The most talked-about aspect of the Equinox renovation has been the restoration of the hotel's golf course by Rees Jones. Building upon the Scottish traditionalist approach taken by the course's original 1927 designer, Walter Travis, Jones has created a superb par-71, 6,451-yard course renamed the **Gleneagles**, after the course at Equinox's sister Guinness property, Scotland's Gleneagles Hotel. Tel: (802) 362-4700.

Just outside the hubbub of Manchester Center, on West Road off Route 7, the **Reluctant Panther Inn and Restaurant** stands out in all its rambling purpleness as one of Manchester's most elegant lodging places. The handsome rooms and suites all have private bath, and some feature Jacuzzis and fireplaces. The restaurant is first-rate (it's open to the public as well as inn guests), with menu offerings such as venison pâté, yellowfin tuna with tomato coulis, locally raised pheasant, and a hearty winter cassoulet. In a somewhat less opulent vein, the **Inn at Manchester**—also located in quieter Manchester Village—offers a selection of cozy rooms and suites in a rambling country house, along with ample breakfasts and a private pool in a meadow.

On Highland Avenue in Manchester Center, the turreted Victorian **Manchester Highlands Inn** is just far enough from town for mountain views, but close enough to serve as a handy base for outlet shopping. Featherbeds, full breakfasts, and fresh-baked afternoon snacks are a plus, as are discount Bromley and Stratton lift tickets. And the **Weathervane Motel**, on Route 7A between the Village and the Center, is a comfortable local standby. In busy seasons, keep in mind Manchester's lodging referral service; Tel: (802) 824-6915.

The downtown cornerstone of Manchester dining has long been the busy, informal **Quality Restaurant** at 735 Main Street. Still showing its sandwich-shop roots—founded in 1920, it was owned for nearly 60 years by the same couple—the Quality has been fancied up a bit, but still does a reliable job with the basics (including not-so-basic desserts like oatmeal chocolate chip pie) from 7:00 A.M. till 9:00 P.M. daily.

A notch farther up the scale, the **Sirloin Saloon** (just east of town on Route 11) is the best place for steak in Manchester, and maybe in Vermont. There's a jolly dark-wood-and-stained-glass-Victorian-good-time atmosphere, a fine salad bar, and, surprisingly for an inland steak house, a deft hand with seafood (Tel: 802/362-2600). Farther east on Route 11, **Garlic John's**, an Italian bistro as hearty and unsubtle as the name implies, has been popular with skiers for 20 years; Tel: (802) 362-9843.

Dorset

Six miles (10 km) north of Manchester Center via Route 30, the archetypal Vermont village of Dorset shares Manchester's history as a favored spot for well-heeled out-of-staters in the late 19th and early 20th centuries: Golf was played here, in cow pastures, as far back as 1893. More democratic now, Dorset nonetheless has few if any rough edges. The town's centerpieces are the **Dorset Playhouse**, a respectable summer-stock venue (Tel: 802/867-5777); and the **Dorset Inn**, one of Vermont's oldest, a chaste white-frame structure with a broad verandah facing the green. The guest rooms are furnished in an old-money country Colonial style; the common rooms combine rural Americana with an English hunt club ambience. The inn's main dining room offers such dishes as poached salmon in dill hollandaise, and wild rice pudding; the menu in the cozy tavern room is hearty and less elaborate.

South from Manchester

You can head south out of Manchester in a hurry—via the new, limited-access Route 7; the interchange is 2 miles (3 km) east of town on Route 11—or at a more stately pace, on Route 7A (old Route 7). Five miles (8 km) south of Manchester Village, along the latter route, turn right for the **Equinox Sky Line Drive**, a 5¼-mile toll road leading to the top of 3,816-foot Mount Equinox, highest peak of the Taconic

Range. The supposed five-state view may be a bit of a stretch (New Hampshire and Maine are a long way off), but the vistas of Vermont, Massachusetts, and New York State are more than worth the trip.

ARLINGTON

Roughly halfway between Manchester and Bennington on Route 7A, Arlington is more a part of the national consciousness than many of us suppose. The reason? For 14 years during the peak of his career this was the home of Norman Rockwell, and Rockwell's neighbors became our own through the painter's use of about 200 of them as models for *Saturday Evening Post* covers and beloved works such as the *Four Freedoms* series. A number of those models are still living, and a few of them work as guides at the **Norman Rockwell Exhibition** (Route 7A in the village; Tel: 802/375-6423). The works on display at the exhibition are all reproductions—but after all, that is how the artist meant us to encounter them.

Afterward, settle into a room at the handsome Greek Revival **Arlington Inn,** just down the street, and reflect on the fact that some places really do look as if they were painted by Norman Rockwell. If that's not enough—well, you're almost back to Bennington, where you can compare reality to the works of Grandma Moses.

THE CHAMPLAIN VALLEY

Lake Champlain defines the "west coast" of New England, and forms nearly two-thirds of Vermont's border with New York State. In less precise but no less important ways, the lake defines the physical, social, and economic character of the western part of the state as well. The broad valley that spreads between the Green Mountains and the lake over its 125-mile length encompasses Vermont's largest concentration of dairy farms, as well as its largest population center, in and around the city of Burlington.

Historically, the isolating effect of the Green Mountains, compounded by the presence of Lake Champlain, has served to link western Vermont more closely with New York than with coastal New England; it was in the Champlain Valley that the encroachments of "Yorker" surveyors were contested most vehemently by Ethan Allen and his Green Mountain

Boys, in the pre–Revolutionary War days when the "New Hampshire Grants"—Vermont's appellation at the time— were sought for annexation by the big colony to the west. Among older Champlain Valley residents, students of regional dialects can still detect speech variants similar to those of upstate New York, whereas the "Vermont Yankee" dialect familiar through countless broad parodies is more characteristic of regions east of the Green Mountains.

Barely wider than a stream at its southern extreme along the border of the Vermont town of West Haven, Lake Champlain widens steadily as it stretches to the north, reaching a breadth of well over ten miles at the Champlain islands north of Burlington. It's big enough for Vermont senator Patrick Leahy to have seriously proposed, a couple of years back, that it be officially designated the sixth Great Lake, an unsuccessful move that would have entitled the lake to a greater share of federal pollution-control money. (At present, the greatest threat to its health is from New York State paper mill effluents.)

As expansive as Lake Champlain is, it was considerably larger during the immediate postglacial era, some 10,000 years ago. Lake Vermont, as geologists have named it, was one of New England's several now-vanished "fingers" of glacial meltwater. This swollen predecessor of Lake Champlain was some 700 feet deeper than the modern lake, the deepest point of which is no more than 300 feet. It flooded Vermont's Winooski River Valley, and linked what are today two separate drainage basins—those of the Hudson and St. Lawrence rivers. Lake Vermont lasted as long as glacial ice blocked the northward path to sea level along the St. Lawrence; once that barrier was removed, the lake emptied into the sea.

But the geological processes of the postglacial era were far from finished with the gentle lowlands that we now call the Champlain Valley. When the ice plug that held in Lake Vermont was pulled from the St. Lawrence, the stage was set not only for the draining of the vast inland sea but for the eventual intrusion of the ocean along the same path. This occurred as the global retreat of glacial ice contributed to the increase in the volume of the earth's oceans. When the level of the Atlantic rose, shoreline areas were flooded— and so were the interior lowlands of the Champlain Valley, as the St. Lawrence became a two-way street.

Lake Champlain was now the saltwater Champlain Sea, an inlet of a greatly swollen Gulf of St. Lawrence that inundated the bottomlands of southern Quebec. But this too was to prove an ephemeral formation; the reason that the sites of Burlington and Montreal did not remain under water is that the earth's crust, relieved of the immense burden of glaciers several miles thick, began to release its compression in the process called isostatic rebound. The Champlain Sea was decanted back into the Atlantic, and the fertile lowlands of today's Champlain Valley appeared. The lake now drains, via the Richelieu River, into the St. Lawrence River and the Atlantic Ocean.

VERMONT'S DAIRY CENTER

Farming will be very much in the foreground as you tour this part of Vermont. The rich soil of the Champlain Valley is one of the state's most vital resources. All along the valley you will enjoy the sort of vistas that suggest the popular image of Vermont as a place where every square foot not covered with ski trails and maple trees is given over to dairying. The Holstein-Friesian cow has become an unofficial state mascot, as you've no doubt noticed if you've visited gift shops in which everything from socks to coffee mugs is done in a black-and-white splotch motif.

The truth is, though, that the open farmland vistas of the Champlain Valley have become more of an anomaly than an accurate emblem of Vermont. A hundred and fifty years ago much of the state was given over to pasture, even the hilly regions that are now so heavily wooded. Since then, Vermont has largely been reforested as the old "hill farms" grew economically less viable. You don't have to walk far into the woods in up-country Vermont to come across old stone walls, cellar holes, and once-cultivated apple trees, all remnants of a time when the state was more pasture than forest. Much of the attrition among dairy farmers has taken place since World War II. The past half-century has seen a spiraling of farm overhead costs, along with the imposition of regulations requiring refrigerated bulk storage of milk—a capital investment far more expensive than the old milk cans. The farmers who survived were the ones milking large herds (100 head or more) on the most productive land. Vermont's overall dairy cattle population of roughly a quarter million hasn't changed appreciably since the 1940s; the big difference is that they now graze on 2,000 farms instead of 20,000. And many of those farms occupy the rich, alluvial soil of the Champlain Valley.

Along with the presence of the lake itself and its ancient terraced shorelines, it is this concentration of dairy farms that creates the Champlain Valley's expansive views. Drive north along Route 22A or 30 or any of the back roads that parallel or connect them, and your immediate environment will be a pastoral foreground, a frame for the Adirondack

Mountains to the west and for the nearer spine of the Green Mountains to the east.

The valley—particularly around the town of Shoreham—is also the headquarters of Vermont's apple-growing industry, a distinction it shares with the Lake Champlain islands to the north. Throughout the region there are numerous pick-your-own orchards, many of which sell their own delicious cider as well. Many a tourist has come home from a September visit to the Champlain Valley badly in need of a good applesauce recipe and a case of mason jars. Once you start picking, it's hard to stop.

TOURING THE CHAMPLAIN VALLEY

To explore the Champlain Valley from the south, start at one of several points west of Rutland along Route 4 (Rutland itself is covered in the Central Vermont section of this chapter). The main north–south artery in this part of Vermont is heavily travelled Route 7, which forms somewhat of a border between the valley and the Green Mountains between Rutland and Middlebury, and is more properly treated as part of our Central Vermont section, below. Routes 30 and 22A, west of Route 7 but parallel to it, are straight, scenic byways with far less traffic. Because 30 and 22A are never more than ten miles apart between Route 4 and Middlebury, it's easy to hop from one to the other while sampling local attractions as well as magnificent views of the Champlain Valley and the Adirondacks to the west.

Castleton to Middlebury

The town of **Castleton** lies along Route 4A (old Route 4, running just south of and parallel to the modern, limited-access route), 2 miles (3 km) east of Route 30. Castleton, home of Castleton State College, is blessed with a wealth of Greek Revival architecture out of all proportion to its size, largely because it was the home of a little-known master of the style named Thomas Dake, who came to Castleton in 1807 and worked here as an architect and builder for nearly 50 years, bringing a wonderfully inventive and idiosyncratic turn of mind to the classical vocabulary. His **Langdon-Cole House**, on Route 4A in the town center, is notable for its unusual recessed portico, with bays flanking graceful twin columns and a Palladian window.

Six miles (10 km) west of Castleton is **Fair Haven**, on the border with New York State. Center of a locally important slate-quarrying industry, Fair Haven has a place-that-time-forgot look about its downtown, a tidy arrangement of brick churches and commercial structures around an expansive common. The **Vermont Marble Inn**, built of marble, strikes a formal, elegant note on West Park Place in town, with its Victorian guest rooms, five-course breakfasts, afternoon tea, and hors d'oeuvres by the fire; at Christmas the inn goes all out with sleigh rides, a tree-trimming party, and a roast goose dinner. The **Fair Haven Inn**, on Adams Street, is more down-home, and offers the unusual—for Vermont—fillip of a restaurant serving Greek specialties.

Lake Bomoseen

Head north on Route 30 out of Castleton Corners (between Castleton and Fair Haven) and you'll soon be driving along the eastern shore of the largest lake (8 square miles) located entirely within the state of Vermont. Bomoseen, a favorite local retreat of bass fishermen and summer cottagers, had a brief fling with fame during the 1920s and 1930s, when critic Alexander Woollcott owned little Neshobe Island, just off the eastern shore opposite Bomoseen State Park. Each summer Woollcott invited members of his Algonquin Round Table crowd from New York City to Neshobe, where the order of the day was fierce competition at croquet. Woollcott sidekick Harpo Marx devoted a funny chapter of his autobiography, *Harpo Speaks,* to Neshobe, surely one of the oddest summer colonies ever to visit itself on the sober Yankee Republic of Vermont.

Neshobe Island remains private, but there is public access to Lake Bomoseen—along with swimming, camping facilities, and rowboat rentals—at **Bomoseen State Park**, located on the lake's western shore and accessible by a secondary road leading north from Route 4A, 1 mile (1½ km) west of the intersection with Route 30. For campsite information, Tel: (802) 265-4242.

Revolutionary War Sites

Near the northern tip of Lake Bomoseen is one of the sites that mark the lower Champlain Valley as an important theater of action in the Revolutionary War. This is the **Hubbardton Battlefield**, 2 miles (3 km) east of the village of Hubbardton via a gravel road (turn right off Route 30). Here, on the morning of July 7, 1777, American forces under the command of Colonel Seth Warner were surprised at breakfast by British and Hessian troops who were pursuing the retreating American general Arthur St. Clair. Warner's men, assigned to protect St. Clair's rear, fought a sharp but losing battle with the larger enemy force. His men did inflict enough casualties on the British and Hessians, however, to stop the British harassment of St. Clair and allow an orderly

American retreat from the fort at nearby Mount Independence. The battle is commemorated today by a small, state-
run **museum** at the site, open Wednesday through Sunday
from late May through mid-October; Tel: (802) 759-2412.

Mount Independence itself is located in Orwell, 6 miles
(10 km) west of the town center off Route 73A (Orwell is 12
miles/19 km north and west of Hubbardton via Routes 30
and 73). Along with New York's Fort Ticonderoga, on the
opposite shore of Lake Champlain, this fortification guarded
the narrow southern throat of the lake, as well as the
approaches to Lake George. Ongoing archaeological excavations have uncovered remnants of the fort's foundations, as
well as parts of the stockade, gun batteries, and hospital. The
site, which includes three miles of hiking trails, is open
during clement weather from Wednesday through Sunday,
late May to mid-October; Tel: (802) 759-2412.

Next to Washington's crossing of the Delaware, perhaps the
most celebrated water-borne foray of the American Revolution was Ethan Allen's attack on **Fort Ticonderoga**, launched
with a force of 83 men from the Vermont side of Lake Champlain near Larabees Point on the morning of May 10, 1775.
Academics with a penchant for demythologizing Allen and his
Green Mountain Boys cast doubt on the legend that he
demanded Ticonderoga's surrender "in the name of the
Great Jehovah and the Continental Congress," but this is one
of those lines that should have been spoken even if it wasn't,
and it's hard not to look across the lake at "Ti" without hearing
its echo.

Actually, you needn't just look. You can follow Ethan
Allen's oar strokes by taking the ferry from Larabees Point (at
the end of Route 74, in the town of Shoreham, 7 miles/11 km
northwest of Orwell) across to Ticonderoga. This southernmost and oldest (1799) of the Lake Champlain ferries operates from 8:00 A.M. to 6:00 P.M. May through October on the
"signal" system—if the boat is on the opposite shore, signal
with your horn and it will come pick you up. Once you're on
the New York side, the big attraction is the fort itself and its
Fort Ticonderoga Military Museum, right on the lake on
Fort Ti Road. The fort has been restored to its late-18th-
century appearance and houses artifacts relating to its role in
both the French and Indian and the Revolutionary wars.

Middlebury

Middlebury, shire town (county seat) of Addison County and
of the Champlain Valley's heartland (30 miles/48 km north of
Route 4 on Route 30), is the home of one of the nation's most
distinguished liberal-arts institutions, **Middlebury College.**

Chartered in 1800, the college followed permanent settlement of the town by only 13 years; even though the local economy owed a good deal to marble quarrying in the early 19th century, and despite Middlebury's stature as the major market town between Rutland and Burlington, few people think of the place without thinking of Middlebury College.

Middlebury plays the role of New England college town with the ease and grace that come of two centuries' experience. The campus, not particularly distinguished architecturally (although 1816 **Painter Hall** does have a chaste, Late Georgian grace), is scattered along a hillside just west of town. Attractions for visitors include the **Johnson Memorial Art Gallery**, in the Fine Arts Building, with sculptures by Auguste Rodin and American 19th-century master—and Vermont native—Hiram Powers; and the **Wright Memorial Theater**, a venue for dance, drama, and concerts throughout the year (Tel: 802/388-3711).

Middlebury's downtown clusters tidily around a village common, highlighted by the 1809 **Congregational church** with its magnificent Palladian window and 136-foot spire. The star of Middlebury's commercial district, which occupies several blocks along Main Street and Merchants Row on and around the green, is the **Vermont Book Shop**. Robert Frost used to shop here when he lived in nearby Ripton, and the shop—still independently owned—does well by the poet's memory, stocking even out-of-print Frost titles. But Frost is just the tip of the iceberg; as befits a college town, the inventory runs broad and deep in fiction and nonfiction alike. There's also a music department, particularly strong in classical and jazz on records, tape, and CD.

The other shop worth seeking out here is the **Vermont State Craft Center** at Frog Hollow, on Mill Street just off Main. The center's juried exhibits, representing the work of several hundred Vermont craftspeople, fill a spacious gallery overlooking the falls of Otter Creek. Jewelry, ceramics, woodwork, and textiles, ranging from country traditional to postmodern whimsical in design, make Frog Hollow a one-stop look into the workshops of artisans throughout the state.

The **Sheldon Museum**, at 1 Park Street between Mill and Main streets, opens a window on Vermont craftsmanship of an earlier era. The 1829 brick structure houses a small but distinguished collection of 19th-century Vermont furniture, paintings, and folk art. Tel: (802) 388-2117.

DINING AND STAYING
IN MIDDLEBURY

Middlebury and its immediate environs begin to make up for the dearth of dining opportunities in the lower Champlain Valley. A venerable favorite, on Dog Team Road off Route 7 just 3 miles (5 km) north of town, is the **Dog Team Tavern**. Nobody does anything clever with raspberry vinegar or kimchi sauce here; the menu is strictly fried chicken, prime rib, baked ham, and seafood, accompanied by home-made relishes and terrific sticky buns. No reservations are taken for parties of fewer than eight, and there's usually a wait for dinner, so have a drink and—as your grandmother would say—don't fill up on cheese and crackers. If she was an old Yankee, you'll find her spirit hovers over this place. Tel: (802) 388-7651.

In downtown Middlebury, try **Amigo's** (4 Merchants Row; Tel: 802/388-3624) for good-timey, college-town Mexican food and ambience. Another locus for casual bonhomie—and great burgers and desserts—is **Rosie's**, just south of town on Route 7 (Tel: 802/388-7052). Or stop in at **Calvi's** (42 Main Street; Tel: 802/388-9338), which has a genuine soda fountain and since the 1950s has occupied this build-ing, which has stood on this site since 1910. Many a pair of saddle shoes must have been scuffed beneath this counter, while romance and final exams occupied the minds above.

The local haute cuisine title, most would agree, belongs to the **Swift House Inn** at 25 Stewart Lane. Built in 1814 and once the residence of a Vermont governor, the Swift House is also a formally elegant place to spend a night. The 19 guest rooms are furnished with Oriental rugs and reproductions of early-19th-century antiques; each has a private bath, with luxurious terrycloth robes provided. The dining room's menu, which the chef changes daily, usually combines well-executed stand-bys with imaginative creations; for instance, recent offerings included filet mignon with three-peppercorn sauce and pan-roasted pheasant with blueberry sauce. Tel: (802) 388-9925.

Overlooking the green is the comfortable, red-brick **Mid-dlebury Inn**, a satisfying anomaly in these days when the lodging industry seems split between self-consciously gor-geous bed-and-breakfasts and cookie-cutter chain hotels. The Middlebury Inn is small enough (75 rooms) to keep its homey character, and large enough to have a decent (if unspectacular) restaurant and a big lobby where the wait-staff will bring martinis to your sofaside table. A tip: Take an upper-floor room in the 1827 main building facing the green, with views of the college and countryside to the west.

THE UNIVERSITY OF VERMONT MORGAN HORSE FARM

Unless you're in a hurry to head north on Route 7 toward Burlington, it's always pleasant to wander north and east out of Middlebury onto back roads that offer some of the prettiest views of Lake Champlain, the valley's farmland, and the Adirondacks. This little corner of the valley also harbors a horse lover's mecca: In Weybridge, 4 miles (6½ km) north of Middlebury just off Route 23, is the University of Vermont Morgan Horse Farm.

Which was the greatest American horse? Racing fans might vote for one of a handful of Triple-Crown winners. But up in Vermont the honors would go straight off to a horse named Figure, who lived at the beginning of the 19th century. A small but powerful bay stallion belonging to Justin Morgan, a Vermont schoolteacher, Figure was a genetic sport (the breeders' term for an animal showing marked change from its parental stock). Most likely part Thoroughbred and part Arabian, he was greater than the sum of his parts. He was the first Morgan.

Every Morgan foaled over the past two centuries can be traced directly to Figure, and many of the finest horses of that lineage have been bred at the University of Vermont's Weybridge farm, which was once a U.S. government facility for raising military horses (valued as cavalry mounts, Morgans had stamina enough to be ridden after hauling artillery into battle). The 150-acre farm today continues in its mission of keeping Morgan bloodlines strong, while offering visitors the opportunity to tour the stables and see some of the best contemporary examples of America's oldest native equine breed, characterized by massive neck musculature, broad shoulders and quarters, and clean limbs that lend the compact Morgans their power and versatility as draft, harness, and riding horses. Open daily from May 1 to October 31; Tel: (802) 388-2011.

Middlebury to Burlington

Beyond Middlebury and Weybridge, all major north–south routes lead to **Vergennes**, a one-square-mile municipality that is the smallest chartered city in Vermont (13 miles/21 km north of Middlebury). Near Route 7 is the **Kennedy Brothers Factory Marketplace**, a collection of shops housed in an old brick factory building and centered upon Kennedy Brothers woodenware outlet. Otherwise, Vergennes is noteworthy principally for its tidy city park and the Victorian, rather than Early American, character of its main street. Just west of the city center, turn right off Route 22A (left if you're driving north toward Vergennes) to reach Button Bay State Park and the Basin Harbor resort.

Button Bay, a state facility with tent sites, lean-tos, boat rentals, and a bathing beach, lies along a protected cove of Lake Champlain. The park gets its name from the curious, button-size pebbles, complete with holes at their centers, that used to appear quite frequently along the beach. For whatever reason, the "buttons" have been turning up less frequently lately, which makes it all the more fun to go looking for them.

Basin Harbor Club, just north of Button Bay, is one of Vermont's premier summer resorts. Owned by the same family since 1886, it comprises 700 acres along the lake, with 77 separate cottages and 44 rooms in the main buildings. Basin Harbor, with its own marina and 18-hole golf course, swimming pool, tennis courts, hiking trails, and formal and casual dining rooms, is virtually a self-contained community. Many of its guests represent the latest of several generations to visit each summer, and they are as likely to tell you that their destination is Basin Harbor as to say Vermont.

A short-term destination right near the big resort is the **Lake Champlain Maritime Museum,** on Basin Harbor Road 5 miles (8 km) west of Vergennes. The museum chronicles the great days of Lake Champlain steam navigation, when Adirondack and Vermont lumber and agricultural products moved to market via water. Maps and archaeological finds (the floor of Lake Champlain is strewn with sunken wooden ships and military artifacts) are on display. Open mid-May to mid-October; Tel: (802) 475-2317.

Although there is no shortage of side roads leading to the lake, Route 7 is the only north–south through route between Vergennes and Burlington. At **Ferrisburg,** 5 miles (8 km) north of Vergennes, Route 7 passes by **Rokeby,** the home of Vermont author Rowland E. Robinson (1833–1900). Largely neglected today, Robinson was a popular exemplar of the regionalist trend in late-19th-century American literature. His specialty was homespun tales written in the phonetically spelled dialect of rural Yankees and French-Canadians—not always easy going for modern readers. He did leave behind a lovely house, however, and it's worth a visit not only because of its collection of two centuries of Vermont furnishings and decorative arts, but because Robinson was an ardent abolitionist who made his home a stop on the Underground Railroad. A secret passage and hiding room offered safety to escaped slaves on this last leg of their run to the Canadian border. Open for guided tours Thursday through Sunday from Memorial Day to mid-October; Tel: (802) 877-3406.

As you head north from Ferrisburg into Charlotte on Route 7 you are passing what is probably the most important invisible boundary in the Champlain Valley. The views of the lake are more beautiful than ever, when the road rises above the surrounding hills, and the village of **Charlotte** itself (just west of Route 7 on F5) is quaint and quiet. But once you reach Charlotte you will doubtless notice that houses on ten-acre lots easily outnumber dairy farms. The lots were farms, or rather parts of them, not so long ago, but now they are the outer marches of Burlington's southern suburbs. This is Chittenden County, where one-fifth of the people in Ver-mont live, and you will have to drive quite a way north of here before it really seems as if you are out in the sticks again. For city dwellers this will seem like pretty tame suburbanization; for Vermonters whose memories go back 20 years or more it's practically New Jersey. All in all, a matter of perspective.

Just before the turn onto Route F5 that brings you into Charlotte village, keep an eye out for the **Vermont Wild-flower Farm**, on the left side of Route 7. This is the largest wildflower seed center in the eastern United States, and it is a gorgeous sight from May through October. Garden tours and seed purchases are available; Tel: (802) 425-3500. And if you do take the left turn into Charlotte and have a little extra time, follow the road down to the lake and take the ferry (with or without your car) to **Essex**, New York, a restored early-19th-century lake port. The scenic trip takes 20 min-utes, with frequent sailings throughout each day from April 1 (if the ice is out) until January 3.

SHELBURNE

Shelburne, the next town north along Route 7, might well seem like little more than a Burlington bedroom commu-nity, were it not for the presence of one of America's pre-mier repositories of folk art, tools, furnishings, and the commonplace impedimenta of 19th-century rural life. This is the **Shelburne Museum**. Opened in 1947, the museum was the lifelong dream of Electra Havemeyer Webb, a sugar heiress who married into Vermont's Webb family of railroad tycoons. An inveterate collector who purchased her first cigar-store Indian when she was in her late teens, Mrs. Webb spent her life acquiring the artifacts of everyday life in preindustrial and steam-age rural and small-town America.

The 45-acre site that she donated for the museum today constitutes the apotheosis of the New England village—an omnium-gatherum dream village of buildings shipped from places around the region and reassembled here. There are period homes, artisans' shops, barns, and a church and school, representing more than two centuries of vernacular design; a covered bridge; a jail; an 1871 Lake Champlain lighthouse; and even the *Ticonderoga,* a 1906 side-wheeler steamboat that plied the waters of Lake Champlain before making its final trip—by rail—to the museum nearly 40 years ago. Although the buildings themselves are part of the collection, they also serve to house more than 80,000 artifacts—paintings, pottery, toys, horse-drawn vehicles, quilts and samplers, farm tools, the world's largest collection of wildfowl decoys on public display, and, of course, cigar-store figures.

Plan on spending a full day at the Shelburne Museum, especially during July and August when there are daily craft demonstrations by artisans using traditional tools. There are also special events during the Christmas season. Open daily late May to late October; Tel: (802) 985-3344.

Until this past decade, the nearby 1,000-acre, Olmsted-designed estate that was the Webb family's private domain remained off-limits to the outside world; occupying virtually all of Shelburne Point between Shelburne Bay and the main body of Lake Champlain, the estate stood behind its entrance gate and pasture fences like something that was in Vermont but not of it (turn left off Route 7 just north of the Shelburne town library to reach the estate). Beginning in the 1970s, however, the Webb family began to make several of the estate's structures available as venues for the **Vermont Mozart Festival** (Tel: 802/862-7352)—most notably, the vast, century-old show barn where musically accompanied dressage events take place.

More recently, a younger generation of Webbs has made something of a going concern of the old family compound. **Shelburne Farms** now produces an award-winning cheddar cheese; tours of the cheese-making operation are offered, as are walks through exquisite formal gardens; Tel: (802) 985-8442. Most spectacularly of all, the working farm's Shelburne House—one of several shingle-style mansions on the property—is now the **Inn at Shelburne Farms**, with 24 guest rooms guaranteed to make each guest feel like an Edwardian magnifico (open mid-May to mid-October), along with tennis, Lake Champlain swimming, and walking trails. The dining room, open to the public as well as to guests (Tel: 802/985-8498), is a lead-crystal, heavy silverware, perfect-roast-rack-of-lamb sort of place, where you can top off dinner with Cognac on the terrace while watching dusk empurple the Adirondacks and discussing, presumably, what a mess T.R. will make of things now that McKinley's been shot.

BURLINGTON

Unless you are coming into Burlington via the ferry from Port Kent, New York, your entrance into the "Queen City"—the commercial, educational, and cultural capital of Vermont—

will unfortunately be less than an edifying experience. The best way to enter a lake city is via the lake; this used to be possible not only by way of the ferry, but also via the waterside Vermont Railway station at the foot of Main Street. Today Amtrak's Montrealer stops 8 miles (13 km) out of town in Essex Junction, and most travellers coming into Burlington are forced to use one of three cluttered back-door entrances, each of which is also fed by I-89 or its extension I-189: Route 7 from the south, Route 2 from the east (and from Burlington International Airport), and Route 15 from the northeast (and the railroad station). Each of these unlovely arteries is lined with strip malls, car dealers, and fast-food places; none of them can possibly prepare the visitor for what a pretty, livable, walkable city Burlington is. Bear with the trip; Burlington's "edge city" commercial suburbs are mercifully small.

Burlington itself is a compact city, built along a hillside facing Lake Champlain and crowned with the spired and turreted halls of the University of Vermont. The founder of the university, Ira Allen (brother of Ethan), was in fact instrumental in founding Burlington. Like many Vermont towns, Burlington had been chartered by New Hampshire governor Benning Wentworth in 1763, and actual settlement began in 1773. But it was during the years immediately following the American Revolution that both Allen brothers, along with Vermont's first governor, Thomas Chittenden, began to promote in earnest the development of the lake-shore near the mouth of the Winooski River through their Onion River Land Company.

At a bend in the river, off Route 127 in the Burlington neighborhood called the "New North End," the recon-structed **Ethan Allen Homestead** stands as a reminder of the community's frontier days. Allen lived here during the last two years of his life, from 1787 to 1789. Interpretive displays explain the patriot-adventurer's life and role in the struggle against New York domination of Vermont and in the Ameri-can Revolution, and illustrate the conditions of life on the far fringes of New England settlement in the late 1700s. Open late April to late October; Tel: (802) 865-4556. (Allen's other local monument is a 42-foot granite shaft over the approxi-mate site of his grave, in Greenmount Cemetery on Col-chester Avenue.)

Despite a perilous position during the War of 1812, due to proximity to hostile Canada and an embargo on shipping, Burlington held on. Its rapid climb to preeminence among Vermont cities began in 1823, with the completion of a canal linking southern Lake Champlain with the Hudson River at Troy, New York. Burlington prospered first as a transship-

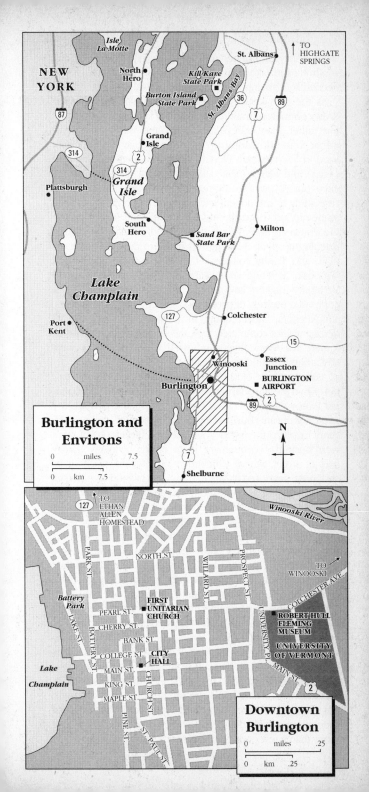

Burlington and Environs

NEW YORK

Isle La Motte

St. Albans

TO HIGHGATE SPRINGS

North Hero

Kill Kare State Park

Burton Island State Park

St. Albans Bay

Grand Isle

Grand Isle

Plattsburgh

South Hero

Milton

Sand Bar State Park

Lake Champlain

Port Kent

Colchester

Winooski

Essex Junction

BURLINGTON AIRPORT

Burlington

Shelburne

N

0   miles   7.5
0   km   7.5

Downtown Burlington

TO ETHAN ALLEN HOMESTEAD

Winooski River

TO WINOOSKI

COLCHESTER AVE.

NORTH ST.

PARK ST.

WILLARD ST.

PROSPECT ST.

Battery Park

FIRST UNITARIAN CHURCH

ROBERT HULL FLEMING MUSEUM

UNIVERSITY OF VERMONT

PEARL ST.

CHERRY ST.

BANK ST.

COLLEGE ST.

CITY HALL

LAKE ST.

BATTERY ST.

UNIVERSITY PL.

MAIN ST.

Lake Champlain

MAIN ST.

KING ST.

CHURCH ST.

MAPLE ST.

PINE ST.

ST. PAUL ST.

0   miles   .25
0   km   .25

ment point for lumber and agricultural products headed south via the lake and canal, and for manufactured goods needed by growing Vermont communities.

As the 19th century progressed, however, the railroads drew commercial traffic away from the lake, and manufacturing rather than transportation became Burlington's economic bulwark. Industry continues to play an important local role—General Electric, IBM, Blodgett (commercial ovens), and a large meatpacker all have plants in or near the city—but Vermont's only real metropolitan area is today a case study in the dependence of an urban economy on the academic, professional, and service sectors. In addition to the University of Vermont, with its medical school and large teaching hospital, Burlington is home to the smaller Champlain and Trinity colleges; St. Michael's is in neighboring Winooski. Banking and insurance also loom large, as do Vermont's biggest law firms. The city's population is not composed entirely of professors, students, doctors, lawyers, shopkeepers, and computer firm employees—nor are its demographics completely upscale—but at times it seems as if there is a decidedly postindustrial, white-collar (or expensive stonewashed denim) feel to the place.

Aside from the election of political independent and self-described socialist Bernard Sanders as mayor in 1980 (Sanders is now Vermont's lone U.S. congressman), perhaps the most significant Burlington phenomenon of the past 15 years involved the north–south **Church Street**, downtown's main business thoroughfare. It had always been a workaday sort of street, where Chittenden County did much of its shopping; anchored at one end by City Hall and at the other by the imposing, elm-flanked Unitarian church that gave it its name, Church Street was lined with department stores, book and stationery shops, and clothing stores.

In the late 1970s, though, Burlington planners decided that the way to compete with the suburban malls was to play the malls' own game. Church Street became an outdoor mall, free of vehicular traffic and devoted largely to specialty, crafts, upscale, and youth-oriented shops, along with sidewalk cafés and, in summer, vendors' pushcarts. What's more, a new indoor mall was built, with a department store anchor and an entrance off Church Street. The net effect was to take an old, red-brick New England downtown—the kind that is dying at the hands of the malls from Bangor to Bridgeport—and make it a destination in itself, greater than the sum of its parts. Love it or hate it, no one can deny that it has brought out the people. Twenty years ago you could have fired a cannon harmlessly down Church Street on most nights and more than a few days. Now it is nearly always abustle.

Around in Burlington

Burlington is a walker's city. All of the areas of prime interest to visitors—downtown, the waterfront, and the university—are within a few blocks of each other. Just remember that walking east to west will require a bit more effort than walking north to south, because of the city's hillside location. The Chittenden County Transportation Authority (Tel: 802/864-0211) provides bus service throughout the city and surrounding area; the main terminus for bus lines is at the corner of Church and Cherry streets, alongside Woolworth's. Also, a College Street "trolley shuttle" (actually a bus done up in turn-of-the-century style) makes the run up and down this east–west street between the waterfront and the university from mid-May to Labor Day; otherwise a university shuttle operates.

THE CHURCH STREET AREA

A good place to begin a walking tour of Burlington is at the corner of Main and Church streets, the southern end of the Church Street Marketplace. Near the southwest corner, at 153 Main Street, is the **Flynn Theater**, a vaudeville theater and early movie palace that operates today—with its Art Deco interior meticulously restored—as a multi-faceted performing-arts facility (Tel: 802/863-5966).

Across Main Street from the Flynn is Burlington's **City Hall**, a 1926 structure designed by the New York firm of McKim, Mead & White in the Georgian Revival style that followed its great Beaux-Arts period. **City Hall Park**, at the building's rear facing Main, Saint Paul, and College streets, is one of the city's more popular outdoor living rooms, and is scheduled—fountain and all—for a major restoration. On Saturdays in late summer and early fall the park is the scene of a popular **farmers' market** featuring fresh produce, baked goods, and preserves.

The car-free **Church Street Marketplace** proper begins at Church and College streets, one block north of Main. The marketplace extends for the next three long blocks, with the entrance to Burlington Square Mall (the indoor shopping area) on the left side between Bank and Cherry streets. Along the way, as you pass the intersection of Church and College, you may hear strains of Edith Piaf or some other vintage bistro music; this would be emanating from **Leunig's**, the indoor-outdoor café on the northwest corner. Tel: (802) 863-3759. Along with the curbside seats at **Sweetwaters** restaurant, across the street, this is one of the best spots from which to watch the Church Street *passeggiata* of students and shoppers. Tel: (802) 864-9800.

It's necessary to raise your sights above the street-level commercial hubbub to appreciate some of the grand-scale vestiges of an earlier Burlington that survive along Church Street. The first of these is the old **Howard Opera House**, on the southwest corner of Church and Bank streets, where **Chassman & Bem** booksellers (see Shopping, below) is now the anchor store and offices fill out the upper floors. Built in 1878 by John Howard for the then-enormous sum of $100,000, this was one of the most important northern New England stopovers for travelling theatrical troupes. It was the Flynn Theater of its day.

At the head of Church Street, where the marketplace ends at Pearl Street, two great brick piles face one another. On the right is the former **Abernethy Clarkson Wright** department store, which now houses a Banana Republic store on its first floor and apartments above; up until two decades ago this turreted turn-of-the-century emporium illustrated the idea of the vertical, rather than horizontal, "marketplace." On the left is the century-old **Masonic Hall**, also with a retail establishment on its ground floor. The Masons built an appropriately foursquare headquarters, topped with a massive roof that resembles nothing so much as a great slate pyramid.

The greatest architectural gem of Church Street stands at its head. This is the 1816 **First Unitarian Church**, a severely elegant Late Georgian structure designed by Peter Banner (architect of Boston's Park Street Church) with some assistance, legend has it, from Charles Bulfinch. Paul Revere cast the original bell at his Canton, Massachusetts, foundry two years before he died; the present bell duplicates the first bell's tone.

Turn left at Pearl Street and head toward the lakefront. Two blocks down, on your left, you will pass two radically different examples of church architecture, both dating from the 1970s. The first, at Pearl and Pine streets, is the Roman Catholic **Cathedral of the Immaculate Conception**; the second, at Pearl and Battery streets, is the Episcopal **Cathedral of St. Paul** (the latter has a superlative hand-built tracker organ). Both of these stark modernist structures replaced Gothic-style cathedrals, destroyed by fire within a few years of each other.

BATTERY PARK AND THE WATERFRONT

Across Battery Street at the end of Pearl is Battery Park, site of an artillery battery that repelled the British during the War of 1812. Author William Dean Howells pronounced the view of the sunset here the finest he had ever seen. Certainly the setting could not be better: Here the lake is almost at its widest point, and the sun has nothing less to sink toward than the grandest peaks of the Adirondacks.

Until the mid-1980s Battery Park was about as close as most people bothered to get to the lakefront at Burlington, unless they were heading down to embark on the ferry to New York State. Since then, however, the former railroad and utility properties along **Lake Street**—the water-level thoroughfare below Battery Street—have steadily been developed for pedestrian and bicycle use. There are now restaurants, a community boathouse, and a pleasant walkway along the stretch between Maple Street (two blocks south of Main) and the Burlington Electric Company site beneath Battery Park. Further public use–oriented development is to follow; at present, debate centers upon the merits of intensive (e.g., retail and housing) versus low-impact planning.

The **ferry** for Port Kent, New York, leaves from the foot of King Street. The Lake Champlain Transportation Company boats operate between mid-May and mid-October, and can accommodate cars as well as pedestrians; the length of the trip is one hour each way. Pedestrian day-trippers should be aware that Port Kent consists of the ferry terminal, a snack bar, a gift shop, and not much else; the nearest community of any size is Plattsburgh, 22 miles (35 km) to the north. For ferry information, Tel: (802) 864-9804.

Another option for cruising the lake is the *Spirit of Ethan Allen,* an excursion boat operating from Perkins Pier at the foot of Maple Street, one block south of the ferry terminal. A schedule of narrated, dinner, and sunset cruises is maintained between late May and late October; durations range from one and a half to two hours. For information, call Green Mountain Boat Lines; Tel: (802) 862-9685.

A vestige of the early days of Lake Champlain navigation, located a short walk from the ferry terminal at 35 King Street, is the circa 1798 **Gideon King House**, now an office building. King was a shipping entrepreneur with a fleet of sailing vessels whose enterprise earned him the title "Admiral of Lake Champlain." As if to underline the close links between shipping and the city's growth, it was in this house, also in 1798, that the grid plan for Burlington's downtown streets was adopted.

The best route for heading back uptown from the lake, whether on foot or via the shuttle trolley, is along **College Street**, which is perpendicular to Church Street. On the right-hand side of the block between Pine and St. Paul streets is an extremely attractive row of four- and five-story brick Victorian commercial buildings, which seem as if they ought to belong to a much bigger city than Burlington; the most impressive, the **Wells-Richardson Building**, at 127 College Street, houses **Bennington Potters North**, a quality housewares outlet (see Shopping, below). And across the street, on the corner of College and St. Paul, the **Vermont Pub & Brewery**, at 144 College, offers an excellent selection of its own beers and ales, brewed on the premises (see Dining, below).

THE UNIVERSITY OF VERMONT

If you're heading east up College Street, you can't miss the university—just draw a bead on the white cupola crowning the hill. That's the Old Mill, oldest of UVM's buildings (the initials UVM stand for the Latin *Universitas Viridis Montis,* or University of the Green Mountains). Once you've left downtown behind, the walk will take you through a residential neighborhood of big Victorian houses, built by the solid Burlington yeomanry of a century ago. Several of them now have Greek letters on their façades, further proof that you're heading in the right direction. Finally, College Street ends at the **University Green**, shaded by some of the tallest and most lovingly protected of Vermont's surviving elm trees.

The University of Vermont was founded in 1791 by Ira Allen, whose statue stands at the center of the green, but classes did not begin until 1800. It is New England's fifth oldest institution of higher learning, and currently enrolls approximately 8,000 undergraduates and 1,600 graduate students.

Although UVM never embarked upon a simultaneous, architecturally cohesive campuswide building program, it has been remarkably fortunate in the aesthetic quality of the structures erected at various times in its history to face the green. The most recent of these, at the extreme left on the corner of Colchester Avenue and University Place, is the 1927 **Ira Allen Chapel**, designed by McKim, Mead & White. Built in a chaste Georgian style, the chapel is joined by a 170-foot brick campanile, which houses a sweet-toned 64-bell carillon. Vermont-born educational philosopher John Dewey (1859–1952, UVM Class of 1879) is buried beneath the chapel wall on the building's left side.

Directly to the right of the Ira Allen Chapel is the one UVM building that aspires to the front rank of American architecture. This is the **Billings Student Center** (formerly Billings Library), designed by Henry Hobson Richardson in his signature Romanesque Revival style and finished after the architect's death in 1885. The elaborate detailing of the rich sandstone exterior is matched by the sumptuous carving of the interior's Georgia pine; if you enter no other UVM building, go inside Billings to see the carved mantel and nearby floor clock, the work of a master carver named Albert Whittekind who came to Vermont from Germany to work on Billings and stayed to ornament many of the city's finest homes.

Next in line, continuing right from Billings, is 1896 **Williams Hall**, a High Victorian edifice with rich terra-cotta ornamentation. Designed by Frank Furness, it was the first completely fireproof building in the United States.

That white cupola you followed from downtown belongs to the **Old Mill**, the original section of which dates from 1825. Architecturally, this gaunt brick building is difficult to pin down, but it has the unmistakable air of a New England college about it; it seems to suggest Virgil and Horace swallowed whole by the light of a whale-oil lamp. The Marquis de Lafayette, on his nostalgic and triumphal American tour of 1825, laid the Old Mill's cornerstone.

Morrill Hall, at the end of University Place on the corner of Main Street, is a blocky 1907 building with a red tile roof that would look more at home on the Stanford University campus in Palo Alto, California. It's noteworthy, though, because of its name: Vermont senator Justin Smith Morrill was the author of the 1862 Land Grant Act that launched state-funded higher education in America.

The University of Vermont's **Robert Hull Fleming Museum**, located on Colchester Avenue around the corner from the Ira Allen Chapel, houses a collection of European, American, and African art and ethnographic material, and mounts a series of changing exhibits. Among its more noteworthy holdings are several fine Hudson River School paintings, including a pair of small Bierstadts, single works by Sargent and Homer, two Corots, and Fragonard's *La Jardinière*. There's even an Egyptian mummy, complete with painted wooden sarcophagus. Closed Mondays; Tel: (802) 656-0750.

SHOPPING IN BURLINGTON

Church Street has long constituted virtually the entirety of Burlington's shopping district; when the street became a pedestrian mall called Church Street Marketplace, the shops were already in place—although, as we noted above, the trend along the street runs less to essentials and more to boutiques as the years go by. Burlington Square Mall, built as an indoor appendage to the outdoor marketplace, features chain outfits such as the Gap and Victoria's Secret—the stuff of malls throughout America—as well as a branch of the Maine-based **Porteous** department store. For shops with a local flavor, though, you should stay out in the weather.

As a college town, Burlington has more than its share of

bookstores. The best for browsing is **Chassman & Bem**, 81 Church Street, which has the finest travel section in the state as well as good depth in contemporary fiction. For used books, especially scholarly titles, spend some time among the 12,000-plus volumes at **Codex**, at 148 Cherry Street, just off Church. **Kids' Ink**, 1 Church Street, has two floors of children's books, games, and toys, but by far the hardest place in town to get a youngster out of is **Thought Works**, a small but crammed emporium of scientific and educational toys, games, and paraphernalia at 57 Church Street.

Vermont has no small reputation as a craftspersons' state, and the **Vermont Craft Center**, 85 Church Street, offers a magnificent selection of specially chosen handicrafts ranging from jewelry, pottery, and glass to metalwork and custom furniture. On the less expensive side, **Bennington Potters North**, 127 College Street, carries not only the handsome, sturdy pottery that made Bennington famous, but also a full complement of the sort of furnishings and incidentals that go well with airy apartments with exposed beams and brick walls. Back up on Church Street, **Once a Tree**, at number 89, features unique wooden housewares and furnishings.

Burlington's most distinctive men's clothing store is **Michael Kehoe**, 117 Church Street, home of a subtly updated traditional style and snappy ties in the Bryant Gumbel mode. In women's clothes, the earthy-casual Vermont look is best represented by **Handblock**, 97 Church Street, purveyors of hand-blocked cotton apparel and household linens.

STAYING IN BURLINGTON
The downtown Burlington lodgings scene is currently the exclusive province of the **Radisson Hotel Burlington**, on Battery Street overlooking Lake Champlain. Modern and architecturally undistinguished but small enough to avoid the chain-hotel cookie-cutter syndrome, the Radisson offers underground parking, an indoor pool, a free airport shuttle, and a respectable restaurant; the only drawback is an uphill hike to the Church Street Marketplace. Pay the extra tariff for a room with a view of the lake and the Adirondacks.

If you don't mind driving to downtown, there is a cluster of reliable chain hotels along Route 2 (Williston Road), just over the hill from the University of Vermont and ten minutes from the airport. The biggest and fanciest is the **Sheraton Burlington Hotel and Conference Center**, which does a sizable conference business; there's an indoor pool and spa, a restaurant and lounge, and an airport shuttle. Here you'll want a room facing Mount Mansfield. The **Holiday Inn** and **Ramada Inn** are nearby; both have outdoor pools (Holiday Inn has an indoor one as well) and full dining and lounge facilities; the Ramada has an airport shuttle. Just off Williston Road and across from the big University Mall shopping center is the **Anchorage Inn**, a good value and perhaps the best pick from among the many local, independent operations that line Routes 2 and 7 in the Burlington outskirts. The Anchorage has an indoor pool, free pastry and coffee in the morning, and an airport van.

If you're not averse to a slightly longer drive into town, or want to be situated for a quick hop into the countryside, the **Inn at Essex**, just past Essex Junction on Route 15 (8 miles/13 km west of Burlington), is a choice alternative. Built a few years ago for the convenience of IBM executives visiting the big plant nearby, the inn offers Colonial elegance in a modern building, at a woodsy off-road location. There's an indoor pool and health club, and a café and restaurant that benefit from association with the prestigious New England Culinary Institute (the restaurant is discussed in the Dining section, below).

Also well out of town, but brand-new and very convenient to I-89, are the **Hampton Inn and Conference Center** and the **Fairfield Inn by Marriott**, both located in Colchester, a ten-minute drive north of downtown Burlington. The Hampton is the more upscale of the two, with an indoor pool and restaurant (and free breakfast); the Fairfield is basic but comfortable, with an outdoor pool and very attractive rates.

DINING IN BURLINGTON

If one word can characterize dining in Burlington and environs, that word is eclectic. Like most college towns, Burlington supports a restaurant scene that is multicultural, informal, and well supplied with inexpensive options; a healthy young professional population, meanwhile, keeps a more upscale selection of establishments in business.

Burlington locals would be the first to admit that two of their most beloved eateries are at the low end of the sophistication scale. **Henry's Diner**, at 155 Bank Street a block from the Church Street Marketplace, is a cheerfully claustrophobic breakfast and lunch joint with rock-bottom prices on its hearty diner repertoire (Tel: 802/862-9010). The **Oasis**, a more traditional diner (it's an actual stainless-steel prefab), sits at 189 Bank Street, a block off Church in the other direction. Stop in for a cup of coffee, keep your ears open, and you'll know everything there is to know about Burlington politics in ten minutes. Don't miss the German chocolate cake. Tel: (802) 864-5308.

Another local tradition is **Bove's**, at 68 Pearl Street, two blocks from Church. Bove's is a 1940s Italian bistro with an Art Moderne façade, Naugahyde booths, and prices straight out of the Truman administration. Cheap Chianti, minestrone, big bowls of spaghetti and meatballs—it'll make you feel like a sophomore on a weeknight date. Tel: (802) 864-6651. Another inexpensive Italian spot, more modern in ambience, is **Alfredo's**, at 79 Mechanics Lane, a little alley off lower Church Street. For the money, a plate of homemade cheese ravioli here makes about the most satisfying lunch in the whole downtown area; at dinner, the veal, seafood, and homemade desserts are more than respectable. Tel: (802) 864-0854.

College towns would be nowhere without their pubs, and downtown Burlington offers two very different takes on the tradition. The **Vermont Pub & Brewery**, a block off Church on College and St. Paul streets, takes the Anglo-American route with a fine selection of beers and ales brewed on the premises, and a hearty menu built around such items as toad-in-the-hole and club sandwiches (Tel: 802/865-0500). At **Leunig's**, however (up on the corner of Church and College streets), you're clearly on the Continent. Leunig's is Burlington's tiny answer to the cafés of Montparnasse, right down to Piaf on the stereo, Beaujolais Nouveau by the glass, *pissaladière* (a French olive-and-onion pizza), and sidewalk seating through three seasons. There's a full menu of pasta dishes, seafood, and daily specials, and an attractive prix-fixe dinner for two with a bottle of wine. Tel: (802) 863-3759.

The **Daily Planet**, 15 Center Street a block east of Church, is another college-crowd favorite, with a decor that's part 1960s reincarnation and part 1990s funk. The chefs have looted the world's cuisines to come up with an appealing, inexpensive menu that ranges from vegetable burritos to Moroccan chicken (Tel: 802/862-9647). **Carbur's**, at 119 St. Paul Street, across from City Hall Park, is the local bastion of the ragtime yard-sale school of decor, with antique advertising signs, musical instruments, and firehouse artifacts hanging on the walls. The stars here are the sandwiches, hefty and imaginative constructions touted in a phone-book-size menu larded with local inside jokes. The bar has an excellent assortment of imported beers and ales (Tel: 802/864-9631). **Sweetwaters**, on College and Church streets catercorner from Leunig's, does business in (and, in summer, outside of) an artfully renovated turn-of-the-century bank. Pasta dishes and meal-size salads (Thai beef and cashew chicken are two standouts) anchor the menu, along with tasty burgers made from locally raised buffalo. Tel: (802) 864-9800.

Burlington's most respected Asian restaurant is the tiny but endlessly ambitious **Five Spice Café**, at 175 Church Street just off Main. The owner-chef of the Five Spice couldn't decide which Asian cuisine to specialize in, so he took on them all—and does an admirable job of it. Chinese, Vietnamese, Indian, Thai, and Indonesian dishes crowd the menu; spices—five and then some—are paramount. On Sunday there's a dim sum brunch (Tel: 802/864-4045). Down at the other end of Church Street, at number 2, **Sakura** concentrates solely on Japanese cuisine—not just the requisite sushi and sashimi, which are done nicely—but generous noodle soups and a wonderfully delicate tempura. Tel: (802) 863-1988.

For Chinese food, the downtown standby is **Hunan**, at 126 College Street, a coolly sedate business-lunch sort of Chinese restaurant notable for cold hacked chicken, tangerine beef, and four treasures in a nest (Tel: 802/863-1023). **China Lite**, out on Dorset Street off Route 2 (across from University Mall), is bigger and splashier (tanks of giant goldfish), and runs a nice buffet at lunch and dinner every day; on Sunday, people come from miles around. Tel: (802) 658-3033.

India House, at 207 Colchester Avenue, near the UVM and Trinity College campuses, does a fine job with the classics of Indian cuisine, and even goes beyond the requisite curries and tandoori dishes to offer an intriguing variety of Indian breads. The Sunday brunch buffet is a particularly good value. Tel: (802) 862-7800.

When the craving for steak or prime rib must be fulfilled, the place to go is **What's Your Beef**, at 1710 Shelburne Road (Route 7), in South Burlington. This Victorian temple of red meat looks out over Shelburne Bay and the Adirondacks, and offers a menu crowned by a 22-ounce New York sirloin. On Sundays there's an all-you-can-eat omelette and waffle bar (Tel: 802/865-3700). At **Perry's**, just down the highway at 1080 Shelburne Road, beef shares the limelight with the freshest seafood in town, including Maine lobster, salmon, trout, and a terrific stew. Tel: (802) 862-1300.

If you've packed along ties and heels, and aren't heading down to the Inn at Shelburne Farms (see above), try the area's other top spot for candlelit formal dining: **Butler's**, at the Inn at Essex, at 70 Essex Way off Route 15 about 3 miles (5 km) from Essex Junction (the inn is discussed above). The restaurant's affiliation with the New England Culinary Institute assures attention to detail and meticulous execution of dishes; recent selections (the menu changes constantly) have included a soup of roasted eggplant and garlic, roast loin of lamb served in a crisp potato basket with green beans and fresh corn sauce, and veal tortellini, with fresh mozzarella and tomatoes. The decor is English country house transposed to a freshly minted suburban hotel. Tel: (802) 878-1100.

Finally, a word about picnics. If you're packing a hamper

and heading for the hills, go first to **Lilydale Bakery**, 1350 Shelburne Road (it's not easy to find, so look for the Talbot's sign), for the best breads in the area. Tel: (802) 658-2422. Although Lilydale can make you sandwiches, it's more fun to match a Lilydale baguette with ingredients from the **Cheese Trader**, at 1186 Williston Road (Route 2), next to the Alpine Shop. The cheese selection here is the best in town; there are also pâtés and wines, and the weekly specials are often astoundingly underpriced. Tel: (802) 863-0143.

ST. ALBANS AND THE
LAKE CHAMPLAIN ISLANDS

Unless you're hurrying straight on to Montreal, try to avoid I-89 and keep to the side roads that reveal the northernmost stretch of the Champlain Valley. There are two options: to stick to the mainland, venturing north via Route 7 toward St. Albans and the border; or to head over the causeway about 8 miles (13 km) north of Burlington onto the Lake Champlain islands of North and South Hero and Isle La Motte. Ideally, you can cover mainland and islands in a one- or two-day loop that will bring you right back to Burlington.

For the mainland route, leave Burlington via either Colchester or Riverside Avenue and cross the Winooski River into **Winooski**, a compact mill town reminiscent of larger southern New England factory cities. Like its bigger counterparts, though, Winooski has left its manufacturing days behind; the red-brick mills that line the riverbank have been rehabbed, on the left into housing and on the right into the **Champlain Mill** retail complex. The mill's wares run from books to clothing to 18th-century reproduction furniture. **The Prime Factor** restaurant (1 Main Street; Tel: 802/655-0300) and **Waterworks** (same address; Tel: 802/655-2044) both occupy choice riverside locations in the mill. Waterworks offers a respectable steak-seafood-pasta-salad-bar menu along with its view (it has a pleasant outside deck).

You may remember Winooski for the mid-1970s notoriety connected with a proposal that it be covered with a plastic dome. Back in those days, when any scheme remotely associated with saving energy could qualify for a grant, somebody spent $50,000 deciding whether it would be feasible to enclose all 795 acres of Winooski and thereby save precious BTUs. The idea sank like a stone, and today nearly everyone agrees that good money was better spent installing bloody Marys in the derelict hulk of the Champlain Mill.

Six miles (10 km) east of Winooski, along Route 15, is

Essex Junction, home of the enormous IBM plant that underpins Chittenden County's economy, of the Champlain Valley Fairgrounds, and of the nearest Amtrak station to Burlington. Unless you're taking the train or going to the Champlain Valley Exposition, though, Essex Junction will probably be just a mall-lined bottleneck along your way to northern Green Mountain destinations. To stay in the Champlain Valley, follow Route 7 north out of Winooski toward St. Albans.

St. Albans and North

St. Albans, 25 miles (40 km) north of Winooski, is a 19th-century railroad town, handsome in a ruddy brick Victorian way but still coping with the fact that the trains and associated concerns have left (except for an Amtrak depot, where the daily Montrealer stops, and the offices of the Central Vermont Railway) and taken a lot of jobs with them. (Ben and Jerry, the lords of premium ice cream, are set to build a new plant in the city, which is about as succinct a commentary on the passage from an industrial to a postindustrial economy as you can find.) St. Albans's downtown is nevertheless stately, almost grand; Taylor Park is a gem, handsomely rimmed by century-old county court buildings and uniform, restored Victorian business blocks.

This main business thoroughfare was the scene of the northernmost engagement of the Civil War—the St. Albans Raid of October 19, 1864. For a number of days prior to that date, 22 Confederate soldiers had slipped unnoticed into the city and secretly contacted each other. At a prearranged moment, separate groups of the infiltrators burst into every bank on Main Street. One local man was killed, several were wounded, and the Confederates escaped to Canada with $200,000. They were apprehended north of the border but acquitted, as a Canadian court ruled that the raid was an act of war rather than a common crime. Canada's Parliament did, however, reimburse St. Albans's bankers to the tune of $50,000, as a hedge against American reprisals.

The best place to dine in St. Albans is the **Old Foundry,** at 3 Federal Street. Occupying an intimate, rambling warren of rooms in what was just that—an 1840s foundry—this is a good prime rib house, whose new owners have nonetheless expanded into subtler fare. They've also added an attractive walled garden for summertime aperitifs. Tel: (802) 524-9665.

St. Albans is the gateway for one of Vermont's more unusual state parks, **Burton Island.** Located in Lake Champlain less than a mile from the tip of St. Albans Point, the park is accessible in summer by a state-run shuttle launch from Kill Kare State Park on the mainland, 6 miles (10 km) west of the city center. (Along the way is St. Albans Bay State Park, not to be confused with Kill Kare). One-square-mile Burton Island has full camping facilities (lean-tos and tent sites; showers), a swimming beach, and nature trails.

North of St. Albans, the remaining 15 miles (24 km) to the Canadian border mark a topographical as well as political boundary. Here the hilly Vermont landscape flattens out, after affording a few last spectacular lake views, and gives way to the broad, open plain of the St. Lawrence Valley. Most travellers pressing north beyond St. Albans on Route 7 or I-89 are heading for points beyond the border. There is, however, one final noteworthy Vermont destination before the Canadian customs agent welcomes you to *la belle province*. This is the **Tyler Place**, a sprawling lakeside family-run resort just off Route 7 in Highgate Springs, 3 miles (5 km) south of the border. The Tyler Place has built a well-deserved reputation as a resort for families with young children; each of the cottages and inn suites has separate kids' bedrooms. There are also outdoor activity programs for six age groups as well as earlier children's dining hours. Adults can enjoy tennis, lake and pool swimming, boating (including sailing and Windsurfing instruction), and golf at three nearby courses. Open Memorial Day to mid-September.

The Lake Champlain Islands

If you've chosen the island route north, either take a leisurely northbound drive out of Burlington on Route 127, along Malletts Bay (later connecting with Route 7 north to the islands), or pick up Route 7 or I-89 at Winooski and head straight for the Champlain Islands exit, Route 2 west.

Just before you enter the causeway heading out onto Grand Isle, keep an eye out for **Sand Bar State Park**, on the right roughly 4 miles (6½ km) past the I-89 exit. Sand Bar (open Memorial Day through Labor Day) has one of Lake Champlain's finest bathing beaches, ideal for small children because of the shallow inshore waters and extremely gradual drop-off. When water levels are low, in fact, you'll begin to wonder if it's possible to wade across to Grand Isle.

GRAND ISLE

Of course, it isn't possible to walk or wade to Grand Isle from Sand Bar, and you will drive over on the causeway. What lies on the other side is Grand Isle County, occupying an elongated archipelago and the southern end of a peninsula that extends southward from Canada between two bays of Lake Champlain. Chamber of commerce brochures extol

Grand Isle as Vermont's fastest-growing county, an alarming statistic until you realize that it wasn't exactly starting with Manhattanesque proportions: The five towns that make up the county barely muster 6,000 souls. Still, there is a fair bit of Burlington bedroom-community development in **South Hero**, at the southerly end of Grand Isle convenient to the causeway, and each year it's necessary to drive a bit farther north to enjoy the uncluttered environment of dairy farms and apple orchards that still predominates in this far northwestern corner of Vermont.

About those names: Along with the towns of Alburg (on the mainland peninsula), Isle La Motte, and Grand Isle, the towns of North Hero and South Hero round out the short list of Grand Isle County communities. Depending on which sources you read, North and South Hero were named for Ethan Allen (the hero of Ticonderoga), or for Ethan and his brother, Ira, who was a hero mainly at hustling real estate—although he did found the University of Vermont. Another version, plausible given the characters involved, is that the Allens named the islands themselves.

Approximately 4 miles (6½ km) after reaching the island via the causeway from the mainland, turn left onto Route 314 and drive 2½ miles (4 km) west if you wish to take the ferry to Plattsburgh, New York. This is the northernmost of the Lake Champlain ferries, and the only one that is open all year. The trip across the channel takes 12 minutes; Tel: (802) 372-5550 for information.

If you're continuing north through the islands, stay on Route 2 as it heads into the town of **Grand Isle** and watch on your right for the **Hyde Log Cabin**, reputed to be the oldest log cabin in the United States. The cabin was built at a nearby site by Jeremiah Hyde, an early Grand Isle settler, in 1783, and moved here in 1945. The interior suggests the loneliness and hardship of frontier life in post-Revolutionary Vermont; in any season, it's impossible to visit the cabin without thinking of the awesome fact of winter in those days. Open early July through Labor Day; Tel: (802) 828-3226.

NORTH HERO

Another causeway carries Route 2 across a narrow inlet called the "Gut" and onto North Hero, the archipelago's northernmost island. North Hero is the most developed of the islands for summer recreation; along a three-mile stretch of Route 2 directly facing the lake (and looking east toward the Vermont mainland), a string of inns, cottages, marinas, and unpretentious restaurants suggests a throwback to the low-key lakeside resort life of 60 or 70 years ago. A fine place to stay here is the **North Hero House**, a restored 1891 inn with water views, tennis, a sauna, boat and bike rentals, and meals served indoors or on the terrace. (Open mid-May to mid-October.) **Shore Acres Inn** is another pleasant islands retreat, with 50 acres of grounds fronting a half mile of lakeshore, plus boat and bicycle rentals. The Green Mountain views are spectacular from the inn's lakeside restaurant, which specializes in steaks and grilled fish and is open to the public (Tel: 802/372-8722).

Of the four state parks on the islands, the most remote, least heavily used, and prettiest is **North Hero State Park**, at the island's northernmost tip 3 miles (5 km) beyond the town's resort strip. Although the swimming beach is small, this is a great place to rent a rowboat and explore either arm of the lake off Stephenson Point. Views of the surrounding countryside and of sailboats on the water are superb.

ISLE LA MOTTE

Staying on Route 2, cross another causeway onto the Alburg peninsula, then follow Route 129 west to Isle La Motte, smallest and most remote of the Lake Champlain islands accessible by car. Here, at the island's northwestern tip, is the **St. Anne Shrine**, an outdoor Roman Catholic shrine built on the site of the first white settlement in Vermont, Fort St. Anne, built by the French in 1666. The shrine has a small century-old chapel, stations of the cross along a pleasant walkway near the lake, a cafeteria (open summer only) and picnic grounds, and a statue of Samuel de Champlain that was sculpted at Montreal's Expo '67. Masses are celebrated on Saturday evenings and Sunday mornings from mid-May to mid-October. From the shrine continue south along the island's west shore for views of the New York State shoreline, then circle back up (the island is only six miles long) to reach the causeway that carries Route 129 back to Alburg and North Hero.

On the way back north, just past the small stone structure that houses the Isle La Motte Historical Society, you'll see in a field on your right the Chazyan coral reef, believed to be the oldest in the world. Formed when Lake Champlain was part of a wide inland sea and Isle La Motte was under water, the 420-million-year-old reef now stands as high as six feet above the surrounding terrain.

Leaving Isle La Motte via Route 129, the only route to the mainland, you can complete the islands–St. Albans loop by heading north for 5 miles (8 km) on Route 2 at South Alburg, then heading east via Route 78 to Swanton. From the Alburg bridge to Swanton Route 78 passes through the **Missisquoi National Wildlife Refuge**, a vast tract of marshes and woodlands at the mouth of the Missisquoi River, where more than 280 species of birds have been spotted. At Swanton you can pick up either Route 7 or Interstate 89 for the trip back to St. Albans and Burlington. If you've been on the Champlain Islands and are heading to Montreal, the best bet is to take Route 2 west across the lake's northern tip to Champlain, New York, where you can connect with Interstate 87, the Adirondack Northway.

CENTRAL VERMONT

The Green Mountains are the central fact of Vermont. Along with the absence of a seacoast, the rugged central interior of the territory was the most important obstacle to early settlement here, which lagged behind that of the surrounding colonies and centered largely upon the more accessible and fertile valleys of the Connecticut River and Lake Champlain. Over the years the mountains came to both inspire and represent the isolation and rugged independence that set Vermont Yankees apart even from other rural New Englanders. By the mid-20th century, when the economically marginal farms of the higher elevations had been largely abandoned, the Green Mountains became not a barrier but an attraction to a new generation of settlers. Once merely the physical backbone of the state, they are now the financial backbone of a vital tourist economy.

The Green Mountains are a northern extension of the Appalachian system, varying in their summit elevations from roughly 2,000 feet to the 4,393-foot crest of Mount Mansfield, the highest point in the state. Created by the folding and elevation of granite and crystalline metamorphic rock some 350 million years ago, their original jagged peaks smoothed and rounded by eons of wind and water erosion, Vermont's mountains were scoured and plucked into their present condition by the mile-high glaciers of the Ice Age 10,000 to 12,000 years ago. Along about the 1930s, humankind learned what to do with them.

Since the days of the Algonquian Indian tribes who once inhabited the region, Vermont was snowshoe territory, and skis were a late arrival. There were a handful of skiing enthusiasts in and around Montreal as early as the 1880s, and by the turn of the century some of the more adventurous Dartmouth men were skiing in and around Hanover, New

Hampshire. From there the sport spread into Vermont, where winter visitors from Boston and New York would putter around farm fields and gentle hills using long, heavy wooden skis and bindings that allowed plenty of heel-and-ankle play for travelling on level ground and climbing uphill—much like today's cross-country bindings.

But in 1934 a group of these winter vacationers relaxing in the lounge of Woodstock's White Cupboard Inn got to talking about how they might climb less and ski more. Pooling the sum of $500, they ordered the construction of Vermont's first rope tow. It was a simple affair involving 1,800 feet of rope and a stationary Model T, but it revolutionized skiing in Vermont. Rope tows began turning up everywhere, and by the end of the decade a chair lift reached nearly to the summit of Mount Mansfield. The Green Mountains had become ski territory, and Vermont's mostly north–south Route 100—the route we'll follow for much of this section—would become its main street. Route 100, along with the byways that branch off into Vermont's "gaps" (high mountain passes), is also a favorite thoroughfare during fall foliage season. And—as it parallels the rugged Long Trail—100 is a hiker's highway as well. (See the discussion of the Green Mountain Club in the Waterbury section, below.)

TOURING CENTRAL VERMONT

The itinerary outlined in this section is really a two-in-one affair; starting at Rutland, we head east along Route 4 and describe jaunts to the north along both Route 100 and Route 12. This approach by no means defines all possibilities for exploring the central Green Mountains (for the sake of convenience, we've covered the southern portion of the range in the "Southern Vermont" section, above); Route 14 between South Royalton and Barre, for instance, also makes for a scenic option. North of Stowe and Smugglers' Notch the choices more and more resemble Robert Frost's roads that "diverged in a snowy wood," and north of Jeffersonville and Morrisville the upper Champlain Valley and the Northeast Kingdom are as readily accessible as the destinations outlined in this section (readers are of course referred to the sections in which those areas are covered).

THE RUTLAND AREA
Rutland

The city of Rutland is a pivotal place, standing at the juncture of the Southern Vermont, Champlain Valley, and Central

Vermont regions outlined in this chapter. As such, it's a convenient jumping-off point for the exploration of any of these areas; a half-hour drive to the east or west would put you, respectively, either at Killington Peak or at the southern end of Lake Champlain. And, given its location astride Route 7, Rutland is also the place to begin a direct drive north to Burlington.

Rutland, Vermont's second-largest city, is an old railroad town—its 19th-century prosperity was built on the twin pillars of the Rutland Railroad and the marble industry—and it still has a largely utilitarian character in its downtown. Ironically, the most interesting building in the city center was the train station, which was torn down in the 1960s and replaced with a shopping mall and accompanying parking lot worthy of any suburb. This hollowness at the core, along with the strip development that lines the main approaches to the city (particularly along Route 7 south), has drawn most visitors' attention to the outskirts rather than the two or three streets that constitute the downtown business district. Rutland's restaurants and accommodations are, in fact, heavily concentrated along Main Street, which is also Route 7 (South Main is south of West Street, which runs through the middle of town, and North Main north); it skirts the city proper and can easily leave a traveller wondering if this is all there is to Rutland.

AROUND IN RUTLAND

Three worthwhile stops along the Route 7 strip are **Charles E. Tuttle**, 28 South Main Street, a bookstore specializing in its own Orientalia titles as well as rare books and Vermontiana; **Boutique Internationale**, 85 North Main Street, stocked with glassware, ceramics, linens, jewelry, and museum reproductions from around the world; and the **Chaffee Art Gallery**, 16 South Main Street, a gallery specializing in works on canvas and paper by Vermont artists. Tel: (802) 775-0356.

For lodgings, many of the big chains—Holiday Inn, Days Inn, and Howard Johnson—are represented along Route 7 and provide a handy backup for late arrivals who haven't booked inn accommodations up at Killington (these are discussed below). For a bit more character that doesn't require your leaving the main drag, try the **Inn at Rutland**, a century-old Victorian mansion with 12 restored to a fare-thee-well rooms with private bath and Continental breakfast.

For decades the best place to eat in Rutland has been **Royal's Hearthside**, at 37 North Main Street. Owner-chef Ernie Royal's deft hand with such classics as prime rib, Chateaubriand, grilled lamb chops, and Indian pudding mark him as a traditionalist, but he isn't afraid to get out the mesquite for chicken or shrimp. This is also the home of the last of the giant popovers, complimentary with each meal. Tel: (802) 775-0856.

Vermont Marble Exhibit

To explore the heart of the Green Mountains, the recommended route out of Rutland is east on Route 4, with a turnoff to the north either at Route 100 near the Killington ski resort, or onto Route 12 farther east at Woodstock. Before leaving the Rutland area, though, you might wish to take a quick jog in the opposite direction for a look at the marble industry. The Vermont Marble Exhibit, 4 miles (6½ km) north of Center Rutland off Route 3, is the world's largest display of its kind (to reach Center Rutland, not to be confused with downtown Rutland, drive 2 miles/3 km west of the city on Route 4). In addition to a film explaining quarrying techniques and a closeup look at factory operations, the exhibit includes a working resident sculptor, a hall of presidential busts, a marble chapel and kitchen, and a gift shop selling slab marble and finished marble products. It's all here, in case you never get to Carrara. The exhibit is open daily except in winter, when it's closed on Sundays; for information, Tel: (802) 459-3311.

SKIING IN THE RUTLAND AREA

Head east out of Rutland on Woodstock Avenue/Route 4 and you'll start climbing almost immediately. You're heading into the massif of Killington Peak, Vermont's second-highest mountain (4,241 feet) and the home of the state's largest ski complex—the largest, in fact, in the eastern United States. Before plunging into the Killington whirl, however, consider a quiet sojourn—complete with extensive cross-country trails on which to limber up for the slopes—at **Mountain Top Inn** in the town of **Chittenden**; turn left off Route 4 at Mendon, 5 miles (8 km) east of Rutland.

Mountain Top occupies 1,000 upland acres in what is, at 46,315 acres, the largest town in Vermont. The inn's setting provides top-of-the-world views of Killington to the south, the Otter Creek Valley to the west, and the main range of the Green Mountains to the north and east. Good food and comfortable lodging, along with a full spectrum of summer activities, have contributed to decades of popularity; but the big draw at Mountain Top is 110 kilometers (68 miles) of cross-country ski trails, 70 kilometers (43 miles) of them machine-groomed and all open to the public for a daily fee. Skating, tobogganing, and horse-drawn sleigh rides round out the winter program.

Killington

Sixteen miles (26 km) east of Rutland via Route 4, Killington, the mountain and the resort, looms over this part of central Vermont. Actually, local boosters once strove to see to it that the great peak would displace Mount Mansfield and loom over the entire state as Vermont's highest point. The time was the 1890s, and Killington's partisans were armed with erroneous U.S. Coast and Geodetic Survey figures pegging Killington at 4,241 feet and Mansfield at 4,071. The problem was that the survey had made its observations from the absolute summit of Killington, but had shortchanged Mansfield by setting up its instruments on the mountain's "nose" rather than its highest point, the "chin." (Mount Mansfield, as we'll see when we get there, has a profile resembling a recumbent human face.) It wasn't until 1901 that the matter was settled and Mansfield finally and permanently recognized as the pinnacle of Vermont.

However, Killington may have the honor of being the place where Vermont got its name—if we can believe the story of Rev. Samuel Peters, an itinerant preacher who claimed to have stood on its summit in 1763 and christened the surrounding territory *Verd-Mont,* or Green Mountain(s). Rev. Peters's claim has been frequently disputed, though, and it is quite likely that French explorers had already come up with the appellation.

Regardless of disputes over summit height rankings and the state's purported baptism, Killington stands secure in its status among the region's ski resorts. The big mountain and its five satellite peaks feature 107 trails and 19 lifts, and a snow-making capability that covers nearly three-quarters of its slopes. (Killington's snow-making prowess, along with an early autumn cold snap, enabled the area to open its 1992 season on October 1.)

If the sheer size of Killington seems daunting, remember that the area is comfortably decentralized. There are five base lodges, along with shuttle-bus transportation connecting the major lifts and several of the overnight accommodations closest to the slopes. The speed and carrying capacity of the lifts, led by a 3½-mile gondola and a pair of brand-new quad chair lifts, also keep things moving: At 35,427 rides per hour, Killington is the leader among Vermont resorts. The lifts' destinations run to a near-even mix of easy and difficult trails. Day care starts at three weeks and ski school at three years.

For general information at Killington, Tel: (802) 422-3333 (golf as well as skiing); for snow conditions, Tel: (802) 422-3261. For information on spring, summer, and fall activities in the vicinity, call the Killington & Pico Areas Association;

Tel: (802) 773-4181. For information on short-term rental of homes and condos in the area, call the Killington Lodging Bureau; Tel: (800) 621-6867 or (802) 773-1330.

Even if the emphasis is on skiing, there is no "off" season at a resort of this size. Mountain biking (rentals are available), tennis, and golf lead the list of summer activities; Killington's 18-hole, par-72 PGA championship course was designed by Geoffrey Cornish. The chair lift to the summit of Killington Peak is open from early June through mid-October, and has become a popular vehicle for foliage viewing.

Pico Ski Resort

Pico Ski Resort, Killington's alter ego (there have been merger talks, but nothing conclusive so far), is somewhat closer to Rutland; the access road is just 2 miles (3 km) west of Route 4's intersection with Route 100. With 40 trails and 9 lifts, Pico has a more laid-back atmosphere than Killington. The area is also more challenging, on average: Fully 80 percent of the runs from the summit are expert and advanced intermediate, although beginners will find acceptable terrain farther down the mountain. And with 82 percent snow-making coverage, Pico is another area that starts its season early and closes late, provided the thermometer cooperates. In summer ride the triple chair lift to the alpine slide, a 3,400-foot winding chute in which each rider controls his or her own wheeled sled on an exhilarating downhill run. For general information at Pico, Tel: (802) 775-4346; for snow conditions, Tel: (802) 775-4345 or (800) 225-7426. For the alpine slide, Tel: (802) 775-4345.

Staying and Dining around Killington–Pico

The Killington–Pico area offers as broad a range of accommodations and as wide a choice of restaurants as any region of Vermont, Stowe and greater Burlington included. For lodgings, top selections include the **Inn of the Six Mountains**, a modern 103-room establishment directly adjacent to Killington's golf course and featuring indoor and outdoor pools; the **Killington Village Inn**, a 29-room luxury lodge just a few minutes' walk from the ski area's main base lodge; and **Cortina Inn**, a short drive west from the Killington access road on Route 4, with eight tennis courts, balconied rooms, an indoor pool, a good restaurant, shuttle service to Killington and Pico, and a lively après-ski lounge with nightly entertainment.

Also on Route 4 (on Cream Hill Road) is the smaller and cozily old-fashioned **Vermont Inn**, a 16-room hostelry 3 miles (5 km) west of Pico and 8 miles (13 km) west of Killington. The inn has an outdoor pool, an indoor hot tub and sauna, great views, and a chef who shows a deft hand with veal, seafood, and pasta. The 22-room **Inn at Long Trail**, practically on the premises of Pico (and astride the famous Long Trail, discussed below), has been serving hikers and skiers for more than 50 years and features an Irish pub with draft Guinness. Spring for one of the fireplace suites.

For nearly two decades **Hemingway's** (Route 4; Tel: 802/422-3886) has enjoyed a reputation as the Killington area's finest restaurant. The decor is intriguing and varied; you can dine at fireside or in the wine cellar of this restored 133-year-old home, and the menu runs to such New American treatments as Vermont lamb with goat's cheese pancakes and pheasant in a basil-Sauternes sauce. **Luigi's Little Naples** (Route 4; Tel: 802/773-4663) is one of the state's premier upscale Italian venues; rack of lamb is served with a rosemary-garlic cream, veal is fork-tender (try the saltim-bocca, made with sage and prosciutto), and fried calamari suggests that you will find the Mediterranean, not the Green Mountains, outside the door. (Both of these restaurants are within a five-minute drive of the intersection of Routes 4 and 100.)

The Gaps North of Rutland

Roughly opposite the Killington access road is Route 4's intersection with Route 100. Here you'll have to decide which route to follow north: Route 100 or, if you continue east on Route 4 to Woodstock, Route 12 (for details of the latter, see The Woodstock Area, below).

Route 100 veers off to the left and makes its northward way close along the eastern shoulder of the Green Mountain Range, linking a number of tiny villages and leading to the ski towns of Warren and Waitsfield, gateways to the resorts of Sugarbush and Mad River Glen. Along the way Route 100 offers the opportunity to traverse the Green Mountains via four passes, or "gaps," as they're called locally, in the range. Given the time—and in the right season—it's pleasant to zigzag back and forth from Route 100 to Route 7 on a couple of the gap roads; there are a number of fine picnic spots along the way. (All four of the gap roads are crossed by the Long Trail, for which see Waterbury, below.)

The southernmost of the passes is **Brandon Gap**, connecting Rochester on Route 100 with Brandon on Route 7 via a 17-mile (27-km) drive along Route 73. At its highest point this two-lane blacktop reaches an elevation of 2,170 feet and opens onto a splendid view of Lake Champlain. (The rather benign-looking peak on your right at this point is 3,216-foot Mount Horrid.)

The next gap to the north is called **Middlebury Gap**, after the college town on Route 7, just 20 miles (32 km) to the west. Beginning at Hancock on Route 100, Route 125—the Middlebury Gap road—passes the state recreation area at **Texas Falls**, one of the prettiest waterfalls in a state not blessed with very many. Some 5 miles (8 km) farther to the west, past the 2,149-foot height-of-land that marks the divide between the Lake Champlain and Connecticut River watersheds, is the famous **Bread Loaf** writing school affiliated with Middlebury College, and the **Robert Frost Wayside Area**. Here a forest trail commemorates the Vermont laureate, who lived for 23 years on a farm in nearby Ripton. The three-quarter-mile path is marked at intervals with plaques bearing Frost quotations.

Lincoln Gap, which connects Warren on Route 100 with Bristol on Route 17, is the most rugged (much of the road surface is gravel) of the four, and the only one not maintained for travel in the winter. The road through Lincoln Gap also reaches the highest elevation (2,424 feet) of any of the passes. From this point, about 4 miles (6½ km) west of Warren, the route through Lincoln Gap descends through deep woods toward the tiny, 200-year-old town of Lincoln and the broad lowlands of the Champlain Valley. To the north loom five peaks reaching or nearly reaching 4,000 feet, among them 4,135-foot Mount Ellen, the third highest of Vermont's mountains.

The northernmost of the gap roads is the paved, year-round link between Irasville, near Waitsfield on Route 100, and Bristol. Designated Route 17, this sharply winding 20-mile (32-km) route crests the **Appalachian Gap** at 2,356 feet and affords several magnificent Champlain Valley views along its descent into Addison County. While you are negotiating the "fiddler's elbow" curves through Buel's Gore, just west of the route's highest elevation, it may be difficult to believe that you are momentarily in Chittenden, Vermont's most populous county.

SUGARBUSH SKI RESORT AND MAD RIVER GLEN

The eastern portion of Route 17 out of Waitsfield is well known as one of Vermont skiing's main highways; it leads to the access roads for both Sugarbush and Mad River Glen. **Sugarbush**, one of the state's largest ski resorts, is really two areas in one. Its 105 trails and 16 lifts are divided between

Sugarbush proper and Sugarbush North. The former, with seven chair lifts and two surface lifts, leans heavily toward expert and intermediate runs; Sugarbush North, which nestles along the east face of Mount Ellen, offers a number of gentle beginner slopes as well as a couple of hair-raisers. The areas are connected by shuttle bus, and about half of the total skiing terrain is covered by snow-making apparatus.

Child care begins at six weeks of age, ski instruction at age four. Indoor and outdoor pools, ice skating, 25 kilometers (16 miles) of cross-country ski trails (at Sugarbush Inn; see below), 35 outdoor tennis courts, and an 18-hole golf course round out the resort's facilities. ("Sugarbush," incidentally, is the traditional Vermont term for a stand of maple trees tapped for the sap used in the making of maple sugar.)

For general information at Sugarbush, Tel: (802) 583-2381 or 583-3333; for snow conditions, Tel: (802) 583-7669. The golf course number is (802) 583-2722. For lodging reservations in the Sugarbush/Mad River Glen vicinity, call Sugarbush Area Reservations at (802) 583-3333 or (800) 53-SUGAR.

Mad River Glen, about 4 miles (6½ km) farther west up Route 17 toward the summit of the Appalachian Gap, is either a traditionalist's paradise or an odd anachronism, depending on your skiing point of view. "Small" and "steep" are the operative words; the 45-year-old area has only 33 runs and four chair lifts, one of them the last single-chair in Vermont. Snow-making is limited to 15 percent of the slope surfaces. Only a quarter of the trails are for beginners or novice-intermediates; fully one-third are rated expert. Mad River Glen's partisans are loyal, and for all the area's challenge it remains family-oriented: Day care starts at three weeks, and lessons are available for ages four and up.

For general information at Mad River Glen, Tel: (802) 496-3551; for snow conditions, Tel: (802) 496-2001 or (800) 696-2001.

Staying and Dining in the Sugarbush–Mad River Glen Area

The Sugarbush–Mad River Glen region is amply served by inns, motels, and restaurants. In fact, given the proximity of the capital district and, just the other side of I-89 to the north, the southern reaches of the Stowe environs, you're never more than a few minutes from comfortable lodgings in this part of Vermont.

For anyone interested in skiing or in taking advantage of Sugarbush's summer activities, the resort's own **Sugarbush Inn** has a location that can't be surpassed; it's adjacent to 25 kilometers (16 miles) of cross-country ski trails and close to the golf course. The inn's own facilities include an indoor pool, tennis courts, and an ice-skating rink. All of these amenities might argue against this establishment's being anything like a country inn in character, but in fact the ambience is as down-home as a 46-room inn can manage, and there are full dining facilities.

Knoll Farm in Waitsfield is more in the family-run, Vermont-country-inn tradition. Set high in the hills with wonderful views and its own small herd of shaggy highland cattle, the inn has four guest rooms (shared baths) and 150 acres of farmland, for about as generous a guest-per-acre ratio as you'll find in the state. Both bed-and-breakfast and MAP (Modified American Plan, i.e., breakfast and dinner included) are available, and the hearty cuisine will keep you in snowshoeing shape.

The **PowderHound**, on Route 100 in Warren, is a reasonably priced establishment offering both inn and condo accommodations. It has its own restaurant and pub, a hot tub, and a Sugarbush shuttle. Another pleasant, low-priced option in the area is the **Grünberg Haus Bed & Breakfast**, 6 miles (10 km) north of Waitsfield village on Route 100 in Duxbury. This Austrian-style chalet has a festive, old-time ski lodge feel to it; there's a bring-your-own pub, a sauna, a grand piano (and owners that play it), and a 100-acre cross-country ski center on the grounds.

The appetites of Sugarbush and Mad River Glen skiers seem to have inspired as eclectic an assortment of restaurants as any region of Vermont can boast. A longtime favorite is the **Common Man** on German Flats Road in Warren, 6 miles (10 km) south of Waitsfield on Route 100. The restaurant, which occupies a sumptuously restored 1860s barn, offers a decidedly uncommon bill of fare: gravlax, rabbit sausage, pan-roasted tuna with an orange-ginger glaze, and that cold-weather favorite, cassoulet. Breads are baked on the premises, and the wine list is superb. Tel: (802) 583-2800.

Also in Warren, up at the top of the Sugarbush access road, the glassy, greenery-filled **Sam Rupert's** dips liberally into the world's cuisines, its ever-changing menu featuring such items as Thai seared scallops, a Basque confit of duck, and fettucine with sun-dried tomatoes and cilantro. Save room even if you dine elsewhere and head for Sam Rupert's lounge for Vermont's most sumptuous desserts. Tel: (802) 583-2421.

The **House of the Two Moons**, right in Sugarbush Village, is high concept at slopeside: a Chinese-Italian eatery. Downstairs, Bella Luna serves up pasta and pizza in a trattoria atmosphere (Tel: 802/583-2001); upstairs, the China Moon does regional Chinese in a, well, Asian trattoria atmosphere. Tel: (802) 583-6666.

Just outside of Waitsfield village on Route 17, **Tucker Hill Lodge** combines a quietly elegant dining room and down-home café. Upstairs, handmade salmon tortellini and pâtés of Vermont-raised pork and veal are the sort of fare you might find; on Monday through Wednesday in the café the star is something called "American flatbread," a Yankee *focaccia* cooked in a stone oven and served with toppings ranging from pheasant to local mozzarella. Tel: (802) 496-3983.

Four miles (6½ km) north of Waitsfield, Route 100 forks into 100 (left) and 100B (right). Follow 100 if you are heading directly toward the Stowe area (which we cover below in The Waterbury Area), or toward I-89 west to Burlington (see the Champlain Valley section, above); take 100B if your destination is the Montpelier–Barre area (covered below following The Woodstock Area).

THE WOODSTOCK AREA

From Rutland, if you continue east on Route 4 past Killington instead of turning north on Route 100 as we've just done, it's a 6-mile (10-km) drive (past the lower terminal of the Killington gondola) to West Bridgewater, where Route 100 forks off to the south. Bear left to stay on Route 4, following the valley of the Ottauquechee River for 14 miles (22 km) to Woodstock. (From Bridgewater Corners, 6 miles/10 km east of Route 100, it's a 6-mile drive south on Route 100A to the Calvin Coolidge birthplace at Plymouth Notch; see Southern Vermont, above.)

As one look at the fast-flowing Ottauquechee will suggest, the Bridgewaters—West Bridgewater, Bridgewater Corners, and Bridgewater—used to be mill towns. Woodenware and woollens were the big items. At **Bridgewater**, 7 miles (11 km) east of the Route 4–100 fork at West Bridgewater, the woollen mills of Vermont Native Industries held on until the early 1970s; today the sprawling riverside factory buildings have been renovated into the **Marketplace at Bridgewater Mills**, a complex of off-price name-brand clothing outlets. The tradition of Vermont manufacturing has been upheld, however, with several floors of the old structure devoted to locally produced woodenware, clocks, specialty foods, marble products, and other items.

Woodstock

Six miles (10 km) east of Bridgewater stands the archetypal Vermont resort town and the state's original skiing destination, Woodstock. No doubt the area's original attraction to "flatlanders" (as outsiders are known to native Vermonters) was its proximity to the Dartmouth College community in and around nearby Hanover, New Hampshire; another plus was the fact that train connections, problematic for many small Vermont towns even during the heyday of rail travel, were available only 15 miles away at White River Junction. But for whatever reason, this is where skiing first made its inroads into Vermont, and where, as we have seen, the first mechanical lift was installed in 1934.

All this history notwithstanding, big-time downhill skiing has passed Woodstock by in favor of the high Green Mountain destinations of Stratton, Killington, Sugarbush, and Stowe. What remains is that much-loved, technically demanding artifact, **Suicide Six**, located 3 miles (5 km) north of town via Route 12 in **Pomfret**. Suicide Six has grown to encompass all of 19 trails now, served by two chair lifts and a surface tow, but 80 percent of its runs are still expert or advanced-intermediate. Still, you shouldn't be put off by the name, a macho souvenir of the early days of downhill skiing. There is enough beginner terrain at the area's lower elevations to make this a family resort, a prospect that is all the more attractive when you consider Suicide Six's affiliation with the Woodstock Inn and the ski package plans the inn offers (see below). For general information at Suicide Six, Tel: (802) 457-1666; for snow conditions, Tel: (802) 457-1622.

Skiing aside, Woodstock has long since become a destination in itself. The town center clusters around the eastern end of a long, manicured green, which is descended from land held in common since Woodstock was first settled in the 1760s; along the green, Federal and Greek Revival domestic architecture predominates, while the more densely built downtown is a cluster of red-brick commercial structures of the 1870s and 1880s that always make a cheerful backdrop for wreaths and snowdrifts.

Downtown (the area is only about four blocks square) runs heavily toward upscale shops featuring such items as designer ski and casual wear, antiques, and Vermont arts and crafts; for the last, visit **Gallery 2** at 43 Central Street. It's always pleasant, by the way, to time your downtown Woodstock peregrinations to coincide with a lunch, dinner, or ice-cream-sundae stop at **Bentley's**, at 3 Elm Street, corner of Central. The decor is in the jolly Victorian-clutter vein and the steaks and burgers are satisfying—as is Sunday brunch, accompanied in winter by live jazz. Tel: (802) 457-3232.

Billings Farm & Museum

Less than a mile north of the town center, on Route 12, the Billings Farm & Museum offers a delightfully comprehensive firsthand look at Vermont agriculture in the age of hand- and horsepower. This was the working farm of Frederick Billings, president of the Northern Pacific Railroad in the 1870s and 1880s and donor of the University of Vermont's Billings Library (see the Champlain Valley section, above). Billings, who was influenced by America's first great conservationist, Woodstock-born George Perkins Marsh (1801–1882), maintained a keen interest in sound farming practices. Today Billings's rich pastures and circa-1890 farm buildings are kept in working order; visitors can observe the milking of Jersey cows, watch butter being made in the creamery, and see draft horses at work. There are exhibits of 19th-century farm implements and home crafts, and even a herd of sheep. The farm and museum are open daily May through October; hours are limited during winter. For information, Tel: (802) 457-2355.

Directly adjacent to the Billings Farm is a lovely 500-plus-acre tract of meadow and forest that is destined to become Vermont's first national park. Currently owned by Laurence Rockefeller, who is married to Frederick Billings's granddaughter, the property has been bequeathed by the Rockefellers for this purpose. The U.S. Interior Department is in the process of making final arrangements for the transfer, which will allow the present owners life tenancy in their home.

STAYING AND DINING IN WOODSTOCK

Another Rockefeller property, the 146-room **Woodstock Inn**, is the current incarnation of a 200-year-old tradition of innkeeping on Woodstock's town green. One of the inn's main attractions is skiing; as the parent resort of both Suicide Six and the **Woodstock Ski Touring Center** (on Route 106, just south of town; Tel: 802/457-2114), the inn offers guests free weekday use of both facilities. Many a nonskier, however, visits this quietly elegant hostelry for its spacious guest rooms (some with fireplaces), tennis, squash, and racquetball courts, 18-hole Robert Trent Jones golf course, and indoor and outdoor pools. The inn has three restaurants ranging from a Colonial tavern to a gracious dining room specializing in a New American treatment of Vermont game.

For pampering on a scale no less lavish but far more

intimate, the eight-room **Village Inn,** on Pleasant Street (Route 4), makes a good choice in Woodstock. Located in a restored Victorian mansion, the inn offers hearty Italian and New England cuisine prepared by the owner-chef. Directly across the street from the Village Inn is Woodstock's best budget bet, the **Shire Motel,** with refrigerators in every room and all of Woodstock within walking distance.

If you aren't dining at your inn, the big night out in Woodstock might best be celebrated at **The Prince & the Pauper,** at 24 Elm Street, where the standout dish is a wonderful boneless rack of lamb in *mille-feuille* pastry with spinach and *duxelles,* finely chopped mushrooms cooked in red wine. The restaurant also has a cozy wine bar with a simpler bistro menu. Tel: (802) 457-1818.

North to Montpelier and Barre

The quickest way to get from Woodstock to the Barre–Montpelier region is to take Route 4 for 11 miles (18 km) east to I-89 and head north. (Even if you aren't taking the interstate, you might want to take a side trip along this route as far as the dramatically narrow and deep **Quechee Gorge,** described in the Connecticut River Valley section of this chapter, below.) But by far the most scenic way to meander up to the capital district is to follow Route 12, which heads north out of Woodstock past the abovementioned Billings Farm and Museum.

Ten miles (16 km) north of Woodstock is the village of **Barnard,** home during the 1930s to Sinclair Lewis and journalist Dorothy Thompson, who were married at the time. A local winter attraction, located near the old Lewis property, is the tiny **Sonnenberg** ski area, with all of 12 trails and two surface lifts; the runs are short, but so are the lines. Tel: (802) 234-9874.

Bethel, located 8 miles (13 km) north of Barnard at the confluence of two branches of the White River, is one of those isolated Vermont towns that make you wonder, at first glance, why it's there. The answer is the river, and the railroad that later followed its valley. Bethel was the first town chartered (1778) by the self-proclaimed Republic of Vermont; later it was a granite-cutting center, until the local quarries were closed in 1925.

At Bethel turn right (east) onto Route 107 if you're headed for the **Tunbridge World's Fair** (take Route 107 to Route 14, then turn north on Route 110 at South Royalton for 2 miles/3 km), which since the mid-19th century has been the tiny village of Tunbridge's bid for international renown. Despite the grandiloquent name, the fair is actually an old-fashioned agricultural and home-arts fair, held each year for three days in the middle of September. For information, Tel: (802) 889-5555. One mile (1½ km) past the Route 110 turnoff, in the town of South Royalton on Route 14, a road on the left leads to the **Joseph Smith Monument**, a granite obelisk placed here by the Church of Jesus Christ of Latter-Day Saints to mark the birthplace of Mormonism's founder, Joseph Smith.

Back on Route 12: Continuing directly north toward Montpelier, Route 12 reaches **Randolph** (8 miles/13 km north of Bethel), central Vermont's principal town on the eastern flank of the Green Mountains. Prior to the selection of Montpelier as state capital in 1805, Randolph's position at Vermont's geographical center made it the other leading contender for the honor; instead, its economy and prestige developed around its location on the Central Vermont Railway. Like many early Vermont communities, Randolph actually witnessed a migration of its main population center— from Randolph Center (the would-be capital site) to the present-day Randolph, at the juncture of Routes 12, 12A, and 66. The latter community has more of a late-19th-century cast about it; for the architectural flavor of the agrarian beginnings of that century, head 4 miles (6½ km) east to **Randolph Center**.

Along the way, if you're looking for lodgings, consider the **Three Stallion Inn**, a big Victorian farmhouse tucked into the 1,300 acres of the Green Mountain Stock Farm. To be sure, there are other inns around here with comfortable, antiques-furnished rooms, chummy little taverns, and decent restaurants; the Three Stallion, however, offers a superb 50-kilometer (30-mile) network of cross-country ski trails, as well as tennis courts and 18 holes of golf. The ski trails are open to the public; for information, Tel: (802) 728-5575.

Hugging the foothills of the Green Mountains, Route 12 continues north out of Randolph past the straggling and completely ungentrified villages of Snowsville and East Braintree into the narrow defile of Brookfield Gulf. To experience an authentic local curiosity, 10 miles (16 km) north of Randolph, turn right onto Route 65, drive east past **Allis State Park** (picnic and tent sites, but no swimming or boating), and cross the I-89 overpass to reach Brookfield's **Floating Bridge**. The bridge, which makes a beeline across Sunset Lake barely a mile east of the interstate, really does float. It was first built on pontoons, the water being too deep for pilings, about 1812; reconstructed every few decades, it now rests on Styrofoam. Cross the bridge (it's closed in winter) and for once you won't be able to blame your car's shock absorbers for the "boaty" feeling as you drive.

Float back over to Route 12 and continue north; in 5 miles (8 km) you'll come to **Northfield** and its **Norwich University**, America's oldest—and only—private military college. Founded in 1819, Norwich (not to be confused with the Connecticut River Valley *town* of Norwich, Vermont, from which it moved in 1867), is in Northfield's town center. Depending on the season, it may be possible to observe cadet parades or other ceremonies. For information on events, as well as tours of the campus and its military collections, Tel: (802) 485-2000.

MONTPELIER

Like most roads in this part of the state, Route 12 leads directly into Montpelier, 11 miles (18 km) north of Northfield. With few more than 8,000 souls, Montpelier is the smallest state capital in the nation. It couldn't have grown much larger if it had wanted to, given its location: The city is shoehorned in along the Winooski River (which backed up behind an ice dam in the spring of 1992, flooding most of downtown) and surrounded by steep hills. From just about any avenue of approach, it's easy to see what Montpelier is all about. The massive golden dome of the State House rises above the west end of State Street, with all the brick and granite of the tiny city center seeming to cluster about its base.

For all its size and grandeur, relative to its location, Vermont's **State House** still has a simplicity about it befitting its original role as the seat of an agrarian democracy. Designed by the Greek Revival master Ammi B. Young (his work includes the original part of Boston's Custom House), the State House was built in 1836 of Barre granite. The rather severe portico is Doric, modeled on the Temple of Theseus in Athens. The dome, which is completely covered in gold leaf, is topped by Larkin Mead's statue of Ceres, the Roman goddess of agriculture—a logical choice in the 1830s, though if the capitol were to be constructed today the goddess of tourism might be more appropriate.

Inside, things get a little more ornate, as a fire necessitated an interior rebuilding in the Early Victorian style of 1859, but the feeling is still far more republican than imperial. In fact, those people you see in the hallways conversing on chairs and sofas are probably legislators and their constituents; Vermont state senators and representatives do not have private offices (Vermont politicians can run, but it's hard for them to hide from their employers). Visitors may walk through the public areas of the State House during business hours, viewing Vermont's collection of Civil War flags and portraits of famous citizens, but for a look at legislative chambers and an informed interpretation of the building, free tours are offered from July through mid-October. Tel: (802) 828-2228 for schedules.

Next door to the State House, at 109 State Street, is a big, mansard-roofed brick building that looks like a High Victorian relic and at the same time appears suspiciously new. It is both. The original **Pavilion Building** was built about 1808 as a hotel, then rebuilt in its present style in 1876. Long the haunt of legislators whose districts were too far from Montpelier to allow them to go home at night, the badly deteriorating Pavilion was demolished in the early 1970s and replaced with the near-exact replica that you see today.

Rather than serving as a hotel, however, the modern structure houses state offices and the museum of the **Vermont Historical Society**. The museum is a rich trove of Vermontiana, encompassing more than 200 years of the state's history in its collections of furniture, agricultural and craftspeople's tools, paintings, toys, costumes, and ephemera. Open afternoons, except Sundays and Mondays. The books, maps, and manuscripts of the adjacent **Historical Society Library** constitute Vermont's finest local history resource and are frequently in demand by the many visitors who claim descent from the Green Mountains' hardy crop of emigrants. Tel: (802) 828-2291.

A six-block walk down State and East State streets from the State House to College Street will take you through the business center of Montpelier, with its shops, cafés, and bookstores, to the city's other principal downtown attraction: the **T. W. Wood Art Gallery** (College Street, on the Vermont College campus; Tel: 802/828-8743), a century-old facility that effectively represents historical as well as contemporary Vermont fine arts. Nineteenth-century portraits and landscape paintings—many of them the work of the museum's founder, Montpelier-born artist Thomas Waterman Wood—reveal the character and environment of the Yankee fastness that was once rural Vermont, and a contemporary gallery reflects the modern diversity of the state's painters and sculptors. Another worthwhile stop in downtown Montpelier is **Bear Pond Books**, now located at 77 Main Street after the disastrous flood of spring 1992 washed out their old location. This is one of northern Vermont's best bookstores, with two floors of titles and particularly strong women's and children's sections.

STAYING AND DINING
IN MONTPELIER

Unfortunately, lodging places are not part of the immediate downtown Montpelier mix; the Days Inn across the street from the State House closed in 1992, and reopening plans, under Days or another name, have not yet been made final. Best bet for staying *almost* in central Montpelier is the **Inn at Montpelier**, located on Main Street, just beyond the business district, in a pair of charming old Federal-style homes that date to the city's earliest days as state capital. Many of the rooms have fireplaces, and, unusual for a small inn, all have televisions and phones. The dining room serves Continental breakfast and full dinners; weather permitting, dinner here really ought to be preceded by a drink on the main building's spacious wraparound porch.

A less elaborate, and less expensive, alternative is **Montpelier Bed & Breakfast** on North Street, a ten-minute walk from downtown. Located in two handsome late-19th-century structures, this B and B offers six rooms with shared bath, and a suite with kitchen and private bath.

Thanks to the presence of a cooking school, the New England Culinary Institute, Montpelier has more good places to eat than most towns its size. The institute's Montpelier showplace is **Tubbs**, tucked into the city's original jailhouse at 24 Elm Street. The atmosphere has been cheered up considerably, and the menu aims high and succeeds: Try the escargots with hazelnuts and Cognac in *mille-feuille* pastry, or the ragout of scallops, leeks, and shiitake mushrooms. Tel: (802) 229-9202.

The institute staff and students also demonstrate their skills at two more casual establishments, the **Elm Street Café** (38 Elm Street; Tel: 802/223-3188) and **La Brioche Bakery & Café** (89 Main Street; Tel: 802/229-0443). At Elm Street the fare runs from "new" (i.e., lighter) New England cookery to Italian, Mexican, and Cajun; at the bakery light meals are complemented by an assortment of terrific breads, pastries, and desserts, as light or as rich as you please. This is a prime stop if you're assembling the ingredients for an elegant picnic.

If you're doing your picnicking indoors, try the lunch or dinner buffet at the **House of Tang**, at 114 River Street. Dinner is the better value, although the chicken wings at lunch are first-rate. Tel: (802) 223-6020.

Barre

The city of Barre, 6 miles (10 km) southeast of Montpelier via Routes 2 and 302, has one thing in common with the capital: Both are company towns. In Montpelier, of course, the business is government; in Barre it's the quarrying and processing of granite.

Barre is built on a vein of granite, four by six miles in area and ten miles deep, formed 335 million years ago. For the past century and a half Barre's stonecutters have hewn granite for monuments, construction, and industry, and today the city's **Rock of Ages** quarries are the world's largest supplier of the durable gray stone. Rock of Ages' quarry tours (off Route 14 south of Barre, open June 1 to mid-October; Tel: 802/476-3115) offer a twist on conventional Green Mountain sightseeing. Here you can look deep into the heart of the hills, where workers niched into the sheer 475-foot walls of the site's E. L. Smith quarry to separate 25-ton blocks from the living rock with 4,200° F "jet torches" and low-velocity explosives.

As a supplement to the shuttle-bus tours of the quarrying operation, visitors are invited to view the finishing of monument-grade granite at the **Rock of Ages Craftsman Center**, located 1 mile (1½ km) from the tour center. Below the elevated walkway at one end of the hangar-size structure, artisans polish huge slabs of granite, which are cut and fashioned into memorial stones, architectural details, and even statuary. On occasion sculptors can be seen working the dense-grained masses of granite with pneumatic chisels and finishing tools.

The Rock of Ages tour is but an introduction to a city infused with the spirit of craftsmanship in granite. Downtown, at the intersection of North Main Street and Maple Avenue, stands Barre's monument to its Italian stonecutters, a granite statue of a mustachioed man in a cap and leather apron, a stout hammer in one hand. And 1 mile (1½ km) north of the city on Route 14, **Hope Cemetery** constitutes a grand display of what the carvers of Barre have done to memorialize one another and their fellow citizens. Don't miss the granite armchair, the granite soccer ball, and the poignant 1903 memorial to carver and labor leader Elia Corti.

THE WATERBURY AREA

From the Barre–Montpelier area take I-89 north and west to Waterbury, where you can either continue west toward Burlington and the Champlain Valley or turn north onto Route 100 for the 10-mile (16-km) drive to Stowe. (The **Bolton Valley** ski resort, a 43-trail, six-lift facility with ample on-site lodging and summer activities that make it a popular family

destination, is located 10 miles/16 km west of Waterbury off
Route 2. For general information at Bolton Valley, including
snow conditions and summer activities, Tel: 802/434-2131 or
800/451-3220.)

Waterbury

Once known primarily as a stopover between Burlington
and Montpelier and as the site of a state hospital, Waterbury
has come into its own of late as a mecca for ice cream fans.
"There is no emperor but the emperor of ice cream," wrote
Wallace Stevens, but in Vermont there are two, and their
names are Ben and Jerry. Ben Cohen and Jerry Greenfield
started selling their homemade ice cream out of a converted
gas station in Burlington in 1977. Building their reputation
on the richness, density, and remarkable textures of their
products (items like nut crunch and chocolate are added not
as minute particles but as massive chunks), Ben and Jerry
also built a mountain of corporate goodwill out of socially
responsible business practices and bountiful donations to
local and global causes.

The old gas station is gone, and in its place is a $100-
million-a-year ice cream giant still led by two guys out to
maximize employee benefits, save the rain forest, and beat
swords into plowshares. Meanwhile, they offer tours of **Ben
and Jerry's** flagship plant in Waterbury (Route 100, 1 mile/
1½ km north of I-89). Visitors can watch the ice cream–
making process from raw materials to finished pints, peek
into the research room to see what new flavors might be
hatching, and—with appetites whetted by a small free
sample—stop in at the plant's own ice cream parlor. In
summer the lawn outside the factory takes on a carnival
atmosphere, with kids taking turns milking cows and cranking old-fashioned ice cream freezers. For tour information,
Tel: (802) 244-TOUR.

Up the road (still Route 100) 2 miles (3 km) from where
Ben and Jerry turn Vermont milk into ice cream, the people
at **Cold Hollow Cider Mill** are busy year-round turning
Vermont apples into a nectar that makes plain apple juice
seem anemic. Two centuries ago cider was a more universal
beverage than water or beer in frontier Vermont; the state
has always been good apple-growing country, and virtually
every farmstead used to have a few trees. Although its
product isn't sold "hard," as was the preference among early
Vermonters (among other qualities, hard cider keeps longer), Cold Hollow still makes cider the old-fashioned way,
crushing and pressing ripe apples. Visitors can watch the
process, abetted now by a big hydraulic press but still

involving wooden racks and cloth strainers, and enjoy a sample of the finished product. In its complex of buildings on Route 100, next to Waterbury Community Church, Cold Hollow also offers retail sales of apple products, baked goods, and other Vermont specialty foods, displays on apple husbandry and maple sugaring, and a cider and coffee bar. Tel: (802) 244-8771.

The Green Mountain Club

About a mile (1½ km) past Cold Hollow, on the opposite (left) side of the road, you'll notice the headquarters of the Green Mountain Club, the organization that supervises maintenance of the **Long Trail**, Vermont's "Footpath in the Wilderness." The trail, which extends for roughly 260 miles along the length of Vermont between the state's borders with Massachusetts and Quebec, was completed in 1928. South of Sherburne Pass, in central Vermont, its route is the same as that of the Maine-to-Georgia Appalachian Trail, but at that point it branches off and follows its own path north. Designed to crest as many as possible of the peaks of the Green Mountain range, the trail can be rough going, but the mountain views and forest solitude it affords are well worth a hiker's effort. Overnight accommodations—lean-tos, huts, and cabins, a few with wood stoves—are provided at intervals. Visitors can drop in at the club's Waterbury headquarters to learn more about the trail; for anyone planning a hike, the organization's *Guidebook to the Long Trail* cannot be too highly recommended. For information on the Long Trail, call the Green Mountain Club at (802) 244-7037.

Stowe

And so to Stowe, 10 miles (16 km) north of Waterbury on Route 100. Killington may claim the most trails, Woodstock the first mechanical tow, but Stowe has long had the cachet of being *the* Vermont ski resort. The town, of course, dates way back to the days when no one went out in the snow except to get to the barn or other necessary outbuildings; it was chartered in 1763 and spent its first century as little more than a hill town in the shadow of Mount Mansfield, distinguished mainly by the white, rapier-like spire of its **Community Church**.

Stowe's first measure of future resort fame came in 1859, with the building of the Summit House hotel near the top of Mount Mansfield. (The hotel survived for exactly a hundred summer seasons, closing in 1958.) The area's winter popularity took a little longer to develop. Swedish immigrant families introduced the town to Nordic skiing, then more a form of transportation than a sport, around 1912; in 1914 a Dartmouth librarian named Nathaniel Goodrich made the first recorded ski descent of Mount Mansfield. Ski jumping was a feature of winter carnivals held during the 1920s, and the downhill sport debuted in earnest when a Civilian Conservation Corps crew cut Mount Mansfield's first official ski trails in 1933 and 1934. These first tentative steps of the 1930s culminated in the organization of the Mt. Mansfield Corporation, which by 1940 had installed, on leased state land, the nation's longest and highest chair lift. The company had also set a standard for serious skiing at the resort by hiring Sepp Ruschp, an Austrian champion who served first as the ski school director, and eventually as the firm's president. Ruschp, who died in 1990, was perhaps more responsible than any other individual for putting Stowe on the ski map.

Considering Stowe's renown as a resort destination—one that is again nearly as popular in summer as in winter—you would think that the town would have a bit more substance and texture to it than first meets the eye. The actual village is a tiny affair, no more than a few blocks along Main Street and a few side lanes; this compact town center bustles with shops and restaurants, but Zermatt or Aspen it isn't. Much of the vacationer's Stowe stretches out along Route 108, the **Mountain Road**, north and west of town. This is the road that leads to the Stowe Mountain Resort, the Mt. Mansfield Corporation's two-mountain ski resort; to the turnoff for the Trapp Family Lodge and its magnificent cross-country trail network; and to most of the lodging establishments and restaurants that cater to ski, summer, and foliage season visitors. (During the months when there is no snow cover, roughly May 1 to mid-November, the Mountain Road is open for travel all the way through Smugglers' Notch and into Jeffersonville, as we'll note later.)

Bicycles are as desirable as skis in Stowe, thanks to the town's 5½-mile paved recreation path, which roughly follows the Mountain Road along the West Branch of the Waterbury River. The path, which is off-limits to motorized vehicles, is popular with cyclists, Rollerbladers, and cross-country skiers. For ski rentals, try the **Mountain Bike Shop**, on the Mountain Road; Tel: 802/253-7919.

STAYING AND DINING IN STOWE

Given the small size of Stowe village, there is an uneven distribution of places to stay between the village and the six-mile, year-round segment of the Mountain Road leading toward Mount Mansfield and the Stowe/Spruce Peak ski area. In town, the best option is the **Green Mountain Inn**, a 54-room establishment (several are suites) that dates to 1833 and is listed on the National Register of Historic Places. Accommodations are furnished with country antiques, and the inn offers both formal and informal dining rooms. Despite the busy Main Street location, there is an outdoor pool tucked in back.

There's more room along the Mountain Road between the town and the ski area, and along with an abundance of motels and small inns there are several full-service resorts. The **Inn at the Mountain**, affiliated with the ski area, is a luxurious property convenient to the slopes, with accommodations ranging from hotel rooms to town houses and detached lodges. Guests enjoy privileges at **Stowe Country Club**, with its 18-hole golf course, along with the resort's own tennis courts and outdoor pool. (The Stowe Country Club golf course is open to the public; for information, Tel: 802/253-4893.)

Another place to stay on the Mountain Road is the **Topnotch Resort & Spa**, where accommodations are also divided between modern inn rooms and town houses. The Topnotch is big on recreation, offering indoor and outdoor pools, indoor and outdoor tennis, cross-country ski trails, and a full health spa. To help counterbalance all this exercise, the resort's restaurants offer a classically simple, splendidly executed menu, running to such dishes as venison medallions, grilled Norwegian salmon, and rack of Vermont lamb.

No mention of resorts with cross-country ski facilities is complete without reference to the venerable **Trapp Family Lodge**, the establishment created by the late Baroness Maria von Trapp and her large family after their escape from Nazi-controlled Austria and emigration to the United States. *The Sound of Music* is the baroness's Hollywood monument, but this is her tangible legacy: 2,000 acres of meadows, mountains, and magnificent views, centered upon a luxurious 93-room lodge and laced with 80 kilometers (50 miles) of cross-country ski trails. Lessons and equipment are available, as are an indoor pool, sauna, and whirlpool for day's end. The main dining room mixes mainstream Continental with more robust *mitteleuropean* dishes (smoked pork chops; Wienerschnitzel with lingonberries), and the Austrian Tea Room, located in a separate chalet, blends mountain scenery, tasty wursts, Austrian wines, and rich *torten* into an experience that Rodgers and Hammerstein couldn't have improved upon.

Among less elaborate establishments, the **Stowe Motel** is a long-standing favorite. Located on the Mountain Road just 2 miles (3 km) out of town, the motel features efficiency units, two-room family suites, chalet accommodations, and even a few units with fireplaces—a rare commodity in a motel. An outdoor pool, tennis court, and free use of bicycles make this an attractive budget summer destination.

Stowe dining runs the gamut from stick-to-your-ribs après-ski fare to some of Vermont's most ambitious cuisine. Two ethnic standbys are **Miguel's Stowe Away** (3148 Mountain Road; Tel: 802/253-7574), home of a locally popular brand of salsa and a full menu of Mexican favorites; and the **China Garden** (Mountain Road; Tel: 802/253-7191), a Szechwan-Hunan establishment where you should preface whatever you choose with cold noodles in sesame sauce.

On the Anglo-Saxon front, try **Mr. Pickwick's Pub** (on the Mountain Road in Ye Olde England Inn; Tel: 802/253-7064), whose fish and chips and savory pies go down nicely to a fine selection of bottled and draft English ales. In Stowe village, skiing's "official" cuisine holds forth at the **Swisspot** (at the corner of Main and School streets; Tel: 802/253-4622). There's fondue, of course, as well as imported Swiss air-dried beef, rich quiches, steak béarnaise, and a raft of Swissed-up burgers.

Quirky spelling aside, **Isle de France** (Mountain Road; Tel: 802/253-7751) often answers the question of where to go for the big night out in Stowe. The classic French repertoire—escargots bourguignon, sole meunière, frogs' legs, and at least a half-dozen sophisticated steak presentations—are executed here with a refreshing absence of gimmickry, and are matched by serenely formal decor in a series of intimate dining rooms.

You'll have to head 6 miles (10 km) back down Route 100 to Waterbury Center (4 miles/6½ km north of Waterbury) for the area's best Italian food at **Villa Tragara** (Tel: 802/244-5288). Pastas and seafood are first-rate, but the star of the menu is a filet mignon pocketed with pancetta and Fontina cheese, finished in a Barolo demi-glacé.

SKIING IN THE STOWE AREA

Skiing at the **Stowe Mountain Resort** means **Mount Mansfield and Spruce Peak**, the big mountain's neighboring hill across the Mountain Road. Forty-five trails and ten lifts, including a new eight-passenger gondola that glides nearly all the way to Mansfield's summit in just over six minutes, provide a broad range of challenges for skiers of all levels. Mansfield itself leans heavily toward advanced and intermediate runs; this is home to the National and the Nosedive, two of American skiing's legendary expert trails. Still, the toll road—open in summer as an auto route to the sub-summit "nose" of Mansfield—offers a gentle route to the base.

Spruce Peak, with five chair lifts of its own, offers nothing but intermediate and beginner runs. (In summer, one of Spruce's lifts serves an alpine slide, with rider-controlled sleds barreling down a looping concrete trough.) In the Sepp Ruschp tradition, instruction programs are extensive, starting at age three and extending through all levels of adult competence. Day care starts at one year.

For general information at Stowe (Mount Mansfield and Spruce Peak), Tel: (802) 253-7311 or (800) 247-8693; for snow conditions, Tel: (800) 637-8693.

There is literally another side to skiing and summer resort activity at Stowe, and it's called **Smugglers' Notch**. Accessible in winter only from the other side of the Mansfield massif via Route 108 from Jeffersonville (from Stowe, take Route 100 north 9 miles/14½ km to Morrisville, then Route 15 west 17 miles/27 km to Jeffersonville), Smugglers' is a self-contained, year-round resort that has built considerable loyalty among a family clientele. Ski trails at Smugglers' fan out over three mountains—Madonna, Sterling, and Morse—with a total of 56 runs and four double-chair lifts plus a rope tow. Except for Morse, which tends primarily toward beginner runs, Smugglers' is largely advanced and intermediate territory. Why the family cachet? Smugglers' has two separate kids' programs, for ages three to six and seven to 12 (day care starts at six weeks); there are also 37 kilometers (23 miles) of cross-country trails and an ice-skating rink.

If anything, things get even livelier at this resort in summer, with a water-slide park and miniature golf in addition to tennis, a pool, and mountain biking. It's all part of the **Smugglers' Notch Resort**, parent organization not only of the ski area but of the Village at Smugglers' Notch, a vacation community with condo-style accommodations, all of the above recreational facilities and more, two restaurants, and a child-care center. (See also Jeffersonville, below, for more lodging options.)

For general information at Smugglers' Notch, including snow conditions and summer activities, Tel: (802) 644-8851 or (800) 451-8752.

SMUGGLERS' NOTCH STATE PARK

Smugglers' Notch is, of course, not only the name of a resort but of a natural feature, the deep gorge through which Route 108 winds its way and which can be navigated by car during the six or seven months of each year when there is no snow cover (plowing this steep succession of hairpin turns would be extremely difficult and expensive). As you drive northwest toward the notch, eventually leaving behind the commercial stretch of the Mountain Road and entering Smugglers' Notch State Park and Mount Mansfield State Forest, the whole majestic east face of **Mount Mansfield** rises on your left. From here, as from the Champlain Valley side, the features of the long summit ridge stand out clearly: forehead, nose, and finally the 4,393-foot-high chin. The nomenclature belongs to the 19th century; difficult as it may sometimes be to puzzle out the contours of a reclining man's face on Mansfield, at least the resemblance is clearer than that suggested by the older Abenaki Indian name, "Mountain with a Head Like a Moose." If you have the time and stamina, you'll find that the Long Trail runs along the length of the profile (see the reference to the Green Mountain Club, above), and can be accessed by a network of side trails on both the Underhill (west) and Smugglers' Notch sides of the mountain, as well as by the automobile toll road.

As for the name "Smugglers' Notch," the story is that the footpath through this defile separating Mansfield from Spruce Peak was used by smugglers defying the ban on commerce between the United States and Canada during the War of 1812. No one has ever conclusively established the truth of these tales, but the dark rocky fastnesses on either side of the pass argue that at least there should have been smugglers lurking around here. To examine this grand and melancholy mountainscape more closely, though, pull off into the parking area at the crest of the notch. Whatever you do, keep your eyes on this road when driving: At places it's barely wide enough for one car, let alone two, and the grades and curves can be harrowing to the uninitiated. There is nowhere you can fall off, though—mountains rise on both sides.

BEYOND SMUGGLERS' NOTCH

After cresting the notch Route 108 descends along a long grade, past the Smugglers' Notch Resort, north into Jeffersonville. **Jeffersonville** is a quiet residential community, little more than two main streets and some commercial frontage along Route 15, but it does offer a couple of dining and lodging choices for travellers who aren't opting for the big resort up at Smugglers' Notch.

The **Highlander Motel**, just outside of town on the Notch Road (Route 108), has an outdoor pool and a fine location in a broad meadow with mountain views. In town, the rambling old **Smugglers' Notch Inn**, partly built in the late 1700s and a hostelry since 1864, has serviceable, if small, rooms and a restaurant with a standard New England menu. The **Windridge Inn** is tiny, but its handful of pretty guest rooms is not what draws a clientele from as far afield as Montreal, New York, and beyond: The Windridge houses **Le Cheval**

d'Or, one of northern Vermont's finest restaurants. Menus at Le Cheval are strictly seasonal and unpredictable, save to say that the chef-owner has found the meeting place of French provincial and New American and made it his own. He's also come up with the single most interesting dessert in New England, a maple soufflé tucked in a crêpe with a spot of ice cream. The Windridge is also open for hearty breakfasts and lunches of straight, old-fashioned New England fare. From spring through fall those meals are served next door to the inn, in an old bakery that turns out the restaurant's breads, muffins, and pies. Tel: (802) 644-5556.

As noted earlier, Route 108 through Smugglers' Notch is a driving option only from late spring through mid-autumn. When snow lies deep in the notch, your route north will take you 9 miles (14½ km) up Route 100 from Stowe to **Morrisville**, the area's chief trading center. Morrisville is a no-frills, workaday town, where you can stock up on travel necessities at the shopping plaza or on lunch at the **Charlmont** restaurant's buffet (junction of Routes 15 and 100). The Charlmont also has weekend dinner buffets, as well as a regular breakfast-through-late-night menu and a lounge with weekend entertainment (Tel: 802/888-4242). Five miles (8 km) east of Morrisville, on Route 12, Lake Elmore at **Elmore State Park** is a fine, scenic spot for a swim.

Jeffersonville is 16 miles (26 km) west of Morrisville on Route 15. Along the way you'll pass through **Johnson**, home of a **Ben and Jerry's** ice cream parlor (serving seconds, but their seconds are better than most companies' firsts) and the **Johnson Woolen Mills** (Main Street), where generations of Vermonters have gone to suit up for winter's worst. In addition to name brands, Johnson sells its own make of heavy woollen trousers, overalls, vests, and jackets, which stand up to the elements as well as to the onslaught of synthetic fibers with a timeless and doughty élan.

To Jay Peak and the Border

At Johnson you can continue on to Jeffersonville if you're heading toward the northern Champlain Valley, but to follow the final northern stretch of the Green Mountains take Route 100C back to Route 100, bearing left at Eden, 9 miles (14½ km) north, onto Route 118. For the next 15 miles (24 km), as you follow Route 118 north to Montgomery Center, you'll see a Vermont characterized by a wild, desolate beauty, quite similar in feeling to the Northeast Kingdom (discussed below; to reach the Kingdom via Newport, just stay on Route 100 at Eden instead of turning onto 118). Civilization turns up again at Montgomery Center, the principal gateway to the ski resort of Jay Peak.

The town of **Montgomery**, of which Montgomery Center is one of two settlements, is Vermont's **covered bridge** champion, with seven of the venerable structures, all of them a short distance off Route 118 (you can get directions at the post office or at any of the local businesses). Before heading off on a bridge-bagging trip, though, stop in at **Kilgore's** (Route 118 in the center of town), a five-story, eclectic barn of a country store that builds superb, meal-size sandwiches on a foundation of delicious homemade breads; there's also an antique marble soda fountain and a bookstore. While construction is under way, browse among one of northern Vermont's most interesting wine selections.

For more formal dining in Montgomery, the place is **Zack's on the Rocks**, on Hazen's Notch Road, where "dinner as theater" is the operating concept. Zack, your host, has done his little retreat up in early Addams Family, with more than a touch of Hollywood camp; usually attired in a loud caftan, he choreographs meals around well-executed basics such as rack of lamb and poached salmon with béarnaise sauce, as well as a changing repertoire of more imaginative entrées and rich, satisfying desserts. It's an experience. Tel: (802) 326-4500.

JAY PEAK

Jay Peak, 7 miles (11 km) northeast of Montgomery Center on Route 242, is Vermont's northernmost, snowiest, and—for its size—least crowded ski area. Jay stands isolated from the main Green Mountain range, and seems to serve as a magnet for snow; given the 200-plus inches (sometimes far more) that fall here in a typical year, it's surprising the management bothered to extend snow-making capability to 80 percent of its terrain. There are 43 trails and six lifts, including a 60-passenger tramway, and a good selection of runs for all experience levels; some of the best intermediate slopes are served by the tram. Lessons begin at age five, day-care at two. Expect your tot to pick up a little French; short of the resorts in the Laurentians, Jay has the Northeast's highest concentration of Québecois skiers.

For general information at Jay Peak, including snow conditions and summer activities, Tel: (802) 988-2611 or (800) 451-4449.

It isn't fancy, but by far the best place to stay in the Jay–Montgomery area is the **Hotel Jay**, at slopeside. With a choice of hotel rooms or fully equipped condo units, this property offers a sauna, outdoor pool, and tennis courts, as well as a complimentary tram ride during the summer and, during the ski season, free day and evening child care and supervised separate dining hours for kids. Some of the room rates include lift tickets.

Don't overlook Jay as a summer or foliage season retreat: The mountaintop views are terrific, you can ride a mountain bike from the summit tram station to the base, and the hotel puts on a fine Sunday brunch. First, stand atop Jay Peak for fresh air to whet your appetite. To the north, the great valley of the St. Lawrence spreads before you toward Montreal and Quebec; to the east, on the other side of the vast Northeast Kingdom, Mount Washington rises from New Hampshire's Presidential Range. Lake Champlain glints in the sun 30 miles to the west, while the southern horizon is crowded with the peaks of the Green Mountains.

THE NORTHEAST KINGDOM

"Northeast Kingdom" is the name coined in the 1930s by then-governor George Aiken for the three northeasternmost counties of Vermont—Essex, Caledonia, and Orleans. In a state where a lot of ink is spilled over which places are authentic and which are self-consciously touristy, the Northeast Kingdom goes authentic one better. This is Ur-Vermont: Not only is much of it not cute, much of it is not settled, and never has been.

Consider Essex County. Bordered on the north and east by the Canadian border and the Connecticut River, respectively, Essex is the outer limits of the Kingdom. With a land area of 671 square miles, its population hovers at about 6,000 souls. That works out to roughly one person for every 65 acres of land—but since most of the people in Essex live along the Connecticut River Valley or in the village of Island Pond, much of the county is actually far less densely settled. The town of Lewis, for example, has no known inhabitants, nor any road access.

Although dairy farming survives along the Connecticut River and in the Green Mountain foothills to the west, much of the Northeast Kingdom is heavily forested. It is part of the great swath of conifer and birch that stretches from northern Maine to New York State's Adirondacks, and—like the northern forests in neighboring states—it is largely owned by big paper companies. This large-scale corporate ownership long ensured the survival of vast, unbroken stands of timber, and unimpeded access for outdoorspeople. Of late, though, the paper firms' accounting departments have been changing their ideas about keeping huge inventories of land, and a North Woods sell-off has begun. Over the next decade, preserving the integrity of the forest in places like the Northeast Kingdom promises to loom as one of northern New England's premier environmental issues. Without a regional planning process, activists argue, subdivision and development are inevitable even in this remote corner of Vermont. Someday even Lewis may have people and roads.

Not all of the Northeast Kingdom is a howling wilderness. The terrain is most rugged in the far northeast, where dozens of 2,000- to 3,000-foot peaks brood in jumbled isolation far from the spine of the Green Mountains, and appear to look instead east across the Connecticut River to the high terrain of northern New Hampshire. Farther west, past a lovely skein of deep glacial lakes, the vistas widen over a patchwork of forest and dairyland: From several of the ridges on the back roads between Barton and Craftsbury in Orleans County you can look west across nearly 30 miles and a thousand shades of green (or one shade of white) to the great massif of Mount Mansfield in the Green Mountains. Most of the Northeast Kingdom's people live in its central valleys, between Essex County's hills and the Green Mountain slopes to the west. The populated axis begins at St. Johnsbury, in the south, and extends to Newport, near the Canadian border on the southern shores of Lake Memphremagog.

Most travellers approach the Northeast Kingdom from St. Johnsbury (which is easily accessible via Interstates 91 and 93) or from the west via Routes 2, 15, or 100. St. Johnsbury offers what is really the only urban experience in the region, and at that we are stretching the term. For the most part, visitors are drawn to this corner of Vermont for the downhill skiing at Burke Mountain; for cross-country skiing at Burke and at Craftsbury; for the country inns of the Craftsbury–Greensboro area; and of course for the fun of driving the back roads or hiking remote trails through the wildest parts of the state. Finally, there's the fishing; Lakes Willoughby, Seymour, and Memphremagog, and Great Averill and Little Averill ponds, offer opportunities for deep-water lake trout and landlocked salmon angling that are seldom equalled even in far larger Lake Champlain.

ST. JOHNSBURY

St. Johnsbury prides itself on being the only St. Johnsbury in the world. The name was taken to honor Michel Guillaume

Jean de Crèvecoeur, a French émigré who, under the pseud-
onym J. Hector St. John, wrote *Letters from an American
Farmer,* which offered Europeans an incisive and sympa-
thetic view of rural American life in the late 18th century.
Although de Crèvecoeur never lived anywhere near the
Northeast Kingdom, his friendship with Ethan Allen, his
general popularity, and some lobbying were enough to
persuade the Vermont legislature of the 1780s to use his
nom de plume when naming its new town.

As anyone who travels the highways of the eastern United
States has probably noticed, de Crèvecoeur is probably the
only French author to have a trucking company inadver-
tently named after him—the St. Johnsbury logo covers the
flanks of many a semitrailer. But it wasn't the trucking firm
that put this little city on the map; it was a local inventor
named Thaddeus Fairbanks. In 1830 Fairbanks patented the
first lever-operated platform scale, an alternative to the earlier balance scales. Since then, the history of St. Johnsbury
has been largely that of the Fairbanks (later Fairbanks-
Morse) Company, and the present-day community of 8,000
continues to owe much of its cultural and architectural
legacy to the 19th-century munificence of the Fairbanks
family. Lambert Packard, the family's favorite architect, was
responsible for one-quarter of all the buildings in the central city, including a number of gorgeously ornate Victorian
mansions.

AROUND IN ST. JOHNSBURY

St. Johnsbury is a valley town, built along the banks of the
Passumpsic River, but the railroad is the conduit that has
shaped its growth. The Canadian Pacific and the Maine
Central, along with local carriers, sent Fairbanks scales to the
world, and the city still hugs the tracks. Passenger service is
long gone, but the old depot still stands on Railroad Street,
where facing rows of Victorian brick buildings house most
of the city's businesses. The most interesting of these are
Northern Lights Books, at number 79 (Tel: 802/748-4463),
with a good inventory of regional-interest titles as well as—
odd enough for a bookstore—St. Johnsbury's best selection
of wines, and **Caplan's Army Store**, number 110–114 (Tel:
802/748-3236), where you can outfit yourself with enough
wilderness paraphernalia to enable you to bushwhack into
Lewis and beyond. And although you probably won't be
shopping for feed grains or agricultural odds and ends, it's
worth a walk down Railroad Street to the St. Johnsbury
Memorial Bridge. Here, between the tracks and the river,
stands a Northeast Kingdom institution: the **E. T. & H. K. Ide
Company**. Owned by six generations of the Ide family since

its founding in 1813, the store is a working reminder of an older Vermont. Tel: 802-748-3127.

St. Johnsbury works on two levels. Its commerce is down by the river and the tracks, while its cultural attractions bracket Main Street, parallel to Railroad Street but three steep blocks farther uphill. Here, at the corner of Main and Prospect streets, is the **Fairbanks Museum and Planetarium**, which shows what an up-country Medici might do if he wanted to establish a northern Vermont version of New York's American Museum of Natural History.

Franklin Fairbanks, scion of the scale family, donated the museum's handsome, Richardsonian Romanesque quarters in 1889, and primed its program of acquisition by donating his own enormous collection of mounted wildlife. Stuffed animals—everything from two polar bears to 300 species of hummingbirds—still make up a large part of the Fairbanks displays, but the place is much more than a taxidermist's morgue. There are considerable ethnographic holdings, including Asian, American Indian, and Pacific Island artifacts; a trove of nostalgic Vermontiana; and, of course, an exhibit of scales. There's a lively children's room (open only in July and August), where kids can handle turtles and take apart a life-size model of a human body, and a working weather station. The tiny planetarium offers accurate star projections, but they are marred somewhat by the amateurish narration of student docents. For either the museum or the planetarium, Tel: (802) 748-2372.

Two blocks south of the Fairbanks Museum, at 30 Main Street, stands the **St. Johnsbury Athenaeum and Art Gallery** (closed Sundays). The red-brick, Second Empire Athenaeum, the 1871 gift of yet another Fairbanks—Horace, governor of Vermont from 1876 to 1878—serves as the city's library, but its principal attraction is the art gallery housed in a wing at the rear of the building. The gallery, also a Fairbanks bequest, has been preserved exactly as it appeared when it was opened, right down to the paint scheme and the ornately geometric Eastlake-style woodwork. Most of the 50-odd paintings on display are the work of 19th-century French academicians like Adolphe Bouguereau, with a scattering of American luminists and Hudson River School artists. But one canvas overshadows all the others and justifies a turnoff from I-91 even if you hadn't planned a stopover in St. Johnsbury: Albert Bierstadt's *Domes of Yosemite,* which takes up the gallery's entire back wall. A depiction of the facing rock walls of El Capitan and Half Dome, with a finely detailed Yosemite Valley sprawling between them, it is a textbook study in the monumental, reverential-awe approach to naturalist painting taken by

Bierstadt and his Hudson River School contemporaries. Spend a few minutes with *Domes,* and the Vermont landscape outside will seem oddly flat.

As you leave the Athenaeum you will see buildings clustered to the left at the south end of Main Street. Many of them belong to St. Johnsbury Academy, a private secondary school that also serves as a high school for students from the city. To turn back to Railroad Street from here, head downhill on Eastern Avenue, where you'll find two of St. Johnsbury's better eating places. Chef-owned **Tucci's Bistro**, 43 Eastern Avenue (Tel: 802/748-4778), is a cheerfully intimate establishment with a sophisticated Northern Italian menu; dinner only. Just across the street is **Granpa's** (Tel: 802/748-8494), an informal spot featuring steaks, burgers, and sandwiches.

Downtown St. Johnsbury would be a pleasant place for an evening's stroll if there were a hotel to stroll to and from. Unfortunately, downtown accommodations went out with the passenger trains, so the modern traveller's best bet is the **Fairbanks Motor Inn**, just off Exit 21 on I-91 at Route 2 east. Some rooms have balconies overlooking the heated outdoor pool; Continental breakfast is included in the price of a room. The **Echo Ledge Farm Inn** is a comfortable bed-and-breakfast, in a 1793 farmhouse (modern touches include private baths) on Route 2 in East St. Johnsbury; children under ten are not accommodated. For a listing of other B and Bs throughout the region, contact the Northeast Kingdom Chamber of Commerce, 30 Western Avenue, St. Johnsbury, VT 05819; Tel: (802) 748-3678.

St. Johnsbury bills itself as the "Maple Capital of the World," a title that might be disputed by the province of Quebec. But when it comes to the sweet by-products of the sap of *acer saccharum,* Vermont has the cachet, and St. Johnsbury has the Maple Grove Farms of Vermont, Inc., which contains the **Maple Museum** and a **maple candy factory**, on Route 2 one mile (1½ km) east of downtown. The tapping of maple trees and the boiling of sap down to syrup—"sugaring," as the whole process is called—is a springtime phenomenon, made possible when warm days and below-freezing nights cause the sap to rise. At Maple Grove, however, it's always sugaring time. When real sap isn't in season, a substitute is used to demonstrate the boiling, or "evaporating," process. There are tours of the factory, which can include the museum when it's open, and a gift shop filled with every conceivable combination of maple. If you're travelling with children, it's only fair to stop here after making them gape at *Domes of Yosemite.* Tel: (802) 748-5141.

North from St. Johnsbury

LYNDONVILLE

Route 5 (or I-91 if you're in a hurry, which the Northeast Kingdom is the last place for) will take you north along the Passumpsic River Valley to Lyndonville, 8 miles (13 km) north of St. Johnsbury. Lyndonville is the home of Lyndon State College, one of three campuses in Vermont's state college system. The school's presence has kept the place livelier than might be expected of an up-country village whose railroad heyday has long since passed, and whose manufacturing base was seriously stricken by the 1992 departure of the Vermont American tool company. The **Bag Balm** factory here makes a product designed for the teats of cows but discovered to be an effective skin softener for people. A tin of the balm makes a dandy souvenir. Lyndonville has a lovely town green, surrounded by well-kept Victorian houses, and a brick-fronted shopping district that looks like something out of a model-train layout. It is also known for its diners, particularly the **Miss Lyndonville**; Tel: (802) 626-9890.

EAST AND WEST BURKE

For most outsiders—aside from parents visiting offspring at Lyndon State—the principal attraction is nearby **Burke Mountain** ski area, 6 miles (10 km) northeast of town in East Burke. Insofar as a 30-trail resort can be "undiscovered," Burke is; it's a favorite among Vermonters and Québecois who'd rather not fight the crowds at the big areas in the Green Mountains. None of which is to say this is a tame, small-time mountain: A number of U.S. Olympians have trained at Burke Mountain Academy. Lift ticket prices are attractive, as are the slopeside condo rentals. Tel: (802) 626-3305.

Burke Mountain also offers 55 kilometers (34 miles) of cross-country ski trails, complete with rentals, instructions, and a café; Tel: (802) 626-8338. In summer and fall the area's access road connects with the hiking trails of the 12,000-acre **Victory Basin Wildlife Management Area**, **Victory State Forest**, and **Darling State Park**. For detailed trail descriptions, consult the Green Mountain Club's *Day Hiker's Guide to Vermont* (see Getting Around, below).

The villages of East and West Burke and environs also offer a good selection of bed-and-breakfasts and country inns. One standout is **Mountain View Creamery**, with seven rooms in a renovated brick creamery on the farm-estate of a 19th-century New York magnifico. If the handmade quilts capture your fancy, sign up for one of Mountain View's on-site quilting classes. The **Old Cutter Inn**, located in East Burke just off

Route 114 less than a mile from the ski area, is a small (10 rooms) establishment that nevertheless offers a modified American plan including full breakfast and a dinner menu influenced by the native cuisine of the Swiss owner-chef. The inn also has a bar and outdoor pool. Somewhat larger, and located off Route 114 between East and West Burke 4 miles (6½ km) from the slopes, is the 23-room **Wildflower Inn**, with an excellent restaurant, outdoor pool, hot tub, sleigh rides, and several suites.

THE ISLAND POND AREA

Although Route 5 is the more direct route to Newport and the Canadian border, bear right onto Route 114 as you head north out of Lyndonville for a fuller Northeast Kingdom circuit. Unless you opt for a dirt-road exploration of deepest Essex County, Route 114 between East Burke and Island Pond will be about as backwoods as you get in the Northeast Kingdom. For a good part of the way you'll follow the East Branch of the Passumpsic northeast through marshland and deep forest in a corner of the town of **Newark**—yes, Newark, one of 28 municipalities in the world sharing the name with the much-maligned New Jersey metropolis. In 1991 an informal association of Newarkians from Newark, Australia, to Newark-upon-Trent, England, gathered here to celebrate Newarkness. The party was held four miles west of Route 114, at a lonely intersection where a church and town clerk's office constitute all there is of Newark village.

There's a good deal more to **Island Pond**, 18 miles (29 km) north of East Burke on Route 114. Island Pond was once a bustling railroad town, a major division point on the Grand Trunk line. In fact, the reason the settlement grew alongside the eponymous pond is that it lies exactly halfway between Portland, Maine, and Montreal by rail. This, along with the fact that it was the birthplace of Rudy Vallee, was about all that put Island Pond on the map until the early 1980s, when a strict, communally oriented fundamentalist religious sect chose the town as its home away from the more egregious manifestations of secular civilization. The group might have gone largely unnoticed, in the Vermont live-and-let-live spirit, had not the then-governor Richard Snelling become alarmed by reports that its doctrines commanded vigorous corporal punishment of children. Determined not to have a revival of the birch-rod era, Governor Snelling had the state police raid the community and remove its children. But a state court ruled that the measure was legally unsupportable, the children were returned, and the Island Pond fundamentalists have largely kept out of the public eye over the past decade. You'll probably see the patriarchially bearded men and kerchiefed women on the streets of the town; they even run a local café. If you get hungry in Island Pond, though, the best place to stop is the **Buck and Doe**, 135 Main Street, on the downtown block facing the old depot (currently undergoing restoration). The menu is conventional down-home American, but everything's homemade, the portions are generous, and it's altogether a lot more restaurant than you have a right to expect this far out in the sticks. Tel: (802) 723-4712.

Before heading out of Island Pond, stop at the **Hudson Trading Post**, at the intersection of Routes 114 and 105 (open late May through mid-November). Aside from being a highly browsable second-hand store, this is an outlet for owner April Hudson's "Hudsonware," a line of incredibly inexpensive blue-and-white glazed molded pottery. The cow pitchers, available in different sizes, are a prime Vermont souvenir.

Three miles (5 km) north of Island Pond you must decide just how deeply into the Northeast Kingdom you care to delve. Bear right and stay on Route 114 (often described as the "roller-coaster road," for obvious reasons) to skirt the Canadian border and loop south, via Route 102, along the Connecticut River Valley. If you choose this option, the only settlement of any size you will encounter will be the furniture-manufacturing community of **Canaan**, near the common border of Vermont, New Hampshire, and Quebec.

A possible destination near the Canadian border on Route 114, 9 miles (14½ km) west of Canaan, is **Quimby Country**, a rustic family resort on **Forest Lake** in Averill. Quimby's 20 cabins (containing one to four bedrooms) and main lodge suggest the ambience Ralph Lauren tries for in his ads; here, however, the effect is more genuine than studied. Celebrating its 100th year in 1993, the resort has a full dining plan, and plenty of activities for children. Quimby Country faces directly on 70-acre Forest Lake; its beach, however, is on **Great Averill Pond**. Water sports include canoeing, rowing, sailing, and windsurfing, as well as fishing for trout and landlocked salmon. On land there are tennis courts, a nearby golf course, and such easygoing activities as shoreside cookouts and browsing through the library.

Heading south on Route 102 past Canaan you'll follow a Connecticut that seems a far cry from the majestic river it becomes as it flows through southern New England; when you catch a glimpse of it as the road winds through the forests and occasional dairy farms of eastern Essex County, it looks like any other mountain stream. Five miles (8 km) south of 102's intersection with Route 105 at Bloomfield

(Bloomfield is 21 miles/34 km south of Canaan), turn onto the access road for **Maidstone State Park** on Maidstone Lake. Maidstone is one of Vermont's most pleasant and secluded state parks, with campsites (lean-tos and tent sites), a swimming beach, rowboat rentals, showers, and walking trails. The lake is stocked with trout. For information, Tel: (802) 676-3930.

The other option, after heading north out of Island Pond, is to bear left onto Route 111 and drive northwest to Newport. Here the forests begin to give way to dairy farms, and the road leads past deep, clear **Seymour Lake**. Seymour is one of a handful of northern Vermont lakes harboring landlocked salmon, and the only one in which these fish are still regularly stocked; the 1,700-acre lake is also known for its lake-trout fishing. There are boat rentals and a guide service at **Seymour Lake Lodge**, on Route 111 in nearby Morgan; the lodge is also a small bed-and-breakfast offering a modified American plan.

Lake Memphremagog

Newport, along with the smaller nearby community of **Derby**, is the commercial center of the border country; local businesses attract a sizable number of Québecois circumventing their province's exorbitant retail sales tax. Otherwise, the main attraction here is its location at the southern tip of Lake Memphremagog, which Vermont shares rather lopsidedly with Quebec: Of the lake's 30-mile north–south length, only the southernmost four miles are in the United States. Bass, northern pike, and landlocked salmon draw fishing enthusiasts, but even if you aren't travelling with tackle this is a big, beautiful lake to explore in an outboard. For boat rentals, there are two choices: The **Memphremagog Marina**, adjacent to the Newport city dock, rents 14-foot fishing boats for $55 a day (open mid-April to November 1; Tel: 802/334-6283). The **Newport Marina**, off Farrant's Street, rents boats for $35–$125 per day (open mid-April to mid-November; Tel: 802/334-5911).

THE CRAFTSBURYS

Leaving Newport, take either Route 5 or Route 105 west to Route 14, and head south through Coventry and Albany to the Craftsburys—Craftsbury Common, Craftsbury, and East Craftsbury, clustered about 20 miles (32 km) south of Coventry. The scenery is more open here, more characteristic of central Vermont than the Northeast Kingdom, with valley pasturelands setting off vistas of the Green Mountains to the

north and west. South of Albany the road rises, and by the
time you reach **Craftsbury Common** it will be apparent that
village locations this good are unusual even in Vermont.
Rather than being tucked into a valley or nestled against a
slope, Craftsbury Common rides a high ridge that gives it
sweeping views on both sides. As for the man-made environment, Craftsbury Common is 200 years old, and every one of
its chaste, white-clapboard houses seems to have been
painted this morning. Add a manicured town green—the
"common" that distinguishes this settlement from just plain
Craftsbury a mile to the south—and you have a perennial
candidate for the prettiest village in Vermont. If you haven't
seen it on a calendar, you've probably been looking at
Weston or Peacham (for which see our Southern Vermont
and Connecticut River Valley sections, respectively).

One of the most common experiences for travellers to
Vermont is to happen upon places like Craftsbury Common,
where there is ostensibly nothing to "do"—no shops, no
theater, no museums or galleries or any of the other things
that make travel itineraries so doggedly purposeful—and
then feel unable to leave. One drastic means of seeing to it
that you stay for a while would be to enroll in the two-year
program at environmentally oriented Sterling College, right
on the green; it's the smallest accredited coed degree-
granting college in the nation (it has 90 students), and
spending a couple of years here would be like living in a
green tower rather than an ivory one.

Short of matriculating, however, you can assuage your
can't-leave-Craftsbury pangs at either of a pair of superb inns
in the area. The **Inn on the Common** occupies a compound
of restored Federal houses on Craftsbury Common's main
street. The ambience is pure English country house, right
down to the croquet course and formal dining room; local
farms stock the larder, and there are tennis courts and a
heated swimming pool on the grounds. Other sporting
activities, including cross-country skiing, sculling, canoeing,
and mountain biking, can be arranged either through the
inn or independently at the nearby **Craftsbury Sports Center**; Tel: (802) 586-7767.

One mile (1½ km) south of Craftsbury Common, the
village of **Craftsbury** proper is only slightly less picturesque;
here there is a gentrified country store, and the 1850
Craftsbury Inn, slightly smaller than its neighbor but with a
similar air of country-squire elegance and a dining room
specializing in farm-raised local game. (Those partial to
partridge, pheasant, and quail can, by the way, order directly
from Craftsbury Common's **Wylie Hill Farm**; Tel: 802/586-
2887.)

To continue your Northeast Kingdom ramble after leaving the Craftsburys, make sure you have a good map—the DeLorme Mapping Company's *Vermont Atlas and Gazetteer,* available at nearly all of the state's bookstores and many general stores, is a must for anyone threading through warrens of back roads such as the ones that meander from Craftsbury northeast to Barton. Along the way, just off I-91 (on Route 122 near the intersection with Route 16) in **Glover**, is the **Bread and Puppet Museum**, a quirky establishment in a ramshackle barn. The Bread and Puppet Theater is a peripatetic outfit that turns up at festivals and holiday gatherings in parts of Vermont where sixties types still people the landscape (this means just about the entire state); its stock-in-trade is malevolent Uncle Sams on stilts and papier-mâché–masked players acting out leftist morality plays. The museum has eclectic and interesting exhibits of mask and puppet craftsmanship—and the political slant will be a comeuppance if you've just spent a few days in the St-Emilion-and-pink-linen world of Craftsbury. Open May through October and by appointment; Tel: (802) 525-3031.

LAKE WILLOUGHBY

The town of **Barton**, 3 miles (5 km) north of Glover on Route 16, is worth a stop if it's August and time for the old-fashioned country fair, or any time you feel like a swim: Nearby **Crystal Lake State Park** has one of Vermont's nicest bathing beaches, complete with a stand where you can rent inflatable sea monsters for the kids. But real connoisseurs of mountain lakes had best press on along Route 16 to Lake Willoughby, touted as everything from an "inland fjord" to the "Lucerne of America," and easily living up to whatever superlatives a tourism bureau could devise. Seven miles long, a mile wide, and 600 feet deep, filling a glacial gash between the sheer rocky slopes of Mounts Pisgah and Hor, Lake Willoughby silences all debate as to which is the most beautiful lake, other than the great Champlain itself, in Vermont. The most dramatic approach is from the north, along Route 5A; if you've come from the west on Route 16 it's worth it to head north for a mile or so on 5A, turn around, and take in the full effect.

Strange as it seems, given the fact that Lake Willoughby still appears to be in the middle of nowhere, this was a popular summer resort a century ago. There were big, rambling wooden hotels, and even steamboats cruising the lake. But the end of the railroad age actually ushered in an era of *un*development at Willoughby; today the state owns much of the shoreline, and even on the loveliest summer days there are only a handful of boats on the lake. Chances are their skippers are out fishing deep for landlocked salmon and lake trout (Vermont's 34-pound record laker was taken from Willoughby in 1981), and there are a couple of liveries along the lake's northeastern shore if you care to join them. Otherwise, Lake Willoughby is best appreciated from the broad verandah of the **WilloughVale Inn**, on Route 5A, where you can take your Cognac after a sophisticated meal. The inn offers nine rooms furnished with up-country New England antiques, as well as four lakeside cottages. Restaurant entrées might include rack of lamb and prime rib, or perhaps a nice curried chicken salad at lunchtime.

From Lake Willoughby a 30-mile (48-km) drive south along Routes 5A and 5 will bring you back to St. Johnsbury. A four-wheel-drive vehicle and another two months, however, will bring you perhaps 10 percent of the way into the hidden heart of the Northeast Kingdom.

THE CONNECTICUT RIVER VALLEY

The Connecticut is the longest of New England's rivers, following a 407-mile course from its source, at the Fourth Connecticut Lake on the border of New Hampshire and Quebec, to its mouth on Long Island Sound. Along the way it forms the entirety of the 200-mile-plus border between Vermont and New Hampshire—a boundary that, many people are surprised to learn, does not extend down the center of the river. Instead, New Hampshire's legal claim runs all the way to the low-water mark on the Vermont side. (The Granite State is kind enough, however, to allow persons holding a Vermont fishing license angling access to the river.)

Long before things like fishing licenses mattered, the Connecticut was one of the most vital of the region's resources. So abundant were the Connecticut's salmon runs that northwestern Vermont's Abenaki Indians made an annual expedition to the river, catching and drying the fish for winter provisions. (Today conservationists are working to restore salmon to the Connecticut.) In Colonial times the Connecticut was an important avenue of settlement. As available fertile land became scarcer in the more heavily populated southern New England colonies, settlers followed the river north to carve out farms and villages along both the Vermont and New Hampshire sides of the valley. Evidence of this trend can be read in the names of many of the valley towns, which were christened by their founders in honor of places left behind in Massachusetts and Connecticut. Lebanon and Haverhill, New Hampshire, and Hartford and Springfield, Vermont, are but a few examples.

Since travellers exploring the upper Connecticut Valley often cross the river a number of times in the course of their journeys, it makes little sense to outline an all-Vermont or all-New Hampshire excursion through the region. In this section we describe a route beginning at Springfield, Vermont, and extending north to Peacham, just south of St. Johnsbury. (South of Springfield, New Hampshire's popular Monadnock region lies well to the east of the Connecticut, and the Vermont side of the river is covered in our Southern Vermont section, above; east of St. Johnsbury, the remotest parts of Vermont's Northeast Kingdom, also discussed above, lie across the river from New Hampshire's rugged Connecticut Lakes region.) In other words, we cover only the central stretch of the Vermont–New Hampshire border here. The route followed, for the most part, is Route 5, which runs along the Vermont side of the river; however, Interstate 91 is always handy for a quicker shunt from one valley locale to another.

SPRINGFIELD TO WHITE RIVER JUNCTION
The Springfield Area

Springfield is an anomaly among Vermont cities; it grew less as a market town for the surrounding countryside than as a manufacturing community with a decidedly big-city specialty: machine tools. The site, on the swift-flowing Black River four miles above its confluence with the Connecticut, attracted water-powered industry as early as the 1770s; a hundred years later Springfield was turning out such a profusion of fine machinery that the city and its surrounding area were known as "Precision Valley." By the early 1900s James Hartness, the polymath part-owner of the Jones & Lamson Machine Company (and eventually governor of Vermont) held 120 patents; and the Fellows Gear Shaping Company was producing the machinery used by Detroit to cut the bulk of America's automotive gears.

Although the machine-tool industry survives in Springfield on a vastly reduced scale (the old Fellows plant now houses the Southeastern Vermont Center for Economic Development, a telling sign of the times), the erstwhile Precision Valley has accustomed itself to a service economy, and makes a pleasant stopover in the course of a Connecticut Valley ramble. The city center is compact, a condition dictated by the tight little valley it occupies, and the city's National Register of Historic Places–listed Main Street manages to combine an old-fashioned, workaday ambience with a 1980s spruce-up. At its center is **Penelope's** restaurant, 30 Main Street, a cheerful, houseplant-filled, circa-1970 sort of place with a hearty, pre-nouvelle approach to American cuisine. Soups, sandwiches, and desserts are the standouts here, but don't overlook the daily blackboard specials. There's outdoor seating in summer, Mexican night on Wednesdays, and a lively adjoining pub called **McKinleys**. Tel: (802) 885-9186.

A superior Springfield hostelry with connections to the city's glory days is the **Hartness House Inn**, set on a 32-acre estate on the outskirts of downtown. Built as the residence of inventor, industrialist, and politician James Hartness in 1904, the Queen Anne–style inn is characterized by the snug formality of the era; fireplaces, Oriental rugs, and candlelight dining make guests feel like up-country magnificoes. Hartness, the magnifico who built it all, was an accomplished astronomer, and his Turret Equatorial Telescope—one of the first of its kind in the United States—still stands in working order on the inn's front lawn. A five-room underground apartment, accessible from the house by a 240-foot tunnel and open to the public, houses a fine collection of telescopes as well as paintings and drawings.

EUREKA SCHOOLHOUSE

Three miles (5 km) southeast of Springfield on Route 11 (1 mile/1½ km west of Route 5), a squat, unprepossessing wooden structure stands as one of Vermont's very few authentic relics of the man-made environment of the 18th century. This is the Eureka Schoolhouse, completed in 1790 and now the oldest one-room schoolhouse in Vermont. Rebuilt, restored to its original appearance, and moved a short distance to its present location during the 1960s, the schoolhouse has been furnished with period antiques. It stands as a reminder of the days when a building such as this offered all the formal education most Vermont frontier children would ever get—although some did get from here to Dartmouth and beyond. Open daily mid-May to mid-October.

FORT NUMBER 4

From the Eureka Schoolhouse it's a short trip across the Connecticut via Route 11 to Charlestown, New Hampshire, and Fort Number 4. Actually a reconstructed palisaded village, looking as it would have in the 1740s, the fort vividly suggests the days when the upper Connecticut Valley was a forbidding wilderness, when English settlers were perpetually on their guard against French or Indian marauders. Within the fort's walls costumed volunteers reenact the daily routines of the era using period tools and furnishings. Open daily from Memorial Day weekend to Columbus Day; closed weekdays the first two weeks of September. Tel: (603) 826-5700.

WEATHERSFIELD CENTER

North of Springfield the Connecticut Valley is broad and relatively featureless; if you're looking to put a few quick miles behind you, this wouldn't be a bad stretch to cover on I-91. For another peek at 18th-century Vermont life, however, stop off at Weathersfield Center, 2 miles (3 km) west of Routes 5 and I-91 on Route 131, then 3 miles (5 km) south (from Springfield drive 6 miles/10 km north via Elm Street). Here you'll find the **Weathersfield Historical Society's museum** of furniture, textiles, and household and farm implements, housed in the town meetinghouse and in the 1785 Reverend Dan Foster House. In an adjacent forge a working smith's furnace and bellows are on exhibit. Open afternoons Wednesday through Sunday late June through mid-October; Tel: (802) 263-5230.

The Windsor Area

Windsor, roughly 15 miles (24 km) north of Springfield via either of the two main roads, bills itself as the "Birthplace of Vermont." The reasons for this sobriquet are sound: On July 8, 1777, representatives of the towns known as the "New Hampshire Grants" (and briefly as "New Connecticut") met at a Windsor tavern and voted to accept a constitution binding their communities into the "Free and Independent State of Vermont"—or, as it became known by its contemporaries and those who still bear a mythic attachment to it today, the Republic of Vermont. It survived as such for 14 years, finally joining the new federal union as the 14th state in 1791. Windsor was not only the little republic's birthplace; it was also the meeting place of its first legislature, in March of 1778.

The Elijah West Tavern, where the constitution was adopted, survives today as the **Old Constitution House**, on

Main Street. Now located a short distance from its original site, the house is a museum of early Vermontiana and a shrine to the spirit of independence that, as much as any of their vaunted Yankee virtues, Vermonters cherish to this day. Not incidentally, the house also summons up images of the days of roadside taverns in New England, where travellers sought a roaring fire and a noggin of ale after an exhausting day on foot or horseback. The house is open daily mid-May through mid-October; Tel: (802) 674-6628.

There were, of course, two American Revolutions: the political upheaval, of which the events played out at the Old Constitution House were a part, and the great Industrial Revolution of the 19th century, of which Windsor also boasts a shrine. This is the **American Precision Museum** (Tel: 802/674-5781), located in the stout brick Robbins & Lawrence Armory and Machine Shop at 196 Main Street. Built alongside Mill Brook, a swift-flowing tributary of the Connecticut, the Robbins & Lawrence plant used water power to build military firearms according to the new "American system" of manufacture, with complete interchangeability of parts. In addition to fulfilling Union army contracts during the Civil War and contracts for the British, the Robbins & Lawrence firm built machine tools and sewing machines; later, the building was used as a cotton mill and a hydroelectric plant.

Since 1966 it has housed the Precision Museum, dedicated to the history of America's development of machine technology from the early 19th century through modern times. If, after spending some time with the museum's fascinating hands-on exhibits, you are daunted by the main gallery's vast collection of machine tools such as turret lathes and drill presses, look beyond the details of the individual artifacts and appreciate the whole of the museum as an homage to a time when no one in the world engaged in the business of making things as heartily and successfully as did Americans. That great era began in the red-brick mills of New England.

Another worthwhile Windsor stop is the **Vermont State Craft Center**, an affiliate of the centers in Burlington and Middlebury, at the Windsor House, also on Main Street. Housed in the state's largest Greek Revival structure (1840), the center showcases and sells the work of more than 250 juried craftspeople working in textiles, wood, ceramics, and other media. Tel: (802) 674-6729.

The most attractive accommodations in the Windsor area are at the **Juniper Hill Inn**, a white, green-shuttered mansion set on 14 acres of grounds atop a hill outside of town. Some of the rooms have fireplaces; all have private baths; and the antiques-filled common rooms are palatial. The inn has an outdoor pool, and pathways through lovely perennial gardens.

Windsor is a good place to cross the Connecticut. The attraction is the crossing itself—New England's longest **covered bridge**, a 468-foot wooden span connecting Windsor with Cornish, New Hampshire. It was built in 1866, to replace a 1796 bridge destroyed by flood. A ten-cent toll was collected on the Cornish bridge as recently as the 1940s; today it's free, and in its best shape in years thanks to a complete restoration in the late 1980s.

AUGUSTUS SAINT-GAUDENS NATIONAL HISTORIC SITE

In Cornish, 2½ miles (4 km) north of the Windsor bridge on New Hampshire Route 12A, look for the road leading to the Augustus Saint-Gaudens National Historic Site (open daily from Memorial Day through October 31; Tel: 603/675-2175). Saint-Gaudens, sculptor of the *Standing Lincoln,* the *Diana* that once stood atop New York's old Madison Square Garden, the *Puritan,* and the renowned bronze memorials to Robert Gould Shaw (Boston) and Mrs. Henry Adams (Washington), spent summers in Cornish and lived here year-round from 1900 until his death at age 59 in 1907.

The story has it that Saint-Gaudens was first steered toward New Hampshire while researching his *Standing Lincoln.* A New York friend of Saint-Gaudens's told the sculptor that he would find "plenty of Lincoln-shaped men" in the Granite State to use as models. Captivated by the beautiful sunsets over Vermont's Mount Ascutney, he purchased an old brick tavern on a hilltop in Cornish to watch them from. He remodeled the tavern into the imposing mansion now preserved, along with his gardens and studios, on the grounds of the national historic site. Saint-Gaudens named his estate "Aspet" after his father's native village in France.

Augustus Saint-Gaudens was in the vanguard of a movement that made Cornish an artists' and writers' colony of considerable repute from 1885 to 1935. Among its luminaries were the novelist Winston Churchill and the painter-illustrator Maxfield Parrish. Parrish built a home and studio in Plainfield, just north of Cornish, in 1898 when he was 28. He died there 68 years later, just as his luminously vivid, fantasy-inspired art was regaining popularity.

The White River Junction Area

From Plainfield, just north of the Saint-Gaudens site, it is roughly 8 miles (13 km) via Route 12A to West Lebanon, where you can recross the Connecticut either via Interstate

89 or Route 4 to reach White River Junction, Vermont, and several nearby points of interest. (In the big shopping center near the I-89 interchange on the West Lebanon side of the river, by the way, you'll find the best-stocked of New Hampshire's state liquor stores. It's pure conjecture, but one suspects the superior selection of wines and spirits at this outlet owes something to the sophisticated tastes of neighboring Dartmouth professors.)

White River Junction, located on the west bank of the Connecticut (the first exit north off I-91, if you've crossed over on I-89), is an old railroad town that grew up where the Central Vermont tracks meet those of the Boston & Maine. Near the old railroad yards, at the intersection of North and South Main streets downtown, there is a preserved, century-old B & M 4-4-0 steam locomotive of the type once used for passenger runs between northern New England valley towns. Another representative of a vanishing breed, the small-city downtown hotel, stands across the square from the old engine. The tidy, fully restored, and up-to-date **Hotel Coolidge** is a remarkably good value (a hotel named for Silent Cal had better be), and a pleasant alternative to characterless motels or pricey accommodations in the vicinity of Dartmouth College. There's also a decent, reasonably priced restaurant on the premises, called **Cashie's.**

There isn't a lot more, though, to downtown White River Junction, unless you've hit town for an event in the performing-arts series at **River City Arts,** housed in the **Briggs Opera House,** a block down South Main Street from the Hotel Coolidge. River City Arts mounts a professional theater season from July through December, and concerts, including folk music and jazz, from January through April. For tickets and information, Tel: (802) 296-2505. Beer aficionados, however, may wish to take the tour at the **Catamount Brewing Company,** at 58 South Main Street, a representative of the burgeoning new trend in up-country microbreweries. The free tour (Saturdays only in winter) is fun just for the language that gets thrown around; are you familiar with the terms "mash tun" and "hopped wort"? For tour information, Tel: (802) 296-2248.

QUECHEE GORGE

Perhaps the greatest single attraction in this part of Vermont is a natural one—Quechee (KWEE-chee) Gorge, about 6 miles (10 km) west of White River Junction on (or rather beneath) Route 4. The 165-foot-deep gorge is a steep, forbidding chasm cut by the fast-flowing Ottauquechee River, a dark canyon of rock and crazy-angled scrub trees that looks like something out of a Hudson River School painting. There are parking areas along the highway near the gorge, as well as picnic tables and foot trails.

The near vicinity of the gorge has also become something of a retail magnet, owing more to the proximity of posh Woodstock (see the Central Vermont section, above) than to the natural phenomenon. Among the more interesting retail establishments are **Scotland by the Yard** (Route 4), purveyors of Scottish knitwear, tartans, books, records, and food; and **Simon Pearce Glass** (The Mill, on Main Street off Route 4), featuring pottery and blown glassware crafted on the premises, as well as giftware, woollens, wooden bowls and boxes, linens, baskets, and furniture. The **Simon Pearce** restaurant, featuring a bistro menu headlined at dinnertime by roast duck, is also in The Mill complex; Tel: (802) 295-1470. At **Timber Village** (Route 4), the entrepreneurial Yankee spirit is represented by a 300-dealer antiques center, a country store, a basket shop, a shop specializing in local crafts, and a working miniature steam train that circles the property.

If you aren't heading west into Woodstock (or if you are, but would prefer to stay on the outskirts), Quechee offers the moderately priced **Friendship Inn at Quechee Gorge**, a motel with an outdoor pool and shuffleboard courts; and the more upscale **Parker House Inn**, a seven-room antiques-furnished hostelry housed in a U.S. senator's mansion (and National Historic Site) built in 1857. Both of these establishments have full-service restaurants.

NORWICH

Five miles (8 km) north of White River Junction via Route 5 is Norwich, Vermont, not to be confused with Norwich University, the military college in Northfield (see Central Vermont, above). Norwich U. was actually located here prior to 1867; today the principal attraction is the **Montshire Museum of Science**, on Montshire Road about a mile (1½ km) from Hanover. The Montshire is a fine stop for travellers with children; there are plenty of hands-on exhibits, salt- and freshwater aquariums, and displays relating to ecology, space, technology, and natural history. The 100-acre wooded site is superb, with nature trails meandering along the Connecticut River. Tel: (802) 649-2200.

Norwich also boasts a first-rate restaurant, **La Poule à Dents**, on the corner of Main and Carpenter streets, a relaxed country bistro with an ever-changing menu firmly anchored in the provincial French tradition. (It's known locally as the 1820 House.) In summer you can dine on the patio—but in winter you're more likely to encounter the cassoulet. Tel: (802) 649-2922.

HANOVER, NEW HAMPSHIRE, AND DARTMOUTH COLLEGE

Norwich is only 1 mile (1½ km) by bridge across the Connecticut from Hanover, New Hampshire, home of Dartmouth College. Though small by the standards of its fellow Ivy League institutions, Dartmouth looms large in a small New England town like Hanover. To outsiders, Dartmouth *is* Hanover, and Hanover Dartmouth. The town does predate the school, though not by very many years. In 1761 New Hampshire governor Benning Wentworth issued a charter for the tract on the east bank of the Connecticut River where Hanover now stands. The parcel was a township in name only for nearly four years, until in the spring of 1765 Colonel Edmund Freeman and his family travelled upriver to carve a farm out of what was still wilderness, marked only by lines on a map in the faraway Colonial capital of Portsmouth. It was Freeman, by most accounts, who gave the new town the name of the ruling English House of Hanover.

Meanwhile, far to the south in Lebanon, Connecticut, the Reverend Eleazar Wheelock was contemplating a move of his own, one that would forever change the fledgling village of Hanover. Wheelock ran a Christian school for young Indians, and had been busy raising funds with which to relocate and expand his mission. He sent one of his former pupils, a Mohegan preacher named Samson Occom, on a speaking tour of England to solicit contributions for this venture. Occom came back with a pledged endowment of 11,000 pounds sterling and the patronage of the Earl of Dartmouth, enabling Rev. Wheelock to begin entertaining invitations from communities that wanted the new school within their borders. Hanover won, through successful use of the same tactic a modern town might use to lure a corporate headquarters to its new office park: It offered land (3,000 acres), money, lumber with which to build, and the manpower of its citizens. What the yeomen hoped for in return were prestige and improved real-estate values.

King George III granted Wheelock the charter for Dartmouth in 1769, and the following year saw the minister arrive in Hanover with his books. The motto adopted later for Dartmouth College—*Vox Clamantis in Deserto* (A Voice Crying in the Wilderness)—is a quite accurate suggestion of what those earliest years must have been like, with Wheelock holding classes in a log cabin built on freshly cleared land. Wilderness though it may have been, few Indians ever showed up for instruction. Before long Dartmouth was a white man's college. It graduated four students at its first commencement exercises in 1771, and by 1791, when the first Dartmouth Hall was built on the site of the present structure of that name, 49 baccalaureates were awarded. From then on the college and the town grew in step with each other.

Dartmouth today is, at its core, the liberal-arts college it has always aspired to be, but it is a protean institution nonetheless. Aside from boasting one of the finest mathematics departments in the country, with computer science especially strong, Dartmouth—though still technically a college and not a university—counts among its graduate facilities the respected Amos Tuck School of Administration and Finance and the Medical School, which is affiliated with two hospitals and a string of community clinics.

THE CAMPUS

A tour of the Dartmouth campus itself might best begin right on the green, and in fact need not stray far from this broad lawn, as most of the buildings of architectural or historic interest border it almost directly. One curious feature of the green, hardly likely to be noticed at all by the casual passerby, is the "senior fence" occupying a short stretch of the walkway along North Main Street. The fence is a simple affair of green wooden rails and granite posts, donated by the Class of 1897 and expanded by the Class of 1923. Traditionally, only seniors are allowed to sit on the rails; today's students are so busy, however, that the fence is almost always empty.

The corner building roughly opposite the senior fence on North Main Street is **Robinson Hall**, noteworthy as the main campus headquarters of the **Dartmouth Outing Club,** as strong an extracurricular outdoor sports organization as can be found in any college in the United States. The club's raison d'être is to make full use of Dartmouth's incomparable location between the Green and White Mountains, and its programs include hiking, climbing, cross-country and downhill skiing, and canoeing. Another Outing Club activity, unheard of on the vast majority of American campuses, is ski jumping. Dartmouth's 45-meter jump is located at the Hanover Country Club, on the northern outskirts of town 1 mile (1½ km) from the green via Route 10. More than 20 American Olympic jumpers have trained here. Spectators can watch the Dartmouth Outing Club's recreational jumpers as well as ski school, high school, and college team members practice on the jump on Monday, Wednesday, and Friday evenings during the winter. For serious competition there's the Roger Burt Memorial Jump, held each January, and the February jump held as part of Dartmouth's time-honored Winter Carnival.

The **Winter Carnival,** a Dartmouth tradition since 1911, is an extravagantly staged throwback to the days when seniors carved their initials in fences. A week-long celebration in February built around parties, dances, and a profusion of winter sports competitions, its most visible manifestation for outsiders is the green's fanciful display of enormous snow sculptures, some of which take three or four days of work on the part of crews fielded by fraternities and other student organizations.

Baker Memorial Library

Turn right from North Main onto Wentworth Street, then left in the middle of the block, and you will be facing the serene Georgian façade of the Baker Memorial Library (Tel: 603/646-2560). Baker, the central library of the Dartmouth campus, is necessarily taken up by stacks and reading rooms, although two areas are of particular interest to visitors. The **Hough Room** (left after you enter the library, then right at the end of the hall) is a sumptuous chamber resembling a 19th-century gentleman's study, its walls lined with the rarest and most valuable books in the Dartmouth College collections. Here are more than 150 volumes of incunabula (books printed before 1501; the word is Latin for "in the cradle" and refers to the infancy of printing with movable type); the Hickmott Shakespeare Collection, including copies of all four folios, nearly 40 quarto volumes, all known pre-1700 editions of *Macbeth,* and much of the playwright's source material; and more than 200 volumes representing the finest achievements of the bookbinder's art. American material includes all first and limited editions of Stephen Crane; a comprehensive Melville collection including important volumes of criticism as well as an exhaustive survey of more than 130 years of editions of *Moby-Dick;* and, in a display case at the center of the room, the first three volumes of the "elephant folio" of John James Audubon's *Birds of America* in the original copies owned by Daniel Webster. (It's speculated that Webster didn't own volume four because he didn't pay Audubon for the first three.)

One flight below the Baker Library's entrance hall, the walls of a **basement reading room** are painted with as remarkable a series of murals as exist in New England. They were painted by José Clemente Orozco between 1932 and 1934, during which time the Mexican artist taught in Dartmouth's art deparment. Executed in an angular, stylized realism, with an expressive use of color, the murals depict the progress (or antiprogress, depending on how one sees it) of civilization in the Americas, from the rise of the Aztecs through the triumph of the European interlopers to the modern ascendancy of an exploitative, technocratic society and the prospects for redemption. An explanatory pamphlet, available at the library, is recommended for anyone who wishes to take more than a cursory look at the Orozco murals.

Webster Hall

The building immediately past Baker Library (clockwise around the Green, on the corner of Wentworth and College streets) is Webster Hall, a 1907 brick Neoclassical auditorium named in honor of the man Dartmouth has always considered to be its greatest alumnus. It was Daniel Webster, Dartmouth Class of 1801, who in the course of successfully defending the school in a landmark court case involving its charter uttered the famous line, "It is, sir, as I have said, a small college, and yet there are those that love it."

Dartmouth Row

The row of structures facing the green along College Street constitutes Dartmouth Row, the best known and most photographed cluster of buildings on campus. Stark white against the lawns and trees of the surrounding landscape, Wentworth, Dartmouth, Thornton, and Reed halls are as beautifully unified an example of collegiate architecture as can be found in America. In their Georgian simplicity they hark back to the vernacular of the New England churches and meetinghouses of Dartmouth's earliest years.

Wentworth and Thornton Halls, built along axes perpendicular to the street, serve as virtual bookends for the serene, 150-foot façade of Dartmouth Hall. This three-story cupola-topped building is a 1904 brick replica of the original Dartmouth Hall, a wooden structure built on this site in 1791 that for many years housed virtually the entire college. Until 1845, in fact, Dartmouth Row comprised the entire campus. When the original Dartmouth Hall burned in 1904, alumni poured in contributions to replace the building immediately.

OFF-CAMPUS HANOVER

College Street ends at Wheelock Street. Here is the entrance to the Hopkins Center, a concert auditorium (Tel: 603/646-2422); and the Hood Museum of Art, housing Dartmouth's fine-arts collections. Housed in a handsome structure designed by Charles Moore, the Hood's collection includes works as diverse as Greek amphorae and fifth-century B.C.

Assyrian bas reliefs, Revere silver, paintings by Winslow Homer and Frank Stella, and a distinguished calendar of visiting exhibitions. Closed Mondays; Tel: (603) 646-2808.

Immediately to the right of the Hopkins Center is the **Hanover Inn**, a posh Dartmouth-owned hostelry that answers the need for a "dorm" for visiting alumni and parents. If the inn's red-brick Georgian architecture seems to fit right in with the campus, there's a good reason: The building's oldest section dates at least to 1780, when it was adapted from a residence into a tavern, and subsequent additions have been in keeping with the Colonial style. The atmosphere inside is clubby and old-shoe comfortable. Nevertheless, the inn's excellent restaurant, the **Daniel Webster Room**, does add a few interesting fillips to its interpretations of American classics—serving celeriac, for example, with its admirable saddle of lamb.

Turn from East Wheelock onto South Main Street, on the corner by the Hanover Inn, to leave the college proper and enter the college town. South Main is abustle with shops, taverns, and restaurants. You'll find hundreds of marked-down volumes on the sidewalk tables in front of the **Dartmouth Bookstore**, at Main and Allen streets. Stop in at **Murphy's Tavern** (on Main Street near West Wheelock; Tel: 603/643-4075) for a Catamount Amber and a burger or Chardonnay and a pasta salad, depending on your disposition, and eavesdrop on scholarly gossip. Another pleasant, informal Hanover dining establishment is **Peter Christian's Tavern** (Edgewood Inn, Main Street; Tel: 603/643-2345), featuring stick-to-your-ribs soups and stews, hefty sandwiches, and scones at teatime.

THE UPPER VALLEY NORTH OF HANOVER
The Lyme Area

Ten miles (16 km) north of Hanover, New Hampshire, Route 10 passes through the town of Lyme, chartered in 1761 and at one time the sheep-raising capital of New England (times have changed; someone is raising caribou in Lyme today). Lyme is the home of the **Dartmouth Skiway**, a small downhill facility open to the public (Tel: 603/795-2143). But the most outstanding attraction here is the village itself, a museum-quality collection of white-clapboard houses clustered around a big, grassy town common and towered over by a white **Congregational church** built in 1812. The big frame house across the street from the church is three years older, and is today the **Lyme Inn**. The inn answers to its archetypal role, no less than the common and the church: If you have a mental image of a quintessential New England hostelry complete with antiques, fireplaces, four-poster beds, and a homey tavern, the Lyme Inn will likely fit it splendidly, and feed you well to boot.

You'll also dine superbly in Lyme at **D'Artagnan** (13 Dartmouth College Highway; Tel: 603/795-2137), specializing in a five-course, fixed-price menu based on a seasonally changing repertoire of updated country French classics. Pâtés, seafood, and desserts are particular standouts, and the streamside patio setting is delightful in summer.

From Lyme you can hopscotch back over the Connecticut into Vermont and follow Route 113 north through a skein of pretty villages such as **Thetford** and **Vershire**. If you turn left (west) on Route 132 at Thetford Center, a short drive will take you to South Strafford and the right-hand turnoff for **Strafford** and the **Justin Smith Morrill Homestead** on the Justin Smith Morrill Highway 2 miles/3 km north of South Strafford (open Wednesday through Sunday from June through mid-October; Tel: 802/765-4484). This handsome, 17-room Gothic Revival cottage was designed by Morrill (1810–1889) as a country retreat, in the midst of a life of public service. A former U.S. representative and senator from Vermont, Morrill is most famous for authoring the Land Grant Act, which endowed state colleges with tracts of federal land in the western territories. (Morrill Hall, at the University of Vermont in Burlington, is named for him.) The house today contains many of the Morrill family's Victorian furnishings and a portion of the senator's library, and many of his own plantings survive in the gardens.

The Orford Area

If you choose to continue north along the New Hampshire side of the Connecticut after leaving Lyme, the next town you reach will be Orford, less than 10 miles (16 km) distant. Orford is the loveliest of all the upper valley towns on the Granite State side; no less accomplished a traveller than Washington Irving called it the most beautiful he had seen in the United States or Europe. The town's outstanding feature is a string of seven Late Georgian and Federal mansions, built between 1773 and 1839 by business and professional men of the town, that line "The Ridge" above Route 10 and the Connecticut River. One, the circa-1815 **General John B. Wheeler House** at the southern end of the row, was designed by Asher Benjamin during his association with Charles Bulfinch, and most of the Ridge's mansions show some Bulfinch influence. All of the houses are private, and are best viewed from Route 10 when the trees are not in leaf.

Lakes Fairlee and Morey

Directly across from Orford, and linked with it by bridge, is **Fairlee**, Vermont. Fairlee stands between the Connecticut River and a 600-foot cliff called the Palisades, but its preeminent natural attraction is a pair of lakes, Fairlee and Morey, which have long been popular as resort destinations. Lake Morey, just outside the village, is the locale of the **Lake Morey Inn Resort**, a sedate hideaway featuring a full array of summer and winter sports, an indoor pool, tennis, and a scenic, just-renovated 18-hole golf course that has long been the site of the Vermont State Open Championship. (The golf course is open to the public; Tel: 802/333-4800.) On a less grand but more whimsical note, the **Fairlee Motel & Drive-In Theater** is a 1950s-style stopover with a twist. In the summer, in-room speakers link the motel units and efficiencies with an adjacent outdoor cinema.

North from Fairlee

If you're sticking to the Vermont side of the Connecticut there is endless meandering to be done north of Fairlee. Route 5 north follows the river through a countryside of rolling farmland, punctuated by a series of unspectacular but pleasant little towns. About 5 miles (8 km) north of Fairlee at **Bradford**, in the middle of an old-fashioned business block, the down-home **Purple Plum Café** (Main Street; Tel: 802/222-5155) is so attuned to the seasons that its June menu often features something called spring greens soup. Just north of Bradford, at South Newbury and Newbury, respectively, the **Peach Brook Inn** and **A Century Past** offer comfortable bed-and-breakfast accommodations. And at **Wells River**, just a few miles beyond South Newbury, where the well-travelled Route 302 crosses the Connecticut into Woodsville, New Hampshire, the main attraction is a downtown that looks as if it could be lifted in its entirety—minus the modern automobiles—and deposited in the Smithsonian Institution as a life-size diorama depicting 1947, right down to the Rexall drugstore and luncheonette.

At Barnet, 10 miles (16 km) south of St. Johnsbury (for which see the Northeast Kingdom section, above), the Connecticut veers off to the east, away from Routes 5 and I-91, and so should you, following the signs marked "Peacham" leading west. **Peacham**, 7 miles (11 km) west of Barnet via

Route 18, comes as close to being the central-casting, picture-perfect Vermont village as—well, as the Northeast Kingdom's Craftsbury, maybe, and hardly anywhere else. Don't look for a great deal of commercial enterprise; business activity in Peacham is just about limited to a crafts shop and a general store, with the tiny **Ha'Penny Gourmet Bed & Breakfast** tucked cozily above the latter. What you will see, in this town first settled in 1776, are beautiful old houses. The Greek Revival style, executed in both clapboard and brick, is the serene hallmark of Peacham's golden age in the early middle years of the 19th century. For the best approach to the town, drive out for a couple of miles on the road leading west toward Route 2, then turn around and head back. The ride along this ridge is like a sail through the clouds, with views in virtually all directions, and the green and white and brick-red gem that is Peacham nestling just ahead.

GETTING AROUND

By Car
Vermont is served by three limited-access highways in the U.S. **interstate** system. I-91 extends from Vernon, in the southeastern corner of Vermont on the Massachusetts border, north along the Connecticut River Valley to St. Johnsbury, from which it extends through the Northeast Kingdom to Derby Line on the Canadian border. The terminal section of I-93 (the main north–south artery in New Hampshire) crosses the Connecticut River from New Hampshire near St. Johnsbury, connecting at that city with I-91. I-89 enters Vermont from New Hampshire at White River Junction, where there is an intersection with I-91; from White River Junction I-89 extends north through east-central Vermont to the state capital of Montpelier, then turns west along the Winooski River Valley to Lake Champlain at Burlington. From Burlington I-89 again turns north, to the Canadian border at Highgate Springs.

Outside of the interstate system, the **main north–south routes** in Vermont are Route 7, which extends along the Champlain Valley from Pownal, in the southwestern corner of the state on the Massachusetts border, to Highgate Springs on the Canadian line; and Vermont 100, which follows a far slower and more meandering (and more scenic) route along the main range of the Green Mountains from Stamford in the south to Newport in the north.

Because of the obstacle presented by the Green Mountains, **direct east–west routes** across Vermont are in short supply. The three primary highways are Route 4, from Fair Haven on the New York State border to White River Junction at the Connecticut River crossing to New Hampshire; Route 2, which descends through the Lake Champlain islands to Burlington, and extends across the state (by way of Montpelier) to the Connecticut River near St. Johnsbury; and Vermont 9, the Molly Stark Trail, which links Bennington and Brattleboro.

The State of Vermont maintains staffed tourist welcome centers in Vernon and Derby Line, on I-91; in Waterford, near St. Johnsbury, on I-93; in Highgate Springs, on I-89; and at Fair Haven, on Route 4. In addition, travel information is available at unstaffed rest stops along the interstates and at chamber of commerce tourist information bureaus in major cities and towns.

Vermont's secondary roads are generally kept in excellent repair, and snowplowing is prompt and thorough. A number of remote, unpaved roads (and several paved routes through high mountain passes) are closed to traffic during the winter, and motorists—even those with four-wheel-drive vehicles—should take these postings at their word. Also, two-wheel-drive vehicles might well avoid unpaved roads during spring "mud season" (late March to early May, depending upon the weather), when melting snows and thawing road surfaces can make for extremely messy and slippery travelling.

By Air
Burlington International Airport, Airport Parkway, South Burlington, is Vermont's only airport serving scheduled commercial carriers. Airlines with flights in and out of Burlington are Continental, United, USAir, Northwest Airlink, and Delta Connection.

By Rail
Amtrak, the nation's intercity passenger rail network, serves Vermont with one daily train, the Montrealer. The Montrealer is an overnight train connecting Washington, D.C., New York City, and Montreal, Quebec. Vermont station stops are at Brattleboro, White River Junction, Montpelier, Essex Junction (Burlington area), and St. Albans. For schedules, fares, and reservations, Tel: (800) USA-RAIL.

By Bus
Major Vermont cities and towns are linked with out-of-state terminals by Vermont Transit, a Greyhound affiliate; Tel: (802) 864-6811.

By Ferry
Four ferries cross Lake Champlain, linking Vermont with New York State. The southernmost crossing is between

Shoreham, Vermont, and Ticonderoga, New York, with continuous six-minute crossings from 8:00 A.M. to 9:00 P.M. in summer and an abbreviated schedule in spring and fall. The ferry does not operate in winter. For information, Tel: (802) 897-7999. The Lake Champlain Transportation Company operates crossings between Charlotte, Vermont, and Essex, New York (20 minutes; May 14 to January 3, depending on ice conditions); Burlington, Vermont, and Port Kent, New York (one hour; mid-May through mid-October); and Grand Isle, Vermont, and Plattsburgh, New York (12 minutes; service year-round). For information, Tel: (802) 864-9804.

Specialty Touring

On foot. The **Long Trail** follows a roughly 260-mile route from the Massachusetts border to Canada; along the way it climbs most of the main peaks of the Green Mountain range. South of Sherburne, the Long Trail's route is the same as the Maine-to-Georgia Appalachian Trail, which branches off to the east at that point. For information on hiking the Long Trail and other Vermont pathways, contact the **Green Mountain Club**, R.R. 1, Box 650, Route 100, Waterbury Center, VT 05677; Tel: (802) 244-7037. The club publishes the invaluable *Guide Book of the Long Trail,* covering mileages, general conditions, and shelter locations, as well as *Day Hiker's Guide to Vermont,* a compendium of routes throughout the state. Also, a hiking-trails information sheet is published by the **Vermont Department of Forests, Parks, and Recreation**, Recreation Division, Waterbury, VT 05671-0601; Tel: (802) 244-8711.

A number of private outfitters offer guided hikes along Vermont trails and back roads, many with inn-to-inn connections. These include **Country Inns Along the Trail**, R.D. 3, Box 3115, Brandon, VT 05733; Tel: (802) 247-3300; **Green Mountain Outdoor Adventures**, H.C.R. 32, Box 90, Montpelier, VT 05602; Tel: (802) 229-4246; **Vermont Hiking Holidays**, Box 750, Bristol, VT 05443; Tel: (802) 453-4816; and **Walking-Inn-Vermont**, P.O. Box 243, Ludlow, VT 05149; Tel: (802) 228-8799.

For a truly unusual hiking experience, try trekking through the Green Mountains accompanied by natives of the Andes. **Northern Vermont Llama Company** offers day-long, half-day, and sunset llama pack trips out of Smugglers' Notch. The llamas carry homemade lunches, snacks, or desserts, depending on the length of the trip. For more information, contact the llama people at R.D. 1, Box 544, Waterville, VT 05492; Tel: (802) 644-2257.

By bicycle. Vermont is ideal bicycling country—you can map out as leisurely or as strenuous a trip as you wish. Just remember that it's not the distance from point A to point B, but the ups and downs in between, that make a Vermont cycling excursion easy or demanding. The *Vermont Atlas and Gazetteer,* published by DeLorme Mapping Company, P.O. Box 298, Freeport, ME 04032, and available in most Vermont bookstores, outlines 21 good routes. Or send for the *Bicycle Vermont Map and Guide,* published by *Vermont Life* magazine, 6 Baldwin Street, Montpelier, VT 05602; Tel: (802) 828-3241.

Bike shops throughout the state offer rentals (of both touring and mountain bikes), as well as maps for self-guided tours; several organizations operate guided group excursions and inn-to-inn tours. Among these are **Bicycle Holidays**, R.D. 3, Box 2394-BL, Middlebury, VT 05753; Tel: (802) 388-BIKE; **Bike Vermont**, P.O. Box 207-GT, Woodstock, VT 05091; Tel: (800) 257-2226; **Craftsbury Sports Center**, P.O. Box 31, Craftsbury Common, VT 05827; Tel: (802) 586-7767; and **Umiak Outdoor Outfitters**, Gale Farm Center, 1880 Mountain Road, #6A, Stowe, VT 05672; Tel: (802) 253-2317.

Cyclists might also check the *Bicycle Touring in Vermont* information sheet published by the Vermont Travel Division, 134 State Street, Montpelier, VT 05602; Tel: (802) 828-3236.

By boat. Travellers bringing boats to Vermont should consult the information on marinas contained in the summer edition of the *Vermont Traveler's Guidebook,* published each year by the Vermont Travel Division (see above, "By bicycle," for address and phone). The guidebook also indicates which marinas offer rowboat and motorboat rentals. A more thorough guide, albeit limited to Lake Champlain and the waterways connecting it to the Hudson and St. Lawrence rivers, is the *Cruising Guide to Lake Champlain,* published by Lake Champlain Publishing, 176 Battery Street, Burlington, VT 05401; Tel: (802) 864-7733 (also available at many Vermont bookstores). For information on boat-launching facilities at Vermont state parks, check the *Official State Map and Touring Guide,* published by the Vermont Travel Division and available at roadside welcome centers or from the Vermont Travel Division. The map also lists those state parks that offer rowboat rentals.

Vermont's mountain lakes, back-country ponds, and winding rivers and streams are ideal for canoeing. Perhaps the best resource for canoeists visiting the state is the Appalachian Mountain Club's New Hampshire–Vermont *River Guide,* available at Vermont book and outdoor-equipment stores or from the AMC at 5 Joy Street, Boston, MA 02108; Tel: (617) 523-0636. A selection of scenic canoe routes is also outlined in the *Vermont Atlas and Gazetteer* (see "By bicycle," above).

Among the many Vermont shops that rent canoes, a number also offer guided trips, many with an "inn-to-inn" theme similar to those organized by outfitters catering to hikers and cyclists. These include **Battenkill Canoe Ltd.**, Historic Route 7A, Arlington, VT 05250; Tel: (802) 362-2800 or (800) 421-5268; **Connecticut River Safari**, Box 3A, Putney Road, Brattleboro, VT 05301; Tel: (802) 254-3908; and **Smugglers' Notch Canoe Touring**, R.R. 2, Route 108, Jeffersonville, VT 05464; Tel: (802) 644-8321 or (800) 937-6266.

Vermont's larger waterways are home to several cruise operators. On Lake Champlain, **Green Mountain Boat Lines** (P.O. Box 2033, South Burlington, VT 05403; Tel: 802/862-8300) operates the *Spirit of Ethan Allen,* a 149-passenger cruise boat, on a regular schedule of scenic, historical, dinner, and sunset cruises out of Burlington harbor. **Connecticut River Tours** (221 Main Street, Brattleboro, VT 05301; Tel: 802/254-7120) offers scenic, historical, and Sunday-brunch cruises on the *Belle of Brattleboro.* And on the Harriman Reservoir, on the Molly Stark Trail (Route 9) near the Massachusetts border, the **Green Mountain Flagship Co.** (R.F.D. 1, Box 51, Wilmington, VT 05363; Tel: 802/464-2975) offers scenic and dinner cruises on a 65-passenger vessel.

Or, run your own cruise. **Vermont Houseboat Vacations** (R.F.D. 1, P.O. Box 90A, Orwell, VT 05760; Tel: 802/948-2330) rents houseboats on Lake Champlain by the day, weekend, and week.

By train. The excursion train Green Mountain Flyer operates along a 26-mile round-trip route between the southern Vermont towns of Bellows Falls (just off I-91) and Chester (junction of Routes 11, 35, and 103). Views include farms, covered bridges, and waterfalls; trains run between late June and Columbus Day. For information contact **Green Mountain Railroad Corporation**, P.O. Box 498, 8 Depot Square, Bellows Falls, VT 05101; Tel: (802) 463-3069. In northern Vermont the **Lamoille Valley Railroad** runs excursions on weekends in summer and daily, except Sundays, during foliage season (mid-September to mid-October) from Morrisville, at the junction of Routes 100 and 15A. Destinations are Johnson (junction of Routes 15 and 100C) and Greensboro Bend (just east of Route 16, north of Route 15); on the latter run trains cross one of the last working covered wooden railroad bridges in the United States. For information contact the Lamoille Valley Railroad at R.F.D. 1, Box 790, Morrisville, VT 05661; Tel: (802) 888-7183.

On horseback. For a complete listing of stables offering trail rides and lessons, as well as hay and sleigh rides, see the State of Vermont's annual *Vermont Traveler's Guidebook* (see above, "By bicycle"). Several stables now offer inn-to-inn horseback excursions, including **Mountain Top Stables**,

Mountain Top Road, Chittenden, VT 05737; Tel: (802) 483-2311; **Kedron Valley Stables**, P.O. Box 168, Route 106, South Woodstock, VT 05071; Tel: (802) 457-1480; and **Vermont Icelandic Horse Farm**, R.R. 1, Box 376-1, Waitsfield, VT 05673; Tel: (802) 496-7141.

By air. **Stowe Airport**, located on Route 100 at the **Morrisville-Stowe** Airport, offers glider rides above the Mount Mansfield/Lamoille Valley area each day from April through early November. Sightseeing tours in powered aircraft can be arranged by reservation. For information contact Stowe Aviation, R.R. 2, Box 6530, Morrisville, VT 05661; Tel: (802) 888-7845. Another glider operation is **Sugarbush Soaring**, at the Warren Airport, offering tours of the Mad River Valley region. Contact Sugarbush Soaring, P.O. Box 123, Airport Road, Warren, VT 05674; Tel: (802) 496-2290. And for something really different, take a long, leisurely drift above the Connecticut River Valley in the gondola of a hot-air balloon. **Boland Balloon**, operating out of Post Mills Airport just north of White River Junction, will take up to 12 people aloft for 1 to 1½ hours, with Champagne after the flight. Contact Brian Boland at P.O. Box 51, Post Mills, VT 05058; Tel: (802) 333-9254.

ACCOMMODATIONS REFERENCE

Unless otherwise noted, the rates given below are projected low- to high-season rates for 1993 for double room, double occupancy. Note that high season may be either winter or summer, with the determination keyed to proximity to ski areas or summer activities. As prices are subject to change, always double-check before booking. The area code for all of Vermont is 802.

Southern Vermont

▶ **Arlington Inn.** Route 7A, **Arlington**, VT 05250. Tel: 375-6532 or (800) 443-9442; Fax: (802) 375-1528. $75–160; includes Continental breakfast.

▶ **Bennington Motor Inn.** 143 West Main Street (Route 9), **Bennington**, VT 05201. Tel: 442-5479 or (800) 359-9900. $46–$68.

▶ **Bromley Sun Lodge.** Bromley Mountain, **Peru**, VT 05152. Tel: 824-6941 or (800) 722-2159; Fax: (802) 824-6290. $75–$120.

▶ **Colonial House Inn & Motel.** Box 138 VW (Route 100), **Weston**, VT 05161. Tel: 824-6286 or (800) 639-5033; Fax: (802) 824-3934. $27–$40; includes Continental breakfast.

▶ **Dorset Inn.** Church and Main streets, **Dorset**, VT 05251. Tel: 867-5500; Fax: 867-5542. $140–$180; includes breakfast and dinner.

► **Echo Lake Inn.** P.O. Box 154, **Ludlow**, VT 05149. Tel: 228-8602 or (800) 356-6844. $100–$150; includes breakfast and dinner.

► **Equinox.** Route 7A, **Manchester Village**, VT 05254. Tel: 362-4700 or (800) 362-4747; Fax: (802) 362-4861. $129–$189 (winter).

► **Four Chimneys.** 21 West Road (Route 9), **Bennington**, VT 05201. Tel: 447-3500; Fax: 447-3692. $75–$125; includes Continental breakfast.

► **Four Columns Inn.** 230 West Street, P.O. Box 278, **Newfane**, VT 05345. Tel: 365-7713. $100–$275; includes dinner and/or breakfast.

► **Hickory Ridge House.** R.F.D. 3, Box 1410, **Putney**, VT 05346. Tel: 387-5709. $45–$80; includes full breakfast.

► **Inn at Long Last.** Box 589, **Chester**, VT 05143. Tel: 875-2444. $160; includes breakfast and dinner.

► **Inn at Manchester.** Route 7A, **Manchester Village**, VT 05254. Tel: 362-1793; Fax: 362-7119. $70–$135.

► **Inn at Weston.** Route 100, **Weston**, VT 05161. Tel: 824-5804. $26–$95; some packages include meals.

► **Inn at Woodchuck Hill Farm.** Middletown Road, **Grafton**, VT 05146. Tel: 843-2398. Call for rates.

► **Kitzhof Lodge.** Route 100, H.C.R. 63, Box 14, **Mount Snow**, VT 05356. Tel: 464-8310 or (800) 388-8310. $84–$128; includes breakfast and dinner.

► **Latchis Hotel.** 50 Main Street, **Brattleboro**, VT 05301. Tel: 254-6300. $34–$68.

► **Londonderry Inn.** Route 100, P.O. Box 301-89, **South Londonderry**, VT 05155. Tel: 824-5226; Fax: 824-3146. $31–$75.

► **Manchester Highlands Inn.** Highland Avenue, Box 1754VWG, **Manchester**, VT 05255. Tel: 362-4565 or (800) 743-4565; Fax: (802) 362-4028. $75–$110; includes full breakfast.

► **Nutmeg Inn.** Route 9 West, **Wilmington**, VT 05363. Tel: 464-3351. $75–$190; includes full breakfast.

► **Okemo Inn.** Routes 103 and 100 North, R.F.D. 1, Box 133VWG, **Ludlow**, VT 05149. Tel: 228-8834 or (800) 328-8834. $170–$190; includes breakfast and dinner.

► **Okemo Mountain Lodge.** R.F.D. 1, **Ludlow**, VT 05149. Tel: (800) 78 OKEMO; Fax: (802) 228-2079. $170–$285.

► **Old Red Mill.** P.O. Box 787 (Route 100) **Wilmington**, VT 05363. Tel: 464-3700 or (800) 843-8483; Fax: (802) 464-8513. $40–$80.

► **Old Tavern at Grafton.** Route 121 and Townshend Road, **Grafton**, VT 05146. Tel: 843-2231; Fax: 843-2245. $95–$150; includes Continental breakfast.

► **Red Shutter Inn.** Route 9 West, **Wilmington**, VT 05363.

Tel: 464-3768 or (800) 845-7548. $88–$155; includes full breakfast.

▶ **Reluctant Panther Inn and Restaurant.** Box 678, West Road, **Manchester**, VT 05254. Tel: 362-2568 or (800) 822-2331; Fax: (802) 362-2586. $160–$300; includes breakfast and dinner.

▶ **Stone Hearth Inn.** Route 11 West, **Chester**, VT 05143. Tel: 875-2525. $60–$120; includes full breakfast.

▶ **Stratton Mountain Resort.** Middle Ridge Road, **Stratton Mountain**, VT 05155. Tel: 297-2500 or (800) 777-1700; Fax: (802) 297-1778. $59–$289.

▶ **Three Clock Inn.** R.R. 59, **South Londonderry**, VT 05155. Tel: 824-6327. $70 per person; includes breakfast and dinner.

▶ **Weathervane Motel.** Route 7A, **Manchester**, VT 05254. Tel: 362-2444; Fax: 362-4616. $24–$85.

▶ **West Dover Inn.** Route 100, **West Dover**, VT 05356. Tel: 464-5207 or (800) 732-0745. $90–$175; includes full breakfast.

▶ **West River Lodge.** R.R. 1, Box 693, **Newfane**, VT 05345. Tel: 365-7745. $65–$75 includes full breakfast; $100–$110 includes breakfast and dinner.

▶ **White House of Wilmington.** Route 9, **Wilmington**, VT 05363. Tel: 464-2135 or (800) 541-2135; Fax: (802) 464-5222. $95–$130; includes breakfast and dinner.

The Champlain Valley

▶ **Anchorage Inn.** 108 Dorset Street, **South Burlington**, VT 05403. Tel: 863-7000 or 658-3351; Fax: 863-7000. $45.95–$72.95; includes Continental breakfast.

▶ **Basin Harbor Club.** Basin Harbor Road, **Vergennes**, VT 05491. Tel: 475-2311 or (800) 622-4000; Fax: (802) 475-2545. $216–$330; includes all meals.

▶ **Fairfield Inn by Marriott.** 15 South Park Drive, **Colchester**, VT 05446. Tel. and Fax: 655-1400 or (800) 228-2800. $29.95–$62.95; includes Continental breakfast.

▶ **Fair Haven Inn.** 5 Adams Street, **Fair Haven**, VT 05743. Tel: 265-4907; Fax: 265-8814. $60.

▶ **Hampton Inn and Conference Center.** 8 Mountain View Drive, **Colchester**, VT 05446. Tel: 655-6177 or 800-HAMPTON; Fax: (802) 655-4962. $72; includes Continental breakfast.

▶ **Holiday Inn.** 1068 Williston Road (Route 2), **Burlington**, VT 05401. Tel: 863-6361 or (800) HOLIDAY; Fax: (802) 863-3061. $59–$106.

▶ **Inn at Essex.** 70 Essex Way, **Essex Junction**, VT 05452. Tel: 878-1100 or (800) 727-4295; Fax: (802) 878-0063. $73–$165; includes Continental breakfast.

▶ **Inn at Shelburne Farms.** Harbor Road, **Shelburne**, VT

05482. Tel. and Fax: 985-8498. $155–$230, private bath; $100–$135, shared bath.

► **Middlebury Inn**. 14 Courthouse Square, **Middlebury**, VT 05753. Tel: 388-4961 or (800) 842-4666; Fax: (802) 388-4563. $75–$144.

► **North Hero House**. P.O. Box 106, Route 2, Champlain Islands, **North Hero**, VT 05474. Tel: 372-8237. $65–$125.

► **Radisson Hotel Burlington**. 60 Battery Street, **Burlington**, VT 05401. Tel: 658-6500 or (800) 333-3333; Fax: (802) 658-4659. $79–$135.

► **Ramada Inn**. 1117 Williston Road (Route 2), **Burlington**, VT 05403. Tel: 658-0250 or (800) 228-2828; Fax: (802) 863-0376. $60–$90.

► **Sheraton Burlington Hotel and Conference Center**. 870 Williston Road (Route 2), **Burlington**, VT 05403. Tel: 862-6576 or (800) 325-3535; Fax: (802) 865-6670. $79–$137.

► **Shore Acres Inn**. Route 2, **North Hero**, VT 05474. Tel: 372-8722. Call for rates.

► **Swift House Inn**. 25 Stewart Lane (at Route 7), **Middlebury**, VT 05753. Tel: 388-9925; Fax: 388-9927. $85–$150; includes Continental breakfast.

► **Tyler Place**. Box 1, **Highgate Springs**, VT 05460. Tel: 868-3301 or 868-4291; Fax: 868-7602. $190–$300 per couple, plus 10 percent service charge. Children $55–$64 each; includes all meals. (Rates are 15 to 30 percent lower before June 26 and after September 4.)

► **Vermont Marble Inn**. 12 West Park Place, **Fair Haven**, VT 05743. Tel: 265-8383. $145–$210; includes five-course breakfast, tea, and dinner.

Central Vermont

► **Cortina Inn**. H.C.R. 34 (Route 4), **Killington**, VT 05751. Tel: 773-3331 or (800) 451-6108; Fax: (802) 775-6948. $80–$180.

► **Green Mountain Inn**. Main Street, **Stowe**, VT 05672. Tel: 253-7301 or (800) 445-6629; Fax: (802) 253-5096. $75–$99. Special packages available.

► **Grünberg Haus Bed & Breakfast**. R.R. 2, Box 1595, **Waterbury**, VT 05676. Tel: 244-7726 or (800) 800-7760. $55–$75; includes full breakfast.

► **Highlander Motel**. Route 108, **Jeffersonville**, VT 05464. Tel: 644-2725. $42–$69.

► **Hotel Jay**. Route 242, **Jay**, VT 05859. Tel: 988-2611 or (800) 451-4449. $86–$300 (includes two meals); condos $215–$290.

► **Inn at Long Trail**. P.O. Box 267, **Killington**, VT 05751. Tel: 775-7181 or (800) 325-2540. $39 with breakfast; $96 with breakfast and dinner.

▶ **Inn at Montpelier.** 147 Main Street, **Montpelier,** VT 05602. Tel: 223-2727; Fax: 223-0722. $93–$143; includes Continental breakfast.

▶ **Inn at the Mountain.** 5781 Mountain Road, **Stowe,** VT 05672. Tel: 253-3000 or (800) 253-4SKI; Fax: (802) 253-7311, ext. 2212. $66–$256.50.

▶ **Inn at Rutland.** 70 North Main Street, **Rutland,** VT 05701. Tel: 773-0575; Fax: ask for extension 12. $70–$150; includes Continental breakfast.

▶ **Inn of the Six Mountains.** P.O. Box 225, **Killington,** VT 05751. Tel: 422-4302 or (800) 228-4676; Fax: (802) 422-4321. $79–$295; includes breakfast.

▶ **Killington Village Inn.** P.O. Box 153, **Killington,** VT 05751. Tel: 422-3301 or (800) 451-4105; Fax: (802) 422-3971. $100; includes breakfast and dinner.

▶ **Knoll Farm.** R.F.D. Box 179, Bragg Hill Road, **Waitsfield,** VT 05673. Tel: 496-3939. From $50 per person.

▶ **Montpelier Bed & Breakfast.** 22 North Street, **Montpelier,** VT 05602. Tel: 229-0878. $25–$60.

▶ **Mountain Top Inn.** Mountain Top Road, Box 432, **Chittenden,** VT 05737. Tel: 483-2311 or (800) 445-2100; Fax: (802) 483-6373. $65–$110.

▶ **PowderHound.** Route 100, **Warren,** VT 05674. Tel: 496-5100 or (800) 548-4022. $50–$110.

▶ **Shire Motel.** 46 Pleasant Street (Route 4), **Woodstock,** VT 05091. Tel: 457-2211. $42–$125.

▶ **Smugglers' Notch Inn.** Church Street, **Jeffersonville,** VT 05464. Tel. and Fax: 644-2412. $46 per person; includes breakfast and dinner.

▶ **Smugglers' Notch Resort.** Route 108, **Smugglers' Notch,** VT 05464. Tel: 644-8851 or (800) 451-8752; Fax: (802) 644-2713. $94 per night, spring and fall; $730 for five-night minimum in winter; includes ski-lift tickets, lessons, activities (various packages available).

▶ **Stowe Motel.** Mountain Road, **Stowe,** VT 05672. Tel: 253-7629 or (800) 829-7629; Fax: (802) 253-7629. $48–$86.

▶ **Sugarbush Inn.** Sugarbush Access Road, **Warren,** VT 05674. Tel: 583-2301 or (800) 451-4320; Fax: (802) 583-3209. $96–$140.

▶ **Three Stallion Inn.** R.F.D. 2, Stock Farm Road, **Randolph,** VT 05060. Tel: 728-5575 or (800) 424-5575; Fax: (802) 728-4036. $75–$90.

▶ **Topnotch Resort & Spa.** Mountain Road, P.O. Box 1458, **Stowe,** VT 05672. Tel: 253-8585 or (800) 451-8686; Fax: (802) 253-9263. $160–$288.

▶ **Trapp Family Lodge.** 42 Trapp Hill Road, **Stowe,** VT 05672. Tel: 253-8511 or (800) 826-7000; Fax: (802) 253-7864. $165–$260; includes breakfast and dinner.

► **Vermont Inn.** Cream Hill Road (Route 4), **Killington**, VT 05751. Tel: 775-0708 or (800) 541-7795. $45–$90 with breakfast and dinner; $30–$75 with breakfast.

► **Village Inn.** 41 Pleasant Street, **Woodstock**, VT 05091. Tel: 457-1255 or (800) 722-4571. $70 off-season (includes breakfast); $290 in-season, two-night minimum (includes two breakfasts and one dinner).

► **Windridge Inn.** Main Street, **Jeffersonville**, VT 05464. Tel: 644-5556. $70; includes breakfast.

► **Woodstock Inn.** 14 The Green, **Woodstock**, VT 05091. Tel: 457-1100 or (800) 448-7900; Fax: (802) 457-3824. $130–$245; suites $295–$495.

The Northeast Kingdom

► **Craftsbury Inn.** Main Street, **Craftsbury**, VT 05826. Tel: 586-2848 or (800) 336-2848. $64–$140; includes dinner and/or breakfast.

► **Echo Ledge Farm Inn.** Route 2, P.O. Box 77, **East St. Johnsbury**, VT 05838. Tel: 748-4750; Fax: 748-1640. $57–$67; includes breakfast.

► **Fairbanks Motor Inn.** 32 Western Avenue, **St. Johnsbury**, VT 05819. Tel: 748-5666. $45–$90.

► **Inn on the Common.** Main Street, **Craftsbury Common**, VT 05826. Tel: 586-9619 or (800) 521-2233; Fax: (802) 586-2249. $220–$260; includes breakfast and dinner.

► **Mountain View Creamery.** Darling Hill Road, **East Burke**, VT 05832. Tel. and Fax: 626-9924. $90–$120; includes breakfast.

► **Old Cutter Inn.** R.R. 1, Box 62, **East Burke**, VT 05832. Tel: 626-5152. $48–$60; M.A.P. rates available.

► **Quimby Country.** Forest Lake Road, **Averill**, VT 05901. Tel: 822-5533. $166–$228 in season (includes all meals).

► **Seymour Lake Lodge.** P.O. Box 61, **Morgan**, VT 05853. Tel: 895-2752 or (800) 828-7760. $50 per person; includes breakfast and dinner.

► **Wildflower Inn.** Darling Hill Road, **Lyndonville**, VT 05851. Tel: 626-8310 or (800) 627-8310; Fax: (802) 626-3427. $65–$130; includes breakfast and afternoon snacks.

► **WilloughVale Inn.** Route 5A, Lake Willoughby, **Westmore**, VT 05860. Tel: 525-4777. $70–$120.

The Connecticut River Valley

► **A Century Past.** Route 5, Box 186, **Newbury**, VT 05051. Tel: 866-3358. $55; includes breakfast.

► **Fairlee Motel & Drive-In Theater.** Route 5, Box 31, **Fairlee**, VT 05045. Tel: 333-9192. $42–$50.

► **Friendship Inn at Quechee Gorge.** Route 4, **Quechee**, VT 05059. Tel: 295-7600 or (800) 732-4376. $54–$72.

▶ **Hanover Inn**. Main Street, **Hanover**, NH 03755. Tel: (603) 643-4300 or (800) 443-7024. $174.

▶ **Ha'Penny Gourmet Bed & Breakfast**. P.O. Box 65, **Peacham**, VT 05862. Tel: 592-3310. $55–$60 (shared bath); includes Continental breakfast.

▶ **Hartness House Inn**. 30 Orchard Street, **Springfield**, VT 05156. Tel: 885-2115 or (800) 732-4789. $60–$105.

▶ **Hotel Coolidge**. 17 South Main Street, P.O. Box 515, **White River Junction**, VT 05001. Tel: 295-3118 or (800) 622-1124. $39.50–$55.

▶ **Juniper Hill Inn**. Juniper Hill Road, **Windsor**, VT 05089. Tel: 674-5273 or (800) 359-2541. $90 with breakfast; $135 with breakfast and dinner.

▶ **Lake Morey Inn Resort**. **Fairlee**, VT 05045. Tel: 333-4311 or (800) 423-1211. $166–$296; includes breakfast, dinner, unlimited golf, and use of all recreational facilities except waterskiing and racquetball.

▶ **Lyme Inn**. **Lyme**, NH 03768. Tel: (603) 795-2222. $65–$95; includes breakfast.

▶ **Parker House Inn**. 16 Main Street, **Quechee**, VT 05059. Tel: 295-6077. $60–$120; includes Continental breakfast.

▶ **Peach Brook Inn**. Doe Hill, **South Newbury**, VT 05051. Tel: 866-3389. $45–$55 with shared bath; $55–$60 with private bath; includes Continental breakfast.

NEW HAMPSHIRE

*By Cynthia W. Harriman, Ann Keefe,
Sara Widness, and Jim McIntosh*

Cynthia Harriman is a longtime resident of Portsmouth. Her travel articles have appeared in the Washington Post, *the* Chicago Sun-Times, *and the* San Francisco Examiner, *and she is the author of* Take Your Kids to Europe. *Ann Keefe writes on international travel from her home in the eastern Monadnock village of Lyndeborough. Sara Widness is a partner in Kaufman/Widness Communications, a New York–based public relations firm. Previously she worked as a journalist and marketing communications specialist in New England, developing an affinity for the region's many roads seldom taken. Jim McIntosh writes frequently about travel and culture in northern New England. For eight years until 1990 he was the editor of* Magnetic North *magazine, a quarterly that celebrated the history and natural attractions of the White Mountains. A 17-year resident of the mountains, he lives in Franconia.*

> Just specimens is all New Hampshire has.
> One each of everything as in a showcase,
> Which naturally she doesn't care to sell.
> —*"New Hampshire," Robert Frost*

The ritual of backwoods commerce begins with the New Hampshire seller professing that, naturally, he doesn't care to sell—a sure sign that a bargain can be struck. This state's character is reflected in the gentle ironies and non sequiturs of its dialect, and Robert Frost often employed these devices to delightful effect in his poetry. His New Hampshire homes numbered two, giving the lie to his "one each of everything,"

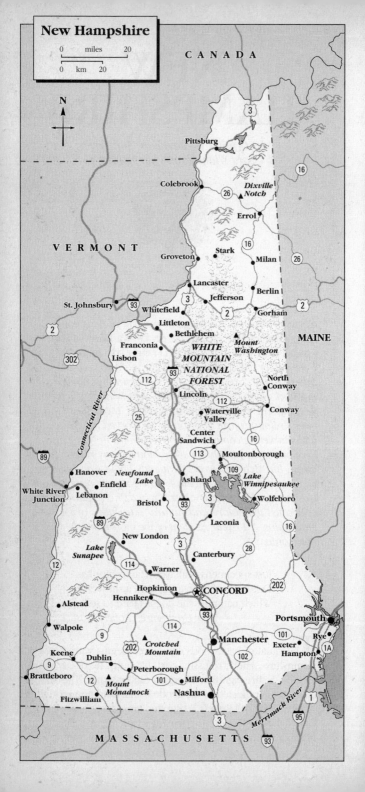

but he would have enjoyed that; he concluded his 400-line poem extolling the character of New Hampshire with the dry throwaway: "At present I am living in Vermont."

Frost loved this state because it defies generalization. A ragged triangle abutting Vermont, New Hampshire is 93 miles wide at the base and 180 miles tall, a mere 9,304 square miles, but with terrain as varied as the fabled elephant in the dark: There are at least six distinct geological divisions, each with a characteristic landscape. This diversity started when the White Mountains formed beneath the Cambrian seas, eons before the glaciers abraded the landscape. When the ice pack began to ebb and flow, these protrusions distorted the flux and created New Hampshire's scores of geologic curiosities.

The coast is an example. South of Maine's rockbound shore, the melting of the vast ice sheets left an 18-mile-long swath of salt marshes and sandy beaches. Eighty miles north of the shore ascend most of New England's highest mountains (the White Mountains), their rocky summits still supporting arctic vegetation sprung from glacier-borne seeds and their valleys embracing the spectacular Crawford, Franconia, and Pinkham notches, the cavernous mountain passes that have awed tourists since the early 1800s. Between the mountains and the sea is a region of dazzling lakes. Ice Age scouring and pot-holing created more than 1,300 lakes in New Hampshire, including immense Winnipesaukee.

Hundreds of icy streams irrigate the state and feed 40 rivers, the most famous of which is the Merrimack, whose valley extends 60 miles from the southern border into the heart of the state. Once a cradle of industry and culture, this valley has become the hypotenuse of the "golden triangle" that is defined by Manchester, Concord, and Nashua, and is host to electronics, service, and retail commerce.

The glaciers' least-esteemed legacy, a thin rocky soil, has confined most agriculture to the broad valleys and rolling uplands typical of the southwestern half of the state and the Connecticut River Valley. Here, the mountains were thoroughly eroded by the glaciers—and later submerged beneath a vast lake of ice—leaving behind a rolling landscape of rugged small hills and shallow valleys dotted by only a few dramatic prominences, notably Mounts Monadnock and Sunapee. Today the state's farms, mostly dairy operations, occupy less than 10 percent of the land area, while forests, more suited to the rocky till, constitute more than 85 percent.

When a Puritan preacher in Colonial Portsmouth—then called Strawbery Banke—asserted that his flock had come to New Hampshire to worship Jehovah, an old man interrupted, ingenuously protesting: "Usn's came to fish!" Settled not by religious fanatics who would impose authoritarian notions of godliness, or by plutocrats who would bind citizens in elaborate systems of economic servitude, New Hampshire's settlers, mostly Scotch-Irish yeomen, sought only dignity, independence, and a chance to prosper in New England's most truculent natural surroundings.

The contrast with Massachusetts is instructive. New Hampshire's settlers saw no profit in persecuting witches. In 1656 a Portsmouth matron accused of witchery was summarily freed by the court. She then sued her accusers for slander and won five pounds plus costs. In Massachusetts she would certainly have been hanged. From the beginning New Hampshire people sought—and expected—tolerance and individual liberty, especially in the realm of commerce. To protest a law against cutting "King's pines," they dressed as Indians and raided a British encampment—this was 35 years before the passage of the 1765 Stamp Act, which led to Boston's far more celebrated Tea Party. New Hampshire was the first colony to declare independence, on January 5, 1776, the same day a state constitution was ratified—also the first in the nation. It was the first of the colonies to declare war on Britain, and it was the first to build and launch a U.S. warship, *The Ranger,* captained by John Paul Jones.

In 1774 a group of New Hampshire men had committed the first overt act of the American Revolution by capturing armaments from a Redcoat armory near Portsmouth. They later deployed these weapons at the Battle of Bunker Hill where, to Boston's eternal chagrin, nearly two-thirds of the Continental soldiers were New Hampshire men. General John Stark, New Hampshire farmer and veteran of Bunker Hill, later led 1,300 New Hampshire troops to defeat Burgoyne in 1777 at the decisive Battle of Bennington. It was Stark, in old age, who penned the words that would become the state motto: "Live free or die, death is not the worst of evils."

New Hampshire Today

Today, while the state's population has swelled to just over a million and its neighbors have strayed from the timeworn Yankee verities, New Hampshire stubbornly adheres to local self-government and civic frugality, generating anachronisms and contradictions that would probably delight Robert Frost but are annoying to progressive souls. No state retains more authority at the township level of government: New Hampshire's 221 towns and cities are often called "little republics," and they continue to sustain the vitality and drama that inspired Thomas Bailey Aldrich's *The Story of a Bad Boy,* Eleanor Porter's *Pollyanna,* Thornton Wilder's *Our Town,* and Grace Metalious's *Peyton Place*. To love New Hampshire is to love small towns.

Long before preservation was fashionable Granite Staters were protecting their scenic and cultural treasures, and today almost two million acres of parkland and forest are held in public trust, as local, state, or federal preserves. It is a typical New Hampshire paradox that the Live Free or Die state, so skeptical of government supervision, has consigned so much land to public ownership. Forty-seven state parks range from historic homesteads to campgrounds to bathing beaches (salt- and freshwater) to picnic areas to public cross-country skiing courses. Half of the coastline is public parkland. The sprawling 770,000-acre White Mountain National Forest, the most accessible wilderness in the nation, covers most of the northern third of the state and offers hundreds of miles of hiking trails. Many local communities maintain their own public museums, parklands, swimming holes, and hiking paths. All of these attractions are impeccably maintained, handy to the highways, and genially unrestricted.

New Hampshire really likes tourists, and always has. It claims the site of America's oldest summer resort in Wolfeboro, where Colonial governor Benning Wentworth built a summer home in the mid-1700s. When railroads reached the lakes and mountains a century later, the tradition of hospitality was further ingrained as grand hotels sprouted from the coast to the Canadian border. The next hundred years witnessed the birth of winter recreation (New Hampshire was home of the nation's first ski school and first ski club), and as the agriculture, textile, and timber industries declined, New Hampshire's cheerful tolerance of visitors became an ardent welcome.

It's a beautiful state, but it is up to the visitor to decide what's most beautiful. Creative people will enjoy this challenge—and likely will find this state curiously stimulating, as Robert Frost and countless others have. They may go to Vermont for repose, but they come to New Hampshire for inspiration. Vermont is a set piece, New Hampshire a pageant. Robert Frost, who loved both states, may have had the last word. In an unguarded moment, he quipped, "Visit unspoiled Vermont. And please spoil it."

At that time he was visiting New Hampshire.

—*Jim McIntosh*

MAJOR INTEREST

Portsmouth
Strawbery Banke open-air museum

Historic South End
Market Square and shopping
Harbor and Isles of Shoals cruises
Restaurants, nightlife, and local inns

Along the Seacoast
Perfectly preserved town of New Castle
Tide pools at Odiorne Point State Park
Rye Harbor restaurants and beaches
Fuller Gardens in North Hampton

Inland from the Coast
Exeter: the academy, history, and shopping
Applecrest Farm Orchards in Hampton Falls

The Monadnock Region
Splendid scenery, especially views of Mount
  Monadnock
Lovely villages and country inns
Music, theater, and arts festivals
Peterborough's architecture and culture
MacDowell Colony for artists, writers, and musicians
Woodland nature walks from Hancock
The gracious village of Francestown
Cross-country and downhill skiing at Temple
  Mountain
Climbing Mount Monadnock, with views of six states

Merrimack Valley
Manchester's Amoskeag Mill Yard and Currier Gallery
  of Art
Concord's historical sights and crafts shops
Canterbury Shaker Village
Country inns and quaint shops in Hopkinton and
  Henniker

The Lakes
Quiet inns and beautiful landscapes
Lake Sunapee
Summer theater in New London
Crystal-clear Newfound Lake
Lovely village of Center Sandwich
Lake Winnipesaukee: boat excursions, beaches, and
  shore towns
Castle in the Clouds
Wolfeboro summer resort

THE WHITE MOUNTAINS
White Mountain National Forest
Autumn foliage

Outdoor pursuits of hiking, skiing, canoeing, fishing, golf, and more

The South: The Pemigewasset Valley
Waterville Valley and Loon Mountain ski areas
Scenic Kancamagus Highway

The Western Slope: Franconia and Sugar Hill
Franconia Notch State Park: hiking, camping, bicycling, skiing
Cannon Mountain Ski Area
The Frost Place, the poet's home for five years

The Western Slope: Route 302 Corridor
Rural towns of Woodsville and Bath: covered bridges
Bethlehem: antiques shops and golf courses
Bretton Woods Ski Area
Mount Washington Hotel
Crawford Notch State Park: hiking, rock climbing
Attitash Ski Area

The Eastern Slope: The Conways
Shopping in North Conway
Country roads and towns south and east of the Conways
Lake Chocorua and Mount Chocorua
Conway village: covered bridges
Echo Lake State Park: hiking, rock climbing, swimming
Mount Cranmore Ski Area

The Eastern Slope: Jackson and Pinkham Notch
Jackson: pretty village and Ski Touring Foundation
Black Mountain Ski Area
Mount Washington and Pinkham Notch: AMC camp and huts, hiking, skiing (Tuckerman Ravine), and Auto Road
Wildcat Ski Area

North Country: Cöos County
Canoeing, fishing, and hunting on county's numerous lakes and rivers
Rural villages along daylong driving circuit, especially Pittsburg
Balsams Grand Resort in Dixville Notch
Moose-spotting

We begin our coverage of New Hampshire in the lively, historic city of Portsmouth and explore the state's abbreviated coastline from there. Next we head west to the town of Peterborough and the bucolic Monadnock region (named for the most-climbed peak in the Western Hemisphere), before turning north along the Merrimack River and passing through the old mill city of Manchester and the state capital, Concord. From there it's on to the so-called lake district, encompassing some of the East's prettiest waters. Finally we enter the northern third of the state, which boasts all of New Hampshire's loftiest mountains, including Mount Washington, the tallest in the East. Note that the border towns along the middle stretch of the Connecticut River Valley (including Hanover, home of Dartmouth College) are covered in the Connecticut River Valley section of our Vermont chapter.

PORTSMOUTH AND THE COAST

Of all the coastal states in the country, New Hampshire lays claim to the shortest stretch of seacoast—just 18 miles sandwiched between Maine and Massachusetts. Yet this short span is a microcosm of New England, with rocky headlands and salt marshes, weathered clapboard homes and regal mansions, and towns as diverse as honky-tonk Hampton Beach and sophisticated, historic Portsmouth.

PORTSMOUTH

In 1623 a ship dropped anchor at the mouth of the Piscataqua River and a small group of English passengers staggered up the slippery, rockbound shore. These people were not seeking religious freedom; in their own simple words, they came to fish. They named their new home Strawbery Banke in honor of the luscious berries so abundant in the area and settled into a boisterous life of fishing and trading.

Such a frontier-town atmosphere existed in Strawbery Banke that when Massachusetts Puritans later moved into town their neighborhood was dubbed the Christian Shore, as it is still called today. Yet the two factions learned to work together, creating a town—soon renamed Portsmouth—that thrived not only on fishing but on shipbuilding and all manner of trade. Just after the Revolution, in fact, Portsmouth was the 12th largest city in the United States. Tall-

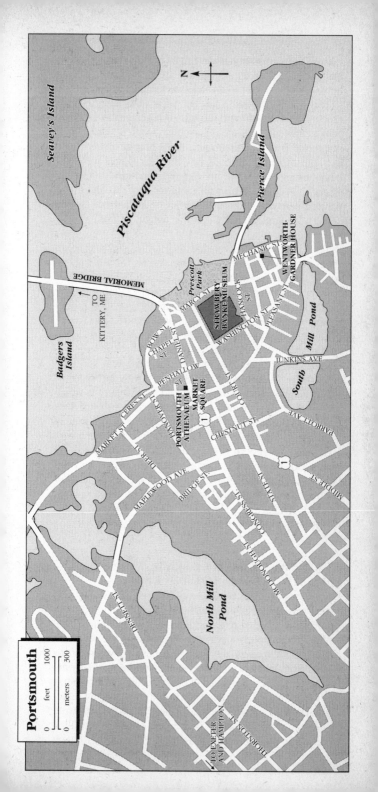

masted ships creaked at anchor in its harbor, elegant Federal mansions stood along its narrow streets, and an ingenious network of wooden pipes carried water to its citizens.

This was Portsmouth's heyday. A few years later, with the Embargo Act of 1807 and the War of 1812, the city began to drift gently into decline. Blue-collar workers at the local breweries and the Portsmouth Naval Shipyard subdivided the ship captains' spacious houses; their wages were just large enough to keep up the old mansions but never enough to replace them with more modern dwellings. As a result, the streets of Portsmouth are still lined with scores of early Federal buildings, to the delight of both visitors and residents.

Yet Portsmouth has avoided the sterile, sanitized atmosphere that preservation often imparts; far from being frozen in time, it's a vibrant town whose best used-book store sits comfortably across the street from Wally's Café, a favorite haunt of local motorcyclists. Ironically, though, most outsiders know of Portsmouth not for its architecture or its vitality, but for its reputation as a great restaurant town, thanks to the quality and variety of its dining options.

Our visit to the Old Town by the Sea, as a late-19th-century Portsmouth writer dubbed it, begins in one of its oldest neighborhoods, the South End, location of the Strawbery Banke open-air museum and street after street of well-preserved private homes. We then continue with a tour of bookstores, bakeries, and boutiques downtown, along with a round-up of several of Portsmouth's best restaurants. Almost all of Portsmouth's historic treasures, shops, and restaurants are concentrated within a half mile of one another in this compact little city, so leave your car in the public garage at the corner of Fleet and Hanover streets and set out on foot.

STRAWBERY BANKE AND THE HISTORIC SOUTH END

Forty years ago the area between Marcy and Washington streets was a maze of junkyards and dilapidated homes built up over the silted-in remains of an ancient tidal inlet called Puddle Dock. A posh subdivision in the 1690s, the neighborhood had thrived in the following century, when goods loaded from its piers were traded all over the world. By the late 1800s, though, the area fell out of fashion as immigrants from Italy, Ireland, and Russia crowded into its aging buildings. Slated for urban renewal, the neighborhood was saved in 1957 by a small group of Portsmouth residents unwilling to let their past be bulldozed. Today 39 buildings dating from 1695 to 1945 make up Strawbery Banke Museum, one of America's oldest continuously occupied neighborhoods.

Strawbery Banke depicts four centuries of ongoing history rather than any particular period. Its eight furnished houses show everyday life in as many different eras, from a shopkeeper's life in the 1790s to that of a Civil War–era governor and even an average 1950s family. Other buildings house displays on architecture, tools, and decorative arts, as well as craftsmen's workshops, including those of a cooper, a potter, and a boat builder.

Be sure to visit the **Dunaway Store** here for local guidebooks, homemade fudge, and colorful patchwork quilts. Also on the grounds is the **Washington Street Eatery**, where you can lunch on salads and sandwiches in the small dining room or outside on picnic tables. Throughout the summer season, special events, such as reenactments of Revolutionary and Civil War soldiers' encampments, are often held at Strawbery Banke. Ask at the ticket office for a schedule and for information on crafts activities and hoop-rolling lessons for kids. Strawbery Banke is open daily from May 1 through October 31. Tel: (603) 433-1100.

Directly across Marcy Street from Strawbery Banke and right on the Piscataqua is **Prescott Park**. Throughout the 1930s and 1940s two civic-minded sisters, Josie and Mary Prescott, used their inherited fortune to buy up seedy waterfront businesses, including brothels, and replace them with a lovely riverside park that today serves as the city's summer living room. Couples wed in the formal gardens, alongside fountains and flowering trees; old men play checkers on boards painted on the granite benches; and kids climb on the whale statue and fish from the pier.

Buy a picnic lunch at one of the pushcarts that line the park in summer and watch the lobster boats unloading at the commercial fish pier opposite the park. In the evenings from early July to mid-August, the Prescott Park Arts Festival hosts concerts and plays on the open-air stage. Spread your blanket on a Friday night and take in a family musical under the stars, or bring a picnic brunch at noon on Sunday (brunch is also served at the park) and listen to classical music or jazz. Locals know that the lawn fills up early, so they come a few hours before any performance, cover themselves with sunscreen or mosquito repellent, and spread out a feast to tide them over until the fun starts. Between performances Prescott Park is a good place for a quiet read of treasures bought from either of two excellent used-book stores, the **Book Guild of Portsmouth** and the **Portsmouth Bookshop**, both located around the corner on lower State Street.

The crooked, narrow streets and centuries-old homes of the South End neighborhood around Strawbery Banke almost compel you to wander on foot. Stop in at the 1760 **Wentworth-Gardner House**, on Mechanic Street, one of the finest examples of Georgian architecture in America, and admire the intricate carving in the front hall and parlor, which took more than 14 months to create. It's open afternoons year-round (closed Mondays); Tel: (603) 436-4406. While you're there ask for a **Portsmouth Trail** walking tour guide, which will direct you to six of the city's most striking houses open to the public.

Next, visit the **Point of Graves Cemetery**, also on Mechanic Street, its tombstones etched with skulls and cherubs dating to at least 1682. If you have young kids in tow take them to the **Children's Museum of Portsmouth**, on top of the hill at 280 Marcy Street, where they can play in a giant yellow submarine or pretend to fish for lobsters. Finally, you might want to rest your feet at **Geno's Coffee and Sandwich Shop** over a bowl of chowder or a lobster roll on the deck overlooking the river, at 177 Mechanic Street. If you want to experience the same seacoast treats at home, the **Olde Mill Fish Market**, at 367 Marcy Street, sells lobsters and the makings for complete clambakes; the nearby **Sanders Lobster Company** (run by the same fishing family), at 55 Pray Street, will ship them anywhere in the country. Call Sanders for details; Tel: (603) 436-3716.

MARKET SQUARE AND DOWNTOWN

Half a mile north of Strawbery Banke and the South End is Portsmouth's downtown area, centered on Market Square. This square, at the junction of Market, Daniel, Pleasant, and Congress streets, was once a chaotic traffic knot lined with parking spaces. Since 1978 wide brick sidewalks and shade trees have funneled traffic into orderly lanes, lending a European feel to the heart of Portsmouth and making Market Square a good place to start exploring the city's restaurants and shops.

The **Portsmouth Athenaeum** anchors the square with dignity. Established as a private library in 1817, this trove of local history and genealogy is open to the public for research on Tuesdays, Thursdays, and Saturdays. Thursday afternoons the members-only Reading Room is open to visitors for viewing the exceptional collection of portraits and oddities, ranging from sailors' valentines made entirely of seashells to a whale's eyeball.

Across the square is **Café Brioche**, a popular bakery and lunch spot. In the best Parisian tradition you can sit at one of the café's many outdoor tables and nibble a *millefeuille* or a croissant sandwich for hours. If Café Brioche is Portsmouth's bakery of the 1990s, **Ceres Bakery**, around the corner at Penhallow Street, is the soul of the 1960s, tending to Birkenstock-clad patrons and specialties such as onion dill bread. While lunch at Ceres is apt to be a nutritious spinach pasta or bean soup, the desserts are shamelessly decadent. The lemon tart is exceptional, but everything, from frangipane and Linzertorte to carrot cake and chocolate chip cookies, is worth the calories.

If you're looking for picnic fare for Prescott Park, Daniel Street is the lunch-to-go center of Portsmouth. **Moe's**, at 22 Daniel just a half block east of Market Square, elevates the simple submarine sandwich to an art form. Across from the post office at number 87 is **Emilio's**, an Italian grocery that dispenses calzones, pizza, and soup with a healthy topping of advice. Emilio Maddaloni, in the beret, makes only two or three dishes every day, and when they're gone, they're gone. But the advice is endless: "How ya doin' today? Ya look a little tired, dear. How about some nice minestrone—it's good for ya."

Shopping Downtown

Portsmouth's main shopping street is Market Street. Although most businesses here cater to tourists, the quality is high and the selection varied, both on Market and on the surrounding side streets. **Harbour Treats**, at 4 Market Square, features handmade chocolate truffles and butter crunch along with an old-fashioned ice-cream fountain. **G. Willikers**, at 13 Market Street, carries classic children's clothes, books, and educational toys. Local crafts are the focus at **Tulips** (19 Market Street) and at **N. W. Barrett Gallery** (53 Market Street), where you can buy everything from model ships to wedding rings to kinetic lobster and fish sculptures. Country collectibles and furniture in the folk-art vein are available at **Old Port Artisans**, 206 Market Street.

Antiques stores are less plentiful in Portsmouth than you might expect, given the town's historic heritage. One of the best is **M. S. Carter's**, at the end of Market Street (number 175), which sells English antiques. If you love old tools, be sure to ask about the toolroom hidden downstairs, where local restoration carpenters often buy the perfect molding plane or saw for period woodworking. **Ed Weissmann**, at 110 Chapel Street, carries high-quality American pieces but is open only by appointment; Tel: (603) 431-7575. The **Doll Connection**, at 117 Market Street, specializes in old dolls and toys. **Partridge Replications**, at 63 Penhallow Street, offers beautifully made reproductions of canopy beds, highboys, and other Early American pieces.

PORTSMOUTH'S MARITIME HERITAGE

Portsmouth's maritime heritage surfaces in delightful and unexpected places. Ten miles off the coast lie the **Isles of Shoals**, first charted by Captain John Smith in 1614, to which you can cruise with the **Isles of Shoals Steamship Company**; Tel: (800) 441-4620. The company offers up to half a dozen sailings per day in summer, all narrated, including whale-watching cruises and stopovers at Star Island, where you'll learn about the history of the fishermen who long populated these islands. Cruises leave from Portsmouth's working waterfront, between the Salt Pier and the Scrap-metal Pier along Market Street Extension. Especially in autumn you might also consider cruises up the Piscataqua with **Portsmouth Harbor Cruises**, whose smaller boat affords a closer look at the foliage and migratory birds of the Great Bay estuary. Harbor cruises leave from a pier on Ceres Street next to the Oar House dock. Tel: (603) 436-8084.

On the Market Street Extension, looking for all the world like a beached whale, is the 205-foot-long **USS Albacore**. Built at the Portsmouth Naval Shipyard (across the Piscataqua on the Maine side) in 1952, this experimental sub served as the prototype for most of our modern submarines. Today it's a museum, where you can tour the cramped quarters its crew of 55 called home. Call for off-season hours; Tel: (603) 436-3680.

DINING IN PORTSMOUTH

Portsmouth's fame as a restaurant town started more than 20 years ago with the opening of chef Jim Haller's **Blue Strawbery** restaurant, at 20 Ceres Street, overlooking the dock where the city's tugboats tie up. Haller has moved on, but this smoke-free restaurant still offers eclectic and imaginative six-course menus featuring such dishes as scallops in Pernod lime butter and beef Wellington with gingered Madeira sauce. Call for reservations and times for the prix-fixe sittings, which vary nightly; Tel: (603) 431-6420. No credit cards accepted.

Vying with the Blue Strawbery for top restaurant honors (and top prices) is **Strawbery Court**, a formal French restaurant on Atkinson Street near Strawbery Banke. The atmosphere is simple and unadorned, almost austere, providing a foil for rich and colorful dishes like roast loin of lamb with rosemary mint pesto and *caneton rôti au cassis,* duckling in a crème de cassis sauce; Tel: (603) 431-7722. For French cuisine that's nearly as good but much more moderately priced, visit **Café Mirabelle**, on Bridge Street, a neighborhood bistro run by an expatriate French chef; Tel: (603) 430-9301.

Two more excellent upper-echelon restaurants are located in the Ceres Street area near the Blue Strawbery. The **Dolphin Striker**, in a 200-year-old tavern at the corner of Bow and Ceres streets, has perhaps the best ambience of any Portsmouth restaurant. The menu emphasizes seafood, from swordfish to scallops, but also includes some meat and poultry; Tel: (603) 436-2377. The **Oar House**, at 55 Ceres Street, is the place to go on a warm summer evening, when its riverside deck offers the best combination of consistently good food and seaport views. (As this book went to press the long-time owner of the Oar House announced his intentions to retire in the very near future, so the fate of this excellent establishment is uncertain.)

A trio of downtown restaurants serves inexpensive but delicious lunches and dinners. **Karen's**, in a light, airy room accented with stenciling at 105 Daniel Street, features fresh California-style cuisine such as grilled tuna Niçoise and smoked chicken in blue cheese Alfredo sauce served over spinach fettucine. The **Grotto Restaurant** and **State Street Saloon**, both near the corner of Pleasant and State streets and under the same ownership, serve imaginative Italian and Greek specialties for less than $10.

One of the Portsmouth area's best restaurants for seafood lies outside of town in Dover Point. **Newick's Restaurant** is a great barn of a building jammed with picnic tables cloaked in red-checked oilcloth. It's noisy and busy but it's true New England, serving mammoth portions of fried and broiled seafood and inexpensive lobsters. Newick's can be tricky to find: From Portsmouth, take the Spaulding Turnpike (Route 16) north about 4 miles (6½ km), cross the General Sullivan Bridge, then take exit 4W, following the signs. Tel: (603) 742-3205.

NIGHTLIFE IN PORTSMOUTH

Portsmouth's downtown is lively on summer nights, with stores open late and crowds of people strolling around, many of them licking homemade Kahlua chip or Swiss chocolate avalanche ice-cream cones from **Annabelle's**, at 49 Ceres Street.

On rainy nights or in the off-season, a cozy alternative is the **Press Room**, a neighborhood pub at 77 Daniel Street run by city council member Jay Smith. On Friday nights local musicians bring their fiddles and penny whistles, and all join in an informal sing-along that ranges from traditional Irish folk tunes to union work songs. Jay is the tenor in the flannel shirt. The **Portsmouth Brewery** is another option. Trading on Portsmouth's history as a brewing center—250,000 barrels of Frank Jones Ale were shipped from Portsmouth every year in the late 19th century—this brew pub serves beer made on the premises, such as Black Cat Stout. Look for the giant beer mug that serves as a sign at 56 Market Street and note the huge copper brewing vats visible through the window in this active and noisy bar.

Theater also thrives in Portsmouth. Check to see what's playing at the **Seacoast Repertory Company**'s steeply tiered modern theater at 125 Bow Street, where shows feature professional performances throughout the year; Tel: (603) 433-4472. The **Music Hall**, on Chestnut Street, one of the last of the grand late-19th-century theaters, is still a showplace for high-caliber performers from Dave Brubeck to Midori to the Peking acrobats; Tel: (603) 436-2400.

STAYING IN THE PORTSMOUTH AREA

The newly built but antiseptic **Sheraton Hotel** is centrally located on lower Market Street, but you'll savor Portsmouth's spirit better in one of several small local inns. The **Inn at Strawbery Banke**, on Court Street, features eight simple Colonial rooms, many with interior wooden shutters and stenciling, all with private bath. Sourdough blueberry pancakes are a favorite item on the breakfast menu. Two blocks west on the same street, the **Sise Inn** is an oak-paneled Victorian mansion with 34 individually decorated, air-conditioned rooms, many with whirlpool baths. Just as close to downtown but across the Piscataqua River in Kittery, Maine, is the **Gundalow Inn,** whose six tranquil rooms have Victorian wallpaper, lace curtains, and brass or iron bed-steads. You can rock on the wide porch while enjoying a book from the owners' copious library.

The **Martin Hill Inn** projects an English country ambience in its seven rooms, despite its location on busy, charmless Islington Street a mile (1½ km) west of downtown. Ask for the so-called Master Bedroom with its curtained canopy bed, or the Library, with pineapple four-poster beds. Even farther out is the **Captain Folsom Inn,** 6 miles (10 km) west in Greenland. Three of the four rooms in this outstanding three-story Federal home have canopy beds; all have fireplaces, quilts, and period furniture, making this a quite romantic getaway. A full breakfast is served in the tavernlike kitchen with its brick baking ovens, and there's a pool for hot summer days.

ALONG THE SEACOAST
New Castle

By far the prettier half of the New Hampshire seacoast is the stretch between Portsmouth and North Hampton. Head southeast out of Portsmouth on Route 1B, a delightful causeway that takes you to the island town of New Castle, about 1 mile (1½ km) away. First settled in 1623, New Castle is a charming collection of weathered old Cape Cod houses and clapboard cottages clinging to the rocks. It's best appreciated if you park your car behind the town hall in the center of town and stroll on foot.

On the island's outer edge lies **Fort Constitution**, where one of the first skirmishes of the Revolutionary War took place. Four months before Paul Revere made his famous ride to Lexington and Concord, he rode here to warn local patriots that the British were marching from Boston to reinforce the fort, then known as Castle William and Mary. Four hundred staunch patriots overwhelmed the British garrison of six and relieved them of 100 barrels of gunpowder. Not far from the fort is **New Castle Common**, a pleasant recreational park with a small, quiet beach and picnic areas overlooking the harbor mouth and the Isles of Shoals.

As you continue along 1B, the road curves back toward the mainland past **Wentworth-by-the-Sea**, one of the last of the great white wooden seaside hotels of the 19th century. Today threatened by demolition, the hotel provided lodging for the Japanese and Russian delegations when they met in 1905 to sign the peace accord after the Russo-Japanese War. The hotel is closed to visitors, but its legacy of fine service lives on in **Ponte Vecchio at the Marina Café**, an excellent Italian restaurant across the street overlooking Little Harbor; Tel: (603) 431-6710. **Wentworth-by-the-Sea Golf Club**, adjoining the hotel complex just off the island of New Castle, allows nonmembers to play on its scenic course at the water's edge. Open April through October; Tel: (603) 433-5010.

Rye

Route 1B ends 1 mile (1½ km) beyond New Castle island, at which point you'll turn south on Route 1A and wend your way through a scenic area of tidal marshes. If you're interested in seashore ecology, stop off at **Odiorne Point State Park**, about 2 miles (3 km) along 1A. Children will enjoy climbing down the rocks and examining tide pools for periwinkles, starfish, and other inhabitants of the Gulf of Maine. Exhibits at the **Seacoast Science Center**, which opened here in 1992, explain your finds.

Route 1A passes through a number of beach communities, many with their views of the sea cut off by a massive rock dike that protects the road from winter storms. Persevere, and you'll soon be rewarded with the lovely beach of **Wallis Sands**, and quaint **Rye Harbor**, with its tiny fishing boats and two good restaurants. To the north of the harbor is **Café Avellino**, serving excellent and moderately priced Italian dinners in a candlelit dining room to the accompaniment of jazz music (Tel: 603/427-2453); to the south, **Saunders at Rye Harbor** offers a traditional surf-and-turf menu in an open, airy building overlooking the harbor and marshes (Tel: 603/964-6466). Farther along are the clean sands of **Jenness Beach**.

North Hampton

About 3 miles (5 km) south of Rye Harbor Route 1A climbs onto the edges of the rocks, affording beautiful views of crashing waves, tankers at sea, and the Isles of Shoals. Now you've arrived at **Little Boars Head**, as locals call this piece of North Hampton that juts into the Atlantic. Here the beach cottages have been replaced by mansions, one of which opens its copious gardens to the public. **Fuller Gardens**, at the corner of Routes 1A and 111, includes rose gardens and a small Japanese garden, both of which invite quiet contemplation. Below Fuller Gardens the area soon succumbs to the boardwalk atmosphere of **Hampton Beach**, a universe of bronzed bodies and fried dough, so you may want to turn your attention inland.

INLAND FROM THE COAST
Exeter

A sleepy town of 12,000, Exeter was the state capital during the Revolution. Now the town, located 13 miles (21 km) southeast of Portsmouth, largely revolves around Phillips Exeter Academy, one of the top preparatory schools in the country.

Exeter's historic past is captured in the **Gilman Garrison**, built before 1690 as a log house fortified to stave off perceived Indian attacks on nearby sawmills. Largely empty of furnishings, the garrison is of special interest to architectural history buffs, who will enjoy seeing how the building made its transition from a frontier outpost to an elegant, richly paneled dwelling as civilization came to Exeter. Daniel Webster boarded here while a student at the nearby academy. The Gilman Garrison is open Tuesday, Thursday, Saturday, and Sunday afternoons from June 1 to October 15.

Also of historical interest in Exeter, at 225 Water Street, is the **American Independence Museum**, newly opened in 1991 and still developing its focus. Its collections in the 1721 Ladd-Gilman house include a number of interesting pieces, including a letter from George Washington, two early drafts of the Constitution, and one of only 25 known original printed copies of the Declaration of Independence.

A half mile south of the center of town is **Phillips Exeter Academy**, whose distinguished alumni include business, government, and literary figures from Gore Vidal to Pierre Du Pont. The campus, immortalized in John Knowles's novel *A Separate Peace,* lines both sides of Front Street with neat Georgian brick buildings, clapboard houses, and a few gems of more recent architecture. Pick up a local paper and check for free concerts and lectures.

The **Inn of Exeter**, at Front and Pine streets, is the place where proud parents take new graduates for a celebratory meal. It serves good food in a proper Bostonian setting of brick walls, small-paned windows, and fine antique reproductions. The inn's 45 rooms are comfortably if rather unimaginatively furnished with Colonial reproduction furniture.

Exeter's small downtown has an all-American Main Street atmosphere, down to the bandstand in the middle of the town square. On lower Water Street are **Water Street Books**, with the good reading you'd expect in an academic town, and **Billingsgate Deli**, a fine place to pick up a sandwich for a picnic along the Squamscott River. Handicrafts, including quilts, weavings, and pottery, abound at both the **League of New Hampshire Craftsmen** (61 Water) and at **Water Street Artisans** (number 20). The **Chocolatier** (number 27) makes all its own candies; the chocolate-covered Oreos are a local favorite. The **Loaf and Ladle**, a restaurant at number 9, is the counterculture alternative to the Exeter Inn. Muffins, whole-grain breads, salads, and delicious soups and stews are served all day long; dinner is accompanied by live folk music Thursday through Sunday.

Stratham and Hampton Falls

We finish up our visit to the seacoast with two out-of-town outings, of interest especially to families. The factory outlet at the **Lindt Chocolate Factory** is tucked away in Stratham not far from the North Hampton line. Take Route 111 north from Exeter until it crosses Route 51; almost immediately take your first left into the Stratham Industrial Park on Marian Way, and follow it to the end. Only truffles are manufactured here, and no factory tours are available, but the Swiss company's entire line of candies can be bought at a large discount on any weekday.

Just south of Exeter via Route 88 in Hampton Falls is **Applecrest Farm Orchards**. Family activities here start in the late spring, when you can pick your own strawberries.

Throughout the summer you can harvest raspberries and blueberries, too, but the orchard is at its peak in autumn, with hayrides, apple bobbing, and pie contests. You can even press your own cider, to take the flavor of New England home with you.

—*Cynthia W. Harriman*

THE MONADNOCK REGION

Paradoxically, the most climbed peak in the Western Hemisphere rises smack from the middle of one of New England's most untrammeled pockets, the serenely bucolic southwestern corner of New Hampshire. Off the beaten path from New York City north to Vermont, but too close to Boston to be considered more than a day's foray, the Monadnock region, named for that mountain peak, retains its water-laced mill villages and steeple-crowned, white clapboard towns, places where pick-your-own apple orchards outnumber touristy gift shops and where all those faded red barns are still just as likely to house a cow as a BMW.

Also surprising, in this down-to-earth Granite State, is the mystical allure Mount Monadnock has exerted on generations of writers, painters, and their patrons, the prosperous "summer people" who first welcomed them here. The tradition of hospitality to artists practiced by those 19th-century Bostonians is maintained by many of their descendants who today are year-round residents of the area. Their support continues to give the hilly, 25-by-35-mile area tucked between the Connecticut and Merrimack rivers its special character as a place where artistry is nurtured and thrives. Hardly a year goes by that a Pulitzer Prize–winning work isn't produced at Peterborough's MacDowell Colony, and the free festival called Monadnock Music transforms a dozen different village churches throughout the area into summer-night concert halls.

So many gods of the late-19th-century literary establishment summered here that Ralph Waldo Emerson declared Mount Monadnock "the new Olympus." Although little more than half the height of northern New Hampshire's 6,000-foot Mount Washington, Monadnock was regarded by James Russell Lowell as "the most high-bred of our mountains." Henry David Thoreau believed that "that New Hampshire bluff— that promontory of a State . . . will longest haunt our dreams."

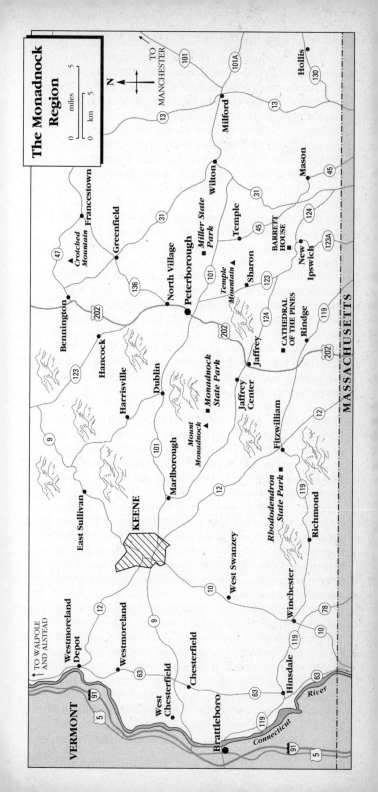

Painters have long been attracted by its symmetry, hikers by its accessibility (two hours' drive from Boston, then two more to the top), botanists by the profusion of flora not found on mountains twice its height. But its greatest attraction is a mystique best described by poets.

Only Japan's Mount Fuji (the Eastern Hemisphere's most-scaled peak) seems to have inspired such veneration. Nathaniel Hawthorne, Rudyard Kipling, and Mark Twain strove to explain Monadnock's mesmerizing charm, and Willa Cather chose to be buried at its foot. Earlier in this century Thornton Wilder called Monadnock "our favorite mountain" in *Our Town,* which he wrote at the MacDowell Colony. His play about the bittersweet dailiness of small-town life was set in Peterborough, home to the artists' colony and fictionalized as Grover's Corners.

Since then other artists-in-residence at that Elysian retreat have racked up 50 Pulitzer prizes for literature and an equal number of Prix de Rome awards for musical composition, painting, and sculpture. Aaron Copland, James Baldwin, Leonard Bernstein, Barbara Tuchman, Alice Walker—it's hard to think of any literary or artistic giant in America who hasn't drawn inspiration from a stay in the woodland studios overlooking Monadnock, the Abenaki Indians' name for "the mountain that stands alone."

TOURING THE MONADNOCK REGION

Pocketed in the state's southwest corner, the Monadnock region has the Dartmouth–Lake Sunapee region as its northern neighbor and the Merrimack Valley to the east. It shares its southern border with Massachusetts and its western border with Vermont.

Route 101 and its continuation, Route 9, bisect the Monadnock region from east to west. Coming down from upstate or north from Boston (50 miles/80 km), most visitors enter the area on Route 101 at Milford, just to the east in the Merrimack Valley. (However, shunpikers, especially those who've been visiting any of the colleges clustered above Springfield, Massachusetts, sometimes meander up Route 202 into Peterborough, New Hampshire.) Route 9 takes over in the west at Keene (the region's only city), then crosses the Connecticut River into Brattleboro, Vermont. Although some of the most enchanting towns lie on capillary roads that branch north and south from this scenic main artery, Peterborough sits right on it. This town of little more than 5,000 people is not the center of the region, but it is its heart.

Just 14 miles (22 km) west of Milford and 38 miles (61 km) east of Brattleboro, at the junction of Routes 101 and 202, is the barn-red cottage of Peterborough Chamber of

Commerce (Tel: 603/924-7234), with a knowledgeable staff and plenty of maps and other information covering the entire Monadnock region. Here, brochures in hand, it's often possible to make an on-the-spot decision as to where to spend the night—or the week (but not in autumn, when cots are set up in school gyms and church halls for the inevitable droves of stranded leaf-peepers who haven't reserved at one of the region's relatively few inns, bed-and-breakfasts, or motels).

For anyone who craves nightlife, even a weekend in the Monadnock region can seem like a month of Sundays. Except in July and August, when classical-music concerts and summer-theater productions abound, there's not much after-dark action. But for those whose pleasures revolve around outdoor daylight activities, and for others who simply yearn to relax in placidly beautiful surroundings, the Monadnock region can fulfill that traditional yen for a month in the country. However, most visitors are satisfied by a stay that falls somewhere between a long weekend and ten days.

While the region is small enough to explore from a single base, those who don't like making circular day trips might prefer an inn-to-inn strategy. Decisions on where to stay often depend on an accommodation's proximity to an attraction or activity. Antiques hunters like to stay in Fitzwilliam; skiers often opt for Temple; mountain climbers tend to favor Jaffrey. In this resolutely noncommercial region the special appeal of a particular hostelry is also an important consideration. In many towns, from dinner time on, the only signs of life are apt to center on the village inn.

PETERBOROUGH

The Monadnock region's most distinguished assemblage of red-brick Federal buildings, capped by belfries, domes, and weather-vaned cupolas, is found in the village of Peterborough. The prosperity suggested by such splendidly maintained architecture now comes less from cattle, farms, and mills than from the town's new role as a publishing center.

Main Street could easily stand alone as a symbol of the region's commitment to culture and the good life. This short thoroughfare begins at the portico of the **Peterborough Town Library**, established in 1833 and the oldest public library in America (after the Library of Congress). The library's downstairs office now serves as headquarters of **Monadnock Music**, whose summertime classical-music concerts are performed in churches and halls throughout the region. Many of the musicians play during colder months with such eminent orchestras as the New York Philharmonic and the Amsterdam Concertgebouw. For schedule information, Tel: (603) 924-7610.

A block up Main Street is the red-brick Unitarian Church, home to the **Monadnock Summer Lyceum**, where a summer series of Sunday-morning lectures is delivered by such nationally renowned authorities as economist John Kenneth Galbraith. After the 11:00 A.M. talk everyone joins the speaker for coffee and chat. Tel: (603) 924-2450.

Across the street, the **New England Marionette Opera**'s theater occupies the former Baptist church. Sitting in red plush seats, the audience listens to recordings of the great operas as the trained fingers of 11 puppeteers bring the scenes to life. Performances are held Saturdays and Sundays from May through December. Reservations suggested; Tel: (603) 924-4333.

The MacDowell Colony

Main Street leads into High Street, where, just north of town, the MacDowell Colony nestles beneath pines. Most days year-round the library and nearby Colony Hall, once the home of the composer Edward MacDowell, are open to visitors. This rustic main building is where colonists congregate for breakfast, dinner, and Ping-Pong. Across the road, the burial place of MacDowell and his wife, who founded the colony in 1907, can also be seen.

But on one special day of the year the 30 artists-in-residence also welcome visitors to their studios, scattered throughout 450 acres of woodland. On all days but this one the only interruption to their work is the silent delivery of a basket lunch. This is Medal Day (by custom the third Sunday of August), when, under an enormous tent, the prestigious MacDowell Award is presented to an outstanding writer, composer, or artist by a speaker who is often someone equally well known for work in the same field. After the ceremony a picnic lunch, complete with splits of wine, can be enjoyed at sun-dappled tables before a stroll to the studios. A reasonable charge for lunch is the only cost for the day's considerable pleasures. Reservations aren't needed for the ceremony, but phone ahead to reserve a picnic basket; Tel: (603) 924-3886.

Peterborough Players

High Street runs directly into Middle Hancock Road and to a meadow, 3 miles (5 km) north of town, that serves as the Peterborough Players' parking lot. From the first week of July through the first week of September mostly light fare—works by Stephen Sondheim or Noel Coward, for example—is given properly sophisticated production. Many actors who are now seen on Broadway and the movie screens, such as William Hurt and Jean Stapleton, first performed here as relative unknowns. Circled by woodland and set in a converted barn, the playhouse, established in 1933, still fulfills every audience's idea of what a summer theater ought to look like. For information, Tel: (603) 924-7585.

DINING AND NIGHTLIFE IN PETERBOROUGH

Prices in the Monadnock region are comparatively low. In top restaurants here, three-course dinners for two often come to less than $40. This is the case even at one of the best, **Latacarta Restaurant** (6 School Street), where chef Hiroshi Hayashi whips up fiddlehead salads, shrimp tempura, and other dishes seldom found on country menus. A classical guitarist plays during dinner on Saturdays. Attached to the restaurant is the tiny **Tensing Theatre**, with sloped seating and a wide screen on which such classic films as *The Red Shoes* are projected Thursday through Sunday evenings. Admission is $4.50, and there's also a $35 dinner-theater package. For movie schedules and/or Latacarta dinner reservations, Tel: (603) 924-6878.

After-dinner folk music is featured most nights at the **Folkway**, at 85 Grove Street, where such deftly prepared vegetarian specialties as angel-hair pasta with mushrooms and herbs are included among the meatier selections. Tel: (603) 924-7484.

Twelve Pine, a takeout place located at 1 Summer Street, is redolent of herbs and baking bread. Picnickers are sure to find something more interesting here than ham on rye.

SHOPPING IN PETERBOROUGH

At 12 Depot Square a former A & P is now home to the **Toadstool Bookshop**, with a stock of more than 30,000 bestsellers, classics, and children's books. **Joseph's Coat**, around the corner at 26 Main Street, is the place to find hand-smocked children's dresses and homemade quilts.

One mile (1½ km) east of the village at the junction of Routes 101 and 123, the **English Gallery**, 6 Old Street Road, exhibits and sells top-drawer work by regional painters and sculptors. Open by appointment only; Tel: (603) 924-9044.

Three miles (5 km) south on Route 123, just over the Peterborough–Sharon line, the **Sharon Arts Center**'s Killian Gallery and Laws House Gallery mount up to nine shows a year of sculptures, photographs, and paintings, many of them for sale, by both local artists and young comers on the national scene. Upstairs, the Crafts Gallery sells one-of-a-kind examples of New England craftspeople's best work in ceramics, blown glass, leather, weaving, toys, jewelry, and clothing. Established in 1946, the center also offers classes in a wide variety of arts year-round. Tel: (603) 924-7256.

On a more prosaic note, **Eastern Mountain Sports**, a huge store 2 miles (3 km) north of town on Vose Farm Road off Route 202, specializes in gear and clothing for the outdoor life.

STAYING IN PETERBOROUGH

Oddly enough, Peterborough itself is lacking in cozy country inns. **Apple Gate Bed & Breakfast**, on Route 123 (Upland Farm Road), neighbor to both an apple orchard and the Sharon Arts Center, dates to 1832 and boasts an enchanting little round staircase among its architectural features. It has only four bedrooms, however. A two-story stack of motel units adjoining the **Salzburg Inn and Motel**, on Steele Road west of the village, has 15 guest rooms. There are no rooms available (or meals served) at the inn building itself (its rooms are rented only on a long-term basis), but the outdoor pool is a draw. **Jack Daniels Motor Inn**, on Route 202, within walking distance of several restaurants in the village, also helps to fill a gap. Be sure to ask for a room with a view of the Contoocook River.

Given these options, it's good to know that in the area *surrounding* Peterborough, inns are almost as integral to the village scene as churches.

NORTH FROM PETERBOROUGH
Hancock

A church built in 1820 and a Greek Revival inn are the two chief gathering places in this tiny, quiet village perched near the edge of a forest laced with nature trails, 10 miles (16 km) north of Peterborough on Route 123. The signature that was writ so large on the Declaration of Independence never appeared on the **John Hancock Inn** guest register here. In fact, Hancock never even saw the town named in his honor—a pity, because its leafy Main Street, lined with red-brick and white-clapboard houses circled with gardens, may be the most charming in the state.

Built in 1789, the ten-room inn, with its two-story-tall front porch, stands catercorner to a bandstand on a bank of Norway Pond, where guests can join townspeople for cooling summer dips. In a recent refurbishment the new owners added optional air conditioning and room phones to such antique features as a room painted with murals by 19th-century itinerant artist Rufus Porter. Dishes to look for on the dining room's menu include Shaker cranberry pot roast, roast pork, and fresh seafood. For dinner reservations, Tel: (603) 525-3318.

The inn is an especially good base for exploring the spruce and white-birch woodlands west of the village. The **Harris Center for Conservation Education** offers guided nature walks on seven miles of paths. Take Route 123 for 2½ miles (4 km) west of Hancock village to a sign on the left that leads to the center's headquarters on King's Highway. A bit farther west along Route 123 a tiny "Audubon Sanctuary" sign on the right directs you to a dirt road, which ends in a footpath that circles Willard Pond. Hearing the cries of the loons here makes it worth the trouble of seeking out this secluded nature trail. Just east of town, the most photogenic of the region's half-dozen **covered bridges** spans the Contoocook River.

Francestown

As a wedding present to his bride, whose beauty has been captured in a John Singleton Copley portrait, Colonial governor Sir John Wentworth named a town in her honor. Appropriately enough, Lady Frances's small village, tucked on a flank of 2,055-foot-high Crotched Mountain, is graced with the most elegantly proportioned old houses in the area. The town general store's shelves are stocked with vintage wines, and the elements of the good life visitors can share with the local gentry include fine dining and golf on a splendidly scenic course.

To reach Francestown, fork off from Route 202 onto Route 136 just 2 miles (3 km) north of Peterborough. Six miles (10 km) northeast, the road skirts the **Greenfield Inn,** a friendly bed-and-breakfast whose nine bedrooms are filled with Victoriana.

Four miles (6½ km) farther along, Route 136 enters the residential village of Francestown, where Federal-era mansions ring the Unitarian church and border Route 47. A right-hand detour here on the New Boston Road leads to **Mill Village Antiques**, just a few yards west. It isn't necessary to be in the market for harvest tables or old fish decoys to enjoy a browse here. A dozen clocks tick-tock in unison under sprigs of bittersweet drying on the barn beams. Open by appointment in the off-season; Tel: (603) 547-2050.

In town Route 47 leads northwest for 2½ miles (4 km) to Mountain Road, where **Maître Jacq Restaurant** perches above the junction. Wide windows beneath beamed ceilings afford good sunset views, while the chef's dinner offerings range from scallops in a sauce of leeks and crème fraîche to a New England version of bouillabaisse with hearty French country bread. Soup, salad, main course, and dessert average only $20; Tel: (603) 588-6655. Across the road is a sweet-scented shop called **Thistledown** that specializes in herbs and dried flower wreaths.

A mile (1½ km) uphill, the **Inn at Crotched Mountain** looks down on endless views of meadows, woods, and mountains far to the north. Small and ivy covered, the inn has a 60-foot swimming pool, two clay tennis courts, a book-lined bar, and a cozy restaurant. Dinner is served Fridays and Saturdays in the off-season, Wednesday through Saturday from May through October; for reservations, Tel: (603) 588-6840.

On Route 47 a short distance west is **Tory Pines Resort**, whose big draw is an 18-hole golf course plus spanking new accommodations that feature working fireplaces and kitchenettes (18 of the 32 rooms are suites). The resort's **Gibson Tavern**, serving three meals a day, offers guests the opportunity to eat out without having to leave the grounds. The emphasis here is on a return to the simplest and freshest kind of American food, made with herbs, vegetables, honey, and maple syrup all produced right in Francestown. For lunch or dinner reservations, Tel: (603) 588-2000. The resort is open from April through November; beginning in 1995 it may remain open year-round.

EAST FROM PETERBOROUGH
Wilton

Twelve miles (19 km) east of Peterborough, Isaac Frye Highway cuts across Route 101 and runs sharply uphill to residential Wilton Center, where expansive, century-old homes share a view of the Monadnock foothills. The turnoff for Wilton village, an especially good base for music, movie, and theater buffs, is another 2 miles (3 km) farther east along Route 101.

One end of this riverbank mill town is dominated by an enormous cupola-topped red-brick town hall that also serves as a movie theater. Decked out with flower boxes, the **Wilton**

Diner marks the other end. This genuine old-fashioned eatery features weekly smorgasbord suppers and pies freshly baked daily (Tel: 603/654-6567).

Less than a mile beyond the diner, still on Main Street, is the old Pine Valley Mill, now home to the **Souhegan Marketplace**. The marketplace consists of three shops that purvey quality toys, crafts, and mineral products, as well as **Café Pierrot**, open for breakfast, lunch, and dinner Tuesday through Saturday and for Sunday brunch. There's a separate cabaret where jazz combos and folk singers entertain on weekends (cover charge is $6) following an all-you-can-eat buffet featuring excellent pastas and rich desserts like shoo-fly pie. Tel: (603) 654-9411.

The **Pine Hill Waldorf Auditorium**, where Monadnock Music's highly professional series of orchestral, chamber-music, and opera concerts takes place each August, is on Abbot Hill Road less than 2 miles (3 km) south of Route 101. (A fee is charged for these, in contrast to the free MM concerts in most area churches.) For tickets, Tel: (603) 924-7610.

Four miles (6½ km) farther east along Route 101 in neighboring **Milford**, Route 13 leads from a traffic oval to the **American Stage Festival**, an Equity playhouse offering top-notch theater—both contemporary plays and revivals of classics—during July and August; Tel: (603) 673-7515.

A ten-room inn called the **Ram in the Thicket** sits on the Milford–Wilton line off Route 101. The pretty bedrooms in this Victorian mansion overlook a field grazed by the inn's namesake sheep. A bar serves as the local pub, while one room in the high-ceilinged restaurant is lit by an immense crystal chandelier. For dinner reservations, Tel: (603) 654-6440.

Those who prefer the intimacy of a bed-and-breakfast will find one called **Stepping Stones**, back in bucolic Wilton Center. Always filled with bouquets of fresh flowers or greenery, this three-bedroom property of a weaver and landscape designer boasts the Monadnock region's most sumptuous blankets and luxuriant gardens.

Davisville Road, the next left-hand turn on Isaac Frye Highway, leads 1 mile (1½ km) north, across a tiny bridge, to **Frye's Measure Mill**. Sequestered beside a woodland waterfall, this wood-shingled mill first began manufacturing wood products in 1858. Today, in addition to the original water-powered machinery, the mill also houses a restored print shop, a wool carding room, a blacksmith's forge, and a store where the mill's noteworthy products, wooden Shaker boxes (known as piggins here) and other decorative boxes, are for sale. Open April 1 to mid-December; Tel: (603) 654-6581.

Mason and New Ipswich

For the ultimate luncheon outing around here the place to go is **Pickity Place**, on Nutting Hill Road in Mason, just south of Wilton. From Route 101, Route 31 runs for 5 miles (8 km) to a blinking light. Turn left here onto Adams Hill Road and follow the signs along woodland roads to a cottage restaurant so picturesque that it once served as an illustration for a book of fairy tales. The five-course meal, redolent of herbs that can be bought in an adjacent greenhouse, is for serious eaters with low cholesterol levels. Reservations are necessary for the three lunch seatings, at 11:30 A.M., 12:45 P.M., and 2:00 P.M. (it's not open for dinner). Tel: (603) 878-1151.

After lunch many people like to drive a few minutes west on Route 124 to **New Ipswich**, where a museum-quality collection of antique furniture still graces the 1800 **Barrett House**, a huge mansion on Main Street complete with a ballroom on its third floor. The rooms may look familiar: In 1978 Merchant-Ivory Productions filmed Henry James's *The Europeans* here. Open Thursday through Sunday afternoons, June to mid-October; Tel: (603) 878-2517.

Temple

Halfway between Wilton and Peterborough on Route 101, Route 45 leads 2 miles (3 km) south to the tiny hamlet of Temple, popular with skiers and with hikers who like to tackle the segment of the mountainous, 21-mile-long **Wapack Trail** that passes through the town.

There are seven bedrooms to accommodate them at the **Birchwood Inn**, set on the edge of the village common. (Henry David Thoreau is said to have stopped at this cozy inn.) The dining room is adorned with frescoes Rufus Porter painted more than a century and a half ago. The inn doesn't have a liquor license, a fact that pleases many guests, who find they can afford better wine when they're able to bring their own to the dinner table. Tel: (603) 878-3285.

The entrance to **Temple Mountain Ski Area** is 3 miles (5 km) west, right on Route 101. A quad chair, a double chair, and T-bars serve 17 downhill trails that are particularly suited to beginning and intermediate skiers. The area has snow-making equipment and is open nights. Twenty kilometers (12 miles) of cross-country trails are also well maintained.

Directly across Route 101 from the slopes is **Miller State Park**, its road snaking up to the top of 2,288-foot **Pack Monadnock Mountain**, second tallest of the peaks that make up the Monadnock range. The view from the picnic tables at the summit is dazzling.

SOUTH FROM PETERBOROUGH
Jaffrey

To reach the top of **Mount Monadnock** itself you'll have to hoof it. The majority of the 125,000-odd people who do this every year choose the trail that begins at **Monadnock State Park** in Jaffrey. Take Route 202 south for 6½ miles (10½ km) from Peterborough to Jaffrey's business district, then Route 124 west 2 miles (3 km) to Jaffrey Center (the bosky, much prettier part of town). From here Dublin Road leads 1½ miles (2½ km) north to the park's entrance.

The small museum at the park's entrance is a good place for first-time climbers to orient themselves to the 40 miles of trails and learn what flora and fauna to look for along the way. Most people, even novices, have no trouble reaching the bald-pate summit in two hours or so. When the weather is right the trails are apt to be thronged with climbers, but the view from the top—its surface is said to have been bared after 19th-century sheep farmers burned out wolves—encompasses all six New England states. As Thornton Wilder declared in *Our Town,* "Yes, beautiful spot up here."

The park's neighbor on Dublin Road is the 18-hole **Shattuck Golf Course**, considered the region's most challenging. Cross-country skiing on the course's cart path in winter is incomparably scenic. (Skiing equipment is available for rent.) Tel: (603) 532-4300.

One and a half miles (2½ km) to the east, on Route 124 in Jaffrey Center, is a meetinghouse raised on the day the Battle of Bunker Hill was being fought. (Carpenters in the steeple are said to have heard the fusillade, 70 miles away.) Willa Cather is buried in its cemetery. Inside, Monadnock Music's virtuoso pianists perform on many Saturday evenings in the summer, and on Friday nights some of the many eminent writers who've chosen to live hereabouts deliver lectures. Called the **Amos Fortune Forum**, the lecture series is named for a freed slave who became a local tanner and whose will helped endow the church.

Cathedral of the Pines is another of the area's open-to-all institutions. Off Route 119 in Rindge, just south of Jaffrey, its pews are open to the sky, facing Mount Monadnock. The parents of an airman killed in World War II dedicated this nonsectarian memorial to the contemplation of God's glory in nature.

STAYING AND DINING
IN JAFFREY

Across Route 124 from the meetinghouse in Jaffrey Center, the gracious old **Monadnock Inn** has a restaurant that serves reliably excellent food. The fish is never frozen, filet mignon is always certified Angus beef, and there's a different freshly made pasta selection every day. With its broad front porch, the 15-room inn looks like a Currier & Ives lithograph. The living room is filled with fresh flowers, English chintz, Oriental rugs, deep armchairs, and a long sofa facing a fireplace that's set to blazing at the first hint of chill in the air. For lunch or dinner reservations, Tel: (603) 532-7001.

Another good lodging choice in Jaffrey is a bed-and-breakfast built in 1853 called the **Benjamin Prescott Inn**, 2½ miles (4 km) east of the village on Route 124 and next door to a dairy farm. Its ten bedrooms are furnished with country antiques.

Fitzwilliam

Southwest of Peterborough on Route 119 lies Fitzwilliam, a favorite Monadnock village among antiques buffs—and the only one that's easily accessible without a car. To drive there, take Route 202 south for 11 miles (18 km) from Peterborough (4 miles/6½ km south from Jaffrey) to its junction with Route 119 in Rindge. Fitzwilliam is another 6 miles (10 km) west on 119. A Greyhound Vermont Transit Line bus from Boston makes two stops a day at the long, leafy common, but the serene little village seems as far away from contemporary urban bustle as Brigadoon.

The bus stops close to the door of the rambling and relaxed **Fitzwilliam Inn**, just as the stagecoach did at the original inn in 1796 (the present establishment was built in 1843). The inn's 28 guest rooms have a homey, old-fashioned charm, but there's an outdoor pool and a pub and restaurant that are open seven days a week. For lunch and dinner reservations, Tel: (603) 585-9000.

The top choice for those who prefer a bed-and-breakfast is just down the road: the Federal–style **Amos A. Parker House**, boasting six wood-burning fireplaces among its comforts. Guests in this outstandingly elegant five-room B and B begin their day with a meal that includes fresh fruit, a meat course, and such tasty surprises as spinach soufflé and cheese blintzes.

There are a dozen antiques shops within an easy stroll of Fitzwilliam's common. The most eclectic collection, with furnishings and whatnots of 43 dealers, is assembled at **Fitzwilliam Antiques**, at the junction of Routes 119 and 12.

Tranquil, bird-filled marshes that branch out from the village offer diversions for serious walkers. **Rhododendron State Park**, especially glorious during the shrubs' mid-July blossoming, is also within the town border on Route 119. A mile-long footpath circles this 16-acre glen; wooden tables in pine groves are fine places to unpack a picnic.

WEST FROM PETERBOROUGH
Dublin and Harrisville

Seven miles (11 km) west of Peterborough along Route 101, Dublin affords the most riveting view of Mount Monadnock, especially on windless days when the mountain is mirrored in Dublin Lake. It's hard to keep your eyes on the road as Route 101 skirts the lake, encircled by the estates that the summer people and the local gentry established during the 19th century. In this, New England's loftiest village (almost 1,500 feet above sea level), *Yankee* magazine and the *Old Farmers Almanac* are published in an appropriately quaint old clapboard building.

It's a measure of just how unspoiled the region remains that there's nowhere at all to stay in Dublin. There is one good place to eat, however: **Del Rossi's Trattoria**, on Route 137 just north of Route 101, favored for homemade pasta and folk music on weekends; Tel: (603) 563-7195.

In **Harrisville**, 4 miles (6½ km) north on the Harrisville Road, there isn't even a place to eat—except for two picnic tables beside a millpond that reflects the entire town center. Awarded National Historic Landmark status as "the best-preserved 18th-century water powered mill village in the nation," Harrisville is also considered the prettiest by the many artists and photographers who flock here.

Marlborough and Keene

Eight miles (13 km) west of both towns Route 101 passes through Marlborough, a village of much more interest to residents than to travellers. However, in the rolling farmland south of this workaday district (via Route 124), Thatcher Hill Road leads to the **Thatcher Hill Inn**, a bed-and-breakfast housed in a smartly restored 18th-century parsonage. Among the inn's antique furnishings is a collection of old music boxes. Be sure to ask for one of the seven bedrooms that afford stunning views of Mount Monadnock, where many trails are open to hikers (see Jaffrey, above).

The inn is also convenient to the more urban attractions

of **Keene**. Five miles (8 km) west of Marlborough on Route 101, this college town has the region's largest population (about 22,000) and a main street so wide that it's more suggestive of the American West than of New England. One of the most absorbing places in town is the **Thorne-Sagendorf Art Gallery**, on the Keene State College campus, where special shows may range from avant-garde photography to antique portraits and oil paintings of Mount Monadnock by the many 19th-century artists who summered in Dublin. (The gallery is open when the campus is open; Tel: 603/358-2720.)

Shoppers head for **Colony Mill Marketplace**, a nicely landscaped mill turned mall at 222 West Street. Most interesting of its myriad shops is **Country Artisans**, which sells Mexican glassware and ceramics as well as silver jewelry, imaginatively patterned hand-knit sweaters, and decorative objects in wood, ceramic, and wrought iron made by New England craftspeople.

Western Monadnock Region

Much of the region's most distinguished Federal-period architecture can be found in **Walpole**. From Keene, Route 12 runs 17 miles (27 km) northwest to a strikingly elegant Connecticut River Valley village characterized by the homes that prosperous, newly expansive yeomen built for themselves after winning the War of Independence. One of the stateliest of the mansions that line Main Street is the **Josiah Bellows House**. Built in 1813 and set on its own six verdant acres, it is now a bed-and-breakfast. Its broad staircase leads from a graciously wide front hall to four exceptionally spacious guest rooms.

But anyone who wonders what life was like for ordinary New Englanders two centuries ago can get an inkling in the Monadnock region's undiscovered, serenely beautiful northwestern corner. Four miles (6½ km) north of Walpole in **Alstead**, a much simpler kind of Early American charm is offered by the **Darby Brook Farm** bed-and-breakfast. The farm's bathroom is shared by three bedrooms, but the compensations are the scent of hay and fresh flowers wafting through the windows, original architectural features such as the wide floorboards and paneling installed when the house was built in 1795, and a remarkably low cost. (From May through October it's just $25 a person, including breakfast.)

The downside is a paucity of places to lunch or dine here in the state's lower Connecticut River Valley. The **Major Leonard Keep Restaurant**, on Route 12 in Westmoreland, 5 miles (8 km) south of Walpole, serves dependably wholesome American fare. The dining room windows overlook the Connecticut River and the hills of Vermont. Open for lunch (every day but Tuesday) and dinner (Saturdays and Sundays only); Tel: (603) 399-4474.

From here you might drive south to the point where Route 63 dips down to meet Route 9, 6 miles (10 km) away. On Route 9 just 2 miles (3 km) short of a green iron bridge that crosses into Vermont, the **Chesterfield Inn** offers something more than comfortable lodging for the night. Once an 18th-century tavern, it has 13 guest rooms, many of which have such amenities as air conditioning, phones, TVs, and wet bars. In three rustic dining rooms, an unpretentious, fair-priced dinner, complete with fresh flowers and snowy linen, adds up to a scene that deserves to be remembered as typical of the Monadnock region. For dinner reservations, Tel: (603) 256-6131.

—Ann Keefe

MERRIMACK VALLEY AND THE LAKES

Central New Hampshire is composed of three loosely defined regions: the Merrimack Valley, which encompasses the state's largest city, Manchester, and its capital, Concord; the Western Lakes, with some of New England's prettiest waters, including Lake Sunapee, quiet villages, and top-notch inns; and the Lakes Region, which is dominated by lively Lake Winnipesaukee to the northeast.

To approach the Merrimack Valley from Massachusetts you may head north on I-93, which bisects the region and passes through Manchester and Concord, two Merrimack River cities that afford visitors the opportunity to dip into the state's history. From Concord we detour briefly northeast to a former Shaker community that once thrived on the strength of its vision. Following the Merrimack Valley comes the pièce de résistance of central New Hampshire: the opportunity to relax along the miles of shoreline provided by refreshingly quiet and pristine lakes, Sunapee and Newfound, that lie to the west of the river. After scooping up these waters we descend from the north for a clockwise loop around Lake Winnipesaukee, the centerpiece of the so-called Lakes Region, northeast of Concord and south of the White Mountains.

While travelling in central New Hampshire, in the southern foothills of the East's most distinguished range—the White Mountains, which we discuss after the Lakes Region—you'll find your perspective is skewed by trees: Fully 90 percent of New Hampshire's nearly 6 million acres are forested. In addition to trees you'll see a lot of the granite that has earned the state its nickname. The prototypes for Robert Frost's "mending wall," knee-high fortresses of granite, snake along the roadsides and coil up through the woods, reminders that this long-overgrown land once served as pasturage for cows and sheep, the latter providing wool for the likes of the Amoskeag Manufacturing Company in Manchester.

The land also supported hay fields, from which the granite stones were removed so horses and plows could furrow their way to harvest. The smaller boulders were used up in stone fences, the larger granite chunks tugged out and chiseled into gravestones. The graves remain, clustered sometimes as few as a half dozen abreast in a plot along the road, sometimes in a larger clutch near a town so small that the only reason for all those graves rests in the village's longevity. When passing through the region, do take a few minutes when the opportunity presents itself to peer through the scrub and pine, to brush dead ferns from gravestones to read weather-worn inscriptions, to scrape away the patina of the late 20th century before slowing down your pace beside one of the region's many lakes.

THE MERRIMACK VALLEY

Because the main attraction of central New Hampshire is its lakes, we suggest just a brief pause in Manchester, a former industrial center, and Concord, which is quieter and more what you would expect a small New England town to be. In just a few hours you can visit the cultural offerings of both and browse along their main streets, which are lined with brick and granite façades. There's no reason to linger too long in either when Yankee hospitality awaits at small village hostelries and country inns in the surrounding regions.

Manchester

Many New England towns and villages are named for places its settlers had known in their native land. (Later many such names appeared on the western prairies and eventually in the far West.) Manchester was optimistically named for England's largest industrial city in the hope that its canal system, which linked it to Boston on the Merrimack River in the early 1800s, would create industrial strength in the new country. The Merrimack River became a major transportation link between northern New England and Boston, and textile mills thrived along its banks, most notably in Manchester. Today that industry has disappeared, but by walking or driving between the rows of factories—all red brick and leaded panes—that parallel I-93 and the river you can still get a good sense of the giant role the mill, and indeed Manchester itself, once played.

The town rises gently from the river with its compact, turn-of-the-century commercial district fanning out into a residential area reminiscent of those of many mill towns.

Amoskeag Mill Yard

Framed in a stairwell of Manchester's Currier Gallery of Art (see below) is a large bronze ram, a weather vane that sat atop mill #1 in the Amoskeag Mill Yard. The ram, whose like grazed neighboring hills, symbolizes the economic clout that the Amoskeag Manufacturing Company enjoyed from 1838 to 1920 as the largest manufacturer of textiles in the world. Once this bronze ram was overlaid with gold leaf, and seemingly so was Manchester, thanks to the mill that employed up to 17,000 workers a year, a hefty percentage of Manchester's population at the time of 70,000.

In 1935, in the wake of the Depression, the mill went bankrupt and closed. Manchester scrambled to diversify its industrial base, but today, almost 60 years later, the town still stands in the shadow of the Amoskeag Mill, which stretches one and a half miles along Commercial Street on the Merrimack River. The complex is slowly being restored, and some of its red-brick buildings are occupied as an adjunct campus by the University of New Hampshire. At present, however, the mills are not open for tours and may be viewed only from the outside.

Science Enrichment Encounters

Within the Amoskeag Mill complex, at 324 Commercial Street, is a children's museum started by physicist Dean Kamen in 1986. Science Enrichment Encounters is a hands-on science center with antigravity machines, angular momentum devices, science and technology puzzles, and more. Kamen also owns most of the millyard overlooking the river. The museum is open daily in the summer and on Thursday nights and weekend afternoons from September through June; Tel: (603) 669-0400.

Currier Gallery of Art

The Currier Gallery of Art, at 192 Orange Street, in a residential neighborhood northeast of the Amoskeag Mill (you'll want to drive; watch for signs), is one of those small museums that surprises and delights: first because of the incongruity of finding a Tiepolo and a Rouault in Manchester, and second because in less than an hour you can be on nodding, if not quite intimate, terms with, among others, Gilbert Stuart, Childe Hassam, George Romney, John Singleton Copley, Lyonel Feininger, Louise Nevelson, Pablo Picasso, Josef Albers, Henri Matisse, and a 13th-century Tuscan Madonna and Child. The museum also houses a collection of Early American furniture and artifacts and has a well-stocked gift shop. A gift to the town by the Moody Curriers, a prominent banking family, the museum opened in 1929 and sits on the site of their former residence.

To reach the Currier Gallery from I-93 take the Wellington Street exit; from I-293 look for the Amoskeag Bridge exit. The gallery, which is open Tuesday through Sunday, stays open till 10:00 P.M. on Thursdays. Through the gallery visitors can arrange to take a tour of a home built by Frank Lloyd Wright known as **Zimmerman House**. Tours are scheduled Thursday through Sunday. En route to the house the tour passes through the mill yards. For information on the gallery and the tours, Tel: (603) 669-6144.

NIGHTLIFE, DINING, AND STAYING IN MANCHESTER

Many of New England's mill cities retain remarkable vestiges of their once-thriving past. One ornate example is the **Palace Theater**, at 80 Hanover Street (Tel: 603/668-5588), with crystal chandeliers that bespeak a bygone elegance. Productions are staged year-round, most notably in July and August with **Stage One Productions** (Tel: 603/669-5511), whose forte is musical theater. In the fall and winter you can catch dinner theater here.

Right in the Amoskeag Mill district, at 75 Arms Park Drive, is **Café Pavone**, serving Italian specialties for lunch and dinner. Dining is alfresco in warm weather; Tel: (603) 622-5488.

Rather than staying in a chain motel or a hotel in Manchester, it's a lot more fun to cozy up under an eiderdown quilt in one of the area's small inns. The **Bedford Village Inn**, just 2 miles (3 km) from Manchester via Routes I-93 south and 101 west, offers a true New England experience. Guest rooms have such traditional furnishings as four-poster beds, enhanced by modern touches like whirlpool baths. Adjacent to the barn that houses the 12 guest rooms is an 18th-century house where you'll find the dining room (open to the public as well as guests), which serves New England fare for breakfast, lunch, dinner, and Sunday brunch. A tavern menu is also available.

Concord

Thirty miles (48 km) north of Manchester on I-93 is Concord, a pleasant town of about 35,000 with a sleepy Main Street that parallels the Merrimack River. The river bisects the town, with most sights of interest within a few blocks of one another on the west side. To get a frame of reference on Concord, browse for a few minutes through the **New Hampshire Historical Society Museum and Library**, at 30 Park Street. A permanent exhibit displays the product of an industry that once flourished here, coach building. One of the buyers of Concord coaches was Wells Fargo. Open year-round; Tel: (603) 225-3381.

The granite, golden-domed **New Hampshire State House**, rising above its neighbors at 107 North Main Street, is the most prominent landmark in town as well as the nation's oldest statehouse still in use. The legislature has occupied the same chambers since 1819. The building's grandeur may serve to remind you that New Hampshire is the state that has, in recent years, produced the courage of a Christa McAuliffe, the eccentricity of a John Sununu, and the still-to-be-plumbed depths of a Justice David Souter. Standing sentry at the statehouse is a statue of the 14th president of the United States, Franklin Pierce, who hailed from nearby Hillsborough.

Pierce, who was elected to the executive office in 1853, lived in Concord from 1842 until 1848. His residence, the **Pierce Manse**, which was moved from its original location on Montgomery Street to 14 Penacook Street, was built between 1838 and 1839, and contains many original family artifacts. It is open to the public daily (11:00 A.M. to 3:00 P.M.) from June 15 to Labor Day. (Penacook Street is at the northern end of Main Street.)

Doubtless when the legislature met years ago many political and other tales were heard by the walls of the old Eagle Hotel, directly across from the statehouse on North Main Street. The hotel is now closed, but its namesake, **Eagle Square**, with a massive Art Deco–style gate, is an award-winning downtown restoration. **Eagle Court**, within the square, is a restaurant popular for its eclectic menu that ranges from stir-fried pork dishes to Italian specialties. Open for lunch and dinner; Tel: (603) 228-1982.

Two fine crafts institutions are located just a short stroll south of Eagle Square on North Main Street: the **Capitol Craftsman**, at number 16, and the Concord shop of the state's **League of New Hampshire Craftsmen**, at number 36. The two shops stock all sorts of crafts, including hand-quilted and hand-woven items, blown glass, pottery, and jewelry.

Christa McAuliffe, the first educator to join a space mission (she was killed in the *Challenger* explosion), is honored at the **Christa McAuliffe Planetarium**, at 3 Institute Drive. In addition to planetarium shows there is an exhibit area that includes hands-on displays. Shows are scheduled afternoons and evenings, every day but Monday. The museum is in a blue-glass structure on the grounds of the New Hampshire Technical Institute. To reach it, take I-93 to exit 15E, then I-393 to exit 1; turn left and go ¾ mile (1¼ km). Reservations are suggested for planetarium shows; Tel: (603) 271-STAR.

DINING IN THE CONCORD AREA

Perhaps because winters are long and cold up here, Concord claims one of New England's best Mexican restaurants. At **Hermanos Cocina Mexicana**, just off North Main Street toward the river, at 8 Pleasant Street, you can dream of being south of the border when the windchill factor brings temperatures down to double-digit figures below zero. Well-travelled patrons donate mementos that decorate the walls. An adjacent shop sells ingredients for making your own spicy meal. No reservations taken.

Off Main Street, toward the river on Depot Street, is another restaurant with a Latin motif, this time Italian, at **Vercelli's Ristorante Italiano**. Osso buco Milanese and *bistecca Fiorentina* are among the offerings here; Tel: (603) 228-3313.

East of Concord, on Pitman Road off Route 126 in Center Barnstead, is the **Crystal Quail Restaurant**, where a select 12 guests per night may bring their own wine to accompany a five-course meal that includes a game dish. Reservations are essential; Tel: (603) 269-4151.

Canterbury

Just 15 miles (24 km) northeast of Concord (exit 18 off I-93) on Shaker Road is Canterbury, a crossroads dominated by a cemetery. Pass through this four corners to reach **Canterbury Shaker Village**, an austere white presence positioned like a child's model village on a hilltop.

Throughout its history, New England has spawned communities that sometimes flourished but more often failed by isolating themselves from the mainstream culture in a framework of moral and religious ideology. Were they similar societal ills that we suffer from today that inspired the Shakers to begin to set themselves apart in isolated communities in the late 1700s?

Some of the answers may be found here in the village, a cluster of 24 white clapboard buildings, five of which are open to the public. This was the sixth of 19 Shaker communities in the United States. By 1860, 100 buildings and 4,000 acres supported 300 people living and worshiping communally here. The last Shaker to live here died in September 1992.

Shaker crafts—boxes, baskets, tin items, woven garments, and furnishings—are still made and sold here, and simply prepared lunches and dinners are served in the village. If you have time, stick around for a candlelight dinner at the village's **Creamery** restaurant, whose menu includes wholesome preparations of seasonal fare from Shaker recipes. There is just one seating for dinner, at 7:00 P.M. For reservations, Tel: (603) 783-9511. The dinner is followed by a candlelit tour of the village in the warmer months and by musical entertainment in cold weather. The village is open daily from May to October, and Friday through Sunday in April, November, and December.

Ten minutes south of Shaker Village is **Wyman Farm**, an ancestral farmhouse with a hilltop vantage where guests have been welcomed in three guest suites (bedroom plus sitting room and private bath) since the late 1800s. Innkeepers Lyford and Judith Merrow serve late-day tea trays with fruit and homemade cookies and made-to-order breakfasts. Call for exact directions; Tel: (603) 783-4467.

West from Concord

HOPKINTON

Hopkinton, 7 miles (11 km) west from Concord on Route 9/202, is a prototypical New England town with the requisite white clapboard homes, a white Congregational church, and sugar maples arching over the streets. The town is best known for its quilting shops, which offer its clients the opportunity to vacation in New Hampshire and at the same time pursue (or build the foundation for) their lifetime hobby. **Country Quilter** is a friendly shop housed in a 200-year-old barn on bucolic College Hill Road. No machine-made quilts are sold here, just the down-home, hand-tied, hand-quilted types that Grandma gathered in her hope chest. Marilyn Hancock is the resident artist, and her husband, Bud, serves as the weekend staff. The shop also sells handcrafted gifts such as miniature quilted dolls pursuing a quilting bee and quilted garments. Yet undiscovered by the public at large, Country Quilter is well known to serious quilters and those wanting to learn the craft; on-premises quilting lessons can be arranged.

Quilters often lodge at the nearby **Windyledge Bed and Breakfast** (off Route 9/202 on Hatfield Road) with hosts Dick and Susan Vogt. The three guest rooms are replete with Oriental carpets, and the inn's elaborate breakfasts energize quilters' fingers for snipping and stitching later in the day.

A neighbor to the quilters on College Hill Road is a 250-year-old barn housing the **Fragrance Shop**, which carries gifts, herbs, and spices. The **Fiber Studio**, on Foster Hill Road in Henniker (see below), offers hand-loomed blankets and scarves in addition to weaving supplies and looms. To get to the Fiber Studio from the Fragrance Shop go east on College Hill Road to Hatfield Road. Turn left on Hatfield, then left again under the bridge to Route 202 west. The Foster Hill Road exit is 1 mile (1½ km) farther. En route you might stop at the **Golden Pineapple** and browse through the store's two floors of country collectibles.

At **Book Farm** (on Old West Hopkinton Road near the corner with Route 9/202), New Hampshire's oldest antiquarian book shop, attention is not lavished—unless it is requested—on browsers. The shop, housed in a building that used to store lumber, specializes in literature, biography, and literary criticism. If you can't find an out-of-print book, they'll undertake a search for you.

The Hopkinton area used to be known for its antiques stores, but many have gone out of business in recent years. Two that remain are **Antiques and Findings**, 835 Main Street (Route 103) in the middle of Contoocook village (part of Hopkinton); and **Boulder Antiques**, on Pine Street in Contoocook. Antiques and Findings closes in the dead of winter, but the owners, Bruce and Audrey Gardner, will open up shop if you give them a call; Tel: (603) 746-5788. Boulder Antiques, which specializes in art pottery and stoneware, closes from October 15 to May 15.

If you've worked up an appetite try the **Horseshoe Tavern**, on Route 103 in Hopkinton, for lunch, dinner, or Sunday brunch. One delicious dish is the salmon *en chemise,* Atlantic salmon topped with lobster, baked in pastry, and served with béarnaise sauce. Tel: (603) 746-4501.

HENNIKER

Some years ago, the quiet college town of Henniker (9 miles/14½ km west of Hopkinton on Route 9/202), once a mill town, went to great lengths to construct a new covered bridge over the Contoocook River in the spirit of preserving an old New England tradition. This kind of civic pride is evidenced in the town's slogan: "The Only Henniker on Earth."

In the town's back yard, on Route 114, is **Pat's Peak** ski area, one of many places in the region where taking winter on its own terms helps mitigate the windchill and shorten a six-month-long winter. The area is open year-round to hikers. Tel: (603) 428-3245.

Dining and Staying in the Henniker Area

The restaurant **Country Spirit**, at the intersection of Routes 114 and 9/202, features barbecues daily and upholds a local tradition: Diners press dollar bills on the ceiling, and the restaurant passes them on to charity. Tel: (603) 428-7007. **Daniel's Restaurant**, overlooking the Contoocook River on Main Street, serves homemade soups, pastas, and seafood for lunch, dinner, and Sunday brunch. Tel: (603) 428-7621.

A 200-year-old farmhouse at 35 Flanders Road (2 miles/3 km south of Henniker via Route 114), the **Meeting House Inn and Restaurant** is the first place locals suggest when it comes to dining out. Such specialties as beef Wellington and brandied seafood have earned the restaurant its reputation. Guests staying overnight in the six antiques-appointed guest rooms have breakfast delivered to them in the morning. For dinner reservations, Tel: (603) 428-3228.

The 16 guest rooms of the **Colby Hill Inn** (follow Route 114 for half a mile south from Route 9/202 and turn right at the blinking light), furnished with simple antiques collected by innkeepers John and Ellie Day, represent 200 years of history. Dinners are prepared by a chef trained at the Culinary Institute of America: One recommended dish is chicken Colby Hill, a chicken breast stuffed with Boursin cheese, lobster, and leeks. For reservations, Tel: (603) 428-3281.

The **Mountain Lake Inn**, on Route 114 about 7 miles (11 km) northwest of Henniker near Bradford, offers guests antiques and quilts in a 200-year-old home on 165 acres with a private sandy beach right on **Lake Massasecum**. Guests can hike on the grounds year-round, swim in and boat on the lake in summer, and snowshoe and cross-country ski in the winter. Dinner is served Friday and Saturday nights, but every day there's a full country breakfast.

WARNER

From Bradford it's an 8-mile (13-km) drive northeast on Route 103 to the **Mount Kearsarge Indian Museum**, on Kearsarge Mountain Road in Warner, a one-street village. (You can also reach it by taking exit 9 off I-89.) The museum houses Bud Thompson's collection of artifacts of Indians of the Northeast woodlands, the Southwest, and the Great Plains. As there are few labels to explain the exhibits, the museum offers guided tours to help shed light on the people who made and used the artifacts. The museum is open May through October, and weekends in November and December; Tel: (603) 456-2600.

From the museum you can continue 4 miles (6½ km) north on Kearsarge Mountain Road to the entrance of **Rollins State Park**, which offers hiking trails to the top of Mount Kearsarge.

On Warner's main street is **Foothills Restaurant**, open daily except Monday for breakfast and lunch. The platter cakes (one-inch-thick pancakes that overflow their plates) are filled with fruit and berries. Tel: (603) 456-2140.

THE WESTERN LAKES

As you head west from the Merrimack Valley you enter the region of the Western Lakes, a cluster of glacial lakes encompassing the northwestern quadrant of the southern half of the state. The pleasures of this water-filled region—with the possible exception of Lake Sunapee, which is well known because of its ski resort—are of a quiet nature, certainly in comparison to those of the raucous Lake Winnipesaukee, in the Lakes Region to the northeast across I-93. Both woods and water vie as the primary attraction here, but diversion is left to the imagination, which opens up such wild possibilities as sitting on a porch reading a book or perhaps even hiking.

Because of the numerous lakes and rivers and the fact that the terrain is suitable for both alpine and cross-country skiing, pursuing outdoor recreation is de rigueur in New Hampshire—and this region is no exception. If you have brought bikes along you may want to consider stopping by cross-country ski centers, as often their trails are excellent for cycling.

Throughout the Western Lakes are villages that exude traditional New England charm, with plenty of cozy inns and interesting shops. We begin our coverage northwest of Concord and the Hopkinton/Henniker area in the Lake Sunapee region with the towns of Sunapee and New London. Then we head northeast through Bristol to Newfound Lake.

Lake Sunapee

Lake Sunapee, ten miles long by three miles wide, is the largest in the Western Lakes cluster. The landscape around

Sunapee (reached by Route 114/103 from Henniker or I-89 from Concord) offers glimpses of lakes, mountains, open fields, and boulder-strewn meadows. Although the two highest mountains in this area—Mount Kearsarge (the mountain that Kate Smith sang about in "When the Moon Comes Over the Mountain") to the east of the lake, and Mount Sunapee, at the lake's foot—aren't the heavyweights you'll find farther north, both offer challenging walks and hikes. The chairlift to Mount Sunapee's summit offers a less strenuous means to see the views in all directions in the summertime and skiing in the winter (see Mount Sunapee State Park, below).

Lake Sunapee is crowded with weekend visitors and seasonal residents in summertime, when excursion boats, windsurfing lessons, and beaches draw the crowds. If you're planning to stay in the region, we recommend you head right to your lodging rather than try to drive around the lake in heavy summer traffic. From your base—in the town of Sunapee on the lake's western shore, or New London, in the northeast—you can make excursions. We cover the lake from south to north, beginning at Mount Sunapee, heading up the western side to Sunapee town, and ending with New London.

A lovely way to see Lake Sunapee is to take advantage of two excursion boats, the *Mt. Sunapee II* (the boat leaves from Sunapee Harbor, in Sunapee town; Tel: 603/763-4030) and the *Kearsarge* (3 miles/5 km east of town on Lake Avenue; Tel: 603/763-5477). Captain David Hargbol charters the *Mt. Sunapee* for parties in addition to giving narrated day tours, and the *Kearsarge* serves buffet suppers on its twice-nightly cruises.

MOUNT SUNAPEE STATE PARK

Mount Sunapee State Park, on Route 103 at the southern end of the lake in Newbury, has a downhill ski area (see Skiing in the Sunapee Area, below), as well as a state park beach on the lake, where there are canoe rentals and a windsurfing school. In August the park hosts the **Annual Craftsmen's Fair**, which claims to be the oldest crafts fair in the nation (1993 will be the 60th year). More than 150 League of New Hampshire Craftsmen representatives compete in a nine-day juried affair of demonstrations and exhibits. For park information, Tel: (800) 258-3530.

SUNAPEE TOWN

Life in Sunapee, north of Route 103 on Route 103B, centers around the harbor. The village population, about 2,500 in the winter, swells to more than 5,000 from the end of June through Labor Day. Coming to Sunapee offers a good excuse to picnic on a grassy knoll near the bandstand overlooking the lake at the harbor. You may wish to linger along the lake in a comfortable inn and perhaps play a little tennis or take day hikes into the nearby mountains.

Dexter's Inn & Tennis Club, on Stagecoach Road, offers three courts (plus a pro) and swimming on 20 acres landscaped with stone walls and gardens. The inn's splendid views take in the lake, Mount Kearsarge, and Mount Sunapee. Guests can choose from among ten rooms in the main house, a two-bedroom cottage, and seven rooms in the annex, which was once a garage housing Model Ts. The room rate includes both breakfast and dinner, with a focused menu that includes just a few carefully prepared entrées. Open May 1 to November 1.

Breakfasts are superb at **Haus Edelweiss**, on Maple Street, a five-room B and B whose hosts lavish a European touch on hearty morning fare.

The **Woodbine Cottage**, a restaurant at 34 River Road, has served up large portions of old-fashioned New England cooking for 65 years under the supervision of the same owner, Mrs. Eleanor W. Hill, who still makes the homemade ice creams and breads herself. This octogenarian monitors quality control for lunch, afternoon tea, dinner, and Sunday brunch in her vine-covered, English-style cottage on the harbor. Tel: (603) 763-2222.

SKIING IN THE SUNAPEE AREA

There are two major alpine ski areas near Lake Sunapee, **King Ridge** (Tel: 603/526-6966), exit 11 off I-89 in New London, and **Mount Sunapee State Park**, off Route 103 in Newbury (Tel: 800/258-3530 or 603/763-2356). King Ridge turns the tables on skiers in the winter: You're outfitted and ticketed at the top of the mountain, where the action is, before skiing down. Mount Sunapee is the larger of the two areas, with a 1,510-foot vertical drop. For cross-country skiers, **Norsk**, on Route 11 in New London, offers 45 miles of trails and is one of the few places in New Hampshire (outside of Jackson in the White Mountains) at an altitude that can guarantee cross-country skiing in warmer-than-average winters, as the past few have been. Tel: 603/526-4685.

New London

New London, a few miles east of Lake Sunapee on Route 114, is the resort hub of this region. This pretty town of white clapboard homes with black shutters bills itself as the "town for all seasons," and for good reason. Its numbers swell from fall to spring with students attending Colby-Sawyer College. In July and August there are band concerts at the **Mary D.**

Haddad Memorial Bandstand in the middle of town, and its summer theater is the best in central New Hampshire. For after-dinner entertainment, the **New London Barn Playhouse**, at 209 Main Street, delivers musicals and comedies from June through August (Tel: 603/526-4631). In the winter skiers flock into town to enjoy the numerous bars and restaurants. The **New London Information Booth** on Main Street (Tel: 603/763-2356) also sells tickets in July and August to a music festival—jazz, folk, and more—at nearby King Ridge.

DINING IN NEW LONDON

The **Millstone Restaurant**, on Newport Road, serves a culinary mix that includes New Zealand venison and Maine mussels. Open daily for lunch and dinner; Tel: (603) 526-4201 or 526-6251.

Peter Christian's Tavern, 186 Main Street, is a branch of the popular pub in Hanover, home of Dartmouth College, midstate on the Connecticut River. Its extensive menu includes lots of grazing items, plus soups, sandwiches, and quiches, and Mexican specials on Tuesdays. Tel: (603) 526-4042.

On the outskirts of town, at Crocketts Corner on Route 11, the **Santa Fe Opera House**, serves Southwestern-style mesquite-grilled lunches and dinners. Tel: (603) 526-8060.

STAYING IN THE NEW LONDON AREA

The late-18th-century, 30-room **New London Inn**, on Main Street, has wraparound porches on both the first and second stories, two living rooms with fireplaces, and lots of antiques and wicker. Its restaurant features seasonal specialties and such Continental standbys as rack of lamb and beef tenderloin. Tel: (603) 526-2791.

Just a few miles out of town there's a resort established in the 1890s that holds onto the concept that three square meals a day make for a happy guest. This is **Twin Lake Village**, on the north side of Lake Sunapee at 21 Twin Lake Villa Road. The resort, open from late June through Labor Day, offers 90 rooms in apartments, cottages, and a hotel; a nine-hole, par-three golf course; three clay tennis courts; shuffleboard; and beach access and boat rentals.

Forget movies, music, bowling, and fast food unless you want to drive great distances from the **Pleasant Lake Inn**, off Route 11 in New London. Guest rooms in this large 1790 farmhouse, which has been an inn since 1878, are comfortable and understated; some have views of Pleasant Lake, as does the dining room. The inn can be hard to find, thanks to local restrictions against signs. The owner describes its location as "one and a half coasting miles down a winding hill through the back roads of New London." More precisely, turn left off Route 11 onto New London's Main Street, drive about 1 mile (1½ km) to a flashing light, and turn right on Pleasant Street. Go about 1½ miles (2½ km) on Pleasant (you'll be at the bottom of the hill by then); you'll see the lodging sign on the left. Guests of the inn are granted privileges at the Slope n' Shore Club, allowing for use of three tennis courts (although court time is very difficult to get) and access to Pleasant Lake.

Northeast of New London and Pleasant Lake is the **English House**, a bed-and-breakfast at the junction of Routes 4 and 11 in the town of **Andover**. Ken and Gillian Smith offer seven English-style guest rooms here, with lots of chintz, handmade quilts, and original artwork made by family members. The breakfast menu changes daily and might offer a soufflé or blueberry pancakes with maple syrup from the Smiths' own trees.

North of Andover by way of Route 4 is the **Inn at Danbury**, an 1850s farmhouse with an attached indoor swimming pool. Hosts George and April Issa offer a cross-country ski program in the winter and encourage their guests (nonsmokers only) to hike, bike, and shop for antiques in the summer. The Issas run the **New England Bicycling Center** on the premises and can suggest easy to rigorous cycling routes. The mood here is casual, as indicated by the red-and-white-checked tablecloths on the dining room tables. The inn enjoys a 70 percent repeat business with nothing but word-of-mouth advertising.

Newfound Lake

Tranquil Newfound Lake, 14 miles (22 km) northeast of Danbury by way of Routes 104 and 3A, is said to be the third cleanest lake in the world. A seven-mile-long glacial font fed by 14 natural springs, it is virtually algae-free and is so clear you can see 180 feet down.

As is typical of New Hampshire lakes, however, it is difficult to gain access to the water unless you're renting a cottage or staying at an inn that offers lake privileges. There is, however, a public beach at the southwestern end and boat rentals are available at the **Newfound Lake Marina**, at 345 North Shore Road in East Hebron (at the northwestern end off Route 3A; Tel: 603/744-3233); a boat equipped with waterskiing gear for four people goes for $250 a day.

On the northern point of the lake on North Shore Road is **Paradise Point Nature Center**, an Audubon Society of New Hampshire preserve near the **Hebron Marsh Sanctuary**. Environmentalists and naturalists are available here in July and August for talks and general information about the Granite State's natural habitat. The center is open weekends in early June and September and daily mid-June to Labor Day, but hiking trails are open year-round. Tel: (603) 744-3516.

DINING AND STAYING
AROUND NEWFOUND LAKE

Just 4 miles (6½ km) south of the lake at the junction of Routes 3A and 104 is the town of **Bristol**. **Abel's Restaurant**, by the Newfound River in Bristol's Central Square, makes a convenient stop for breakfast, lunch, or dinner. Its wide-ranging menu offers such choices as pastas, stir fries, and enchiladas; Tel: (603) 744-8072. The **Homestead**, a restaurant on Route 104 in Bristol, was just that, belonging to a former Revolutionary soldier circa 1788. There's a slight Mediterranean flavor to the ambitious menu, with an emphasis on seafood; Tel: (603) 744-2022.

On Route 3A in **Bridgewater** (between Bristol and East Hebron) is the **Pasquaney Inn on Newfound Lake**, which owns 300 feet of private sandy beach on the southeastern shore of the lake. Rooms are sparingly appointed, hearkening back to a time when bedrooms were for sleeping only, not for lounging. The restaurant features French/Belgian cuisine prepared by Bud Edrick, who trained at the French Culinary Institute and teaches French cooking techniques at the inn on weekends from October through June (excluding January, when the restaurant is closed). Guests at the inn are extended a 10 percent discount on the *Moonlight Miss,* which departs Pasquaney Inn Pier for hour-long cruises of the lake. For dinner reservations, Tel: (603) 744-9111.

Less expensive fare is accompanied by a DJ and music at **Ryan's Loft**, at the Whittemore Inn, just south of the Pasquaney Inn on Route 3A (still in Bridgewater). Folks flock here for Sunday brunch and Wednesday and Saturday night buffets. There's live music on Friday and Saturday nights. Tel: (603) 744-3518.

A fraction of a mile up a steep dirt road off Route 3A (ask the Bristol Chamber of Commerce representative, which maintains a booth on Route 3A, for directions) is **Cliff Lodge**, a 20-seat restaurant where breezes off Newfound Lake fan a kitchen stacked high with fresh produce. Meals here rival the sunsets. The very popular Sunday brunch comes with complimentary Champagne and "morning glory" muffins. Reservations recommended for all meals; Tel: (603) 744-8660. Cliff Lodge also has seven rustic, unheated cabins (sleeping two to eight) available from late May to late September.

THE LAKES REGION

The Lakes Region is defined by a 72-square-mile, glacier-carved, spring-fed lake called Winnipesaukee (translated from the Indian as "Smile of the Great Spirit" or "Beautiful Water in a High Place"), which stretches 28 miles from Center Harbor in the north to Alton Bay in the south. The lake has some 283 miles of coastline and 365 islands. Mountains surround it, with the Sandwich Range to the northwest, the Belknap Mountains to the south, and to the northeast the Ossipee Mountains, harboring a number of pristine state parks that skirt well-travelled Route 16 (which leads to the factory-outlet shopping oasis of North Conway, covered in the White Mountains section, below). In the Ossipees, off Route 16 in Tamworth, is Chocorua Lake, a beautiful setting of peaks and water (also discussed in the White Mountains section).

The Lakes Region was once more of a resort area than it is today. Many of the cottages once available to the public have been bought by individuals, and condominiums have sprung up all around the shore. It's still a vacation mecca, however, as the amusement-park atmosphere of Weirs Beach and the bustle of Wolfeboro across the lake attest. You'll have to do some searching for the same peace and quiet here that you experienced so effortlessly in the Western Lakes.

Our coverage of the Lakes Region in effect describes a complete circle. It begins with the Squam lakes, due east of Newfound Lake and north of Winnipesaukee. Then we move northeast to Center Sandwich, perhaps one of the most charming tiny villages in all of New England. From Center Sandwich we proceed clockwise around Lake Winnipesaukee, with a stop at Castle in the Clouds for an overlook of the region, then on to the old summer resort town of Wolfeboro, around the lake to Weirs Beach on the western shore, and on up to Center Harbor, at the lake's northern tip—not far from Squam Lake and Center Sandwich, where we began. (The next section after that will begin a discussion of the southern quadrant of the White Mountains, just to the north of Center Harbor and Squam Lake.)

ENTERING THE LAKES REGION

The least scenic way to enter the Lakes Region from the south is via I-93, exiting at Tilton (exit 20). Your compensation for taking this route is **Pauli's Restaurant**, at 170 Main Street in Tilton. If you like big breakfasts, this is your kind of place: Owner Steve Nicholson claims the breakfasts here are the biggest you'll ever have. Lunches include deli-style sandwiches served on homemade breads. Pauli's is also open for dinner Wednesday through Friday nights; Tel: (603) 286-7081. From Tilton you can head northeast up Route 3 to Laconia and Weirs Beach on Winnipesaukee's western shore.

Another way to gain access to the area is to stay on I-93 north and take exit 24 at **Ashland**. (If you are coming from Newfound Lake take Route 104 east from Bristol to I-93 north to Ashland.) From here you can connect with Routes 3 and 113, which wind around the Squam lakes. The **Common Man Restaurant**, on Main Street in Ashland, is a good place to fuel up and chow down on an eclectic menu with the locals (Tel: 603/968-7030).

However, another tack into the Lakes Region, bypassing the Squam lakes (you can return to them later, after Center Sandwich or after circling Lake Winnipesaukee) and entering from the north between the White Mountains and the lakes, offers a much more scenic introduction and provides a sense of the magnitude of the mountains that shape the northern part of the state. To enter the area this way, continue north on I-93 to the Campton exit (10 miles/16 km north of Ashland). Near the entrance to the White Mountain National Forest on Route 49 in Campton there's a back road (marked on some maps) known as the **Sandwich Notch Road**. Under no circumstances should you attempt to drive this 11-mile (18 km) stretch without first checking with locals to determine that it's passable (it's usually O.K. in summer and fall). With the go-ahead, this is an adventure in back-country driving, revealing high-country farms, stunning views, and the wonderful village of Center Sandwich at the end (covered below).

Squam and Little Squam Lakes

These two pretty lakes just miss being part of their giant neighbor to the south, Winnipesaukee, from which they are separated by just a couple of miles. The **Inn on Golden Pond** in **Holderness** (the first town you'll come to heading east from Ashland) has country-comfortable guest rooms overlooking Little Squam Lake and the Holderness (incorporated in 1771) town hall. *On Golden Pond* was filmed on Squam Lake, and touches of Fonda and Hepburn seem to linger on at the inn, a casual place where a partially worked puzzle of a loon on the lake may be lying on a card table in the den. A short stroll down the road from the inn is the **Squam Lakeside Farm**, which sells irresistible homemade ice cream.

Also in Holderness, on Shepard Hill Road and Route 3, is an ornate, turn-of-the-century summer mansion that is now the **Manor on Golden Pond**, a 17-room inn with tennis courts and its own 300-foot beach on Squam Lake. Some of the rooms have four-poster beds, fireplaces, and views of the lake. The room rate includes a full breakfast and dinner, and nonlodging guests are also welcome to dine here. For restaurant reservations, Tel: (603) 968-3348.

The **Science Center of New Hampshire at Squam Lake**, on Route 113 in Holderness, encompasses 200 acres with a ¾-mile trail system designed for a self-guided tour. Indigenous species of animals, including bald eagles, otters, and black bears, that for one reason or another are unable to live in the wild, live in outdoor enclosures here. The center is open daily from May to November; Tel: (603) 968-7194.

If you're interested in fishing Squam Lake for landlocked salmon and lake trout or taking a boat ride, call Captain Joe Nassar, who has fished here for 30 years; Tel: (603) 968-7577.

From Holderness take Route 113 north toward Center Sandwich (Squam Lake will be on your right), 12 miles (19 km) away. Just a few minutes out of Holderness watch for signs for **Rattlesnake Mountain**. There will be a parking lot on the left and a path across the road that takes you on a 20-minute hike affording lovely views of Squam Lake.

Center Sandwich

Stone walls, white birch forests, and occasional beaver dams are part of the landscape along the drive to Center Sandwich, the middle village in a cluster that also includes North Sandwich and Sandwich (named after England's earl of Sandwich) on the north border of the Lakes Region just south of the White Mountain National Forest. When you consider the wilderness that you passed through if you took the Sandwich Notch Road and that you will see on the immediate outskirts of Center Sandwich, you will begin to appreciate the fortitude and courage required to maintain a semblance of civilized life in these mountains centuries ago.

Settled in 1767, Center Sandwich is a picturesque, seemingly miniature village with brick and white-frame churches, a crossroads with white signposts, and the handsome **Corner House Inn**, built in 1849. The inn's four guest rooms display a restrained, countrified Victorian decor, and the dining room draws people from miles around. The menu may include homemade breads and soups, duckling, and a scalloped seafood dish. Sunday brunches here are especially popular. Because you are in a territory where life is defined by the seasons, it is suggested that you call for information on when the dining room is open; Tel: (603) 284-6219.

Up here foliage season is a season all its own, sometimes beginning as early as late August and merging with autumn just as mud season merges with spring. On Columbus Day weekend, when the foliage is at its peak, Center Sandwich hosts its annual agricultural show, the **Sandwich Fair**. You can expect to see the usual country fair sights: youngsters tending proudly displayed exhibits of rabbits, chickens, and garden produce, a mix of country folk and city slickers, and lots of fried dough. It's one of the last true old-fashioned country fairs in New England, where jelly judging is still a big event.

Artisans flourish in Center Sandwich, among them Robert and Roberta Ayotte, both graduates of the Rhode Island School of Design. **Ayottes' Designery**, housed in an 1856 building on Maple Street (Route 113) that used to be a high school, has been in the business of weaving and selling clothes and furnishings for 27 years. The Ayottes also proffer crafts, quality yarns, and looms.

Among other artisans and antiques dealers, the League of New Hampshire Craftsmen has a shop here on Maple Street called **Sandwich Home Industries**, founded in 1926 and garnering a respect for traditional crafts long before Sharon Rockefeller began collectivizing Appalachian quilters.

The Sandwich Historical Society's **Elisha Marston House**, also on Maple Street/Route 113, offers free admission to its collection of antique toys, children's clothing, and period furnishings. It is open June through September; Tel: (603) 284-6269.

If you continue northeast on Route 113 you'll bump into the **Strathaven Bed and Breakfast**, in North Sandwich, where innkeepers Betsy and Tony Leiper will be pleased to direct you to **Potholes**, recognized as one of the country's best swimming holes, and to **Durgin Bridge**, a covered bridge dating to 1828 that is a pleasant drive away through stone-fenced woods past a Quaker meetinghouse. The Strathavens' four comfortable guest rooms and welcoming dining and living rooms are lovely. Betsy tends an English-style garden that is popular for weddings and is something of an embroidery guru, giving instruction to small groups throughout the year.

Lake Winnipesaukee

As you head south on Route 109 from Center Sandwich you can clearly see that what the Granite State lacks in coastline it makes up for in freshwater lakes and rivers, most of which are concentrated in this area. Dominant here, of course, is Lake Winnipesaukee, which has two state beaches open to those who aren't lucky enough to be staying right on the lake: **Ellacoya State Park** on Route 11 in Gilford on the western shore, and **Wentworth State Park**, on Route 109 in Wolfeboro on the eastern shore.

MOULTONBOROUGH

A fire department, a church, and a country store make up the main square of Moultonborough, just 5 miles (8 km) south of Center Sandwich at the junction of Routes 25 and 109. Residents of older homes in this tiny town likely as not are relatives of the first people who occupied them. Despite its small size, Moultonborough is a typical New England village, with the advantage of lots of lake frontage.

Moultonborough is one of several towns in the Lakes Region from which you can take a sightseeing tour on an airplane. Because the terrain here is so heavily forested and sprawling, it is difficult to get a true picture of the immensity of Winnipesaukee and the wildness of the surrounding landscape from the ground. An aerial tour allows you to focus on just how rugged this terrain is, how few open working farms have survived the encroachment of the northeastern forest, and how important tourism is to the economy—witness the countless lakeside and island dwellings. Chris Dodge runs 25-minute sightseeing tours with running commentary through **Dodge Air**, at the Moultonborough Airport. Open year-round; Tel: (603) 476-8801. Charter flights are also offered on the opposite side of Winnipesaukee by **Emerson Aviation** (open year-round; Tel: 603/293-7980), at the Laconia Airport off Route 11 in Laconia, and **Seaplane Services** (Tel: 800/541-6923 year-round, or 603/524-0446 from May to mid-October), Route 3 in Weirs Beach.

Staying and Dining in Moultonborough

The **Kona Mansion Inn**, a turn-of-the-century former country estate connected to the Jordan Marsh family, is situated on 125 acres just off Moultonborough Neck Road. The inn offers accommodations with hilltop views, a nine-hole golf course, tennis, and lakefront access. The house specialty in the dining room (open to the public for breakfast and dinner) is Kona chicken, a chicken breast with cream cheese and spinach. For reservations, Tel: (603) 253-4900.

The **Woodshed Restaurant**, ½ mile (1 km) off Route 109 on Lee Road, specializes in prime rib and surf-and-turf combinations. Open for dinner only; Tel: (603) 476-2311.

The northern Italian and French specialties at the **Sweetwater Inn**, on Route 25 in Moultonborough, include steak *au poivre* and lobster ravioli; the Portuguese-style paella is also popular. Sunday brunch is served in summer. Tel: (603) 476-5079.

CASTLE IN THE CLOUDS

Sprinkled throughout many remote areas of New England are vestiges of long-forgotten dynasties, whose grand dwellings, fortunately, have been preserved. If not on the scale of Hearst Castle, they still represent a grandeur that evokes the robber barons of the past.

One such reminder is Castle in the Clouds, reached by heading south on Route 109 to Route 171 and following signs for the castle, which owes its existence to millionaire industrialist Thomas Plant, who reputedly hired 1,000 Italian masons to carve the stone from which his home was built in the early 1900s high above the eastern shore of Lake Winnipesaukee. The approach to the mansion and its 5,200 acres of grounds takes you through a gatehouse and up a steep, private road that passes a 50-foot waterfall and winds through woods opening into meadows in which visitors can picnic, browse, enjoy horse-drawn wagon rides, or ride horseback on 85 miles of trails.

The mansion, recently renovated, is typical of its time, with heavy dark woods dominating in the octagonal rooms and inlaid floors with motifs that meet at the center of the oddly shaped rooms. The stone-covered house sits atop a granite mountain affording views of Winnipesaukee and the surrounding landscape.

On the property is the **Castle Springs** bottling facility, launched recently to quench the growing thirst Americans have for pristine, from-the-source water. A tour of the bottling plant is included in the admission fee to the house. Allow 45 minutes for each. The castle and grounds are open on weekends from mid-May to early June, and daily from mid-June to mid-October; Tel: (800) 729-2468 or (603) 476-2352.

WOLFEBORO

Heading down the southeastern shore of the lake on Route 109 you reach the **Libby Museum**, perched on an inlet of Winnipesaukee called Mirror Lake. Although the museum's founder, a dentist born in 1850, is long gone, his speeches and writings remain to cast a new light on the traditional stereotype of the laconic New Englander: "When I was forty, life began anew for me, or rather the man I was to be was born. It was then that I began to see and feel the force and beauty of Nature. . . . I commenced to collect things, much as a child, for my study of the cycle of life began with butterflies and moths."

Mr. Libby's legacy lies in his museum, which opened in 1912, doubtless a big attraction for summer visitors to Wolfeboro, the oldest summer resort in America. (Wolfeboro, just a couple of miles farther down the lakeshore, was once linked to Boston by train.) His collection includes Abenaki Indian relics, mounted birds, and Early American farm and home artifacts. Open Memorial Day through September.

Wolfeboro was named for General James Wolfe, who died after defeating the French under Montcalm at the Battle of Quebec. Although he purportedly never came through the town, legend has it that over many mugs of ale and rum in a Portsmouth tavern in 1759, three men decided he was an appropriate hero after which to name the new town.

From just about anywhere in Wolfeboro, which today draws such extremely wealthy families as the Marriotts and the Kluges, you can get a glimpse of the water, which lends a festive air to the town. Physically Wolfeboro is reminiscent of a village on Cape Cod—minus the salt air and to some extent the traffic, which is eased by a trolley that runs through town. Wolfeboro visitors are known to dip into Winnipesaukee early in the year—in late June—even though the air temperature may be only in the 60s.

Staying and Dining in Wolfeboro

Some of the 43 rooms of the **Wolfeboro Inn**, on the corner of North Main Street and Sewall Road, date to 1812, and some afford views of Wolfeboro Bay across the landscaped grounds. The hotel offers lake jaunts on its boat, the *Judge Sewall,* holding up to 75 passengers (the cruise is included in the room rate, but nonguests may go for a modest fee). Cruises, an hour to an hour and a half long, board at the town docks in downtown Wolfeboro and proceed along the shoreline.

The Wolfeboro Inn's dining room, presided over by chef Gary Brockney, serves traditional country cuisine. The inn's New England clam chowder has been the winning entry in a local culinary contest twice. (Remember that even though you're in the mountains, it's only a short hop to the Atlantic Ocean, so this is a good place to indulge a fancy for little-neck clams and other seafood.)

The menu at the inn's **Wolfe's Tavern** is a sociological insight unto itself, with the Ploughman's Lunch, the Big Barndoor, the Barber Pole, and the Graveyard among its more whimsical offerings. Referring to Montcalm's Revenge, a whopping sandwich, the house claims: "If you eat one of these all by yourself at one sitting, you not only get a free entrée the next time you come by, but your name will be forever memorialized on our tavern wall as a General Wolfer." Tel: (603) 569-3016.

An extensive collection of 78s and a Victrola to play them on are among the turn-of-the-century indulgences for guests of the **Tuc' Me Inn**, on North Main Street. Not necessarily an indulgence are the inn's spirits. While sitting in a rocking chair you might find your socks mysteriously tugged, or while walking upstairs your shoulder tapped. Other mysterious happenings here include the appearance of balls of light and doors slamming shut that were already closed. But innkeeper Ernie Foutz promises his ghosts are benign. Look for homemade touches of intricately carved fretwork around the windows here; Ernie's a jigsaw artist! A full country breakfast is served every morning.

The American fare in the dining room of the **Lakeview Inn**, at 120 North Main Street, is a staple for Wolfeboro's summer folks. Fourteen rooms are available in the adjacent motor court and three in the inn itself. The Lakeview often hosts musical entertainment, including cabaret, on various nights. Tel: (603) 569-1335.

The entertainment at **Rumors Café**, on the water at 6 North Main Street, includes having a beer and watching boats maneuver into slips. The witty menu was no doubt contrived during the long New Hampshire winter. Hard-rock bands perform on weekend evenings. Tel: (603) 569-1201.

WEIRS BEACH AREA

As you dip around the southern tip of Winnipesaukee and then head north on Routes 11 and 11B on the western side of the lake the traffic thickens. You're approaching Weirs Beach, a community dedicated to amusement whose star is a huge water slide. The *Mount Washington* cruises Lake Winnipesaukee from Weirs Beach from May to October. Daytime cruises lasting two hours and 15 minutes or three hours and 15 minutes sail from Weirs Beach to Wolfeboro and other parts. En route the boat skirts some of the 365 islands, many of which are privately owned and inhabited, that dot the lake. If you happen to be out on a tranquil day it's hard to imagine the force of the wind that skips through here in a storm, kicking up waves and posing a hazard to small boats. The *Mount Washington* also offers evening sailings with theme dinner dances and live bands (the evening dress code is dressy casual—collared shirt required for men). Tel: (603) 366-2628.

Just a few miles south of Weirs Beach, at 76 Lake Street in Laconia, is the **Margate on Winnipesaukee**, a modern resort offering beachfront lodging, indoor and outdoor swimming pools, tennis, and a fitness center. The specialty of the resort's restaurant, **Blackstone's Lounge**, is prime rib, and there's dancing and live entertainment in the nearby lounge.

MEREDITH

Route 3 leads north from Weirs Beach to the town of Meredith, which rises terrace-like above its harbor. The old part of town, up on the hill, has seen better times, and these days most of the activity takes place right on the lakeshore and across the street at the **Mill Falls Marketplace**. This retro-fitted structure with gleaming, wide-plank floors and beamed ceilings is refreshingly eclectic—a mélange of 20 shops, including book and crafts shops; restaurants, such as the **Millworks Restaurant** (Tel: 603/279-4116), serving clam chowder and Maine lobster; and the 54-room **Inn at Mill Falls**, all under one roof. The hotel is so neatly tucked into this historic edifice that until you go upstairs and discover the front desk you'd hardly know you're at an inn. The guest rooms are spacious and tastefully decorated in a country-Colonial style.

As background noise the marketplace enjoys the roar of falling water that the controlled turbulence of the old millrace makes as it descends from an underground canal, culminating in a 40-foot waterfall that pours into Lake Winnipesaukee. The power generated was used to run the mechanisms by which linen towels and other items were produced at this mill, which at its height employed some 150 people.

In July and August you might catch productions of the Alley Cat Players at the **Lakes Region Theatre**, located at the Inter-Lakes High School in Meredith on Route 25. After a ten-year hiatus summer theater was relaunched in the region in 1992. Tel: (603) 279-9933.

The **Old Print Barn**, just west of Meredith (take Route 104 west from its intersection with Route 3 for 1½ miles/2½ km and turn right onto Winona Road), is a restored 19th-century barn with hand-hewn beams, the perfect setting for displaying reproductions of lithographs, etchings, and engravings of masters spanning the 14th through the 20th centuries. Prints from estate collections are sometimes available. The adjoining gallery is open daily year-round, though the barn is closed in winter.

CENTER HARBOR

If you continue northeast on Route 25 you will come to Center Harbor, south of Squam Lake.

Near the town, high atop a knoll with views of Squam Lake and the White Mountains, is the **Red Hill Inn** (reached by a winding road off Route 25B and College Road). Guest rooms are spread out among the antiques-appointed lodge and in rustic cottages and a farmhouse, all part of the complex. In the winter the inn grooms two miles of ski trails on and about its 60 acres. The ambitious menu at the restaurant includes roast rabbit and pheasant and baked brie served with crackers and jam. Reservations are essential for dinner; Tel: (603) 279-7001.

—*Sara Widness*

THE WHITE MOUNTAINS

This is the Notch of the White Hills. Shame on me that I have attempted to describe it by so mean an image— feeling as I do, that it is one of those symbolic scenes which lead the mind to the sentiment, though not to the conception, of Omnipotence.

—*Nathaniel Hawthorne on Crawford Notch*

The northern third of New Hampshire claims less than a tenth of the state's one million citizens but all of its famous notches—mountain passes or gaps—and all of its big mountains: 48 peaks in excess of 4,000 feet, and Mount Washington, at 6,288 feet the loftiest in the Northeast. The highways are corridors of green and granite punctuated by sheer cliffs, covered bridges, waterfalls, country inns, and grand hotels. Half of the region is protected as national forest and the other half is rural or even wild. The rivers that wrought much of New England's prosperity originate here: the Connecticut, the Androscoggin, the Saco, and the Merrimack. As this rugged landscape shaped human endeavor, it not only limited development but demanded endurance and proportion, the qualities that define the White Mountains' abiding charm.

When the intellects of the young nation first dared to dream, they dreamed of a romanticized wilderness, which, for Ralph Waldo Emerson, Nathaniel Hawthorne, John Greenleaf Whittier, Henry David Thoreau, and Henry Wadsworth Longfellow, meant the White Mountains. The transcendentalists celebrated the "gothick" wonders, civilized hospitality, and amusing rusticity they discovered here. America's first crop of landscape artists sought "the sublime" in these rugged hills. At the same time, the canvases of Thomas Cole, Benjamin Champney, Albert Bierstadt, and Jasper Francis Cropsey captured their "terrible grandeur" in images that heralded an American style distinct from European conven-

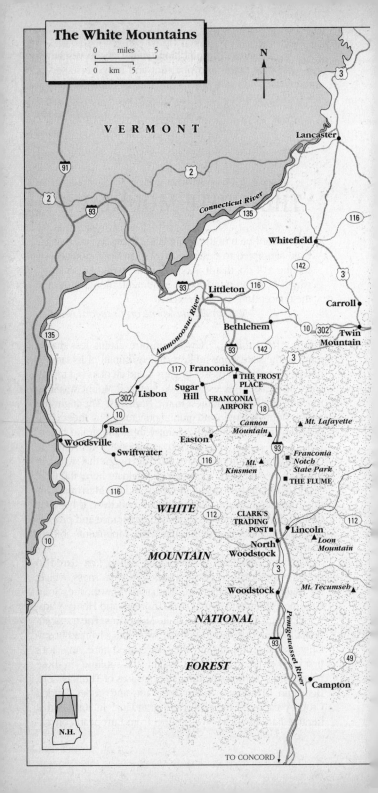

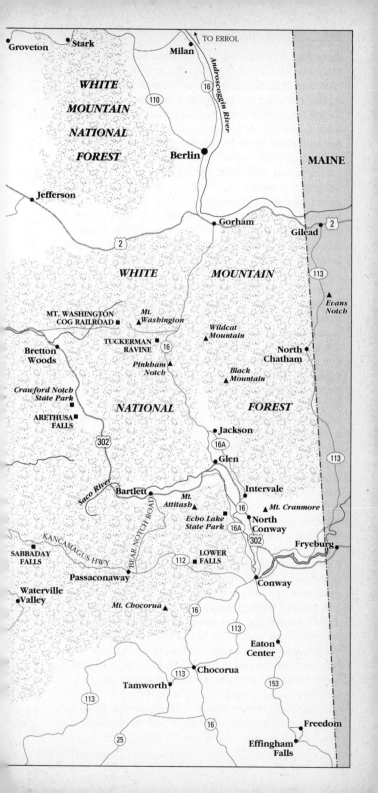

tions. (Art historians call it the White Mountains School.) When the Old World first took notice of American culture, the White Mountains were in the foreground.

This romantic pother served as excellent publicity for a region that, frankly, never has been suited for any enterprise save recreation. As poets stumbled along the mountain paths, Yankee farmers fled the shallow, bony soil; for a century they had raised sheep—pointy-nosed ones, they bitterly jested, that could nibble between the rocks. In the wake of this Yankee exodus, farmhouses that were not engulfed by forest became country inns. This lovers' quarrel between man and forest set the pattern for future episodes, and although the forest would always prevail, human endeavor would always leave a reminder. In no other part of New England do so many relics of so many epochs survive and coexist.

The new railroads bore the farmers away and brought the beneficiaries of the Gilded Age, the prosperous half century following the Civil War when newly wealthy and mobile bourgeois arrived at gingerbread depots to be greeted by acres of fields—scenic vistas sprouting grand new hotels, golf courses, and opulent cottages. The reforestation of the White Mountains accelerated, only to be interrupted by an interval of rapacious logging in the 1880s. The culture of the lumberjacks—river drives, cozy camps, and narrow-gauge railroads—joined the lore of the mountains, whereas their irresponsible forestry practices spurred the establishment of the White Mountain National Forest in 1911.

Not since the 1820s have the White Mountains been greener than today. Valleys and foothills that a century ago were 85 percent bare are now 90 percent wooded—but with a difference. The old evergreen fir and spruce have yielded to a second growth of white birch, yellow birch, and maple, the species that produce the most dazzling fall foliage.

The impact of the automobile age has been less than one might expect. As Laura and Guy Waterman explain in *Forest and Crag:* "Though many *more* visitors now came to the mountains, the irony is that quicker and cheaper transportation enabled them to spend *less* time there." The state built superb roads to the mountains, but visitors trod more lightly and left fewer scars. The old wooden hotels were abandoned. Always easy targets for lightning (and later vandalism), they succumbed to flames, often spectacularly, and the forest reclaimed their proud lawns. Although automobiles, ski resorts, and condominiums have arrived in the White Mountains, impressive Victorian hotels survive, as do rambling farmhouses, hushed villages, and the romantic vistas that thrilled a young nation's soul.

WEATHER AND SEASONS

It was not only rocky soil that sent the farmers west. The growing season is a fleeting 60 to 90 days, and although precipitation is evenly distributed throughout the year, "normal climate" in the White Mountains is an unpredictable mix of what are usually considered to be abnormal weather conditions. High elevations are one factor, but the main culprits are low-pressure systems that converge in a howling vortex on Mount Washington.

From mid-June to the end of August temperatures range from the 50s to the 80s F, with only a half dozen days in the 90s. Showers are common, but rain seldom lasts for more than a day. Wildflowers are at their best from mid-June to mid-July. Berries appear in late August, apples in September.

Anthony Trollope, travelling through Crawford Notch in autumn, marveled that the giant hotels were boarded up. Happily, this is no longer so; today's hotels are filled to capacity during this beautiful time. Foliage season lasts from three to five weeks, from mid-September to mid-October, just as drier Canadian air disperses summer's haze. The temperature drops ten degrees in September, then to the 50s in October when the last leaves turn color. November, when the locals take *their* holiday, is of interest only to hunters. Daylight hours diminish and temperatures plunge to the 30s.

Ski season starts in mid-December, except for a few resorts that open in November more for publicity than for skiing. By Christmas the "Canadian high" starts to dominate, with dry, polar air and temperatures in the 20s, dropping to the teens in January and February. Seasonal snow accumulation averages 100 inches. The closer to Mount Washington, the deeper the snow.

Spring comes late, but sap is running by March for the sugar makers. This may be "mud season" for mortals, but for the skier it is heaven: no crowds, lengthening days, and the camaraderie of die-hard virtuosos. Sunny days in the 60s are not uncommon, although extreme swings are the rule. April temperatures generally hover in the 40s as skiing ends and many inns and restaurants close. May enters with fog and mud and goes out with sunshine and black flies. The insect plague lasts from mid-May to the end of June, and although it persists all summer at higher altitudes and in certain northern precincts, insect repellent is effective.

THE WHITE MOUNTAIN NATIONAL FOREST

The WMNF encompasses 1,200 miles of hiking trails, 20 campgrounds, and a scattering of backwoods lean-tos and tent sites. Ranger stations, administrative offices dispensing maps and information, are located in Bethlehem, Gorham, and Conway. Unlike the national park system, whose role is primarily recreational, national forests emphasize forestry. The 770,709-acre tract is managed not as a pristine preserve—although five areas, for a total of 114,932 acres, have been designated as permanent wilderness—but as an economic resource, balancing recreation, development, and logging interests.

Off-road and all-terrain vehicles are prohibited in the WMNF because of the damage they cause, but snowmobiles are allowed in some areas. Campfires are also permitted— rangers call this the "asbestos forest"—but check for specific prohibitions; a few fragile high-altitude ecosystems are designated as restricted-use areas.

Bethlehem's Ammonoosuc Ranger Station, on Trudeau Road (a link between Route 3 and Route 302), is open from 7:00 A.M. to 4:30 P.M. weekdays and from 8:00 A.M. to 4:30 P.M. weekends; Tel: (603) 869-2626. Conway's Saco Ranger Station, at the junction of Route 16 and the Kancamagus Highway, is open from 8:00 A.M. to 4:30 P.M. all week; Tel (603) 447-5448. Gorham's Androscoggin Ranger Station, on Route 16 a half mile (1 km) south of Route 2, is open from 7:30 A.M. to 4:30 P.M. weekdays; Tel: (603) 466-2763.

HIKING AND MOUNTAINEERING

Clearly marked by roadside signs, hiking trailheads beckon throughout the White Mountains, and nobody should resist their lure. However, *The White Mountain Guide,* published by the Appalachian Mountain Club (AMC), is indispensable for anyone who goes into the woods here. The 25th edition, published in 1992, costs $16.95 and includes a set of topographical maps that clearly show the major trails—more than 400 of them—while the 638-page text describes each one in detail, ending with the trail's estimated length and duration. Double the "book time" for round trips; bring a canteen, sweater, and windbreaker; and always pack the AMC guide.

Don't be deceived by modest elevations and underestimate the steepness of these mountains; mountaineers accustomed to high-altitude ranges, like the Rockies, should calculate the difference in elevation from trailhead to summit. There is a respectable gain in altitude. Secondly, the tree line—the point beyond which trees cannot grow—is at a mere 4,000 feet because of the area's demented weather. Even in summer, freezing temperatures and ferocious gusts can ambush exposed hikers. The hikes described in this narrative vary from brief strolls to strenuous climbs; they are but a meager sample of the maintained paths in this region, and the descriptions cannot begin to suggest the enormous aesthetic and recreational benefits these happy trails provide.

AMC Backwoods Huts

In addition to providing information and maps about hiking in the White Mountains and maintaining hundreds of miles of trails, the Appalachian Mountain Club operates a network of shelters, tent sites, and eight alpine huts. "In New England the term hut is normally reserved for that unique backcountry building where a resident crew provides the food and does the cooking," explain the Watermans in *Forest and Crag,* but the AMC backwoods huts also provide bunks and blankets, allowing hikers to travel very lightly. Accommodations are rustic (coed dorms, gaslights, and pit toilets), the staff consists mostly of students, and the guests are mostly white-collar families. You can generally rent a hut for a large group or just reserve one bunk, and the food is always good.

SKIING IN THE WHITES

The archetypal New England ski trail is a narrow, tree-lined corridor that weaves in and out of the fall line. This design, perfected in the 1940s, protected precious natural snow from being blown away and also encouraged graceful, rhythmic skiing. The late Seldon Hannah, the foremost trail designer of that era, insisted that such trails "have a pulse in them and a pattern in their life." Some beauties survive on Cannon, Wildcat, and Cranmore mountains, evoking the days of "hickory wings." In the 1960s, when man-made snow was invented, trail designers cut wider trails, worrying less about wind and more about attracting skiers.

The White Mountains boast some of the largest snowmaking operations in North America. You will not encounter bare ground here, but neither will you find much natural powder. The most common surface is packed powder, a fast, groomed surface that demands edge control. In December and March icy patches are common. Skiers accustomed to these slopes adjust their style as the packed powder softens to loose granular in the midday sun, then cools to speedy packed granular in the afternoon.

TOURING THE WHITE MOUNTAINS

This region may be divided into quadrants, with Mount Washington as the benchmark. The southern quadrant includes the **Pemigewasset River** area, which runs north to south along I-93 south of Franconia Notch. The Pemi encompasses the towns of Waterville Valley (also a ski area), Lincoln, and Woodstock. The scenic Kancamagus Highway

(Route 112), which starts at Lincoln, is the only east–west road in this quadrant. A good winter destination, the Pemi has plentiful modern accommodations.

The **Western Slope** of Mount Washington embraces Franconia Notch and the Ammonoosuc River towns. For our purposes we've further divided the region into the Franconia–Sugar Hill area and the Route 302 corridor from Woodsville north and east to Bretton Woods. The north–south artery of this area is still I-93. Easy access to the rest of the region makes this a good touring base; its country inns, B and Bs, and proximity to hiking and skiing make it a favored destination in itself.

The **Eastern Slope** is divided into the commercialized Conway area and the more serene Jackson–Pinkham Notch area farther north. Both are accessed by Route 16 from the south or by Route 302 from the west. With its retail outlets and range of accommodations, the Mount Washington Valley, as the Conway area is known, is a popular shopping destination. As a touring base, Jackson's quiet inns are nearer the heart of the mountains.

The northernmost and final quadrant is **Cöos County**, bordered on the east by Route 16 and the Androscoggin River Valley and on the west by Route 3 and the Connecticut River Valley. These two north–south highways are linked by Route 2 in the lower county and Route 26 in the upper county; together these four roads describe a daylong loop. Cöos County is a destination only for fishermen, hunters, and habitués of the splendid Balsams Grand Resort.

Your best bet is to base yourself in the Western Slope, close to the important mountains and the less crowded ski trails and golf courses. Staying here also allows for day trips to the various notches, the Conways, and Cöos County.

Because a large percentage of motorists enter the region from the south, the majority on I-93, this narrative begins with the Pemigewasset Valley and proceeds north on I-93 through Franconia Notch into the Franconia–Sugar Hill area. At this point we follow the Route 302 corridor across the state from the Connecticut River east to the Maine border. Because many travellers to the Eastern Slope enter via Route 16, we follow that road north through the Conways to Jackson and Pinkham Notch. Cöos County, which caps the region, is described in brief.

THE PEMI AREA

Route I-93 parallels the Pemigewasset (a.k.a. Pemi) River, the fount of the Merrimack and the engine of commerce for this rural region since the 1760s. The deep valley affords the northbound traveller progressively more dramatic views— the highway between Waterville Valley and Lincoln won awards for its design—as ever-steeper hills give way to cloud-capped mountains. Unlike the northern Whites, these southern ranges lack the eye-catching glacial anomalies that enchanted 19th-century tourists, and the resort trade was further frustrated when the railroad's arrival in the 1880s made logging and paper making profitable. The valley hamlets of Lincoln, Woodstock, and Campton became bleak mill towns populated by laborers and lumberjacks. The hillsides were stripped and the river was fouled.

Full recovery arrived only in the last decades of this century. The mills closed, the waterways revived, the ski areas opened, and the allure of the mountains reemerged. Lacking the timeworn cachet of destinations north of Franconia Notch, the Pemi resorts have invented their own, focusing on their skiing lifestyle (modern and sporty, with an emphasis on convenience) and their muscular lumberjack legacy (casual and rugged, with a fun-loving bent). In the 1980s speculators built thousands of hotel and condominium units (many condo suites are available as hotel-style lodgings) that have obliterated the residual blight of the mills. Happily, these new structures are dwarfed by the soaring hills.

Waterville Valley

Waterville Valley is an incorporated town with 250 year-round citizens. The town of Waterville was founded in 1829, but in the mid-1960s the expanding resort permeated the tiny village (which had a pre-resort population of fewer than 30 people), and citizens changed its name to Waterville Valley. Today only tax attorneys know what is civic and what is private. Town and resort are loosely termed the Valley or Waterville Valley or just plain Waterville.

Waterville Valley could not be called the Aspen of the White Mountains—there is no such thing—but as the major ski resort closest to Boston (two hours via I-93 and Route 49, the latter running ten miles northeast along the Mad River), it does attract an affluent crowd salted with political and media figures from that city. The valley's developer, Tom Corcoran, is a friend of the Kennedys, and when he launched the resort in 1966 their patronage helped shape its stylish image. A Dartmouth graduate who had competed on three consecutive U.S. Olympic Ski Teams, Corcoran had worked in Aspen for two seasons when, in 1965, he bought an old inn and 425 acres in Waterville Valley. He returned to his native New England and cut Western-style trails on Mount Tecumseh: wide, steep, and fast, with plenty of room for turns. Mount Tecumseh quickly became World Cup headquarters for the White Mountains.

Skiing conditions are usually good in Waterville and they are amply advertised; consequently, on winter weekends the valley attracts capacity crowds with many day-trippers. To prevent long lift lines, ticket sales are limited. Either arrive early or go on weekdays. Four-thousand-foot Tecumseh has 53 trails on 255 skiable acres serviced by 13 lifts, including a detachable four-person chair (quad) that runs from base to summit. The vertical drop is 2,020 feet, and snow making covers 96 percent of the trails. The terrain is rated 19 percent beginner, 58 percent intermediate, and 23 percent expert. The ski school is excellent. For more information, Tel: (800) GO-VALLEY or (603) 236-8311; for ski conditions, Tel: (603) 236-4144.

There are also 65 miles of Nordic ski trails in Waterville. The **Cross Country Center**, located at the dining and shopping complex called Town Square within the resort, can furnish rentals, tune your boards, and arrange for a lunch in the woods (Tel: 603/236-4666). Other winter amusements at Waterville include a large skating rink and horse-drawn sleigh rides.

An old missionary hymn describes a land where "every prospect pleases and only man is vile." Certainly every prospect in Waterville Valley pleases. A mountainous cul-de-sac cups a small lake circled by neat clapboard-and-shingle buildings—lodges, hotels, and condominiums—that adhere to a strict code of proportion and ornamentation. They are linked by bridges, bus shuttles, and footpaths (cross-country ski trails) to the ski area, the golf course, the Sports Center (see below), and **Town Square**. This three-story, U-shaped structure opens onto the lake shore, which pleasantly mitigates the mall-like shops with their identical fronts. A bandstand and other picturesque embellishments make this a soothing venue. Summer recreation at Town Square revolves around 18 clay tennis courts and a nine-hole golf course. The lake has been outfitted with boats and a swimming beach, while horseback riding and hiking can get you into the woods.

The **Sports Center** is located a short walk from Town Square. While in winter a 25-meter indoor pool is the main attraction, the facility also has steam rooms, saunas, a weight room, a tanning salon, a running track, and five indoor courts: two tennis, two racquetball, and one squash. Less vigorous clientele can enjoy video games, table tennis, or a Mexican meal upstairs in the hangar-like building (see below).

TOURING THE WATERVILLE AREA

Outside of the resort itself, Waterville Valley is relatively undeveloped, and most visitors confine themselves to Route 49 bordering the rocky Mad River. The hilly terrain, under its carpet of trees, reveals the gargantuan rubble typical of glacial flows. The ice dragged boulders from hills to the north and dropped them here, as the melted water cut deep, irregular valleys. In this neighborhood it seems as though the Ice Age ended yesterday.

The easiest hike in the area with the best views is a 4.4-mile, three-hour loop over Welch and Dickey mountains. First find Upper Mad River Road, off Route 49 midway between I-93 and the resort. Go north about ¾ mile (1¼ km) on Upper Mad River Road to Orris Road and follow that about half a mile (1 km) to the trailhead, which will be on the right. The footpath forks immediately; the right fork leads to the summit of Welch (1.9 miles, or one hour forty-five minutes). Descend into the woods and climb to the summit of Dickey Mountain, half a mile farther. As you complete the loop there are many fine overlooks. The views of the Campton Valley are great, but the ledges on the summit may be slippery in wet weather.

Nonhikers may prefer to drive the gravel **Tripoli Road** (pronounced "TRIPLE-eye"), which leads through wild country typical of the Pemi area. It begins in the resort, snakes between Mount Tecumseh and Mount Osceola through Thornton Gap, and emerges at the interstate highway (exit 31). Sections follow the bed of the short-lived (1909–1914) Woodstock and Thornton Gore Railroad. (The road is not plowed in winter.)

Another summer-only route, **Sandwich Notch Road**—not recommended for the new car and never after dark—leaves Route 49 midway between the resort and I-93 (well marked, about 5 miles/8 km from either point). It climbs a ridge and descends to Center Sandwich, about 8 miles (13 km) south (see the Lakes Region section of this chapter, above). This abandoned country road has primitive underpinnings that were not intended to carry modern auto traffic, but spooky house foundations and tunnel-like vegetation will entertain the adventuresome. For the fit, it is a good mountain-bike trek.

DINING AND STAYING IN WATERVILLE VALLEY

Within the resort complex, at Town Square, the **Brookside Bistro** serves good Northern Italian cuisine in a Milanese-style café with outdoor tables when weather permits; Tel: (603) 236-4309. Sharing the plaza, the **Yacht Club** has a nautical atmosphere to gratify homesick Bay Staters and a range of seafood dishes to meet their high expectations; Tel: (603) 236-8885. Town Square has a snack bar and, for condo dwellers who wish to microwave a meal, a small grocery. At the Sports Center **Chili Peppers** has Mexican food, but it's a long way from Guadalajara; Tel: (603) 236-4646.

Seven miles (11 km) southwest of the resort complex, on the right (north) side of Route 49 in Thornton, is the **William Tell**, whose Swiss owner and chef Franz Dubach is known for his homemade strudels, fondues, and Wiener schnitzel. The freestanding fireplace is cozy, the rustic decor a respite from the Valley's relentless charm (reserve; Tel: 603/726-3618). Boston celebrities may be seen here or cruising the **Mad River Tavern & Restaurant**, 3 miles (5 km) beyond the William Tell and a quarter mile from I-93. The smoky bar is studded with taxidermy, and the casual restaurant has a good grill. The prices and friendly service make this a favorite of ski bums and local folks. Tel: (603) 726-4290.

Accommodations around here tend to be modern rather than charming or cozy. The closest to cozy may be the 30-room **Silver Squirrel Inn**, the earliest of Waterville Valley's inns, built in 1967. The more ambitious **Snowy Owl Inn** has 80 rooms, half with wet bars, refrigerators, and whirlpool tubs. It has an outdoor pool and an octagonal indoor pool under a timbered dome. Hot chocolate is served in the knotty-pine lobby, where a fieldstone chimney soars two and a half stories above five fireplaces and an array of comfy chairs.

The **Black Bear Lodge** is called a condominium because it has suites with kitchens and dining–sitting areas; the suites accommodate four to six people and are favored by families with children. The Black Bear provides saunas and whirl-pools downstairs, along with a heated pool that extends outdoors for swimming polar bear–style. The newest condo-minium, the top-flight **Golden Eagle**, is vaguely patterned after an imaginary "grand" hotel with Romanesque touches and four round towers housing opulent suites. The lobby decor, proudly described by the staff as "not very modern," maladroitly mixes Tudor half-timbers, formal balustrades, and Tuscan columns, while the 139 large suites are inexplica-bly Colonial. Some have Jacuzzis, and some—unique in Waterville Valley—are reserved for nonsmokers. There are an indoor pool, whirlpools, and saunas. All of these accom-modations include access to the Sports Center.

The Lincoln–North Woodstock Area

As you head north from the Waterville turnoff along I-93 you'll see to the northwest the rounded Kinsman Range, while the serrated Franconia Range looms straight ahead. At exit 32, which leads to Lincoln and the Kancamagus (a.k.a. Kanc) Highway (Route 112), is the two-story White Mountains Visitors Center; Tel: (603) 745-8720.

The communities of Lincoln and North Woodstock, which border each other on either side of I-93, are linked by two roads, Route 112 and Route 3, and by two rivers, the main stem and the East Branch of the Pemi. In the 1800s North Woodstock hosted its share of fine hotels and served as a base for Franconia Notch tourism, while Lincoln was a hardscrabble town where woodsmen pitched logs into the Pemi. Today both towns favor recreation and tourism. Surrounded by national forest, they are very much mountain communities, but Lincoln, home of Loon Mountain Ski Area (discussed below), is geared to automobiles, malls, and condominiums, while North Woodstock is an old-fashioned village where the splash of the Pemi is always within earshot. Together they offer a fine balance of convenience and tradition.

LINCOLN

Lincoln and North Woodstock, with a year-round combined population of less than 3,000, have an astounding visitor capacity of 13,000 guest pillows in motels, inns, and condos. These pillows are waiting for Loon's expansion to South Mountain, a project that will increase skier capacity from fewer than 6,000 skiers per day to more than 9,000. The expansion has been delayed by a complicated environmental controversy, but expect South Mountain by the winter of 1994–1995. Meanwhile, lodging in the area remains relatively inexpensive.

Staying in Lincoln

Two miles (3 km) west of the ski area, on Route 112, the old Franconia Paper Mill has been given new life as the **Mill at Loon**, a complex incorporating three hotels, 32 shops, three restaurants, and a summer theater. Most facilities at the Mill are linked by covered walkways and horse-drawn trolleys, and a complimentary shuttle bus connects it to Loon Mountain Ski Area. The 96-room **Mill House Inn**, built in 1986 and popular with European package tours, offers indoor and outdoor heated pools and Jacuzzis plus an exercise room with sauna. Plush suites with private decks, kitchen facilities, and in-room Jacuzzis are found at the **Rivergreen Condominium Hotel** on the banks of the Pemi behind the Mill House Inn. Rivergreen has three clay tennis courts, and guests also have access to the Mill House Inn's pools and other facilities. The **Lodge at Lincoln Station**, a quarter mile upriver, has its own indoor and outdoor pools, saunas, tennis courts, and a game room, but offers more modest condos that attract budget-minded families. The **North Country Center for the Arts**, in a building that once housed a mammoth paper machine, stages musicals and comedies in the summer (Tel: 603/745-2141).

At exit 33 of I-93, 1¼ miles (2 km) north of Route 112, is a strip of well-established motels and amusements. Once a main drag, the strip shows symptoms of having adjusted to the completion of the Notch Parkway (see Franconia Notch State Park, below) less than a decade ago. Businesses that survived the bypass are thriving, however, a testimony to their good value and their cultivation of a loyal clientele. Motels with indoor and outdoor pools, dining, cocktail lounges, and the like include (from south to north) Woodward's Motor Inn, the Beacon, and the Indian Head, perfect bases for exploring Franconia Notch.

The **Beacon** is the largest, with cottages, suites, and motel rooms totaling 136 units. It offers four pools (two indoors) and two indoor tennis courts; a steady stream of bus tours testifies to its popularity. The **Indian Head Motel**, with 98 units, including fireplace cottages, is also on the bus itinerary. Its landmark observation tower is not necessary to view the face-like rock formation on Mount Pemigewasset, but it's fun to climb. With less of a package-tour atmosphere but equivalent amenities, **Woodward's Motor Inn** has 80 spotless motel units and the **Open Hearth Restaurant**, an honest beef and chicken place.

(See also North Woodstock, below.)

Dining in Lincoln

The best place for breakfast or a sweet snack in the area is **Jassman's**, on the Mill's upper level, which offers six kinds of French toast, three varieties of eggs Benedict, 20 flavors of coffee, 80 different pastries, coffee cakes, tea breads, pies— you get the idea. Jassman's will pack box lunches for picnickers; Tel: (603) 745-2329. The **Tavern at the Mill** is a multilevel restaurant and lounge accented by structural timbers that reveal the building's origin as a huge woodshed. The fixed-price menu is determinedly international, with items like *fajita flameado,* scallops Gloucester, and blackened prime rib sharing space with competently prepared Italian and Oriental dishes; Tel: (603) 745-3603.

There are three popular restaurants on Main Street (Route 112), between Loon Mountain and the Mill. Nearest to Loon, on the corner of Main Street and Pollard Road, **The Common Man** has a casual ambience, and the food—American fare—is fresh, although the menu is self-consciously cute with items like Almost Escargots (mushroom caps); Tel: (603) 745-3463. For steaks and lobster try **Gordi's Fish & Steak House**, operated by two former Olympic skiers and decorated accordingly. It's in a nearly vacant retail strip on Route 112, diagonally across from Pollard Road; Tel: (603) 745-6635. Across the street and nearer the Mill in a small mall called Lincoln Square, **Chieng Gardens** serves the best Chinese food in New Hampshire. It is hidden on the second floor but worth discovering. The management is young, but "the cook is very old." Tel: (603) 745-8612.

The romantic **Café Lafayette**, an 80-ton 1924 Pullman dining car stationed at the Hobo Railroad (discussed below), on Route 112 just east of exit 32, embarks on a 15-mile round trip at 7:00 P.M. on weekends from Memorial Day through April 1, and Wednesday through Sunday between Memorial Day and December 31. Delicacies such as caviar, pâté, filet mignon, and key lime pie are served amid sumptuous decor accented by mahogany paneling, white linen, brass lamps, and lace curtains. Expect to pay $40 to $50 per person for a five-course meal, train fare, gratuity, and drinks. Reservations are advised, as the car holds only 50 guests; Tel: (603) 745-3500.

(See also North Woodstock, below.)

Shopping in Lincoln

The Mill at Loon's enclosed mall, the **Millfront Marketplace**, is decorated with photos and relics of Lincoln's industrial past. The **Innisfree Bookshop** here is a good place to browse, especially for regional books about nature and history. The **Original Design Company** sells locally crafted silk-screened clothing, while the **Country Carriage** carries limited-edition Lizzie High Dolls, toiletries from Crabtree and Evelyn, and high-quality gift items from sources such as Buyer's Choice.

Across the street from the Mill on Route 112, **Pinestead Quilts** specializes in fabrics and threads, patchwork potholders, place mats, and pillows. For hiking and skiing supplies, try **Lahout's Country Clothing and Ski Shop, Inc.**, a sports and apparel store where there is always a sale, and **Rodgers Ski & Sport**, offering comparable values on clothing as well as used equipment and rentals. Lahout's and Rodgers are also on Main Street.

NORTH WOODSTOCK

Heading west from Lincoln, Route 112 ducks under I-93 and in less than a mile (1½ km) intersects with Route 3 at the village of North Woodstock, the center of local commerce. Scaled to pedestrians, the one-stop village has a pleasant green and a cluster of shops and restaurants housed in 19th-century buildings. Park on Main Street (Route 3) and visit **Hilliard's Candyland** for sweets made on site. Behind Hilliard's there's a beautiful riverside park. **Fadden's General Store** here is genuinely general and is not a tourist trap.

Dining and Staying in North Woodstock

North Woodstock's best casual year-round restaurant is **Truants Tavern**, on Main Street. Prime rib, homemade pasta, and sandwiches are served in two rustic dining rooms (one nonsmoking) or in a friendly pub with Guinness on draft. Expect to find an easygoing crowd of ski bums and local characters in the pub, families in the dining rooms; Tel: (603) 745-2239. The **Woodstock Inn**, two blocks north of the traffic lights, offers bed-and-breakfast–style lodging in a 19th-century house with frilly Victorian rooms and clawfoot tubs. (The Riverside annex across the street is more conventional.) The **Clement Room**, the inn's enclosed front porch, offers formal dining in the evening; the Caesar salad and beef dishes are superb (Tel: 603/745-3951). And behind the inn is **Woodstock Station**, a hodgepodge of high-ceilinged rooms linked to a genuine railroad station that serves lighter meals and appetizers; Tel: (603) 745-3951.

About 2 miles (3 km) west of the village on Lost River Road (Route 112) is **Govoni's Italian Restaurant**, perched over rocky Agassiz Basin on the Moosilauke Brook, next to Indian Leap—all of which are nice distractions while you wait to be seated. A very short walk permits a glimpse into a scoured granite bowl (the basin) beneath the walls of a miniature gorge (the leap). The veal here is superb, but Govoni's takes no reservations and the unscheduled throngs can be irritating.

LOON MOUNTAIN SKI AREA

Sherman Adams worked in the woods for the Lincoln mill before becoming governor of New Hampshire and kingmaker to Dwight Eisenhower during the first New Hampshire presidential primary in 1952. After serving as Ike's White House chief of staff he returned to Lincoln and, in 1966, started Loon Mountain.

Loon opened the same year as Waterville Valley and, like its southern neighbor, features wide trails and good snow making. But Loon is geared more to the intermediate skier and enjoys prodigious popularity in this biggest of markets. Loon limits ticket sales based on the number of trails in service, eliminating long lift lines; however, weekend tickets sell out very early. An unusual midweek option, new in 1992, allows you to pay only for the runs that you take. Purchase any quantity of "LoonPoints," which are printed in bar code on a ticket, and a scanner at each lift deducts the points for that run from the ticket. This system lets skiers carry over points to subsequent weekdays, allowing them flexibility in coping with weather or faltering stamina.

Loon's 234 skiable acres support 41 trails serviced by nine lifts, including a four-passenger gondola. (As mentioned in the Lincoln section above, Loon is expected to expand to South Mountain by the winter of 1994–1995, greatly increasing skier capacity here.) The summit elevation is 3,050 feet, the vertical drop 2,100 feet, but it cannot be skied in one run. Snow making covers 85 percent of the trails, of which 11 are novice, 20 are intermediate, and 10 are expert. Light meals, beer, and wine are available at lodges on the summit and mid-mountain. Tel: (603) 745-8111; for ski conditions, Tel: (603) 745-8100.

Staying and Dining at Loon Mountain

Situated slopeside on the Pemi's East Branch is the expansive, 240-unit **Mountain Club on Loon**, which includes 100 plush suites, each with a kitchen, two baths, and a balcony with mountain view. Designed for convenience to all ski facilities, the club complex includes a heated indoor pool, outdoor pool, and courts for racquet sports. Nonguests may avail themselves of the rental shop, gift shops, snack bars, lounges, and **Rachel's**, the club's casual restaurant; Tel: (603) 745-8111. **Govoni's Italian Restaurant** is also slopeside, but is open only in winter (their summer establishment is in North Woodstock); Tel: (603) 745-8042. A quarter mile downriver the Governor Adams Lodge serves the mountain's west slopes with a cafeteria and bar (no overnight accommodations here). Designed for maximum views, it is linked to the main complex by a passenger steam train that operates year-round.

Summer at Loon Mountain

Ski areas try to minimize idle capacity by developing summer activities, and Loon, like Waterville, has been assiduous in this regard. A summer stay at Loon might include gondola rides to the summit, guided hikes, horseback riding, mountain biking, trap shooting (using laser guns), cookouts, lectures (for information, Tel: 603/745-8111, ext. 5535), summer theater (contact the North Country Center for the Arts, Tel: 603/745-2141), concerts (notably the **North Country Chamber Players** in Bethlehem; Tel: 603/869-3154), and even roller skating. All that's missing is golf. Be that as it may, a ski resort without snow, like an ocean liner without an ocean, is indefinably disconcerting.

CLARK'S TRADING POST AND THE HOBO RAILROAD

Nostalgic for low-tech theme parks? Clark's Trading Post and the Hobo Railroad are quirky, old-fashioned, family-owned institutions with an authentic regional flavor. Edward P. Clark began the former as a dog show in 1928; bears were added as an attraction later. His sons, Ed and Murray, rescued and restored an array of New England artifacts and transformed the park into a mecca for steam train buffs. A wood-fired steam locomotive takes passengers across a Vermont covered bridge, while back at the Post, Murray, all the while maintaining a stream of dry patter, leads pampered bears through a charming performance. An 1880s fire station complex shelters several working player pianos, and the funhouses are delightfully hokey. The Trading Post is located at the junction of Routes 3 and 3A, 1 mile (1½ km) north of North Woodstock village; Tel: (603) 745-8913.

The Hobo Railroad is the project of Ed's son, "young Eddie." (Impossible to miss, it's on Route 112, just east of the interchange of I-93 and Route 112.) The excursion down the Pemi Valley runs every two hours during the summer, less frequently during spring and fall. The railroad's name is not an apt one—hobos surely never had it so good. Passengers view the rugged landscape from plush velour seats while box lunches are served with a "bindle stick." Tel: (603) 745-2135.

THE KANCAMAGUS HIGHWAY

New England's wildest scenic highway was a muddy backwoods road until 1959, and it was not plowed for winter traffic until 1968. It climbs out of Lincoln for 6 miles (10 km) to the Kancamagus Pass at 2,855 feet, then rolls eastward for another 28 miles (45 km) to Conway. There are neither motorist services on this road nor human habitations. It transects some of the White Mountain National Forest's least hospitable country. Except for seasonal logging camps, no human dwelling ever sprouted in these extraordinarily steep and rocky hills. A landowner in these parts once complained that his property was "not fit to hold the rest of the earth together." For visitors, however, it holds considerable fascination.

Just 2 miles (3 km) east of the Loon Mountain Ski Area, on the left just beyond Hancock Campground, is the entrance to the **Pemigewasset Wilderness Area**, a 40-square-mile irregular bowl rimmed by towering 4,000-foot crags. The floor, laced with numerous streams, is at an elevation of about 1,500 feet. It is a happy irony of history that this once-ravaged domain is now entirely reforested and graced by a network of paths set along the roadbeds of former logging railroads. Forest Service rangers at the seasonal information booth at the area's entrance can suggest foot excursions of varying difficulty, but at the very least wander across the suspension bridge and stand in the verdant right-of-way of the East Branch & Lincoln Railroad (1893–1948). The rails ran from Lincoln to here and then followed the East Branch of the Pemi ten miles into the wilderness, flinging out miles of branch lines dotted by lumber camps.

Hiking the **Wilderness Trail** (which follows one of these old logging trails from the parking lot at the wilderness area entrance) along the East Branch to **Franconia Falls** also conveys the flavor of the Pemi wilderness without much effort. It takes three hours round-trip and follows an easy grade on the former railroad track, identified by its hemlock ties. At 2.8 miles you'll come to a bridge and the Franconia Brook Campsite (formerly Logging Camp number 7). Just before the bridge take a left turn onto a well-marked spur trail and walk half a mile to an acre of pools, chutes, whirlpools, and cascades. Bathing is permitted. As a cross-country ski trip in winter, the Wilderness Trail is hushed and isolated.

Another short hike (two and a half hours round-trip) to the **Greeley Ponds Scenic Area** rewards picnickers and fishermen. The trailhead for the Greeley Ponds Trail is 2 miles (3 km) east along the Kancamagus from the head of the Wilderness Trail. The trail, which is not dauntingly steep, crosses a number of bridges that lead to secluded ponds. Beavers, birds, and the occasional moose will keep you company on this jaunt.

The Kancamagus makes a couple of hairpin bends at the height of land (Kancamagus Pass) where you leave the Pemigewasset watershed and enter the Saco River watershed. The road then descends for 8 miles (13 km) following the Swift River. **Sabbaday Falls**, a favorite subject of 19th-century artists, is located on the south side of the road, a short walk from the well-marked Sabbaday picnic area (no swimming at these falls). The **Passaconaway Historic Site**, east of the Sabbaday Falls turnoff and just before the intersection with Bear Notch Road, is less interesting for its history (the 1831 cottage has a prosaic past) than for the **Rail 'N' River Trail**, a half-mile self-guided walk that leaves from the Forest Service's visitors' center here and follows an old railroad grade through woods and swamp. Signs identify the plants and trees common to the region.

The stretch of the Kancamagus from Passaconaway to Conway, along which the Swift River tumbles 700 feet, is punctuated by inviting turnouts. About 3 miles (5 km) east of Bear Notch Road, on the north side of the highway, is **Rocky**

Gorge, where the force of the river has sculpted the steep walls of granite. **Lower Falls**, a couple of miles farther east, is a boulder-strewn cataract in the spring and a popular swimming hole in the summer. Just beyond Lower Falls and 6 miles (10 km) west of Conway is the **Albany Covered Bridge**, located at the Covered Bridge Campground. The Dugway Road, which runs parallel to the Kanc, leads motorists across this much-modified 1850 bridge. Also at the site are a nature trail and some facilities. The eastern terminus of the Kanc is marked by the **Saco Ranger Station** (Tel: 603/447-5448), a good spot to pick up information on the area, at the town of Conway (Conway itself is discussed below).

From Conway, or from Bear Notch Road, you can pick up Route 302 and follow it northwest to Route 3 and on down to Franconia Notch, our next destination. (The Route 302 Corridor is discussed below.) Or you can approach Franconia Notch from the south via Route 3 from Lincoln and North Woodstock.

THE WESTERN SLOPE: FRANCONIA AND SUGAR HILL

From his Franconia farmhouse, Robert Frost looked out over the entrance to the notch. Watching vapor drift mysteriously from the deep gap, he would tell his daughters that it was the breath of a sleeping dragon.

To travel through that chasm of granite known as Franconia Notch is to embark as though from a mainland port to an island—the transition is palpable. As you leave the broad Pemi Valley, enter the mountains, and climb to 2,000 feet, cliffs tower and mountains cast broad shadows. The small towns north of the notch beckon as safe havens.

Franconia Notch was too rugged to be a railroad route. The old coach road was notoriously rough, and the paved highway was not plowed in winter until 1925. A dozen miles north communities developed along rivers and were served by the railroad's valley lines, but Franconia and Sugar Hill remained isolated and uncommercial. They are a good base for touring the region, but it's difficult to find better destinations in and of themselves: two mountain ranges, Franconia Notch State Park, miles of national forest, country inns, lakes and streams for swimming and boating, a legendary ski area, a lifetime's variety of hiking trails, and a concentration of fine dining. At a minimum, set aside a day for Franconia Notch and a picnic tour of the pretty villages of Franconia and Sugar Hill.

Franconia Notch State Park

In Hawthorne's story "The Great Stone Face," a farm boy who lives in the shadow of a prominent rock formation waits for a man to appear whose features will match it. By the tale's end it is apparent that the boy has become that man. The Old Man's home is a U-shaped mountain pass—Franconia Notch—a geological smorgasbord of talus cliffs, mile-long slides, mountain lakes, and bare summits. The recorded history of Franconia Notch begins in 1805, when white men building the first road through this defile discovered the striking stone formation. Subsequently, the notch supported three hotels, but the last and most ambitious, the 400-room Profile House, burned in 1923.

Man-made attractions in 6,440-acre Franconia Notch State Park include the Franconia Notch Parkway itself, which provides access to the park area, Cannon Mountain Aerial Tramway, Cannon Mountain ski area, both of which are discussed below, and a nine-mile-long bicycle path. The parkway, which is actually the 8-mile (13-km) stretch of I-93 that goes through the notch (completed in 1988), is more pretty than safe. The awkward layout encourages U-turns (there are no median barriers), and drivers are often distracted by the scenery. The paved **bicycle path** (no roller skating permitted), which extends the length of the notch with several access points, serves in winter as a cross-country ski trail. It slopes gently downhill from north to south through woods and past lakes. Bike rentals are available at exit 2 off the parkway or in Franconia village.

Northbound motorists on the parkway are treated to progressively more dramatic vistas. The treeless summits of Mount Flume and Mount Liberty emerge to the right; then, as the road climbs, the rest of the ridge comes into view: Haystack Mountain, Mount Lincoln, and finally Mount Lafayette, with its shelf of crags known as Eagle Cliffs. Simultaneously, Cannon Mountain's talus slope (steep fields of rubble beneath a sheer rock wall) appears on the left. At the top of this slope three rock ledges form a human visage—the Old Man of the Mountain—that comes into view as the road passes Profile Lake. But these are only the Notch's most obvious natural features. The rewarding details are best enjoyed by stopping at the several parkway turnouts.

TOURING THE NOTCH

There are three visitors' centers in the park: at the Flume (parkway exit 1), a hiking information center at Lafayette Place East (between exits 1 and 2), and at the Cannon Mountain Aerial Tramway (exit 2).

At the southern entrance to the park, the **Flume** (again, parkway exit 1) is a 700-foot gorge where Flume Brook cascades between narrow walls of granite, which are criss-crossed by walkways, paths, and a covered bridge. (Pedestrians are cautioned to stay on the paths; there is no swimming or wading.) In winter the ice makes sublime sculptures, in spring Avalanche Falls is fearsome, in autumn the foliage is spectacular, and in summer there's a small admission charge. A half-mile (1-km) walk north of the Flume Visitor Center is a **covered bridge** overlooking the Pool, a glacial pothole more than 100 feet in diameter and 40 feet deep. Two miles (3 km) north of the Flume along the parkway is a scoured granite bowl rather prosaically called the **Basin**. Don't be taken in by its ho-hum name—the real attraction here is the **Basin Cascades Trail**, which runs alongside Cascade Brook as it sheets across broad ledges of granite, trickles through mossy stones, and plumes over sculpted rocks.

Lafayette Campground, with 97 tent sites, is the base for several important trails (see Hiking, below). Located on the west side of I-93, it is accessible to northbound motorists by exiting at the tramway farther north at exit 2 and doubling back. A second option is to park at Lafayette Place East and take a pedestrian tunnel to the other side. **Boise Rock**, at the first turnoff north of the campground, memorializes a Franconia gentleman named Boise who became stranded in a snowstorm and, to keep from freezing, skinned his horse, wrapped himself in the hide, and crawled beneath the otherwise unremarkable boulder. The next morning rescuers chopped him out of the frozen skin and found him unharmed. There is a good potable spring here, but otherwise there's nothing to see.

The **Old Man of the Mountain**, a natural rock formation 1,200 feet above Profile Lake that served as the inspiration for Hawthorne's story, can be viewed from a turnout across from Profile Lake (just beyond Boise Rock as you're travelling northbound), or by continuing to the tramway (exit 2). The former vantage is fine for a quick snapshot, while the latter offers better photographic opportunities, an interpretive center, and toilet facilities. Better still, it is connected by a short driveway to the extensive facilities at the tramway (see below). Stroll to **Profile Lake**, the source of the Pemigewasset River, where you may fish but not swim, and see the Old Man, then either walk or drive north 300 yards to the tramway.

First designed as a summer-to-fall tourist attraction, Cannon Mountains' original **Aerial Tramway** predated the ski area; a new tram was constructed in the 1980s. The five-minute 2,000-foot ascent to the summit in the 80-passenger enclosed cable car can be entertaining, but unless the clouds are quite high your view at the top will be limited to a fogged-in cafeteria. On a good day the views are striking, especially south and east across the yawning notch to glacier-scoured Mount Lafayette and Eagle Cliff. The **Rim Trail**, a half-mile loop around the 4,077-foot summit, affords glimpses of some unusual alpine vegetation, notably diapensia and dwarf white birch.

The tram's base—a complex of lawns and picnic areas bordering ski trails and Echo Lake—offers the notch's widest selection of activities. In the base building there are snacks, a gift shop, and toilets. In the parking lot a **Franconia Sports Shop** tailgate concession rents bicycles for the bike path and sells fishing licenses and bait. There is a boat-launch ramp at Echo Lake for private boats. (Bathing beach and boat rentals are at parkway exit 3.) The **New England Ski Museum**, at the north end of the parking lot, will entertain even those who have never taken to the slopes. The audiovisual presentations and other exhibits, although planned around the history of skiing, skillfully illuminate the region's cultural heritage, and the gift shop has items that are unavailable elsewhere, including replicas of 1940s ski posters and tee-shirts bearing their designs. There is always a lively video on the screen and admission is free. Closed mid-October through Christmas.

The tram base is also the approximate site of the immense Profile House, built in 1852 and enlarged until it could accommodate more than 400 guests, among them P. T. Barnum, who said the notch was the "second greatest show on earth." A narrow-gauge railroad served the hotel from Bethlehem Junction to the north. Except for some stonework in the bushes, the Profile House has entirely vanished, but Barnum would recognize the soaring cliffs and swooping hills.

The northernmost parkway exit is exit 3, which leads directly to the good bathing beach at **Echo Lake** and the Peabody Base Lodge (the base lodge is one of two serving Cannon's skiers; see below). Echo Lake offers good views of Eagle Cliff and Cannon's eastern slopes, where bears reside. Canoes and other nonmotorized craft are permitted on the lake and may be rented here. The parking lot has hookup facilities for recreational vehicles, and the beach has a bathhouse, snack bar, and picnic tables.

HIKING IN THE NOTCH

All Franconia Notch summits involve strenuous hikes of at least three hours and three miles, one way. Even on mild days Franconia Ridge can be whipped by winds that drop the temperature to below freezing. Besides outerwear, bring your AMC *White Mountain Guide*.

For an easy hike with terrific views head across Route 18 from Peabody Base Lodge at exit 3 and then cross a gravel parking lot to the well-marked **Bald Knob Trail**, a quarter-mile climb to a bare protuberance resembling a miniature summit (sometimes called Bald Mountain, although it's only 2,340 feet). The views of Echo Lake and Cannon Mountain are far better than this mere 15-minute climb deserves. A side trail leads to **Artist Bluff**, another fine overlook, which connects to Echo Lake beach by another trail.

At Lafayette Place East, across from Lafayette Campground, the steep **Falling Waters Trail** repays a partial ascent with several nice falls. The best route to **Mount Lafayette**'s rocky cone is a loop that ascends the Falling Waters Trail and descends the less arduous **Old Bridle Path**—or vice versa. Both trails meet at the **Franconia Ridge Trail**, which links the five summits of the Franconia Range—Mount Flume (4,328 feet), Mount Liberty (4,459 feet), Little Haystack Mountain (4,760 feet), Mount Lincoln (5,089 feet), and Mount Lafayette (5,260 feet)—and is arguably the most scenic path in the White Mountains: wilderness to the east, plummeting cols to the west, and the Presidentials to the north.

Across the parkway, beginning right at the campground, the **Lonesome Lake Trail** climbs to pristine Lonesome Lake (elevation 2,743 feet), on the shoulder of Cannon Mountain. The 1.6-mile hike (one way) follows a moderate grade and takes 90 minutes. There's an AMC hut at Lonesome Lake, a pleasant mid-hike stop. Another, more difficult trail that climbs Cannon Mountain begins at the tramway area, but because Cannon is served by the tramway it is perhaps less fun to conquer.

Mount Liberty and **Mount Flume** can be scaled from trailheads at the Flume Visitor Center at exit 1. Take the Whitehouse Trail from the Flume parking lot until the summit trails branch and follow the **Liberty Spring Trail** (part of the Appalachian Trail) to the more interesting summit of Liberty, with its views east over the Pemi Wilderness, north to Mount Lafayette, and south to Loon Mountain and beyond.

CANNON MOUNTAIN SKI AREA

Cannon lacks hotels, hot tubs, and haute couture—and doesn't apologize. It's a skiers' mountain, and a legendary one. The lower trails, with a few exceptions, are wide, but the summit has some steep serpentine defiles dating to the 1930s. (No adept skier should miss Upper Cannon, the classic 1930s ski trail.) Cannon attracts fewer families and is seldom crowded except on peak weekends. By taking the tram you can ski the entire vertical drop of 2,146 feet in one run, selecting either intermediate swoops or expert drops. Cannon has 32 trails on 140 skiable acres serviced by six lifts, including the tram. Snow making covers 87 percent of the trails, of which 18 percent are novice, 50 percent are intermediate, and 32 percent are expert. Two base lodges and a summit lodge serve cafeteria-style food. A sports shop, pub, ski rentals, and ski school are found at the "new" (1960s) Peabody Base Lodge at exit 3. Tel: (603) 823-7751; for ski conditions, Tel: (800) 552-1234.

Cannon is state operated and, until recently, has not competed effectively against private areas. A reorganization in the 1980s wrought wonders with morale and infrastructure, resulting in a new expert trail, more snow making, a new quad chair, and more.

Franconia and Sugar Hill

This corner of the western slope was fashionable during Cannon's heyday, from the 1930s until the 1960s, when more modern resorts exerted their flashy appeal. "Good taste never goes out of style" was the response of Franconia and Sugar Hill. These towns, 6 miles (10 km) northwest of Franconia Notch via I-93, have not changed much since the 1950s, and that is an important part of their charm. For a frenetic vacation, go elsewhere; the Franconia–Sugar Hill area offers not just a change of scenery, but a relaxing getaway.

Named circa 1760 by homesick German settlers for its breathtaking alpine views (Franconia, or Land of the Franks, is in northern Bavaria), Franconia has as its governing natural feature the Gale River, which gurgles the entire length of the village (exit 38 off I-93). Between the Gale and I-93 is Main Street (Route 18), a half-mile strip consisting of a modest commercial district and town offices. The town's power lines were buried in 1992, so the mountain views from here are uncluttered. At the I-93 exit in the middle of the village, Route 116 begins by crossing Main Street and the Gale River, then follows a pretty stream, the Ham Branch, to rural Easton. At the north end of the village Route 117 leaves Route 18 and climbs to the village of Sugar Hill. A motor tour outlined below introduces these towns and covers their main features.

At the **Quality Bakery**, across from the Franconia Post Office on Main Street, Mike Valcourt grinds whole grains for his Grateful Bread, which he ships all over New England. The **Franconia Sport Shop**, on Main Street near its intersection with Route 116, sells hiking, skiing, and fishing gear. This is also the place to rent mountain bikes and roller skates; owner Kim Cowles can suggest itineraries. The chamber of commerce booth (seasonal), located on Main Street between the town hall and the library, dispenses a good local map.

Franconia's downtown architecture includes some typically rambling New England homes with stables attached by ingenious ells, but the **Abbie Greenleaf Library** and the **Dow Academy** are quite distinguished. The former, on Main Street a block south of the Route 116 intersection, was built in 1913 by the Profile House hotelier and named for his wife. The "eyebrow" fenestrations on the tile roof are typical of the Romanesque architecture of Henry Hobson Richardson, designer of Boston's Trinity Church. The interior boasts tile floors, stained-glass windows, marble fireplaces, and mahogany columns. Facing the library across the river is the Dow Academy. A community school until the late 1950s (Robert Frost served on the school board), it is now a luxury condominium. Its handsome Georgian-style exterior, which dates to around 1903, was sensibly preserved. The north end of Main Street was the center of town from approximately 1810 to 1850 during the operation of the Franconia Iron Works. Ore was mined atop Sugar Hill and hauled by oxen to the charcoal-fired stone iron furnace, the remains of which are just across the river from a small park near the Route 117/18 junction.

A FRANCONIA – SUGAR HILL
DRIVING TOUR

The appeal of these picturesque communities is evident in a 14-mile (22-km) loop that samples museums, farms, mountain views, a maple sugar operation, gift shops, and several historic sites. From downtown Franconia, proceed north on Route 18 (Main Street) to where Route 117 begins by crossing the Gale River and ascending to the hamlet of Sugar Hill.

A half mile (1 km) up Route 117 from the turn off Route 18 you'll come to Iris Farm and incomparably serene views: a bucolic foreground and a panorama of the mountains in the background. A little farther along a state historical marker indicates the site of the country's first ski school. **Polly's Pancake Parlor**, in an 1830s former carriage house, is another half mile beyond. Open for breakfast and lunch, Polly's has great atmosphere and pretty views. The seating is family-style and the pancakes are made from stone-ground flours; Tel: (603) 823-5575.

Less than a mile (1½ km) past Polly's, as you crest the hill, take a left onto Sunset Lane at the Homestead Inn (see Staying in Franconia–Sugar Hill, below) and **Sugar Hill Sampler**, a white farmhouse and a red barn owned by descendants of the original settlers and operated as a B and B and gift shop. Besides housing a barn-size selection of fine gifts, cheeses, maple syrup, and the like, the Sampler includes a three-room museum of family memorabilia and farm implements. Continue another half mile to the Sunset Hill House hotel (closed at this writing) to enjoy 180-degree vistas of the Franconia and Kinsman ranges. Opposite the hotel, the **Sunset Hill Golf Course**, a nine-hole hilltop jewel, is still operating (Tel: 603/823-5522). Return to Route 117, turn left, descend a quarter mile to a sharp bend, and enter the village.

Named for its sugar maples, **Sugar Hill** (population 418) was a mining and agricultural community from its settlement in 1780 until the 1860s, when the trees were all cut for charcoal and the views became apparent. For the next 100 years it was a prestigious summer resort with five hotels and numerous elaborate cottages. (Joyce Kilmer wrote "Trees" while summering here.) Although still a wealthy community, Sugar Hill has no more hotels.

Sugar Hill lost 14 homes in an 1893 fire, so Main Street, though charming, lacks real antiquity. Still standing, however, are the picturesque 1884 Community Church at the hamlet's upper end and the 1831 Village Meeting House at the lower end. In between, with a background of rolling fields, is the Hilltop Inn, a bed-and-breakfast with an ambitious kitchen (see Dining, below), and **Harman's Cheese & Country Store**, proffering aged Cheddar and maple products. The **Sugar Hill Museum**, opposite Harman's on the village green, is a repository of rural artifacts, some horse-drawn vehicles (including a rare hearse), and interesting old photos. Call for open hours or to make an appointment; Tel: (603) 823-8142.

A quarter mile downhill from the museum on Route 117, at an intersection called Five Corners, two roads enter on the left. Take Easton Road, the second left, for 1¼ miles (2 km) through the woods until rows of roadside maples and stone walls announce **Charlie Stewart's Sap House**. Typical of many older hillside farms, Stewart's agricultural activities are now mostly confined to manufacturing maple syrup for mail-order outlets, but he'll sell you some from the farmhouse if you knock and holler. A half mile beyond the farm, Easton Road forks at Toad Hill Road, where a swampy pond is frequented by moose and herons. Turn right onto Toad Hill Road, climb a quarter mile, and turn left at the stone house onto Easton Road (unmarked) to enjoy a 3-mile (5-km) descent with views of Mount Kinsman and the Easton Valley.

The village of **Easton**, on Route 116 5 miles (8 km) south of Sugar Hill on the Ham Branch River, is mostly national forest and is sparsely populated (140 souls); by the time you reach Route 116 you'll have travelled about half its system of town roads. Easton folk have fought over roads since the town was part of neighboring Landaff. An 1876 dispute over building "Bunga Road," intended to carry lumber from Landaff to Bath, resulted in a town meeting brawl that prompted residents of eastern Landaff, who opposed the road, to secede and form the new town of Easton. The local people still call the isolated junction of Route 116 and Route 112, near the Landaff–Easton town line, Bunga (or Bungy or Bungay) Corner, though you won't find the name on signposts or maps. (Easton has a couple of very good bed-and-breakfasts; see Staying in Franconia–Sugar Hill, below.)

The sign marking Easton Road at the junction with Route 116 says "Sugar Hill Road" (the New England convention of naming one end of a road for the town at the other end is worth noting). Turn left on Route 116 back toward Franconia. Along the road in the shadow of the Kinsman Range are working farms and some that are barely working. This is the valley of the Ham Branch, a small river that joins the Gale in Franconia village. A broad expanse of fields terminates at a sizable house; Coppermine Road will be on the right.

Park in a designated area on Coppermine Road and take the **Coppermine Trail**, a 2.5-mile hike along splashy Coppermine Brook to **Bridal Veil Falls**. Bette Davis fans will detour about three-quarters of a mile up the trail to where the land slopes sharply down to the brook in a piney grove. On the trail side of the brook an auto-size boulder extends into the water; attached to the boulder and facing downstream is a plaque that reads: "In Memoriam to Arthur Farnsworth 'The Keeper of Stray Ladies'—Pecketts 1939—Presented by a Grateful One." The tale is that, knowing that Farney would find her, a certain Ruth Elizabeth Davis Nelson (better known as Bette Davis) deliberately wandered away from a Peckett's Inn picnic (Peckett's has since closed). She erected the plaque in the 1960s.

North toward Franconia on Route 116 is the **Franconia Airport**, a grassy field from which you can soar in gliders. Opposite is the Franconia Inn (discussed below), with stables and cross-country ski trails. Two miles (3 km) north of the inn (turn left onto Bickford Hill Road and cross the bridge) is the **Frost Place**, Robert Frost's home year-round from 1915 to 1920. You can tour the farmhouse and enjoy mountain views from its disproportionately broad porch. In addition to a daily open house, summer programs include poetry readings and workshops. Open Memorial Day through Columbus Day, weekends only, except during July and August, when the farm is open daily except Tuesdays.

Still unknown as a poet when he lived in Franconia, the 40-year-old Frost earned a local reputation as a comically inept farmer. But during his five years in these hills he wrote the book that won him international recognition, *Mountain Interval,* which included such poems as "The Road Not Taken" and "Birches." In his next book, *New Hampshire,* the poet seems to season his trademark iambic pentameter with the cadences of Franconian dialect (a hypothesis with proud support hereabouts); in any event, the title poem does contain a number of specific references to the old neighborhood.

DINING IN FRANCONIA – SUGAR HILL

Restaurants sporting graciously set, candle-lit tables outnumber neon and Formica eateries in this valley where *chefs de cuisine* are inclined to move from kitchen to kitchen. **Lovett's Inn**, 2 miles (3 km) south of Franconia village on Profile Road by Lovett's Brook, serves Continental cuisine with a regional flavor; try the homemade relishes and the blueberry or black bean soup. Tel: (603) 823-7761. The **Franconia Inn**, 4 miles (6½ km) west of town on Route 116, is somewhat more expensive than Lovett's but has more adventurous veal and seafood dishes. The ambience seems more formal here, although the staff is not more sophisticated. Tel: (603) 823-5542. The **Horse and Hound Inn**, on Wells Road, south of Franconia village, favors liberally and imaginatively sauced Continental cuisine; veal and duck are good bets here. The paneled dining room is cozy and restful. Tel: (603) 823-5501.

The **Hilltop Inn**, a newcomer to the area, is a homier place on Main Street (Route 117) in Sugar Hill village. It has a following among local foodies for dishes like vegetable lasagna and paella made with homemade pork sausage. Tel: (603) 823-5695. The latest to enter the game is the **Sugar Hill Inn**, a quarter mile west of Franconia village on Route 117. The Sugar Hill's dining room met with immediate success when it began accepting nonguest dining reservations in 1992. Its entrées usually include a fresh seafood dish and are always accompanied by homemade bread. *Yankee* magazine extolled the apple pie. Tel: (603) 823-5621.

(All the above restaurants are discussed as accommodations below.)

More modest family-style dining is the norm at Franconia village restaurants. The Red Coach Inn's **Coachmen Restaurant** is new, clean, and relatively inexpensive. Steaks and chicken have predominated here, but the chef has promised (and is capable of) more adventurous fare. (The inn itself is discussed below; Tel: 603/823-7422.) The **Hillwinds**, overlooking the river just south of the village, emphasizes charcoal-broiled fare (its midweek specials are good buys). Entertainment at the lively lounge runs to rock bands.

STAYING IN FRANCONIA – SUGAR HILL

With an indoor pool, restaurant (discussed above), exercise room, and more, the **Red Coach Inn**, at exit 38, is the sole modern hotel in town. It's clean, new, and friendly. The dependably clean and friendly **Gale River Motel**, north of the village on Route 18, has a great view of Mount Lafayette. Besides the motel units, it offers three cottages and a summer-only, heated outdoor pool.

There are two country inns in the area with extensive grounds laced with babbling brooks and cross-country ski trails; outdoor (seasonal) pools; cocktail lounges; and fine dining rooms. **Lovett's Inn** has the better range of accommodations, with terraced cottages and a remodeled carriage house for groups in addition to the country inn, while the **Franconia Inn** excels in entertaining guests with sleigh rides, horseback riding, bicycling, and tennis. Both inns have 30 or more rooms (their restaurants are discussed above).

The scale of the **Sugar Hill Inn**, a restored farmhouse, is smaller, the atmosphere warmer and more intimate. Its 15 rooms are spread out among the inn and several cottages. The Sugar Hill is a white building on Route 117, near Franconia village; look for the wagon on the lawn. The **Horse and Hound Inn**, built in the 1830s and 1840s, is smaller still, with just ten rooms, and seems more geared to dining than lodging (see Dining, above).

The area's best bed-and-breakfast might be the **Bungay Jar**, 5½ miles (8½ km) south of Franconia village on Route 116. With its views of Mount Kinsman, spacious suites, fireplaces, skylights, and private balconies, the Bungay Jar is in a special category all its own. This rebuilt 18th-century barn is a refreshing change from the usual Laura Ashley Victorian decor so often favored among bed-and-breakfasts.

Additions completed in 1898 gave the **Homestead Inn** a Victorian veneer, but its core is an 1802 farmhouse, one of Sugar Hill's earliest and occupied by the Aldrich family and descendants for seven generations. Faithful to its name, the low-ceilinged inn is homey, the service informal, and the antique furnishings notable for being here since they were new. Rooms with private baths are available in an annex across the street, and there are two rental cottages on the grounds. The location is enviable; the inn is bordered by fields on the corner of Sunset Lane and Route 117, 2½ miles (4 km) west of Franconia village.

Well known for its creative kitchen, the Victorian-era **Hill-top Inn** also has six guest rooms, all with baths, ceiling fans, antiques, flannel sheets, extra-firm mattresses, quilts, and electric blankets. The rambling white house has a deck and two porches with rocking chairs. Breakfast here always includes smoked salmon, French toast, and offbeat surprises, some prepared in a wood-fired oven. It's located on Route 117 in the center of Sugar Hill village.

On Route 116 in Easton, 5 miles (8 km) south of Franconia village on the left, is a white farmhouse with green shutters. Named for a pet cat belonging to the proprietors, **Blanche's Bed & Breakfast** has no private baths for its five immaculate rooms, but hospitality here is especially genteel and personal. Guests who share the owners' cultural bent will enjoy the antique furnishings, which include many family heirlooms. A graphic design studio, the owners' second business, occupies a portion of the parlor.

THE WESTERN SLOPE: THE ROUTE 302 CORRIDOR

The Ammonoosuc and Saco rivers traverse the heart of the White Mountains, and Route 302 travels their valleys (Ammonoosuc and Saco are Abenaki Indian names that translate as "narrow fishing river" and "outlet," respectively). Our coverage follows this route from the town of Woodsville on the Vermont border north through Littleton and Whitefield (briefly leaving Route 302), passing through covered bridges and pretty, rural towns before turning back south and east through Bethlehem and the Carroll–Twin Mountain area, and on into the White Mountain National Forest. On all sides peaks march into the distance; the most prominent, flanking Mount Washington north to south, make up the bare-topped Presidential Range: Mount Jefferson, Mount Monroe, Mount Madison, Mount Pierce, Mount Eisenhower, two Mount Adamses, and, nonpresidentially, Mount Franklin. The corridor can be driven in a hasty two hours, but for side trips to examine a covered bridge, hike to a waterfall, or sample the shopping in Littleton, allow at least eight hours.

Within the national forest, Route 302 takes us to the Bretton Woods Ski Area, New Hampshire's newest, and the grand, fantastically situated Mount Washington Hotel. Finally we travel south between the sheer cliffs of Crawford Notch and along the forested banks of the Saco River to pass the Attitash Ski Area in Bartlett, just west of the Conways—the subject of our next section.

Woodsville and Bath

The oldest documented covered bridge in New Hampshire is found on Route 135 just east of the Vermont border in Woodsville, which is 20 miles (32 km) southwest of Franconia village via Routes 117 and 302. In the center of this former railroad town, turn left (north) onto Route 135, across from the handsome Opera Block, and drive beneath the railroad bridge. The road immediately narrows to cross the Ammonoosuc on the one-lane 1827 Bath/Haverhill covered bridge, a 278-foot Town lattice truss with a roofed sidewalk. Beyond, the road curves around an enormous ledge with fine views of the river.

This bridge's distinctive crisscrossed plank walls are a series of overlapping triangles that serve as trusses to distribute the weight along the length of the structure, a design patented in 1820 by Ithiel Town of New Haven, Connecticut. The Town truss was popular because it was easier to build than the slightly older Burr truss, which incorporated a tricky arch and vertical posts with diagonal supports on each side. The most prevalent surviving design in the White Mountains is the Paddleford truss, a somewhat later development pioneered by a Littleton man. Like the Burr, it has vertical posts, but only one diagonal brace and a patented series of reverse braces tied into the chords (the horizontal weight-bearing members). The Paddleford required master carpenters to form the many joints but was favored for its strength. These three designs are remarkable, not only because of their wooden components but also because they display an advanced understanding of mechanical physics. Every timber serves a purpose. Even the roof, besides protecting the wood from ruinous dampness, serves to control lateral stress. Other designs, notably the Howe truss, a transitional style that used steel cables, also survive in this region, and although renovations such as the addition of arches and steel plates have affected the absolute authenticity of some covered bridges, their utility and charm are intact.

Three miles (5 km) east of Woodsville, turn right (southeast) from Route 302 onto Route 112 and follow the Wild Ammonoosuc River to the tiny town of **Swiftwater**, with its granite-ledged swimming hole shaded by a 174-foot, 1849 Paddleford truss. (Unspoiled Route 112, especially beautiful in the autumn, will please shunpikers, but it's fraught with bumps—locally known as frost heaves—in spring and winter.)

Quaint **Bath Village**, about 1 mile (1½ km) north of the Route 112 turnoff, is a toy town with a fire station, church, town hall, and village green all within hailing distance of each other. Bath's farmers enjoy the fertile valleys of three major rivers—the Connecticut, the Ammonoosuc, and the Wild Ammonoosuc—but in the early 1800s this was a mining and mill town. A huge 392-foot Burr truss, dating to 1832, is just off Route 302/10 and adjacent to the 1804 **Brick Store**, the oldest continuously operating general store in the country (there has been a store on the site since 1796).

Over the hill on Route 302/10 are **Upper Bath Village** and a cluster of striking Federal-style houses, the legacy of the Jeremiah Hutchins family, prosperous farmers, publicans, and attorneys. Local brick was used to build these homes, several of which date to 1816, the nightmarish year when there was no summer.

Lisbon

As you continue along Route 302/10 keep in mind that all the villages along the Ammonoosuc at some time looked a lot like Lisbon, 6 miles (10 km) north of Bath. Lisbon's industrial structures and mill housing may seem drab, but they bear witness to a continuing vitality and enterprise that once characterized other villages that are now merely picturesque. Main Street is home to shoe, wire, and wood mills, but just a block away are country lanes and hillside farms. Emerging from the village the road enters a meadowland. About a mile (1½ km) out of town, on the left, is a four-story porched building, the former **Young-Cobleigh Tavern**. Built in the 1780s, this rare survivor was a stagecoach stop for a century but has been a privately owned farmhouse for a century since.

Route 117 intersects Route 302/10 in the Salmon Hole neighborhood, where Ogontz Brook enters the Ammonoosuc, creating a shallow bathing area on the north side of Route 302 (no facilities) and some interesting fishing (but no salmon) on the south side. Across the bridge is the turn to the **Ammonoosuc Inn**, a restored 19th-century farmhouse with restaurant, an outdoor pool, tennis courts, and a very scenic nine-hole golf course. The inn has nine rooms with private baths and five new condominiums in the carriage house. **Cobblers Restaurant** here is competent and casual, with a menu geared to a year-round local clientele; Tel: (603) 838-6118.

Littleton

Eleanor Porter, author of *Pollyanna,* grew up in Littleton, 11 miles (18 km) northeast of Lisbon. With a population of 5,800, Littleton is the region's "big city." That is, it has a hospital, a traffic light, and a placid self-regard evident in 2,500 pages of immensely detailed town histories published over the last 100 years. Main Street presents the canny visitor with a few good restaurants and a couple of fine ones (discussed below). Retailers lure tax fugitives from Vermont and Canada with good prices and friendly service. Pollyanna would still recognize the place.

You'll enter town on Route 302/10, here a commercial strip, and climb a hill; you might want to park your car in one of the free off-street lots and tour the town on foot.

The Littleton Historical Society runs a small museum in the Town Building, a towered pile at 2 Cottage Street. Of special interest are the exhibits of 19th-century stereoscopic views (postcards intended for mounting in binocular viewers) manufactured in Littleton at the once-famed Kilburn Brothers Stereoscopic View Factory.

SHOPPING IN LITTLETON

Across from Thayers at 127 Main Street is **Parker's Marketplace**, a rehabilitated mansion doing service as a boutique mall: **Duck Soup** sells kitchenware, **Sport Thoma** sports attire and equipment, and the **Elephant's Trunk** women's fashions. For outdoor attire and gear, visit the **Outlet**'s two locations—across from the Marketplace at 126 and 82 Main Street, the former, called **North Country Outfitters**, with a rock-climbing wall for customers. Open seven days a week at 88 Main Street is the **Village Book Store**, whose exhaustive collection includes books on local subjects. The **Booklady**, two doors down, is a quirky, comfortable place with a mix of rare collectibles and affordable used books. For a wide selection of periodicals visit **Rae's Gifts**, at 44 Main Street. The **Littleton Bicycle Shoppe**, at the traffic light, is the only bike facility on the Western Slope.

Before purchasing outdoor gear be sure to visit Lahout's, as well as Sport Thoma and the Outlet. The three stores have competed for decades, and the rivalry can save you money. **Lahout's** is at 96 Union Street (Route 116), a half mile (1 km) past the lights, in an old Grange Hall that was purchased by a Lebanese immigrant named Herbert Lahout in 1922. The third generation of Lahouts has modernized the inventory, but the store retains a zesty mix of Levantine warmth and Yankee thrift.

STAYING AND DINING IN LITTLETON

Littleton claims a handful of good eating places and two tiny venues for fine dining. The **Beal House Inn** is an 1833 Federal–Renaissance farmhouse at the corner of Main (Route 302) and West Main (Route 18). It seats only 20, but the Belgian mâitre d', a former sommelier, has put up more than 200 Californian and French wines. The menu changes bi-weekly; among recent offerings were noisettes of lamb served with garlic red-currant sauce topped with toasted pine nuts, and, for dessert, maple bourbon soufflé glacé and poached pears with *crème anglaise.* Reserve; Tel: (603) 444-2661. The Beal House is also Littleton's best bed-and-breakfast, with high ceilings, four-posters, and breakfast served on blue willow china. The game room is furnished with antique toys, the breakfast room with porcelain dolls made by local artists. Each of the nine guest rooms has a private bath. Some of the antiques are for sale, but not conspicuously so.

The four-story, colonnaded **Thayers Inn**, at 136 Main Street, was built in 1850 and represented a great advance from the era typified by Lisbon's Young-Cobleigh Tavern. The management of Thayers has restored one of the inn's rooms as a "museum" in mid-19th-century style, but its guest rooms are more up-to-date, with private baths, telephones, and TVs. At street level, **Daddy Thayers** offers breakfast, while the **Back Street Café** serves sandwiches downstairs.

Tim-Bir Alley, at 28 Main Street, down an alley across from the Methodist church, is where foodies go for such delights as salmon with hazelnuts and citrus-Champagne sauce or sautéed shrimp on corn pancakes with tomato salsa. (The restaurant's name is a sort of combination of the owners' first names, Tim and Biruta.) Seating here is also limited, so phone ahead; Tel: (603) 444-6142.

For tuna pea wiggle try the **Littleton Diner**, at 170 Main Street diagonally across from the post office; Tel: (603) 444-3994. At I-93 exit 42 on Dells Road is the **Clamshell**, a high-volume, mid-range seafood restaurant with a reputation for freshness and consistency (Tel: 603/444-6445), while at exit 41, on Route 302/116, the restaurant at the **Eastgate** motel serves prime rib and "luxury at prices a working man can afford" (Tel: 603/444-3971).

Whitefield

About 11 miles (18 km) northeast of Littleton via Route 116 is Whitefield, a picturesque town with an excellent summer theater and an exclusive resort. Although Whitefield is technically in Cöos County (our final, northern quadrant), its cultural compass points to the Western Slope, so we include it here.

On the way to Whitefield, on Route 116 just 6 miles (10 km) north of Littleton, is **Forest Lake State Park**, with a nice beach. A mile (1½ km) beyond is Parker Road; turn left here and you'll come to **Maxwell Haus**, a mid-1800s Greek Revival–style bed-and-breakfast surrounded by 32 acres of private forest. Inside there are six Victorian-style rooms with shared baths. Maxwell Haus is operated with zest by an energetic young couple who host theme weekends around such topics as gourmet cooking, hiking (with picnics), cross-country skiing, and slimming down. Four miles (6½ km) farther along Route 116, at the bottom of the steep hill where the road intersects Route 3, is the Whitefield village green, complete with hatbox bandstand. Completing the village, which is often featured on calendars, are a mill stream, white churches, and friendly—not touristy—shops. Visit **Frank's** for good buys on brand-name clothing. The proprietor's name is Dave.

Two miles (3 km) north up the hill on Route 3, a red barn houses the **Weathervane Theatre** (performances in summer only). Comedies and musicals are favored by the enthusiastic, mostly Equity cast, and the repertoire of productions is scheduled so that the same show is not performed on consecutive nights. For schedule information, Tel: (603) 837-9322. Conveniently located adjacent to the theater is the **Inn at Whitefield**, open year-round and, judging by the scallops oreganata, a cut above most north-of-the-notch Italian restaurants. Tel: (603) 837-2760.

A stone's throw north of the Weathervane is Mountainview Road, which leads to the **Spalding Inn** and the grand old Mountain View House. The latter is in suspended animation, its yellow towers peeling and broad porches vacant since 1988. The Mountain View's spectacular views and golf course (nine holes, par 70) have survived nicely, however, and are enjoyed by Spalding Inn guests quartered a furlong up the road.

Lawn bowling and the gentry that followed this rarefied sport were emblematic of the Spalding Inn during the post–World War II years, but as the white-clad aristocrats of yore are now nourishing lawns rather than bowling on them, the Spalding seems to have been left with a cachet in search of a clientele. "More like a fine country estate than a hotel," says the brochure for this 58-room inn, with its 12-room carriage house, fireplaced cottages, poolside grill house, sports house, and four spacious public rooms. Four clay tennis courts, a putting green, and the pampered bowling green keep the new (1991) owners busy. The dining room has a reputation for finger bowl formality and the fanciest cuisine between Littleton and Cöos County's Balsams Grand Resort. Tel: (603) 837-2572.

Bethlehem

About 5 miles (8 km) east of Littleton via Route 302, Bethlehem rests on a shoulder of Mount Agassiz (2,378 feet). In the 1880s a narrow-gauge railroad linked Bethlehem village with the main line, and 34 hotels sprang up here. Most of them have vanished in the last 50 years, leaving odd gaps along Main Street. The lure of this lofty (elevation 1,440 feet) town was its air, reputed to be nearly pollen free. Henry Ward Beecher and others publicized the miracle. In the 1920s New York doctors prescribed Bethlehem vacations for their hay-fever patients (at one point the town was the headquarters of the American Hay Fever Association), and the town developed a Jewish colony that remains a vital presence.

No other town can match Bethlehem's collection of late-19th and early-20th-century summer homes. Many are closed to the public, but most can be admired from the road. The broad stone walls at the intersection of Route 302 and I-93 (exit 40), 3 miles (5 km) west of town, belong to the **Rocks**, an estate built by the former International Harvester's Glessner family and now owned by the Society for the Protection of New Hampshire Forests. Visitors are welcome. Although the main house was demolished in the 1940s, about 20 other buildings, including three houses and several barns, remain as part of an educational project. Tel: (603) 444-6228.

The junction also marks the entrance to the **Adair—A Country Inn**, a bed-and-breakfast down the road near the small information booth. Built in 1927, Adair was the summer home of a Washington, D.C., lawyer. In 1992 it became a year-round country inn with eight spacious guest rooms in a three-story white clapboard house. The public areas are roomy, and all of the guest rooms have private baths (two have working fireplaces). The 200-acre grounds include dramatic gardens, large maples, and rolling lawns landscaped by Frederick Law Olmsted, designer of Manhattan's Central Park.

As Route 302 climbs into town, the **Bethlehem Country Club Golf Course** appears on the left (Tel: 603/869-5745). Both of Bethlehem's courses were designed around 1898 by Donald Ross (the other, the Maplewood Golf Course, is discussed below). Past the clubhouse on the right is Strawberry Hill Street, with three notable homes. The one on the west corner, built in 1918 by Sylvanus D. Morgan, was clearly influenced by Frank Lloyd Wright. Behind it is the **Bells**, an amusing pagoda-style Victorian built in 1892 by a retired clergyman that is now a romantic bed-and-breakfast. (The cupola bedroom is a favorite with honeymooners.) The house on the east corner was built in 1873 by Henry Howard, governor of Rhode Island, and is considered to be Bethlehem's first summer cottage. Its embellished gables are typical of the Stick Gothic style. Only the Bells is open to the public, and it is restricted to patrons (open summers only).

A row of antiques shops, each quite distinct, leads along Route 302 to the Route 142 intersection (the center of town), a grassy swath marked by a tiny gazebo where stood, until a 1978 fire, the enormous Sinclair Hotel. A quarter mile farther east on 302 is the vintage 1870s Maplehurst Hotel. The **Mulburn Inn**, a quarter mile beyond that, is a Tudor-style "cottage" built in 1913 by the Woolworth family. Another Sylvanus Morgan design, it has rounded wings, a roomy interior (huge bathrooms), and rich appointments (maple, mahogany, ash, and oak); today Mulburn is a very attractive bed-and-breakfast. (Cary Grant and Barbara Hutton slept here.) The inn affords views of both Mount Washington and, perhaps of more interest to some, the 18-hole golf course of the **Maplewood Casino & Country Club**, which spreads on both sides of the road (Tel: 603/869-3335), anchored by a local landmark, the 1886 Casino clubhouse, restored in 1986. The stone-towered casino was an outbuilding of the 750-room Maplewood Hotel, which burned in 1963.

Route 302 descends to the Pierce Bridge neighborhood, where, in the 19th century, the main line of the railroad sprouted two narrow-gauge spurs, one to Bethlehem and one to the Profile House hotel in Franconia Notch. The latter spur is now Trudeau Road, location of the U.S. Forest Service Ammonoosuc Ranger District headquarters. All that remains of the busy junction is the **Wayside Inn**, built in 1825 by a nephew of President Franklin Pierce. The accommodations are ordinary, but the restaurant, which has a pretty view of the river, is above average, specializing in such Swiss dishes as *Geschnatzeltes und Rosti.* Tel: (603) 869-3364.

The Carroll Area

"Would there ever be a town in the State of New Hampshire that would house five great hotels of the national and international prominence of these?" asks George McAvoy in *And Then There Was One,* his book about the grand hotels of

Carroll. The answer is "no," but a better question is "Where is Carroll?"

Maps usually omit Carroll in favor of Twin Mountain, Fabyan, Bretton Woods, and Crawford, all former railroad stops marking vanished hotels in this now sleepy, but still scenic town. Given by legislative fiat in 1832 in honor of Charles Carroll, a signer of the Declaration of Independence, the name was never embraced by townspeople, who preferred Haven (never officially adopted) or the older king's-grant designation of Bretton Woods (for the grantee's ancestral home in England). Even today the name Carroll is seldom used by residents, and for visitors, what the place is called is less important than the sudden proximity of the mountains. The skyline presents surprises at every river bend. Many famous people travelled this road to Carroll's grand hotels. McAvoy's partial list mentions, in no particular order, Princess Margaret, Winslow Homer, Henry Ward Beecher, Harriet Beecher Stowe, Anthony Eden, John Kenneth Galbraith, Alfred Hitchcock, Rudy Vallee, Carl Sandburg, Ulysses S. Grant, Winston Churchill, Joan Crawford, Samuel P. Colt, and Thomas Edison.

TWIN MOUNTAIN

In Twin Mountain, 8 miles (13 km) west of Bethlehem at the junction of Routes 302 and 3, a modest tourist strip has grown around the site of the Twin Mountain House. Razed in 1960, the inn was the first New Hampshire property to be developed by the Barron brothers, whose descendants started up *The Wall Street Journal*—but that's another story. In recent years Twin Mountain has promoted itself as a destination for snowmobiling and has earned year-round popularity among enthusiasts of that sport.

West of the junction the surroundings get more rural as you enter the White Mountain National Forest. The **USFS Zealand Campground**, right at the forest's entrance, derives its name from a logging town owned by J. E. Henry, a notorious logging entrepreneur, or "woods baron," during the interregnum of rapacious cutting in the 1880s. Detested by the hoteliers and pursued by forest fires, Henry literally moved the town—railroad, buildings, people, and livestock—to Lincoln in 1892, and Zealand became green again. Zealand's broad gravel road has three distinct campgrounds—Zealand Campground at the junction of Route 302, and the two Sugarloaf Campgrounds a half mile (1 km) up the road—for a total of 73 woodsy campsites: fire pit, water, and toilets, but no hookups. For information, Tel: (603) 869-2626; for reservations, Tel: (800) 283-2267.

A picnic area beside the Ammonoosuc on Route 302 offers an information billboard describing hikes, fishing spots, and the like. The **Zealand Trail**, marked by waterfalls, wildflowers, and a population of beavers, follows an old railroad bed from the campground on an easy grade to the AMC (Appalachian Mountaineering Club) Zealand Falls Hut. The 5.6-mile, three-and-a-half-hour round-trip trail is also good for cross-country skiing. Details on hikes in the area are available at the campground. Tel: (603) 869-2626.

BRETTON WOODS

The biseasonal community of Bretton Woods, 6 miles (10 km) east of Twin Mountain along Route 302, comprises the Bretton Woods Ski Area, the Mount Washington Hotel, and the base station for the Mount Washington Cog Railway. Across Route 302 from the ski area, Fabyan's Station, once a junction for a branch line to the Cog Railway, now houses an eponymous restaurant (discussed below) in its restored depot. These enterprises have their own ZIP code and telephone exchange and, since 1991, are linked administratively. The Ammonoosuc River becomes Ammonoosuc Brook here, threading its way toward its source at the Lakes of the Clouds, high on Mount Washington's west flank.

Bretton Woods Ski Area

New Hampshire's newest ski area has wide, easy trails and great views of Mount Washington. When it opened in 1973 it virtually stole the beginner market from steeper mountains. The spacious base lodge has a second-story pub where parents can watch their youngsters on the slopes. Also in the lodge is a branch of the **Sport Thoma** chain of stores, with clothing, accessories, and gear; a cafeteria; and a less casual restaurant. Across the parking lot is a health club with an indoor pool and racketball. There are slopeside condos for rent, but the nocturnal snow-making crew with their roaring guns and snarling snowmobiles may discomfit some sleepers. For more information, Tel: (800) 258-0330 or (603) 278-1000.

Bretton Woods's vertical drop is only 1,500 feet down the gentle slope of Mount Rosebrook (elevation 3,007 feet), but a speedy detachable quad chair compensates, allowing for frequent runs. There is a total of five lifts and 30 trails (31 percent beginner, 46 percent intermediate, and 23 percent expert) on 165 skiable acres. Good natural snowfall is supplemented by snow making on 98 percent of its trails. Bretton Woods offers night skiing (one slope, two nights a week), which, like the snow-board half pipe, thrills teenagers. A ski school offers weekday package deals that include either lift ticket, lesson, and lunch or lift ticket, lesson, and ski rental for around $30. For more information, Tel: (603) 278-5000; for ski conditions, Tel: (603) 278-5051.

The trail mileage at the **Bretton Woods Touring Center,** the cross-country facility here, is rivaled only by that of Jackson's Ski Touring Foundation (see Jackson, below), but Bretton Woods is less crowded on weekends and has two distinctive features: a biathlon range where spectators may watch ski-riflery teams compete in this unusual Olympic sport, and a five-mile, fully groomed, intermediate mountain run accessed via the ski lifts at the alpine ski area. A total of 53 miles (85 km) of trails lace the hotel complex; the touring center's hub—ski school, waxing clinic, and other services—is located in the stables. Guided tours, picnics, and rentals are also available. Tel: (603) 278-5181.

A half mile (1 km) east of the Bretton Woods Ski Area, Route 302 bends left to reveal one of the most photographed scenes in the mountains: the entrance (left) to the mile-long driveway leading to the Mount Washington Hotel.

The Mount Washington Hotel

"The location," marveled the hotel's first manager, "is unique ... in the center of a plain, on an eminence, with a great circle of mountains all about. As far as the view goes, every room is a front room...." This five-story white palace, built in 1902 with red turrets, elaborate cornices, and broad verandahs, is a vibrant anachronism that was promised to be "a hotel in which nothing will be lacking that experience can suggest or the liberal use of money provide."

The money belonged to Joseph Stickney, and he was lavish with it. (The Pennsylvania Railroad magnate died in 1903, barely a year after the hotel opened.) Every convenience was supplied, from a stable of horses specially trained to share roadways with newfangled automobiles to a water-powered printing press that produced the *Bretton Woods Bugle,* a daily newspaper. In a town that boasted three other grand hotels, the Mount Washington was the ne plus ultra. Appropriately, this monument to prosperity hosted the 1944 Bretton Woods Monetary Conference, which laid the foundation for the World Bank and the International Monetary Fund, and launched Europe's postwar recovery.

Although strictly a summer operation, the Mount Washington Hotel complex—we describe the hotel itself in more detail below—embraces several year-round enterprises that are owned and managed by the same principals; at times, some of these offer tie-ins with the hotel's amenities. First, across Route 302 from the entrance to the hotel, is the **Lodge at Bretton Woods,** a modern 50-unit motel with indoor pool and private balconies facing the Presidential Range across the hotel's lawns. The Lodge also houses **Darby's**, a family restaurant with a flair for dishes like shrimp sauté with pistachio pesto. **Fabyan's Station** is a restaurant and lounge located a half mile (1 km) west on Route 302, opposite the ski area; burgers and pasta dishes are safe bets here. Tel: (603) 846-2222.

In the shadow of the hotel and reached by the hotel's driveway is the **Bretton Arms Inn**, an 1896 country inn that was thoroughly renovated in 1986 to offer 34 up-to-date rooms and suites. Dining at the Bretton Arms is exceptionally good; roast rack of wild boar and venison steak sauced with Jack Daniel's are representative offerings from this daring kitchen. On the hotel's western grounds are **Townhome Rentals at Bretton Woods**, 65 furnished one-story town houses with full kitchens, built within the past decade. In winter all of these facilities nicely complement the Bretton Woods Ski Area and are connected to the slopes by shuttles.

The main event, however, is the hotel itself: five dining rooms with a seating capacity of 700, a casual restaurant, a nightclub, six cocktail lounges, a ballroom, 11 function rooms, 177 guest rooms, 12 clay tennis courts, indoor and outdoor pools, an equestrian center, and two golf courses. But if the size is impressive, the perfect proportions of the place are enchanting. If it were any smaller it would be dwarfed by the mountains; any bigger and it would be vulgar. Even if you do not plan to stay here, at least stroll the quarter-mile-long verandah or take a guided tour.

All that said, it must be admitted that in 1990 the Federal Deposit Insurance Corporation had to spend $1.2 million on restoration before a savvy group of Littleton businesspeople took ownership. This is a very big old hotel that will never appeal to all tastes. As the *Boston Globe* observed: "This is luxury turn-of-the-century style. Instead of a Jacuzzi, you sink up to your neck in a gleaming claw-foot tub. Instead of staring at a TV, you focus on the mountains." The appointments that impressed pre–World War I visitors may seem depressingly retro to some visitors. But why stay in your room? Downstairs is the **Cave**, a notorious Prohibition-era lounge with lively music, and the pillared ballroom usually hosts a big band or similar entertainment. Then there's dining. Try sautéed cinnamon trout with strawberry and kiwi sauce in the hotel's huge, octagonal main dining room as the orchestra plays chamber music. Jackets are required of gentlemen after 6:00 P.M. More casual dining can be found downstairs at **Stickney's** in the hotel concourse. This former billiard parlor has a genteel Edwardian charm that unfortunately does not always extend to the food or service.

Daytime recreation in the complex itself entails golf, mountaineering, or railroading. Behind the hotel the **Mount Washington Golf Club**, an 18-hole Donald Ross course (par 71), spreads toward the Presidentials. Completed in 1915, it is the permanent site of the New England PGA Pro-Am Festival. In front of the hotel and lining the river, the nine-hole **Mount Pleasant Golf Links** was reopened in 1991 after extensive restoration. For both courses, Tel: (603) 278-1000.

Hiking

All the hiking trails around the hotel are too numerous to list, but the best route up **Mount Washington** is the steep, 4.5-mile **Ammonoosuc Ravine Trail**, a four-and-a-half-hour (one-way) hike marked by waterfalls and pools. A mile below the summit is the safe haven of the AMC Lakes of the Clouds Hut. This is the most famous of the Appalachian Mountain Club alpine lodges, a network of backwoods bunkhouses where hefty meals are served to weary trampers (see the Appalachian Mountain Club in the Pinkham Notch section, below). Although an overnight stay requires reservations, the 1915 stone building is open to day-trippers who want to get out of the wind, refresh their canteens, buy a candy bar, and consult with the staff about the weather before attacking the summit cone. The tiny Lakes of the Clouds are located next to the hut at an elevation of 5,050 feet; these two rock bowls of icy water are the source of the Ammonoosuc River. (The summit of Mount Washington is discussed below.)

Descend Mount Washington the same day via the less-precipitous **Jewell Trail**, which offers a breathtaking glimpse over the rim of the Great Gulf, a glacial cirque (U-shaped canyon) on Mount Washington's northern shoulder where steep walls plunge 1,600 feet to a flat, forested floor. Take the Gulfside Trail at the summit to connect with the Jewell Trail near the Great Gulf. Total descent: 5.1 miles. Well-marked trailheads for the Ammonoosuc Ravine Trail and the Jewell Trail are 6 miles (10 km) from the hotel: 1 mile (1½ km) west on Route 302 to Fabyan and right onto the 5-mile (8-km) road to the Cog Railway Base Station (discussed below). At the end of this road a new parking lot serves both trails.

The summit of **Mount Eisenhower** can be reached in three hours by three-mile **Edmands Path**; the trailhead is on Mount Clinton Road, a 15-minute drive from the hotel; follow the same Base Road almost all the way to the Cog Railway but turn right on the Mount Clinton Road and proceed one mile (1½ km) to the conspicuous trailhead. Climb Eisenhower to see Washington.

Mount Washington Cog Railway

Since the Mount Washington Cog Railway opened in 1869 and carried Ulysses S. Grant to Mount Washington's summit, it has carried 50,000 tourists annually on the same trip from the Base Station, 5 miles (8 km) off Route 302. Perhaps the world's only coal-powered cog railroad steam engine, it pulls itself uphill by means of a gear (cog) that grabs teeth in a slotted track. The engine consumes a ton of coal during each ascent and hauls cars up grades as steep as 37.4 percent, thrilling rail buffs and others who enjoy paleotech. But it's a smoky way to climb Mount Washington; if you like trains, take the cog ($32 round-trip), but if you like mountains, walk. Closed Columbus Day through early May. For schedule, Tel: (603) 374-2272.

Crawford Notch State Park

It costs nothing to stop at the old **Crawford Railroad Station**, 4½ miles (7 km) east of the Mount Washington Hotel on Route 302, to examine the historical exhibits and visit, across the highway, two-acre **Saco Lake**, the source of the Saco River. Fishing and canoeing are permitted, but no swimming. Picnic spots abound up and down the railroad tracks and in the woods on all sides. Built in 1891 to service the stately Crawford House hotel (1859–1977), which was located 200 yards north of here, the station was restored during the 1980s to serve as an information kiosk (open 9:00 A.M. to 5:00 P.M. daily in summer, irregularly off-season). Two notable hiking trails originate here: the **Crawford Path**, the oldest continuously maintained footpath in the United States (since 1819); and the **Mount Willard Trail**, affording the best views for the least effort. Take the former on a tolerable grade as far as Mount Clinton's 4,324-foot summit (3 miles, two and a half hours one way), or the latter to the ledgy summit of 2,804-foot Mount Willard (1.6 miles, one and a quarter hours one way) for a spectacular view down the notch from tiered outcroppings. Shorter hikes lead to pleasant overlooks and falls, notably **Gibbs Falls**, ten minutes up Crawford Path.

The descent into Crawford Notch on Route 302 is dramatic, with cliffs soaring on either side—Mount Webster on the north and Mount Willard on the south—amid waterfalls, rock slides, and spindly railroad trestles. (The tracks are no longer used.) The next 11 miles (18 km) of highway have no services and no recreational facilities save hiking trails. This notch and its environs were the haunt of the legendary Crawford family. Innkeepers to Hawthorne and Thoreau, the Crawfords were pioneering trail builders who opened up the mountains for their guests' exploration.

At the bottom of the hill between perpendicular valley walls and beside a pleasant pond is the **Willey House**, important not so much for its gruesome history—in 1826 a landslide narrowly missed the house but killed the Willey family, who were outside at the time—as because the tragedy attracted the first cultural tourists, painter Thomas Cole and writer Nathaniel Hawthorne, both of whom publicized the incident. (Hawthorne's story about the landslide is "The Ambitious Guest.") The death of the Willeys marked the birth of White Mountains tourism; it was the spark that ignited the romantic passion for the region. The state park operates a snack bar here, and visitors often relax beside a small lake and gaze at the fatal hillside while picnicking.

Exactly 1 mile (1½ km) southeast of the Willey House, off Route 302, is the **Ripley Falls** trailhead, a half-mile uphill walk leading to a 100-foot waterfall. The trailhead for 176-foot **Arethusa Falls**—the highest in the state—is 2 miles (3 km) beyond that to Ripley Falls. The 1.3-mile trail to the falls is rather steep, but both this trail and that to Ripley Falls are as pretty as their destinations. The Arethusa Falls trailhead is marked by the **Frankenstein Cliffs**, named not for Mary Shelley's hapless scientist but for Godfrey N. Frankenstein (1820–1873), a landscape painter who followed Cole to the area. The cliffs attract experienced rock climbers and hikers.

The **Notchland Inn**, a stone mansion built in 1862 by a Boston dentist, is a couple of miles (3 km) beyond the cliffs. The 400-acre estate has been an inn for many years, and, under the latest owners, a toney but entertaining one. Eleven large guest rooms include four two-room suites. Each room has a bath, a fireplace, and period antiques. The Map Room, one of the public parlors, is an early example of the Arts and Crafts style. The dining room's menu is limited but alluring, usually offering a beef, a chicken, and a fish choice. The proprietors possess the personal touch you might expect from people who maintain a refuge for rare and endangered species of domestic animals, including goats, llamas, and miniature horses.

The Bartlett Area

The 6 miles (10 km) between Notchland and the village of Bartlett (still on Route 302) offer many picnic sites beside the Saco River. The road follows the river through the attenuated town of Bartlett: first the village of Bartlett, then Attitash Ski Area, and finally Glen, a precinct that seems to belong more to Jackson or Conway, which we discuss after Glen.

Bartlett is a former railroad town that has become a quiet bedroom community for the bustling Conways. Seasonal **Bear Notch Road** begins here and winds through pleasant hills with scenic overlooks. An express route south, the Bear Notch terminates at Route 112 (the Kancamagus Highway, discussed above), bypassing busy North Conway.

You can always find good snow at **Attitash Ski Area**, 3 miles (5 km) east of Bartlett village and 9 miles (14½ km) west of North Conway. A snow drought in the early 1980s led the owners to install a top-flight snow-making system that uses Omicron guns to make light, naturalistic snow over 98 percent of the terrain. The depth is ample, the grooming is unequaled, and the season is long. Although Attitash is a newish ski area (1965), its somewhat narrow trails have a classic feel. There is no central hotel, but **Top Notch Vacation Rentals**, in Attitash Marketplace in Bartlett, offers lodging in motels and rental condominiums; Tel: (800) 762-6636.

Mount Attitash, which attracts a loyal clientele of committed skiers, has a vertical drop of 1,750 feet from the 2,300-foot summit. Six lifts service 28 trails (25 percent beginner, 46 percent intermediate, and 29 percent expert) on 220 skiable acres (Tel: 603/374-2368; for ski conditions, Tel: 603/374-0946). The roadside base lodge has a ski school, day care, rentals, ski shop, cafeteria, and lounge. Attitash offers the option of purchasing a Smart Ticket worth from 75 to 450 points, which are deducted by computerized scanners at ski lifts. Smart Tickets can be shared or transferred, and are valid for two years from date of purchase. **Horsefeathers** restaurant, across the road, is good for sandwiches and self-consciously hip specialties; Tel: (603) 374-0808.

In addition to horseback riding and a chairlift to a summit view, Attitash runs a water slide and so-called "mountain slide" during the summer season. The latter is a wheeled cart that hurtles down a half-pipe conduit.

As the road nears Glen it offers another opportunity to bypass the North Conway traffic. Exactly 1½ miles (2½ km) beyond Attitash is an inconspicuous right turn onto West Side Road, which parallels the Route 16/302 bottleneck.

On Route 302, just before the turn for West Side Road, is **I Cugini**, an Italian restaurant with a local following; Tel: (603) 374-1977. Serious foodies will stay on Route 302 and visit the **Bernerhof Inn**, half a mile (1 km) past the West Side Road. The Bernerhof runs a cooking school that attracts the best New England chefs. Accommodations are plush here. Six of the nine units have two-person spa tubs, and one suite has a private sauna. Still, the emphasis here is on dining; the menu features Swiss dishes amid a changing array of Continental specialties.

The village of **Glen**, 1½ miles (2½ km) east of the Bernerhof, clusters around the junction of Routes 302 and 16; it serves as the local shopping district for Bartlett and Jackson, offering, among other shops, a supermarket and a thriving state liquor store. It is also home to **Margaritaville** (Tel: 603/383-6556) and the **Red Parka Pub** (Tel: 603/383-4344), both casual and popular eateries. The former has the best Mexican dishes in the White Mountains (no credit cards), while the latter is an après-ski steakhouse.

At Glen you may continue south and east to the Conways and the Mount Washington Valley (discussed next) or turn north on Route 16 to Jackson and Pinkham Notch (discussed after that), two very different areas.

THE EASTERN SLOPE: THE CONWAYS

The Conways have been tagged with a spate of promotional monikers: the Eastern Slope, the Mount Washington Valley, and, simply, North Conway. We will use the last to refer to the three-mile commercial strip extending south from the village of North Conway. Incorporated in 1765, Conway bloomed along the Saco River Valley with an agricultural village here, a mill town there, and clusters of stores everywhere. A good map will show the villages of Conway, Center Conway, North Conway, Intervale, Kearsarge, and Redstone, and there is also a South Conway and an East Conway. (Local historians also fondly cite the vanished bailiwicks of Fag End, Dolloftown, and Pigwacket.) For most purposes, remembering Conway, North Conway, and Intervale is sufficient.

Shopping here is unmatched in the state, but be warned: Route 16/302, the major thoroughfare linking the towns, is an anachronistic two-lane road. The 12-mile (19-km) stretch through Conway, North Conway, and on up to Intervale can be a vexing bottleneck of shoppers flooding the scores of factory outlets that line the North Conway strip, especially on rainy days and weekends. While it's true that the emphasis in the Conways is frankly commercial, there are also covered bridges, swimming holes, and waterfalls a few blocks away, wooing the jaded shopper with canoeing, skiing, and biking. Accommodations and dining in the area, too, are among the best in the mountains.

The mountains stop at Conway, giving way to sandy, rolling uplands, but the change is so abrupt that peaks to the north and west literally loom over the town. Coach travellers had long stopped at Conway's taverns to brace for the mountain passage, but the town's transition from way station to destination began in 1827, when Thomas Cole arrived to paint the scene of the tragic Willey landslide in Crawford Notch (see above). He returned to paint Mount Chocorua, Mount Washington, and the Saco River, thereby publicizing the region for other painters and cultural tourists. Most prominent among Cole's followers was Benjamin Champney (1817–1907), who made North Conway his permanent residence. At least one 19th-century valley innkeeper proffered emoluments to artists who advertised the area, and this tradition of good-natured promotion has carried into the 20th century.

The heart (if not the soul) of the valley may be the North Conway shopping strip, but surrounding the bustle on all sides await pleasures of a more bucolic nature. First, to the south, is the Tamworth/Chocorua area, which encompasses those pretty towns themselves as well as impressive Mount Chocorua (hiking) and Lake Chocorua (swimming). Also south of the Conways is a lovely stretch of Route 153, with more unspoiled villages and lakes. Conway village itself, still south of North Conway, remains untouristy and claims two 19th-century covered bridges. Even closer to North Conway to the west and north are several good golf courses, Echo Lake State Park (swimming and hiking), and Mount Cranmore Ski Area, a sunny mountain with night skiing. Finally, a detour east of the Conways brings us over the Maine border to Fryeburg and Evans Notch, linked by Route 113, a less-travelled road that follows an old railroad bed.

South of the Conways

Bypassed by most travellers, the pretty town of Tamworth, southwest of the Conways via Routes 16 and 113, is a lovely place to visit, and includes the village of Chocorua, with its famous mountain of the same name. To the east, Route 153 remains happily neglected as it winds north–south through quiet villages. Both detours from the Conway area are dotted with inn-style lodgings and fine restaurants.

ROUTE 153
Pick up Route 153 in Effingham Falls, 13 miles (21 km) south of Conway, and follow it north to the white-painted village of Freedom. The main part of the village is just east of Route 153 on Freedom Village Road. The rolling countryside is a broad glacial deposit of sand and gravel that has rewarded farmers for more than two centuries. In season, farm stands

abound. Glittering ponds and lakes are numerous in this rich lowland. Another 4 miles (6½ km) north in East Madison are Purity Lake and the **Purity Spring Resort**, a year-round self-contained resort that caters to active families. Manicured grounds, white buildings with black shutters, a baseball diamond, and tennis courts border a spring-fed lake of great clarity. Accommodation here, all under one management, varies from New England inn to private cottages to rustic lodges. Dinner guests are welcome in the summer. The **King Pine Ski Area**, part of the resort, is a tiny mountain with a vertical drop of only 350 feet (the vertical drop at all other White Mountains ski areas starts at 1,000 feet), but its ski school is one of the best around for beginners.

Three miles (5 km) north of Purity Lake, Route 153 curves sharply right at Crystal Lake and enters the unspoiled village of **Eaton**, which hides a handful of country inns. Go around the lake, watch for the right turn (Fire Lane number 37), and continue 1 mile (1½ km) to Snowville and the **Snowville Inn**, with good views of the mountain ranges to the north and overlooking apple trees and flower gardens. The hillside buildings, red with white trim, that make up the inn include a house built in 1916 and originally used as a writer's retreat, a handsome annex with fireplaces in every room, and a converted barn—18 rooms in all, each named for an author and furnished with country antiques. Guests enjoy lake swimming, tennis, or cross-country skiing. Meals are served to the public by reservation; Tel: (603) 447-2818. Snowville is also home to **Sleighmill Antiques**, which specializes in 19th-century lamps and shades.

Five miles (8 km) north of Eaton Route 153 rejoins Route 16 at the traffic lights in Conway village.

TAMWORTH AND CHOCORUA

Travellers on Route 16, the most popular northbound route to the Conways, often overlook the out-of-the-way 19th-century resort community of Tamworth village, situated on an adjoining secondary road (Route 113), while Chocorua village, on Route 16, has postcard views that deserve a pause.

As you enter the Tamworth town limits on Route 16 from the south, on your left will be **White Lake State Park**, with tall pitch pines, a sandy beach, and campsites; for reservations, Tel: (603) 323-7350. This popular campground has 173 tent sites, and when 173 campfires are lit, it is smoggy. But do see the 72-acre stand of pines, which are a national landmark. Two woodsy miles (3 km) farther north on Route 16, on the left, is the **Country Primrose**, a rambling barn with aisles of gifts and antique quilts.

In another mile (1½ km), a waterfall and millpond mark the tiny village of **Chocorua** (shuh-COR-rew-a) at the junction of Route 113. Only a seasonal ice-cream shop lures the Conway-bound, but the tranquillity of the scene makes this an arresting photo stop. Tamworth village is 2½ miles (4 km) west on Route 113.

If on the way to Tamworth you turn right off Route 113 onto Philbrook Neighborhood Road you'll come to **Staffords in the Field**, at the bottom of a hill and surrounded by fields. Staffords, a year-round bed-and-breakfast, has 17 cozy rooms, six with private bath, all furnished with antiques. The dining room is highly regarded locally; try the curried pumpkin soup. Tel: (603) 323-7766.

Tamworth village has more the flavor of tranquil lakes than of the rugged mountains that border it north and south; it lies in a sandy plain, eight miles wide, that is speckled with dozens of ponds and marshes. Gracefully straddling the Swift River, the village has been a refined summer colony for a century. President Grover Cleveland summered here and his grandson founded the **Barnstormers Playhouse**, which has operated for more than 60 summers, on Tamworth's Main Street. An Equity cast performs musicals and popular plays in July and August; Tel: (603) 323-8500.

Also on Main Street, across from the theater, is the 1833 **Tamworth Inn**, a year-round country inn beside the Swift River with 15 rooms, all with private bath. The inn houses a pub, a library, and a very good restaurant with a diverse menu featuring items like curried lamb and smoked trout. (Dinners only; Tel: 603/323-7721.) Outdoor activities include summer swimming at the inn's pool and fly fishing on the Swift River. In winter there's skating on the Swift and nearby ponds.

LAKE CHOCORUA AND MOUNT CHOCORUA

Chocorua was a Sokosis chief who met his end on the mountain named for him—either by suicide or murder, depending on your choice of legend—while uttering a curse on the white man. The chief's demise was depicted by Cole and has since been amply celebrated in poetry and painting. The dramatically bare 3,475-foot summit is a few miles north of the lake, which is itself just north of Chocorua village on Route 16. There is a swimming area at the north end of the lake but no facilities. Mount Chocorua can be climbed on foot from several directions and by several trails, none of them less than six hours round-trip and all of them strenuous. One trailhead is 3 miles (5 km) north of the lake at Piper Trail Cabins.

Stop at the U.S. Forest Service Saco Ranger Station, 10 miles (16 km) north of the lake at the junction of Route 16 and the Kancamagus Highway (Route 112), for maps, hiking routes, and information. The **Robert Gordon Gallery**, 100 yards down the Kanc from the ranger station, exhibits and sells fine landscapes of local scenes by Robert Gordon.

Conway Village

Just north of the ranger station a summer information booth welcomes you to Conway village, a residential area that is also home to the sprawling regional school, the town hall, and other civic facilities. Having conceded the hotel trade and outlet stores to frenetic North Conway, this village, with its tree-lined side streets, is less touristy but just as pretty, and noticeably friendlier. What to do here? Visit two covered bridges and two bookstores, and lunch at one of the modest eateries.

The covered bridges are on Washington Street; turn left at the lights at the junction of Route 153. The **Saco Covered Bridge** is a 240-foot, double-span Paddleford truss built in 1890 on the site of an earlier bridge that was demolished when the old Swift River Bridge floated downstream into it. The "new" **Swift River Bridge**, a 144-foot single-span Paddleford truss, is less than a mile (1½ km) down the same road. It was built in 1869 using timbers salvaged from both bridges.

Back at the lights, the **Book Warehouse** offers a quirky selection of discounted titles, but you will first want to try **Campbell's Books**, a third of a mile (½ km) north on Route 16 in the Conway Outlet Center, with uncatalogued overstock books selling for two dollars apiece.

Avoiding the Traffic

If you don't care to see the valley's commercial strip, take Washington Street from Conway; there will be no other alternate route. Continue past the covered bridges, following the west bank of the Saco, and you'll pass through farmland and residential neighborhoods as the throughway becomes West Side Road. Six miles (10 km) north, at Echo Lake State Park (discussed below), West Side Road meets River Road, which turns east to North Conway village. West Side Road continues north to Route 302 in Bartlett (discussed above).

Otherwise, follow Route 16 for 4 miles (6½ km) north of Conway village where it merges with Route 302 to create the North Conway strip, a three-mile stretch of road lined by outlets that ends in the village of North Conway.

North Conway

Cradled among hills of great beauty, dozens of name-brand outlets line the North Conway strip. Here the term "outlet" may not necessarily denote a factory-owned store that sells overproduced or slightly flawed goods at wholesale prices. Generally, these stores have the same goods as more conventional retailers but at lower prices (and, of course, New Hampshire has no sales tax); at the same time, customers are given somewhat scantier service.

The following is a partial inventory of stores with a distinctly local flavor or ones that vacationers find particularly useful, from south to north on the strip. **Yield House Industries**, a local company on the west side of the road at the Route 302 junction, sells gifts, unfinished furniture, and furniture kits. **Settlers' Green**, on the east side of the strip just north of Route 302, consists of a Sheraton hotel, five restaurants, and an "Outlet Village" of 30 shops, including **Banana Republic**, **Eddie Bauer**, and a general-interest bookstore, **White Birch Booksellers**. On the same side, just north of Settlers' Green, are the well-known **L. L. Bean** and **Chuck Roast** outlets, the former a Maine institution, the latter a North Conway manufacturer of warm, durable outdoor clothing and backpacks.

Gralyn Antiques has two locations on the west side of the highway, both of which, open "by chance or by appointment" (Tel: 603/356-5546), offer prints, paintings, and collectibles. Also on the left is a **League of New Hampshire Craftsmen** store, with fine pottery, pewter, jewelry, and other crafts juried for quality and made locally. Founded in 1932, the league was the first state-supported arts and crafts organization in the United States and has a reputation for exacting standards. Within walking distance of the league, toward North Conway village, is **Richard M. Plusch Antiques**, with a carefully chosen selection of fine antiques.

North Conway village, at the north end of the three-mile strip, is a colorful neighborhood of brightly painted older storefronts lining broad sidewalks. Shopping is on a more intimate scale here; parking is plentiful around Schouler Park, the village green, which is fronted by a Victorian railroad depot. The chamber of commerce has a small information booth across the street from the park.

At the traffic light a brick building houses **Annalee's Gift Shop**, noted for collectible dolls. Next door is the women's apparel store that started the town's retail boom in the 1930s, **Carroll Reed**. On the next block north, across from the public library, is **Bye the Book**, purveying works on local and regional subjects. Another block north is **Dondero's Rock Shop**, for jewelry and minerals. Finally, the impressive-looking Eastern Slope Inn (discussed below) houses **Eastern Mountain Sports**, a shop to equip the casual mountaineer.

Across Main Street from the inn is **International Mountain Equipment**, a mountaineers' outfitting shop that includes a climbing school (Tel: 603/356-7013). On the same block, **Saco Bound** can arrange tours or rentals amid a sampling of merchandise from the larger Center Conway store (see East of the Valley: Fryeburg and Evans Notch, below). Finally, visit **Joe Jones Ski and Sports**, on the corner of Main and Mechanic streets, for all-seasons gear; they also rent bicycles.

IN AND AROUND NORTH CONWAY

Ride a train, visit a museum, golf, or bike—all within a block of the village green. Diesel or steam-powered engines make an 11-mile, one-hour round trip through the Mount Washington Valley every two hours daily in the summer from the **Conway Scenic Railroad**, an 1874 station on Route 16/302 that also houses a free rail museum. Closed weekdays in spring and late fall; Tel: (800) 232-5251. The **North Conway Country Club**, an 18-hole, par-72 course, is right next to the railroad station (Tel: 603/356-9391). Just south on Main Street are the League of New Hampshire Craftsmen store discussed above and the **Mount Washington Observatory Resource Center**, which displays White Mountains memorabilia, notably Mount Washington summit photos that graphically depict the world's worst weather. (Note that within North Conway village Route 16/302 is also known as Main Street.)

Swimming, hiking, and more golf are available across the Saco. Just north of the Eastern Slope Inn, take a left onto River Road and continue 1 mile (1½ km) to **Echo Lake State Park** on, naturally, Echo Lake (with a swimming beach). The park is dominated by the steep prominences of **Cathedral Ledge** and **White Horse Ledge**. The former can be ascended by auto road, but both cliffs may be scaled by rock climbers or hiked via less precipitous routes. A 4.2-mile loop to White Horse Ledge begins in the parking lot. Allow three hours and bring a map, as other trails converge at the top.

Golfers should take West Side Road to **Hale's Location Golf Course**, part of the White Mountain Hotel and Resort at Hale's Location (discussed below). It's about half a mile (1 km) past the turn for Old West Side Road (the sign is small for such a big hotel). This is a new (1990) course with nine holes (par 72) dramatically set between cliffs and rolling hills. Nonguests may play; Tel: (603) 356-2140.

On the way to Intervale, which is just 2 miles (3 km) north of the village on Route 16/302, you'll pass the red-shuttered **Scottish Lion Import Shop**, purveyor of tweeds, tartans, and other gifts from the British Isles; it's located just before and almost opposite the entrance to Memorial Hospital. A quarter mile past the hospital on the east side of the road, flies, reels, and rods are displayed and sold alongside wildlife art at the **North Country Angler**. They provide lessons and guide service, too; Tel: (603) 356-6000. Also on the way to Intervale, just 1 mile (1½ km) out of North Conway, is the lapidary Stonehurst Manor, a hotel and restaurant with a medieval feel (discussed below). An excellent stop 1½ miles (2½ km) north of the village is the **Antiques and Collectibles Barn**, where 40 dealers display antique jewelry, dinnerware, prints, and rare quilts.

Intervale's rest area has a roadside view of the Saco Valley that was Champney's favorite. This is also a staging area for two driving tours. The short 2½-mile (4-km) **Intervale Resort Loop**, a country road with several pretty inns (see below), follows Route 16A and returns you to Route 16.

A longer, more ambitious tour starts on **Hurricane Mountain Road**, nearly opposite the rest area. The first leg is a rugged 6 miles (10 km) east along the shoulder of 2,100-foot Hurricane Mountain toward Chatham (population 230). Turn south (right) at the stop sign and continue 3½ miles (5½ km) through the quiet farm community of East Conway to Route 113. In 6 or 7 miles (10 or 11 km) Route 113 returns to Route 302, which you follow west to Route 16 and back through North Conway.

Mount Cranmore Ski Area

To get to Mount Cranmore head east at the lights in North Conway village on Kearsarge Road. When the valley was known more for skiing than shopping, Austrians Benno Rybizka and Hannes Schneider fled the Nazis and found employment here as ski instructors. Cranmore was launched just before the war, amid the yodeling refrain of "Bend ze knees! Two dollars, please!" Although the jaunty Austrian gemütlichkeit has faded and slopeside condos have arrived, some lovely, narrow winding trails remain from that era.

Cranmore has 100 percent snow-making coverage and the best night skiing in the area; the vertical drop from the summit is 1,167 feet. During the day the mountain's southern exposure makes it marginally warmer than its neighbors. It has four wide, pasture-like slopes and 28 trails (eight beginner, 13 intermediate, seven expert) served by five lifts. In addition to housing a cafeteria, ski shop, and rental facilities, the base lodge is linked to a condominium with such amenities as a health club, swimming pool, tennis courts, and a climbing wall for rock climbers. Tel: (603) 356-5543.

STAYING AND DINING
IN THE CONWAYS

North Conway's range of accommodations has widened in recent years as resort hotels have supplemented the traditional inns and strip motels. The **Sheraton Inn North Conway** is typical, with an indoor pool, a restaurant, tennis courts, exercise facilities, and more. Also offering the same amenities are the **Best Western Fox Ridge** and the **Red Jacket Mountain View**. The three hotels are found in this sequence (south to north) on the North Conway strip. As part of the Settlers' Green shopping complex, the 200-room Sheraton, newest of the three, overlooks lawns, promenades, and an elaborate bandstand in a village-like setting. On a hillside surrounded by 300 wooded acres, Fox Ridge has 136 rooms, most with good views of the western Whites from private balconies. Also hillside with good views, the 150-room Red Jacket has the best dining among these three resorts.

The **White Mountain Hotel and Resort at Hale's Location**, on West Side Road, does not have an indoor pool, but the outdoor pool is heated for year-round use. Its setting is more secluded and it has a new nine-hole par-72 golf course. The hotel's restaurant is still finding its niche, but the brunch is good and the setting splendid, with excellent views.

The **Eastern Slope Inn**, on Main Street in North Conway village, is billed as a resort but is primarily a time-share complex including attractive town houses. It has an indoor pool and exercise room, while the **New England Inn and Resort**, a genuine, family-owned inn on Route 16A (the Intervale Loop, discussed above), has neither but is more secluded, with lawns and trees surrounding white clapboard buildings and an outdoor pool. The 38 guest units range from Colonial-style rooms with four-poster beds in the original 1809 inn, to cottages with fireplaces. Cross-country ski trails begin at every door, and tennis is popular here. (In the early 1980s, when the Volvo Tennis Tournament was headquartered in North Conway, world champions stayed here and practiced on the three clay courts.) The kitchen, under new management, sustains its reputation for unpretentious but interesting dining; the Shaker cranberry pot roast tops a menu of local specialties (Tel: 603/356-5541).

The Valley has more than a dozen bed-and-breakfasts, ranging in appeal from the courtly to the casual. The genteel **Buttonwood Inn** is 2 miles (3 km) east of town on the secluded Mount Surprise Road (off Kearsarge Road). Croquet, an outdoor pool, hiking trails, and cross-country ski trails provide relaxing entertainment while the nine guest rooms, three with private baths, are individually decorated with antiques. The **Cranmore Inn**, a block from town at 24 Kearsarge Street (as opposed to Kearsarge Road), has a long history (in business since 1863) and an authentic feel. Its 23 rooms have private baths and country decor; a pool and lawn sports are supplemented by guest privileges at the Mount Cranmore Recreation Center, one-third of a mile away.

The **Cranmore Mountain Lodge**, on Kearsarge Road near the ski resort, is more like a hostel: Most rooms share baths, and there is a dormitory for groups. This is an athletically inclined place—appropriately, as it was frequented by Babe Ruth and once owned by his daughter. Besides a 40-foot swimming pool and outdoor Jacuzzi–hot spa, there are facilities for volleyball, basketball, tennis, skating, cross-country skiing, and tobogganing. Families are welcome. The **Nereledge Inn** on River Road, near the village, attracts an active clientele of rock climbers, guides, and the like with its fine views of Cathedral Ledge. Eiderdowns and rocking chairs grace its nine rooms, some with private baths. At day's end, cliff-hanging moments are relived over backgammon or cribbage in the English-style pub. Beer and wine, but not liquor, are served in the White Horse Pub, connected to the inn.

Valley folks are spoiled by the number and variety of restaurants—more than 30—ranging from national chain eateries to dining rooms of distinctive quality. The latter category is led by the **1785 Inn**, also a hostelry with beautiful views, located on Route 16 at scenic Intervale. Private baths for 12 guest rooms and an outdoor swimming pool are welcome concessions to the 20th century, while the inn's 18th-century origins (1785) are impressively evident in the older dining room's hand-hewn beams, giant fireplace, and beehive brick oven. In the other dining room a wall of windows overlooks rolling uplands that halt dramatically at Mount Washington. The wine list is the most extensive in the valley, and the classical menu the most acclaimed; coquilles St. Jacques may be followed by sherried rabbit or Black Angus sirloin. Although pricier than other Italian restaurants in the area, **Bellini's**, on Seavey Street, across from Schouler Park, has the best food; the portions are large and the atmosphere authentic. Tel: (603) 356-7000.

Stonehurst Manor, 1 mile (1½ km) north of North Conway village in a stone mansion, will surprise and delight you with grilled turkey steak and apple cranberry chutney, but the accent here is on wood smoke: Fragrant salmon, duck, and beef emerge from a miniature smokehouse while a wood-fired oven yields offbeat "designer pizzas" with toppings such as smoked salmon, pesto, and eggplant. The dining room is formal and spacious enough for guests to loll in wicker chairs, while the library of this three-story stone mansion is a gentlemanly lounge with oak woodwork and leaded-glass windows. Fourteen large guest rooms are in the main building and ten more in an attached motel section. Rooms have private baths and TVs, and the 33-acre grounds include a swimming pool and tennis courts. Tel: (603) 356-3113. The **Scottish Lion Inn and Restaurant,** 1½ miles (2½ km) north of North Conway village, on the left, is under new ownership but still serves bridies and syllabub to delight homesick Caledonians. (Bridies are pastries filled with spiced ground beef and lamb; syllabub is a creamy, frozen lemon dessert.) The Inn's Black Watch Pub has 60 blended scotches and 24 single malts.

Of the more casual eateries that abound hereabouts, three deserve mention. The **Scarecrow Pub,** on Route 16 between Intervale and Glen, can't make money on its tasty Italian dishes and grill, and seems to survive on its cheerful atmosphere. Other ski hangouts used to be like this before they were discovered by the voguish (no credit cards). The **Big Pickle,** on Seavey Street a block from Main, is a neighborhood favorite for reasonably priced deli sandwiches at a fair price (open for breakfast or lunch). Go one block over to Kearsarge Street for cannolis, éclairs, and Neapolitans—the **Country Fresh Bakery and Deli** is a rare find in the mountains.

(See also Tamworth and Chocorua, above.)

East of the Valley:
Fryeburg and Evans Notch

For an offbeat day trip from the Conways take Route 302 east to the Maine border and follow Route 113 north through Evans Notch. You'll then take Route 2 west and return to the valley via Route 16 south.

Seven miles (11 km) east of the bottom of the Conway strip on Route 302 in Center Conway is **Saco Bound,** a soup-to-nuts canoe outfitter. The Saco River is flat and gentle for 43 miles into Maine, and Saco Bound will put you in and pick you up. Canoe rentals cost less than $30 per day; guided day trips with lunch are less than $25 per person. Overnight tours and other options are very tempting, but keep in mind that weekdays are less crowded (and less expensive) than weekends. Saco Bound is not bound to the Saco, either. They will arrange rafting expeditions on such wilder rivers as the Kennebec and Penobscot. Saco Bound also runs a white-water school on the Androscoggin River in Errol, where they can provide guided day tours in kayaks. For more information on the expeditions and the school, Tel: (603) 447-2177.

Fryeburg Academy, a private prep school, sets the tone for **Fryeburg**, Maine, 5 miles (8 km) east of Center Conway. "Perhaps no street in the county possesses such a wide range of building types and styles as does Main Street in Fryeburg Village," writes Randall Bennett in the authoritative *Oxford County, Maine: A Guide to Its Historic Architecture*. Routes 302, 5, and 113 merge into a broad, mile-long avenue lined with sizable 19th-century homes, a tiny 18th-century stone schoolhouse, the handsome brick campus of Fryeburg Academy, and a half dozen other eye-catching structures. Primarily an agricultural community since its settlement in the 1760s, Fryeburg today has a remarkable cultural diversity because of its location on the major market route to Portland, as well as the presence of the academy (founded in 1792). Future admiral Robert E. Peary lived here for two years after graduating from Bowdoin College. Daniel Webster lived here, too, while serving as headmaster of the academy. But few residents were more beloved than Clarence Mulford, author of Western novels, including the Hopalong Cassidy series; the town's public library displays Mulfordiana in its Hopalong Cassidy Room. Across the street, near Mulford's house (he used to fire six-shooters in the back yard), is the **Oxford House**, a restaurant with venturesome cuisine and an elegant table; Tel: (207) 935-3442. The **Fryeburg Fair**, an old-fashioned country fair with lots of animals, is a major regional event held in early October (1993 dates: October 3–10).

At the northern end of Fryeburg village at the academy campus, Route 302 forks east. Continue straight ahead (north) on Route 5 for 3 miles (5 km), passing the West Oxford Agricultural Society Fairgrounds, home to the Fryeburg Fair, and turn left onto Fish Street. Until a canal was completed in 1820, the Saco River often overflowed this neighborhood—the northern end of Fish Street is still called Fryeburg Harbor—but today it is dry, flat farmland as Fish Street travels 3 miles (5 km) to its terminus at Route 113. Turn right and continue north 9 miles (14½ km), passing through tiny Stow, Maine (population 180), crossing into New Hampshire, and arriving in North Chatham. This remote farming village marks the entrance to **Evans Notch** and the craggy valley of the Wild River. Because the valley floor is so low the mountains seem higher than they are: The Royce Range on the west and Spruce Hill to the east are less than 4,000 feet. Picnic spots and hiking trails abound on this seldom-travelled road, which is closed to winter travel and lies entirely within the White Mountain National Forest. The road re-enters Maine, climbs 5 miles (8 km) to Evans Notch, then descends 3 miles (5 km) to Hastings.

Now a U.S. Forest Service campground, **Hastings** is the site of a vanished logging town and the place where in 1885 Leon Leonwood Bean, age 13, shot his first deer. Years later, after inventing his famous boots and founding his store and mail-order catalogue, L. L. Bean still scouted these woods and enjoyed his backwoods camp ("Dew Drop Inn") on a stream near the village. Hastings' population peaked at 1,000 around 1895. When the national forest purchased it in 1929, the village was deserted, and its buildings were then re-moved. Except for an interval in the 1930s when a Civilian Conservation Corps camp was located here, Hastings has remained hushed and uninhabited.

North of Hastings Route 113 follows the bed of the Wild River Railroad (1890–1903) and in 3 miles (5 km) terminates at Route 2 in the old railroad town of Gilead, Maine. Turn west on Route 2 and travel 10 miles (16 km) along the Androscoggin River through Shelburne to Gorham (see the Cöos County section, below). In Gorham, take Route 16 south 20 miles (32 km) through Pinkham Notch (see below) back to Route 302 in Glen, and then east 5 miles (8 km) back to Conway.

THE EASTERN SLOPE: JACKSON AND PINKHAM NOTCH

According to Pennacook Indian legend, the remains of Chief Passaconaway were borne to Mount Washington on a flam-ing sleigh drawn by wolves. Today, more orthodox vehicles travelling west from the Conway area on Route 302 turn off onto Route 16 in Glen and drive north on this road that nearly broke the heart of Daniel Pinkham.

One of Jackson's earliest settlers, Pinkham contracted with the State of New Hampshire to build a road through the mountain pass to Gorham. He worked two years but aban-doned the project when the rainstorms of 1826 (the same that triggered the fatal Willey Slide in Crawford Notch) inundated his road with tons of mud and stone. By the time people started calling the valley—framed by the Presidentials to the west and the Carter-Moriah Range to the east—Pinkham Notch, its namesake had moved to Lancaster and taken up farming. A year-round road was not established until the 1920s, and the passenger railroads never ventured here; the notch is now served by an excellent two-lane highway.

Despite, or perhaps because of, its persistent wildness, Pinkham Notch has become the most popular approach to Mount Washington. Not only does Jackson provide a perfect base for exploring the most storied and lofty of peaks in the eastern United States, but at the mountain's base the Appalachian Mountain Club provides paths, programs, and lodging at Pinkham Notch Camp, a resource unequaled elsewhere in the White Mountains. This year-round attraction is complemented by the exhilarating trails of the Wildcat Ski Area, the thrilling Mount Washington Auto Road, and the popular Dolly Copp Campground, the state's largest U.S. Forest Service camping facility.

Route 16 leaves Route 302 in Glen, and 3 miles (5 km) north is Route 16A to Jackson village, while Pinkham Notch and Mount Washington are 8 miles (13 km) farther north on Route 16. In Gorham, another 12 miles (19 km) north, Route 16 joins Route 2, a major east–west highway. For a driving tour, allow a half day for Jackson and a half day for a drive to the summit. Upon becoming acquainted with the AMC's facilities, visitors often extend their stay for another day to enjoy a hiking excursion.

Jackson

Route 16 brushes off the glitter of North Conway when it leaves Route 302 and bends north toward Jackson. Within a mile there are two pretty good amusement parks, Storyland and **Heritage New Hampshire**, the latter a fine rainy-day diversion with indoor dioramas portraying Granite State history. Two miles (3 km) farther a much-photographed covered bridge spanning the Ellis River welcomes you to the village of Jackson.

Just before the bridge is the chamber of commerce office, which dispenses detailed maps outlining driving routes, cross-country ski tours, and walking paths. The main road through Jackson is 16A, which loops through the village and returns to Route 16. A secondary road, 16B, wanders into the hills beyond Jackson.

Strict zoning regulations have limited Jackson's commercial development and earned the town a reputation for snobbishness. However, there is no prettier town in the White Mountains, and no place does a better job of welcoming visitors. There is meager shopping, except for a few modest art galleries. Casual visitors will have to be content with exploring and photographing the village. A longer stay allows you to golf, ski, and dine in fine restaurants while based at one of the area's several B and Bs, country inns, or hotels.

An Auto Loop

The following 6-mile (10-km) auto loop surveys the town's scenic features and introduces four notable hostelries (others are discussed in Staying Elsewhere in the Jackson Area, below). If you like what you see, you will like the rest of Jackson.

Drive north along Route 16A through the **covered bridge** (a 138-foot Paddleford truss dating to the 1870s) and stop in at the **Myke Morton Gallery** next on your right. Ms. Morton's naturalistic watercolors, acrylics, prints, and note cards depicting local subjects are available for purchase here. The road then curves left to "downtown" Jackson, marked by the landmark **Wildcat Inn & Tavern**, right on Route 16A. Although it offers 12 rooms in country-style decor—10 with baths and most arranged as smallish suites—the Wildcat is best known for its restaurant. Home-baked breads and desserts accompany dishes like Mondo Chicken, cooked in apricot brandy with Italian sausage. Across the street the **Jackson Ski Touring Foundation** presides over 95 miles of groomed trails, the largest touring network in New England. You may ski inn to inn, take lessons, learn to wax, or tour with a group (Tel: 603/383-9335). Next door, ski gear and garb are available for rent or purchase at the **Jack Frost Shop**.

At the schoolhouse follow Route 16B (Black Mountain Road) for less than a mile (1½ km) as it ascends to the **Christmas Farm Inn**. Parts of the original Cape-style building date to the late 1700s; it belonged to Rufus Pinkham, brother of the would-be roadbuilder. Subsequent additions, including the attachment of an abandoned Free Will Baptist Church, have resulted in a pleasantly rambling, white and red colony of 37 rooms, five with Jacuzzis, as well as six cottages, all with fireplaces. The name Christmas Farm was coined in 1941 when a Philadelphia man gave the property to his daughter for Christmas. Shortly afterward it became an inn and is now operated by the family of Bill Zeliff, one of New Hampshire's two congressmen. The decor is Christmasy: elfin flourishes, rooms named for Santa's reindeer, and so on. The dining room's menu—an unfocused selection of kabobs, curries, teriyakis, and fettuccine and other Italian dishes—omits venison. Beyond Christmas Farm, bear right at the fork and ascend to Black Mountain Ski Area, 1¾ miles (nearly 3 km) from the village.

Black Mountain Ski Area is an affordable, family-oriented place where a southwestern exposure and sunny, sheltered trails make snow making (95 percent coverage) a necessity. Although not challenging (vertical drop 1,100 feet), Black is a fun mountain. It has four lifts and 20 trails (seven beginner, nine intermediate, and four expert), plus the "Cowabunga" snowboard half-pipe. The modest lodge has a nursery, rentals, ski shop, cafeteria, and the like. The ski area's views of Mount Washington are rivaled only by Wildcat's (see below). Tel: (603) 383-4490; for ski conditions, Tel: (603) 278-5051.

To the left of the ski area is **Whitney's Inn**, originally the Moody Farm, where in 1935 George Morton, legendary inventor (and grandfather of Myke Morton), erected a steel cable with little ropes hanging from it—the country's first overhead ski tow. The Whitneys purchased the farm in 1936 and pioneered Jackson's winter hospitality industry by opening their inn to skiers. (They later replaced the little ropes with shovel handles.) The inn—a main building as well as cottages with fireplaces—remains a favorite of downhill and cross-country skiers, especially families with children.

A sharp left in front of Whitney's begins a 1½-mile (2½-km) forested traverse along Route 16B that ends with a stop and sharp left turn at a bridge, where Route 16B continues as Carter Notch Road. This leg follows the Wildcat River back to the village, passing the **Eagle Mountain Resort**, another notable inn. The white four-story 1920s façade remains, but this 94-room hotel was modernized in the late 1980s and is now owned by Colony Hotels. A nine-hole golf course, outdoor heated swimming pool, and two tennis courts make this a small-scale grand hotel. New England fare is served at the hotel's **Highfields** restaurant; Tel: (603) 383-9111.

As you descend on Route 16B from the hotel you'll see on the left the cascades of **Jackson Falls**, a delight to picnickers and bathers. As described by Bruce and Doreen Bolnick in their book *Waterfalls of the White Mountains,* "Jackson Falls is not so much a waterfall as a maze of cataracts and pools spread across an enormous ledge of beautiful pink granite. . . . The ledge is so large that if pulled flat and smoothed over it could easily accommodate landing aircraft. So there is plenty of room for exploring." They also note the falls' uniquely in-town location and its southern exposure, which warms the water—"at least in comparison to most other mountain streams."

At the base of the falls, where Route 16B rejoins Route 16A, is the **Wentworth Resort**, with all the amenities of a grand hotel plus an 18-hole golf course. The central structure, three stories with green-roofed towers, dates to 1883 but has been extensively modernized. Rooms may have Jacuzzis or fireplaces, and condominium cottages all have kitchens. In summer guests can swim in the outdoor pool or walk to Jackson Falls; in winter sleigh rides, skating, and cross-country skiing are available (the resort is linked to the Jackson Ski Foundation's trails). Meat dishes seem to be favored on the hotel's menu; rack of lamb is the chef's specialty.

The loop ends a stone's throw from "downtown," in front of the Wentworth Resort. Turn right here onto Route 16A and drive past the golf course to the **Thompson House Eatery**, the best place around for casual dining. Whether indoors by the fireplace or under the striped awning on the outdoor deck, diners will find the menu distinctive and the food fresh. Chef Larry Baima excels at Italian dishes, but a lunch favorite is Mexicali Blues, a spicy salad topped with salsa made from scallions, black olives, and pepperoncini. Evening fare is more elaborate and equally inventive. T.H.E. has a personal touch and caters to special diets. Tel: (603) 383-9341.

STAYING ELSEWHERE IN THE JACKSON AREA

The ten-room **Inn at Thorn Hill**, an 1895 Stanford White creation, is supplemented by three cottages and a seven-room carriage house. The new owners are expected to maintain its Victorian decor and reputation for fine dining. The half-dozen bed-and-breakfasts in the area include the 16-room **Village House**, centrally located on Route 16A, with a pool and tennis courts; some of the rooms have kitchenettes, and there is a year-round outdoor Jacuzzi. Up nearby Dinsmore Road is seven-room **Nestlenook Farm**, a Queen Anne–style house extravagantly ornamented but subtly modernized; Jacuzzis have replaced the claw-foot tubs, for example. The extensive grounds sport gazebos, topiary shrubs, miniature arched bridges, and wishing wells. Guests enjoy horseback riding, skating, fishing, swimming, and Clydesdale-drawn sleigh rides courtesy of a pair named Currier and Ives. Daily tours of the inn are also available. (The tours and sleigh rides are also available to nonguests.)

Mount Washington
and Pinkham Notch

When Captain John Smith glimpsed Mount Washington from the ocean in 1614 he called it the "twinkling mountain of Angososico." Seen at dawn from Pinkham Notch, 7 miles (11 km) north of Jackson, the dewy summit still twinkles above the scooped depths of Huntington and Tuckerman ravines. To drive up Mount Washington, continue to the Auto Road (discussed below), but to explore its astounding ecology, stop at the AMC's Pinkham Notch Camp, at the base of the mountain.

Begun in 1876 as a hiking club for Bostonians, the Appalachian Mountain Club pioneered modern trail maintenance and pushed for the establishment of the White Mountain National Forest. It has developed into a well-endowed 50,000-member club that promotes four overlapping programs: education, politics, trail maintenance, and recreation.

AMC PINKHAM NOTCH CAMP

The Pinkham Notch Camp is open year-round for information, cafeteria dining, and dormitory lodging at the **Joe Dodge Lodge**. Nature books and mountain maps are sold here as well. There is ample cross-country skiing around the base camp. Call in advance to participate in a guided hike, day program, or educational workshop tied to such themes as wilderness survival, geology, photography, or ornithology. The club also sponsors overnight canoeing adventures, snowshoeing treks, and backwoods skiing. Year-round lectures and seminars draw a well-educated, ardently green audience. Tel: (800) 262-4455 or (603) 466-2727.

In addition to the accommodations at the camp's Joe Dodge Lodge, there are also two AMC backwoods huts within hiking distance. To get to the **Carter Notch Hut** follow the Nineteen-Mile Brook Trail from its trailhead 3½ miles (5½ km) north of Pinkham Notch Camp via Route 16. The hut, which is 3.8 miles along the trail, has a couple of natural pools that are good for swimming. The second hut, **Lakes of the Clouds**, is on Crawford Path, which is accessible from the Tuckerman Ravine Trail (discussed below). For more information on both, call the numbers listed above for Pinkham Notch Camp.

Short hikes abound near the camp. Visit **Crystal Cascade**, a pretty 80-foot drop an easy third of a mile behind the camp. A short drive south of the camp and conspicuously signposted, the splendid **Glen Ellis Falls** reward an even easier excursion.

The camp is the trailhead for the shortest, most popular path to the summit of Mount Washington: the famous **Tuckerman Ravine Trail**, 4.2 miles and four and a quarter hours one way. (Skiing Tuckerman Ravine has been a springtime ritual since the 1920s. Starting in March a youthful crowd carries skis, boots, and poles two and a half miles uphill to a steep bowl where the snow lasts through June. Early in the season it's possible to ski all the way back to camp, but as the snow melts, skiers frequent the bowl, sunbathe on flat boulders, and watch others negotiate the head wall.) For a longer, more rugged climb with fewer companions try the five-hour, 5-mile (one way) **Nelson Crag Trail**. Talk to the staff at the AMC before setting out, and never climb this mountain alone or unprepared.

MOUNT WASHINGTON

At 6,288 feet above sea level, Mount Washington's summit elevation is not impressive, but dozens of people have died from exposure on its slopes. The AMC calls it "the most dangerous small mountain in the world." The highest wind ever recorded (231 mph) was clocked here on April 12, 1934, and the summit temperature rarely reaches 70° F. The U.S. Special Forces and several Himalayan expeditions have used the mountain for survival training. Yet this is the most accessible big mountain in the country, and thousands ascend it annually.

"No other mountain," writes Peter Randall in *Mount Washington: A Guide and Short History,* "can boast of having, in its history, a carriage road, railway, daily newspaper, four different hotels, two weather observatories, a radio station, and a television station, in addition to miles of hiking trails." There is a **museum** at the summit where visitors can trace this rich history, but, when the weather is favorable, the summit is best enjoyed outdoors. Canada, New York State, and the Atlantic can be descried on certain days. Hike down to the **Alpine Garden**, east of the summit (ask directions), to see alpine azalea, Lapland rosebay, dwarf fir balsam, and glorious diapensia (blooming in late June)—precious marvels of endurance in this cruel climate.

WILDCAT SKI AREA

One mile (1½ km) north of the AMC camp via Route 16 is the Wildcat Ski Area, a challenging mountain that was first skied in the 1930s on trails carved by President Roosevelt's Civilian Conservation Corps. Some of these classic trails remain—indeed Wildcat Mountain rivals Cannon for steep, narrow trails with a traditional New England flavor—and the views of Mount Washington's eastern exposure are unequaled. Wildcat's high base elevation (1,950 feet) and proximity to Mount Washington have given it a reputation for good natural snow (plus 98 percent snow making) but chilly temperatures.

The vertical drop is 2,100 feet, and the 4,100-foot summit is reached by a two-passenger gondola. Lift lines are rare. Four triple chairs and a double chair serve 30 trails (six beginner, nine intermediate, and 15 expert). The lodge was expanded in 1992 and is now adequate. There is a ski school, two cafeterias, a new lounge and dining area, rentals, sport shop and nursery, but no lodging. Tel: (603) 466-3326.

MOUNT WASHINGTON AUTO ROAD

On the Mount Washington Auto Road, the access to which is located 2½ miles (4 km) north of the AMC camp and 1½ miles (2½ km) north of Wildcat on Route 16, you can drive yourself or take a chauffeured van ($18) approximately 8 miles (13 km) to the summit. A toll is charged ($14 for car and driver, $5 for other passengers), and certain vehicles, such as big campers, are banned. Hailed as an engineering marvel when it opened in 1861, the "carriage road" carried elaborate stage-coaches from the Glen House hotel, which once operated at its base. People have raced up the road on foot, on bicycles, unicycles, wheelchairs, skis, dogsleds, and, of course, in automobiles. Such races are still a feature on the historic road, which is open May to October, weather permitting.

Three and a half miles (5½ km) north of the Auto Road is the entrance to **Dolly Copp Campground**, the largest in the state with 176 campsites operated year-round by the U.S. Forest Service in characteristic Spartan style; for reservations, Tel: (800) 283-2267. It surrounds the site of the Copp homestead, where Dolly and her husband, Hayes, settled in the 1830s amid utter wilderness. When the Glen House opened in 1852, Dolly's handicrafts were sought by tourists and she became a quaint local attraction. She is best remembered for her 50th wedding anniversary pronouncement: "Fifty years is long enough to live with any man"—upon which she left Hayes and moved to Maine.

NORTH COUNTRY: CÖOS COUNTY

"Cöos" derives from the Abenaki Indian word for pine, coo-ash, corrupted to cohoss and finally cöos, which is properly pronounced COH-oss. (It gets tougher. Milan, just south of Lake Umbagog [Um-BAY-gog] and north of Berlin [BURR-lin], is pronounced MY-lin.)

The interstate highways never reached Cöos County, New Hampshire's northernmost quadrant, where the paper industry has prospered more than the hospitality industry. Except for a couple of enclaves—most notably the Balsams Grand Resort in Dixville Notch—the 20 towns of the Cöos region do not lure travellers with quaint inns or modern condos. Hunters and snowmobilers seek modest digs, while fishermen retreat to rustic lakeside camps. New Hampshire's largest (one million square miles) but least populous county (34,000 and declining) is mostly wooded, wild, and raw.

A day is all that's required to tour Cöos County—we outline a daylong driving circuit below—but do see it, especially in autumn. The prettiest sections are found along the rivers (the Connecticut and Androscoggin, which more or less define the county's western and eastern borders, respectively) and in the northern precincts of Dixville and Pittsburg (PITCH-burg).

Gorham and Shelburne

Gorham, 10 miles (16 km) north of Pinkham Notch, is the crossroads of Routes 2 and 16, both major commercial routes that merge for two miles to form a prosperous Main Street. Gorham has been a crossroads since the 1850s, when the Grand Trunk Railroad linked lines from Portland, Boston, Burlington, and Montreal at this Androscoggin River town. Population quadrupled in a decade, and when the Mount Washington Carriage Road (now the Auto Road) opened in 1861, daily passenger trains began to come up from Boston, depositing tourists who would transfer to horse-drawn carriages bound for the now-defunct Glen House. As the century drew to a close, regiments of immigrant laborers flocking to the paper mills in Berlin joined the lumberjacks, trappers, travelling merchants, and Boston dandies who swarmed Gorham's sidewalks.

Twentieth-century Gorham has become a quiet bedroom community for industrial Berlin; tourism is low key, and commercial activity is restricted to Main Street. However, a spacious common at the southern junction of Routes 16 and 2 is good for picnicking; a local history museum has taken root in the adjacent railroad station (irregular hours); and twice daily in summer the chamber of commerce sponsors bus tours that start at the common's information booth. The afternoon tour includes close-up views of the enormous paper mill in Berlin; the evening tour features a moose watch. For information, Tel: (603) 466-2340 or (800) 992-7480, ext. 6.

A dozen eateries line Main Street. A block past the common, at 16 Exchange Street, is the **Café**, with modestly priced and competently prepared Continental specialties; Tel: (603) 466-5640. Farther north, on Main Street just beyond McDonalds, the **Yokohama** is a popular Asian-Pacific restaurant. Always fresh, the food—Japanese, Chinese, and Hawaiian—pleases American tastes; Tel: (603) 466-2501. As for lodging, Gorham's motels are friendly and budget minded, notably the **Mount Madison Motel** on Main Street, but unfortunately the aroma wafting down from Berlin's pulp mill, five miles upstream on the Androscoggin, is redolent of rotten eggs (the smell of money, according to locals). Depending on how the wind blows, you may prefer to sleep a few miles east in or near the tiny border town of Shelburne.

On Route 2 a mile (1½ km) east of Gorham toward Shelburne, the **Town and Country Motor Inn**, a 160-room family-owned resort, is a favorite of travellers from Ontario and the Canadian Maritimes, who constitute about 60 percent of the trade. Well-maintained facilities include an indoor pool, a health club, and, across the street, the 18-hole **Androscoggin Valley Golf Club**. Locals consider the dining room a posh place; it has nice views and the prime rib is served with a smile; Tel: (603) 466-9468.

As you proceed east on Route 2 toward Shelburne, note the Mahoosuc Range rising to the north. The Appalachian Trail traverses these humps, which are noted for their alpine bogs—swamps on the summits—and their hiking difficulty. Appalachian Trail hikers who are used to ten or twenty miles' progress a day discover that six Mahoosuc miles are plenty.

Take the second North Road turn (left) after you pass the grove of birches and the rest area with the information building. North Road bridges the Androscoggin and turns right into **Shelburne** and **Philbrook Farm Inn**, a white three-story clapboard farmhouse with green shutters that has been an unpretentious inn since 1861. Philbrooks still live here amid 19 guest rooms (including cottages) and family heirlooms. A dinner bell announces a one-entrée meal (roast beef or chicken), with homemade bread, vegetables, and more, but bring your own spirits, as there is no bar. Outdoor recreation at the inn includes horseshoes and swimming in summer, and showshoes and cross-country skiing in the winter. But it's not the broad porch and quiet lawns that put this place in a class by itself; it is the unreserved warmth and frank courtesy of the innkeepers.

Cöos Auto Loop

You may commence this daylong driving loop anywhere on the 120-mile circuit (we begin in Berlin), but plan to take lunch in Gorham, Berlin, at the Balsams Resort in Dixville Notch (on Route 26), or in Lancaster (at the junction of Routes 2 and 3, on the Vermont border). Local eateries are few and far between. The tour winds through mountains impressive less for their elevation—few exceed 3,000 feet—than for their abundance and their conifers. The *AMC White Mountain Guide* extols these dense woods as part of the "great band of boreal forest" that extends across northern Maine and covers much of Ontario and Quebec, while noting their relative lack of recreational hiking trails. Paper companies own most of the acreage and operate mills in Berlin and Groveton, the only sizable towns on this loop. Yet amid this lumberjacks' domain are found the state's most famous resort hotel and its prettiest covered bridge.

BERLIN TO ERROL

Once the site of substantial falls, the Androscoggin was dammed at **Berlin**, at the junction of Routes 16 and 110, in the 1870s. Raw materials for the mills—first timber logs and then pulp logs—choked the river. Under the reign of Brown Paper Company, the city's population surged to more than 20,000 and sprouted neighborhoods of Finnish, Russian, Irish, Italian, and Québecois immigrants. Solidly blue-collar and unionized, this is the only city in the White Mountains, although its population has shrunk to 12,000 and commerce has substantially departed the downtown district. The odiferous and promethean James River Corporation's mill is an inescapable presence. However, more cosmetically pleasing communities might envy the friendly atmosphere and resolute pride of this "City That Trees Built."

Route 16 enters Berlin on a commercialized strip that begins north of the Route 2 intersection. The most interesting store, 1½ miles (2½ km) from the intersection, is **Labonville, Inc.**, a lumberjack outfitter where rugged, warm clothing is sold at reasonable prices amid snowshoes, chainsaws, axes, cant dogs (a hooked tool used to roll logs), and other logging gear.

On the hill to the left you'll see the gold onion domes of the **Orthodox Church of the Holy Resurrection**, at 20 Petrograd Street. Built in 1915, it is on the National Register of Historic Places, as is the imposing **St. Anne's Catholic Church**, on Route 16 at the north end of the downtown district; this red-brick Gothic-style structure, dedicated in

1900, sits on a ridge that overlooks the city. The huge mill complex dominates the western horizon as the road winds north along the river. The last log drive on the Androscoggin was in 1966, but the stone piers that secured booms remain regularly spaced up the center of the stream.

A mile (1½ km) out of town is the **Northland Restaurant and Dairy Bar**, a super place for lunch. Famous for its fried foods and bilingual waitresses (French/English), it is Berlin's only real restaurant (Tel: 603/752-6210). Another 3 miles (5 km) north, the Nansen Ski Jump looms on the left, a relic of the days when Scandinavian immigrants sponsored national events. There is now a park here with benches and a boat-launching ramp across the road, but the 262-foot-high (80-meter) ski jump is idle and awaits restoration. The only real tourist attraction in the farming community of **Milan**, (again, MY-lin), 9 miles (14½ km) north of Berlin, is a fire tower (open to the public) and some picnic tables at Milan Hill State Park, a short drive up Route 110B.

The **Thirteen-Mile Woods Scenic Area**, north of Milan and just south of Errol, is a particularly scenic stretch of Route 16 as it closely follows the Androscoggin through an uninhabited plain. Visited by canoeists, fishermen, and moose, this is a relatively unfrequented treasure, accessible to the sportsman and a delight for motorists. The river can build a canoeist's confidence with long stretches of flat water, but three intervals of Class II white water require rock-dodging, and one stretch of Class III rapids at Pontook Dam is for experts only. Rent a canoe or kayak from **Saco Bound** in Center Conway (Tel: 603/447-2177), which has a whitewater school and rental facilities in Errol, the last village on Route 16, where our loop turns west.

At the junction of Routes 16 and 26, **Errol** (population 313) is the location of the dam that made the log drives possible. Errol's village is anchored by a hardware store and a couple of nondescript eateries-cum-convenience stores that are frequented by sportsmen, truckers, and loggers. **Saco Bound Whitewater School**, located on Route 26 a third of a mile (½ km) east of the intersection of Routes 16 and 26, provides instruction along with kayak and canoe rentals.

Eight-mile-long **Lake Umbagog**, a fisherman's paradise and home to bald eagles, is not visible from town, nor is the dam. To glimpse a portion of the lake, drive 7½ miles (12 km) east on Route 26 to a state-operated boat launch. Canoeists usually drive a mile (1½ km) north from Errol Center on Route 16 along the Magalloway River, select one of several roadside launching spots, and paddle less than a mile to where Magalloway empties into Umbagog at the dam. Serious sightseeing and exploration will require a boat or canoe.

BALSAMS GRAND RESORT

Nine miles (14½ km) of two-lane Route 26 lead west from Errol and Route 16 to small, craggy **Dixville Notch** (1,871 feet) and the Balsams Grand Resort, the region's finest. The setting of this miniature castle—beside a lake cupped by hills and cliffs—is perfect, but it is the service that wins awards. Four hundred trained employees staff 215 guest rooms and maintain facilities for tennis, golf (27 holes), swimming, and skiing, downhill as well as 43 miles (70 km) of cross-country trails, most of them groomed. Day-trippers are welcome to lunch (summer only), an extraordinary buffet that but dimly adumbrates the evening's repast. The hotel's Ballot Room, where Dixville citizens vote, is the first place in the nation to cast ballots and announce results in national elections.

The **Wilderness Ski Area** here is open to the public, but most of its patrons are hotel guests and some locals. Serviced by three lifts, the dozen trails (three beginner, six intermediate, three expert) are never crowded. There is usually natural snow at this northernmost of New Hampshire's ski areas, but 85 percent snow making ensures a decent surface. The requisite cafeteria, ski school, nursery, rentals, and the like are all provided in the cozy base lodge. At this 1,000-footer, skiing is part of the total resort experience, rather than the reverse.

The town of **Colebrook,** another 12 miles (19 km) west along Route 26, has a nine-hole golf course, but little else to tempt the traveller, unless you count the stuffed remains of a two-headed calf displayed in the Mobil station.

PITTSBURG

The 800 people who reside in Pittsburg (again, PITCH-burg) are outnumbered by moose. At dusk motorists line the shoulder of Route 3 to watch half-ton beasts slurp swampweeds seasoned by road salt. If you go to Pittsburg, you will see moose.

A half hour north of Colebrook via Route 3 or Route 145, Pittsburg counts 60 lakes on its 400 square miles of woods, which are accessible via private gravel roads sans road signs. This is Spartan country more reminiscent of the backwoods of Maine than the White Mountains, which cannot be seen from here. Rather, on the eastern horizon is Mount Magalloway. In winter ice fishing and, especially, snowmobiling are popular. In summer rent a boat, hire a guide, and wet a line. Stay on the First Connecticut Lake, just north of Pittsburg on Route 3, at **The Glen,** which is comfortably rustic, with maid service for its brown cottages, some with screened porches and several set at the edge of the lake. Among Pittsburg's numerous fishing-camp colonies, this may be the most patrician and traditional. Staying here is like stepping into the cover of a 1948 edition of *Field & Stream*.

The headwaters of the Connecticut River rise at Fourth Lake, a fly-infested swale, notable only because, in 1842, its moisture determined the international border. The history of the uncertain border was comically punctuated in 1832, when 300 Pittsburg residents, resentful of simultaneous taxation by Canada and the United States, declared independence from both and formed the Republic of the United Inhabitants of Indian Stream Territory. They elected a president, adopted a written constitution, established courts, formed a militia, and authorized coinage (none was issued). The Crown and Congress took little notice for three years, but then a prolonged brawl between Canadian and U.S. sympathizers (immortalized as the Indian Stream War despite its lack of fatalities) drew the attention of New Hampshire's governor, who sent the state militia in October 1835. By spring the republic had dissolved and the president moved to Wisconsin.

COLEBROOK TO LANCASTER

Route 26 ends at Route 3 in Colebrook, where our loop turns south to follow the Connecticut River. The views of the river are better from the Vermont side on Route 102. (In Colebrook go north one block, take a left onto Bridge Street, and follow it to Route 102.) You can braid your way down to Lancaster by crossing the infrequent bridges. A covered bridge (1912 Howe truss) crosses from Lemington, Vermont, to Columbia, 4 miles (6½ km) south of Colebrook.

The Connecticut River was used for log drives until the turn of the century, when hydroelectric dams ended the colorful era. The valley villages, mostly sawmill and railroad towns, suffered many fires; consequently, few buildings of distinction remain. However, the countryside claims some classic farmhouses, and the geology of the river's sweep is quite dramatic. Traffic is sparse.

At **Groveton**, on the New Hampshire side 26 miles (42 km) south of Colebrook, the Upper Ammonoosuc flows into the Connecticut from **Stark**, a village so picturesque that it is a White Mountains icon. At the junction south of downtown Groveton take Route 110 and drive 6 miles (10 km) east to view the unspoiled scene of church, farmhouse, and bridge. The bridge is a much-modified Paddleford truss erected in 1862. The white house with green shutters is a bed-and-breakfast called the **Stark Village Inn**. It offers two double rooms and one single, all with private baths and furnished in Colonial style. The adjoining barn houses a small antiques shop. Two miles (3 km) east of the inn is the site of a World War II German P.O.W. camp, of which Stark residents are quite proud.

Stark's **Nash Stream Wilderness** has yet to draw many sightseers, although it rivals many better-known wilderness attractions. The precious preserve of forests and waterfalls is accessible by an 11-mile (18-km) gravel road. Take Emerson Road (one of Stark's three roads) to North Road and follow the markers. The dilapidated buildings along the way are the remains of lumberjack camps; the narrow stream was used to drive logs. Since 1989 the 39,000-acre tract has been managed by the state.

About 4 miles (6½ km) south of Groveton and below the Guidhall bridge is the **Potato Barn**, one of the more interesting antiques shops in the county, noted especially for old tools and postcards. The **Lancaster Fairgrounds**, to the south on the outskirts of Lancaster, await the first week of September, when an agricultural fair draws thousands. A mile (1½ km) beyond, Route 3 joins Route 2 and turns sharply east to become Lancaster's Main Street.

Lancaster, the county seat, is a handsome town with a broad Main Street lined with fine old homes. The 1780 **Wilder-Holton House**, at the north end of town (intersection of Routes 2 and 3), was a stop for escaped slaves on the Underground Railroad to Canada; today it is a museum of settlers' artifacts and also displays items, such as gears and wagons, that were once manufactured here. Open by appointment; Tel: (603) 788-3004.

The downtown district is the social and commercial center for western Cöos County, so there are many stores and restaurants geared to local tastes. **Old Susannah's**, at 70 Main Street, is a cheerful eatery that is regarded as hip. A "light" menu is available. Evening entertainment in an affiliated hall includes live music, comedy, and karaoke; Tel: (603) 788-2933. The **Double SS Diner**, at 60 Main Street, is authentic; the coffee's good, the food is filling, and it's open 24 hours; Tel: (603) 788-2802. The weekly *Cöos County Democrat* is always literate and often witty.

Lancaster has one beautiful 288-foot **covered bridge** over the Connecticut River, a 1911 Howe truss, 5 miles (8 km) south of town on Route 135; and a 108-footer over Israel's River, an 1862 Paddleford truss located in town on Mechanic Street.

Detour a couple of miles (3 km) south of town on Route 3 to visit **Weeks State Park** and the mountaintop summer home of the senator who authored the 1911 National Forest Act. The views from the top of Mount Prospect, to which you can drive in the summer, are terrific.

JEFFERSON

South of Lancaster Route 2 rolls east over smooth hills and past a string of family-oriented shops and amusements. After 8 miles (13 km) you come to the town of Jefferson, and the Presidentials and southern Whites rise sharply on the horizon. Jefferson seems a perfect setting for a hotel, and indeed a fine one once stood here. The Waumbek Inn was razed in the 1980s, leaving a huge gap in the fabric of this community. The 18-hole, par-71 golf course still operates as the **Waumbek Country Club**, Tel: (603) 586-7777. Across the street is the modest **Jefferson Inn**, built in 1896 as an overflow cottage for the Waumbek and nicely renovated during the 1980s. It's a year-round B and B with 13 rooms, all with bath, and a suite. Inn patrons enjoy the old stone swimming pool across the street. Also a relic of the Waumbek Hotel complex, it is maintained by townspeople and has a sandy beach for children.

The 18 miles (29 km) from Jefferson back to Gorham, the start of our Cöos County tour, are punctuated with frequent views of Mount Washington and the northern Presidentials, but Berlin-bound trucks barrel along this two-laner and drivers of lesser vehicles are best not distracted.

—Jim McIntosh

GETTING AROUND

New Hampshire has the best-built roads in northern New England, and, in winter, the best-maintained ones. Near-freezing conditions are the most dangerous because icing can occur unexpectedly. Collisions with moose are frequent in spring and fall when the males are rutting, but moose are a danger any season and especially, with their dark coloration, at night.

Portsmouth and the Coast

Though limited commuter airline service to Portsmouth is scheduled to begin in 1993, most travellers to New Hampshire's seacoast will choose to fly to Boston's Logan Airport. Buses run regularly from both downtown Boston and Logan, stopping either in Portsmouth's Market Square (Greyhound) or at Pease International Tradeport (Trailways), 3 miles (5 km) west of the city. Unless you plan to restrict your visit solely to the walkable center of Portsmouth, however, you're better off renting a car. Extremely limited public transportation on the seacoast means you cannot explore the coast or travel inland to Exeter without your own wheels.

Approaching Portsmouth from Boston, drive north on I-95. Take exit 5, turn right onto the Market Street Extension, and drive east half a mile (1 km) directly into Portsmouth. The public parking garage (25¢ an hour) is just 200 feet from the corner of Market and Hanover streets. It's best to park and proceed on foot, as downtown Portsmouth is a somewhat confusing muddle of one-way streets.

To reach Exeter from either Boston or Portsmouth, take I-95 to exit 2 (the Hampton toll plaza) and head west on Route 51 for about 2 miles (3 km). Then drive west on Route 111 south almost 3 miles (5 km), until you reach the center of town. Small public parking lots are clearly marked throughout the town.

Monadnock Region

By Car. For anyone who wants to see more than a town or two of the Monadnock region, a car is a necessity. Fifty miles (80 km) north of Boston, Route 101 enters the area from Milford in the Merrimack Valley, and continues westward to Keene, the region's only city. West of Keene Route 9 crosses the Connecticut River into Brattleboro, Vermont, 50 miles from Milford. Peterborough, Dublin, and Keene sit right on this main east–west artery, but most of the region's prettiest villages lie on country roads that branch off north and south.

By Air. **Keene Dillant Hopkins Airport** is served by Skymaster (Tel: 800/553-9021), a commuter airline with two flights daily on weekdays and one flight a day on weekends from both Boston and Newark. Avis has a car-rental facility at the airport; Tel: (800) 562-3156 or (603) 624-4000. National has an office nearby and will deliver a car to the airport on request; Tel: (800) 227-7368 or (603) 357-4045.

Merrimack Valley and the Lakes

By Bus: The Manchester Transportation Center (Tel: 603/668-6133), at Canal and Granite streets in Manchester, and the Concord Bus Terminal (Tel: 603/228-3300), on Storrs Street in Concord, are both served by Concord Trailways (Tel: 603/228-3300) and Vermont Transit (Tel: 603/228-3300). Manchester is also serviced by Peter Pan Bus Lines (Tel: 800/237-8747 or 603/228-3300) and First Class Limousine (Tel: 603/626-5466), which offers limousine service to and from Logan Airport. Concord Trailways also runs from Logan Airport into Laconia, New Hampton, Meredith, and Plymouth in the Lakes Region. New London is serviced several times daily by

Vermont Transit (Tel: 800/451-3292 or 802/864-6811), which stops at the New London Pharmacy on Main Street.

By Plane: Both Manchester and Concord are served by the **Manchester Airport** (603/624-6539), with daily flights on USAir, United, Northwest, Business Express, TW Express, and Continental. Car rentals are available through Avis, Budget, Hertz, and National. **Lebanon Municipal Airport** (Tel: 603/298-8878) in West Lebanon is serviced by Delta Business Express and Northwest Airlink. **Laconia Airport** in the Lakes Region, on Route 11 in Guilford, is served by Skymaster airlines. For the airport, Tel: (603) 524-5003; for Skymaster, (800) 553-9021 or (603) 524-7784.

By Train: Amtrak (Tel: 800/872-7245 or 802/295-7160) stops in White River Junction, Vermont, across the Connecticut River from Lebanon.

The White Mountains

There is no scheduled rail or air service to the White Mountains. Concord Trailways (Tel: 603/228-3300 or, in New Hampshire, 800/639-3317) operates daily buses from Boston and Manchester to major towns along I-93 as far as Littleton, and along Route 16 to Gorham. There is no public transportation within the mountains. Cars can be rented in Conway, Gorham, and Littleton, while resorts (in Lincoln, for example) provide shuttle service for visitors who arrive by bus. Eighty percent of motorists enter the region from the south. Rest areas at the state border have helpful staff members and provide free road maps.

ACCOMMODATIONS REFERENCE

Unless otherwise noted, the rates given below are projections for 1993 for double room, double occupancy. As prices are subject to change, always double-check before booking.

In New Hampshire's White Mountains, high season is winter; off-season periods generally are March through May and October 15 through December 15. Some White Mountains hotels offer American Plan (AP), which includes three meals, or Modified American Plan (MAP), which includes breakfast and dinner. Some AP and MAP rates are per person rather than double occupancy.

During the foliage season (roughly September through mid-October) some hotels may impose a surcharge of $10 to $30 per room and require reservations; the same caution may hold for winter holidays and weekends. New Hampshire's room and meals tax of 8 percent should be added to these rates. The area code for New Hampshire is 603.

Portsmouth and the Coast

▶ **Captain Folsom Inn.** 480 Portsmouth Avenue (Route 151), **Greenland**, NH 03840. Tel: 436-2662. $70–$85; includes breakfast.

▶ **Gundalow Inn.** 6 Water Street, **Kittery**, ME 03904. Tel: (207) 439-4040. $75–$95; includes breakfast.

▶ **Inn of Exeter.** 90 Front Street, **Exeter**, NH 03833. Tel: 772-5901 or (800) 782-8444. $68–$100; suites $165.

▶ **Inn at Strawbery Banke.** 314 Court Street, **Portsmouth**, NH 03801. Tel: 436-7242 or (800) 428-3933. $70–$85; includes breakfast.

▶ **Martin Hill Inn.** 404 Islington Street, **Portsmouth**, NH 03801. Tel: 436-2287. $78–$98; includes breakfast.

▶ **Sheraton Hotel.** 250 Market Street, **Portsmouth**, NH 03801. Tel: 431-2300 or (800) 325-3535; Fax: (603) 433-5649. $95–$125.

▶ **Sise Inn.** 40 Court Street, **Portsmouth**, NH 03801. Tel: 433-1200 or (800) 232-4667. $99–$175; includes Continental breakfast.

Monadnock Region

▶ **Amos A. Parker House.** Route 119, Box 202, **Fitzwilliam**, NH 03447. Tel: 585-6540. $65–$110; includes breakfast.

▶ **Apple Gate Bed & Breakfast.** 199 Upland Farm Road, **Peterborough**, NH 03458. Tel: 924-6543. $60–$70; includes breakfast.

▶ **Benjamin Prescott Inn.** Route 124, **Jaffrey**, NH 03452. Tel: 532-6637. $60–$130; includes breakfast.

▶ **Birchwood Inn.** Route 45, **Temple**, NH 03084. Tel: 878-3285. $59–$70; includes breakfast.

▶ **Chesterfield Inn.** Route 9, **West Chesterfield**, NH 03466. Tel: 256-3211 or (800) 365-5515; Fax: (603) 256-6131. $99–$149; includes breakfast.

▶ **Darby Brook Farm.** Hill Road, **Alstead**, NH 03602. Tel: 835-6624. $50 (shared bath); includes breakfast.

▶ **Fitzwilliam Inn.** **Fitzwilliam**, NH 03447. Tel: 585-9000. $45–$55.

▶ **Greenfield Inn.** Box 400, **Greenfield**, NH 03047. Tel. or Fax: 547-6327. $49–$99; includes breakfast.

▶ **Inn at Crotched Mountain.** Mountain Road, **Francestown**, NH 03043. Tel: 588-6840. $70 with breakfast; $120 with breakfast and dinner.

▶ **Jack Daniels Motor Inn.** Route 202 north, **Peterborough**, NH 03458. Tel: 924-7548. $68–$78; includes Continental breakfast.

▶ **John Hancock Inn.** Main Street, **Hancock**, NH 03449. Tel: 525-3318; Fax: 525-9301. $85–$105; includes breakfast.

► **Josiah Bellows House.** P.O. Box 818, North Main Street, **Walpole**, NH 03608. Tel: 756-4250. $70; includes breakfast.

► **Monadnock Inn.** P.O. Box 249, **Jaffrey Center**, NH 03452. Tel: 532-7001. $65.

► **Ram in the Thicket.** 24 Maple Street, **Milford**, NH 03055. Tel: 654-6440. $75; includes breakfast.

► **Salzburg Inn and Motel.** Steele Road, **Peterborough**, NH 03458. Tel: 924-3808. $47–$75.

► **Stepping Stones Bed and Breakfast.** Bennington Battle Trail, **Wilton Center**, NH 03086. Tel: 654-9048. $50; includes breakfast.

► **Thatcher Hill Inn.** Thatcher Hill Road, **Marlborough**, NH 03455. Tel: 876-3361. $68–$88; includes breakfast.

► **Tory Pines Resort.** RR 1, Box 655, Route 47, **Francestown**, NH 03043. Tel: 588-2000; Fax: 588-2275. $65–$100.

Merrimack Valley and the Lakes

► **Bedford Village Inn.** 2 Old Bedford Road, **Bedford**, NH 03110. Tel: 472-2001. $95–$185.

► **Cliff Lodge.** Route 3A, **Bristol**, NH 03222. Tel: 744-8660. $50–$80.

► **Colby Hill Inn.** 3 The Oaks, P.O. Box 778, **Henniker**, NH 03242. Tel: 428-3281. $85–$140; includes breakfast.

► **Corner House Inn.** Box 204, **Center Sandwich**, NH 03227. Tel: 284-6219. $60–$70; includes breakfast.

► **Dexter's Inn & Tennis Club.** Stagecoach Road, P.O. Box 7032, **Sunapee**, NH 03782. Tel: 763-5571 or (800) 232-5571. $130–$182; includes breakfast and dinner.

► **English House.** Main Street, P.O. Box 162, **Andover**, NH 03216. Tel: 735-5987. $75; includes breakfast.

► **Haus Edelweiss.** 13 Maple Street, P.O. Box 368, **Sunapee**, NH 03782. Tel: 763-2100. $50–$60; includes breakfast.

► **Inn at Danbury.** Route 104, **Danbury** NH 03230. Tel: 768-3318. $49–$89; includes breakfast.

► **Inn on Golden Pond.** Route 3, P.O. Box 680, **Holderness**, NH 03245. Tel: 968-7269. $85–$95; includes breakfast.

► **Inn at Mill Falls.** Mill Falls Marketplace, Route 3, **Meredith**, NH 03253. Tel: 279-7006 or (800) 622-6455. $75–$140.

► **Kona Mansion Inn.** Box 458, **Center Harbor**, NH 03226. Tel: 253-4900. $65–$160.

► **Lakeview Inn.** 120 North Main Street, **Wolfeboro**, NH 03894. Tel: 569-1335. $50–$85; includes breakfast.

► **Manor on Golden Pond.** Shepard Hill Road and Route 3, Box T, **Holderness**, NH 03245. Tel: 968-3348. $105–$170 with breakfast; $155–$220 with breakfast and dinner.

► **Margate on Winnipesaukee.** 76 Lake Street, **Laconia**, NH 03246. Tel: 524-5210. $45–$164; includes breakfast.

▶ **Meeting House Inn and Restaurant.** 35 Flanders Road, **Henniker,** NH 03242. Tel: 428-3228. $65–$93; includes breakfast.

▶ **Mountain Lake Inn.** Box 443, **Bradford,** NH 03221. Tel: 938-2136. $85; includes breakfast.

▶ **New London Inn.** 140 Main Street, P.O. Box 8, **New London,** NH 03257. Tel: 526-2791. $60–$90; includes breakfast.

▶ **Pasquaney Inn on Newfound Lake.** Route 3A. **Bridgewater,** NH 03222. Tel: 744-9111. $76–$146; includes breakfast.

▶ **Pleasant Lake Inn.** P.O. Box 1030, 125 Pleasant Street, **New London,** NH 03257. Tel: 526-6271. $65–$90; includes breakfast.

▶ **Red Hill Inn.** Route 25B and College Road (RFD 1, Box 99M), **Center Harbor,** NH 03226. Tel: 279-7001. $65–$125; includes breakfast.

▶ **Strathaven Bed and Breakfast.** Route 113, **North Sandwich,** NH 03259. Tel: 284-7785. $55–$60; includes breakfast. (No credit cards.)

▶ **Tuc' Me Inn.** Route 109 north, 68 North Main Street, P.O. Box 657, **Wolfeboro,** NH 03894. Tel: 569-5702. $57–$73; includes breakfast.

▶ **Twin Lake Village.** 21 Twin Lake Villa Road, **New London,** NH 03257. Tel: 526-6460. $315–$550 per person weekly; includes three meals daily.

▶ **Windyledge Bed and Breakfast.** Hatfield Road, RFD 3, **Hopkinton,** NH 03229. Tel: 746-4054. $45–$75; includes breakfast.

▶ **Wolfeboro Inn.** 44 North Main Street, **Wolfeboro,** NH 03894. Tel: 569-3016 or (800) 451-2389. $77–$207.

▶ **Wyman Farm.** RFD 13, Box 163, **Concord,** NH 03301. Tel: 783-4467. $45–$65; includes breakfast and tea tray.

The White Mountains: Pemi Area

▶ **Beacon.** Route 3, **Lincoln,** NH 03251. Tel: 745-8118 or (800) 258-8934 (outside New Hampshire); Fax: (603) 745-3783. $65–$150.

▶ **Black Bear Lodge.** **Waterville Valley,** NH 03215. Tel: 236-4501 or (800) 468-2553. $69–$209.

▶ **Golden Eagle.** Snows Brook Road. **Waterville Valley,** NH 03215. Tel: 236-4551 or (800) 468-2553; Fax: (603) 236-4551. $80–$220.

▶ **Indian Head Motel.** Route 3, **North Lincoln,** NH 03251. Tel: 745-8000 or (800) 343-8000; Fax: (603) 745-8414. $59–$119.

▶ **Lodge at Lincoln Station.** Kancamagus Highway, **Lin-**

coln, NH 03251. Tel: 745-3441 or (800) 654-6188; Fax: (603) 745-6777. $75–$160.

► **Mill House Inn.** Kancamagus Highway, P.O. Box 696, Lincoln, NH 03251. Tel: 745-6261 or (800) 654-6183; Fax: (603) 745-6896. $79–$149.

► **Mountain Club on Loon.** Kancamagus Highway, Lincoln, NH 03251. Tel: 745-8111 or (800) 229-7829; Fax: (603) 745-2317. $69–$219.

► **Rivergreen Condominium Hotel.** Kancamagus Highway, Lincoln, NH 03251. Tel: 745-2450 or (800) 654-6183; Fax: (603) 745-6777. $70–$275.

► **Silver Squirrel Inn.** Waterville Valley, NH 03215. Tel: 236-8325 or (800) 468-2553. $50–$100.

► **Snowy Owl Inn.** Village Road, Waterville Valley, NH 03215. Tel: 236-8383 or (800) 766-9969; Fax: (603) 236-4890. $49–$269; includes Continental breakfast.

► **Woodstock Inn.** 80 Main Street, North Woodstock, NH 03262. Tel. and Fax: 745-3951. $45–$135; includes breakfast.

► **Woodward's Motor Inn.** Route 3, Lincoln, NH 03251. Tel: 745-8141 or (800) 635-8968; Fax: (603) 745-3408. $58–$89.

The White Mountains: Franconia–Sugar Hill

► **Blanche's Bed & Breakfast.** Easton Valley Road, Franconia, NH 03580. Tel: 823-7061. $60; includes breakfast.

► **Bungay Jar Bed and Breakfast Inn.** P.O. Box 15, Easton Valley Road, Franconia, NH 03580. Tel: 823-7775; Fax: (603) 444-0100. $60–$110; includes breakfast.

► **Foxglove Country Inn.** Main Street, Sugar Hill, NH 03585. Tel: 823-8840. $85–$95.

► **Franconia Inn.** 1300 Easton Road, Franconia, NH 03580. Tel: 823-5542 or (800) 473-5299; Fax: (603) 823-8078. $56–$103; $120–$168 MAP.

► **Gale River Motel.** 1 Main Street, Franconia, NH 03580. Tel: 823-5655 or (800) 255-7989. $38–$75.

► **Hilltop Inn.** Main Street, Sugar Hill, NH 03585. Tel: 823-5695. $60–$110; includes breakfast.

► **Homestead Inn.** Route 117, Sugar Hill, NH 03585. Tel: 823-5564. $50–$80.

► **Horse and Hound Inn.** 205 Wells Road, Franconia, NH 03580. Tel: 823-5501. $60–$80.

► **Lovett's Inn.** Route 18, Franconia, NH 03580. Tel: 823-7761 or (800) 356-3802. $115–$138 MAP.

► **Red Coach Inn.** P.O. Box 729, Wallace Hill Road, Franconia, NH 03580. Tel: 823-7422 or (800) 262-2493; Fax: (603) 823-5638. $70–$170; includes Continental breakfast.

► **Sugar Hill Inn.** Route 117, Sugar Hill, NH 03585. Tel: 823-5621 or (800) 548-4748. $90–$115; includes breakfast.

The White Mountains: Route 302 Corridor

▶ **Adair—A Country Inn.** P.O. Box 359 (I-93 exit 40), **Bethlehem**, NH 03574. Tel: 444-2600. $85–$175; includes breakfast.

▶ **Ammonoosuc Inn.** Bishop Road, **Lisbon**, NH 03585. Tel: 838-6118. $50–$80 (includes Continental breakfast); $120–$150 MAP.

▶ **Beal House Inn.** 247 West Main Street, **Littleton**, NH 03561. Tel: 444-2661. $55–$85; includes breakfast.

▶ **Bells Bed and Breakfast.** Strawberry Hill Street, **Bethlehem**, NH 03574. Tel: 869-2647. $65–$90.

▶ **Bernerhof Inn.** Box 240, Route 302, **Glen**, NH 03838. Tel: 383-4414 or (800) 548-8007; Fax: (603) 383-0809. $69–$119; includes breakfast.

▶ **Bretton Arms Inn.** Bretton Woods, NH 03575. Tel: 278-1000 or (800) 258-0330; Fax: (603) 278-1000. $75–$140.

▶ **Lodge at Bretton Woods.** Bretton Woods, NH 03575. Tel: 278-1000 or (800) 258-0330. $80–$335.

▶ **Maxwell Haus Bed & Breakfast.** Parker Road, **Whitefield**, NH 03598. Tel: 837-9717 or (800) 776-9719. $60–$85; includes breakfast.

▶ **Mount Washington Hotel & Resort.** Bretton Woods, NH 03575. Tel: 278-1000 or (800) 258-0330; Fax: (603) 278-3457. $165–$250 MAP.

▶ **Mulburn Inn.** Main Street, **Bethlehem**, NH 03574. Tel: 869-3389. $55–$80; includes breakfast.

▶ **Notchland Inn.** Route 302, **Hart's Location**, NH 03812. Tel: 374-6131 or (800) 866-6131. $136–$210 MAP.

▶ **Spalding Inn.** Mountainview Road, **Whitefield**, NH 03598. Tel: 837-2572 or (800) 368-8439. $150–$310 MAP. Open June through October.

▶ **Thayers Inn.** 136 Main Street, **Littleton**, NH 03561. Tel: 444-6469. $30–$50.

▶ **Townhome Rentals at Bretton Woods.** Bretton Woods, NH 03575. Tel: 278-1000 or (800) 258-0330. $60–$95.

▶ **Wayside Inn.** Route 302 at Pierce Bridge, P.O. Box 480, **Bethlehem**, NH 03574. Tel: 869-3364 or (800) 448-9557. $48–$54.

The White Mountains: The Conways

▶ **Best Western Fox Ridge.** Route 16, P.O. Box 16, **North Conway**, NH 03860. Tel: 356-3151 or (800) 843-1804; Fax: (603) 356-9089. $99–$129.

▶ **Buttonwood Inn.** Mount Surprise Road, **North Conway**, NH 03860. Tel: 356-2625 or (800) 258-2625. $40–$90; includes breakfast.

▶ **Cranmore Inn.** 24 Kearsarge Street, **North Conway**, NH 03860. Tel: 356-5502 or (800) 526-5502. $67–$79.

▶ **Cranmore Mountain Lodge.** Kearsarge Road, **North Conway,** NH 03860. Tel: 356-2044 or (800) 356-3596. $81–$91; $99–$109 MAP.

▶ **Eastern Slope Inn.** Main Street/Route 16, **North Conway,** NH 03860. Tel: 356-6321 or (800) 862-1600. $66–$220 (high end for town houses).

▶ **Nereledge Inn.** River Road, **North Conway,** NH 03860. Tel: 356-2831. $59–$85; includes breakfast.

▶ **New England Inn and Resort.** Route 16A, Intervale, Box 428, **North Conway,** NH 03860. Tel: (800) 826-3466; Fax: (603) 356-2191. $104–$128; includes breakfast.

▶ **Purity Spring Resort.** Route 153, **East Madison,** NH 03849. Tel: 367-8896 or (800) 367-8897. $132–$198 AP; $90–$110 MAP (in fall).

▶ **Red Jacket Mountain View.** P.O. Box 2000, Route 16, **North Conway,** NH 03860. Tel: 356-5411; Fax: (603) 356-3842. $89–$139; $225 town houses.

▶ **1785 Inn.** P.O. Box 1785, **North Conway,** NH 03860. Tel: 356-9025 or (800) 421-1785. $79–$129; includes breakfast.

▶ **Sheraton Inn North Conway.** Settlers' Green, Route 16/302, **North Conway,** NH 03860. Tel: 356-9300 or (800) 648-4397 (outside New Hampshire); Fax: (603) 356-9300, ext. 515. $79–$135.

▶ **Snowvillage Inn.** Stuart Road, **Snowville,** NH 03849. Tel: 447-2818 or (800) 447-4345. $90–$130, includes breakfast; MAP available.

▶ **Staffords in the Field.** Philbrook Neighborhood Road, **Chocorua,** NH 03817. Tel: 323-7766 or (800) 446-1112. $120–$170 MAP.

▶ **Stonehurst Manor.** P.O. Box 1937, Route 16, **North Conway,** NH 03860. Tel: 356-3113 or (800) 525-9100 (in New England). $96–$156.

▶ **Tamworth Inn.** Main Street, Box 189, **Tamworth,** NH 03886. Tel: 323-7721 or (800) 642-7352. $110–$160; includes breakfast.

▶ **White Mountain Hotel and Resort at Hale's Location.** West Side Road, Hale's Location, P.O. Box 1828, **North Conway,** NH 03860. Tel: 356-7100 or (800) 533-6301; Fax: (603) 356-7100, ext. 418. $50–$140.

The White Mountains: Jackson–Pinkham Notch

▶ **AMC Joe Dodge Lodge.** AMC Pinkham Notch Visitor Center, **Gorham,** NH 03581. Tel: 466-2727 or (800) 262-4455. $44 per person for bunk, supper, and breakfast; $34, breakfast only.

▶ **Christmas Farm Inn.** Route 16B, **Jackson,** NH 03846. Tel: 383-4313 or (800) 443-5837. $70–$100 per person MAP.

▶ **Eagle Mountain Resort.** Carter Notch Road, **Jackson,** NH

03846. Tel: 383-9111 or (800) 777-1700; Fax: (603) 383-0854. $65–$155.

▶ **Inn at Thorn Hill.** Thorn Hill Road, **Jackson**, NH 03846. Tel: 383-4242 or (800) 289-8990; Fax: (603) 383-8062. $100–$182, includes breakfast; MAP available.

▶ **Nestlenook Farm.** Dinsmore Road, **Jackson**, NH 03846. Tel: 383-8071 or (800) 659-9443. $145–$250. (No children under 12.)

▶ **Village House.** Route 16A, P.O. Box 359, **Jackson**, NH 03846. Tel: 383-6666 or (800) 972-8343. $55–$120.

▶ **Wentworth Resort.** Route 16B, **Jackson**, NH 03846. Tel: 383-9700 or (800) 637-0013; Fax: (603) 383-4265. $49–$109.

▶ **Whitney's Inn.** Route 16B, **Jackson**, NH 03846. Tel: 383-8916 or (800) 677-5737. $49–$84 per person MAP.

▶ **Wildcat Inn & Tavern.** Route 16A, **Jackson**, NH 03846. Tel: 383-4245 or (800) 228-4245. $75–$99; includes breakfast.

The White Mountains: Cöos County

▶ **Balsams Grand Resort.** **Dixville Notch**, NH 03576-9710. Tel: 255-3400 or (800) 255-0800 (in New Hampshire), (800) 255-0600 (United States and Canada); Fax: (603) 255-4221. $142–$195 AP; $112–$162 (January to March).

▶ **The Glen.** First Connecticut Lake, **Pittsburg**, NH 03592. Tel: 538-6500 or (800) 445-4536. $60–$80 per person AP.

▶ **Jefferson Inn.** Route 2, **Jefferson**, NH 03583. Tel: 586-7998. $44–$70.

▶ **Mount Madison Motel.** 365 Main Street, Routes 2 and 16, **Gorham**, NH 03581. Tel: 466-3622. $48–$58.

▶ **Philbrook Farm Inn.** North Road, **Shelburne**, NH 03581. Tel: 466-3831. $97–$127 MAP.

▶ **Stark Village Inn.** RFD 1, Box 389, **Stark**, NH 03582. Tel: 636-2644. $45.

▶ **Town and Country Motor Inn.** Route 2, P.O. Box 220, **Shelburne/Gorham**, NH 03581. Tel: 466-3315 or (800) 325-4386; Fax: (603) 466-3315, ext. 207. $48–$82.

Long-Term Rentals

For long-term accommodations on Lake Winnipesaukee, contact: **Preferred Vacation Rentals**, Route 25, Box 161, Center Harbor, NH 03226. Tel: (603) 253-7811.

MAINE

*By Christina Tree and Mimi Steadman
with Cynthia Hacinli*

*Christina Tree is the editorial consultant for this guidebook.
Mimi Steadman is, along with Christina Tree, the author of*
Maine, An Explorer's Guide *and a contributing editor for*
Boston Magazine's New England Travel Guide. *The director
of an advertising agency specializing in the worldwide yacht-
ing industry, she lives by the sea in the heart of Maine's
Midcoast. Cynthia Hacinli served as restaurant critic for* The
Maine Times *from 1988 to 1990 and now writes about food
and travel for such publications as* The New York Times,
and Travel & Leisure, Yankee, *and* Philadelphia *magazines.
She is also the author of* Down Eats: The Essential Maine
Restaurant Guide.

The typical photograph of Maine is of a lighthouse on a
cliff, a lobster boat in a cove, or a sailboat in a yachting
harbor. Interestingly enough, the more you explore Maine,
the better these clichéd images work. The picture of water
meeting land holds as well for the vast, lake-stippled interior
as for the coast. In addition to 3,500 miles of coast and some
2,000 islands, Maine claims 6,000 lakes and ponds and
32,000 miles of rivers and streams. And while coastal roads
wind down peninsulas, leading to coves and points from
which small ferries serve islands, inland routes tend to
follow rivers and lead to lakes.

Maine's distinctive blend of land and water is a legacy of
the Ice Age. As the glaciers receded they scoured myriad
inland lakes and ponds and drowned many miles of coastal
hills—which now form all those islands and the peninsulas
stretching south from Route 1, which runs "down east" along
the coast.

Maine's other symbol—the pine tree—is also a fitting
one. Planted firmly in the middle of the state flag, the tree

represents not only Maine's most pervasive plant life but also its prime industry. In 1816 Massachusetts, its coffers at their usual low, permitted Maine to secede from the state only on the condition that an even division of all previously undeeded wilderness be part of the separation agreement. These woodlands—which still account for almost half the state of Maine—were quickly sold by the Massachusetts legislature to the new state for 12½ to 28 cents per acre. They never did become towns; today these "unorganized townships," as they were called then, remain largely privately owned working woodland.

Maine is, of course, almost as big as the other five New England states combined, yet its residents add up to less than half the population of Greater Boston. It's no wonder that the acquisition of public lands historically has been less of an issue here than in the other New England states—there always seemed to be so much land and so few people.

So it happens that 95 percent of Maine is privately held, leading modern visitors to complain that access to all that water—salty and fresh alike—is severely limited. However, all of Maine's major sandy beaches are not only public but conveniently located south of Portland. Because of these circumstances more than half the state's annual visitors converge on the south coast's beach towns. Yet another large percentage—some five million visitors a year—drive the Park Loop Road in Acadia National Park, the most dramatic stretch of Maine's rocky coast and the only substantial piece open to the public.

Far too many visitors drive straight from the south coast to Acadia. While it's just 162 highway miles (259 km) from Kennebunkport north and east to Bar Harbor, Acadia's gateway, more than 1,500 miles of coast intervene, thanks to all those ragged peninsulas. It is precisely these peninsulas that harbor some of Maine's most picturesque villages and satisfying places to stay.

Whether you head inland or stick to the coast you will truly experience Maine only when you get out on the water. Inland you can plunge through dramatic gorges on rubber rafts or glide out at dawn or dusk on magnificent lakes to look for moose. Along the coast, day sailers, sightseeing boats, and puffin- and whale-watching excursions are all readily available, and dozens of sea-kayaking outfitters offer guided day and multiday trips that require no prior experience.

If you have one week for Maine, there can be no more rewarding way of spending it than aboard a traditionally rigged windjammer, sailing through Penobscot Bay and putting into small coves and islands. If you have just a few days, be sure to board a ferry for an island such as Monhegan or

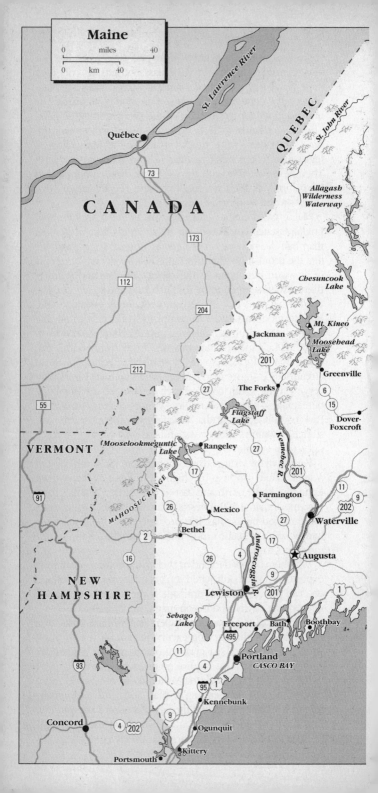

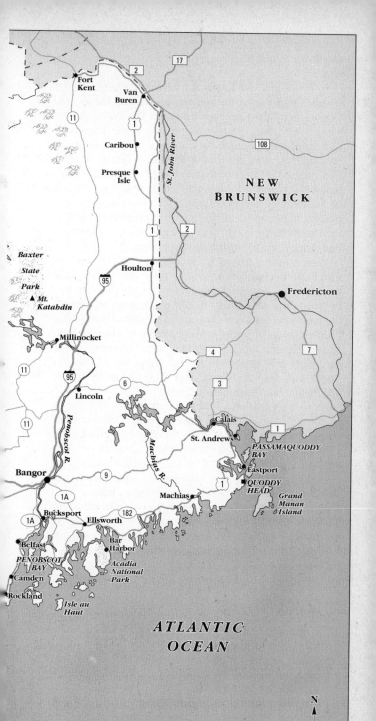

Isle au Haut, one with coastal paths that run through pine stands.

To combine a visit to Maine with one to Quebec city or Canada's Maritime Provinces makes good sense. The route to Quebec is up the Kennebec Valley, via The Forks, Maine's white-water rafting center, not far from majestic Moosehead Lake. The scenic route to the Maritimes lies beyond Acadia National Park, along the coast of Washington County (Maine's easternmost) to Campobello Island, and then via small ferries across Passamaquoddy Bay to the New Brunswick resort town of St. Andrews and the island of Grand Manan. It's also possible to take an overnight car ferry from either Portland or Bar Harbor to Yarmouth, Nova Scotia, ideally going from the one Maine town and returning to the other.

Maine's tourist season is the shortest in all of New England. Warm weather arrives in June and lingers only through mid-October. September is usually the sunniest, brightest, and least foggy month of the year, and prices plummet after the Labor Day exodus of families with school children. Lodging prices in Maine are lower during foliage season than they are in New Hampshire and Vermont, but the colors are equally spectacular. Maine has its share of maple and other deciduous trees that contrast beautifully with firs on both mountains and coast.

Maine is also known for its ski resorts, two in particular. In northwestern Maine there's Sugarloaf/USA, a self-contained village at the base of a mountain capped with snowfields and surrounded by other mountains. Sunday River, nearer Portland and lower in elevation, claims the country's most efficient snow-making system, offering consistent snow cover on six interconnecting peaks throughout the winter.

Increasingly, Maine's two major airports—in Portland and Bangor—serve as winter as well as summer gateways to northern New England. Visitors who allot just a couple of days for this vast, varied state inevitably return for more, whatever the season.

—Christina Tree

MAJOR INTEREST

The South Coast
Lively summer communities
Sandy beaches and coastal footpaths
Boat tours and whale-watching excursions
Grand old hotels and inns
Shopping at factory outlets in Kittery
Visiting 18th-century buildings in York village
Splendid Ogunquit Beach

Shops, restaurants, and fishing boats in Ogunquit's Perkins Cove

Nature trails and wildlife refuge in Wells

Dock Square, Kennebunkport's downtown hub

Cape Porpoise's seafood restaurants

Portland

Shopping and dining in the Old Port Exchange

Portland Museum of Art

Victorian Morse-Libby House and 18th-century Wadsworth-Longfellow House

Portland Head Light in South Portland

Inns and restaurants in the Western Promenade

Casco Bay

Excursions to the bay's islands

Shopping at L. L. Bean and outlet stores in Freeport

Bowdoin College museums in Brunswick

Drives along the Harpswell peninsulas

The Midcoast

Exploring peninsulas, coves, and islands

Unspoiled fishing villages

Sailing and tour-boat excursions

Windjammer trips in Penobscot Bay

Shopping for crafts and antiques

Bath's shipyard and maritime history

Early-19th-century sea captains' mansions, house-museums, and antiques shops in Wiscasset

Boothbay Harbor for shopping and dining

Monhegan Island's artists' colony

Farnsworth Art Museum and Homestead in Rockland

Camden's lovely harbor and hillside location

East Penobscot Bay

Small harbor towns

Elegant mid-19th-century houses in Castine

Blue Hill's galleries, inns, and restaurants

Galleries and the Haystack Mountain School of Crafts on Deer Isle

Sea kayaking off Stonington

Hiking on Isle au Haut

Wooden Boat School in Brooklin

Mount Desert Island

Acadia National Park

Spectacular scenery: mountains, lakes, and rocky coastline

Hiking, bike-riding, and boat excursions

Bar Harbor's shops, restaurants, and gracious inns

Northeast Harbor's galleries
Excursions to the Cranberry Isles

Down East and Passamaquoddy Bay
Blueberry barrens
Machias Seal Island for puffin watching
The Burnham Tavern in Machias
Lubec's Quoddy Head for whale watching and shore
  walks
Campobello Island: FDR's house, scenic drives and
  hikes, whale watching
Ferry to Deer Island
Bird-watching and bicycling on Grand Manan Island
Shopping in St. Andrews-by-the-Sea, New Brunswick
Fishing and canoeing in the St. Croix Valley
Eastport for sailing, fishing, and whale watching

Inland Maine
Skiing at Sugarloaf/USA, Saddleback Mountain, and
  Sunday River
White-water rafting on the Kennebec, Dead, and
  Penobscot rivers
Fishing at remote sporting camps
Hiking and camping
Sabbathday Lake Shaker community and museum
Moosehead Lake for moose watching and boat
  excursions
Canoeing in Allagash Wilderness Waterway
Hiking and camping in Baxter State Park in the north
  woods

TOURING MAINE

In the chapter that follows we have divided the state of
Maine into distinct regions, each of which can be visited on
its own or as part of a larger tour. Our coverage goes up the
coast, from the south to the north and east ("down east"),
and then explores inland Maine, generally south to north.

The **south coast**, the sandiest and most easily accessible
stretch of shore, contains the state's largest concentration of
places to stay and to dine. Known for century-old beach
resorts like Ogunquit and Kennebunkport, it also harbors
Maine's oldest village (York) and many miles of conservation
land laced with trails.

Portland and the Casco Bay area support Maine's largest
resident population. A decade ago few tourists would have
stopped in Portland for anything more than lunch in its Old
Port, but the recent expansion of its art museum and increase in pleasant places to stay—as well as the proliferation
of outlet stores in nearby Freeport—invite a longer stay.

North of Casco Bay the coastline shreds into a series of ragged peninsulas—the spines of mountains submerged in the Ice Age. The westernmost series of these peninsulas is known collectively as the **Midcoast**. Boothbay Harbor and Camden are the well-known resort towns here, and there are many less famous but equally picturesque villages and inns scattered along quiet coves and on the off-shore islands of Monhegan, Vinalhaven, and Islesboro.

Penobscot Bay, known as one of the best sailing grounds in the Western Hemisphere (board a Maine windjammer if you don't have your own yacht) divides the Midcoast from **East Penobscot Bay**, where a many-sided, low-key peninsula and its off-shoot islands (connected by causeways and bridges) are studded with Maine's highest concentration of art and crafts galleries.

Most visitors stop at coastal Maine's better-known resorts, using them like stepping stones to reach Bar Harbor, where myriad inns, motels, bed-and-breakfasts, and campgrounds serve visitors to Acadia National Park. Both Acadia and Bar Harbor are on **Mount Desert Island** (connected to the mainland by causeways), known for its high mountains, hiking and biking paths, and ocean views.

A small fraction of visitors explore the rugged coastal fishing villages east of Mount Desert, in the area known as **"down east."** Lodgings down east are limited, but inns and B and Bs are slowly popping up in the lobster and blueberry country that runs along the Atlantic to the town of Lubec. There the coast turns the easternmost corner of the United States and heads inland up along **Passamaquoddy Bay**. Narrowing to the width of a broad river, this bay forms a centerpiece for the Maine and New Brunswick towns on its opposite shores, which are connected by small car ferries via Deer Island.

Inland Maine is our final destination. Most famous for its vast northern woodlands, it also contains rushing rivers, such as the Kennebec, ski resorts, and old sporting camps that predate any of coastal Maine's resorts. This vast area, wedged between tall mountains and pristine lakes, seems to stretch endlessly northward into the acres of unpeopled forest—most of it without roads—owned by paper companies.

THE SOUTH COAST

From the moment you cross the Piscataqua River from Portsmouth, New Hampshire, you are unmistakably in Maine. Right away on Kittery Point you will find distinctly Maine houses, their yards filled with lupin; quiet coves; and weathered docks piled high with lobster traps. Follow the shore into York and you'll come to Maine's oldest village center, surprisingly intact. You can travel hundreds of miles farther "down" (actually north and east) the coast and find no more picturesque grouping of fishing and sailing boats than those in York Harbor and few shore paths more appealing than that along the York River, through Steadman Woods, and over the so-called Wiggly Bridge.

Maine's relentlessly rocky coast softens into sand south of Portland. More than 90 percent of the state's public beaches fringe the 50-odd miles of coastline between Kittery and Casco Bay, and more than half of its summer visitors generally can be found within walking distance of these strands. Ogunquit and Kennebunkport are the south coast's best-known and most established beach resorts, but the neighboring towns of Kittery, York, and Wells also offer ample space to walk or sun by the sea.

The south coast's sand was considered so much useless wasteland until the mid-19th century, when its potential as a seaside vacation spot began to emerge. In the 1870s, for one example, a Boston development group bought the five-mile stretch of coast from the western end of Kennebunk Beach to Cape Porpoise, and the area subsequently spawned 30 huge hotels and hundreds of large summer cottages by the turn of the century.

Each of the coastline's beach resorts evolved a distinct look and following. York Harbor, Ogunquit, and Kennebunkport catered to the wealthy, while York Beach, Wells, and Old Orchard Beach became havens for day-trippers (these last towns were accessible by trolley from Boston as well as Portsmouth) and working-class families.

Today almost all of the grand hotels are gone and the social lines have blurred, but these towns still look entirely different from one another. Several villages—York Harbor, York Beach, Ogunquit, Kennebunk Beach, and Kennebunkport—retain a distinct turn-of-the-century feel. In summer open-sided trolleys on wheels circle through all these towns, ferrying visitors to and from lodging places, beaches, and gathering spots such as Perkins Cove in Ogunquit and Dock

Square in Kennebunkport—narrow, water-oriented gathering places never meant for cars. Other towns, namely Kittery and Wells, have suffered from the touristic encroachment, with motel strips and freeways destroying their calm. Nonetheless, even they retain some of the scenic beauty that first attracted visitors to this coast.

TOURING THE SOUTH COAST

The south coast, which for our purposes extends from Kittery to Kennebunkport, is best approached by Route 1. It takes less than an hour to drive the 50 or so miles (80 km) on parallel I-95, but you should plan to spend a day along Route 1, which runs closer to the shore. By far the most heavily travelled section of the state, it is also one of the most varied, offering a sampling of everything you would find the length of the coastline: rugged promontories like Bald Head, rocky shoreline, such as that along the drive from Kennebunkport to Cape Porpoise, salt marshes between Kittery Point and York, and, of course, beaches.

If you have only two or three days to spend in Maine a good argument can be made for positioning yourself somewhere between Kittery and Kennebunkport (many lodging places demand a two- or three-day minimum in summer) and allowing one day to relax on a beach, walk, or take a boat excursion (whale-watching, sailing, deep-sea fishing, and sightseeing cruises are available); one day to sightsee and shop in the coastal towns; and a third to travel to Portland's museums, Freeport's shops, or Portsmouth, New Hampshire.

DINING ON THE SOUTH COAST

Dining on the south coast has its pitfalls. The hordes of visitors that descend every summer and fall make the area tourist-trap heaven. To be safe, beware of places with cutesy names or gimmicks, which are generally the rule on Route 1. Of course there are exceptions, and you can find a good, even great, meal here. There's a little bit of everything—from the simplest lobster shack to atmospheric country inns to some of the most ambitious dining rooms in Maine. The Kennebunks, Perkins Cove, and Ogunquit are especially well endowed with restaurants, and it is in these places that you will find the full range—the best and worst of the lot.

KITTERY

Maine's southeasternmost town (right across the Piscataqua River from Portsmouth, New Hampshire), Kittery is best

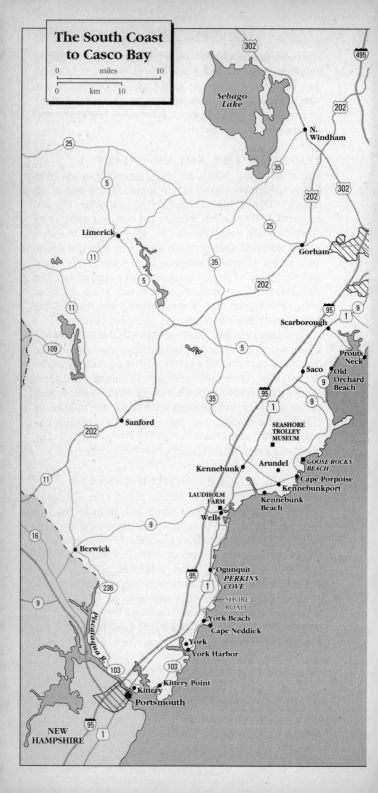

The South Coast to Casco Bay

miles 0 — 10

km 0 — 10

Sebago Lake

302

495

N. Windham

202

35

25

Limerick

11

5

Gorham

25

202

35

202

Scarborough

95

9

1

Prouts Neck

Saco

9

Old Orchard Beach

5

Sanford

202

35

SEASHORE TROLLEY MUSEUM

Kennebunk

Arundel

GOOSE ROCKS BEACH

Cape Porpoise

Kennebunkport

LAUDHOLM FARM

Kennebunk Beach

11

Berwick

9

Wells

16

Ogunquit

PERKINS COVE

95

1

SHORE ROAD

236

York Beach

Cape Neddick

York

York Harbor

9

Kittery Point

103

103

Kittery

Portsmouth

Piscataqua R.

NEW HAMPSHIRE

95

1

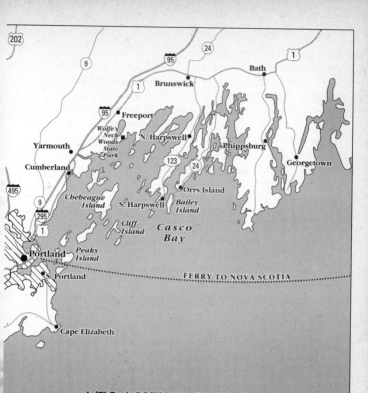

known for its factory outlets. More than 100 discount stores are grouped in a series of malls along Route 1 within little more than a mile of each other. Less famous than the Freeport "off-price" stores (see Casco Bay, below), the Kittery collection boasts just as many outlets, including big names like Dansk, J. Crew, Calvin Klein, Samsonite, Lenox (china and crystal), American Tourister, Corning/Revere, and Brooks Brothers. If you are interested solely in shopping, take exit 3 off I-95 and head north on Route 1.

Most shops in Kittery's dozen or so malls purport to offer between 20 and 70 percent off retail prices. Bostonians think nothing of driving to Kittery for savings on clothing, china, luggage, and shoes in particular. Shops are generally open daily in summer from 9:30 A.M. to 9:00 P.M. and until 6:00 P.M. on Sundays. The anchor store here (and a local landmark since the 1920s) is the **Kittery Trading Post**, the third complex on your left heading north up Route 1, a sprawling place selling sportswear, fishing and camping gear, firearms, shoes, and more.

The village of Kittery itself has been shredded by highways and rotaries. Its best and most natural approach is by the Memorial Bridge (also known as the Route 1 Bridge) from Portsmouth, though you can also come in over the I-95 Bridge (the High Level Bridge). Beware of hitting Kittery at the beginning or end of the workday, when the thousands of employees of the country's oldest government shipyard— the **Portsmouth Naval Shipyard** (PNS, on Seavey Island in the mouth of the Piscataqua, to the right as you cross the bridge)—drive through town. It was here that ships ranging from John Paul Jones's sloop-of-war *Ranger* to the first experimental American submarine, the *Albacore,* were built and here that the treaty ending the Russo-Japanese War was signed in 1905. The **PNS Command Museum** at the yard is open to the public one day a week and also by appointment (Tel: 207/438-3550). The **Kittery Historical and Naval Museum**, less than a mile from the navy yard on Route 1, just north of the Route 236 rotary, displays relics from the navy yard's past as well as from the shipbuilding and seafaring history of this stretch of the coast. (Open daily from May through October; Tel: 207/439-3080.)

KITTERY POINT

Back at the rotary follow Route 236 just a short distance southeast (it's marked "east," however) to Route 103 east and follow that along the harbor for less than a mile; park your car by the white wooden **Congregational church** and the small green across from the splendid **Georgian house**. This is Kittery Point. The church, built in 1730, is the oldest in Maine; the parsonage out back dates to 1729; and the graveyard, overlooking the harbor across the street, is filled with old, thin slate stones. The house (now private) was built in 1760 for the widow of Sir William Pepperrell, the French and Indian War hero who was the first American to be knighted, in honor of his part in the capture of the Louisburg, Nova Scotia, fortress from the French in 1745.

Just up the road on the right is **Fort McClary**, a hexagonal blockhouse built in the mid-19th century (and originally called Fort Pepperrell) overlooking Portsmouth Harbor— unfortunately the picnic tables are across the road and do not afford views of the ocean, though they are set in a pine grove adjoining a lily pond. Everyone in **Pepperrell Cove**, the next huddle of houses along the shore, seems to be named Frisbee. Indeed five generations of Frisbees have operated the general store, **Frisbee's Supermarket**, located on Kittery Point Town Wharf and proclaimed to be "North America's oldest family store, est. 1828." Members of the family also run the neighboring **Cap'n Simeon's Galley**, specializing in fresh fish and water views. Just far enough off the track to depend on locals and summer residents for its patrons, this is a moderately priced find, open for both lunch and dinner. Tel: (207) 439-3655.

The next turn off Route 103 follows Chauncey Creek Road, a winding waterside road that ends at **Seapoint Beach**, a relatively short, soft, silvery strand that belongs to the town (there is no admission charge, but visitors must park a half-mile back and walk in). Along the way you'll pass the **Chauncey Creek Lobster Pound**, right on the water. Because it's geared to locals the prices are good, but all you get is lobster, chowder, and steamers; most patrons bring their own salad, bread, and wine. Tel: (207) 439-1030.

STAYING IN KITTERY

The **Gundalow Inn**, a 19th-century brick house at 6 Water Street that has been restored and furnished with imagination and care, offers some water views and makes a comfortable base from which to explore New Hampshire's old port city as well as Maine's south coast. The inn's six bedrooms all have private baths. (**Warren's Lobster House**, nearby at 9 Water Street, has genuine 1940s decor and features fish both fried and broiled, an immense salad bar, and water views. Tel: 207/439-1630.)

A small sign by the graveyard in Kittery Point indicates the way to **Harbour Watch B & B**, hidden down Follett Lane and positioned on the very tip of Kittery Point overlooking the mouth of Portsmouth Harbor. The 18th-century white-clapboard house has been in owner Marian Craig's family since an ancestor bought it in 1797; many of its antiques were brought from England on sailing vessels. All three guest rooms overlook the water, and the view and lawn chairs will tempt you to sit all day watching the boats go by.

THE YORKS

York, just across the York River from Kittery via Routes 103 and 1A, is composed of so many distinct villages that residents refer to their town as "the Yorks." Bemused by its many post offices, Mark Twain, who summered here in the 1890s, wrote: "It is difficult to throw a brick . . . in any one direction without danger of disabling a postmaster."

YORK VILLAGE

Twain was part of a circle of intellectuals who devoted themselves to restoring York Village's Colonial-era buildings. Kittery Point summer resident William Dean Howells, then editor of the *Atlantic Monthly,* suggested turning the village's 1719 **Old Gaol** into a museum. Today its fascinating displays relate the community's history, from its beginnings as an Indian settlement called Agamenticus to its prominence in the 1640s as America's first chartered city (it was then known as Georgeana), its subsequent destruction by Indians, and finally the gradual evolution of the Colonial town as a way station between Portsmouth and the northern frontier.

The Old York Historical Society (Tel: 207/363-4974) maintains a half-dozen buildings right in York Village, including the Old Gaol, all of which are worth seeing (one ticket allows entrance to all). All six sights are closed from October to mid-June, except for the library in the George Marshall Store.

Begin with **Jefferds Tavern**, at the junction of Route 1A and Lindsay Road, a 1759 structure in which costumed guides orient visitors to the village and the other buildings. The **Emerson-Wilcox House**, also in the middle of the village, contains period rooms depicting the building's varied uses since the mid-18th century. The house is best known for its elaborate bed hangings, which were embroidered in York in 1745. The **George Marshall Store**, on Lindsay Road, is occupied by a local historical research library, while on the opposite side of the York River, but still on Lindsay Road, the **Elizabeth Perkins House** is a 1730s farmhouse filled with Colonial antiques and with the spirit of Miss Perkins, a real powerhouse and the founder of the historical society. The sixth building is the **Hancock Warehouse**, also on the river in York Village, with exhibits that illustrate 18th-century life and industry on the York River.

Historic houses aside, York Village is a crossroads community for which **Rick's All Season Restaurant**, at 240 York Street, forms the breakfast and lunchtime gossip center. Dinner is served only on Wednesdays and Thursdays; Tel: (207) 363-5584. **Fazio's**, hidden away next to the post office at 38 Woodbridge Road, is worth seeking out for dinner. Annette Fazio's pastas are made from scratch, and entrées, such as seafood Tecchia (linguine with scallops and shrimp sautéed with lemon butter and diced plum tomatoes) are moderately priced; pizzas, vegetarian dishes, and children's meals are also served. Reserve for five or more; Tel: (207) 363-7019.

YORK HARBOR

The shore beyond York Village acquired its present name, York Harbor, after the first hotel opened here in 1871. Soon other hotels opened and were surrounded by gracious shingled summer cottages. Around the turn of the century York Harbor was said to rank third, after Newport and Bar Harbor, as New England's fashionable summer address. It is still a fashionable address, and very low key: mostly 19th-century houses scattered around a sheltered harbor filled with fishing and lobstering boats and pleasure craft.

The 1970s **Stage Neck Inn**, a low-slung complex of 58 rooms and formal common rooms, sits on its own little peninsula, and all four exposures look over water. Its grounds encompass a small, curving black-sand beach, tennis courts, and a modest spa. The inn's **Sand Pipers Grill**, less formal than the dining room and overlooking the beach, is a favored local dining spot; try the blackened Maine crab cakes.

Dockside Guest Quarters, on spacious grounds on Harris Island, also overlooking the harbor, includes the 19th-century Maine House, scattered contemporary cottages, and a restaurant. Some of the Maine House's cozy rooms open onto either a second-floor balcony or the first-floor porch (where many guests take breakfast), but not all rooms have private baths. Closed from Columbus Day to late May.

A number of spacious former summer cottages in York Harbor are now bed-and-breakfasts. Among them is **Hutchins House**, at 209 Organug Road, a splendid 19th-century home with large, bright rooms and a Jacuzzi. It overlooks the York River, and a canoe is available for use by guests. (Closed December to March.) The **Inn at Harmon Park** is another shingled Victorian house, this one within walking distance of a small beach. The five rooms (three with private bath) are large and airy, and guests are welcomed by Tico, a miniature pig. Both bed-and-breakfasts are just steps from **Fisherman's Walk**, a mile-long path along the York River beginning at Hancock Warehouse and running through shady Steadman Woods and across a miniature suspension bridge—the **Wiggly Bridge**—through the front yard of the **Sayward-Wheeler House**, an early-18th-century house now preserved by the Society for the Protection of New England Antiquities as a house museum (closed mid-October to mid-June). The path continues sketchily along the shore.

Guests of the **York Harbor Inn**, which sits on Route 1A across from the harbor, also have easy access to Fisherman's Walk. A low-beamed 1637 house, one of several that were floated across from the Isles of Shoals (in the Atlantic just off Portsmouth) in the 18th century, serves as the inn's lobby. Some of the 32 guest rooms (most with private bath) have fireplaces and ocean views. The dining rooms, also with ocean views, offer a menu that's a cut above the norm. This is a local gathering place for both lunch and dinner, and the locals know enough to go with chef Gerry Bonsey's nightly specials—which always include milk-fed veal, fresh seafood, and a creative pasta dish. Sunday brunch is popular as well.

YORK BEACH

There may be no village line in the country more visibly drawn than that between York Harbor and York Beach, about 3 miles (5 km) north via Route 1A. The harbor imposed some of the earliest zoning regulations in the country, a reaction to the trailer camps established in the 1930s on the shore just over the line in York Beach. Beyond the campgrounds stretches two-mile **Long Sands Beach**, backed by Route 1A (here called Shore Road) and a long line of small beach cottages (there's also a public bathhouse). The 178-room **Anchorage Inn**, across from the beach, offers standard motel rooms, most with ocean views; with its indoor pool, this is a haven for families.

Beyond the beach turn right onto Nubble Road and out on the cottage-packed peninsula to Sohier Park, a rocky promontory with parking, rest rooms, and an information booth overlooking the **Cape Neddick Light** (a.k.a. **Nubble Light**), an 1879 lighthouse positioned just offshore on its own island. Note the "No Diving on Sunday" sign: This is a popular spot for deep-sea diving (divers' cars sometimes clog the small parking area).

Beyond "the Nubble," on Route 1A, is **Short Sands Beach**,

with a lively boardwalk at the far end. The **Goldenrod**, a century-old restaurant, marks the center of York Beach. The group in front of the restaurant's big plate-glass windows changes constantly, but there's always one there, watching multicolored saltwater taffy being stirred, pulled, and stamped into "Goldenrod kisses." Owned by the Talpey family, who opened it in 1896—just before the arrival of the first streetcars from Portsmouth—the restaurant remains a great place for a quick sandwich or some ice cream at the old-fashioned soda fountain (the two dozen or so flavors of ice cream are all made on the premises) or a full dinner at one of the time-polished wooden tables around the fieldstone fireplace in the dining room. Closed Columbus Day to early May; Tel: (207) 363-2621. The parking lot (reasonably priced meters) and bathhouse for Short Sands Beach are just across the street, as is a game arcade. **York's Wild Kingdom**, a block away, is a combination amusement park and zoo with exotic animals. Closed Columbus Day to early May; Tel: (207) 363-4911.

FROM YORK BEACH TO OGUNQUIT

From York Beach, continue northeast on Route 1A. Within a mile (1½ km) veer left onto Route 1 to visit the **Cape Neddick Inn**, in Cape Neddick, which would be considered an unusual restaurant anywhere. Sculptures, paintings, and objets d'art fill the two-level dining room of this old farmhouse. Aside from the oversize abstract pieces, there's nothing else to distract you—nothing except the food, which is as interesting as the room. Grilled lamb kabobs with Persian vegetables and couscous, curried-beef wontons, and chateaubriand on herbed French toast are examples of the chef's inventiveness. The menu is moderate to expensive. Closed Mondays and Tuesdays during winter; Tel: (207) 363-2899.

Continue east (actually northeast, but the roads here are marked "east") along Shore Road until you see signs for Bald Head Cliff and the **Cliff House**. The hotel, perched on a cliff overlooking the ocean, welcomes visitors for lunch and dinner as well as overnight. The hotel's Cliffscape Building was opened in 1990 to recapture the lost splendor of the original resort, which was inaugurated in 1872 by the great-grandmother of the current owner, Kathryn Weare. It houses a two-story lobby and dining room as well as an indoor pool and a spa. Accommodations here reflect a variety of eras, but all have ocean views and access to facilities, which include tennis, pools, and golf privileges at the nine-hole course across the road. A trolley shuttles guests back and forth to Ogunquit's beach and shops.

OGUNQUIT

Ogunquit, best and most scenically approached from York
by Shore Road, is synonymous with sand. The three-mile
beach here is backed not by road or private houses (as are
most of Maine's major beaches) but by dunes and the tidal
Ogunquit River. It's a splendid beach, firm enough for kite-
flying, calm and warm enough for toddlers, yet long enough
for everyone to find ample space.

By the turn of the century Ogunquit had its share of big
wooden summer hotels, and in the 1920s it became known
as a summer artists' colony. The opening of the **Ogunquit
Playhouse** in 1933 furthered its reputation as an arts center.
Now air-conditioned and billing itself as "America's Foremost Summer Theater," the 750-seat playhouse features big-
name stars in productions staged every evening except Sunday from late June through early September; matinees are
held Wednesdays and Thursdays (Tel: 207/646-5511). The
1930s and 1940s also brought dozens of motor courts—
basically cottage clusters—along Route 1 between Ogunquit
and Wells, and the 1980s have added condo-like motel units
geared to families as well as more art galleries, restaurants,
and boutiques.

From early July through Labor Day Ogunquit is one of
New England's liveliest resort towns. Its open-sided trolley
(circulating every 10 minutes between Route 1, Perkins
Cove, and the beach) averages an impressive 12,000 passengers per day.

Your first stop in Ogunquit should be the **Ogunquit Museum of American Folk Art**, right on the Shore Road. Built
to maximize its view of Perkins Cove, the museum always
displays a few canvases by Henry Strater, Reginald Marsh,
and other "local" artists from its permanent collection, in
addition to staging changing exhibitions. (Closed mid-
October through April; Tel: 207/646-4909.)

Perkins Cove, Marginal Way, and Ogunquit Beach
The first right turn off Shore Road after the museum brings
you right to Perkins Cove, a quaint fishing cove harboring
excursion boats and a number of small shops and restaurants (discussed below) housed in picturesquely weathered
lobster shacks. What distinguishes Perkins Cove from every
other Maine inlet is its much-photographed and -painted
pedestrian drawbridge. (Note that there are few parking
spaces on the dock, and from early June through Columbus
Day they are nearly always taken. If they are, you may pay to
park in the lot on Shore Road, just beyond the turnoff.)

At the beginning of the cove is the entrance to the **Marginal Way**. Running more than a mile along the rocky shore, from Perkins Cove into the middle of Ogunquit Village, the Marginal Way is Maine's single most popular stroll. Benches have been positioned along the path, and the ocean-smoothed rocks below invite exploration.

In the 1920s York farmer Josiah Chase gave the Marginal Way to the village of Ogunquit—*after* he had sold off all the sea-view lots behind it for a handsome sum. By keeping the path public Chase preserved his own right-of-way. You can walk the Marginal Way into the middle of Ogunquit Village, which consists of a gathering of shops, two vintage-1940 movie houses, and a dozen inns and restaurants along Shore Road between Perkins Cove and Route 1. Continue along Wharf Lane down to Ogunquit Beach, or take the longer way up to the corner of Shore Road and Route 1, then Beach Street back down to the water. Whenever you feel tired, just hop a trolley.

Parking at the main entrance to **Ogunquit Beach** costs $2 per hour. If you are not staying in town, park at one of the town lots ($6 per day), which are within walking or trolley distance, or at a lot behind Town Hall on Cottage Street ($4 per day) that is about a half mile from the beach. There are changing facilities, rest rooms, and restaurants on the cement walkway along the beach.

Ogunquit Beach is also accessible by driving north along Route 1 toward Wells and turning onto either Ocean Street (with $6 per day parking at Footbridge Beach) or Eldridge Road (with $6 per day parking at the Moody Beach entrance).

STAYING IN OGUNQUIT

Most of Ogunquit's best places to stay are an easy walk from the Marginal Way, Perkins Cove, and the beach. The **Beachmere Inn** is a large Victorian mansion right on the Marginal Way overlooking Ogunquit Beach. Rooms here range from suites with working fireplaces to motel units with balconies; all are equipped with private bath and kitchenette. (Closed mid-December to late March.) Also on the Marginal Way overlooking the beach is the **Sparhawk**, a deluxe motor-inn complex that replaced the town's grandest old hotel in the 1960s. (Closed late October to early April.) The family that owns the **Riverside Motel**, on Shore Road and commanding the best view of Perkins Cove, used to own a classic old hotel on the same site. The Riverside's 41 motel units overlook the cove, and there are also a few rooms in an 1847 house on the property (closed late October to late April).

The **Aspinquid**, just across the river from the beach, is yet another modern accommodation that has replaced a big wooden hotel, and is also still under the same ownership (closed November to mid-March). Units range from standard motel rooms to two-room apartments; facilities include a pool, lighted tennis court, a sauna, and a spa.

Dozens of bed-and-breakfasts and small inns line Shore Road and neighboring streets. **Marginal Way House and Motel**, hidden away at 8 Wharf Lane, offers efficiency apartments by the week as well as pleasant old-fashioned rooms (closed November to late April). The non-smoking **Pine Hill Inn** is a Victorian summer cottage with five bedrooms (three with private bath), a large living room, and a screened porch on quiet Pine Hill Road South, within walking distance of Perkins Cove. Easy access by trolley; closed mid-October to mid-May.

DINING IN OGUNQUIT

Ogunquit is known for its many restaurants. Chef-owner Richard Perkins of **Poor Richard's Tavern**, on the corner of Pine Hill Road and Shore Road, prides himself on his lobster stew. Tel: (207) 646-4722. Across Shore Road, the **Cove Garden** is known for chef-owner Osvaldo Coolidge's authentic pastas, despite the restaurant's pagoda-like shape. Tel: (207) 646-3509.

Arrows, off Route 1 on Berwick Road, has what must be one of the loveliest garden settings in the state. Nearly every table affords views of the expansive English flower beds outside the windows. The artistically presented food is pan-ethnic, with hints of East Asia, India, the Southwest, and the West Coast. Daring and wonderful combinations abound: a lobster spring roll with spicy cucumber sauce, applewood-roasted salmon with a nest of deep-fried sweet potato slivers, and homemade mint ice cream in a pure chocolate cone. It's expensive. Closed December through mid-May; Tel: (207) 361-1100.

Summer camp is what the **Ogunquit Lobster Pound** is all about. Located on Route 1 about a mile north of Ogunquit Square amid a stand of pines, the pound serves up a measure of nostalgia along with plump steamers, perfectly cooked lobsters, crunchy fried clams, and delectable deep-dish fruit pies. Outdoor picnic tables and benches are painted summerhouse green, and the mammoth stone lobster steamer adds a rustic touch. The pound has tables indoors as well, in a somewhat impersonal hangar of a dining room. Though prices can be steeper than you would expect in this casual setting, the crowds don't seem to care, making the pound a routine lunch or dinner stop on the way north. Closed November through mid-May; Tel: (207) 646-2516.

Barnacle Billy's, right at Perkins Cove, is the big lobster restaurant in the cove; you order at the counter and grab a table on a deck or near a fireplace, depending on the weather, while waiting for your number to be called. Closed mid-October through mid-April; Tel: (207) 646-5575. The **Lobster Shack**, near the end of the cove, is a reasonably priced 1940s-style place with picnic tables (the way all real lobster places used to look). Tel: (207) 646-2941. Also at the cove and less crowded than Barnacle Billy's is **Oarweed Cove Restaurant**, a good spot for a seafood lunch; it also offers free parking. Closed mid-September through mid-June; Tel: (207) 646-4022.

Despite its suggestive moniker, **Hurricane Restaurant**, also at Perkins Cove, is really a rather serene spot—unless a nor'easter happens to be blowing through. The two smallish dining rooms wrapped in windows afford breathtaking vistas of rocks and surf. White tablecloths and fresh flowers complete the clean, spare look. Food is modern and imaginative, though occasionally disappointing: roast duck with wild-rice pancakes, veal *crostini,* and daily fish specials at dinner; and fancy burgers and unusual salads and soups at lunch. Desserts, which also live up to the view, include fantasy creations like crème brulée, tiramisù, espresso cake, and flavored cheesecakes. Open daily year-round for lunch and dinner; Tel: (207) 646-6348.

Wells

The strip of motels, cottages, restaurants, and shops stretches along Route 1 without any visible change from Ogunquit through the length of Wells, a very old town (incorporated in 1640) but one that lacks a center. Its seven-mile beach, separated from Route 1 by tidal marshes, is backed by a road and a long line of small beach cottages and motels.

But don't dismiss Wells too quickly. In recent years it has become a mecca for book-lovers and bird-watchers; the wetlands here are said to attract some 250 species of birds. An unusual number of **antiquarian booksellers** are scattered along Route 1 between such unlikely seasonal neighbors as the **Wells Auto Museum** (displaying more than 80 cars; Tel: 207/646-9064) and **Wonder Mountain** (miniature golf). The largest of these bookstores, **Douglas Harding Rare Books**, boasts some 4,500 feet of rare and old books, maps, and prints. Each of a half-dozen smaller places has its own specialties.

Bird-watchers will want to turn off Route 1 at the blinking light onto Laudholm Road, which leads to **Laudholm Farm**. The former summer estate of a Boston & Maine Railroad president, this is now the information center for a seven-mile system of walking trails that meander through fields, woods, and wetlands. One trail leads to a stretch of barrier beach where swimming is permitted but not encouraged, because this is a habitat for endangered bird species. Parking costs $5 in July and August, but is free the rest of the year. For information on guided walks during summer months, Tel: (207) 646-1555.

The Laudholm farm trails are part of the 2,000-acre Wells National Estuarine Research Reserve, a coastal wildlife refuge that also includes acreage managed by the adjoining **Rachel Carson Wildlife Refuge**, reached from the manager's office on Route 9, which bears right off Route 1.

The fastest way to Kennebunkport is to fork right onto Route 9 beyond Laudholm Road rather than continuing north on Route 1. It's 9 miles (14½ km) from the Routes 1 and 9 junction to the bridge linking Kennebunk Lower Village (east of Kennebunk proper) and Kennebunkport. Park as soon as you can; the municipal lot is just across the bridge on your left behind the Congregational church.

THE KENNEBUNKS

"The Kennebunks" are geographically confusing. The Kennebunk-Kennebunkport Chamber of Commerce (Tel: 207/967-0857) information center at Cooper's Corner, at the junction of Routes 9 and 35 in Kennebunk Lower Village, dispenses free maps to help you understand the township's layout. Briefly, Kennebunk Beach is a shorefront village in the town of Kennebunk, while Kennebunkport is the neighboring shore town, with Cape Arundel, Cape Porpoise, and Goose Rocks all distinct areas within it. Arundel is a town in its own right between Kennebunk Beach and Kennebunkport. From late June through Labor Day open-sided trolleys circulate through Kennebunk, Kennebunkport, and Arundel, precluding the need to drive. We begin our coverage of the Kennebunks with Kennebunkport.

KENNEBUNKPORT

Dock Square, right in "downtown" Kennebunkport, is the resort hub of the Kennebunks and the single liveliest summer spot on Maine's south coast. From early morning until late at night cars nudge their way through the constant flow of tourists eating ice-cream cones and browsing in the shops that now fill the weathered old riverside buildings.

The second-floor back porch of the **Kennebunkport Book Port**, housed in a 1775 structure at 10 Dock Square, with a table to picnic on, commands a view of the harbor; inside the store a couch overlooks the square, inviting customers to sit and read a while. The Book Port specializes in books about Maine and the ocean. Dozens of boutiques fill adjacent blocks. Standouts include **Port Canvas**, selling totes, hats, and suitcases made in town (closed January to March); and the **Good Earth**, specializing in stoneware mugs, vases, and bowls.

The **Satellite Grill**, upstairs in the yellow Federal house known as the Weinstein Building, is another vantage point from which to survey the square. You can lunch on a Dinner Dog or dine on broiled swordfish with fruit salsa. Tel: (207) 967-0202.

Alisson's, right on Dock Square, is popular with both locals and tourists, which is why there's often a wait in high season. The great burger menu, which ranges from classic blue cheese and mushrooms to a "loaded" Mexican with jalapeños, guacamole, and Monterey Jack, and the easy-to-swallow prices are the draws here. Along with burgers Alisson's has good fries and onion rings, and soups, salads, sandwiches, and theme-of-the-day dinner specials—Italian, Cajun, New England. The regular dinner roster runs from steak to seafood to pizza. The restaurant does a little bit of everything—breakfast, lunch, dinner, and bar business—in its several small dining rooms. The noise level makes it ideal for a family party, and greenery, butcher-block tables, and framed maps make it a lot more pleasant than a fast-food joint. Tel: (207) 967-4841.

The **Arundel Shipyard**, by the Dock Square drawbridge, remains the south coast's prime departure point for **whale-watching cruises** and the boarding place for the excursion boat *Elizabeth 2,* which heads down the Kennebunk River every two hours or so, daily from May through October. Captain Wayne Showalter's narration aboard the *Elizabeth 2* is funny and informative (he'll tell you that Kennebunk is an Indian word meaning "Long Water Place"), and from the water you can see how neatly the river divides Kennebunk Beach (a long firm stretch of sand backed by cottages and inns) from Kennebunkport and the rocky, mansion-lined shore of Cape Arundel. You'll pass the hotels and yachts on the Kennebunkport shore and the green grounds of **St. Anthony Franciscan Monastery and Shrine**, a 40-acre compound open to visitors, on the Beach shore. (The monastery is accessible on land by the Beach Road in Kennebunk Beach.)

Before George Bush, Showalter explains, the big names in town belonged to writers: historic novelist Kenneth Roberts, novelist Margaret Deland, and Booth Tarkington, who liked to write on his schooner, moored at a weathered dock that still juts far out into the river. The dock is attached to the author's former home, which now bears a sign that says "Maritime Museum and Antiques Shop." Tarkington's 1930 novel *Mirthful Haven* is set in a Kennebunkport filled with large summer hotels that all close "with a visible abruptness" on Labor Day. By the 1920s the Kennebunks had almost 40 of these summer-only hotels. (A few of them have been given new life, and are discussed below. See Staying in the Kennebunks.)

Suddenly the *Elizabeth 2* is in the open ocean, and looking back you'll see the long row of large, elaborate Victorian mansions rising above the rocky shore of Cape Arundel. The most palatial mansion of all is on **Walker's Point**, a privately owned peninsula reaching out from the shore. Built in 1903 by George Herbert Walker, grandfather of former president George Bush, it is surrounded on three sides by water, uncannily suited to its use during Bush's term as a summer White House. The boat continues northeast to the mouth of Cape Porpoise Harbor and then returns to the river.

Of course you can follow this same shoreline by land: From Dock Square drive, walk, or bike south along Ocean Avenue. Roughly a mile (1½ km) down the avenue, just beyond a small cove, is **Mabel's Lobster Claw**, a small but popular restaurant favored by summer residents, including George Bush. Reservations are a must; Tel: (207) 967-2562. The neighboring **Green Heron**, a recently renovated little inn (ten rooms with private baths plus a cottage) that has an enthusiastic following, is known locally as *the* place to breakfast. Though the sunny dining room is really for overnight guests, locals often stop by to see what's cooking. Usually something offbeat such as creamed eggs with potato and cheddar pancakes or Mexican-style eggs is offered along with the standard breakfast fare. Tel: (207) 967-3315.

As Ocean Avenue rounds the corner onto the open ocean, note the series of turnoffs in which you can usually find short-term parking. This small piece of the shore is **Henry Parsons Park**; a path along the rocks leads to **Spouting Rock** and **Blowing Cave**, both of which you can really see only at mid-tide. But whatever the tide, it's a nice walk.

CAPE PORPOISE

If you're in a car or on a bike (it's too far to walk), continue along Ocean Avenue past Walker's Point and turn right on the Wildes District Road, following it into Cape Porpoise. The sheltered harbor here is usually filled with lobster boats and draggers in the evening, the time of day when most visitors converge on the village to eat. **Nunan's Lobster Hut**, a shed-like landmark on Route 9 in the village, is the place around here for a real feed: just steamers and lobster with plenty of melted butter—and sinks to wash in before you tackle the pie. Tel: (207) 967-4362.

Seascapes, on Pier Road overlooking the harbor, is Cape Porpoise's fancy restaurant. Tel: (207) 967-8500. Locals dine at the **Wayfarer**, also on Pier Road, a pleasant, informal place featuring moderately priced seafood pies and pastas and "tonight's roast"; bring your own bottle from the general store across the street. Tel: (207) 967-8961.

ELSEWHERE IN THE KENNEBUNKS

Seashore Trolley Museum

From Dock Square follow North Street to Log Cabin Road and the Seashore Trolley Museum, the world's oldest and largest trolley museum, maintained by the New England Electrical Railway Historical Society, a nonprofit group dedicated to preserving, exhibiting, and operating trolleys and similar vehicles from the last century and a half. The museum dates to 1939, when the last of the open-sided trolleys to run between nearby Biddeford and Old Orchard Beach was retired, and admirers placed it in an open field that straddles the rail bed of the old Atlantic Shore Line, which linked Kennebunkport to Biddeford from 1903 to 1927.

The Seashore Trolley Museum now owns 300 acres and more than 225 cars, ranging from a spooky green 19th-century horse bus used to transport prisoners from jail to court to a double-decker trolley that ran until 1955 in Blackpool, England.

From the museum's large, station-like visitors' center you can board an open-sided car and clatter out across woods and fields for a couple of miles before it's time to reverse the cane seats, clang the bell, and head back in. The museum is open daily from May through mid-October; Tel: (207) 967-2800.

Kennebunk

On a rainy day or on your way out of town, don't fail to stop by the **Brick Store Museum**, at 117 Main Street in Kennebunk, about 4 miles (6½ km) west of Kennebunkport via Route 9A/ 35 (a.k.a. Summer Street). Built in 1825 as a store, it is now a fine small museum with changing historical exhibits and an extensive permanent collection of artifacts and textiles. (Closed Sundays and Mondays in summer; Tel: 207/985-4802.) The **Taylor-Barry House**, two blocks away at 24 Summer Street, is an 1803 house furnished to the period that retains some original stenciling. (Open June through September, Tuesday through Friday; Tel: 207/985-4802.)

Summer Street is lined with a number of other early houses, the most famous among them the privately owned **Wedding Cake House**, a handsome yellow Federal house garnished with an elaborate confection of white Gothic-style flourishes and wooden tracery. According to local legend a sea captain about to be married was ordered away on an emergency from the very altar to the sea. Because his wife never got to eat her wedding cake he gave her one to live in.

The **1810 Eatery**, probably the best place to eat in downtown Kennebunk (17 Main Street), is almost too good to be true. Here is a casual restaurant that serves excellent Italian food, has an interesting wine list, and is charming *and* reasonable. The only catch is that it can get crowded in season. Dining early or late is one way to beat the problem. But even if you're here during the rush, the fine eggplant Parmesan, fettuccine Alfredo, vegetable lasagna, and the changing roster of specials are worth waiting for. Garlic bread and salads with good Parmesan pepper dressing come with the meal. The outdoor deck is especially appealing in summer, but the indoor rooms are pleasant as well, with pine floors, track lighting, and stenciled walls. Closed Sundays; Tel: (207) 985-2858.

Arundel

Back in the days when **Tilly's Shanty** was on the Cape Porpoise pier, George Bush used to tool over in his high-speed launch to pick up a pint or two of chowder for Barbara. Now that Tilly's has moved to Route 1 (north from Kennebunk in Arundel), he has to drive. Tilly's is a lobster shack with all the usual suspects on the menu: creamy lobster stew, steamers in broth, fried seafood, steamed lobster, french fries, and onion rings. There are also a few items like grilled chicken for landlubbers. Unlike most lobster shacks, Tilly's has waitress service and a large cedar-paneled indoor dining room. But its prices are in the low to moderate range. Desserts lean toward pie—peanut butter, blueberry, apple—served à la mode, the way it should be. Tel: (207) 283-1548.

Old Orchard Beach and Maine Aquarium

Families may also want to check out the 1906 carousel and the Palace Playland rides on the old-fashioned boardwalk in Old Orchard Beach, seven miles of white sandy beach (with lifeguards) that is a 20-minute drive north of Kennebunkport on Route 9. The Maine Aquarium, with a small petting zoo and penguins as well as marine exhibits, is also north of the Kennebunks on Route 1 in Saco, just west of Old Orchard Beach. Tel: (207) 284-4511.

BEACHES AND GOLF
IN THE KENNEBUNKS

The softest sand in town is at **Goose Rocks Beach**, a few miles east of Cape Porpoise on Route 9. **Kennebunk Beach**, Kennebunk's shorefront west of the Kennebunk River, is a long wide strip of sand backed by Beach Avenue, private houses, and a few inns. To discourage day-trippers the Kennebunks limit beachside parking to those with passes, which you can purchase at the town hall (weekdays only) if you're not staying locally. All Kennebunkport inns offer beach privileges. Note that there are no rest rooms or changing facilities at the beaches.

Golf is almost as big in the Kennebunks as going to the beach. The **Cape Arundel Golf Club** in Kennebunkport (Tel: 207/967-3494), the **Webhannet Golf Club** in Kennebunk Beach (Tel: 207/967-2061), and the **Dutch Elm Golf Course** in Arundel (Tel: 207/282-9850) are all 18-hole courses open to the public.

STAYING IN THE KENNEBUNKS

Kennebunkport and Kennebunk Beach

Before Kennebunkport became known as the site of the summer White House it was already one of Maine's foremost summer resorts. In addition to the few hotels that survive from its gilded era, the village offers Maine's largest concentration of elegant inns and bed-and-breakfasts.

Note that Kennebunkport inns generally stay open until early December, longer than in most coastal Maine resorts, in part to accommodate the many guests who come for **Christmas Prelude**, a series of concerts and special events held annually the first weekend in December. For information and a calendar of events, write to the Chamber of Commerce, P.O. Box 740, Kennebunk, ME 04043.

The **Captain Lord Mansion**, at the corner of Pleasant and Green streets, is a striking three-story Federal mansion topped by a widow's walk. It's a good bet off-season as well as in, if you can secure one of the 11 rooms with working fireplaces. Many of the three suites and 12 rooms (all with private bath) in the **Captain Jefferds Inn**, on Pearl Street, might qualify as works of art, so carefully and imaginatively are they furnished with a combination of original art and antiques (closed midwinter).

In the neighboring blocks the **Inn on South Street**, the **Kylemere Inn** (also on South Street), and the **Captain Fairfield Inn** (Pleasant and Green streets) are accommodations in former sea captains' homes dating from the 1820s, an era when hundreds of schooners and clipper ships were produced in dozens of shipyards along the Kennebunk River. All three are elegantly furnished Federal mansions, and all have considerable charm.

Two other survivors of Kennebunkport's gilded era are the century-old **Nonantum Resort**, renovated and expanded to include condo-style units, and the neighboring **Breakwater Inn**, a comfortable, moderately priced complex composed of parts of two old hotels and known for its dining room. The white bulk of the **Colony**, the town's last truly grand hotel, rises above its own beach at the mouth of the Kennebunk River. Open only from late June to mid-September, this is a classic old place with wide corridors and verandahs, a saltwater pool, a private beach, and a dress code. It has been owned by the Boughton family since 1948. Also hidden away down by the Kennebunk River are a number of handsome old summer cottages, one of which, **Bufflehead Cove**, is now an unusually attractive B and B with five guest rooms (all with private bath) and six riverside acres.

Among Ocean Avenue's line-up of bed-and-breakfasts is the non-smoking **Welby Inn**, a turn-of-the-century gambrel-roofed summer house with 7 bright, comfortably furnished rooms (all with private bath) and ambitious breakfasts. The neighboring **Green Heron Inn**, recently renovated, draws a loyal clientele and is known locally for its fantastic breakfasts (discussed above).

The **Kennebunkport Inn**, just off Dock Square, combines a convenient location with tastefully furnished rooms (all with private baths), a small pool, and a first-rate dining room. Non-smoking rooms are available. The **White Barn Inn**, on Beach Street in Kennebunk Beach, has been accommodating overnight guests since 1865. It's been elegantly refurbished and is highly rated and priced (all 27 rooms are non-smoking). The inn's rustic wood-timbered dining room is known for elaborate New American feasts with a New England influence. Grilled veal with morel sauce and baked halibut with sliced fennel and pepper are two dishes you might find on the changing menu. **Maine Stay Inn and Cottages**, on Maine Street within easy walking distance of Dock Square, is a good choice for families; rates include a full breakfast and an afternoon snack.

Cape Porpoise and Cape Arundel

The place to stay in Cape Porpoise is the non-smoking **Inn at Harbor Head** on Pier Road. Most rooms have views of the harbor, all five have private baths, and one has a fireplace. The Summer Suite offers as fine a combination of view and decor as any room in Maine. (Closed January through March.)

Old Fort Inn, hidden away on the site of a big old resort on Cape Arundel, has 16 pleasant rooms (all with private bath) in a former carriage house, as well as a common gathering space, a pool, and a tennis court. (Closed mid-December to mid-April.)

—*Christina Tree*

PORTLAND AND CASCO BAY

Portland, Maine's largest and most appealing city, sits on Casco Bay and is suffused with the smell and sense of the sea. The commercial area of Portland is a peninsula, enveloped in the waters of Back Cove on its north side, Casco Bay to the east, and Portland Harbor to the south. The waterfront on the harbor remains the city's focal point, a place to stroll, shop, and dine, and the boarding point for ferries to the small islands in Casco Bay and points north, such as Nova Scotia.

Sheltered by islands, Casco Bay is a wide arc of water stretching from Cape Elizabeth, just south of Portland, to the twin peninsulas known as the Harpswells, north of the city. The Casco Bay area includes Freeport, Maine's shopping mecca, and Brunswick, its college town, both north of Portland. Until the 1980s the Casco Bay area was a place to pass through on the way to somewhere else. It's just within the past decade that the Portland Museum of Art has quintupled in size, that Portland's Old Port Exchange has coalesced to the visitor attraction that it is, and that more than 100 outlet stores have surrounded the L. L. Bean flagship store in Freeport, about 10 miles (16 km) north of Portland.

Portland's motto, *Resurgam* ("I shall rise again"), is eerily apt. In the 17th century the settlement here was eradicated twice by Indians, and during the Revolution the town was burned by the British. In the 1820s the community prospered as Maine's first capital and continued to thrive as a shipping and rail center into the first half of the 19th century. Then in 1866 the entire waterfront area was destroyed by fire. It was sturdily rebuilt in brick, but by the 1960s the Old Port Exchange, the area along the harbor, was a shambles, and the entire city seemed dispirited and shabby. Its importance as a shipping center had been devalued by the opening of the St. Lawrence Seaway in 1959, and rail service had atrophied. The immense Grand Trunk Station was demolished in 1966.

Fortunately the rail station was the only major architectural casualty. In the 1970s artists and craftspeople began moving into the derelict buildings in the Old Port area, attracted by the intrinsic beauty of the structures and by low rents. Building by building they restored a five-block-square area and young people began moving into town, opening and patronizing shops and restaurants.

Today Portland is considered one of the country's most desirable cities in which to live. With a population of 66,000, it's big enough to sustain year-round theaters and a symphony, some 40 restaurants, and small, individually owned shops and galleries that complement all those big-name discount outlets in nearby Freeport. Yet it's small enough to be relatively uncongested, unhurried, and friendly.

Brunswick, just a few miles beyond Freeport, is another cultural center for the Casco Bay area. In the academic year Bowdoin College stages frequent theatrical productions, concerts, and lectures, and in summer the town hosts three summer theaters and the Maine Arts Festival, the state's largest and most colorful cultural happening. The Harpswells, the peninsulas that stretch southward into the bay from Brunswick, are perhaps best known for their restaurants but also harbor attractive bed-and-breakfasts, most of them right on the water.

TOURING THE CASCO BAY AREA

If you have only a few days to explore the coast of Maine you might just swing by Portland for a visit to the Portland Museum of Art followed by lunch in the Old Port Exchange, moving on from Portland to the shops of Freeport, dinner in Brunswick or on the water on Casco Bay's Bailey Island, and an overnight at a bed-and-breakfast in the Harpswells.

An extra day or two, however, will not be wasted in and around Portland. The city rewards visitors who take the time to explore its historic sights and its neighborhoods, such as the 19th-century residential streets around the Western Promenade, the string of shops and museums along Congress Street, and the Old Port Exchange. Just a 20-minute ferry ride from the Portland waterfront is Peaks Island, where you can rent a bike or try sea kayaking. You can also take a sailboat ride through Casco Bay or a boat to Eagle Island, one-time home of Arctic explorer Admiral Robert Peary and, though no longer a roost for eagles, a good place to spot other birds of prey.

The Portland area, moreover, offers some interesting places to stay, ranging from downtown hotels and old-fashioned inns to an inn on Chebeague Island and waterside resorts on Cape Elizabeth and Prouts Neck, both south of the city. You may also simply want to base yourself in a bed-and-breakfast on one of the picturesque points or coves in the Harpswells, visiting Portland from there.

Finally, if you've seen the Portland area's sights and still have a few free days, hop an overnight car ferry to Nova Scotia, return by car ferry to Bar Harbor, and drive back to the city along the coast.

PORTLAND

Portland is a hilly peninsular city with most of its business concentrated in the center just inland of Portland Harbor, and its residences clustered on its eastern and western ends. Visitors are drawn to the elaborate 19th-century Old Port buildings housing shops and restaurants and to the harbor ferries and excursion boats lining waterfront Commercial Street. Congress Street, which runs east–west along the ridge that forms the spine of the peninsula and is lined with buildings from the 18th to the 20th century, is the city's longest and its prime business street. While it has lost many of its shops to the Old Port area in recent years, it is still a pleasant walk, especially from the Wadsworth-Longfellow House (just above the Old Port) west to the Portland Museum of Art.

Flanking the peninsula's commercial core on both the east and the west are residential areas. The park-like Western Promenade is fronted by handsome blocks lined with elaborate Victorian, Queen Anne, and Romanesque Revival houses backed by streets of 19th-century brick row houses. Inland of the Eastern Promenade, the east end of town is, by contrast, filled with shabby, closely packed wooden buildings gathered around the old cemetery and observatory on Munjoy Hill.

COMMERCIAL STREET

Begin a visit to Portland where the city began: the waterfront (the route is clearly marked from I-295). Park along Commercial Street near the Convention and Visitors Bureau of Greater Portland, at number 305. At the center you can pick up a copy of the annually revised *Greater Portland, Maine, Visitors Guide,* useful for its map and current listings, as well as copies of the self-guided walking tours published by Greater Portland Landmarks.

Parking is more problematical as you enter the Old Port Exchange around the bottom of Exchange Street, which runs perpendicular from Commercial Street and the waterfront.

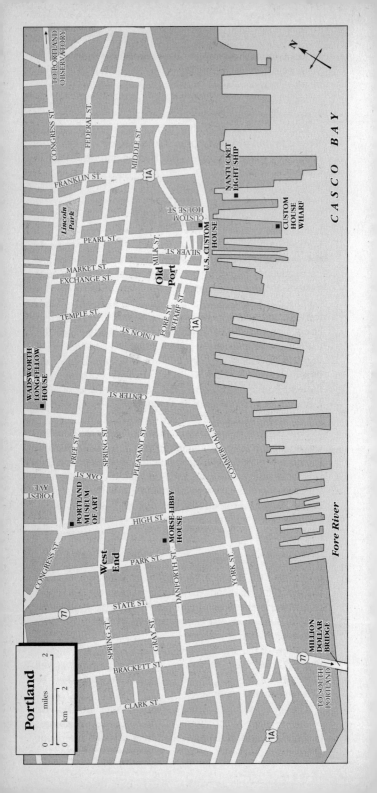

Portland

miles 0 — 2
km 0 — 2

TO PORTLAND OBSERVATORY

CONGRESS ST.
FEDERAL ST.
MIDDLE ST.
FRANKLIN ST.
1A

Lincoln Park

PEARL ST.
CUSTOM HOUSE ST.
MARKET ST.
EXCHANGE ST.
SILVER ST.
MILK ST.
Old Port
FORE ST.
WHARF ST.
U.S. CUSTOM HOUSE
TEMPLE ST.
UNION ST.
1A

WADSWORTH-LONGFELLOW HOUSE

CENTER ST.

FREE ST.
SPRING ST.
OAK ST.
PLEASANT ST.
FOREST AVE.

PORTLAND MUSEUM OF ART

HIGH ST.
MORSE-LIBBY HOUSE
West End
PARK ST.
DANFORTH ST.
YORK ST.
COMMERCIAL ST.

CONGRESS ST.
77
STATE ST.
SPRING ST.
GRAY ST.

BRACKETT ST.

CLARK ST.

MILLION DOLLAR BRIDGE
77
TO SOUTH PORTLAND
1A

NANTUCKET LIGHT SHIP

CUSTOM HOUSE WHARF

CASCO BAY

Fore River

N

If you can't find a spot on Commercial Street, head for one of the neighborhood's reasonably priced garages (see Getting Around, below).

Before getting too far from the waterfront you might want to stroll east along Commercial Street and step inside the opulent **United States Custom House** (1871) to take a look at the chandeliers, the painted and gilded ceilings, the woodwork, and the marble floors. At the next wharf is the **Nantucket Light Ship**, which floated up and down the New England coast lighting the waters for 40 years; it's now open to the public for 45-minute tours. The sleek new **Casco Bay Lines** terminal (with ample parking) is next door at 56 Commercial Street. (Casco Bay cruises are discussed below.)

OLD PORT EXCHANGE

Inevitably the Old Port is no longer the trove of unusual, reasonably priced art and craft work that it was 20 years ago. Some of those idealistic young artists and entrepreneurs who helped restore this area are still prospering here, but now that the Old Port is a tourist stop along the Maine coast, souvenir shops, clothing boutiques, and high-priced crafts and art galleries have moved in, along with a confusing array of restaurants.

Still, almost every building in this five-block area (bounded by Commercial Street on the waterfront, Congress Street on the north, Franklin Street on the east, and Exchange Street on the west) deserves a second look. As you walk up Exchange Street you can't help but notice the arched entrances and windows of the **Merchants Bank Block** (at number 34) and the **Preble Heirs Block** (numbers 41–49), both built right after the fire in 1866. Also built in 1866 and also impressive is the large Gothic window in the **Seaman's Club**, around the corner at 373–375 Fore Street. (The Seaman's Club is now occupied by a restaurant.) The most striking pre-fire building is the **Mariner's Church**, across the street from the Seaman's Club at 366–376 Fore. A one-block-square Federal and Greek Revival building, it was built of granite in 1828 and was the largest building in the new capital of a new state (Maine had just separated from Massachusetts in 1820). It now houses the **Maine Potters Market**, a 14-member cooperative store.

Shopping in the Old Port

The Old Port is Portland's best shopping neighborhood for unusual crafted items. Among the best crafts shops are the **Nancy Margolis Gallery** (367 Fore Street), **Abacus/Handcrafters Gallery** (44 Exchange Street), and the **Stein Gallery** (20 Milk Street), which displays stunning art-glass pieces.

Clothing stores include **Joseph's** (410 Fore Street), proferring elegant clothing and accessories for men and women, and **Amaryllis** (41 Exchange Street), good for unusual, reasonably priced women's clothing. Across the street is **Books, Etc.**, a well-stocked bookstore. The **Whip & Spoon**, at the corner of Market and Commercial streets, represents what is probably Maine's most complete source of cookware as well as gourmet foods and wines. Last but not least, the **Bottle Shop** (428 Fore Street), owned for the past 58 years by Sam Kaman, sells old bottles and is a wonderful holdout against the neighborhood's gentrification.

Also within these five square blocks are stores selling records, tobacco, wooden gifts, antiques, posters, games, herbs, art materials, Celtic jewelry, recycled cards, coffee, toys, fish, and a lot more.

Lunching in the Old Port

There are three good lunchtime spots in the Old Port (the neighborhood's restaurants are discussed in detail in the Portland dining section, below): **Baker's Table**, at 434 Fore Street, especially good for soups (Tel: 207/775-0303); **Walter's**, at 15 Exchange Street, currently considered one of Maine's best, and discussed further below; and the **Porthole**, on the old Custom House Wharf on Commercial Street, as genuine as a greasy spoon can be and still one of the best bets in town for a lunch of chowder and fried fish (also discussed below).

WEST OF THE OLD PORT

The **Portland Museum of Art**, at the corner of Congress and High streets (High runs one way up from Commercial Street), is just far enough from the Old Port area that you will probably want to drive there. Look for parking just west of the museum on or off Congress Street.

Thanks largely to local art collector and philanthropist Charles Shipman Payson and his wife, Joan Whitney Payson (whose personal collection was absorbed by the museum just last year), this is one of the major art collections on the East Coast. Unfortunately, just a small percentage of the museum's holdings may be displayed at any one time. Look for watercolors and oils by such Maine-based painters as Winslow Homer, Edward Hopper, and Andrew Wyeth. Picasso, Renoir, and Degas, among many others, are also represented. Closed Mondays; Tel (207) 775-6148 or 773-ARTS.

Also in the west end of town, just a few blocks south from the art museum at 109 Danforth Street (corner of Park), is the **Morse-Libby House**, also known as the Victoria Mansion. This Italianate brownstone mansion, built in 1859 by architect Henry Austin, is truly Victorian, with ornately frescoed walls and ceilings, a staircase with 377 banisters handcarved from Santo Domingo mahogany, huge gold-leaf mirrors, marble mantels, and stained glass. Open from June to mid-October; Tel: (207) 772-4841.

The **Wadsworth-Longfellow House**, just a few blocks east of the art museum at 487 Congress Street, is a classic Federal brick mansion built in 1786 by General Peleg Wadsworth, a Revolutionary War hero and grandfather of Henry Wadsworth Longfellow. The poet's boyhood home, it is interesting primarily as an illustration of the style in which prominent Portland families lived in the mid-19th century. Allow 45 minutes for the guided tour, which offers perhaps more insight into the city than into the poet. The house closes at 4:00 P.M. Tel: (207) 772-1807.

EAST OF THE OLD PORT

East across town on Congress Street is the **Portland Observatory**, at number 138. Built on Munjoy Hill in 1807, this was the tower that local women climbed to catch sight of their husbands' homebound ships. Climb the 102 steps and you will be rewarded by great views east to the coast and west to the mountains. Open Memorial Day to Halloween, whenever the flags are flying.

A few blocks west of the observatory at Congress Street and Washington Avenue is the **Eastern Cemetery**, where more than 4,000 souls are interred in nine acres, with headstones dating back to the mid-17th century.

PORTLAND HEAD LIGHT

After visiting the museums and historic houses of downtown Portland you may be ready for a little fresh air and the harbor view from South Portland's **Museum at Portland Head Light**. Head south on State Street (Route 77) and cross the Million Dollar Bridge to South Portland; turn left on Broadway and then right on Cottage Road, which turns into Shore Road. (The distance from Congress Street to the lighthouse is 4 miles/6½ km.) Portland Head Light adjoins **Fort Williams Park**.

The oldest lighthouse in Maine, Portland Head was commissioned by George Washington, completed in 1791, and manned until 1989, when it was automated; the decommissioned keeper's house opened in 1992 as an elaborate six-room museum depicting the history of lighthouses around the world (dating back to early Egyptian times) as well as the evolution of Portland Head Light itself. One exhibit locates all 52 lighthouses in Maine and others depict local maritime commerce and history. Tel: (207) 799-5251.

You might want to bring a picnic and enjoy the view from

this rocky promontory; there are picnic tables in surrounding Fort Williams Park.

CASCO BAY ISLANDS

Before it went bankrupt in 1980, the Casco Bay Lines claimed to be the country's oldest continually operated ferry company. Presently reconstituted as the **Casco Bay Island Transit District** (Tel: 207/774-7871), the outfit looks and works much as it always has, its bright yellow-and-red boats ferrying freight and passengers to islands in Casco Bay. The terminal, with ample parking, is on the Portland waterfront at 56 Commercial Street.

According to 17th-century explorer John Smith, who named the islands in Casco Bay the Calendar Islands, there was one for every day of the year. No one seems to agree on just how many there are, but four of them—Peaks, Great Diamond, Cliff, and Eagle islands—invite exploration: three via Casco Bay Lines and one by Eagle Tours. A car may be ferried to only one of these islands (Peaks), but the island is so small that a car is unnecessary. (See also Getting Around, below, for more information on boat excursions.)

Peaks Island, just a 20-minute ferry ride from Portland (boats leave frequently), is a flat island circled by a paved road; its harbor side—with great views of downtown Portland—is residential, while its ocean side is mostly undeveloped. A former resort island that once claimed a number of summer hotels and a large amusement park, today it is a pleasant place to bike and a popular base from which to try sea kayaking. Bike rentals are available from **Peaks Island Mercantile**, on Island Avenue, while **Maine Island Kayaking** offers introductory day and overnight trips in Casco Bay, ideal waters to practice in as you can test both sheltered water and open ocean (Tel: 207/766-2373). **Will's**, a chic and inexpensive café on Island Avenue, offers fantastic views of the Portland waterfront and skyline. Open for lunch and dinner (see Dining in Portland, below).

Great Diamond Island, just north of Peaks Island and another frequent ferry stop, is the site of 19th-century Fort McKinley, an elaborate 1890s brick structure now occupied by a resort complex known as **McKinley Estates**. The fort's officers' and soldiers' quarters and the commander's house are now condominiums. Town houses can be rented for a minimum of two days, which you can pass by strolling the landscaped grounds and walking paths, playing tennis, and going to the small beach. The Estate's restaurant, **Diamond's Edge Restaurant**, is *the* summertime "in" spot of Portland, both for lunch and dinner (see Dining in Portland, below). Reservations are essential; Tel: (207) 797-5904 or 766-5804.

Cliff Island, more than an hour's ride from the waterfront, is a lovely place to bring a picnic and explore the sandy roads leading to quiet beaches (the beaches are within walking distance of the ferry). With a small year-round population and a number of summer cottages, Cliff Island has the feel of a place you would expect to find hundreds of miles farther down east (that is, northeast). Ferries run only a couple of times a day.

Eagle Island, accessible via an Eagle Tours excursion boat from Portland's Long Wharf (Tel: 207/774-6498; from late June through September only), is the former home of explorer Robert Peary. The only building on the island, the admiral's house, facing the northeast on a rocky bluff that resembles the prow of a ship, is restored to look lived in, as though Peary just stepped out for a walk. The three-sided living room has a hearth made from Arctic quartz crystals. The small island, webbed with paths, is delightful. While there are no eagles, it's a good place to spot osprey and horned owls.

STAYING IN THE PORTLAND AREA

Downtown Hotels

Lodging choices in the Portland area are the most varied in all of Maine, and include two distinctive downtown hotels. The 202-room, 12-story **Sonesta Portland Hotel**, at 157 High Street, was built in 1927 as the Eastland Hotel, then the pride of the city. It sits conveniently across the street from the Portland Museum of Art and, while it caters to conventions and business meetings, offers comfortable, well-furnished rooms with unbeatable views of the city, as well as a fitness center with a sauna. The 95-room **Portland Regency Hotel**, at 20 Milk Street, is housed in a century-old armory in the Old Port area, one block west of the water. Rooms are furnished with antique reproductions, and the hotel's restaurant is the Market Street Grill. Facilities include a full-service health spa.

Inns and Bed-and-Breakfasts

The outstanding B and B in town—some would say in all of Maine—is the **Pomegranate Inn**, at 49 Neal Street in the Western Promenade neighborhood. Interior designer and former antiques dealer Isabel Smiles has transformed the interior of a plain-faced 19th-century house into a work of art. Walls are hand-mottled or -painted in bright, bold designs and hung with original art, mostly contemporary; furnishings are an eclectic mix of one-of-a-kind creations and antiques. If this all sounds a bit much, it isn't: The effect is relaxing and fun. All eight guest rooms have private baths, phones, and small TVs. Guests meet at a breakfast worthy of the decor.

Also in the West End (the area just east of the Western Promenade), at 46 Carleton Street, the **Inn on Carleton** has its own enthusiastic following. The graciously restored 1860s town house has seven rooms furnished with Victoriana and equipped with marble-top sinks (three have private baths). The gathering around the morning breakfast table is usually warm and lively.

The **Inn at ParkSpring**, at 135 Spring Street, is an 1835 town house handy to the Portland Museum of Art and to Congress Street offices and shops. It tends to cater to single business travellers. The seven guest rooms are elegantly furnished and a Continental breakfast is set out in the kitchen.

Beyond Portland Proper

The **Black Point Inn**, about 8 miles (13 km) south of the city in **Prouts Neck**, is Maine's last truly grand seaside resort. Built in 1876 as an extension of the exclusive summer community here (the inhabitants of which included Winslow Homer), the Black Point remains so much a part of the local scene that guests are permitted to use the Prouts Neck Country Club's 18-hole golf course and 14 tennis courts in addition to the inn's own indoor and outdoor pools and fine, sheltered beach. Guests are shuttled into Portland in black taxis similar to those used in London. Still, the inn's real draw is its location: Views from the dining room (proper attire required for dinner) extend down the coast of Cape Elizabeth and from the lounge back to Pine Point and Old Orchard Beach. A little-publicized path leads around the peninsula of Prouts Neck itself, and other paths lead through a bird sanctuary that was established by Charles Savage Homer, Winslow's brother.

The **Inn by the Sea**, south of Portland in **Cape Elizabeth** near Portland Head Light, faces the Atlantic on a rise above superb Crescent Beach (the other end of this strand is accessible through Crescent Beach State Park). A contemporary (1980s) grand resort, the Inn by the Sea is a low-slung structure with a small marble lobby and a variety of room choices, including one- and two-bedroom garden and loft suites and cottages fanning out on both sides above the beach. All units have kitchens, living-dining area, TVs, and VCRs. Facilities include a dining room and a heated outdoor pool.

While it's not particularly luxurious, the **Chebeague Inn-by-the-Sea**, an old three-story, flat-roofed summer hotel, appeals to island-lovers. (**Chebeague Island** is accessible by ferry from Portland as well as by a far more convenient ferry from Cousins Island, linked by a bridge to the town of Cumberland, just north of Portland.) The hotel, with its exposed-beamed lobby, living rooms, and dining room, and the long porch with its line of rockers, is a throwback to a simpler time. A nine-hole golf course adjoins the hotel. Bicycles, which guests may rent from the hotel, allow exploration of the island, the largest in Casco Bay, with a varied terrain of hills, promontories, and hidden beaches.

DINING IN THE PORTLAND AREA

Portland may not be on the roster of great restaurant cities of the world, but for a town its size the pickings are impressive. In addition to down-home favorites and trendy upscale addresses, there's a panoply of ethnic choices, Thai, Afghan, and Indian among them. That's not to say there aren't a few glitches—this isn't the place to find great Mexican or Chinese, for example—but in the main you can eat well here. Although the Old Port has the densest concentration of restaurants, other parts of town are worth exploring, too. There are restaurant rows right outside the Old Port on the east end of Middle Street and on Pleasant Street. Both areas are an easy walk from Exchange Street. Farther afield, the residential West End and busy Forest and Washington avenues also have their share of good eating. South Portland also has some worthy dining spots as well, and the drive there, across the Million Dollar Bridge (Route 77), takes only a few minutes. For those with more time, there are appealing choices on Peaks Island and Great Diamond Island, accessible by public ferry from downtown Portland or by private launch.

Prices in Portland, in general, are gentler than those in larger East Coast cities. At inexpensive spots entrées cost less than $10 and the moderate places generally charge $10 to $15 per dish. Even in the most expensive dining rooms entrées are usually well under $25. The telephone area code for Portland is 207.

Old Port

Down on the waterfront at 20 Custom House Wharf, the **Porthole** is a genuine Portland institution. Lobstermen fill the counter stools in the early morning hours, while counter-culture types wander in later on for brunch. But the best reason to mosey over is Friday's all-you-can-eat all-day fish fry, an invitation to gluttony with mountains of golden-crusted fish-and-chips, and coleslaw there for the asking. A big part of the Porthole's charm is its dedication to reverse chic: mismatched chairs and tables, faded walls, and that all-around greasy-spoon demeanor. This is no yuppie creation, though—it's the real thing. Prices, as you might expect, are low. Tel: 773-9348.

Street & Company, right on a cobblestone alley known as Wharf Street (at number 33), has a way with pasta and seafood. This subterranean restaurant with an open kitchen and outdoor tables is a true trattoria—casual and not too rough on the wallet. Dried herbs hang in bunches from the rafters, and shiny copper tables and pine floors give a rustic feel to the place. The fare is simple: oysters on the half shell (in season), mussels marinara, sole Français, and linguine with shrimp and capers, all with an ample shot of garlic. Fresh seafood doesn't need much embellishment, which is precisely the point here. Tel: 775-0887. Also at number 33 is the **Wharf Street Café,** an inexpensive soup and sandwich spot at lunch and BYOB restaurant by night. Don't be deceived by the homespun trappings—butcher's paper on the tables, calico throws disguising the soda machine. The evening crew champions clever new wave cooking on the order of pecan-crusted salmon with soba noodles, grilled tenderloin with crunchy fried onion rings and gruyère potatoes gratin, and gossamer lobster ravioli with a grape-studded Champagne sauce. Dinner here is one of the best deals in town, and the kids can color on the tables too. Tel: 773-6667.

Raphael's, at 36 Market Street, offers regional Italian cuisine in an elegant setting. Done in pale tones and polished wood, the Art Deco–style dining room is on the formal side, with cushioned chairs and white linens. The whole effect is very private—this would be an ideal spot for a tryst. Pastas, seafood, and veal dominate the menu. Combinations on the seasonally changing menu are creative; for example, a sauté of grilled sausage, littleneck clams, garlic, tomatoes, and red onions makes the most of fresh local seafood. There's also an extensive list of Italian and California wines. Prices are moderate to expensive. Tel: 773-4500.

Gritty McDuff's, at 396 Fore Street, is Portland's only brew pub, and as such has a rabidly loyal following. House-made ales, stouts, and bitters are the mainstays here, along with such classic British pub fare as mulligatawny, fish-and-chips, and shepherd's pie. The long, narrow barroom and annex are both done in dark gleaming wood and decorated with rugby souvenirs. Windows let a bit of light into this cool, dark space, as well as a view of Casco Bay in the distance. Tel: 772-2739.

An eclectic menu and a central location have made **Walter's Café** the popular lunch and dinner stop that it is. On busy lower Exchange Street at number 15, this two-story restaurant specializes in nouvelle cuisine, with an emphasis on pasta dishes. High ceilings, exposed brick, terra-cotta planters, and an open kitchen give the room the feel of a big-city bistro, while shiny-crusted pies add a touch of nostalgia. Unusual main-course salads, burgers, pastas, and offbeat sandwiches fill the lunch menu. Dinner is more upscale—grilled lamb steak, sautéed lobster with angel hair pasta—though there are a few lighter (and less expensive) choices as well. Tel: 871-9258.

There's something very satisfying about eating Afghan food in the middle of Yankee country. Lunch or dinner at the **Afghan Restaurant**, at number 88 on upper Exchange Street, is a political and cultural experience as well as a culinary one. Tapes of Afghan pop music play in the background and a mural of the homeland and newspaper articles grace the walls of this family restaurant. *Mantu* (ultra-thin ravioli filled with beef, onions, and peas) and *caraie* (a mixture of egg white, onions, and ground beef) are two specialties. For those who like to graze, the combination plate with a dab of everything is probably the way to go. Though the food is highly seasoned with cumin, cardamom, cinnamon, and cilantro, it is not spicy-hot. Best of all, it's a real bargain. Tel: 773-3431.

On the ground floor of One City Center, **Thai Garden** is an attractive spot at which to ponder the complexities of Thai cuisine. The split-level dining room is sleek and soothing with cool green walls and matte-black tables. Coconut milk, lemongrass, basil, garlic, coriander, ginger, and hot red chiles are the flavors here, and there's a good balance of hot and not-so-hot dishes. *Pad Thai,* the classic rice-noodle dish, is extremely well done, as are the sliced beef with lemongrass, mint, coriander, and chiles, and the red, green, and yellow curries. In summer tables are set up on the outdoor promenade so diners can watch all of Portland go by. Prices are in the inexpensive to moderate range. Tel: 772-1118.

Middle Street

Café Always, at 47 Middle Street, has long been considered one of the top choices in town. Despite its diminutive size, tables are well spaced against a backdrop of sunny hues. Everything seems to revolve around a faux column with a dramatic floral arrangement. The food (moderate to expensive in price) picks up where the decor leaves off: creative without being precious, and sometimes a little quirky. An antipasto platter looks like an artist's palette with lemony squid salad, eggplant caviar, and tiny white beans. Influences are multicultural and their manifestations run from Japanese beef scallion rolls to a lobster and goat's cheese burrito to apple-and-prune-stuffed pork loin. Tel: 774-9399.

Across the street and a few doors down at number 78, the **Pepperclub** offers inexpensive quasi-vegetarian dishes in a casual, smoke-free environment. Homemade soups, rice-and-bean casseroles, and grilled fish dishes are listed on the mobile blackboards. Even the lone meat choice is politically correct: an organic beef burger served on a whole-wheat bun. The hip, contemporary feel is probably due to the music (world beat to classical guitar), the changing exotic beers list, and the vivid, painted walls. Tel: 772-0531.

A few more doors down Middle Street at number 88, in a funky setting reminiscent of a curio shop, **Hugo's** serves such updated Irish and British classics as herb-crusted rack of lamb with a hint of honey and soy sauce as well as New American dishes and pasta. Vintage lamps and odd antiques give the place a homey feel, and despite the stylish, modern cuisine prices are generally moderate. The savvy beer list, which changes with the season and tends toward Irish labels, is a real bonus. Tel: 774-8538.

Northwest of the Old Port

The **Back Bay Grill** gets some of the loudest raves despite its out-of-the-way location on Portland Street (at number 65), northwest of the Old Port. A modish wood-and-steel bar, open kitchen, and enormous wall mural of the city are the focal points in the spare white-washed dining room. Food is stylish—Portland's take on New American—and fairly expensive. Venison with blueberry and lingonberry relish, pork loin with red-pepper coulis, and lobster with Thai curry-cream represent the range on the changing menu. Just about the only constant is the addictive crème brulée. Tel: 772-8833.

A few blocks away, next to the Portland Performing Arts Center at 23 Forest Avenue, the **Madd Apple Café** walks the line between Southern and Louisiana cooking. Mauve walls, flickering candles, giant white rice-paper spheres, and Duke Ellington make for a playful, romantic mood. This is the rare restaurant where the music is up to the cuisine, which ranges from moderate to expensive. It's also the place to try such bayou mainstays as escargots in brandy cream sauce, sautéed soft-shell crabs, barbecued sausage with red beans and rice, chicken livers in Madeira, and frogs legs meunière. Tel: 774-9698.

Pleasant Street and the West End

Hi Bombay, at 1 Pleasant Street (at the corner of Center Street), is a casual Indian restaurant in a storefront setting with burnt-orange velour cushions, Taj Mahal wall hangings, and the recorded twangs of a sitar to dine by. Appetizers such as *samosas* and *pakoras* and breads such as *poori* and *keema paratha* (lamb and pea-filled) are standouts. *Biryanis, tandoor* roasts, curries, and kabobs are excellent here, too. Prices range from low to fairly high, and service can be aggressively helpful—so practice saying "No" before taking the plunge. Tel: 772-8767.

A few doors away at 21 Pleasant Street, **Alberta's Café** has long been a favorite with locals. One of the first restaurants to bring New American cooking to Portland, Alberta's has evolved into the place to see and be seen during the lunch and dinner hours. Dishes are imaginative: greens with cornmeal-coated fried oysters, eggplant terrine, and the café's signature pan-blackened chicken with remoulade in a flour tortilla. (This last is imitated by many around town but equaled by none.) Bare wood tables keep things casual, but rosy sponge-painted walls and fresh flowers add a bit of festivity. And the scene is low key enough that a well-behaved toddler wouldn't raise any eyebrows. Entrées are in the moderate to expensive categories. Tel: 774-0016.

Katahdin, 106 High Street (at the corner of Spring Street), is a funky outpost turning out a mix of such old-time favorites as Yankee pot roast and buttermilk biscuits as well as more contemporary fare like grilled scallops with spicy lime-and-vegetable vinaigrette, goat's cheese tart, and a killer of a dessert called "chocolate mountain." Named for Maine's highest peak, the restaurant is a veritable museum of "camp" memorabilia. Adding to the general kitschiness are vintage salt shakers (no two are alike) and crockery. Prices are easy, too. Tel: 774-1740.

Tucked in a residential neighborhood at 58 Pine Street, the **West Side** does an all-day business. In the morning look for textbook-perfect eggs Benedict, homemade muffins, and designer omelets. Lunch is a mix of crepes, main-course pastries, and offbeat salads. Dinner covers a wide range—in both price and cuisine—from a basic lamb burger to pan-blackened tuna with cherries. In summer the tented back patio is the place to be as long as it's not too muggy. Inside, a potbellied stove, abstract collages, and blooms in glass vases lend character to the two-level dining room. Tel: 773-8223.

Portland Environs

It may be way off the beaten path, but **Marshall's Southern Restaurant**, a ten-minute drive from downtown at 14 Veranda Street, off Washington Avenue (reached via Congress Street or Route 295 south), is where locals go when they get a craving for soul food and Caribbean specialties. This no-frills operation—low ceilings, vinyl booths, plastic placemats—is a cholesterol-watcher's nightmare, but it's *the* place to scarf down Southern-fried chicken and all the appropriate sides, such as collards, yams, and rice and peas. On the Caribbean end of the menu, West Indian chicken curry and fried fish topped with a pile of sweet and spicy onions, peppers, and tomatoes are the ticket. The adventurous might want to dabble with serious soul standards like pigs' feet and chitterlings (chitlins), but for most, Miles Davis on the jukebox and a Jamaican Red Stripe at the bar are enough. Tel: 773-8964.

Uncle Billy's Southside, at 60 Ocean Street in South Portland, is more than worth the trip across the Million Dollar Bridge, a.k.a. Route 77. (Once you're over the bridge it's only a couple of minutes' drive around the Route 77 loop to the restaurant.) The draw here is Texas soul food with a dash of Cajun thrown in. Porcine memorabilia cover nearly every inch of wall space, and barbecue, right from the sideyard smoker, is the theme: ribs, brisket, pork shoulder, chicken. Corn bread, slaw, and spicy baked beans are all a little offbeat and very tasty. But save room for dessert: The Death-by-Chocolate ice cream studded with real chocolate shavings is out of this world. Tel: 767-7119.

Lobster is Maine soul food, and the **Lobster Shack**, off Route 77 at 225 Two Lights Road in Cape Elizabeth (about 5 miles/8 km from the bridge), is the quintessential spot to indulge. Outdoor picnic tables perch above craggy rocks and crashing surf. Inside it's just as informal, with bare wood tables and nautical antiques. Service is cafeteria-style on cardboard trays. You get a number, grab a table, and wait. Lobster is the point here, but if the steamed crustacean seems daunting in its entirety, try the lobster roll: large chunks barely moistened with mayonnaise and piled into a split, grilled hot-dog bun. Tel: 799-1677.

At 78 Island Avenue on Peaks Island, a 20-minute ferry ride from downtown Portland, is **Will's Restaurant**, a stylish, inexpensive café with umbrella-shaded tables on the deck and a tiny dining room inside. On a clear day the Portland skyline is visible at lunch; in the evening the lights of the city glow. The fare is a mixed bag of everything from burgers and a chicken burrito to fancier dishes such as salmon with lime-ginger sauce and sautéed scallops with white wine and capers—with an equally wide range of prices. Wines by the glass and by the bottle may be limited, but they are well chosen and reasonably priced. Tel: 766-3322. Catch the ferry at Casco Bay Lines, at 56 Commercial Street in Portland (Tel: 774-7871); Will's is a two-block walk from the ferry landing.

Diamond's Edge Restaurant at Diamond Cove on Great Diamond Island is somewhat more formal and expensive.

The airy dining room and outdoor deck have a Caribbean feel, though the menu is decidedly New American regional. Pork tenderloin in a garlic-peanut crust and Champagne lobster are the sorts of imaginative dishes you can expect at dinner; lunch and brunch are more straightforward, but still have culinary dash. Desserts like chocolate toffee torte are almost too pretty to eat, and wines (by the glass and bottle) are fairly unusual. Tel: 797-5904 or 766-5804. Casco Bay Lines has ferries to Great Diamond as well; see above. (Some, however, stop at the other end of the island. A van will be sent to pick you up if this is the case—reservations are required.) The ferry trip from Portland to Diamond Cove is half an hour; the restaurant is about 100 yards from the dock. The Water Taxi, $25 for up to six people one way, is another option; Tel: 233-0456.

—*Cynthia Hacinli*

SIDE TRIP TO NOVA SCOTIA

The Prince of Fundy Cruises' MS *Scotia Prince* leaves from Portland from May through October at 9:00 P.M. daily and arrives 12 hours later in Yarmouth, Nova Scotia. After spending some time in Nova Scotia you may return instead to Bar Harbor on the Marine Atlantic Bluenose Ferry boats and drive back along the coast to Portland (161 miles/258 km)—or vice versa. (See also Getting Around, below, for further ferry and cruise information.)

Nova Scotia, two-thirds the size of Maine, demands at least a week for thorough exploration. Almost completely surrounded by water (it's connected to New Brunswick by a narrow spit of land), the Canadian province boasts some of North America's most beautiful coastal scenery, a particularly spectacular stretch of it on Cape Breton Island, the most remote part of the province.

Nova Scotia is too big and its attractions too varied and far-flung to cover comprehensively here; for more complete coverage of Nova Scotia, see *The Berlitz Travellers Guide to Canada*.

CASCO BAY
Freeport

Freeport, 17 miles (27 km) northeast of Portland on Route 1, has always simply been a convenient crossroads, the point at which travellers have to decide whether to turn inland toward Augusta or to continue up the coast toward Bar Harbor. It was probably for this reason that the agreement separating Maine from Massachusetts was signed in the Jameson Tavern here in 1820 and surely for this reason that Leon Leonwood Bean positioned his store here to catch hunters and fishermen headed for the backwoods corners of Maine.

There isn't much more to the town of Freeport than the Route 1 shopping strip, which is Freeport's Main Street. A word of warning before you hit the strip: Watch where you park, because time limits vary on spaces, and the Freeport meter maids are ever vigilant.

SHOPPING IN FREEPORT

New England's most famous store and Maine's chief tourist attraction, **L. L. Bean** is said to attract 3.5 million customers annually (more than twice the population of Maine). It all began in 1912 when Leon Leonwood Bean began selling his own invention—a hunting boot with a rubber bottom and leather top—and then began keeping his shop open around the clock to cater to hunters and fishermen headed north.

It's now impossible to find the original boot factory hidden at the heart of the sleek, double-tiered store on Main Street (Route 1), dwarfed only by the company's huge office and warehouse complex (devoted to fulfilling L. L. Bean catalog orders) on the edge of town. (There's also a no-frills L. L. Bean factory store in one of the vast Main Street parking lots, which always seem to be full.)

So is L. L. Bean all it's cracked up to be? Yes. Whether it's a canoe or kayak, a tent or rocking chair, a doormat or book, a sweater or pair of pants, a flowerpot or a pair of boots, the store still stands behind the quality of what it sells with liberal return policies. It's also just plain fun to shop at Bean's, especially if you happen to be passing through in the middle of the night (you'll be amazed at all the other people here, too).

Amazing as it seems—given the number of stores lined up along Route 1—it has been only a decade since a sizable number of retailers have cashed in on the flow of consumers lured by Bean. While the other stores—which now number more than 100—haven't gone so far as to stay open 24 hours, they are generally open from 10:00 A.M. to 10:00 P.M. in summer and from 10:00 A.M. to 7:00 or 8:00 P.M. off-season (closing at 6:00 P.M. on Sundays off-season). Although they are discount shops, these are not the old-fashioned no-frills outlets you find in mill towns; many of them are quite sleek. Among the big-name clothiers here are Laura Ashley, Benetton, Polo/Ralph Lauren, Calvin Klein, Carroll Reed, Cole-Haan, the Gap and Gap Kids, Carter's Childrenswear, J. Crew, and Brooks Brothers—all claiming to offer discounts of a minimum of 20 percent off prices in their regular retail stores. Household items (sheets, towels, and cookware), luggage, handbags, lingerie, cosmetics, and, especially, shoes are also Freeport specialties. The old Eastland Outlet—the only factory outlet in town ten years ago—is now Banister Shoe, and of course Bass, Dexter Shoe, and Reebok/Rockport are also represented here.

ELSEWHERE IN FREEPORT

Freeport offers plenty of parkland where you can walk off a spending binge. You can get directions at the L. L. Bean information desk or the Maine Publicity Bureau welcome center in Yarmouth (just south of Freeport) to the 100-acre **Mast Landing Sanctuary**, maintained by the Maine Audubon Society, the 600-acre waterside **Wolfe's Neck Farm**, and the 244-acre **Wolfe's Neck Woods State Park**. Also nearby is the **Desert of Maine**, a 35-acre tract of sand that was once a farm. Created by blatant mismanagement of the land for a century, it is indeed a desert, though its sand is unusually rich in mineral deposits. (Head west from the first I-95 Freeport exit; closed mid-October to mid-May.)

DINING AND STAYING IN THE FREEPORT AREA

Predictably, restaurants and inns have appeared to feed and lodge Freeport's shoppers. McDonald's and the ubiquitous street vendors aside, there are some attractive lunch spots.

At 115 Main Street, the **Jameson Tavern**—the same brick building in which Maine gained its independence from Massachusetts in 1820—is a good place for sandwiches and light meals. Tel: (207) 865-4196. The **Blue Onion Tavern**, an atmospheric spot at the southern end of Main Street, offers soups and salads as well as more substantial fare, such as scampi. Tel: (207) 865-9396. The **Muddy Rudder**, south of the shopping strip on Route 1, overlooks the water from both the dining room and deck; the menu features sandwiches and a wide selection of seafood. Tel: (207) 846-3082. The elegant place to dine in Freeport is **Fiddlehead Farm** (Independence Drive and lower Main Street), a Greek Revival house with two dining rooms. The dinner menu ranges from veal to pasta to fresh seafood; this is also a good bet for lunchtime soups and salads. Tel: (207) 865-0466.

On a nice summer day head for **Harraseeket Lunch and Lobster Company**, a dockside lobster pound in South Freeport (turn off Route 1 south of the shopping strip at the giant Indian, then turn right at the stop sign several miles down).

You order lobster and clams at one window, fried food at another, and eat at picnic tables (if you can obtain one) in the middle of the Harraseeket boat yard while watching sailing and fishing boats come and go in the harbor. Tel: (207) 865-4888.

The **Cannery Restaurant**, at Lower Falls Landing in Yarmouth (just off Route 1 south of Freeport), offers a weatherproofed view of Casco Bay. Housed in a herring processing plant built in 1913, it's an attractive place specializing in seafood dishes such as crab cakes and bouillabaisse. Tel: (207) 846-1226. (The Cannery is part of a shopping complex that also includes **Harbour Books**, a well-stocked store with soft music, and **Maine Cottage Furniture**, featuring Maine-made furnishings and a constantly changing inventory of artwork.)

The **Harraseeket Inn**, within walking distance of all the shops, at 162 Main Street, is the largest and fanciest place to stay in the village of Freeport. Many of the rooms have canopy beds, Jacuzzis, and fireplaces, and all are furnished with reproduction antiques. The Harraseeket's dining room, the most expensive place to dine in town, serves Continental cuisine in a formal setting. The inn's **Broad Arrow Tavern**, in contrast, has a pubby atmosphere and menu to match.

The **Isaac Randall House**, an old farmhouse at 5 Independence Drive just minutes from the shopping drag but surrounded by five acres of woods, offers antiques-furnished, air-conditioned guest rooms, and a full breakfast. **Atlantic Seal B&B**, at 25 Main Street in South Freeport, is just a five-minute drive from the stores but feels far removed from the commercial bustle, with views of Freeport Harbor from all three non-smoking guest rooms (one has a private bath). Innkeepers Thomas and Gaila Ring also operate the 40-foot excursion boat *Atlantic Seal,* which cruises through Casco Bay making twice-daily trips to Eagle Island (discussed above).

Brunswick

Beyond Freeport I-95 and Route 1 split from their parallel path along the coast. The interstate heads due north, following the Kennebec River inland to Augusta, the state capital. Coastal travellers continuing northeast on Route 1 find themselves on a motel- and gas station-lined strip, one they tend to equate with Brunswick. Most travellers don't bother to leave Route 1 to explore this handsome college town, but it takes just a few extra minutes to drive straight up Pleasant Street instead of doglegging left with Route 1. If you're passing through in early August, you might want to attend the **Maine Arts Festival**, held at Thomas Point Beach in Cooks Corner, just east of Brunswick. Usually a four-day event, the festival offers continuous entertainment on several stages, including music and dance groups from around the world, as well as exhibits of local crafts, food, and art.

Driving down Pleasant you'll pass the Brunswick Area Chamber of Commerce, distributing pamphlets and information at number 59, and the **Maine Writers and Publishers Alliance** bookstore, featuring Maine poetry and fiction, at number 12. Turn right on Maine Street and drive along the **town mall**, a long, thin green with a bandstand in the middle that is the site of Tuesday and Friday farmers' markets and Wednesday-night concerts (summer only). Near the mall the **Pejepscot Museum**, at 159 Park Row, focuses on local history, while the **Skolfield-Whittier House**, an adjoining 1858 Italianate mansion, contains the furnishings of two prominent families who lived here in the late 19th century (both are open weekdays year-round, plus Saturdays in summer). The **Joshua L. Chamberlain Civil War Museum**, at 226 Maine Street, exhibits memorabilia of one of the most remarkable figures in the Civil War, who was also a state governor and president of Bowdoin (open Memorial Day to Labor Day; closed Mondays).

Bowdoin College

The Bowdoin College campus begins around the curve of Maine Street beyond the town mall. One of the country's top colleges, as well as one of its oldest (established in 1794), Bowdoin has remained a small school (1,350 men and women). The center of the campus is still the venerable brick quad on which Henry Wadsworth Longfellow and Nathaniel Hawthorne lodged. (Tours of the 110-acre campus begin at Moulton Union, posted from Maine Street.)

The **Bowdoin College Museum of Art**'s Walker Art Building exhibits a distinguished collection of works by such artists as John Sloan, Mary Cassatt, Gilbert Stuart, and Rockwell Kent. Tel: (207) 725-3275. The **Peary-MacMillan Arctic Museum** in neighboring Hubbard Hall displays mementos from expeditions to the North Pole by Bowdoin alumni Robert Edwin Peary, generally recognized as the first man to reach the North Pole, and Donald Baxter MacMillan, Peary's assistant who went on to further explore the Arctic. Tel: (207) 725-3416. Finally, the college's Packard Theater provides the stage for the **Maine State Music Theater**, a series of summer musicals, as well as for numerous concerts, productions, and lectures throughout the academic year.

STAYING AND DINING IN BRUNSWICK

Brunswick Bed & Breakfast, at 165 Park Row, is a nicely restored Greek Revival home with floor-to-ceiling windows overlooking the green, within walking distance of Maine Street shops and the campus. **Stowe House**, the Federal-era home in which Harriet Beecher Stowe wrote *Uncle Tom's Cabin* while her husband was an instructor of religion at Bowdoin, is now a large restaurant serving lunch and dinner; it's at 63 Federal Street, parallel to Maine and just one block east of the town mall. Tel: (207) 725-5543. At 42 Maine Steet, the **Great Impasta** is a first-rate northern Italian restaurant with good antipasti, homemade bread, and a variety of dishes combining fresh produce and seafood, pasta, and garlic. Tel: (207) 729-5858.

The **Captain Daniel Stone Inn**, the most elegant place to stay in town, is farther up the street from Stowe House (Federal becomes Water Street after crossing Route 1). The inn is housed in a Federal-era home, but the 25 rooms and suites are thoroughly modern, with color TVs and VCRs; seven of the rooms have whirlpool baths. The inn's **Narcissa Stone Restaurant** serves all three meals and features a musical dinner-theater cabaret. Tel: (207) 725-9888.

The Harpswells

The three narrow fingers of land that stretch south into Casco Bay from Brunswick and several bridge-linked islands collectively form the town of Harpswell. Because the "town" is divided into so many sections by water, it's generally referred to as "the Harpswells." These quiet communities have a returning summer population and less of the transient trade found in the coastal areas closer to Portland.

From Brunswick's Maine Street follow Route 24 (at the curve) just a block south and turn right onto Route 123. You'll pass by **Richard's**, a restaurant known for its imported beer and German dishes (open for lunch and dinner; Tel: 207/729-9673) and through **Harpswell Center**, little more than a grouping of a mid-18th-century town hall and church with a matching white-clapboard general store. A right turn here on Lookout Point Road brings you to a working lobster cove and to the **Harpswell Inn**, an 1850s boardinghouse turned B and B, furnished with an unusual number of antiques and blessed with water views. Four of the 12 rooms have private baths.

A half-dozen crafts studios are salted around this corner of town, among them **Ma Culley's Old Softies**, a store full of soft-sculpture characters so whimsical and lifelike that their creator, Colleen Moser, prefers to sell them individually herself rather than marketing them to other stores. Look for her sign on Allen Point Road just beyond J. **Hathaway's Restaurant and Tavern**, a locally popular dining spot known for fish-and-chips, barbecued spareribs, homemade soups, breads, and desserts. Tel: (207) 833-5305.

Water views increase as the peninsula narrows, but it's difficult to make yourself stop and enjoy them. So follow the signs off Route 123 to the **Dolphin Marina and Restaurant** at Basin Point, a combination chandlery and coffee shop divided by a model boat from a more formal eating area. This is the perfect place to savor chowder or lobster stew while watching the fishing boats come and go. Tel: (207) 833-6000. On Route 123, **Estes Lobster Barn** offers waterside dining indoors as well as out (picnic tables are set up across the road from the restaurant). Tel: (207) 833-6340.

Continue south on Route 123 to **Potts Point**, a gathering of multicolored 19th-century summer cottages on the rocks. This is one of the most picturesque spots on the entire coast, though relatively few tourists come here.

Drive back up Route 123 through Harpswell Center and turn right on Mountain Road to Route 24 and head south. Immediately you'll notice an increase in traffic—you're back on the tourist trail. Route 24 crosses a small bridge onto Orrs Island and continues across an unusual **cribstone bridge** (the granite blocks are constructed in a honeycomb pattern to ease tidal flow) onto **Bailey Island**. The most famous in the lineup of restaurants here is **Cook's Lobster House & Pound**, adjacent to a working fishing pier (closed mid-September to Memorial Day; Tel: 207/833-2818). Be forewarned that a Casco Bay liner full of hungry excursionists from Portland arrives here every day at noon in July and August. (You can board the boat at Cook's for an hour-and-a-half cruise around Eagle Island and through the north end of the bay while its passengers chow down at the restaurant.)

Route 24 continues along an ever-narrowing spit of land, past picturesque Mackerel Cove. The **Mackerel Cove Restaurant** takes in this lovely sight (closed mid-October to April). The coffee shop here, open from 6:00 A.M., caters to fishermen, and the pine-paneled, reasonably priced restaurant serves all three meals. Tel: (207) 833-6656.

Driftwood Inn and Cottages, a classic old Maine resort owned by the same family for more than 50 years, is hidden away off Route 24 across from Mackerel Cove. Most guest rooms are in three shingled houses set on a rocky point, but there are also five housekeeping cottages. Guests gather for meals in the central lodge's dining room and around a small pool set into the rocks. (Closed mid-October to mid-May.) Continue beyond Mackerel Cove to **Land's End**, where there's a small parking area, a beach, and a statue dedicated to lobstermen.

Little Island Motel, reached by driving back up Route 24 to Orrs Island, sits on its own tiny island off Orrs. There are just nine units, each with a small refrigerator and color TV and access to the homey reception area, where a full buffet breakfast is served. (Closed late October to mid-May.)

To get back to the mainland from Orrs Island, head north on Route 24 to Cooks Corner. If you are heading farther up the Maine coast toward Bath, follow Route 24 north to Route 1 just beyond Cooks Corner. If you are returning to Brunswick you can pick up Route 1 south here.

—Christina Tree

THE MIDCOAST: BATH TO CAMDEN

You can drive the 50 miles (80 km) along Route 1 from Bath to Camden, Maine's so-called Midcoast, in just about an hour (unless you're stuck in one of July and August's seemingly endless traffic tie-ups), or you can spend many a delightful day wandering winding roads along the peninsulas and around the tiny villages, coves, and islands that give this region its true character. On Friday and Sunday afternoons in summertime when cars come to a standstill along Route 1, taking the back roads is certainly a stress-reducing—and very possibly a timesaving—alternative as well.

Be sure to include at least a day in your itinerary for poking down some of the craggy, glacier-sculpted fingers that extend into the sea. It is spectacular country—not to be missed on a tour of Maine. As you gaze across a perfect blue-and-green vista, perhaps coveting a particularly stunning seafront dwelling or imagining what it would be like to live here in your own dream house, consider that just 200 years ago, after the American Revolution, the nascent government auctioned off vast tracts of this marvelous real estate for the grand sum of about $2.75 an acre.

To explore the area, just follow almost any of the roads that lead south from Route 1—yes, *south*. Take a look at a map and you'll see that, contrary to what you might expect, this coast, and Route 1, actually run mostly east–west rather than north–south. The roads down the peninsulas and the

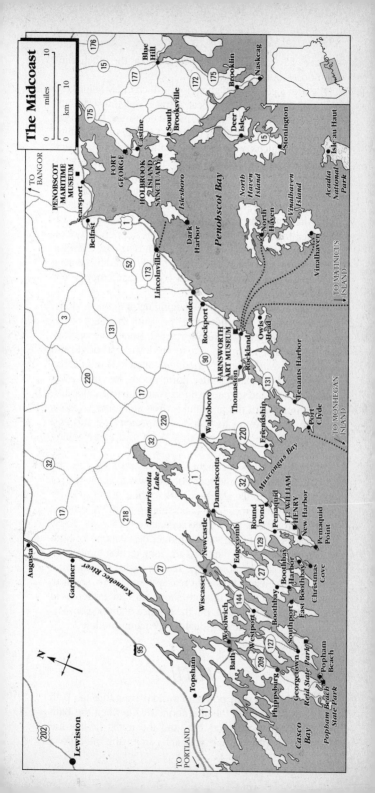

The Midcoast

miles 10

km 10

0

TO BANGOR

176

15

Blue Hill

177

172

175

Brooklin

Naskeag

175

PENOBSCOT MARITIME MUSEUM

Searsport

FORT GEORGE

Castine

South Brooksville

HOLBROOK ISLAND SANCTUARY

Islesboro

Deer Isle

15

Stonington

Belfast

1

Dark Harbor

Penobscot Bay

52

173

Lincolnville

North Haven Island

Vinalhaven Island

Acadia National Park

Isle au Haut

3

131

Camden

Rockport

North Haven

TO MATINICUS ISLAND

220

90

Rockland

Owls Head

17

FARNSWORTH ART MUSEUM

Thomaston

Vinalhaven

Waldoboro

220

131

Tenants Harbor

Port Clyde

TO MONHEGAN ISLAND

32

Friendship

Damariscotta Lake

220

Muscongus Bay

Damariscotta

32

17

218

Newcastle

Round Pond

Pemaquid

FT. WILLIAM HENRY

New Harbor

Augusta

27

Edgecomb

129

Pemaquid Point

Gardiner

Kennebec River

Wiscasset

27

144

Boothbay

Boothbay Harbor

East Boothbay

Christmas Cove

95

Topsham

Woolwich

Bath

Westport

Southport

209

127

Phippsburg

Georgetown

Reid State Park

202

Lewiston

1

TO PORTLAND

N

Casco Bay

Popham Beach

Popham Beach State Park

saltwater bays and rivers between them, on the other hand, run north–south.

The area's convoluted geography, which today helps keep much of this coast off the beaten track, was the very thing that made the region a magnet in past centuries. Easy access by sea and dozens of deep, protected harbors drew fishing parties from such countries as the Netherlands, England, and Portugal as early as the late 1500s. Making intermittent peace with the local Indians, they set up colonies (many of them seasonal) among the inlets and on several of the offshore islands, including Monhegan. The settlement at Pemaquid, about halfway along the Midcoast near Damariscotta, was well established even before the Pilgrims stepped ashore on Plymouth Rock. In fact, had the Massachusetts Bay colonists not sent a boat to the Maine colony to buy salted fish during their first brutal winter, there's a good chance they would not have survived.

To some the Midcoast is the beginning of the real "down east" region, for it is here that the sandy beaches of the southern coast give way to the rugged, stony outcroppings for which Maine is famous. The term "down east" originated in the 1800s when trading schooners sailed to Boston carrying lumber from Maine's great north woods, ice cut from its coastal ponds, and granite from its island quarries. Because of the direction of the prevailing winds along here, vessels heading from Boston to Maine sailed *down*wind and *east* along the Maine coast; thus they were said to be sailing down east.

By the early 1900s overnight steamboats were also heading down east, whisking America's nobility away from the heat of Boston, Philadelphia, and New York to their grand summer "cottages." Artists, too, have been smitten by the Midcoast's wild beauty, among them three generations of Wyeths. Today the region is one of the state's premier destinations for both visitors on week-long vacations and long-term summer residents. The area's popularity has brought considerable change, with elegant bed-and-breakfasts and hotels, sophisticated restaurants, and upscale shops now in evidence in practically every borough. But the essence of the region—its intractable nature, its individuality—remains undiluted.

BATH

Do everything in your power to avoid driving through Bath on Route 1 at 4:00 in the afternoon: This is when the **Bath Iron Works** day shift lets out, and the traffic tie-ups are legendary. If you do find yourself part of this miles-long creep of cars, however, you'll have plenty of time to contemplate Bath's long and noble shipbuilding tradition, today most evident in the collection of navy cruisers and frigates in various stages of completion on the Kennebec River just below the Carleton Bridge, alongside the ironworks. Towering above it all like a giant praying mantis is the yard's crane, said to be the tallest such contraption on the East Coast.

America's boat-building tradition began on the Kennebec in what is now Phippsburg (south of Bath, and discussed below) with the launching in 1607 of the pinnace *Virginia,* the first vessel built by Europeans in the New World. With the deep Kennebec's easy access to the sea, its banks sloping at the perfect angle for laying keels and launching ships, and a nearby supply of timber, the location was ideal for shipbuilding. Even after the local forests had been exhausted through exportation of masts and spars to Europe, the industry continued to flourish because of the renowned skills of the many shipwrights who had become established here. The skills passed from generation to generation, and by the 1840s swift clipper ships were sliding down the ways where sturdy cargo carriers had gone before. In the 1870s the clippers were replaced by downeasters (a cross between the fast but small-capacity clippers and the old-style freighters). In the early 1900s impressive multimasted schooners designed to carry coal, ice, granite, and lime were the toast—and the bread and butter—of the Kennebec.

The **Maine Maritime Museum**, on lower Washington Street in Bath, chronicles much of this history, beginning with a model of the *Virginia* and continuing through to an extensive exhibit on the Bath Iron Works. There is a particular focus on the era beginning in 1862, when a whopping 80 percent of American-flagged full-rigged ships were built in Maine, almost half of them at Bath's 16 shipyards. Adjacent to the museum's large brick exhibition hall is the **Percy & Small Shipyard**, the country's last extant yard in which large wooden ships were built, and the **Apprenticeshop**, where the skills for building traditional wooden boats are still imparted to dedicated young apprentices. Visitors with even just a passing interest could easily spend a full afternoon at the museum, especially in summer when the Nova Scotia fishing schooner *Sherman Zwicker* and other old-timers tie up at the dock for tours. Tel: (207) 443-1316.

The far-flung success of Bath shipbuilders a hundred years ago made fortunes for many of the town's families. One of the most prominent was the Sewalls, whose yard built the majority of the world's four-masted barks—steel-hulled, sail-powered vessels that carried grain from California, Oregon, and Washington to Europe. Through their trade in the Pacific, the Sewalls also became deeply involved in efforts to annex the Hawaiian Islands to the United States. They and the city's other wealthy shipbuilding families erected mansions on and around upper Washington Street, leaving behind an impressive architectural heritage now preserved in a historic district. Several of the many grand homes within the historic district are now B and Bs (see Staying in Bath, below).

Just down Washington Street from the historic district is the cocoa-colored **Center for the Arts at the Chocolate Church**, where musical and theatrical performances are presented throughout the year; there is also an art gallery here (Tel: 207/442-8455).

At 21 Elm the charming little storefront **Truffles Café** serves unusual lunchtime salads, soups, and desserts. Tel: (207) 442-8474. A couple of blocks up, at the corner of Center and High Streets, is **Kristina's**, a sophisticated, relaxed restaurant particularly well known for its voluptuous cheesecakes and pastries. Tel: (207) 442-8577.

STAYING IN BATH

If you're a nautical-history buff you'll find convenient lodging at the **Front Porch**, a homey B and B practically across the road from the Maine Maritime Museum. Built at the turn of the century by a shipyard foreman, this small house has just two guest rooms and an efficiency apartment, which, says hostess Barbara Boyland, means she's able to give each guest personal attention.

Among the bed-and-breakfasts in the historic district is the particularly welcoming **Inn at Bath**, a rambling structure built in 1810 with an elegant interior including twin parlors with matching black-marble fireplaces. All five guest rooms have private baths and are non-smoking. The surroundings are formal, but innkeeper Nick Bayard, a former Wall Streeter, has created an atmosphere that is friendly and personalized. Just a block beyond is **1024 Washington**, an imposing Victorian edifice built in the 1850s by Captain Gilbert Patten, who brought all of its rosy bricks from England as ballast in his ship. Inside, the sweeping staircase and towering ceilings recall a grand lifestyle; the claw-footed tubs in the capacious bathrooms (shared or private) invite long, leisurely soaks.

Just around the corner from Washington Street at 45 Pearl Street is the **Packard House**, a gracious Georgian of an earlier vintage. Built in 1790, it was later owned by Benjamin Packard, partner in one of the world's most successful shipbuilding companies. Today Vincent and Elizabeth Messler offer three guest rooms with period furnishings, and generous food and conversation at breakfast.

High Street leads north from the center of town to the **Fairhaven Inn** (turn left onto Whiskeag Road and then right onto North Bath Road). Set on 27 acres of forest and meadow near the Kennebec, this long, low 1790 farmhouse welcomes guests to enjoy the outdoors as well as the fireplace in the living room, and the cozy tavern room and library. There are seven guest rooms (private and shared baths) carefully decorated with antique and country furniture. About a mile (1½ km) away is **Merrymeeting Bay**, an important stopover on the Atlantic flyway; in spring and fall it buzzes with migratory bird activity.

Phippsburg Peninsula

Head south on Route 209 from the center of Bath 7 miles (11 km) to the town of **Phippsburg**, which encompasses a clutch of tiny villages spread across the entire wooded peninsula. Lapped to the west by Casco Bay and to the east by the Kennebec River, this long finger of land is especially rich in history, with traces of Viking, Indian, and Early American inhabitants still bearing witness in old burying grounds, settlement sites, forts, and even what may be runic stones. It was here that hardy souls made the first attempt at an English settlement on America's northeast coast in 1607, just months after their counterparts arrived in Jamestown, Virginia. They weathered a winter and built the pinnace *Virginia,* but, discouraged by illness and the harsh climate, they set sail in her and returned to England the following year.

The town was later named for Sir William Phips, arguably the New World's first millionaire. Phips was born in the mid-1600s in Woolwich (just east of Bath) and grew up to be a successful entrepreneur and sea captain. Among many notable accomplishments, he found and retrieved from a Spanish galleon sunk in the Bahamas some 300,000 pounds of gold and silver, which he presented to his English monarch; he was knighted in return.

TOURING THE PENINSULA

Plan a leisurely drive down Route 209 along the peninsula, enjoying the saltwater vistas along the way. Stop at the inviting shop at **Dromore Bay Herb Farm** for homemade candies, jellies, pickles, herbal vinegars, and dried herbs as well as unusual teas and small accessories for the house and garden. A short way farther on, look for the sign indicating a left turn onto Parker Head Road to the pocket-size white-clapboard village of **Phippsburg Center**. Headquartered in an 1859 schoolhouse on the left, the **Phippsburg Historical Society Museum** exhibits memorabilia from three centuries of shipbuilding as well as artifacts from Indian and Colonial times (open weekdays during the summer and by appointment year-round; Tel: 207/442-7606). Just beyond and also on the left is a white, steepled 1802 **Congregational church**.

STAYING ON THE
PHIPPSBURG PENINSULA

The small lane that leads up to the church circles around to **Riverview**, one of the earliest Cape Cod cottages in the area (ca. 1830). Perched at the river's edge, it is now a B and B that offers three homey rooms, one with private bath; all are furnished in period style. Smoking is not allowed.

A short distance farther, on the left, is the driveway to the **Captain Drummond House**, Phippsburg's oldest house and now an unpretentious B and B (closed November to April). There's nothing fancy about the non-smoking accommodations in this secluded home (built ca. 1770), but the genuine welcome offered by Donna Dillman and Ken Brigham, and the view of the water and islands from its perch atop a 125-foot bluff, make this an exceptionally pleasant place to stay. Originally a tavern frequented by ship captains and shipwrights, the low-ceilinged building has five fireplaces. Of the suite and three guest rooms, the River Room, with a private balcony overlooking the seascape, is favored among guests, many of whom return year after year. Mr. Brigham, who is a Coast Guard–licensed captain, also takes guests on afternoon and overnight cruises aboard his 37-foot O'Day sloop *Symbion*.

Back on Route 209, the way curves around to **Sebasco Lodge**, a genteel, 650-acre summer resort (open late June to early September) with golf, tennis, sailing, and swimming in a saltwater pool or at a private beach. The main driveway leads past Sebasco's nine-hole golf course and its assortment of guest cottages to **Rock Gardens Inn**, which successfully combines the intimacy of a casual country inn with access to all of the resort activities next door (for a fee). Its guest rooms are spread out among several buildings, some so close to the water that your first morning gaze out the window may make you feel as though you've slept aboard a boat. (Open mid-June to September.)

POPHAM BEACH

Beyond here Route 209 winds through salt marshes and salty seascapes—and the site of the 17th-century Popham Colony—all the way to **Popham Beach State Park**. Though Popham Beach never enjoyed the cachet of Bar Harbor, 100 years ago guests passed the summer in rambling hotels and boardinghouses here, spending languid days in sailing regattas and square dances and promenading along kerosene-lighted boardwalks in the evening. Today you can stroll the broad expanse of sand, wade through tide pools and scramble over the rocks, or have a picnic while monitoring the boating traffic entering and leaving the Kennebec. For lobster in the rough try **Spinney's Restaurant**, a good, old-fashioned beachfront joint with a tankful of lobsters awaiting your selection. Tel: (207) 389-1122. Just around the point is **Fort Popham**, which has stood watch over the broad mouth of the river since the early 1860s. In the Revolutionary War some 1,000 men under the command of Benedict Arnold (in his pre-traitor days) set off from near here on their disastrous march up the Kennebec to Canada to take over Quebec.

Georgetown Island

The next "finger" to the east is Georgetown Island, connected to the mainland by bridge just beyond Bath (turn right on Route 127 after crossing the Carleton Bridge from Bath, and continue on, crossing a small bridge onto the island). Drive down through Arrowsic and stop at **Arrowsic Pottery**, where Nan Kilbourn-Tara captures the colors of nature in her functional wares. The road then takes you across the small bridge to Georgetown and **Georgetown Pottery**, whose flower- and bird-bedecked pieces include soap dishes, ingenious butter keepers, and hummingbird feeders. A short distance beyond, turn left on Robinhood Road to Robinhood Marina. Here, in an unlikely location in the middle of a working boat yard, is the **Osprey**, widely regarded as one of this region's finest restaurants. The dining room and porch overlook the harbor and the namesake osprey nest. The menu is ambitious, but the chef is up to it, turning out exceptional dishes featuring local seafood presented in unusual ways. Perhaps the only drawback is the penchant for heavy sauces. Tel: (207) 371-2530.

Continue a short distance on Route 127 until you see a large American flag painted on a rock on your right. Turn right here onto Seguinland Road, named for a wonderful old 1901 summer hotel that is now called the **Grey Havens Inn** (open mid-May to mid-October). It's hard to tear yourself away from the front porch and what is certainly one of the most spectacular views offered by any Maine inn. Spread out below you in a sweeping panorama are Sheepscot Bay and its many islands. Seguin Island, rising high above the water, is crowned by one of the country's oldest lighthouses (1795); at 188 feet above sea level, it's also the highest on the Maine coast. When you do go inside you'll be drawn to the inn's relaxing living room, its ceiling adorned with antique baskets, and an imposing popplestone fireplace commanding center stage on the far wall. The Grey Havens also boasts the first picture window in Maine, delivered here by a very careful barge crew. The same Mr. Reid who built this turreted ark of a summer hotel donated vast acres of adjoining shorefront property to the state for what is now **Reid State Park**. Its three sandy beaches offer a choice of open surf or more protected backwater.

East from Bath

When you are able to wrest yourself away from the idylls of Georgetown, return to Route 1 and head north. Soon you'll see signs for the **Woolwich Historical Society Museum** on your right. While modern traffic speeds by on Route 1 just beyond the windows of this 1910 farmhouse, take the time to study the museum's exhibits from a slower-paced era, including a commendable collection of antique clothing, unusual quilts (many with unique embroidery and other fancy work), and memorabilia of local sea captains. Tel: (207) 443-4833.

Also on Route 1 in Woolwich is **Montsweag Farm**, an authentic, no-frills, very reasonably priced restaurant especially good for families. Housed in an old apple barn (the apple press is still here), it was opened by former Maine governor Sumner Sewall in the 1950s and is still owned by the descendants of this famous Bath shipbuilding family. Be sure to take a look at the governor's official blue-and-gold china displayed in a glass-fronted vitrine in the second dining room. Tel: (207) 443-6563. The nautical antiques and decor may inspire you to explore the **Montsweag Flea Market**, a jumble of parasol-shaded tables in a meadow close by the restaurant (closed in winter).

A bit farther along turn right off Route 1 onto Route 144 and follow the signs to the **Maine Yankee Energy Information Center**, at Maine's only nuclear power plant. Whether or not you are a proponent of generating electricity with nuclear power, this collection of hands-on exhibits, including a control-room simulator, offers an excellent opportunity to increase your understanding of it. Tel: (800) 458-0066.

In sharp contrast to this state-of-the-art technology is the **Squire Tarbox Inn** (open May through October), hidden away down winding Route 144 on the island of **Westport** (about 8 miles/13 km from Route 1). Karen and Bill Mitman's exceptional inn is steeped in country hospitality, offering authentic 18th- and 19th-century architecture, three parlors, 11 exceptionally comfortable rooms in the Federal main house and older attached barn, and a wonderfully restorative setting. Adding to the appeal are the artful four-course fireside dinners served in a very atmospheric barn dining room beneath ceiling beams that were once ship timbers (the dining room is open to the public by reservation; Tel: 207/882-7693). Before dinner you're invited to enjoy a drink and nibble on a selection of goat's cheeses made right here at the inn. Top off the evening with a visit to the goat barn at milking time—the small herd of Nubians are delightfully engaging creatures.

WISCASSET

All traffic headed along this stretch of Route 1 must pass through the center of Wiscasset (11 miles/18 km beyond Bath), making for notoriously slow going on weekend afternoons in summer. A block away from this patience-testing bottleneck, however, neighborhoods of 19th-century white-clapboard mansions sleep quietly under a canopy of trees, seemingly as removed from today's bumper-to-bumper snarl as they were from yesteryear's riverfront bustle. In Wiscasset's heyday at the start of the 1800 as many as 35 square-riggers home-ported here, setting sail down the Sheepscot River to the sea, carrying masts and spars to Europe and salted fish to the Caribbean. In Europe the masts were exchanged for salt crucial to the fish business. From the Caribbean vessels that had borne the fish and more lumber to the islands returned down east brimming with kegs of molasses and rum. One young boy who stood on the waterfront here in 1806 before embarking on a transatlantic voyage was James Fenimore Cooper; he later recounted his adventure in *Tale of the Sea*.

Local shipyards flourished in support of this sea trade, and both industries brought scores of seamen and lumbermen here in search of their fortunes. For the hard-living and hard-drinking among them, a secure jail house was built in 1811. Today in the **Old Jail Museum**, on Federal Street (Route 218), visitors may tour the jailer's house and the original dank cells, making note of the window bars and heavy metal doors as well as 19th-century graffiti scratched on the thick granite walls. Tel: (207) 882-6817.

The more prominent members of the community lived far more comfortably, and today Wiscasset is rich with its heritage of early-1800s sea captains' houses, giving it the basis for its claim to be the prettiest village in Maine. At the bend in the road as you come through town you'll see the handsome 1835 edifice of the **Bailey Inn** on your left. Long known as The Ledges, it had grown tired in recent years until new owners Joe Sullivan and Sue Rizzo renovated, renamed, and reopened it in 1992. Good, reasonably priced breakfasts, lunches, and dinners are served in the carriage-house pub and the more formal dining rooms. The seven bedrooms (all with private bath) on the second and third floors are currently being redone.

One 19th-century pillar of local society even fancied living in a copy of a Scottish castle, which he built in 1807. **Castle Tucker,** a couple of blocks off Route 1 at the corner of Lee and High streets, is especially notable for its elegant curving portico, freestanding elliptical staircase, and original wallpapers. It's open only in July and August, but you're welcome to walk the grounds when it's closed (Tel: 207/882-7364). The 1852 sea captain's house that has become the **Musical Wonder House** is just up High Street, where you can see and listen to one of the world's finest antique music box collections (open daily from June to mid-October; for guided tours, Tel: 207/882-7163). On Route 1 (at the corner of Main and Federal streets) is the **Nickels-Sortwell House,** a classic Federal mansion with a beautiful elliptical staircase. It is owned and administered by the Society for the Preservation of New England Antiquities. (Open Wednesday through Sunday afternoons from June through September; Tel: 207-882-6218.)

In keeping with Wiscasset's grand captains' homes and heritage of elegant living, the town has a number of very good antiques shops. As you browse through the shops, keep in mind that you may even stumble onto a particularly precious piece once owned by Marie Antoinette. Stories persist about Wiscasset sea captain Stephen Clough and his thwarted plans to spirit the doomed French queen to safety here. It's said a nearby house was prepared for her, and her furniture was even sent on ahead (to end up as treasured heirlooms in old Wiscasset family homes).

Among the town's fine shops is the **Marston House,** on your left at the corner of Main Street (Route 1) and Middle Street, in a white house whose front porch is always bedecked with flags and bunting. Dealers Sharon and Paul Mrozinski also operate a small, pleasant B and B in a separate carriage house behind the main house (open May through November). For almost three decades **Marine Antiques,** also on Route 1, has specialized in ship models, figureheads, sea chests, whaling journals, and the like. Folk art and Americana are the stock-in-trade at the **Coach House,** on Pleasant Street just off Main.

Just before Route 1 crosses the Sheepscot River bridge to Edgecomb, turn right onto Water Street, where you'll find **Le Garage,** a good choice for lunch or dinner (ask for a table on the glassed-in porch). Overlooking the Sheepscot River and

what's left of the schooners *Hesper* and *Luther Little,* this
1920s-era garage is a favorite of locals as well as travellers
(reservations are a very good idea in season; Tel: 207/882-
5409). Its extensive menu is highlighted by local lamb and
seafood dishes, and this is one of the few places you'll find
authentic finnan haddie—salty smoked haddock in cream
sauce. For lighter meals and snacks, including delicious
home-baked goods, try **Sarah's Pizza and Café**, on Main
Street (Tel: 207/882-7504). If you're in the mood for a picnic
you can purchase delicious supplies at **Treats**, also on Main
Street, and then follow Route 1 across the bridge, taking an
immediate right at the other end. This will bring you to **Fort
Edgecomb Memorial**, an 1809 octagonal blockhouse with
picnic tables overlooking the water.

On Route 1 in **Edgecomb**, in a handsome building on the
left, is **Sheepscot River Pottery**. In addition to the flowered
pottery made right here you'll find a pleasing assortment of
jewelry and furniture. Also on Route 1 in Edgecomb, a bit
farther on and still on the left, is the huge, yellow, peaked-
roof barn of **Partridge Antiques**. The unusually fine paintings and furniture that Londoners Tatiana and Jack Partridge
display in their three-room gallery draw serious antiques
hounds from far and wide.

THE BOOTHBAY REGION

From Route 1 the Boothbay region lies off to your right,
down Route 27 (turn soon after crossing the Sheepscot River
bridge into Edgecomb). Three miles (5 km) south along
Route 27 is **Edgecomb Potters**, which has grown like Topsy
as its business has increased. Inside this complex of barn-
red buildings you'll find beautiful handcrafted jewelry as
well as finely made pottery. After crossing the town line into
Boothbay you'll pass by a bit of Maine history preserved at
the **Boothbay Railway Village**, where the nearly 100-year-old
cars of the narrow-gauge Wiscasset, Waterville and Farmington Railroad trace a circular track through a miniature New
England village. Open early June through early October; Tel:
(207) 633-4727.

Just beyond the Boothbay Region Information Center on
your right, Route 27 curves around to the left, where you'll
see the driveway leading up to a shady knoll and the 200-year-
old pillared white edifice of the **Kenniston Hill Inn**. There are
ten non-smoking guest rooms here, four with fireplaces, and
all with appropriate period furnishings and private bath. Like
the Kenniston Hill Inn, the **Five Gables Inn** (open June
through October) in nearby **East Boothbay** offers a quiet

retreat just enough removed from the bustle of downtown Boothbay Harbor. To reach East Boothbay, continue on Route 27 around the Boothbay town common and down the road, turning left across from the Shop 'n' Save plaza onto Route 96. The Five Gables is on Murray Hill Road (turn right at the East Boothbay General Store, which, by the way, claims to have one of the best wine selections in the area). The region's last remaining old summer hotel, the Five Gables was completely renovated into a luxurious small inn in 1988. Five of the 15 rooms (all with water views) have working fireplaces, and all are pleasingly furnished with handsome reproduction antiques and fine fabrics.

East Boothbay has long enjoyed high regard as a boat-building town, its yards having built sturdy working vessels and patrician yachts, including the famous *America*. Also here is the **Andersen Studio**, whose lifelike stoneware animal sculptures are prized by collectors. Practically next door is **Lobstermen's Wharf**, a seafood restaurant popular with the locals, especially on summer Sunday afternoons when a band plays outside on the dock. Tel: (207) 633-3443.

Route 96 continues all the way to the end of the peninsula and **Ocean Point**. It's a peaceful, scenic drive along the shore of Linekin Bay to this quiet, old-fashioned summer colony where the view from small rocky beaches takes in the broad expanse of the Atlantic, dotted with historic islands. Among them is storied Damariscove, where a ghost is said to wander on dark and stormy nights. Monhegan Island is also visible from here on all but cloudy or foggy days.

Boothbay Harbor

Around the next point is Boothbay Harbor (retrace your way back up Route 96, then go south on Route 27), originally an unassuming fishing and boat-building village just like its neighbors. Hordes of summer visitors over the years have changed all that, and today cars stream down Route 27 to the harbor bringing tourists to shop, take sightseeing boat rides, and stroll the docks enjoying all the waterfront attractions. Things slow right down off-season, however, and in the quieter months the real Boothbay Harbor emerges once more from the caricature it assumes in the summertime.

The waterfront is the center of activity in Boothbay Harbor because it is the gateway to the sea, the primary element in the town's personality. (It was also here, on the docks of the east side of the harbor, that the movie *Carousel* was filmed.) Join the crowd and climb aboard an excursion boat, whether power or a more leisurely sail. There are numerous boats to choose among, all with ticket desks set up on the dock (it's wise to reserve a space a few hours in advance). Even a short trip of a couple of hours will take you across the outer harbor and past spruce-clad islands and impressive summer homes to the open ocean. You can also opt for a daylong trip aboard the *Balmy Days II* (Tel: 207/633-2284) out to rugged **Monhegan Island**, artists' colony, lobstermen's community, and wildlife sanctuary (Monhegan is discussed further under Port Clyde, below). Another vessel, the *Argo*, goes to **Cabbage Island** twice a day for old-fashioned clambakes with all the trimmings (Tel: 207/633-7200).

Boothbay Harbor's web of narrow streets is lined with shops vending everything from amusing tee-shirts to fine crafts and gifts. Two especially noteworthy shops are the **Village Store** and **Lupine Court**, both on Townsend Avenue. The former has a tasteful selection of home furnishings, while the latter offers unusual crafts, many of them with a cat theme. Just down and across the street, **A Silver Lining** sells delicate gold, vermeil, and silver jewelry fashioned after flowers and wildlife. Around the corner on McKown Street, **Abacus Gallery** showcases a delightfully clever array of contemporary crafts.

DINING AND STAYING IN BOOTHBAY HARBOR

For a quick snack, look for **Brud**, who's been selling wieners from his hot-dog cart for decades—he's usually somewhere near the intersection of McKown and Townsend. For more substantial dining in Boothbay Harbor there are innumerable choices, and while most menus were once heavy with fried seafood and, of course, steamed lobster, you can now find a far more stimulating variety. The **Black Orchid**, on the Byway (across from the funky old bowling alley), serves creditable Northern Italian cuisine in a pleasant setting of linen tablecloths and candlelight (open mid-May through mid-October; Tel: 207/633-6659). The **Bocce Club** upstairs offers a raw bar and an atmosphere more like that of a trattoria. Nearby, just off Townsend Avenue at the entrance to the municipal parking lot, is **No Anchovies**, a less formal eatery also specializing in Italian dishes (Tel: 207/633-2130). The **Russell House**, on Route 27 on the way to the harbor, is another pleasant choice, offering romantic dining in the atmosphere of a small inn (Tel: 207/633-6656).

For a fancier evening drive out Atlantic Avenue, on the eastern side of the harbor, to the **Spruce Point Inn**. The formal dining room here caters both to the guests of this grand old summer resort and to the public (reservations required; Tel: 207/633-4152). The chef has won awards for his Continental presentations of the freshest local seafoods. The inn is open from late May through late October.

The Spruce Point Inn is also one of the more gracious places to stay in the Boothbay region. Situated on its own 100-acre peninsula, it has been fashionable for years, especially when the Kennedys used to come here. Recently it has undergone a thorough renovation that has dressed it up but left unchanged its feeling of relaxed elegance.

The dozens of other lodging choices range from motels and cottages, to unpretentious family resorts on the water, to a gaggle of in-town B and Bs. Among the last, the **Welch House** has a very convenient location, perched atop McKown Hill overlooking the town and the sea. If you're lucky, innkeeper Martha Mason will be making her special chocolate-raspberry-ripple muffins for breakfast the day you're here. (Open mid-April through mid-October.)

Two especially appealing lodging choices on nearby Southport Island are the **Lawnmeer Inn**, just across the bridge to the island, and the **Newagen Seaside Inn**, at the island's southern tip. The Lawnmeer has rooms both in the old inn and in a motel annex, plus one in a tiny former smokehouse (perfect for honeymooners). Everyone here looks forward to a leisurely afternoon spent doing absolutely nothing but sitting in one of the Adirondack lawn chairs watching the boats pass by on Townsend Gut. (Open mid-May to mid-October.) Summer guests at the Newagen have been enjoying the inn's setting on a mile of bold coastline for nearly a century. Among the pastimes here are swimming in a heated freshwater or saltwater pool, tennis, and traditional lawn games. **Robinson's Wharf**, across from the Newagen Inn, is a good place to have lobster in the rough. The dockside picnic tables overlook the boats that bring the catch ashore (Tel: 207/633-3830). There are also several similar places along the eastern waterfront in Boothbay Harbor.

NEWCASTLE AND DAMARISCOTTA

If time allows, continue on to Newcastle and Damariscotta via River Road rather than Route 1. To do this, retrace your steps up from Boothbay Harbor on Route 27 to the **Basket Barn of Maine** (great selection of baskets and wicker imported from around the world). Just beyond, turn right onto River Road, which follows the Damariscotta River for approximately 12 miles (19 km) until it brings you to the villages of Newcastle and Damariscotta, perched on opposite banks of the river and linked by a small bridge. About halfway along River Road keep an eye peeled for the distinctive black-and-gold sign on the left marking the driveway for **David and Susan Margonelli Fine Furniture**. In their small showroom you'll see examples of their master cabinet-making and you can order a special piece for your home.

River Road also passes by the front door of the highly acclaimed **Newcastle Inn**. An inn for decades, it has come into its own under the loving care of keepers Ted and Chris Sprague. The common rooms are welcoming, with wing chairs, a fireplace, a stenciled floor, and wicker furniture on the glassed-in porch; most of the bedrooms feature four-poster or canopy beds, and all are non-smoking. But it is Chris's inspired cooking that brings people here from far and wide. In the intimate dining room, every evening in summer and on weekends in winter, diners are dazzled by five exquisitely flavored and beautifully presented courses (the dining room is open to the public by reservation; Tel: 207/563-5685). It's no wonder the inn has been lauded in *Yankee* magazine, *Food & Wine,* and several other publications. Chris shares her love of cooking and her recipes in her *Newcastle Inn Cookbook,* which you can buy either at the inn or at the **Maine Coast Book Shop**, an excellent bookseller on Main Street in Damariscotta.

A wide variety of fancy foods is offered by **Weatherbird Trading Company**, a block from Main Street, where you'll also find appealing accents for the home and women's clothing. Downstairs is **Damariscotta Pottery**, whose bold colors and primitive designs are reminiscent of majolica. Two other shops to browse before leaving the area are the **Victorian Stable**, on Water Street, where the work of some 100 Maine craftspeople is displayed in what were formerly this big old stable's box stalls; and **Kaja Veilleux Antiques**, close by the Newcastle Inn. Here, in a handsome old brick building that was once a shipping company's office, are three floors of fine antiques.

The **Chapman-Hall House**, at the opposite end of the Main Street business district, is the area's oldest house. Built in 1754, it's been restored and is open on summer afternoons. In addition to the authentic interior, there are an herb garden and 18th-century rosebushes on the grounds.

PEMAQUID TO WALDOBORO

Just across the street from the Chapman-Hall House, Routes 129 and 130 lead down to tiny waterside villages clinging to the two fingers of the peninsula that form the eastern side of the Damariscotta River. Just outside Damariscotta the two routes separate, with 129 bearing off to the right, taking you to the lobstering and boat-building community of **South Bristol**. The historic old Thompson ice house on Route 129 is under restoration, funded in part by an ice-cream social held every summer. At the tip of this finger is **Christmas Cove**, visited and named by Captain John Smith on Christmas day, 1614. One of the tiny hamlet's most famous modern visitors is Walter Cronkite, who always stops here when cruising down east on board his boat *Wyntje.* In his book *North by Northeast,* Cronkite calls the **Shore Restaurant and Dory Bar** (Tel: 207/644-8540) at the **Coveside Inn** "a mandatory stop for cruising yachtsmen"—and his saying so has surely helped to make it so. A look at the worldwide assortment of signal flags and burgees hung from the ceiling of the bar indicates that sailors from all over have donned their brick-red pants and come ashore to talk about the day's winds over a rum at the bar and to enjoy seafood or steak in the dining room overlooking the harbor. For lodging, the Coveside offers a choice of waterfront motel units or simpler rooms in a big red Victorian inn across the road (open June through mid-September).

Pemaquid

Route 130 wanders down the other finger of the peninsula to the Pemaquid area. Turn right on 130 to **Pemaquid Harbor**, where the **Pemaquid Fishermen's Co-op**, the oldest such cooperative in the country, offers lobsters in the rough. **Pemaquid Beach** is a pleasant sandy stretch, an exception along this rockbound coast. This is also the site of Maine's "Lost City," where today the **Colonial Pemaquid Restoration** maintains one of the world's few on-site archaeological museums open to the public. Excavations have uncovered early-1600s foundations of homes, a tavern, a jail, and the custom house where all ships travelling between the Kennebec and St. Croix rivers were required to check in. A diorama in the museum explains the entire layout of the 1620 settlement. Nearby is **Fort William Henry**, a 1907 replica of the third in a series of three English forts built here in past centuries.

At the very tip of this peninsula is **Pemaquid Point**, with its oft-photographed lighthouse standing firm above spectacular crashing surf. Climb about the rocks, but be careful, as more than one unwary soul has been swept to his death here. The lighthouse is now the **Fishermen's Museum**, displaying a simple but engaging collection of local seafaring memorabilia. In the **Pemaquid Art Gallery**, across the way, you'll find works by local artists; requested donations go toward art scholarships for local high-school students.

Just outside the entrance to the lighthouse parking lot is the **Hotel Pemaquid**, a lovely, sleepy old summer hotel (recently restored) with irresistible front-porch rockers. (Open mid-May through mid-October.) The **Bradley Inn**, practically across the street and also recently restored, offers a similarly lazy old-time Maine atmosphere. It has 12 non-smoking guest rooms (all with private bath) and a cottage.

New Harbor and Round Pound

When you leave Pemaquid Point, go a short way back up Route 130 and turn right on Route 32 north to the small fishing village of New Harbor. There the *Hardy III* offers daily excursions to Monhegan Island (see below), plus trips to see the puffins on Eastern Egg Rock. **Shaw's**, with a balcony above the harbor, is a favorite place for eating lobster in the rough (Tel: 207/677-2200).

Route 32 continues on to the charming village of Round Pound, so named because of its curving harbor. After a day at Pemaquid Point, this is a perfect place to spend the night. The **Briar Rose B & B** here has two rooms on the second floor (shared bath), while the entire third floor is a reasonably priced suite with its own sitting room. All rooms are non-smoking. Downstairs, host Anita Palsgrove maintains a small antiques shop. Across the street from the Briar Rose is the **Granite Hall Store**, whose inventory includes penny candy, ice cream, toys, books, local pottery decorated with blueberries; woollens from Ireland, Scotland, and Maine; and antiques and baskets.

You'll find a variety of appealing artisans' shops in the village, too, including **Pemaquid Floorcloths, Heirloom Woodworkers** (rocking horses and Shaker furniture), the **Scottish Lion Blacksmith, Laberge Stained Glass Design, Village Weavers, Blueledge Studio Pottery,** and **Wingset**, makers of working decoys.

Waldoboro and Friendship

Route 32 continues from Round Pond through Medomak to Waldoboro, named for Bostonian Samuel Waldo, who in the mid-1700s secured a large tract along this part of the coast and settled it by importing 40 German families. Their 1772 meetinghouse still stands (on Route 220), and a marker in the adjacent graveyard tells their bleak story: "This town was settled in 1748 by Germans who immigrated to this place with the promise and expectation of finding a prosperous city, instead of which they found nothing but wilderness."

If you're an aficionado of Oriental rugs, pop into **Central Asian Artifacts**, at the corner of Main and Jefferson streets. Very pleasant overnight accommodations are offered nearby at the **Broad Bay Inn**, a restored 1830 Colonial that also has a small art gallery in its barn. Hosts Jim and Libby Hopkins enjoy discussing their enduring love of the arts with guests over tea and Sherry in the afternoon or a generous breakfast in the morning. They have five guest rooms sharing three baths (closed in January). For dinner, try the **Snow Turtle Inn**, at Route 32 and Old Route 1. Innkeeper Aileen Allen is the chef, preparing everything from veal Marsala, roast duck, and raspberry chicken, to blackened red snapper and Cajun scallops. There are two candle-lit dining rooms in this 1803 sea merchant's house, plus a sun porch for the warmer months. Tel: (207) 832-4423. (The pleasant guest rooms upstairs include the Christmas Room, complete with a decorated "evergreen" tree at the head of the bed.) If you're more in the mood for down-home cooking like meat loaf and corned-beef hash (or even tripe), there's the classic choice for road food, **Moody's Diner**, up on Route 1. Tel: (207) 832-7468.

The lobstering town of **Friendship** is 10 miles (16 km) south of Waldoboro on Route 220. Famous for its Friendship sloops, which have been built here since 1753, it hosts an annual Friendship Sloop Days celebration every summer (there's also one in Boothbay Harbor). A road sign recites the engaging names and distances of some other Maine communities: "Freedom 45; Liberty 3; Harmony 96; Unity 52; Union 20; Hope 27. Friendship is here."

THOMASTON, TENANTS HARBOR, AND PORT CLYDE

In 1840 there were only seven millionaires in the entire country, and Thomaston was home to two of them. Route 1 runs right through the middle of town, with stately mansions from that boom time gracing both sides of the street. Some of them are early-1800s Federals, while others are confections from the Victorian era. Once stunning in their white-clapboard and dark-green-shuttered finery, some of these elegant ladies have become a bit tattered over time as a result of a decline in the local shipbuilding business, but they remain as proud and beautiful testimony to the wealth of the local citizenry a century ago. With the incongruous backdrop of a huge cement plant, **Montpelier** stands at the head of the street. It is a replica of the mansion built in 1794 by General Henry Knox, the rotund (five feet six inches, 300 pounds) Bostonian who became a Revolutionary War hero and then America's first secretary of state. Married to the granddaughter of Samuel Waldo, who owned all of this area, he built himself a pretentious mansion complete with oval dining room, high ceilings, and semi-flying staircase. By 1871 it had fallen into disrepair and was torn down, then rebuilt in the 1930s through the generosity of Camden summer resident Cyrus Curtis. Alas, the replica has now also become shabby, like some of her less flamboyant sisters down the street.

Route 131 leads past Montpelier down toward the sea and the village of **Tenants Harbor**—little more than a bend in the road—where the **East Wind Inn**, originally a sail loft, proffers simple hospitality, harbor-view bedrooms, and salty breezes. The dining room, with windows overlooking the working harbor, serves Continental preparations of local seafood (Tel: 207/372-6366). In summer the wraparound porch is a pleasing spot for a cocktail.

Beyond Tenants Harbor is **Port Clyde**, where artist Andrew Wyeth summered as a child. Stop into the **Port Clyde General Store**, surely the embodiment of everyone's fantasy of the perfect little country store.

Monhegan Island

The mail boat *Laura B* travels between Port Clyde and Monhegan Island, where Andrew Wyeth's son Jamie now spends summers in a home that previously belonged to artist Rockwell Kent. Monhegan has always appealed to artists, who come here for visual inspiration and spiritual renewal. Many of them hang out shingles with hours during which they'll welcome you into their studios. On Monhegan the deer run freely in the woods, and islanders say you'll find fairy houses beneath moss-covered tree stumps. Take time to walk the path from the tiny harborfront village across the island to the other side. Here, as you stretch out for a rest or a picnic on high, rocky headlands, you can look down at crashing surf and out to a wide open sea that reaches all the way to Spain.

Overnight lodging on Monhegan is limited, and early reservations are essential during July and August. Before your boat even docks you'll spot the turreted **Island Inn** keeping watch above the harbor. It's an old-fashioned no-frills summer hotel (open June through September) with small, simple rooms; all of them have lovely views of either the harbor or the meadow (the harbor-view rooms are a bit more expensive). The dining room serves three unpretentious meals a day to guests and the public (Tel: 207/596-0371). **Tribler Cottage** and **Shining Sails** both offer very nice efficiency apartments and are open year-round.

ROCKLAND

Rockland, about 15 miles (24 km) northeast of Port Clyde at the western head of Penobscot Bay, has long claimed to be the "Lobster Capital of the World," with a big Seafood Festival every August to celebrate its number-one industry. Now this broad, busy harbor also lays claim to the title "Windjammer Capital of the World." Few can argue, for more windjammers hoist their sails here than in any other port. Every week during summer and fall passengers climb aboard almost a dozen schooners—some old and some authentic reproductions—to sail among the islands of Penobscot Bay and drop anchor each evening in a new harbor. (For brochures on various vessels in the fleet, call the Maine Windjammer Association; Tel: 800/MAINE-80.) The hospitality is genuine, the accommodations simple, the food hearty, and the camaraderie irresistible. It's also one of the last great vacation bargains. All of which explains why so many people come back year after year to go windjamming. If you can't join them, walk out to the lighthouse at the end of the **Rockland Breakwater** on the eastern side of the harbor on a Monday morning and watch as they sail by. You may also spot the jaunty motor vessel *Pauline,* a converted sardine carrier that now takes passengers on week-long cruises in a bit more luxury than on the windjammers (Tel: 800/999-7352).

Farnsworth Art Museum and Homestead

Certainly the greatest cultural treasure in Rockland is the Farnsworth Art Museum and Homestead, on Elm Street. Among the highlights of its collection are works by N. C., Andrew, and Jamie Wyeth, as well as paintings by Winslow Homer and American marine impressionist William Partridge Burpee, and the largest collection anywhere of sculptures by Louise Nevelson, who moved here as a child with her family from Ukraine. The elegant Georgian Revival library has an extensive collection of reference materials, and there's also a good museum shop.

Across the garden from the museum is the Farnsworth Homestead, the 1850 Greek Revival mansion where Lucy

Farnsworth, the maiden daughter of a wealthy businessman, lived as a virtual recluse until her death at the age of 96. Her father enjoyed great success in the local lime industry and from his fleet of ships and other ventures, including the area's first water and gas company. The house is as Miss Farnsworth left it, filled with High Victorian velvet, lace, satin furnishings, and clumsy, machine-made American furniture that Mr. Farnsworth had brought from Boston on his ships. Hung on the walls are chromolithographs, cheap copies of oil paintings; the fireplace mantel is not marble but rather glass painted to look like it; and doors and wood trim are painted to effect fine wood grains. This striking lack of fine furnishings seems odd in the home of a woman who was to leave all of her money for the establishment of an art museum. Rather a strange soul, Miss Lucy hardly ever let anyone into the house, collecting monthly rent from her tenants at the dining-room window. She put the cash in the soup tureen and in other hiding places throughout the house, creating what later became a treasure hunt for curators.

Because of the Farnsworth Museum's close ties with the Wyeths, it recently has been given the Olson house, subject of Andrew Wyeth's renowned painting *Christina's World*. Located 17 miles (27 km) south of the museum in Cushing, it was donated by Apple Computer CEO John Sculley. Plans are to open it to the public on a limited basis in the summer of 1993. (Call the Farnsworth for information; Tel: 207/596-6457.)

Elsewhere in the Rockland Area

Another museum of note in Rockland is the **Shore Village Museum**, 104 Limerock Street, with a fine collection of lighthouse memorabilia, antique clothing, and dolls. Down at the town of **Owls Head**, 2 miles (3 km) from Rockland on Route 73, the **Owls Head Transportation Museum** boasts an outstanding collection of antique autos and planes; on summer weekends it hosts spectacular air shows. **Jessica's**, on Route 73 at the Rockland–Owls Head line, is a "European bistro" in a restored Victorian house that's become a favorite among local connoisseurs of fine dining (Tel: 207/596-0770). For a picnic in the area there's no better place than the rocks surrounding the 1825 **Owls Head Lighthouse** (go north from the Transportation Museum to a dirt road that leads to a parking area and walk in from there). You'll dine with spectacular views of the islands of the Muscle Ridge Channel. A good place to pick up sandwiches is the **Brown Bag**, at 606 Main Street, just north of the center of Rockland. The homemade breads they use are delicious, and in addition to the usual BLTs, egg salad, and such, they offer hummus and veggies, a falafel pocket, and a lentil burger. This is also an excellent place to have breakfast. Tel: (207) 596-6372.

Vinalhaven and North Haven Islands

At the Rockland ferry terminal you can catch shuttles several times daily to two nearby islands that, despite their proximity to each other, offer quite different Maine island experiences. The long, large island of Vinalhaven is the place for spending a barefoot summer in a simple cottage (request a list of rentals from the Rockland Chamber of Commerce; Tel: 207/596-0376), while North Haven has long been an exclusive summer resort.

VINALHAVEN

Vinalhaven's heritage is one of working-class folk, beginning with the fishermen who settled it, and followed by the European stonecutters who came here in the 19th century to work the granite quarries (several of which are now excellent swimming holes). Vinalhaven granite was carried aboard Maine downeasters and multimasted schooners to New York and other mainland cities, where it helped build some of their most impressive municipal buildings, including most of New York's Greenwich Village and Boston's North End. (The granite walls of the library in the main village of **Carver's Harbor** are the island's only construction of local stone, a gift to the community from Andrew Carnegie.)

Other industries that once flourished here include ice cutting, fishing, shipbuilding, farming, and one of the country's biggest fishing net factories. In the years just after the Civil War the island's population reached a peak of 4,000. Today, however, things are far quieter, and only the shabby Victorian buildings in Carver's Harbor speak of the old glory days. Most notable among current residents is *LOVE* artist Robert Indiana, who lives right in the center of town in the former Masonic temple. You can see some of his work at the **Fog Gallery**, a short walk from the ferry landing.

If you come to Vinalhaven for just a night or a weekend, you'll find a hospitable welcome at several B and Bs in Carver's Harbor. Closest to the harbor is the **Libby House**, a handsome white Victorian furnished with solid carved beds, fainting couches, and even a love seat in one of the bathrooms. (Open summer and fall.) The **Morning Glory** combines Victorian architecture with furnishings collected by innkeeper Gloria Strazar as she has worked and travelled in South America, Europe, Asia, and Africa. (Open April through December.) A couple of blocks away is the **Fox Island Inn**, with simple and pleasant accommodations sparked by an extensive collection of fox portraits. (Open May through October.)

There's also a very nice motel right on the harbor called the **Tidewater Inn**, which offers a choice of rooms or efficiencies, most with sun decks right over the water. The Tidewater also rents bicycles on a daily basis.

NORTH HAVEN
In contrast to neighboring Vinalhaven, North Haven has long been a summer retreat for the wealthy, including the likes of IBM founding father Tom Watson and several generations of others among America's industrial and financial gentry. Their lifestyles are very low-key, however, and the island's simple nature has not been changed by their presence. In the main town of North Haven, where the ferry puts into port, **North Island Yarn Shop** sells beautiful hand-knitted sweaters with pastoral scenes from wool sheared, spun, and dyed right on the island. Across the street is an artists' gallery in the old general store.

A couple of miles (3 km) outside of town is the **Pulpit Harbor Inn**, a small country inn (open May through October) with a good dining room (by reservation; Tel: 207/867-2219). If you don't have a car, call and the innkeepers will be glad to fetch you from town. The rooms here are brightened with antiques, quilts, and paintings by local artists; the dinners are accompanied by freshly picked home-grown vegetables.

ROCKPORT

From downtown Rockland follow Route 1 half a mile (1 km) north. Look for Waldo Avenue and signs for the right-hand turnoff to the **Samoset**, a full-service resort with a golf course that's been hailed by *Golf Digest* as one of the country's most scenic. The Samoset's guest rooms, many with water views, are comfortable and modern in decor. **Marcel's**, the resort's restaurant, is a pleasant place for lunch with a view of the blue expanse of Penobscot Bay. At dinner, more formal service emphasizes table-side preparation (Tel: 207/594-2511).

Nearby is the road to the **Rockland Breakwater**, a long stone wall atop which you can walk out to the **Rockland lighthouse**. At the intersection of Routes 1 and 90 (at the flashing light) is the **Market Basket**, with exceptional sandwiches, salads, wines, and prepared foods that are ideal if you've planned a picnic.

Turn right onto Route 90, which takes you into the village

of Rockport, cited by Charles Kuralt in a recent *TV Guide* article as one of his five favorite places "on the road." Route 90 dead-ends in front of an old general store that's now **L. E. Leonard**, a gallery of unusual furnishings from such places as Indonesia and northern China. If you turn right here, and then left, you'll come to the **Artisans School**, where wooden boat–building skills are kept alive through the construction of traditional craft. You may watch the work under way from a visitors' balcony.

If you turn left at L. E. Leonard and continue across the bridge you'll come into the center of Rockport, with its picture-postcard harbor down to your right. Old lime kilns, remnants of a booming 19th-century industry, can still be seen on the harborfront. An extremely volatile cargo (if wetted, it burst into flames), lime from Rockport was carried aboard local downeasters and schooners to the Caribbean. Reminiscent of those times is the lovely *Timberwind,* the only windjammer sailing from here today. Tel: (800) 624-6013.

The headquarters for the highly regarded **Maine Photographic Workshops** is in the middle of Rockport. Professional photographers, and those who would like to be, flock here from all over the country to enroll in courses taught by some of the field's most outstanding artists (Tel: 207/236-8581). Down toward the water is the **Sail Loft**, unfailingly good for fresh seafood prepared simply and elegantly at lunch and dinner. Tel: (207) 236-2330.

Out on Route 1 in Rockport is **Maine Sport Outfitters**, a "mini L. L. Bean" with a wide selection of camping and outing equipment and a full schedule of classes in sea kayaking and other outdoor pursuits. If you don't plan to stop here, a far more scenic route from Rockport to Camden follows Rockport's Main Street up the hill, past the **Rockport Opera House** on your right (the **Bay Chamber Concerts** held here were founded by members of the Curtis, Bok, and Zimbalist families; Tel: 207/236-2823). Bear to the right here, stopping at the **Maine Coast Artists Gallery**, which houses excellent changing exhibitions of contemporary art by Maine artists all summer long, in an old firehouse. Just beyond on the right is **Ann Kilham**'s gallery, with appealing Advent calendars and brightly colored postcards featuring hand-drawn scenes of the Maine coast. One of her postcards depicts the black-and-white-striped "Oreo cookie cows" you'll pass by in the meadows of Aldemere Farm, which boasts the country's largest herd of Belted Galloways, a breed of Scottish beef cattle.

Continue on to Camden either straight along upper Chestnut Street or turn right just beyond the graveyard and follow leafy, winding upper Bayview Street. Both roads take you past marvelous shingled summer "cottages"; and the latter route offers tantalizing snippets of sea views through the stone gates and winding driveways. Summer residents of this impressive neighborhood include John Sculley of Apple Computer as well as descendants of old, established Philadelphia and Boston families, like the Boks and the Curtises, who first erected their stylish summer homes here in the earlier part of the century.

CAMDEN

Camden shipwrights built their first schooner in 1796 and later set a record by producing the world's first six-master, the *George W. Wells.* Today more yacht repair than actual shipbuilding takes place here (mostly at the large Wayfarer Marine yard on the east side of the harbor), including major refits on luxury yachts that come here from the Caribbean for the summer. There aren't any six-masters around, but a number of **passenger-carrying windjammers** do grace the harbor with their traditional beauty. Some offer short day sails, while others take guests on week-long cruises. There are also a couple of former lobster boats that offer sightseeing among the islands of Penobscot Bay plus a close-up look at lobster trap hauling; you'll find their sign-up desks beneath parasols on the town landing (*Lively Lady,* Tel: 207/ 236-6672; *Belselma,* Tel: 207/236-2101).

Famous for the stunning juxtaposition of its harbor and hills, Camden figured in many of FitzHugh Lane's most beautiful paintings. Climb to the top of **Mount Battie** (in **Camden Hills State Park**)—by car if not by foot—for the best view of the harbor, bay, and islands; locals chuckle over the fact that when *Peyton Place* was filmed here, this well-known lookout was used as Allison's "secret place." Nearby Mount Megunticook's distinctive profile is visible from such a distance that it was used as a navigational landmark by Champlain and fellow explorers searching for the Northwest Passage. Today's cruising yachtsmen also navigate their way across beautiful Penobscot Bay to Camden, among them baby guru Dr. Benjamin Spock and actor Christopher Reeve, who keeps his sailboat *Sea Angel* here.

Working mills once stood along the banks of the Megunticook River, harnessing its force as it rushed through town and over a waterfall into the harbor. Today one of the old mills has been reborn as a complex called **Highland Mill,** with offices, shops, and a small motel, the **Highland Mill Inn,** at the corner of Washington and Mechanic streets. The inn has seven high-ceilinged, Victorian-styled rooms, each with private bath and a balcony over the river and its old water wheel. Also in Highland Mill are **Rooster Brothers**, a wine and gourmet food shop featuring Maine-made mustards and jams, and the **Camden Bakery**, with delicious old-fashioned treats and a chalkboard menu of unusual and tasty lunch dishes.

One of the largest of Camden's mills has emerged from its chrysalis as the **Center for Creative Imaging**, which draws design, printing, and photography professionals to its state-of-the-art courses in the computerized manipulation of illustrations and photographs. The adjacent gallery displays digitally altered images as well as changing exhibitions of the work of such acknowledged masters of photography as Richard Avedon. Another nearby mill is slated to reopen in 1993 as a small brewery and tavern.

Today, of course, one of Camden's main industries is tourism, and the town is well equipped for the business, with a wide assortment of shops, restaurants, and lodging choices for every taste and pocketbook, plus plenty of activities to fill many leisure hours.

SHOPPING IN CAMDEN

Shopping is one of the major pastimes here, and for good reason: Camden offers more quality and less kitsch than most other coastal tourist destinations. If you fancy precious, one-of-a-kind jewelry, for example, you've come to the right place. Among the local jewelry designers who have won international recognition is **Etienne**, whose store is right on Main Street in the middle of town. At **Good Hands Gallery**, a few blocks from Main Street on Bayview, there's a tempting array of the work of many of the local goldsmiths. **p.b. las goldsmith** shares an upstairs studio on Main Street with creative clothing designer **Rosamund**, and just below them is a company store for another Maine designer, **Kirsten Scarcelli**, whose colorful, unfitted cotton and woollen knit separates sell for much more in New York. For clothing you might also stop at **Planet**, on Main Street, with a small but casually stylish selection; the **Grasshopper Shop**, on Bayview Street, for young, trendy fashions; and **The Admiral's Buttons**, farther along Bayview, for classic men's and women's resort wear.

As you wander the shops look for exceptional interior furnishings at **Margo Moore**, on Route 1 just south of the center of town; country accents for the home at **The Right Stuff**, on Main Street; and, across the street, small antiques and unusual greeting cards at **Star Bird**. **Ducktrap Bay Trading Co.**, on Bayview Street, is a gallery of the finest hand-carved decoys and bird and animal sculptures, and **Once a Tree**, farther down Bayview, offers just about every sort of wooden item except decoys.

Also on Bayview Street are two very good bookstores, the **Owl & Turtle** and, for younger readers, **A Children's Bookstore** (just off Bayview Street on Willey's Wharf). **Surroundings**, farther along the way, has unusual and very fairly priced items for home and garden, and across the street is the well-respected **Pine Tree Shop and Bayview Gallery**, which specializes in the work of Maine artists.

DINING AND STAYING IN CAMDEN

Tucked in among the shops on Main Street are two informal restaurants with loyal local followings. **Cappy's Chowder House**, at the crossroads in the center of town, is the closest thing here to a neighborhood pub, where everyone gathers to share the latest gossip over generous drinks and good, reasonably priced meals at breakfast, lunch, and dinnertime. Tel: (207) 236-2254. **Mama & Leenie's**, up Main and across the street, draws a breakfast crowd with its home-baked treats and also offers light lunches; eating on the tiny outdoor patio is very pleasant in warm weather. Tel: (207) 236-6300.

But on a soft summer afternoon there's no better place for a good meal with a terrific harbor view than the deck of the **Waterfront**. The menu features overly generous entrée salads at lunchtime, plus fried and broiled seafood, pastas, steaks, and boiled lobster. Tel: (207) 236-3747. For an exceptional lunch or dinner, try tiny **Cassoulet**, on Main Street, whose "country French" menu always includes a namesake *cassoulet*. Tel: (207) 236-6304. The dining room of the **Belmont**, a small inn on Belmont Avenue (turn off Main Street at the flashing light south of town), has a well-deserved reputation for one of the area's finest kitchens; despite the sophistication of the New American menu, the atmosphere is relaxed and unpretentious. Upstairs from the Belmont's cool and airy dining rooms are quiet, pleasant bedrooms for guests. (Closed December to May; Tel: 207/236-8053.)

Camden brims with lodging establishments that range from economical to very elegant. At the height of the summer, however, most hang out their "No Vacancy" signs early in the day, so plan ahead. The **Lord Camden Inn**, tucked away upstairs above Main Street shops, combines upscale accommodations (nice period reproductions and balconies) with a convenient location in the middle of town. This is where Joan Lunden stayed when *Good Morning America* broadcast its program from beside Camden Harbor; it's also where Mel Gibson slept when he came to town to consider filming *The Man Without a Face* here. He liked what he saw and returned to spend most of the summer of 1992 working on the movie in Camden and Rockport.

Inviting B and Bs line Route 1 from one end of town to the other. There isn't a disappointing one in the bunch, but favorites include the low-key, countrified **Blue Harbor House** (also serving dinner to guests by reservation; Tel: 207/236-3196), on your left as you enter Camden from the south; and, just north of the town center, the elegant Victorian **Hawthorn Inn**, with six rooms in the house and four mountain-view suites with private Jacuzzis in the carriage house. A block beyond the Hawthorn, on the opposite side of the street, is the handsome white-clapboard **Maine Stay**, where you just may be serenaded in three-part harmony by the very hospitable innkeepers, a retired navy captain, his wife, and her twin sister. Four of the eight rooms have private baths. Ask for the Maine Stay's newest room, which opens onto its own patio at the back of the house. All three B and Bs are non-smoking.

The **Whitehall Inn**, another block or so along, is a wonderful old "summer in Maine" hotel, complete with rocking chairs on the front porch. The dining room (Tel: 207/236-3391), open to the public, is elegant in a self-assured, old-fashioned way. As a young girl Edna St. Vincent Millay was a chambermaid here and was "discovered" by a guest one evening as she recited her poetry to an after-dinner gathering. The guest, a graduate of Vassar College, was so impressed that she arranged for Millay to get a scholarship. There's a monument to the poet atop Mount Battie, overlooking the view she described in "Renascence," and a second statue in town looking out to those "three islands in a bay" mentioned in the poem.

Just north of town on Route 1, on your right, is the landmark **Norumbega**, a turreted Victorian pile built by Joseph Sterns, inventor of duplex telegraphy, which provided the technology for Western Union. Before it became a posh B and B in 1984, it also belonged to foreign-affairs commentator W. Hodding Carter III for a short while. Today guests retire to their bedrooms up an ornate staircase outfitted with its own fireplace and built-in love seat halfway up.

Across from Norumbega is a jewel box of a Victorian inn called **A Little Dream**. All ribbons and furbelows, its five rooms (all with private bath and all non-smoking) are a feast for the eyes, with romantic groupings of such things as leather-bound books of poetry, teddy bears, and silver and china artfully arranged on almost every surface. Just beyond, set back on a hilltop, the **Edgecombe-Coles House** is rimmed by a wicker-bedecked porch and is beautifully decorated inside with the owners' intriguing collections and handsome antiques. Three of the six rooms (all with private baths) have ocean views, as do the porch and the common rooms.

A short distance farther on, the **Lodge at Camden Hills** (open year-round) and the **High Tide Inn** (open May to October) both offer all the convenience and privacy of a deluxe motel coupled with the personal attention of an inn. The former offers a choice of standard motel rooms or fancier suites with fireplaces and Jacuzzis, while the latter comprises inn rooms, motel units, a duplex, and four cottages all set on seven landscaped acres that slope to the water. Finally, the oceanfront **Inn at Sunrise Point**, just over the town line in Lincolnville Beach (turn right on Fire Road 9), has very comfortable modern accommodations (three rooms in the main house and four cottages) with fireplaces in every room.

LINCOLNVILLE AND ISLESBORO

At the northern end of Camden's business district, instead of continuing on Route 1 to Belfast, Searsport, and East Penobscot Bay, you can elect to veer off Route 1 and go more or less straight onto Route 52, which takes you out of town and up over a rise to reveal a lovely vista of Megunticook Lake. Just a bit farther, at the intersection of Route 52 and Youngtown Road, is the **Youngtown Inn**, a pleasant escape from the Camden crowds. Guest rooms are simple and pleasing (shared baths). Downstairs the two dining rooms and pub are especially welcoming on a cool evening when fires burn in the fireplaces. The cuisine is prepared with skill by the French innkeeper. Tel: (207) 763-4290.

There's more French food at **Lincolnville Beach**, just north of Camden on Route 1. **Chez Michel** doesn't offer any atmosphere to speak of, but its bouillabaisse is a happy marriage of Gallic culinary skill and local seafood (Tel: 207/789-5600). Across the street is the **Lobster Pound**, the place everyone has been going to for years for a roll-up-your-sleeves-and-dig-in lobster feed (Tel: 207/789-5550). You can also park here to enjoy an hour or two on the small beach.

Ferries leave from here for the island of **Islesboro** several times a day (you may bring your car, which you'll need, but try to reserve space as the ferry is small; Tel: 207/789-5611 or 734-6935). Described by Sidney Sheldon in his gossipy novel *Master of the Game* as "the jealously guarded colony of the super-rich," Islesboro's **Dark Harbor** remains a summer enclave of old money and nouveau trying to look old. It's one of the few places where you're still likely to see white-ruffled nannies pushing prams down country lanes to grand summer "cottages." One of these "cottages" is now the **Dark Harbor House**, a yellow hilltop mansion built in 1895 by a Philadelphia banker. The living room, library, and ten upstairs guest rooms and suites retain an atmosphere of low-key elegance appropriate to the house's birthright. (Open mid-May through mid-October.) A nearby "cottage" had been operated as the Islesboro Inn, but it was purchased a couple of years ago by TV's "Cheers" star Kirstie Alley and her husband, Parker Stevenson, and returned to its original status as a summer home. Alley's buddy John Travolta has since bought a neighboring cottage. When planning a winter retreat for friends recently, Travolta reportedly called ahead to inquire whether snow-making machines could be brought in to correct nature's failure to deliver any white stuff. The town fathers respectfully declined.

—Mimi Steadman

EAST PENOBSCOT BAY

Penobscot Bay and the Penobscot River meet in a narrow reach of water between the Route 1 towns of Belfast and Searsport to the west and the Blue Hill Peninsula, which forms the eastern shore of Penobscot Bay. Most travellers pass right through Belfast and Searsport and across the top of the peninsula on their way from Camden to Bar Harbor— which is just fine with most residents of East Penobscot Bay, and with its fervent out-of-state following.

The heart of this region is the wide, spreading Blue Hill Peninsula. On a map it resembles a huge pendant dangling from the ten-mile length of Route 1 between Bucksport and, to the east, Ellsworth. Easy to miss from the highway, the peninsula is one of the most tranquil yet sophisticated stretches of the Maine coast. There are no resort towns, just proud, Federal-era communities such as Castine and Blue Hill, and Stonington, a fishing village at the tip of Deer Isle, which is attached to the peninsula by a bridge and causeways.

Instead of commercial attractions the Blue Hill area offers galleries and crafts studios, tucked away among the kinds of deep coves and lupin-lined inlets usually thought of as "typical Maine." Together, Blue Hill and Deer Isle harbor the largest concentration of craftspeople in New England.

Hiking trails lace the Holbrook Island Sanctuary on Blue Hill's Cape Rosier and on Isle au Haut, an island off Ston-

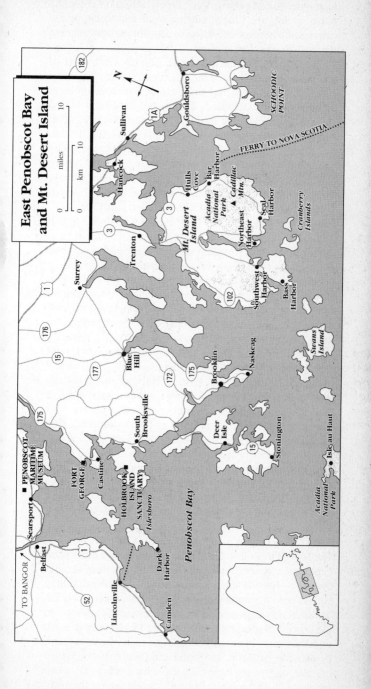

East Penobscot Bay and Mt. Desert Island

ington accessible only by ferry. Restaurants and inns, while not plentiful, are varied, ranging from reasonably priced eateries and bed-and-breakfasts to some of the best places to stay and dine in New England.

The Blue Hill Peninsula has quite a history. Castine, set on its own mini-peninsula at the confluence of the Penobscot and Bagaduce rivers, has been claimed by four different countries (France, Holland, Britain, and the United States) since its founding early in the 17th century. Known as Fort Pentagoet to the Pilgrims, who traded here, it fell in 1667 to the young French nobleman Baron de Saint Castine, who married a Penobscot Indian princess and governed eastern Maine as a combination feudal lord and Indian chief. During the Revolution Castine went its own way, its Loyalist residents welcoming the British who occupied it in 1779.

All of East Penobscot Bay prospered as a shipbuilding hub in the 19th century, and in the 1870s Stonington boomed as the center for quarrying and shipping Deer Isle's distinctive pink granite. The 1880s brought steamboats and summer people, but a less showy breed than those who settled on Mount Desert, the next peninsula to the east. Because there were already so many fine houses in Castine and Blue Hill, through the years summer people tended to buy and restore them rather than build new ones. Several rustic 1880s resorts are run by the descendants of their founders, who still cater to descendants of their first guests.

But the thing for which Blue Hill became nationally known is pottery. Some 60 years ago summer resident Adelaide Pearson held a conversation about pottery with Mahatma Gandhi, prompting her to begin producing it in the house she had inherited here in 1898. Her intention was to use local craftspeople and local materials: clay and glazes gathered from the town's abandoned copper mines, quarries, and bogs. Pearson's Rowantrees Pottery continues to produce distinctive pieces, and to sell them in the pottery shed behind the house in Blue Hill (discussed below).

TOURING EAST PENOBSCOT BAY

The Blue Hill peninsula and Deer Isle area resist methodical exploration. Route 15 runs all the way—more than 40 miles (64 km)—from Route 1 south through the village of Blue Hill on down to Stonington, crossing the soaring suspension bridge across Eggemoggin Reach and several causeways in the process. If you simply follow Route 15, however, you will miss the beauty of the shore roads and such villages as South Brooksville, Brooklin, and wonderful Castine. It would be a mistake to try to see everything if you have only a day or two for this remarkable area. Instead, concentrate on the highlights. You might stay in Castine the first night and in Blue Hill or Stonington the second; allow a third day for hiking on Cape Rosier or Isle au Haut.

The loop described below begins with the Route 1 towns of Belfast, Searsport, and Bucksport, then follows Route 175 south to Castine on the Blue Hill Peninsula. From Castine we head east across the peninsula to the village of Blue Hill, then take Route 15 to Route 175/176 in a loop around the Brooksville area and on down to Deer Isle and Stonington, which is the departure point for Isle au Haut. Finally, we detour through the town of Brooklin back on the mainland before following Route 172 back up into the Blue Hills and on to Route 1 at the town of Ellsworth. This adds up to roughly 120 miles (192 km), but seems far longer as you twist and turn around coves and inlets.

BELFAST TO BUCKSPORT
Belfast

Route 1 skirts Belfast (take the Belfast exit), a small city with a brick Victorian downtown and Federal-era captains' homes ranged above it. Its slightly down-at-the-heels look is almost refreshing after Camden's relentlessly bright paint and high prices. Both **Gallery 68** (68 Main Street) and the **Frick Gallery** (139 High Street) show and sell works of the region's top artists; **90 Main**, at the corner of High and Main, is a good lunch stop. In summer months the **Belfast and Moosehead R.R. Co.** operates an excursion train from the waterfront north to the village of Brooks. The two-hour round-trip ride is sure to include at least one simulated train robbery.

Just north of the Belfast turnoff on Route 1, **Perry's Tropical Nut House** is an unabashed tourist trap. It was begun in the 1920s by a local entrepreneur who travelled through South America collecting nuts (there's a display) as well as exotic animals, now stuffed and also displayed. It's all a bit funky but fun, especially if you like nuts.

Searsport

Searsport, just 5 miles (8 km) up Route 1, opens a window on the Age of Sail of the 1870s and 1880s. Nowhere else along the coast are so many handsome houses strung so evenly and so far. The **Penobscot Marine Museum** in the middle of the village explains why: In the late 19th century Searsport boasted more deep-water sea captains than any town its size in the country. The museum, which occupies the old (1845) town hall and several restored sea captains' houses, displays models, paintings, souvenirs, and photographs of the era, when dozens of town residents captained square-riggers, many bringing their families along on multi-year voyages. Some of the photographs show Searsport families meeting in Far Eastern ports. Open Memorial Day to mid-October; Tel: (207) 548-2529.

Searsport is now known for antiques and bed-and-breakfast inns. A dozen antiques dealers line Route 1, and the **Searsport Flea Market**, held every summer weekend, is a big event.

STAYING AND DINING IN SEARSPORT

Searsport is well positioned as a way station between Camden and Bar Harbor, and more than a dozen former captains' houses in town now welcome overnight guests. Prices in these inns are relatively low, and quality is generally high. The **Homeport Inn**, an 1861 captain's mansion with a widow's walk and flower gardens right on Route 1, has ten cozy, well-decorated rooms, some with bay views and private baths. All three guest rooms at the **Captain Green Pendleton Inn**, set on a small hill above Route 1 on 80 wooded, trail-laced acres, have fireplaces. There's a pond for swimming, boating, or ice skating.

Thurston House Bed & Breakfast, an 1830s house right in the village, is informal and friendly; the Carriage House room accommodates a family of five. The **Capt. Butman Homestead**, an 1830s farmhouse set on five and a half acres, is also informal and geared to families (open only from Memorial Day to Labor Day). The **Hichborn Inn**, just beyond Searsport in the old shipbuilding village of Stockton Springs, is an Italianate mansion built by one of the area's most prolific shipbuilders. There are four guest rooms (two with private bath) in this non-smoking inn. It's been nicely restored, and is occupied by friendly ghosts, one of whom is said to be N. G. Hichborn, who built the house in 1849.

The landmark restaurant along this stretch of Route 1 is the **Nickerson Tavern**. Not surprisingly, it's housed in an 1838 sea captain's house with a beamed dining room and fresh flowers on polished wooden tables, and is rated among the top restaurants in the state. Chef-owner Tom Weiner is known for combining meats and fruits in dishes like raspberry hazelnut chicken (Tel: 207/548-2220). Dependable local eateries include **Light's Diner**, right on Route 1 in Searsport (with good daily specials and custard pie; Tel: 207/548-2405), and **Sail Inn**, a Route 1 diner high on the bluff overlooking the Penobscot River and Verona Island, just before the suspension bridge (Tel: 207/469-3850).

FORT KNOX AND BUCKSPORT

Follow Route 174 north from Route 1 instead of crossing the bridge to Bucksport and you'll come to **Fort Knox State Park**, a massive granite defense complex built *after* the signing in 1842 of the peace treaty ending a boundary battle between Canada and the United States. (Open May to November.)

Bucksport, just across the bridge on Route 1, is a paper-mill town with several good lunch spots. **McCloeds**, on Main Street, open for both lunch and dinner, has a comfortable, fern-bar atmosphere and entrées such as chicken and shrimp Dijonnaise. Tel: (207) 469-3963.

Just beyond Bucksport, note the Route 46 turnoff for the **Alamoosook Lodge**, less than 3 miles (5 km) off Route 1. All six of the simple guest rooms at this non-smoking inn have private baths. Alamoosook Lake's waters—blessedly warmer than the Maine ocean—are good for swimming and canoeing (the lake is also open to non-guests).

BLUE HILL PENINSULA
Castine

The next turnoff from Route 1 is Route 175 south to Castine, quite possibly Maine's most dignified town. Stately old elms, destroyed by Dutch elm disease almost everywhere else in New England, arch high above streets lined with elegant houses sheathed in immaculate white clapboard, most dating from Castine's mid-19th-century shipbuilding era— when it claimed to be the second wealthiest town per capita in the country.

This is a town to walk around in. A pamphlet called "Walking Tour of Castine," available at almost any inn or shop, tells the town's long history, which includes the 1779 attempt by the Commonwealth of Massachusetts to punish Castine's resident Tories. No fewer than 1,000 troops and 400 marines attacked Castine's tiny British Fort George— and lost. The survivors, Paul Revere included, were forced to walk back to Boston.

Fort George, occupied by redcoats again during the War of 1812, is today a peaceful grassy earthworks that children enjoy rolling down. The fort is near the Maine Maritime Academy campus on Battle Avenue, from which Main Street slopes downhill to the town dock. Moored at the dock is the *State of Maine,* a 1952 training ship for the academy's cadets. Huge and gray, totally out of scale and character with the town, it's open for tours.

On sunny summer days life in Castine eddies around the **town dock**, where picnic tables and benches invite lingering with coffee or fried clams taken out from the **Breeze**, a neighboring place that merits its loyal following. **Dennets Wharf**, a large waterside restaurant on Sea Street (off the town dock), boasts "the world's largest oyster bar."

Another focal point of this interesting town is the **Castine Inn**, a third of the way up Main Street from the dock to Battle Avenue. Innkeepers Mark and Margaret Hodesh are passionate about food, gardening, and art. The dining rooms of this old 1890s summer hotel serve as a town meeting place at breakfast and a gathering spot for cognoscenti up and down the coast at dinner. Crabmeat cakes in mustard sauce are the specialty, and local seafood and produce are always featured on the changing menu. A mural of Castine by Margaret Hodesh covers all four walls of the dining room, and French doors overlook the inn's formal gardens and the harbor beyond. The garden is Ms. Hodesh's gift to the town— everyone is invited to come sit. Many of the 20 guest rooms (all with private baths) overlook both the garden and water, and a number of original artworks brighten walls throughout.

A couple of good shops in Castine are **Water Witch**, on Main Street, specializing in Dutch Java batiks and Maine woollens; and the **Four Flags Chandlery**, overlooking the harbor, a good place to browse for nautical books and gifts from an eclectic selection. The **Wilson Museum**, on Perkins Street, houses an interesting display of Indian artifacts and changing art exhibits at a splendid waterside location. The Native American and ancient artifacts were collected by summer resident J. Howard Wilson, who donated the building for the museum. Also housed here is a local historical collection of old tools, farm equipment, a kitchen from 1805, a Victorian parlor, and a blacksmith's shop. Open from Memorial Day to October.

Finally, perhaps to walk off a meal, search out **Dyce's Head Light** at the western end of town (where Perkins Street and Battle Avenue meet) and follow the trails leading to the ledges below, overlooking Penobscot Bay.

Blue Hill

Over the entrance to the Bagaduce Lending Library in Blue Hill (16 miles/26 km east of Castine via wooded Routes 199 and 177) a mural depicts the village as the center of concentric circles of creativity rippling over the peninsula and islands. It's a concept to which many residents and visitors readily ascribe.

The village of Blue Hill, a cluster of early-19th-century buildings between rounded Blue Hill and Blue Hill Bay, still resembles the portrait painted of it by its first resident minister, Jonathan Fisher (the portrait hangs in Rockland's Farnsworth Museum). A gifted journal keeper and inventor as well as artist, Parson Fisher was the first of literally hundreds of creative people to be drawn to—and to thrive in and around—Blue Hill.

The Haystack Mountain School of Crafts on Deer Isle (to the south) has been a factor in attracting many nationally known artisans to the area. But that doesn't explain why so many have stayed on to make this their year-round home, or why writers, ranging from essayist E. B. White to naturalists Helen and Scott Nearing, have done the same. And what about the musicians? Blue Hill's Bagaduce is a sheet-music library, one of the few in the country, and the village's Kneisel Hall Chamber Music Festival attracts top faculty and students each summer. Its radio station (WERU) and Left Bank Café are stops on the national folk-music and jazz circuits, and local music groups range from big band to opera.

Blue Hill is the kind of crossroads village you can drive through in a minute if you don't know any better. Most of the interesting shops and inns are all on side streets that turn into country roads in a block or two.

For a first-hand look at some of Blue Hill's famous pottery, as well as a chance to buy some, stop by **Rowantree's Pottery** on Route 177, which turns into Union Street as it nears the village center. The house looks so private that if the sign weren't hanging out front, above the picket fence, you would hesitate to walk back through the garden. The pottery shed is immense, one floor for production (visitors are welcome to watch pieces being hand thrown) and a second, a showroom, filled with deeply colored tableware and decorative pieces displayed against bright prints by local artist Frank Hamabe. Tel: (207) 374-5535.

Toward the middle of the village on Route 172 is **Rackliffe Pottery**, a family-owned business that, like Rowantree's, specializes in local, deeply colored glazes. The **Liros Gallery**, on Main Street, specializes in antique prints and maps, while **Handworks Gallery**, just off Main Street above the Blue Hill Department Store, showcases unusual handwoven clothing, jewelry, furniture, pottery, and rugs created on Blue Hill Peninsula and Deer Isle. If the work of any craftspeople in particular catches your fancy, you might want to pick up a copy of "The Maine Cultural Guide" (available free here and in most galleries) and use it to find their studios.

The **Leighton Gallery** on Parker Point Road (turn off Main Street at the library) features the work of more than 40 contemporary artists as well as whimsical animal sculptures by local octogenarian Eliot Sweet. The two-story gallery, with its extensive sculpture garden, stages frequently changing and widely reviewed exhibits (open June through October).

The **Holt House**, a Federal-era mansion right in the middle of the village on Water Street, is known for its stenciling (open July and August only). The **Parson Fisher House**, about half a mile (1 km) south of the village on Route 15, while less impressive than the Holt House from the outside, offers a more interesting collection comprising Jonathan Fisher's possessions, writings, and artworks (open July to mid-September).

STAYING, DINING, AND ENTERTAINMENT IN BLUE HILL

The **Blue Hill Inn**, just down Union Street (Route 177) from Rowantree's Pottery, is an 1830s double house with 11 tastefully furnished non-smoking guest rooms, some with fireplaces and all with private baths, and spacious downstairs sitting rooms. A six-course prix-fixe dinner is served nightly (except midweek in winter) in the low-beamed, candle-lit dining room. Guests may be seated family-style. (The dining room is open to non-guests by reservation; Tel: 207/374-2844.)

Two of the region's best restaurants are around the corner. The **Firepond**, along toward the middle of Main Street, is so famous up and down the coast that you may be surprised at the simplicity of the dining room. Ask for a table on the porch, from which you can hear the rush of a mill stream. You might begin with a soufflé of local sea urchin and then dine on roast duckling with raspberries and Chambord. Tel: (207) 374-2135.

Jonathan's, a few doors up Main Street, serves lunch as well as dinner in two pleasant dining rooms. House specialties include shrimp Scorpio: flaming shrimp bathed in ouzo and served with feta cheese over linguine. Chef-owner Jonathan Chase recently coauthored *Saltwater Seasonings,* a glossy cookbook with recipes requiring coastal Maine ingredients. Tel: (207) 374-5226.

The **John Peters Inn** is hidden away just east of the village on Peters Point. It's a multi-chimneyed, white-columned 1825 mansion with a lawn, a garden, and a meadow that sweeps down to Blue Hill Bay. All 14 rooms have private baths and are non-smoking; many have fireplaces and some have decks. The most romantic rooms are in the main house, but the spacious carriage house units with kitchenettes are also appealing. (Open mid-May to November.)

Blue Hill Farm Country Inn, north of the village on Route 15, is an informal, relaxing haven, a rambling farmhouse with seven non-smoking guest rooms (shared baths) and an attached barn that has been cleverly converted into a two-story breakfast area and lounge and seven more guest rooms with private baths. The inn's 48 acres include walking/cross-country skiing trails and a trout pond.

During the **Kneisel Hall Chamber Music Festival**, early July through mid-August, brief chamber-music concerts are held regularly on weekdays at the Blue Hill, John Peters, and Blue Hill Farm Country inns. These are actually practice sessions for the formal concerts in Kneisel Hall on Pleasant Street (Route 15 north), Friday evenings and Sunday afternoons. (For further information, Tel: 207/374-2811.)

On summer weekends Blue Hill offers a choice of live entertainment. The **New Surry Theater and Acting School** will most likely be staging a production either in the school or in their own theater (Tel: 207/374-5057), and the **Surry Opera Company** may be mounting a production in its barn 7 miles (11 km) up Route 172 (Tel: 207/667-8919). There is sometimes contredanse or big-band music at the town hall.

Finally, check to see who is performing at the **Left Bank Café**, a small house behind a big vegetable garden just north of the village on Route 172. Open daily from 7:00 A.M., the Left Bank offers some of the best bagels, peasant breads, hearty soups, beef Stroganoff, and spinach pies in Maine. A published poet and former educator, owner Arnold Greenberg does the baking, supervises the cooking, and schedules the nightly performances, which often feature nationally known folk, jazz, and blues artists as well as poetry readings (winter Sundays at 4:00 P.M.). Afternoon children's and chamber-music concerts are also held here. Tel: (207) 374-2201.

South from Blue Hill

Turn your car radio dial to 89.9 FM (WERU) as you head south toward Deer Isle. This nonprofit community station, housed in a former chicken coop in Blue Hill Falls owned by folksinger Paul Stookey of Peter, Paul, and Mary, airs jazz, folk, and reggae music as well as poetry readings.

There are three routes south from Blue Hill; the one you take depends on your time limits and where you are going. If you are hurrying to Deer Isle to catch the mail boat from Stonington to Isle au Haut, stick to Route 15. Otherwise, you may veer off on Route 172 down the Blue Hill Bay (east) side of the peninsula to Brooklin; or take Routes 175 and 176 on a 15-mile (24-km) loop around the mini-peninsula that's the town of Brooksville. We do the last of these three options first, then head south to Deer Isle, and pass through Brooklin on our way back north.

BROOKSVILLE AND CAPE ROSIER

The stretch of Route 176 that leads through North Brooksville is particularly scenic; **Bagaduce Lunch**, right on Route 176 in town, offers picnic tables and fried clams overlooking the Bagaduce River's reversing falls.

If you take Route 176 beyond North Brooksville to the turnoff for Cape Rosier—a small peninsula off Brooksville—be prepared for a narrow road. A side trip to Cape Rosier is (or should be) at least a half-day expedition. Follow signs along the Cape Rosier road to the **Holbrook Island Sanctuary**, a 1,230-acre state-maintained wildlife preserve with picnic benches and trails that run along the shore and to the top of Backwoods Mountain. **Hiram Blake Camp**, signposted from the tiny village of Harborside near the sanctuary, is a rustic resort that has been run by the same family for more than 75 years. Cottages are spread out below the central lodge along the shore of Penobscot Bay, and there are rowboats to use, trails to hike, and a recreation room for foul-weather days. The dining room in the central lodge doubles as a library: Thousands of books are filed by category in the ceiling. (Open mid-May to mid-October.)

Past the Cape Rosier turnoff Route 176 continues into South Brooksville and **Buck's Harbor**. Almost perfectly round, this small harbor is filled with home-based as well as visiting sailing craft. The small yacht club above the harbor is a turn-of-the-century period piece. In summer months you can lunch at the **Buck's Harbor Café**, a takeout place overlooking the harbor. The **Landing Restaurant**, upstairs in the same building, starts serving dinners of local fish and produce from 3:00 P.M. (open May to November; Tel: (207) 326-4166). The neighboring **Buck's Harbor Inn**, informal and friendly, offers simply but well-furnished sea-bright rooms and shared baths. Dinner is served on Saturday nights from November to April 1, when the Landing Restaurant is closed.

SOUTH TO DEER ISLE

From Buck's Harbor follow Route 176 back around to Route 15 and head south for Deer Isle. As the road reaches its highest point, you'll see a turnout on your right: This is **Caterpillar Hill**, affording a memorable view across a series of lesser hills, ponds, coves, and bays.

The road dips down into Sargentville, notable chiefly for a lovely old resort called **Oakland House**. Watch for the sign and turn right at the big tree. Oakland House has been in present owner Jim Littlefield's family since 1889 and today counts descendants of its original guests among its clientele. This is not to suggest that there's anything snooty about the place—there isn't. It's a family-oriented establishment on

Eggemoggin Reach with ten bedrooms in the main house and 15 shorefront, wooded cottages (most with fireplaces and some with up to four bedrooms), a private lake, and a central lodge and recreation hall.

Deer Isle

The high, unnervingly narrow suspension bridge across Eggemoggin Reach just south of Sargentville links the Blue Hill Peninsula with a chain of islands connected by causeways and bridges. Known collectively as "Deer Isle," it includes the towns of Deer Isle and Stonington, as well as the villages of Little Deer Isle, Deer Isle, Sunset, and Sunshine.

The Eggemoggin Reach Bridge leads to Little Deer Isle, where the volunteer-run Deer Isle–Stonington Chamber of Commerce booth, on Route 15, serves as a gatehouse of sorts for the area. If you are lucky enough to find it open, pick up a local map/guide. If it's after 5:00 P.M. you could do worse than follow the signs to Blastow's Cove, site of **Eaton's Lobster Pool**, the area's premier lobster pound; it's a shade more formal than most, with indoor dining and a full menu. Tel: (207) 348-2383.

THE VILLAGE OF DEER ISLE

A causeway leads to the island and village of Deer Isle, the latter a crossroads of shops and galleries that seem to have gathered around the **Pilgrim's Inn**. Said to have been built in Newburyport, Massachusetts, in 1793 and shipped up to Deer Isle, the inn is known for its fine cuisine (the restaurant is open to the public by reservation; Tel: 207/348-6615). Guests meet over hors d'oeuvres at 6:00 P.M. in the four large common rooms, where a house-party atmosphere prevails. The 13 non-smoking guest rooms are furnished with carefully chosen antiques and original art, and all have water views. Many rooms have fireplaces; the five on the third floor share one shower. (Open mid-May to mid-October.)

Another lodging choice on Deer Isle is the **Inn at Ferry Landing**, a converted 1850s farmhouse with a superb view of Eggemoggin Reach from the common room as well as the seven guest rooms, four with private bath and all non-smoking. (Turn left on Old Ferry Road, just after the bridge.)

The **Turtle Gallery**, across from the Pilgrim's Inn (open June through September), showcases the work of local artists and craftspeople, as do the **Blue Heron** and the **Deer Isle Artists Association**, both just south of the village center on Route 15. The **Haystack Mountain School of Crafts**, 7 miles (11 km) east of the village (turn left at the Gulf gas station on Route 15 south of town), is worth visiting if only to see the way it has been built to blend with its dramatic site, a steep hillside overlooking Jericho Bay. The school was chartered in 1950 and is named for its former location, inland on Route 3 west of Belfast. It gained a national reputation by the early 1960s, when it moved to its present site. Some 80 students are enrolled in a series of three-week sessions scheduled between mid-June and Labor Day. Call before visiting to check the time of tours and special events; Tel: (207) 348-2306.

STONINGTON

Stonington, at the southern tip of Deer Isle, probably qualifies as the most picturesque fishing village in Maine. Its buildings date from the 1880s and 1890s, a boom time when Deer Isle pink granite was quarried and shipped by schooner around the country. The distinctive rock continues to be quarried on a small scale, and such landmarks as the Pilgrim Monument in Provincetown, Boston's Museum of Fine Arts, and New York's Radio City Music Hall all feature Stonington granite. The town's surviving wooden houses and shops, most with mansard roofs and many hedged with flowers, are scattered irregularly around the harbor.

Stonington remains a working fishing town, and the hardware store, chandlery, cannery, supermarket, and fish pier are still the busiest spots. The harbor is the town's focus, rather than its backdrop. Lobster boats, trawlers, a now-rare sardine carrier, and often two or three windjammers and several smaller sailboats maneuver among dozens of small pink-granite fir-topped islands. On nearby Crotch Island a quarrying crane still rises above the trees.

Kayaks are also an increasingly common sight here, because the harbor, along with Merchant Row and the Deer Island Thoroughfare just beyond it, are considered among the best paddling areas on the East Coast. **Explorers at Sea**, a widely respected sea-kayaking outfit headquartered on East Main Street, offers introductory lessons and guided day and multiday trips (May to mid-September only). Tel: (207) 367-2356.

For visitors, Stonington's Main Street has become a shopping mecca of sorts. The **Eastern Bay Gallery** (open mid-May to Christmas) showcases and sells the work of 50 local craftspeople, including clothing, pottery, and jewelry. The **Island Supply Co.** (open June to October) sells the natural-fiber clothing that owner Kathyrn Butler spends winters buying in Greece, the South Pacific, South America, India, and the Far East.

On West Main Street, **Dockside Books and Gifts** offers an

exceptional selection of books about Maine and a view of the harbor from the deck, on which patrons are encouraged to sit and read. The best harbor view, however, is from the porch of the **Overlook Building**, set high above West Main Street, up granite steps. It's now a complex of shops and galleries; look for Jill Hoy's bold, bright oils.

Stonington is also a good place to grab a bite to eat. From **Penobscot Bay Provisions** you might want to buy a sandwich or freshly baked bread and Maine goat's cheese and amble down to the harbor or out to the **Crockett Cove Woods Preserve**, a 100-acre property west of town owned by the Nature Conservancy, or to **Ames Pond** to the east. **Austin Wood's Ice Cream** (open May to early December) features Hancock Creamery ice cream and a harbor view. For a heartier meal try **Fisherman's Friend Restaurant**, on School Street; what it lacks in views it more than compensates for with excellent chowder, crabmeat rolls, and fishermen's platters.

There are two appealing bed-and-breakfasts in the village of Stonington. **Pres du Port**, uphill from the harbor at the western end of the village, is friendly and comfortable, offering three bright guest rooms with decks and harbor views. The **Ocean View House** (near the mail boat dock), built in the 19th century to board quarry workers, also has three attractive guest rooms with water views (both open July and August only). **Captain's Quarters Inn and Motel**, a lineup of several old waterfront buildings, offers a wide variety of accommodations, from basic rooms to efficiencies with working fireplaces. You can buy lobsters at the co-operative here, boil them in your room, and eat them on the inn's expansive deck, right on the harbor.

SUNSET

If you're not continuing on to Isle au Haut (discussed next) you can just continue around Deer Isle on Route 15 via the town of Sunset. The drive isn't particularly rewarding, but one worthwhile detour is a walk along the shore path in the Crockett Cove Woods Preserve (discussed above; turn left on Whitman Road beyond Burnt Cove). Also along this route is **Goose Cove Lodge**, a family- and nature-oriented resort (open May to mid-October) comprising a cluster of cottages around a central lodge (open to the public for evening dining by reservation; Tel: 207/348-2508). Guests of the resort are permitted to walk out on the wide sandbar to the **Barred Island Preserve**, a two-acre island that's good for hiking.

ISLE AU HAUT

For many visitors Stonington is just the departure point for the mail boat to Isle au Haut (pronounced "aisle a ho"). Unusually mountainous, this six-mile-long island offers some of the most scenic coastal hiking trails in Maine, the majority maintained as part of **Acadia National Park**. Most of the trails are accessed from Duck Harbor at the far end of the island from the village, a special mail-boat stop during the summer. Five Adirondack-style shelters are also maintained by the national park, and the island's former lighthouse, near the village, is now an inn called **Keeper's House** (open June through October). The huts, available from May 15 to October 15, can be reserved by writing to Acadia National Park, P.O. Box 177, Bar Harbor, ME 04609. Reservation requests, which are not accepted before April 1, must be accompanied by a $5 reservation fee. For more information, Tel: (207) 288-3338.

North from Deer Isle

If time permits on the drive back from Deer Isle to Blue Hill and the mainland, explore the eastern side of the peninsula. North of Eggemoggin Reach Bridge, turn east onto Route 172/175 and follow it to the village of **Brooklin**; take another right between the general store and the tiny **Morning Moon Café** (a good bet for breakfast and lunch, and also open for dinner Thursday through Saturday; Tel: 207/359-2373). The **Wooden Boat School** (open June to November) is signposted a few miles down on the right. A spinoff of *Wooden Boat Magazine,* the school offers more than 60 one- or two-week summer classes in building and navigating boats (from kayaks and canoes to sailing yachts) as well as in such related coastal pleasures as drawing. Visitors are welcome to tour the facilities, which include a shop, an extensive library in a former mansion, and paths leading down to the boathouse. Tel: (207) 359-4651.

As you continue north on Route 175 along Blue Hill Bay note the turnoff for Flye Point, a narrow land finger pointing into Herrick Bay, site of the **Lookout**. A summer hotel since 1891, the Lookout is an unpretentious extension of a home that's been in the Flye family since 1800. Three of the inn's five rooms have water views, as do all seven cottages. The inn closes from mid-October to mid-May, but a cottage or two remain open all winter. The dining room, featuring fresh fish and produce from the garden, is open to the public for dinner by reservation; Tel: (207) 359-2188.

On the way back to Blue Hill pause to watch the water churn through the narrows at the village of Blue Hill Falls.

From there take Route 172 north, which brings you by the
Surry Inn, serving good, reasonably priced dinners with a
view of Contention Cove (Tel: 207/667-5091). From Surry it's
just a few miles to Route 1 at Ellsworth, the gateway to
Mount Desert Island and Acadia National Park.

—Christina Tree

MOUNT DESERT ISLAND

In 1947, when *Le Figaro* reported that fire had destroyed
17,000 acres of forest in Maine and much of the town of Bar
Harbor, the newspaper implied that the fire had been set by
local "peasants" in protest against the opulence of the area's
many estates. (It is not known, in fact, how the fire started.)

Bar Harbor, which occupies a corner of the eastern side of
Mount Desert Island, itself east of Blue Hill peninsula, still
evokes images of wealth and social status—although today
it's a motley, tourist-clogged town, the gateway to the only
major piece of the Maine coast that's public. Luckily, it's the
most beautiful piece of all.

The 35,000 acres (58 square miles) of **Acadia National
Park** that cover half of Mount Desert Island (other lands
belonging to Acadia can be found on Isle au Haut, covered
in the East Penobscot Bay section, and Schoodic Peninsula,
discussed further below) encompass more than a dozen
mountains rising from the sea and from the shores of five
large lakes. Magnificent at first glance, Acadia rewards those
who take the time to delve deeper with a beauty composed
of numberless small details: masses of seashells, blankets of
wildflowers, and hundreds of species of birds and marine
fauna.

The island of Mount Desert, which is about five times the
size of Manhattan, has much to offer both inside and outside
the park's boundaries. The summit of Cadillac Mountain,
literally the high point of the island and the park, yields a
360-degree view of the area's island-dotted bays, coves and
inlets, forests and beaches, and small fishing villages.

Since 1836 Mount Desert (pronounced dez-ERT) has
been linked to the mainland by bridge, which made little
difference to the visitors of the 1870s known as "rusticators,"
who all arrived by steamboat. By the turn of the century,
however, the large volume of visitors—easily filling a dozen
huge hotels as well as many mansion-size "cottages" in

season—came by express train from Philadelphia, New York, and Boston.

Cars were not allowed on Mount Desert until 1915, and then only after heated debate. Summer resident John D. Rockefeller—whose own fortune had been fueled by oil—was among those who approved the ban. He responded to the arrival of the automobile by commissioning more than 50 miles of carriage roads, deftly designed to blend into the natural lay of the land yet to maximize views—and guaranteed to be forever off-limits to cars. These carriage trails remain, and so it happens that visitors of all enterprise and energy levels can still appreciate Acadia's beauty to their own satisfaction. Today's five million annual visitors can choose among driving the 27-mile Park Loop Road, which follows some superb shoreline and leads to the top of Cadillac Mountain, renting a mountain bike or taking a horse-drawn carriage ride along Rockefeller's paths, or hiking some of the 100 or so miles of walking trails, which range from gentle to difficult.

Rockefeller is just one of many philanthropists to have shaped Acadia. Fearing that lumbering and development would erode the island's natural beauty, several of its wealthiest and most influential summer residents formed the Trustees of Public Reservations in 1903, a time when public parks were still novelties. After patiently and steadily amassing land for a decade, the cadre used all its lobbying skills and social clout finally to convince President Woodrow Wilson to accept the land it had accumulated for a public park in 1916. In this spirit of noblesse oblige land contributions continued for several decades.

In addition to land, the private sector left many other legacies to Acadia National Park. The Robert Abbe museum displays a fine collection of early New England Indian artifacts compiled by a New York surgeon, and the adjacent Sieur de Monts Spring was one of the first purchases by George Dorr, a Boston textile heir who devoted his life and fortune to the park. In Northeast Harbor the Asticou Terraces and Thuya gardens, along with the Asticou Azalea Garden, are the work—and gifts—of two noted landscape architects of the time.

VISITING MOUNT DESERT ISLAND
Mount Desert itself is relatively free from the commercial clutter that usually surrounds the world's major tourist attractions. But Acadia is the second most heavily visited national park in America, and, as you would expect, a strip of self-styled factory outlets and "museums" lines the 9 miles (14½ km) of Route 3 south from Route 1 at Ellsworth to the

causeway at the island's entrance. It peters out in a lineup of cottages and motels along the stretch of Route 3 that leads to Hulls Cove, where signs route you to the Acadia National Park Visitor Center and the Park Loop Road or to Route 3 and Bar Harbor. (If you know that you don't want to drive the Loop Road or visit Bar Harbor, or if you just want to do some hiking first, you might stop at the Thompson Island Information Center, just over the causeway in Acadia, and pick up some maps and get some advice first thing.)

If you enter the Park Loop Road from the visitor center, you will find yourself on a one-way 27-mile circuit around much of the eastern half of the island (there are several opportunities to exit the road once you're on it).

The village of Bar Harbor, a tight grid of streets lined with shops, restaurants, and lodging places, is just beyond Hulls Cove via Route 3. Turn-of-the-century mansions, many of them now inns, still line waterside West Street, overlooking Bar Island (accessible at low tide), and the Shore Path, overlooking the Porcupine Islands. Route 3 continues through Bar Harbor—its name changes from Eden Street to Mount Desert, to Main Street, and back to Route 3—and then leads south and west to Seal Harbor and on through Northeast Harbor.

Northeast Harbor, at the mouth of Somes Sound (on the eastern side), is a 1990s version of Bar Harbor in the 1890s, with a prestigious inn and a shopping street lined with art galleries that cater to the very rich and their guests, most of whom arrive by sailing yacht at this small village's large marina. Many of the town's mansions overlook **Somes Sound**, a narrow, steep-banked arm of water said to be the only true fjord on the Eastern seaboard. It divides Mount Desert Island almost in two.

From Bar Harbor it's also possible to bypass the Park Loop Road area entirely and to cut through the heart of the island on Route 233, past park headquarters, and on to the "quiet side" of Mount Desert, as residents of Southwest Harbor and Bass Cove are fond of calling their western half of the island. Some of Mount Desert's most rewarding hiking paths are here, on mountains overlooking Seal Cove and Long ponds as well as Echo Lake, and some of the best views of Cadillac Mountain and its rounded, pink-granite neighbors are from Southwest Harbor.

But assuredly the finest views of the mountains are from the water. Whether you take a day sail out of Bar Harbor on three-masted schooner *Natalie Todd,* a mail boat to the Cranberry Isles, or an excursion in a sea kayak or a rental punt, don't fail to get out on the water and see the bald cliffs as Samuel de Champlain saw them in 1604, prompting him to christen the island L'Isle des Monts Deserts.

Many visitors still catch their first—or last—view of the island from the Marine Atlantic Bluenose Ferry, which makes the run from Bar Harbor to Yarmouth, Nova Scotia, in just six hours (June to late September). For many years the only car ferry from Maine to Canada's Maritimes, the Bar Harbor service now complements Marine Atlantic's alternate route from Portland. One strategy for exploring Maine and the Canadian Maritimes is to drive along the Maine coast as far north as Bar Harbor, then hop the ferry to Yarmouth, and return from Yarmouth to Portland (or vice versa).

Mount Desert offers plenty of space to get away from the crowds that converge in July and August, when lodging prices soar. From September through mid-October, though, even Bar Harbor is less crowded and expensive and the island is just as beautiful. The rest of the year is considered off-season; if you come then be sure to find lodgings with a fireplace.

Finally, what the brochures don't mention about Bar Harbor and points east is weather. Bright, sunny days are precious on this foggy, wind-scoured coast. In allotting your time, throw in an extra day or two for "fog time."

Ellsworth and Environs

Ellsworth, on Route 1 northeast of the Blue Hill Péninsula and due north of Mount Desert, is a crossroads town that serves as the commercial center for much of eastern Maine. The **Grand**, the town's classic Main Street theater, draws an audience for its live performances and films from up to 100 miles around; Tel: (207) 667-9500. The **Mex** restaurant, also on Main Street at number 185, is good for bean soup and enchiladas, but service can be slow; Tel: (207) 667-4494. **Maidee's**, the gentrified diner across the street, offers Asian and standard American fare; Tel: (207) 667-3640.

Deep in the strip of malls along Route 1, beyond the old downtown, is **Willy's**, a local clothing store that's grown into eastern Maine's version of L. L. Bean, while the real thing, an **L. L. Bean** outlet, is just across the highway.

Also on Route 1, just south of town, is the **Big Chicken Barn**, Maine's largest used bookstore. Most book and antiques lovers will stop in their tracks, unwittingly drawn into the former chicken house by its 110,000 used books and magazines and a cooperative of more than 30 antiques dealers.

At the southern fringe of town, off Route 1 on Route 172 (just before the bridge into Ellsworth proper), is Ellsworth's real treasure. Built in the 1820s by a wealthy land agent, the **Colonel Black Mansion** is a consummately graceful brick house with floor-to-ceiling windows and a spiral staircase, appropriately furnished and set in 150 landscaped acres (open daily except Sundays from May to mid-October; Tel: 207/667-8671).

From Ellsworth the commercial strip continues south along Route 3 most of the way into Bar Harbor. Roughly a mile (1½ km) south of the junction of Routes 1 and 3 a small sign on the right signals the entrance to the **Stanwood Homestead and Birdsacre Sanctuary**. This was the home of Cordelia Johnson Stanwood (1865–1958), a pioneering ornithologist and nature photographer. Trails web the 130-acre grounds, where owls, hawks, and other injured birds are housed in cages. The mid-19th-century house contains a collection of stuffed birds, eggs, and photographs; picnickers are welcome.

It's easy to scorn the go-cart tracks, miniature golf, and other commercial attractions along Route 3, but one person's junk is another's treasure: These diversions can be lifesavers for people travelling with children on those inevitable foggy days. And for some reason the clutch of lobster pounds around the entrance to Mount Desert Island charge the lowest prices for lobster dinners in all of Maine.

MOUNT DESERT ISLAND AND ACADIA NATIONAL PARK

The Acadia National Park Visitor Center, a sleek stone-and-glass building on Route 3 at Hulls Cove in the northeastern part of the island, shows an introductory film to the park and provides both an excellent map/guide to the park's driving, biking, and walking trails and copies of the "Acadia Beaver Log," which describes the park's extensive program of cruises, guided walks, lectures, and demonstrations. Where you go from the visitors' center may depend on the weather. If it's a beautiful day, grab it: Drive the Loop Road or go for a hike or boat excursion. Otherwise you might head south into Bar Harbor to search out indoor diversions.

Bar Harbor

Bar Harbor is a bustling place filled with shops and restaurants, and is best reserved for a rainy day. Most of Bar Harbor's streets seem to slope down to the **town pier**. The dock for excursion boats, private yachts, and fishing vessels, the pier is a good place to begin your visit; above it, **Agamont Park** offers an overview of the action. Shops and restaurants run uphill from the pier along Main Street. **Bayside Landing**, a new complex of shops at number 53, houses **Testa's**, a Bar Harbor dining landmark that has served three square meals a day (pretty standard fare) in one shape or another since 1934; Tel: (207) 288-3327. **Island Artisans**, at number 99, is a cooperative run by 24 area craftspeople whose work—pottery, wooden birds and carvings, jewelry, woven clothing, silk-screened fabrics, stained and blown glass—is of very good quality. **Caleb's Sunrise**, at number 115, carries well-chosen leather, wood, clay, fiber, and metal crafted work from many places, as well as graphic art.

Restaurants and shops also line several blocks of adjoining Cottage Street. **Bubba's**, at number 30, and the **Island Chowder House**, at number 38, are both good for lunch; if you are in a real rush try cafeteria-style **Epi's Sub & Pizza**, serving freshly baked calzones and salads. The 1932 Art Deco **Criterion Theater**, on Cottage Street, presents first-run and art films (Tel: 207/288-3441).

The **green**, at the corner of Main and Mount Desert streets (parallel to Cottage), is a good people-watching spot. The former comfort station here now houses the **Island Association of Museums and Historical Societies** with exhibits and information on the area's nonprofit museums (as opposed to commercial attractions that bill themselves as museums). Just beyond the green, in the basement of the Jesup Memorial Library at 34 Mount Desert Street, the **Bar Harbor Historical Society** exhibits photographs of 19th-century hotels, steamers, the old cog railway, and the 1947 fire and its aftermath. (Open daily except Sundays from mid-June to November; Tel: 207/288-3838.) **St. Saviour's Episcopal Church**, across the street, is fitted with 1870s Tiffany windows.

Finally, for a bit of old Bar Harbor head to **J. H. Butterfield**, back at the green at 156 Main Street. The store, decorated with stuffed stag heads and a tile floor, has been the town's purveyor of "fancy foods" since 1887. Buy a sandwich and a slice of lemon cake here and head down Albert Meadow to Grant Park, overlooking the harbor, then follow the Shore Path back to Agamont Park.

DINING IN AND AROUND BAR HARBOR

Bar Harbor boasts more than 40 restaurants, all of which seem to be mobbed for dinner in July and August. The best-known dining room is the **Reading Room**, part of the Bar Harbor Inn, which in the 1880s served as a men's club. Service is formal, the specialties are steak and seafood, and the music is smooth. Tel: (207) 288-3351.

George's Restaurant doesn't advertise, but there it is hidden away at 7 Stephen's Lane, just off Main Street behind the First National Bank, serving dinner from 5:30 P.M. until midnight. The cuisine is creative Greek, with specialties like seafood strudel and seafood sausage, Greek wines, and homemade ice creams. Open mid-June to November; Tel: (207) 288-4505.

The **Porcupine Grill**, 123 Cottage Street, is furnished in old oak, its walls hung with photographs of the Porcupine Islands, which are just offshore from Bar Harbor. Dishes are a blend of reverently prepared fresh vegetables and entrées such as homemade chicken and veal sausage, roasted salmon, and crab cakes. Breads are served warm. Closed in midwinter; Tel: (207) 288-3884.

At the leafy, quiet end of Cottage Street, **124 Cottage Street** has a 55-item salad bar and features spicy seafood dishes such as Szechwan shrimp, mussels marinara, and bouillabaisse; Tel: (207) 288-4383. Next door at 122 Cottage, the **Quiet Earth** serves vegetarian dishes and seafood (Tel: 207/288-3696), while **Miguel's Mexican Restaurant**, at 51 Rodick Street, is generally considered to have the best Mexican food in Maine (open 5:00 to 10:00 P.M. nightly; Tel: 207/288-5117).

On the Park Loop Road (see below), just north of the turnoff to Route 3, are **Jordan Pond** and the **Jordan Pond House**. Afternoon tea with popovers at the Jordan Pond House is such a popular ritual that it can be a bit of a nightmare due to the crowds. Built originally in the 1870s, destroyed by fire and rebuilt in 1979, the Jordan Pond House is as basic a stop on the loop as the top of Cadillac Mountain. It's less crowded for lunch and dinner, and the legendary popovers go with any meal. Tel: (207) 276-3316.

If you're looking for the area's premier dining experience, you'll have to head out of Bar Harbor to Hancock, about a 20-minute drive north of Bar Harbor on Route 1 by way of Marlboro. **Le Domaine**, which resembles a French country inn, is frequently rated the best restaurant in all of Maine, period. Chef-owner Nicole Purslow, a graduate of the Cordon Bleu, carries on a tradition begun by her mother, who ran an inn in Les Baux, Provence, before fleeing to the United States during World War II. Purslow's specialties include a memorable pâté, *lapin aux pruneaux,* and *escalope de saumon à l'oseille.* Tel: (207) 422-3395.

Lobster Pounds

Maine is the place to eat lobster, and the place to eat lobster in Maine is a lobster pound. A "pound" is a Maine institution wherein you select your crustacean from a tank and then sit down at a plank table (outdoors, the proper place to consume lobster and clams) to a Styrofoam cup of chowder or a paper plate of steamers while awaiting the lobster, which should be steamed, not broiled.

While not a true lobster pound (you don't choose your own lobster, and other types of seafood are served), **Fisherman's Landing**, at 47 West Street in Bar Harbor, does have outside tables right on the water; Tel: (207) 288-4632. **Oak Point Lobster Pound**, in Trenton (4½ miles/7 miles from the bridge to Mount Desert via Route 3), is the local favorite; Tel: (207) 667-8548. The **Tidal Falls Lobster Pound**, half a mile (1 km) off Route 1 in Hancock, also fulfills all the requirements (bring your own wine or beer; Tel: 207/422-6818).

Around the Island

THE PARK LOOP ROAD

Once you have paid your $5 entrance fee (again, good for one week) at the entrance station south of Bar Harbor, you are free to follow the Loop Road on its 27-mile circuit around the eastern half of Mount Desert Island. Or you may prefer to rent a bike in Bar Harbor and explore the carriage roads, which are also accessible by horse-drawn tours led by **Wildwood Stables**, just off the Loop Road about half a mile (1 km) south of Jordan Pond House. (Tel: 207/276-3622). Our coverage here follows the loop all the way south, then exits it to head west to Northeast Harbor and the rest of Mount Desert Island.

Cadillac Mountain, the first sight of interest on the Loop Road south of the Hulls Cove Visitor Center, is a good place to start a tour of Acadia National Park. You may choose to drive or hike up—either way, bring a picnic. Said to be the highest mountain on the Atlantic shoreline north of Brazil, it affords wonderful views of the entire area. Like many high-profile tourist attractions, Cadillac is often crawling with people, but if you imagine what it would be like if you came on it all alone on a clear day you can more fully appreciate its grandeur. The smooth rocks invite you to explore and linger, looking off across Frenchman Bay, stippled with islands. With water stretching before you in every direction you have the sense of being in the prow of a ship. Unfortunately, when reality intrudes you find yourself in just another busy people-watching spot.

After visiting Cadillac Mountain backtrack a fraction of a mile to the point where one-way traffic begins and follow the Loop Road southeast to the **Robert Abbe Museum of Stone Age Antiquities**, one of New England's few collections of Indian artifacts. The Abbe Museum's holdings include a canoe fashioned from a single piece of birch bark as well as numerous ornaments, tools, and baskets, some dating back 5,000 years (open April to November; Tel: 207/288-3519). Right next door is the entrance to the stone-canopied **Sieur de Monts Spring**, one of George Dorr's first purchases and the symbolic core of the park that grew up around it. The adjacent **Wild Gardens of Acadia**, maintained by the Bar Harbor Garden Club, displays neatly labeled specimens of 300 species of local flora.

As you continue south along the Loop Road you'll see signs indicating various trailheads and natural attractions. Among the latter are **Sand Beach**, which is actually composed of tiny shells (there are a lifeguard and changing rooms here, but the water is usually very cold), and **Thunder Hole**, a small cave through which water rushes noisily in and out.

We leave the Park Loop Road at its southern end (the rest of the loop is relatively uninteresting), but you may choose to continue around it to Jordan Pond House (see Dining in and around Bar Harbor, above), a traditional spot for tea a little farther north on the loop.

ROUTE 3 TO NORTHEAST HARBOR

Exit the Park Loop Road at the Stanley Brook entrance and you'll soon come upon **Asticou Terraces** (modestly marked on the left side of Route 3 between Seal Harbor and Northeast Harbor), designed and donated to the park by landscape architect Joseph Henry Curtis (1841–1928). Curtis's series of fir-shaded stone terraces have transformed the hillside into a superb place to sit, stroll, and take in the views. Walking up the terraces you'll reach **Thuya Lodge**, Curtis's former home and now a botanical library. Formal perennial gardens designed by landscape architect Charles Savage stretch behind the house (the house and gardens are open from July to Labor Day). A short distance farther along Route 3, near its junction with Route 198, is the **Asticou Azalea Garden**, a very different example of Savage's work. Oriental in theme, the garden is especially splendid in June, when the azaleas are in bloom.

The **Asticou Inn**, between the two gardens, is the island's grandest hotel, very elegant in a low-key sort of way. The formal dining room is open to the public, but be forewarned that the best tables are reserved for regular guests; Tel: (207) 276-3344. Nonguests are also welcome in the lobby and on the porch, which runs the length of the inn, overlooking formal gardens and the harbor. (Open early May to late December.)

NORTHEAST HARBOR

The obvious point of entry to downtown Northeast Harbor (at the mouth of Somes Sound), whether you arrive by yacht or car, is the **marina**, where there are parking spots, rest rooms, an information center (with a reading room and showers for yachtsmen), tennis courts, and a public phone. From the marina competing companies run out to **Great Cranberry** and **Little Cranberry Isles**, both dotted with private residences. The **Islesford Historical Museum** on Little Cranberry offers insights into Maine history from the perspective of these small islands. Open daily in summer; closed October through early June. Tel: (207) 288-3338. Park rangers lead tours from Northeast Harbor's marina to remote, uninhabited **Baker Island** to examine the delicate fauna there.

Northeast Harbor's Main Street is short but studded with boutiques and the island's best art galleries; **Smart Studio & Art Gallery** and the **Wingspread Gallery** are among the best in Maine. The Old Firehouse, also on Main Street, is now occupied by the **Great Harbor Collection**, an eclectic assortment of exhibits ranging from a restored country kitchen to a fire engine (open Memorial Day through Columbus Day).

A hidden oasis in Northeast Harbor is the **Outback Café & Deli**, tucked in the back of the **Pine Tree Market** (Tel: 207/276-3335), a grocery with an unusual stock of wines and liquor that makes deliveries to the marina and to the mansions squirreled away on the harbor and along Manchester Road, overlooking the entrance to Somes Sound.

SOMESVILLE

At the end of Main Street bear left as far and as long as you can, following Manchester Road onto **Sargent Drive**, which hugs the sound for several miles before rejoining Route 198. Then follow Route 198 north and west to Route 102 and turn south into the tiny village of Somesville. Somesville's former general store is now the **Port in a Storm Bookstore**, two floors of books, compact disks, and cassettes; sofas are positioned to overlook the water. The former Masonic Hall now houses the **Acadia Repertory Theater**, a resident group that performs Tuesday through Sunday in July and August. Tel: (207) 244-7260.

SOUTHWEST HARBOR

Follow signs south from Somesville along Route 102 to Southwest Harbor, a small village with a relaxing atmosphere, neither as upscale as Northeast Harbor nor as busy as Bar Harbor. Half the village's acreage lies within Acadia National Park.

The harbor, more than a mile (1½ km) down Clark Point Road from the village, is the site of the **Mount Desert Oceanarium**, whose exhibits include 20 tanks displaying sea life (open mid-May to mid-October; Tel: 207/244-7330); and **Beal's**, a stand selling crabmeat and lobster rolls on the pier.

Southwest Harbor is also home to the **Claremont**, the most old-fashioned—and oldest—of the island's hotels (open from late May to late October). The 24 units in the main hotel and the 12 cottages (each with a living room and fireplace, and most with private bath) are non-smoking and meticulously maintained. Still owned by one of the park's founding families, the Claremont is friendly but dignified (though not at all stuffy), with a strong sense of its place in the island's history. Facilities include a dining room in which every table commands a view, a long verandah lined with green rockers, clay tennis courts, and rowboats and motorboats. The informal **Boathouse** restaurant, overlooking the mountains across the water, is popular for lunch. The hotel's social season revolves around the August Croquet Classic.

The **Drydock Café**, at 108 Main Street in the middle of Southwest Harbor, is an informal place to lunch or dine on *quesadilla* or Cajun chicken (Tel: 207/244-3886 or 244-5842), while the **Clark Point Café**, on Clark Point Road, is good for vegetarian dishes as well as filet mignon or seafood stew (Tel: 207/244-5816).

A final lunch option is to choose from the 22 varieties of sandwiches at **Deacon Seat**, at the junction of Clark Point Road and Route 102, and picnic on top of nearby **Beech Mountain** (an easy hike), followed by a dip in **Echo Lake** (north of the village); or at the **Seawall Picnic Area** south of the village on Route 102A. The nearby Wonderland and Ship Harbor hiking trails offer a bucolic blend of woods and shore.

BASS HARBOR

Bass Harbor, just down Route 102 from Southwest Harbor, is a working fishing village, not particularly pretty but lively and authentic, without the gussied-up look that other villages have taken on. It's also the departure point for **Swan's Island**, six miles offshore, a flat island good for biking (you can rent a bike in Southwest Harbor). Besides the usual lobster wharves, fishermen, and small summer community, there is the **Swan's Island Education Society** museum, in the Seaside Hall, less than a mile (1½ km) from the ferry (open seasonally; Tel: 207/526-4350). Its displays include an old-fashioned store, a school, and old tools and photographs.

Bass Harbor also claims two of the better places to dine on Mount Desert. The **Seafood Ketch**, a family-run restaurant open for all three meals, is known for homemade breads and very fresh seafood (open May to December; Tel: 207/244-7463). At the end of the Swan's Island ferry road, the **Deck House Restaurant** is in a class of its own: The serving staff, drawn from top music schools, begins singing cabaret numbers around 8:30 P.M. The menu consists of basic seafood and Continental dishes, but they are especially well prepared here. Reservations required; Tel: (207) 244-5044. (Open seasonally.)

ELSEWHERE ON THE ISLAND
Antique-car lovers should ferret out the little-publicized **Seal Cove Auto Museum**, north of Bass Harbor via Route 102, then left on Pretty Marsh Road. The life's work of a private collector, the museum displays 100 vintage cars and more than 30 motorcycles (open daily 10:00 A.M. to 5:00 P.M., June to October; Tel: 207/244-9242). Another hidden treasure in this northwestern corner of the island is the **Blagden Preserve**, a 110-acre nature conservancy tract with inviting walking trails leading to a prime spot for seal watching. North of Somesville, look for Indian Point Road and follow it to the end; the entrance is signposted.

STAYING ON MOUNT DESERT
Although Mount Desert claims one of the largest concentrations of inns and bed-and-breakfasts in the state, you do not want to arrive here without reservations in July and August. You *will* probably find a room, but it may cost more than $300. Yes, $300. Over the past decade a couple dozen former mansions have been converted to inns, their guest rooms fitted with whirlpool baths and canopy beds. Mansion inns with water views fetch prices (in summer) equaled within New England only by the best Boston hotels. Mansions without views form the next echelon.

Bar Harbor and Environs
The **Inn at Canoe Point** in Hulls Cove, 2 miles (3 km) north of Bar Harbor near the entrance to the park visitors' center, is a tastefully restored, imaginatively decorated 1889 Tudor-style house with five guest rooms, most with water views and all with private baths. The master suite has its own fireplace and deck and may just be the most romantic room on the island.

The nearby **Bay Ledge Inn & Spa** is a newer, plainer house, but it does have a small, heated pool with a spellbinding view of Frenchman's Bay and a very private pebble beach at the bottom of 79 steps (with landings to break the climb). Facilities include a hot tub and exercise machines;

off-season a full spa program is offered. The **Manor House Inn**, one of Bar Harbor's renovated mansions, has exceptional detailing (especially the woodwork) to recommend its 14 non-smoking rooms, several with working fireplaces and all with private baths. (Open May through October.)

Elsewhere in Bar Harbor three more deftly restored cottages offer real luxury. **Nannau Seaside Bed and Breakfast**, vintage 1904 and right on Compass Harbor (south of the center of town), has three reasonably priced non-smoking guest rooms with shared baths. (Open May through October.) The **Tides**, on West Street (handy to offshore Bar Island as well as downtown shops and restaurants), has three guest rooms, all with private baths, and a suite with a fireplace. All rooms have ocean views. This non-smoking inn is open from Memorial Day through October. At **Breakwater**, a 1904 Tudor cottage under the same ownership, wicker porch rockers overlook a lawn sweeping to the Shore Path and the water. The six non-smoking guest rooms all have a private bath, fireplace, and queen-size bed.

The **Bar Harbor Inn** is one of the few downtown lodging places with water views that is geared to families. Its core, now occupied by its restaurant (discussed under Bar Harbor, above), was built in the 1880s to house the village's elite summer men's club, and its 51 guest rooms represent the first lodging space in town after the 1947 fire. A modest 15-unit motel was added later and has since been upstaged by a 64-unit oceanfront lodge with large, well-decorated rooms, each with its own balcony overlooking the bay. The complex is set in seven manicured acres with a pool and a playground. Its only drawback is that it caters to bus groups.

Beyond Bar Harbor

The island's two grand old resorts—the **Asticou Inn** and the **Claremont**—are discussed under Northeast Harbor and Southwest Harbor, respectively. Also among the island's best lodging options, both in Northeast Harbor, are the **Harbourside Inn**, an expansive 1880s "cottage" set in two wooded acres with 14 non-smoking guest units (some are suites and many have working fireplaces); and the **Maison Suisse**, another elegant turn-of-the-century mansion, with ten guest rooms (including four suites), in the middle of the village. Both are closed November through April.

Southwest Harbor claims a number of attractive, reasonably priced bed-and-breakfasts. Among them are three neighbors in the middle of the village: Penury Hall, Inn at Southwest, and Kingsleigh House. **Penury Hall** was the first B and B on Mount Desert, and its owners, Toby and Gretchen Strong, are longtime local residents who pride themselves on steering their guests to all the right places. The three rooms share two baths. Extras here include a sauna, a canoe, a 21-foot sloop, and a Windsurfer. **Kingsleigh House**, across the street, is a spacious Colonial Revival with eight rooms (all with private baths and non-smoking) and a suite occupying the entire third floor. The **Inn at Southwest**, next door, is Victorian style, with nine rooms (all with private baths and all non-smoking) furnished in antiques and Waverly wallpapers. (Open March to November.)

Between the village and harbor is the non-smoking **Harbor Cottage Inn**, built in 1870 as an annex to a now-vanished inn. Its eight rooms have private baths, some with claw-footed tubs, others with whirlpools. For families, **Seal Cove Farm**, a century-old farmhouse on Route 102 with plenty of animals, also bears mention. It overlooks a lake and has four spacious, pleasant rooms, two with private bath and all non-smoking.

Finally, **Crocker House Country Inn** in Hancock, on Route 1 about 5 miles (8 km) from Bar Harbor, is a true country inn with stenciled rooms, handmade quilts, private baths, and not too many frills. There's room to relax downstairs in the three-story 1880s inn proper as well as in the carriage-barn library, off the hot-tub room. (Closed January to late April.) The town dock and tennis courts are across the way.

—*Christina Tree*

DOWN EAST MAINE AND PASSAMAQUODDY BAY

"Down east," as we have explained, is a nautical term referring to the way Maine's coastal winds blow dependably from the southwest, easing sailing vessels ever eastward "down" the coast. Geographically the term refers somewhat ambiguously to the easternmost stretch of the Maine coast, from Bar Harbor on up. Purists discount even Bar Harbor's claims to down east status, insisting that only the coast of Washington County (up from Steuben) is truly down east, while others would bestow down east status on even the Midcoast.

Washington County, which reaches as far east as you can get in the United States, is a throwback to Maine as it was 40 years ago. Lobster boats still outnumber yachts along its 921 miles of coastline, and the shore trails still see just a smatter-

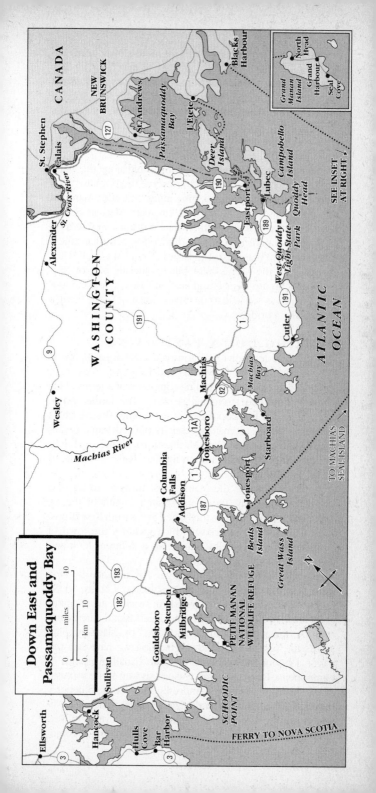

ing of hikers. Time seems to move more slowly here, and you'll find yourself slowing your pace to match it. The only visitor attractions are small historical museums, such as the 18th-century Burnham Tavern in Machias, the 1818 Ruggles House in Columbia Falls, and the Old Sardine Village Museum in Lubec. Since there is little reason to rush from one attraction to the next, you'll find yourself talking to the locals more than in other parts of coastal Maine.

Birding, especially puffin watching, is big along the Atlantic coast here; the best place to observe the brightly billed birds is Machias Seal Island, nine miles off Cutler. Managed as a lighthouse station and bird sanctuary, Machias Seal is one of four islands just off the Maine coast that were erased from most American maps (and added to Canadian ones) more than 150 years ago. The largest, Grand Manan, lies just 15 miles off the Maine coast but is officially part of New Brunswick, as are Deer Island, just off Eastport, and Campobello, which is so close to the Maine town of Lubec that it's attached by a bridge.

TOURING DOWN EAST MAINE

This piece of coast divides into two distinct areas. Between Sullivan (just east of Ellsworth) and Lubec the coast runs along a fairly clean diagonal line composed of a series of fir-topped peninsulas stretching seaward. The farther down east you go, the less populated these become. Anyone who's searching for the ultimate sparsely populated Maine peninsula should drive east from Machias through the small lobstering village of Cutler and on through Bailey's Mistake to West Quoddy Light.

At this lighthouse the Maine coast turns a corner into Passamaquoddy Bay, the island-spotted mouth of the St. Croix River, which divides the United States from New Brunswick. This part of the coast, which includes the town of Eastport and Campobello Island, has a different look and feel than that facing the Atlantic.

Passamaquoddy Bay is not large. The distance by land from Machias, county seat of Washington County, to St. Andrews, the Bar Harbor of New Brunswick, is just 80 miles (128 km). In summer, when the Deer Island ferries are running, the journey can be shortened by island-hopping across the bay. In the following section we have ignored national boundaries and included the Canadian islands of Campobello, Deer, and Grand Manan, as well as the sophisticated old resort town of St. Andrews, a foil for the blueberry barrens, secluded lakes, and rugged coastal walks of Washington County. The state of Maine and the province of New Brunswick have similarly come together to mount a promotional effort to link Washington County and New Brunswick points of interest in a unified destination—in effect bridging an artificial political division of a natural geographic area. They have called this area—essentially the roughly 90-mile stretch of Route 1 from Machias to Blacks Harbour, New Brunswick—the Quoddy Loop.

More than 90 percent of the visitors who travel as far down east as Bar Harbor get no farther. What you notice first about the stretch of Route 1 beyond Bar Harbor is the relative lack of traffic. You may also notice the way the sky seems to loom larger above the blueberry barrens, which are literally blue with berries by early August, russet in September. But here, as is true in the rest of Maine, you won't fully absorb the beauty of your surroundings unless you leave the highway to wander down the peninsulas that extend along tidal rivers and out into the Atlantic and the Cobscook and Passamaquoddy bays.

The wave of new inns and bed-and-breakfasts that flooded most of the Maine coast in the 1980s was a mere ripple by the time it reached Washington County. But it did bring a dozen or so interesting and widely scattered places to stay, enough to double the number of such establishments already here and to turn what had been a "pass-through" region into a genuine destination.

The Quoddy Loop as we've defined it above is doable in two days, but it's most enjoyable if you take the time to stray off the highway, to walk on Great Wass Island and Quoddy Head, and to spend a day each in St. Andrews and on Grand Manan Island, New Brunswick. Fishermen should also allow at least a day to test the backcountry lakes north of Calais.

Plan to spend at least one night in Addison or Jonesport, another in the Machias area or on Campobello Island, one on Grand Manan, the next in St. Andrews, and a final night in Eastport, an old sardine-packing port on Moose Island. While geographically Eastport is in the middle of our itinerary, its haunting, end-of-the-world feeling makes it a fitting conclusion to our tour of Passamaquoddy Bay.

THE ATLANTIC COAST OF WASHINGTON COUNTY
Sullivan to Machias

The rusty iron bridge on Route 1 separating the towns of Hancock and Sullivan, 14 miles (22 km) east of Ellsworth, is generally recognized as the gateway to down east Maine. Just east of the bridge in Sullivan a road sign points back along a wooded road to the **Barter Family Art Gallery**, a couple of rooms in Philip Barter's modest home filled with the original furniture and primitive, bold paintings for which this artist is known. (Closed from January to mid-May; Tel: 207/ 422-3190.) A few miles up Route 1 from Sullivan the view across Frenchman Bay to the mountains of Mount Desert Island is so splendid that a pullout area (near Dunbar's store) has been provided. The aptly named **Island View Inn**, set well back from Route 1, is a spacious turn-of-the-century shingled cottage that also enjoys this panorama. Large, sea-bright common rooms downstairs complement the seven comfortable guest rooms, five with private bath.

Farther along on Route 1 at the neck of the **Schoodic Peninsula** is **Gouldsboro**, a town that values its privacy. Its large old summer homes are sequestered off Route 186 facing Cadillac Mountain and its rounded neighbors across Frenchman Bay. Note the sign for **Bartlett Maine Estate Winery**, Maine's oldest and most highly rated fruit winery. Tours are available from June through mid-November; Tel: (207) 546-2408.

Eleven miles (18 km) down the peninsula on Route 186 from the Gouldsboro town center (marked by the general store) is another section of Acadia National Park. A loop road circles **Schoodic Point**, affording nice views of Mount Desert, and a short trail leads to Schoodic Head's rocky summit. You needn't pack a picnic: The fishing village of **Winter Harbor**, near the park entrance, has three good eateries. The **Donut Hole**, down by the water, is the local hangout, best for its namesake and, oddly, fried fish. **Chase's Restaurant** serves a decent chowder, and **Fisherman's Inn** excels at steamed local crabmeat in butter; both are on the village's main street.

Just beyond Gouldsboro on Route 1 is **Steuben**, the first town in Washington County. Bird-watchers may want to turn off Route 1 here and follow Pigeon Hill Road south 6 miles (10 km) to the **Petit Manan National Wildlife Refuge**, where trails lead out to rocky Petit Manan Point.

The next town up Route 1 is **Milbridge**, home of Jasper Wyman and Sons, among Maine's oldest blueberry processors (established in 1874), a Christmas wreath factory, and one of the state's few surviving sardine canneries. Victorian houses line Main Street (Route 1) north and south of the general store and the Milbridge Theater, which features first-run films and the best popcorn in the county.

Milbridge is a good place to stop for lunch or dinner, at either **Milbridge House**, in the middle of the village (try a slice of their pie; Tel: 207/546-2020), or at the **Red Barn**, just beyond the village on Route 1, with deep booths and a big salad bar (Tel: 207/546-7721). **Hands On**, a small shop on the water side of Route 1 in Milbridge, showcases the work of 35 local craftspeople, including soft, bright woven and woollen clothing as well as jewelry, striking quilts, pillows, and pottery.

Route 1 dips inland beyond Milbridge, so you may want to opt for the shorter coastal route, 1A. Either route will bring you through **Columbia Falls**, a small village gathered around waterfalls, and the **Ruggles House**, one of the most elegant Federal-style buildings in all of New England. Built in 1818 for lumber dealer Thomas Ruggles, it is known for its graceful flying staircase and for both the abundance and the delicacy of its carved detailing (open June to mid-October; no phone). Next door, **Columbia Falls Pottery** sells the bright, sophisticated terra-cotta creations made in a studio on the premises by April Adams and Alan Burnham.

From Columbia Falls you may want to continue the extra couple of miles (3 km) south on Route 187 into Addison and down along the Pleasant River to **Pleasant Bay Bed & Breakfast**, a 100-acre working llama farm with wooded paths along the water. The house, recently built along traditional lines, has three tastefully decorated guest rooms (one has a private bath and all are non-smoking) with views of Pleasant Bay and ample common space.

From Addison you can continue southeast along the peninsula on Route 187 to **Jonesport**, a genuine lobstering and fishing port with a fine little marina sequestered off Sawyer Square. The non-smoking **Moose-A-Bec House**, overlooking the marina, offers two gracious rooms that share a bath (open May through October). **Tootsie's Bed and Breakfast**, a lobsterman's house at the other end of the village, has three rooms with a shared bath. The place to eat here—despite its unpromising exterior—is **Tall Barney**, near the bridge. Inside it's spanking clean and lined with booths. The service is quick and friendly and the specials are usually good. The middle table in the front room is reserved for local lobstermen. Tel: (207) 497-2403.

Together Jonesport and **Beals Island**, just across the bridge, claim Maine's largest lobstering fleet; the bridge serves as a viewing stand for Fourth of July lobster-boat races. A causeway connects the other end of Beals to **Great Wass Island**, a 1,540-acre nature preserve with tall pines and a two-mile path along the shore to Little Cape Point. The walk makes a great family outing, especially if you stop afterward at the **Islander**, on Alleys Bay Road. A takeout place with a deck overlooking the water, this is a good spot for fried clams and soft ice cream. (Open seasonally from 3:00 to 9:00 P.M.; Tel: 207/497-2000.)

Jonesport is also the departure point for Barna Norton's

Machias Seal Island puffin-watching expeditions. Machias Seal is the only place in Maine where you can watch puffins through a blind on dry land. Since the 1940s Norton, now assisted by his son John, has been bringing bird-watchers to the island, which, he claims, was granted to his family by Canada in 1865. (Canada maintains the island still belongs to it.) Norton emphasizes his views on the subject by bringing along an umbrella with an American flag on top. Tours are offered to a limited number during the nesting season, which runs roughly from May to August; Tel: (207) 497-5933.

MACHIAS

Machias, 17 miles (27 km) northeast of Columbia Falls on Route 1, looks funky, even shabby from Route 1 (Main Street), but it is a village of many charms. Its handsome **Congregational church** was built in 1826, and late-19th-century houses line the hilly residential streets. The falls in the middle of town gave Machias its name, which is said to mean "bad little falls"; they are accessible by footpaths and can be seen from the suspension footbridge accessible from Route 92.

Today the seat of Washington County, Machias was a hot-bed of patriotic zeal at the outbreak of the Revolution. A tour of the 1770 **Burnham Tavern**, which looks as if it might have been transported here from Newport's Colonial quarter, illuminates the events behind the first naval victory of the war, when the British man-of-war *Margaretta* was captured on June 12, 1775, by Machias men in the sloop *Unity*. The smallish yellow-clapboard, gambrel-roofed tavern, hidden behind the town's old-fashioned five-and-dime, contains period furnishings and mementos of the battle. (Open weekdays mid-June through Labor Day; Tel: 207/255-4432.)

Thanks to the presence of the University of Maine at Machias, the town's year-round calendar includes frequent concerts, plays, and other live performances. Among the shops in Machias is **Eastern Maine Books**, specializing in books both new and used about Maine. It's just off Route 1 at the northern end of town.

Staying and Dining in Machias

Once second only to Bangor as a lumber port, Machias retains many handsome old houses, two of which—the **Clark Perry House** and **Halcyon Days**—are now bed-and-breakfasts. The Clark Perry House, a mid-19th-century mansion nicely renovated by Robin and David Rier, has three guest rooms. All share a bath, but the Riers provide many small niceties for their guests' comfort. Halcyon Days features a wonderful view of Machias from its deck and a pleasant eat-in kitchen, which forms the heart of the household.

Machias is a scheduled stop on many bus tours from Bar Harbor to Campobello; they break for pie at **Helen's**, also on Route 1 and very well marked. Although this landmark has doubled its size and lost much of its original atmosphere over the years, the fruit pies topped with whipped cream are still outstanding. Open from 5:00 A.M. to 10:00 P.M., Helen's is, in fact, a good bet for all meals (no liquor served; Tel: 207/255-6506).

In nearby Machiasport (bear right on Route 92 before the bridge leading to downtown Machias), the oldest and most picturesque of the villages that make up the town of Machias, is **Micmac Farm**, considered Washington County's best restaurant. Occupying two low-beamed rooms of a house built in 1776 by a patriot who fled here from Nova Scotia, the restaurant usually offers a dinner menu of five entrées that Barbara Dunn manages to create in her minute kitchen. Prix-fixe dinners, including soup, salad, and delectable desserts, cost from $14 to $18 (bring your own wine). For reservations, Tel: (207) 255-3008 (closed Sundays and Mondays). Micmac Farm also offers three small efficiency guest cabins overlooking the river (open May to mid-October).

Farther down the peninsula on Route 92 are two more attractive bed-and-breakfasts: the **Gutsy Gull**, a deftly decorated 1850s house (five rooms with shared bath) with views of the Machias River and a hot tub; and **Starboard Cove**, Marion Davis's cozy home with a two-floor, two-person apartment overlooking the cove. Between the two B and Bs is **Jasper Beach**, an expanse of wave-tumbled and -polished pebbles of jasper and rhyolite (the water here is too cold for swimming).

From Machias you can continue down east along the coast to Cutler via Route 191 (our route), and proceed directly to Campobello Island via Routes 1 and 189; or take the high road, Route 1, to New Brunswick.

Cutler and Lubec

Cutler, 12 miles (19 km) down Route 191 from East Machias, is a lobstering village known throughout the world in intelligence circles. Just beyond the village is a navy communications center, said to be the world's most powerful radio station, providing communication to all units of the U.S. fleet in the North Atlantic, the Arctic, and Europe. Fortunately, the 26 antenna towers are not visible from **Little River Lodge**, an

1870s hotel turned country inn and restaurant in the middle of the village. At present the lodge is up for sale, and whether it will continue to be as pleasant as it is now remains to be seen (reserve for dinner; Tel: 207/259-4437). Cutler is also the base for Captain Andrew Patterson's **Bold Coast Charter Company**, which offers seasonal trips to Machias Seal Island (discussed above) and to the wildlife refuge on Cross Island in Machias Bay. Captain Patterson also offers cruises that run the length of this unspoiled coast, and, for a price, he will run groups out to Grand Manan (discussed below). Tel: (207) 259-4484.

Route 191 continues another 14 miles (22 km) through unspoiled bogs and woodlands, rejoining the road from Machias to Campobello (Route 189) 6 miles (10 km) west of Lubec.

Lubec was once Maine's sardine-canning capital, but the Peacock Company, the surviving cannery, is now processing salmon, as the strong currents in the bay seem to favor salmon farming. They also seem to attract whales, frequently visible in the warm-weather months from **Quoddy Head** in **West Quoddy Head State Park** (take South Lubec Road, marked from Route 189 just west of town). Open mid-April through October, this park is worth a visit, whales or no. The red-and-white-striped 1858 lighthouse is a beauty, and a two-mile trail to Carrying Place Cove hugs the cliffs.

If you happen to pass by between June and mid-October, the **Old Sardine Village Museum**, just beyond the turnoff for Quoddy Head on Route 189, may (or may not) be open. A large warehouse filled with genuinely interesting displays about Lubec's sardine-canning industry and era, the museum is run as a hobby by Barney Rier. Tel: (207) 733-2822.

While Lubec's downtown has virtually vanished, the village, like Machias, retains some handsome homes set high on its hill. One of them, now the **Home Port Inn**, houses what is widely recognized as the best restaurant around. All three meals are served at just eight well-spaced tables in the dining room at the back of the inn. The specialty is seafood, in such preparations as scampi served over linguine and creamed haddock with artichoke hearts. (Reserve for dinner; Tel: 207/733-2077.) The inn also offers seven antiques-furnished rooms, all with private bath.

Your best bet for lunch in Lubec is the **Hillside Restaurant**, on Route 189. As there's no view from the restaurant, buy some chowder and a lobster sandwich and take your lunch down to the town landing beneath the FDR Memorial Bridge, overlooking the "Sparkplug," as the curiously shaped Lubec Channel Light is known. Tel: (207) 733-4223.

AROUND PASSAMAQUODDY BAY

A WORD ON FOG

Weather is a factor in your explorations of Passamaquoddy Bay. To describe Campobello, Deer Island, Grand Manan, and West Quoddy Head, for that matter, as if you could count on blue skies and long views, would be misleading. The major reason this beautiful corner of the world is so little touristed isn't just its distance from points west: What the realtors and chambers of commerce don't mention is fog. While fog is endemic to most of the Maine coast, it is thicker and more abundant the farther you travel down east. It's even worse offshore. So it's probably a good thing that you can't reserve for the ferries to Deer and Grand Manan islands. Watch the weather forecast carefully before you set off.

Campobello Island

Billed as a yachting center and a haven from hay fever, Passamaquoddy Bay's Campobello Island (in New Brunswick, but linked to Lubec by bridge) was a fashionable resort in the 1880s. It was to stay in one of the island's big hotels that Franklin Delano Roosevelt's parents first came to Campobello. They subsequently built themselves a summer home, which they replaced in 1910 with a grand "cottage" that they later presented to Franklin and Eleanor. This is the 34-room house that forms the centerpiece for the 2,800-acre **Roosevelt Campobello International Park**, encompassing a third of the island. The terrain here is beautiful in the way that northern islands often are: rocky shores, quiet coves, dense woods, and long, undeveloped stretches.

A visitors' center shows a 15-minute film that depicts FDR's relationship to the island in his days before polio and the presidency, as does the house, which is charged with the spirit of the dynamic family. The Hubbard Cottage next door offers another glimpse of 1890s summer life on the island.

The park includes a network of drives modified from old carriage roads as well as many miles of hiking trails to scenic vistas. The walk to the **East Quoddy Head Lighthouse**, a popular whale-watching spot, is a bit of an expedition, possible only at low tide. The clubhouse of the nine-hole **Herring Cove Golf Course**, also within the park, features water views and the island's best fried fish. The course is open to the public; Tel: (506) 752-2922.

The place to stay on Campobello is the **Owen House** (open May to October), in Welshpool, in the middle of the island's north shore. Built in 1829 by Admiral Fitzwilliam Owen, son of the British captain to whom the island was granted in 1769, it is furnished with homey antiques, handmade quilts, and original art. The nine guest rooms are non-smoking and five have private baths. Innkeeper Joyce Morrell is an artist, an avid birder, and a source of local lore. The ferry to Deer Island leaves from the neighboring dock.

Deer Island

If the ferry is running—as it does hourly from mid-June to mid-September—the 45-minute ride from Campobello to Deer Island is a delightful way to get out on Passamaquoddy Bay (ferries also leave for Deer Island from Eastport, Maine, discussed below). The boat takes 15 cars and passengers to the southern tip of the island; from there a winding road runs for 9 miles (14½ km) along the western shore. One of the first places in the world to farm salmon, Deer Island boasts the world's largest lobster pound and offers several bed-and-breakfasts and takeout lunch spots with water views.

The free provincial ferry (also carrying just 15 cars) for L'Etete, New Brunswick, on the eastern shore of Passama-quoddy Bay, leaves from the northern tip of the island. Reservations are not permitted for either Deer Island ferry.

Grand Manan Island

Grand Manan, accessible by ferry year-round from Blacks Harbour, 16 miles (26 km) east of L'Etete, is a birding and bicycling haven. John James Audubon put the island on the birding map in 1833 when he came to verify the rumor—which proved true—that Grand Manan gulls nest in trees.

Fifteen miles long and six miles across at its widest, Grand Manan is flat enough to invite bicycling but varied enough in its terrain to offer exceptional hiking. Walking trails lead to the **Castalia Marshes**, breeding grounds for a variety of shorebirds; to the 360-foot-high cliffs at North Head, where eagles nest; and along the length of the cliff-walled western shore.

Grand Manan's villages—North Head, Grand Harbour, and Seal Cove (from north to south)—are on the sheltered eastern side of the island, linked by the island's main road, Route 776. Only tiny Dark Harbour huddles in the shadow of the high cliffs on the western shore. Herring is still smoked on Grand Manan in long wooden smokehouses, and the harbors are filled with draggers, trawlers, and lobster boats. Grand Mananers also gather and package dulse, a seaweed that is consumed in New Brunswick like popcorn.

Stuffed birds, representing most of the 340 species that visit the island annually, are displayed in the **Grand Manan Museum**, in Grand Harbour, one of the island's few "sights." Housed in the small home of one of the island's first settlers, the museum also displays the typewriter and table on which American novelist Willa Cather wrote many of her books. The cottage (private) in which she summered for 20 years still stands on nearby Whale Cove.

There are no big hotels on Grand Manan, but a dozen inns and B and Bs are scattered around North Head and Grand Harbour. The **Compass Rose**, two shingled houses in North Head, offers nine rooms with water views (all shared baths) and antique pine furnishings, and a dining room. Feast here on a large homemade bun stuffed to overflowing with thick chunks of succulent, freshly caught thin-shelled Bay of Fundy chicken lobster. Grand Manan is one of those places where the simple life can also be truly luxurious.

St. Andrews-by-the-Sea

With its many Federal-era homes and arching elms, St. Andrews (at the tip of a peninsula jutting into Passamaquoddy Bay 21 miles/34 km northwest of L'Etete via Routes 1 and 127) looks uncannily like Castine, Maine, and there's a reason. The town was founded in 1783 by Loyalists who fled here from Castine, many unpegging their houses and bringing them along. To demonstrate its approval of such loyalty, England granted the refugees a superb site and sent army engineers to dig wells, construct a fort, and lay out the town—with generous housing lots in a neat grid—across a gentle slope rising from the bay. The result is the most gracious town north (and east) of Castine.

St. Andrews's pride is the Tudor-style **Algonquin Resort**, the last of the grand old coastal hotels in the Northeast (open May through October). Built originally in 1889 and rebuilt after a fire in 1915, the six-story, 200-room, turreted Algonquin offers ample public space to sit and sip tea while enjoying views of the formal gardens. The resort's two golf courses (one nine-hole and one 18) are the oldest and widely considered the best in New Brunswick. Dining options at the resort range from dinner in the intimate and formal Van Horn Room to Sunday brunch in the main dining room, an event with a different theme every week—and an enticingly low price.

St. Andrews is so blessed with shops, snug eateries, and

inns that it's effectively fogproof. It's also the only New Brunswick town to offer Sunday-afternoon shopping. Water Street, the main commercial street, is lined with shops selling British woollens and china as well as crafts, antiques, and gifts. **Cottage Craft Limited**, on Town Square, has been in business since 1915, selling yarn, bolts of tweed and woollen cloth, skirt and sweater kits, and finished clothing, as well as distinctive throws made in homes throughout Charlotte County.

The finest restaurant along the waterfront is **L'Europe Dining Room and Lounge**, at 63 King Street, with an à la carte menu featuring local fish and seafood (reserve; Tel: 506/529-3818). The **Gables**, at 143 Water Street, is a moderately priced place that also specializes in local seafood and offers a wide selection of beers (Tel: 506/529-3440). **Passamaquoddy Fish and Chips**, out on Market Wharf, is the place for fried fish.

The **Ross Memorial Museum**, at the corner of King and Montague streets, is St. Andrews's token Federal-era mansion-museum, displaying an unusually fine collection of American decorative art amassed by Henry Phipps Ross, an Ohio-born heir to the Dun & Bradstreet fortune. (Open May through September Tel: 506/529-3906.)

The house built by Henry and Juliette Ross sits several miles east of town on Route 127. The boxy, three-story mansion is now the **Rossmount Inn**, a High Victorian hostelry popular locally for dinner as well as for afternoon tea; it also serves as the ideal setting for the murder-mystery weekends offered here off-season. The 840-acre grounds include Chamcook Mountain, the highest point in the Passamaquoddy Bay area. It's said that on a clear day you can see Mount Katahdin in Maine's north woods from Chamcook's summit (accessible only by foot).

Calais and the St. Croix Valley

From St. Andrews it's a 26-mile (42-km) drive back up Route 1 to the rather ugly towns of St. Stephen, New Brunswick, and Calais, Maine, the border towns on the St. Croix River that constitute the shopping center for Passamaquoddy Bay. **Ganong Brothers**, a large, old-fashioned shop on Milltown Boulevard in St. Stephen near the border crossing, claims to be the birthplace of the world's first chocolate bar. Just across the border in Calais, **Angelholm** is a good stop for basic diner food, while the chef-owned **Chandler House**, at 20 Chandler Street, is dependable for dinner and specializes in seafood (Tel: 506/454-7922).

Calais's shops offer the basics of a frontier town supplying the wilderness to the north, as well as New Brunswick residents attempting to avoid Canada's steep taxes. Be warned that the border crossing heading north—back into New Brunswick—can jam up at lunchtime and at 5:00 P.M., when Canadians head home after doing their daily grocery shopping. (Note that U.S. citizens need to show a driver's license or other proof of citizenship at border crossings. Residents of other countries should bring a passport.)

Fishermen and canoeists may well want to explore the St. Croix Valley north of Calais. The village of **Grand Lake Stream**, 20 miles (32 km) northwest of Calais on a river connecting West Grand and Big lakes, offers access to a chain of lakes known for their stock of landlocked salmon, lake trout, and smallmouth bass. Fishing is best in May, June, and September, but **Weatherby's**—a rambling 1870s lodge featuring ample meals and log cabins with stone fireplaces—is a pleasant haven even if you don't fish (open May through September).

The St. Croix River itself, which forms the border between Canada and the United States, is a popular canoe route. **Sunrise Canoe Expeditions**, based on Cathance Lake (about 20 miles/32 km southwest via Routes 9 and 191), offers camping trips from May to early October; Tel: (207) 454-7708.

Calais to Eastport

South from Calais, Route 1 follows the St. Croix River, which widens into Passamaquoddy Bay at **Robbinston**; a boat launch with picnic tables marks the spot. It's worth pausing here for the view across the river toward St. Andrews, which seems very near. Across the road from the boat launch stands the 1830s **Brewer House**, a columned inn affording views of the bay from its three non-smoking guest rooms (one with private bath). Chicago antiques dealers David and Estelle Holloway recently renovated the inn and furnished it with very fanciful Victorian pieces.

To reach Eastport turn off Route 1 onto Route 190 at the Trading Post in Perry, 8 miles (13 km) south of Robbinston. Perry's gas station and general store, the **Wigwam**, is run by the Passamaquoddy Indian tribe, more than 500 members of which live in Perry, most of them on the Pleasant Point Indian Reservation, farther down Route 190. The **Waponahki Museum** here offers a glimpse into both the historic and current lifestyles of the Passamaquoddy people (closed weekends; Tel: 207/853-4001).

EASTPORT

Eastport, across from Deer and Campobello islands on the west shore of Passamaquoddy Bay, is occasionally compared to other end-of-the-road fishing villages like Provincetown and Key West, but the country's easternmost city (it shares this claim with Lubec) has resisted most attempts to soften its hard edges for tourists. The most prosperous store in town remains an old-fashioned (and genuinely old) five-and-dime, and the busiest eatery is still the **Waco Diner** (Tel: 207/853-4046).

The 1880s commercial buildings along Eastport's Water Street were obviously built in the city's heyday as a sardine-canning center and deep-water port. These buildings are more elaborate and more abundant than this city of fewer than 2,000 seems to warrant. A number stand vacant, but some now house art galleries, notably the **Eastport Gallery and Art Center**, at the corner of Water and Dana streets, a cooperative showcase for more than 20 artists; and **Studio 44**, at 44 Water Street, displaying paintings by owner Philip Harvey and the work of several local potters.

Eastport was occupied by the British from 1814 to 1818, a story told, along with pictures of Eastport in its heyday, in the **Barracks Museum**, at 79 Washington Street (open Tuesday through Sunday from Memorial Day to Labor Day). If the yellow flag is flying at **J. W. Raye & Co.**, just up Washington Street at number 83, it means that mustard is being ground and that visitors are welcome. Billed as the country's only surviving stone-ground mustard mill, this red wooden factory has been in business since 1903. The mustard for myriad Maine sardines canned in mustard sauce has come from Raye's. The mill's pantry store offers samples on pretzels. Tel: (207) 853-4451.

The other souvenir worth bringing home from Eastport is smoked salmon, which you can pick up at **Jim's Smoked Salmon**, 37 Washington Street. Eastport is headquarters for Maine Pride, the county's largest salmon packer. You can see their pens in both Cobscook and Passamaquoddy bays if you stroll up the mile-long trail at **Shackford Head** (marked from Route 190 just north of town).

Staying in Eastport

Despite its lack of concessions to tourists, Eastport does offer three fine places to stay. **Weston House**, two blocks west of Water Street, is a Federal-style house built in 1810, with five spacious guest rooms, all with shared bath and one with a working fireplace. **Todd House**, at Todd's Head near the Deer Island ferry landing (see below), is a cozy 1770s Cape with two large guest rooms and views of the bay. The third option is the **Motel East**, a nicely furnished two-story structure with all units overlooking the water.

Boat Excursions

Eastport grows on you, especially if you take a day sail on the *Anna,* a shallow-keeled sailboat patterned on the traditional Bay of Fundy scow sloops, once the workhorses of this bay (end of June through mid-September, later if the weather is good; Tel: 207/726-5151). Or you might take a ride on George and Butch Harris's *Janna Marie,* a 56-foot fishing and whale-watching boat (Tel: 207/853-4303). Of course, you can also take the Deer Island ferry, with or without your car, just for the ride out into the bay. Contrary to rumor, the ferry, which is simply a fishing boat lashed to a barge, does not cross the Old Sow whirlpool, billed as the second largest in the world. Located in the bay off the western shore of Deer Island, Old Sow's vortex sometimes dips as much as six feet below the surrounding surface.

—*Christina Tree*

INLAND MAINE

The view from the Height O' Land lookout south of Rangeley in western Maine is a spread of high mountains and large lakes etched, depending on the weather, in various shades of blue and green. It's this combination of mountains and lakes—along with the East Coast's only remaining wilderness—that sets inland Maine apart from the rest of the state and, indeed, from New England.

The big mountains are Katahdin, in the north, centerpiece for 200,000-acre Baxter State Park; and Sugarloaf, in the west, focus of one of the state's largest self-contained ski resorts. The big lakes are Sebago and Long lakes in the south; the Rangeley chain, near Sugarloaf Mountain, known in spring and fall for trout and landlocked salmon; and Moosehead, the largest lake entirely within New England.

Inland Maine is varied as well as vast and divides into several clearly defined regions. The first is the **western lakes and mountains region,** which includes the state's most accessible resort areas: large lakes like Sebago, lined with children's camps and summer cottages; the handsome old town of Bethel, a long-established hub for hiking and more recently for skiing in the more mountainous country to the north; the ever-steeper and more heavily wooded country of the Rangeley Lakes, for which the village of Rangeley serves

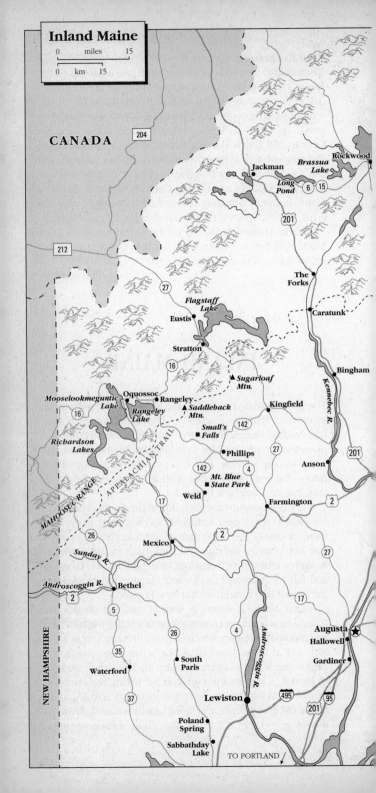

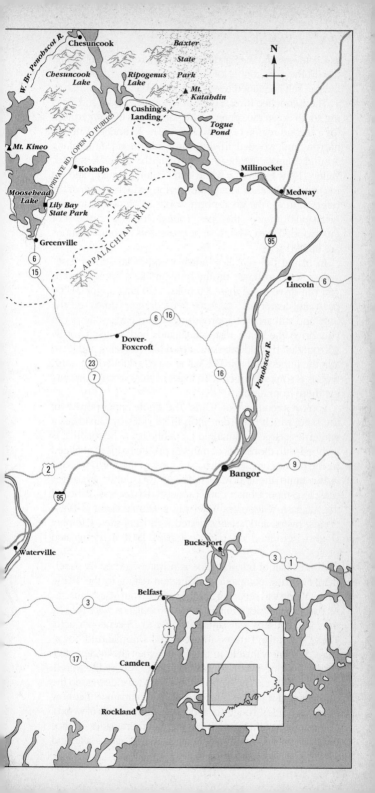

as a gateway; and the Carrabassett Valley, remote lumberland that in the past couple of decades has evolved into a four-season, self-contained resort, Sugarloaf/USA.

The Kennebec River, rising in Moosehead Lake and flowing south down the center of the state, forms the centerpiece for a second region of inland Maine. The **Kennebec Valley** is narrow and wooded in the north and broad and rolling around Augusta. We head up through the upper Kennebec Valley (New England's white-water rafting center) and on into the Moosehead/Katahdin region, which is generally referred to as "the great north woods." (We do not include Aroostook County—the open, rolling farmland northeast of this wooded area—because at present its accommodations are limited.)

In Maine the so-called **north woods**, like "down east," always seem to hover on the horizon like a mirage. Just as you can drive more than 200 miles (320 km) up the Maine coast and learn that you have been driving "down" all the time and still are just approaching "down east," so, too, can you drive the same distance inland, find yourself totally surrounded by wilderness in a town like Rangeley, and learn that the unpeopled third of Maine usually dubbed the north woods is somewhere else. To make matters worse, you can't get there from here.

Look at a road map of Maine. The whole upper portion of the state, which is bordered on three sides by Canada, is a wilderness largely unmarked by public roads. (Actually it is webbed with thousands of miles of private roads maintained by the paper companies that own most of the north woods.)

But amid these private fiefdoms two public preserves cater to campers, hikers, and canoeists: Baxter State Park and the Allagash Wilderness Waterway, a 92-mile chain of lakes, ponds, rivers, and streams dotted with campsites. Camping is also permitted on paper-company land in designated places.

Almost half of inland Maine is privately owned by paper-manufacturing companies, a situation dating to the 1820s, when Maine was securing independence from Massachusetts. As part of the agreement, unsettled woodlands were sold by the Massachusetts legislature for 12½ to 28 cents per acre. These vast inland tracts, the so-called Unorganized Townships, became valuable in the 1840s, when the ancient process of making paper from wood fibers was rediscovered.

About 150 years of corporate mergers have decreased the number and increased the size of the companies that now maintain roads through six-and-a-half million acres of woods. The number of these roads has increased dramatically since the 1970s, when log drives—floating the logs across lakes and sending them down rivers—ended. After a century and a half the tannic acid from the logs was visibly destroying the rivers, and ecologists and fishing lobbyists were successful in getting the practice stopped. Instead of the annual spring drives, huge log trucks now lumber (literally) over the rough company roads year-round, altering the feel of the north woods, and of their "sporting camps."

An 1860s invention, sporting camps generally consist of log cabins grouped around a central rough-hewn lodge deep in the wilderness. The camps have been catering to "sports"—urbanites who hire a guide to help them hunt or fish—since trains from New York and Boston first reached the towns of Greenville and Rangeley. Roughly three dozen such camps survive, widely scattered from the Rangeley Lakes area north and east to the Allagash Wilderness Waterway. Long accessible only by canoe and then by air, many are now reached primarily over unpaved roads from the nearest town.

In winter, skiers head like homing pigeons for Maine's biggest ski areas, taking the shortest routes from Boston and Portland to Bethel (Sunday River), Rangeley (Saddleback), or the Carrabassett Valley (Sugarloaf/USA). But summer is a very different story. Not only are the distances between these three areas short, but the drive itself is quite beautiful; possible in three days, it's far more satisfying if stretched to a week. Moosehead Lake and Baxter State Park demand at least another three days.

TOURING INLAND MAINE

The most pleasant gateway from Portland to western Maine is Route 26, which climbs quickly into the high lake country and Sabbathday Lake, passing by the country's last working Shaker community on the way to Bethel. The old commercial hub of a large, sparsely populated farming and logging community, Bethel offers some of the best places to stay, dine, and shop in western Maine; it's also the natural base from which to explore the lake region to the south and to take advantage of some splendid hiking in the neighboring White Mountain National Forest (see the New Hampshire chapter) and in the Mahoosuc Range. (Note that it's less than 25 miles/40 km from Bethel to Gorham, New Hampshire, which means that that state's Mount Washington is also within easy striking distance.)

From Bethel we follow the Androscoggin River north through a broad valley to Mexico, a classic brick paper-mill town where you pick up Route 17 north to Rangeley and the Rangeley chain of lakes. In all, there are seven lakes in the Rangeley chain, and it's not difficult to find an inn or camp with access to water. (Of course you can head back to the coast or points south from Rangeley via Routes 4 and 27 to Augusta, which is right on I-95.)

From Rangeley our next destination is the Carrabassett Valley, accessible by two routes. The shortest, just 19 miles (30 km), follows Route 16 north to Stratton, basically a knot of shops and restaurants servicing hikers and loggers, then another 6 miles (10 km) south to Sugarloaf/USA, a modern, self-contained ski resort that can put up 5,000 guests in its inns and condominiums. The valley was remote lumber land until the last two decades, when Sugarloaf was established in the town of Carrabassett. In summer the focus shifts from skiing to golf.

If you don't play golf there's little reason to visit Sugarloaf in summer—in which case it's better to follow Route 4 southeast from Rangeley along the Sandy River, stopping to view the series of cascades known as Small's Falls and perhaps to spend a day on Lake Webb in Weld, south of Route 4 on Route 142. Kingfield, north on Route 142, is, like Bethel, a handsome old commercial center with a variety of lodging, dining, and shopping options.

From Kingfield (on the Carrabassett River) we continue on to Maine's north woods via The Forks, Maine's white-water rafting center, and then from Jackman to Rockwood, a year-round resort village dramatically situated at the narrows of Moosehead Lake across from the sheer cliffs of Mount Kineo. Greenville, at the toe of Moosehead, is New England's largest seaplane base and a jumping-off point for the sporting camps, many of them a century old, that can be found throughout the north woods.

From Greenville hikers may want to head for Baxter State Park and Mount Katahdin, the terminus of the Appalachian Trail. The highest mountain in Maine, Katahdin is unquestionably the most dramatic and one of the most difficult New England peaks to climb. Canoeists may well want to head for Chesuncook, a former lumber camp on Chesuncook Lake, just west of Baxter State Park, that now offers two inns yet retains a splendid sense of isolation. Either path from Greenville follows the so-called Golden Road, a private road (open to the public) owned by Georgia Pacific paper company. Simply pay the toll and yield to moose and fast-travelling paper trucks.

The shortest way home from Baxter State Park is via I-95 and Bangor (from which you can get to Bar Harbor and points east via Alternate Route 1). However you get back to the coast or Portland, be sure to stop en route in Augusta and see the best-maintained state museum in all of New England.

WESTERN LAKES AND MOUNTAINS

SABBATHDAY LAKE

Gently rolling lake country begins just northwest of Portland. Follow Route 26 (leave the Maine Turnpike at Gray) as it climbs steadily into the hills. It's just 8 miles (13 km) from the turnpike to the Sabbathday Lake Shaker community, an 18th-century meetinghouse set amid orchards on one side of the road and a multistory dwelling and other buildings on the other.

The oldest and most successful of America's many 19th-century communal religious sects, the Shakers once numbered 6,000 celibate brethren and sisters scattered in 18 self-contained villages from Maine to Ohio. Today the number of practicing Shakers can be counted on your fingers, and they are all here. You're welcome to sit on the "world's people" benches in the meetinghouse at 10:00 A.M. any summer Sunday and listen as the six Shaker sisters and two brothers speak in response to the psalms and Gospel readings. Each observation is affirmed with a Shaker song, of which there are said to be 10,000.

Tours of six of the village's 17 buildings are offered Monday through Saturday from Memorial Day to Columbus Day; rooms are either furnished or filled with exhibits to illustrate periods or products of Shaker life. One of the buildings houses a shop that sells, among other things, herbs and herbal teas, yarn from the community's sheep, and a cookbook by community leader Frances Carr.

Unless you come to Sunday meeting, however, chances are you won't meet a Shaker on a tour. They tend to be busy with printing, tending the sheep, cultivating the herb gardens, cooking, sewing, and knitting, and with work in the library, where 63,000 documents are carefully catalogued and preserved (open by appointment; Tel: 207/926-4597).

POLAND SPRING

Welcoming the World's People has been part of summer at Sabbathday Lake since the community's inception in 1794. For more than a century guests from the neighboring Poland Spring resort flocked to the Sunday service.

The huge resort, once one of the largest in Maine, has now all but vanished. Visitors are still welcome to wander its grounds to see the State of Maine Building from the 1893 World's Columbian Exposition in Chicago, an ornate Victorian building moved here for hotel guests to enjoy as combination reading rooms and art gallery (open June through

September; Tel: 207/998-4142). The spring water for which
the resort has long been known continues to be bottled on
the premises.

THE PARIS AREA

Route 26 continues its climb northwestward, leveling into a
commercial strip of shops and eateries in South Paris.
Shaner's Family Dining, in South Paris at 193 South Main
Street, is a good place to stop for fried chicken, liver and
onions, or other home-cooked specials as well as the area's
widest and creamiest array of ice-cream flavors. Tel: (207)
743-6367.

Another 9 miles (14½ km) up the road is a deceptively
small and old-fashioned-looking house (yellow clapboard
with green trim) signposted **Perham's of West Paris**. In
business since 1919, Perham's is Maine's rockhounding
mecca. In addition to selling locally mined amethyst, tourma-
line, and topaz jewelry, the store dispenses maps to four
local quarries where visitors are welcome to try their own
luck.

Bethel

An old farming and trading center on the Androscoggin
River, Bethel (16 miles/26 km northwest of West Paris on
Route 26) has been a summer resort since the train from
Portland to Montreal began stopping here in the 1850s.
Visitors stayed in local farmhouses, feasting on homegrown
produce and walking on mountain trails.

The **Bethel Inn**, built as a spa in 1913 by a pioneering
therapist, stressed exercise as a cure for depression. Guests
were encouraged not only to walk but to chop down trees to
clear a golf course—which has since been expanded to 18
holes. With 57 guest rooms and 40 two-bedroom suites, the
clapboard inn has a large, old-fashioned dining room and
gracious living rooms. It remains the heart of the town.

Surrounded by its mansion-like annexes, town houses,
and sports center, the Bethel Inn anchors a corner of the
long town **common**, which is framed entirely by handsome
clapboard houses. These include the Federal-style **Moses
Mason House**, known for its murals by early-19th-century
itinerant artist Rufus Porter and maintained by a lively local
historical society (open June through August; Tel: 207/824-
2175); and two bed-and-breakfasts, the elegant but comfortable **Hammons House** and the family- and hiker-geared
Chapman Inn. Hammons House has two spacious double
rooms with shared bath, a two-room suite with private bath,

formal gardens out back, and a two-story conservatory where breakfast is served. Chapman Inn offers an unusual range of rooms, from carefully furnished doubles with private baths to reasonably priced apartments to dorm-style rooms, rented to single hikers and groups.

Bethel has several agreeable restaurants and shops. Chef Irv Skaff has put the **Sudbury Inn**, a friendly, comfortable 1870s hotel (all with private bath and all non-smoking) on lower Main Street (Route 26), on Maine's culinary map—on which **Mother's** (Tel: 207/824-2589), also on Main Street, has long been included. The Sudbury is open for all meals, and seems to serve everything, from pizzas and salads to chicken Marsala and flamed tenderloin au poivre.

Bethel's sloping, mile-long Main Street rewards strollers with a number of intriguing shops. **Bonnema Potters**, across from the Sudbury Inn, produces and sells multi-hued stoneware ranging from dinnerware to lamps and garden furniture. **Mainely Fibers**, housed in a carriage house behind a Main Street home, sells locally spun yarns as well as general knitting supplies, and **Maine Line Products** stocks locally made tee-shirts and souvenirs like Maine Woodsman's Weathersticks, as good a weather forecaster as any. The **Mount Mann** shop, also on Main Street, is a source of local rockhounding information as well as the exceptional jewelry made with local stones that Jim Mann mines, cuts, and sets.

Sunday River Ski Area

Not just a summer resort anymore, Bethel is a lively ski town. The Sunday River Ski Area, 6 miles (10 km) north of town on Route 5/26, has quadrupled in size over the past few years, a boon to Bethel's shops, restaurants, and lodging places. For general information, Tel: (207) 824-3000.

Boasting "the most dependable snow in North America" (meaning man-made) and with trails for all levels of skiers, Sunday River covers more than 70 trails spread over six peaks with man-made snow from much of December through March. Condo-style lodges, each with an indoor swimming pool, accommodate some 4,800 overnight guests, and on most winter weekends Sunday River draws more than 10,000 skiers a day, mostly from Portland, Boston, and Rhode Island. Facilities include three base lodges and the new 147-room **Summit Hotel and Crown Club**, whose amenities include a heated outdoor pool, a health club, a restaurant and lounge, and a game room. For lodging information and reservations at Sunday River, Tel: (800) 543-2SKI.

Even in pre-snow-making days Bethel was recognized as a sort of magnet for natural snow. The **Sunday River Ski**

Touring Center, based at the **Sunday River Inn**, a homey ski lodge near but not connected with the ski area (closed in April, July, August, and November), offers 40 kilometers (25 miles) of trails through the woods, and there are three other cross-country centers in town.

In summer the ski area offers a lift-serviced network of trails for mountain biking. Day treks and multiday expeditions from the **Telemark Inn and Llama Farm**, a rustic retreat sequestered in the wooded semi-wilderness of West Bethel, also draw people from around the country. But hiking in nearby **Grafton Notch State Park** and in the White Mountain National Forest (see the New Hampshire chapter, above) remain the area's chief summertime draw. Grafton Notch, a relatively small but dramatic cul-de-sac in the Mahoosuc Range, is popular for its short hikes to scenic waterfalls, caves, and up Old Speck, the third highest mountain in the state. Tel: (207) 824-2912.

AROUND BETHEL

The hub of all local roads, Bethel is also a logical place from which to explore the Mount Washington Valley (it's just 30 miles/48 km from the middle of town to the Mount Washington Auto Road; see the New Hampshire chapter) and the Long and Sebago lake areas to the south. Or you might just drive 18 miles (29 km) down Routes 5 and 35 to **Lake House**, in Waterford, a graceful, tastefully restored old stagecoach inn with five guest rooms (with private bath) and a dining room known for dishes like lobster in fennel and cream (Tel: 207/583-4182), or to **Westways on Kezar Lake**, in Center Lovell (15 miles/24 km west of Waterford on Route 5A), a millionaire's silver-shingled summer estate built in the 1920s that has low-beamed, luxuriously furnished public rooms and upstairs guest rooms with lake views. Tel: (207) 928-2663.

North from Bethel follow Route 2 about 27 miles (43 km) along the Androscoggin River to the mill town of Mexico, where you turn onto Route 17 north. Just 34 miles (54 km) long, Route 17 is the kind of road that deserves a song. First it threads a mountain-hemmed valley that has obviously been farmed for centuries, and then, beyond Byron (where a state-run picnic site straddles a waterfall), the woods close in and your ears begin to pop as the road climbs to meet the Appalachian Trail. A series of pullouts serve as vantage points at the so-called **Height O' Land**, and a bit farther on, the Rangeley Lake Overlook yields yet another panorama of mountains and lakes in the opposite direction.

Rangeley Lakes Region

Route 17 ends in the Rangeley Lakes village of Oquossoc, at a nondescript crossroads with a tiny post office and three restaurants (try one of the daily specials at the **Four Seasons Café**; Tel: 207/864-5291). The interesting part of Oquossoc begins a mile (1½ km) to the north at Haines Landing on **Mooselookmeguntic Lake**. The big 19th-century Mooselookmeguntic House itself is gone, but its log cabins can still be rented (Tel: 207/864-3627). Alternatively, just a short distance down the shore road are the 1890s **Bald Mountain Camps** (open mid-May to October). Lodging is in old-style log cabins, most sharing a continuous porch overlooking the lake, and meals are served at tables set with linen and fresh flowers in the log-sided dining room.

The Maine classic *We Took to the Woods*, written by Louise Dickinson Rich around 1940 near Lower Richardson Lake (which flows into Upper Richardson, which then flows into Mooselookmeguntic), conveys a sense of the splendid isolation still possible in this area at traditional sporting camps such as **Grant's Kennebago Camps** (on Kennebago Lake; open Memorial Day to Columbus Day), at **Bosebuck Mountain Camps** (on Aziscohos Lake; open May through November), and at **Lakewood Camps** (open from May to September), described in Rich's book, at Middledam on Lower Richardson. Sporting camps are a Maine phenomenon that began to appear in the 1860s, about the time railroads put the Maine woods within easy reach of the East Coast's major cities. Patrons would be met at the rail depots in Rangeley and Greenville by guides who would paddle them to remote "camps," invariably a cluster of lakeside log cabins around a central lodge in which three daily meals were served. The camps served—and continue to serve—as bases from which to hunt and fish. Today most sporting camps are accessible by logging roads, and fishing for trout and landlocked salmon is a favored preoccupation.

VILLAGE OF RANGELEY

The village of Rangeley, 6 miles (10 km) east of Oquossoc via Route 4/16, has the look of an outpost. A sign in front of Doc Grant's Restaurant proclaims that it's 3,107 miles from both the North Pole and the equator. The town's hub in summer is the **Rangeley Sport Shop**, a source of fishing licenses, equipment, tips about where the fish are biting, and information about local guides. The town's only brick building, formerly the jail and now the **Rangeley Lakes Historical Society** (open June through August), displays pictures of the turn-of-the-century heyday when Rangeley's huge hotels were filled with New Yorkers and Philadelphians who came by train in the summer and when steamers toured the lakes.

The big blue-shingled **Rangeley Inn**, in the middle of the village, dates from this era. Originally an annex to a far larger hotel, its pillared lobby, old-fashioned check-in desk, and tin-ceilinged dining room have been preserved by innkeepers Fay and Ed Carpenter. Many guest rooms in the inn retain the original claw-footed tubs (all have private baths), while some of those in the motor lodge, overlooking Haley Pond in back, have been outfitted with wood stoves, whirlpool baths, and kitchens. Moreover, the inn's dining room is the region's finest (the chef specializes in seafood); save room for one of the elaborate but light desserts. Tel: (207) 864-3342.

You can also sign up for a morning **moose watch** at the inn. These excursions depart at 5:00 A.M. and include a three-hour canoe trip on the Kennebago River. It might be said that you haven't really arrived in Rangeley until you've been out in a boat one way or another. Most lodging places are either on, or overlooking, the water.

The **Country Club Inn** (closed April and November), just beyond the village, is set back behind the 18-hole (public) **Mingo Springs Golf Course**, overlooking Rangeley Lake. Built by a millionaire sportsman in the 1920s, the inn has an atmosphere that can only be described as clubby. Guests gather around massive stone fireplaces in the living room, in the friendly pub, and in the bright dining room, which is dominated by its view of the lake. The menu changes nightly. Tel: (207) 864-3831.

Mallory's Bed and Breakfast Inn, a gracious old home right on Rangeley Lake, offers boating, as do most of the rental cottages listed with the Rangeley Lakes Region Chamber of Commerce. Tel: (207) 864-5364 or (800) MT-LAKES.

Saddleback Mountain

Saddleback Mountain is just a 15-minute drive from the village but seems far removed; it keeps the lowest profile of any New England ski area of its size. The 4,116-foot mountain, the centerpiece of a semicircle of mountains surrounding a small lake, affords spectacular views of a number of lakes and mountains. Despite Saddleback's 40 trails and fairly dependable snow conditions (best late February through March), it caters to a relatively small but enthusiastic following. Lifts and snow-making facilities have not been upgraded to compete with nearby Sugarloaf/USA, and just two condominium complexes, jointly called **Saddleback Ski and Summer Lake Preserve**, are squirreled away on a slope above the base lodge (the condos are unusually large and luxurious, and many have hot tubs; Tel: 207/864-5671).

Saddleback's 30 kilometers (20 miles) of cross-country ski trails are another well-kept secret. Billed as the highest touring network in the East, they meander off above the condominiums into the woods around isolated Rock and Midway ponds, and are tracked as much by wildlife as by machines.

South from Rangeley

If you want to return to the coast, Portland, or Boston and points south from Rangeley, take Route 4 southeast 29 miles (46 km) to Farmington and Route 27 another 23 miles (37 km) to Augusta, which is on I-95. En route you pass through Belgrade Lakes, an old summer-home community and the inspiration for the novel and movie *On Golden Pond*.

AUGUSTA AND ENVIRONS

Augusta is a very small city dominated by the dome of its capitol building and divided by the Kennebec River. Augusta's **Maine State Museum** is unquestionably the best state museum in New England and possibly the country. A real sleeper, it isn't even signposted. From I-95 follow Western Avenue (Route 11/17/20) to the rotary and go three-fourths of the way around to State Street (Route 201/27 south). The museum is just past the domed State House (designed by Charles Bulfinch) in the massive Maine State Library and Archives. Plan to spend at least an hour.

Artfully mounted displays, which trace 12,000 years of humankind's history in Maine, include reproductions of pictographs, genuine arrowheads, and amazingly intricate ancient tools, baskets, and beadwork. Early explorations and the study of antiquities in the state are also chronicled, while still other exhibits are devoted to Maine's natural landscape and industries. Tel: (207) 289-2301.

Unfortunately, there really isn't a restaurant to be recommended in Augusta, but **Burnsie's Homestyle Sandwiches** is a standout (several doors down from the State House on State Street). If the weather is good, choose a sandwich from the dozen or so combinations named for local political figures and take it down to the picnic tables across the Kennebec in the riverside park adjoining **Fort Western Museum**. Built in 1754, this 16-room, 100-foot-long garrison house served as a combination fort, trading post, and way station for travellers while providing protection for the locals. It has been restored to look the way it did in the late 18th century. Tel: (207) 626-2385.

If you want to continue on to the coast from here, take Route 3 about 44 miles (70 km) east to Belfast (see the Midcoast section of this chapter) and, if it's a hot day, stop about halfway for a swim at Lake St. George State Park. If you are headed for Portland and points south, follow Route 27 south from Augusta along the Kennebec 3 miles (5 km) to the town of Hallowell, its streets lined with quaint 19th-century commercial buildings, antiques stores, and restaurants. Slate's, at 167 Water Street, has a pleasant coffeehouse atmosphere, good food, and live music (open for all meals, except Monday dinner; Tel: 207/622-9575), while Freemont and Julien, across the way at 152 Water Street, is a combination café/bookstore serving espresso and light meals (Tel: 207/626-3256).

However, you may want to save your appetite for the A1 Diner, at 3 Bridge Street in Gardiner, just a few miles south. This is a classic 1946 Worcester diner complete with gleaming chrome and a neon "Time to Eat" clock. While the menu includes dishes you'd expect to find in an old vinyl-and-Formica diner—eggs and hash, split pea soup, and tapioca—other intriguing possibilities include orange poppyseed waffles, salmon with salsa, and "chicken noble." Wine and beer are served. (Open from 5:00 A.M. weekdays and from 6:00 and 7:00 A.M. on Saturdays and Sundays, respectively; Tel: 207/582-4804.) Walk off your meal down Gardiner's handsome 19th-century Main Street. The way to I-95 is clearly marked.

North and East from Rangeley

Ideally, you should be able to drive due northeast from Rangeley to The Forks, the center of Maine's rafting industry, and on to Baxter State Park. Unfortunately, because of the dearth of public roads in the area, this is one of those cases of "you can't get there from here." You can drive north 19 miles (30 km) to Stratton and then 5 miles (8 km) northwest to Eustis. The Forks lie less than 20 miles (32 km) east from Eustis, but to get to them you must drive a total of 85 miles (136 km): back through Stratton, southeast through the Carrabassett Valley to Kingfield, and north through the Kennebec Valley. Alternatively, you can take a 74-mile (118-km) route southeast from Rangeley along the Sandy River over back roads that pass through the towns of Phillips and Weld and on into the upper Kennebec Valley. Happily, both ways are scenic. We follow the former route first, as it takes us to the Stratton–Eustis area, where scenic beauty, rustic sporting camps, great trout fishing, and the skiing and golfing mecca of Sugarloaf/USA provide a variety of diversions. Later we cover the scenic Sandy River route and quiet Weld and pretty Phillips.

STRATTON AND EUSTIS

Unless you count the knot of houses that make up the town of Dallas, Route 16 north from Rangeley is wooded all the way to Stratton, a crossroads outpost with a first-rate eatery called **Cathy's Place**, good for all three meals (try the peanut butter pie). Tel: (207) 246-2922. Northwest of Stratton, Route 27 crosses a corner of Flagstaff Lake; just beyond are the **Cathedral Pines**, a majestic stand of pines and a good place to picnic, with the Bigelow Range in the background.

Tim Pond Wilderness Camps, billed as "the oldest continuously operating sporting lodge in America," are hidden 12 miles (19 km) down a logging road off Route 27 in **Eustis**. Founded in the 1860s, the rustic resort consists of 11 log camps around a lodge in the only clearing on mile-long Tim Pond, which is surrounded in turn by 4,450 acres of wilderness. The pond, which has never been stocked, is famous for its square-tailed trout, far more prized among fishermen than their hatchery-bred kin. Because August is low season for fishing, the camp closes the first two weeks of that month, reopening in mid-month with programs that cater to families rather than serious fishermen. (Closed from November to spring thaw.) On the same logging road are **Tea Pond Camps**, six 1890s log cabins grouped around a central log dining hall by Tea Pond.

For those less interested in roughing it, Eustis has a good restaurant, the **Porter House**, which sits by itself on Route 27. With candlelight dining in four small rooms, it specializes in soups, breads, and desserts made from scratch and, of course, porterhouse steak. Open for dinner only; for reservations, Tel: (207) 246-7932.

Sugarloaf/USA

In stark contrast to these old-fashioned sporting camps is Sugarloaf/USA, Maine's largest self-contained ski resort, less than 20 miles (32 km) southeast of Eustis on Route 27.

Clustered on a steep slope of the Carrabassett Valley, Sugarloaf's inns and condominiums routinely accommodate 5,000 skiers each night in winter and a small fraction of that number in summer, when the focus shifts from skiing to the 18-hole public **golf course** designed by Robert Trent Jones, Jr. Hiking, mountain biking (rentals available), and the spa facilities at the Sugar Tree Spa at the condo complex are also part of the summer scene. For lodging information, Tel: (207) 237-2000 or (800) THE-LOAF.

Sugarloaf is a mighty mountain, with a 2,837-foot vertical drop and a 4,237-foot summit crowned with snowfields. The 91 trails add up to 45 miles of skiing, and 90 percent of the mountain is covered—by snow-making if not the real thing. Facilities include an unusually well-designed base lodge and skiing instructions tailored to children of all age groups, from toddler through teenager.

In addition to the forest of condominiums below the base area (connected by a feeder chair lift), slopeside lodging options include the **Sugarloaf Inn**, a luxurious ski lodge with its own restaurant and living room; and the large (119 rooms), seven-story, towered and gabled **Sugarloaf Mountain Hotel**, right next to the base lodge. **Arabella's at the Gladstone** is considered the best of the restaurants in the condo complex. Tel: (207) 237-2262.

KINGFIELD

Kingfield, 20 miles (32 km) southeast along Route 27 from Sugarloaf is, like Bethel, a long-established farming, logging, and commercial center. Basically one uneven street of clapboard buildings, it nonetheless offers some first-rate restaurants and lodgings. At **One Stanley Avenue** Dan Davis uses local produce to create such regional dishes as lobster seasoned with dill served on zucchini, maple cider chicken, and sage-spiced rabbit with raspberry sauce. Dinner guests gather for drinks in the Victorian parlor or in the gazebo in the back garden while waiting for their orders to be prepared. (Closed November and May.) Davis also offers attractive lodgings (33 guest rooms, all with private baths) in neighboring **Three Stanley Avenue**, whose guests may use the ornate living room next door.

The **Herbert Hotel**, right on Main Street, is Kingfield's second fine restaurant and a 33-room hotel as well. Built along what were considered palatial lines in 1918, the Herbert has been restored to its role as the center of town. The rooms are simple but tasteful, there's usually a fire in the hearth beneath the moose head in the living room, and there are always comfortable places to sit and watch the town pass by through the big plate-glass windows.

Kingfield bears the stamp of its most inventive sons, Francis Edgar (F. E.) and Freeland Oscar (F. O.) Stanley. The **Stanley Museum** displays a sleek Stanley Steamer, the steam- and gas-powered car for which the twins are chiefly remembered. You also learn here that F. E. invented the airbrush in the 1870s and a dry plate process that speeded photographic production. Turn-of-the-century photographs of the area taken by the Stanleys' sister, Chansonetta, are also fascinating. (Open Tuesday through Sunday in summer; Tel: 207/265-2729.)

WELD AND PHILLIPS

The alternate way to get to Kingfield and beyond from Rangeley is to take Route 4 about 22 miles (35 km) southeast via Phillips. Kingfield lies 15 miles (24 km) northeast of Phillips via Route 142. The highlights of this route are walking along Small's Falls, stopping by the Phillips Historical Society (if it's open), and hiking up Mount Blue and bedding down by Lake Webb, both in nearby Weld.

At **Small's Falls**, 12 miles (19 km) south of Rangeley on Route 4, the Sandy River drops through a small but deep gorge that is edged by paths with guardrails. This is a popular picnic spot and a swimming hole for those crazy enough to dare it. A short trail leads to a waterfall.

Four miles (6½ km) farther down Route 4 you might consider turning south on Route 142 and driving another 12 miles (19 km) to **Weld**, a quiet village at the entrance of 6,000-acre **Mount Blue State Park** (open May to mid-October). The park encompasses 3,187-foot Mount Blue itself, popular with hikers, and Lake Webb, a great fishing lake with a beachside campground. The **Kawanhee Inn**, situated in the pines above a beach on the lake, is a classic north woods–style lodge with a large, pine-sided dining room and an open-beamed lobby with a central fireplace. There are plenty of places to relax here, such as a screened porch lined with rockers overlooking the lake. Rooms in the lodge are simple but comfortable, and there are lakeside cabins as well.

The **historical societies** for both Weld and **Phillips**, a gracious old town back on Route 4 just east of the Route 142 turnoff, are both outstanding but, unfortunately, open just on Friday and Saturday afternoons from 2:00 to 4:00 during the month of August.

From Phillips you can head north on Route 142 to Kingfield or take a shortcut to the Kennebec River along rural back roads (Routes 149 and 234) to North Anson. This is the open, rolling farm country of mid-Maine. Head north on Route 16 from North Anson along the Kennebec River, crossing over to Solon at the junction with Route 201. If you are getting hungry, hold out for **Thompson's Restaurant**, in Bingham, 8 miles (13 km) up Route 16 from Solon. Open from 5:30 A.M. year-round, Thompson's serves road food at its best: pea soup, baked beans, homemade doughnuts, and custard pie as well as fresh fish and wine. The decor, which consists of red booths, red awnings, and the original moose head, hasn't changed much since the place opened in 1939.

THE UPPER KENNEBEC VALLEY

Above Bingham Route 201 snakes along the Kennebec as it widens into Wyman Lake. The drive is distractingly beautiful, so beware of the many logging trucks that roll down this particular road at sometimes alarming speeds.

For more than two centuries Maine rivers served as transport for the logs harvested in the north woods, and this stretch of the Kennebec was one of the last to do so. Until 1976 the Kennebec Log Driving Company was moving 300,000 cords of wood a year from the woods to the mill well below here.

Logs were, in fact, still hurtling treacherously through the rapids on a spring day in 1976 when Wayne Hockmeyer, a Rockwood-based fishing guide, first tried riding them in a rubber raft. Hockmeyer had been looking for a new fishing hole when he happened on the isolated but dramatic Kennebec Gorge and sensed its appeal—rafting was already big on the Colorado River and in West Virginia. Hockmeyer secured a raft and talked eight bear hunters from New Jersey into coming along for the ride in a driving rainstorm.

What a ride! Below the Harris Hydroelectric Station they found themselves shooting releases that we now know gush up to 8,000 cubic feet of water per second. Hockmeyer knew enough to position himself at the back of the raft and to try to steer it with a canoe paddle (he had seen the 1954 movie *River of No Return,* in which Robert Mitchum steers Marilyn Monroe down the Salmon River this way), but basically they were out of control through the entire 12-mile gorge.

Hockmeyer knew he was on to a good thing, especially when environmentalists managed to secure a law prohibiting log runs on the Kennebec later that year. He bought a second-hand cattle truck and herded clients to the put-in spot; in 1977 his newly founded Northern Outdoors company rafted 600 clients through Kennebec Gorge. Word of the wildest raft ride in the country quickly spread, and soon competitors were vying for time on the river. Today this time is regulated, and almost 20 different outfits raft some 50,000 people a year in Maine, 30,000 of them on this river.

You begin seeing signs for white-water rafting outfits in Caratunk, 16 miles (26 km) north of Bingham, and on up the river. Empty as the upper Kennebec Valley may have seemed when the first rafters began to arrive in the 1970s, this was not the area's first brush with resort status—indeed, it was a famous beauty spot in the 19th century. In the 1860s the three-story, 100-room Forks Hotel was built in the middle of **The Forks**, the village at the confluence of the Kennebec and

Dead rivers (although liquor was illegal in Maine at the time, the hotel, now gone, was famed for its flow).

White-Water Rafting Companies

The Forks remains the hub of Maine's rafting industry, the nearest village to put-in places on both the Dead and Kennebec rivers, and also to such natural attractions as Moxie Falls, just a few miles east of The Forks. Many of the rafting outfits offer their patrons places to stay (for an extra charge) and other facilities and activities in addition to the rafting trips. All rafting outfits serve patrons a meal on the river after they've run the rapids.

New England Whitewater Center (Tel: 800/766-7238 or 207/672-5506), which offers expeditions on the Penobscot, Kennebec, and Dead rivers, puts up rafters at the Sterling Hotel in Caratunk, a 19th-century stage stop, and at the Morgan House in The Forks. **Wilderness Expeditions** (Tel: 800/825-WILD or 207/534-2242), specializing in white-water trips on the Kennebec, maintains a lodge in The Forks in which patrons can dine and relax. Platform tents are available here for overnight stays; otherwise Wilderness Expeditions rafters stay at The Birches in Rockwood (see Moosehead Lake, below). **Northern Outdoors** (Tel: 800/765-RAFT or 207/663-4466) has turned its large, elaborate lodge in The Forks into the centerpiece for a year-round resort featuring horseback riding, platform tennis, mountain biking, snowmobiling, and cross-country skiing as well as rafting trips on the Kennebec and Dead rivers.

Two companies in The Forks, **Crab Apple White Water**, which has converted an 1830s village house into an inn, and **Voyagers Whitewater**, offering a few rooms in the house from which it is based, encourage guests to explore more than the river. Sue Varney, chef for Voyagers, has written *Take a Hike,* a slim but informative guide to local hiking options (she also offers patrons far more than the standard "river steak" at the end of their run).

A growing number of people are combining a couple of days in The Forks area with a visit to Quebec city, just 112 miles (180 km) north.

The Moose River Valley

The 26-mile (42-km) stretch of Route 201 north from The Forks to **Jackman**, a knot of shabby north country shops and houses at the junction of Routes 201 and 15, is heavily wooded. Watch for moose and for the one well-marked rest area on your right, with picnic tables and a superb view of the chain of Attean, Holeb, and Big Wood ponds off to the west and of the high mountains beyond. These lake-size "ponds" are linked by the Moose River to form a 42-mile canoe route that brings you back to the place where you started, eliminating the need for a shuttle. This so-called **Moose River Bow Trip** is well known among canoeists and is spotted with wilderness campsites; canoes can be rented in Jackman. The Jackman-Moose River Chamber of Commerce maintains an information booth on Route 201 in Jackman, north of the junction with Route 15. Tel: (207) 668-4094.

Your best bet for a meal in Jackman is **Briarwood Mountain Lodge**, a motel with a large dining room hidden away in its rear, with windows overlooking the spread of woods and mountains to the east. Tel: (207) 668-7756.

Turn east on Route 6/15 in Jackman and follow the Moose River—known for brook trout and salmon fly-fishing—as it threads Long Pond and then Brassua Lake and ultimately flows into Moosehead Lake at Rockwood.

Moosehead Lake

Forty-mile-long Moosehead Lake is the largest lake totally within any one New England state. It is, besides, visually impressive, especially from the village of **Rockwood**, right where Route 6/15 runs into the lake, with Mount Kineo rising abruptly from the water just across the narrows, and the rounded humps of the Spencers (Big Spencer and Little Spencer mountains) beyond.

This is the view from the front porches of the 17 rough-hewn cabins at **The Birches**. Scattered through the woods right on the lakeshore in Rockwood, these are traditional sporting camp cabins, each with the distinctive Maine woods overhang on the front and wood stoves or a fireplace for heat. In addition to the cabins, guests may choose to stay in cabin tents or in the four rooms upstairs in the log lodge. During the high summer season all three meals are served in the lodge, with its massive fireplace and, of course, lake views. Warm-weather sports include rafting and canoeing, while in winter cross-country skiing is offered on an extensive touring system. From spring through fall there are also moose cruises.

The biggest craze to hit this area since rafting is **moose watching**. Of course the moose have always been here, but moose watching seems to be a 1990s phenomenon. In the past few years no fewer than four excursion boats have begun offering moose-watching cruises at dawn and dusk. For details contact the Moosehead Lake Region Chamber of Commerce (Tel: 207/695-2702), which sponsors "Moose Mania Month" (mid-May to mid-June) with many special events.

In 1992, 1,361 moose sightings were reported in the area for the month.

Mount Kineo is said to resemble a huge moose rising from the lake, and of course there is an Indian legend to this effect. Virtually an island (access through a thin neck of land on the shore opposite Rockwood has been blocked), Kineo was once the site of Maine's grandest hotel. A recently revitalized **golf course** (nine holes, open to the public) and several Victorian annexes are all that survive to suggest that the Mount Kineo House ever existed. A steep but rewarding hiking path leads to the watchtower atop a cliff. (The Kineo Shuttle boat leaves from Rockwood twice daily; Tel: 207/534-7577.)

GREENVILLE

Many people have lost their shirts trying to revive the Mount Kineo House, but the last duo to do so didn't just turn their backs on Moosehead Lake in defeat. Instead, Leigh Turner and Mariette Sinclair opened the **Road Kill Café**, 20 miles (32 km) down Route 15 in Greenville Junction.

This small restaurant, which opened in 1992, was an instant international sensation. Leigh's press releases were witty enough to spark newspaper stories as far away as Australia and Japan. Road Kill Café tee-shirts are currently the hottest souvenir from Maine. So what's all the fuss? The menu, for starters. It's blazoned with the slogan "Where the food used to speak for itself." Skidbits include "pail o' nightcrawlers," subtitled "French fries with that off the road patina," and you can lunch on "Route 15 soup du jour" ("what the UPS man found on his way here from Guilford") or a "fungus burger" and dine on "probably pork ribs" or "mooseballs." Huge draft beakers of beer as well as wine are served, and the food is actually quite good. Not surprisingly, the decor runs to hubcaps, road signs, and license plates. (Closed April to mid-May; Tel: 207/695-2230.)

Unbelievable as it may seem, Canadian VIA Rail Service stops in tiny Greenville Junction en route from Halifax, Nova Scotia, to Montreal; it's possible to walk from the train to **Curriers Flying Service** (Tel: 207/695-2778), just around the corner, and fly off to a sporting camp deep in the north woods.

Greenville, just 2 miles (3 km) east of Greenville Junction on Route 6/15, is New England's largest seaplane base; **Folsom's Air Service** (Tel: 207/695-2921), founded by Dick Folsom in 1946 and now headed by his son Max, offers charter service to Portland as well as dozens of widely scattered camps. Both flying services will also transport canoes, reserve camps, furnish guides, or simply give scenic flights.

Greenville looks the part of a wilderness outpost even more than does Rangeley. Like Rangeley, it was once far more of a resort, accessible directly by train from New York and Philadelphia, and it, too, had its share of wooden hotels and a flotilla of steamboats that met trains to ferry guests off to lakeside retreats. The SS *Katahdin,* a jaunty 115-foot 1914 steamboat, was restored with volunteer effort a few years ago and now circles the lake daily in summer. Even if you don't take a cruise, look in on its home base, the **Moosehead Marine Museum** in Greenville, with displays devoted to the lake's steamboat era. Tel: (207) 695-2716.

The **Indian Store**, in the white Victorian building at the corner of Main Street and Pritham Avenue, dates from the early 20th century. Since 1929 Ida Faye has sold baskets, feathers, candy, and an astounding array of knickknacks, and the place has changed little over the years. The **Maine Guide Fly Shop and Guide Service**, just up Main Street, is another landmark, stocking more than 300 different flies and a wide variety of gear. The Moosehead Lake Region Chamber of Commerce, midway between the two stores, is unusually helpful and well stocked (open year-round; Tel: 207/695-2702).

The **Greenville Inn**, set high on a hill just beyond town on Norris Street (with a magnificent view down the length of the lake), is a classic 1890s lumber-baron's mansion, with rich paneling, pressed tin walls, a half-dozen working fireplaces, and an immense leaded-glass window depicting a spruce tree. Thanks to Austrian-born chef Elfie Schnetzer, dining here is superb; specialties include grilled lamb chops with garlic and herbs and apricot-glazed roast duckling.

Eastern River Expeditions, on Route 15 on the outskirts of Greenville, is another of Maine's leading rafting companies, offering day trips on both the Kennebec and Penobscot rivers. Tel: (800) 634-7238 or (207) 695-2512.

It is possible to leave Maine's interior in Greenville and head home from here, just as you could from Rangeley, Kingfield, or Phillips. The most direct route is Route 6/15 south to Abbot Village, where you pick up Route 16 east to Route 23/7, then follow Route 11 to I-95 at Newport. Having come so far, however, it would seem a shame for you not to go the rest of the way—but only if you have the right car for it. Motorcycles, large all-terrain vehicles (longer than 44 feet), and bikes are not permitted on paper-company roads.

NORTH FROM GREENVILLE

Along the eastern shore of Moosehead, the blacktop ends 8 miles (13 km) north of town, just beyond **Lily Bay State Park,** good for both swimming and camping. The road surface is hard-packed dirt, and it's a pretty drive for the next 10 miles (16 km), climbing Blair Hill (with views off over the lake) and tunneling into the woods all the way to **Kokadjo**, a former lumbering station. In Kokadjo there are a general store and the **Northern Pride Lodge**, an inn with simply furnished guest rooms and innkeeper-guide Paul Wade's trophies (which include a stuffed black bear) arranged around the common rooms.

One of Maine's most traditional sporting camps, it should be mentioned, is a 10-mile (16-km) drive into the woods from Kokadjo, east along First Roach Pond. First opened as a moose-hunting lodge in 1880, **West Branch Ponds Camps** offers cabins weathered to a silvery gray that overlook the pond and Whitecap Mountain, a square bell-topped lodge, and Carol Stirling's legendary cooking.

Continuing north on the "main" road you soon hit the first Georgia Pacific checkpoint (a user fee is charged May through November) and are handed a list of rules of the road, the most important of which is "Trucks have the right-of-way. Watch for log trucks and pull over when you see one."

THE GREAT NORTH WOODS
West Branch of the Penobscot

Because the West Branch of the Penobscot River is a longer drive from Eastern cities than the Kennebec, it has a smaller—though equally enthusiastic—following of canoeists. You enter the river at Ripogenus Dam, north of Kokadjo, and career for two miles through dramatic Ripogenus Gorge, then through rapids with names like Exterminator.

The West Branch originates in Seboomook Lake, just north of Moosehead, flows east into long, completely wilderness-locked Chesuncook Lake, and runs on into Baxter State Park, a 201,000-acre island of public lands in a 2.8 million-acre sea of green paper-company land. It's this vast tract of private and public woods, traversed only by private roads, that is usually equated with the "great north woods," the last major wilderness area in the Northeast.

Twenty miles (32 km) north of Kokadjo you hit the **Golden Road**, a 98-mile (158-km) private logging road that runs from Quebec province in the west to Millinocket in the east. Turn east (right). In just a couple of miles (3 km) you'll come to Cushing's Landing, at the foot of **Chesuncook Lake**, where you'll find a woodsman's memorial hewn from a post and doorway of a Bangor tavern, decorated with logging tools and an iron bean pot. In *The Maine Woods* Henry

David Thoreau describes canoeing up Chesuncook Lake, stopping by the lumbermen's village of Chesuncook—which has survived to an amazing degree, despite the absence of roads leading to it. In summer guests come by boat or plane, in winter by snowmobiles. You can stay here in one of the 12 gas-lit guests rooms at the **Chesuncook Lake House** and dine handsomely on well-sauced dishes prepared by Maggie McBurnie, the Parisian wife of Chesuncook native Bert McBurnie. If you don't have your own canoe, Bert will pick you up at Cushing's Landing.

The turnoff from the Golden Road for **Ripogenus Dam** is just beyond the eastern rim of Chesuncook Lake. Go by Pray's Store and drive across the dam itself on Telos Road for a view of the gorge. Continue on Telos Road and you'll eventually come to the **Allagash Wilderness Waterway**, a 92-mile-long chain of lakes, ponds, rivers, and streams with wilderness camping areas, accessible only by canoe. (See Getting Around for details.)

The good news is that the Golden Road is paved from "Rip" Dam all the way to Millinocket. It continues east through woods (more prime moose-spotting territory), skirting Baxter State Park.

Baxter State Park

You may wonder why you have seen no signs for Baxter State Park, which seems to discourage visitors. It has to do with the park's history and mandate. As governor of Maine between 1920 and 1925, Percival Baxter urged acquisition of the land around Mount Katahdin—to no avail. Finally he invested much of his personal fortune to purchase the park's present acreage, donating it to the state with the proviso that it remain "forever wild."

So it happens that both the park's roads and hiking trails—of which there are 180 miles—are rough, and access to the park is strictly limited. To secure one of the 1,200 campsites you must send the fee with your request (see Getting Around), and unless you arrive early on peak summer days, you may not even get a chance to pay the gate fee. (Baxter State Park averages 115,000 visitors a year compared with Acadia National Park's five million.) The park also closes from mid-October to December 1 and again from April 1 through mid-May, the most dangerous hiking seasons.

Mile-high **Mount Katahdin** is the highest and most distinctive (it's long and high shouldered) mountain in Maine and is considered one of the world's great mountains to climb. However, it's just one of 47 peaks in the park. Because its trails are far more heavily travelled than those on neighboring mountains, and because you can't see Katahdin from Katahdin, most park habitués advise heading up another mountain.

The serenity to be found in the park's campgrounds, on its ponds (rental canoes are available), and on its trails is well worth the planning it takes to get there. Campgrounds are plentiful on the rim of the park, both at its **Togue Ponds Gate**, a half-hour's drive west of Millinocket, and at the **Matagamon Gate**, accessible from Shin Pond, north of Patten. For help with finding local lodging, contact the Millinocket Chamber of Commerce, P.O. Box 5, Millinocket, ME 04462; Tel: (207) 723-4443.

If you are heading directly to Baxter State Park from the Maine coast, and are planning to bypass the other inland places described in this chapter, the shortest route from the south is I-95 to the Medway exit, then 25 miles (40 km) northwest to the Togue Ponds entrance. On the way home you might stop in Bangor, 70 miles (112 km) south of Medway on I-95.

BANGOR

The Bangor that boomed during Maine's lumbering era burned down in 1911, and what fire didn't destroy fell to 1960s urban renewal. All that remains of that time is **West Market Square Historic District**, a mid-19th-century block of shops that includes the **Quality Inn–Phenix**, a restored four-story building from 1873 furnished with reproduction antiques; and the Broadway neighborhood, with its many lumber-barons' mansions, including the turreted, spooky-looking home of novelist Stephen King (it's the one with the bat-and-cobweb fence).

Take the Broadway exit off I-95 and stop at the **Bangor Historical Society Museum** to see its collection of spinning wheels and local memorabilia, at 159 Union Street (corner of High Street). Closed mid-December to February; Tel: (207) 942-5766. For great delicatessen food try the **Bagel Shop**, at 1 Main Street (in West Market Square), and if you like garlic have dinner at **Seguino's Italian Restaurant**, 737 Main Street; Tel: (207) 942-1240. If you would rather not stay right in town, **Hamstead Farm**, set in 150 acres a few minutes from downtown, is a homey retreat for guests as well as for some 70 turkeys, 40 cows, 15 sows, 100 pigs, one black sheep, and many kittens.

From Bangor you may return via I-95 and Augusta to Boston or head for the coast, either 25 miles (40 km) southeast along Route 1A to Ellsworth (and from there to

Mount Desert) or 20 miles (32 km) due south via another Route 1A (we don't understand this route designation either) to Stockton Springs and thence south along the coast.

—*Christina Tree*

GETTING AROUND

The South Coast

The most common approach to the south coast is up I-95 from New Hampshire and Massachusetts. Kittery is just one hour north of Boston. Exits off I-95 are limited to Kittery, York Village, and Kennebunk. The York and Ogunquit information centers are both on Route 1: The York Chamber of Commerce (Tel: 207/363-4422) maintains a walk-in information booth at the light near the I-95 access road, and the Ogunquit Chamber of Commerce (Tel: 207/646-2939) maintains one just south of the village (north of the Ogunquit Playhouse). Both are sources of local maps, town brochures, local menus, and information about boat excursions; both close in the dead of winter (hours vary in other seasons).

The Kennebunk-Kennebunkport Chamber of Commerce (Tel: 207/967-0857) dispenses maps at its information center at the junction of Routes 9 and 35 in Kennebunk Lower Village. The Kennebunk narrated excursion aboard *Elizabeth 2* lasts one and a half hours and is offered frequently throughout the day from May through October; Tel: (207) 967-5595. **Whale-watching cruises** from Kennebunkport are offered May through October aboard the *Nautilus* (Tel: 207/967-5595) and by Indian Whale Watch (Tel: 207/967-5912).

Portland and Casco Bay

By air. Each year more and more visitors are discovering the ease of using Portland as a gateway to New England. The **Portland International Jetport** (Tel: 207/774-7301) resembles a small town airport, yet it is served by Continental Airlines, Delta Airlines, Northwest Airlink, and USAir. Direct flights link Portland to Boston, New York, Newark, Quebec, Chicago, Philadelphia, and Washington. Just off I-95, it's quite accessible, and just minutes from downtown Portland. Metro City Buses connect the airport with the city, though most visitors choose to rent a car. Car-rental firms represented at the airport include American International Rent-a-Car, Avis, Budget Rent-A-Car, Hertz, and Thrifty Car Rental. It's possible to return most of these rental cars at Boston's Logan International Airport, if you plan to fly out of Boston after touring Maine.

By ferry. The idea of entering one place and exiting by another also works well with the Canadian ferries. It's quite possible to take the **Prince of Fundy Cruises'** MS *Scotia*

Prince (Tel: 800/341-7540 from outside Maine or 800/482-0955 in-state) on its overnight passage to Yarmouth, Nova Scotia, and to return from Yarmouth via the **Marine Atlantic Bluenose Ferry** (Tel: 800/341-7981) to Bar Harbor, and then to drive back along the coast to Portland (or vice versa). The MS *Scotia Prince* departs from Portland at 9:00 P.M., arriving in Yarmouth at 9:00 A.M. the following day (May through October). The ferry accommodates 1,500 passengers in 800 cabins and can carry 250 cars. The cruise company packages the crossing itself as a 23-hour cruise featuring a buffet dinner, dancing, and a full casino with gaming tables and slot machines. It also puts together Nova Scotia tours of any length and scope.

Far better organized than the New England tourism industry, the **Nova Scotia Department of Tourism and Culture** offers a toll-free number through which to secure its lengthy free guide and to make reservations at any inn or hotel in the province; Tel: (800) 341-6096. There's also a Nova Scotia Provincial Tourist Information Center in Portland, right in the Old Port at 136 Commercial Street. Tel: (207) 772-6131.

By car. Most visitors to the Casco Bay area are, of course, driving up I-95. Many stop at the Kittery Information Center (open daily except Christmas and Thanksgiving) maintained by the Maine Publicity Bureau on I-95 northbound, just a few miles beyond the New Hampshire line (Tel: 207/439-1319). This is the most elaborate visitors' center in all of New England; it's worth a stop just to see the exhibits representing various regions within Maine. While the information racks are filled with literally thousands of brochures, be sure to ask if you can't find enough about your destination— there are even more brochures behind the desk. You might request the *Greater Portland, Maine, Visitors Guide,* for instance, rather than waiting to pick it up at the Convention and Visitors Bureau of Greater Portland information center, in downtown Portland at 305 Commercial Street (Tel: 207/772-5000).

The most common approach to Portland from I-95 is by the waterfront. Take exit 6A off the interstate to Route 295 and follow signs for the waterfront and ferry. If you cannot find a parking space on Commercial Street, follow "P" signs to the Fore Street Garage (439 Fore Street), the Custom House Square Garage (25 Pearl Street), or the Casco Bay Garage (Maine Street Pier). All have nominal rates.

Casco Bay Lines offers excursions as well as ferry service (frequently the latter, disguised as the former) to islands in Casco Bay (Tel: 207/774-7871). **Eagle Tours, Inc.** (Tel: 207/774-6498), based on Portland's Long Wharf, offers tours to Eagle Island and a variety of other excursions. **Bay View**

Cruises (Tel: 207/761-0496), based at Fisherman's Wharf, specializes in narrated harbor cruises. Cruises to Eagle Island are also offered aboard the *Atlantic Seal* out of South Freeport (Tel: 207/865-6112).

North from Portland follow Route 295 to I-95; take exit 20 or 21 for Freeport and Route 1 to Brunswick.

Midcoast

The best way to explore the nooks and crannies of the Midcoast is by car. If you are flying to Boston you can rent a car and head up Routes 95 and 1 to the region. Alternatively, you may fly into Portland or Bangor, Maine, both good-size airports with major car-rental desks right in the terminal and just off-site. Both airports are also served by regular limousine service to the Midcoast area. Just south of Rockland is the Knox County Airport at Owls Head, with daily commuter flights from Boston. Once you are in the area you'll find that Route 1 is the central artery along the coast, with smaller routes taking you down the peninsulas and inland to rolling countryside.

To reach the island of **Monhegan** you have three choices during the summer: the daily morning departures of the sightseeing boat *Balmy Days II* from Boothbay Harbor (Tel: 207/633-2284), the daily trips on the *Hardy III* from New Harbor (Tel: 207/677-2026 days, 882-7909 evenings), and the twice-daily crossings on the mail boat *Laura B* from Port Clyde (Tel: 207/372-8848; reservations usually necessary). Off-season only the *Laura B* offers regular trips to the island. (You cannot take your car to Monhegan.)

Ferries depart daily to the islands of **Vinalhaven** and **North Haven** from the Maine State Ferry Terminal in Rockland (Tel: 207/596-2202), and the Maine State Ferry offers daily service to **Islesboro** from Lincolnville Beach (Tel: 207/789-5611 or 734-6935).

The area's chambers of commerce offer a wealth of information, such as lists of weekly and monthly rentals. They include: Boothbay Harbor Region Chamber of Commerce, P.O. Box 356, Boothbay Harbor, ME 04538, Tel: (207) 633-2353; Damariscotta Chamber of Commerce, P.O. Box 13, Darmariscotta, ME 04543, Tel: (207) 563-8340; Rockport-Camden-Lincolnville Chamber of Commerce, P.O. Box 919, Public Landing, Camden, ME 04843, Tel: (207) 236-4404; and Rockland Chamber of Commerce, P.O. Box 508, Rockland, ME 04841, Tel: (207) 596-0376.

East Penobscot Bay and Blue Hill

The obvious approach to this area is up Route 1 from Camden, but the fastest route from Portland and points south is via I-95 to Augusta and Route 3 to Belfast. For nearby air service, see Mount Desert Island, next.

The **Isle au Haut Company** (Tel: 207/367-5193) runs a mail boat from Stonington, on Deer Isle, to Isle au Haut at least twice daily (except Sundays) year-round. Boats run to Duck Harbor, at the southern end of the island, on Saturdays and Sundays from late June through Labor Day.

Mount Desert Island

By air. Air service to the **Hancock County/Bar Harbor Airport** in Trenton, just north of Bar Harbor, is offered from Boston and Rockland by Colgan Air (Tel: 800/272-5488). **Bangor International Airport** (Tel: 207/947-0307), the area's major airport, 20 miles (32 km) north of Ellsworth, is served by Delta Business Express, Continental Express, Northwest Airlink, and United Airlines with flights from New York, Washington, Boston, and Portland. Air Belgium and Bal Air (Swiss) flights also service Bangor. Avis, Budget, and Hertz have offices here.

By ferry. Marine Atlantic's **Bluenose Ferry** (Tel: 800/341-7981) carries passengers and cars from Bar Harbor to Yarmouth, Nova Scotia, daily from late June to late September, three times per week in shoulder seasons, and twice per week in winter. The trip takes six hours. Note that the Prince of Fundy Company provides ferry service from Yarmouth to Portland (see Portland, above).

By car. There are three routes to Bar Harbor from points south. The slowest—also the most popular and the most scenic—is up Route 1 along the coast. The most direct route is I-95 and the Maine Turnpike to Bangor, then Route 1A to Ellsworth. A compromise is to take I-95 to Augusta, then Route 3 to Belfast, and coastal Route 1 north.

Organized tours. **National Park Tours** offers two-and-a-half hour narrated bus tours of Acadia National Park's Loop Road, departing from Testa's at 53 Main Street in Bar Harbor; Tel: (207) 288-3327.

Wildwood Stables offers two-hour horse-drawn tours of Acadia's carriage roads; Tel: (207) 276-3622.

Consult local listings for the numerous boat excursions offered from Bar Harbor and Northeast Harbor.

Down East Maine

Down east, as we've defined it in this chapter, begins in the town of Sullivan, 14 miles (22 km) east of Ellsworth on Route 1. Colgan Air (Tel: 800/272-5488) flies from Boston to the **Hancock County-Bar Harbor Airport,** 7 miles (11 km) south of Ellsworth. **Bangor International Airport** (see Mount Desert Island, above) offers connections with all parts of the country. It's an hour's drive from Bangor to Calais on Route 9, and about an hour and a half from Bangor to Machias on Route 1. Hertz, Avis, and Budget car-rental agencies serve both airports.

Around Passamaquoddy Bay. Route 1 is the high road down east, but there are many possible detours down the coast's peninsulas. Our suggested itinerary around the **Quoddy Loop** takes you over the international bridge from Lubec to Campobello Island, then aboard the seasonal **East Coast Ferry** (Tel: 506/747-2159) to Deer Island and the (free) Deer Island–L'Etete Ferry (506/453-2600) to L'Etete, New Brunswick. Both of these are 15-car ferries that run hourly, and neither accepts reservations. The **Coastal Transport Ltd. Ferry** from Blacks Harbour to Grand Manan Island transports passengers and cars year-round, six times daily (four times on Sundays), to North Head on Grand Manan; no reservations are accepted. Tel: (506) 662-3724.

We then head back through St. Andrews, New Brunswick, and around through Calais, Maine, to Eastport. The shorter, more scenic way back to Maine is to take the ferry from L'Etete to Deer Island again and go back across Deer Island to the ferry for Eastport, which departs from the same place as the Campobello ferry. Both are owned by the East Coast Ferry company.

Seasons and weather. Season and weather are big factors here in northeasternmost Maine. From October through mid-June, when the East Coast ferries are not running, the 95-mile (152-km) land route around Passamaquoddy Bay from Machias to Blacks Harbour is your only choice.

Clear weather, moreover, is a key but elusive ingredient in appreciating the beauty of this area. Your best chances for good weather are from July through October, but May and June can also be fine. Bring rubber boots, a heavy sweater, and a slicker just in case.

Also be aware of the time difference between the Maine and New Brunswick sides of Passamaquoddy Bay. New Brunswick is on Atlantic standard time, one hour ahead of Maine, which is on eastern standard time.

Canadian taxes. Canadian taxes are another phenomenon to consider. You begin to notice their effect as far south of the border as Machias, where gas prices begin to climb. New Brunswick residents drive many miles south to escape Canadian taxes on gas, cigarettes, and basics. The **Canadian Goods and Services Tax** (GST) is known locally as "Going South Today." Visitors must pay the GST as well but can get most of it back (providing they have spent $100 on goods and short-term accommodations) by filling out a Revenue

Canada application (available at border crossings and in stores), including itemized receipts.

For further information, the Quoddy Loop Regional Tourism Office (Tel: 207/454-1579; Box 688, Calais, ME 04619) is located downstairs in the year-round Calais Information Center (Tel: 207/454-2211), at 7 Union Street, Calais. For Washington County the best information source is the Machias Bay Area Chamber of Commerce; open year-round, it also maintains a seasonal information center in the Emporium shopping complex on Route 1 (Main Street); Tel: (207) 255-4402.

Inland Maine

Hikers intent on climbing Mount Katahdin, rafters who have come from afar simply to raft the Kennebec or Penobscot rivers, or canoeists who've come just to "do" the Allagash or St. Croix may well want to fly directly into **Bangor International Airport** (see Mount Desert Island, above).

The route we have followed in this chapter simply links inland Maine's most scenic and accommodating sights. Obviously you can choose to do only one segment or another, or you might choose to just drive up Route 26 from Portland to Bethel and continue on via Route 2 to Gorham, New Hampshire. Another possibility is to take I-95 to Augusta and then Route 201 through the upper Kennebec Valley to Quebec city.

I-95 serves as a quick way out of the woods whenever you want to take it. The Maine Turnpike, incidentally, is not precisely the same thing as I-95. While the two begin as one toll road in York, the Maine Turnpike (I-495) diverges just north of Portland. To pick up Route 26 you must take I-495 for 3 miles (5 km) to Gray. But if you are heading up to, or back from, Augusta, take I-95 instead—it's cheaper and faster.

For information and camping reservations in Baxter State Park, write to the **Baxter State Park Authority**, 64 Balsam Drive, Millinocket, ME 04462; Tel: (207) 723-5140. Reservation requests must be accompanied by a camping fee, which is currently $6 per person in a bunkhouse, $5 in a lean-to, $15 in a campsite, and $3 at group campsites. The gate fee to the park is $8.

To find out more about canoeing the **Allagash Wilderness Waterway**, contact the **Bureau of Parks and Recreation**, State House Station 22, Augusta, ME 04333; Tel: (207) 289-3821.

For white-water rafting information and reservations, contact **Raft Maine**, an association representing most of the major outfitters; Tel: (800) 359-2106.

North Maine Woods, a consortium of the major landowners of 2.8 million acres of forest, publishes a map/guide to the region's roads and campsites, as well as a canoeing guide to the St. John River; Tel: (207) 435-6213.

One major canoe outfitter not mentioned in the text deserves special mention here. **Sunrise Canoe Expeditions**, based at Cathance Lake (Grove Post Office, ME 04638), offers guided trips down the Grand Lake chain and the St. John and St. Croix rivers; Tel: (207) 454-7708.

ACCOMMODATIONS REFERENCE

Unless otherwise noted, the rates given below are projections for 1993 for double room, double occupancy. As prices are subject to change, always double-check before booking. The area code for all of Maine is 207.

The South Coast

▶ **Anchorage Inn.** Long Beach Avenue, **York Beach**, ME 03910. Tel: 363-5112; Fax: 363-6753. $85–$220.

▶ **Aspinquid.** P.O. Box 2408, **Ogunquit**, ME 03907. Tel: 646-7072. $95–$110; apartments $170.

▶ **Beachmere Inn.** P.O. Box 2340, **Ogunquit**, ME 03907. Tel: 646-2021 or (800) 336-3983; Fax: (207) 646-2231. $75–$180; includes Continental breakfast.

▶ **Breakwater Inn.** Ocean Avenue, **Kennebunkport**, ME 04046. Tel: 967-3118. $75–$135; includes breakfast.

▶ **Bufflehead Cove.** P.O. Box 499, **Kennebunkport**, ME 04046. Tel: 967-3879. $75–$130; includes breakfast.

▶ **Captain Fairfield Inn.** P.O. Box 1308, **Kennebunkport**, ME 04046. Tel: 967-4454. $65–$105; includes breakfast.

▶ **Captain Jefferds Inn.** P.O. Box 691, **Kennebunkport**, ME 04046. Tel: 967-2311. $85–$135; suites $135–$145; includes breakfast.

▶ **Captain Lord Mansion.** P.O. Box 800, **Kennebunkport**, ME 04046. Tel: 967-3141; Fax: 967-3172. $149–$199; includes breakfast.

▶ **Cliff House.** P.O. Box 2274, **Ogunquit**, ME 03907. Tel: 361-1000. $120–$305; includes breakfast.

▶ **Colony.** Ocean Avenue and Kings Road, **Kennebunkport**, ME 04046. Tel: 967-3331 or (800) 552-2363. $155–$260; includes all meals.

▶ **Dockside Guest Quarters.** P.O. Box 205, Harris Island Road, **York**, ME 03909. Tel: 363-2868. $58–$89; cottages $89.50–$138.

▶ **Green Heron Inn.** Ocean Avenue, P.O. Box 2578, **Kennebunkport**, ME 04046. Tel: 967-3315. $60–$86; includes breakfast.

▶ **Gundalow Inn.** 6 Water Street, **Kittery**, ME 03904. Tel: 439-4040. $75–$95; includes breakfast.

▶ **Harbour Watch B & B.** 6 Follett Lane, **Kittery**, ME 03904. $65; includes breakfast.

▶ **Hutchins House.** 209 Organug Road, **York**, ME 03909. Tel: 363-3085. $85; includes breakfast.

▶ **Inn at Harbor Head.** R.R. 2, Box 1180, **Kennebunkport**, ME 04046. Tel: 967-5564; Fax: 967-8776. $105–$185; includes breakfast.

▶ **Inn at Harmon Park.** Route 1A, P.O. Box 495, **York Harbor**, ME 03911. Tel: 363-2031. $40–$69; includes breakfast.

▶ **Inn on South Street.** P.O. Box 478A, **Kennebunkport**, ME 04046. Tel: 967-5151. $85–$155; includes breakfast.

▶ **Kennebunkport Inn.** P.O. Box 111, **Kennebunkport**, ME 04046. Tel: 967-2621 or (800) 248-2621; Fax: (207) 967-3705. $79–$159; includes breakfast.

▶ **Kylemere Inn.** P.O. Box 1333, **Kennebunkport**, ME 04046. Tel: 967-2780. $90–$115; includes breakfast.

▶ **Maine Stay Inn and Cottages.** P.O. Box 500A, Maine Street, **Kennebunkport**, ME 04046. Tel: 967-2117; Fax: 967-8757. $85–$185; includes breakfast.

▶ **Marginal Way House and Motel.** 8 Wharf Lane, P.O. Box 697, **Ogunquit**, ME 03907. Tel: 646-8801; 363-6566 in winter. $68–$112; apartments $875–$1,050 weekly.

▶ **Nonantum Resort.** Ocean Avenue, P.O. Box 2626, **Kennebunkport**, ME 04046. Tel: 967-4050. $95–$125.

▶ **Old Fort Inn.** P.O. Box M, **Kennebunkport**, ME 04046. Tel: 967-5353 or (800) 822-FORT. $125–$230; includes breakfast.

▶ **Pine Hill Inn.** 14 Pine Hill Road South, P.O. Box 2336, **Ogunquit**, ME 03907. Tel: 361-1004. $65–$85; includes breakfast.

▶ **Riverside Motel.** P.O. Box 2244, **Ogunquit**, ME 03907. Tel: 646-2741. $50–$110; includes Continental breakfast.

▶ **Sparhawk.** P.O. Box 936, **Ogunquit**, ME 03907. Tel: 646-5562. $125–$185; includes breakfast.

▶ **Stage Neck Inn.** York Harbor, ME 03911. Tel: 363-3850 or (800) 222-3238; Fax: (207) 363-2221. $135–$195; includes breakfast.

▶ **Welby Inn.** Ocean Avenue, P.O. Box 774, **Kennebunkport**, ME 04046. Tel: 967-4655. $60–$90; includes breakfast.

▶ **White Barn Inn.** P.O. Box 560C, **Kennebunkport**, ME 04046. Tel: 967-2321. $110–$260; includes breakfast.

▶ **York Harbor Inn.** Route 1A, P.O. Box 573, **York Harbor**, ME 03911. Tel: 363-5119 or (800) 343-3869; Fax: (207) 363-3545, ext. 295. $84–$135; includes breakfast.

Portland and Environs

▶ **Black Point Inn.** 510 Black Point Road, **Prouts Neck**, ME 04074. Tel: 883-4126 or (800) 258-0003; Fax: (207) 883-4126. $250–$330 (plus 15 percent gratuity); includes breakfast and dinner.

▶ **Chebeague Inn-by-the-Sea.** P.O. Box 492, **Chebeague Island**, ME 04107. Tel: 846-5255; from October to April, 774-5891. $70–$130; includes breakfast.

▶ **Inn on Carleton.** 46 Carleton Street, **Portland**, ME 02102. Tel: 775-1910. $60–$90.

▶ **Inn at ParkSpring.** 135 Spring Street, **Portland**, ME 04101. Tel: 774-1059. $75–$105.

▶ **Inn by the Sea.** 40 Bowery Beach Road (Route 77), **Cape Elizabeth**, ME 04107. Tel: 799-3134. $85–$375.

▶ **McKinley Estates. Great Diamond Island**, P.O. Box 3572, Portland, ME 04104. Tel: 797-6241; Fax: 797-0253. $120 per night; $1,000–$1,200 weekly.

▶ **Pomegranate Inn.** 49 Neal Street, **Portland**, ME 04102. Tel: 772-1006 or (800) 356-0408; Fax: (207) 773-4426. $85–$125; suites $150.

▶ **Portland Regency Hotel.** 20 Milk Street, **Portland**, ME 04101. Tel: 774-4200 or (800) 727-3436; Fax: (207) 775-2150. $95–$140.

▶ **Sonesta Portland Hotel.** 157 High Street, **Portland**, ME 04101. Tel: 775-5411 or (800) 777-6246; Fax: (207) 775-2872. $80–$135; suites $100–$210; includes breakfast.

Casco Bay Area

▶ **Atlantic Seal B&B.** P.O. Box 146, 25 Main Street, **South Freeport**, ME 04078. Tel: 865-6112. $65–$125; includes breakfast.

▶ **Brunswick Bed & Breakfast.** 165 Park Row, **Brunswick**, ME 04011. Tel: (207) 729-4914. $69–$79; includes breakfast.

▶ **Captain Daniel Stone Inn.** 10 Water Street, **Brunswick**, ME 04011. Tel: 725-9898; Fax: ask for extension 102. $65–$165.

▶ **Driftwood Inn and Cottages. Bailey Island**, ME 04003. Tel: 833-5461. $65–$75; cottages $300–$500 weekly.

▶ **Harpswell Inn.** 141 Lookout Point Road, R.R. 1, Box 141, **South Harpswell**, ME 04079. Tel: 833-5509 or (800) 843-5509 $55–$105.

▶ **Harraseeket Inn.** 162 Main Street, **Freeport**, ME 04032. Tel: 865-9377 or (800) 342-6423; Fax: (207) 865-1684. $135–$225.

▶ **Isaac Randall House.** 5 Independence Drive, **Freeport**, ME 04032. Tel: 865-9295. $70–$110.

▶ **Little Island Motel.** R.D. 1, Box 15, **Orrs Island**, ME 04066. Tel: 833-2392. $88–$108.

The Midcoast

▶ **Bailey Inn.** Main Street, **Wiscasset**, ME 04578. Tel: 882-4214. $70–$90.

▶ **Belmont.** 6 Belmont Avenue, **Camden**, ME 04843. Tel: 236-8053 or (800) 238-8053. $70–$145; includes breakfast.

▶ **Blue Harbor House.** 67 Elm Street, **Camden**, ME 04843. Tel: 236-3196 or (800) 248-3196; Fax: (207) 236-6523. $85–$125; includes breakfast.

▶ **Bradley Inn.** Route 130, MC 61, 361 Pemaquid Point Road, **New Harbor**, ME 04554. Tel: 677-2105. $90–$135; includes Continental breakfast.

▶ **Briar Rose B & B.** P.O. Box 27, Route 32, **Round Pond**, ME 04564. Tel: 529-5478. $55–$68; includes breakfast.

▶ **Broad Bay Inn.** P.O. Box 607, Main Street, **Waldoboro**, ME 04572. Tel: 832-6668. $40–$70; includes breakfast.

▶ **Captain Drummond House. Phippsburg**, ME 04562. Tel: 389-1394. $65–$130; includes breakfast.

▶ **Coveside Inn. Christmas Cove**, HC 64, Box 150, South Bristol, ME 04568. Tel: 644-8282; Fax: 644-8204. $65–$80.

▶ **Dark Harbor House.** Box 185, Main Road, **Dark Harbor**, ME 04848. Tel: 734-6669. $95–$225.

▶ **East Wind Inn.** P.O. Box 149, **Tenants Harbor**, ME 04860. Tel: 372-6366, 372-6367, or (800) 241-VIEW. $74–$110; includes Continental breakfast.

▶ **Edgecombe-Coles House.** 64 High Street (Route 1), HCR 60, Box 3010, **Camden**, ME 04843. Tel: 236-2336; Fax: 236-6227. $115–$165; includes breakfast.

▶ **Fairhaven Inn.** North Bath Road, **Bath**, ME 04530. Tel: 443-4391. $60–$75; includes breakfast.

▶ **Five Gables Inn.** Murray Hill Road, **East Boothbay**, ME 04544. Tel: 633-4551 or (800) 451-5048. $80–$120; includes breakfast.

▶ **Fox Island Inn.** P.O. Box 421, Carver Street, **Vinalhaven**, ME 04863. Tel: 863-4618. $45–$60; includes breakfast.

▶ **Front Porch.** 324 Washington Street, **Bath**, ME 04530. Tel: 443-5790. $45–$50; includes Continental breakfast.

▶ **Grey Havens Inn.** Seguinland Road, **Georgetown Island**, ME 04548. Tel: 371-2616. $90–$150; includes Continental breakfast.

▶ **Hawthorn Inn.** 9 High Street, **Camden**, ME 04843. Tel: 236-8842. $90–$225; includes full breakfast.

▶ **Highland Mill Inn.** P.O. Box 961 (corner Mechanic and Washington streets at the Highland Mill Mall), **Camden**, ME 04843. Tel: 236-1057 or (800) 841-5590; Fax: (207) 236-6553. $109–$139.

▶ **High Tide Inn.** Route 1, **Camden**, ME 04843. Tel: 236-3724. $60–$150; includes Continental breakfast.

▶ **Hotel Pemaquid.** Route 130, HC 62, Box 421, **Pemaquid Point**, ME 04554. Tel: 677-2312. $54–$105.

▶ **Inn at Bath.** 969 Washington Street, **Bath**, ME 04530. Tel: 443-4294. $65–$90.

▶ **Inn at Sunrise Point.** P.O. Box 1344 (Route 1, Lincolnville), **Camden**, ME 04843. Tel: 236-7716 or (800) 43-LOBSTER. $150–$300; includes breakfast.

▶ **Island Inn. Monhegan**, ME 04852. Tel: 596-0371. $110–$162; includes breakfast and dinner.

▶ **Kenniston Hill Inn.** P.O. Box 125, Route 27, **Boothbay**, ME 04537. Tel: 633-2159 or (800) 992-2915. $65–$95; includes breakfast.

▶ **Lawnmeer Inn.** P.O. Box 505, **West Boothbay Harbor**, ME 04575. Tel: 633-2544 or (800) 633-SMILE. $65–$110.

▶ **Libby House.** Water Street, **Vinalhaven**, ME 04853. Tel: (207) 863-4696 or winter, (516) 765-3756. $60–$79; $90 for an apartment; $135 for a two-bedroom suite. Open June through fall.

▶ **A Little Dream.** 66 High Street (Route 1), **Camden**, ME 04843. Tel: 236-8742. $95–$139; includes breakfast.

▶ **Lodge at Camden Hills.** P.O. Box 794 (Route 1), **Camden**, ME 04843. Tel: 236-8478 or (800) 832-7058. $95–$150.

▶ **Lord Camden Inn. Camden**, ME 04843. Tel: 236-4325 or (800) 336-4325; Fax: (207) 236-7141. $128–$175; includes Continental breakfast.

▶ **Maine Stay.** 22 High Street, **Camden**, ME 04843. Tel: 236-9636. $75–$100; includes breakfast and afternoon tea.

▶ **Marston House.** P.O. Box 517, Main Street, **Wiscasset**, ME 04578. Tel: 882-6010 or (800) 852-4137. $75; includes Continental breakfast.

▶ **Morning Glory.** Pleasant Street, P.O. Box 580, **Vinalhaven**, ME 04863. Tel: 863-2051. $50–$70; includes breakfast.

▶ **Newagen Seaside Inn.** Box 68, **Newagen**, ME 04552. Tel: 633-5242 or (800) 654-5242. $85–$150; includes breakfast.

▶ **Newcastle Inn.** River Road, **Newcastle**, ME 04553. Tel: 563-5685 or (800) 832-8669. $85–$125, with breakfast; $145–$185, with breakfast and dinner.

▶ **Norumbega.** 61 High Street (Route 1), **Camden**, ME 04843. Tel: 236-4646; Fax: 236-0824. $145–$260; penthouse $395; includes breakfast and afternoon wine and cheese.

▶ **Packard House.** 45 Pearl Street, **Bath**, ME 04530. Tel: 443-6069. $65–$80; includes breakfast.

▶ **Pulpit Harbor Inn.** Pulpit Harbor, **North Haven Island**, ME 04853. Tel: 867-2219. $75–$100; includes Continental breakfast.

▶ **Riverview.** Church Lane, **Phippsburg**, ME 04562. Tel: 389-1124. $55; includes Continental breakfast.

▶ **Rock Gardens Inn. Sebasco Estates**, ME 04565. Tel: 389-1339. $148–$190; includes breakfast and dinner.

▶ **Samoset Resort.** Rockland Breakwater, **Rockport**, ME 04856. Tel: 594-2511 or (800) 341-1650. $180–$235.

▶ **Sebasco Lodge. Sebasco Estates**, ME 04565. Tel: 389-1161 or (800) 225-3819. $150–$210; includes breakfast and dinner.

▶ **Shining Sails.** Box 344, **Monhegan**, ME 04852. Tel: 596-0041. $65–$90; includes Continental breakfast.

▶ **Snow Turtle Inn.** Route 32 and Old Route 1, **Waldoboro**, ME 04572. Tel: 832-4423. $50–$65; includes breakfast.

▶ **Spruce Point Inn. Boothbay Harbor**, ME 04538. Tel: 633-4152 or (800) 553-0289. $220–$292; includes breakfast and dinner.

▶ **Squire Tarbox Inn.** R.R. 2, Box 620, **Wiscasset**, ME 04578. Tel: 882-7693. $70–$150, with breakfast; $120–$200, with breakfast and dinner.

▶ **1024 Washington.** 1024 Washington Street, **Bath**, ME 04530. Tel: 443-5202. $50–$125, includes breakfast.

▶ **Tidewater Inn.** Vinalhaven, ME 04863. Tel: 863-4618. $55–$82.

▶ **Tribler Cottage. Monhegan**, ME 04852-0307. Tel: 594-2445. $60–$90; $370–$550 weekly.

▶ **Welch House.** 36 McKown Street, **Boothbay Harbor**, ME 04538. Tel: 633-3431. $55–$90.

▶ **Whitehall Inn.** 52 High Street, **Camden**, ME 04843. Tel: 236-3391. $125–$160; includes breakfast and dinner.

▶ **Youngtown Inn.** Route 52 and Youngtown Road, **Lincolnville**, ME 04849. Tel: 763-4290. $50–$95; includes breakfast.

East Penobscot Bay and Blue Hill

▶ **Alamoosook Lodge.** P.O. Box 16, **Orland**, ME 04472. Tel: 469-6393. $64–$72; includes breakfast.

▶ **Blue Hill Farm Country Inn.** Box 437, **Blue Hill**, ME 04614. Tel: 374-5126. $68–$78; includes breakfast.

▶ **Blue Hill Inn.** P.O. Box 403, Union Street, **Blue Hill**, ME 04614. Tel: 374-2844. $120–$160; includes breakfast and dinner.

▶ **Buck's Harbor Inn.** Box 268, **South Brooksville**, ME 04617. Tel: 326-8660. $60–$70; includes breakfast.

▶ **Capt. Butman Homestead.** Route 1, **Searsport**, ME 04974. Tel: 548-2506. $45; includes breakfast.

▶ **Captain Green Pendleton Inn.** Route 1, **Searsport**, ME 04974. Tel: 548-6523. $55–$65; includes breakfast.

▶ **Captain's Quarters Inn and Motel.** P.O. Box 83, **Stonington**, ME 04681. Tel: 367-2420. $20–$90.

▶ **Castine Inn.** P.O. Box 41, Main Street, **Castine**, ME 04421. Tel: 326-4365. $75–$110; includes breakfast.

▶ **Goose Cove Lodge. Sunset**, ME 04683. Tel: 248-2508. $150–$196; includes breakfast and dinner.

▶ **Hichborn Inn.** Church Street, P.O. Box 115, **Stockton Springs**, ME 04981. Tel: 567-4183. $40–$85; includes breakfast.

▶ **Hiram Blake Camp.** P.O. Box 59, Harborside, **Cape Rosier**, ME 04642. Tel: 326-4951. Cottages $400–$700 weekly.

▶ **Homeport Inn.** Route 1, **Searsport**, ME 04974. Tel: 548-2259 or (800) 742-5814. $37–$75; includes breakfast.

▶ **Inn at Ferry Landing.** Old Ferry Road, R.R. 1, Box 163, **Deer Isle**, ME 04627. Tel: 348-7760. $55–$80; suite $90; includes breakfast.

▶ **John Peters Inn.** Peters Point, **Blue Hill**, ME 04614. Tel: 374-2116. $85–$135; includes breakfast.

▶ **Keeper's House.** P.O. Box 26, **Isle au Haut**, ME 04645. $240.75; includes all meals.

▶ **Lookout.** Flye Point, **North Brooklin**, ME 04661. Tel: 359-2188. $56–$75, includes breakfast; cottages $350–$700 weekly.

▶ **Oakland House.** Herrick Road, **Sargentville**, ME 04673. Tel: 359-8521 or (800) 359-RELAX. $259–$623 per person weekly; includes breakfast and dinner daily.

▶ **Ocean View House.** Box 261, **Stonington**, ME 04681. Tel: 367-5114. $60; includes breakfast.

▶ **Pilgrim's Inn. Deer Isle**, ME 04627. Tel: 348-6615. $160; cottage $180; includes breakfast and dinner.

▶ **Pres du Port.** Box 319, **Stonington**, ME 04681. Tel: 367-5007. $40–$60; includes breakfast.

▶ **Thurston House Bed & Breakfast.** 8 Elm Street, **Searsport**, ME 04974. Tel: 548-2213. $40–$60; includes breakfast.

Mount Desert Island

▶ **Asticou Inn.** Route 3, **Northeast Harbor**, ME 04662. Tel: 276-3344. $195–$260; includes breakfast and dinner.

▶ **Bar Harbor Inn.** Newport Drive, **Bar Harbor**, ME 04609. Tel: 288-3351 or (800) 248-3351; Fax: (207) 288-5296. $80–$195.

▶ **Bay Ledge Inn & Spa.** 1385 Sandpoint Road, **Bar Harbor**, ME 04609. Tel: 288-4204 or (800) 848-6885. $65–$185; includes breakfast.

▶ **Breakwater.** 45 Hancock Street, **Bar Harbor**, ME 04609. Tel: 288-2313 or (800) 238-6309. $175–$250; includes breakfast.

▶ **Claremont.** Claremont Road, **Southwest Harbor**, ME 04679. Tel: 244-5036. $150–$165, includes breakfast and dinner; cottages $110–$140.

▶ **Crocker House Country Inn. Hancock Point**, ME 04640. Tel: 422-6806; Fax: 422-3105. $65–$90; includes breakfast.

▶ **Harbor Cottage Inn.** Box 258, **Southwest Harbor**, ME 04679. Tel: 244-5738. $85–$125; includes breakfast.

▶ **Harbourside Inn. Northeast Harbor**, ME 04662. Tel: 276-3272. $90–$140; includes breakfast.

▶ **Inn at Canoe Point.** Box 216, Hulls Cove, **Bar Harbor**, ME 04609. Tel: 288-9511. $105–$195; includes breakfast.

▶ **Inn at Southwest.** P.O. Box 593, **Southwest Harbor**, ME 04679. Tel: 244-3835. $70–$105; includes breakfast.

▶ **Kingsleigh House.** Box 1426, 100 Main Street, **Southwest Harbor**, ME 04679. Tel: 244-5302. $55–$155; includes breakfast.

▶ **Maison Suisse.** P.O. Box 1090, **Northeast Harbor**, ME 04662. Tel: 276-5223 or (800) 624-7668. $95–$225.

▶ **Manor House Inn.** 106 West Street, **Bar Harbor**, ME 04609. Tel: 288-3759 or (800) 437-0088. $80–$150; includes breakfast.

▶ **Nannau Seaside Bed and Breakfast.** Box 710, Lower Main Street, **Bar Harbor**, ME 04609. Tel: 288-5575. $95–$135; includes breakfast.

▶ **Penury Hall.** Box 68, Main Street, **Southwest Harbor**, ME 04679. Tel: 244-7102. $60; includes breakfast.

▶ **Seal Cove Farm.** HCR 62, Box 140, **Mount Desert**, ME 04660. Tel: 244-7781. $53.30–$64.20; includes breakfast.

▶ **Tides.** 119 West Street, **Bar Harbor**, ME 04609. Tel: 288-4968. $145–$195; includes breakfast.

Down East and Passamaquoddy Bay

The rates for accommodations in New Brunswick are given in Canadian dollars. In New Brunswick an 11 percent provincial tax is charged for accommodations, and a 7 percent GST (Goods and Services Tax) is superimposed on that for larger hotels.

▶ **Algonquin Resort. St. Andrews**, N.B., Canada E0G 2X0. Tel: (506) 529-8823 or, in U.S., (800) 828-7447. $181.

▶ **Brewer House.** Route 1, P.O. Box 94, **Robbinston**, ME 04671. Tel: 454-2385. $50–$75; includes breakfast.

▶ **Clark Perry House.** 59 Court Street, **Machias**, ME 04654. Tel: 255-8458. $35–$55; includes breakfast.

▶ **Compass Rose.** Route 776, North Head, **Grand Manan**, N.B., Canada E0G 2M0. Tel: (506) 446-5906. $55; includes breakfast.

▶ **Gutsy Gull.** P.O. Box 313, Route 92, **Machiasport,** ME 04655-0313. Tel: 255-8633. $50–$65.

▶ **Halcyon Days.** 7 Freemont Street, **Machias,** ME 04654. Tel: 255-4662. $30–$50; includes breakfast.

▶ **Home Port Inn.** 45 Main Street, **Lubec,** ME 04652. Tel: 733-2077 or (800) 457-2077. $50–$75.

▶ **Island View Inn.** HCR 32, Box 24, **Sullivan Harbor,** ME 04664. Tel: 422-3031. $100–$150; includes breakfast.

▶ **Little River Lodge.** Box 237, **Cutler,** ME 04626. Tel: 259-4437. $40–$75; includes breakfast.

▶ **Micmac Farm Guest Cabins. Machiasport,** ME 04655. $45–$60; $350–$375 weekly.

▶ **Moose-A-Bec House. Jonesport,** ME 04649. Tel: 497-2607. $55; includes breakfast.

▶ **Motel East.** 23A Water Street, **Eastport,** ME 04631. Tel: 853-4747. $70–$85.

▶ **Owen House.** Welshpool, **Campobello,** N.B., Canada E0G 3H0. Tel: (506) 752-2977. $55–$65.

▶ **Pleasant Bay Bed & Breakfast.** P.O. Box 222, West Side Road, **Addison,** ME 04606. Tel: 483-4490. $45–$60; includes breakfast.

▶ **Rossmount Inn. St. Andrews,** N.B., Canada E0G 2X0. Tel: (506) 529-3351; Fax: 529-1920. $95.

▶ **Starboard Cove.** HCR 70, Box 442, **Bucks Harbor,** ME 04618. Tel: 255-4426. $40.

▶ **Todd House.** Todd's Head, **Eastport,** ME 04631. Tel: 853-2328. $45–$80.

▶ **Tootsie's Bed and Breakfast.** R.F.D. 1, Box 575, Trynor Square, **Jonesport,** ME 04649. Tel: 497-5414. $25–$40; includes breakfast.

▶ **Weatherby's. Grand Lake Stream,** ME 04637. Tel: 796-5558. $146; includes breakfast and dinner.

▶ **Weston House.** 26 Boynton Street, **Eastport,** ME 04631. Tel: 853-2907. $48.15–$69.55; includes breakfast.

Inland Maine

▶ **Bald Mountain Camps.** P.O. Box 332, **Oquossoc,** ME 04964. Tel: 864-3671 or 864-3788. $75 per person; includes all meals.

▶ **Bethel Inn. Bethel,** ME 04217. Tel: 824-2175 or (800) 654-0125; Fax: (207) 824-2233. $160–$260; includes breakfast and dinner.

▶ **The Birches. Rockwood,** ME 04478. Tel: 534-7305. $60, includes breakfast; cottages, $455–$875 weekly.

▶ **Bosebuck Mountain Camps. Wilsons Mills,** ME 04293. Tel: 243-2945. $65–$70 per person; includes all meals.

▶ **Chapman Inn. Bethel,** ME 04217. Tel: 824-2657. $55–$95.

► **Chesuncook Lake House.** Box 656, Route 76, **Greenville**, ME 04441. Tel: 745-5330 or 695-2821. $82 per person; includes all meals.

► **Country Club Inn.** P.O. Box 680, **Rangeley**, ME 04970. Tel: 864-3831. $134–$154; includes breakfast and dinner.

► **Crab Apple White Water. The Forks**, ME 04985. Tel: 663-2218 or (800) 553-RAFT. $35 per person; includes breakfast.

► **Grant's Kennebago Camps.** P.O. Box 786, **Rangeley**, ME 04970. Tel: 864-3608 in summer; 282-5264 in winter, or (800) 633-4815. $90 per person; includes all meals.

► **Greenville Inn.** P.O. Box 1194, Norris Street, **Greenville**, ME 04441. Tel: 695-2206. $75–$90; includes breakfast.

► **Hammons House.** P.O. Box 16, **Bethel**, ME 04217. Tel: 824-3170. $55–$80.

► **Hamstead Farm.** R.F.D. 3, Box 703, **Bangor**, ME 04401. Tel: 848-3749. $40; includes breakfast.

► **Herbert Hotel.** P.O. Box 67, **Kingfield**, ME 04947. Tel: 265-2000 or (800) THE-HERB. $47–$80; includes breakfast.

► **Kawanhee Inn. Weld**, ME 04285. Tel: 585-2000; in winter 778-3809. $60; cabins from $400 weekly.

► **Lake House.** Routes 35 and 37, **Waterford**, ME 04088. Tel: 583-4182 or (800) 223-4182. $69–$115.

► **Lakewood Camps. Middledam**, ME 04216. Tel: 243-2959; in winter 392-1581. $82 per person.

► **Mallory's Bed and Breakfast Inn.** Box 9, Hyatt Road, **Rangeley**, ME 04970. Tel: 864-2121, 864-5326, or (800) 722-0397. $98–$124; includes breakfast.

► **New England Whitewater Center.** Box 21, **Caratunk**, ME 04985. Tel: 672-5506 or (800) 766-7238. Sterling Inn $40 per person; rafting trips $75–$95 per person.

► **Northern Outdoors.** P.O. Box 100, Route 201, **The Forks**, ME 04985. Tel: 663-4466 or (800) 765-7238. $50 per person.

► **Northern Pride Lodge.** HCR 76, Box 588, **Kokadjo**, ME 04441. Tel: 695-2890. $76 per person; includes all meals.

► **Quality Inn–Phenix.** 20 Broad Street, West Market Square, **Bangor**, ME 04401. Tel: 947-3850 or (800) 4-CHOICE; Fax: (207) 947-3550. $63–$78.

► **Rangeley Inn. Rangeley**, ME 04970. Tel: 864-3341 or (800) 666-3687; Fax: (207) 864-3634. $65–$105.

► **Saddleback Ski and Summer Lake Preserve.** Box 490, **Rangeley**, ME 04970. Tel: 864-5671. $130–$350.

► **Sudbury Inn. Bethel**, ME 04217. Tel: 824-2174 or (800) 395-7837. $80–$100; includes breakfast.

► **Sugarloaf Inn.** R.R. 1, Box 5000, **Kingfield**, ME 04947. Tel: 237-2000 or (800) THE-LOAF. $82–$195.

► **Sugarloaf Mountain Hotel.** R.R. 1, Box 2299, **Carrabassett Valley**, ME 04947. Tel: 237-2222 or (800) 527-9879; Fax: (207) 237-2874. $90–$140.

▶ **Sunday River Inn.** R.F.D. 2, **Bethel**, ME 04217. Tel: 824-2410; Fax: 824-3181. $78–$146; includes breakfast and dinner.

▶ **Summit Hotel and Crown Club.** P.O. Box 450, **Bethel**, ME 04217. Tel: 824-5500 or (800) 543-2SKI. $99–$139.

▶ **Tea Pond Camps.** P.O. Box 349, **Stratton**, ME 04982. Tel: 244-2943. $60 per person; includes all meals.

▶ **Telemark Inn and Llama Farm.** R.F.D. 2, Box 800, **Bethel**, ME 04217; Tel: 836-2703. Lodging $75 per person; trips $100 per person daily.

▶ **Three Stanley Avenue.** P.O. Box 169, **Kingfield**, ME 04947. Tel: 265-5541. $50–$60.

▶ **Tim Pond Wilderness Camps. Eustis**, ME 04936. Tel: 243-2947. $95 per person; includes three meals.

▶ **Voyagers Whitewater.** Route 201, **The Forks**, ME 04985. Tel: 663-4423 or (800) 289-6307. $35–$50 per person; includes breakfast.

▶ **West Branch Ponds Camps.** Box 35, **Greenville**, ME 04441. Tel: 695-2561. $82 per person; includes three meals; cabins $28–$30 per night.

▶ **Westways on Kezar Lake.** Route 5, Box 175, **Center Lovell**, ME 04016. Tel: 928-2663. $99–$159; includes Continental breakfast.

▶ **Wilderness Expeditions.** P.O. Box 41, **Rockwood**, ME 04478. Tel: 534-7305, 534-2242, or (800) 825-WILD. $185 per person; includes rafting trip, two nights' lodging, and meals.

CHRONOLOGY
OF THE HISTORY
OF NEW ENGLAND

The last of the Ice Age glaciers receded from New England circa 10,000 B.C., leaving behind much of the region's characteristic topography: rocky soils, low drumlin hills, kettlehole ponds, and the terminal moraine that forms much of upper Cape Cod. Little is known about the paleo-Indians who first peopled New England during the years following the retreat of the glaciers. By some accounts they were related to modern Eskimos; later they were supplanted by a pre-Algonquian culture related to the now-extinct Beothuk people of Newfoundland.

The Indians inhabiting New England from roughly 2000 B.C. through historical times were primarily members of the Algonquian language group of Eastern Woodland peoples. Among the Algonquian tribes of New England, who subsisted through hunting, farming, and fishing were the Pennacooks, Nipmucs, Massachusetts, Wampanoags, Narragansetts, Pequots, Mohegans, and Abenaki; along the region's western boundary war with the Iroquois was more or less perpetual. Alien diseases carried by European fishermen decimated the coastal tribes even before the era of formal English settlement; as the colonists moved inland the Indians either moved west before them or remained to gradually assimilate and survive in isolated cultural pockets. Thus there remain groups of Penobscots in Maine, Pequots in Connecticut, Wampanoags on Cape Cod, and Abenakis in Vermont.

- **circa A.D. 1000:** Coastal New England is quite possibly visited by the Norse adventurer Leif Ericson, and later by his brothers Thorvald and Thorstein. Attempts to positively identify "Vinland," mentioned in the Icelandic sagas, as Maine, Massachusetts, or Rhode Island, have never proven conclusive.

- **1602**: The English explorer Bartholomew Gosnold sights Cape Cod and Martha's Vineyard.

- **1609**: Striking south from the St. Lawrence Valley, French explorer Samuel de Champlain becomes the first European to lay eyes on Lake Champlain and the future state of Vermont. Attacking a band of Iroquois on behalf of his Algonquian companions, he casts the die of future European and Indian alliances: French/Algonquian and English/Iroquois.

- **1614**: Captain John Smith cruises along the coast of New England; his book *A Description of New England,* containing some of the first reliable maps of the region, is published two years later. Dutch navigator Adriaen Block becomes the first European to explore the Connecticut River.

- **1620**: Blown off course on its way to Virginia, the *Mayflower,* carrying a group of religious dissidents, lands at Provincetown on Cape Cod. The group settles—and establishes the first permanent English colony in New England—across the bay in what is now Plymouth. Under Governor William Bradford, the Plimoth Colony agrees to live by the Mayflower Compact, a root document of the American democratic tradition.

- **1623**: The first English settlements are established in New Hampshire at the coastal sites of Portsmouth and Dover. The Dorchester Adventurers' Company establishes a settlement at Gloucester, on the tip of Cape Ann, Massachusetts. Gloucester grows to become one of New England's preeminent fishing ports.

- **1630**: The ship *Arbella* and an accompanying fleet bring the first major contingent of English settlers to the mouth of the Charles River, where they found the city of Boston, part of the Massachusetts Bay Colony.

- **1633–1636**: First European settlement of Connecticut, by Dutch traders near Hartford (1633; abandoned 1654) and English colonists at Wethersfield, Windsor, and Hartford (1634–1636).

- **1635**: Boston Latin School founded; now part of the city's school system, it is New England's oldest public educational institution. Religious and political dissident Roger Williams is expelled from the Massachusetts Bay Colony; the following year he founds a new colony in Rhode Island.

- **1636**: Harvard College is founded at Newtown (later Cambridge), Massachusetts. It is named for Reverend

John Harvard, a Cambridge University graduate who willed his library to the new college.

William Pynchon leads a group of settlers from the Massachusetts Bay Colony to the banks of the Connecticut River, where they found the town of Springfield (known as Agawan prior to 1640).

- **1637**: The Pequot War: In New England's first major confrontation between settlers and Indians, Captain John Mason and his men annihilate a Pequot encampment following the Pequots' massacre of settlers at Wethersfield, Connecticut.

- **1640**: The *Bay Psalm Book,* first book published in New England, is printed at Cambridge, Massachusetts.

- **1642**: Darby Field makes the first recorded climb of what is now known as Mount Washington, New Hampshire, New England's highest peak.

- **1662**: Connecticut receives its Colonial charter from King Charles II.

- **1663**: The colony of Rhode Island is chartered by King Charles II.

- **1675–1676**: King Philip's War: In this final and most decisive of the New England Indian wars, the Wampanoag chief Metacomet (also known as King Philip) and his Narragansett allies are defeated by an English Colonial militia.

- **1679**: King Charles II grants New Hampshire its Colonial charter.

- **1685**: King Charles II revokes the charters of the New England colonies, proposing that the entire region be ruled as the Dominion of New England by a royally appointed governor, rather than as semi-autonomous chartered entities.

- **1689**: One year after England's so-called Glorious Revolution and the deposing of James II, New England lifts the yoke of viceregal government, ridding itself of the autocratic governor Sir Edmund Andros.

- **1692**: The Colonial charter of Massachusetts is restored. The Salem witchcraft hysteria results in the trial and execution of 20 men and women accused of consorting with the devil in the Massachusetts village of Salem and surrounding communities.

- **1701**: The Collegiate School within Connecticut is founded by Congregationalist ministers at Killingworth and Saybrook. In 1745 it is moved to New Haven and renamed after benefactor Elihu Yale.

- **1704**: The *Boston News-Letter,* first successful newspaper in the American colonies, begins publication. In the Great Deerfield Raid, Indians allied with the French massacre the inhabitants of the western Massachusetts town and carry off more than 100 to captivity in Canada.

- **1724**: The first English settlement in what is now Vermont is founded, at Fort Dummer near present-day Brattleboro.

- **circa 1734**: The "Great Awakening," New England's first important indigenous religious revival, gathers force under the evangelical leadership of Jonathan Edwards, a Congregationalist pastor of Northampton, Massachusetts.

- **1754–1763**: The French and Indian War pits Great Britain and her American colonies against the French in Canada, and results in the loss of New France (present-day Quebec and the Maritimes, with a string of forts down through part of present-day Ontario into the Ohio Valley) to the British.

- **1755**: Williams College is founded at West Hoosuck, Massachusetts, according to the will of Colonel Ephraim Williams, which also stipulates that the town's name be changed to Williams.

- **1764**: Rhode Island College is founded; it moves to Providence in 1771, and is renamed Brown University in 1804 after benefactor Nicholas Brown.

- **1765**: Britain imposes the Stamp Act on its American colonies. Vigorously opposed in New England, the act seeks to raise revenue through mandatory affixing of tax stamps to publications and legal documents.

- **1769**: Dartmouth College, an outgrowth of an Indian school established by Eleazer Wheelock, is founded at Hanover, New Hampshire.

- **1770**: British soldiers posted outside the seat of Colonial government in Boston fire upon a taunting mob; five die in what becomes known as the Boston Massacre.

- **1770**: Ethan Allen organizes the Green Mountain Boys, dedicated to fighting New York's designs on the territory later to become the state of Vermont.

- **1773**: Outraged over British taxes on tea, Bostonians led by Samuel Adams disguise themselves as Indians and stage the Boston Tea Party, tossing crates of the commodity into the harbor.

- **1774**: The Boston Port Bill: In one of the final provocations prior to the outbreak of the American Revolution, Britain closes the port of Boston. On the night of April 18 Paul Revere and William Dawes ride from

Boston to warn outlying towns of the approach of British regulars. Early the following morning, the battles of Lexington and Concord signal the start of the American Revolution.

- **1775.** On May 10 Ethan Allen and the Green Mountain Boys seize the British Fort Ticonderoga, on the New York side of Lake Champlain. Cannon taken from Ticonderoga are later used by George Washington to lay siege to Boston. On June 17 British troops win a costly victory over entrenched American forces at the Battle of Bunker Hill in Charlestown, Massachusetts. (The battle was actually fought on nearby Breed's Hill.) Two weeks after Bunker Hill, Washington takes command of the Continental army at Cambridge, Massachusetts.

- **1776:** With artillery placed above the city on Dorchester Heights, Washington routs the British from Boston.

- **1777:** On August 16 Colonel John Stark and his New Hampshire and Vermont militiamen defeat a detachment of British and Hessian troops sent to seize stores at Bennington, Vermont. The Battle of Bennington helps turn the tide of war in western New England and the Hudson River Valley. Vermont declares its independence as the Republic of Vermont; it does not join the Union until 1791. Massachusetts's Springfield Armory begins production of muskets for the Continental army. The armory's line of production extends through the M-1 era and World War II.

- **1783:** The Treaty of Paris formally ends the Revolutionary War.

- **1786–1787:** Shays's Rebellion: Revolutionary War veteran Daniel Shays leads an insurrection of western Massachusetts farmers demanding relief from the oppressive economic policies of Boston business interests.

- **1787:** The Constitution of the United States is approved in convention and sent to the states for ratification. Rhode Island is the only state of the original 13 not to send a delegate to the Constitutional Convention; later, it was the last state to ratify the document.

- **1791:** Vermont becomes the 14th state.

- **1793:** Samuel Slater builds America's first water-powered cotton mill at Pawtucket, Rhode Island. Slater circumvented a British ban on textile technology exports by recalling from memory the layout of an English mill.

- **1797:** The 44-gun frigate USS *Constitution,* later revered as "Old Ironsides," is launched in Boston.

Victorious against the Barbary pirates and in the War of 1812, it is saved from scrapping by an 1830 campaign led by Oliver Wendell Holmes, Sr.

- **1807**: President Thomas Jefferson's embargo on trade with France and Britain, a retaliation for their interference with American shipping, plunges the economy of coastal New England into depression.

- **1809**: The forerunner of the Amoskeag mills, destined to become the world's largest textile enterprise, is founded on the Merrimack River in Manchester, New Hampshire.

- **1812–1814**: The War of 1812 further depresses New England's maritime economy.

- **1812**: Seth Thomas, whose name is to become synonymous with clocks, establishes his factory at Plymouth Hollow (later Thomaston), Connecticut.

- **1820**: Maine, formerly part of Massachusetts, is admitted to statehood.

- **1822**: The Merrimack Manufacturing Company is established at Lowell, Massachusetts. Lowell grows to become the quintessential New England mill city.

- **1830–1836**: New England's first railroads reach out from Boston to Lowell, Worcester, and Providence.

- **1831–1865**: In Boston, Massachusetts native William Lloyd Garrison publishes *The Liberator,* a leading organ of the New England–based radical abolitionist movement.

- **1832–1840**: A U.S.–Canada boundary dispute results in the northernmost corner of New Hampshire declaring independence as the "Republic of Indian Stream." When the boundary is settled the territory reverts to U.S. control.

- **1836**: Ralph Waldo Emerson publishes his essay *Nature,* a cornerstone of the transcendentalist movement. In the same year the Transcendental Club first meets in Boston.

- **1837**: Mount Holyoke, the first women's college in the United States, is founded by Mary Lyon at South Hadley, Massachusetts.

- **circa 1845–1850**: Driven by the potato famine, thousands of Irish immigrants arrive in Boston. Within a generation the city's ethnic complexion is radically altered.

- **1845**: Henry David Thoreau begins a two-year sojourn in the woods near Walden Pond in Concord, Massachusetts.

The New England whaling industry, originally centered on Nantucket but increasingly headquartered in New Bedford after the War of 1812, reaches its peak. New Bedford whalers bring in 158,000 barrels of sperm oil, 272,000 barrels of whale oil, and three million pounds of whalebone. Twelve years later the industry is forever undermined by the discovery of petroleum in Pennsylvania.

- **1847**: Samuel Colt, inventor of the revolver, establishes his Colt Patent Arms Company in Hartford.
- **1861–1865**: New England sends thousands of its sons to the battlefields of the Civil War. Vermont suffers the highest casualty ratio of any northern state.
- **1861**: The Massachusetts Institute of Technology is established in Boston; later, the campus is moved across the Charles River to Cambridge.
- **1864**: On October 19 Confederate infiltrators stage the St. Albans Raid, escaping from the Vermont city to Canada with $200,000 in bank robbery proceeds.
- **1876**: The Appalachian Mountain Club is founded in Boston. In 1888 the AMC opens the first of its hikers' huts in the White Mountains of New Hampshire, where it assumes a major conservation and wilderness management role.
- **1885**: Hugh O'Brien is elected the first Irish mayor of Boston.
- **1891**: The Trustees of Reservations, a landholding conservation organization that prefigured organizations such as the Nature Conservancy and Britain's National Trust, is founded in Boston. The trustees currently own and manage 72 Massachusetts properties, totaling 18,000 acres.
- **1892**: Lizzie Borden is arrested for the axe murders of her mother and father in Fall River, Massachusetts. She is later acquitted, and the case remains officially unsolved.
- **1901**: The Boston Pilgrims, soon renamed the Red Sox, take their place among the teams of baseball's American League.
- **1910**: The Green Mountain Club is founded. The club built and maintains Vermont's 260-mile Long Trail, which extends from the state's border with Massachusetts to its border with Quebec.
- **1911**: The federal government establishes New Hampshire's 70,000-acre (later expanded) White Mountain National Forest. Vermont's Green Mountain National Forest follows during the 1930s.
- **1912**: Textile workers angered by a proposed wage reduction stage the great strike in Lawrence, Massa-

chusetts. Managed by the Industrial Workers of the World (IWW), the so-called Bread and Roses strike results in a modest wage increase.

- **1914:** With his election as mayor of Boston, James Michael Curley begins a four-decade career as the lovable rogue of machine politics.

- **1918:** The Boston Red Sox win their last World Series. Two years later the team's owner sells Babe Ruth to the New York Yankees.

- **1919:** The Boston police strike: The strike is eventually broken by Massachusetts governor (and Vermont native) Calvin Coolidge, who rises to national prominence as a result. Acadia National Park is established on Maine's Mount Desert Island.

- **1921:** Two Italian anarchists, Nicola Sacco and Bartolomeo Vanzetti, are arrested for a payroll robbery and murder in Dedham, Massachusetts. The pair become a cause célèbre in the struggle between progressives and establishment forces; their 1927 execution sparks widespread protest.

- **1934:** New England's first ski tow is installed in Woodstock, Vermont.

- **1935:** The Amoskeag Manufacturing Company closes its textile mills in Manchester, New Hampshire. The closure is part of a massive shift of textile jobs from New England to the South.

- **1936:** Carroll Reed and Hannes Schneider open America's first ski school in North Conway, New Hampshire.

- **1938:** In September New England is devastated by the worst hurricane ever to strike the region. Coastal towns are inundated; salt spray encrusts windows as far inland as Vermont.

- **1946:** A Boston congressional district sends 29-year-old John F. Kennedy to the U.S. House of Representatives. William Loeb buys New Hampshire's *Manchester Union Leader;* over the next three decades he turns the newspaper into a major ultraconservative political force.

- **1950s:** A new era begins in New England's economic life, with the rise of such high-technology companies as Polaroid, Raytheon, Wang Laboratories, and Digital Equipment Company. Massachusetts's Route 128 is nicknamed "America's Technology Highway."

- **1952:** New Hampshire holds its first presidential primary.

- **1960:** Massachusetts senator John F. Kennedy is elected president of the United States. Among Kennedy's efforts on behalf of his native region is the creation of the Cape Cod National Seashore, permanently protecting the fragile dunelands of the Outer Cape from development.

- **1962**: Maine's ex-governor Percival Baxter completes the acquisition of 201,000 acres in the state's north woods, including Mount Katahdin, which he donates to the public as Baxter State Park.

- **1970**: Vermont's Act 250 sets stringent statewide standards for land development; increasingly, the state is seen as a trendsetter in environmental legislation.

- **mid-1970s**: Boston is torn by controversy surrounding court-ordered school busing to achieve racial integration.

- **1978**: Two transplanted New Yorkers, Ben Cohen and Jerry Greenfield, start selling homemade ice cream in Burlington, Vermont.

  A powerful nor'easter ravages coastal New England with fierce winds, high tides, and heavy snowfall. The "Blizzard of '78" remains the region's worst winter storm of the century.

- **1988**: Citing his association with the "Massachusetts Miracle" of booming, high technology–based economy, Massachusetts governor Michael Dukakis makes an unsuccessful bid for the U.S. presidency.

- **1989**: New England reels under the effects of the nationwide recession. The region's economy is especially weakened by the slowdown in Massachusetts-based computer industries.

- **1991**: Cape Cod and much of the southern New England coast is hammered by Hurricane Bob, and by a fierce, unnamed nor'easter that strikes later in the autumn.

- **1992**: The entire six-state region, including the traditional Republican bastions of Maine, New Hampshire, and Vermont, places its electoral votes solidly behind Democratic presidential candidate Bill Clinton. Maine is the only state in the nation to give more than 30 percent of its vote to independent candidate Ross Perot.

—William G. Scheller

INDEX